CONCISE
ENCYCLOPEDIA OF
COMPUTER SCIENCE

CONCISE ENCYCLOPEDIA OF COMPUTER SCIENCE

Editor:

Edwin D. Reilly

WILEY

Other Wiley Editorial Offices

John Wiley & Sons, Inc., 111 River Street,
Hoboken, NJ 07030, USA

Jossey-Bass, 989 Market Street,
San Francisco, CA 94103-1741, USA

Wiley-VCH Verlag GmbH, Boschstr. 12,
D-69469 Weinheim, Germany

John Wiley & Sons Australia, Ltd, 33 Park Road,
Milton, Queensland, 4064, Australia

John Wiley & Sons (Asia) Pte Ltd, 2 Clementi Loop #02-01,
Jin Xing Distripark, Singapore 129809

John Wiley & Sons Canada Ltd, 22 Worcester Road,
Etobicoke, Ontario, Canada, M9W 1L1

Wiley also publishes its books in a variety of electronic formats. Some content that appears in print may not be available in electronic books.

Library of Congress Cataloguing-in-Publication Data

Concise Encyclopedia of Computer Science/Editor, Edwin D. Reilly.
    p. cm.
  Includes bibliographical references and index.
  ISBN 0-470-09095-2 (pbk.)
1. Computer science–Encyclopedias. I. Reilly, Edwin D.
  QA76.15.C654 2004
  004'.03–dc22

2004009421

British Library Cataloguing in Publication Data

A catalogue record for this book is available from the British Library

ISBN 0-470-09095-2

Typeset in 9.5/12.5pt AGaramond by Laserwords Private Limited, Chennai, India.
Printed and bound in Great Britain by Biddles Ltd, King's Lynn.
This book is printed on acid-free paper responsibly manufactured from sustainable forestry in which at least two trees are planted for each one used for paper production.

Contents

Contributors

(Numbers after each name indicate the pages at which articles by each author begin.)

John N. Ackley, Ackley Communications Enterprises 793

Ole Agesen, VMware   117

David H. Ahl, Writer   173

James F. Allen, University of Rochester   548

Jonathan Allen, deceased   714

Charles Ames, Composer   189

Charles G. Ames, Tulsa Community College   89

Scott E. Anderson, Sony Pictures Imageworks Inc.   306

Ross Anderson, University of Cambridge, UK   273

Deane Arganbright, University of Tennessee-Martin 717

Malcolm P. Atkinson, University of Glasgow, UK   281, 510

Geoffrey Austrian, Writer   362

Algirdas Avižienis, University of California at Los Angeles   7, 38, 668

Jean-Loup Baer, University of Washington   208, 538, 545

David W. Barron, University of Southampton, UK—retired   209, 443, 682

Tim Bell, University of Canterbury, New Zealand   231

Hal Berghel, University of Nevada at Las Vegas   804

Laurent Bernardin, Waterloo Maple Inc., Canada   131

Valdis A. Berzins, Naval Postgraduate School   704

Raj Bhatti, University of Greenwich, UK   671

Michael Bieber, New Jersey Institute of Technology 363

Adrienne Bloss, Roanoke College   437, 603, 735

Marjory S. Blumenthal, CSTB   113

Ronald F. Boisvert, National Institute of Standards and Technology   640

Daniel Boneh, Stanford University   526

Kathleen H. V. Booth, Autonetics Research Associates, Canada   512

David H. Brandin, IMI Group LLC   416

Allan G. Bromley, deceased   27, 253

Heather Brown, University of Exeter, UK   251

Peter J. Brown, University of Kent, UK   480, 703

Richard A. Buckingham, deceased   48

Mark Burgess, Oslo College, Norway   775

Katie Burke, Desktop.com   299

Alice R. Burks, Writer   48

Arthur W. Burks, University of Michigan   48

Martin Campbell-Kelly, University of Warwick, UK 521, 654

George S. Carson, GSC Associates   179

John Case, University of Delaware   50

Paul E. Ceruzzi, Smithsonian Institute   258, 809

Janice F. Cerveny, Florida Atlantic University   298

Sreejit Chakravarty, Intel Corporation   160

Ned Chapin, Consultant   329

Srisakdi Charmonman, Assumption University of Thailand, Bangkok   289

Surajit Chaudhuri, Microsoft Research   243

Joseph Chlamtac, University of Texas   523

Keith L. Clark, Imperial College, London, UK   458

Billy G. Claybrook, Claybrook Enterprises   325

William R. Cockayne, Microsoft Research   787

I. Bernard Cohen, deceased   485

Robert P. Colwell, Intel Corporation   512

Preface

The *Encyclopedia of Computer Science* has evolved through four editions, the most recent having been published in July 2000. This *Concise Encyclopedia of Computer Science* contains a shorter version of 60% of the articles in the full Fourth Edition, the principal omissions being highly mathematical articles and others that were thought to be of limited interest to most readers of this volume. Eight articles have been added on important topics that have arisen over the past four years. The intent is that this edition be useful to anyone wishing a more portable, less expensive reference than the full Encyclopedia. In particular, high school and college students or professionals in noncomputer fields should find that this Concise Encyclopedia fulfils most of their needs.

An effort has been made to preserve the essence of each original article. The shortened articles retain their authors' sentences except for editorial changes which provide either transitions that replace deleted material or updates regarding recent developments. Like the full Encyclopedia, this concise edition is a general reference to computer science and engineering, as well as a broad picture of the discipline, its history, and its direction.

The organization of this volume is alphabetical by article titles. Titles have been chosen so that the first word is generally the one likely to be selected by the reader in searching for a particular topic. In addition, there are cross-reference entries when the reader might have sought more than one word in a title, or when the article could have been given an alternative synonymous title.

There are five additional aids to the reader. The first aid is the Classification of Articles, which follows this Preface. This classification is intended to guide the reader to clusters of related articles. It may also help readers to follow a coherent self-study regime in a particular subfield. The second such aid is the list of cross-references to closely-related articles at the beginning of each article, and the third aid is the frequent use of the notations (*q.v.*) and "*See*" in articles to refer to an article related to the point under discussion.

The three appendixes constitute the fourth aid— Abbreviations and Acronyms, Notation and Units, and a Timeline of Significant Milestones in Computing.

The fifth aid is the Index. In a dictionary or glossary, all terms being defined appear as entries, making an index superfluous. But in an encyclopedia only the most important terms are used as article titles or even main cross-references, making a comprehensive index essential. The index to this work contains not only article titles, but also the names of persons cited and references to subcategories and important words in general usage. Thus the index will often provide pointers to unfamiliar terms whose exploration the reader might find useful and interesting.

Edwin D. Reilly   *reilly@cs.albany.edu*   **July 2004**

Classification of Articles

This classification of articles embodies a taxonomy that should be helpful to the reader in grasping the scope and interrelationships of this volume's 382 articles. Articles are classified under nine categories:

1. Hardware
2. Computer Systems
3. Information and Data
4. Software
5. Mathematics of Computing
6. Theory of Computation
7. Methodologies
8. Applications
9. Computing Milieux

Each article appears at least once in this classification, and some more than once in order to avoid the clutter of cross-references. Most classification headings are themselves article titles, in which case the title is followed by the page on which it begins. Headings preceded by an asterisk (*), however, are not actual titles but rather were invented to provide coherence to the classification.

1. *HARDWARE

2. *COMPUTER SYSTEMS

3. *INFORMATION AND DATA

Trademarked Items Mentioned in Articles

Item	Principal Article	Original Owner
Alpha	Intermediate Languages	Digital Equipment Corporation
Alta Vista	World Wide Web	Digital Equipment Corporation
Apple	Apple; Personal Computing	Apple Computer, Inc.
Aptiva	IBM PC	IBM
AutoCAD	CAD/CAM	AutoDesk, Inc.
Axiom	Computer Algebra	Numerical Algorithms Group
Buddy List	Online Conversation	America Online
C#	Microsoft	Microsoft
Chem	Computer Science	NASA
DataGlove	Virtual Reality	VPL Research
DB-2	Computer Science	IBM
dBase	Computer Science	dBase, Inc.
DECNET	Computer Science	Digital Equipment Corporation
Deep Blue	Computer Chess	IBM
Derive	Computer Algebra	SoftWarehouse
Eispack	Computer Science	Netlib
Excel	Spreadsheet	Microsoft
Hypercard	Hypertext	Apple Computer, Inc.
IBM PC	IBM PC	IBM
iBook	Apple	Apple Computer, Inc.
ICQ	Online Conversation	Mirabalis
iMac	Apple	Apple Computer, Inc.
Ingres	Relational Database	Computer Associates
Instant Messaging	Online Conversation	America Online
IntelliMouse Explorer	Mouse	Microsoft
Java	Java	Sun Microsystems
JavaScript	Java	Sun Microsystems
Jaz	Memory: Auxiliary	Iomega Corporation
Lego	LOGO	Lego Corporation
Linux	Linux	Linus Torvalds
Listserv	Electronic Mail	L-Soft International

Item	Principal Article	Original Owner
Lotus 1-2-3	Spreadsheet	Lotus
Lotus Notes	Word Processing	IBM
Macintosh	Apple	Apple Computer, Inc.
MacOS	Apple	Apple Computer, Inc.
Macsyma	Computer Algebra	Macsyma, Inc.
Majordomo	Electronic Mail	Great Circle Associates
Maple	Computer Algebra	Waterloo Maple Software
Mathematica	Computer Algebra	Wolfram Research, Inc.
Microsoft Messenger	Online Conversation	Microsoft
Microsoft Word	Word Processing	Microsoft
MouseMan	Mouse	Logitech, Inc.
MPIOC	Input–Output Operations	MasPar
MS-DOS	Operating Systems	Microsoft
Multics	Time Sharing	Honeywell
Netscape Communicator	Markup Languages	Netscape Communications Corporation
NewWave	Text Editing Systems	Hewlett-Packard
Omnipage Pro	Optical Character Recognition	Caere Corporation
OS/2	Personal Computing	IBM
PageMaker	Desktop Publishing	Adobe
PageMill	Markup Languages	Adobe
Pentium	Microcomputer Chip	Intel
Photoshop	Digital Photography	Adobe
Portége	Portable Computers	Toshiba
PostScript	PostScript	Adobe
PowerPC	Apple	IBM
Red Hat	Linux	Red Hat Software
Rolodex	Word Processing	Borel Corporation
Quattro Pro	Spreadsheet	Corel Corporation
Sparc	Intermediate Languages	Sun Microsystems
System R	Relational Database	IBM
T$_E$X	T$_E$X	American Mathematical Society
Thinkpad	IBM PC	IBM
Unix	Unix	AT&T
Visicalc	Spreadsheet	Trellix Corporation
Visual Basic	Basic	Microsoft
Windows	Window Environments	Microsoft
WordPerfect	Word Processing	Corel Corporation
Yahoo! Messenger	Online Conversation	Yahoo!
Zip	Memory: Auxiliary	Iomega Corporation
Zip+4	Optical Character Recognition	US Postal Service

A

ABSTRACT DATA TYPE

For articles on related subjects, *see*

+ Class
+ Data Type
+ Data Structures
+ Encapsulation
+ Information Hiding
+ Object-Oriented Programming
+ Program Specification
+ Software Reusability
+ Structured Programming

An *abstract data type* (ADT) is a programmer-defined data type, comprising a specification and at least one implementation. The specification gives an abstract description of the behavior of instances of the type, independently of any particular implementation. The provider of an abstract type implementation is obliged to ensure that it obeys the specification perfectly. So long as this is the case, users of the type need understand only the specification, rather than the implementation, to know how values of the type will behave.

The purpose of ADTs is to allow the modular construction of software systems through the composition of components whose individual behavior is well understood. This approach to software construction has a number of advantages. The specification may be given in a language other than the one used to implement it, and, in particular, an axiomatic specification language such as Z or Vienna Definition Language may be used. This allows the user of an ADT to gain a very clear understanding of its operational behavior without having to understand the lower-level details of its implementation. Different implementations can be substituted, for example for performance reasons, without affecting the user code. The implementation itself consists of a concrete representation, a set of operations that may be performed on that representation, and an interface to those operations. It is a critical requirement for an ADT that the interface operations provide the only access by which the concrete representation is manipulated.

Some programming languages provide explicit support for ADTs, some provide implicit support, and some provide no support at all. However, the concept of abstract typing may be usefully thought of as a programming discipline rather than a syntactic construct, and it is possible to program in this discipline in many languages that do not possess explicit syntactic support, as well as in those that do. Languages that explicitly support pure models of ADTs include Alphard, CLU, Euclid, ML, Napier88, and Quest. Commercial languages with at least some support for the key concepts include Ada (*q.v.*), C++ (*q.v.*), Java (*q.v.*), and some dialects of Pascal (*q.v.*).

An Example ADT

Consider an abstract definition of a simple counter. The abstract interface consists of the operations

a
b
c
d
e
f
g
h
i
j
k
l
m
n
o
p
q
r
s
t
u
v,w
x,y
z

"click," "look," and "reset." "Click" and "reset" have no argument or result; the former has the effect of incrementing the counter, while the latter zeros it. "Look" also has no argument, but returns a natural number, representing the current value of the counter.

The specification is completely independent of the programming language used for coding. However, although the definition might be completely abstract, it is still necessary to find sufficient commonality between the specification and coding languages for the interface operations to be defined in both. In this case we can manage with any language that provides procedures and integers; here is an obvious implementation in an imaginary language:

```
Let counterRep := 0
procedure click() ; counterRep :=
                      counterRep + 1
procedure reset() ; counterRep := 0
procedure look() -> integer ;
                    return( counterRep )
```

However, this implementation of the abstract description does not qualify as an abstract type because the operational interface can be compromised by a change to the variable counterRep from another context without using click or reset.

First-Order and Second-Order Information Hiding

There are two ways in which the concrete representation of an ADT can be protected from unlawful manipulation: by making it incapable of being denoted in the language, or by giving it a type that precludes illegal operations. Mechanisms in these classes are known respectively as *first-order* and *second-order information hiding*. The critical difference is that second-order mechanisms allow instances of the abstract type itself to appear in the operational signature (the specification of the types of the operations in terms of the types of their operands and return values). The use of first-order information hiding is thus restricted to state transformation models, in which the abstract instance is hidden behind interface operations that affect and report aspects of its state. Second-order hiding is more flexible, as it allows abstract values to be passed around along with operations that may be applied to them.

To introduce a second-order example, we will continue to model the concept of a counter, but slightly change the abstract definition to model a collection of such counters. Each has the same interface operations, modeled now as procedures that operate on counters, and two new interface functions are introduced: one to create a counter and one to test whether one counter has a greater value than another. Given the identifier counter to represent the type of the new counter, the abstract interface is as follows:

```
Structure
(
newCounter : procedure() -> counter,
click      : procedure( counter ),
reset      : procedure( counter ),
look       : procedure( counter )
                          -> integer,
greater    : procedure( counter, counter )
                          -> boolean
)
```

The procedure greater exemplifies one of the major differences in expressive power between the two classes of information hiding, in that second-order hiding allows the neat definition of operators that act over more than a single instance of the type. With first-order information hiding, as in the pure object-oriented paradigm, such operators do not fit neatly and can only be expressed artificially, either asymmetrically or by using the published interface at a different level of abstraction. Second-order hiding, however, allows the definition of arbitrary abstract algebras (mathematical systems of operations on the types). There are three well-known mechanisms in this category: the abstract type model first used by the language ML, the existential types model proposed by Mitchell and Plotkin (1988), and the class abstraction of many object-oriented programming languages.

Object-Oriented Information Hiding

Another well-known mechanism that allows the abstraction required for second-order information hiding is the *class* mechanism of object-oriented languages. Such mechanisms control the scoping of instance variables and methods, and can be used to describe ADTs. The converse is not the case, however, and many classes described in such languages cannot usefully be regarded as abstract types because they lack the necessary static properties.

Object-oriented information hiding is an interesting mix between first- and second-order models. The concept of an object is essentially a first-order model and is normally used in the state transformation paradigm. However, the scoping rules for method definition can allow the coding of second-order models by giving access to the internal state of more than one object of the same class, as in the above example. This is a common paradigm in the languages C++ and Java.

Bibliography

1988. Mitchell, J. C., and Plotkin, G. D. "Abstract types have existential type," *ACM Transactions on Programming Languages and Systems* (TOPLAS), **10**(3), 470–502.

1994. Schmidt, D. A. *The Structure of Typed Programming Languages.* Cambridge, MA: MIT Press.

1996. Paulson, L. *Standard ML for the Working Programmer*, 2nd Ed. Cambridge, MA: Cambridge University Press.

1999. Henning, M., and Vinoski, S. *Advanced CORBA Programming with C++.* Reading, MA: Addison-Wesley.

Richard Connor

ACCESS TIME

For articles on related subjects, *see*

+ Diskette
+ Hard Disk
+ Memory: Auxiliary

Access time is the elapsed time between the initiation of a request for data and receipt of the first bit or byte of that data. Direct-access devices require varying times to position a read–write head over a particular record. In the case of a moving-head hard disk drive, this involves positioning the *comb* (head assembly, as in Fig. 1) to the designated *cylinder* (all tracks of the same number), plus rotation of the selected track to the desired record.

For a disk, total access time is the sum of comb-movement (seek) and rotational times to reach a particular record (plus the time to switch from reading or writing one surface to another; however, since this is done at electronic speeds, it contributes almost nothing to the access time). There is a different access time for each record retrieved at random from a disk drive, since it is necessary to move from cylinder C_1 to cylinder C_2 (Fig. 2) and then await rotational positioning of record R.

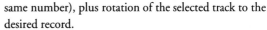
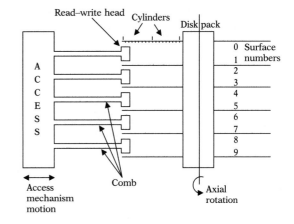
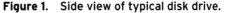

Figure 1.   Side view of typical disk drive.

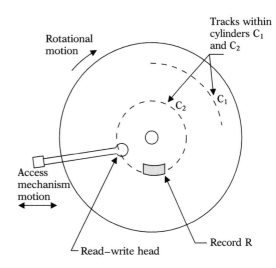

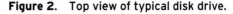

Figure 2.   Top view of typical disk drive.

a
b
c
d
e
f
g
h
i
j
k
l
m
n
o
p
q
r
s
t
u
v,w
x,y
z

Consider an 18-GB disk drive (which might have 16 384 cylinders) that rotates at 7200 rpm, or 8.3 ms/rotation. Typical times for comb-movement are 20 ms maximum, 9 ms average, and 2 ms minimum seek times. Thus the *maximum access* time for this disk is $20 + 8 = 28$ ms, the *average access time* is 13 ms (half a rotation $+$ 9 ms), and the *minimum access time* for data on an adjacent cylinder is 2 ms. The last time is also called the *track-to-track* seek time. Of course, the minimum access time for successive records on a single cylinder approaches 0.

Average access time is an important parameter for analytical planning of a real-time computer application, for example an online inquiry system. Minimum access time is more important for sequential usage of disk drives. The dominant component of delay for sequential retrieval of records from a disk drive is the average time for a half rotation (4.17 ms for the drive described).

David N. Freeman

ACM

See ASSOCIATION FOR COMPUTING MACHINERY (ACM).

ACTIVATION RECORD

For articles on related subjects, *see*

+ Block Structure
+ Calling Sequence
+ Parameter Passing

An *activation record* consists of all of the information pushed onto the system stack (*q.v.*) during execution of a procedure call in a high-level block-structured language. The activation record has only transient existence during execution of the called procedure. Typically, the record contains arguments used by the programmer as part of the procedure's *calling sequence*, current contents of important system registers (*q.v.*) pushed by the machine command used to invoke the procedure, and local variables pushed by the procedure itself.

Figure 1, adapted from Calingaert (1979), shows schematically in part (a) the static structure (nesting of blocks) of a portion of a block-structured program and its corresponding activation record stack. Assume that blocks A, B, C, D, and E are activated in that order and that E is a procedure that calls itself recursively. In addition to key parametric information, the stacked activation records of Fig. 1(b) must contain *static links*

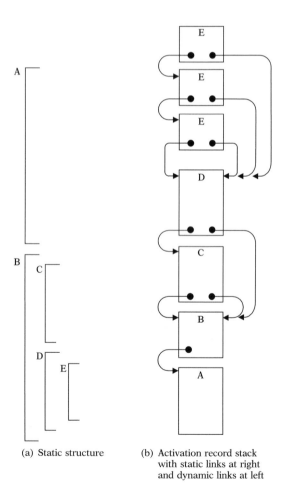

(a) Static structure

(b) Activation record stack with static links at right and dynamic links at left

Figure 1. Run-time representation of nested procedures.

that indicate which procedure encloses (or precedes) a given activation record's procedure and *dynamic links* that point to the activation record of the procedure that called a given stacked record's procedure. Static links, shown at the right of Fig. 1(b), are needed to allow access to local and nonlocal identifiers. Dynamic links are shown at the left in the same figure. The stacked activation records do not contain executable machine code; single reentrant copies of each procedure are stored elsewhere in memory.

Suppose that, on the Digital Equipment Corporation VAX, a main program calls *proc1*, which then calls *proc2*, which in turn calls *proc3*. Figure 2 shows how the stack would then appear. Each activation record results from execution of a procedure call, and each called procedure terminates execution by executing a *return* command,

which removes the topmost activation record from the stack (by merely resetting the stack pointer, SP, in the figure). As first *proc3* and then *proc2* and finally *proc1* finish, their corresponding activation records will be removed from the stack, and thus the stack will return to its status prior to the call of *proc1*. Among the important registers saved by each procedure call is the PC, the program counter, a dynamic link which is needed so that the corresponding *return* can transfer control to exactly the right place in the calling routine. The registers labeled AP and FP, called the argument pointer and the frame pointer, are static links used by the procedure in order to reference procedure arguments and local variables respectively, and, by following the FP chain of links, nonlocal variables that lie within the scope defined by usual block structure rules.

In Fig. 2, the second and third nested procedures are called *proc2* and *proc3*, but the essence of the figure would be no different if those procedures happened to be later activations of *proc1* itself. This is equivalent to picturing how the stack would look just after recursive procedure *proc1* has called itself twice (*see* RECURSION). As far as the recursive logic is concerned, additional activation records may be created indefinitely, bounded only by the amount of memory available to enlarge the stack. But lack of such a resource is exactly what usually causes a runaway recursive procedure to abort. A properly written recursive routine will contain terminal conditions and an inductive step that relates to those conditions in such a way that the stack will accumulate activation records only until a terminal condition is reached, and then recede to its original status as each successive stage feeds information back to the stage that called it.

Bibliography

1979. Calingaert, P. *Assemblers, Compilers, and Program Translation*. Potomac, MD: Computer Science Press.

1991. Federighi, F. D., and Reilly, E. D. *VAX Assembly Language Programming*. New York: Macmillan.

1996. Sethi, R. *Programming Languages: Concepts and Structures*, 2nd Ed. Reading, MA: Addison-Wesley.

Edwin D. Reilly

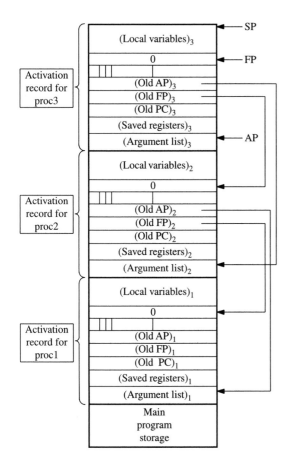

Figure 2. VAX activation records on a stack.

ADA

a

b

c

d

e

f

g

h

i

j

k

l

m

n

o

p

q

r

s

t

u

v,w

x,y

z

For articles on related subjects, see

+ Abstract Data Type
+ Concurrent Programming
+ Embedded System
+ Information Hiding
+ Object-Oriented Programming
+ Package
+ Programming Languages
+ Real-Time Systems
+ Structured Programming

History

Ada was initiated with the intent that it would supersede the hundreds of languages then in use in the US Department of Defense (DoD) for critical systems. It was the outcome of an engineering project initiated and technically managed at the Office of the Director of Defense Research and Engineering. The rationale of the initiative was that (1) the use of a high-level language (HLL) reduces programming costs; increases the readability of programs and the ease of their modification; and facilitates maintenance, and (2) a new HLL was needed to let real-time, parallel, and input–output portions of programs be expressed at that level rather than in assembly language inserts that destroy program readability and transportability.

The DoD High Order Language Working Group (HOLWG) was chartered in 1975 to formulate the requirements, to evaluate existing languages against those requirements, and to implement the minimal set (perhaps one) of high-level computer programming languages appropriate for DoD-embedded computer systems. David Fisher, acting as Secretariat for the HOLWG, assembled, sifted, correlated, and integrated the requirements. This was not a research effort; HOLWG was a committee of users, not language designers.

An initial requirements document (STRAWMAN) was circulated to the military departments, other government agencies, the academic community, and industry, including technical experts outside the USA.

Requirements proceeded through further generations with worldwide technical input (WOODENMAN, TIN-MAN, IRONMAN, to STEELMAN). The final name, Ada, was chosen to honor Augusta Ada Byron (*see* LOVELACE, COUNTESS OF).

The next phase of the program was the award of contracts for the design. Four contractors were funded to produce competitive prototypes. A first-phase evaluation reduced the designs to two (Cii Honeywell-Bull and Intermetrics), which were continued through a second phase. A number of teams representing various interests, applications, and organizations, analyzed reports from many reviewers. On 2 May 1979, a meeting of the HOLWG, including the representatives of the UK, France, and Germany, unanimously selected the design (code-named "Green") of the international Cii team led by Jean Ichbiah, "the designer of Ada." The cost of the program from the beginning through final language selection and the beginning of the validation effort was $4.1 million.

The DoD established an Ada Joint Program Office (JPO), a follow-on to the HOLWG, to continue support of Ada. Through the usual Ada open process, the definition was refined to MIL-STD 1815A, and this was endorsed by ANSI (American National Standards Institute) in February 1983, and as ISO (International Organization for Standardization) Standard 8652 in 1987.

As required by the Standard's processes, an "Ada 9X" project was launched to update Ada. The project leader at the primary contractor, Intermetrics, was Tucker Taft. The principal thrust was to facilitate object-oriented programming while remaining almost entirely compatible with the existing 1983 Ada. In February 1995, the ISO adopted the revision of Ada as ANSI/ISO/IEC 8652:1995. The ANSI adopted the new standard, called Ada 95, in April 1995. The original became Ada 83, and "Ada" now generally refers to Ada 95.

The Language

Although the early Ada development was heavily influenced by Pascal (*q.v.*), extensive syntactic changes and semantic extensions make it a very different language. The major additions to the basic Pascal block-structured model include:

- module structures and interface specifications for large-program organizations and separate compilation;
- encapsulation (*q.v.*) facilities and generic definitions to support abstract data types;
- support for concurrent processing; and
- control over low-level implementation issues related to the architecture of target machines.

There are three major abstraction tools in Ada. The *package* (*q.v.*) is used for encapsulating a set of related definitions and isolating them from the rest of the program. The *type* determines the states (values) an object (variable or data structure) may take on and its predefined behaviors (set of valid operations). The *generic* definition allows many similar instances of a definition to be generated from a single template. There is also support for parallel processing (*q.v.*), including concurrently executable code segments called *tasks* and language facilities for synchronization.

Bibliography

1986. Ichbiah, J. D., Barnes, G. P., Firth, R. J., and Woodger, M. *Rationale for the Design of the Ada Programming Language.* Washington, DC: Ada Joint Program Office.

1996. Whitaker, W. A. "Ada—The Project: The DoD High Order Language Working Group," in *History of Programming Languages* (eds. T. J. Bergin Jr., and R. G. Gibson), Ch. V, 173–232. Reading, MA: Addison-Wesley.

1998. Feldman, M. B. "Ada 95 in Context," in *Handbook of Programming Languages*, Vol. 1, Chapter 10. London: Macmillan Technical Publishing.

1998. Taft, S. T., and Duff, R. A. *Ada 95 Reference Manual.* New York: Springer-Verlag.

William A. Whitaker and Michael Feldman

ADA, AUGUSTA

See LOVELACE, COUNTESS OF.

ADDER

For articles on related subjects, *see*

+ **Arithmetic, Computer**
+ **Arithmetic-Logic Unit (ALU)**
+ **Central Processing Unit (CPU)**
+ **Computer Circuitry**
+ **Logic Design**
+ **Pipeline**

An *adder* is a logic network that forms the sum of two or more numbers represented by digit vectors (strings of digits). The simplest adder is the binary one-position adder, or *full adder* (FA) (*see* Fig. 1), in which the ith

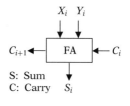

(a) Diagram

X_i	Y_i	C_i	S_i	C_{i+1}
0	0	0	0	0
0	0	1	1	0
0	1	0	1	0
0	1	1	0	1
1	0	0	1	0
1	0	1	0	1
1	1	0	0	1
1	1	1	1	1

(b) Function (truth) table

Figure 1. The binary full adder (FA).

bits of two summands (X_i, Y_i) and the carry C_i from the (previous) stage $(i-1)$ are added to form the ith sum bit S_i and the carry C_{i+1} to the (next) stage $(i+1)$. A *ripple-carry adder* for two n-bit binary numbers is formed by connecting n full adders in cascade (Fig. 2). The addition time of the ripple-carry adder corresponds to the worst-case delay, which is n times the time required to form the C_{i+1} (carry) output by one full adder, plus the time to form the S_i output, given the C_i input. Higher speed for two-operand addition can be attained by the use of *carry-completion sensing, carry-lookahead, carry-select,* and *conditional-sum* techniques (Koren, 1993). In these techniques, additional logic elements are employed to reduce the carry propagation delay in the adder network.

One-position adders for a higher radix r (for example, 4, 8, 10, or 16) are similar to the full adder of Fig. 1. The digits X_i and Y_i assume values 0 to $r-1$, and they are represented by two or more binary variables. The values of S_i and C_{i+1} for any radix $r \geq 2$ are determined by the following expressions:

$$C_{i+1} = \begin{cases} 0 & \text{if } X_i + Y_i + C_i \leq r-1 \\ 1 & \text{if } X_i + Y_i + C_i \geq r \end{cases}$$

$$\text{for } i = 0, 1, ..., n-1 \text{ with } C_0 = 0$$

$$S_i = X_i + Y_i + C_i - r \times C_{i+1}$$

$$\text{for } i = 0, 1, ..., n-1 \text{ with } S_n = C_n.$$

The adder speed-up techniques discussed for radix 2 also apply to two-operand addition of higher radix numbers.

Fast summation of three or more operands can be accomplished by the use of *carry-save adders* (CSA). A binary three-operand n-bit CSA is shown in Fig. 3. The third n-bit operand Z is entered on the C_i inputs of n binary full adders. The C_{i+1} outputs form a second output result $C = (C_n C_1)$ and the sum of the three input operands X, Y, Z is represented by two output results, C and $S = (S_{n-1} S_0)$. The time required to form C and S is equal to the time required by one binary full adder. The final sum, which is the sum of C and S, is then obtained in a two-operand adder, which may employ any of the speed-up techniques discussed above. CSAs are frequently employed to implement fast multiplication by means of multiple-operand summation. A *pipeline* (*q.v.*) may also be used to improve the effective speed of CSA utilization.

A *signed-digit adder* is a two-operand adder in which numbers are stored in a form such that carry propagation is not needed and the addition time is independent of the length of the operands. The addition of two signed-digit numbers of *any* length requires only the time needed to add two one-digit numbers (Avižienis, 1990). Signed-digit (SD) numbers for radix $r \geq 3$ are digit vectors in which the digits (X_i, Y_i) assume a set of values $\{-a, \ldots, -1, 0, 1, \ldots, a\}$, with $r-1 \geq$

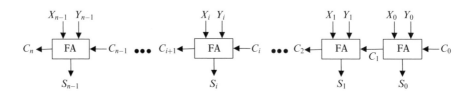

Figure 2. Binary ripple-carry adder.

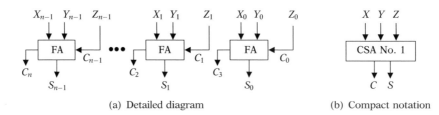

(a) Detailed diagram   (b) Compact notation

Figure 3. Three-operand binary carry-save adder.

$a \geq \lfloor r/2 + 1 \rfloor$ and with the place values corresponding to powers of the radix as with conventional radix r numbers. Thus, not only may there be more than one value of a for a given r but, in addition, there may be more than one SD number corresponding to a single radix r number. For example, with $r = 10$ and $a = 6$, the decimal number -2396 may be expressed in SD form as $-2\ -4\ 0\ 4$ or $-3\ 6\ 0\ 4$. However, the conversion algorithm assigns a specific SD number to each radix r number. Thus radix 10 may use the set $\{-a$ to $a\}$ with $a = 6, 7, 8$ or 9 and radix 16 may have $a = 9$, 10, 11, 12, 13, 14 or 15 but radix 4 must have $a = 3$. Radix 2 is a special case with the digit values $\{-1, 0, 1\}$.

Similar to CSAs, pipelining can be used in SD addition to increase the rate at which the sums are generated. Since signed-digit addition can be carried out left to right starting with the most significant digits, it has found useful application in, among other places, systolic arrays.

Bibliography

1990. Avižienis, A. "Signed-digit Number Representations for Fast Parallel Arithmetic," in *Computer Arithmetic* (ed. E. E. Swartzlander Jr.), Vol. II, 54–65. Los Alamitos, CA: IEEE Computer Society Press. (Reprinted from *IRE Trans. El. Comp.*, **EC-10** 1961, 389–400).

1993. Koren, I. *Computer Arithmetic Algorithms*. Upper Saddle River, NJ: Prentice Hall.

Algirdas Avižienis

ADDRESSING

For articles on related subjects, *see*

HARDWARE ASPECTS

A typical computer instruction must indicate not only the operation to be performed but also the location of one or more *operands*, and the location where the result of the computation is to be stored. All parts of the instruction must be either explicitly or implicitly given. We consider only storage in which each location has associated with it a sequentially assigned numerical address.

Historically and presently, computer hardware allows addresses to be specified in a variety of ways. The most straightforward approach would be to put the entire address directly into the instruction, representing a specific location of a word or part of a word in storage. As the amount of main memory increases, however, and the number of bits needed to represent an address becomes large relative to the size of the instruction, it is no longer feasible to represent an entire address each time it occurs. This is especially true when the address part of an instruction must be able to accommodate the largest possible storage that might be attached to a particular model of computer, even though a particular computer configuration might currently have only a small part of that storage.

Several hardware devices are employed to obtain, from one of a small number of larger registers, most of the information needed to specify an address, with the instruction itself containing only the information needed to complete the address. A number of these methods were employed as early as 1959 in the CDC 160 and 160A computers, early small machines that started out with 4096 12-bit words of storage. In the CDC 160, six bits were used for the operation code, while the other six bits (with only 64 possible values) were used in the determination of an address. By choosing an appropriate operation code, the address would be interpreted to be in one of five modes: direct address (d); indirect address (i); relative address forward (f) and backward (b); and no address (n).

In the direct addressing mode (d-mode), the address referred to an operand in one of the first 64 words of storage. Relative addressing provided for operand addresses and jump addresses that were near the storage location containing the current instruction. In relative addressing forward (f), the 6-bit address portion was added to the current contents of the program counter (PC–*q.v.*). This register held the full 12-bit address of the current instruction. The new value was then used for obtaining the operand or to jump to one of the 63 addresses forward from the address holding the instruction that was being executed. For relative addressing backward (b), the operand or jump address was obtained by subtracting the 6-bit address from the current contents of the PC. In the no-address mode (n), which is usually now referred to as the *immediate address* mode, the 6-bit address part was not treated as an address, but as a constant to be used in the actual computation.

Indirect Addressing

One way of addressing a memory larger than what the address part of an instruction allows is to have the instruction address point to another address that contains the operand address. This facility, called *indirect addressing* or *deferred addressing*, was available on the CDC 160 and on many subsequent computers up to the advent of reduced instruction set computers (RISC—*q.v.*). Figure 1 illustrates this situation on a hypothetical 16-bit computer with a 7-bit instruction field and a 9-bit address field that permits the direct addressing of only 512 ($=2^9$) memory locations. Indirect addressing can be used to address a memory of up to 65 536 words. In the example in Fig. 1, the program has placed the (octal) operand address 021326 at a specific address (125) in the first 512 words of memory. If the instruction is, for example, an "add indirect" instruction, indirect address 125 points to the address stored at 125 (namely, 021326), which becomes the *effective address*.

Index Registers

The concept of an *index register* (*q.v.*) grew out of the B-register (named, in contrast to the accumulator, the *A-register*), introduced on some of the earliest Manchester University computers (*q.v.*). Index registers are hardware registers that can be set, incremented, tested, and so on, by machine instructions. Each instruction contains an indication as to whether its address is to be added to (or subtracted from) the contents of a designated index register to form the effective address. One of the main purposes was to allow the effective address to be used as an index into a set of contiguous memory locations commonly referred to as an *array*. Without changing the part of the address that was in the instruction itself, one could refer to one after another of the contiguous locations merely by successively adding 1 to the contents of the index register.

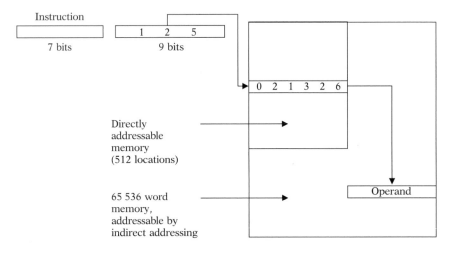

Figure 1. Extension of addressing through indirect addressing.

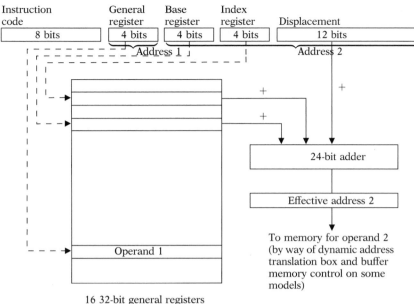

Figure 2.   Effective address calculation on the IBM 360.

The use of index registers eliminated the need for modification of the instruction itself by allowing the index register to be modified by special instructions for that purpose. With the advent of *multiprocessing* (*q.v.*) and *multitasking* (*q.v.*), in which more than one job (*q.v.*) or task may be executing the same instructions at the same time, it has become vital that instructions not be modified during execution (*see* REENTRANT PROGRAM).

General Registers

The use of variable-length instructions became widespread in the 1960s and 1970s. The IBM System/360/370/390, for example, uses instructions that may take one, two, or three half-words for their representation. In the System/360, 16 *general registers* are provided, each capable of acting as an arithmetic register, a base register for relative addressing, or as an index register. An instruction might refer to only one or two of these registers, in which case only four bits would be needed in the instruction for each one, and it could fit in a half-word (16 bits). A full-word instruction could accommodate one reference to a general register (4 bits)

and a reference to a storage address. The latter could be a combination of a base register (4 bits), an index register designation (4 bits), and a 12-bit displacement, which could be used as a local offset from the contents of the base register. Figure 2 illustrates the determination of an effective address from a System/360 instruction.

Relocation Registers

Many computers have one or more hardware *relocation registers*, which aid in the implementation and running of multiprogramming (*q.v.*) systems. An example is the CDC Cyber series. A number of different programs may be in the computer memory, each occupying a contiguous area. Thus, program A might occupy the area from 40 000 to 67 777, but this program (as well as all other programs in memory) is written and loaded into memory as if the area it occupies actually has the addresses 0 to 27 777. When program A is given control, the address 40 000 is stored in the hardware relocation register, and this constant is automatically added to all memory reference addresses while program A is running. The program could have been loaded anywhere else in memory, and can be loaded into

a

different areas at different times. It will always produce the correct memory addresses, since all addressing is automatically made relative to the starting address of the area into which the program has been loaded. In computers of this type, another hardware register will contain the *field length* or program size. Any attempt to reference beyond the area occupied by the program will be trapped, and an error condition will be signaled.

A relocation register is quite different in nature from an index register or a register used as a base for relative addressing. It is a special hardware register whose contents can be accessed and changed only through the use of privileged instructions under the control of the operating system.

Bernard A. Galler and Saul Rosen

SOFTWARE ASPECTS

Corresponding to each hardware-addressing mode, there must be one or more techniques by which the programmer specifies addresses in the program.

Absolute Addressing

In the earliest and most elementary programming systems, a programmer would assign instructions and data to locations in memory, and instructions would refer to absolute locations in memory. Thus, using a decimal computer for convenience, a programmer might write 267 ADD 3256 and, as a result of the eventual loading process, the instruction ADD 3256 would appear in location 267. It was the responsibility of the programmer to make sure that the appropriate data word was in location 3256 at the time the program was to be run. These are absolute addresses, in that 267 always represents the same physical location in memory and 3256 similarly represents a specific physical location.

Relative Addressing

The first significant advance in programming involved permitting the programmer to write programs or parts of programs without having to be aware of the absolute physical locations where the instructions and

data were to be stored. One of the early approaches to this goal was by way of regional or relative programming. The program would be divided into a number of regions, A, B, C, D, and so on. Addresses would then be relative to the start of a region. A programmer might write 5 ADD B15 to specify that an instruction located in the fifth location in region A is to add (to the accumulator) the data located in the fifteenth location in region B. A translator and loader would eventually take all regional addresses and convert them into absolute addresses. There are a number of important advantages to this procedure. The programmer does not have to make arbitrary decisions about how large the regions are going to be. Separate sections of the program can be written independently, and unexpected or undesirable interactions can be avoided.

Indirect Addressing

In a computer that allows indirect addressing, the assembly language programmer typically indicates an indirect address by adding a character such as * to the absolute or symbolic address, or by enclosing it in parentheses. Thus, ADD ALPHA* would indicate that the effective address is not ALPHA, but is in the location specified by ALPHA.

Indexing

If an index register is to be used in calculating an effective address, this is normally specified following the instruction address. For example, ADD A, 4 indicates that the contents of index register 4 is to be added (subtracted on some computers) to A to determine the effective address. Indexing can be combined with indirect addressing so that ADD A*, 4 would specify the effective address as the sum of the contents of location A and index register 4.

Overlays

Many programs are too long to fit into the space in main memory that can be allocated to them at run time. In a uniprogramming system, this will be true when the amount of space required by the program is greater than the total memory available to problem programs. In a multiprogramming system, it may be true because the amount of space that is needed is more than what the operating system is willing to allocate to this particular program. In either case, it becomes necessary to break the program up into sections, segments, or overlays so that the entire program need not be in main memory at the same time. The term *folding* has sometimes been used for this process.

There have been a number of efforts to produce software systems that provided automatic folding of programs. In such systems, a programmer would write a program as if there were enough main memory to contain the whole program, and the software system would organize the program into overlays to fit into the actual amount of storage that was available. Efforts to produce software systems of this type date back to the earliest computers, but none was particularly successful until the advent of the so-called *virtual memory* (*q.v.*) systems that first made their appearance around 1959, became increasingly common in the 1970s, and became ubiquitous in the 1990s.

Bibliography

1996. Hamacher, C. V., Vranesic, Z. G., and Zaky, S. G. *Computer Organization*, 4th Ed. New York: McGraw-Hill.

1982. Siewiorek, D. P., Bell, C. G., and Newell, A. *Computer Structures: Principles and Examples*. New York: McGraw-Hill.

Saul Rosen

AIKEN, HOWARD HATHAWAY

For articles on related subjects, see

✛ Digital Computers, History of: Early
✛ Hopper, Grace Murray
✛ Mark I, Harvard

Howard Hathaway Aiken (Fig. 1) was born on 8 March 1900 in Hoboken, NJ, and died on

Figure 1.   Howard Aiken.

14 March 1973 in St Louis, MO. He grew up in Indianapolis, where he attended Arsenal Technical High School. In 1923, he received his B.A. degree from the University of Wisconsin. He then went to work for Madison Gas where he became chief engineer.

In 1935, he returned to study first at the University of Chicago and then at Harvard. His doctoral thesis at Harvard, resulting in a Ph.D. in 1939, was on the theory of space-charge conduction. The research required laborious calculations of nonlinear differential equations. This experience led him to investigate the possibility of performing these types of calculations with machine assistance. With the encouragement of two Harvard professors, Harlow Shapley and Ted Brown, and the knowledge that IBM had the necessary technology, Aiken approached Thomas Watson Sr. A contract was signed in 1939, whereby IBM would build the Automatic Sequence Controlled Calculator (Harvard Mark I). The machine was running in 1944, and Aiken and Grace Hopper described it in a paper in *Electrical Engineering*, reprinted in Randell (1982). The Mark I was followed by the Mark II (a relay machine completed in 1946), the Mark III (an electronic machine completed in 1950), and the Mark IV (an electronic machine delivered to the US Air Force in 1952).

It is difficult to evaluate precisely the impact of Aiken's work at the Harvard Computation Laboratory, which he founded. He was a great teacher as well as an innovator. The Harvard catalog of his period provides clear evidence of the existence of courses in "computer science" a decade before the emergence of this program at most universities.

After Aiken retired from Harvard in 1961, he formed Aiken Industries in Florida and joined the faculty at the University of Miami. He was clearly a man of rare vision, whose insights have had a profound effect on the entire computing profession.

Bibliography

1982. Randell, B. (ed.) *The Origins of Digital Computers*, 3rd Ed. New York: Springer-Verlag.

1984. Williams, M. R. "Howard Aiken and the Harvard Computation Laboratory," *Annals of the History of Computing*, **6**(2), 157–159.

1984. Hurd, C. C. "Aiken Observed," *Annals of the History of Computing*, **6**(2), 160–162.

1999. Cohen, I. B. *Howard Aiken: Portrait of a Computer Pioneer*. Cambridge, MA: MIT Press.

Henry S. Tropp

ALGOL

For articles on related subjects, see

+ Block Structure
+ Procedure-Oriented Languages
+ Programming Languages

The development goal for the programming language *Algol* was to establish a notation for programs that would be a suitable carrier of algorithms and programs among computers of different types and capabilities. Algol was the result of a collaboration of American and European committees. When the work was initiated in 1956, the computing scene in Europe was still dominated by one-of-a-kind computers, while in the USA the most commonly used computers were from manufacturers' standard series.

The problems of designing adequate programs were becoming acute everywhere. One approach to overcoming these problems was to replace the cumbersome machine languages by more convenient notations. The selection of such notations was guided by the applications of computers in science and engineering. Numerical techniques build principally on operands that are numerals in floating-point form. Thus, programming notations came to be inspired by the algebraic notations that had a long tradition in mathematical analysis.

The idea of establishing a programming notation that would be equally suitable in programming computers of different makes and types was first proposed in Europe in 1955, and it became the subject of a working group of GAMM (Gesellschaft für Angewandte Mathematik und Mechanik). In 1957, this group joined a similar effort conducted within the Association for Computing Machinery (ACM—*q.v.*). In June 1958, a GAMM-ACM working conference in Zurich worked out a proposal for an algebraic programming language, Algol 58, designed for use in programming a variety of computers, as well as for describing algorithms in publications. As a result of intense public discussion, a 13-person committee met in Paris in January 1960, where a new version of the language, Algol 60, was discussed and agreed upon. Some minor corrections to Algol 60 were published in the *Revised Report on the Algorithmic Language Algol 60* in 1962.

The problems discussed and solved during the development of Algol were those that were imposed so that the resulting notation would be suitable both for wide communication and for programming of many different computers. This implied the requirements that both the meaning of the computational processes described in the notation and the description of the notation itself would be clear and unambiguous. An induced requirement was that, for reasons of expediency, the computational processes made available to the user of the notation had to allow effective description in brief terms. Mechanisms made available to the user of the notation had, as far as possible, to be describable in terms of a few rules that were generally valid, without exceptions.

The first proposal for the language, Algol 58, solved many of the problems. It introduced the idea that there would be three *representations* of the language (reference, publication, and hardware) such that the meaning of texts expressed in the language would only be defined in terms of the reference representation, while the typographical forms used in the publication and hardware representations were left to be chosen by users and implementers.

In Algol 58, as in earlier programming languages such as Fortran (*q.v.*), the meaning of each identifier used in a program had to be defined in an explicit or implicit *declaration* (*q.v.*). In Algol 58, each identifier could be declared to denote either an integer or real quantity (intended to be implemented as a floating-point representation), an array of integers or reals having fixed subscript bounds, a label, a switch, a function, or a procedure. The functions and procedures of Algol 58 were designed to be effective in communicating computational processes in publication. Thus, they provided for flexible control through parameters of a variety of types and forms. The problems raised by Algol 58 and solved in Algol 60 were mostly induced by the incompleteness and ambiguity of Algol 58. However, it was found that the most effective solutions of the problems might be achieved, not by minor corrections of the earlier description, but through radical redesign, aiming at generality and simplicity of both the language mechanisms and of their description.

The major part of the redesign of the language mechanisms related to the following:

- *The scope of identifiers*: to allow programs to include procedures taken from a library, the language had to provide means for restricting the meaning and use of any identifier to the text of one procedure;

- *Dynamic declarations*: while Algol 58 provided only for arrays whose size was fixed with the program, Algol 60 provided for arrays whose size depended on quantities calculated by the program;
- *The structure of programs*: solving the problems of the scope of identifiers and the dynamics of declarations depended on establishing suitable static and dynamic program structures;
- *The static and dynamic handling of procedure parameters.*

The solutions adopted in Algol 60 rested on a static program structure of nested blocks. Each declaration of the meaning of an identifier belonged statically to a block, being valid for any inner nested blocks unless superseded by another declaration of the same identifier within that inner block. The dynamic meaning of a declaration was determined at the moment of entry of program control into the block in which the declaration belonged.

The dynamic meaning of a procedure parameter might be determined by the programmer either at the moment of the procedure call (call by value) or at the moment of reference to the parameter (call by name). As an incidental consequence of the solutions adopted for the program and procedure structures, Algol 60 provided for *recursion* (*q.v.*). The description of Algol 60 employed a formal notation of productions, later called Backus–Naur form (BNF–*q.v.*). With this notation, the syntactic descriptions of language constructs were coupled to the descriptions of their dynamic meanings through the use of identical designations.

The influence of Algol 60 on many later programming language developments is visible both in the capabilities of such languages and in the terminology employed in describing them. Several significant later languages, such as Simula and Pascal (*q.v.*), extended Algol 60 by providing additional operand types.

Bibliography

1963. Naur, P. (ed.) "Revised Report on the Algorithmic Language ALGOL 60," *Communications of the ACM*, **6**(1), 1–17. Reprinted in 1987. *Programming Languages: A Grand Tour* (ed. E. Horowitz), 3rd Ed., 44–60. Rockville, MD: Computer Science Press.

a

1981. Perlis, A. J. *The American Side of the Development of ALGOL*, 75–91; Naur, P. *The European Side of the Last Phase of the Development of ALGOL 60*, 92–139; in Wexelblat, R. (ed.) *History of Programming Languages*. New York: Academic Press.

Peter Naur

ALGORITHM

For articles on related subjects, *see*

+ Algorithms, Analysis of
+ Algorithms, Design and Classification of
+ Algorithms, Theory of
+ Program Verification
+ Searching
+ Sorting
+ Turing Machine

In discussing problem solving, we presuppose both a problem and a device to be used in solving it. The problem may be mathematical or nonmathematical in nature, simple or complex. The basic requirements for a well-posed problem are that (1) the known information is clearly specified; (2) we can determine when the problem has been solved; and (3) the problem does not change during its attempted solution. The device to be used for problem solution may be human or machine, or a combination of the two.

Definition

Given both the problem and the device, an *algorithm* is characterized by these properties:

1. Application of the algorithm to a particular input set or problem description results in a finite sequence of actions.
2. The sequence of actions has a unique initial action.
3. Each action in the sequence has a unique successor.
4. The sequence terminates with either a solution to the problem or a statement that the problem is unsolvable for that set of data.

We illustrate these concepts with an example: "Find the square root of the real number x." As stated, this problem is algorithmically either trivial or unsolvable, owing to the irrationality of most square roots. If we accept $\sqrt{2}$ as the square root of 2, for example, the solution is trivial: the answer is the square root sign ($\sqrt{}$) concatenated with the input. However, if we want a decimal expression, then the square root of 2 can never be calculated exactly since the requirement of a finite number of actions would be violated.

A modified statement of the problem is more suited to our purposes: "Find the positive square root of the real number x to four decimal places." This statement has three useful properties:

1. It explicitly names the *positive* square root as the desired one, whereas the earlier statement left that quality ambiguous.
2. It eliminates the string $\sqrt{x}$ as a problem solution.
3. By stating "four decimal places" (or any other fixed number of places), it provides a test for termination.

A conceivable but questionable method of solution is as follows:

1. Choose a number y and compute y^2.
2. If $|y^2 - x| < 5 \times 10^{-5}$, the solution is y; if not, return to step (1).

This method fails to be an algorithm, since no procedure is specified for choosing either the initial value y or subsequent values. And, even if there is a solution, there is no guarantee that this method will find it.

Now consider another method:

1. Let $y = 1$.
2. Compute y^2.
3. If $|y^2 - x| < 5 \times 10^{-5}$, the solution is y, HALT; if not, continue with step 4.
4. Replace y by $((x/y) + y)/2$; go to step 2.

This procedure is a special case of a general technique known as the Newton–Raphson method, which has the precise definition of each step required of an algorithm. Moreover, whenever applied to a nonnegative real number x, the method will produce the proper solution in a finite number of steps. However, whenever applied to a negative number, the method will endlessly recompute y without recognizing the futility of the task. This is typical of a class of methods called *semialgorithms*: they will halt in a finite number of steps if the problem posed has a solution, but will not necessarily halt if there is no solution.

To transform this method into an algorithm, two things must be done:

1. Add a step, (0); if $x < 0$, there is no solution; HALT; and
2. Rewrite the given method in a notation suitable for the proposed device. In pseudocode, for example,

```
Input x
Output y          [An approximation to √x̄]
Algorithm SquareRoot
  print Find the square root of x
  if x ≥ 0 then
      y ← 1
    repeat until |y² − x| < .00005
        y ← ((x/y) + y)/2
    endrepeat
    print The square root of x is y.
  else
    print There is no real square root for x.
  endif
```

This algorithm requests input data and then responds with the square root of the input, or a message that there is no real square root. Although this algorithm concerns the solution of a numerical problem, algorithms can be applied to a wide variety of nonnumerical problems, for example, searching (*q.v.*) and sorting (*q.v.*).

Quality Judgments on Algorithms

Any computer program is at least a semialgorithm, and any program that always halts is an algorithm. (Of course, it may not solve the problem for which the programmer intended it.) Given a solvable problem, there are usually many algorithms (programs) to solve it, not all of equal quality. The primary practical criteria by which the quality of an algorithm is judged are time and memory requirements, accuracy of solution, and generality. Questions of the minimal time and storage requirements posed by a given class of problems, and of

the time and storage requirements of any proposed algorithm, have, despite the increasing speed of computers and decreasing cost of storage, become increasingly important (*see* COMPUTATIONAL COMPLEXITY).

Bibliography

1990. Cormen, T. H., Leiserson, C. E., and Rivest, R. L. *Introduction to Algorithms*. Cambridge, MA: MIT Press.
1992. Sedgewick, R. *Algorithms in C++*. Reading, MA: Addison-Wesley.
2000. Berlinski, D. *The Advent of the Algorithm*. New York: Harcourt Brace.

Robert R. Korfhage

ALGORITHMS, ANALYSIS OF

For articles on related subjects, *see*

+ Algorithm
+ Algorithms, Design and Classification of
+ Algorithms, Theory of
+ Computational Complexity
+ Graph Theory
+ NP-Complete Problems
+ Searching
+ Sorting

Analysis of algorithms consists of algorithm complexity and problem complexity. The former analyzes the behavior of a specific algorithm with respect to the amount of memory space, time, or other resources needed for a problem. The latter analyzes the minimum requirements of space and time or other resources for the class of *all* algorithms for that problem.

With each problem, we associate an integer called the *size* of the problem. For example, the size of a matrix inversion problem is the dimension of the matrix, the size of a graph problem is the number of edges, and so on. The growth rate of the execution time of the algorithm is determined as a function of the size of the problem. The limiting behavior of the growth rate

a

is called the *asymptotic growth rate*. For example, the asymptotic behavior of the function $17 + 5n + 2n^2$ is $2n^2$, since, for sufficiently large n, $2n^2$ approximates $17 + 5n + 2n^2$ to arbitrary accuracy. For $n > 100$, the lower-order terms account for less than 3%.

The asymptotic growth rate of an algorithm is expressed in terms of functions whose domain is the set of natural numbers. We measure the asymptotic running time by *upper bounds* and *lower bounds*. We denote an *asymptotic upper bound* for a function by O-notation to give an upper bound on the function to within a constant factor. Given a function $g(n)$, $O(g(n))$ is defined as $O(g(n)) = \{f(n) |$ there exist positive constants c, n_0 such that $0 \le f(n) \le cg(n)$ for all $n \ge n_0\}$. Intuitively, $f(n)$ is in $O(g(n))$ if the graph of $f(n)$ lies on or below the graph of $cg(n)$ for all values of n greater than n_0. We denote an *asymptotic lower bound* for a function by Ω-notation to give a corresponding lower bound on the function. Given a function $g(n)$, $\Omega(g(n))$ is defined as $\Omega(g(n)) = \{f(n) |$ there exist positive constants c, n_0 such that $0 \le cg(n) \le f(n)$ for all $n \ge n_0\}$. Intuitively, $f(n)$ is in $\Omega(g(n))$ if the graph of $f(n)$ lies on or above the graph of $cg(n)$ for all values of n greater than n_0.

On small problems, the asymptotic growth rate is unimportant and most algorithms perform reasonably well. However, on a high-speed computer, the problem size normally encountered is large and the asymptotic growth rate becomes important. Given two algorithms with growth rates $O(n^2)$ and $O(2^n)$ and similar values of c, for problems up to size 6, the difference in execution times is never more than a factor of 2. If the problem size is 100, though, the $O(n^2)$ algorithm is easily executed, whereas the $O(2^n)$ algorithm would require centuries to compute.

Algorithm Complexity

Space and Time

Economies of space and time are the most important aspects of algorithm complexity. An algorithm that requires relatively little memory space may have a greater running time than another algorithm that requires more space, while both algorithms may provide a solution to the same problem. Thus, there is frequently a trade-off between space and time.

Frequency Analysis

A *frequency analysis* of an algorithm reveals the number of times certain parts of the algorithm are executed. Such an analysis indicates which parts of the algorithm consume large quantities of time and, hence, where efforts should be directed toward improving the algorithm. Consider, for example, the polynomial evaluation problem of the preceding article. The asymptotic running time for evaluating the polynomial expression as originally written is $O(n^2)$, but the expression rewritten in accord with Horner's Rule runs in just $O(n)$.

Execution Time

To determine the actual execution time of an algorithm requires knowledge of the operation times for each instruction of the computer on which the algorithm is to be executed and how the compiler generates code. It is customary to find upper and lower bounds c_1 and c_2 such that the execution time of every instruction is between c_1 and c_2. Then the execution time of an algorithm can be estimated from a count of the number of operations that are executed. This frees the analysis of the algorithm from peculiarities of individual computers.

Frequently, the time required by an algorithm is data dependent. In this case, one of two types of analyses is possible. The first is called the *worst-case analysis*, in which that set of data of given size requiring the most work is determined and the behavior of the algorithm is analyzed for that specific set of data. The other alternative is to assume a probability distribution for the possible input data and compute the execution time as a function of the input distribution. Usually, this computation is so difficult that only the expected or average execution time as a function of size is computed. This is called the *average-case analysis*.

Problem Complexity

In problem complexity, we are concerned with analyzing a problem rather than an algorithm. The analysis provides us with lower bounds on the amount of time and space required for a solution to the problem, independent of the algorithm used. The lower bounds may be either worst-case or average-case bounds. These lower bounds can serve as an indication of how well an algorithm fits the problem and whether it can be improved. For example, such an analysis shows that any algorithm that evaluates an arbitrary n-degree polynomial represented by its coefficients requires at least n multiplications and n additions. Thus, Horner's rule cannot be improved upon.

On the other hand, an analysis of matrix multiplication gives a lower bound of order $\Omega(n^2)$ operations for multiplying two matrices of dimension n. The usual matrix multiplication algorithm has an asymptotic growth rate of $O(n^3)$. Thus, there is substantial interest in trying either to find a better lower bound or to improve on the current matrix multiplication algorithms. Currently, the asymptotically fastest known algorithm has a growth rate of $O(n^{2.376})$.

A major difficulty with problem analysis is that it is concerned with the class of all algorithms for a given problem. One can no longer postulate a computer with a given structure and instruction set. Instead, one must envision an abstract computer that is sufficiently general to encompass *any* physically implementable algorithm. The difficulties involved are of such magnitude that one is forced to obtain bounds for certain limited classes of programs. For example, sorting n integers can be shown to require $n \log n$ operations if restricted to the class of algorithms that sort by binary (two at a time) comparisons. Almost all known lower bounds are either linear in the size of the problem or have been obtained by restricting the classes of algorithms. One of the major goals of computer scientists working in the analysis of algorithms is to close the gaps in our knowledge of problem complexity.

Bibliography

1974. Aho, A. V., Hopcroft, J. E., and Ullman, J. D. *The Design and Analysis of Computer Algorithms.* Reading, MA: Addison-Wesley.

1997, 1997, 1998. Knuth, D. E. *The Art of Computer Programming*, Vols. 1 (3rd Ed.), 2 (3rd Ed.), 3 (2nd Ed.). Reading, MA: Addison-Wesley.

2001. Cormen, T. H., Leiserson, C. E., Rivest, R. L., and Stein, C. *Introduction to Algorithms*, 2nd Ed. Cambridge, MA: MIT Press.

John E. Hopcroft and Daniela Rus

ALGORITHMS, DESIGN AND CLASSIFICATION OF

For articles on related subjects, *see*

+ Algorithm
+ Algorithms, Analysis of
+ Algorithms, Theory of
+ Computational Complexity
+ Graph Theory
+ Searching
+ Sorting

Introduction

Although it is very difficult to determine that *no* algorithm exists to solve a particular problem, the challenge is to find one. Once one is found, it can then be analyzed for its time and space efficiency. But that leads to the question of whether a still better algorithm for this problem exists. So, algorithm design is just as important as algorithm analysis. Though there are thousands of algorithms, there are very few design techniques.

Divide-and-Conquer

With the *divide-and-conquer* strategy, a problem is split into subproblems, which are somehow solved, and then the solutions are combined into a solution for the original problem. The subproblems can usually be solved recursively in the same way—by splitting, solving, and combining (*see* RECURSION). An ideal example of divide-and-conquer is *mergesort*, a method for sorting a set of numbers or character strings. First, divide the set into two approximately equal size sets. Then sort each set individually. Next, take the resulting sorted subsets and merge them to produce a single sorted set for the entire data. The algorithm is recursive so that to sort one-half of the data, that data is again divided into two roughly equal parts, sorted in the same manner, and then merged. A recursive Pascal (*q.v.*) version of this algorithm is shown in Fig. 1.

Greedy Method

The *greedy method* is possibly the simplest of the design techniques. Consider an *optimization problem* that has

```
Procedure mergesort (var x: afile; low, high: integer)
{the consecutive elements (x[low],…,x[high])are sorted.}
var mid: integer;
begin
  if low < high then
   begin
    mid: = (low + high) div 2;
    mergesort (x, low, mid);{apply algorithm recursively}
    mergesort (x, mid + 1, high); {apply algorithm recursively}
    merge (x, low, high); {merge the two results}
   end
end; {mergesort}
```

Figure 1.   A Pascal version of mergesort.

n inputs and requires an algorithm that finds a subset of the inputs that satisfy a certain constraint. Any subset that satisfies these constraints is called a *feasible solution*. The goal is to find not only a feasible solution, but one that either maximizes or minimizes a given objective function. A feasible solution that does this is called an *optimal* solution. Often it is easy to determine feasible solutions, but much harder to determine optimal solutions. The greedy method constructs a feasible solution in stages, at each stage adding the most promising element to what had previously been chosen. In some cases, greedy algorithms will produce the optimal result. In other cases, they can be used to derive approximate solutions when programs based on the optimal algorithm take intolerably long times to execute.

Optimal Greedy Solutions

The greedy strategy leads to a simple sorting algorithm that works this way: look at the remaining elements to be sorted, select the smallest, and place it at the end of the list of already sorted elements. This is called *selection sort*, and its computing time on n elements is $O(n^2)$. Though it is simple to conceive and to write, it is not very efficient.

Another problem for which the greedy method does produce an optimal solution is the problem of making change using the fewest number of coins. For example, if the cost of an item is 37 cents and the customer hands the clerk a one-dollar bill, then the clerk might return a 50-cent coin, a 10-cent coin and 3 pennies. These five coins are the *minimum* number of coins that could be used to make up the difference between one dollar and 37 cents. The greedy strategy leads us to postulate an algorithm that at each stage returns the largest coin possible without going over the one-dollar limit. A proof that this strategy yields the minimum number of coins is not hard.

Approximate Greedy Solutions

As an example of how the greedy method can be used to create an approximation algorithm, suppose you have m machines, all identical, and you have a set of n jobs that need to be carried out on the machines, $n > m$. The times for the n jobs vary. You want to schedule the jobs on the machines so as to complete all the jobs in the shortest time possible. The best-known algorithm that always finds the optimal (shortest time) assignment of jobs to processors for arbitrary m, n, and job times takes exponential time. For most reasonably sized problems, that makes the exact solution infeasible. The greedy method provides an algorithm that produces a reasonably good approximation quickly. It considers the jobs in order from the longest to the shortest and assigns one job at a time to the next processor that becomes free. This greedy *heuristic* will always produce an answer that is within four-thirds of the optimal result.

Further examples of successful greedy algorithms are optimal storage on tapes, Huffman codes (*see* DATA COMPRESSION), and finding minimal spanning trees or a shortest path on a graph (*see* GRAPH THEORY).

Dynamic Programming

Dynamic programming arises when an algorithm works by enumerating all possible configurations of the given data and testing each one to see if it is a solution. An essential idea is to keep a table of all previously computed configurations and their results. If the total number of configurations is large, the dynamic programming algorithm will require substantial time and space. However, if there are only a small number of distinct configurations, dynamic programming avoids recomputing the solution to these problems over and over.

To determine that there are only a small number of distinct configurations, one needs to detect when the so-called *principle of optimality* holds. This principle asserts that every decision that contributes to the final solution must be optimal with respect to the initial state. When this principle holds, dynamic programming drastically reduces the amount of computation by avoiding the enumeration of some decision sequences that cannot possibly be optimal.

As a simple example, consider computing the nth Fibonacci number, F_n, where $F_n = F_{n-1} + F_{n-2}$ and $F_0 = F_1 = 1$. The first few elements of this famous sequence are 1, 1, 2, 3, 5, 8, 13, 21, 34, ... The obvious recursive algorithm for computing F_n suffers from the fact that many values of F_i are computed over and over again. The total time for this recursive version is exponential. However, if we follow the dynamic programming strategy and create a table that contains all values of F_i as they are computed, a linear time algorithm results.

Some examples of dynamic programming algorithms are optimal binary search trees, optimal matrix arrangements, and the shortest path problem for all pairs of vertices in a graph.

Basic Traversal and Search

Often, complex objects are stored in a computer using a data structure (*q.v.*) composed of nodes that contain fields. These fields may contain either data or pointers to some other nodes. Thus, a particular instance of some object may include many nodes, all connected in an intricate pattern. Some typical examples of objects would be lists, trees (*q.v.*), binary trees, and graphs.

Often, one wants an algorithm that computes a function of the data object. The traversal-and-search strategy for developing such an algorithm is to move along the data structure from node to node and collect information. After all nodes have been reached, the final answer should be known. Some examples are traversals of binary trees, evaluation of postfix expressions, breadth-first and depth-first traversal of graphs, code optimization, "and/or" graphs of artificial intelligence (*q.v.*), and finding connected and biconnected components of a graph.

Backtracking

Backtracking is an appropriate algorithm design strategy when the desired solution is expressible in the form $(x_1, \ldots, x_n)$, in which each of the x_i is chosen from a finite set S_i. Often, the problem calls for finding one vector that maximizes, minimizes or satisfies some criterion function. Sometimes it seeks all such vectors. If the size of S_i is m_i, there are $m = m_1 \times \cdots \times m_n$ n-tuples that are possible candidates. The brute force approach would generate all of these n-tuples and evaluate each one. The idea of backtracking is to build up the vector one component at a time, using functions to test whether the vector being formed has any chance of success. Backtracking becomes most efficient when these functions are able to eliminate large sets of possible vectors.

A classic combinatorial problem is to place eight queens on an 8×8 chessboard so that no two "attack," that is, so that no two of them are in the same row, column, or diagonal. Assume that the rows and columns of the chessboard, as well as the eight queens, are numbered 1 to 8. We see that each queen will be on a separate row, so we can represent a solution to this problem by a vector, $(x_1, \ldots, x_8)$, in which x_i is the column on which queen i is placed. There are $8^8 = 16\,777\,218$ tuples, so if an algorithm attempts to enumerate all of these and requires 1/10 of a second to generate each one, the algorithm will require over 19 days to get its answer.

The backtracking solution makes use of two important facts that help prune the number of vectors it must consider. No two x_i can be the same (all queens in different columns). This reduces the number of tuples to $8! = 40\,320$. Also, no two x_is can be on the same diagonal. The backtracking algorithm will proceed by generating a tuple so that, if $(x_1, \ldots, x_i)$ has already been picked, x_{i+1} is chosen so that $(x_1, \ldots, x_{i+1})$ represents a chessboard configuration in which no two queens are attacking.

Figure 2 shows a chessboard on which queens have been placed in columns 1 to 5. But with the configuration shown, no queen can be placed in column 6. So we *backtrack* to column 5 and move the queen down column 5 looking for another "safe" square. However, none exists and so we backtrack again to column 4 and move the queen in this column down to row 7, which is also safe. Then we try again to put a queen in column 5, and so on. Eventually, we find a solution: $(1, 1), (5, 2), (8, 3), (6, 4), (3, 5), (7, 6), (2, 7), (4, 8)$. This is one of 92 solutions, only 12 of which

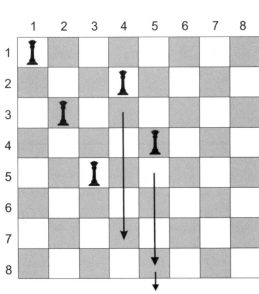

Figure 2. Backtracking in the eight queens problem.

are really distinct (i.e. not related to each other by some type of symmetry). All 92 solutions could be found by continuing as above by backtracking to column 7 after each solution is found.

Randomization Algorithms

The randomization algorithm design strategy is based on the principles of probability theory. The general idea is to use a random number generator (called a *randomizer*) to produce a set of inputs. The inputs are given to an algorithm that tests for the result. Probability theory is used to establish the fact that the algorithm is likely to find the correct result of reasonably quickly.

Suppose we toss a coin and watch how many times heads or tails appears. For three tosses of a coin there are eight possible outcomes {HHH, HHT, HTH, HTT, THH, THT, TTH, TTT}, in which H stands for Head and T for Tail. There are 2^8 possible events (i.e. combinations of possible outcomes), for example, the probability of the event {HHT, HTT, TTT} is 3/8. In general, the probability of an event is the ratio of the number of possible events divided by the total number of events that could occur, termed the *state space*. If one flips a coin 100 times, then the probability that the first outcome is T is 1/2. The probability that the second outcome is also T is 1/4, and the probability of obtaining 100 Ts in a row is $(1/2)^{100}$.

There are two categories of randomized algorithms. A *Las Vegas algorithm* always produces the same (correct) output for the same input, but its execution time depends upon the output of the randomizer and may vary widely. *Monte Carlo algorithms* may produce outputs that differ from execution to execution despite the same input, but they generally execute in the same (relatively short) time. For a Monte Carlo algorithm, we require that the probability of an incorrect answer be low (*see* MONTE CARLO METHOD).

A Simple Example

Consider an array of n numbers that has $n/2$ distinct elements and $n/2$ copies of another element. Any deterministic algorithm to discover the repeated element will require $(n/2) + 2$ comparisons in the worst case. A *Las Vegas algorithm* works as follows: two random elements are chosen and compared for equality. One must check that the random array *indices* are distinct before checking that the array *elements* are distinct. It is easy to show that the probability that the algorithm terminates in 10 iterations or less is greater than 0.94. The probability that the algorithm does not terminate in 100 iterations for $n > 20$ is about $(3/4)^{100}$ or approximately 3×10^{-13}, a very small number.

Randomized algorithms are generally simple and more efficient than the deterministic version. In many cases, the probability of producing an incorrect answer is smaller than the probability of the computer's hardware failing. For problems such as primality testing they are ideal.

Other Algorithm Design Techniques

Some other design techniques that we describe only briefly are

Branch-and-bound: This design strategy is similar to backtracking in attempting to find one or more vectors that satisfy some criteria. Instead of generating a solution vector element by element, however, all possible candidates for the next entry are produced and stored in a set. With effective bounding functions to prune the set, branch-and-bound can be quite efficient.

Transformation of domain: Sometimes it is easier to transform the data for a problem into another domain, solve the problem in the new domain, and then transform the solution back into the original domain. Examples of domain transformation include translating decimal numbers to binary notation before doing computer arithmetic, the fast Fourier transform, and algebraic operations such as polynomial arithmetic, greatest common divisor calculations, and factorization.

Preconditioning: If we have an algorithm that we know will be executed many times, sometimes we can improve its speed by precomputing a set of values that are reused in all or most of the problem cases. With proper preconditioning, only two comparisons

are needed to answer the question of ancestry in a binary tree. Other examples of successful use of preconditioning are repeated evaluation of a polynomial and searching for a pattern within a string (*see* STRING PROCESSING).

Bibliography

1984. Bentley, J. "Programming Pearls: Algorithm Design Techniques," *Communications of the ACM*, **27**(9), 865–871.

1988. Brassard, G., and Bratley, P. *Algorithmics: Theory and Practice*. Upper Saddle River, NJ: Prentice Hall.

1997. Horowitz, E., Sahni, S., and Rajasekaran, S. *Computer Algorithms in C++*. New York: Computer Science Press, imprint of W. H. Freeman and Co.

Ellis Horowitz

ALGORITHMS, THEORY OF

For articles on related subjects, *see*

+ Algorithm
+ Algorithms, Analysis of
+ Computational Complexity
+ Formal Languages
+ NP-Complete Problems
+ Turing Machine

In order to have a *theory of algorithms*, we need a mathematically precise definition of algorithm. We adopt that of Hopcroft and Ullman (1979): "*A procedure* is a finite sequence of instructions that can be mechanically carried out, such as a computer program. . . A procedure which always terminates is called an *algorithm*."

The recognition of whether or not a sequence of instructions is a procedure or an algorithm is subjective. All algorithms provide a solution to *some* problem, but not necessarily the one of interest to us. In the theory of computation, one is mainly concerned with algorithms that are used either for computing functions or for deciding predicates.

A function f with domain D and range R is a definite correspondence by which there is associated with each element x of the domain D (referred to as the "argument") a single element $f(x)$ of the range R (called the "value"). The function f is said to be *computable* (in the intuitive sense) if there exists an algorithm that, for any given x in D, provides us with the value $f(x)$. An example of a computable function is one that associates, with any pair of positive integers, their greatest common divisor. It is computable by the Euclidean algorithm (Knuth, 1997).

A *predicate P* with domain D is a property of the elements of D that each particular element of D either has or does not have. If x in D has the property P, we say that $P(x)$ is true; otherwise, we say that $P(x)$ is false. The predicate P is said to be *decidable* (in the intuitive sense) if there exists an algorithm that, for any given x in D, provides us with a definite answer to the question of whether or not $P(x)$ is true. An example of a decidable predicate over the set of integers greater than 1 is the predicate that determines whether a number is or is not *prime*. An algorithm for implementing this predicate is described by Hopcroft and Ullman (1979).

The computability of functions and the decidability of predicates are very closely related notions because we can associate with each predicate P a function f with range $\{0, 1\}$ such that, for all x in the common domain D of P and f, $f(x) = 0$ if $P(x)$ is true and $f(x) = 1$ if $P(x)$ is false. Clearly, P is decidable if and only if f is computable. For this reason we will hereafter restrict our attention to the computability of functions.

In order to show that a certain function is computable, it is sufficient to give an algorithm that computes it. But, without a precise definition of an algorithm, all such demonstrations are open to question. In order to avoid uncertainty, we need a mathematically precise definition of a computable function. One way of making the concept precise is to define an appropriate type of machine, and then define a function to be computable if and only if it can be computed by it. The machine usually used for this purpose is the *Turing machine* (*q.v.*). This simple device has a tape and a read–write head, together with a control that may be in one of finitely many states. The tape is used to represent

numbers. A function f is called computable if there exists a Turing machine which, given a tape representing an argument x, eventually halts with the tape representing the value $f(x)$.

The claim that a function is computable in the intuitive sense if and only if it is computable by a Turing machine is usually referred to as *Church's thesis* or the *Church–Turing thesis*. Such a claim can never be "proved," since one of the two notions whose equivalence is claimed is mathematically imprecise, but an overwhelming majority of workers in the theory of algorithms accept its validity.

Given a precise definition of a computable function, it is now possible to show for particular functions whether they are or are not computable.

Example 1   Consider the following problem. Give an algorithm that, for any Turing machine, decides whether or not the machine eventually stops if it is started on an empty tape. This problem is called the "blank-tape halting problem." The required algorithm would be considered a *solution* of the problem. A proof that there is no such algorithm would be said to show the (effective) *unsolvability* of the problem. The blank-tape halting problem is in fact unsolvable.

Example 2   Our second example indicates that there are unsolvable problems in classical mathematics. The following problem is known as "Hilbert's tenth problem" (after the German mathematician David Hilbert, 1862–1943):

Given a Diophantine equation (an equation of the form $E = 0$, where E is a polynomial with integer coefficients; e.g. $xy^2 - 2x^2 + 3 = 0$) with any number of variables, give a procedure with which it is possible to decide after a finite number of operations whether or not the equation has a solution in integers. This problem was stated by Hilbert in 1900. In 1970, the Russian mathematician Yuri Matiyasevich showed it to be unsolvable.

That there are clearly defined problems that cannot be solved by any computer-like device is probably the most striking aspect of the theory of algorithms. A whole superstructure has been built on such results (*see* Rogers, 1967).

Suppose we had a device that, for any given Turing machine, told us whether or not the Turing machine would eventually stop on the blank tape. Can we write an "algorithm" that makes use of this device and solves Hilbert's tenth problem? It has been known for some time that such an "algorithm" exists. In this sense, Hilbert's tenth problem is *reducible* to the blank-tape halting problem. It is the proof that the reverse is also true that gave us the unsolvability of Hilbert's tenth problem. Problems that are reducible one to the other are said to be *equivalent*. Most of the theory of algorithms has, until recently, concerned itself with questions of the reducibility and equivalence of various unsolvable problems. Much of the activity in the theory of algorithms has been concerned with computable functions, decidable predicates, and solvable problems.

Bibliography

1967. Rogers, H. *Theory of Recursive Functions and Effective Computability*. New York: McGraw-Hill.
1979. Hopcroft, J. E., and Ullman, J. D. *Introduction to Automata, Languages, and Computation*. Reading, MA: Addison-Wesley.
1990. Cormen, T. H., Leiserson, C. E., and Rivest, R. L. *Introduction to Algorithms*. Cambridge, MA: MIT Press.
1997. Knuth, D. E. *The Art of Computer Programming: Fundamental Algorithms*, 3rd Ed. Reading, MA: Addison-Wesley.

Gabor T. Herman

ALU

See ARITHMETIC-LOGIC UNIT (ALU).

ANALOG COMPUTER

For an article on a related subject, *see*

+ Simulation

Introduction

The word *analog* is derived from the Greek *ana-logon*, meaning "according to a ratio." Simply, it means a similarity in proportional relationships transcending structure or material. For example, the wing of an airplane, a submerged hydrofoil, and a sail filled with wind are different in structure, but analogous in function in the way they transfer physical forces. In an electronic *analog computer*, the output voltage of an operational amplifier varies in response to its input signals analogously to how a variable in the physical system being *modeled* responds to its conditions.

The use of analog computation goes back to antiquity. The areas of irregularly shaped tracts of land were "measured" by cutting pieces of paper similar in shape to the land and weighing them, thus obtaining an analogous measure of the total land. A number of physical principles have been used throughout the ages for analog computations, such as marks on a burning candle and the streaming sand in an hourglass to indicate the passage of time. Slide rules were analog devices that juxtaposed sliding scales to add or subtract logarithms. Cutting and weighing paper pieces and using the slide rule represented, at best, *static analog computing*. But such methods offered little or no help in solving differential equations, the principal means for expressing scientific and technical knowledge. For this, the process of integration was required and is carried out by *dynamic analog computing*.

Early Developments

The emergence of dynamic analog computing may be dated from the invention of the mechanical integrator by Professor James Thomson in 1876 (Fig. 1) and its immediate adaptation to scientific problem-solving by his brother, Sir William Thomson, later Lord Kelvin. Kelvin's setup included two mechanical integrators in series. Implicit in Kelvin's analysis was the discovery of the *closed-loop principle*, with the output of an integrating device fed back to form its inputs. This feedback principle is the key to all dynamic analog computing. Lord Kelvin discovered, "that the general differential equation ... may be rigorously, continuously, and in a single process solved by a machine."

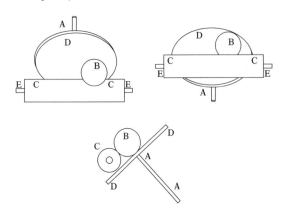

Figure 1. James Thomson's mechanical integrator (reproduced from the article Harmonic Analyzer, in *Proceedings of the Royal Society of London*, Vol. XXVII, London 1878, 371–373). A–Input drive shaft, the turning of which represents the independent variable; B–Heavy ball transferring, by friction, the rotation of the disk D to the cylinder C; C–Receiving cylinder firmly attached to shaft E, the turning of which represents the dependent variable (the integration result); D–Integrator disk coupled firmly to shaft A.

Within a few years, Kelvin had constructed several analyzers and had determined the periodicity of naturally occurring phenomena, most notably the tides. This allowed him to construct accurate tide predictors that turned out to be very valuable for ships sailing out of English ports. Mechanical integration was also the principle of several gun-directing systems used in US Navy ships through the Second World War. The inventor, Hanniball Ford, constructed a complete *mechanical analog computer* in 1918.

The next notable mechanical integrator development occurred in 1931 at the Massachusetts Institute of Technology (MIT), where Vannevar Bush announced the completion of a purely mechanical equation solver that he called a *differential analyzer*. Containing six mechanical integrators, it was capable of integrating with respect to six independent variables and thus could solve any combination from six first-order linear differential equations to one sixth-order equation.

The Electronic Integrator

In an electronic analog computer, differential equations are solved in much the same way as Kelvin first proposed. The key difference is the use of real time as the independent variable, progressing linearly from an initial value to the desired end point. To carry out the required integrations from higher to lower-order terms, a series of electronic integrators is used. Each integrator is an adaptation of a high-gain operational amplifier in which a capacitor is the only feedback element.

Solving Differential Equations in Real Time

Electronic analog computers solve differential equations in accordance with the feedback principle discussed earlier. The possibility of solving sets of simultaneous differential equations emerged with the availability of many integrators in one computer. In addition, some large analog computers operated in so-called *real time*, that is, when one second of clock time equals one unit of time of the independent variable.

Solutions carried out in real time lasted minutes or hours, sometimes even days, and rendered output signals that agreed closely with the physical variables they *simulated*. In many cases, the analog computers were connected to specific hardware and involved so-called *person-in-the-loop* applications. Several key NASA studies in the early 1960s were of this kind, putting pilots or astronauts into capsules that were "flown" in simulated orbits or under the sea. Such person-in-the-loop simulations were very effective in evaluating engineering solutions in which it would be too risky or too costly to experiment directly.

High-Speed Analog Computers

Several specialty firms produced electronic real-time analog computers in the 30 years after the Second World War. Such computers were generally large and assembled to form integrated systems made up of many analog consoles. A large system typically contained dozens of real-time integrators and hundreds of operational amplifiers. Early American producers of large systems were Reeves Electronics of New York; Electronic Associates Inc., of West Long Branch, NJ;

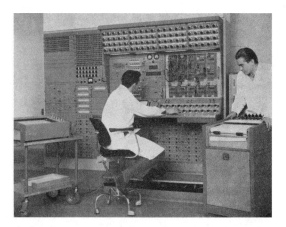

Figure 2. The EAI 231-R electronic analog computer from Electronic Associates. This was one of the first and most important analog computers and provided the capabilities for extensive and complex simulations of process dynamics, spaceflights, airplane stability analysis, and medical (drug) evaluations from about 1956 to the late 1960s.

Berkley Division of Beckman Instruments, Los Angeles; Applied Dynamics, Inc. of Ann Arbor, MI, among others. Smaller electronic analog computers were made for teaching purposes or more limited engineering simulations. Typical of these were the desktop analog computers made by Donner Associates, Inc. of Los Angeles and Computer Products Corp. of Newton, MA, and by Electronics Associates (Fig. 2).

Hybrid Computers

During the period from the early 1960s to the early 1970s, electronic analog computers were increasingly combined with a digital computer in *hybrid systems*. The idea was to combine the easy programmability of a general purpose digital computer with the ability of a large electronic analog computer to solve substantial, complex problems, notably large sets of nonlinear differential equations, or to simulate challenging spaceflights and "person-in-the-loop" situations in real time. A number of specialty hybrid systems emerged in the mid- to late 1960s and early 1970s. An unusual such system was the Trice digital analog computer developed

by the Packard Bell Company and used by NASA for spaceflight simulation.

The End of an Era

Analog and hybrid computers were generally phased out during the late 1970s, the end of an era, brought on by the ever-increasing speed, power, and memory capacity of digital computers. By the late 1970s, digital solutions became faster—and considerably more accurate and convenient to use—than even high-speed analog or hybrid computers. The paradigm shift occurred with the advent of digital computer programs written in special programming languages such as the Continuous System Modeling Program (CSMP), Simscript, and a number of others that allowed users to solve sets of differential equations with ease and accuracy.

Bibliography

1972. Korn, G. A., and Korn, T. M. *Electronic Analog and Hybrid Computers*, 2nd Ed. New York: McGraw-Hill.

Per A. Holst

ANALYSIS OF ALGORITHMS

See ALGORITHMS, ANALYSIS OF.

ANALYTICAL ENGINE

For articles on related subjects, *see*

+ Babbage, Charles
+ Difference Engine
+ Digital Computers, History of: Origins
+ Lovelace, Countess of

The Analytical Engine, designed by Charles Babbage between 1833 and 1846, anticipated many features of electronic computing devices invented in the 1940s and 1950s. Although mechanical in all its operations, the

Analytical Engine could carry out calculations of arbitrary complexity under the control of punched cards. Conditional branching was possible, and Babbage had prepared test programs that included elaborate calculations based on nested loop structures. In a beautiful anticipation of twentieth-century thinking, Babbage showed that, given sufficient time, any finite calculation could be carried out by the Analytical Engine.

Babbage commenced work on the design of the Analytical Engine in 1833 after the collapse of the project to build his Difference Engine (*q.v.*). Babbage had realized that the second difference of the sine function is proportional to the sine itself. If the difference engine could be rearranged so that the tabulated value of the sine could be "fed back" to become the second difference, the sine could be calculated directly without an intermediate polynomial approximation. This image of the engine "eating its own tail" led Babbage to place the number stores of the Difference Engine around a set of central gear wheels that served as a "data bus" to transmit numbers from one store, or "register," to another.

Babbage's *anticipating carry*, a mechanical equivalent of carry-lookahead, greatly speeded multiplication. But its complexity led Babbage to separate the Analytical Engine into two distinct parts—the *store*, in which numbers are normally kept, and the *mill*, to which they are brought for calculations.

Division needs little more calculating apparatus than multiplication, but its control is more complex, as division is inherently a trial-and-error process. To control the Analytical Engine, Babbage developed *barrels*, similar in principle to a music box, in which each row of pins puts into gear those parts of the calculating mechanism that must act during one cycle of the drive shaft. In effect, the barrel is a microprogram store, and complex operations are implemented by microprograms represented by rows of pins on the barrel. But in June 1836, Babbage borrowed from the Jacquard pattern-weaving loom the idea of a sequence of punched cards to provide a more flexible alternative to this "user program" barrel.

By late 1837, Babbage had developed all of the essential ideas for a flexible programmed calculating machine. Much of his additional work was applied to the "architecture" of the Analytical Engine—the functional arrangement of the component mechanisms and the all-important microprograms for multiplication, division, and other operations.

Some of Babbage's microprograms are remarkably sophisticated. Signed addition, for example, is "pipelined" so that several additions are in progress simultaneously. Each stage of the pipeline is controlled by its own barrel. These step independently through their own microprograms while cooperating to maximize the flow of operands through the pipeline. It would be an impressive piece of technical design even today.

Disenchanted by the attempt to build the Difference Engine, Babbage did not attempt to build the Analytical Engine in the late 1830s, but treated the design as merely an intellectual pursuit. In the mid-1850s, however, Babbage returned to the analytical engine and simplified it so that it might be built within his own means. Although this period showed remarkable technological innovation, and a test piece using diecast components was nearing completion at the time of his death in 1871, the brilliance of the earlier years was missing.

Bibliography

1987. Bromley, A. G. "The Evolution of Babbage's Calculating Engines," *Annals of the History of Computing*, **9**, 113–138.

1990. Bromley, A. G. "Difference and Analytical Engines," *Computing Before Computers* (ed. W. Aspray), 59–98. Ames, IA: Iowa State University Press.

1998. Collier, B., MacLachlan, J. H., and Gingerich, O. C. *Babbage and the Engine of Perfection*. Oxford: Oxford University Press.

Allan G. Bromley

ANIMATION

See COMPUTER ANIMATION.

APL

For an article on a related subject, *see*

+ Functional Programming

APL (A Programming Language) was first developed as a notation for teaching in a master's program in *Automatic Data Processing* introduced at Harvard University by Professor Howard Aiken (*q.v.*) in 1955, and was first implemented at IBM in 1965. Its early development is documented in *The Design of APL* (Falkoff and Iverson, 1973) and *The Evolution of APL* (Falkoff and Iverson, 1978).

APL is distinguished by three main properties:

1. the use of functions that apply to arguments of a single type, called *arrays* of various ranks;
2. the use of *operators* (in the sense of Heaviside) that apply to functions to produce-related functions (as do adverbs to verbs in natural languages); and
3. the systematic use of *ambivalent* functions, modeled on the use of the minus sign in mathematics for both subtraction ($x - y$) and negation ($-y$) (*see* OPERATOR OVERLOADING).

As is characteristic of any functional language, when APL is given an expression that is not being assigned a variable, the value of the expression is printed. Thus,

```
 ⍳6          ⍝ "iota 6" => print the
             ⍝ 1st 6 integers starting at 0
 0 1 2 3 4 5

 a←2 3 5 7   ⍝ a is (assigned) a rank-1
             ⍝ array (vector)

 a+a
 4 6 10 14

 +/a         ⍝ / is an operator; +/ is the
             ⍝ sum-over function

 17
 a +.× a     ⍝ Outer product operator
 4   6 10 14 ⍝ +.× produces rank-2 (matrix)
 6   9 15 21
 10 15 25 35
 14 21 35 49
```

```
 a * a            ⍝ Example of ambivalence
 4 27 3125 823543 ⍝ (* => power for dyadic
                  ⍝              case)

 *a               ⍝ Exponential (* a => exp(a))
 7.38906 720.0855 ⍝ for monadic case)
 148.413 71096.63
```

A convenient (but overemphasized) mnemonic characteristic of APL is the use of nonstandard characters (such as ← for assignment, × for times, {⍝ for *comment*, and Greek letters for certain operators) made possible by use of a special type font ball on the IBM Selectric typewriter (newly available at the time of the first implementation). The implementation developed into a general-purpose programming language widely available on time-sharing systems within IBM. Commercially available dialects were developed in many other companies, beginning in 1969. The language J (Iverson, 1991) is a major new implementation that simplifies and extends the original design. Unlike APL, J uses the normal ASCII character set. The addition of a few additional facilities make J a fully functional language that supports tacit definitions, definitions in which no explicit mention is made of the arguments of the function being defined.

The uses of APL have been widely varied. Special interest groups have formed in many countries, and APL journals have been established, notably *APL Quote Quad* (Association for Computing Machinery—*q.v.*) and *Vector* (British Computer Society—*q.v.*).

Bibliography

1973. Falkoff, A. D., and Iverson, K. E. "The Design of APL," *IBM Journal of Research and Development*, **17**(4), (July) 324–334.

1978. Falkoff, A. D., and Iverson, K. E. "The Evolution of APL," *ACM Sigapl*, **9**(1), (September) 30–44.

1991. Falkoff, A. D. "The IBM Family of APL Systems," *IBM Systems Journal*, **30**(4), 416–432.

1991. Iverson, K. E. "A Personal View of APL," *IBM Systems Journal*, **30**(4), 582–593.

Kenneth E. Iverson

a

b

c

d

e

f

g

h

i

j

k

l

m

n

o

p

q

r

s

t

u

v,w

x,y

z

APPLE

For articles on related subjects, *see*

+ Digital Computers, History of
+ Personal Computing

Foundation

Apple Computer, Inc., familiarly just *Apple*, was the first mainstream vendor of personal computers (PCs). The company was born out of the desire of two spirited innovators, Steve Wozniak and Steve Jobs (Fig. 1). Stephen G. Wozniak was a regular attendee of the Homebrew Computer Club that began meeting in 1975 in Menlo Park, CA, at the northern edge of what was already called Silicon Valley. It was at a Homebrew meeting that Wozniak heard about the first PCs that were being offered as mail-order kits. By mid-1976, Wozniak, 26, had written a Basic (*q.v.*) programming language interpreter for a new microprocessor from MOS Technology, the 6502, and designed a computer to run it.

Steven P. Jobs, aged 21 in 1976, shared Wozniak's passion for computers. The two had collaborated on several electronics projects, including creating the video game *Breakout* for Atari, Inc., where Jobs worked. Jobs persuaded his friend to sell the Apple I kits to other hobbyists. They sold Jobs's Volkswagen van and

Figure 1.   Apple cofounders Steve Wozniak (left) and Steve Jobs with the original motherboard of the Apple I (courtesy of Apple Computer Inc.).

Figure 2.   The popular Apple IIGS Computer–the last of the Apple II line–which launched Apple Computer in 1977 (courtesy of Apple Computer Inc.).

Wozniak's programmable calculator to raise enough money to get started. Jobs then landed an order for 50 Apple I computers from one of the first computer retail stores in the country, and, on the strength of that order, the two men secured credit at an electronic parts house. In the garage of Jobs's parents' home in Cupertino, CA, Apple went into business.

Wozniak began designing a second computer that would be far superior to the Apple I, incorporating a keyboard, power supply, color graphics, and Basic. Former Intel marketing guru A. C. "Mike" Markkula, only 33 himself, wrote a business plan for the company, invested in it, and joined Apple when it incorporated in January 1977. Thereafter, he served in various executive positions, including president. Apple blossomed during that first year. It introduced the Apple II (Fig. 2) at the first West Coast Computer Faire and finished its first fiscal year with $774 000 in sales and a $42 000 profit.

An Industry Grows Up

By the end of 1982, more than 100 companies were manufacturing PCs, including Atari, Commodore, Tandy, and a host of start-ups. Apple contributed key products that catalyzed the development of software for the Apple II, including the Disk II floppy disk drive and disk operating system, and several programming languages and aids. As a result, landmark programs, including VisiCalc (*see* SPREADSHEET) and other business-oriented applications, were developed first for the Apple II. Of the 130 000 Apple II computers sold by September 1980, an estimated 25 000 were purchased specifically to run VisiCalc.

Apple improved its Apple II line with the Apple II Plus in 1979, the Apple IIe in 1983, and the Apple IIc in 1984. Beginning in 1979, Apple awarded grants to schools and individuals for the development of educational software. At one point, more than 50% of computers used in US primary and secondary schools were Apple computers.

Apple revenues continued to grow at unprecedented rates, reaching $583.1 million for fiscal 1982, the company's fifth year of operation. The company's initial public stock offering—in December 1980—was one of the largest in Wall Street's history, raising approximately $100 million. In 1983, Apple entered the Fortune 500 and gained additional Wall Street renown by recruiting Pepsi-Cola's president John Sculley as its new chief executive.

The IBM PC (*q.v.*), introduced in August 1981, stirred up a frenzy in the industry, as software and accessory developers rushed to create products compatible with it. Development for the Apple II and Apple III, though still strong, dwindled by comparison. In early 1983, Apple launched its fourth computer, the Lisa. But the Lisa was slow and lacked network capability. Lisa failed in the marketplace, but it paved the way for the similar but smaller Macintosh. The Macintosh graphical user interface (GUI), introduced in January 1984, included icons, windows, pull-down menus, and a mouse (*q.v.*), and set new standards for ease of use.

In 1985, Steve Wozniak resigned from the company to start a new video electronics business. Macintosh and Apple II sales fell dramatically. Apple eliminated 1200 jobs, sharply cut operating costs, and closed three factories. The company sustained its first quarterly loss. In September 1985, founder Steve Jobs quit Apple, forced out by John Sculley, whom he had hired only two years before. However, sales did pick up in 1986 as some businesses bought Macintoshes, spurred by

Figure 3. The Macintosh Plus, one of the earliest Macintosh computers (courtesy of Apple Computer Inc.).

introduction of the faster and more powerful Macintosh Plus (Fig. 3), enhancements to the Apple II, dozens of software and accessory products from Apple and third-party developers, and the new desktop publishing (*q.v.*) applications.

From 1987 through 1991, Apple continued to introduce new versions of the Macintosh that made it faster, more powerful, and more able to network with computers based on MS-DOS. By 1991, Apple's share of the business market was barely 10%, with low-priced IBM clones proving to be extremely tough competition. After years of pursuing a strategy of high gross margins, Apple realized it would remain a niche player unless it lowered its prices and expanded its market share.

In October 1990, Apple instituted an aggressive strategy to gain share in all segments of the market with the introduction of lower-priced Macintosh systems—The Macintosh Classic, the Macintosh LC, and the Macintosh IIsi and lower-priced laser printers. As a result, Apple's market share began to increase despite an overall industry downturn. The downturn, which continued into 1991, and overspending inside Apple led to the company's second massive layoff in a decade when, again, 1200 people lost their jobs. In May 1991, Apple began delivery of System 7, a new version of its proprietary operating system.

The Alliance

In October 1991, Apple reached an agreement with its rival IBM. In an alliance called Taligent, the companies planned to create new technologies, especially cross-platform operating systems, which both companies believed were crucial to their futures. Both companies invested dollars, staff, and intellectual property in the hope of competing with competitors like Microsoft (*q.v.*). But cultural differences and technological difficulties got in the way, and Taligent became an IBM subsidiary in December 1995. Other parts of the IBM-Apple partnership survived. They agreed to create, with the help of Motorola, Inc., a new family of reduced instruction set computing (RISC–*q.v.*) microprocessors optimized for PCs and entry-level workstations. Derived from IBM's single-chip implementation of its Power RISC architecture, the PowerPC chips are made by Motorola and IBM for both Apple Macintosh and IBM computers and successfully marketed by both. They form the basis for the current Apple product line.

In October 1991, two years after introducing an ill-fated "luggable" 15-pound Macintosh Portable, Apple introduced its PowerBook laptop line. That was followed in the late 1990s with the G3 portable, considered a formidable high-end machine, but Apple now needed a low-end strategy. By the end of fiscal 1991, Apple reported net sales of $6.3 billion, a 14% increase over fiscal 1990. In 1992, Apple entered the personal digital assistant (PDA) business with its Newton handheld computer. On the basis of the ARM RISC chip, the device permitted data entry by handwriting recognition and offered note taking, address book, and calendar functions. But the machine's technology was premature and faulty, especially its initial handwriting recognizer, and the product was discontinued in 1998.

In June 1993, John Sculley moved up to Chairman. He was succeeded, as Chairman and CEO, by Michael Spindler. Soon, Sculley would move on, following his vision in other parts of the information industry.

On 14 March 1994, apple introduced its first PowerMac based on the IBM PowerPC RISC chip. Sales were brisk. PowerMac sales buoyed Apple's market share so that, in the third quarter, Apple was reported to be Number One in overall PC sales in the USA, with over 13% market share. It would be the last good news for quite some time.

Apple's 1995 announcements included an Apple Internet Server for the World Wide Web (*q.v.*). New PowerBooks, PowerMacs, and Newtons were announced, as well as a new version of the Newton operating system.

In early 1996, Gilbert Amelio succeeded Spindler as CEO and President of Apple. In this period, Apple became the first major vendor to support Linux (*q.v.*), both with activities at the Open Software Foundation (OSF—*see* FREEWARE AND SHAREWARE) and also with the announcement of a product that September. Amelio needed to find a new operating system for Apple and in choosing to acquire that of NeXT (Steve Jobs's company), he probably caused his own undoing. Not only did he find himself presiding over a debacle with valuable employees fleeing, market share melting, and attempts to integrate the NeXT OS floundering, but Jobs was also in position to take his place. Amelio resigned in July 1997, and Jobs rejoined the Apple Board of Directors.

In August of 1997 at MacWorld, Jobs announced an alliance with Microsoft. Microsoft would provide a next-generation version of Macintosh Office, allegedly better than that on the Windows platform, and guarantee future versions. It would also make a $150 million investment in Apple. In turn, Apple would use the Microsoft Internet Explorer browser on the Macintosh and cross-license patents, in part to settle prior litigation. It was a brilliant strategy and has served Apple well, getting it both cash and required software, as well as convincing others to write for the platform.

A few months later, Jobs agreed to become interim CEO of Apple, a position he held until January 2000 when he agreed to drop the "interim." Apple then acquired Power Computing (an Apple clone manufacturer) for $100 million, bringing to an end the competition of the clones and the hope that Apple might succeed, through licensing, to build a broader market.

In 1998 and 1999, Apple brought G3 and G4 desktops, servers, and PowerBooks to the market, based on the powerful new PowerPC chip. This provided processor speeds of up to 600 MHz. This was followed later with the *i*Mac focused on the consumer market. More than 800 000 were sold in only five months. The iBook that followed, a G3-powered notebook computer with a unique clamshell design, also proved very popular (*see* Fig. 4). The OS X Server (with the long-promised integration of NeXT and Macintosh technologies) was also announced, as well as hints of a low-cost mobile product for the consumer and education markets soon.

As of 2003, Apple's premier product was the PowerMac G5 with 64-bit architecture that supports up to 8 GB of RAM. At 4 GHz, the G5 is rated as twice as fast as the most powerful Pentium machine. But the software advantage of IBM-compatible PCs and the widespread familiarity with its Windows operating system makes it unlikely that the G5's appeal will extend beyond those who like to boast of owning a personal supercomputer. Apple's future is likely to be more closely tied to its less expensive iMac line, and perhaps to its MP3 music products.

Bibliography

1995. Levy, S. *Insanely Great: The Life and Times of Macintosh, the Computer that Changed Everything.* London: Penguin.

1997. Carlton, J. *Apple: The Inside Story of Intrigue, Egomania, and Business Blunders.* New York: Harper-Business.

1999. Hall, T. "Poor Little Lisa," *American Heritage of Invention and Technology,* **15**(1) (Summer), 64.

1999. Linzmayer, O. W. *Apple Confidential: The Real Story of Apple Computer.* San Francisco: No Starch Press.

Mary A. C. Fallon and Amy Wohl

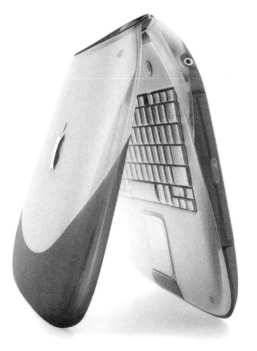

Figure 4. The iBook (courtesy of Apple Computer Inc.).

APPLICATIONS PROGRAMMING

For articles on related subjects, *see*

+ **Programming Languages**
+ **Software**
+ **Systems Programming**

Applications programs are programs written to solve specific problems, to produce specific reports, or to update specific files. The term is used in contradistinction to *systems programming*, which deals with the development of the software tools that the applications programmer uses. The programming languages that are used most often in applications programming are Fortran, Ada, and C (or C++) for scientific applications and Cobol for data processing applications. (*See* the articles on those languages.)

Applications programs make use of *program libraries* (*q.v.*) and special packages such as sort–merge systems and database management systems (*q.v.*). There are very large applications systems such as airline reservations systems and online banking and merchandising systems in which many considerations of systems programming and of applications programming are intermixed. Increasingly, such applications are programmed in an object-oriented language such as C++ or Java (*q.v.*).

Saul Rosen

APPLICATIVE PROGRAMMING

See FUNCTIONAL PROGRAMMING.

ARCHITECTURE, COMPUTER

See COMPUTER ARCHITECTURE.

ARITHMETIC, COMPUTER

For articles on related subjects, *see*

+ Arithmetic-Logic Unit (ALU)
+ Complement
+ Numbers and Number Systems
+ Precision

Computer Storage of Numbers

A memory *cell* is the smallest unit of addressable computer memory. Older word-oriented computers typically used large cell sizes, such as 60 or 64 bits. Newer computers address memory in small 8-bit units called *bytes*. In word-oriented computers, a number is stored in one word, while in byte-oriented computers, a number is stored in multiple bytes (2, 4, 8, and 16 bytes have been commonly used). "Single-precision" numbers typically occupy 32 bits of storage (4 bytes) and "double-precision" numbers occupy 64 bits (8 bytes). A given number may be stored in one of two formats: *fixed-point* or *floating-point*.

Fixed-Point Representation

Figure 1 illustrates the storage of two numbers, 0.15625 and 57.8125, as fixed-point numbers in a 32-bit format. Throughout this article, numbers in the text will be cited in decimal but their stored representations will be shown in binary. For convenience, only positive numbers will be used in examples. Storage of negative numbers can be either by absolute value and sign form or as complements (*q.v.*).

Consider Fig. 1:

1. The left-hand bit (S or bit 0) represents the sign of the number; 0 is used for positive numbers and 1 for negative numbers.

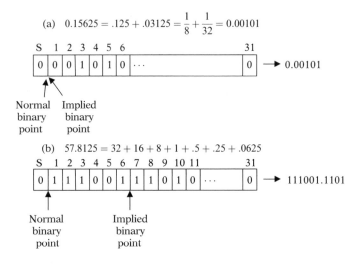

(a) $0.15625 = .125 + .03125 = \frac{1}{8} + \frac{1}{32} = 0.00101$

(b) $57.8125 = 32 + 16 + 8 + 1 + .5 + .25 + .0625$

Figure 1.   Fixed-point numbers.

2. The normal binary point (radix point) is assumed to be at the left end of the number, just to the right of the sign bit. The programmer, however, may choose a different or *implicit binary point*, so long as computation is done consistently with respect to the chosen alternative position. A computer calculating with fixed-point numbers assumes that the binary point is always in the same, fixed location—hence the name "fixed-point." Most computers now assume the binary point to be at the right-hand end of the number, that is, as *integers*. But for the sake of this article, placement is as shown in Fig. 1.

Doing arithmetic on fixed-point numbers creates several major problems.

1. How could numbers with magnitudes of 1 or greater be handled? Such numbers can be stored as fixed-point numbers, but when using these numbers in computations, programmers must be careful to keep track of the implicit locations of the radix point.

2. More significant problems occur when two numbers have implicit radix points in different positions. How could these be added?

As an example, consider adding the numbers in Figs. 1a and 1b. Before bit-by-bit addition can be done, one of the numbers must be shifted relative to the other. The term *scaling* is used for the twin activities of shifting the numbers and choosing the location of the implicit binary point. Numbers are usually scaled before they are stored or used in computations. Doing this can be difficult and tedious for all but the simplest calculations, and led to the introduction of floating-point hardware.

Floating-Point Representation

Numbers stored in "floating-point" format closely resemble "scientific notation." A number in scientific notation is represented as $f \times R^E$, where f is a fraction in the range $0 \leq f < 1$, R is the radix (usually 10), and E is the signed integral power (exponent) of the radix. Thus, the number 57.8125 in Fig. 1b would be represented as 0.578125×10^2, where 0.578125 is the fraction, 10 is the radix, and 2 is the exponent. Using floating-point terminology, the fraction 0.578125 is called the *mantissa*. The term *floating-point* is used because the radix point is not fixed, but can move, or "float," depending on the value of the exponent.

To store a single-precision floating-point number in a byte-addressable memory, separate portions of the four bytes must be assigned to the sign bit, the exponent, and the fraction. A floating-point format for N bits is labeled (X, Y), where

1. $X + Y + 1 = N$
2. X bits are allocated to the exponent
3. Y bits are allocated to the mantissa.

For any fixed number of bits N, increasing X increases the range of representable numbers but decreases their precision, while decreasing X produces a greater precision but smaller numeric range. Figure 2

(a) .15625 in (7, 24) Format

$$= 0.101 \times 2^{-2} = 0.15625$$
Bias-64 exponent

(b) 57.8125 in (8, 23) Format

$$= .1110011101 \times 2^6 = 57.8125$$
Bias-128 exponent

Figure 2.   Floating-point numbers.

displays 32-bit binary floating-point formats for 0.15625 and 57.8125. Figure 2a shows 0.15625 in (7, 24) format, and Fig. 2b shows 57.8125 in (8, 23) format. Two pertinent comments are as follows:

1. As with fixed-point numbers, the binary point of the mantissa is assumed to be in the same place, usually at the left end. The sign bit (S or bit 0) always represents the sign of the mantissa.
2. Special techniques are needed to represent exponents, which may be zero, positive, or negative. One technique is to let bit 1 denote the sign of the exponent, but, more commonly, "biased" exponents are used. The format in Fig. 2a uses "bias-64" to represent any signed exponent -64 to $+63$ by using unsigned numbers 0 to $2^7 - 1 = 127$. Thus 1000000 represents the exponent 0, 1000001 represents 1, 0111111 represents -1, and so forth. Figure 2b uses "bias-128" and can represent any signed exponent from -128 to $+127$.

Floating-point mantissas are usually stored as *normalized* numbers in which the most significant digit is nonzero. Double-precision floating-point numbers typically are stored in 64-bits; common formats include (7, 56), (8, 55), and (11, 52). "Extended" implementations include 80-bit (15, 64) and 128-bit (15, 112) formats.

In 1985, the Institute of Electrical and Electronics Engineers (IEEE) proposed a standard format for floating-point representations, which has now been generally adopted by computer manufacturers.

Fixed-Point Arithmetic

Fixed-point arithmetic is done essentially like ordinary binary arithmetic, except for the restriction that negative numbers are generally stored in some complement form. However, some aspects of fixed-point arithmetic need to be considered explicitly. In the following examples, we assume that fixed-point numbers are binary fractions of magnitude less than 1 and that the binary point is at the left.

Fixed-point addition and subtraction are subject to the exceptional condition known as *overflow*. Since not only the two addends but also the result in addition and subtraction must be less than 1 in magnitude, a

result greater than 1 will not be correctly handled. To be precise, when adding positive numbers *overflow occurs when bit-1 has a carry-out*. In some computers, this carry-out bit is discarded, while in others it replaces the sign bit, resulting in an artificial negative number. In any case, the result is incorrect, and most computer architectures maintain an overflow bit, which allows a programmer to test for overflow by using a Branch-On-Overflow instruction.

Overflow cannot occur in fixed-point multiplication, since the product of two factors less than 1 in magnitude must be less than 1. But multiplying two n-bit numbers produces a $2n$-bit product, which cannot be accommodated in an n-bit register. Normally, the least significant n-bits are placed in a second register. Figure 3 shows such a multiplication, assuming a word length of 5 bits. Normally only the rounded results are kept, as shown in Fig. 3.

Fixed-point division can result in overflow if the dividend has magnitude as great or greater than the divisor. A fixed-point divide overflow causes an exceptional condition (different from fixed-point addition overflow) that is usually testable by programmers.

The dividend in fixed-point division is usually double-length (or precision) and occupies two paired registers. The single-precision quotient is commonly placed in one register and the remainder in another, as illustrated in Fig. 4.

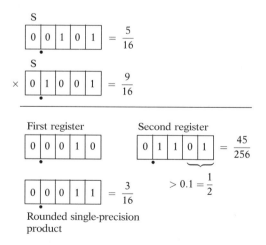

Figure 3. Fixed-point multiplication.

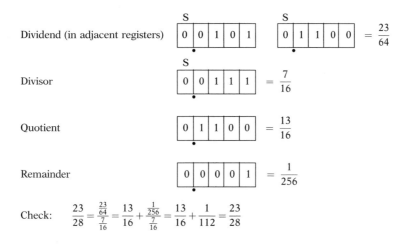

Figure 4.   Fixed-point division.

(a)

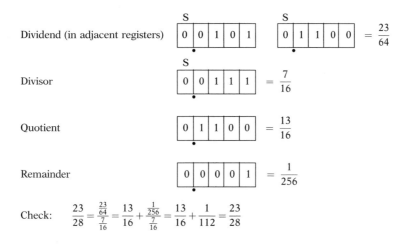

A = .15625 = $.101 \times 2^{-2}$

B = 57.8125 = $.1110011101 \times 2^{-6}$

Step 1 $E_c = 10110$
Step 2 $F_a = 0000000010$ (Note the loss of precision)
Step 3 $F_c = 1110011111$
Step 4   Nothing to be done   (Answer already normalized)

(b)

A = .8125 = $.1101 \times 2^{-0}$

B = .5625 = $.1001 \times 2^{-0}$

Steps 1 and 2   Nothing to be done in these steps

Step 3 $F_c = \boxed{1}$ 01100   00000   (Note the overflow)

Step 4   Normalize

Figure 5.   Floating-point addition.

Floating-Point Arithmetic

To add or subtract two floating-point numbers, the exponents must be the same. If the rightmost mantissa digit of a floating-point number is 0, shifting the mantissa one digit to the right and increasing the exponent by one produces an equivalent floating-point number. The following algorithm for floating-point addition uses this shifting technique. Suppose A and

B are to be added, producing C as a result. Let the exponent and fractional parts be denoted by E_a, E_b, and E_c; and F_a, F_b, and F_c, respectively.

Step 1. Set E_c = the larger of E_a and E_b. (Assume in what follows that $E_a \geq E_b$.)

Step 2. Align the exponents. Shift F_b to the right $E_a - E_b$ places (which causes F_a and F_b to have the same exponent, but may cause a loss of precision).

Step 3. Add the mantissas. Set $F_c = F_a + F_b$.

Step 4. Normalize. Shift F_c to make its most significant bit 1, and adjust E_c accordingly.

This four-step algorithm is illustrated in Fig. 5, assuming a hypothetical computer with a binary (5, 10) floating-point format using bias-16 exponents. Note that Step 3 of Fig. 5(b) results in overflow. No error results because the "overflow" bit is always retained and shifted right in Step 4. The calculation in Fig. 5a has no overflow, and normalization is not necessary in Step 4.

Overflow can occur in any floating-point operation where the magnitude of the result exceeds the floating-point capacity. *Underflow* results from an attempt to produce a nonzero result smaller in magnitude than the smallest possible positive floating-point number. The usual method of handling underflow is to generate a zero result, but sometimes an underflow indicator is also set, which the programmer can test.

Floating-point multiplication and division techniques do not require exponent alignment. Instead, the appropriate operation is performed on the mantissas, the result rounded, the exponents added (for multiplication) or subtracted (for division), and then the result normalized, if necessary.

Bibliography

1989. Levy, H. M., and Eckhouse, R. H. Jr. *Computer Programming and Architecture*, The VAX, 2nd Ed. Bedford, MA: Digital Press.

1991. Goldberg, D. "What Every Computer Scientist Should Know about Floating-point Arithmetic," *ACM Computing Surveys*, **23**(1), (March), 5–48.

1991. Swartzlander, E. E. Jr. *Computer Arithmetic*, Vols. I and II. Los Alamitos, CA: IEEE Computer Society Press.

Thomas J. Scott

ARITHMETIC-LOGIC UNIT (ALU)

For articles on related subjects, *see*

+ Arithmetic, Computer
+ Bus
+ Central Processing Unit (CPU)
+ Complement
+ Instruction Set
+ Numbers and Number Systems
+ Register

The *arithmetic-logic unit* (ALU) is that functional part of the digital computer that carries out arithmetic and logic operations on machine words that represent operands. It is usually a part of the central processing unit (CPU—*q.v.*). The three fundamental attributes of an ALU are its operands and results, functional organization, and algorithms.

Operands and Results

The operands and results of the ALU are machine words of two kinds: *arithmetic words*, which represent numerical values in digital form, and *logic words*, which represent arbitrary sets of digitally encoded symbols. Arithmetic words consist of digit vectors (strings of digits). Conventional radix r number representations allow r values for one digit: $0, 1, \ldots, r - 1$. Practical design considerations have limited the choice of radices to the values 2, 4, 8, 10, and 16. The value of every digit is represented by a set of bits. Radices 2, 4, 8, and 16 employ binary numbers having lengths of 1, 2, 3, and 4 bits, respectively, to represent the values of one digit (*see* NUMBERS AND NUMBER SYSTEMS). Radix-10 digit values are represented by 4 bits. Most commonly used is the four-bit BCD (binary-coded decimal) encoding (*see* CODES).

Two methods have been employed to represent negative numbers. In the sign-and-magnitude form, a separate sign bit is attached to the string of digits to represent the $+$ and $-$ signs. (Usually, 0 represents the $+$ sign, and 1 represents the $-$ sign.) Alternatively, the negative value $-x$ is represented as the complement (*q.v.*) with respect to A of the value x; that is, $-x$ is represented by $A - x$. The value of A used is either $A = r^{n+1}$ or $A = r^{n+1} - 1$, when x is represented by n digits in the sign-and-magnitude form (*see* COMPLEMENT). The choice of $A = r^{n+1}$ is called *range* (or *radix*) complement; in binary arithmetic ($r = 2$) it is usually called *twos complement*. It is the prevalent choice in contemporary ALUs. The choice of $A = r^{n+1} - 1$ is called *digit* (or *diminished radix*) complement, usually called *ones complement* for $r = 2$. It has the disadvantages of an "end-around carry" in modulo A addition and two zero representations ($+0$ and -0), and is little used in contemporary ALUs. The use of complements to represent negative values makes it possible to replace the subtraction algorithm in an ALU by a complementation followed by an addition modulo A; therefore, a subtractor is not needed in the ALU.

Functional Organization of an ALU

A typical ALU consists of three types of functional parts: storage registers, operations logic, and sequencing logic.

The inputs and outputs of the ALU are connected to other functional units of the CPU, such as the cache memory and the program execution control unit. At one time a bus (*q.v.*) was used as the means of connection, but in current microprocessors the ALU and other CPU elements are all on a single chip.

The input information received by the ALU consists of operands, operation codes, and format codes. The operands are machine words that represent numeric or alphanumeric information. The operation code identifies one operation from the set of available arithmetic and logic operations, and also designates the location (within local storage) of the operands and of the results. The designation of operands is omitted in ALUs with limited local storage; for example, an ADD operation code in a single-accumulator ALU always means the addition of the incoming operand to the operand in the accumulator, which retains their sum.

The output information delivered by the ALU consists of results, *condition codes*, and *exception codes*. The results are machine words generated by the specified operations and stored in the local storage registers. The condition codes are bits or sets of bits that identify specific conditions associated with a result, such as that the value of the result is positive, negative, zero; that the result consists of all zeros, all ones, and so on. The exception codes indicate that the specified

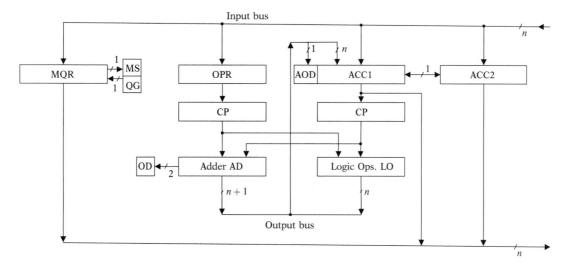

Figure 1. Organization of a fixed-point ALU.

a

operation does not yield a representable result. Examples of exceptions are *overflow*, that is, the value of the result exceeds the allowed range; attempted division by zero; excessive loss of precision in floating-point operations; and error caused by a logic fault. Exception codes usually set a flag bit in the machine status register.

Internally, the ALU is composed of storage registers, logic circuits that perform arithmetic and logic algorithms, and logic circuits that control the sequence of inter-register transfer operations within the ALU. A diagram of a simple ALU is shown in Fig. 1. The ALU contains four registers: the Operand register, OPR; a double-length Accumulator, ACC, composed of shift registers ACC1 and ACC2; and a multiplier-quotient shift register, MQR.

An ALU may be bit-serial, byte-serial, or parallel, depending on how many digits are processed simultaneously in the adder (or logic operator) circuits. In a serial ALU, the adder adds one pair of digits at once; in a byte-serial ALU, it adds a pair of bytes; in a parallel ALU, it adds two full machine words. Machines with variable word length have byte-serial ALUs, since the words consist of a varying number of bytes. The time required to complete one addition in the adder circuits is a basic time unit of ALU operation.

Bibliography

1990. Avižienis, A. "Signed-digit Number Representations for Fast Parallel Arithmetic," in *Computer Arithmetic*, (ed. E. E. Swartzlander Jr.), Vol. II, 54–65. Los Alamitos, CA: IEEE Computer Society Press. (Reprinted from IRE Trans. El. Comp., EC-10 (1961), 389–400.)

1993. Koren, I. *Computer Arithmetic Algorithms*. Upper Saddle River, NJ: Prentice Hall.

1994. Ercegovac, M., and Lang, T. *Division and Square Root*. Boston: Kluwer Academic Publishers.

Algirdas Avižienis

ART, COMPUTER

See COMPUTER ART.

ARTIFICIAL INTELLIGENCE (AI)

For articles on related subjects, *see*

+ Artificial Life
+ Cognitive Science
+ Computer Chess
+ Computer Games
+ Computer Music
+ Computer Vision
+ Expert Systems
+ Genetic Algorithms
+ Knowledge Representation
+ Machine Learning
+ Machine Translation
+ Natural Language Processing
+ Pattern Recognition
+ Robotics
+ Searching
+ Speech Recognition and Synthesis
+ Turing Test
+ Turing, Alan Mathison

Introduction

Artificial Intelligence (AI) is a field of computer science concerned with the computational understanding of what is commonly called *intelligent behavior*, and with the creation of artifacts that exhibit such behavior. This definition may be examined more closely by considering the field from three points of view: computational psychology, computational philosophy, and machine intelligence.

Computational Psychology

The goal of computational psychology is to understand human intelligent behavior by creating computer programs that behave in the same way that people do. For this goal it is important that the algorithm expressed by the program be the same algorithm that people actually use, and that the data structures used by the program be the same data structures used by the human mind. The program should do quickly what people do quickly, should do more slowly what people have difficulty doing, and should even tend to make mistakes where people tend to make mistakes.

Computational Philosophy

The goal of computational philosophy is to form a computational understanding of human-level intelligent behavior, without being restricted to the algorithms and data structures that the human mind actually does use. By "computational understanding" is meant a model that is expressed as a procedure that is implementable on a computer. By "human-level intelligent behavior" is meant behavior that, when engaged in by people, is commonly taken as being part of human intelligent cognitive behavior, even though the implemented model performs some tasks better than any person would.

Machine Intelligence

The goal of machine intelligence is to expand the frontier of what we know how to program. This goal led to one of the oldest definitions of AI: the attempt to program computers to do what, until recently, only people could do. This is a perpetually self-defeating goal in that, as soon as a task is conquered, it no longer falls within the domain of AI. Two examples are computer algebra and response to database queries. Thus, AI is left with only its failures; its successes become other areas of computer science.

The goal of machine intelligence differs from that of computational psychology and computational philosophy in being task-oriented rather than oriented toward the understanding of general intelligent behavior. A machine intelligence approach to a task is to use *any* technique that helps accomplish the task, even if the technique is not used by humans and would probably not be used by generally intelligent entities.

Subsymbolic AI

The key assumption of symbolic AI is that knowledge is represented by structures of semantically meaningful symbols, each symbol representing some entity, be it abstract or concrete, that the intelligent system or agent is discussing, observing, reasoning about, or operating on. On the contrary, the key assumption of subsymbolic AI is that intelligent behavior can be attained without semantically meaningful symbols. Much of subsymbolic AI is included in the field of *soft computing*. In contrast to the traditional hard computing, soft computing is tolerant of imprecision, uncertainty, and partial truth. The goal of soft computing is to exploit this tolerance to achieve tractability, robustness, and lower solution cost. The principal constituents of soft computing (SC) are fuzzy logic (FL–*q.v.*), neurocomputing (NC), and genetic algorithms (GA–*q.v.*). The principal contribution of FL is a methodology for approximate reasoning and, in particular, for computing with words; that of NC is curve fitting, learning, and system identification; and that of GA is systematized random search and optimization (Zadeh, 1995).

Heuristic Programming

AI researchers are more interested in *heuristics* than *algorithmics*. A *heuristic* is any problem-solving procedure that fails to be an algorithm, or that has not been shown to be an algorithm. The most common reasons that a heuristic H fails to be an algorithm are that it does not terminate for some instances of P, it has not been proved correct for all instances of P because of some problem with H, or it has not been proved correct for all instances of P because P is not well defined. An example of a heuristic AI program is any natural language understanding program or interface. Since no one has any well-defined criteria for whether a person understands a given language, there cannot be any well-defined criteria for programs either.

Early History

AI was born at a conference held at Dartmouth College in the summer of 1956. The conference was organized by Marvin Minsky and John McCarthy, and McCarthy coined the name "Artificial Intelligence" for the proposal to obtain funding for it. Among the attendees were

a

Herbert Simon and Allen Newell, who had already implemented the Logic Theorist program at the Rand Corporation.

The first AI text was *Computers and Thought*, edited by Edward Feigenbaum and Julian Feldman, and published by McGraw-Hill in 1963. This is a collection of 21 papers by early AI researchers. Most of the papers in this collection are still considered classics of AI, but of particular note is a reprint of Alan M. Turing's 1950 paper in which the Turing Test (*q.v.*) was introduced.

AI-Complete Tasks

There are many AI subtopics. Several of these broad areas can be considered *AI-complete*, in the sense that solving the problem of the area is equivalent to solving the entire AI problem—producing a generally intelligent computer program. The following sections discuss some of these areas.

Natural Language

The AI subarea of *natural language processing* (*q.v.*) is the overlap of AI and computational linguistics. The exceedingly ambitious goal is to form a computational understanding of how people learn and use their native languages, and to produce a computer program that can use a human language at the same level of competence as a native human speaker.

Problem Solving and Search

The distinctive characteristic of the area is its approach of seeing tasks as problems to be solved, and of seeing problems as spaces of potential solutions that must be searched to find the true one or the best one.

Knowledge Representation and Reasoning

Knowledge representation (*q.v.*) is an AI-complete area concerned with the formal symbolic languages used to represent the knowledge (data) used by intelligent systems, and the data structures (*q.v.*) used to implement those formal languages. The goal is to use explicitly stored knowledge to produce additional explicit knowledge, the process called *reasoning*.

Learning

Learning is often cited as the critical characteristic of intelligence, and is, potentially at least, the easiest way to produce intelligent systems. Why build an intelligent system when we could just build a learning system and send it to school? Learning includes all styles of learning, from rote learning to the design and analysis of experiments, and all subject areas. If the ultimate learning machine is ever created, it will acquire general intelligence, which is why *machine learning* (*q.v.*) is AI-complete.

Vision

Vision, or image understanding, has to do with interpreting visual images that fall on the human retina or the camera lens. If we take "interpreting" broadly enough, it is clear that general intelligence may be needed to do the interpretation, and that correct interpretation implies general intelligence, so *computer vision* (*q.v.*) is another AI-complete area.

Robotics

Robotics (*q.v.*) is concerned with artifacts that can move about in the actual physical world and/or that can manipulate other objects in the world. Intelligent robots must be able to accommodate to new circumstances, and to do this they need to be able to solve problems and to learn. Thus, intelligent robotics is also an AI-complete area. The most direct work on the problem of generally intelligent systems is to use a robot that has vision and/or other senses, plans and solves problems, and communicates via natural language. Periodically, research groups have assembled such integrated robots as tests of the current state of AI.

Autonomous Agents

Autonomous agents are computer systems that are capable of independent action in dynamic, unpredictable environments. Autonomous agents are like integrated robots, except that they need not have physical bodies nor need they operate in the real, physical world. Instead, they may be completely software agents, sometimes called "*softbots*" or just "*bots*," and may operate in the world of the Internet, crawling around from file to file, collecting information for their human clients. To do this well, softbots may need general-purpose reasoning.

Applications

Throughout inception, AI research has produced spinoffs into other areas of computer science. Programming techniques developed by AI researchers have found application to many programming problems, particularly those in the AI subarea known as *expert systems* (*q.v.*). After many years of being criticized as following an impossible dream, AI has been recognized by the general public as having applications to everyday problems.

Bibliography

1950. Turing, A. M. "Computing Machinery and Intelligence," *Mind*, **59**, (October), 433–460.

1963. Feigenbaum, E. A., and Feldman, J. (eds.) *Computers and Thought*. New York: McGraw-Hill.

1990. Kurzweil, R. *The Age of Intelligent Machines*. Cambridge, MA: MIT Press.

1991. Shapiro, S. C. (ed.) *Encyclopedia of Artificial Intelligence*, 2nd Ed. New York: John Wiley.

1995. Zadeh, L. Foreward to inaugural issue of the E-journal *Intelligent Automation and Soft Computing*, `http://wacong/autosoft/autosoft-zadeh_forward.html`

Stuart C. Shapiro

ARTIFICIAL LIFE

For articles on related subjects, *see*

+ Artificial Intelligence (AI)
+ Biocomputing
+ Cellular Automata
+ Computer Animation
+ Computer Art
+ Computer Graphics
+ Genetic Algorithms
+ Machine Learning
+ Robotics

Introduction

As defined by Langton (1992), "*Artificial Life* (AL, or *Alife*) is a new discipline that studies 'natural' life by attempting to recreate biological phenomena, from scratch, within computers and other 'artificial' media. AL complements the traditional analytic approach of traditional biology with a synthetic approach in which, rather than studying biological phenomena by taking apart living organisms to see how they work, one attempts to put together systems that behave like living organisms."

AL amounts to the practice of "synthetic biology," which attempts to recreate biological phenomena in alternative media. It is the study of *life-as-it-could-be*, rather than the biological *life-as-we-know-it*. Its goal is not only better theoretical understanding of the phenomena under study but also practical applications of biological principles in the technology of computer hardware and software. AL draws researchers from different disciplines such as computer science, physics, biology, chemistry, economics, and philosophy. The issues raised in AL research pertain to existing biological phenomena as well as to complex systems in general. Thus, AL pursues a two-fold goal: (1) an increased understanding of reproduction in nature; and (2) an enhanced insight into artificial models with a view to improving their performance.

Reproduction

An example of the first goal is the research of John von Neumann (*q.v.*) who, in 1966, wondered whether an artificial machine could create a copy of itself, which in turn could create still more copies, in analogy to nature. Levy (1993) gives a good description of von Neumann's (positive) answer to his own question. von Neumann defined a formal reproductive process that uses assembly instructions in the form of computer code and data interpreted by a robotic device executing a computer program. Other biological phenomena studied are models of the origin of life, evolution, cell construction, animal behavior, and ecology.

Evolution

An example of the second goal, improving the performance of artificial models such as programming tasks, is software development through evolution (genetic programming), as done by Koza *et al.* (1999). While a programmer develops a single program, attempting to perfect it as much as possible, genetic programming involves a population of programs. Generations of programs are formed by evolution so that in time the population comes to consist of fitter programs (more suitable to solve a given problem), using genetic operators such as mutation, crossover, and selection. The evolution proceeds without human intervention. After the task is set, an initial population is generated at random and evolution continues until a satisfying result is found.

Evolutionary programming is advantageous not only in solving difficult problems but also in offering better adaptability. Current computer programs are well known for their brittleness; that is, they are not *robust*. Evolution offers the possibility of adaptation to a dynamic environment; when an unforeseen event occurs, the system could, by analogy with nature, evolve and adapt to the new situation.

Emergence

Along with evolution, a second process called *emergence* is essential to AL. By *emergence* is meant that phenomena at a certain level arise from interactions at lower levels. In physical systems, individual molecules possess neither temperature nor pressure; such system attributes are higher-level emergent phenomena.

AL systems consist of large collections of simple, basic units whose interesting properties are those that emerge at higher levels. One example is the work of Craig Reynolds (1987) on flocking behavior. To investigate how flocks of birds fly without apparent coordination of a central guiding mechanism, Reynolds created a virtual bird with basic flight capability, called a *boid*. He populated a computerized world with a collection of boids, flying in accordance with three rules: collision

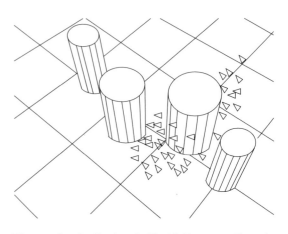

Figure 1. A flock of "boids" separating to avoid obstacles.

avoidance (avoid collisions with nearby boids), velocity matching (attempt to match velocity with nearby boids) and flock centering (attempt to stay as close as possible to the perceived center of mass of nearby boids). These three rules sufficed for the emergence of flocking behavior even though none of them specifically directs the formation of an orderly flock. The boids fly in a cohesive group and when obstacles appear in their way they spontaneously split up into two subgroups, without any central guidance, rejoining again after clearing the obstruction (*see* Fig. 1). The boids model has been used to produce photorealistic imagery for the feature motion pictures *Batman Returns*, *The Lion King*, and *Cliffhanger*.

Artificial Intelligence and Artificial Life

The underlying principles of artificial life stand at the core of the work of Rodney Brooks (1991). His method for building sophisticated robots demonstrates the AL approach. His robots possess "brains" comprising a hierarchy of layers, each one performing a more complex function than the one beneath. This scheme allows incremental construction of robots by adding to existing layers, thus enabling some form of robotic evolution. Artificial intelligence (AI) employs a top-down methodology in which complex behaviors are identified and an attempt is made to build a system that presents all the details of a behavior (e.g. chess playing—*see* COMPUTER CHESS). Artificial life operates in a bottom-up manner, starting from simple elemental units, gradually building its way upward through evolution and emergence. AL and AI investigate different issues. Whereas AI has traditionally concentrated on complex human functions, AL concentrates on basic natural behaviors, emphasizing survivability in complex environments.

Websites and Recent Projects

The Website `http://www.genarts.com/karl/evolved-virtual-creatures.html` describes Karl Sims' work entitled, *Evolved Virtual Creatures*. A population of several hundred creatures is created within a supercomputer (*q.v.*), and each creature is tested for its ability to perform a given task, such as swimming in a simulated water environment. Those that are most successful survive, and their virtual genes containing coded instructions for their growth, are copied, combined, and mutated to make offspring for a new population. As cycles of variation and selection continue, creatures with more and more successful behaviors emerge.

Bibliography

1966. von Neumann, J. *Theory of Self-Reproducing Automata* (ed. A. W. Burks). Urbana, IL: University of Illinois Press.

1987. Reynolds, C. W. "Flocks, Herds, and Schools: A Distributed Behavioral," *Computer Graphics*, **21**(4), (July), 25–34.

1991. Brooks, R. A. "New Approaches to Robotics," *Science*, **253**(5025), (September), 1227–1232.

1992. Langton, C. G. Preface to *Artificial Life II* (eds. C. G. Langton, C. Taylor, J. D. Farmer, and S. Rasmussen), *SFI Studies in the Sciences of Complexity*. Volume X: xiii–xviii. Redwood City, CA: Addison-Wesley.

1993. Levy, S. *Artificial Life*. New York: Vintage Books.

1999. Koza, J. R., Bennett, F. H., Keane, M. A., and Andre, D. *Genetic Programming III: Darwinian Invention and Problem Solving*. San Francisco: Morgan Kaufmann.

Anthony Liekens

ASCII

See CHARACTER CODES.

ASSOCIATION FOR COMPUTING MACHINERY (ACM)

For articles on related subjects, *see*

+ Institute of Electrical and Electronic Engineers–Computer Society (IEEE-CS)
+ International Federation for Information Processing (IFIP)
+ Turing Award Winners

The *Association for Computing Machinery* (ACM) is an international scientific and educational association of computer professionals that traces its beginnings to the founding of the Eastern Association for Computing Machinery (EACM) in 1947, followed in 1954 by the incorporation of ACM. With a current membership of 85 000, ACM was formed to advance the art, science, engineering, and application of information technology, serving both professional and public interests by fostering the open interchange of information and by promoting the highest professional and ethical standards. To these ends it annually sponsors or cosponsors over 100 conferences, meetings, workshops, and symposia and engages in an extensive publication program. Its publications include periodicals, books, monographs, tutorials, transactions, and conference proceedings.

The leading ACM periodicals are its monthly *Communications of the ACM*, which contains general articles and news about computing as well as some technical articles, and which goes to all ACM members; its bimonthly *Journal*, which is a research journal covering a wide swath of computer science; the quarterly *Computing Surveys*, which provides tutorials on a wide range of computing topics; and the monthly *Computing Reviews* (CR), which for more than 25 years was the only periodical printing critical reviews of the literature of computing. In addition to publishing transactions in 12 different subject areas, ACM cooperates with the IEEE Computer Society in the publication of *Transactions on Networking*.

Technical activities are carried out by 36 semiautonomous Special Interest Groups (SIGs) whose subject areas are given at the Website www.acm.org. ACM conducts an active awards program honoring technical achievements and service to the profession, society, and ACM itself (*see* TURING AWARD WINNERS). It has 125 professional chapters, almost a third outside the USA, and 420 student chapters, including 45 outside the USA, all of which can benefit from the ACM Lectureship Program, which provides speakers on a wide variety of topics.

On 1 January 1999, ACM, as an international organization, became a full member of the International Federation for Information Processing (IFIP—*q.v.*) having previously been one of the two members (with the IEEE-CS) of FOCUS, which until 31 December 1998 represented the USA in IFIP. ACM is also is a constituent society of the Institute for Certification of Computing Professionals, and is a professional member of the Internet Society. ACM has joint membership arrangements with the IEEE-CS and with 24 computing societies outside the USA. The ACM headquarters is at One Astor Place, 1515 Broadway, New York, NY 10036-5701.

Eric A. Weiss

ASSOCIATIVE MEMORY

For articles on related subjects, see

+ **Addressing**
+ **Cache Memory**
+ **Memory Hierarchy**
+ **Virtual Memory**

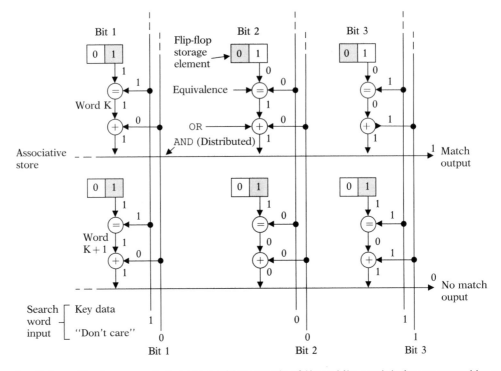

Figure 1. Schematic of an associative store of two words of three bits, each being accessed by match on two bits and by "don't care" on one.

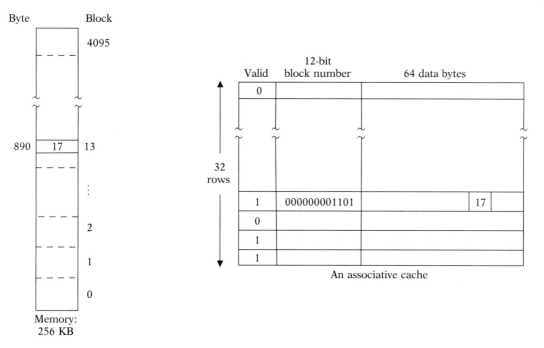

Figure 2. A cache organized as 32 rows, each holding 64 data bytes. The block number (tag) is formed from the high 12 bits of a memory address, and the low 6 bits of the address specify the position of a byte within a cache row. Byte 890 (000000001101 111010 in binary) is in block 13, at position 58 within the cache row, and contains 17. The cache valid bits indicate which rows currently hold data.

Data in an *associative or content-addressable memory* is looked up by properties of its value, rather than by its address as in conventional memory (*see* Fig. 1). Such a property might be a pattern of bits at the start of a word or set of words of storage, for example, that serves as an identifying tag. Associative memory is used in multilevel memory systems (*see* MEMORY HIERARCHY), in which a small fast memory such as a cache may hold copies of some blocks of a larger memory for rapid access (*see* Fig. 2).

To retrieve a word from associative memory, a search key (or *descriptor*) must be presented that represents particular values of all or some of the bits of the word. This key is compared in parallel with the corresponding lock or tag bits of all stored words, and all words matching this key are signaled to be available.

Associative memory is expensive to implement as integrated circuitry (*q.v.*). Other approaches have recently been studied. A massively parallel processing system with small processors and efficient message-broadcast mechanisms can function associatively. If each processor holds a line of text, for example, a broadcast query, "Where does 'associative' appear?," will get affirmative responses from nodes whose text includes that word. Neural networks can model associative memory in a slightly different sense of the term, providing the ability to retrieve information associated with a given input. Such associations might be similarities of meaning in natural language processing (*q.v.*) or pattern similarities in pattern recognition (*q.v.*).

Bibliography

1997. Krikelis, A., and Weems, C. C. (eds.) *Associative Processing and Processors*. Los Alamitos, CA: Computer Society Press.

Kenneth C. Smith and Adel S. Sedra

ATANASOFF-BERRY COMPUTER

The Atanasoff–Berry Computer, or ABC, named for its inventor, John V. Atanasoff, and his graduate assistant, Clifford E. Berry, was the world's first electronic computer. Atanasoff conceived the basic plan of the ABC during the 1937–1938 academic year at Iowa State College, where he was a professor of both physics and mathematics. He and Berry completed a successful model of the computer's central apparatus by December 1939, and the computer itself by May 1942.

The digital (binary) ABC was designed to solve systems of up to 29 simultaneous linear equations (*see* Fig. 1). On the basis of Gaussian elimination, it used repeated additions and subtractions, sign sensing, shifting, and automatic sequential controls for the main step of eliminating a designated variable from a pair of equations. The binary digits of such a pair of equations were represented as high or low charges on capacitors housed in two drums on a common axle. As the drums rotated, their signals were transmitted in parallel to the separate arithmetic unit, in which 30 add–subtract mechanisms, together with an associated carry–borrow drum, performed the appropriate additions or subtractions and sent the results back to the memory drum.

In practice, I/O errors spoiled results for sets of more than five equations, a difficulty Atanasoff and Berry were unable to resolve before they left Iowa for war research positions in 1942. The capacitor memory and the vacuum tube arithmetic unit worked exactly as intended, however, and established the feasibility of electronic computing, as well as many of its principles, for all time.

The electronic switching principles of the ABC were used throughout the ENIAC (*q.v.*), and its principles of both regenerative storage and logical switching adders were also used in the ensuing EDVAC (*q.v.*). Later computers have used all of these principles, plus those of mechanically rotated memories and capacitor memory elements. Atanasoff's priority over J. Presper Eckert (*q.v.*) and John W. Mauchly, whose ENIAC had been unveiled as the first electronic computer in 1946, was not established until 1973, when Federal District Judge Earl R. Larson ruled in Atanasoff's favor in the now famous Honeywell vs Sperry Rand legal suit.

In his later years, Atanasoff received many honorary degrees and other citations, culminating in the 1990 National Medal of Technology "for inventing the electronic digital computer." A replica of the ABC was built at Iowa State University and was first demonstrated in October 1997.

Bibliography

1988. Burks, A. R., and Burks, A. W. *The First Electronic Computer: The Atanasoff Story*. Ann Arbor, MI: University of Michigan Press.

1988. Mackintosh, A. R. "Dr. Atanasoff's Computer," *Scientific American*, **259**(2), 90–96.

Arthur W. Burks and Alice R. Burks

Figure 1.   The ABC computer.

ATLAS

For articles on related subject, *see*

+ Digital Computers, History of: Early
+ Manchester University Computers

Atlas was the third in a series of early computers designed in the UK by a team under Tom Kilburn in the Department of Electrical Engineering, University of Manchester, in association with Ferranti Ltd. Previous systems were the Ferranti Mark I and Ferranti Mark II (Mercury).

The designing of Atlas began in 1958, and ultimately three systems, known as Atlas 1, were constructed and installed at the University of Manchester (1962), the University of London (1963), and the Atlas Laboratory, Chilton, next to the Atomic Energy Research Establishment at Harwell (1963). All were operated until the early 1970s, with the Chilton machine being the last to be switched off in March 1973.

Atlas was the first major system designed for multiprogramming (*q.v.*) and was provided with a composite memory consisting of ferrite cores and magnetic drums linked to provide the user with a one-level memory (*see* VIRTUAL MEMORY). This was achieved by a paging system in which page switching was controlled by a simple learning program, or swapping algorithm. There was also a ferrite rod ("hairbrush") memory of 8000 words to hold the supervisor, a very early *operating system* (*q.v.*). The standard word length was 48 bits, equivalent to one single-address instruction with two modifiers and allowing for up to 2^{20} addresses. Additionally, 128 index registers (*q.v.*) were provided. Instructions were normally executed at an average rate of 0.5 ms, about a hundred times faster than the Mercury computer.

The magnetic tape system used 1-inch tapes, although standard 0.5-inch tapes could also be used. Magnetic disks were not standard, but were fitted later to the Manchester and Chilton machines. Multiple I/O channels (*q.v.*) provided for both paper-tape and punched-card peripherals, as well as line printers.

A modified version of Atlas, known as Atlas 2, was produced with increased core memory and no magnetic drums (thereby dispensing with paging), the prototype being the Titan computer at the University of Cambridge, which was taken out of service at the end of 1973.

Bibliography

1961. Kilburn, T., Howarth, D. J., Payne, R. B., and Sumner, F. H. "The Manchester University Atlas Operating System; Part I, Internal Organisation," *Computer Journal*, **4**, 222–225; "Part II, Users' Description," *Computer Journal*, **4**, 226–229.

1984. Hendry, J. "Prolonged Negotiations: The British Fast Computer Project and the Early History of the British Computer Industry," *Business History*, **26**, 280–306.

Richard A. Buckingham

AUTHENTICATION

For articles on related subjects, *see*

✚ Cryptography, Computers in
✚ Digital Signature
✚ Password
✚ Pretty Good Privacy (PGP)

Authentication is used to refer to several distinct, though related, processes. The earliest use, as described in Needham and Schroeder (1978), is to arrange that two entities engaged in communication, generically referred to as principals, should each be confident as to the other's identity. A more demanding requirement is for each to be able to convince a referee or arbiter that a certain transaction was performed by the other—generally known as *nonrepudiation*. Finally, document content may need to be authenticated in the sense that its integrity is guaranteed in addition to original authorship. In theory, authentication is quite distinct from confidentiality, but in practice they often go together.

Authentication is usually made on the basis of knowledge of something, or by possession of a token or a by combination of the two, as in the use of passwords, physical keys, or an ATM card with a secret PIN number. There are many different protocols (*q.v.*), but they all depend on a very simple principle: if I receive a message that shows unequivocal knowledge of

a

something that only Joe knows, then it came from Joe. Cryptography is used only to demonstrate knowledge of Joe's secret, without advertising the secret itself. In detail there are differences. If we are dealing with symmetric cryptography, the reasoning is usually "Only Joe and I know X, and I didn't send this message so Joe did," and if we are dealing with asymmetric cryptography it will be "Only Joe knows the X needed to send that which I can unpick with X^{-1} (the inverse of X)."

This principle may be simple, but the detail is not. Authentication protocols are subject to numerous errors of design, and it is quite remarkable how many of them, typically programs of no more than five statements long, are incorrect. It is not unknown for insecurities to be noticed 10 years after publication of a protocol.

Authentication protocols are not necessarily appropriate to convincing a third party of anything—for example, for A to convince an arbiter in a dispute that an action really had been undertaken at B's request. This is the second form of authentication.

Yet another kind of authentication is done by computing a "one-way function" of the content, and authenticating it by digital signature. Such one-way functions have to have the property that, given a message and its signed *digest*, as such functions are usually called, it is impracticable to construct a different message with the same digest. Designing digest functions is difficult, and the field is moving very fast.

Bibliography

1995. Meadows, C. "Formal Verification of Cryptographic Protocols—A Survey," *Advances in Cryptology—AsiaCrypt 95*, 133–150. New York: Springer-Verlag.

1996. Abadi, M., and Needham, R. M. "Prudent Engineering Practice for Cryptographic Protocols," *IEEE Transactions on Software Engineering*, **22**(1), (January), 6–15.

1996. Schneier, B. *Applied Cryptography*, 2nd Ed. New York: John Wiley.

Roger M. Needham

AUTOMATA THEORY

For articles on related subjects, *see*

+ **Cellular Automata**
+ **Formal Languages**
+ **Quantum Computing**
+ **Turing Machine**

Introduction and Definitions

Automata theory is a mathematical discipline concerned with the invention and study of mathematically abstract, idealized machines called *automata*. These automata are usually abstractions of information-processing devices, such as computers, rather than of devices that move about, such as robots, mechanical toys, or automobiles.

The automata to be discussed here process strings of symbols from some finite alphabet of symbols. Let A be any alphabet. For example, A might be $\{a, b, c, \ldots, z\}$ or $\{0, 1\}$. We write A^* to mean the set of *all* finite strings of symbols chosen from A. If A is $\{a, b, c, \ldots, z\}$, then A^* contains strings representing English words, such as "cat" and "mouse," along with nonsense strings such as "czzxyh." If A is $\{0, 1\}$, then A^* contains the strings representing the nonnegative integers in binary notation $(0, 1, 10, 11, 100, \ldots)$ and also these same strings but with extra zeros on the left (e.g. 00010).

Automata generally perform one (or both) of two symbol-processing tasks. They compute partial functions from X^* to Y^* for some finite alphabets X and Y, or they *recognize* languages over some alphabet X. A *partial function* f from X^* to Y^* is a correspondence between some subset D of X^* and the set Y^* that associates with each element of D a unique element in Y^*. D is called the *domain* of f, that is, $D = \{x \in X^* | f(x) \text{ is defined}\}$. For example, let $X = Y = \{0, 1\}$ and let D be the elements x of X^* such that x begins with 1 or consists of a single 0. If f associates with x the string in Y^* that denotes the binary number representing twice the binary number represented by x, then f is a partial function from X^* to Y^*.

We say that an automaton α *computes* a partial function f from X^* to Y^* when, if α is given any input x in X^* such that $f(x)$ is defined, α eventually produces an output $y \in Y^*$ such that $f(x) = y$, and otherwise α produces no output. Automata usually receive their inputs on a linear tape, which they may read one symbol at a time. The manner in which they read symbols on an input tape (left to right, back and forth, with or without changing symbols, etc.) depends on the particular class of automata under consideration.

A *language* over an alphabet X is just a subset of X^*. For example, if $X = \{a, b, c, \ldots, z\}$, then $\{a, aa, aaa, \ldots\}$ and $\{x \in X^* | x$ is a word in the English language$\}$ are both languages over X. We say that an automaton α *recognizes* a language L over X if, when α reads an input $x \in X^*$ on its input tape in the manner of automata of its type then, if $x \in L$, α eventually performs some particular act of recognition. Examples of such acts of recognition are (1) halting, (2) entering a special internal state called a *final*, or *accepting*, state, or (3) emptying a designated storage tape, for instance a *pushdown store*. If $x \notin L$, then α, on input x, never performs such an act of recognition. Exactly what constitutes an act of recognition depends on the particular class of automata under consideration. Generally, there are many results of the form: the languages recognized by a particular class of automata are exactly those formal languages generated by a particular class of grammar. For example, *pushdown automata* are capable of recognizing the valid syntactic classes of all Algol-like languages.

Automatic *theorem proving* is also concerned with language recognition. The language to be recognized is the set of propositions derivable from some set of axioms. Automatic theorem proving has been applied to discover new mathematical theorems, to question-answering systems, and to robotics (*q.v.*).

Types of Automata

Most types of automata are special cases of the *Turing machine* (*see* Fig. 1). Turing machines may be operated either to recognize languages or to compute partial functions. A Turing machine is a finite-state deterministic device with read and write heads (which read or write one symbol at a time) attached to one or more tapes. *Finite state* means that the number of

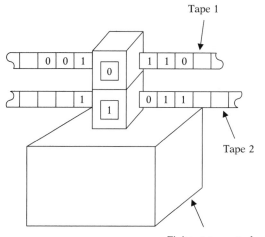

Figure 1. A two-tape Turing machine. Each tape is scanned by a single read–write head. Tape 1 contains the string of nonblank symbols 0010110, with the underlined 0 currently being read. Tape 2 contains 11011, with the underlined 1 being currently read. If the tapes can move in only direction, the same diagram would depict a two-tape finite automaton.

distinguishable internal configurations of the device is finite, and *deterministic* means that the next state of the device and its subsequent action (writing or motion) on the tapes is completely determined by its current state and the symbols it is currently reading on its tapes.

Turing machines were first introduced independently by Turing (*q.v.*) and Post in 1936 to give a precise mathematical definition of *effective procedure*. There is considerable evidence that the partial functions computed by (languages recognized by) Turing machines are exactly those computed (recognized) by informal effective procedures or algorithms (*q.v.*). Any computation or recognition problem for which there is a known informal algorithm can be handled by a Turing machine. Turing machines with many (in general, n-dimensional) tapes and read–write heads can compute and recognize no more than can Turing machines with a single one-dimensional tape and single read–write head, although they may compute and recognize more efficiently.

Finite Automata

A *finite automaton* is a deterministic finite-state device equipped with a read (only) head attached to a single input tape. A special subset of the finite set of states of a finite automaton is designated as the set of *final*, or *recognition*, states. A finite automaton α processes a string of symbols thus: α begins in a special initial, or start, state and automatically reads the symbols of x (on its tape) from left to right, changing its states in a manner depending only on its previous state and the symbol just read. If, after the last (rightmost) symbol of x is read, α goes into a final state, α recognizes x; otherwise, α does not recognize x. Let $A = \{0, 1\}$. It is possible, for example, to design a finite automaton α such that α recognizes that $L = \{x \in A^* | x$ ends in two consecutive 1s and does not contain two consecutive 0s$\}$; *see* Fig. 2. On the other hand, it can be shown that *no* finite automaton can recognize $L' = \{x \in A^* | x$ consists of a consecutive string of n^2 1s, for some positive integer $n\}$, though a Turing machine can.

In Fig. 2, the circles represent the different states of α, and the number inside each circle is a name for the state that circle represents. Hence, 0 is the start state of α and 4 is its only final state. An arrow from one state to another means that if α is in the first state while scanning the alphabet symbol that labels the arrow, then it goes next into the second state. For example, if is in state 1 scanning a 0, it goes next into state 2; whereas, if it is in state 1 scanning a 1, it goes next into state 3. If α is given the input string 010111, beginning in state 0, the successive states into which it is thereafter driven are (in order) 1, 3, 1, 3, 4, 4. Since 4 is a final state, α (correctly) recognizes the input string 010111. If α is given 10011, beginning in state 0, the successive states into which it is thereafter driven are (in order) 3, 1, 2, 2, 2. Since 2 is *not* a final state, α (correctly) fails to recognize 10011.

A *nondeterministic finite automaton* is a device just like a finite automaton except that the next state is not completely determined by the current state and symbol read. Instead, a *set* of next possible states is so determined. A nondeterministic finite automaton α may be thought of as processing a string of symbols x, just like an ordinary finite automaton, except that it has to be run over again several times so that each of the different possible state-change behaviors is eventually realized. Proceeding in that fashion, a nondeterministic finite automaton α is said to *recognize x* if at least *one* of the possible ways of running α on input x results in getting α into a final state after the last symbol of x has been read.

Interestingly, it can be shown that nondeterministic finite automata cannot recognize any broader class of languages than do ordinary finite automata. Turing machine recognizers that operate nondeterministically can also be defined, but they, too, cannot recognize more languages than can ordinary Turing machines. But it is often conceptually easier to program or design machines that operate nondeterministically. For many types of automata, nondeterministic machines are significantly more compact, succinct, or powerful than the corresponding deterministic ones. Furthermore, many practically important recognition tasks can be solved by nondeterministic Turing machines that run in time bounded by a polynomial in the size of their input strings. A famous open question in computer science asks whether these tasks can be done at all in polynomial time by deterministic Turing machines

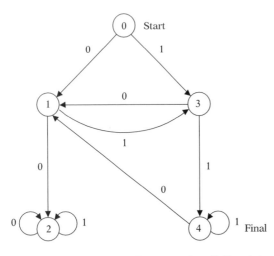

Figure 2. The state diagram of a finite-state automaton for recognizing {$x \in \{0, 1\}^* | x$ ends in two consecutive 1s and does not contain two consecutive 0s}.

(see COMPUTATIONAL COMPLEXITY and NP-COMPLETE PROBLEMS).

Neural Nets

In 1943, McCulloch and Pitts introduced nets of formalized neurons and showed that such neural nets could realize the state-change behavior of any finite automaton. These nets were composed of synchronized elements, each capable of realizing some Boolean function such as *and, or,* or *not*. In 1948, von Neumann added to the computational and logical questions of automata theory by introducing new questions pertaining to construction and self-replication of automata. The iterated arrays of interconnected finite automata that he introduced have also been used to study pattern processing for patterns of symbols, including one-dimensional strings of symbols, among others.

Linear-Bounded-Automata

A *linear-bounded automaton* (LBA) is a (possibly nondeterministic) one-tape Turing machine whose read–write head is restricted to move only on the section of tape initially containing the input. Special end markers are placed on each side of an input string to prevent the tape head from leaving this restricted section of tape. A form of deterministic LBA was first studied by Myhill in an attempt to find models of computation more realistic than the completely general Turing machines. (A deterministic LBA is logically equivalent to an ordinary stored-program computer with finite memory.) Later, it was shown that LBAs recognize all (and only) the *context-sensitive* languages, an important and natural class of languages that is more restricted than the languages recognizable by Turing machines but more general than the *context-free* languages. It is an open question whether a (nondeterministic) LBA can recognize more languages than a deterministic LBA.

Pushdown Automata

A *pushdown automaton* is a (possibly nondeterministic) finite automaton with a special sort of auxiliary tape called a *pushdown store* (or *stack–q.v.*). A pushdown store is a tape quite like the stack of plates found on a spring in cafeterias. It is a *last in, first out* store. A special read–write head always scans the top symbol on the pushdown store. Pushdown automata recognize a string x by one of two conventions. Either x is recognized by the device as it gets into one of its final states or by the pushdown store as it empties just after the rightmost symbol of x is read. The class of languages recognized by emptying the pushdown store is the same as that recognized by final states. Let $A = \{0, 1\}$. For $x \in A^*$, let x^R be x written backwards. For example, 001110^R is 011100. A string x is a *palindrome* if x and x^R are the same; for instance, 0 and 1001 are palindromes. The language $L = \{x \in A^* | x$ is a palindrome$\}$ is recognizable by a suitable nondeterministic pushdown automaton, but L is *not* recognizable by a deterministic pushdown automaton.

Bibliography

1966. von Neumann, J. *Theory of Self-Reproducing Automata* (edited and completed by A. W. Burks). Urbana, IL: University of Illinois Press.

1967. Minsky, M. *Computation: Finite and Infinite Machines.* Upper Saddle River, NJ: Prentice Hall.

1979. Hopcroft, J. E., and Ullman, J. D. *Introduction to Automata Theory, Languages, and the Theory of Computation.* Reading, MA: Addison-Wesley.

1998. Lewis, H., and Papadimitriou, C. *Elements of the Theory of Computation,* 2nd Ed. Upper Saddle River, NJ: Prentice Hall.

John Case

AUTOMATION

For articles on related subjects, *see*

+ Automata Theory
+ Computer-Aided Design/Computer-Aided Manufacturing (CAD/CAM)
+ Cybernetics

a

b
c
d
e
f
g
h
i
j
k
l
m
n
o
p
q
r
s
t
u
v,w
x,y
z

+ Management Information Systems (MIS)
+ Robotics
+ Telerobotics

Automation is the conversion of a work process, a procedure, or equipment to automatic rather than human operation or control. Automation does not simply transfer human functions to machines, but involves a deep reorganization of the work process. Early automation relied on mechanical and electromechanical control devices. Modern automation is usually associated with computerization.

Phase I: Mechanization and Rationalization of Labor

The mechanization of machine tools for production began during the Industrial Revolution at the end of the eighteenth century with the introduction of the Watt steam engine, the Jacquard loom, the lathe, and the screw machine. Mechanization replaced human or animal power with machine power; those mechanisms, however, were not automatic but controlled by factory workers. The factory system, with its large-volume, standardized production, and division of labor, replaced the old work organization, where broadly skilled craftsmen and artisans produced small quantities of diverse products.

In the late nineteenth century, Frederick W. Taylor rationalized the factory system by introducing the principles of "scientific management." He viewed the body of each worker as a machine whose movements had to be optimized in order to minimize time required to complete each task and thus increase overall productivity. "Scientific management" strictly separated mental work from manual labor: workers were not to think but to follow detailed instructions prepared for them by managers. The rationalized factory system gave birth to a new managerial class and large clerical bureaucracies.

Taylor's principles served as a basis for Henry Ford's system of mass production. In 1913, the Ford Motor Company introduced a moving assembly line, drastically cutting assembly time. The assembly line imposed a strict order on production by forcing workers to keep pace with the motion of the conveyor belt. Mass production relied on the standardization of components and final products and routinization of manufacturing and assembly jobs.

Phase II: Automation of Production

In 1947, the Ford Company brought the term "automation" into wide circulation by establishing the first Automation Department, charged with designing electromechanical, hydraulic, and pneumatic parts-handling, work-feeding, and work-removing mechanisms to connect standalone machines and increase the rate of production. In 1950, Ford put into operation the first "automated" engine plant. Although early automation was "hard," or fixed in the hardware, and did not involve automatic feedback control, this concept provoked great public enthusiasm for "unmanned factories" controlled by "buttons that push themselves," as well as causing growing concern about the prospects of mass unemployment.

To meet US Air Force demands for a high-performance fighter aircraft whose complex structural members could not be manufactured by traditional machining methods, a technology of Numerical Control (NC) of machine tools was developed in the early 1950s. NC laid the foundation for programmable, or "soft," automation, in which the sequence of processing operations was not fixed but could be changed for each new product style. Commercial NC machines for batch production appeared in the mid-1950s.

Phase III: Computer-Aided Manufacturing (CAM)

The first industrial applications of digital computers occurred in the electrical power, dairy, chemical, and petroleum refinery industries for automatic process control. In 1959, TRW installed the first digital computer designed specifically for plant process control at Texaco's Port Arthur refinery. Early applications were open-loop control systems: gathering data from measuring devices and sensors throughout the plant, the computers monitored technological processes, performed calculations, and printed out "operator guides"; subsequent adjustments were made by human operators. In the 1960s, closed-loop feedback control systems appeared. These computers were connected directly to servo-control valves and made adjustments automatically (*see* CYBERNETICS).

In the late 1960s, with the development of time sharing (*q.v.*) on large mainframe computers, standalone NC machines were brought under Direct Numerical Control (DNC) of a central computer. DNC systems proved vulnerable to frequent failures due to malfunctioning of the central computer and the interference of factory power cables with the data transmission cables of the DNC system. With the introduction of microprocessors in the 1970s, centralized DNC systems in manufacturing were largely replaced by Computer Numerical Control (CNC) systems with distributed control, in which each NC machine was controlled by its own microcomputer.

Robotics combined the techniques of NC and remote control to replace human workers with numerically controlled mechanical manipulators. The first commercial robots appeared in the early 1960s. Robots proved very efficient in performing specialized tasks that demanded high precision or had to be done in hazardous environments. To approach the human level of flexibility, robots were supplied with sophisticated techniques of feedback, vision and tactile sensors, reasoning capabilities, and adaptive control.

Hierarchical Numerical Control Systems combined DNC and CNC features: they linked each standalone computer controller to a central computer that maintained a large library of CNC programs and monitored production. This approach aspired to replace the human operator's expertise by engineering knowledge formalized in CNC programs. In such systems, human operators generally no longer programmed CNC equipment on the shop floor, and production was brought under remote supervision of a central management-controlled computer.

Phase IV: Automated Engineering

In the 1960s, large aerospace manufacturers, such as McDonnell-Douglas and Boeing, developed proprietary computer-aided design (CAD) systems, which provided computer graphics (*q.v.*) tools for drafting, analyzing, and modifying aircraft designs. In 1970, Computer-Vision Corporation introduced the first complete turnkey commercial CAD system for industrial designers, which provided all the necessary hardware and software in one package. While CAD systems are often packaged and standardized, CAM (Computer-Aided Manufacturing) applications tend to be industry-specific and proprietary. With the introduction of Computer-Aided Engineering (CAE) systems for standard techniques of engineering analysis, a whole range of engineering tasks became automated, blurring the distinction between blue-collar and white-collar jobs.

Phase V: Automated Management

Among the earliest applications of information technology was the automation of information-processing tasks. The first stored-program digital computer purchased by a nongovernment customer was UNIVAC I (*q.v.*), installed by GE in 1954 to automate basic transaction processing: payroll, inventory control and material scheduling, billing and order service, and general cost accounting. Large clerical bureaucracies, which processed huge amounts of data generated in mass production and mass marketing, became a primary target of automation and job reduction in the 1960s and 1970s. By 1970, the profession of bookkeeper was almost completely eliminated in the USA. In the mid-1960s, the first management-information system (MIS–*q.v.*) appeared, providing management with data, models of analysis, and algorithms for decision-making.

Phase VI: Computer-Integrated Manufacturing (CIM)

In the late 1980s, an integration of the automated factory and the "electronic office" began. Computer-Integrated Manufacturing (CIM) combines flexible automation (robots, numerically controlled machines, and flexible manufacturing systems), CAD/CAM systems, and management-information systems to build integrated production systems that cover the complete operations of a manufacturing firm.

a

b
c
d
e
f
g
h
i
j
k
l
m
n
o
p
q
r
s
t
u
v,w
x,y
z

Social and Economic Dimensions of Automation

Views of automation range between two extremes—unabashed optimism and utmost pessimism. The optimists believe in a technological utopia, an imagined bright future in which machines will relieve people of all hard work and bring prosperity to humankind. The pessimists view machines as instruments of subjugation and control by a ruling elite, argue that automation leads to the degradation of human beings, and depict the future as a grim technological dystopia. Both sides view automatic technology as an autonomous force determining the direction of human history. Automation itself, however, is a social process shaped by various social and economic forces. This process may take various directions and may have diverse consequences depending on the socioeconomic and organizational choices made during automation.

Bibliography

1967. Bright, J. R. "The Development of Automation," in *Technology in Western Civilization*, (eds. M. Kranzberg, and C. W. Pursell Jr.), Vol. II, 635–654. New York: Oxford University Press.

1996. Kling, R. (ed.) *Computerization and Controversy: Value Conflicts and Social Choices*, 2nd Ed. San Diego, CA: Academic Press.

1997. Rochlin, G. I. *Trapped in the Net: The Unanticipated Consequences of Computerization*. Princeton, NJ: Princeton University Press.

Slava Gerovitch

AUXILIARY MEMORY

See MEMORY: AUXILIARY.

BABBAGE, CHARLES

For articles on related subjects, *see*

+ Analytical Engine
+ Difference Engine
+ Digital Computers, History of: Origins
+ Lovelace, Countess of

Charles Babbage (Fig. 1) was born in London on 26 December 1791. He went up to Cambridge University in 1810 where he acquired a high mathematical reputation that increased with the years. In 1828, he was appointed Lucasian Professor, a position that Newton himself had held.

Babbage was a polymath, but his dominating interest was calculating machinery. While still a student, he began to work on his *Difference Engine*, intended to facilitate the production of accurate mathematical tables. His own attempt at implementation failed, but another one by Georg and Edvard Scheutz, who had read of his ideas in a magazine, was more successful.

It is his work on the *Analytical Engine* that gives Babbage his greatest fame. This was to have been an automatically sequenced, general-purpose computer, a profoundly original concept. The real breakthrough came in 1834 and the years immediately following, but Babbage continued to work on the subject for the remainder of his life.

Babbage thought of the Analytical Engine as being entirely mechanical, with no suggestion, even

Figure 1. Charles Babbage (courtesy of the Mary Evans Picture Library).

in later years, that electricity might be used. The Engine's decimal numbers were to be stored on wheels, with 10 distinguishable positions, and transferred by a system of racks to a central *mill*, or processor, where all arithmetic would be performed. He planned storage capacity for one thousand 50-digit numbers. He studied exhaustively a wide variety of schemes for performing the four operations of arithmetic, and he invented the idea of *anticipatory carry*, which, in a mechanical computer, is much faster than carrying successively from one stage to another.

Punched cards laced together as in a Jacquard loom were to be used both for sequencing the Analytical Engine and for the input of numbers. For sequencing, Babbage proposed to have two independently stepping card mechanisms, one for operation cards controlling the mill, and one for variable cards controlling the store. Thus, he had operation codes and addresses that became associated at run time, but not the concept of combining them into a stored instruction; the Analytical Engine was not a stored-program computer.

Much of what we know about how the Analytical Engine would have functioned derives from an account written in French by L. F. Menebrea of a series of presentations given by Babbage in Turin in 1842. This was ably translated into English by Lady Lovelace, the daughter of Lord Byron, who added extensive notes written under Babbage's close supervision, including the outline of a program for computing Bernoulli numbers.

Although Babbage had skilled machinists in his employ until the end of his life, he failed to implement the Analytical Engine. We can only conclude that he was a perfectionist, temperamentally incapable of carrying the project through. His detailed design studies lay buried in his unpublished notebooks and were forgotten for years. He died in London on 18 October 1871.

Bibliography

1864. Babbage, C. *Passages From the Life of a Philosopher.* London; facsimile edition, London, 1968; reprint (ed. M. Campbell-Kelly), London: Pickering & Chatto, 1994.

1971. Wilkes, M. V. "Babbage as a Computer Pioneer," *Report of the Babbage Memorial Meeting*, British Computer Society. Reprinted in *Historica Mathematica*, **4**, 415, 1977.

1982. Hyman, A. *Charles Babbage.* Princeton, NJ: Princeton University Press.

1989. Campbell-Kelly, M. (ed.) *The Works of Charles Babbage*, 11 Vols. London: Pickering & Chatto.

Maurice V. Wilkes

BACKUS-NAUR FORM (BNF)

For articles on related subjects, *see*

+ Algol
+ Expression
+ Metalanguage
+ Procedure-Oriented Languages: Survey

Backus–Naur Form, named for John W. Backus of the United States and Peter Naur of Denmark and usually written BNF, is the best-known example of a *metalanguage* (*q.v.*), that is, one that syntactically describes a programming language. Using BNF it is possible to specify which sequences of symbols constitute a syntactically valid statement in a given language.

A *metalinguistic variable* (or *metavariable*), also called a *syntactic unit*, is one whose values are strings of symbols chosen from among the symbols permitted in the given language. In BNF, metalinguistic variables are enclosed in brackets, ⟨⟩, for clarity and to distinguish them from symbols in the language itself, which are called *terminal symbols* or just *terminals*. The symbol ::= is used to indicate metalinguistic equivalence; a vertical bar (|) is used to indicate that a choice is to be made among the items so indicated; and concatenation is indicated simply by juxtaposing the elements to be concatenated.

For an example, here is how the definition of an Algol integer is built up. First, we define a *digit* as

```
⟨digit⟩ ::= 0 | 1 | 2 | 3 | 4 | 5 | 6 | 7 | 8 | 9
```

Next we have a statement that an unsigned integer consists either of a single digit or an unsigned integer followed by another digit:

```
⟨unsigned integer⟩ ::= ⟨digit⟩
                     |⟨unsigned integer⟩⟨digit⟩
```

This definition may be applied *recursively* to build up unsigned integers of any length. Since there must be a limit on the number of digits in any actual computer implementation, this would have to be stated separately in conjunction with each particular implementation or, as in some extensions to BNF, by an addition to the definition of *unsigned integer* (e.g. placing [10] above ::= could indicate a limit of 10 digits). Finally, the definition of an integer is completed by noting that it may be preceded by a plus sign, a minus sign, or neither:

```
⟨integer⟩ ::= ⟨unsigned integer⟩
            | + ⟨unsigned integer⟩
            | - ⟨unsigned integer⟩
```

An extended version of BNF (EBNF) is used in the *Pascal User Manual and Report* (Jensen *et al.*, 1985) and in the definition of Modula-2 (Wirth, 1985). An EBNF specification of the syntax of a programming language consists of a collection of rules (*productions*), collectively called a *grammar*, that describe the formation of sentences in the language. Each production consists of a nonterminal symbol and an EBNF expression separated by an equal sign and terminated by a period. The nonterminal symbol is a *meta-identifier* (a syntactic constant denoted by an English word), and the EBNF expression is its definition. An EBNF expression is composed of zero or more terminal symbols, nonterminals, and metasymbols, summarized in Table 1.

The superficial difference between BNF and EBNF is that, in the former, nonterminals need to be delimited (by angle brackets) and terminals are allowed to stand for themselves, whereas in EBNF, terminals must be delimited (by quotation marks) and nonterminals are allowed to stand for themselves. The more profound difference is that the bracket and brace notation of EBNF allows a simpler presentation of definitions that must be expressed recursively in BNF. Consider, for example, these contrasting definitions of a Pascal ⟨identifier⟩:

Table 1. Metasymbols in EBNF.

Metasymbol	Meaning
=	is defined to be
|	alternatively
.	end of production
[X]	0 or 1 instance of X
{X}	0 or more instances of X
(X|Y)	a grouping: either X or Y
"XYZ"	the terminal symbol XYZ
MetaIdentifier	the nonterminal symbol MetaIdentifier

```
BNF: ⟨identifier⟩ ::= ⟨letter⟩
                    | ⟨identifier⟩ ⟨letter⟩
                    | ⟨identifier⟩ ⟨digit⟩
```

Meaning: an identifier is either a single letter or else something that is already a valid identifier followed by either a letter or a digit.

```
EBNF: Identifier = Letter
                   {Letter | Digit}.
```

Meaning: an identifier is a single letter followed by any number of letters or digits, possibly none.

The information conveyed through an EBNF production can be displayed pictorially through the use of *syntax diagrams* (*railroad diagrams*), a technique popularized by the Pascal report of Jensen *et al.* (1985). The syntax diagram for a Pascal identifier is shown in Fig. 1a. A more complex syntax diagram, one that defines a ⟨signed real⟩ number in Pascal, is shown in Fig. 1b. The diagram can be used to show that such

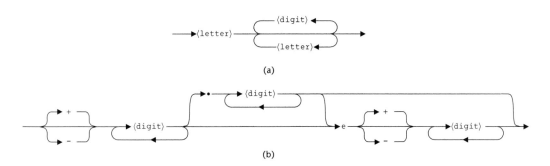

Figure 1. (a) ⟨identifier⟩ (b) ⟨signed real⟩.

character strings as 5.7, -19.0, +3.9, -7.36e-3, and 123e4 are valid signed real numbers but that -7., .2, and 123.e4 are not.

Bibliography

1985. Jensen, K., Wirth,   N., Mickel,   A. B.,   and Miner, J. F. *Pascal User Manual and Report*, 3rd Ed, ISO Pascal Standard. New York: Springer-Verlag.

1985. Wirth, N. *Programming in Modula-2* (third corrected edition). New York: Springer-Verlag.

Daniel D. McCracken

BANDWIDTH

For articles on related subjects, *see*

+ Baud
+ Communications and Computers
+ Data Communications
+ Ethernet

The *bandwidth* of an analog communication network is a measure of the range of frequencies it can transmit at maximum power levels. Within the preserved range, however, there is still attenuation, since the power of signals passing through a transmission system is reduced. A typical measurement of attenuation on the US telephone network is shown in Fig. 1, which indicates that somewhere below 300 Hz and above 3 to 4 kHz, the attenuation rises very rapidly. The range of frequencies in which the power level stays at above one-half its peak value (the so-called 3 dB (decibel) points) is the *nominal bandwidth* of the circuit. This is typically 3 kHz in a switched telephone line.

In digital communications, bandwidth has become a synonym for what had been known as the information *transfer rate*. For example, the bandwidth or capacity of an Ethernet network may be 100 (or more) Mb/s. The digital bandwidth of a channel, or *capacity*, depends directly upon the analog or "electrical" bandwidth of the communication medium and the channel's

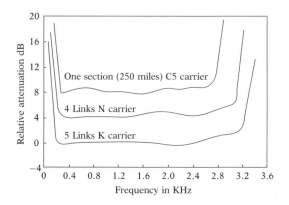

Figure 1. Attenuation for frequency division multiplexing (FDM) systems (reproduced from *Communication-Networks for Computers* by D. W. Davies and D. L. A. Barber, New York: Wiley, 1973, Fig. 2.16).

noise levels. The channel capacity is governed by the Hartley–Shannon law of information theory (*q.v.*).

Bibliography

1999. Bateman, A. *Digital Communications: Design for the Real World*. Reading, MA: Addison-Wesley.

Vicky J. Hardman and Peter T. Kirstein

BAR CODE

See UNIVERSAL PRODUCT CODE.

BASIC

For articles on related subjects, *see*

+ Programming Languages
+ Procedure-Oriented Languages
+ Structured Programming
+ Time Sharing

The Birth of Basic

Basic (Beginner's All-purpose Symbolic Instruction Code) was invented at Dartmouth College in 1964 by John Kemeny and Thomas Kurtz to allow students to write simple programs. The students used Basic on a time-sharing system, which allowed them to reach the computer using terminals in their dorms. The computers of that era were expensive and hard to use and there were only a few computer languages to choose from, Fortran (*q.v.*) and Algol (*q.v.*) being two of the most common. Basic came into being partly because these other languages seemed too hard for most students to learn.

Basic Principles

The design of Basic followed these criteria:

1. *Free form input and default output.* Fortran required key-punching numbers into fixed fields on cards, and also required stating how to print the output numbers. Basic allowed numbers to be entered as the user pleased and printed its output to reasonable precision without explicit formatting rules.

2. *English words rather than punctuation.* Fortran and Algol both used tricky punctuation with semicolons or commas. Basic used English words chosen to suggest what was actually going on. Compare the Fortran loop statement with those of Algol and Basic:

```
Fortran:     DO 200,I=1,100,3
        200  SUM=SUM+X(I)
Algol:       for i := 1 step 3 until 100 do
               sum := sum + x(i);
Basic:   FOR I = 1 TO 100 STEP 3
           LET SUM = SUM + X(I)
         NEXT I
```

3. *One line = one statement.* A statement in a computer language is like a sentence in a written language. Fortran allowed statements longer than could be punched onto one card. Algol allowed short statements to be bunched on the same line. Basic used the simple rule that one line equals one statement.

4. *Each statement starts with a keyword.* In most languages all statements except assignment statements like X = X + 1 start with a keyword. Basic unified the practice through use of LET, as in LET X = X + 1.

5. *Formulas like ordinary algebra.* The only differences were that fractions had to be on a single line (using the /) and exponents followed the ^ character used as a left *delimiter* (*q.v.*).

6. *Only one number type.* Basic used double-precision floating-point as its only numerical *data type* (*q.v.*).

7. *Line numbers double as GO TO targets.* Each line had to begin with a line number. Since Basic used GO TO statements for looping, the line numbers also served as GO TO targets. This design feature of the original Basic quickly disappeared. Word processors now allow writing a program just as you might write a paper, and structured programming (*q.v.*) has taught us how to avoid the use, and therefore the misuse, of GO TO statements.

Personal Computers

In the late 1960s and early 1970s, Basic was the most common language on time-sharing systems, and most dialects were patterned after the original Dartmouth Basic. So when personal computers of limited memory arrived in the early 1980s, interpretive versions of Basic rather naturally became their language of choice. Two of the most common embellishments were graphing commands and number typing. A third addition were the PEEK and POKE instructions, which allowed access to particular memory cells. LET became optional.

Modern Basic

All modern versions of Basic now are fully structured, that is, you don't have to use GO TO statements (*see* STRUCTURED PROGRAMMING). All have sophisticated ways to organize large programs using subroutines and modules. The original Basic included a simple subroutine structure using the GOSUB statement along with line numbers. Parameters (arguments) were not allowed. Named subroutines with parameters are now allowed.

Most of the modern features are contained in Standard Basic, a direct descendant of the original Dartmouth Basic. But the most popular version of Basic today is Microsoft's Visual Basic. Of the original design criteria, only 1, 2, and 5 remain in all versions of Basic. Most versions allow some form of line continuation for very long statements, and some versions allow more than one statement on a line.

Bibliography

1968. Kemeny, J. G., and Kurtz, T. E. "Dartmouth Time Sharing," *Science*, **162**, 223–238.
1981. Kurtz, T. E. "BASIC," in *History of Programming Languages* (ed. R. L. Wexelblat), 515–549. New York: Academic Press.

Thomas E. Kurtz

BAUD

For articles on related subjects, *see*

+ Bandwidth
+ Communications and Computers
+ Data Communications

The *baud* is a unit of signaling speed and refers to the number of times the state (or condition) of a data communication line changes per second. It is the reciprocal of the length (in seconds) of the shortest element in the signaling code. Historically, it is a contraction of the surname of the Frenchman J. M. E. Baudot, whose five-bit code was adopted by the French telegraph system in 1877. By contrast, a bit is the smallest unit of information in a binary system. The baud rate is therefore equal to the bit rate only if each signal element represents one bit of information.

Unfortunately, in much of today's literature, the terms "baud" and "bits per second" are used synonymously. This is correct in cases where pure two-state signaling is used, but is incorrect in general. For this reason, the term "baud" is gradually being replaced by "bits per second," since the latter is independent of the coding method and truly represents the information rate.

John S. Sobolewski

BINARY ARITHMETIC

See ARITHMETIC, COMPUTER; COMPLEMENT; and NUMBERS AND NUMBER SYSTEMS.

BINARY CODED DECIMAL (BCD)

See CHARACTER CODES.

BINARY SEARCH

See SEARCHING.

BINARY TREE

See TREE.

BINDING

For articles on related subjects, *see*

+ Compile and Run Time
+ Compiler
+ Expression
+ Language Processors
+ Linkers and Loaders
+ Machine- and Assembly-language Programming
+ Programming Languages

Binding means translating a program expression into a form immediately interpretable by the machine on which the program is to run; *binding time* is the moment at which this translation is achieved. An expression is *completely* bound, therefore, when translated into an absolute machine representation at a fixed location in a storage device. When the context so indicates, however, *binding* can refer to an intermediate point in this process, and *binding time* can mean the point at which the translator has gone as far toward binding the expression as it can. For example, a compiler may intentionally leave the binding of some class of expressions to be completed by a linker, or even defer binding of some to run time. Many programming languages require that such type attributes as *real, integer, string,* and so on, be assigned when a variable is introduced, thus enabling the compiler to test statements involving the variable for formal correctness as they are encountered at compile time.

In general, early binding means more efficient processing of a source program, usually at some cost in flexibility and potentially useful information. The information sacrificed might have supported the use of arrays whose dimensions could vary at run time, or the issuing of more informative error messages, or the ability to compile the same program for various configurations of the target system.

A compiler may offer the choice of optimizing a program once it is believed to be correct, or of preserving more of its original form to facilitate debugging (*q.v.*). In many respects, the history of software development is the history of ever-later binding time, with user convenience and program adaptability given progressively greater emphasis, but also with the security of early binding still provided. A language with polymorphic functions (*see* FUNCTIONAL PROGRAMMING) will still check at compile time that the function treats its arguments consistently. Likewise, object-oriented programming (*q.v.*), which makes run-time resolution of attributes and linkages a major feature, preserves static (early) checking of type attributes. The OOP feature called *inheritance* is, in effect, a systematic approach to distinguishing those attributes of an object that are to be bound at compile time from those to be bound at run time.

Bibliography

1996. Pratt, T. W., and Zelkowitz, M. V. *Programming Languages: Design and Implementation.* Upper Saddle River, NJ: Prentice Hall.

Mark Halpern

BIOCOMPUTING

For articles on related subjects, *see*

+ Artificial Life
+ Computer Graphics
+ Data Mining
+ Genetic Algorithms
+ Image Processing
+ Medical Imaging
+ Scientific Applications
+ Simulation
+ Virtual Reality

Modeling Living Systems

The very complexity that makes life difficult for experimental biologists intrigues mathematicians and has led to the formation of the field of *mathematical biology*. As computers become more cost-effective, simulation modeling is increasingly being used for incorporating the necessary biological complexity into original, often simplified, mathematical models.

Visualization

The life sciences are visual in two ways: (1) directly, in that they handle data from images (X ray, molecular modeling, computational chemistry); and (2) indirectly, in that they handle complex data and transform it to a visual representation. In a sense, the computer becomes the laboratory, and, as a consequence, what was once done *in* the tube is now being done *on* the tube.

Imaging

A natural use of computers for visualization is the handling of patient image data and the construction or reconstruction of medical image data for clinical diagnosis and analysis. Imaging includes three major problem classes: (1) simple rebuilding of two-dimensional (2D) graphics data into a useful screen image, (2) reconstruction of 3D images from 2D scans, and (3) visualization of an image in a real-time interactive mode. In the areas of noninvasive medicine and image reconstruction, CAT, PET, and MRI scanners now inhabit most hospital complexes. With these systems, physicians are now able to simulate a surgical procedure before it is performed, thereby minimizing potential hazards and increasing surgical accuracy.

Computational Genetics and Molecular Biology

The surge in molecular information associated with the human genome and other animal genome sequencing projects has two computational foci: (1) a field that is referred to as *computational biology* and which we have chosen to think of as "computational molecular biology and genetics"; and (2) *molecular informatics*. These fields deal with the issues of data analysis and data management problems arising in the experimental domain of gene sequencing and molecular analysis.

As experimental molecular biology sequences more and more of the genes in various species, we have a greater database of information that can be used to study evolutionary biology. Tree search algorithms, implemented on parallel computers and on networks of smaller workstations, can assist scientists in evaluating genetic evolutionary trees. At the gene sequencing level, mathematical and computational algorithms are used to align gene sequences, match them, reconstruct them from sequence fragments, and to construct theoretical 3D structures based on those sequences.

Computational Chemistry

Computational chemistry subsumes three major topics: (1) *biophysical properties*, such as crystallographic reconstruction and molecular visualization, (2) *molecular*
biochemistry, which encompasses such areas as structure/function studies, enzyme/substrate studies, and protein dynamics and their properties, and (3) *Pharmacokinetics/pharmacodynamics*, which encompasses such areas as interactive molecular modeling, drug design and interactions, binding site properties, structure/function relationships as applied to drug effectiveness, and cell receptor structures. All of these areas involve intensive numeric computation and subsequent real-time graphics for visualization. Neural nets are being used to learn to identify similar protein structures based upon recognition of pattern representations for the 3D structure of proteins. Typically, the work is performed on a vector supercomputer.

Computational Cell Biology

The dynamics of cell populations is of interest to both biologists and clinicians. A mathematical model of cellular processes could be used to test cancer and AIDS treatment protocols and regimens before they were actually implemented. Early work in this area was performed by Morrison, Aroesty, and Lincoln at the Rand Corporation. More recently, mathematical models of cell population growth for the purposes of studying AIDS progression and treatment have been developed and studied by Webb at Vanderbilt University; cancer progression and treatment by Tucker and Zimmerman at M. D. Anderson Cancer Center; aging and its interplay with cancer development and progression by Witten at the University of Michigan; cell cycle progression by Tyson at Virginia State; and by many others.

Computational Physiology

Human physiology attempts to explain the physical and the chemical factors that are responsible for the origin, development, and progression of human life. Humans are complex machines built from equally complex systems (immune system, digestive system, nervous system, etc.). These systems contain multiple parts or organs. Realistic models of these systems can lead to deeper understanding of the basic biology of these interacting bodily systems.

Reproductive Biology

Of the approximately 500 000 follicles present in the two ovaries at birth, only about 375 will eventually develop into ova (eggs). Mathematical models of the development of a follicle have been made by Lacker at the Courant Institute for Mathematical Sciences, Gosden *et al.* (UK), and Witten. The basic premise of these models is that the follicle undergoes a series of stages or steps in its growth that can be modeled by differential equations. Witten's system involves the solution of anywhere from 50 000 to over 200 000 nonlinear differential equations describing a probability distribution for a given number of follicles in each stage of development. Male reproductive biology can also be addressed. Mathematical models of swimming tails (sperm without heads) have been studied by Fauci at Tulane University. The solution of a swimming object in a viscous fluid is a numerically intensive problem in computational fluid dynamics.

Cardiac Dynamics

Arthur Winfree of the University of Arizona has been studying circulating, vortex-like excitation in the heart as it is related to the onset of fibrillation. Winfree has shown that 2D and 3D vortices arise in excitable media such as heart muscle and that they do so in ways that are predicted by his theory. At the University of Calgary, Wayne Giles heads a research team that is investigating the electrical energy of the heart and its effect upon the organ's natural rhythm. Charles Peskin of the Courant Institute for Mathematical Sciences has been performing 2D and 3D modeling of the heart, including valves, ventricles, atria, and other vessels. This complex model involves a coupled system of equations modeling the wall, the blood, and the valve motion.

The Nervous System

The human brain is estimated to contain approximately 10^{12} neurons. Many of these neurons are connected to 10 000 other neurons. Thus, in many ways, the brain is itself a sophisticated supercomputer. At the single neuron level, Steve Young and Mark Ellisman of the

Laboratory for Neurocytology at UC, San Diego are using a supercomputer to reconstruct single neurons. The neurons are frozen, sliced into sections 0.25 to 5 µm thick, and photographed through a high-voltage electron microscope. The computer is then used to reconstruct the slices and to subsequently view them on a graphics workstation (*q.v.*).

T. D. Lagerlund of the Mayo Clinic has been examining the effects of axial diffusion, via mathematical modeling and computer simulation, on oxygen delivery in the peripheral nerves. It is known that victims of diabetes often suffer changes in their system of blood vessels. These changes reduce the supply of oxygen and nutrients to the tissue and subsequently damage the kidneys, retinas, and nerves.

Computing the Kidney

Don Marsh of the University of Southern California School of Medicine is leading a group of investigators in large-scale mathematical modeling and simulation of the kidney. They have looked at two problems: (1) the concentrating mechanism of the inner medulla of the kidney; and (2) the oscillation in tubular pressure initiated by the kidney's nonlinear control mechanism. The concentrating mechanism was modeled using a 3D model of the kidney structure. It included longitudinal symmetry, tubules, and blood vessels. They were able to demonstrate that the longitudinal symmetry played no part in the concentrating mechanism of the kidney. In their study of the oscillation in tubular pressure, they use a sophisticated system of partial differential equations to describe the physiological control of the kidney tubular pressure. They have been able to show the existence of what appears to be a chaotic attractor in the system and that there is a period-doubling bifurcation in the development of hypertension (*see* FRACTALS).

Modeling the Dynamics of the Body

Mathematical and computer models of limb motion are of importance in areas from robotics (*q.v.*) to biomechanics. Karl Newell of the University of Illinois Urbana-Champaign simulates limb movements using spring–mass models. Such models are currently used as a metaphor for the neuromuscular organization of limb motion. At the cellular level, Cy Frank and Raj Rangayyan of the University of Calgary are examining ligament injuries and methods of treatment. Collagen fibrils, the basic building blocks of normal healthy ligament, are in nearly parallel arrangement when the ligament is healthy. In injured tissue, the arrangement is highly random. The randomness of the distribution depends upon the nature of the injury sustained and the stage of healing. As the tissues heal, the collagen fibrils realign in a process called *collagen remodeling*. Using a supercomputer for sophisticated and intense image processing, these investigators are attempting to interpret the realignment stages and to use such knowledge to treat trauma to the limbs more accurately.

Patient-based Physiological Simulation

Computerized surgery systems are currently in place at the Washington University of St Louis Mallinkrodt Institute and at the Mayo Clinic. Facial reconstruction and surgical simulation are now a practiced reality.

At the VA Medical Center Minneapolis, T. K. Johnson and R. L. Vessella are developing a patient-based simulation of radioactive decay in the organs of the body. Such a problem is computer-intensive in that it requires the mapping of the 3D spatial distribution of radio-labeled compounds.

Project DaVinci at the University of Illinois is attempting to build a 3D simulation of the human body. Witten has examined the problem of ultra-large-scale simulation of cellular systems and the interaction between aging cellular systems and cancerous ones.

Project Human

Beyond the complexity of such ultra-large-scale simulations and models is the goal of an ultra-large-scale simulation of a human being. Such a simulation would rely upon the patient's image data, noninvasive measurements of physiological functions, and assorted clinical tests. One can begin to hypothesize scenarios in which chemotherapy can be simulated, in a given patient, before the therapy is performed. Radical and new drug treatments can also be simulated and the results examined and evaluated based upon an integrated model and patient system. Eventually, one can envision the possibility of actually testing newly designed drugs in computer-based large-scale simulations.

Computational Population Biology

The study of populations, particularly human populations, is called *demography*. Models, in this area, are generally hyperbolic partial differential equations. Given the increasing cost of health care and the increase in the aged population, it is important to understand the dynamics of the human population in an effort to hold down the cost of health care. In addition, models of this type arise in the study of toxicological effects of the environment (ecotoxicology).

Mathematical modeling of diseases, particularly of such diseases as AIDS and Lyme disease, requires the use of computational methods. The models are routinely complex, often stochastic in nature, and quite frequently intractable analytically. Epidemiology and biostatistics study population dynamics and characteristics from a probabilistic perspective. Clinical trials often generate large data sets. Statistical analysis of these data sets is often intense, because of the sample size and the complexity of the interactions.

Computational Dentistry

Many dental schools are collaborating with mechanical and biomedical engineers for the purpose of finite element modeling of the jaw (e.g. Michael Day at the University of Louisville). The resultant models are then applied to examining the problems of orthodonture and of computer-automated patient-based, dental prosthetics design. Numerous researchers have used high-performance computing methods to study dental implant design.

The Matrix of Biological Knowledge

Hidden within the complete database of published biological experiments—*the matrix of biological knowledge*—lies the potential for developing a new and powerful tool for the investigation of biological principles. Many databases of biological information already exist. Perhaps the best known of these is GenBank, the database of all known gene sequences. This project is an outgrowth of the Human Genome Project, which requires massive computer support in such areas as numerical computation, searching algorithms, and database design. One can envision user interfaces (*q.v.*) incorporating knowledge engineering, advanced graphics and mathematical capabilities, and simulation engines. The future of biocomputing is one of great excitement and potential.

Bibliography

1987–1989. Witten, M. (ed.) *Advances in Mathematics and Computers in Medicine*, Vols. 1 and 2. New York: Pergamon Press.

1990. Bell, G. I., and Marr, T. G. (eds.) *Computers and DNA*. Reading, MA: Addison-Wesley.

1995. Schulze-Kremer, S. *Molecular Bioinformatics*. Berlin: Walter de Gruyter.

1997. Panfilov, A. V., and Holden, A. V. (eds.) *Computational Biology of the Heart*. Chichester, UK: John Wiley.

Tarynn M. Witten

BIOS

For articles on related subjects, *see*

+ IBM PC
+ Kernel

The *basic input output system* (BIOS) of the disk operating system (DOS) for a typical microcomputer is the portion of the operating system (*q.v.*) that provides an interface between the kernel and the underlying hardware. The *kernel* is the portion of an operating system closest to the application software. It is responsible for process control, memory management, file management, and peripheral support. The kernel passes commands from the application software to the BIOS for translation into hardware-specific requests.

The BIOS consists of two parts. The *firmware* (*q.v.*) portion is encoded in PROM chips that cannot be erased by the user. This portion is essentially a table of interrupts (*q.v.*) and some executable code for servicing the interrupt requests. A changeable and extensible portion of the BIOS sits in files, usually hidden, on the boot disk (*see* BOOTSTRAP). On IBM PCs (*q.v.*), these files are named IO.SYS or IBMBIO.COM.

The BIOS is responsible for system checking at startup time. It is also the module that translates commands to specific peripherals and devices into a language that the hardware can handle. The original IBM BIOS for the PC also contained part of the language Basic (*q.v.*), but this is no longer common.

To avoid copyright infringement, manufacturers of IBM-compatible micros emulate the functions of the IBM BIOS without copying the actual code. The relative ease with which this can be done was a major factor in the rise of so many vendors capable of producing low-cost microcomputers that are 100% compatible with the IBM PC. As long as software operates through the BIOS and only through the BIOS, compatibility can be assured.

The BIOS, however, does not support all of the hardware's capabilities. Hardware designers cannot conceive all the uses that software might want to make of new devices. The BIOS is also quite slow at many tasks, especially video graphics. Many software authors choose to bypass the BIOS and program the hardware directly. This leads to increased performance, but there is then a danger that the program will not work on all machines, especially ones whose plug-in boards and other devices are slightly nonstandard.

Devices that were not available when BIOS code was originally burned into PROM can be accommodated by DEVICE commands in CONFIG.SYS files, commands that access the extensible portion of the BIOS that resides on disk.

More recently, BIOS code has been made extensible by the use of *flash memory chips*. These chips are normally divided into blocks. Each block can be erased and programmed independently. Blocks can also be locked to prevent accidental reprogramming. This ability to program the BIOS after it has been installed forestalls the obsolescence of BIOS chips as new hardware features are installed. In this way the BIOS can be updated by modem (*q.v.*) or directly from a diskette (*q.v.*) to bring the code in line with new hardware capabilities.

Modern BIOS chips must be able to perform the basic set of boot instructions; carry out Power On Self Tests (POST); track system date and time; test memory parity; set the boot sequence, display type, and keyboard type; set CPU speed; set sign-on password (*q.v.*); provide boot sector virus protection; manage multiple processors and configurations; and even sense and update new *Plug and Play* devices in which I/O ports, interrupts, and DIP switch settings no longer need to be set by the user. They are written directly to the BIOS by the Plug and Play system.

BIOS chips also assist in *local area network* (*q.v.*) management using the Desktop Management Interface (DMI). System administrators use this interface to gather information about clients and server system hardware, software, and use for individual computers over the network.

As add-on cards have become more sophisticated and been equipped with their own special CPUs, BIOS chips have been installed to track and manage the variety of settings native to these peripheral and control cards. Thus, high-performance PCs and workstations no longer use a single BIOS chip; they have as many as they have CPUs.

Stephen J. Rogowski

BLOCK STRUCTURE

For articles on related subjects, *see*

+ Activation Record
+ Class
+ Control Structures
+ Procedure-Oriented Languages
+ Programming Languages
+ Structured Programming

Block structure is a programming language concept that allows related declarations and statements to be grouped. When used judiciously, it can help transform a large, unwieldy program into a disciplined, well-structured, easy-to-understand program. Block structure, first used in Algol (*q.v.*), is found in some form in most procedural programming languages developed thereafter.

Use of Block Structure in Programming

Block structuring is used to partition a large program into smaller and more manageable *blocks*. Since a block may contain nested subblocks, block structure can be used to decompose a large program into an orderly hierarchy, resulting in increased program clarity and elegance.

A programming language-specific notation indicates the start and end of a block. Algol 60 and Pascal (*q.v.*) use the reserved words **begin** and **end**. C uses the braces { and }.

Block structure is used for two purposes:

1. It allows a sequence of executable statements to be grouped into a single *compound statement*. This allows the compound statement to be used in places where the programming language allows only a single statement (e.g. in any branch of an **if-then-else** statement).
2. It allows the programmer to control where symbols can be modified and used. Each block introduces a new *scope*, a domain for the definition of symbols. Symbols declared within a block (i.e. *local* to the block) may be used only within that block (and within any contained block). This provides a degree of data security (*q.v.*), since a programmer can use a block to "hide" variables (*information hiding–q.v.*) and thereby make them inaccessible outside of this block.

Conceptually, storage is allocated for variables declared in a block when the block is entered and is deallocated when execution leaves the block. This

```
begin     comment first block - main program;
    integer sumx, sumxx, xxsize;
    interger array x[1:100];
    real array y[1:50];
    . . .
    begin     comment second block;
        integer p,y;
        integer array xx[1:xxsize];
        sumx := sumxx := 0;
        for p := 1 step 1 until 100 do
              begin  comment third block;
                  sumx := sumx + x[p];
                  xx[p] := x[p] * x[p];
                  sumxx := sumxx + xx[p]
              end;
    . . .
    end
end;
```

Figure 1. An Algol program demonstrating block structure.

means that data objects with dynamically determined sizes (e.g. arrays with bounds that are determined by run-time values) can have a different size each time that the block containing the object is entered during program execution.

The Algol 60 code segment in Fig. 1. illustrates the use of block structure. The first block is used to declare the global variables *sumx, sumxx, x, xxsize,* and *y*. The second block is used to introduce the new variables *p, y,* and *xx*. These variables may be used only during execution of the second block. The size of the array *xx* is determined from the value of the global variable *xxsize*. The third block is used to group three assignment statements so that they behave as one statement in the body of the **for** loop.

Scope Rules

A block *body* is a sequence of executable statements and a block is itself an executable statement. Therefore, blocks may be nested to any depth. This has several consequences:

1. Although an identifier may be used only once as the name of an object in a block, the same identifier may be used to name different objects in different blocks.
2. If the same identifier is used to name objects in several nested blocks, the programming language's

scope rule is used to disambiguate references to the identifier. The Algol 60 scope rule starts at the point where the identifier is used and searches blocks starting with the block containing the use of the identifier and working outward through containing blocks toward the main program block until a declaration of the identifier is found.

The C program of Fig. 2 illustrates these points. The identifier *b* is used to name variables in both the first and fourth blocks. In the second block (body of the function *P*), the variable *x* declared in the first block is inaccessible because the identifier *x* was also used to name a formal parameter of *P*; the variable *c* declared in the first block is inaccessible in the body of *P* because another variable named *c* is declared there. In the assignment statement in the body of *P*, the identifier *c* refers to the variable *c* declared in *P*, the identifier *x* refers to a formal parameter of *P*, and the identifier *b* refers to the variable *b* declared in the first block. In the fourth block, the variable *b* declared in the first block is inaccessible because a local variable *b* has been declared there.

Blocks provide a hierarchical method for controlling access to variables. Other programming language

```
/* global declarations--first block */
double c, b, x ;
/* declaration of function p */
int p(double x, float y)
      {/* second block - body of p */
      float c ;
      . . .
      b = x + c ;
      . . .
      }       /* end of p */
main() /* third block */
      {. . .
      if ( c <= x ) /* fourth block */
            {float b ;
            b = c ;
            c = x ;
            x = b ;
            }

      . . .
      }
```

Figure 2. C block structure example.

mechanisms, for example modules and classes (*q.v.*), provide more structured access control.

Bibliography

1964. Randell, B., and Russell, L. S. *Algol 60 Implementation*. New York: Academic Press.

1996. Pratt, T. W., and Zelkowitz, M. *The Design and Implementation of Programming Languages*, 3rd Ed. Upper Saddle River, NJ: Prentice Hall.

                                   David B. Wortman

BNF

See BACKUS–NAUR FORM (BNF).

BOOLEAN ALGEBRA

For articles on related subjects, *see*

+ Arithmetic, Computer
+ Discrete Mathematics
+ Logic Design
+ Logic Programming

The concept of a Boolean algebra was first proposed by the English mathematician George Boole in 1847. The relationships between Boolean algebra, set algebra, logic, and binary arithmetic have given Boolean algebras a central role in the development of electronic digital computers.

Set Algebras

A *Boolean algebra* is a finite or infinite set of elements together with three operations—negation, addition, and multiplication—that correspond to the set operations of complementation, union, and intersection, respectively. Among the elements of a Boolean algebra are two distinguished elements: 0, corresponding to the empty set; and 1, corresponding to the universal set. For any

Table 1.

Distributivity:	$a(b + c) = ab + ac$
	$a + (bc) = (a + b)(a + c)$
Idempotency:	$a + a = a$
	$aa = a$
Absorption laws:	$a + ab = a$
	$a(a + b) = a$
DeMorgan's laws:	$(a + b)' = a'b'$
	$(ab)' = a' + b'$

Table 2.

a	b	a·b	a	b	a + b
0	0	0	0	0	0
0	1	0	0	1	1
1	0	0	1	0	1
1	1	1	1	1	1

given element a of a Boolean algebra, there is a unique complement a' with the property that $a + a' = 1$ and $aa' = 0$. Boolean addition and multiplication are associative and commutative, as are ordinary addition and multiplication, but otherwise have somewhat different properties. The principal properties are given in Table 1, where a, b, and c are any elements of a Boolean algebra.

Since a finite set of n elements has exactly 2^n subsets and the finite Boolean algebras are precisely the finite set algebras, each finite Boolean algebra consists of exactly 2^n elements for some integer n. For example, the set algebra for a set of four elements corresponds to a Boolean algebra of 32 elements. Table 2 defines the Boolean operations for a Boolean algebra of two elements.

Propositional Calculus

The two-element Boolean algebra can be identified with elementary logic or propositional calculus. A *proposition* is a statement that can be said to be either true or false. We will denote propositions by letters such as p, q, and r.

The connectives "and" and "or" combine two such propositions into a new one. If we consider two

Table 3.

p	q	0	1	2	3	4	5	6	7	8	9	10	11	12	13	14	15
T	T	T	T	T	T	T	T	T	T	F	F	F	F	F	F	F	F
T	F	T	T	T	T	F	F	F	F	T	T	T	T	F	F	F	F
F	T	T	T	F	F	T	T	F	F	T	T	F	F	T	T	F	F
F	F	T	F	T	F	T	F	T	F	T	F	T	F	T	F	T	F

propositions, p and q, each may, independently of the other, assume the value true (T) or false (F). Hence, together, the ordered pair $\langle p, q \rangle$ may assume $2 \times 2 = 4$ combinations of truth values: $\langle T,T \rangle$, $\langle T,F \rangle$, $\langle F,T \rangle$, and $\langle F,F \rangle$. If $\circ$ denotes a binary operator, then $p \circ q$ may be either T or F independently for each of these four T–F combinations. Thus, we can define $2^4 = 16$ distinct binary logical operators, as shown in Table 3. Of the 16 so-called "binary" logical operators that can be defined, six are not really binary because either they depend on neither p nor q (columns 0 and 15), or else they are unary operators that depend on only p or q or their negation (columns 3, 5, 10, and 12). The remaining ten are "and" (column 7), "or" (column 1), "exclusive or" (column 9), "implication" (column 4), "is implied by" (column 2), and the negation of each.

The "negation" or "not" operation, $\neg p$ is defined to form a proposition that is true precisely when the proposition p is false, and false whenever p is true. If we equate the truth values "true" and "false" with the Boolean values 1 and 0, respectively, then we find that negation corresponds to Boolean complementation. That is, $\neg p$ replaces the value "true" with "false," and vice versa, just as p' replaces the value "1" with "0," and vice versa. (In Table 3, column 12 is $\neg p$ and column 10 is $\neg q$.)

The logical "conjunction" or "and," $p \wedge q$, forms a proposition that is true precisely when both p and q are true, and is false otherwise. This corresponds to the Boolean operation of multiplication, with the Boolean expression pq having the value 1 if and only if both p and q have the value 1. (See Table 3, column 7.)

In ordinary usage, the word "or" has two distinct meanings, referred to as the "inclusive or" and the "exclusive or." In the inclusive sense, the statement "p or q" is true if p or q or both are true; in the exclusive sense, the same statement is true if either p or q, but not both, is true. The logical "disjunction" or "or," $p \vee q$, is defined to be the inclusive "or." That is, $p \vee q$ is true precisely when at least one of the statements p and q is true. Thus, this operation corresponds to Boolean addition as we have defined it. (See Table 3, column 1.) The "exclusive or," $p \neq q$, is also called *inequivalence*, since it defines a proposition that is true precisely when p and q have opposite or inequivalent truth values. This corresponds to any of several more complex Boolean operations such as $pq' + p'q$, and $(p + q)(pq)'$. (See Table 3, column 9.)

The remaining widely used logical operator is the *conditional* or *implication*, $p \Rightarrow q$, corresponding to the statement "if p then q." The conditional proposition $p \Rightarrow q$ takes the value "false" if p is true and q is false, and takes the value "true" otherwise. Thus, it corresponds to the Boolean operation $p' + q$. If p is false, then $p \Rightarrow q$ is true, regardless of the value of q. This corresponds to the statement that one can prove anything (q, whether true or false) from a false hypothesis (p). (See Table 3, column 4.)

All logical operators can be defined in terms of one basic operator, either the "nand" or the "nor" operator, the negations of the conjunction and disjunction operators, respectively. (See Table 3, columns 8 and 14.) In circuitry terms, our toolkit need consist of only "nand" gates or only "nor" gates.

Truth Tables

A *truth table* gives the truth values of a logical expression for each combination of the truth values of its variables. Thus, for a logical expression in n variables, the truth table contains 2^n lines, one for each combination of the truth values of its variables. The truth table for an unknown logical function can be used to generate an expression for that function. The expression thus generated is called a *disjunctive normal form* or, in Boolean algebra, a *sum of products form*. The development of a typical expression is illustrated in Table 4. For each line of the table wherein the unknown function has the value "true," an expression is formed by taking the conjunction of all variables that are true in that line and the negations of all variables that are false in that line. The expression for the function f is then the disjunction of all expressions formed for the single lines. At the bottom of Table 4, f is given first in Boolean algebraic form, then in sum of products form, and then in a shorter form developed by direct inspection of the function values. (Equivalence, $\equiv$, is defined by column 6 of Table 3.)

The development of the disjunctive normal form shows that the logical operators conjunction, disjunction, and negation are sufficient to develop an expression

Table 4.

pqr	$f(p, q, r)$	Generated expression
T T T	F	−
T T F	T	$P \wedge q \wedge \neg r$
T F T	T	$P \wedge \neg q \wedge r$
T F F	F	−
F T T	T	$\neg p \wedge q \wedge r$
F T F	F	−
F F T	F	−
F F F	T	$\neg p \wedge \neg q \wedge \neg r$

$$f(p, q, r) = (p \wedge q \wedge \neg r) \vee (p \wedge \neg q \wedge r)$$
$$\vee (\neg p \wedge q \wedge r) \vee (\neg p \wedge \neg q \wedge \neg r)$$
$$f(p, q, r) = pqr' + pq'r + p'qr + p'q'r'$$
$$f(p, q, r) = p \equiv (q \neq r)$$

Table 5.

	$\wedge, \neg$	$\vee, \neg$
$\neg p$	$\neg p$	$\neg p$
$p \wedge q$	$p \wedge q$	$\neg(\neg p \vee \neg q)$
$p \vee q$	$\neg(\neg p \wedge \neg q)$	$p \vee q$
$p \Rightarrow q$	$\neg(p \wedge \neg q)$	$\neg p \vee q$
$p \equiv q$	$\neg(\neg(p \wedge q) \wedge \neg(\neg p \wedge \neg q))$	$\neg(p \vee q) \vee \neg(\neg p \vee \neg q)$

Table 6.

	|	$\downarrow$
$\neg p$	$p\|p$	$p \downarrow p$
$p \wedge q$	$(p\|q)\|(p\|q)$	$(p \downarrow p) \downarrow (q \downarrow q)$
$p \vee q$	$(p\|p)\|(q\|q)$	$(p \downarrow q) \downarrow (p \downarrow q)$

for any logical function. Furthermore, we may use DeMorgan's laws (Table 1) to transform conjunctions to disjunctions, or vice versa. Thus, any logical function can be developed from the operators negation and either conjunction or disjunction. Table 5 shows the development of the five common logical operators in terms of these two minimal combinations of operators. In turn, Table 6 shows the development of negation, conjunction, and disjunction in terms of both the "nand" and the "nor" operators, thus indicating that every logical operator can be defined in terms of either one of these latter two operators.

Duality

There is a symmetry in the operations of addition and multiplication with a Boolean algebra, which is captured in the Principle of Duality:

> If a given proposition holds in a Boolean algebra, then so does the formula obtained by interchanging addition and multiplication, and the elements 0 and 1 throughout the given formula.

The properties of commutativity and associativity, together with those shown in Table 1, are all examples of the Principle of Duality. Some dual pairs are as follows:

$$a + 1 = 1 \qquad a0 = 0$$
$$0' = 1 \qquad 1' = 0$$
$$a + a' = 1 \qquad aa' = 0$$
$$a + (a'b) = a + b \quad a(a' + b) = ab$$

Logical Design

Logical design is the development of computer circuitry to perform the desired functions for a particular computer. Of the various devices designed to systematize study of the needed logic, the *Venn diagram* and *Karnaugh map* are particularly simple and highly effective for functions of two to five variables. However, the use of these devices becomes increasingly difficult as the number of variables increases beyond five. The Venn diagram consists of a rectangle, representing the universe, containing a circle or other simple closed curve for each variable represented. The interpretation is that within the circle the given variable has the value 1, while outside it has the value 0. These circles are arranged in such a way as to include all possible combinations of 1s and 0s for the variables. The Venn diagram for a three-variable problem is given in Fig. 1, with the various regions labeled in Fig. 1a and certain regions shaded to represent the Boolean function $pq + pr + p'r$ in Fig. 1b. But the Venn diagram is relatively ineffective for logical analysis when four or more variables are involved.

The Karnaugh map is a practical modification of the Venn diagram, with each region of the diagram represented by a square within a larger rectangle. The Karnaugh maps for two-, three-, and four-variable problems are given in Fig. 2. The region represented by each square is determined by the product of the

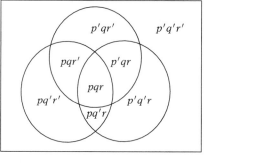

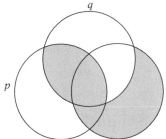

(a)   (b)

Figure 1. Venn diagram.

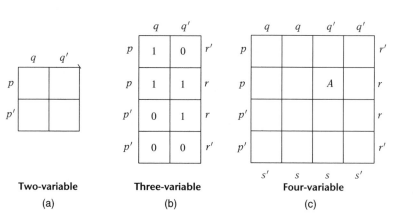

Two-variable   Three-variable   Four-variable
(a)   (b)   (c)

Figure 2. Karnaugh maps.

letters on the edges of the rectangle. For example, the square marked A in Fig. 2c represents the region $pq'rs$. To represent a Boolean function, say $pq + pr + q'r$, on a Karnaugh map, first expand each term of the function to include all variables present:

$$pq + pr + q'r$$
$$= pq \cdot 1 + p \cdot 1 \cdot r + 1 \cdot q'r$$
$$= pq(r + r') + p(q + q')r + (p + p')q'r$$
$$= pqr + pqr' + pqr + pq'r + pq'r + p'q'r$$
$$= pqr + pqr' + pq'r + p'q'r.$$

Then mark each square corresponding to a term in the expanded expression. Thus, the Boolean function $pq + pr + q'r$ is represented by the squares marked "1" in Fig. 2b, while 0s fill those squares not included in the representation. Note that $pq + q'r$ is also represented by the same four marked squares, and hence is equivalent to the given function. It is also possible to label a square d, denoting "don't care," if the value of that square is irrelevant to the particular function being represented.

Minimization of Boolean Functions

In the interest of economy, it is often desirable to use the simplest possible expression for a Boolean function in the design of computer circuitry. The determination of the simplest expression equivalent to a given one is known as *minimization*. When computers were constructed from discrete individual logic components, minimization of the number of components or *gates* was a significant task. However, with the development of integrated circuit technology and the shift to Very Large Scale Integration (VLSI), the importance of the individual logic gates in the overall cost of the computer has much diminished. In VLSI technology, each computer chip may contain hundreds or thousands of logic gates. Hence the focus of minimization effort has shifted away from individual gates toward the problem of finding the best combination of logic gates to fit on a chip to perform a given set of functions.

Bibliography

1984. Korfhage, R. R. *Discrete Computational Structures*, 2nd Ed. New York: Academic Press.
1995. Whitesitt, J. E. *Boolean Algebra and its Applications*. New York: Dover Publications.
1998. Maurer, S. B., and Ralston, A. *Discrete Algorithmic Mathematics* (second corrected edition). Wellesey, MA: A. K. Peters.

Robert R. Korfhage

BOOTSTRAP

For an article on a related subject, see

+ BIOS

To *bootstrap*—more commonly, just *boot*—is to accomplish a task by means of a procedure that gives its user a "free" head start. The term was first used in computing to describe the process whereby a loader program, whose job it is to get other pieces of software into a machine, is itself loaded. This task was made possible by a very simple loader, wired into the hardware, that was just adequate to load a more extensive loader program, which then loaded everything else. From this beginning, *bootstrapping* has become a generic term for the use of any procedure that requires its user to do only some relatively trivial part of a task, with the procedure itself then doing the rest.

Bootstrapping is also used to describe the programming of a complete translator for some language L by means of an already-implemented translator for a small subset of L that is adequate—not necessarily good—for writing a translator. Such a subset can be used for the programming of a complete language-L translator, with the resulting translator run through the subset-translator to yield a running translator of the whole language, bootstrapped into existence by means of the already running fragment.

On the hardware side, the term is commonly used now to denote bringing a computer to an operational state—that is, a state in which it accepts user commands—from either an unpowered state, or a powered but unresponsive state. Booting a PC, for example, from an unpowered state—a *cold boot*—is initiated simply by switching the PC on—a one-touch operation that initiates a great deal of hardware testing and loading of software. Booting from a powered state—a *warm boot*—is usually initiated by pressing one or more keys or a button on the computer casing. It is normally done only to recover from a condition in which the computer is not behaving properly, for example, a "frozen" screen and unresponsive keyboard. A warm boot is also called a *reboot* or *restart*.

Mark Halpern

BRITISH COMPUTER SOCIETY (BCS)

For articles on related subjects, see

+ Association for Computing Machinery (ACM)
+ Institute of Electrical and Electronic Engineers–Computer Society (IEEE-CS)
+ International Federation for Information Processing (IFIP)

The British Computer Society (BCS), formed in 1957, has 35 000 members and is the chartered body in the UK for all information technology professionals. Society membership is limited to those who have satisfactorily passed a two-part examination. A 1984 Royal Charter gives the BCS unique and exclusive responsibilities and authority. It takes responsibilities for education and training, for public awareness, and for standards, quality, and professionalism, and issues and enforces both a code of conduct and a code of practice. It advises Parliament and the government and their agencies as well as the Banking and Building Society Ombudsmen. It examines and pronounces on topical issues concerning computers.

It inspects university and polytechnic courses in computer science and information technology (*q.v.*) and conducts its own examinations. It is the UK member of the International Federation for Information Processing. It organizes an ambitious Professional Development Scheme for young professionals and established practitioners. It is represented on the advisory committees of national examining and educational bodies.

The BCS publishes seven journals. *The Computer Bulletin* is a general interest publication, which goes to all members. The others are *The Computer Journal* (which covers computer science broadly), and five more specialized journals: *Software Proceedings, Formal Aspects of Computing, Interacting with Computers, Journal of Digital Information, and Distributed System Engineering Journal*. In tandem with its hard copy publications, the BCS increasingly publishes electronically. The Society and its special interest groups publish several series of books and monographs.

Fifty-five BCS specialist groups and 41 local branches conduct conferences and meetings, a dozen or two each month, that insure that the influence of BCS is felt throughout Britain and elsewhere through its overseas sections (in Hong Kong, Malta, Sri Lanka, The Netherlands, and Switzerland) and international conferences. The address of the BCS is 1 Sanford Street, Swindon SN1 1HJ, UK, www.bcs.org.uk.

Eric A. Weiss

BROWSER

See MARKUP LANGUAGES; and WORLD WIDE WEB.

BUFFER

For an article on a related subject, see

+ Cache Memory

A *buffer* is an area of storage that temporarily holds data that will be subsequently delivered to a processor or I/O peripheral. Buffers exist as an integral part of many peripherals, for example, bits arriving serially over a communications line are collected in a buffer before the character is presented to a processor. Similarly, the bits representing a given character remain in a buffer while being serialized for transmission.

A technique called *double buffering* permits one set of data to be used while another is collected. It is used with graphics displays, where one frame buffer holds the current screen image while another acquires the bits that will make up the next image. When it is ready, the buffers are switched, the new screen is displayed, and the process continues.

In a typical situation, a processor will be capable of producing data several orders of magnitude faster than a peripheral can accept it. In order to make most efficient use of the processor, the data will be placed in a buffer and its location made known to the peripheral. The peripheral then proceeds to empty the buffer while the processor is freed for other work.

As random access memory (RAM) has become less expensive, designers have increased average buffer size. This helps I/O response and throughput (*q.v.*) by exploiting local referencing patterns and the use of a *cache memory* (*q.v.*). Mainframe systems use very large "extended" RAM memories as caches to optimize this effect to the greatest extent possible.

Robert W. Taylor

BUG

For articles on related subjects, *see*

+ Debugging
+ Program Verification

A *bug* is an error in either the syntax or the logic of a computer program or circuit. Because the story has been retold so often by well-meaning people, many believe that the term originated when a moth was removed ("debugged") from an errant Mark I (*q.v.*)

relay circuit in the early 1940s. Though this may very well have happened, the term *bug* was used in exactly its current context by Thomas Edison in an 1878 letter to Theodore Puskas.

Syntactical bugs can be detected during the translation from the symbolic languages that programmers use into the (binary) language that is eventually executed. For example, the assignment operator in the Ada (*q.v.*) programming language is :=, and if a programmer writes x=x+1 as if it were an assignment statement, the Ada compiler will detect the syntax error and print a diagnostic message.

It is a more serious error if the programmer writes the legal Ada code x:=x-1 when x:=x+1 was intended. This is a bug in program logic, and no compiler can catch it. Such errors can be found only through exhaustive testing, comparing output with results known to be correct (*see* DEBUGGING).

Program bugs can be so extremely subtle that they may resist great efforts to eliminate them. The number of possible paths through a large computer program is enormous, and a particular path containing a bug may not be followed in actual production runs for a long time (if ever) after the program has been certified as correct by its author or others.

Fred Gruenberger

BUS

For articles on related subjects, *see*

+ Channel
+ IBM PC
+ Open Architecture
+ Personal Computing

Introduction

A *bus* is an electronic highway in a digital computer that provides a communication path for data to flow between the CPU and its memory and between and among the CPU and the various peripheral devices. A bus contains one wire for each bit needed to specify the address of a device or location in memory, plus additional wires that distinguish among the various data transfer operations to be performed. A bus can transmit data in either direction between any two components of the computing system. Without a bus, a computer would need separate wires for all possible connections between components—clearly an intolerable situation.

Mainframe and Minicomputer Buses

There are a number of proprietary bus systems used on mainframes (*q.v.*) and minicomputers (*q.v.*). Examples are the Digital Equipment Corporation *Unibus* and the Intel *Multibus*. The Unibus, used on the PDP-11 and VAX series computers, has 56 bidirectional lines and a transfer rate of almost 3 MB/s. Another widely used bus is the General-Purpose Interface Bus (GPIB) defined by the standard ANSI/IEEE 488–1978. Bus-Tech, Inc. and Harbor Systems Management, Ltd market a bus that provides data movement between S/390 mainframes and large enterprise servers such as IBM RS/6000, HP/UX, Sun Solaris, and Windows NT at transfer rates in excess of 10 MB/s. But since the diversity of buses intrinsic to large computers does not seem to have played a pivotal role in industry competitiveness, the remainder of this article is devoted to the evolution of the microcomputer bus.

Microcomputer Buses

On a microcomputer, the bus is usually called an *expansion bus* because its design determines the degree to which the minimum configuration of the system can be expanded with regard to memory, processing speed, graphics capability, and peripheral support. The expansion bus is the collection of wires, paths, connectors, and controllers responsible for distributing the data and instructions from the microprocessor to the peripheral expansion cards. *Slots* connected to the bus provide places to plug those cards in, and the bus then provides a mechanism for communicating with them.

S-100 Bus

When Altair introduced its 8080 computer in 1974, it came with an expansion bus with a published specification that used common parts and connectors. This *open architecture* soon became a standard. One hundred pins were provided for various signals on what became known as the S-100 bus. This meant that new video cards, more memory, and serial and parallel ports could be added to the computer as needed. At the height of its popularity, more than 100 companies manufactured S-100 products.

ISA Bus

In 1981, IBM announced its new personal computer, the IBM PC (*q.v.*). The machine was a success, due in no small part to its open architecture and the flexibility of its expansion bus, whose design details were placed in the public domain. The new IBM bus came to be known as the Industry Standard Architecture (ISA) bus. The ISA bus was processor-specific and its edge-triggered interrupts meant that each expansion card could have only one interrupt (*q.v.*). An entire industry flourished in the shadow of IBM, making products that could be placed in the expansion slots of IBM PCs and compatible machines.

ISA AT Bus

By 1984, IBM announced its Advanced Technology (AT) machine, built around the 16-bit Intel 80286 chip, which could be run as fast as 12 MHz. An additional connector was added next to the 8-bit ISA connector, which allowed additional address and control signals while maintaining downward compatibility with ISA expansion boards. A *wait state* generator was added to allow the microprocessor to cope with bus components that might be too slow. Information could be transferred at up to 2 MB/s on this bus, but its rating of 8 MHz ultimately proved to be too slow.

Micro-Channel Architecture (MCA)

In April 1987, IBM announced the Personal System/2 (PS/2), featuring a new expansion bus based on a concept called *Micro-Channel Architecture* (MCA), which IBM intended to license. The MCA increased data throughput to 20 MB/s, more than 10 times the speed of the AT ISA bus. The PS/2 was still an *open* architecture (*q.v.*) machine in some sense, but emulation would no longer be cost-free to the clone makers. The MCA bus was a full 32-bit bus, but its standard never caught on.

Extended Industry Standard Architecture (EISA)

Not surprisingly, clone makers were reluctant to pay IBM royalties on every card and machine made. A group of computer manufacturers formed the "Gang of Nine": Wyse, AST, Tandy, Compaq, Hewlett-Packard, Zenith, Olivetti, NEC, and Epson. They agreed to develop a joint standard, publish it, and stick to it. EISA, which remained compatible with the old ISA boards, was a 32-bit standard, even faster than the MCA, with a maximum transfer rate of 33 MB/s. Only the 80386 and 80486 chips can use EISA since Pentium (80586) interrupts are not edge-triggered and can be shared.

NU-Bus

Apple (*q.v.*) recognized the benefits of open architecture when it introduced its NU-Bus in the late 1980s for use with the Mac II. Until then, the Macintosh had been a closed machine. Nu-Bus operates on a 10 MHz synchronous clock, providing access to all main logic board resources through six Euro-DIN connectors.

Local Bus Architectures

As computers became more powerful, two competing architectures evolved—VESA and PCI. The Peripheral Component Interface (PCI) is a 32/64-bit local bus architecture developed by DEC, IBM, Intel, and others that is widely used in Pentium-based PCs. The PCI bus provides a high-bandwidth data channel between the system-board components such as the CPU and devices such as hard disks and video adapters. The VL-Bus or VESA Local Bus architecture was developed by the Video Electronics Standards Association—a consortium of computer manufacturers responsible for the SVGA video standard—and is primarily used in older 80486 PCs. The PCI bus is currently the dominant bus structure. It accommodates a 100-MHz

data rate and supports Plug and Play, Hot Plug, Bus Power Management, bus mastering, error detection, and CPU independence. The PCI bus can be designed into portable or desktop machines and is backward compatible with 8- and 16-bit ISA expansion cards.

Other Buses

The Small Computer Systems Interface (SCSI—pronounced "scuzzy") was standardized in 1986, and updated in 1994 to SCSI-2. SCSI is a high-speed interface, originally designed for disk drives and now used for devices such as CD-ROMs and scanners as well. It is the standard disk interface on Apple Macintoshes and on Unix workstations, as well as on Intel PCs that are used as servers. The original SCSI, now SCSI-1, had a clock speed of 5 MHz and a data transfer rate of 5 MB/s. SCSI-2 now runs at 10 MHz and, with a 16-bit rather than 8-bit datapath, has a transfer rate of 20 MB/s. SCSI devices are connected in a serial *daisy chain* to an SCSI controller, which can manage seven devices. As of 1999, SCSI-3 standards are being developed.

The Universal Serial Bus (USB) is a new PC bus designed to make it easy to attach low-speed peripheral devices to a computer. With the USB, devices do not need separate bus interface cards with switches that need to be set correctly. Multiple devices can be attached to an external USB socket or *hub*. The USB has a bandwidth of 1.5 MB/s, which is shared among all devices connected to it.

Bibliography

1997. Schmidt, F. *The SCSI Bus and IDE Interface: Protocols, Applications and Programming*. Reading, MA: Addison-Wesley.

1997. Anderson, D. *USB System Architecture*. Reading, MA: Addison-Wesley.

2000. Buchanan, W. *Computer Buses*. Boca Raton, FL: CRC Press.

Stephen J. Rogowski

BUSINESS APPLICATIONS

See DATABASE MANAGEMENT SYSTEM (DBMS); ELECTRONIC COMMERCE; ELECTRONIC FUNDS TRANSFER (EFT); MANAGEMENT INFORMATION SYSTEMS (MIS); and SMART CARD.

a

b

c

d

e

f

g

h

i

j

k

l

m

n

o

p

q

r

s

t

u

v, w

x, y

z

C

For articles on related subjects, see

+ C++
+ Java
+ Linux
+ Procedure-Oriented Languages
+ Programming Languages
+ Structured Programming
+ Systems Programming
+ Unix

C is a general-purpose programming language featuring economy of expression, basic control flow and data structure capabilities, and a rich set of operators and data types. C was originally best known as the primary language of the Unix operating system, but it has become in effect the *lingua franca* of computing: most programmers know C and many large programs are written in C or a descendant like C++ or Java.

C was originally designed and implemented by Dennis Ritchie in 1972–1973 for the DEC PDP-11. C has its roots in an early language called BCPL in much the same way that, for example, Pascal (*q.v.*) sprang from Algol (*q.v.*). C is the successor to a short-lived BCPL-like language called B. C is a traditional procedural language. It is compact, oriented toward systems programming, and easily compiled. Its data types (*q.v.*) and operations map directly into the

capabilities of conventional computers, so compilers are small and generated code is efficient. C relies on library routines for input–output and other interactions with an operating system (*q.v.*). C is not tied to any particular hardware or operating system, and C compilers run on virtually all machines. The Unix operating system itself, which is largely written in C, has been ported to a variety of computers with relatively modest effort. An ANSI/ISO standard for C and its basic libraries was defined in 1988. The standard reference on C is Kernighan and Ritchie (1988); detailed information on the history of the language may be found in Ritchie (1995).

Language Components
Control Flow

Control flow in C is relatively conventional:

```
if (expr) stat1 else stat2
while (expr) stat
for (expr1; expr2; expr3) stat
do stat while (expr)
switch (expr) {
    case const1: stat1
    case const2: stat2
    ...
    default: stat
}
```

In each of these, *expr* is an expression and *stat* is a statement, either simple or a group of statements enclosed in braces. Within a loop, **break** causes an immediate exit and **continue** causes the next iteration to begin; **break** also terminates cases of a **switch** statement.

Data Types

The basic data types in C are char (usually an eight-bit byte); int, short, and long; and float and double (floating-point numbers). Integer types come in signed and unsigned variants. An int usually corresponds to the natural word size of the machine (32 or 64 bits), while short is often 16 bits and long the longest possible integer. In addition, there is a conceptually infinite hierarchy of derived types. If T is a type, then there are pointers (*q.v.*) to objects of type T, arrays of Ts, and structures and unions (records and variant records, in Pascal terminology) that may contain Ts. There are also pointers to functions, and enumeration types (i.e. ones whose discrete members are explicitly listed by the programmer). C does not have a string data type; strings are represented as arrays of chars, usually with a null byte as terminator, and manipulated by library functions.

Pointer arithmetic is an integral part of C, and the use of pointers to create and access dynamic data structures is one of its most characteristic features. Pointers are more constrained than mere machine addresses, however. Pointers to different types cannot be assigned or combined without explicit coercion (*q.v.*). If *p* is of type pointer to T, and currently points to an element of an array of Ts, then $p + 1$ is a pointer to the next element of the array. That is, arithmetic operations on pointers are scaled by the size of the object to which the pointer points; the programmer is not (and should not be) concerned with the actual size.

Operators and Expressions

In addition to the usual +, −, and so on, C has a relatively rich set of operators. Any binary operator such as + has a corresponding "assignment operator" (here + =) so that the statement

```
v = v + expr;
```

can be more concisely written

```
v += expr;
```

The unary operators ++ and −− increment or decrement their operand:

```
v++; or ++v;
```

is the preferred way to write

```
v = v + 1;
```

An expression (*q.v.*) may be coerced (converted or *cast*) to another type by preceding the expression with a type name, as in

```
x = sqrt( (double) integer expression);
```

The coercion in this example converts the *integer expression* into double precision, the type required by the function sqrt. Standard coercions (for example, integer type to floating-point type or vice versa) are performed implicitly, so in this example the cast is unnecessary.

Program Structure

A *C* program is a set of declarations of variables and functions in one or more source files that may be compiled separately. Function definitions may not be nested, but variables may be declared or redeclared within any block (*see* BLOCK STRUCTURE).

Functions or external variables at the top level are declared either global (i.e. available to all functions) or visible only within the source file where they are declared. Variables internal to a function are either *automatic* (they appear when the function is entered and disappear when it is exited) or *static* (they retain their values from one call of the function to the next). Variables may be initialized at the point of declaration.

All functions may be called recursively. Function arguments are passed by value, but passing a pointer provides call by reference when necessary (*see* PARAMETER PASSING). Function arguments and return values may have any basic type or may be pointers, structures, unions, and enumerations. Arrays are passed as a pointer to their first element.

An Example

The following program computes and prints the powers of 2 up to 2^{30}. Execution begins at main. The standard library function printf does formatted output conversion according to the specification in its first argument. Here, %d signals an ordinary integer and %ld a long integer; \n is a newline character.

```
#define LIMIT 30
void main() /* test power function */
{
    int i;
    long power(int, int);
    for (i = 0;i <= LIMIT; ++i)
        printf("%d %ld\n", i,power(2,i));
}
long power(int x, int n)
        /*raise x to nth power; n >= 0*/
{
    int i ;
    long p ;
    p = 1;
    for (i = 1; i <= n; ++i)
        p = p * x;
    return p;
}
```

Assessment

The C language has remained remarkably stable and unified compared with those of similarly widespread currency, for example, Pascal and Fortran, and has remained freer of proprietary extensions than other languages. Although C was not originally designed with portability as a prime goal, it has been used to write programs, even operating systems, on machines ranging from the smallest personal computers to the mightiest supercomputers. Ultimately, C has succeeded because it has satisfied a need for a system implementation language sufficiently abstract and fluent to describe algorithms and interactions in a wide variety of environments, yet efficient enough to displace assembly language.

Bibliography

1978. Ritchie, D. M., Johnson, S. C., Lesk, M. E., and Kernighan, B. W. "UNIX Time-sharing System: The C Programming Language," *Bell Sys. Tech. J.*, **57**(6), 1991–2019.

1988. Kernighan, B. W., and Ritchie, D. M. *The C Programming Language*, 2nd Ed. Upper Saddle River, NJ: Prentice Hall.

1995. Ritchie, D. M. "The Development of the C Language," in *History of Programming Languages II* (ed. T. J. Bergin, and R. G. Gibson), 671–687. Reading, MA: Addison-Wesley.

Brian W. Kernighan and Dennis M. Ritchie

C++

For articles on related subjects, *see*

+ Abstract Data Type
+ C
+ Class
+ Object-Oriented Programming
+ Programming Languages
+ Procedure-Oriented Languages: Survey

Chronology

C++ was designed and originally implemented by Bjarne Stroustrup at the Bell Labs Computer Science Research Center, Murray Hill, NJ. The work on what became C++ started in 1979 and led to a first commercial release from AT&T in October 1985. C++ added better type checking, support for data abstraction, and support for object-oriented programming to the C programming language. The early versions of C++ were called "*C with Classes.*" The name C++, signifying "incremental improvement of C" and "successor to C," came into use in 1984.

After its initial commercial release in the form of a highly-portable compiler front-end, C++ became widely used and supported by many implementations on all major kinds of computers—including the then newly prominent personal computers (PCs). Up through 1992, Stroustrup refined C++ based on user feedback.

In late 1989, formal standardization of C++ under the auspices of the American National Standards Institute (ANSI) started. In 1991, this effort became international, leading to an ISO standard in 1998 (×3 Secretariat, 1998) and the resulting language, standard library, and the primary programming techniques supported by Standard C++ were documented (Stroustrup, 1997).

The Initial Design of C++

A programming language has two roles:

1. It serves as a medium in which a programmer can express ideas as a means of communication among programmers.

2. It serves as a means of instructing computers to perform specific actions.

The Simula 67 language with its support for object-oriented design and programming was a good match for the first role. The C programming language was a good match for the second role. Thus, C++ was designed to provide Simula's facilities for program organization together with C's efficiency and flexibility for systems programming (*q.v.*).

Abstraction and Efficiency

Consider designing a simulation of traffic flow through a city to estimate response times for emergency vehicles or commute times. We use concepts such as road, hospital, traffic light, car, motorcycle, and ambulance as we think about our problem. In our program, we want to represent these concepts as directly and as conveniently as possible. A major design aim of C++ was to allow the programmer to specify concepts such as `road`, `hospital`, `traffic_light`, `car`, `motorcycle`, and `ambulance` as user-defined types. Such user-defined types, called *classes*, receive the same degree of support from the language as do built-in types such as integers and characters. Thinking in terms of user-defined types and hiding implementation details within the implementations of these types is commonly called *data abstraction*. Enabling a style of programming based on efficient user-defined data types was a major aim of C++. The benefits are comprehensibility, maintainability, and easier debugging.

However, just having classes doesn't raise the level of programming to the level at which we use concepts. For example, we talk of vehicles, rather than always listing the various kinds of vehicles. Thus, C++ had to provide the programmer with the tools to specify relationships among concepts. For example, it is easy to specify that a `motorcycle`, a `car`, and an `ambulance` are `vehicles`, and that an `ambulance` and a `police_car` are `emergency_vehicles`. Representing commonality among concepts in a hierarchical fashion leads to what is referred to as *class hierarchies*. For example, in a program, it is then possible to specify an action such as "the vehicle turns right" without listing the kinds of vehicles that we want to turn; each individual vehicle performs the action appropriate for its type. This style of programming is called *object-oriented programming*, and can be used to design very flexible and extensible systems.

Bibliography

1994. Stroustrup, B. *The Design and Evolution of C++.* Reading, MA: Addison-Wesley.

1996. Stroustrup, B. "A History of C++: 1979–1991," in *The History of Programming Languages* (eds. T. J. Bergin, and R. G. Gibson), 699–754. Reading, MA: Addison-Wesley.

1997. Stroustrup, B. *The C++ Programming Language*, 3rd Ed. Reading, MA: Addison-Wesley.

Bjarne Stroustrup

CABLE MODEM

For articles on related subjects, see

+ Baud
+ Channel
+ Modem
+ Networks, Computer

A *cable modem*, more formally a *Data Service Unit/Channel Service Unit* (DSU/CSU), serves the same function for digital data service communication (DDS) lines as a modem does for conventional analog communication lines. The cable modem is an external device that converts the digital data stream from a computer, most typically now a personal computer (PC) equipped with an internal Ethernet (*q.v.*) card, into a format suitable for transmission over the digital communication line. That line is typically a Digital Subscriber Line (DSL)—(*see* INTEGRATED SERVICES DIGITAL NETWORK (ISDN))—or the fiber optics (*q.v.*) line that delivers cable TV service. The CSU terminates the digital line and performs line conditioning functions, ensures network compliance to FCC rules, and responds to remote commands for control and loop-back testing.

John S. Sobolewski

CACHE MEMORY

For articles on related subjects, *see*

Introduction

A *cache memory* is a small, high-speed buffer used for temporary storage of those portions of the contents of some larger memory that are (believed to be) currently in use. The most common use of a cache memory is in the CPU of a computer system, where it holds or buffers the contents of main memory. Cache memories can also be used to hold the contents of the disk (a disk cache) or mass storage (e.g. a tape cache).

A cache memory is normally both significantly faster and significantly smaller than the memory whose contents it caches. Like any component of the memory hierarchy, it is useful only if it can satisfy a large fraction of the references to the larger memory. In practice, caches are very effective in a wide variety of situations because of the *principle of locality* (*see* WORKING SET), which is an empirical observation that most of the time the information in use is either the same information that was recently in use (temporal locality), or is information "nearby" the information recently used (spatial locality). Thus, a cache typically operates by retaining copies of blocks of storage, each containing recently used information.

Caches are usually transparent or invisible to the processor. The CPU generates a main memory address when it wishes to read or write data. When a cache is added to this design, it is interposed between the CPU and the main memory. The cache thus receives the main memory address, and determines, through some sort of associative search using the main memory address as the key, whether it already holds the data corresponding to that address. If so, in the case of a read, it replies to the CPU with the data, and the main memory is not referenced. When the data sought is retrieved from the cache, there is a cache *hit*, otherwise a cache *miss*.

Cache Operation

A CPU (central processing unit) typically consists of three major components: the *instruction unit*, which fetches and decodes instructions (*see* INSTRUCTION DECODING); the *execution unit*, which executes the instructions; and the *storage unit*, which contains the cache, the TLB (translation lookaside buffer), and the translator. The operation of the cache is inseparable from the operation of the rest of the storage unit, and we discuss the cache in that context.

Figure 1 is a diagram showing the CPU and main memory. Figure 2 presents a very simple design for a CPU cache memory, showing that the cache consists of a number of entries. Each entry consists of an address tag, a valid bit, and a *line* or *block* of data. If the valid bit is set to 1, the data is a copy of the data held in the main memory locations identified by the address tag. If the valid bit is set to 0, then the corresponding data field does not currently hold valid data as a result of changes to the contents of main memory. When the instruction (I) or execution (E) units of the CPU generate a main memory address, that address is presented to the cache, which associatively and simultaneously compares the address with the address field of each entry for which the valid bit is on. If a match is found (a *hit*), on a read, the cache then replies to the I- or E-unit with the requested information. If there is no match, then the cache fetches the line containing the desired information from main memory, extracts the target information and

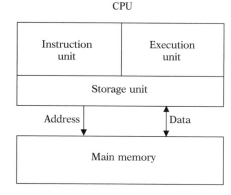

Figure 1. A CPU and main memory.

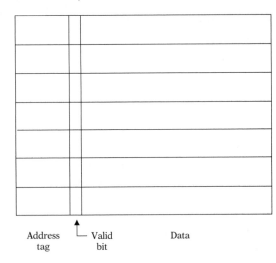

Address   Valid   Data
  tag   bit

Figure 2. Elements of a simple cache memory.

sends it to the I- or E-unit, and also stores the line in a cache entry, replacing the previous contents of that entry. In the case of a write, the data in the cache is updated and, concurrently, the write is also transmitted to main memory, where the main memory copy of the data is updated.

Typically, CPU cache memories will experience 95–99.9% hits and TLBs generally will have 98–99.9% hits, depending on the cache size, line size, and workload.

Other Types of Cache

Caches can be used in numerous ways in computer systems. A common type of cache is the *disk cache*. The disk cache holds portions of the material on the disk in some sort of faster storage, usually semiconductor storage. The disk cache can be located within the disk enclosure, in which case it is managed by the (single) disk controller in a file server or multidisk controller, or the CPU can do the disk caching itself by using a portion of main memory for that purpose. Disk caches are reasonably effective, with typical read hit ratios in the range of 70–90%. Issues in disk cache design are similar to those for CPU caches; the designer must consider the cache size, the cache location (CPU, server, disk controller), the write policy (write-through, copy-back), replacement algorithm, fetch algorithm, and block size. A particularly important consideration in disk cache

design is the problem of reliability in the case of system failure or power loss. In general, an operating system assumes that data written to disk is completely safe and immune to system failure. If data "written" to disk is actually in the disk cache, this assumption is violated, with potentially severe consequences for system integrity. Either write-through or battery backup is typically used for disk caches in systems that are expected to be highly reliable.

Database systems almost always do some amount of caching; typically, they maintain a region in main memory, which is used to hold recently referenced blocks of data. This is similar in concept and operation to disk caching.

Caching is used within operating systems to avoid lengthy and redundant computations. For example, the directory structure is used to translate file names to file descriptors, and frequently the same name is translated repeatedly. By caching recently performed translations, use of the directory structure can be avoided.

Caching is used in various ways in accessing the World Wide Web (*q.v.*). A Web browser caches recently used pages locally at the user's computer. Typically, a Web server will also cache recently referenced pages, so that it isn't necessary to retrieve popular pages from disk each time they are referenced.

Bibliography

1982. Smith, A. J. "Cache Memories," *ACM Computing Surveys*, **14**(3), 473–530.

1997. Uhlig, R. A., and Mudge, T. N. "Trace-driven Memory Simulation: A Survey," *ACM Computing Surveys*, **29**(2), 128–170.

1999. Peir, J.-K., Hsu, W., and Smith, A. J. "Implementation Issues in Modern Cache Memories," *IEEE Trans. on Computers*, **48**(2), 100–110.

Alan Jay Smith

CAD/CAM

See COMPUTER-AIDED DESIGN/COMPUTER-AIDED MANUFACTURING (CAD/CAM).

CAI

See COMPUTER-ASSISTED LEARNING AND TEACHING.

CALCULATING MACHINES

For articles on related subjects, see

+ Calculators, Electronic and Programmable
+ Leibniz, Gottfried Wilhelm
+ Museums, Computer
+ Pascal, Blaise

A *mechanical calculator* is a device that has three properties: a mechanism that will act as a register to store a number; a mechanism to add a fixed amount to the number stored in that register; and an addition mechanism having the ability to deal automatically with any carry, from one digit to the next, that is generated during the addition process.

The first known device of this kind (Fig. 1) was produced by the German scholar Wilhelm Schickard (1592–1635) in 1623 as a response to a request for calculating help from the astronomer Johann Kepler. The upper portion of the machine contains a multiplication table in the form of cylindrical Napier's bones with slides that allow one row at a time to be seen. The lower part contains a very simple register, much like an automobile odometer, each digit of which contains a single tooth which, when it rotates from 9 to 0, will cause the next wheel on the left to rotate one-digit position.

The next major advance in mechanical calculation came 19 years later when Blaise Pascal (*q.v.*) invented an adding machine with a gravity-assisted carry mechanism (Fig. 2). Difficulties with the Schickard single-tooth carry were overcome in *Pascaline*, as he called his machine, by having a weight lift up as the digits of the register rotate. When a carry was necessary, the weight would fall and "kick" the adjacent digit of the register over one position.

During one of his trips to France as a German diplomat, mathematician Gottfried Wilhelm Leibniz (*q.v.*) saw a copy of the Pascal machine and became intrigued with the concept. When he attempted to build a machine like it, but with extra gearing added to implement multiplication, he discovered that the internal mechanism was not capable of simultaneous action on all digits at once. To correct this deficiency, he invented the *Leibniz stepped-drum principle*, which was to become the basic pattern for many mechanical calculating machines for the next 300 years. A working Leibniz machine (Fig. 3) was first constructed during the summer of 1674.

In about 1820, Charles Xavier Thomas (1785–1870), also known as Thomas de Colmar, a French insurance executive, designed and sold

Figure 1. Schickard's calculator.

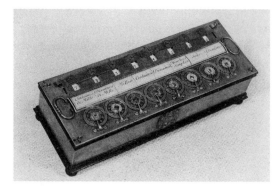

Figure 2. Pascal's calculating machines (photograph courtesy of IBM Archives).

Figure 3. The Leibniz calculating machine (photograph courtesy of IBM Archives).

Figure 4. A Brunsviga Calculator. (Courtesy of Smithsonian Institution.)

a workable mechanical calculator. The Thomas Arithmometer was based on the Leibniz stepped-drum principle, but had a fully working carry mechanism. It was first demonstrated to the French Academy of Science in 1820, and several thousand were sold in Europe until about 1900.

The major problem with any machine based on the Leibniz stepped drum was that it was both large and heavy. The Leibniz drum essentially provided a gear with a variable number (0–9) of teeth, but at the cost of size and weight. A number of attempts at producing a better variable-toothed gear that would literally change the number of teeth protruding from its surface were unsuccessful until the solution was found, essentially simultaneously, by Willgodt T. Odhner (1845–1905), a Swede working in Russia, and Frank S. Baldwin (1830–1925), an American, in about the year 1874.

Odhner first produced his "pin wheel" calculator in 1874 at a factory in St. Petersburg. The concept quickly spread and soon the famous Brunsviga firm was producing them in Germany, the Baldwin calculators were being made in America, and the original Odhner firm was continuing to produce them in Russia. By 1912 the Brunsviga firm alone had produced over 20 000 machines (Fig. 4).

The only significant advance on the technology of the variable-toothed gear was the key-driven adding machine. Dorr E. Felt (1862–1930), an American, produced the first workable system in 1886, which he named the Comptometer (Fig. 5). By combining the action of entering a number with the action of actually adding it to a mechanical register, the process of performing simple addition was speeded up by several orders of magnitude.

Figure 5. An early Comptometer. (Courtesy of Smithsonian Institution.)

There were many improvements to these basic devices over the years. The addition of a printing mechanism allowed users to keep track of their computations. The replacement of human motive power by electric motors allowed both faster computation and less fatigue for the operator. The improvements in engineering technology shrunk the size and weight of the machines to the point where the Curta calculator (Fig. 6) could be used by holding it in one hand. Designed by Curt Herzstark (1902–1988) in 1943 while imprisoned in Buchenwald, over 14 000 Curta calculators were sold from 1948 to 1972. It will undoubtedly remain the smallest *mechanical* calculator ever built.

Figure 6. The Curta. (Courtesy of Smithsonian Institution.)

By the mid-twentieth century, electromechanical desktop calculating machines manufactured by Brunsviga, Facit, Friden, Marchant, and Monroe, among others, were widely used but, with the advent of the handheld electronic calculator, they were gradually relegated to museum pieces and collectors' items.

Bibliography

1914. Horsburgh, E. M. *Handbook of the Napier Tercentenary Celebration on Modern Instruments and Methods of Calculation.* Edinburgh: The Royal Society of Edinburgh. (Reprinted by MIT Press and Tomash Publishers, 1982).

1921. Turck, J. V. A. *Origin of Modern Calculating Machines.* Chicago: The Western Society of Engineers.

1989. Aspray, W. (ed.) *Computing Before Computers.* Ames, IA: The Iowa State University Press.

Michael R. Williams

CALCULATORS, ELECTRONIC AND PROGRAMMABLE

For articles on related subjects, *see*

+ Calculating Machines

+ Digital Computers, History of

+ Portable Computers

Prior to the 1950s, desktop calculators were either key driven or used a rotating drum to enter sums punched into a keyboard. The invention of the transistor in 1948 and the integrated circuit in 1964 were the two events that formed the basis for the electronic calculator. Miniature solid-state electronics enabled calculators to progress past the basic four arithmetic functions to the point where they are capable of performing almost any function that can be expressed as a programmable sequence or a mathematical formula.

By 1974, calculators using modern electronic technology cost less than $50 and could outperform mechanical calculators that had once sold for up to $1500. Today, some handheld calculators can be purchased for less than $5; and $100 will buy an extremely sophisticated one.

Some electronic calculators are intended for desk use, but since 1970 numerous hand models have been available, some as small as a credit card. At the same time, solar or other long-life batteries brought about calculators that can operate for thousands of hours without energy source replacements. Nearly all calculators have internally programmed microinstructions; their circuitry can do any of several different things depending on coded commands stored in the system. Some electronic calculators may be programmed externally.

Texas Instruments now uses *flash technology* (reprogrammable *read-only memory*—*q.v.*), so their models 83 and 92 calculators can be upgraded (Fig. 1). Casio calculators use three colors in their graphing mode and the Sharp EL9600c has some unique features such as Slide Show and EZ modes to facilitate teaching. The calculators of all three companies can use adapters to collect data such as motion, temperature, and voltage from actual experiments.

Electronic calculators are designed to perform their functions using either algebraic notation or RPN—Reverse Polish Notation (*see* POLISH NOTATION). Algebraic notation permits entry of calculations as normally written (e.g. $\boxed{2}\boxed{+}\boxed{3}$) with the arithmetic function between the two numbers—infix notation.

Figure 1. The TI-92 Plus scientific calculator (courtesy of Texas Instruments).

With RPN, the operator is placed after the two numbers, ($\boxed{2}\,\boxed{3}\,\boxed{+}$), and therefore the operator is input *after* both numbers have been entered (postfix notation). The former requires parenthesizing for all but the simplest calculations, whereas RPN allows any sequence of calculations to be entered without parentheses.

Calculators typically compute nonzero numbers in a range from 10^{-99} to 10^{99} and print from 8 to 12 digits in the display. If the answer is larger than the display, many calculators will automatically express the answer in scientific notation. A typical advanced nonprogrammable electronic calculator would normally include the following scientific functions: x^2, $\sqrt{x}$, $1/x$, y^x, $x\text{–}y$ interchange, normal and inverse trigonometric functions, logarithms to the bases 10 and e, e^x, 10^x, $x!$, and degree to radian conversions. Statistical functions often included are summation, mean, and standard deviation. Other common calculator capabilities are the ability to store a number in memory, to add to memory, to multiply or divide a number saved in memory, and to exchange the display with memory.

Handheld technology, especially graphing calculators, is becoming a necessity in the high schools and colleges in the USA. Mathematics and science teachers are adapting their curricula to use the calculators. The Scholastic Aptitude Test (SAT) administered by the Educational Testing Service now permits the use of graphing calculators. This test is used by many colleges and universities in the USA as part of their entrance requirements. The New York State Regents Exam in mathematics (Test B), given after three years of high school mathematics, is to require the use of a graphing calculator after June 2001. Texas Instruments, Sharp, and Casio provide extensive support through conferences, workshops, and educational materials to aid teachers. Addison-Wesley and Holt, Reinhart, Winston are two US publishers who are publishing textbooks that integrate the use of the graphing calculator.

Texas Instruments has produced the TI-73 graphing calculator and Casio the fx7400 for middle-school mathematics applications. The TI-73 has 25K RAM and graph functions, as well as support for statistical calculations, such as mean, standard deviation, and linear and quadratic regressions, among others. It has list capabilities and is able to graph statistical data in pie chart, histogram, pictorial, and line form. It is programmable and is still able to work with fractions and trigonometric functions. These calculators are available for under $80.

Special-purpose calculators have been designed for many professions and hobbies, including finance, statistics, business, mathematics, science, economics, accounting, real estate, sports, and time management. An inexpensive calculator developed by Sharp Electronics, the EL-509RH, supports all usual arithmetic functions plus the ability to calculate two-variable statistics.

Jerald L. Mikesell and Charles G. Ames

CALLING SEQUENCE

For articles on related subjects, see

+ Activation Record
+ Parameter Passing
+ Subprogram

A *calling sequence* is the precise sequence of one or more commands or statements needed to invoke a subordinate procedure. In a high-level language like Pascal, procedures are called by stating their name, followed by a parenthesized list of the actual parameters that the procedure needs to do its work. An example is

```
search(haystack,150,'needle',locations)
```

which invokes a procedure that searches an array of 150 character strings called *haystack* and places in an array called `locations` the indices (subscripts) of all *haystack* locations that contain `'needle'`.

The single-statement calling sequence cited is properly formed only if it contains exactly the right number of parameters expected by the called procedure, the parameters are specified in the expected order, and the *data type* (*q.v.*) of each parameter (integer, real, string, etc.) is what is expected.

The mechanism used for *parameter passing* (*q.v.*) may limit the form of the expression used to cite actual parameters. For example, if the second parameter used with procedure `search` is to be an integer passed by value, then the actual parameter used in this position could be an expression such as $n - j + 2$, just as well as a particular number like 150. But if the first and last parameters are passed by reference (VAR parameters in the vocabulary of Pascal), the actual parameters used in those positions must be variable names, as they are in the example given. (When a parameter is passed "by reference," the address where it may be found is transmitted rather than the value stored at that address.)

The term *calling sequence* predates the use of high-level languages. In assembly language, the most common form of calling sequence consists of loading certain machine registers with specified parameters prior to transfer of control to the subprogram that will process them.

Edwin D. Reilly

CARD, PUNCHED

See PUNCHED CARD.

CD-ROM

See OPTICAL STORAGE.

CELLULAR AUTOMATA

For articles on related subjects, *see*

+ Automata Theory
+ Parallel Processing

A *cellular automaton,* or *polyautomaton*, is a theoretical model of a parallel computer, subject to various restrictions to make formal investigation of its computing powers tractable. All versions of the model share these properties: each is an interconnection of identical cells, where a cell is a model of a computer with finite memory—that is, a finite-state machine. Each cell computes an output from inputs it receives from a finite set of cells forming its neighborhood, and possibly from an external source.

All cells compute one output simultaneously and each cell computes an output at each tick of a clock, that is, after each unit time step. The output of a cell is distributed to its neighborhood and possibly to an external receiver.

A version of the cellular automaton model exists for each set of choices in the following dichotomies: an infinite or a finite number of cells; a uniform interconnection scheme (all cells have neighborhoods of the same shape, that is, that in Fig. 1) or a nonuniform scheme (Fig. 2); deterministic or nondeterministic cells

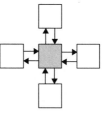

Figure 1.   A cell (tinted) and its neighborhood.

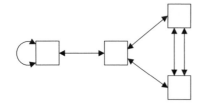

Figure 2. A cellular automation with nonuniform neighborhood.

(a choice of exactly one output value at each unit time step or a set of several values); the absence or presence of an external input (output), and, in the case of an external input (output), connecting it to all cells or to only a subset; Moore-type or Mealy-type cells (unit time or zero time required, respectively, between inputs and the associated output); a static or dynamic interconnection scheme (neighborhood does or does not remain fixed in time). Some of the names associated with one or more of these versions are cellular automaton, cellular space, tessellation automaton, modular array, iterative automaton, intelligent graph, Lindenmayer system, and cellular network.

Historically, the first version of the cellular automaton was the cellular space obtained by selecting the first choice in each dichotomy above, but with no external input or output. It can be visualized in two dimensions as an infinite chessboard, each square representing a cell. It has been used to prove the existence of nontrivial self-reproducing machines, is capable of computing any computable function with only three states per cell and the four nearest cells as the neighborhood (Fig. 1), and can exhibit *Garden of Eden configurations*; that is, patterns of cell states at one time, which can never arise in a given cellular space except at time zero. If an external input is assumed distributed to each cell, then the cellular space becomes what is usually called a *tessellation* space.

The cellular automaton is obtained from the cellular space by admitting only a finite, connected set of cells on the chessboard. A cell with a neighbor missing has a special boundary signal substituted instead. The cellular automaton is particularly useful as a pattern recognizer, where the pattern comprises the states of the cells at time zero, especially if nondeterministic cells are allowed. A famous problem for the (deterministic) cellular automaton, the Firing Squad problem, calls each cell a soldier with one of them as the general—that is, all cells but one are "off" initially—and asks if all soldiers can begin firing simultaneously by going into the same state. The Firing Squad theorem, which solves this problem, guarantees a yes.

The infinite chessboard cellular automaton gained much public popularity in the 1970s as the basis for the so-called *Game of Life* (Gardner, 1971). A resurgence of interest in the 1980s accompanied application of simple two-state, one-dimensional cellular automata (now often abbreviated CA) to fractals (*q.v.*) and dynamic chaos, rich new subjects that arose during that decade, propelled by inexpensive computer graphics (*q.v.*).

Bibliography

1968. Codd, E. F. *Cellular Automata, ACM Monograph Series*. New York: Academic Press.

1971. Gardner, M. "On Cellular Automata, Self-reproduction, the Garden of Eden, and the Game of Life," *Scientific American*, **224**, 112–117.

1986. Wolfram, S. (ed.) *Theory and Applications of Cellular Automata*. Singapore: World Scientific.

Alvy Ray Smith

CENTRAL PROCESSING UNIT (CPU)

For articles on related subjects, see

+ Adder
+ Arithmetic-Logic Unit (ALU)
+ Computer Architecture
+ Digital Computer
+ Instruction Decoding
+ Memory: Main
+ Stored Program Concept

The *central processing unit* (CPU) of a digital computer carries out the essential data manipulation, arithmetic, and control tasks at the heart of the computer. The principal element of the CPU, its *arithmetic-logic unit* (ALU), is designed to operate on a pair of numbers and apply to them the processes of addition, subtraction, multiplication, and division, as well as logical operations on individual bits of numbers. It can compare numbers and determine whether one is greater or whether they are equal.

The other important element of the CPU is the *control unit* required to supervise the functioning of the machine as a whole. It receives the program instructions one by one in sequence, interprets them, and sends appropriate control signals to various other units. When the control unit recognizes special signals (e.g. that the result of a subtraction is negative), it can depart from the strict sequence of program instructions and "jump" to a different part of the program that is designed to deal with those circumstances.

The arithmetic and the control units depend heavily on a third element of a computer, the memory unit. Memory is not part of the CPU *per se*, but together with the CPU it forms the *processor subsystem.* The arithmetic unit needs numbers on which to operate and needs to store intermediate results until the end of the calculation. The control unit needs program instructions in rapid succession. Both data and instructions are held in memory.

With the advent of microprocessors, entire CPUs are now contained on a single integrated circuit chip ("CPU on a chip"). These CPUs are faster and more powerful than those that once required entire cabinets of hardware.

Graham J. Morris

CHANNEL

For articles on related subjects, see

+ Bandwidth
+ Baud
+ Buffer
+ Bus
+ Input-Output Operations
+ Interrupt
+ Memory: Auxiliary
+ Multiplexing
+ Multitasking
+ Polling
+ Port, I/O

Introduction

In the sense of this article, a *channel* is a processor that performs I/O for a mainframe computer. Additionally, the channel provides overlap of I/O processing with logical and arithmetic processing, thereby obtaining high throughput (*q.v.*) by performing different operations in parallel. The channel also provides a standard interface for a range of I/O devices that may be connected to a processor.

Autonomous Channel Operation

The availability of buffered peripherals calls for the fast transfer of data to and from those peripherals. If these transfers were controlled by the central processing unit (CPU—*q.v.*), much time would be lost since character transfer is slow compared with other CPU operations. Methods of autonomous transfer were needed whereby a whole block of data is transferred rapidly, word by word, to and from the main store, the cycles of the storage time taken for the word transfer being "stolen" from those available to the CPU. This *cycle stealing* usually causes only a slight hesitation of the CPU, whose storage cycle time of 10–50 ns should be compared with that of a high-speed disk drive whose transfer rate is, at best, about 100–200 ns per byte.

To facilitate block transfers directly between the store and the peripheral units, a controller called a *data channel* was introduced. A large mainframe (*q.v.*) has several such channels. A data channel is essentially a small, special-purpose computer. An I/O operation is initiated by the processor that selects a channel and a device to be connected to it. The channel then accesses a unique location in main memory where the processor has stored the address of the first instruction to be issued to the channel. Usually, a list of instructions called a _program_, is set up in storage. Each instruction is a particular operation that the channel must execute. The CPU sends to the channel the address of the block of consecutive storage words (or bytes) to be transferred and the number of words to be transferred. If the channel is not already busy and the channel equipment is available and ready to operate, the channel initiates the transfer.

Channel Capacity

The rate at which a channel can transmit data to or from an I/O device, or to or from main storage, is called the _transfer rate_ or _channel capacity_. This is usually given in megabytes per second (MB/s). The channel capacity must, of course, be great enough to service the fastest I/O device connected to it. The maximum rates given for discrete channels may also be degraded by the operation of other channels with which they are _multiplexed_ and by relative channel priorities.

Since _multiplexer_ or _selector_ channels are essentially independent computers controlling I/O, they will, of course, have their transfer rates affected by the way they are programmed. If the data is entered into a contiguous area of storage, the effective data transfer rate will be greater than if it is entered into a noncontiguous set of areas, where all sorts of addresses must be computed and the CPU notified as to which storage area is being affected. This use of noncontiguous memory for a data set is known as _data chaining_. Of course, data chaining creates more conflict with the CPU, slowing either data transmission or processing or both.

Channel Commands

A computer program consists of a set of instructions that are decoded and executed by the CPU. _Channel commands_ are instructions that are decoded and executed by the I/O channels. A sequence of commands constitutes a channel program. Commands are stored in the main storage just as though they were instructions. They are fetched from main storage and are common to all I/O devices, but modifier bits are used to specify device-dependent conditions. The modifier bits of the command may also be used to order the I/O device to execute certain functions that are not involved in data

transfer, such as tape rewinding or repositioning of a hard disk (_q.v._) access arm.

During program execution, the CPU will initiate relevant I/O operations. A command will specify a channel, a device, and an operation to be performed, and perhaps a storage area to be used, and perhaps also some memory protection information about the storage area involved. All this information may appear in the command word, or the command may tell the channel in which locations in memory to seek the necessary information. Upon receipt of this information, the multiplexer channel will attempt to select the desired device by sending the device address to all I/O units (including controllers) attached to the channel. A unit that recognizes its address connects itself logically to the channel. Once the connection is made, the channel will send the executable command to the I/O device. The device will respond to the channel, indicating whether it can execute the command and make this information available to the CPU.

Bibliography

1978. Kuck, D. J. _The Structure of Computers and Communications_. New York: John Wiley.

Trevor Pearcey and Milton Pine

CHARACTER CODES

For articles on related subjects, see

+ Codes
+ Error Correcting and Detecting Code
+ Punched Card
+ Typefont
+ Universal Product Code

Since computers are binary machines, they must represent the characters as sequences of 1s and 0s. Various schemes have been developed to encode them.

BCD

Binary-Coded Decimal (BCD) was an early and widely used code for representing single decimal digits in binary form. Table 1 shows the 4-bit equivalent of each decimal digit in BCD.

EBCDIC

The Extended Binary-Coded Decimal Interchange Code (EBCDIC) was an 8-bit code developed by IBM for use in its System/360 and later computers. EBCDIC has been superseded on all computers, even those of IBM, by ASCII.

ASCII

The American Standard Code for Information Interchange (ASCII) is a 7-bit code also known as the USA Standard Code for Information Interchange (USASCII). Table 2 exhibits ASCII; blank cells are reserved for the control character codes that are used in computer communications. The leftmost three bits and their decimal equivalents are shown at the top, while the

Table 1. BCD. Each combination is the binary representation of the corresponding digit.

Digit	BCD combination
0	0000
1	0001
2	0010
3	0011
4	0100
5	0101
6	0110
7	0111
8	1000
9	1001

Table 2. ASCII codes for letters, numbers, special characters, and some control characters. All codes with first digit 0 or 1 are for control characters. The meanings of those shown are: BS—Backspace, HT—Horizontal Tab, LF—Line Feed, VT—Vertical Tab, FF—Form Feed, CR—Carriage Return and DEL (in location 7F)—Delete. Also, SP in location 20 is the space character. For the complete ASCII character set see http://webopedia.internet.com/TERM/A/ASCII.html.

Bit positions 4, 5, 6, 7	Hexadecimal digit	000 0	001 1	010 2	011 3	100 4	101 5	110 6	111 7	Bit positions 1, 2, 3 Decimal digit
0000	0			SP	0	@	P	`	p	
0001	1			!	1	A	Q	a	q	
0010	2			"	2	B	R	b	r	
0011	3			#	3	C	S	c	s	
0100	4			$	4	D	T	d	t	
0101	5			%	5	E	U	e	u	
0110	6			&	6	F	V	f	v	
0111	7			'	7	G	W	g	w	
1000	8	BS		(	8	H	X	h	x	
1001	9	HT		)	9	I	Y	i	y	
1010	A	LF		*	:	J	Z	j	z	
1011	B	VT		+	;	K	[	k	{	
1100	C	FF		,	<	L	\	l			
1101	D	CR		-	=	M	]	m	}	
1110	E			.	>	N	^	n	~	
1111	F			/	?	O	—	o	DEL	

rightmost four bits and their hexadecimal equivalents are shown at the left.

Because 8-bit bytes are common on computers, ASCII is commonly embedded in an 8-bit field in which the high-order (leftmost) bit is either used as a parity bit or is set to zero. There are various extensions of ASCII to 8 bits, among which are the IBM extended character set with characters for elementary graphics and the ISO 8859 standard, which includes Latin-1 (the standard ISO 8-bit extension to ASCII (ISO 8859) for Western European alphabets). Since even 8-bit ASCII is capable of encoding only 256 characters, it is unsuitable for the large number of characters and symbols needed with the many languages which do not use the Latin alphabet or which (like French and German) have an effective alphabet of more than 26 characters because of the use of accents, umlauts, and so on.

Unicode

Unicode is a 16-bit code and can therefore represent 2^{16} or 65 536 characters. Blocks of codes in Unicode have been assigned to various languages and special character groups (e.g. a block of 94 codes for the Latin alphabet, 104 for Greek (including 14 Coptic characters), 76 for punctuation and 242 for mathematics symbols). Extensions of Unicode to 20 bits enable the representation of 2^{20} or 10 48 576 characters. The 2003 version, Unicode 4.0, has encoded 2 36 029 characters from the world's alphabets, ideograph sets, and symbol collections. These characters cover the principal written languages of the Americas, Europe, the Middle East, Africa, India, Asia, and the Pacific.

Unicode distinguishes *characters* and *glyphs*. A glyph is a visual depiction of a character. A character itself has no inherent image. This distinction is in contrast to the common understanding that equates these two concepts. For example, a *font* is often described as being composed of characters. In contrast, by Unicode, a font contains glyphs, not "characters." Therefore, a character set should not encode glyphs, since the number of glyphs is much larger than the number of characters that should be encoded.

Bibliography

2003. Aliprand, J. (ed.). *The Unicode Standard, Version 4.0.* Reading, MA: Addison Wesley. (*See also* http://www.unicode.org.).

Stephen J. Rogowski

CHARACTER SET

See CHARACTER CODES.

CHECKPOINT

For articles on related subjects, *see*

✦ Debugging
✦ Job
✦ Programming Support Environments

A *checkpoint* is a designated place in a program at which normal processing is interrupted so as to preserve the status information necessary to allow resumption of processing at a later time. The purpose of a checkpoint is to avoid repeating the execution of a program from its beginning should an error or malfunction occur during processing. This is especially important in runs involving several hours of machine time, although such durations are becoming exceedingly rare.

A checkpoint is implemented by a procedure that captures the status of the program at the particular instant when it stopped and copies it to auxiliary storage. This data includes the contents of special registers, storage locations associated with the program, and other information relating to the status of I/O devices. Later, a *restart routine* can reset the system to resume processing by reading and restoring the checkpoint information.

In a sense, multiprogramming (*q.v.*) operating systems implement an automatic form of checkpoint/restart. Depending on the scheduling algorithm used, a particular process may be interrupted to make its storage and other resources available to other processes. The status of the interrupted process is saved so that the process can be continued at a later time.

Seymour V. Pollack and Ron K. Cytron

CHESS, COMPUTER

See COMPUTER CHESS.

CHIP

See INTEGRATED CIRCUITRY; MICROCOMPUTER CHIP; and MICROPROCESSORS AND MICROCOMPUTERS.

CHOMSKY HIERARCHY

For articles on related subjects, *see*

+ Automata Theory
+ Formal Languages
+ Machine Translation
+ Turing Machine

For the mathematician, an *alphabet* is a set of symbols and a language is a set, finite or infinite, of strings formed from that alphabet. A *grammar* is a finite system that characterizes a language. Grammars work by substitution. Take the alphabet (or, as it is usually called, the *terminal* alphabet) of the language V_T, add a *nonterminal* alphabet V_N, and a special symbol S that belongs to neither V_T nor V_N. A *production* or rule of substitution, R, is an ordered pair of strings, $R = T_1 \rightarrow T_2$. A grammar is a system, $G = \langle V_N, V_T, P, S \rangle$, where P denotes the set of allowable productions. To use the grammar, start with S and find a rule (i.e.

a production) $S \rightarrow T_1$ and substitute T_1 for S. Find another rule $S_1 \rightarrow T_2$, such that S_1 matches part or all of T_1, and substitute T_2 for the matched part of T_1. Continue with any member of P until the result is a string that contains only terminal symbols. This sequential process is called the *derivation* of the string, and the final string belongs to the language. The language consists of exactly the strings that can be so derived.

If, in a grammar, every rule has the form $n \rightarrow nt$, $n \rightarrow t$, or $n \rightarrow \varepsilon$, where n is a nonterminal symbol, t is a terminal symbol, and ε is the empty string, the grammar is *regular* and characterizes a *regular language*. If every rule has the form $n \rightarrow T$, where T is a string over the combined terminal and nonterminal alphabets, the grammar is *context-free* (the substitution $n \rightarrow T$ can be made wherever n occurs). A context-free grammar generates a context-free language. If every rule has the form $S'nS'' \rightarrow S'TS''$, where S' and S'' are strings over the combined alphabet of terminal and nonterminal symbols, the grammar is *context-sensitive* (the substitution $n \rightarrow T$ can be made only in the context $S' \ldots S''$). A context-sensitive grammar characterizes a context-sensitive language.

Changing the restrictions on the forms of rules changes the power of the grammar. Without restrictions on the form of rules, a grammar can characterize any *recursively enumerable* set of strings, that is, any language that can be characterized at all. Call this class of languages type 0. Not every recursively enumerable set (type 0 language) is a context-sensitive language, but every context-sensitive language is a recursively enumerable set. Call the context-sensitive systems type 1. Again, the context-sensitive systems characterize all context-free languages, but the context-free systems (type 2) cannot characterize some context-sensitive languages. Finally, a regular language can be characterized by a system of any type, but regular grammars (type 3) cannot characterize all context-free languages. The hierarchy of types 0, 1, 2, 3 is commonly called the *Chomsky hierarchy* (*see* Fig. 1), named after the linguist Noam Chomsky, who described it in 1956.

To each type of grammar corresponds a kind of machine that *produces* or *accepts* a language of

Class of grammar, G_i	Grammatical characterization	Machine characterization
Type 0	Unrestricted (or phase structure)	Turing machines
Type 1	Context-sensitive	Linear-bounded automaton
Type 2	Context-free	Pushdown automaton
Type 3	Regular (or right linear)	Finite-state machine

Figure 1. The Chomsky hierarchy. Each class of grammars in the hierarchy contains all lower levels. Thus, $G_3 \subset G_2 \subset G_1 \subset G_0$.

the given type: Turing machines (type 0), linear-bounded automata (type 1), nondeterministic pushdown automata (type 2), and finite-state machines (type 3).

The following example illustrates differences among the four classes. If the terminal alphabet is $\{0,1\}$, then $\{0^n 1^m\}$, the set of strings with any number of 0s followed by any number of 1s, is a regular language. The set of strings with any number of 0s followed by the *same* number of 1s, $\{0^n 1^n\}$, is context-free but not regular, because an accepting automaton for this language would have to be capable of counting arbitrarily high, which no finite-state machine can do. A pushdown automaton has an unbounded *stack* (*q.v.*) and can record any count of initial 0s and match that with the count of 1s. However, the language with any number of 0s followed by the same number of 1s and then by the same number of 0s again, $\{0^n 1^n 0^n\}$, would require two such matching mechanisms. That exceeds the power of a pushdown automaton, and thus this language is context-sensitive.

Strictly type 0 languages arise in the theory of Turing machines and of recursive functions (*see* RECURSION). Every Turing machine with the alphabet $\{0,1\}$ can be encoded in a unique way as a string of 0s and 1s. It is then possible to define a universal Turing machine that, given the encoding of any such Turing machine M joined with an input string I, will accept that concatenated string just in case M would halt on input I. The set of strings accepted by this universal Turing machine is of type 0 but is not context-sensitive.

Bibliography

1956. Chomsky, N. "Three Models for the Description of Language," *IRE Trans. Information Theory*, **IT-2**, 113–124.

1969. Salomaa, A. *Theory of Automata*. Oxford: Pergamon Press.

1997. Sudkamp, T. A. *Languages and Machines*, 2nd Ed. Reading, MA: Addison-Wesley.

David G. Hays

CIRCUITRY

See COMPUTER CIRCUITRY; and INTEGRATED CIRCUITRY.

CLASS

For articles on related subjects, *see*

+ Abstract Data Type
+ Block Structure
+ Data Structures
+ Data Type
+ Declaration
+ Object-Oriented Programming

The concept of *class* was introduced in the programming language Simula 67 as an extension to the block structure and procedure mechanisms of Algol (*q.v.*). As a technique for structuring programs, it is an alternative to the strict nesting of blocks. More recently, the class concept has been used in C++ (*q.v.*) and Java (*q.v.*), primarily as a mechanism for building abstract data types.

Classes in Simula 67

A Simula 67 class declaration resembles a procedure declaration in Algol 60. It was the inspiration for the *abstract data type* mechanism that is an important feature of several modern programming languages. A class may have formal parameters like a procedure. In general, a class declaration includes declarations for variables, functions, and procedures that are local to the class, followed by the body of the class, which is usually a block. An example of class declaration is given in Fig. 1. A class declaration does not by itself cause storage to be allocated or executable code to be compiled; it is a *template* that can be used to create instances of the class. In Simula 67, these class instances are called *objects*. Simula 67 allows the declaration of variables that are references to objects. The built-in operation **new** is used to create objects (class instances). For example, if Z is a variable that is a reference to the class C declared in Fig. 1, then the statement $Z := $ **new** C (100) would create an instance of the class C. The formal parameter n of the class is used to specify the

characteristics of the object created from the class (e.g. the upper bound of the array A).

There may be many objects of a given class, each with its own set of variables. Each object has its own copy of the class variables. When an object is created, control is transferred to the executable statements in the body of the class. Three situations are possible:

1. Control passes through the class definition to the end of the block; the object is terminated; execution cannot reenter the object, but its local storage remains allocated. This possibility is usually used to initialize class variables.

2. A **detach** statement is executed in the body of the object; in this case, the object becomes an independently executing entity; its lifetime may exceed that of the block in which it was created, allowing objects to be used to create *processes*. Thus, a multiprocessing system can be structured as a set of cooperating concurrently executing class objects.

3. A **resume** statement is executed in the body of the object. Execution of the body is suspended at the point of the **resume** statement until it is reactivated by a **resume** statement from outside of the object. For example, if the class *C* in Fig. 1 is used to create the object named Z, as shown above, then the statement **resume** (Z)A: would cause execution to continue in the body of the object Z at

```
class C(n);
      integer n;
      begin
            integer array A[1:n];
            integer k;
            procedure clear;
                  begin
                        integer i;
                        for i:=1 step 1 until n do
                              A[i] := 0
                  end;
            . . .
            comment end of declarations;
            comment execution of class object starts here;
            k := 0;
            resume;
            k := k + 1;
            . . .
      end;
```

Figure 1. Simula 67 class declaration.

the statement **k := k + 1**. This allows coroutine (*q.v.*) structures to be built using objects.

Simula 67 Subclasses

The power and flexibility of the class concept is enhanced by the ability to declare subclasses. A subclass is formed by logically concatenating the formal parameters, local variables, procedures, and executable statements of an existing class with those of a class being declared. A subclass is created when the name of a class is used as a prefix to a class declaration.

Classes in C++

In C++, classes are used primarily as a tool for building abstract data types. A mechanism called *inheritance* allows subclassing as in Simula 67 so that the programmer can control the functionality, from none to all, that the subclass inherits from its base class. C++ extends the class concept of Simula-67 in several ways:

- The designer of a class has explicit control over access to variables declared in the class. Variables can be declared to be accessible (**public**), accessible only to inheriting classes (**protected**) or inaccessible (**private**).
- The designer of the class can provide a *constructor* function that can be used to guarantee that variables in a class are properly initialized. The designer can also declare a *destructor* function to deallocate data no longer needed.
- A **template** mechanism allows classes to have value parameters as in Simula 67 and class (i.e.

```
template <class T, int size>
          class Stack
          {
          public:
                    push (T newVal);
                    pop (void);
                    T top (void);
                    int isEmpty(void);
          private:
                    T s[size];
                    int sp;
          }
     . . .
   Stack <int,1024> intStack;
   Stack <float, 512> floatStack;
```

Figure 2. C++ class template example.

type) parameters that can be used to determine the types of variables declared in the class.

Figure 2 illustrates the use of a template class declaration to create a family of bounded data stacks.

Bibliography

1973. Birtwistle, G. M., Dahl, O. J., Myhrhaug, B., and Nygaard, K. *SIMULA Begin*. Philadelphia: Auerbach.

1990. Ellis, M. A., and Stroustrup, B. *The Annotated C++ Reference Manual*. Reading, MA: Addison-Wesley.

1996. Gosling, J., Joy, B., and Steele, G. *The Java Language Specification*. Reading, MA: Addison-Wesley.

David B. Wortman

CLIENT-SERVER COMPUTING

For articles on related subjects, *see*

+ Distributed Systems
+ Electronic Commerce
+ Internet
+ Operating Systems
+ Time Sharing
+ TCP/IP

Introduction

Client–server computing is a distributed computing model in which *client* applications request services from *server* processes. Clients and servers typically run on different, though interconnected, computers. Any use of the Internet is an example of client–server computing, but the concept is more frequently associated with *enterprise computing*, which makes the computing resources of an organization available to every part of its operation.

A *client* application is a process or program that sends messages to a server via a network. Those messages request the server to perform a specific task, such as looking up a customer record in a database or returning a portion of a file on the server's hard disk (*q.v.*). The client manages local resources such as a display, keyboard, local disks, and other peripherals. The *server* process listens for client requests and performs actions such as database queries and reading files. The client–server model is an extension of the *object-based (or modular)* programming model, where large pieces of software are structured into smaller components that have well-defined interfaces. This decentralized approach helps to make complex programs maintainable and extensible. Components interact by exchanging messages or by *Remote Procedure Calling* (RPC—*see* DISTRIBUTED SYSTEMS). The calling component becomes the client and the called component the server.

Design Considerations

Some important design considerations are as follows:

- **Fat vs thin client:** A "thin" client receives information in its final form from the server and does little or no data processing. A "fat" client does more processing, thereby lightening the load on the server.
- **Stateful vs stateless:** A *stateless* server retains no information about the data that clients are using. However, applications where clients need to acquire and release locks on the records stored at a database server usually require a *stateful* model, because locking information is maintained by the server for each individual client.
- **Authentication:** In a networked environment, an unauthorized client may attempt to access sensitive data stored on a server. Authentication of clients is handled by using cryptographic techniques such as *public key encryption* (see CRYPTOGRAPHY, COMPUTERS IN) or special *authentication* (*q.v.*) servers such as in the OSF DCE system described below.
- **Fault tolerance:** Applications such as flight-reservation systems and real-time market data feeds must employ *fault-tolerant computing* (*q.v.*). This means that important services remain available in spite of the failure of part of the computer system on which the servers are running (high availability), and that no information is lost or corrupted when a failure occurs (consistency).

Distributed Object Computing

Distributed object computing (DOC) is a generalization of the client–server model. Object-oriented modeling and programming are applied to the development of client–server systems. Objects are pieces of software that encapsulate an internal state and make it accessible through a well-defined interface. In DOC, the interface consists of object operations and attributes that are remotely accessible. Client applications may connect to a remote instance of the interface with the help of a naming service. Finally, the clients invoke the operations on the remote object. The remote object thus acts as a server. This use of objects supports heterogeneity since requests sent to server objects depend only on their interfaces and not on their internals. It permits autonomy because object implementations can change transparently, provided they maintain their interfaces.

Standards are required for objects to interoperate in heterogeneous environments. One of the widely adopted vendor-independent DOC standards is the OMG (Object Management Group) CORBA (Common Object Request Broker Architecture) specification. CORBA consists of the following building blocks:

- **Interface Definition Language:** Object interfaces are described in a language called IDL (Interface Definition Language), a purely declarative language resembling C++ (*q.v.*). It provides the notion of interfaces (similar to *classes-q.v.*), of interface inheritance, of operations with input and output arguments, and of data types (*q.v.*) that can be passed along with an operation.
- **Object Request Broker:** The purpose of the ORB (Object Request Broker) is to find the server object for a client request, to prepare the object to receive the request, to transmit the request from the client to the server object, and to return output arguments back to the client application.
- **Basic Object Adapter:** The BOA (Basic Object Adapter) is the primary interface used by a server object to gain access to ORB functions. The BOA exports operations to create object references, to register and activate server objects, and to authenticate requests. An object reference is a data structure that denotes a server object in a network.

A server installs its reference in a *name server* so that a client application can retrieve the reference and invoke the server.

- **Dynamic Invocation Interface:** The DII (Dynamic Invocation Interface) defines functions for creating request messages and for delivering them to server objects.
- **Internet Inter-ORB Protocol:** The Internet Inter-ORB Protocol (IIOP) allows CORBA ORBs from different vendors to interoperate via a TCP/IP connection. IIOP is a simplified RPC protocol used to invoke server objects via the Internet in a portable and efficient manner.
- **Interface and Implementation Repository:** The CORBA Interface Repository (CIR) is a database containing type information (interface names, interface operations, and argument types) for the interfaces available in a CORBA system.

Client–Server Toolkits

Client–server toolkits such as CORBA are referred to as *middleware*. Other examples are OSF DCE, DCOM, message-oriented middleware, and transaction processing monitors.

- **OSF DCE:** The Open Software Foundation (OSF) Distributed Computing Environment (DCE) is a *de facto* standard for multivendor client-server systems. DCE is a collection of tools and services that help programmers in developing heterogeneous client-server applications.
- **DCOM:** Distributed Component Object Model (DCOM) is Microsoft's object protocol that enables *ActiveX* components to communicate across a network. An ActiveX component is a remote accessible object that has a well-defined interface and is self-contained. ActiveX components can be embedded in Web documents, so that they download to the client automatically to execute in the client's Web browser (*see* WORLD WIDE WEB).
- **MOM:** Message-Oriented Middleware (MOM) allows the components of a client-server system to interoperate by exchanging general-purpose messages. A client application communicates with a server by placing messages into a *message queue*. After the client has placed a message into the queue, it continues other work until the MOM informs the client that the server's reply has arrived. This is called *asynchronous messaging*, since client and server are decoupled by message queues. MOM functions much like electronic mail (*q.v.*), storing and forwarding messages on behalf of client and server applications.
- **Transaction Processing (TP) Monitors:** Transaction processing monitors allow a client application to perform a series of requests on multiple remote servers while preserving consistency among the servers. Such a series of requests is called a *transaction*. The TP monitor ensures that either all requests that are part of a transaction succeed, or that the servers are *rolled back* to the state they had before the unsuccessful transaction was started.

Bibliography

1995. Mowbray, T. J., and Zahavi, R. *The Essential CORBA*. New York: John Wiley.

1997. Shan, Y.-P., Earle, R. H., and Lenzi, M. A. *Enterprise Computing With Objects: From Client/Server Environments to the Internet*. Reading, MA: Addison-Wesley.

1998. Orfali, R., and Harkey, D. *Client/Server Programming with Java and CORBA*, 2nd Ed. New York: John Wiley.

Silvano Maffeis

CLUSTER COMPUTING

For articles on related subjects, *see*

- Client-Server Computing
- Cooperative Computing
- Database Management System (DBMS)
- Distributed Systems
- Multiprocessing
- Networks, Computer
- Parallel Processing
- Supercomputers

Introduction

A cluster of computers, or simply a *cluster*, is a collection of computers that are connected and used as a single computing resource. Clusters have been used since the late 1950s as a straightforward way to obtain greater capacity and higher reliability than a single computer can provide. Often they have not been built by computer manufacturers but rather assembled by customers on an *ad hoc* basis to solve a problem at hand. An exception occurred in the early 1980s when the Digital Equipment Corporation coined the term *cluster* for a collection of software and hardware that made several VAX minicomputers (*q.v.*) appear to be a single time-sharing (*q.v.*) system called the VAXcluster.

In the early 1990s, scientific computer users began replacing expensive supercomputers with clusters of workstations (*q.v.*). Alternatively, so-called *Beowulf clusters* were formed whose individual elements were just off-the-shelf microprocessors. These became the standard form of supercomputers by the mid-1990s.

In February 1998, a very large, highly diffuse and informal cluster—using spare time on approximately 22 000 personal computers owned by volunteers, connected only occasionally though the Internet—succeeded in decoding a "challenge" message encrypted using the Data Encryption Standard (DES) system with a 56-bit key (*see* CRYPTOGRAPHY, COMPUTERS IN). The answer was found by simply trying one after another of the 63 quadrillion possible keys; success came after taking only 39 days to examine 85% of the keys. Appropriately, the decoded message read, "Many hands make light work." But this is more appropriately called *cooperative computing* (*q.v.*); "cluster" more accurately implies use of an aggregate of a specific number of colocated processors.

Many hands make light work only if they all work on different parts of the job. If there is a single large problem to solve, such as decoding a message or simulating the airflow over an airplane, techniques must be used that break the problem down into many separate parts that can be worked on separately by the different computers in a cluster. Such techniques are described in PARALLEL PROCESSING: ALGORITHMS, and can lead to the ability to use massive numbers of computers on the same problem. For example, the decryption problem mentioned above was broken into parts by simply giving to each computer a different set of keys to test.

Related Concepts

Sometimes a cluster is formed from individual workstations connected by a local area network (LAN—*q.v.*). Unused capacity on such systems can be effectively used this way. In practice this is useful, but usually needs to be supplemented by a rack full of centralized workstations or servers dedicated solely to cluster computing. This is often enhanced by adding a fast communications network within the rack. The entire collection, including the rack of systems, is then called a NOW (*network of workstations*) or COW (*cluster of workstations*).

The term *massively parallel processor* (MPP) refers to any parallel computer containing a very large number of computing elements, typically 500 or more, and often thousands. As of the late 1990s, the computing elements in most such systems were whole computers, effectively making such systems clusters.

Nonuniform memory access (NUMA) systems are sometimes confused with clusters, but are not clusters. NUMA systems connect what seem to be separate computers through their memory subsystems, allowing direct access from any processor to memory anywhere in the complex; the term "nonuniform" is used because it is faster to access nearby memory than remote memory. The processors in clusters, in contrast, have no direct access to nonlocal memory; communication is only by messages.

Bibliography

1994. Almasi, G. S., and Gottlieb, A. *Highly Parallel Computing*, 2nd Ed. New York: Benjamin/Cummings.

1998. Hwang, K., and Xu, Z. *Scalable Parallel Computing: Technology, Architecture, Programming*. New York: WCB/McGraw-Hill.

1998. Pfister, G. F. *In Search of Clusters*, 2nd Ed. Upper Saddle River, NJ: Prentice Hall.

Gregory F. Pfister

COBOL

For an article on a related subject, *see*

+ Programming Languages

A Short History of Early Cobol

Cobol (common business-oriented language) was created by a committee; no one person can be described or listed as the "developer" or "creator" of Cobol. From 28 to 29 May 1959, a meeting was held at the Pentagon. It was chaired by Charles A. Phillips, then Director of the Data Systems Research Staff, Office of the Assistant Secretary of Defense (Comptroller). About 50 people attended, including representatives of seven government organizations, 11 users, and 15 manufacturers. I was present as the senior of two representatives from Sylvania Electric Products.

The meeting was called to consider the potential need for a common business language. The Department of Defense (DoD) was concerned about the inability to run the same business data processing (BDP) programs on differing computers (e.g. UNIVAC I (*q.v.*), IBM 705). BDP programs involved a lot of data and datafiles, but relatively little calculation. The only programming language in significant use, Fortran (*q.v.*), did not have the necessary capabilities.

The four most important results of the meeting were the following:

1. The development of a list of desired characteristics of a proposed common business language based on the use of English rather than mathematical symbolism.
2. The creation of three committees with short-, medium- and long-range objectives, and an executive committee to coordinate the efforts of these groups.
3. A mission for the short-range committee.
4. The creation of CODASYL (committee on data systems languages) and its executive committee.

Phillips's report of the meeting stated the Mission of the Short-Range Language Committee as, "To report by September 1, 1959, the results of its study of the strengths and weaknesses of existing automatic compilers (especially AIMACO, FLOWMATIC, and COMTRAN); and to recommend a short-range composite approach to a common business language for programming digital computers. . ." The wording of this sentence is ambiguous, and it was not clear that we were directed to create a *new* language.

The Short-Range Committee consisted of representatives from six computer manufacturers (Burroughs, Honeywell, IBM, RCA, Sperry Rand, Sylvania), and three government organizations (Air Force, David Taylor Model Basin, National Bureau of Standards). After several meetings of the Committee, it was clear that we were bogged down by its size. In October, a six-person subcommittee was appointed to try to produce a set of specifications. The six persons were Gertrude Tierney and William Selden (IBM), Howard Bromberg and Norman Discount (RCA), and Vernon Reeves and Jean Sammet (Sylvania). This subcommittee did the bulk of the work in creating the Cobol specifications; the full Short-Range Committee then reviewed and modified their work to produce the final set of specifications. In December 1959, the specifications for Cobol were given to the CODASYL Executive Committee, which accepted the report "for publication and recommended its adoption for usage by the entire data processing community. . ." Frances (Betty) Holberton then did some editing and the specifications were released as a government report in April 1960.

Technical Characteristics of Cobol

The major concepts embodied in Cobol were as follows:

1. Creation of four divisions in a program: PROCEDURE, DATA, ENVIRONMENT, and IDENTIFICATION. The PROCEDURE Division contained the statements (i.e. commands) and was (meant to be) machine-independent. The DATA Division contained a description of the data to be used, and was moderately machine-independent. The ENVIRONMENT Division was completely machine-dependent and listed the computer, compiler, and so on, to be used by the program. The IDENTIFICATION Division just contained information

needed to identify the programmer, date, and so on.

2. Use of the English language throughout for commands, and data names, including allowance of 30 characters for data names. (This allowed the writing of `SOCIAL-SECURITY-NUMBER` rather than an abbreviation.)

   Commands were of the form

   ```
   MOVE data-name-1 to data-name-2
   IF data-name-3 IS GREATER THAN
            data-name-4 THEN READ file-name
   ```

3. Data could be organized into files that contained records (*q.v.*), then subrecords, and fields within (sub)records; each level could be named and described. One method of describing fields was by using a `PICTURE` clause indicating the number and type of characters, location of a decimal point (if any) and other characteristics. For example,

   ```
   ALPHA PICTURE 9(12)
   ```

   meant that a field named `ALPHA` had 12 digits. (The number 9 was used to denote a digit.)

   ```
   BETA PICTURE A(2)
   ```

   indicated a two-letter field.

   ```
   GAMMA PICTURE $$,$$9.99
   ```

   means that `GAMMA` is an edited character string. Its value is a series of characters representing a price from $0.00 to $99 999.99.

4. As a by-product, the committee developed a metalanguage (*q.v.*) that has been widely used for programming language definition ever since.

Later Versions and Standardization

Cobol has changed significantly over the years, while still maintaining its basic structure. Even before the Cobol-60 specifications were released, a committee went to work on some improvements, resulting in Cobol-61. This was the first version to be widely implemented. This was followed by Cobol-61 Extended (issued in 1962), and Cobol-65. The first Cobol ANSI standard was issued in 1968, based on Cobol-65; it set the

precedent for later standards of not making changes to the specifications but possibly removing some of the language features or reorganizing the specifications. Later, standards were issued in 1974 and 1985, and the latest was approved by the International Organization for Standardization (ISO) in September 2002 and published in December 2002.

Bibliography

1981. Sammet, J. E. "The Early History of Cobol," in *History of Programming Languages* (ed. R. L. Wexelblat), Ch. V, 199–276. New York: Academic Press.

1985. Sammet, J. E., and Garfunkel, J. "Summary of Changes in Cobol, 1960–1985," *Annals of the History of Computing*, 7(4), (October), 342–47.

1985. *Annals of the History of Computing* (Special Cobol 25th Anniversary Issue), 7(4), (October).

Jean E. Sammet

CODES

For articles on related subjects, *see*

+ Character Codes
+ Error Correcting and Detecting Code
+ Universal Product Code

The term *code* has a particular meaning in cryptography, and is sometimes also used as a synonym for *program* or part of a program. But for the purpose of this article, a *code* is a nonsecret mapping between a symbol of an alphabet (e.g. our alphabet of letters) and a number of digits of a number system (e.g. six bits for base 2). The mathematician would say that a code is a pair $(\Sigma; \Pi)$ where Σ is the symbol space (the set of symbols to be coded) and the Π are numeric combinations (the codes). Suppose that S is some symbol in the symbol space Σ and P is one of the permutations of the digits in a numeric counting system Π. We might say "S is mapped into P" or that "S is represented by P," using the symbols

$$S \to P \text{ or } S \equiv P \qquad (1)$$

Each P in Π is called a *combination*. When P consists of n digits, it can be written as

$$P = P_1 P_2 P_3 \ldots P_n \qquad (2)$$

where P_i is any digit of the counting system with radix r, that is,

$$P_i = 0, 1, 2, \ldots \text{ or } r - 1. \qquad (3)$$

Let us examine the case where the symbol space Σ_A consists of letters of the alphabet. Let each combination P consist of two decimal digits; thus, $r = 10$ and $n = 2$. A very simple code might assign numbers consecutively to the letters so that we would have

$$A \equiv 01, B \equiv 02, C \equiv 03, \ldots, Z \equiv 26 \qquad (4)$$

The notation $|s|$ is used for the number of elements in a set, that is, its *cardinality*. For example,

$$|\Sigma_A| = 26 \text{ and } |\Pi| = 100. \qquad (5)$$

Since there are many more elements in Π than there are symbols in the symbol space, many numeric combinations are unassigned. These are sometimes called *forbidden combinations*.

Decimal Codes

A decimal code provides a representation for the decimal numbers in binary. To summarize their characteristics

$$|\Sigma_D| = 10, \quad r = 2, \quad n \geq 4 \qquad (6)$$

There are two principal ways to associate symbols with combinations:

1. *Weighted codes* assign different weights to each bit in the combination.
2. *Transition rules* may be created to indicate how the code for the successor number is created from the code for any given number.

Four-Bit Codes

Weighted Codes

Let us label the bits of the combination that represents a decimal digit. Unlike (2), where the subscripts increase from left to right, we will now order the subscripts 1 through 4 in reverse, going from right to left. Thus, if D is a decimal digit, we have

$$D \equiv b_4 b_3 b_2 b_1. \qquad (7)$$

A weighted code associates a weight W_i with each bit b_i, which might be stated symbolically as

$$b_i \leftrightarrow W_i i = 1 \text{ to } 4. \qquad (8)$$

The requirement of the weighted code is that, when each bit is multiplied by its weight and the products are totaled, the sum must be equal in value to the digit. Stated symbolically,

$$D = \sum_1^4 b_i W_i = b_4 W_4 + b_3 W_3 + b_2 W_2 + b_1 W_1.$$
$$(9)$$

Some restrictions arise in setting up the weights:

1. For each digit to be encoded, there must be a combination of bits and their corresponding weights, whose total is equal to the value of the digit.
2. When two combinations exist that, when substituted into (9), yield the same digit D, then another rule must be provided to decide which combination will be used.

8421 Code

The weighted 8421 code is illustrated in column 1 of Table 1. From left to right, weights 8, 4, 2, and 1 are assigned to the bits that make up the combination. When the bits are set to 0 or 1, the resulting number is shown in the left column of the table.

The sequence of combinations for the 8421 code is the same sequence in which these binary numbers occur in the binary counting system, hence, the

Table 1.   Weighted codes.

Weights digits	(1) 8 4 2 1 Code	(2) 7 4 2 1 Code	(3) 7 4 2 −1 Code	(4) XS 3 Code
0	0000	0000	0000	0011
1	0001	0001	0011	0100
2	0010	0010	0010	0101
3	0011	0011	0101	0110
4	0100	0100	0100	0111
5	0101	0101	0111	1000
6	0110	0110	1001	1001
			(0110)	
7	0111	1000	1000	1010
		(0111)		
8	1000	1001	1011	1011
9	1001	1010	1010	1100
*(A)	1010	1011	1101	1101
*(B)	1011	1100	1100	1110
*(C)	1100	1101	1111	1111
*(D)	1101	1110	1110	–
*(E)	1110	1111	–	–
*(F)	1111	–	–	–

*Forbidden combinations.

appellation *binary-coded decimal*, or simply BCD, for the code of column 1.

7421 Code

Column 2 presents the 7421 code, which has six forbidden combinations. The bits that constitute each combination are calculated so that equation (9) will yield the digit value. There are two combinations, 1000 and 0111, both of which yield the value 7. An auxiliary rule is required to settle this difficulty: use the combination with the least number of 1s in it (i.e. 1000).

742-1 Code

The code for these weights is presented in column 3. One or more of the weights may be negative as long as the weights fulfill the requirement that all digit values must be created. This time we find that there are two combinations that yield the digit value 6. Since both

have the same number of 1s, we choose the combination with the 1 in the least significant place.

XS 3 Code

Not all codes require weights explicitly. Consider the XS 3 (excess-3) code presented in column 4. The rule for generating this code requires that we use the BCD code for a digit, call it n_D, and add the binary number 0011 (i.e. 3 in decimal) to it:

$$D \equiv n_D + 0011 \qquad (10)$$

This has two advantages:

1. No proper combination consists of all zeros; therefore, no combination will be mistaken for a null transmission or *vice versa*.
2. It is a self-complementing code.

A *self-complementing* code is very valuable because it possesses the property that the combination for the complement of a digit is the complement of the combination for that digit. The complement of a number is needed when we do subtraction by addition and complementation. For decimal arithmetic, this requires that we subtract the value of the digit from 9. In our binary code, the complement of a combination b_D is taken with respect to the largest valued combination; for a four-bit code, this would be 1111. Then, our definition for a self-complementing code is one for which the following holds:

$$9 - D \equiv 1111 - b_D \qquad (11)$$

As an example of how XS 3 fulfills this requirement, we have

$$2 \equiv 0101, 9 - 2 = 7, 1111 - 0101 = 1010,$$
$$7 \equiv 1010 \qquad (12)$$

Hexadecimal

Programmers often deal with data in units of a byte, which consists of eight bits or two *nibbles*, each nibble consisting of four bits. If the combination for each nibble has a different symbol to represent it, then this simplifies the description. The binary values with decimal equivalents 10 through 15 are usually assigned the upper case letters A through F, as shown in Table 1 in parentheses. Thus, the programmer can describe the byte consisting of 10110101 in hexadecimal as B5.

Other Decimal Codes

If we do not restrict ourselves to four-bit decimal codes, we can provide one or more of the following advantages:

1. Error detection.
2. Simplicity of combination construction.
3. Simplicity of implementation in hardware.

2-Out-of-5 Code

The 2-out-of-5 code is illustrated in column 1 of Table 2. Every five-bit combination that represents

Table 2.   Other decimal codes.

Digit weights	(1) 2-out-of-5 Code 74210	(2) Biquinary Code 50 43210	(3) Gray Code n.a.
0	11000	01 00001	0000
1	00011	01 00010	0001
2	00101	01 00100	0011
3	00110	01 01000	0010
4	01001	01 10000	0110
5	01010	10 00001	0111
6	01100	10 00010	0101
7	10001	10 00100	0100
8	10010	10 01000	1100
9	10100	10 10000	1101
10	–	–	1111
11	–	–	1110
12	–	–	1010
13	–	–	1011
14	–	–	1001
15	–	–	1000

a digit contains exactly two 1s. Since there are 10 such combinations, this works out well. To assign each combination, we establish a set of five *pseudoweights*. One of these weights, W_1, is 0, and the bit corresponding to this weight, b_1, should be set to 1 when the value of the digit being encoded corresponds to precisely one of the nonzero weights; this is true for the digits 1, 2, 4, and 7. The weights work out for all digit values except 0; this digit uses bits with weights 7 and 4, which obviously do not sum to 0; hence the term "pseudoweights."

Biquinary

The biquinary code is a seven-bit code using exactly two 1s; it is illustrated in column 2 of Table 2. One of the 1s is chosen from the left two bits; the other is chosen from the right five bits. The weights are used as would be expected. This code provides error detection whenever more than one 1 appears in either half of a combination, and also provides a logical progression from one combination to the next, which is useful for implementing arithmetic.

Gray Code

The Gray code, invented by Frank Gray, was developed to fill a particular requirement. At one time, many devices designed to convert analog (i.e. continuous) data depended on the mechanical position of a shaft. Attached to the shaft was an encoder that produced electromechanical or optical signals corresponding to the shaft rotation. This created a transition problem. Column 1 of Table 1 shows that the combination for 7 is 0111 and that for 8 is 1000. As the shaft rotated, the apparatus for reading out the position could not be depended upon to change simultaneously in each bit position. Thus, totally erroneous readings occurred. If b_4 goes to 1 before the other bits change in going from 7 to 8, the output would be read as 15.

To overcome this transition difficulty, successive Gray code values change in one bit position only. Column 3 of Table 2 displays a 4-bit Gray code in which successive values change by only one bit at a time. The transition from one code value to the next is described by this rule: If B_i is the binary equivalent of the integer $i, i = 0, 1, \ldots, 2^n - 1$ and if B'_i is the result of shifting B_i to the right one place (inserting a zero in the left), then $G_i = B_i \oplus; B'_i$, where $\oplus;$ represents the exclusive OR operation, is a Gray code. A similar transformation exists such that given G_i, one can compute B_i.

Though a 4-bit example is given here, Gray codes can be extended to any length, so they were discussed here rather than in the earlier section that discussed the strictly 4-bit codes of Table 1.

Error Detection and Correction

In the case of biquinary, we saw how a code can be constructed with error detection properties. The simplest means for detecting errors is to attach an extra bit to each combination of the code, called a *parity* bit. This bit is set to 0 or 1, according to the scheme used: for *odd* parity, the total number of 1s, including the parity bit, must be odd; for *even* parity, the total number of 1s, including the parity bit, must be 0 or even. For example, the ASCII encoding of the letter Z is 90, which is 1011010 in binary. With an even-parity rule, this would be 01011010; with odd parity, it would become 11011010. For information on more complex error detection codes, *see* ERROR CORRECTING AND DETECTING CODE.

Bibliography

1961. Peterson, W. W. *Error Correcting Codes*. Cambridge, MA: MIT Press.

1977. McEliece, R. J. *The Theory of Information Coding, Vol. 3 of the Encyclopedia of Mathematics and Its Applications*. Reading, MA: Addison-Wesley.

1997. Honary, B., Darnell, M., and Farrell, P. (eds.) *Communications Coding and Signal Processing*. New York: John Wiley.

Ivan Flores

COERCION

For articles on related subjects, *see*

+ Expression
+ Procedure-Oriented Languages: Programming

Many programming languages provide a mechanism for automatically converting from one data type to another in expressions. This automatic type conversion is called *coercion*. A familiar example of coercion occurs in arithmetic expressions containing both integer and floating point operands, as in $K + 3.5$, where K is of type integer. The integer variable K is first automatically converted to floating point, and then the addition is performed in floating-point mode. If the language does not have such coercion, the programmer must make the conversion explicit (e.g. FLOAT(K) + 3.5).

The kind of coercion that must be applied to an operand depends on the type of that operand, as well as on the type of operand required by the context. Consider the expression $X + K$, where K is again of type integer. If X is also of type integer, no coercion need be performed; if X is of type floating-point or complex, K must be coerced to the same type as X before the addition can be performed.

In Snobol4 and AWK, an expression such as $K+$ '01.50' is permitted, since '01.50' may be coerced from type string to type floating-point. Other common coercions are from decimal to binary (PL/I), and scalar to array (APL-*q.v.*). The term *coercion* was first used in this context in Algol 68.

Andrew S. Tanenbaum

COGNITIVE SCIENCE

For articles on related subjects, *see*

+ Artificial Intelligence (AI)
+ Knowledge Representation
+ Machine Learning
+ Parallel Processing
+ Turing Test

Definition

Cognitive science is the interdisciplinary study of cognition. Cognition includes mental states and processes such as thinking, reasoning, remembering, language understanding and generation, visual and auditory perception, learning, consciousness, and emotions. Cognitive science can also be defined as, roughly, the intersection of the disciplines of computer science (especially artificial intelligence), linguistics, philosophy, psychology, cognitive anthropology, and the cognitive neurosciences. In most other academic disciplines, a common methodology is usually brought to bear on a multitude of problems. By contrast, in cognitive science, many *different* methodologies—those of the several cognitive sciences—are brought to bear on a *common* problem: the nature of cognition.

Cognition and Computation

According to the computational view of cognitive science, (1) there are mental states and processes intervening between input stimuli and output responses, (2) these mental states and processes either *are* computations or else are computable, and—hence—(3) mental states and processes are capable of being investigated scientifically (even if they are not capable of being directly observed). The proper methodology of cognitive science is to express theories about (human) cognition in a computer program and then compare the program's behavior with (human) cognitive behavior.

History of Cognitive Science

Cognitive science can trace its origins to two major lines of investigation. First, there was the development of symbolic logic at the turn of the century and McCulloch and Pitts's application of logic to the analysis of the behavior of neural networks (1943). Second, there were Turing's analyses of computation (1936) and, using the Imitation Game (Turing Test–*q.v.*), of whether computers could think (1950).

Cognitivism burst upon the scene in 1956. In (or very near) that year, the following cognitive theories appeared: George Miller's theory of human short-term memory, Chomsky's analysis of formal grammars, Jerome Bruner and colleagues' study of thinking, and Newell and Simon's Logic Theorist—the first artificial intelligence program. In 1979, the journal *Cognitive Science* appeared, and two years later the first annual meeting of the Cognitive Science Society was held. Other major cognitive science journals include: *Behavioral and Brain Sciences, Cognition, Linguistics and Philosophy, Mind and Language, Minds and Machines,* and *Philosophical Psychology.* Finally, there has been a recent surge of research centers and institutes of cognitive science, as well as graduate and undergraduate degree programs, including university departments of cognitive science.

Bibliography

1936. Turing, A. M. "On Computable Numbers, with an Application to the Entscheidungsproblem," *Proceedings of the London Mathematical Society, Series 2,* **42**, 230–265.

1950. Turing, A. M. "Computing Machinery and Intelligence," *Mind,* **59**, 433–460; reprinted in *Minds and Machines* (ed. A. R. Anderson) 4–30. Upper Saddle River, NJ: Prentice Hall.

1990. Searle, J. R. "Is the Brain's Mind a Computer Program?" *Scientific American,* **262**(1), 20–25.

1992. Dreyfus, H. L. *What Computers Still Can't Do: A Critique of Artificial Reason.* Cambridge, MA: MIT Press.

William J. Rapaport

COLLATING SEQUENCE

For articles on related subjects, *see*

+ Character Codes
+ Sorting
+ String Processing

Given a set of symbols, a *collating sequence* for that set is a sequential ordering of those symbols which, through mutual agreement of a group of users of those symbols, is used to determine the *lexicographic* order of symbol strings whose constituents are chosen from the set.

The simplest example of lexicographic order is alphabetization, through which the strings Jones, Brown, Ryan, and Cohen are commonly placed in the ascending order Brown, Cohen, Jones, and Ryan. But this ordering depends on the centuries old agreement that the 26 letters of the English alphabet in their standard order is used as a collating sequence. We seldom, if ever, dwell on this, but this sequence is just an arbitrary choice of one of the 26! permutations (about 4×10^{26}) of our alphabet that might have been chosen. This particular ordering is closely related to that used for corresponding letters of the Greek alphabet, which in turn is believed to have its origins in Egyptian hieroglyphics.

There are innumerable other symbol sets for which someone has had to decide on a collating sequence. For example, in the card game Bridge, the four suits have increasing value in the order clubs, diamonds, hearts, and spades. Within a suit, the ace is usually considered to have the highest value, above the king, but in the most common form of solitaire it has the value 1; that is, it ranks below the 2.

In defining a collating sequence for a symbol set that contains characters in addition to the alphabet, such as digits and punctuation, one must decide on their rank with respect to the alphabet. For that matter, one must decide on whether uppercase letters collate above or below lowercase letters, and where the digit sequence 0 to 9 collates with respect to either grouping. In ASCII and Unicode, the ascending order of these groups is digits, uppercase alphabet, lowercase alphabet (with certain special characters placed between the groups), but in the older EBCDIC, the ranking of these groups is exactly the reverse. This means that character strings written to a file in lexicographic order ("sorted") by, say, a late 1960s vintage IBM mainframe (*q.v.*) that used EBCDIC would not be considered in proper order if the file were to be read on a more recently designed computer that uses ASCII or Unicode (*see* CHARACTER CODES).

Once a collating sequence is chosen for a set of *n* characters, the resulting rank of each character is said to have an *ordinal value,* a number that ranges from

0 for the first character to $n - 1$ for the last. In fact, what we consider to be characters are actually stored in memory as ordinal values of type integer of usual size one byte (EBCDIC and extended ASCII), two bytes for the original Unicode, and 20 bits for Unicode 4.0.

Edwin D. Reilly

COLOSSUS

For articles on related subjects, *see*

+ Cryptography, Computers in
+ Digital Computers, History of: Early
+ Turing, Alan Mathison

Colossus was the first large programmable electronic computer (*see* Fig. 1). It was developed at the British Post Office Research laboratories at Dollis Hill in North London at great speed and in complete secrecy during the Second World War to help break top-level German Lorenz machine ciphers. Design started in March 1943 and the Mark 1 Colossus, with 1500 vacuum tubes, was working by December 1943. It was then dismantled and transported to Bletchley Park, in north Buckinghamshire, home of the Government Codes and Ciphers School. After reassembly, it was operational in January 1944 and was successful in its first attempt at breaking a German Lorenz message. A successor, the Mark II with 2500 vacuum tubes, was operational on 1 June 1944, five days before D-Day. Eight more Colossi followed, making them 10 in all before the end of the war. Because of engineering improvements and evolving cryptographic principles, no two were identical.

As early as 1939, British cryptanalysts working at Bletchley Park, and led by Alan Turing, had invented an analog device, "The Bombe," to break the rotor cipher of the German Enigma machine. This was a substitution cipher in which the actual substitution for each input letter was achieved in a very complex manner through wiring inside the rotors in the Enigma machine. Radio signals enciphered using much more difficult teletype

Figure 1. The Colossus computer at Bletchley Park, 1943. (Courtesy of the Bletchley Park Trust/Science and Society Picture Library.)

ciphers were intercepted in 1940. These teletype ciphers used an additive method devised by Gilbert Vernam at AT&T in 1918. The Lorenz company devised a cipher machine for the German Army high command based on the Vernam principle.

By 1942, when mathematics professor Max Newman arrived at Bletchley from Cambridge University, cryptanalysts led by Bill Tutte had worked out the logical structure of the Lorenz machine. Newman set up a team of mathematical specialists to mechanize part of the decipherment task and speed up the breaking of messages. Their early work led to the development of the "Heath Robinson" machines, which compared two punched paper tapes at rates of up to 1000 characters per second. One tape contained the intercepted cipher text, the other contained the streams of patterns that the cryptanalysts had worked out by hand. Mechanical problems with the Robinsons pushed Newman and his team toward radical innovations. Newman approached Dollis Hill for help and T. H. Flowers, an engineer from the Post Office Research Station, proposed building a Colossus, a machine with 1500 vacuum tubes, almost three times the number in any contemporary machine.

Colossus read punched tape at 5000 characters per second using a projection lamp and photocells, a truly impressive speed even by post-war standards. Programming was done with plugboards and switches.

When installed at Bletchley, each Colossus filled a large room in one of the wartime buildings. (It was 7.5 ft tall by 15 ft wide by 8 ft deep.) Its logic circuits operated in parallel at 5000 pulses per second and it had electronic decimal counting circuits, electronic ring pattern generators that were changeable by an automatically controlled sequence of operations, and typewriter output. The Mark II Colossus could process data five times faster than the Mark I.

Colossus went on line two years before ENIAC (*q.v.*). Colossus, though built as a special-purpose logical computer, proved flexible enough to be programmed to execute a variety of tasks, including decimal multiplication, but only at a slower clock speed. Although it was the ENIAC group that made the final leap toward the modern general-purpose digital computer with the design for EDVAC (*q.v.*), Colossus stands as an impressive pioneering achievement in its own right. Colossus undoubtedly inspired Alan Turing to proceed rapidly in 1945 with his designs for the ACE computer and inspired Allen Coombs, one of the designers of Colossus, to design MOSAIC for the Post Office. Eight of the original 10 Colossi were dismantled in Bletchley Park at the end of the war in 1945. The remaining two lasted until about 1960, but the very existence of Colossus was kept secret until the 1970s.

A fully working rebuild of Colossus has now been completed at Bletchley Park and demonstrates the high speed and parallel nature of the original 1944 machine. This rebuild, which took three years, had to be done from just eight wartime photographs of Colossus and some fragments of circuit diagrams that survived.

Bibliography

1977. Randell, B. "Colossus: Godfather of the Computer," *New Scientist*, 10 February. Reprinted in *The Origins of Digital Computers—Selected Papers*, (ed. B. Randell), 3rd Ed, 1982, 349–354. New York: Springer-Verlag.

1980. Randell, B. "The Colossus," in *A History of Computing in the Twentieth Century* (eds. N. Metropolis, J. Howlett, and G. C. Rota), 47–92. New York: Academic Press.

1997. Fox, B., and Webb, J. "Colossal Adventures," *New Scientist*, **154**, (10 May), 2081.

Tony Sale

COMMUNICATIONS AND COMPUTERS

For articles on related subjects, *see*

+ Bandwidth
+ Baud
+ Data Communications
+ Electronic Commerce
+ Internet
+ Mobile Computing
+ Network Architecture
+ Network Protocols
+ Networks, Computer
+ Packet Switching
+ Privacy, Computers and
+ World Wide Web

Computing is increasingly inseparable from *communications*. This linkage, referred to as *convergence*, is driven by technology and amplified by business trends. Convergence has fostered diversity in the devices used for communications: conventional computers, telephones, and televisions persist, while previously unnetworked devices (such as household appliances) are taking on communications capabilities, and entirely new kinds of devices are emerging.

The Internet as Catalyst

Convergence is epitomized and driven by the Internet. The Internet, conceived for communication among computers and relying on packet switching of digitized information, draws on decades of experimentation that generated its underlying technologies. The early years (the 1970s and 1980s) of the forerunners of the Internet (e.g. Arpanet) were paralleled by other developments that helped set the stage for turn-of-the-century integration of computers and communications. These included

- growth in data communications telephony in the relatively closed environments of large business and government organizations;
- the adoption of personal computers and private branch exchanges (PBXs);
- computer support for telephone service, local area networks (*q.v.*), and wide area networks;
- deployment by telephone companies of digital, value-added networks that applied third-party computers and communications to support inter-enterprise communication and wide area networking for a single enterprise ("intranets");
- cable and satellite television "broadcasts" to closed audiences;
- widespread use of facsimile (fax) transmission over public telephone lines using specialized modems.

Fundamental Network Infrastructure Trends

The rapid growth of the Internet and associated business activity has fueled the deployment of the networking infrastructures that underlie it. Computing has accelerated communications, and vice versa. One of the earliest indicators of this trend was the mid-1990s linkage of cable television system upgrading, which pushed fiber optic (*q.v.*) cable further into cable TV distribution networks, and into high-speed Internet access via cable modems. Cable Internet support has grown with the rise of national cable-oriented systems linked to the Internet (e.g. Time Warner's *Road Runner* in the USA).

Regulatory change also furthered the 1990s deployment of international submarine cables and Low-Earth Orbit (LEO) satellite systems, designed to support different kinds of use (high and low bandwidth, stationary and mobile users). Major satellite and cable consortia are international, and they are expected to promote international networking in general and Internet access in particular. Very small aperture terminal (VSAT) systems (typically supported by geosynchronous orbit (GEO) satellites)

are being used to diffuse telephony and Internet access into remote areas, notably in developing nations.

Competition associated with regulatory relaxation and the Internet has promoted the upgrading of wireline telephony networks, but the trends there have been particularly unstable. Before the takeoff of the Internet, first Integrated Services Digital Network (ISDN—*q.v.*) technology in the 1980s and then in the early 1990s Asynchronous Transfer Mode (ATM) were touted as bandwidth- and capability-enhancing improvements for telephony. The Internet has shown these technologies to fall far short of the promise. ATM is found primarily in network backbones, enabling gigabits per second traffic flow. Of the family of digital subscriber line technologies (xDSL), the most familiar variant is asymmetric or ADSL, originally advanced as a means for video delivery via the telephone network and providing up to a few megabits per second. These are relatively easy ways to increase bandwidth for local access to the Internet, but growing deployment of fiber optic cable has excited interest in all-optical networks using wave-division multiplexing.

Internet telephony (or IP telephony) is emblematic of the turn-of-the-century convergence. Its early growth took advantage of the sheltering of Internet communications from the kind of telephony regulation that had made long-distance and especially international telephone calls relatively expensive. Demonstrations of Internet telephony have fostered growth of the more general capability supporting audio, video, and collaboration (e.g. conferencing).

Mass Market Measures

Traditionally, discussions of computers and communications revolved around business applications: data communications among units of an enterprise, among workers and between workers and an employer, and to a limited extent among enterprises for specific transactions (order submission and tracking between buyers and suppliers who have agreed to standard formats and technologies—the underpinnings of electronic data interchange (EDI) and electronic funds transfer (EFT—*q.v.*) among financial institutions).

The spread of data communications was seen as a trickle-down process affecting first large organizations, then smaller ones, and eventually feeding home applications.

Convergence and growth in home computing and home-based network-connected devices is inspiring development of home networking technologies, including support for linking multiple devices within the home (e.g. microcellular wireless networks) to streamlined support for multiple kinds of network services going into and out of the home. Some of these services will support people's communications, some will be associated with telemetry (e.g. utility meter monitoring, medical device monitoring), and some may be influenced by strategies for controlling flows of content (e.g. set-top boxes or the equivalent). Computers in the home are as likely to be embedded in various devices as to be standalone.

Maturing Environment

Internet growth has made growth itself a source of concern and technology development. Although the Internet was designed for large-scale use, the proliferation of users, connected devices, and bandwidth-intensive applications raises questions about congestion. Responses to congestion include increasing capacity—most notable in network backbones and also in access ports and lines supported by Internet service providers (ISPs)—and exploration of protocol modifications to support a larger address space (the next generation of the Internet Protocol, IP v6, does this) and to facilitate differential treatment of different kinds and priorities of traffic.

The spread of the Internet and networking generally has spawned a growing number of jobs and groups concerned about the structure and management of networks. On the supply side, ISPs are proliferating, providing new competition for traditionally monopolistic telecommunications providers. At the same time, there is a trend toward ISP consolidation, which makes small ISPs less competitive except in hard-to-serve areas where large companies may be reluctant to invest in deployment.

Computers, Communications, and Public Policy

Government policies have generally served to promote networking. Internet-related technologies were developed with government-supported research and development investments, and R&D support continues because networking fosters cost-sharing and collaboration in research and because research applications continue to push the frontier of possibility for both computation and communications. For example, in the USA, the Next Generation Internet initiative and private counterpart Internet2 emerged in the late 1990s, contributing to the formulation of the 1999 Information Technology for the twenty-first century (IT^2) initiative. In Europe, the Trans-European Network program has advanced bandwidth support for researchers in several countries and the Information Society Technologies Programme provides coordinated support for research.

Information policy includes protection of privacy, intellectual property rights, and freedom of speech. Privacy refers to the protection of information about persons, and the spread of databases containing personal information and their connection to networks, which may contribute to problems from embarrassment to identity theft and harassment.

The central intellectual property issue associated with networking is copyright (*see* LEGAL PROTECTION OF SOFTWARE). Digitized information is very easy to copy. The growth of the Internet aggravates these concerns because not only is text affected, but music, images, and video are increasingly easy to copy, and new forms of "documents" can involve syntheses of previously generated and potentially owned content.

Freedom of speech, even more than other aspects of information policy, is colored by ideology. Even in the USA there are disagreements over whether some kinds of speech over the Internet should be controlled, as they have been in broadcast radio and television contexts.

The future of computers and communications depends on a mix of technology, business, and public policy. Early 1990s attention to information infrastructure focused policy attention on promotion of deployment and capability, spurring business investments in network deployment and new kinds of networkable devices that depend on computer technology. The attention to electronic commerce (*q.v.*) over the last decade has focused attention on the use of computers and communications, including the balance between capability proliferation and safeguards for the infrastructure as a complex super-system intended for the use of the earth's whole population.

Bibliography

1996. Computer Science and Telecommunications Board. *The Unpredictable Certainty; Information Infrastructure Through 2000*. Washington, DC: National Academy Press.

1997. Computer Science and Telecommunications Board. *The Evolution of Untethered Communications*. Washington, DC: National Academy Press.

1999. Blumenthal, M. S. "Networks of the World: Unite!," in *Global Networks: Vision and Reality* (ed. J. R. Schement), 1–52, Washington, DC: Aspen Institute.

Marjory S. Blumenthal

COMPACTION

See DATA COMPRESSION.

COMPATIBILITY

For articles on related subjects, *see*

+ Emulation
+ Open Architecture
+ Open Systems Interconnection
+ Simulation
+ Software
+ Software Portability
+ Transparency

Two compilers or language translators are said to be *compatible* if source programs written for a compiler on one computer will compile and execute successfully on the other. Similarly, two versions of the same compiler (on the same computer) are said to be compatible if a source program written for one version of the compiler will successfully compile and execute using the other version. If the compatibility extends in only one direction, we speak of "upward" (older to newer) or "downward" (newer to older) compatibility.

Occasionally, specific programs will be said to be compatible with specific computer systems when they can be compiled or assembled and executed correctly using that computer system; but the more common use of compatibility in computing is applied to two machines, two configurations, two operating systems, or two software packages with respect to the ease with which programs or data can be converted from one to the other. The term normally applied to a program to describe the ease with which it can be converted from one system to another is *portability*.

Hardware component compatibility is an intensely competitive area. Since many peripheral devices are hooked to the computer by a relatively small number of cables (usually with a plug, in fact), so-called *plug-to-plug compatible* peripherals have been developed by some competitive firms. Their practice is to build one that works exactly the same (and even has identical plugs on the ends of the cables) as the original, but which can be profitably marketed at a lower price. Thus, potential customers exist wherever the original equipment is installed.

Chester L. Meek

COMPILE AND RUN TIME

For articles on related subjects, *see*

+ Binding
+ Compiler
+ Diagnostic
+ Language Processors

✚ Object Program

✚ Source Program

The complete process of running a program that has been written in a high-level language such as Pascal (*q.v.*) or C++ (*q.v.*) is accomplished in two steps:

1. Translation of the *source program* as written by the programmer into a machine-executable form (a process commonly referred to as *compilation*).
2. Execution of the generated form; that is, the *running* of the compiled or *object program*.

To distinguish between certain actions that may occur during one of these phases, the period of compilation is known as the *compile time* and the succeeding period as the *run time* or *execution time*. These two phases are usually distinct and may be temporally separated—the object program may be rerun many times without need for recompilation of the source program. In an interpretive system, however, the two phases *are* intertwined, since execution of each source program statement follows immediately after its translation (*see* LANGUAGE PROCESSORS).

Typically, errors in a program are related to compile time or run time. Where the error is an error of language (i.e. incorrect syntax), then the system can recognize this at compilation time; on the other hand, errors in logic or arithmetic (i.e. semantic errors) are normally discovered (if at all) at run time.

J. A. N. Lee

COMPILER

For articles on related subjects, *see*

✚ Backus–Naur Form (BNF)

✚ Declaration

✚ Expression

✚ Formal Languages

✚ Intermediate Language

✚ Language Processors

✚ Linkers and Loaders

✚ Source Program

✚ Statement

A *compiler* is a program that translates programs expressed in a *source language* into equivalent programs expressed in a *target language*. Usually, but not always, the source language is high level, such as C++ (*q.v.*) or Java (*q.v.*), and the target language is low level, such as assembly language or even pure machine code. A good compiler must tolerate and report errors in source programs, generate target programs that make efficient use of resources, and provide information about the translated programs to other tools such as *debuggers* (*see* DEBUGGING), and *linkers* (*see* LINKERS AND LOADERS).

Compilers consist of two parts: a front end, mainly responsible for *analyzing* the source programs, and a back end, mainly responsible for generating or *synthesizing* the target programs; *see* Fig. 1. The front end translates the source program into an *intermediate representation* (IR) from which the back end generates the target program.

The Front End

The front end takes source programs, reads from text files, analyzes them, makes sure there are no errors, and then builds an IR that can be passed on to the back end. Most compilers employ three phases to map a program source file into the IR: *lexical analysis, parsing,* and *semantic analysis*. Each of these phases performs extensive error checking.

The first phase, lexical analysis, groups the individual characters in the input source program into *tokens*. The tokens constitute the basic meaningful units of the source program such as identifiers, reserved words, and separators. Some portions of the input, called *whitespace*,

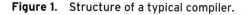

Figure 1.   Structure of a typical compiler.

do not contribute to the tokens and are discarded. Examples are tabs, line terminators, and spaces.

The second phase, parsing, matches the tokens with the *grammar* of the programming language. A grammar represents the syntactic structure of a programming language. The result of parsing is a *parse tree*—a *data structure* (*q.v.*) that captures how the input tokens are assembled to match the grammar.

The third phase, semantic analysis, analyzes the parse tree. This phase involves checking the source language rules that are not captured directly in the syntactic description of the language. For example, the semantic analyzer may verify that variables are declared before their first use, and that operators are applied only to operands of the right type.

Context-Free Grammars

Consider a simple programming language, in which programs consist of the keyword begin, a list of declarations, a list of statements, and terminated by the keyword end. A declaration introduces a single new integer variable. A statement is either an if-then-else statement or an assignment statement, which sets a variable to the value of an expression. Expressions are made up of variables and numbers, and may use addition, multiplication, relational operators, and parentheses. The following is a *context-free grammar* for this language:

```
program ::="begin" {declaration}
            {statement} "end"
declaration ::= "int" ID ";"
statement ::=assignment | ifthenelse
assignment ::= ID "=" expression ";"
expression ::= term [relop term]
relop ::= "<" | "<=" | ">" | ">="
            | "==" | "!="
term ::=factor {"+" factor}
factor ::= primary {"*" primary}
primary ::= ID | NUM | "(" expression ")"
ifthenelse ::= "if" expression "then"
            statement "else" statement
```

The grammar consists of a list of rules, one per line. Each rule defines a *nonterminal* on the left-hand side of the "::=" operator in terms of possible expansions on the right-hand side. In this grammar, the nonterminals are program, declaration, statement, assignment, expression, relop, term, factor, primary, and ifthenelse. The rule for the assignment nonterminal specifies that it can be expanded into an identifier token ID followed by the "=" token, followed by any expansion of the expression nonterminal, followed by a ";". The rule for primary specifies three alternatives, separated by the "|" operator: primary can be expanded into an identifier ID, a number NUM, or a parenthesized expression "(" expression ")". Each alternative is known as a *production* for the nonterminal. Nonterminal definitions are often recursive, for example, expression has a recursive definition involving term, factor, primary, and then expression itself.

The other entities that appear on the right-hand sides of productions include *terminals* (so named because they cannot be expanded). Terminals match the tokens produced by the lexical analyzer. There are two kinds of terminal in the above grammar: constant strings such as "int" or ";", and variable strings such as ID and NUM. The details of ID and NUM are not defined in the grammar; instead their definition is part of the lexical token specification.

Grammar definitions use parentheses for grouping symbols and may use special notation to specify repeated or optional constructs. In the above grammar, a sequence of symbols enclosed in "{" and "}" may be repeated zero or more times, whereas a sequence of symbols enclosed in "[" and "]" (as in the rule for expression) may be included at most once. (This notation is known as EBNF, or Extended Backus–Naur Form). Thus, the nonterminal program can include zero or more declarations followed by zero or more statements in its expansion.

Regular Expressions

Regular expressions, like context-free grammars, are a specialized notation to describe languages. Regular expressions, however, are simpler than context-free grammars in that they disallow recursive EBNF definitions. This simplification makes them well suited to describing the lexical structure (tokens) of programming languages, since the absence of recursion enables construction of very efficient lexical analyzers.

The following example uses regular expressions to define a token for the simple grammar shown earlier. It defines ID to be a letter followed by zero or more letters and digits, and NUM to be any sequence of one or more digits:

```
ID ::= LETTER {LETTER | DIGIT}
NUM ::= DIGIT {DIGIT}
LETTER ::= "A" | "B" | ... | "Z" |
           "a" | "b" | ... | "z" |
DIGIT ::="0" | "1" | "2" | "3" | "4" |
          "5" | "6" | "7" | "8" | "9" |
```

Lexical Analysis and Parsing

Lexical analysis matches character sequences to regular expression descriptions of tokens, while parsing matches token sequences to context-free grammar descriptions of programming languages. For performance and convenience, most compilers separate lexical analysis and parsing. Lexical analysis is the most performance-critical part of the front end, since it is the only phase that processes each individual character in the input source program. The use of nonrecursive regular expressions in the lexical specification allows construction of fast lexical analyzers, without which the front end could spend a lot of time grouping individual characters into tokens. The separation matches how humans use natural language (reading words rather than individual letters). Moreover, the lexical analysis/parsing interface is the ideal place to discard whitespace, since whitespace appears between tokens.

Example 1 (no errors)   Consider the program:

```
begin
 int i;
 i = 0;
end
```

The lexical analyzer converts the program into the following sequence of tokens:

```
BEGIN INT ID SEMICOLON ID
  ASSIGN NUM SEMICOLON END
```

While we identify tokens simply by name, some tokens contain additional information that later stages of the compiler need. For example, an ID token contains the text image (the actual letters in the identifier), and a NUM token contains the numerical value.

The parser matches these tokens with the grammar as follows:

```
program → BEGIN declaration statement END
  declaration → INT ID SEMICOLON
  statement → assignment
  assignment → ID ASSIGN expression
                   SEMICOLON
    expression → term
    term → factor
      factor → primary
        primary → NUM
```

The sequence of tokens generated by the lexical analyzer constitutes the leaves of a parse tree, while the interior nodes constitute the nonterminals involved in producing the token sequence from the topmost nonterminal program.

Parsing algorithms used in compilers fall into two general categories: *bottom-up* and *top-down*, also known as LR and LL parsers, respectively. LR and LL parsers offer different trade-offs between ease of specifying certain language constructs, speed of parsing, size of parsers, and conceptual complexity. Bottom-up parsers build parse trees from the leaves (the bottom), progressing up towards the root, while top-down parsers build parse trees from the root (the top), progressing down towards the leaves. For performance reasons, both bottom-up and top-down parsers restrict the context-free grammars that they can process. The restrictions typically allow parsers to select productions from the grammar by looking ahead at most k tokens at each step, where k is a small positive constant. Parsers satisfying such constraints are referred to as "look-ahead k" parsers, or more briefly LR(k) and LL(k) parsers. In practice, $k = 1$ suffices for parsing most programming languages.

Example 2 (syntax error)   Suppose the first semicolon is omitted from the program in Example 1:

```
Begin
 int i
 i = 0;
end
```

In this case, the lexical analyzer produces these tokens:

```
BEGIN INT ID ASSIGN NUM SEMICOLON END
```

Now the parser can no longer match the token with the grammar rules and consequently reports an error.

Example 3 (lexical error)   Suppose the first semicolon in Example 1 is changed into a colon:

```
Begin
  int i:
  i = 0;
end
```

Upon encountering the colon character on the input, the lexical analyzer is unable to find a match with any of the regular expressions, and therefore reports an error.

Semantic Analysis

The semantic analyzer receives the completed parse tree from the parser and verifies that it contains no *semantic* errors—errors that the language specification requires be reported at compile time, but which cannot be detected by the lexical analyzer or parser. An example of a program with a semantic error is the following:

```
Begin
  int i;
  j = 0;
end
```

In this program, the variable j is used without a preceding declaration. The program passes the lexical analyzer and parser despite the error, since neither the lexical specification or the grammar requires that variables be declared before their first use. This error must be caught in the semantic analysis phase.

The Intermediate Representation

Some compilers use a parse tree, annotated by the semantic analyzer, as the main representation in the back end. More commonly, however, the parse tree is converted into a more convenient IR before being passed to the back end. A possible IR for the parse tree that corresponds to Example 1 is shown in Fig. 2. This IR discards unimportant details of syntactic appearance and remnants of the parsing process such as the terminals

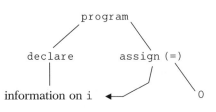

Figure 2.   Possible IR for the parse tree.

BEGIN, END, INT, and SEMICOLON while retaining the essential information, including the semantic link from the use to the declaration of the variable i.

The IR serves to bridge the gap from the source to the target language and therefore is designed to (1) be easy to generate from the parse tree of the source program, (2) include sufficiently low-level constructs to expose all computation for optimization, and (3) be easy to use to generate target code. Figure 3 gives examples of two kinds of IR for an if statement.

The Back End

The back end generates the target program from the information it receives from the front end. In the simplest case, the target program is constructed directly from the IR. More commonly, though, the back end consists of a number of phases that operate on the IR (or even multiple IRs), allowing the program to be optimized as part of the compilation.

The phases gradually transform the intermediate representation of the program into one that is closer to the low-level target language. The use of multiple phases, in addition to enabling more optimization, improves the organization of the compiler itself. Phase separation increases modularity (each phase can concentrate on a single task), maintainability (phases can be modified individually), and retargetability (the target machine-dependent parts can be isolated in a few phases rather than permeating the whole compiler).

Optimization

An optimizer works on the IR, transforming the program into one that computes the same result,

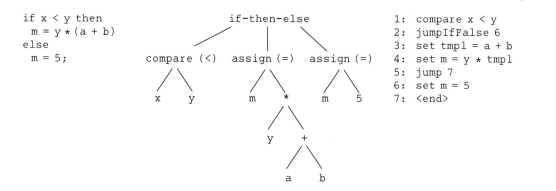

```
if x < y then                  if-then-else          1:  compare x < y
    m = y * (a + b)           /      |      \         2:  jumpIfFalse 6
else                                                  3:  set tmp1 = a + b
    m = 5;        compare (<)  assign (=)  assign (=) 4:  set m = y * tmp1
                    /  \        /  \        /  \      5:  jump 7
                  x     y     m     *      m    5     6:  set m = 5
                                  /  \                7:  <end>
                                 y    +
                                    /  \
                                   a    b
```

Figure 3. Source program fragment (left), abstract syntax tree IR (center), and pseudo-assembler IR (right).

but does so more efficiently according to some measure, such as execution time or memory consumption. Two trends have greatly increased the importance of optimization: new programming paradigms make modern languages harder to implement efficiently (e.g. object-oriented and logic-programming languages), while modern computers sustain peak performance only when programmed carefully (e.g. factors like pipelining, multi-instruction issue, register usage, and data layout for high cache rates must all be considered).

Every optimization involves two steps: first the optimizer proves that the contemplated optimization is correct (meaning-preserving) for the specific program, and then it performs the optimization by transforming the IR. For example, if the optimizer can prove that the variable y in Step 4 of Fig. 3 will always have the value 2, it can replace the multiplication set m = y * tmp1 by a faster addition, set m = tmp1 + tmp1, without changing the meaning of the program. This simple optimization is just one of many kinds that have been developed. Commonly used optimizations are: *dead code elimination* (delete code that can never be executed), *constant folding* (perform computation at compile time instead of run time), *constant propagation* (track variables that have a constant value), *common subexpression elimination* (avoid recomputing expressions that occur multiple times), *strength reduction* (replace certain expressions that depend on loop counters by more efficient ones),

and *code motion* (e.g. hoist loop-invariant expressions out of loops).

Optimization can be performed at different scopes. *Local* optimization operates on one *basic block* at a time, where a basic block is a maximal piece of straight-line code (e.g. in Fig. 3 the three basic blocks are 1–2, 3–5, and 6). *Loop* optimization improves a single loop or a nest of loops. *Global* optimization operates on multiple basic blocks and loops within a procedure. Finally, *interprocedural* optimization operates on multiple procedures or even whole programs.

Code Generation

The code generator transforms the optimized IR into an equivalent target program. Code generation is best understood in terms of several subproblems: *register allocation instruction selection*, and *instruction scheduling*. The subproblems are highly interdependent, making optimal code generation infeasible except in restricted cases. Typically, code generators compromise by solving the subproblems in a particular order, for example, doing most register allocation before instruction scheduling, and using heuristics to predict the effects on later subproblems.

Commonly, code generation is followed by *peephole optimization* to eliminate local inefficiencies in the target code. An example of a local inefficiency could be an instruction that stores the contents of a CPU register $R1$

into a memory location M followed by an instruction that loads the contents of M into a register $R2$. In this case, the peephole optimizer can replace the second instruction by a faster register-to-register transfer or entirely eliminate the instruction if the two registers are the same. In general, a peephole optimizer looks at fixed-length sequences of target instructions (hence the name "peephole"), trying to replace them by faster sequences. It may eliminate redundant instructions, short-circuit jumps to jumps, and substitute complex instructions for sequences of simpler instructions.

Bibliography

1986. Aho, A. V., Sethi, R., and Ullman, J. D. *Compilers— Principles, Techniques, and Tools.* Reading, MA: Addison-Wesley.

1994. Bacon, D. F., Graham, S. L., and Sharp, O. J. "Compiler Transformations for High-performance Computing," *ACM Computing Surveys,* **26**(4), (December), 345–420.

1997. Muchnick, S. S. *Advanced Compiler Design and Implementation.* San Francisco, CA: Morgan Kaufmann.

Ole Agesen and Sriram Sankar

COMPLEMENT

For articles on related subjects, see

+ Arithmetic, Computer
+ Numbers and Number Systems

In ordinary arithmetic, we represent negative numbers by a minus sign followed by the absolute value (i.e. magnitude) of the number (e.g. −6.42). In computers, we can represent negative numbers this way also, and sometimes this is actually done, but more often a *complement* representation is used.

Consider the addition of two numbers expressed in sign–magnitude form. Before the operation can be carried out, the signs of the numbers must be compared. If they are the same, the two numbers can be added; if they are different, the smaller in magnitude may be subtracted from the larger and the correct sign appended to the result. The use of complements avoids this complication.

Definitions

There are two kinds of complements, *radix complements* and *diminished radix complements*, where *radix* refers to the base of the number system being used. Let x be a positive decimal number. Then the diminished 10s complement of x, which we denote by $\bar{x}$ and which is generally called the *9s complement*, is formed by subtracting every digit of x from 9. Thus, if $x = 426.3091$, $\bar{x} = 573.6908$. The *10s complement* $\tilde{x}$ is defined as the result of adding 1 in the least significant place of $\bar{x}$ or, equivalently, as the result of subtracting x from 10^n, where n is such that the 1 in 10^n is one place to the left of the most significant digit of x. Using the above example, $\tilde{x} = 573.6909 = 1000.0000 - 426.3091$. Both the quantities $\bar{x}$ and $\tilde{x}$ may be used as representations of the quantity $-x$.

The other complements of practical importance are those in the radix 2, or binary, system. If x is now a positive binary number, its *1s complement* $\bar{x}$ is formed by changing all 0s in x to 1s and 1s to 0s (i.e. subtracting all bits of x from 1) and the *2s complement* $\tilde{x}$ is formed by adding 1 in the least significant place of $\bar{x}$ or, equivalently, subtracting x from 2^n with n chosen as above. Thus, if $x = 10.1101$, then $\bar{x} = 01.0010$ and $\tilde{x} = 01.0011 = 100.0000 - 10.1101$.

Properties of Complements

Consider a computer whose arithmetic operations are to be performed on 8-bit 2s complement operands, the first of which is a sign indicator (0 for plus, 1 for minus). To add two such operands, we may treat them as 8-bit positive integers (i.e. treat the sign as another bit of the number), add them, and discard any carry to the left of the eighth position (*see* Fig. 1). Thus, we are able to ignore both the sign and relative magnitudes of the two numbers. With negative numbers in the 1s complement form, there is the slight additional complication that carries to the left of the eighth position must be added into the first (i.e. least significant) position (*see* Fig. 2).

Let $x = 00001000$ (decimal 8)

       $y = 00010101$ (decimal 21)

Then $\tilde{x}$ 11111000 (decimal -8)

       $\tilde{y} = 11101011$ (decimal -21)

Then $x + \tilde{y} = 00001000$

          $+\ 11101011$
          $\overline{}$
          11110011

which is the 2s complement of 13 in decimal (00001101 in binary); and

    $\tilde{x} + \tilde{y} = 11111000$

          $+\ 11101011$
          $\overline{}$
          11100011

which is the 2s complement of 29 in decimal (00011101 in binary).

Figure 1.   Addition of numbers using 2s complements.

Let $x = 00001000$
     $y = 00010101$
     $\bar{x} = 11110111$
     $\bar{y} = 11101010$
Then $x + \bar{y} = 00001000$
          $+\ 11101010$
          $\overline{11110010}$

which is the 1s complement of 13 in decimal (00001101 in binary); and

    $\bar{x} + \bar{y} = 11110111$
          $+11101010$
          $\overline{11100001}$
              1
          $\overline{11100010}$

which is the 1s complement of 29 in decimal (00011101 in
binary).

Figure 2.   Addition of numbers using 1s complements.

Both methods can be proved correct by writing complemented numbers as 2^n minus the corresponding positive number (minus 1 for 1s complements).

One interesting property of the 1s complement form is the existence, as in sign–magnitude representation, of two zeros, one with a positive sign and one with a negative sign. This follows because the 1s complement of 0000 0000 to is 1111 1111 (-0). With 2s complements, however, there is only one n-bit zero (namely, 0000 0000 for $n = 8$), since the 2s complement of 0000 0000 is 10000 0000,

which has nine bits, the first of which is discarded. (Of the other 255 different 8-bit patterns, only one is its own 2s complement: 1000 0000 [-128].) In 2s complement representation, 1111 1111 is the complement of 0000 0001.

Since 1s complements are generated merely by changing 0s to 1s, and vice versa, it is very easy to build a circuit to generate the 1s complement of a number. It is somewhat more difficult, but not very hard, to build a circuit to generate 2s complements. Therefore, it is easy to perform subtraction by first

Let $x = 00001000$
      $y = 00010101$

Then $x - y$ is found by first forming

$\tilde{y} = 11101011$

and then adding $x + \tilde{y}$, as in Fig.1, to get 11110011, which is the 2s complement of 13 in decimal.

Figure 3.   **Subtraction using 2s complements.**

complementing the minuend and then adding (*see* Fig. 3).

Although 1s complement computers were once common, 2s complement arithmetic is used on most recent computers, the chief advantage being the unique 0.

Anthony Ralston

COMPLEXITY

See COMPUTATIONAL COMPLEXITY; and NP-COMPLETE PROBLEMS.

COMPRESSION, DATA

See DATA COMPRESSION; and IMAGE COMPRESSION.

COMPUTATIONAL COMPLEXITY

For articles on related subjects, *see*

+ Algorithms, Analysis of
+ Algorithms, Theory of
+ NP-Complete Problems
+ Sorting
+ Turing Machine

Once we have developed an algorithm for solving a computational problem and analyzed its worst-case time requirements as a function of the size of its input, it is inevitable to ask: "Can we do better?" In a typical problem, we may be able to devise newer algorithms for the problem that are more efficient. But, eventually, such research often seems to reach a level beyond which improvements are very difficult, seemingly impossible, to achieve. At that point, algorithm designers inevitably start to wonder if there is something *inherent* in the problem that makes it impossible to devise algorithms that are faster than the current one. They may try to develop mathematical techniques for *proving formally* that there can be no algorithm for the given problem that runs faster than the current one. Such a proof would be valuable, as it would suggest that it is futile to keep seeking improved algorithms for this problem. The realm of mathematical models and techniques for establishing such impossibility proofs is called *computational complexity*.

For example, sorting n keys is a computational task that can be easily accomplished in $O(n^2)$ time by naive exchange algorithms such as *bubblesort*, while more sophisticated techniques such as *quicksort* and *mergesort* bring the time requirements down to $O(n \log n)$. Can we do better, or is $n \log n$ an unsurpassable milestone for sorting by comparison of keys? Another example is matrix multiplication. It was long assumed that n^3 operations are needed to multiply two $n \times n$ matrices. But, in 1969, Volker Strassen showed that two $n \times n$ matrices can be multiplied in $O(n^{2.81})$ operations! Over the past 30 years, this exponent has undergone a sequence of reductions and now stands below 2.4. Where will this end? Can we multiply two matrices in $O(n^2)$ time? Can we prove a lower bound of the form $n^2 \log n$, or, even more ambitiously, $n^{2.2}$, for the matrix multiplication problem?

A third example is the *traveling salesman problem* (Fig. 1), a popular well-studied problem that is notorious for its difficulty. Given a traveling salesman problem with n cities, it is trivially possible to find the optimum tour in time $O(n!)$—just check all possible permutations of the cities. This algorithm, is, of course, all but unusable for any but the smallest instances: even for a modest instance with $n = 30$ cities, the number of tours to be examined is greater than the age of the universe

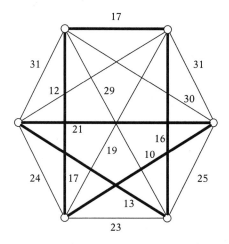

Figure 1. In the traveling salesman problem we are given a set of cities and the distances between them, and we seek the shortest closed tour that visits all cities. The optimum tour in this simple example is shown in bold, with total length 94. Because of the simplicity of its statement, its obvious appeal, and its maddening complexity, the traveling salesman problem has been studied extensively for decades, and it has been the testbed of every new algorithmic technique. Still, all algorithms known for it require exponential time in the worst case.

in picoseconds. It took several decades from the time the problem was posed in the 1920s to find a faster algorithm, one requiring "only" $O(n^2 2^n)$ steps. This algorithm, discovered by Michael Held and Richard M. Karp, uses a *dynamic programming* technique (*see* ALGORITHMS, DESIGN AND CLASSIFICATION OF) that patiently solves the problem for larger and larger subsets of the cities, using the results from smaller subsets to crack the larger ones, until the optimum tour of the set of all cities is finally identified.

Can we do better? To this date, there is no known algorithm that is guaranteed to solve the traveling salesman problem exactly for *n* cities faster than the dynamic programming algorithm. There are algorithms that are known *empirically* to solve quite large typical instances of the traveling salesman problem reasonably fast, and there are fast algorithms that somehow

approximate the optimum solution, but there is no known algorithm that is guaranteed to return the optimum, and to do so in time that is *polynomial* in *n*—an algorithm with a running time such as $O(n^2)$, or $O(n^5)$. It is thus tempting to conjecture, and try to prove, that *the traveling salesman problem requires exponential time for its solution*, that all algorithms that solve it must spend exponential time for some infinite collection of instances.

The task of proving *negative results*, or *lower bounds* on the complexity of a problem, is usually a lot more intricate mathematically than just devising an efficient algorithm. Coming up with an efficient algorithm, however ingenious it may be, requires only that the algorithm be specified and analyzed. Proving a lower bound, however, necessitates that the prover must consider *the whole spectrum of all possible algorithms for the problem in hand*, and show that none of them does better than the specified bound; the difficulty of the task is obvious.

General Models

The barrier separating polynomial algorithms from exponential ones is significant. Polynomial-time algorithms, algorithms whose running time is bounded by a function like $O(n)$, $O(n^3)$, and so on, form a substantial and important class of computations, broadly considered akin to the empirical concept of "practically feasible computation." Naturally, an $O(n^{1000})$ algorithm would hardy deserve to be called "practical," but such extreme polynomials never come up in practical situations.

The process of proving a lower bound on the complexity of a problem must start with a precise mathematical model for algorithms and their complexity. There are several useful mathematical models of algorithms, starting with the many variants of the Turing machine, proceeding to more down-to-earth models such as the *random access machine* (an abstraction of the von Neumann machine—*q.v.*), pointer machines, and many others. For each such model, we have a way of evaluating the time required for the solution of an instance (in the case of the Turing machine, this is simply the number of steps the machine takes to come up with the final answer). This confusing diversity of models appears to add another layer of difficulty, besides the fundamental mathematical one, to the development of a theory of computational complexity.

Complexity Classes

In computational complexity, we classify computational problems into *complexity classes*. The most important complexity class is the set of all problems that can be solved by polynomial-time algorithms (by Turing machines, or algorithms in any other one of a broad set of standard models). This important complexity class is denoted P, for polynomial-time. Actually, complexity classes are composed not of problems, but of *languages*, that is, sets of strings in some fixed alphabet such as {0.1} (*see* FORMAL LANGUAGES). Any computational problem of interest can be transformed into a corresponding language in a way that captures its complexity. For example, the traveling salesman problem can be captured by the language L_{TSP}, consisting of all strings of 0s and 1s which encode an $n \times n$ matrix of nonnegative integers (the distances between the cities) plus another integer B, such that there is a tour of the n cities of total length equal to B or less.

It is widely conjectured that the language L_{TSP} is not in P. However, it does belong in a broader, albeit somewhat less natural, complexity class called NP, for *nondeterministic polynomial*. Any language in this class can be decided by a polynomial *nondeterministic Turing machine*, a hypothetical device that has the ability to make correct guesses. For example, to recognize a string in L_{TSP}, a nondeterministic Turing machine would correctly guess the optimum tour of the instance encoded, and check that its length is indeed below the given bound. A language belongs in the class NP if such a recognition algorithm—a guessing phase, followed by a polynomial-time checking phase—exists. This important class contains, besides all of P, the traveling salesman problem and many other notoriously difficult problems. It is widely believed that the class P is strictly included in the class NP (i.e. that there are problems in NP not in P); this conjecture, as yet unproven, is the most central, important, and well-studied problem

in computational complexity. (*See* NP-COMPLETE PROBLEMS.)

Complexity classes go beyond NP. The class EXP contains, informally, all problems solvable by exponential-time algorithms. By a straightforward quantitative extension of the diagonalization proof which establishes that the *halting problem* is undecidable, it can be shown that there are problems in EXP that are not in P. EXP itself is a proper subset of the decidable languages. And it is known that EXP contains all of NP.

Complexity classes also deal with resources other than time, most significantly *space*. In analogy to P, PSPACE is the complexity class of all languages that can be recognized by a computer using an amount of memory (e.g. number of Turing machine tape squares) that is bounded by a polynomial in the size of the input. Memory is a resource that is more powerful and robust than time (obviously, you can compute more things with 1 000 000 memory words and unlimited time, than you can with 1 000 000 instructions and unlimited memory). For example, PSPACE contains both P and NP (but is contained in EXP). Also, another sign of the robustness of space is that nondeterminism makes no big difference in the space domain, and nondeterministic machines can simulate deterministic ones with only *quadratic* increase in space (but exponential increase in time)—hence the absence of an NPSPACE class.

There is an important and intriguing connection between space and *parallel time*: it turns out that, again within a broad range of "reasonable" models of sequential and parallel computation (*see* PARALLEL PROCESSING), the computational tasks that can be accomplished with a given amount of memory are closely related to the tasks that can be carried out in the same amount of parallel time—assuming that there are no limitations on the number of processors that are available. Another complexity class, called NC, is supposed to model feasible parallel computation more accurately: it includes all problems that can be solved in $O((\log n)^k)$ parallel time, for some fixed integer k, on polynomially many processors. This class is a subset of P, and is in fact believed to be a *proper* subset of P—as there seem to be many tasks that can be solved efficiently on sequential computers but cannot

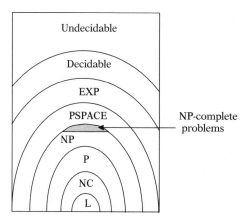

Figure 2. The complexity classes introduced in this article are depicted here as regions arranged according to the currently most prevalent view among experts in computational complexity. If a region A contains another region B, then the corresponding classes are known to contain one another in the same way. However, whether the containment is *proper*–that is, whether there is any space inside region A and outside region B–is for most of this map currently a subject of conjecture. There are a few known proper containments–for example, we can prove that EXP properly contains L, and that EXP is properly contained in the class of decidable problems.

be successfully parallelized beyond some level. Alas, as with most of our more interesting insights related to complexity classes, that NC is different from P is currently yet another unproven conjecture.

Figure 2 depicts the various complexity classes and their inclusions.

Bibliography

1979. Garey, M. R., and Johnson, D. S. *Computers and Intractability: A Guide to the Theory of NP-completeness.* New York: W. H. Freeman.

1992. Harel, D. *Algorithmics: The Spirit of Computing*, 2nd Ed. Reading, MA: Addison-Wesley.

1994. Papadimitriou, C. H. *Computational Complexity.* Reading, MA: Addison-Wesley.

Christos H. Papadimitriou

COMPUTATIONAL LINGUISTICS

See FORMAL LANGUAGES; MACHINE TRANSLATION; and NATURAL LANGUAGE PROCESSING.

COMPUTER-AIDED DESIGN/ COMPUTER-AIDED MANUFACTURING (CAD/CAM)

For articles on related subjects, *see*

+ Computer Animation
+ Computer Graphics
+ Robotics
+ Workstation

Introduction

Since the 1960s, computers have aided the closer integration of design activities with the actions required to manufacture goods, and the systems used to provide these aids have been called *CAD/CAM* systems. Initial CAD systems were directed at *computer-aided design* (CAD), with the resulting computer models used to aid manufacturing activities. As the benefits of *computer-aided manufacturing* (CAM) were recognized, the need for tighter integration of the two functions led to CAD/CAM systems where the design result (a model of the item) could be used directly to create the manufacturing information for the item. In addition to manufacturing information, the CAD/CAM database is often supplemented to aid in tracking inventories of materials and costs.

Design

Design is primarily a creative activity in which a person takes an esthetic or functional idea and expresses it in some medium in a way that can be understood by someone else. The most common example is engineering design, where the ideas of the designer include both geometric descriptions and notes, sometimes on paper as engineering drawings, but increasingly as electronic files. The essence of CAD is the marriage between the strengths and capabilities of computers and the skill and ingenuity of the designer. Most often, a designer works with a number of previously defined elements that are selectively included in the design of a item. For example, the designer of an electrical circuit selects circuit elements and places them into the design. Even at the level of designing the elements, geometric entities such as circles and lines are used to "build up" the element. This selection process is well suited to computer assistance, since computers can store large numbers of elements and allow designers rapid access to them.

Manufacturing

Manufacturing frequently involves the positioning of parts and subsequent operations, such as cutting, milling, drilling, forming, and finishing. In all of these, the geometry of the part is critical, particularly if the operations are carried out by computer-driven tools, often termed NC (*numerically controlled*) tools. When the same basic geometry is used for both design and manufacturing, parts fit together with great precision. The creation, storage, and interface of 3D geometric data among various disciplines (e.g. engineering and manufacturing) provide communication that is helpful in increasing both the precision with which parts are made and the ease of specifying the manufacturing steps to be carried out. The same geometric model is accessed and used by designers, part programmers (people who describe machine tool movements to create parts), structural engineers, tool designers, and quality assurance personnel. CAD/CAM systems allow this data to be captured during the construction phases of design.

Application Areas

The most obvious examples of CAD/CAM uses are in engineering design activities such as the design of structures, highways, machine parts, printed circuit boards, plants, piping, assembly lines, airplanes, transportation vehicles, and consumer products. In addition, CAD/CAM is often thought of as including the use of computers to aid in a design and analysis process, such as structural analysis following the

actual design work, although this is more properly called *computer-aided engineering* (CAE). The main strengths of computers—speed, accuracy, and repeatability—are particularly well matched to these kinds of design activities.

Computers as an Aid

Until about 35 years ago, almost all engineering design was done on the drafting board. Selection of elements was implemented by tracing, drawing from templates, or pasting the elements onto the drawing of the design of each element. Iteration was obtained by sequential use of pencil, eraser, pencil, eraser, and so on. The only way to improve productivity was to provide better templates or paste-ons, to use less iteration, or to speed up the humans in some way. The recognition that significant gains in productivity could result from using computers to aid the process led to CAD systems.

The Process

The essence of CAD/CAM design functions is geometric construction. Geometric entities are typically built through repeated selection of "functions" or "tasks" to be performed from a menu of possibilities. A menu, function keyboard, mouse (*q.v.*), or other input devices are used for selection of *elements* for insertion and positioning. These devices are also used to select tasks that permit a designer to move elements or items from location to location (translations and rotations), to create a blown-up view of a portion of the drawing (*windowing*), and to permit easy annotation or dimensioning of the drawings. Using these and other functional capabilities, the user builds the database interactively—a database composed of both geometric and alphanumeric information.

Construction of the design is not the only way in which data can be captured, however. An automatic laser scanner can be used for 2D data capture, with data automatically entered into the database. This data is then available for further modification (or editing). In addition to this type of scanner, handheld or movable scanning (or "digitizing") devices are available. These allow the locations of points to be input. They can be moved to various points on 2D or 3D models. At a desired point, the user has the device sense the location of the point and enter it into the database. After the points are entered, CAD functions can be applied to create smooth lines, curves, or surfaces between the points. These lines, curves, or surfaces can then be used with the points for further design or for interfacing with CAM functions (*see* Fig. 1).

A digital definition of the product that can be viewed from any angle or projected into any plane is the end product. It replaces the traditional drawing, which usually shows the principal orthographic views (front, top, and side) and a 3D view. The drawing is just a by-product, obtained if desired. Integration of CAD with CAM has further proceeded to integration with business and technical environments, since such environments are often present on the same personal computer as the CAD/CAM system.

The primary benefit of CAM is the use of the computer description of a part to drive cutting, forming, and other operations in a manufacturing environment. Manufacturing personnel are concerned with deciding how the part will be manufactured. One of their concerns is the determination of tools, materials, and methods that will be used to cut, form, and/or finish the part. In addition, databases for CAD/CAM systems need to provide information about stock to form or cut the part.

CAD/CAM integrated systems allow users to create "virtual products"—products designed (with CAD) that exist in digital models for which manufacturing information (CAM) exists so the product can be "built" (and "broken," if necessary, for analysis) using the virtual model, before a physical manifestation of the product exists. This capability is sometimes part of what is called a "master model" environment, in which the digital model is passed from design to other disciplines (e.g. tooling, analysis, manufacturing) that add value to the model.

Hardware

Pioneering CAD systems were developed in the 1960s, using large mainframe (*q.v.*) computers attached to graphics terminals. These systems were primarily used in automotive and aerospace organizations, industries that required large amounts of data storage for their CAD data. The large centralized mainframe systems were the only systems that could provide this needed

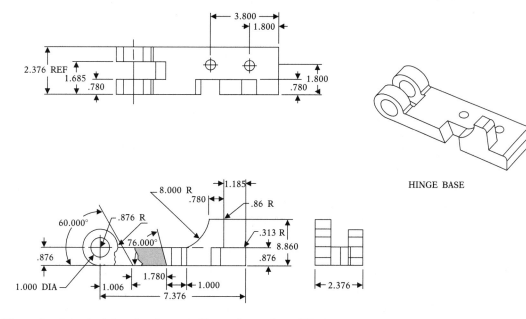

HINGE BASE

Figure 1. A typical drawing format—three views plus a 3D view.

Figure 2. A surface representation of a face, serving as the start of the design of a fire protection mask. The physical sculpted model was digitized (scanned) to produce 3D data points, which were then used to create surfaces. The display shows the computer-generated surfaces.

data storage. In addition, the large mainframes were the only source of sufficient computing power for the geometric and display calculations required. The advent of personal computers and workstations has broadened the way that CAD/CAM capabilities can be delivered. Applications are now available on every type of hardware, with the specific type of application varying depending on the computing power and sophistication of the graphics device.

Software

Initial CAD/CAM models grew from 2D systems representing drawings to 3D systems representing objects defined by lines, curves, circles, and points

located in space. Actual surfaces on the part were defined in second-generation systems in the 1970s; the surfaces allowed the design and manufacturing of more complex shapes as the CAD/CAM data was used to model smooth-flowing surfaces where accuracy was critical. Designing with solid shapes has always been attractive due to the ability of solids to define an object unambiguously and to present a complete definition of their outside surfaces. The drawbacks of solid-based modeling systems had once been the large amount of computing resources they require and the inability to represent free-form surfaces such as those shown in Figure 2. With the advent of high-powered technical workstations and personal computers, sufficient computing power is now available to allow systems that model solids to support general surfaces.

There is a trend toward even tighter ties between CAD and CAM, because systems are starting to incorporate aids to enforce rules of manufacturability during the design process. These aids are inspired by artificial intelligence work in expert systems (*q.v.*). These systems ensure that manufacturing constraints are not violated, that parts can be produced by an organization with the tools it has on hand, and that classes of products can be designed once, with parameters distinguishing the individual particular members of the classes.

NC Applications

The use of CAD data to program NC machines was one of the first manufacturing application areas. This area of activity was pioneered by the aerospace industry, using the Automatically Programmed Tool (APT) language (*see* PROBLEM-ORIENTED LANGUAGES). This is a language used to describe the operations and path of a machine tool or NC lathe in the cutting of a part from a piece of stock. Modern CAM software allows the cutter path to be programmed, using graphic aids without the use of a separate language. With increased use of surface and solid models, artificial intelligence methods are used to help develop manufacturing programs with minimal user involvement. These techniques are based on the recognition of features in the object, such as drilled holes, machined pockets, and specified tolerances; the features require specific operations that are automatically invoked.

Assemblies

CAD/CAM objects are often part of larger assemblies, made up of a number of objects obtained from several different designers and manufacturers. The assembly of a first prototype can involve time-consuming fitting and adjustment of these individual parts so that they can become part of a more complex assembly. This problem is compounded when the assembly involves complex motions at high speeds or high stress levels, such as the paper-handling mechanism in a copier or the steering and suspension of a front-wheel-drive automobile. Assembly modeling lessens redesign and improves the performance of the assembly, while reducing the need for prototype test fitting. The emphasis in assembly modeling is on avoiding physical mockups or models, using "digital" instead of "physical" "looks" at the full assembly. In addition, by identifying parts that make up an assembly while they are being designed, complete bill of materials processing can be performed, which later produces benefits in purchasing and scheduling.

Bibliography

1996. Farin, G. E. *Curves and Surfaces for Computer-Aided Geometric Design: A Practical Guide*, 4th Ed. New York: Academic Press.

1997. Combs, S. B., and Zirbel, J. H. *Fundamentals of Autocad*. Upper Saddle River, NJ: Prentice Hall.

1999. Mortenson, M. E. *Mathematics for Computer Graphics Applications: An Introduction to the Mathematics and Geometry of CAD/CAM*. New York: Industrial Press.

Barry Flachsbart, David Shuey, and George Peters

COMPUTER ALGEBRA

PRINCIPLES

For an article on a related subjects, *see*

✛ Symbol Manipulation

Computer algebra is a branch of scientific computation that differs from traditional numerical analysis in three ways: (1) Computer algebra involves computation in algebraic structures, such as finitely presented groups, polynomial rings, rational function fields, algebraic and transcendental extensions of the rational numbers, or differential and difference fields. (2) Computer algebra manipulates formulas. Whereas in numerical computation the input and output of algorithms are basically just numbers, the input and output of computer algebra algorithms are generally formulas. So, typically, instead of computing

$$\int_0^{1/2} \frac{x}{x^2 - 1}\, dx = -0.1438$$

an integration algorithm in computer algebra yields

$$\int \frac{x}{x^2 - 1}\, dx = \frac{\ln|x^2 - 1|}{2}.$$

(3) Computations in computer algebra are carried through exactly (i.e. no approximations are applied at any step). So, typically, the solutions of a system of algebraic equations such as

$$x^4 + 2x^2y^2 + 3x^2y + y^4 - y^3 = 0$$
$$x^2 + y^2 - 1 = 0$$

are presented as (0, 1), $(\pm\sqrt{3/4}, -1/2)$, instead of $(\pm 0.86602\cdots, -0.5)$.

Applications of Computer Algebra
The Piano Movers Problem

Many problems in robotics (*q.v.*) can be modeled by the piano movers problem: finding a path that will take a given body *B* from a given initial position to a desired final position. The additional constraint is that along the path the body should not hit any obstacles, such as walls or other bodies. A simple example in the plane is shown in Fig. 1. The initial and final positions of the body *B* are drawn in full, whereas a possible intermediate position is drawn in dotted lines. J. T. Schwartz and M. Sharir have shown how to reduce this problem to

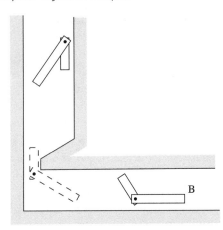
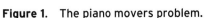

Figure 1. The piano movers problem.

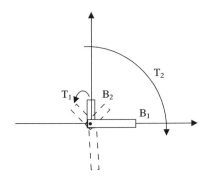

Figure 2.

a certain problem about semialgebraic sets that can be solved by Collins's cylindrical algebraic decomposition (cad) method.

Semialgebraic sets are subsets of a real m-dimensional space R^m that can be cut out by polynomial equations and inequalities. That is, start with simple sets of the form

$$\{(x_1, \ldots, x_m) | p(x_1, \ldots, x_m) = 0\}$$

or

$$\{(x_1, \ldots, x_m) | q(x_1, \ldots, x_m) > 0\},$$

where p, q are polynomials with real coefficients, and allow the construction of more complicated sets by means of intersection, union, and difference. Any subset of R^m that can be defined in this way is called a *semialgebraic set*.

Consider a two-dimensional problem, as in Fig. 1. Starting from some fixed position of the body B (say P at the origin, where P is the point at which the parts of B are joined together) in R^2, obtain an arbitrary position of B by applying a rotation T_1 to part B_2, a rotation T_2 to B (Fig. 2), and afterwards a translation T_3 to B. Since T_1, T_2 can be described by 2×2 matrices and T_3 by a vector of length 2, any such position of B can be specified by 10 coefficients (i.e. a point in R^{10}). Some of these possible positions are illegal, since the body B would intersect or lie outside of the boundaries. If the legal positions $L(\subset R^{10})$ can be described by polynomial equations and inequalities, then L is a semialgebraic set.

The piano movers problem is now reduced to the question of whether two points P_1, P_2 in L can be joined by a path in L (i.e. whether P_1 and P_2 lie in the same connected component of L). This question can be decided by Collins's cad method, which makes heavy use of computer algebra algorithms.

Algorithmic Methods in Geometry

Often, a geometric statement can be described by polynomial equations over some ground field K, such as the real or complex numbers. Consider, for instance, the statement, "*The intersection of its altitude with the hypotenuse of a right-angled triangle and the midpoints of the three sides of the triangle lie on a circle*" (Fig. 3).

Once the geometric figure is placed into a coordinate system, it can be described by polynomial equations. For instance, the fact that E is the midpoint of

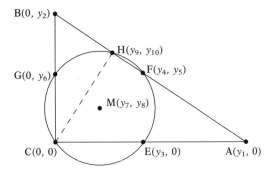

Figure 3.

the side AC is expressed by the equation $2y_3 - y_1 = 0$; the fact that the line segments EM and FM are of equal length is expressed by the equation $(y_7 - y_3)^2 + y_8^2 - (y_7 - y_4)^2 - (y_8 - y_5)^2 = 0$; and so on. In this way, the system $h_1 = \cdots = h_m = 0$ of polynomial equations in the indeterminates $y_1, \ldots, y_n$ determines the geometric figure. Call these polynomials the *hypothesis polynomials*. The equation $(y_7 - y_3)^2 + y_8^2 - (y_7 - y_9)^2 - (y_6 - y_{10})^2 = 0$ then states that the line segments HM and EM are also of equal length. Call this polynomial the *conclusion polynomial*.

The problem of proving the geometric statement is now reduced to the problem of proving that every common solution of the hypothesis polynomials (i.e. every valid geometric configuration) also solves the conclusion polynomial (i.e. the statement is valid for the configuration). Various computer algebra methods can be used for proving such geometry statements, such as characteristic sets or Gröbner bases.

Modeling in Science and Engineering

In science and engineering, it is common to express a problem in terms of integrals or differential equations with boundary conditions. Numerical integration leads to approximations of the values of the solution functions. But, as Richard Hamming (*q.v.*) has written, "the purpose of computing is insight, not numbers." So, instead of computing tables of values, it would be much more gratifying to derive formulas for the solution functions. Consider, for example, the system of differential equations

$$-6\frac{dq}{dx}(x) + \frac{d^2 p}{dx^2}(x) - 6\sin(x) = 0$$

$$6\frac{d^2 q}{dx^2}(x) + a^2 \frac{dp}{dx}(x) - 6\cos(x) = 0$$

subject to the boundary conditions $p(0) = 0$, $q(0) = 1$, $p'(0) = 0$, $q'(0) = 1$. Given this information as input, any of the major computer algebra systems will derive

the formal solution

$$p(x) = -\frac{12\sin(ax)}{a(a^2 - 1)} - \frac{6\cos(ax)}{a^2} + \frac{12\sin(x)}{a^2 - 1} + \frac{6}{a^2},$$

$$q(x) = \frac{\sin(ax)}{a} - \frac{2\cos(ax)}{a^2 - 1} + \frac{(a^2 + 1)\cos(x)}{a^2 - 1}$$

Some Algorithms in Computer Algebra

Polynomial arithmetic with coefficients in a field, like the rational numbers, presents no problem. These polynomials form a Euclidean domain, so we can carry out division with quotient and remainder. Often, however, we need to work with polynomials whose coefficients lie in an integral domain like the integers. Addition, subtraction, and multiplication are again obvious, but division with quotient and remainder is not possible. Fortunately, we can replace division by a similar process, called *pseudo-division*. If $a(x) = a_m x^m + \cdots + a_1 x + a_0$ and $b(x) = b_n x^n + \cdots + b_1 x + b_0$, with $m \geq n$, then there exists a unique pair of quotient $q(x)$ and remainder $r(x)$ such that $b^{m-n+1}a(x) = q(x)b(x) + r(x)$ where either r is the zero polynomial or the degree of r is less than the degree of b.

Good algorithms are needed for computing the *greatest common divisor* (gcd) of polynomials. If we are working with polynomials over a field, we can use Euclid's algorithm, which takes two polynomials $f_1(x)$, $f_2(x)$ and computes a chain of remainders $f_3(x), \ldots, f_k(x)$, $f_{k+1}(x) = 0$, such that f_i is the remainder in dividing f_{i-2} by f_{i-1}. Then $f_k(x)$ is the desired greatest common divisor. For polynomials over the integers we can replace division by pseudo-division, and the Euclidean algorithm still works. The problem, however, is that, although the inputs and the final result might be quite small, the intermediate polynomials can have huge coefficients. This problem of coefficient growth is ubiquitous in computer algebra, but there are some general approaches for dealing with it.

The most efficient algorithm for computing gcds of multivariate polynomials is the *modular algorithm*. The basic idea is to apply homomorphisms to the coefficients, compute the gcds of the evaluated polynomials, and use the *Chinese remainder algorithm* to reconstruct the actual coefficients in the gcd.

Decomposing polynomials into irreducible factors is another crucial algorithm in computer algebra. A few decades ago, only rather inefficient techniques for polynomial factorization were available. Research in computer algebra has contributed to a deeper understanding of the problem and, as a result, has created much better algorithms. Let us first consider univariate polynomials with integer coefficients. Since the problem of coefficient growth appears again, one usually maps the polynomial $f(x)$ to a polynomial $f_{(p)}(x)$ by applying a homomorphism H_p, p a prime. $f_{(p)}$ can now be factored by the *Berlekamp algorithm*, which involves some linear algebra and computations of gcds.

To integrate a rational function $A(x)/B(x)$, where A, B are polynomials with integral coefficients, we could split the polynomial B into linear factors in a suitable algebraic extension field, compute a partial fraction decomposition of the integrand, and integrate all the summands in this decomposition. The summands with linear denominators lead to logarithmic parts in the integral. Computations in the splitting field of a polynomial are very extensive; if n is the degree of the polynomial, the necessary algebraic extension has degree $n!$. So the question arises as to whether it is really necessary to go to the full splitting field. For instance, for $x \geq \sqrt{2}$

$$\int \frac{x}{x^2 - 2} \, dx = \int \frac{\frac{1}{2}}{x - \sqrt{2}} \, dx + \int \frac{\frac{1}{2}}{x + \sqrt{2}} \, dx$$
$$= \tfrac{1}{2}[\ln(x - \sqrt{2}) + \ln(x + \sqrt{2})]$$
$$= \tfrac{1}{2} \ln(x^2 - 2).$$

The example shows that although we had to compute in the splitting field of the denominator, the algebraic extensions actually disappear in the end. A deeper analysis of the problem reveals that, instead of factoring the denominator into linear factors, it suffices to compute a so-called *square-free factorization*—that is, a decomposition of a polynomial f into $f = f_1 f_2^2 \ldots f_r^r$, where the factors f_i are pairwise relatively prime and

have no multiple roots (square-free). The square-free factorization can be computed by successive gcd operations. Now if A and B are relatively prime polynomials over the rational numbers, B is square-free, and the degree of A is less than the degree of B, then

$$\int \frac{A(x)}{B(x)} \, dx = \sum_{i=1}^{n} c_i \log v_i$$

where the $c_1, \ldots, c_n$ are the distinct roots of the resultant of $A(x) - cB'(x)$ and $B(x)$ w.r.t. x, and each v_i is the gcd of $A(x) - c_i B(x)$ and $B(x)$. In this way, we get the smallest field extension necessary for expressing the integral.

A very common class of integrands is that of elementary functions. We get this class by starting with the rational functions and successively adding exponentials ($\exp f(x)$), logarithms ($\log f(x)$), or roots of algebraic equations, where the exponents, arguments, or coefficients are previously constructed elementary functions. Not every elementary integrand has an elementary integral (e.g. $\int e^{x^2} \, dx$ cannot be expressed as an elementary function). However, there is an algorithm (the *Risch algorithm*) that can decide whether a given integrand can be integrated in terms of elementary functions, and if so, produce the integral.

The discrete analog of the integration problem is the problem of summation in finite terms. We are given an expression for a summand a_n, and we want to compute a closed expression for the partial sums of the infinite series $\sum_{n=1}^{\infty} a_n$. That is, we want to compute a function $S(m)$ such that

$$\sum_{n=1}^{m} a_n = S(m) - S(0).$$

For instance, we want to compute

$$\sum_{n=1}^{m} nx^n = \frac{mx^{m+2} - (m+1)x^{m+1} + x}{(x-1)^2}.$$

For the case of hypergeometric functions, *Gosper's algorithm* solves this problem. There is also a theory of summation similar to the theory of integration in finite terms.

Representation of Expressions

Dynamic data structures are necessary for representing the computational objects of computer algebra. Most computer algebra programs represent objects as lists. An integer is represented as a list of digits. For more complicated objects, the choice of representation is not that clear. So, for instance, we can represent a bivariate polynomial recursively as a polynomial in a main variable with coefficients in a univariate polynomial ring, or distributively as pairs of coefficients and power products in the variables. For example:

Recursive representation:

$$p(x, y) = (3x^2 - 2x + 1)y^2 + (x^2 - 3x)y + (2x + 1)$$

Distributive representation:

$$p(x, y) = 3x^2y^2 - 2xy^2 + x^2y + y^2 - 3xy + 2x + 1$$

For both these representations, we can use a dense or a sparse list representation. In the dense representation, a polynomial is a list of coefficients, starting from some highest coefficient down to the constant coefficient. So the dense recursive representation of p is

$$((3 -2 1)(1 -3 0)(2 1))$$

For the dense distributive representation of p, we order the power products according to their degree and lexicographically within the same degree. So p is represented as

$$\begin{pmatrix} 3 & 0 & 0 & 0 & -2 & 1 & 0 & 1 & -3 & 0 & 0 & 2 & 1 \\ x^2y^2 & x^3y & x^4 & y^3 & xy^2 & x^2y & x^3 & y^2 & xy & x^2 & y & x & 1 \end{pmatrix}$$

If only a few power products have a coefficient different from 0, then a dense representation wastes a lot of space. In this case we really want to represent the polynomial sparsely (i.e. by pairs of coefficients and exponents). The sparse recursive representation of p is

$$((((3 2)(-2 1)(1 0)) 2)(((1 2)(-3 1)) 1)$$
$$(((2 1)(1 0)) 0))$$

and the sparse distributive representation of p is

$$((3(2 2))(-2(1 2))(1(2 1))(1(0 1))(-3(1 1))$$
$$(2(1 0))(1(0 1)).$$

For different algorithms, different representations of the objects are useful or even necessary. In general, a computer algebra program has to provide many different representations for the various algebraic objects along with transformations that convert one form to another.

Bibliography

1989. Akritas, A. G. *Elements of Computer Algebra.* New York: John Wiley.

1996. Winkler, F. *Polynomial Algorithms in Computer Algebra.* New York: Springer-Verlag.

1997. Bronstein, M. *Symbolic Integration I—Transcendental Functions.* Berlin: Springer-Verlag.

Franz Winkler

SYSTEMS

The goal of a symbolic computation system is to provide facilities for general mathematical calculations, typically those of arithmetic with exact fractions, polynomial and rational function arithmetic, factorization of integers and of polynomials, exact solution of linear and polynomial systems of equations, closed forms for summations, simplification of mathematical expressions, and differentiation and integration of elementary functions.

Special-purpose computer algebra systems are designed to solve problems in one specific area of mathematics, for example, celestial mechanics, general relativity, or group theory. These systems use special notations and data structures (*q.v.*). Such systems will normally excel in their respective areas, but are of limited use in other applications. Examples are: Magma (formerly Cayley) for group theory and algebraic geometry, GAP for discrete algebra and group theory, Macaulay 2 for algebraic geometry and commutative algebra, or Pari for number-theoretic computations. We will restrict our attention to general-purpose computer algebra systems which are designed to cover many diverse application areas and which have sufficiently rich data types, data structures, and functions to do so.

Computation

All computer algebra systems have the ability to do mathematical computations with unassigned variables. For example

```
> t := x ^ 2 * sin(x);
                    t := x² sin(x)
> diff(t, x);
            2 x sin(x) + x² cos(x)
```

computes the derivative of an expression, where x is an unassigned variable.

Computer algebra systems have the ability to perform exact computation, that is, arbitrary precision rational arithmetic, algebraic arithmetic, finite field arithmetic, and so on. For example

$$\frac{1}{2} + \frac{1}{3} \rightarrow \frac{5}{6} \qquad \frac{1}{(\sqrt{2}+1)^3} \rightarrow 5\sqrt{2} - 7$$

rather than 0.8333... and 0.07106 .... of course, an arbitrarily precise numerical approximation can be computed on demand.

Computer algebra systems often produce complex symbolic results of unpredictable size. This implies the use of dynamic memory management (e.g. garbage collection—$q.v.$), the main reasons why Lisp ($q.v.$) is so often used as an implementation language.

Correctness

In most current symbolic computation systems, simplifications such as $(x+y)/(x+y) \rightarrow 1$ are performed automatically, without considering that x must not be equal to—y for this to make sense. Computer algebra systems must be allowed to make an occasional mistake in order to produce efficient simplification in the great majority of cases. Another example is the automatic simplification $0 \times f(1000) \rightarrow 0$ before evaluation of $f(1000)$. This simplification is obviously desirable except when $f(1000)$ may be undefined, or infinity. The user should be aware that all systems will perform some simplifications that are not safe 100% of the time.

The Systems

All systems to be described are interactive general-purpose computer algebra systems that provide the following three key capabilities:

- *Symbolic computations*: all systems provide routines for expansion and factoring of polynomials, differentiation and integration (definite and indefinite), series computation, solving equations and systems of equations, and linear algebra.
- *Numeric computations*: all systems support arbitrary precision numerical computation including computation of definite integrals, numerical solutions of equations, and evaluation of elementary and special functions.
- *Graphics*: all systems except Reduce allow plotting of two- and three-dimensional graphics.

Additionally, each system has an associated programming language that allows the user to extend its operations.

Macsyma

The Macsyma (Macsyma Inc., 1995) project was founded by William Martin and Joel Moses of MIT. Macsyma was built upon a predecessor MIT project, Mathlab 68, an interactive general-purpose system. The Macsyma system internals were first implemented in Maclisp, a systems programming dialect of Lisp ($q.v.$) developed at MIT. PC and Unix versions of Macsyma are now distributed by Macsyma Inc. The Macsyma kernel is currently written in Common Lisp. The external math libraries are written in Common Lisp or the Macsyma language. Macsyma users can translate programs into Lisp. This allows interpretation by the Lisp interpreter (instead of the Macsyma language interpreter, which itself is coded in Lisp). The Lisp compiler can be applied to the translation to take the further step of compiling the program into machine code.

Reduce

Reduce, by Anthony Hearn, was originally written in Lisp to assist symbolic computation in high energy physics in the late 1960s. Its user base grew beyond the particle physics community as its general-purpose facilities were found to be useful in many other mathematical situations. Reduce 2 was ported to several different machines and operating systems during the 1970s, making it the most widely distributed system of that time, and one of the first efforts in Lisp portability. Reduce 3, written in the "Standard Lisp" dialect, is a further refinement and enhancement. Reduce, like Macsyma, has a simple syntax for the basic mathematical commands (expression evaluation, differentiation, integration, etc.), and a Fortran-like programming language.

Derive

Derive (Rich *et al.*, 1994) was developed by Albert Rich and David Stoutemyer and is marketed by Soft Warehouse Inc. It is also implemented in Lisp and will run on any IBM PC compatible. Derive is the successor to μMath and is menu-driven. Many commands and operations can be carried out with just two or three keystrokes. In addition to μMath, it has a powerful graphics package that can plot functions in two and three dimensions. One can plot more than one function on the same graph and use multiple windows for easy comparisons. Derive supports all basic symbolic mathematics, such as factorization, integration, and differentiation. It also understands matrices and vectors and can do basic vector calculus. Although Derive is less capable than other general-purpose computer algebra systems, the extent of its power based on such minimal hardware is remarkable. Nonetheless, it lacks, for example, procedures for solving systems of nonlinear equations, computation of eigenvectors of matrices, and special features such as Laplace transforms, Fourier transforms, and Bessel functions.

Mathematica

The development of Mathematica (Wolfram, 1996) was started by Stephen Wolfram in 1986. The first version of the system was released by Wolfram

Research, Inc. in 1988. Mathematica was designed to be a computer algebra system with graphics, numerical computation, and a flexible programming language.

In Mathematica, patterns are used to match classes of expressions with a given structure. Pattern matching and transformation/rewrite rules greatly simplify the programming of mathematical functions because one need only define replacements for patterns. For example, consider the definition of the logarithm of a product or a power:

```
In[1] := log[x_y_] := log[x] + log[y]
In[2] := log[x_^y_] := y log[x].
```

These definitions are global rules. Such a rule is applied to all expressions automatically if the left-hand side of the rule matches the expression, that is, the heads are equal and the arguments match. This is in contrast to rewrite rules, which are applied on demand. Pattern matching is structural, not mathematical, so b^2 is not recognized as the product b × b. However, the pattern matcher recognizes that multiplication is associative:

```
In[3]:= f[log[2ab^2]]
Out[3]= f[log[2] + log[a] + 2 log[b]]
```

Mathematica's colorful plotting features are very good. It provides two- and three-dimensional graphs, along with flexibility to rotate and change the viewpoint easily. The plot in Fig. 1 was generated with the command

```
Plot3D[Sin[xy], {x, 0, 3}, {y, 0, 3},
        PlotPoints -> 31, Boxed -> False]
```

Maple

The Maple (Waterloo Maple Inc., 1996) project was started by Keith Geddes and Gaston Gonnet at the University of Waterloo in November 1980. Maple is distributed by Waterloo Maple Inc. It followed from the construction of an experimental system (named "wama") which proved the feasibility of writing a symbolic computation system in system implementation

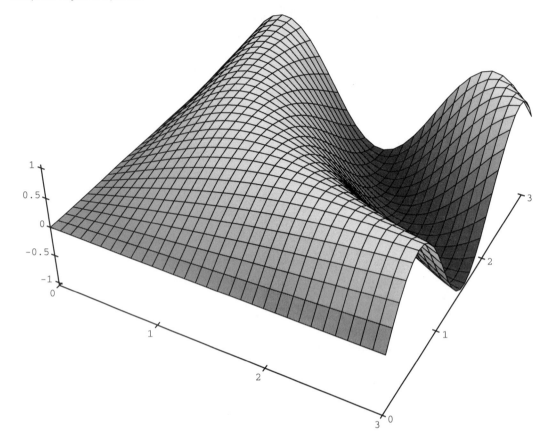

Figure 1.   Mathematica plot of the function sin(xy).

languages and running it in a crowded time-sharing environment.

Maple was designed and implemented to be a pleasant programming language, as well as being compact, efficient, portable, and extensible. Maple is reminiscent of Algol 68 (*q.v.*) without declarations, but also includes several functional programming (*q.v.*) paradigms. The internal mathematical libraries are written in the same language provided to users. Maple's kernel interprets this language relatively efficiently. Most higher-level functions or packages, about 95% of the functionality (e.g. integration, solving equations, normalization of expressions, radical simplification, and factorization), are all coded in the user language. Primitive functions, like arithmetic, basic simplification, polynomial division, manipulations of structures,

series arithmetic, and integer gcds, are coded in the kernel.

Maple supports a large collection of specialized data structures: integers, rationals, floating-point numbers, expression trees, series, equations, sets, ranges, lists, arrays, tables, and so on. All of these are objects that can be easily type-tested, assembled, or disassembled. Maple V incorporates a new user interface for the X Window system that includes 3D plotting and separate help windows, allows editing of input expressions, and maintains a log of a Maple session.

Axiom

Axiom (Jenks and Sutor, 1992) is a system developed at the IBM Thomas J. Watson Research Center and presently distributed by the Numerical Algorithms Group (NAG). Axiom is implemented in Lisp and runs on all major Unix (*q.v.*) platforms as well as on PCs.

Axiom is both a language for casual algebraic computing and an object-oriented programming language complete with abstract data types (*q.v.*), and information hiding (*q.v.*) designed to allow description and implementation of mathematical code at a high level. Axiom also includes a compiler that can be used to extend the system with user-defined functions and data types.

Examples

In this section, we present some examples which define the boundaries of what computer algebra systems can and cannot do. The successful results we call "remarkable," are so in the sense that it is surprising that computer algebra systems can obtain them. In the future, systems might evolve that will be able to solve the ones we now call "difficult/impossible."

Difficult/Impossible Problems

- For which values of n is $\int dx/(x^n\sqrt{1-x^3})$ integrable in closed form?
- Let H be a Banach space. . . (computer algebra systems cannot handle such abstract concepts at present).
- Test whether the expression $\varsigma(3/2) + 4\pi\varsigma(-1/2)$ is or is not equal to zero, where $\varsigma(s)$ is the Riemann zeta function.
- Solve the nonlinear differential equation $y''(x) - 2y^2(x)/x = 0$.

Remarkable Solutions

- Series expansion of

$$R(s) = \int_0^\infty \frac{\ln(1+st)}{1+t^2}\,dt$$

```
> series ( int ( ln (1 + s * t)/(1 + t ^ 2), t=0..infinity), s = 0);
```

$$(-\ln(s)+1)\,s + 1/4\,Pi\,s^2 + (1/3\,\ln(s) - 1/9)\,s^3 - 1/8\,Pi\,s^4$$
$$+ (-1/5\,\ln(s) + 1/25)\,s^5 + O(s^6)$$

- We define $\{x_n\}$ to be the sequence of iterated sines, i.e. $x_{n+1} = \sin(x_n)$. What is the asymptotic expansion of x_n for $n \to \infty$?

```
> asympt (rsolve (x(n + 1) = sin (x(n)), x), n);
```

$$\frac{3^{1/2}}{n^{1/2}} + \frac{\_C - 3/10\ 3^{1/2}\ln(n)}{n^{3/2}} + O(1/n^2)$$

where $\_C$ is a constant which depends on the value of x_0.
- $\int \tan(\arctan(x)/3)\,d\,x$ in terms of tangents and arctangents:

```
integrate( tan(atan(x)/3), x)
```

$$(1)\quad \frac{8\log\left(3\tan\left(\frac{atan(x)}{3}\right)^2 - 1\right) - 3\tan\left(\frac{atan(x)}{3}\right)^2 + 18x\tan\left(\frac{atan(x)}{3}\right) + 16}{18}$$

```
Type: Union (Expression Integer, List Expression Integer)
```

Bibliography

1992. Jenks, R., and Sutor, R. *AXIOM: The Scientific Computation System*. New York: Springer-Verlag.

1994. Rich, A., Rich, J., and Stoutemyer, D. R. *DERIVE Version 3 User Manual. Honolulu*, HI: Soft Warehouse, Inc.

1995. Hearn, A. C. *REDUCE User's Manual*, Version 3.6. Report CP 78, RAND.

1995. Macsyma, Inc. *Macsyma User's Guide*, 2nd Ed. Arlington, MA: Macsyma, Inc.

1996. Waterloo Maple Inc. *Maple V Learning Guide*. New York: Springer-Verlag.

1996. Wolfram, S. *The Mathematica Book*, 3rd Ed. Cambridge: Wolfram Media/Cambridge University Press.

Gaston H. Gonnet, Dominik W. Gruntz, and Laurent Bernardin

COMPUTER ANIMATION

For articles on related topics, *see*

+ Artificial Life
+ Computer-Aided Design/Computer-Aided Manufacturing (CAD/CAM)
+ Computer Art
+ Computer Games
+ Computer Graphics
+ Entertainment Industry, Computers in the
+ Image Processing
+ Scientific Applications
+ Simulation
+ Virtual Reality

Animation can infuse a sequence of inert images with the illusion of motion and life. Creating this illusion is not easy. Traditionally, animation has been created by drawing images at certain key points in the action. These images, known as *keyframes*, outline the motion for the sequence. Later, the images between the keyframes are filled in to complete the sequence, in a process called *in-betweening*. For example, to keyframe hitting a ball, the animator would draw several key moments in the sequence such as the impact of the bat on the ball and the follow-through of the swing. The remaining images would be filled in later, perhaps by a different animator.

The most basic computer animation tools automatically interpolate between the keyframes of images or models. Animation tools have also been developed to assemble ("*composite*") multiple layers of an animated scene in much the same way that layers of *cels* are used in traditional animation. Other, more powerful, techniques make use of computer graphics algorithms that render the images from geometric descriptions of the scene. These techniques change the task from drawing sequences of images by hand to using computer tools effectively to specify how the images should change over time.

Complex computer animation techniques are either two-dimensional (2D) or three-dimensional (3D). Although there is some overlap, 2D techniques tend to focus on image manipulation while 3D techniques build virtual worlds in which characters and objects move and interact.

Two-Dimensional Animation

The impact of 2D techniques can be as spectacular as the addition of ET to a shot of the moon or as subtle as the removal of the guide wires used to suspend Superman. These techniques provide the tools used for blending or morphing between images, embedding graphical objects in video footage, or creating abstract patterns from mathematical equations.

Morphing refers to animations where an image or model of one object is metamorphosed into another. In Michael Jackson's music video *Black or White*, the animators at Pacific Data Images created morphs between people with strikingly different facial characteristics. This work is remarkable because the faces in the intermediate images appear natural and human-like. Unfortunately, morphing is labor intensive because the key elements of each image must be specified by hand.

Embedding graphical objects into an existing image allows new elements to be added to a scene. For example, the ghosts in *Casper* and many of the dinosaurs in *Jurassic Park* were computer generated and then composited into existing footage. Objects can also be removed from a scene. The bus in *Speed* flies over a gap in a bridge that was created by digitally removing a span from footage of an intact bridge. Mathematical equations are often used to create abstract motion sequences. When the values of the mathematical functions are mapped into color space and varied with time, the motion of the underlying structures can be quite beautiful. Fractals (*q.v.*), such as those shown in that article, are an example of functions that create attractive patterns.

Three-Dimensional Animation

With 3D techniques, the animator constructs a virtual world in which characters and objects move and interact. Using a virtual 3D world to generate images for an animation involves three steps: *modeling*, animating, and rendering. Modeling deals with the task of setting up the elements in a scene and describing each of them, while *rendering* deals with converting the descriptions of objects and their motions into images.

Modeling Requirements

To animate motion, the user needs both a static description of an object and information about how the object can move. One common way to specify this additional information is to use an *articulated model* such as the one shown in Fig. 1. An articulated model is a collection of objects connected by joints in a hierarchical, tree-like structure. The location of an object is determined by the location of the objects above it in the hierarchy. For example, the motion of the elbow joint in a human model will affect not only the position of the lower arm but also the position of the hand and fingers. The object at the top of the hierarchy, or the root of the tree, can be moved arbitrarily, affecting the position and orientation of the entire model.

A second type of model is a *particle system* or collection of points. The motion of the particles through space is determined by a set of rules. The laws of physics provide a basis for the motion so that the particles will fall under gravity and collide with other objects in the environment. Systems that are well modeled by particle systems include water spray, smoke, and even flocks of birds.

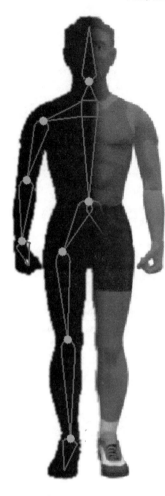

Figure 1.   An articulated model of a human male: the structure of the joint hierarchy is shown on the left while the right side shows the graphical model used for rendering.

Deformable objects are a third type of model and include objects that do not have well-defined articulated joints but still have too much structure to be represented easily with a particle system. Water, hair, clothing, and fish are among the systems that have been successfully modeled as deformable objects.

Rendering Requirements

Motion blur is a rendering technique that is required for animation, but not for most still images. Without motion blur, rapid motion of an object in a series of frames creates unpleasant strobing effects or causes objects, such as stagecoach wheels in old westerns, to appear to rotate in the wrong direction. To solve this problem, a fast-moving object can be rendered in several of the positions it had during the period of time represented by each frame. This rendering technique creates a blurred representation of the object and mimics the exposure of film by a camera shutter that is open for short period of time.

Motion Generation

Even animating a simple object like a bouncing ball can present problems. In part, this task is difficult because humans are very skilled at observing motion and can quickly pick out motion that is unnatural or implausible. In many situations, the animator must be able to specify subtle details of the motion in order to convey the personality of a character or the mood of an animation in a compelling fashion. All available tools require a trade-off between automation and control. *Keyframing* allows fine control but does little to insure naturalness. *Procedural methods* and *motion capture* generate motion automatically but offer little control over fine details.

Keyframing

Keyframing requires that the animator specify key positions for the objects being animated. The computer then interpolates to determine the positions for the in-between frames. The interpolation algorithm is an important factor in the appearance of the final motion. The simplest form of interpolation, *linear interpolation*, often results in motion that appears to be jerky because the velocities of the moving objects are discontinuous. Better interpolation techniques, such as *splines* (*q.v.*), can be used to produce smoothly interpolated curves.

The specification of keyframes can be made easier with techniques such as *inverse kinematics*. Inverse kinematics aids in the placement of articulated models by allowing the animator to specify the position of one object and then have the positions of the objects above it in the articulated hierarchy computed automatically. For example, if the hand and torso of an animated character must be in particular locations, inverse kinematics allows the computer to calculate the angle at the elbow and shoulder.

Procedural Methods

Current technology is not capable of generating motion automatically for arbitrary objects; however, it is possible to build algorithms for specific types of motion or objects. These techniques are called *procedural methods* because a computer procedurally follows an algorithm to generate the motion. Procedural methods have two main advantages over keyframing techniques: they make it easy to generate a family of similar motions, and they can be used for complex systems that would be too difficult to animate by hand, such as particle systems or flexible surfaces.

Physically based simulation refers to a class of procedural methods that make use of the laws of physics, or an approximation to those laws, to generate motion. Simulated motion is inherently realistic and for many applications that is an advantage. Simulations can be divided into two categories: *passive and active*. Passive systems have no internal energy source and can move only when an external force acts on them. Passive systems are well suited to physically based simulation because once the physical laws have been encoded correctly and the initial conditions of the animation have been specified, the method is ready for use. Pools of water, clothing, hair, and leaves have been animated using passive simulations. Active systems have an internal source of energy and can move on their own. People, animals, and robots are examples of active systems. These systems are more difficult to model because in addition to implementing the physical laws, the behavior of the simulated muscles or motors must be specified.

Procedural methods can also be used to generate motion for groups of objects that move together. Flocks of birds, schools of fish, herds of animals, or crowds of people are all situations where algorithms for *group behaviors* can be used. In Walt Disney's animated version of *The Hunchback of Notre Dame*, most of the crowd scenes were computer animated using procedural models. This animated film is particularly impressive because computer and hand animation are seamlessly combined to create very detailed scenes.

Motion capture

A third technique for generating motion, *motion capture*, employs special sensors, called *trackers*, to record the motion of a human performer. The recorded data is then used to generate the motion for an animation. Alternatively, special puppets with joint angle sensors can be used in place of the human performer. The technology used for motion capture makes it difficult to capture some motions. One class of sensors are magnetic but metal in the environment creates noise in the data. Another class of sensors requires that the actor be connected to the computer by an "umbilical cord," thereby restricting the actor's motion. All sensing technologies have a relatively small field of view, limiting the kinds of actions that can be captured.

Bibliography

1996. Kerlow, I. V. *The Art of 3-D Computer Animation and Imaging*. New York: Van Nostrand Reinhold.

1996. Taylor, R. *The Encyclopedia of Animation Techniques*. London: Quarto.

1997. Gianbruno, M. *3D Graphics and Animation: From Starting Up to Standing Out*. Indianapolis, IN: New-Riders Publishing.

Jessica K. Hodgins and James F. O'Brien

COMPUTER ARCHITECTURE

For articles on related subjects, *see*

+ Addressing
+ Arithmetic-Logic Unit (ALU)
+ Bus
+ Cache Memory
+ Central Processing Unit (CPU)
+ Channel
+ Digital Computer
+ Index Register
+ Input–Output Operations
+ Instruction Decoding
+ Instruction-Level Parallelism
+ Instruction Set
+ Interrupt
+ Memory
+ Memory Hierarchy
+ Memory-Mapped I/O
+ Microprogramming
+ Network Architecture
+ Parallel Processing: Architectures
+ Program Counter
+ Reduced Instruction Set Computer (RISC)
+ Register
+ von Neumann Machine

Introduction

Computer architecture is concerned with the physical or hardware structure of computer systems, the attributes of their various parts, and how these parts are interconnected. For the purpose of this article, two fundamental aspects of computer architecture will be identified:

1. *System architecture*: the functional behavior and conceptual structure of a computer system as seen by an assembly language programmer. Characteristics considered are word length, number base, arithmetic modes (1s vs 2s complement), primitive data types, operand addresses per instruction (0 to 4), addressing modes, registers, and command repertoire (instruction set–*q.v.*).

2. *Implementation architecture*: those characteristics affecting the relative cost and performance of a computer system and which are of concern to the semiconductor designer or electronic engineer, such as logic design, memory *bandwidth* (*q.v.*), and device technology.

Subsystems

The three major subsystems of a computer are memory, processor(s), and its input–output and communication subsystem. We discuss each of these from both the system and implementation architecture perspectives. Except where otherwise noted, a classic von Neumann stored-program machine design is assumed.

Storage

The *storage*, or *memory*, of a stored-program computer system contains both the data to be processed by the system and the instructions indicating what processing is to be performed. Three levels of storage are generally identified: registers, main random-access memory (RAM), and secondary or auxiliary storage (*see* MEMORY: AUXILIARY). Table 1 indicates the general characteristics of each of these. Regardless of the level, the fundamental unit of binary digital computer storage is the *bit*, having one of two distinct values: 0 or 1. Aggregates of bits are combined into larger units, such as *nibbles* (4 bits), *bytes* (8 bits), and *words* (anywhere from 16 to 64 bits or more). As a rule, the longer its word length, the more powerful the computer.

Early computer systems organized memory as fixed-length words, where each word was referenced as a unit by a single memory address, and the individual bits of a word were transferred as a group between a computer's main memory and its registers or secondary storage. Each word would contain a single instruction or datum. The *arithmetic–logic unit* (ALU) would operate on one word of data at a time.

A contemporary computer, by contrast, might address data in groups of 8 bits, transfer data to registers in groups of 16 bits, transfer data to secondary storage in groups of 64 bits, operate arithmetically on data "words" of 32 bits, have variable-length instructions ranging from 16 to 48 bits, and use a 24-bit memory address. What, then, is the computer's word length? The most commonly accepted definition is that it is the length of a typical arithmetic register. This is usually equal to the number of bits operated on in parallel by the arithmetic unit, and may or may not be equal to the

number of bits needed to hold a single-precision integer. A related quantity, the number of bits transferred in parallel from the main memory to the processor, is called the *data path*.

Registers

Registers were once the fastest and most expensive memory units in a computer. Today, because of advances in semiconductor technology, main memories and registers can be essentially equal in cost and performance, but their functions remain distinct. Registers are a computer's most frequently used memory units, playing a role in the execution of every instruction. They also tend to be few in number, both to enhance performance by keeping them physically "close" to the processing elements, and to make possible a shorter addressing scheme in the instruction format.

The minimum complement of registers is one: an arithmetic register or *accumulator* that serves to hold the intermediate results of computations or other data processing activities. (Although usually part of the system architecture, accumulators may be hidden from the software in some designs such as those using a *stack* (*q.v.*) for computation). Most current computers have multiple accumulators so that several intermediate results may be maintained. Other registers usually found in contemporary computers include a *status register*, indicating the current condition of the various hardware components and computational results; and a *program counter*, indicating the location in main memory of the next instruction to be executed. In addition to these, many computers have *index registers* for counting and for "pointing" into tables; *address or base registers*, containing addresses of blocks of main or secondary memory; a *stack pointer*, containing the address of a

Table 1.

Type	Access time	Number or capacity	Use
Registers	10–50 ns	1–4096	Data, status, control info, current instruction
Cache memory	10–100 ns	512 KB–16 MB	Frequently used instruction and data
Main Memory	20–100 ns	64 MB–4 GB	Programs, data
Auxiliary memory	10–250 ms	100 MB–1 TB	Long-term storage

special block of registers or main memory, which is treated like a pushdown stack; and various *special-purpose registers*, whose functions depend on the details of the particular computer.

Main memory

The main memory contains programs and data that are ready for processing by the computer. It consists of a linear sequence of "words," each individually address-able and each capable of being read or overwritten. The performance of a computer depends on the size and speed of its main memory. The total number of words in a memory is typically a configuration decision, with upper and lower limits determined by both the system and implementation architectures. The speed of memory is determined by implementation and cost factors, and is also influenced by size in the sense that very large memories must be physically more distant from the processor and therefore take longer to access. Numerous techniques have been used to increase the effective speed of a memory system. *Caching and interleaving* are the two most popular.

Caching is a technique whereby a small, high-speed memory is used to contain the most frequently used words from a larger, slower main memory. If the "hit ratio" (percentage of memory references found in the small *cache memory—q.v.*) is high, the average speed of the entire memory is substantially increased.

With *interleaving* (*q.v.*), two or more independent memory systems are combined in such a way that they appear as one faster memory system. In one approach, all words with even addresses come from one memory bank, and all words with odd addresses come from another. When an even-numbered word is fetched, the next-higher odd-numbered word is fetched simultaneously from the other memory system, on the theory that it is likely to be the next word requested.

The form in which memory is presented to the software by the system architecture is sometimes called the *logical address space* or the *virtual address space*. In the most straightforward designs, the logical address space is a *linear* sequence of words or bytes containing the programs being executed and the data to be acted upon. It will differ from the physical memory (implementation) mainly in size (number of words). Two potential drawbacks of a linear approach are that large memories require use of large effective addresses, which costs more to implement, makes instructions longer, and generally makes processing slower (it takes n bits to address 2^n words); and that it may be awkward to partition a linear space into several parts that have different purposes.

To deal with these drawbacks, certain system architectures provide a more complex logical address space. In one design, the address space is perceived by software as a set of *pages*. Each page is a sequence of words; all pages are the same in size (usually a power of two); and each page has a distinct identification number or page number. A memory address consists of two parts: a page number and a word offset or displacement within the page (*see* VIRTUAL MEMORY).

Another approach is the *segment* design, in which there are several independently numbered blocks called segments, but with no requirement that they all be the same size. This permits each software module to be placed in whatever size segment is most suitable. Segment and page designs may be combined so that each segment contains several pages and the size of a segment is a multiple of the page size.

Memory mapping

Memory mapping is the translation between the logical address space and the physical memory. The objectives of memory mapping are (1) to translate from logical to physical address, (2) to aid in memory protection (*q.v.*), and (3) to enable better management of memory resources. Mapping is important to computer performance, both locally (how long it takes to execute an instruction) and globally (how long it takes to run a set of programs). In effect, each time a program presents a logical memory address and requests that the corresponding memory word be accessed, the mapping mechanism must translate that address into an appropriate physical memory location. The simpler this translation, the lower the implementation cost and the higher the performance of the individual memory reference.

There are two fundamental situations to be handled. When the logical address space is smaller than the physical address space (common to microcontrollers, microprocessors, and older mini- and mainframe computers, mapping is needed to gain access to all of physical memory). When the logical address space is larger than the physical address space, mapping is used to insure that each logical address generated corresponds to an existing physical memory cell.

The size of the logical address space is determined by the number of bits in a memory address. Typically, the size of an address is limited by the word length of the computer. On a typical 1980s vintage computer with a 16-bit word, only 2^{16} or about 65 000 words could be addressed. Technology now permits such systems to be attached physically to many times this memory, but there is no direct way to address it without redesigning the instruction set. Thus, the primary purpose of a memory mapping mechanism on such a system is to enable the logical address space to be assigned to a desired portion of a larger physical address space.

In paging, the logical address space is divided into a set of equal-sized blocks called *pages*, and each is mapped onto a block of physical memory called a *page frame*. Each page must begin at a page frame boundary in physical memory. The primary advantage of paging is that it allows a contiguous logical address space to be split into several noncontiguous physical frames. This permits sharing of some of a program's pages among multiple processes without complete overlap of physical addresses. The page map file is often kept in a cache memory.

Segmenting breaks the logical address space into several blocks, but does not require them to be of any particular size or to be mapped into any particular physical frames. Physical addresses are obtained by biasing the individual segments. This approach is the most flexible but also the most costly, both in hardware and performance. It requires both a segment table and an extra addition operation per memory reference.

Auxiliary memory (secondary storage)

Auxiliary memory is the lowest-cost, highest-capacity, and slowest-access storage in a computer system. It is where programs and data are kept for long-term storage or when not in immediate use. Such memories tend to occur in two types—sequential access (data must be accessed in a linear sequence) and *direct access* (data may be accessed in any sequence). The most common sequential storage device is the magnetic tape, whereas direct-access devices include rotating drums, disks, CD-ROMs and DVD-ROMs (*see* OPTICAL STORAGE).

Virtual memory and memory hierarchies

The idea of virtual memory is to give the programmer the illusion of a very large main memory, even though a lesser amount of main memory is actually available. This is achieved by placing the contents of the large, virtual memory on an auxiliary storage device and bringing parts of it into the main memory, as required by the program, in a way that is transparent to the program. Virtual memory is prevalent in systems with large word lengths (large logical address sizes), although it is found in systems of all sizes.

A concept related to virtual memory is that of *hierarchical memory* (*see* MEMORY HIERARCHY). In its simplest form, this means that there is a hierarchy of memory types ranging from "large and slow" to "small and fast." The important idea, however, is to give the programmer access to only one type of logical memory (typically, "main" memory), with unseen implementation techniques making this memory appear both fast and plentiful. Caches and interleaving (*see* MEMORY: MAIN) are popular techniques for achieving a high apparent speed, and virtual memory techniques are used to achieve a large apparent size.

Processing

The processing unit of a computer system consists of two parts: the control unit, which governs the operation of the system, and the arithmetic–logic unit (ALU), which carries out the computational and processing functions. In addition to the register set, key issues in processing unit architecture are the instruction set and the extent of parallelism.

Instruction set

An instruction occupies one or more words of storage, and its purpose is to specify an operation to be performed by the processor. An instruction (Fig. 1) consists of an *operation code* (*op code*), which indicates the general nature of the function to be performed; possibly one or more *flags*, denoting special modes of operation; and possibly one or more *addresses*, which specify the operands or data to be operated upon. An instruction format is usually characterized by the number of such operand specifiers, and although a given processor will usually support several instruction formats, one will tend to predominate. Most common today is the "three-address" format, although small processors have "one-address" and "two-address" instruction formats. Consider a typical instruction, "integer add," which requires three operands: two integer numbers to be added, and one integer result. With a three-address format, the location (address) of all three operands would be specified directly. With a two-address format, one of the three would be implicit—typically, a register or the top of a stack. A one-address format would have two implicit operands, and so forth.

The field of an instruction that identifies an operand may contain several subfields, and may require a significant amount of computation just to determine the location of the operand. The various ways of identifying an operand are called addressing modes. A representative set of *addressing modes* is as follows:

Operation	Flags

Zero address (data implicit)

Operation	Flags	Address 1

One address

Operation	Flags	Address 1	Address 2

Two address

Operation	Flags	Address 1	Address 2	Address 3

Three address

Figure 1. Typical instruction formats.

In addition to the format of a computer's instructions, the architect must consider their semantics, that is, what functions they perform. For example, one issue is how to compare different values. In one approach, a "compare" instruction compares the values of two operands and sets a *condition code*, indicating whether the first operand is less than, equal to, or greater than the other. This code can be tested or stored for later use. An alternative approach is to simply subtract one item from the other and test the sign and value of the result. The condition code approach is more flexible, especially for comparing nonnumeric quantities, but it is also more expensive to implement (*see* INSTRUCTION SET).

CISC and RISC

For many years, instruction sets were designed on the basis of the register set, word length, technology characteristics, and the designer's concept of how programs would be written (generally based on assembly language programming styles). The functions performed were quite simple, such as controlling the sequence of instruction execution, shifting data, adding numbers together, and comparing values. Among the first "higher-level" features found in instruction sets were instructions to perform floating-point calculations.

In the mid-1970s, more designers began to examine what actual programs do. Initially, this work led to direct instruction set support for such "high-level" functions as procedure calling, list searching, and complex array access. As the computers of this period developed more and more complex features, they came

**Operand specifier format
(in address field of instruction)**

type	designator

Type	Operand class	Designator interpretation
0	Immediate	Operand is designator itself
1	Direct	Designator is address of operand
2	Indirect	Designator is address of memory cell containing address of operand
3	Register	Designator indicates a register containing the operand

to be known eventually as Complex Instruction Set Computers (CISC). The trend was toward even more complex architectures that provide direct support for high-level languages.

However, another trend was quietly developing among those trying to develop better microprocessors and microcomputers—entire processors and/or computers on a single, very large-scale integrated circuit (VLSI) (*see* INTEGRATED CIRCUITRY). Some of the more complex CISC instructions perform functions that can be accomplished just as well, if not better, by short sequences of simpler instructions. This observation led to reduced instruction set computers (RISC), which have only a few carefully selected instructions but a large number of registers.

Tagged architectures

In the von Neumann type of instruction set, there is no distinction made in storage between instructions and data. That is, it would be possible to perform an addition operation on a bit pattern representing an instruction and, although the results might be meaningless, the computer would probably not detect any problem. Such cases are the cause of numerous programming errors. To avoid this, some computers use a *tagged architecture*, in which each memory word consists of two parts: the "data" part, which contains conventional data or instruction, and the "tag" part, which is a few extra bits that describe the data part. Because the type of data is implied by the word containing the data, it is no longer necessary to have separate instructions for each data type supported by the machine. Instead of "integer add," "floating-point add," and "decimal add," a tagged architecture needs only a single "generic" instruction: "add." The tag fields indicate the specific type of addition to be performed.

Microprogramming

One technique for implementing processing units is *microprogramming* (*q.v.*). In this technique, each instruction can be thought of as a "subroutine call" to a program written in a lower-level language whose domain includes the data paths and registers of the processor. An advantage of microprogramming is that

hardware design errors can be corrected by simply revising the microprograms instead of changing the circuitry. This is a particularly important advantage because the entire processing function may be embedded in a single silicon circuit. Normally, microprograms are stored in a "read-only" memory device (ROM), both to reduce cost and to avoid loss of information during a loss of power.

Parallelism

The speed with which instructions can be processed is determined by two factors: how fast the circuitry can perform a single instruction, and how many instructions can be performed in parallel. Circuit speed is largely determined by system cost, as limited by the available circuit technology, which now is limited by the fundamental laws of physics. Thus, to achieve the speed desired in high-performance systems, efforts are made to achieve high degrees of parallelism.

Parallelism requires the use of multiple processors, and one of the first design issues is whether they should share the same main memory (tightly coupled) or have their own separate memories (loosely coupled). Either way, each processor generally has its own registers, and they generally share at least some of the secondary storage and peripherals.

A second issue is whether to use a small number of very powerful processors or a very large number of simple processors (massive parallelism). The latter approach generally involves tight coupling and an intricate design for the memory access mechanism. Algorithm design plays an important role in the effective use of massively parallel processors.

A third issue is whether to associate processors in a "pipeline" or "assembly line" fashion, with each stream of data passing through several processors, or whether to assign each processor to work on a separate stream of data.

Input-Output and Communication

I/O devices share certain characteristics with auxiliary storage devices. I/O devices have relatively low access speed and are usually capable of operating more or less independently of the main processing unit. Thus, a complex "loosely coupled" connection to the processor and main memory is required. Because of their relatively low speed, it is desirable to keep these devices in continuous operation, so that their maximum performance potential can be realized. Low speed and independent operation make it attractive to allow several devices to operate simultaneously. The fundamental issues of I/O architecture relate to the means of transferring data between these devices and main memory, and to the process of coordinating and synchronizing multiple devices.

Communication paths

A peripheral or storage device must be connected to either the processor or the main memory. A *data path* is a collection of wires or other connecting medium that accomplishes this task. More capable data paths may involve their own special-purpose processing units. Data paths are generally grouped into three types: *simplex* paths allow data to flow in only a single direction; *half-duplex* paths allow data to flow in either direction, but only one at a time; *full-duplex* paths allow data to flow in both directions simultaneously. A simplex path might be used to connect an input-only device (e.g. a keyboard) to the computer or to connect the computer to an output-only device (e.g. a display or printer). A half-duplex path would be used to connect a device that does both input and output, but only one at a time (e.g. a tape drive). A full-duplex path is necessary when the device needs to do both input and output at the same time or requires rapid switching between input and output modes.

A *channel* (*q.v.*) is a data path connecting a peripheral device directly to a memory system. If more than one device is required, each may be connected to a different channel, or there may be a way for several devices to share the same channel. Simple shared channels permit only one device to transmit data at a time, whereas multiplexor channels allow interleaved data transfers from several devices. *Multiplexing* (*q.v.*) can be performed by dividing the channel into several parallel subchannels or by time multiplexing, in which units of data from different devices alternate.

A *bus* is a data path that connects devices in parallel, more or less like a party line. Any device can use the bus, but one of the devices is designated as a master, and it controls access to the bus by issuing authorization signals. Information is transmitted across a bus in two parts: address and data. Each device is associated with a specific address or range of addresses, and when an address comes down the bus the associated device is designated to receive or send the associated data. An advantage of the bus is simplicity in connecting things to the main memory system. Only one bus-to-memory connection need be made. All contention (*q.v.*) for memory access is resolved with the bus, rather than with the memory interface. This permits memory access to remain fast and simple, while allowing many devices to have direct access to memory.

Control

Control of input and output must accomplish initiation of the transfer, synchronization of communicating devices, and completion reporting. Three potential "players" in this process are the main processor, the main memory, and a peripheral or secondary storage device. The data path is the medium of communication, and it often handles much of the synchronization.

The most straightforward approach to controlling the transmission of data is *program-controlled* I/O. Under such a scheme, the processor directs the input and output activity. In one approach, an *explicit instruction* initiates the transfer by commanding a device to accept a small amount of data (typically one word or byte) for display or storage (output) or to transmit a small unit of data to the processor (input).

An alternative to the use of explicit instructions is *memory-mapped I/O* (*q.v.*). This technique has the processor direct activity by writing to certain reserved cells in its logical memory space called *control words*. Control words may actually be implemented as reserved main memory cells or may be implemented within the device itself. The act of writing into a control word causes the address of that word to be sent out across the memory bus.

The memory-mapped approach simplifies the control interface and the instruction set. Its main drawbacks are that it puts "holes" in the logical address space (i.e. sections of the address space that cannot be used as genuine memory cells), and it complicates caching and virtual memory.

Direct memory access (DMA) is a technique for reducing processor involvement during the transfer of blocks of data. This technique incorporates specific concepts of both control and communication. DMA not only allows transmission directly between devices and memory, as the name implies, but, as commonly defined, it eliminates the high processor control overhead described earlier. With DMA, the main processor will initiate the transfer of a block of data, with the "completion" notification coming only when the entire block has been moved. Meanwhile, while data is still flowing, the processor can do other useful work.

Interrupts and traps

These two techniques are very similar, and some designs do not distinguish between them. Both are methods of notifying the processor of an event. A *trap* signals an abnormal event within the processor, such as an arithmetic fault, illegal instruction, or power failure. An *interrupt* notifies the processor of an external event, such as completion of an I/O operation. Traps generally force the processor to stop what it is doing and deal immediately with the event. Interrupts usually signal events that are less urgent than traps, and the processor need not always respond immediately. Vectored interrupt schemes often associate a distinct priority with each distinct interrupt address. There remains some dispute as to whether this degree of priority distinction is really necessary for most applications. Too many priority levels can lead to excessive "context switch" overhead as one device interrupts another.

Bibliography

1990. Hennessy, J. L., and Patterson, D. A. *Computer Architecture: A Quantitative Approach*. San Francisco, CA: Morgan Kaufmann.

1993. Hwang, K. *Advanced Computer Architecture: Parallelism, Scalability, Programmability*. New York: McGraw-Hill.

1996. Stallings, W. *Computer Organization and Architecture*, 4th Ed. Upper Saddle River, NJ: Prentice Hall.

1998. Patterson, D. A., and Hennessy, J. L. *Computer Organization and Design*, 2nd Ed. San Francisco, CA: Morgan Kaufmann.

Dennis J. Frailey

COMPUTER ARITHMETIC

See ARITHMETIC, COMPUTER; COMPLEMENT; and NUMBERS AND NUMBER SYSTEMS.

COMPUTER ART

For articles on related subjects, *see*

+ Computer Animation
+ Computer Graphics
+ Entertainment Industry, Computers in the
+ Fractals
+ Image Processing
+ Multimedia
+ Virtual Reality

A New Visual Order

The computer deeply affects the way today's art is produced, disseminated, and valued. Until recently, images were created through acts of human perception either through skills based on eye–hand coordination or through the lens of copying processes such as photography, cinematic film, or video where what is seen is recorded through various chemical or electronic processes. Increasingly, however, images reside only in the database of a computer, causing a break with the visual means of representation available to artists for creating art since the Renaissance.

The potential for intervention and interaction in an artwork challenges notions of a discrete work of art, one that is authored by the artist alone. By means of an appropriate *user interface (q.v)*, an *interactive* art work may use a navigation system of branched databases to create a work of connective links and nodes. The viewer may now participate in the work's ultimate unfolding of meaning by choosing directions within the artwork. Interactivity challenges the role of the artist, who now assumes a different function, one similar to a systems designer.

Early Use by Artists

By 1965, computer research into the simulation of visual phenomena had reached a significant level, particularly at Bell Labs in Murray Hill, NJ. Here the pioneer work of Bela Julesz, A. Michael Noll, Manfred Schroeder, Ken Knowlton, Leon Harmon, Frank Sinden, and E. E. Zajac led them to understand the computer's possibilities for visual representation and for art. That same year, Noll and Julesz exhibited the results of their experiments at the Howard Wise Gallery, New York, concurrent with Georg Nees and Frieder Nake's exhibition of digital images at Galerie Niedlich, Stuttgart, Germany. Research in Germany at the Stuttgart Technische Universität was conducted under the influence of the philosopher Max Bense, who coined the terms "artificial art" and "generative esthetics," terms which grew out of his interest in the mathematics of esthetics.

By the early 1970s, a new generation of artists began to emerge who were able to retain their intuition and sensitivity while exercising the logical, methodical approach to work demanded by the use of digital equipment. For example, Manfred Mohr and Duane Palyka began to program their own software as a result of frustration with existing programs and systems which did not serve their creative needs. They represented a class of "hybrid" artists who have made important contributions to the field of visual simulation. The need for new software development has led many artists, especially those interested in interactive applications, to collaborate with engineers or scientists, or to study computer science for themselves.

Use of the computer still seems threatening to many artists who fear they may lose control to a machine that has a powerful agenda of its own. However, its presence

Figure 1. Joseph Nechvatal, *The Informed Man*, 1986. Computer/robotic-assisted Scanamural (acrylic on canvas 82"×116". Degraded information patterns are printed via airbrush guns guided by computer-driven robotic arms onto a canvas support (collection: Dannheisser Foundation).

is so ubiquitous that it is creeping into every artist's studio as a tool for some functions (much as the camera eventually did), raising questions about what aspect of it can be used for their work, although most still do not contemplate its use as a medium in itself (but *see* Fig. 1).

The First 35 Years

In the short 35-year history of computer use in the visual arts, the first 10 years ("first wave" 1965–1975) were dominated by computer scientists with easy access to equipment. In the "second wave," significantly larger numbers of artists began to gain access to computers and realize their potential benefit for their work. Many of these were interested in kinetic and interactive aspects of the computer. Some artists used the computer as a means of programming their kinetic sculptures, which emphasized interactivity between optics, light displays, and motorized controlled movement, such as those by Thomas Shannon, Jean Dupuy, and Hilary Harris among many others in both Europe and the USA.

The use of the computer as a medium by artists has until recently brought the same rebuff by critics as earlier reactions to photography, which was rejected as a mainstream art form from the 1850s to the

a
b
c
d
e
f
g
h
i
j
k
l
m
n
o
p
q
r
s
t
u
v, w
x, y
z

1960s. However, wide dispersal and greater access to greatly improved equipment for a far broader group of artists, and to the development of much more "friendly" technology, has created important new conditions. More and more artists are able to access flexible, powerful, and challenging computer hardware and software at lower cost. New forms and esthetic values are developing as a broader range of artists come to electronic tools with training in the visual arts rather than in computer science. Art schools are rapidly integrating digital tools into their curricula.

The computer allows rapid visualization of complex spatial concepts. Many programs have been developed, which allow complex layering of imagery and ease of decision-making about color and composition, and which permit the creation of film and printer output. A variety of sophisticated color printers using laser, ink-jet, sublimation, and other technologies make high-quality prints on a variety of papers and print media. Interactive installations, CD-ROMs and the World Wide Web (q.v.) create a realm where a different set of abstract relationships can be brought into play, which expand avenues for art-making, challenging both artist and viewer. Major museums now acquire works that incorporate computer influence as part of their photography, video, and sculpture collections—works such as Jon Kessler's kinetic sculptures, Jenny Holzer's computer-controlled electronic message boards, and Bill Viola's video installations. These works tend to integrate rather than isolate the computer aspect and enhance the overall conception.

Artists, the Interface and Interaction

Originally, interactive media grew out of developments in electronic computer games in the 1970s and 1980s. Because of the popularity of these games, the early technology became so well developed that many artists decided to use the concept of branched-out situations to involve the audience in a different kind of experience. Among others, Jane Veeder, Nancy Burson, Myron Krueger, and Ed Tannenbaum created different genres of interactive works.

Harold Cohen thinks of the computer as an "interface for the creation of his work—a collaborator, and an assistant in the drawing phase." Cohen's drawing program is what he terms a formal distillation of the rules and habits a human artist follows during the process of drawing. The computer sifts through these programmed rules and drives an artist-built drawing machine (a *turtle*—*see* LOGO) by steering it with separate commands.

Lyn Hershman is one of the first artists to have taken interactive laser disc technology beyond commercial exploitation. Her 1984–1986 *Lorna* represents an important beginning artistic involvement with a potentially powerful interactive medium. Hershman's film *Conceiving Ada* (1996) makes use of virtual sets. It is a cyber-fantasy based on the true story of Augusta Ada Byron (*see* LOVELACE, COUNTESS OF), who in a major collaboration with Charles Babbage (*q.v.*) created software concepts for the Analytical Engine (*q.v.*), a direct forerunner of the modern computer.

It takes enormous skill to craft work where there are pathways, nodes, links, networks, and connecting loops between databases of visual narrative elements with sound and text. Multifaceted procedures and coding require interdisciplinary collaboration. Most common interactive multimedia (*q.v.*) works are designed for presentation on computer screens. Creating a CD-ROM is similar to organizing a film production in its use of theatrical lighting, scriptwriting, working with actors, music, and storyboard. A work on CD-ROM or DVD-R is not a linear narrative, although it may be a meta-narrative based on a database of narrations, and so does not evoke the suspension of disbelief that is the goal of many films.

A major feature is the interface with the viewer: experimental investigations for developing new ways to compress and represent complex information and the procedural tools needed for the users/audience to navigate are rapidly being developed, particularly in relation to the Internet and the World Wide Web (*q.v.*). How does communication take place to indicate how interaction should occur? How can the viewer be motivated to interact and to want to continue? What most interactive producers have found is that the interaction itself must be intuitive, meaningful, simple, attractive, familiar-feeling, and noticeably responsive to the user.

Simulations

A variety of simulation techniques *called texture mapping, ray-tracing, three-dimensional modeling,* and *figure animation interpolation* grew out of high-level research, which puts mathematics at the service of the quest for a "new realism." One of the most formidable tasks the computer can accomplish is to simulate a three-dimensional shaded model. Once all the physical measurement information about the object has been fed into the computer's data bank, the simulated object then materializes on the screen. It can then be rotated, skewed, and made to zoom in and out of space in perspective, with a choice of where the light source originates.

Powerful Silicon Graphics machines have been designed to capture the essential character of real forms and textures through the programming of digital instructions designed to simulate, for example, the diminishing size of tree branches as the trunk rises from the ground. An enormous number of such algorithms are required for realistic simulation of mountains, clouds, and water. The team at Lucasfilm has even been able to recreate the blur of motion that is caused by a wave striking the shore or two billiard balls colliding. Various computer programs that build in a randomness factor have been developed to make images seem more lifelike.

Monsters of Grace, the first full-length 3D computer animation, is in the form of an opera based on the poetry of the thirteenth century Persian poet Jalaluddin Rumi. The film is a collaborative work by composer Philip Glass and theatrical producer Robert Wilson, who worked with the computer animation firm of Kleiser-Walczak. Wearing 3D glasses, the audience is assailed by unexpected juxtapositions of unusual objects or events seeming to move forward in the space between screen and viewer. Although there have been many 3D digital animations exploring new aspects of imaging over the years since the early 1980s, this rich and satisfying artwork potentially allows the expansion of esthetic values. The slow-moving animations are suggestive of a meditative inner world, rather than an outer one; of

sudden appearances and mysterious disappearances; and of changes in scale.

The Immersive Artwork

Virtual reality hardware now exists for head and hand motion; for the use of body characteristics such as touch, motion, eye focus, gesture/speech, and brainwaves. A small band of artists in Europe and North America are harnessing the potential of virtual reality by exploring it as imaginary space. Although sophisticated VR technology was developed by the military during the Cold War, it was directed at the concept of a sedentary operator following the movement of a vehicle through a 3D virtual world. Most artists approaching VR want to create an open immersive space where they can control all the objects or all the spatial coordinates in order to achieve an esthetic effect. Some project their "virtual images" in space; some employ head-gear or gloves connected to sensing devices which control the flow and placement of images within the space.

Films and videos are now being designed for insertions of animated figures with live photographed ones in the most complex interactions of reality and fiction yet attempted. Computer-simulated graphic images or animated passages can be encoded as a video signal and inserted into a work as part of its totality, or entire video passages can be digitized and edited, reformulated, manipulated, and again reformatted as a video signal. This provides an unprecedented expansion of pictorial variety and texture. In the future, the computer may play a greater role than the camera in filmmaking.

At MIT, Pattie Maes has created *Alive, An Artificial Life*, a virtual immersive environment. The goal of *Alive* is to present an environment in which a real participant can interact in natural and believable ways with autonomous semi-intelligent artificial agents whose behavior appears to be equally natural and believable. Normally, navigation through a virtual space requires the wearing of gloves, goggles, or a helmet—cumbersome equipment tethered to a computer workstation. However, in *Alive*, a single CCD (charge-coupled device) camera obtains color images of a person that are then inserted into a 3D graphical world,

a
b
c
d
e
f
g
h
i
j
k
l
m
n
o
p
q
r
s
t
u
v, w
x, y
z

which contains the position of various body parts. This composite world is then projected onto a large video wall, which gives the feeling and effect of a "magic mirror."

Art in Cyberspace

Interactive telecommunications systems empower the individual to connect with others globally and vastly increase the possibilities for inventing expanded forms for art. These include satellite transmissions, online network programs, ISDN, and fax projects. Artists choosing to work with computer telecommunications often choose subjects that focus reflexively on the inherently structural aspects of their medium such as exploiting concepts that focus on the interdependence of world communities. Artists in five different countries might collaborate on a drawing that is faxed and embellished at sites in each country; participants in a global online electronic mail conference are invited to share views about online artworks; via videophone, artists in art cafes in three different cities participate in a teleperformance opera. Artists often critique manipulation of the public mind through information manipulation itself. They invent ways to use browsers as a way of entering people's living spaces.

Software such as CU-SeeMe transmits live digitized video with an uplink feed to the Internet. An example of live imagery being uplinked to the Web is *Alice Sat Here*, a project by Emily Hartzell and Nina Sobell in conjunction with computer scientists and engineers from NYU's Center for Digital Multimedia. On entering the gallery, the live viewer is invited to sit on a motorized throne that has a telerobotic (*q.v.*) eye mounted on it. The viewer navigates within the gallery—or in the street—by steering the vehicle. The goal of the piece is to send what a telerobotic videocam "eye" sees to a page on the Internet. This "in effect" turns the Web inside out to create a real physical 3D-space, which Web users can explore through a collaborative navigation with people who are actually in that place. What this "eye" sees is monitored and controlled by the viewer on the Web. Passers-by on the street are able to interact with this process through a touch screen system surrounding a monitor located in the gallery's front window. A combination of software and hardware is used to create an interface which gives Web users control over an aspect of this physical environment. Feedback comes through the use of video monitoring, which shows physical visitors the shape of the piece.

An Online Electronically Produced Public Artwork

An online, electronically produced artwork is transmitted and disseminated like television. But it is completely different from TV because of its interactive potential. Accessibility changes the work itself because it must be created with a broader audience in mind, one which is much larger than the aggregate of those reached through conventional exhibition.

Sherrie Rabinowitz comments that the implications of the new technological conditions are that we must begin to imagine a much larger scale of creativity, one which opens up the possibility of new communication across all disciplines and boundaries. Linking this idea of using the interactive potential of the medium to empower other people instead of one's self creates a powerful opening for a new role for the artist and a new kind of public art—one with all the constraints and freedoms to communicate within a wider sphere. It implies a new way of being and communicating in the world. Viewers become collaborators in an interactive dialogue, adding notes, drawings, and comments at the site of the exhibition or printing out sections of images or texts for exchange or discussion.

The impulse to create art to involve the public is very different from merely placing artwork on the Net. Such Internet exhibition activities, however, do allow artists to bypass cultural gatekeepers and power brokers. Exhibitions of conventional artwork have been placed in Websites on the Internet and can be downloaded through a normal computer printer complete with the artist's biography and the price of the original. These are rapidly becoming accepted in everyday cultural practice.

Bibliography

1967. Noll, M. "The Digital Computer as a Creative Medium," *IEEE Spectrum*, **4**(10), (October), 89–95.

1984. Wallis, B. (ed.). *Art after Modernism: Re-Thinking Representation*. New York: New Museum.

1996. Moser, M. A., and MacLeod, D. (eds.) *Immersed in Technology: Art and Virtual Environments*. Cambridge, MA: MIT Press.

1997. Lovejoy, M. *Postmodern Currents: Art and Artists in the Age of Electronic Media*, 2nd Ed. Upper Saddle River, NJ: Prentice Hall.

Margot Lovejoy

COMPUTER-ASSISTED LEARNING AND TEACHING

For an articles on a related subject, *see*

+ Logo

The impact of computers on *teaching* and *learning* activities at all levels of education is considerable, and the extent of use increases as computers become less expensive and more convenient to use. Every area of postsecondary education is affected. A medical student practices diagnosis and prescription on hypothetical patients simulated by computer programs. A group of engineering students uses computer assistance to solve problems in analysis and design that otherwise would be unapproachable. A student aide develops a program to help a professor of chemistry evaluate the effectiveness of questions on a multiple-choice quiz. A laboratory technician confirms newly acquired skills using a terminal on a hospital information system (HIS).

Computing is also quite visible in education in schools, homes, and community centers. School science students collect and analyze data on water quality in a stream near their school, and then share their results with similar working groups elsewhere in the world. An English literature student programs a computer to generate poetry. A child explores mathematics and problem solving by writing computer programs that direct a robot to draw spirals or solve mazes.

When the computer system is appropriate for educational uses and the programs are properly written, learners should find the assistance to be responsive to their needs; patient and not punitive while they learn; accurate in assessment of answers and problem solutions; individualized in a useful way; realistic in the presentation of training or testing situations; and helpful with many information-processing tasks. Teachers find computer assistance valuable for keeping accurate records, summarizing data, projecting student-learning difficulties, assembling individualized tests, and retrieving information about films or other learning resources.

A Brief History of Computer-Assisted Instruction (CAI)

Use of the computer as a tool for problem solving in education began in US graduate schools in about 1955, and a few years later moved into the classroom with the initiation of curriculum development projects in engineering and science. Computers used as teaching machines date from 1958; early developments took place at IBM's Watson Research Center, System Development Corporation, and the University of Illinois. The topic of computers in education became popular for meetings in 1965; separate conferences were held on computers in American education, higher education, and physics teaching. In the next 10 years, major conferences were organized for computers in mathematics teaching, chemistry education, computer science education, science education, the undergraduate curriculum, and high school counseling.

Also, in the 1960s a group of engineers and educators in the Computer-based Education Research Laboratory at the University of Illinois, Urbana, designed a computing system (PLATO) for effective and efficient teaching. It was a large system that provided instructional computing to about 1000 simultaneous users throughout the university and other colleges and schools in Illinois. The design included notable advances in the technology for display and communications. PLATO was once marketed commercially by the Control Data Corporation.

At about the same time, Stanford University operated a CAI system to distribute instructional computing to a number of centers throughout the country. A large-scale service operation using long-distance telephone communications, clusters of terminals, and some standalone computer systems, the remote centers were usually associated with elementary school demonstration projects and special education institutions. The service operation was conducted in parallel with an extensive program of research and development at the Institute for Mathematical Studies in the Social Sciences, Stanford University. Curriculum materials were prepared for young children (elementary school mathematics and reading), learners with special difficulties, and university courses for learning a second-language. Introduction of the personal computer in 1977 greatly reduced the cost of computers in education. Tools for desktop publishing (*q.v.*), laboratory instrumentation, music, graphic art, and manipulation of media introduced in the 1980s increased the scope and depth of applications.

When "instruction," in the acronym CAI, is replaced by "learning," as in CAL, the combination connotes greater emphasis on activities initiated by the learner than on the instructional materials created by a teacher-author. When "learning" is replaced by "education" to obtain CAE (or CBE, computer-based education), the implication is a greater variety of computer uses, including administrative data processing and materials production as well as student use of computers. If the role of the computer is to assist the teacher in managing instruction, for example, in retrieving and summarizing performance records and curriculum files, the label used is CMI: computer-managed instruction.

Instruction and the Learning Process

The most visible use of computers in instruction is to provide direct assistance to learners and to assist teachers, administrators, and educational technologists in helping them. The users may work individually or in groups, online or offline, typing text, scanning images, speaking words, singing or playing an instrument, and many other options. Some typical labels within this category of use are drill, skills practice, programmed tutorial, testing and diagnosis, dialogue tutorial, simulation, gaming, information retrieval, computation, problem solving, construction of procedures as models, and display of graphic constructions. A very popular use of the computer is for simulation of a decision-making situation, as in resource management, pollution control, business marketing, or medical testing.

Management of Instruction Resources and Process

Computer aids help teachers to supervise the instructional process, and similar assistance is provided directly to students without the intervention of teachers and managers. Information management services are readily extended to potential users of learning resources outside traditional educational institutions. The essential information in the various files for management of instructional resources concerns student performance, learning materials, desired outcomes, job opportunities, and student interests.

Preparation and Display of Materials

Materials may be generated in "real time" (i.e. as needed by a student in a seminar or by a teacher during a lecture). Text and problems may also be assembled by computer in advance of scheduled use so that individualized material may be distributed at less expense than through individual computer stations. Computers assist writers of materials in many ways—for example tools for generating films and graphics; data collection during trial of materials under development; procedures for automatically editing and analyzing text materials for new uses, and information structures for representing new organizations of knowledge; hierarchies of instructional objectives; and libraries of learning materials.

Means and Goals
Diversity of Resources

Many different kinds of computer and software systems are being used effectively (*see* Fig. 1). Desktop and laptop machines can be used by one or a few students

Figure 1. Boy using a multimedia personal computer at home to learn French. The computer screen is showing the training package's introductory title page, with the French flag and Eiffel tower. Multimedia (*q.v.*) computers are able to make sounds as well as produce pictures. The combination of a spoken work with a colorful graphical image can help students to memorize it. Multimedia training packages also have the advantage of allowing the user to progress at a comfortable speed (courtesy of Damien Lovegrove/Science Photo Library).

to access stored programs (usually drills or simulations), collect data in the field, or assemble resources collected by searches using the Internet. Workstations (*q.v.*) offer tools for scholarly and creative work conducted by students individually and in groups.

Programming languages and systems (software) exhibit even more diversity than computing equipment (hardware). More than 100 languages and dialects have been developed specifically for programming conversational instruction, although many programs have been written in general-purpose languages, such as Fortran, Pascal, C, and Basic. The characteristics of different subject areas necessitate different language features. Appropriate design of display screens, user control, and input devices can be of great

help compensating for disabilities (*see* DISABLED, COMPUTERS AND THE) and reduces the need for the user to learn computing tools and languages that are incidental to the learning and performance tasks.

Instructional materials (*courseware*) have been written in nearly all subject areas and for many age levels. While some of the materials use the computer as an information-processing device, others use it as a presentation medium in competition with less expensive modes, such as books or videotapes.

Computer Contributions

The value of computer assistance for self-instruction depends on many factors: organization of the subject matter, the purposes of the author or institution, convenient means for interacting with the subject, and the characteristics of the student. Self-study material in text format has been adapted for computer presentation with the following computer contributions proposed. First, the machine evaluates a response constructed by the student (the author must provide a key or standard); an automated procedure prints out discrepancies, tallies scores, and selects remedial or enrichment material. Second, the machine conceals and, to some extent, controls the teaching material so that the author can specify greater complexity in a strategy of instruction and assume more accuracy in its execution than is possible when the student is expected to find a way through the branching instructions in the pages of a large booklet (the scrambled text format for programmed instruction). Third, the computer carries out operations specified by the student, who uses a simple programming language or CAD/CAM system. Fourth, the author or researcher obtains detailed data on student performance (and perhaps attitude) along with a convenient summary of student accomplishment ready for interpretation. Fifth, the author is able to modify the text on the basis of student use and prepare alternative versions with relative ease.

Some of the limitations imposed by the present computer technology involve the unreliability of processing lengthy verbal constructions and the inaccuracy of interpreting bodily gestures or vocal intonations. Computing costs are decreasing even while capabilities are increasing, but one of the most difficult problems remaining is lack of organization of the subject matter. Human teachers manage to be reasonably successful in spite of vague goals and material poorly organized for learning; instructional computing seems to require specific text materials and clear guidelines for successful use.

Major Approaches
Educational Technology

Educational technology and instructional psychology have been the main sources of one kind of development activity. Specific programming of computer-based lessons characterizes this first approach to computer use. In some curriculum development projects, the content has been assembled in files separate from the logic of the computer program (the strategy of instruction). Elements of the curriculum can thereby be varied without rewriting many lines of instructions to the computer, and different strategies can be tried on the same file of learning materials. This arrangement helps the instructional psychologist give full attention to the design of effective instructional strategies and helps the subject expert avoid the distraction of programming procedures.

Computing and Information Sciences

Major advances in instructional use of computers may occur through significant developments in artificial intelligence (*q.v.*), natural language processing (*q.v.*), speech recognition (*q.v.*), and virtual reality (*q.v.*) The results of computer science research may be an important source of suitable models for instruction strategies, information structures, and representations of knowledge (*see* KNOWLEDGE REPRESENTATION). Projects giving particular attention to educational applications have adapted tools from computing and information science, and formulated new models of human learning and information processing.

Computing Technology Engineering and "Common Sense"

A third category includes all other approaches, particularly those characterized by the engineering of technology helpful to learning and creative work. Engineers design and build systems suited to a range of purposes: educational technologists present programmed instruction, instructional psychologists conduct research on teaching and learning, professors prepare a computer presentation of a lecture or laboratory, and computer specialists build information-processing aids for learning and scholarly work. Specialists in computers and education devise various programming languages (e.g. Logo and LogoWriter) and equipment (computer-controlled "turtle," music player, and construction kits) for computer-related learning activities. Children write simple programs for controlling robots, drawing and animating pictures, generating speech and music, and the like. Interest in enhancing such capabilities motivates a new approach to mathematics and heuristics (*q.v.*) in which programming languages provide a powerful conceptual framework.

Trends

A major trend in the design of computer-based exercises has been a shift from programmer to learner control. The designer of the exercise invests less effort in a careful diagnosis and prescription accomplished by some automated instructional strategy, and instead provides information and tools by which the student can explore the topic and assess his or her own learning. The teacher is now more likely to see computer-managed instruction as an aid to human management than as a replacement for it.

Bibliography

1996. Gooden, A. R. *Computers in the Classroom: How Teachers and Students are Using Technology to Transform Learning.* San Francisco: Jossey-Bass.

1997. Sandholtz, J. H., Ringstaff, C., and Dwyer, D. C. *Teaching with Technology: Creating Student-Centered Classrooms.* New York: Teachers College Press.

1997. Schank, R. C. *Virtual Learning: A Revolutionary Approach to Building a Highly Skilled Workforce.* New York: McGraw-Hill.

Karl L. Zinn

COMPUTER CHESS

For articles on related subjects, *see*

+ Artificial Intelligence (AI)
+ Computer Games

Chess tournaments exclusively for computers have been held since 1970. Until 1978, these tournaments were dominated by David Slate and Larry Atkin's program, first called *Chess 3.0* and, after many revisions, *Chess 4.9*. It earned a rating on the international rating scale of about 2050 in 1978. It was developed at Northwestern University and ran on CDC's Cyber 176 in the late 1970s. Chess 4.9 carried out a sequence of incrementally deeper exhaustive depth-first searches, examining approximately 5000 chess positions per second.

The first international computer chess championship, organized by the International Federation for Information Processing Societies (IFIPS-*q.v.*) in 1974, was won by the Russian program *Kaissa* running on an ICL 4/70. In 1976, the program *Chess 4.5* written by Lawrence Atkin, David Slate, and Keith Gorlen of Northwestern University was the first to earn an expert rating. An improved version of the program won the IFIPS tournament of the following year.

At the 1977 World Championship in Toronto, the International Computer Chess Association (ICCA) was formed to provide a framework for activities in computer chess and to encourage advances in the field. In 2002, the Association's mission was broadened and the name changed to the International Computer Games Association (ICGA) (*see* www.cs.unimass.nl/icga). There are currently about 700 members. It publishes the *ICGA Journal*, the leading publication in the field.

In 1979, Daniel and Kathe Spracklen wrote a program embodied in the base of an actual chessboard and marketed it as the *Fidelity Chess Challenger*, which gave the casual player the first opportunity to play computer chess. Successively, more powerful versions of the *Challenger* were sold over the next 10 years until the popularity of PC software dried up the demand. As of this writing, the most powerful such program is a Mattel product called *Chessmaster 8000* that embodies the *King v3.11* "chess engine" written by Johan de Koning (whose last name means "king"). The same engine is embodied in products made by the Dutch company Tasc. Only grandmasters can hold their own against the King program when it is allowed to play at its highest level on a 1-GHz PC or better.

In 1978, British International Master David Levy won a wager of several thousand dollars by defeating Chess 4.7 in a match in Toronto. In 1968, Levy had wagered four computer scientists that no computer would defeat him in a match during the next 10 years. Levy won the match with a 3.5–1.5 score. Following the match, *Omni* magazine offered a prize of $5000 to the authors of the first program to defeat Levy. (The prize was not won until 1989 when an IBM program called *Deep Thought* defeated Levy with a perfect 4–0 score.)

Belle, developed at Bell Laboratories by Ken Thompson and Joe Condon, ruled the world of computer chess from 1979 through 1983. It was the first program to be awarded the title of Master by the United States Chess Federation (USCF). Belle examined 150 000 chess positions per second and ran on special-purpose chess circuitry.

In the 1980s, endgame databases were created by Ken Thompson and Larry Stiller. All five-piece endgames have been solved as well as a number of six-piece endgames. The databases are built using retrograde analysis: starting with a database of won or drawn positions and then working backwards to all other positions, each position is assigned a win, loss, or draw, and a count of the number of moves to the end of the game, or to another simpler endgame. It had long been known that a bishop, knight, and king could checkmate a lone opponent king, but not whether such a win could be forced or could only result from imperfect defense.

But a computer has now shown that the mate can indeed be forced, and how to do so.

In 1983, *Cray Blitz*, developed at the University of Southern Mississippi by Robert Hyatt, Albert Gower, and Harry Nelson, won the world computer chess championship while running on a 4-processor Cray XMP supercomputer. The program successfully defended its title in 1986. *Hitech* appeared in 1986, winning the Pennsylvania State Championship two years in a row and established new levels of performance in human play, obtaining a USCF rating in the neighborhood of 2400. Hitech was developed at Carnegie Mellon University by Carl Ebeling, Hans Berliner, Gordon Goetsch, Murray Campbell, Andy Gruss, and Andy Palay. It searched approximately 200 000 positions per second.

By 1989, Deep Thought, the victor over Levy, had established itself as the world's best program and began defeating grandmasters in tournament competition and earning a rating of approximately 2600. It won the World Computer Chess Championship that year. But later in 1989, it lost a two-game match to Garry Kasparov, the human world champion. Work on Deep Thought began at Carnegie Mellon University. Subsequently, the programming team joined IBM's T. J. Watson Research Center. The team was originally led by Feng-Hsiung Hsu and has included Murray Campbell, Thomas Anantharaman, Mike Browne, Andreas Nowatzyk, Joe Hoane, and Jerry Brody, with Chung-Jen Tan serving as the project leader beginning in 1992.

In 1994, *Deep Thought II*, an improved Deep Thought, was renamed *Deep Blue*. The program ran on a 32-node IBM RS6000 SP computer with each node containing a special-purpose chess circuit. Deep Blue examined in excess of 200 000 000 chess moves per second. Two years later, Kasparov defeated Deep Blue in the six-game $500 000 ACM Computer Chess Challenge match by a score of 4–2. But in a rematch of the following year, Deep Blue defeated the world champion in a six-game $1 000 000 match sponsored by IBM by a score of 3.5–2.5. The six games from this historic match are presented in the full Encyclopedia. Kasparov had a rating of 2828 entering the match. On the basis of the result, Deep Blue would earn an even higher rating.

A good computer chess program, even a PC version, is intimidating to all but a handful of human players. No advantage can be gained early in a game because of the program's huge repertoire of well-analyzed opening moves. No advantage not already earned can be exploited in the end game because the program knows the standard algorithms for perfect play when there are six or fewer pieces left. That leaves only the middle game, where the computer's brute force search deep into the game tree tends to prevail over humans whose ability to look ahead seldom matches that of the computer. The only weakness, and a very small one, is that a human's evaluation of a given position may be superior to that of a computer that must rely on a possibly fallible arithmetic score. But the computer is relentless, has no feeling, does not tire, and never makes an outright blunder such as failing to protect a major piece or overlooking a fork. Attention can now turn to the more complex game of *Go*, which should keep AI researchers busy for at least another 50 years.

Bibliography

1990. Levy, D. N. L., and Newborn, M. *How Computers Play Chess*. New York: W. H. Freeman.

1991. Hsu, F. -H., Anantharaman, T., and Nowatzyk, A. "A Grandmaster Chess Machine," *Scientific American*, **263**(4), (October), 44–50.

1997. Newborn, M. *Kasparov Versus Deep Blue: Computer Chess Comes of Age*. New York: Springer-Verlag.

Monty Newborn and Edwin D. Reilly

COMPUTER CIRCUITRY

For articles on related subjects, *see*

+ Adder
+ Boolean Algebra
+ Integrated Circuitry
+ Logic Design

✦ Microcomputer Chip
✦ Microprocessors and Microcomputers

Introduction

Electrical principles first found application in digital computers in the form of electromechanical relays. The most prominent examples are the Bell Labs relay machines and the Mark I (*q.v.*). Even while these machines were under construction in the early 1940s, it was recognized that an *electronic* computer would offer great advantages in terms of computational speed. Electronic computers use electronic circuits that interconnect electronic components called *gates*. Gates implement basic operations called *Boolean* or *logic functions*.

The physical realization of electronic gates has undergone considerable change since the 1940s, when vacuum tubes were used as the first electronic components. Electronic computers built since the late 1960s have used *metal-oxide semiconductor* (MOS) transistors. Prior to that, bipolar junction transistors (BJT) gates were used. The earliest semiconductor computer circuits consisted of gates mounted on printed circuit boards connected by copper wires. Today gates and interconnection wires are integrated into a single silicon wafer in VLSI (Very Large Scale Integration) technology (*see* MICROCOMPUTER CHIP).

Boolean Algebra

Boolean algebra deals with functions and variables that take on only two values, commonly denoted by either T and F or 1 and 0. Using the axioms of Boolean algebra, it can be shown that any Boolean function can be composed from at most three primitive operations: *and*, *or*, and *not*. This set of logic operations is therefore said to be *functionally complete*. In fact, there are two primitive operations widely used in the design of computer circuitry that are functionally complete in themselves. These are *nand* (equivalent to a *not* following an *and*) and *nor* (equivalent to a *not* following an *or*). Thus, one needs only to design circuits for a functionally complete set of Boolean operations in order to have the basic building blocks for an entire digital computer.

The association made between an abstract Boolean operation and circuitry that implements that operation is through voltage level. That is, digital circuitry is designed to respond to two voltage levels, designated high and low (e.g. +5 volts and 0 volts). The conventional method uses the high voltage (or V_{dd}) to represent a 1 and the low voltage (or *Gnd*, for Ground) to represent a 0.

MOS Logic Gates

Circuits that implement the most primitive Boolean functions are called *gates*. The symbols that are used to implement the commonly used gates are shown in Fig. 1. A small circle used in conjunction with the output of any gate denotes negation of that gate's function.

Variations of MOS technologies are currently used to implement computer logic. Logic gates are built using *controlled switches*. As shown in Fig. 2, such switches consist of three terminals and can be either "*n*-type" or "*p*-type" ('*n*' for negative and '*p*' for positive). In an *n*-type switch, if G equals 1, terminal S is connected to terminal D. If G equals 0, then terminal S is disconnected from terminal D. In a *p*-type switch, if G equals 1, terminal S is disconnected from terminal D. If G equals 0, then terminal S is connected to terminal D. Physically, the "*n*-type" switch is an *n*-type field-effect transistor (*n*FET) and the "*p*-type" switch

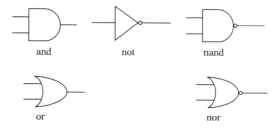

and   not   nand

or   nor

Figure 1.   Symbols for logic gates.

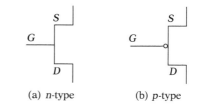

(a) *n*-type   (b) *p*-type

Figure 2.   Symbols for FETs.

is a *p*-type field-effect transistor (*p*FET). As shown in Fig. 3, such switches may be interconnected to form a network having two distinct terminals, X and Y. The connection pattern of Fig. 3a is a series connection, and the pattern of Fig. 3b is a parallel connection. These elementary connection patterns can be used to build larger networks, as shown in Fig. 3c.

We say that a network N of switches is *activated* if and only if the two terminals X, Y of N are connected through a set of switches. For example, in Fig. 3a, if $A = B = 1$, both switches are closed and X is connected

to Y. Therefore, the network of Fig. 3a is activated by the assignment $A = B = 1$. If $A = B = 0$, the network of Fig. 3c is activated.

MOS logic gates are constructed by using networks of switches. As shown in Fig. 4, there are two distinct models of logic gates. The *type-a* gate uses two networks of switches—*pullup* and *pulldown* networks. The pullup network consists only of *p*FETs and the pulldown network consists only of nFETs. These gates are designed so that, for any assignment of values to the input variables, only one of the two networks is activated. If

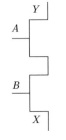
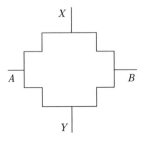
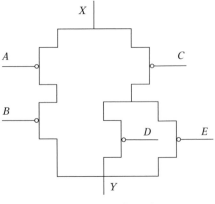

(a) Series connection   (b) Parallel connection   (c) Series–Parallel graph

Figure 3.   Series-Parallel connections.

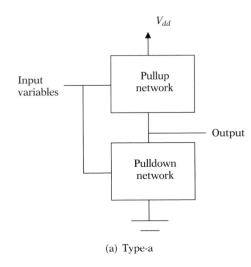
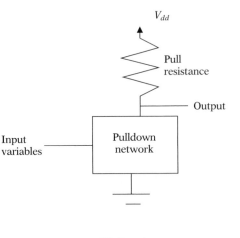

(a) Type-a   (b) Type-b

Figure 4.   Structure of MOS gates.

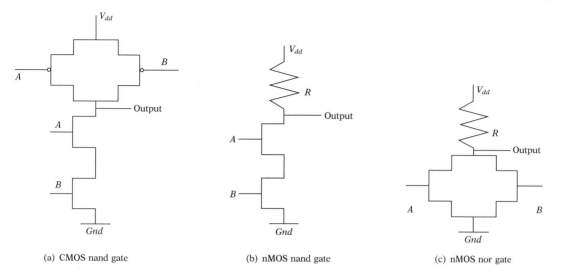

(a) CMOS nand gate (b) nMOS nand gate (c) nMOS nor gate

Figure 5. Examples of MOS gates.

the pullup (pulldown) network is activated, the output of the gate is set to the logic value 1 (0). Figure 5a is an example of a type-a gate. If $A = B = 1$, the pulldown network is activated and the output is set to 0. If $A = B = 0$, then the pullup network is activated and the output is set to 1. The gate of Fig. 5a implements the *nand* function. For any assignment of values to the input of *type-b* gates, the output is set to 0 if and only if the assignments activate the pulldown network. Figure 5b is a type-b *nand* gate, and Fig. 5c is a type b *nor* gate.

Type-a gates in which the pullup network consists only of pFETs and the pulldown network consists only of nFETs are known as CMOS (*complementary metal-oxide semiconductor*) gates. Circuits consisting of CMOS gates are known as CMOS circuits. Type-b gates in which the pulldown network consists only of nFETs are known as *nMOS* gates. Circuits consisting of nMOS gates are known as nMOS circuits. Historically, nMOS circuits preceded CMOS circuits because nMOS circuits, unlike CMOS circuits, require only one type of switch. However, technological innovation has made CMOS an equally feasible technology, and today almost all circuits are CMOS circuits.

Other Logic Families

Although MOS, more specifically CMOS, is now the dominant technology, a number of technologies have

been used for manufacturing computers. The logic families that we will discuss here use *bipolar junction transistors* (BJTs) as the switching device. Like FETs, BJTs are also three-dimensional devices. We use the symbol of Fig. 6a to represent a BJT in which G is the *base*, E is the *emitter*, and C is the *collector*. If the voltage at C is "sufficiently higher" than the voltage at E, terminal C is electrically connected to terminal E (the switch is ON); otherwise, terminal C is disconnected from terminal E (the switch is OFF). BJT logic gates are similar to type-b gates. In *resistor-transistor logic* (RTL), only *nor* gates are available for designing circuits. It is for this reason that RTL is said to be "nor logic" A two-input RTL *nor* gate is shown in Fig. 6b.

In *diode-transistor logic* (DTL), unlike RTL, only *nand* gates are available for designing the circuits. These *nand* gates use both *diodes* and *transistors* as active devices. The symbol for a diode is shown in Fig. 6c. A diode is a unidirectional two-terminal device. If the voltage at X is higher than the voltage at Y, terminal X is electrically connected to terminal Y; otherwise, X is disconnected from Y. A DTL *nand* gate is shown in Fig. 6d. To understand the operation of this gate, note that if $A(B)$ has the logic level 0 (i.e. voltage 0), diode d1 (d2) conducts. This implies that the voltage at P is 0. $V-$ is a negative voltage. Therefore, diodes d3, d4

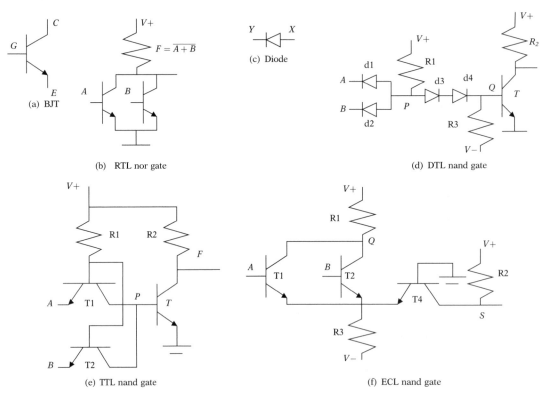

Figure 6.   Implementation of some universal gates using BJT-based logic families.

conduct and Q is at a negative voltage (by adjusting the resistance value R3). This cuts T, the *driver* transistor, OFF and the output F is at logic level 1. If $A = B = 1$, diodes d1, d2 do not conduct. Diodes d3, d4 conduct and Q is at a positive voltage (adjusted by resistances R1, R3). The driver T is ON and the output F is pulled down to logic level 0.

In *transistor-transistor logic* (TTL), the only gates available are *nand* gates. A TTL *nand* gate is shown in Fig. 6e. It is very similar to a DTL *nand* gate, but is faster than either RTL or DTL. If either A or B is at logic level 0, there is enough base-to-emitter voltage difference at either T1 or T2 to turn one or both of them ON. This brings down the voltage of P to a sufficiently low value to cut T OFF. The output F is therefore at logic level 1. When both A, B are 1, then both T1 and T2 are cut OFF and P returns to a high voltage. This turns T ON and the output F is pulled to logic level 0.

In DTL and TTL, there is a driver BJT and circuitry is added to the base of this BJT to implement the *nand* function. In *emitter-coupled logic* (ECL), the base of the driver BJT is grounded and circuitry is added to its emitter to implement the *nor* function. ECL circuits are potentially faster than RTL, DTL, or TTL because, unlike those logic families, the driver BJT is never driven into saturation and can therefore switch much faster from one state to another. If either A or B in Fig. 6f is at logic level 1, either T1 or T2 conducts. Therefore, there is current through R1. This brings Q to logic level 0. The emitter of T4 is now at either 0 or a small positive voltage (depending on the values of R1 and R3) and this cuts T4 OFF. S is therefore at logic level 1. When both A, B are 0, neither T1 nor T2 conducts. Q is at logic level 1. The emitter of T4 is at a negative voltage (close to 0). T4 conducts and S is set to logic level 0. Note that Q and S are complements.

One advantage of using logic gates implemented using BJTs is that they have faster switching speeds than gates using MOS devices. However, the low-power dissipation of MOS gates, among other reasons, made it easier to integrate MOS devices. Nevertheless, many BJT devices are still in use for special-purpose circuits or where higher driving capabilities are required.

Classes of Computer Circuits

Depending on the functions they implement, computer circuits are divided into two classes: *combinational circuits* and *sequential circuits.* Combinational circuits are the simpler of the two classes and, along with other circuit elements, are used in the design of sequential circuits. To understand the difference between these circuits, *see* Fig. 7a. The time interval is divided into subintervals $I1, I2, \ldots$ of equal size. The intervals are marked by a periodic logic signal known as *clock.* The *period* of clock is equal to the length of the interval. Every interval is divided into two parts. During the first part, clock is 1, and during the second part, clock is 0. We will refer to them as the *one* and *zero* periods of the interval. Every such circuit can be represented as shown in Fig. 7b. Computation proceeds as follows. During the *one* period, the values of the inputs change. During *zero* period, the logic values at the outputs change and settle down to their steady-state value. This is known as *single-phase clocking.*

Combinational circuits are circuits whose output, during any time interval, depends only on the values of the inputs during the current time interval and is independent of the values of the inputs during the preceding time intervals. The output of *sequential circuits*, during any time interval, on the other hand, depends on *both* the values of the inputs during the current interval, as well as the values of the inputs during the preceding time intervals.

Combinational Circuits

Boolean functions are functions over Boolean variables whose result can be only one of the two Boolean values 0, 1. Combinational circuits implement Boolean functions. An example of such a function is the *odd parity function* P_n of n variables. P_n equals 1 if and only if an odd number of the n input variables equal 1.

Boolean functions are defined using *truth tables.* Such a table defines the value of the function for each combination of values of the input. The truth table of the *parity function* of three variables is shown in Table 1. Circuits with multiple outputs can also be specified using truth tables.

Figure 8 is a description of a circuit for the parity function. Such a pictorial representation is a *gate level description* of the circuit. A simple, but not necessarily efficient, way to derive a *gate* level description from a truth table is as follows. An input variable X_i or its

Table 1.

X_1	X_2	X_3	P_3
0	0	0	0
0	0	1	1
0	1	0	1
0	1	1	0
1	0	0	1
1	0	1	0
1	1	0	0
1	1	1	1

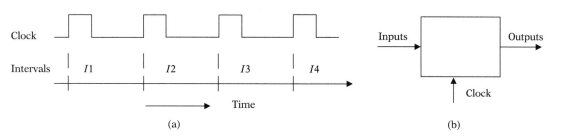

(a)　　　　(b)

Figure 7. Global clock.

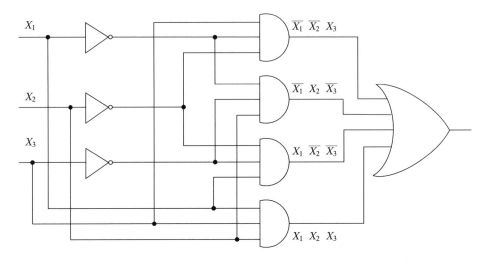

Figure 8. Example of sum-of-product circuits.

complement (i.e. negation) $\bar{X}_i$ is known as an *input literal*. A conjunction of literals is known as a *term*. Corresponding to each row of a truth table, we have a term. For example, for row 1 of Table 1, we have the term $\bar{X}_1 \cdot \bar{X}_2 \cdot \bar{X}_3$ ("." denotes the "and" operation). The term corresponding to a row of a truth table for a Boolean function f is a *one-term* for f if and only if the value of f for that input combination is 1. A *zero-term* is similarly defined. From Table 1, $\bar{X}_1 \cdot \bar{X}_2 \cdot \bar{X}_3$ is a zero-term and $\bar{X}_1 \cdot \bar{X}_2 \cdot \bar{X}_3$ is a one-term for P_3.

Let $a_1, \ldots, a_t$ be the one-terms of a function f. Then, $a_1 + a_2 + \cdots + a_t$ ("+" denotes the *or* operation) is a *sum-of-products* expression for f. From Table 1, we get the following sum-of-products expression P_3 : $P_3 = \bar{X}_1 \cdot \bar{X}_2 \cdot X_3 + \bar{X}_1 \cdot X_2 \cdot \bar{X}_3 + X_1 \cdot \bar{X}_2 \cdot \bar{X}_3$. From such an expresssion, we get the gate level description shown in Fig. 8. Note that, for each term, we have an *and* gate and there is one *or* gate that is driven by all the *and* gates.

Programmable Circuits

The gate level description is a description of the circuit that is used for fabricating it. Prior to fabrication, the physical location on a silicon wafer of the devices (such as FETs, resistors, etc.) has to be determined (*placement*). This is followed by determining how the devices are to be interconnected (*routing*). For circuits using a small number of devices, placement and routing can be done manually. For larger circuits, the entire process has to be automated. Many of the steps of placement and routing can easily be automated if the circuit topology is regular. Moreover, the integration process becomes simpler and more cost-effective if a variety of circuits can be physically implemented by minor variations (or *programming*) of a "master piece." These factors have led to the evolution of a number of design styles such as *programmable logic arrays* (PLAs), *Weinburger arrays, gate matrix arrays*, and so on. Such design styles are being used extensively. To gain insight into these styles, we will have a brief look at nMOS PLAs.

Let $X_1, \bar{X}_2, X_3$ be input variables. The *nor* expression $\overline{(X_1 + \bar{X}_2 + X_3)}$ can be implemented logically as shown in Fig. 9a. To implement this expression physically, if there are n input variables, we have a physical row of $2n$ nFETs. For every input variable X_i, there exist two nFETs, one driven by X_i and the other driven by $\bar{X}_i$. An example is shown in Fig. 9b. For this row of nFETs, some of the "links" are "broken." This effectively removes some of the FETs from the circuit, resulting in the desired gate shown in Fig. 9c. This is the basic idea used in a PLA.

A PLA is shown in Fig. 10. It consists of two parts, an AND-PLANE and an OR-PLANE. Each of these two parts is a two-dimensional array of FETs. Every row

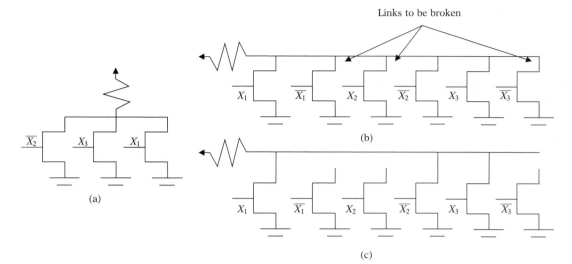

(c)

Figure 9. Programmable NOR gate.

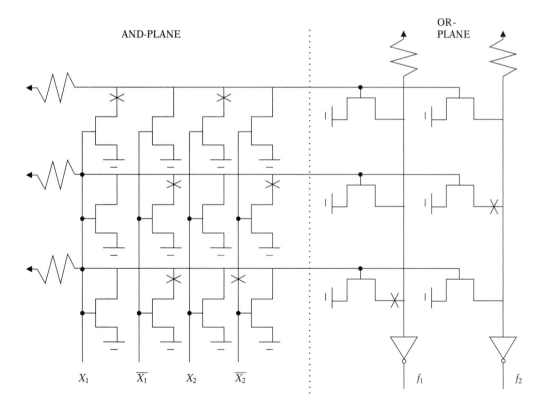

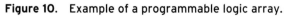

Figure 10. Example of a programmable logic array.

of the AND-PLANE is arranged to form a potential *nor* gate. All FETs in a column of the AND-PLANE are driven by the same input literal. Every column of the OR-PLANE is arranged to form a potential *nor* gate. The inputs of the FETs in a row of the OR-PLANE are driven by the output of the same *nor* gate of the AND-PLANE. Given such an array of FETs, a set of sum-of-products expressions is implemented by "selectively disconnecting" some of the FETs from the circuit. For example, to implement the following Boolean functions, the FETs to be disconnected are shown by "×" in Fig. 10.

$$f_1 = X_1 X_2 + \overline{X_1 X_2}$$

$$f_2 = X_1 X_2 + \overline{X}_1 X_2$$

Sequential Circuits

Consider a circuit with one input X and one output Y, defined as follows. Let n_j be the number of intervals, including and up to I_j, during which X had the value 1. At the end of I_j, Y is set to 1 if and only if n_j is divisible by 3. We call such a circuit *MOD-3*.

In order to compute the value of Y during the interval I_j, MOD-3 must remember some characteristics of the pattern of 0s and 1s during the intervals 1 to I_{j-1}. It is enough for the circuit to remember the value of $r_{j-1} = n_{j-1} \bmod 3$, which is nothing but the remainder left after dividing n_{j-1} by 3. Also note that if X, during I_j, equals 1, then $r_j = (r_{j-1} + 1) \bmod 3$; and if r_j equals 0, then Y is to be set to 1. Therefore, at the end of any

interval, we need to remember if the remainder was 0, 1, or 2.

Another way to express this behavior of MOD-3 is with the help of the *state diagram* of Fig. 11b. Since we need to know if r_j is 0, 1, or 2, we say that the circuit, at the end of I_j, is in state S_0 if r_j is 0, S_1 if r_j is 1, and S_2 if r_j is 2. The arrow marked a/b, which starts at S_i and ends at S_t, is to be interpreted as follows: if, at the end of the interval I_{j-1}, r_{j-1} is i and during interval I_j the value of X is a, then, at the end of interval I_j, the value of Y should be b and r_j should be t.

While designing a circuit from a state diagram, we have to make sure that the circuit "remembers" the state of the system. In order to do that, the states are *encoded* using two *state variables* a_0, a_1 as: $S_0 = (a_0 = 0, a_1 = 0)$; $S_1 = (a_0 = 0, a_1 = 1)$; and $S_2 = (a_0 = 1, a_1 = 0)$. The circuit now needs to remember the values of the state variables. In other words, the circuit should be capable of remembering *two bits of information*. This leads to the question: how exactly does a circuit remember two or more bits of information?

As they did for logic gates, circuit designers have devised circuit elements called *flip-flops*. A flip-flop can store (i.e. remember) one bit of information. The structure of a flip-flop is shown in Fig. 12a and we will use the symbol of Fig. 12b to represent such a flip-flop. Here Q is the output of the flip-flop and $\bar{Q}$ is another output, such that the value of $\bar{Q}$ is always the complement of the value of Q. D is the input to the flip-flop. When CLOCK is 1 and D is 1, Q is set

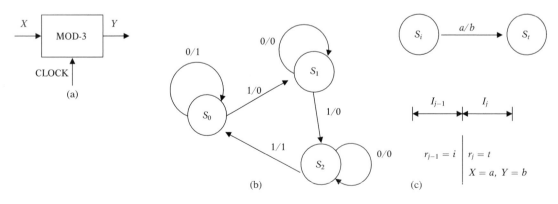

Figure 11.   Example of a state diagram.

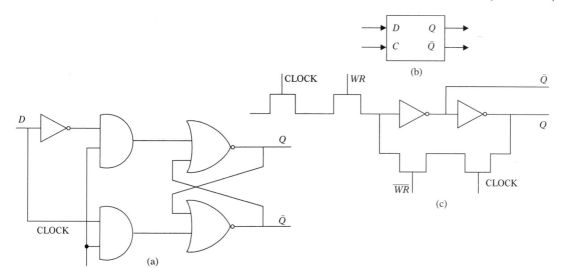

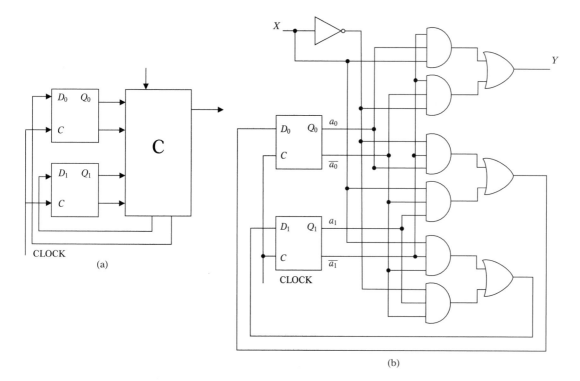

(b)

(c)

(a)

Figure 12. Structure of a flip-flop.

(a)

(b)

Figure 13. Implementation of the state diagram of Fig. 11.

Table 2.

Input X	S_i		S_t		Output Y
	a_0	a_1	D_0	D_1	
0	0	0	0	0	1
1	0	0	0	1	0
0	0	1	0	1	0
1	0	1	1	0	0
0	1	0	1	0	0
1	1	0	0	0	1
0	1	1	dc	dc	dc
1	1	1	dc	dc	dc

dc–don't care.

to 1. When D is 0 and CLOCK is 1, then Q is set to 0. When CLOCK is 0, the value of Q or $\bar{Q}$ cannot change. What we have just described is a D flip-flop. There are a number of other classes of flip-flops such as SR flip-flop, JK flip-flops, and so on. Figure 12c depicts a slight variation of a D flip-flop that uses nFETs. In this case, in order to modify the values of Q and $\bar{Q}$, both CLOCK and WR have to be 1.

The state table for our example, derivable from the state diagram, is shown in Table 2. For each edge in the state diagram, we have a row in the state table. The pair $\{a_0, a_1\}$ defines the state S_i of Fig. 11c; $\{D_0, D_1\}$ defines the state S_t; X defines the value a; and Y defines the value b. Note that D_0, D_1 will become the new value of a_0, a_1 at the start of the next interval. In order for that to happen, the circuit should be of the form shown in Fig. 13a, in which C must satisfy the conditions of the state table (Table 2). Since there is no state S_3, the case $a_0 = a_1 = 1$ cannot arise; hence there are "don't care" values in these rows. The complete circuit is shown in Fig. 13b. Note that Table 2 is like a truth table for the combinational block C of Fig. 13a. This is a simple, but not necessarily an efficient way to implement sequential circuits.

Bibliography

1998. Unger, S. H. *The Essence of Logic Circuits*, 2nd Ed. Upper Saddle River, NJ: Prentice Hall.

1998. Wolf, W. *Modern VLSI Design—Systems on Silicon*, 2nd Ed. Upper Saddle River, NJ: Prentice Hall.

2000. Wakerly, J. F. *Digital Design: Principles and Practice*, 3rd Ed. Upper Saddle River, NJ: Prentice Hall.

Sreejit Chakravarty

COMPUTER CRIME

For articles on related subjects, *see*

+ Electronic Commerce
+ Hacker
+ Legal Protection of Software
+ Virus, Computer

Introduction

Business, economic, and white-collar crimes have changed rapidly as computers proliferate. Computers have engendered a different form of crime. The Internet (*q.v.*), in particular, provides many new avenues for crime, such as identity theft and spreading computer viruses. Computers have been involved in fraud, theft, larceny, embezzlement, bribery, burglary, sabotage, espionage, conspiracy, extortion, attempted murder, manslaughter, distribution of pornography, trespassing, violation of privacy, and kidnapping.

US state and federal criminal codes contain at least 54 statutes defining computer crime. Any violations of these specific statutes are computer crimes; in some contexts it is also customary to include alleged violations of these statutes as computer crimes. Computer-related crimes—a broader category—are any violations of criminal law that involve a knowledge of computer technology for their perpetration, investigation, or prosecution. Although computer-related crimes are primarily white-collar offenses, any kind of illegal act based on an understanding of computer technology can be a computer-related crime, even violent crimes that destroy computers or their contents and thereby jeopardize human lives. Computer larceny—the theft and burglary of computers—is spreading rapidly as computers shrink in size to the point where security similar to that for jewelry must be applied. The victims and potential victims of computer crime include all organizations and people who use or are affected by computer and data communication systems, including people about whom data is stored and processed in computers. Those using the Internet are particularly vulnerable to computer crime.

Categories

Computer crime involves computers in one or more of four roles:

- *Object* Destruction of computers or of data or programs contained in them or of supportive facilities and resources.
- *Subject* A computer can be the site or environment of a crime or the source of or reason for unique forms and kinds of assets lost, such as a pirated computer program. A fraud perpetrated by changing account balances in financial data stored in a computer makes the computer storage the subject of a crime.
- *Instrument* A computer can be used actively, such as in automatically scanning Internet message packets for passwords and credit card numbers, or passively

to simulate a general ledger in the planning and control of a continuing financial embezzlement.

- *Symbol* A computer can be used as a symbol for intimidation or deception. This could involve an organization falsely claiming to use nonexistent computers.

Not all crimes involving a computer are *computer* crimes. If a computer is stolen in a simple theft where, based on all circumstances, it might just as well have been a washing machine or VCR, the thief needs no knowledge of computer technology and the act would not be a computer crime.

SRI International Inc.'s Computer Abuse Methods Model considers a classification system for computer abuses that is summarized in Fig. 1. The model is more of a system of descriptors than a taxonomy in the usual sense, in that multiple descriptors may apply in any particular case. For visual simplicity, this model is depicted as a simple tree, although that is an oversimplification—the classes are not mutually disjoint. The order of categorization depicted is roughly from the physical world to the hardware to the operating system (and network software) to the application code. The leftward branches all involve misuses, while the rightward branches represent potentially acceptable use

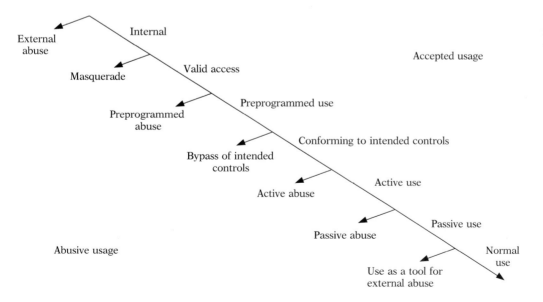

Figure 1. Computer abuse methods model.

until a leftward branch is taken. Every leftward branch represents a class of vulnerabilities that must be defended against and detected at the earliest possible time, but the techniques for doing so differ from one branch to the next.

History

The first recorded computer abuse occurred in 1958 (Parker *et al.*, 1973). The first federally prosecuted computer crime in the USA, identified as such, was the alteration of bank records by computer in Minneapolis in 1966.

In 1976, Senator Abraham Ribicoff and his US Senate Government Affairs Committee became aware of computer crime and the inadequacy of federal criminal law to deal with it. The committee produced two reports on its research (US Senate, 1976, 1977), and Senator Ribicoff introduced the first Federal Systems Protection Act Bill in June 1977. These legislative efforts evolved into House Bill 5616 in 1986, which resulted in the Computer Fraud and Abuse Act of 1987, established as Article 1030, Chapter 47 of Title 18 Criminal Code.

On the state level, Florida, Michigan, Colorado, Rhode Island, and Arizona were the first to adopt computer crime laws based on the first Ribicoff bill. Current legislation on computer crime exists in all US states and many other countries. The Computer Fraud and Abuse Act was modified in the early 1990s to make the creation and spreading of computer viruses a crime.

Computer crime has been portrayed fictionally in several novels, motion pictures, and television dramas. The British Broadcasting Corporation dramatized the computer crime aspects of a massive insurance fraud. NBC TV News and the CBS show "60 Minutes" have had special segments. The motion pictures *War Games* and *Sneakers* were the first to portray computer hacking. Unfortunately, public interest and sensationalism associated with computer crime, particularly the malicious hacker (*q.v.*) cases that peaked in 1982 and more recent computer virus cases, have made folk heroes of the perpetrators and embarrassed the victims.

Bibliography

1973. Parker, D. B., Nycum, S. H., and Oura, S. *Computer Abuse*. Menlo Park, CA: SRI International. Report distributed by National Technical Information Service, US Department of Commerce, Springfield, VA.

1976. Parker, D. B. *Crime by Computer*. New York: Charles Scribner's Sons.

1991. Hafner, K., and Markoff, J. *Cyberpunk: Outlaws and Hackers on the Computer Frontier*. New York: Simon and Schuster.

1992. Sterling, B. *The Hacker Crackdown: Law and Disorder on the Electronic Frontier*. New York: Bantam.

1997. Littman, J. *The Watchman (The Hacker Crimes of Kevin Poulson)*. New York: Bantam.

Donn B. Parker

COMPUTER ENGINEERING

For an article on a related subject, *see*

+ Computer Science

Computer engineering, as differentiated from *computer science*, focuses on the implementation aspects of the discipline, and the trade-offs required to produce viable computing systems. Like computer science, computer engineering is concerned with all elements of information-processing systems, including the application environment (e.g. visualization of the results of a computation, artificial intelligence, computational science, and perceptual and cognitive processes), paradigms for representing information (e.g. algorithms for numeric and nonnumeric applications, symbol manipulation, and language processing), paradigms for processing information (e.g. distributed computing, information storage and retrieval, programs for managing computing resources, programs for transforming source programs, hardware execution models, programming languages and compilers, and networks that interconnect pieces of a computer system and those that connect complete systems), and tools for designing and measuring the effectiveness of computer systems (e.g. CAD design tools and performance measurement and analysis tools). Also, like computer science, computer engineering is concerned with the human–machine interface, computer vision (*q.v.*), robotics (*q.v.*), computer graphics (*q.v.*), reliable computer systems, logic circuits, hardware devices and structures, and application-specific computers.

The discipline of computing is characterized by three recurrent themes: theory, abstraction, and design (Denning *et al.*, 1989). Computer engineering and computer science both involve all three, but design is the preeminent domain of computer engineering, while theory is central to computer science. Abstraction, by which we master complexity, has an important role in both: it helps the engineer to crystallize thoughts to achieve a better design, and it helps the scientist to crystallize ideas to achieve a more robust theory.

As in the relationship between science and engineering in general, the science may yield results that become important for engineering. Theories of data abstraction may fall under computer science, but abstract data types (*q.v.*) are now essential for good software engineering (*q.v.*). Computer engineering and computer science are coupled particularly tightly; for example, much work in programming languages has been motivated by the need for reliable software engineering design methods.

Computer engineering and computer science are not at all differentiated by whether they involve hardware or software, since each involves both. Rather, computer engineering is more concerned with the implementation of ideas, while computer science is more concerned with the formal structure of those ideas.

Bibliography

1989. Denning, P. J., Comer, D. E., Gries, D., Mulder, M. C., Tucker, A. B., Turner, A. J., and Young, P. R. "Computing as a Discipline," *Communications of the ACM*, **32**(1), (January), 9–23.

1992. Chen, C. H. (ed.) *Computer Engineering Handbook.* New York: McGraw-Hill.

Yale Patt

COMPUTER GAMES

For articles on related subjects, *see*

+ Artificial Intelligence (AI)
+ Computer Chess
+ Videogames

HISTORY

Computers were not invented to play games. In the 1950s and 1960s, with computer time both scarce and expensive, writing games for fun was actively discouraged at most computing centers. Nevertheless, there were many other reasons for writing computer games: exploring the power of the computer; improving understanding of human thought processes; producing educational tools; simulating dangerous environments; and providing the means for discovery learning.

In some sense, the association of computers and games started in 1950 when Alan Turing proposed his famous *imitation game* in the article "Computing Machinery and Intelligence," published in *Mind* magazine (*see* TURING TEST). Never programmed by Turing himself, a variation of Turing's game called *Eliza* was put in the form of a computer program 13 years later by Joseph Weizenbaum at MIT.

The first military simulation games were programmed in 1952 by Bob Chapman and others at the Rand Air Defense Lab in Santa Monica. In the same year, a number of simple games such as Nim and tic-tac-toe were programmed for several early computers. Also in 1952, a computer was specially designed to play Hex, a game with no exact solution, by E. F. Moore and Claude Shannon at Bell Labs in New Jersey. In 1953, Arthur Samuel first demonstrated his Checkers program for the IBM 701. The next year, the first primer on game theory, *The Compleat Strategyst* by J. D. Williams, was published by Rand Corporation. The first computer game of blackjack was programmed in 1954 for the IBM 701 at the Atomic Energy Lab at Los Alamos, NM. Also in 1954, a crude game of pool—perhaps

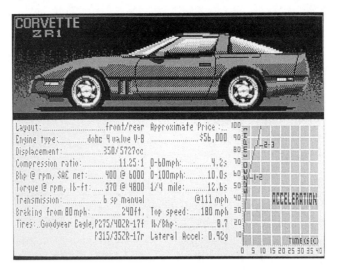

Figure 1. In "Test Drive," players can choose to drive various cars on a variety of demanding tracks and courses. (Courtesy Accolade, Inc.)

Figure 2. In "Yeager," a typical flight simulator, players must learn to land on a carrier deck, tough even for seasoned pilots. (Courtesy Electronic Arts, Inc.)

the first nonmilitary game to use a video display—was programmed at the University of Michigan.

In 1958, a tennis game was designed for an analog computer at Brookhaven National Laboratory by Willy Higinbotham. This game, played on an oscilloscope display, was significant in that it was the first videogame to permit two players to control the direction and motion of the object (the ball) moving on the screen.

With the delivery in 1959 of the first Digital Equipment Corporation (DEC) PDP-1 with its 15-in. video display, the continuing evolution from text-only games to videogames was hastened. Written by Slug Russel, Shag Gratz, and Alan Kotok, the first game for

Figure 3. "Hardball," a baseball simulation, provides realistic player animation, instant replays, complete player and team statistics, and five field perspectives. (Courtesy Accolade, Inc.)

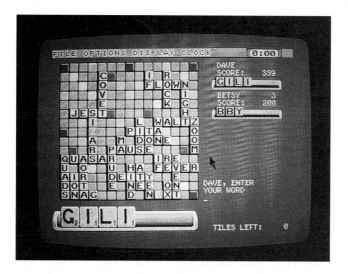

Figure 4. Computer versions of virtually every card and board game, such as this version of Scrabble, are available for one or more players. (Courtesy Hasbro Interactive, Inc.)

the PDP-1 was "Spacewar," first demonstrated at an MIT open house in 1962.

Various types of graphics displays from many manufacturers were introduced in the mid-1960s. Thus, we find a video pool game developed at RCA (1967), a ball-and-paddle game by Ralph Baer at Sanders Associates (1967), later to become the Magnavox Odyssey home videogame in 1972, a rocket car simulation by Judah Schwartz at MIT (1968), a graphic flight simulation by Evans and Sutherland (1969), a lunar lander game at DEC (1969), and a device to permit computer output and standard television video on the same display at Stanford (1968). In the October 1970 issue of *Scientific American*, Martin Gardner devoted his "Mathematical Games" column to a description of John Conway's "Game of Life" (*see* CELLULAR AUTOMATA). Easily programmed, it began to appear on virtually every video computer terminal in the country within weeks.

In 1971, Nolan Bushnell rewrote "Spacewar" as a coin-operated arcade game called "Computer Space," which was marketed by Nutting Associates. Only 1500 units were sold, but a year later, Bushnell's next project, the Pong arcade game, was considerably more successful and led to the foundation of the Atari Corporation. In 1972, Willy Crowther and Don Woods wrote a game for the DEC PDP-10 that they simply called "Adventure." The game, the first in the interactive role-playing fantasy genre, was unbelievably addictive and players consumed vast amounts of time-shared computer time on whatever system it was loaded.

Atari introduced the home version of Pong in 1975 and it was followed a year later by literally hundreds of imitators. Removable-cartridge home games were first introduced by Fairchild in 1976, followed by Bally, Atari, and others a year later. By 1982, over 100 companies had entered the market with game systems or cartridges.

The kit era of personal computers lasted only two years and by 1977 manufacturers of self-contained, assembled computers such as Commodore, Apple, and Radio Shack took the market by storm. This opened the computer game floodgates, as the cost of entry was so low. In more than one case, bright teenage programmers started game companies and hired their parents as employees. For a glimpse at the aftermath, *see* VIDEOGAMES.

David H. Ahl

TRADITIONAL GAMES

There are several reasons to study game playing by computers. The first relates to the popular conception of computers as "giant brains." Even the earliest digital computers could do arithmetic and make decisions at a rate thousands of times faster than humans could. Thus, it was felt that computers could be set up to perform intelligent activities, such as to translate French to English, recognize sloppy handwriting, and play chess. A new scientific discipline arose from these considerations and became known as *artificial intelligence* (*q.v.*).

A second reason involves the understanding by humans of their own intelligence. It is conjectured that computer mechanisms for game playing bear a resemblance to human thought processes. If this is true, game-playing computers can help us understand how human minds work.

Another reason for studying games is that they are well-defined activities. Most games use very simple equipment and have a simple set of rules. Usually, the ultimate goal (winning) can be very simply defined. A computer can be easily programmed to follow the rules of any board or card game. This allows the computer scientist to devote more effort to the problem of getting the computer to play an intelligent game.

Basic Techniques

The fundamental reason for the ability of computers to play a variety of games is that computers have the ability to represent arbitrary situations and processes through the use of symbols and logic operations. For example, one can set up a chess position inside a computer by means of an 8×8 array of integers, and tentative moves can be made by computer instructions that change the positions of the numbers in the array (Fig. 1). This capability is extremely general. That is, the symbols could represent checker pieces, or with a slight rearrangement, they could be playing cards for poker or bridge.

Figure 1 also shows the representation of derived information. The values of the pieces are stored in another 8×8 array for use by the computer. In effect, they are part of the computer's "knowledge" of the values of chess pieces.

Since symbols can be used to represent the objects of a particular game, computer instructions can be written by a programmer to specify the procedures for playing the game according to the rules and also for playing the game according to a strategy. The game of tic-tac-toe,

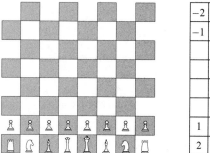

-2	-3	-4	-5	-6	-4	-3	-2
-1	-1	-1	-1	-1	-1	-1	-1
1	1	1	1	1	1	1	1
2	3	4	5	6	4	3	2

-5	-3	-3	-9	$-\infty$	-3	-3	-5
-1	-1	-1	-1	-1	-1	-1	-1
1	1	1	1	1	1	1	1
5	3	3	9	∞	3	3	5

Figure 1. Computer representation of a chess position. In the second array, numbers are used to represent the various pieces. The third array represents the values of the pieces for use by the computer in evaluating trades.

for example, can be played perfectly by the following algorithm, in which the word "row" refers to a row, column, or diagonal.

Algorithm A (the computer plays X)

A1. Perform the first applicable step that follows.

A2. Search for two Xs in a row. If found, then make three Xs in a row.

A3. Search for two Os in a row. If found, then block them with an X.

A4. If there are Os at opposite corners, place an X in a side square if one is vacant.

A5. Search for two rows that intersect with an empty square, each of which contains one X and no Os. If found, then place an X on the intersection.

A6. Search for two rows that intersect at an empty square, each of which contains one O and no Xs. If found, place an X at the intersection.

A7. If there is an O in a corner and the center is empty, place an X there.

A8. Search for a vacant corner square. If found, then place an X on the vacancy.

A9. Search for a vacant square. If found, then place an X on the vacancy.

The algorithm is perfect in the sense that it will find a forced win if it exists and it will never lose. This algorithm may be called a *rejection scheme* because the first applicable step (following A1) is to be performed and all other steps are rejected (Fig. 2).

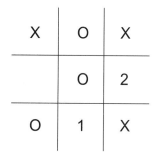

Figure 2. In the position shown here, algorithm A would choose a move at square 2 for a win rather than at square 1, to block the opponent win. This is done because step A2 precedes step A3.

For another example, consider the following game, a special case of Nim. It is played with 13 matches; two players remove matches in turn until one player is forced to take the last match. A player may remove only one to three matches in a single turn, and the player who removes the last match is the loser. This is an algorithm for perfect play.

Algorithm B (the computer plays second)

B1. Let n be the number of matches taken by the opponent at the last turn.

B2. Remove $(4 - n)$ matches.

B3. If the game is not over, go to Step B1.

Both tic-tac-toe and Nim are simple examples of a large number of games classed as two-person games of skill. An essential feature of these games is that both players have perfect information about the current state of the game. Chess, checkers, and Go are well-known games of pure skill. In order to show that an optimal strategy exists for such two-person games of skill, the principle of *minimax* must be explained. If the state of a game is represented by a circle and the moves from that state are represented by lines, then a tree can be obtained that represents the set of all possible games. The leaves of this tree (Fig. 3) can all be labeled with the terms *win*, *loss*, or *draw* for the first player. Now consider any node that is followed only by labeled nodes. If that node corresponds to the first player's move and it is connected to a node labeled *win*, then it may be labeled with the term win. It may be labeled *draw*, if it is connected to a node labeled draw, otherwise, it is labeled *loss*. If it is the second player's move from a position, then a loss (for player 1) is most preferred. This procedure can be repeated to back up the values W, L, and D to the top of the lookahead tree. Optimal strategy consists of each player choosing the path corresponding to the label W, D, or L at the node for the current move, once all nodes up to the top have been labeled. In the tree of Fig. 3, the best outcome for player 1 is a draw, and that is also the best outcome for player 2 once player

1 has made the optimal first move. In other words, a player makes the best move, based on the assumption that the opponent will make the best reply, and the opponent's reply assumes that the player will make the best counter-reply, and so on.

Thus, since all possible chess games can be expressed in a tree, it is known that there is a perfect strategy for chess that guarantees a win or a draw for one player. Of course, the strategy has never been found. It is the combinatorics of game playing that prevent the discovery of perfect strategies. In chess, when it is a player's turn to move, that player has, on average, 30 legal moves resulting in 30 different positions. If the opponent also has 30 replies to each of these moves, then 900 positions result. This sort of calculation gives an estimate of 10^{125} as the size of the lookahead tree for chess (the number of paths from the top of the tree to the terminal positions). If a computer could examine a billion positions per second, it would still take 10^{108} years to examine the entire lookahead tree to determine the optimal strategy.

A second class of games involves no skill at all, and a player's success depends only on chance. Examples are craps and roulette, in which the roll of dice or drop of a ball determines whether a bet is won or lost. A third and most important class of games involves a mixture of skill and chance of varying degrees. This includes games

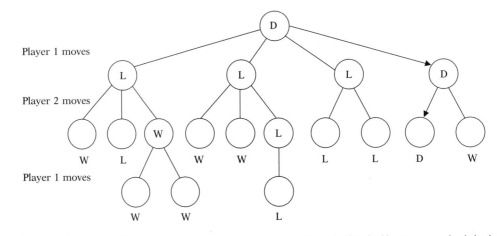

Figure 3. Illustration of the minimax procedure. The values at the bottom are calculated by an evaluation function. The backed-up values in circles reflect the result of optimal play. The arrows show the path of optimal play.

such as poker, bridge, backgammon, and Monopoly, which are affected by the distribution of cards or the roll of dice, although these randomizing features are generally overcome in the long run by the skill of a player. Computers can be set up to play these games of chance, but it is usually more difficult to represent the tree for a game when probabilistic factors are present.

Game-Playing Programs

The first improvement that can be made for computer play is to establish an evaluation function for game positions that are not final. This allows the computer to examine part of the game tree and apply minimax to the terminal search values, resulting in a move. A refinement is alpha–beta minimax, which applies the principle "If a move is refuted, don't try to refute it even more." For the computer, this involves setting cutoff values for each search node based on values achieved at a given point in the search.

An early and very successful game-playing program is Arthur Samuel's (1967) checker player, which was able to play a world champion to a draw. More recently, Jonathan Schaeffer has developed Chinook, a checker player that is considered unbeatable by any human player. Backgammon has been programmed at world champion level by Hans Berliner. Othello (or Reversi) has also been conquered by computer.

Go-Moku has become an extremely popular subject for computerization. It is essentially a game of the tic-tac-toe type, with each player trying to achieve five in a row on a 19×19 board. Since 1975, a North American computer Go-Moku tournament has been held, and, since 1977, there has also been a European tournament.

The more complex game of Go is played by placing black and white stones on a 19×19 grid, and the most important feature of play is the emergence of groups or armies of similarly colored stones. Human perception can rapidly see the groups, but computers have trouble simulating human pattern matching. The best programs are still 20 levels below world champion level, even though computer tournaments have been held since 1985.

Bridge is an especially interesting case, since there are two distinct phases of play—bidding and trick taking.

Anthony Wasserman has produced a bridge bidder that achieves an expert level of skill. An unusual feature of his program is that it knows all standard, bidding conventions and therefore, can be adjusted to be an ideal partner for any player. Wasserman's approach was to use a base language, Algol, to implement primitive elements of bridge bidding; for example, a routine FIVECARDMAJOR[NORTH] that returns TRUE or FALSE, depending on the north hand cards. Higher-level routines are built in layers over the primitives.

Of all games programmed for computers, more time and effort has been devoted to computer chess (*q.v.*) than to any other. A recent trend is the emergence of microcomputer-based games on the mass market. The quality of play varies, with backgammon, checker, and chess programs playing quite well and bridge programs playing at a lower level. Rapid improvements in the quality and variety of these games may be expected.

Bibliography

1980. Berliner, H. J. "Backgammon Computer Program Beats World Champion," *Artificial Intelligence*, **14**, 205–220.

1990. Hsu, F., Anantharanum, T., Campbell, M., and Nowatzyk, A. "A Grandmaster Chess Machine," *Scientific American*, **263**(4), 44–50.

1996. Schaeffer, J., Lake, R., Lu, P., and Bryant, M. "Chinook: The Man–Machine World Checkers Champion," *AI Magazine*, **17**(1), 21–29.

1997. Schaeffer, J. *One Jump Ahead: Challenging Human Supremacy in Checkers.* New York: Springer-Verlag.

Albert L. Zobrist

COMPUTER GRAPHICS

PRINCIPLES

For articles on related subjects, see

+ Artificial Life
+ Cellular Automata

+ Computer-Aided Design/Computer-Aided Manufacturing (CAD/CAM)
+ Computer Animation
+ Computer Art
+ Computer Games
+ Computer Vision
+ Entertainment Industry, Computers in the
+ Fractals
+ Image Processing
+ Interactive Input Devices
+ Medical Imaging
+ Monitor, Display
+ Pattern Recognition
+ User Interface
+ Videogames
+ Virtual Reality
+ Workstation

Computer graphics consists of two steps: describing an image and then displaying it. There are a number of other issues that also come into play. Is the image an individual one or part of a series of images in an animation? Is the image to be static, or can a computer user interact with a software package to change it? Is the goal of the image to be highly realistic because it will be viewed at length, or is it just to give a quick impression of the scene?

In the past, graphics was limited to narrow applications. Documents were entered as text with special formatting codes and only seen in their final form when printed. Objects in images were very simple and appeared highly artificial. Now, graphics is an expected part of every software package. Word processors use graphics technology to display documents as they are being created, so given that both characters and images are just arrays of pixels, it is no harder to display one than the other. Computer users expect graphical user interfaces (GUI) as part of modern software packages. Images in games and educational software are highly realistic.

There are two different views of computer graphics. A graphics system user is interested in what images are produced, what they mean, and how they can be manipulated. A graphics system programmer is interested in how to write graphics-based applications programs for those users. This article is about the latter.

Areas related to computer graphics are image processing, and image analysis or computer vision. In image processing, the input and output are both images. The work that is done on these images is to enhance the information that they contain. This process may improve the balance of the image colors, or may sharpen the contrast. In image analysis or computer vision, the process is the reverse of what is done in graphics, since an image is analyzed and a description of the environment it depicts is created.

Interactive vs Noninteractive Graphics

The choice between interactive and noninteractive computer graphics depends on the application. Interactive graphics is used for systems in which the user plays a significant and active role in the system. A *computer-aided design/computer-aided manufacturing* (CAD/CAM-*q.v.*) system must be interactive since the user must create the object and its components as they are viewed on the computer monitor. CAD/CAM developed out of the 1960s realization that the computer could help with these drawing intensive activities. Projects were developed to help with car (General Motors) and lens design (Itek). Visualization systems are also frequently interactive so that the user can replay animation sequences, magnify parts of the image that appear interesting (*zooming*), and alter colors used so that different phenomena are highlighted. Applications that by their nature require frequent user input are programmed as interactive systems.

Noninteractive graphics systems are primarily those that are so computationally complex that the production of a single image takes longer than the time even the most patient user would wait. The production of realistic imagery using techniques of *radiosity* and *ray tracing* and the production of animated sequences can be very time-consuming. In these cases, the user will define the environment for the image using some preprocessing system. This definition then serves as the input for the *image generator*, which can be run in background mode. The resulting images are usually stored in a file and viewed at a later time using a device-dependent postprocessor. Some complex animation sequences of a few minutes duration take many hours of compute time to prepare.

Some Representative Uses of Computer Graphics

Data Visualization

Data visualization is a very broad term that includes the creation of images for science, business, and many other applications. The basic idea is to use color theory and design to present information in a way that efficiently and effectively displays large amounts of data to improve understanding, reveal trends, or display phenomena. Visualization allows a user to capture and display data in such a way as to give the scientist a better understanding of the forces at work. For example, an animated sequence of warm and cold water mixing can represent direction of water movement with an arrow, water velocity by the arrow size, and temperature by arrow color for various data collection locations.

Games

Computer games have shown great progress from the simple ball and paddle games of the 1970s. Today, computer games have high-quality graphics, produced in real time, along with fast-paced user interaction. These games are produced as either stand-alone units for arcades, tabletop units that connect to a television or monitor, or software for use on a computer. Examples include computer versions of popular board games or television game shows, sports or athletic competitions, and combative games that are frequently in futuristic settings. *See also* VIDEOGAMES.

Virtual Reality

Computer graphics plays a large role in virtual reality systems, as do sound and movement. The intent is to create the illusion that the user is in another environment—through the use of images, movements, and sounds—and can interact with it through specialized input devices.

Graphical User Interfaces (GUIs)

Computer users now expect that software will have an interface that makes it easy to use. Interaction with computers is now commonly done through GUIs that present files and directories as *icons*, that allow data to be moved or copied by dragging icons around the screen, and that request information through buttons and check boxes on dialog boxes that pop up when needed. *See* USER INTERFACE and WINDOW ENVIRONMENTS.

Animation

Animated movies are only one of the uses of computer animation. Computer-generated animation is also part of training simulators and videogames. Animation is affecting the legal system as litigants design animations, based on physical evidence, that show a jury what allegedly happened. *See* COMPUTER ANIMATION.

Art

Some artists use a computer for tasks throughout the entire artistic process, from sketching or ideation, through the production of prototypes or drafts, and then for the final work, which can be a traditional sculpture or painting, a computer print, or an interactive installation. *See* COMPUTER ART.

The Early History of Graphics Technology

From the earliest days of computing, people were interested in having computers draw pictures. Graphs of data were constructed on line printers by carefully printing spaces and symbols on successive lines. Computer-driven cathode ray tube (CRT) displays were a part of the output of MIT's Whirlwind (*q.v.*) Computer (1950) and the Sage Air Defense System (mid-1950s). Input devices that were precursors to the mouse and lightpen were also part of early computer systems. Ivan Sutherland was an interactive computer graphics pioneer when he developed his *Sketchpad* drawing system in 1963.

In the 1960s, displays were monochrome and vector-based, with all images drawn as a set of lines. A full display system consisted of a display processor, a display list, and a CRT. The display list stored a series of points representing the ends of the lines to be drawn and the sole task of the display processor was to draw those lines repeatedly on the CRT. Changing the image on the screen required changing the points stored in the display list. CRTs, both then and now, create an image with a phosphor and an electron beam. To draw a line on the screen, the electron beam is deflected along the path of the line. As the electrons strike the phosphor, it is energized and made to glow. Over time, light from the line diminishes as more and more energy is released. Thus, each line must be refreshed at least 30 times a second or the viewer will be able to perceive the dimming of the phosphor and the image will appear to flicker.

Modern Graphics Hardware

There are two kinds of graphics hardware: softcopy and hardcopy. The first category includes devices that produce output that can change. Display and projection units are in this category because the image that is drawn on the screen is not permanent. The second category includes devices that produce fixed output, typically on paper and film, such as printers, plotters, and film recorders.

Display devices used today have their origin in the mid-1970s, and use a technology called *raster graphics*. As in television technology, an image is created by lighting discrete spots of phosphor, each called a *pixel* (picture element), and letting the eye merge them into a picture. In a monochrome monitor, these pixels have only one color phosphor, but in an RGB color monitor, each pixel is a triad of Red, Green, and Blue phosphor (*see* MONITOR, DISPLAY). The image on the screen is composed of pixels in a grid typically about 640 rows of 1024 pixels each, though monitors are available that can display over 16 times this number. Monitors will typically refresh the image 30 to 60 times a second.

Hardcopy technology also includes both vector and raster devices. Plotters will create their output as a series of lines in much the same way as a vector display. These high quality drawings are typically used in design, architecture, and artistic applications. Printers and film recorders operate like raster devices, producing discrete locations of color on paper or film.

Realistic Image Generation

The creation of a realistic computer graphics image involves a number of steps. The coordinates of the "world" are chosen, objects are defined and placed into this world, the location of the "viewer" is set, and a window is specified identifying the part of the scene that is visible. Once this is done, software will now determine what part of the world can be ignored because it is not visible, and then draw the rest of the objects on the basis of their definitions. The first stage of this process, the description of the world, is called *modeling*. The second stage, the drawing of the world, is called *rendering*.

Modeling
Concepts

Before a computer can create an image, descriptions must be developed for all of the objects that are to appear in it. Model descriptions can be created by hand using a plain text editor to enter the model data or by software that allows interactive specification while a crude depiction of the model is displayed. Many of the models used in graphics are highly mathematical and rely on the equations of lines, planes, circles, spheres, ovals, and complex curves and surfaces. Models can be hierarchical, defining a collection of simple objects and then using those to define larger and more complex objects. An example of this would be a model of a bicycle that had a simple wheel object defined that was then replicated for the front and back wheels.

Object attributes

Each displayed object has parameters that determine its position and size, as well as others that determine its appearance. For simple objects drawn as lines, attributes specify the color and whether the lines are solid or dashed in some fashion. Text attributes include the font type (e.g. Courier, Helvetica) and the character style (e.g. bold, italic). *See* TYPEFONT.

As objects become more complex, more parameters must be specified. For 3D objects, the following types of properties are typically specified:

- *Reflectivity* What portion of light that strikes an object reflects off it? Is the reflection sharp like a mirror (specular) or dull like metal? Does the reflection stay focused, or does it diffuse and spread?
- *Refractivity* What portion of light that strikes an object refracts through it? How much does the refraction shift or bend the light (as a pencil in a glass of water appears bent)? Is the object transparent like clear glass or translucent like tracing paper?
- *Absorptivity* How much of the light energy striking an object is absorbed by the object and neither reflected nor refracted?
- *Texture* Does the object have a smooth or rough surface? If rough, is there a pattern to the roughness or is it random?

Additional properties may be specified for objects on the basis of the needs of the model type or on the rendering method to be used.

Modeling two-dimensional objects

Two-dimensional (2D) objects include simple objects such as circles, lines, and polygons, as well as more complex curves described through mathematical equations. Circles can be specified by their center point and radius. An arc is a portion of circle, and so has the additional parameters of starting and ending radii. An oval or ellipse can be specified by two centers of curvature and a length. All points whose sum of distances to both centers is equal to the specified length are on the ellipse. Lines can be specified as a starting and ending point, or as the coefficients of the equation of a line. A polygon is specified as a list of points that are the vertices of the polygon.

Modeling three-dimensional objects

Simple 3D objects can be defined like their 2D counterparts. A sphere can be defined by specifying its center and radius. A box can be defined by specifying the locations of its eight vertices. If we place restrictions on the orientation of the box, so that all of its faces must be perpendicular to either the x, y, or z axis, then we need to specify only two vertices that are opposite each other, because the other six vertices can be derived from these two. A planar surface can be uniquely defined by

specifying three noncollinear points. This plane can be considered infinite in all directions or can be triangular-bounded by the lines connecting these three points. That is, three points (P_1, P_2, and P_3) uniquely specify a plane with the equation $Ax + By + Cz + D = 0$. Curved surfaces can be defined mathematically, or by a set of small planar patches. For highly curved surfaces, this approximation can get quite large, since the planar patches must be small if the result is to look reasonable.

Solids modeling

Objects described by their outer surfaces are fine for applications that require only the production of images, but systems designed to manipulate or test created objects need an alternative representation. Solids modeling treats all objects as solids, clearly identifying the inside and outside of each object, which allows tests for stress and obstruction as well as production of parts lists. This is the underlying model for CAD/CAM systems. In solids modeling, the system has a collection of primitive objects that can be scaled, rotated, and translated. Complex objects are built by applying Boolean operations to simpler objects. A washer can be created by subtracting a short narrow cylinder from a short wide one. A door hinge pin can be created through the logical union of a wide, short cylinder with a tall, narrow one.

Rendering

Windowing

Since large drawings cannot fit in their entirety on display screens, they can either be compressed to fit, thereby obscuring details and creating clutter, or only a portion of the total drawing can be displayed. The portion of a 2D or 3D object to be displayed is chosen through specification of a rectangular window that limits what part of the drawing can be seen. A 2D window is usually defined by choosing a maximum and minimum value for its x- and y-coordinates, or by specifying the center of the window and giving its maximum relative height and width. Simple subtractions or comparisons suffice to determine whether a point is in view. For lines and polygons, a *clipping* operation is performed that discards those parts that fall outside of the window. Only those parts that remain inside the window are drawn or otherwise rendered to make them visible.

Lighting models

As a prelude to discussion of shading models, we discuss the way in which the effects of incident light can be quantified for image production. The first type of illumination to be considered is *ambient light, I_a*, present in the environment. Since ambient light has no focus or direction, this is treated as an additive factor for all objects. The second type of light is *reflected light*, which varies depending on the location of the light source, the object, and the viewer. From Lambert's cosine law of physics, we know that the intensity of the diffusely reflected light is related to the scalar (dot) product of the surface normal, **N**, and a unit vector pointing toward the light source, **L**. The last type of illumination is *specular reflection,* which produces the highlights on an object. Specular reflection (Fig. 1) depends on the angle between the reflected vector, **R**, and the vector pointing at the viewer's position, **V**. If these two coincide, the highlight is bright; the further apart they are, the dimmer the highlight.

Painter's and Z-buffer algorithms

In the Painter's Algorithm, each object is broken into planar piece approximations that are arranged as separate units, according to their distance from the viewer. The algorithm now works like a painter applying paint to a canvas—if something is blocked by an object in front, the painter just paints the foreground object over it.

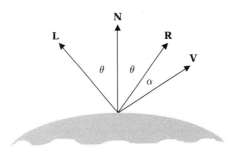

Figure 1. Specular reflection.

The piece farthest from the viewer is drawn, then the second farthest, and so on. If a piece will ultimately be visible, nothing will be drawn over it; however, if it is not entirely visible, a piece drawn later will cover all or part of it. So the picture is drawn back to front.

In the Z-Buffer Algorithm, there is a Z- or *depth-buffer* that has one value for each pixel in the frame buffer. These values represent the depth of the object of which the pixel is a part. For example, if an area of four pixels square is part of the first object, which is 4 units away from the viewer, all of the Z-buffer values for these pixels would be set to 4. As each new piece is drawn, its depth at the pixel location is compared with the Z-buffer value. If the buffer value is greater, this piece is in front and can be drawn (and the Z-buffer value is updated). If the buffer value is smaller, the old object is closer, so the current one is not drawn at that point. The benefit of the Z-buffer algorithm is that it is not necessary to sort the pieces, as the Z-buffer does that implicitly.

These two algorithms show the common space vs time trade-off of computer science. The Painter's Algorithm is slower because of the sorting, but it doesn't require the extremely large memory of the Z-buffer. With the low cost of computer memory, however, many graphics controllers include extra memory specifically for the Z-buffer.

Flat shading

A problem with the Painter's and Z-Buffer Algorithms is that they ignore the effects of the light source and use only the ambient light factor. Flat shading goes a bit further and includes the diffuse reflections as well. For each of the planar pieces, an intensity value is calculated from the surface normal, the direction to the light, and the ambient light and diffuse coefficient constants. Since none of these change at any point on the piece, all of the pixels in that piece will have the same intensity value. The resulting image will appear to be faceted, with ridges running along the boundaries of the pieces that make up an object (*see* Fig. 2a).

Figure 2. (a) Flat shading; (b) Gouraud shading; (c) Phong shading. (Courtesy of David Weimer and Gary Bishop, AT&T Bell Laboratories.)

Gouraud shading

In 1971, Henri Gouraud developed an interpolation method that removed some of the discontinuities between pieces and also produced more realistic highlighting (Fig. 2b). The problem with the previous method is that a single normal is used for a patch that approximates a curved surface. Gouraud's method keeps the normal vector from the actual surface for each vertex of every piece. This means that the normals at the vertices of a patch can be different from each other, but that the normals where two patches touch will be the same since they come from the actual surface at that point.

Phong shading

Gouraud shading improved on the images that were produced by flat shading, but the highlighting was still off. In 1975, Bui-Tuong Phong improved on Gouraud shading by interpolating the normals across the surface, as opposed to the intensities (Fig. 2c). This leads to finer and more precise highlights.

Ray tracing

In the methods examined so far, all objects are assumed to have a matte or dull finish. None is reflective, translucent, or transparent, because the previous methods are not able to handle these types of objects. *Ray tracing* takes the previous methods one step further in allowing rays of light that strike a surface

to reflect and refract among all the objects in the scene. When the viewer location and pixel location on the screen are considered, they define a line or ray into the scene to be rendered. This ray is traced into the scene, in which it can strike a matte surface object, and the pixel color is determined as in Phong shading. If the ray strikes a reflective or refractive surface, the laws of optics are used to determine the new direction of one or more rays that would result. These new rays are then traced recursively until they leave the scene or strike another surface.

Texture mapping

Early computer-generated images used shaded objects that had unnaturally smooth surfaces. To produce a textured surface using the techniques discussed would require creating an excessive number of surface pieces that follow all of the complexities of the texture. An alternative to the explosion of surfaces would be to use the techniques of *texture mapping*. Texture mapping is a technique used to paint scanned images of a texture onto the object being modeled. Through an associated technique, called *bump mapping*, the appearance of the texture can be improved still further.

Animation

Animated cartoons were the hallmark of Walt Disney, whose studio produced a number of classic films. This work, called *cel animation*, first requires the production of an overall storyboard. From that, individual scenes are created, with the *animator* drawing only key frames, an *in-betweener* drawing the frames connecting the key frames, and an *inker* adding the proper colors. The characters are drawn on acetate sheets called cels that are laid over the background and photographed to make the animated scene, a very labor-intensive process. Computers help by automating in-betweening and inking, or even more commonly, by controlling the whole process (*see* COMPUTER ANIMATION).

Conclusion

Computer graphics has a unique role in computer science because of its ability not only to illuminate information, simulate complex processes, and make computers easier to work with, but also to entertain. Graphics professionals will continue to advance the abilities of computers to create realistic images, making it difficult to decide what is real and what is created by computer. The impact of this on law, business, and human relationships will be far-reaching.

Bibliography

1990. Foley, J., van Dam, A., Feiner, S. K., and Hughes, J. F. *Computer Graphics: Principles and Practice*. Reading, MA: Addison-Wesley.
1990. Hill, F. S. *Computer Graphics*. New York: Macmillan.
1993. Watt, A. H. *3D Computer Graphics*. Reading, MA: Addison-Wesley.
1994. Foley, J., van Dam, A., Feiner, S. K., Hughes, J. F., and Phillips, R. *Introduction to Computer Graphics*. Reading, MA: Addison-Wesley.

Jeffrey J. McConnell

STANDARDS

For articles on related subjects, *see*

+ Image Compression
+ Multimedia
+ User Interface
+ Window Environments

Introduction

Computer graphics standards serve one of several purposes. *Application Programming Interfaces* (APIs) provide a foundation on which to build graphics applications. They typically provide toolkits of useful primitive graphical elements and thereby relieve the application of the burden of managing both graphical data and physical graphics devices. Historically, the goals of such APIs were to support application portability across computing systems and support operability of applications with different graphics devices (often called "device independence"). Today both goals are less important because APIs (and applications) are typically platform dependent and because graphics devices in common usage are less diverse. *Graphical file formats* (also called *graphical metafiles*), on the other hand, provide a way to describe graphical objects such as pictures or interactive virtual worlds so that different platforms that exchange descriptions can create equivalent pictures and behavior from them. In addition, specialized graphical interfaces and metafile formats can be defined at any of several levels of abstraction between applications and graphical devices.

Computer Graphics Reference Model

The Computer Graphics Reference Model (CGRM) is a special International Standard intended to be a model for the development of future standards. A reference model is an authoritative basis for the development of standards. It provides a pattern or set of principles that they must adhere to. The CGRM defines computer graphics as the creation of, manipulation of, analysis of, and interaction with pictorial representations of objects and data using computers. The CGRM itself consists of a set of models that explain important aspects of computer graphics. Figure 1 is one of these models that describes the interfaces between computer graphics and external objects. The four important external objects in this model are the application, operator, data capture metafile, and audit trail metafile. The first of these permits external software to control the graphics system through an API; the second allows human operators to interact with the system; and the last two permit the storage and retrieval of graphical information.

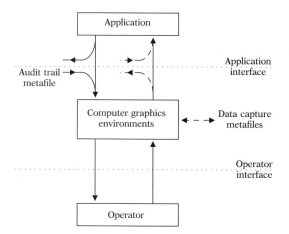

Figure 1. Computer graphics.

Graphical Kernel System

The Graphical Kernel System (GKS) is the oldest of the computer graphics standards. Although the standard claims to include "all the capabilities that are essential for a broad spectrum of graphics, from simple passive output to highly interactive applications," GKS is, in fact, an API for 2D graphics and is best suited for display of static images and applications requiring primarily discrete input. A 3D version of GKS has been defined as an international standard, but it is little used.

Computer Graphics Metafile

The Computer Graphics Metafile (CGM) is the most widely used computer graphics standard. CGM is a data capture metafile that provides a means to store and transfer descriptions of 2D pictures in a device-independent manner for use by graphics production systems and applications. It contains elements for describing vector primitives such as lines, arcs, and ellipses as well as raster primitives and the appearance of primitives through a system of attributes such as edge width, edge color, and edge style. The CGM standard as a whole contains a rich set of elements from which an appropriate set for a particular class of applications can be selected by means of a *profile*.

CGM supports three types of encoding: character, binary, and clear text. The character encoding (to be eliminated in the next republication of the standard) provides an encoding of minimum size that may be transmitted through character-oriented communications services. The binary encoding provides a representation that optimizes speed of generation and interpretation. The clear text encoding provides a representation that may be easily read and edited by humans. It is intended that CGM data will be interpreted by the application rather than by other standards, as the particular device used to render a picture may not have the exact complement of features as used for the picture description. The applications programmer, who presumably understands the class of display devices available, is then responsible for making trade-off decisions regarding the rendering of the picture.

Programmer's Hierarchical Interactive Graphical System

The Programmer's Hierarchical Interactive Graphical System (PHIGS) is an API that specifies a set of two- and three-dimensional functions for the definition, display, and modification of geometrically related objects and graphical data. Whereas GKS, CGM, and CGI are oriented towards static pictures, PHIGS is designed to provide dynamic interpretation of geometrical relationships inherent in a hierarchical model. As such, PHIGS is much more suited for applications that require animated display of structured objects, particularly computer-aided design. It is also more suited to and makes better use of the advanced graphics capability of sophisticated computer graphics workstations.

Presentation Environment for Multimedia Objects

The Presentation Environment for Multimedia Objects (PREMO) International Standard defines a middleware framework for distributed multimedia, encompassing synchronization and other fundamental multimedia services; interoperation of media processes across a heterogeneous network; and integration of synthetic graphics with other digital media. PREMO consists of four parts called components and was designed from the outset to be extensible by creating new components. The standard is described using object-oriented terminology. The object type provides services (in the form of operations that can be invoked by clients), or has a passive role, for example as in data *encapsulation* (*q.v.*).

Virtual Reality Modeling Language

The Virtual Reality Modeling Language (VRML) is a data capture metafile format for describing interactive 3D objects, behaviors, and worlds. VRML may be used on the Internet, intranets, and local client systems. In particular, it is the 3D graphics format for the World Wide Web (*q.v.*). It is intended to be a universal interchange format for integrated 3D graphics and multimedia. VRML may be used in a variety of application areas such as engineering and scientific visualization, multimedia presentations, entertainment and educational titles, Web pages, and shared virtual worlds.

Portable Network Graphics

Portable Network Graphics (PNG) is an extensible file format for the lossless, portable, well-compressed storage of raster images. PNG provides a patent-free replacement for GIF (Graphics Interchange Format) and can replace many common uses of RGB indexed and truecolor TIFF (Tagged Image File Format). Indexed-color, grayscale, and truecolor images are supported, plus an optional alpha channel for transparency information. Sample depths range from 1 to 16 bits. The PNG International Standard is designed to work well in online viewing applications, such as the World Wide Web, and is based on a specification developed by the World Wide Web Consortium (W3C).

Bibliography

1986. Hopwood, F. R. A., Duce, D. A., Gallop, J. R., and Sutcliffe, D. C. *Introduction to the Graphical Kernel System (GKS)*. New York: Academic Press.

1990. Arnold, D. B., and Duce, D. A. *ISO Standards for Computer Graphics*. London: Butterworth.

1993. Henderson, L. R., and Mumford, A. M. *The CGM Handbook*. New York: Academic Press.

George S. Carson

COMPUTER LANGUAGES

See PROCEDURE-ORIENTED LANGUAGES; PROGRAMMING LANGUAGES; and language sections of FUNCTIONAL PROGRAMMING; LOGIC PROGRAMMING; LIST PROCESSING; and STRING PROCESSING. See also names of particular languages.

COMPUTER LITERACY

For articles on related subjects, *see*

+ Personal Computing
+ Power User
+ Word Processing
+ World Wide Web

A *computer literate* person is one who has acquired the skills needed to use computers effectively. More important, the computer literate person is comfortable in the computer age. Technical expertise is not required. Familiarity, experience, and understanding create comfort.

Computer literacy has five characteristics:

1. The ability to use the computer as a tool for problem solving.
2. An understanding of what computers can and cannot do (the function of hardware and software).
3. Nontechnical experience with computer software.
4. Experience in using the Internet (*q.v.*), particularly the World Wide Web (*q.v.*), as an information-gathering tool.
5. The ability to evaluate the societal impact of computers.

When the only effective way to use a computer was to program it yourself, programming knowledge was considered an integral part of computer literacy. With today's vast array of off-the-shelf software products, such knowledge is unnecessary. An understanding of and experience in using readily available software is more important than knowing how to program. The computer literate person should have experience with computer software tools for writing, communicating, and processing information.

People frequently become computer literate through courses taught in schools, colleges, community centers and computer stores, but many individuals choose to learn on their own. More and more, children are amassing considerable computer knowledge and, for all intents and purposes, are computer literate by the time they leave elementary school.

Bibliography

1998. Kershner, H. G. *Computer Literacy*, 3rd Ed. Dubuque, IA: Kendall/Hunt Publishers.

Helene G. Kershner

COMPUTER MUSEUMS

See MUSEUMS, COMPUTER.

COMPUTER MUSIC

For articles on related subjects, see

+ Computer Art
+ Entertainment Industry, Computers in the
+ Speech Recognition and Synthesis

Historically, the first application of *computers to music* resulted in compositions such as Hiller and Isaacson's famous 1957 *Illiac Suite* for string quartet. In this work, a mainframe computer was used to emulate stochastically well-known musical stylistic rules, and derive some of its own in a very loosely constrained random compositional procedure. Shortly thereafter, in the late 1950s and early 1960s, Max Mathews and his colleagues at Bell Laboratories introduced the first programs for digital sound synthesis. Today, computers participate in all aspects of music making, including composition, live performance processing, the study of music cognition, musicology, music notation and score printing, sound production, studio editing of digitized audio signals, and sound reproduction.

Digital Sound Synthesis

Computer sound synthesis is based on analog-to-digital (A/D) and digital-to-analog (D/A) conversion. This technology transforms a continuous audio signal into discrete *samples*, each of which quantifies the signal's amplitude at an instant in time. The number of samples per second is known as the *sampling rate*, while the number of bits accorded to one sample is the *quantization* or resolution. Both of these factors significantly affect sound quality. The frequencies represented in any digitized signal are limited to half the sampling rate R, since samples are required to represent both the "up" and "down" phases of an oscillation. This is often referred to as the *Nyquist frequency*, because of the Nyquist Theorem that describes it. Any attempt to digitize frequencies above this ceiling—including upper harmonics of complex timbres—leads to *foldover* (also called *aliasing*); the out-of-range frequencies are reflected back down below $R/2$. Digitized waveforms also suffer from distortions owing to imprecise quantization. Rudimentary sound synthesis, such as that used in early video games, employs 8-bit quantization at sampling rates around 10 KHz for a maximum frequency barely exceeding the highest pitch on the piano. Currently, quality audio processing employs 16-bit, 24-bit, or higher quantization at a minimum 48 KHz per channel (although 44.1 KHz is the 1999 commercial standard), which fully accommodates the ear's conventionally given frequency limit of 20 KHz.

Most computer sound synthesis environments have been based on a conventional paradigm for music: the score/instrument model. These environments implement software simulations of devices employed in "classical" electronic music studios. They use what is commonly referred to as the *unit generator model*. Devices are simulated by software modules written as *reentrant programs* (*q.v.*). In Mathews' programs and their contemporary descendants, a control language enables the user to describe a computer-simulated musical "instrument" as a coupling of signal (or unit) generators (e.g. oscillators and noise generators) and signal modifiers (e.g. mixers, amplifiers, filters, and reverberators).

Digital *oscillators* store a single cycle of a waveform in a digitized table; they then produce different fundamental frequencies by stepping through this table at variable rates. More complex waveforms can be produced by amplitude, frequency, and timbral modulation, in which signals are multiplied together. *White noise* is simulated by generating random values for each sample; *low-pass noise* is simulated by interpolating linearly between random values chosen at a specified rate. Digital *mixers* simply add source samples together, while digital *amplifiers* multiply each source sample by a gain factor. Such a gain factor might typically be supplied by an *envelope generator*, which computes attack, decay, sustain, and release contours by interpolating between specified magnitudes over specified intervals of time. Digital *filtering* is implemented using second-order difference equations. Digital *reverberation* (or *echo*) is accomplished by diverting samples through a *delay line* and feeding them back into the signal.

Acousticians most commonly describe instrumental tone production in terms of an active *source* phase coupled to a passive *transfer* phase, and the source–transfer model provides the foundation for many sound synthesis strategies. The source phase describes how energy is introduced into the vibrating system. Sometimes, the source is pitched, as in the glottal vibrations of the human voice or the buzzing of lips into a trumpet mouthpiece; sometimes the source is unpitched, as in the rasping of a bow against a violin string. The transfer phase accommodates the various resonances present in the system. *Harmonic* resonators, such as strings and tubes, nurture specific source overtones, thus producing clear-pitched tones. *Formant* resonators, such as the cavities of the vocal tract or the sounding body of a stringed instrument, nurture wider frequency bands.

Analog-to-digital converters provide the option of incorporating "real-world" sources into computer music compositions. The most straightforward approach—direct sampling—treats a source signal very much like a digital oscillator with an extremely long waveform. Theoretically, direct sampling has been possible from the earliest days of computer sound synthesis, but it became practical only with the introduction of large-memory computers. Source signals may be analyzed and resynthesized using Fourier and other methods. With current commercial technology, sampling has become perhaps the primary esthetic and technological resource for composers and sound artists.

An efficient way of reducing real-world sources is *linear predictive coding* (LPC), which effectively strips the pitch information from a signal, leaving only the timbre, in the form of an optimized set of filter coefficients. In a process sometimes referred to as *cross synthesis*, this extracted formant information may subsequently be used to make an instrumental source, such as a string orchestra, "sing" the poem. Composers who have pioneered the use of this technique include Charles Dodge and Paul Lansky.

There are a number of common techniques for sound processing and transformation, which may be roughly classified as either *time* or *frequency* domain. Time domain techniques include modulations, enveloping, editing, and reordering of sounds. *Granular synthesis*, a technique first suggested by Gabor (in the 1940s), involves the use of short sound *grains* in the analysis/resynthesis process. The density, intergrain distance, and shape of the grains are among a number of parameters that may be controlled to alter source sounds. Composers such as Iannis Xenakis, Barry Truax, and Curtis Roads have explored this technique in detail.

Frequency domain techniques for sound transformation have often made use of the *phase vocoder* model, based on implementations of the *Fast Fourier Transform* (FFT), explicated and pioneered in computer music by researcher Mark Dolson. Popular FFT-based environments have included the Carl system developed by F. Richard Moore at the University of California at San Diego, the Composer's Desktop Project (Wishart and others), the work of Xavier Rodet and others at IRCAM, Paul Lansky's Cmix program, and the widely-used program Soundhack by Tom Erbe (Fig. 1). Other more recent frequency domain techniques have included *wavelet*, or time–frequency domain approaches, and the

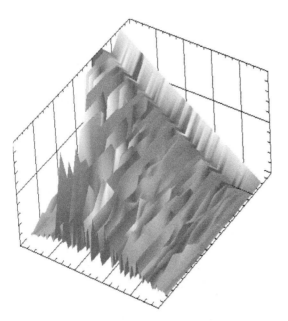

Figure 1. Waterfall plot of a spectral interpolation from a sawtooth shaped spectrum to a slightly randomized triangular one. The *y*-axis is spectral band amplitude, the *x*-axis is spectral band, and the *z*-axis is time. This process is derived from Erbe and Polansky spectral morphing functions implemented in the program *Soundhack*. (From Erbe and Polansky "Spectral Mutation in Soundhack," *Computer Music Journal*, **20**(1), 92–101, 1995).

use of McAulay–Quatieri (MQ) analysis, in which an FFT is further processed, by an algorithm that eliminates redundant and *masked* frequency information (similar to human cochlear processing) to form a set of *spectral tracks*.

MIDI

MIDI, or *musical instrument digital interface*, was established by the synthesizer industry during the mid-1980s. Initially conceived as a set of industry standards for communicating performance data between synthesizers, MIDI was quickly exploited as a means of bringing synthesizers under computer control. The key to this control has been the MIDI *sequencer*, software that enables musicians to record,

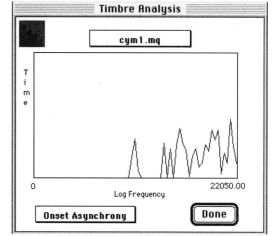

Figure 2. A window from the timbral analysis program *Past* showing the analysis of the onset asynchrony of a sound. (From Langmead, C. J., "A comparison and Modification Based on a Perceptual Model of Timbre," Proceedings of the ICMC, Alberta, Canada, 475–480, 1995.)

play back, splice, overdub, and otherwise manipulate performance data. The MIDI sequencer does more than coopt tasks that formerly could be undertaken using only expensive multitrack recorders. With a MIDI sequencer, one can, for example, selectively change tempo without affecting transposition and vice versa.

Automated Composition

The first generation of composing programs, produced during the 1960s, emphasized two general approaches: (1) *serialism*, in which basic motifs are subjected to a variety of systematic manipulations (e.g. inversion, retrograde, transposition, and rotation), and (2) *random selection*, including ball-and-urn-type statistical procedures and Markov-style conditional probability.

The introduction of online computer systems in the 1970s inspired hybrid computer–synthesizer environments that greatly enhanced the rate of interaction between musicians and computers, permitting composers to evaluate a composition aurally at each stage in its genesis. Serialism and randomness were augmented by interactive score-processing and score-editing tools—the direct forerunners of today's MIDI sequencers and graphic score editors.

One of the first alternatives to first-generation serialism and randomness was top–down *recursion* (*q.v.*). Recursive concepts of musical structure had been advocated by musical theorists (e.g. Lorenz and Schenker) since the early twentieth century, and this internal tradition received added impetus from three external influences: Chomsky's formal grammars, Gestalt psychology, and fractal geometry (*see* FRACTALS). More recent ways for applying mathematical constructs to composition have included the use of nonlinear dynamics, genetic algorithms (*q.v.*), neural nets, group theory, multi-dimensional scaling, game theory, and many other topics.

An important innovation for composing programs during the 1980s was the adoption of artificial intelligence (AI-*q.v.*) search techniques. Instances include Ebcioglu's 1980 program for species counterpoint, the programs for Ames's 1981 composition *Protocol*, Ebcioglu's 1984 chorale harmonization program, Hiller and Ames's tune-writing program Mix or Match, Thomas's 1985 Vivace, Schwanauer's 1986 MUSE, and Ames's 1987 Cybernetic Composer. Such programs made a significant leap by formalizing not just compositional procedures but also the principles underlying these procedures.

Bibliography
Journals

Computer Music Journal, Cambridge, MA: MIT Press Journals. The primary source for articles on computer music.

INTERFACE: Journal of New Music Research. Lisse, The Netherlands: Swets Publishing Service. Emphasizes computer applications to composition and analysis. Articles are typically more detailed than in CMJ.

Books and Articles

1969. Mathews, M. V., Miller, J. E., Moore, F. R., Pierce, J. R., and Risset, J. C. *The Technology of Computer Music*. Cambridge, MA: MIT Press. The classic book on digital sound synthesis, still valuable for its discussion of basic principles.

1987. Ames, C. "Automated Composition in Retrospect: 1956–86," *Leonardo*, **20**(2), 169–185.

1990. Moore, F. R. *Elements of Computer Music*. Upper Saddle River, NJ: Prentice Hall.

1995. Roads, C. *The Computer Music Tutorial*. Cambridge, MA: MIT Press.

1997. Dodge, C., and Jerse, T. *Computer Music: Synthesis, Composition, and Performance*, 2nd Ed. New York: Schirmer Books.

Charles Ames and Larry Polansky

COMPUTER NETWORK

See INTERNET; LOCAL AREA NETWORK (LAN); NETWORK ARCHITECTURE; NETWORK PROTOCOLS; NETWORKS, COMPUTER; and SENSOR NETWORK.

COMPUTER SCIENCE

For articles on related subjects, *see*

+ Computer Engineering
+ Cybernetics

The computing profession is the people and institutions that have been created to take care of other people's concerns in information processing and coordination through worldwide communication systems. The profession contains various specialties such as computer science, computer engineering, software engineering (*q.v.*), information systems, domain-specific applications, and computer systems.

The discipline of computer science was born in the early 1940s with the confluence of algorithm theory (*see* ALGORITHMS, THEORY OF), mathematical logic, and the invention of the stored-program electronic computer. Examples are the works of Alan Turing (*q.v.*), Alonzo Church, and Kurt Gödel in the 1930s about algorithms and their realizations as machines or rule systems (*see* TURING MACHINE), the algorithms created by Augusta Ada (Countess of Lovelace–*q.v.*) 60 years earlier, the analog computers built by Vannevar Bush in the 1920s, and the electronic computers built by Howard Aiken (*q.v.*) and Konrad Zuse (*q.v.*) in the 1930s. The writings of John von Neumann (*q.v.*) gave considerable intellectual depth to the emerging discipline by the late 1940s. By the early 1960s, there was a sufficient body of knowledge to merit the first academic departments and degree programs. This discipline is also variously called *computer science and engineering, computing,* and *informatics.*

The Domain of Computer Science

Even though computer science addresses both natural and human-made information processes, the main effort in the discipline has been directed toward the latter. Much of the work of the field until the mid-1980s concerned computers as tools for number crunching, symbol manipulation (*q.v.*), and data processing (*q.v.*); but personal computing (*q.v.*) and the Internet (*q.v.*) have since enlarged the focus to include coordination and communication. Much of the body of knowledge of computing concerns the digital computer (*q.v.*) and the phenomena surrounding it—the structure and operation of computer systems, principles underlying computer system design and programming, effective methods for using computers for information processing, and theoretical characterizations of their properties and limitations. The field is grappling with new questions arising from interactions with other fields, where computers are tools but not the objects of study, and where other considerations such as transparency, usability, dependability, hardware and software reliability, and software safety are paramount.

Standard Concerns of the Field

The digital computer plays the central role in the field because it is a universal computing machine: with enough memory, a digital computer is capable of simulating any information-processing system, provided the task can be specified as an unambiguous set of instructions. If such a specification is possible, the task can be represented as a program that can be stored in the memory (*q.v.*) of a computer. Thus, one machine is capable of exploring and studying an enormous variety of concepts, schemes, simulations, and techniques of information processing. Practitioners of the discipline should be skilled in four basic areas: algorithmic thinking, representation, programming, and design.

Representation goes beyond knowing how to organize data for efficient information retrieval (*q.v.*) or processing. It deals with knowledge representation (*q.v.*), ways of encoding phenomena to allow algorithmic processing. Examples include representing a mathematical expression so that it can be differentiated (*see* COMPUTER ALGEBRA), representing a document so that "What you see [on the screen] is what you get [on the printer]" (WYSISWYG); representing handwritten postal codes for processing by optical character recognition (*q.v.*); representing encoded speech so that one can talk to a computer or so that the computer can talk back (*see* SPEECH RECOGNITION AND SYNTHESIS); representing an engine part so that it can be shown on the graphics screen and then can be manufactured automatically (*see* COMPUTER-AIDED DESIGN/COMPUTER-AIDED MANUFACTURING (CAD/CAM))).

Programming enables people to take algorithmic thinking and representations and embody them in software (*q.v.*) that will cause a machine to perform in a prescribed way. This skill includes working knowledge of different programming languages (*q.v.*); program development tools that aid testing, debugging (*q.v.*), modularity, and compatibility; and operating systems (*q.v.*) that control the internal operations of computers.

Design connects the other three skills to the concerns of people through the medium of systems that serve them. Design includes many practical considerations such as engineering tradeoffs, integrating available components through use of component software, meeting time and cost constraints, and meeting safety and reliability requirements.

Principal Subdivisions of the Field

The subject matter of computing can be broadly divided into two parts. The first studies information-processing tasks and their related data representations. The second studies structures, mechanisms, and schemes for processing information. Within the field, these two parts are called *applications* and *systems*, respectively, and programming that relates to these areas is called, respectively, applications programming (*q.v.*) and systems programming (*q.v.*). A major goal of computing education is to elucidate the relationships between applications and computer systems.

Computer applications can be subdivided into numerical and nonnumerical categories. Numerical applications are those in which mathematical models and numerical data are dominant; they are supported by numerical analysis, optimization methods, simulation (*q.v.*), program libraries (*q.v.*), computational geometry, and computational science (*see* SCIENTIFIC APPLICATIONS). Nonnumerical applications are those in which problems and information are represented as symbols and rules; they are supported by artificial intelligence (*q.v.*), multimedia (*q.v.*) and hypertext (*q.v.*) systems, language processors (*q.v.*), computer graphics (*q.v.*), mathematical expression systems, database management systems (*q.v.*), information retrieval (*q.v.*), and combinatorial processes.

Computer systems can be subdivided into software systems and hardware systems. *Software systems* are concerned with machine-level representations of programs (*q.v.*) and data; schemes for controlling program execution; assemblers, compilers (*q.v.*), and language processors (*q.v.*) for intermediate languages (*q.v.*), programming support environments (*q.v.*), operating systems (*q.v.*), and data communications (*q.v.*) and management (*see* NETWORKS, COMPUTER). *Hardware systems* are concerned with logic design (*q.v.*), machine organization, processors, memory, and devices in various technologies such as VLSI, silicon, and GaAs (*see* INTEGRATED CIRCUITRY). Computer architecture (*q.v.*) and computer engineering (*q.v.*) are concerned with both software and hardware. Most systems areas are also concerned with task environments, practices of the application area, and modes of human interaction.

Relationships with Other Disciplines

Computer science has, by tradition, been more closely related to mathematics than to physics, chemistry, and biology. This is because mathematical logic, the theorems of Turing and Gödel, Boolean algebra (*q.v.*) for circuit design, and algorithms for solving equations and other classes of problems in mathematics played strong roles in the early development of the field. Conversely, computer science has strongly influenced mathematics, many branches of which have become concerned with demonstrating algorithms for constructing or identifying a mathematical structure or carrying out a function. For these reasons, some observers like to say that computing is a mathematical science.

The bond between engineering and computer science is much stronger than between many natural science disciplines and their engineering counterparts—for example, chemical engineering and chemistry, aircraft design and fluid dynamics, pharmacy and biology, and materials engineering and physics. This is because computer science has a strong heritage in electrical engineering and because many algorithmic methods were originally designed to solve engineering problems. Examples include electronic circuits (and hence now computer circuitry–*q.v.*), data communications (*q.v.*), engineering graphics, engineering design, systems engineering, fabrication, and manufacturing. Conversely, computers have become indispensable in many engineering disciplines—for example, circuit simulators, finite-element simulators, flow-field simulators, graphics, CAD/CAM systems, computer-controlled tools, and flexible manufacturing systems. For these reasons, some observers like to say that computing is an engineering science.

A new bond is forming between the physical sciences and computer science. Leaders of physics, chemistry, biology, geology, seismology, astronomy, oceanography, and meteorology have brought to prominence certain very hard "grand challenge" problems that demand massive high-speed computations, performed on new generations of massively parallel computers (*see* PARALLEL PROCESSING) with new kinds of algorithms. These problems include crystalline structure, quantum electrodynamics, calculation of chemical properties of materials from the Schrödinger equation, Monte Carlo (*q.v.*) reactor calculations, electromagnetic scattering, simulation of aircraft in flight, exploration of space, global climate modeling, oil exploration, cosmological models of the universe, long-range weather forecasting, earthquake prediction, turbulent fluid flow, and human genome sequencing. Many leaders of science now say that computation has emerged as a third paradigm of science, joining theory and experimentation. For these reasons, some observers identify computing with computational science.

Who is right? All are, demonstrating the richness of the discipline and its heritage in older sciences and engineering. In addition to the influences of mathematics, engineering, and science woven into the discipline itself, computing interacts closely with many other disciplines. Among them are library science, management science, economics, medicine and biology, forensics, psychology, linguistics, philosophy, and the humanities.

Processes

Mathematics, science, and engineering have special historical relationships with computing, roots revealed through three major paradigms:

- *Theory*: building conceptual frameworks and notations for understanding relationships among objects in a domain and the logical consequences of axioms and laws.
- *Experimentation*: exploring models of systems and architectures within given application domains and testing whether those models can predict new behaviors accurately. This paradigm is sometimes called *abstraction* by computer scientists.
- *Design*: constructing computer systems that support work in given organizations or application domains.

In areas of rapidly developing technology, such as databases, human interfaces, and Web-based systems,

theoreticians aim mainly at bringing order into a rapidly accumulating mass of experience through broad conceptual frameworks, taxonomies, and analytic methods. In mature areas such as computational complexity (*q.v.*), algorithms (*q.v.*), data structures (*q.v.*), automata theory (*q.v.*), switching theory, graph theory (*q.v.*), combinatorics, and formal languages (*q.v.*), theoreticians focus on deeper, comprehensive analyses of phenomena for which formal models exist.

Experimenters construct models of phenomena or of possible systems; the models generally suppress detail and enable fast predictions. Examples are measurement of programs and systems, validation of hypotheses, software prototyping (*q.v.*) to extend abstractions to practice, logic simulation, simulations of systems and of physical processes, testing of protocols (*q.v.*), system performance analysis, and comparisons of different architectures. Experimental computer science relies heavily on laboratories. It often stimulates new developments in computer design and use. More attention is being paid to experimental computer science because human intuition often does not work well with complex systems.

Designers are concerned with building systems that meet clear specifications and satisfy their customers. They boast many significant accomplishments, such as program development systems, simulators, microchip design systems, VLSI, CAD, CAM, graphics, databases, and supercomputers (*q.v.*).

In addition to the three processes and the specialists who practice them, the discipline of computing has a number of broad concerns that touch all the subfields. The main ones are parallel processing (*q.v.*) and distributed systems (*q.v.*), performance analysis, reliability, safety, security, and computer ethics.

Subareas of the Field

Computer science can be divided into a number of coherent subareas, each with substantial theoretical, experimental, and design issues, and each with its own version of the shared concerns. The chart below depicts the discipline as a matrix with 12 subareas as rows and the three processes as columns. Though it is not done here, each of the boxes could be filled in with detailed descriptions of that category of the subarea's activities and accomplishments.

		Theory	Abstraction	Design
1	Algorithms and data structures			
2	Programming languages			
3	Architecture			
4	Operating systems and networks			
5	Software engineering			
6	Databases and information retrieval			
7	Artificial intelligence and robotics			
8	Graphics			
9	Human computer interaction			
10	Computational science			
11	Organizational informatics			
12	Bioinformatics			

Algorithms and Data Structures

The theory of algorithms encompasses computability theory (*see* NP-COMPLETE PROBLEMS), computational complexity (*q.v.*), information-based complexity, concurrency theory (*see* CONCURRENT PROGRAMMING), probabilistic algorithms, the theory of deductive and relational databases (*q.v.*), randomized algorithms, pattern-matching algorithms (*see* PATTERN RECOGNITION), graph and network algorithms, algebraic algorithms, combinatorial optimization, and cryptography. It is supported by discrete mathematics (*q.v.*) such as graph theory, recursive functions (*see* RECURSION), recurrence relations, and combinatorics, and by calculus, induction, predicate logic, temporal logic, semantics, probability, and statistics.

Experimentation has been found very useful with complex algorithms and heuristics for which no tractable theoretical analysis is known. Algorithms can be evaluated by applying them to suites of test cases and analyzing their performance. Testing has yielded valuable characterizations of certain methods such as divide-and-conquer, greedy algorithms, dynamic programming, finite-state machine interpreters, stack (*q.v.*) machine interpreters, heuristic searches, and randomized algorithms. Testing has yielded significant insights into the performance of parallel and distributed algorithms.

Programming Languages

This area deals with notations for virtual machines that execute algorithms and with notations for algorithms and data; the sets of strings of symbols that are generated by such notations are called *languages*. It also deals with efficient translations from high-level languages into machine codes through language processors such as a compiler. Fundamental questions include: What are possible organizations of the virtual machine represented by the language, data types, operations, operands, control structures (*q.v.*), and extensible language (*q.v.*) mechanisms for introducing new types and operations)? How are these abstractions implemented on computers? What notation (syntax) can be used effectively and efficiently to specify what the computer should do? How are functions (semantics) associated with language notations (*see* BACKUS–NAUR FORM (BNF))?

The theory of programming languages studies models of machines that generate and translate languages and of grammars for expressing valid strings in the languages. Examples include models of formal languages, automata theory, Turing machines (*q.v.*), Post systems, lambda calculus, pi calculus to model concurrency, and propositional logic. The theory deals with semantics, the study of the relationships between strings of the language ("well-formed formulas") and states of the underlying virtual machines such as that which exists between a regular expression and a finite-state machine (*see* CHOMSKY HIERARCHY). It deals with types, which are classes of objects. Related mathematics is predicate logic, temporal logic, modern algebra, and mathematical induction.

The modelers have developed classifications of languages based on their syntactic and semantic models, for example, static typing, dynamic typing, functional programming (*q.v.*), procedure-oriented language design vs object-oriented analysis and design, logic specification, message-passing, and dataflow. They have developed classifications by application, for example, (business) data processing, simulation, list processing (*q.v.*), and computer graphics (*q.v.*). They have developed classifications by functional structure, for example, procedure hierarchies, functional composition, abstract data types (*q.v.*), and communicating sequential processes (*see* CONCURRENT PROGRAMMING). They have developed abstract implementation models for each major type of language including imperative, object-oriented, logic and constraint, concurrent, and distributed.

Programming language designers have developed many practical languages including procedural languages such as Cobol, Fortran, Algol, Pascal, Ada, and C (*see* COBOL, FORTRAN, ALGOL, PASCAL, ADA, and C); object-oriented programming (*q.v.*) languages such as Clu, Smalltalk, C++ (*q.v.*), Eiffel, and Java (*q.v.*); functional languages such as Lisp (*q.v.*), ML, and Haskell; dataflow languages such as Sisal, Val, and Id Nouveau; and logic (Prolog), string (Snobol, Icon), and concurrency languages such as Concurrent Pascal, Occam, SR, and Modula-3.

Architecture

This area deals with methods of organizing hardware (and associated software) into efficient, reliable systems. The fundamental questions include: What are good methods of implementing processors, memory, and communication in a machine? How does one design and control large computational systems and convincingly demonstrate that they work as intended despite errors and failures? What types of architecture can efficiently incorporate many processing elements that can work concurrently on a computation? How can performance measurement and evaluation best be implemented? Can hardware devices mimic selected human sensors such as eyes and ears?

The theory of computer architecture (*q.v.*) includes: digital logic, Boolean algebra, coding theory (*see* CODES), and finite-state machine theory. Supporting mathematics include statistics, probability, queuing theory, reliability theory, discrete mathematics, number theory, and arithmetic in different number systems (*see* ARITHMETIC, COMPUTER and NUMBERS AND NUMBER SYSTEMS).

Computer architecture is replete with successful designs. These include arithmetic function units, cache memory (*q.v.*), the so-called von Neumann machine (*q.v.*), reduced instruction set computers (RISCs–*q.v.*), CISCs (Complex Instruction Set Computers), efficient methods of storing and recording information and of detecting and correcting errors (*see* ERROR CORRECTING AND DETECTING CODE); error recovery, computer-aided design (CAD) systems and logic simulations for the design of VLSI circuits, reduction programs for layout and fault diagnosis and silicon compilers (compilers that produce instructions for manufacturing a silicon *microcomputer chip–q.v.*). They also include major systems such as dataflow, tree, Lisp, hypercube, pipeline, vector, and multiprocessors (*see* MULTIPROCESSING); and supercomputers, such as the Cray, Cyber, and IBM (*q.v.*) RS/6000 series machines. Architects have collaborated with other scientists to design prototypes of devices that can imitate human senses.

Operating Systems and Networks

This area deals with control mechanisms that allow multiple resources to be coordinated efficiently in computations distributed over many computer systems connected by wide area and local area networks (LANS–*q.v.*). Fundamental questions include: at each level of temporal granularity (e.g. microsecond, minute, hour, or day) in the operation of a computer system, what are the visible objects and permissible operations on them? For each class of resource (objects visible at some level), what is a minimal set of operations that permit their effective use? How can user interfaces (*q.v.*) be organized so that users deal only with abstract versions of resources and not with physical details of hardware? What are effective control strategies for job scheduling, memory management (*q.v.*), communications, access to software resources, communication among concurrent tasks, reliability, and security? What are the principles by which systems can be extended in function by repeated application of a small number of construction rules? How should distributed computations be organized, with the details of network protocols (*q.v.*), host locations, bandwidths (*q.v.*), and resource naming being mostly invisible? How can a distributed operating system be both a program preparation and execution environment?

Major elements of theory in operating systems include: concurrency theory (synchronization, determinacy, and mutual exclusion–*q.v.*); scheduling algorithms; program behavior and memory management theory; network flow theory; performance modeling and analysis. Supporting mathematics include bin packing, probability, queuing theory, communication and information theory (*q.v.*), temporal logic, and cryptography.

Software Engineering

This area deals with the design of large software systems that meet program specifications and are safe, secure, reliable, and dependable. Fundamental questions include: what are the principles behind the development of programs and programming systems? How does one make a map of the recurrent actions people take in a domain and use the map to specify a system of hardware and software components to support those actions? How does one prove that a program or system meets its specifications? How does one develop specifications that do not omit important cases and can be analyzed for software safety? By what processes do software systems evolve through different generations? By what processes can software be designed for understandability and modifiability? What methods reduce complexity in designing very large software systems? Reflecting the importance of these questions, seven articles in

this *Concise Encyclopedia* have titles that begin with SOFTWARE, and several additional articles pertain to the subject.

Three kinds of theory are used for software engineering: program verification (*q.v.*) and proof (which treats forms of proofs and efficient algorithms for constructing them), temporal logic (which is predicate calculus extended to allow statements about time-ordered events), and reliability theory (which relates the overall failure probability of a system to the failure probabilities of its components over time). Supporting mathematics include predicate calculus and axiomatic semantics.

Database and Information Retrieval Systems

This area deals with the organization of large sets of persistent, shared data for efficient query and update. The term database is used for a collection of records (*q.v.*) that can be updated and queried in various ways. The term *retrieval system* is used for a collection of documents that will be searched and correlated; updates and modifications of documents are infrequent in a retrieval system. Fundamental questions include: What models are useful for representing data elements and their relationships? How can basic operations such as *store, locate, match*, and retrieve be combined into effective transactions? How can the user interact effectively with these transactions? How can high-level queries be translated into high-performance programs? What machine architectures lead to efficient retrieval and update? How can data be protected against unauthorized access, disclosure, or destruction? How can large databases be protected from inconsistencies because of simultaneous update? How can protection and performance be achieved when the data is distributed among many machines? How can text be indexed and classified for efficient retrieval?

A variety of theories have been devised and used to study and design database and information retrieval systems. These include relational algebra and relational calculus (*see* RELATIONAL DATABASE), concurrency theory, serializable transactions, deadlock prevention, synchronized updates, statistical inference, rule-based inference, sorting (*q.v.*), searching (*q.v.*), indexing, performance analysis, and cryptography as it relates to ensuring privacy of information and authentication of persons who stored it or attempt to retrieve it.

Artificial Intelligence and Robotics

This area deals with the modeling of animal and human cognition, with the ultimate intention of building machine components that mimic or augment them. The behaviors of interest include recognizing sensory signals, sounds, images, and patterns; learning; reasoning; problem-solving; planning; and under-standing language. Fundamental questions include: What are basic models of cognition and how might machines simulate them? How can knowledge of the world be represented and organized to allow machines to act reasonably (*see* KNOWLEDGE REPRESENTA-TION)? To what extent is intelligence described by search, **heuristics**, rule evaluation, inference, deduc-tion, association, and pattern computation? What limits constrain machines that use these methods? What is the relation between human intelligence and machine intelligence? How are sensory and motor data encoded, clustered, and associated? How can machines be orga-nized to acquire new capabilities for action (machine learning–*q.v.*), make discoveries, and function well despite incomplete, ambiguous, or erroneous data? How might machines understand natural languages, which are replete with ambiguities, paraphrases, ellipses, allusions, context, unspoken assumptions, and listener-dependent interpretations (*see* NATURAL LANGUAGE PROCESSING)? How can robots see, hear, speak, plan, and act (*see* COMPUTER VISION, ROBOTICS, and TELEROBOTICS)?

Nine major branches of theory have been developed for artificial intelligence. (1) Logic systems for mechanical reasoning such as first-order logic, fuzzy logic (*q.v.*), temporal logic, nonmonotonic logic, probabilistic logic, deduction, and induction. (2) Formal methods for representing and translating knowledge including objects, grammars, rules, functions, frames, and semantic networks. (3) Methods for searching the very large spaces that arise when enumerating solutions to problems; these include branch-and-bound, alpha-beta, tree pruning, and genetic algorithms (*q.v.*). (4) Theories of learning including inference, deduction, analogy, abduction, generalization, specialization, abstraction, concretion, determination, and mutual dependency. (5) Neural networks deal with neural interconnection structures, computing responses to stimuli, storing and retrieving patterns, and forming classifications and abstractions. (6) Computer vision. (*q.v.*) (7) Speech recognition and synthesis (*q.v.*). (8) Machine translation (*q.v.*) of natural languages. (9) Robotics (*q.v.*). All branches of the theory draw heavily on the related disciplines of structural mechanics, graph theory, formal languages, programming linguistics, logic, probability, philosophy, and psychology.

Computer Graphics

Computer graphics is concerned with processes for representing physical and conceptual objects and their motions visually on a two-dimensional computer screen or in a three-dimensional hologram. Fundamental questions include: what are efficient methods of representing objects and automatically creating pictures for viewing? For projecting motions of complex objects onto the viewing screen in real time? For displaying data sets to aid human comprehension? For virtual reality (*q.v.*), that is, simulation of real situations that are difficult to distinguish from the actual thing?

The theory of computer graphics draws heavily on computational geometry. It studies algorithms for projecting objects onto the viewing surface, removing hidden lines from the projection, ray-tracing, shading surfaces, showing reflections, and rendering translucent surfaces. It has yielded new algorithms for computing geometric forms. It has used chaos theory to create efficient algorithms for generating complex structures resembling natural formations such as trees, coastlines, clouds, and mountains (*see* FRACTALS). Graphics theory also uses color theory, which relates colors formed from light on screens to colors formed from pigments on printed surfaces. Sampling theory is used to reconstruct images from noisy data, filter out unwanted effects, and remove spurious patterns caused by displaying sampled data on pixel-oriented screens. Important supporting areas are Fourier analysis, sampling theory, linear algebra, graph theory, automata theory, physics, analysis, nonlinear systems, cybernetics (*q.v.*), and chaos.

Models have been essential for practical graphics systems. Extensive studies have yielded efficient algorithms for rendering and displaying pictures including methods for smoothing, shading, hidden line removal, ray tracing, hidden surfaces, translucent surfaces, shadows, lighting, edges, color maps, representation by, rendering, texturing, antialiasing, coherence, computer animation (*q.v.*), and representing pictures as hierarchies of objects. Models for virtual reality (*q.v.*) and distributed interactive simulation are among the most recent additions.

Human-Computer Interaction

This area deals with the efficient coordination of action and transfer of information between humans and machines via various human-like sensors and motors, and with information structures that reflect human conceptualizations. Important contributors to this field are computer graphics and user interfaces. Fundamental questions include: What are effective methods for receiving input or presenting output? How can the risk of misperception and subsequent human error be minimized? How can graphics and other tools be used to understand physical phenomena through information stored in data sets? How can people learn from virtual worlds simulated for them?

Theory in human–computer interaction involves cognitive psychology and risk analysis. Cognitive psychology is important to understanding how humans perceive displays and react; it gives designers the means to evaluate whether humans will misinterpret information presented to them, especially in times of stress. Risk analysis is important because many user interfaces control and monitor complex, safety-critical systems. Important supporting areas are statistics, probability, queuing theory, and coordination theory.

Computational Science

This area deals with explorations in science and engineering that cannot proceed without high-performance computation and communications. Computation is seen as a third approach to science, joining the traditional approaches of theory and experiment. It is being used to address very hard problems, sometimes called "grand challenges." On the computing side, this area deals with general methods of efficiently and accurately solving equations resulting from mathematical models of physical systems; examples include airflow around wings, water flow around obstacles, petroleum flow in the Earth's crust, plasma flow from stars, weather progression, and galactic collisions (*see* SCIENTIFIC APPLICATIONS). Fundamental questions include: How can continuous or infinite processes be accurately approximated by finite discrete processes? How can algorithms minimize the effects of errors arising from these approximations? How rapidly can a given class of equations, partial differential equations for example, be solved for a given level of accuracy? How can symbolic manipulations on equations, such as integration, differentiation, and reduction to minimal terms, be carried out (*see* COMPUTER ALGEBRA and SYMBOL MANIPULATION)? How can the answers to these questions be incorporated into efficient, reliable, high-quality mathematical software packages? How can data sets generated by these models be most effectively visualized for human comprehension?

Organizational Informatics

This area deals with information and systems that support the work processes of organizations and coordination among people participating in those processes. Information systems are essential to the success of commerce and business in the growing global marketplace. Because most of the work of organizations occurs in human processes, information systems must be designed with an understanding of human work. Therefore, this has been a major area of collaboration between computing people, systems engineering, and people in organization disciplines such as management, marketing, decision sciences, management sciences, organizational systems, and anthropology.

Management Information Systems (MIS–*q.v.*) is a long-standing commercial arena in which computing systems consisting of workstations (*q.v.*), databases, networks, and reporting systems are deployed in organizations to assist them in their work. Many decision support systems are available commercially; they range from simulation and mathematical models that forecast market, economic, and competitive conditions to cooperative work systems that assist people in reaching decisions as groups that collaborate over a network.

Bioinformatics

This is an emerging area of intimate collaboration between computing and the biological sciences. Investigators are exploring a variety of models and architectures that can revolutionize computing, biology, and medicine. Examples: (1) DNA chemistry has been used to encode and solve combinatorial problems, opening the possibility of chemical computation (*see* MOLECULAR COMPUTING). (2) New string-analyzing algorithms are searching through base-pair sequences in the sprawling network of databases compiled in the Human Genome Project, attempting to construct the overall genome from many fragments (*see* BIOCOMPUTING). (3) Computer architects and physicians have produced cochlear implants that restore hearing and prototypes of silicon retinas, opening the possibility of practical, bionic prostheses. (4) Computer analyses are used extensively in genetic engineering to determine the proper chemical structures of enzymes to treat medical conditions. (5) New kinds of organic memory devices are being studied that would be capable of storing data at a thousand times current densities or more.

Bibliography

1970. Wegner, P. "Three Computer Cultures—Computer Technology, Computer Mathematics, and Computer Science," in *Advances in Computers 10* (ed. W. Freiberger), Ch. 2, 7–78. New York: Academic Press.

1997. Denning, P., and Metcalfe, R. (eds.) *Beyond Calculation: The Next 50 Years of Computing*. New York: Copernicus Books.

1998. Denning, P. "Computing the Profession," *Educom Review*, **33**(Nov–Dec), 26–39, 46–59.

1999. Denning, P. *Talking Back to the Machine: Computers and Human Aspiration*. New York: Copernicus Books.

Peter J. Denning

COMPUTER SCIENCE EDUCATION

See EDUCATION IN COMPUTER SCIENCE.

COMPUTER SECURITY

See COMPUTER CRIME; DATA SECURITY; and VIRUS, COMPUTER.

COMPUTER VIRUS

See VIRUS, COMPUTER.

COMPUTER VISION

For articles on related subjects, *see*

+ Image Processing
+ Medical Imaging
+ Pattern Recognition
+ Robotics

Computer vision is the process whereby computers are used to extract from images useful information about the physical world, including meaningful descriptions of physical objects. Computer vision has many applications, including robotics, industrial automation, document processing, remote sensing, navigation, microscopy, medical imaging, and the development of visual prostheses for the blind.

Terminology

There are various terms used to refer to the field of computer vision: machine vision, computational vision, image understanding, robot vision, image analysis, and scene analysis. Each term has a different historical perspective, and some retain a difference in emphasis. For example, the term "machine vision" is most commonly used in engineering disciplines. The term "computational vision" arose from interdisciplinary research by computer scientists, physicists, and neuroscientists. There are two goals of computational vision: one concerns the creation of computer systems that can "see," and the other concerns understanding biological vision. The unifying principle is the concept that it is possible to understand vision independent of whether it is implemented in computer hardware or in biological "wetware." More specifically, the goal of computational vision is to express the process of vision in terms of computations, though not necessarily numerical computations.

Related Fields

Computer vision is closely related to *image processing*, which involves image-to-image transformations; *computer graphics* (*q.v.*), which involves description-to-image transformations (the inverse of computer vision's image-to-description transformations); and *pattern recognition*, which involves pattern-to-class transformations. Computer vision is a subfield of artificial intelligence (AI—*q.v.*), but vision requires in addition significant perceptual preprocessing of visual input before cognitive analysis.

Levels of Computer Vision Processing

Computer vision processing is generally divided into two levels: *early vision* and *scene analysis*. Early vision, otherwise known as *low-level vision*, involves the first stages of processing required for a visual task. One aspect of this first stage is *feature analysis*, whereby information about color, motion, shape, texture, stereo

depth, and intensity edges is extracted. Another aspect of early vision is *image segmentation*, whereby the featural information is used to segment the image into regions that have a high probability of having arisen from a single physical cause. For example, suppose a scene consisted of a single orange resting upon an infinitely large flat white surface that is illuminated by a diffuse light source. An image of this scene could be segmented based on color information alone to form two regions—one corresponding to the orange and the other corresponding to the flat surface.

The second level of processing, scene analysis, involves taking the featural descriptors generated by early vision and constructing higher-level descriptions of the scene. Some components of this task are *shape analysis, object recognition*, and *object localization*. This level is also referred to as *high-level vision*, and involves more knowledge-based processing than early vision. In the example image of an orange, scene analysis would involve recognizing that the circular orange-colored region was an image of an orange. This recognition must be based on the system having knowledge about the nature of oranges, and the ability to make inferences based on the visual information.

Dynamic Vision

While much of computer vision deals with the analysis of static images, the subfield of dynamic vision (active vision) stresses the importance of considering vision as part of an active agent interacting with its environment. Many vision problems that are difficult to solve using static images become easier to solve in an active vision system where the agent has the ability to move the camera or in other ways interact with a dynamic scene in order to resolve ambiguities.

Why Computer Vision is Difficult

Computer vision is difficult because it is underconstrained. For example, an image is a two-dimensional (2D) projection of a three-dimensional (3D) scene, but there can be infinitely many 3D scenes that project the same 2D image. For example, the image in Fig. 1a appears to depict a rectangle, but the

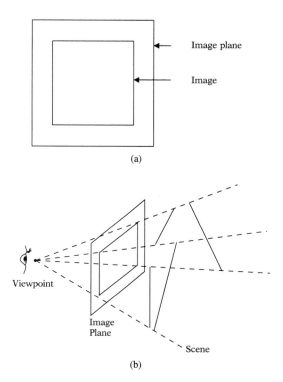

(a)

(b)

Figure 1. The sides of the apparent "rectangle" in 2D image (a) may actually be projections of four skewed lines in the 3D space depicted in (b).

actual scene from which this image arose (Fig. 1) consists of four thin wires that do not touch. Of course, the image in Fig. 1a *could* have been the projection of a scene containing a rectangle since it is possible to have two or more 3D scenes that project to the same 2D image. But the image in Fig. 1a does not *appear* to be ambiguous. Thus, humans either use some additional high-level information about the world to interpret images unambiguously (e.g. knowledge about rectangles), or they use some general constraints to rule out multiple interpretations.

Determining Constraints for Vision

One of the primary tasks in computer vision is to find a set of constraints that would allow a computer to interpret images unambiguously. There are four main techniques for doing so: the engineering approach, the statistical approach, the biological approach, and the physical approach.

Engineering Approach

The engineering approach relies on the intuitions, introspections, and prior knowledge of the system designer as to what the important image features should be and how they should be interpreted.

Statistical Approach

The basic idea of the statistical approach is that it is possible to design a system that can "learn" what the constraints are simply by observing the world through sensory input. This is the approach used in statistical pattern recognition, and more recently in artificial *neural networks*.

Biological Approach

The third approach to finding useful image constraints involves studying biological vision systems with the aim of uncovering the constraints that they use in image interpretation. In some cases, the biological solution may be constrained by the neurophysiological implementation mechanisms, and in such cases the biological approach may fail. However, in other cases the biological solution may be constrained by the general problem of vision and may provide useful insights for computer vision. In one sense, all computer vision uses the biological approach, as vision is defined in terms of the human visual sense. But since most stages of visual processing are not open to conscious introspection, other means of determining how the mammalian visual system functions must be used.

Physical Approach

In the physical approach, the basic idea is to determine properties of the physical world that can be used to constrain image interpretation. This has been a very successful approach and has led to many useful constraints. For example, David Marr (1982) frequently used continuity as a constraint, making use of the fact that the physical world is basically continuous. Thus, neighboring image points have a high probability of having arisen from the same physical entity.

Another example of a frequently used constraint is the assumption of a general viewpoint. This assumption is based on the fact that for a given scene, as the viewpoint changes slightly, there will generally be only slight changes in the projected image, and thus many properties of the projected image will remain constant over most viewpoints.

Bibliography

1982. Marr, D. *Vision*. San Francisco: W. H. Freeman.

1992. Haralick, R. M., and Shapiro, L. G. *Computer and Robot Vision*. Reading, MA: Addison-Wesley.

1995. Jain, R., Kasturi, R., and Schunk, B. G. *Machine Vision*. New York: McGraw-Hill.

1997. Davies, E. R. *Machine Vision*. San Diego, CA: Academic Press.

Deborah Walters

COMPUTERS, HISTORY OF

See DIGITAL COMPUTERS, HISTORY OF; and SOFTWARE HISTORY.

CONCURRENT PROGRAMMING

For articles on related subjects, *see*

+ Ada
+ Contention
+ Coordination Languages
+ Distributed Systems
+ Guarded Command
+ Monitor, Synchronization
+ Multiprocessing
+ Multiprogramming
+ Multitasking
+ Mutual Exclusion
+ Operating Systems
+ Parallel Processing

Concurrent programming concerns programs in which several actions may be performed at the same time. A concurrent program is composed of multiple processes or computational *threads*, each of which is a sequential computation, that is, a linearly ordered series of steps.

Concurrency—the execution of concurrent programs—arises in many contexts. Multiprocessors, parallel processors, and distributed systems, all of which have multiple CPUs (*q.v.*), naturally run concurrent programs. A multitasking operating system runs concurrent programs even on a single CPU (also called *multiprogramming*). Time-sharing (*q.v.*) operating systems that support many users are multitasking, but so are modern personal computer operating systems. It is also common for input and output devices to be handled through concurrent programming; thus embedded systems (*q.v.*) and real-time systems (*q.v.*) use concurrency. Finally, concurrent programming is a design technique that is useful for modular programming (*q.v.*) even in intrinsically sequential computations.

When two parts of a concurrent program actually execute at the same time they are *physically* concurrent. Physical concurrency is not possible on a uniprocessor, but we say that processes are *logically* concurrent if *time slicing* selects one or another for execution by the single CPU, though all are capable of executing. Logically concurrent processes behave like physically concurrent processes that run on relatively slower CPUs than the actual one.

One standard model of concurrency is based on *interleaving*, in which execution of concurrent instructions is regarded as equivalent to *some* sequential interleaving of the instructions of the different threads. There are many possible such interleavings, of course, and as models of a concurrent program they are all equivalent. Suppose two threads execute the following sequences concurrently:

thread a	thread b
x := x*y	m := m-n
y := y+1	n := n*n

One of the six possible interleavings is $x := x+y$, $m := m-n$, $n := n*n$, $y := y+1$; another is $m := m-n$, $n := n*n$, $x := x*y$, $y := y+1$. Since the threads operate on different variables, all interleavings produce the same final values.

Concurrent programming is more difficult than sequential programming. A sequential program is correct if it produces correct results for all possible *inputs*. A concurrent program must produce correct results not only for all possible inputs but for all possible *timings* (interleavings) of concurrent statements. Consider a program in which two threads both increment a variable that is a shared counter. Even an elementary programming language instruction like $x := x+1$ is implemented by several assembly language instructions that fetch a value into a private CPU register, increment it, and store it back, so that the two threads execute

thread a	thread b
`load r1,x`	`load r1,x`
`add r1,r1,1`	`add r1,r1,1`
`store r1, x`	`store r1,x`

Suppose that both threads attempt to increment the counter. If one thread executes its `store` before the other executes `load`, the counter will go up by 2. Otherwise each will add 1 to the old value of x and each will store its new value; that is, one of the two increments is lost! This error is an example of a *race condition*, in which the precise timing of instructions affects the result of a computation. Concurrent programs with race conditions may appear to work correctly for quite some time before an interleaving occurs that reveals the error.

To prevent race conditions certain sequences of instructions must be *atomic*; that is, indivisible. If the three-instruction sequence that updates the counter x above were atomic, whichever thread began an update would finish it before the other could start. A block of code that must be atomic to guarantee correct execution is called a *critical section*, and are implemented by providing *mutual exclusion* through a locking mechanism.

Solutions to the problem of providing mutual exclusion depend on some minimal kind of atomicity at the hardware level. In a uniprocessor system,

it is achieved by disabling interrupts, thus making all instruction sequences atomic until interrupts are reenabled. In a multiprocessor, it normally requires an "interlock" that prevents two processors from addressing the same memory cell at the same time. Mutual exclusion can then be achieved if the processors have instructions that can atomically exchange a value in a CPU register with the value in a shared memory cell. Suppose a memory cell, lock, is initialized with a 1, representing permission to proceed, and that two (or more) threads running on different processors seek permission to use a critical section by putting a 0 in a register and then atomically exchanging it with the lock. If two attempt this operation at once, the atomicity of the exchange operation insures that one will get the 1; the other, a 0 (Fig. 1). In the following pseudocode `mutexbegin` causes a thread to wait, continually retrying to obtain the lock, until it gets the 1 representing permission to use the critical section, which it returns in `mutexend`.

```
                  reg := 0
mutexbegin: repeat
                  exch reg, lock
            until reg = 1
            {critical section}
mutexend:   exch reg, lock
```

The atomic exchange operation guarantees an invariant property of the system: there is exactly one copy of the value 1 at all times; it is impossible for two processors both to get a copy in their private registers.

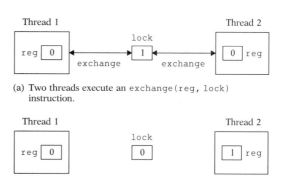

(a) Two threads execute an `exchange(reg, lock)` instruction.

(b) After the two exchanges, thread 2 has acquired the lock value.

Figure 1. Using an atomic exchange instruction for mutual exclusion.

The implementation of mutual exclusion with an atomic exchange instruction has the defect that a processor must idle while a process is waiting. *Semaphores* are a common operating system construct that provides an equivalent atomic locking mechanism, and lets a process suspend execution while waiting for another to signal it, thus allowing another process to execute (*see* MUTUAL EXCLUSION). Semaphores are a low-level construct from a programming standpoint, however. They cause transfers of control akin to the goto of sequential programming: a process that issues a *wakeup* semaphore operation will cause execution to resume in some other part of the program (the part that did the semaphore *wait* operation). Furthermore, a process might neglect to issue the *wakeup* or execute a *wakeup* operation on the wrong semaphore.

Concurrency in Programming Languages

A concurrent programming language must provide a means to start multiple processes and to synchronize them. Process synchronization includes both mutual exclusion (*cooperating* processes) and *condition synchronization*—used when one process must wait for another process to make some condition true, at which point it is notified that it may resume execution. Since condition synchronization generally involves some exchange of data, processes that use it are sometimes called *communicating* processes.

Concurrent processes can be started by a `fork` statement that lets a process invoke a new one, like a subprogram (*q.v.*) call except that the called routine runs in parallel with the caller; such an operation is part of the Unix operating system (*q.v.*). In Java (*q.v.*), a thread can be started by a similar `threadname.start()` call. Other languages, like Algol 68 (*q.v.*), have a `cobegin-coend` construct; `cobegin S1; S2; S3; coend` would start three statements executing as separate threads, and all would have to terminate before execution continued beyond the `coend`.

Shared Variables

When processes have shared variables, a convenient construct for both mutual exclusion and condition synchronization is the *conditional critical region* (CCR), which has the syntax **region** R **when** B **do** S. Any named region provides mutual exclusion, which means that a process can evaluate the condition B atomically and when it is true, continue on to execute S before any other process can change the value of the condition. As an example, suppose that a queue holds a number of resources shared by several processes, and that there are standard operations on the queue: `empty`, `put`, `get`, which test for an empty queue and add or remove an item from the queue. Each process would execute

```
region Resource when not empty(Resource_Q)
        do get(item)
{ use the item}
region Resource when true do put(item)
```

The first use of the critical region lets a process acquire a copy of the resource without interference, once one is available; the second, which never causes a wait, returns the copy.

An important characteristic of CCRs, as of some other synchronization constructs, is that they are nondeterministic. That is, if several processes await the same condition, when it becomes true one of them will resume execution, but which one is not specified. An implementation might provide a first come, first served ordering, but need not, though a common requirement is that it be fair in the sense that a waiting process will eventually resume if its condition repeatedly becomes true. This nondeterminism, also found in the *guarded command* (*q.v.*) of sequential programming, separates abstract specification of behavior from implementation details.

An alternative to CCRs is the *monitor* (*see* MONITOR, SYNCHRONIZATION). It provides *encapsulation* (*q.v.*) of critical data, giving access to it only through operations declared as public; thus, it is like a *class* (*q.v.*) in object-oriented programming (*q.v.*). It adds mutual exclusion, allowing only one activation of any of its routines at a time; that is, only one calling process at a time may be "in" the monitor and have access to its data.

Message Passing

Another approach to concurrency provides mutual exclusion and condition synchronization through *message passing*. Message passing is essential in distributed systems or others in which concurrent processes do not share memory, but it is a useful abstraction even when there is shared memory. In the former case messages require data to be copied from one place to another; in the latter, message passing may simply be a transfer of *access rights*. Message passing uses `send` and `receive` primitives, which provide mutual exclusion in access to messages, and which synchronize by making a receive operation delay its caller until a message is present.

In another form of message passing, the sender waits for the receiver to reply to the message. This produces a transfer of control in which the sender stops, the receiver (re)activates, and when the receiver completes its message-handling operation it stops and the sender resumes. That is, it is akin to the transfer of control in an ordinary subprogram call in which the calling program transfers control to the called subprogram, which transfers it back with a *return* statement, so this message passing is called *remote procedure call*. In one form of remote procedure call a new process is created to execute each call of a procedure; for example, many Unix *daemon* processes like the one that manages printing work this way. Ada uses a form of remote procedure call, which it calls *rendezvous*, in which a single process handles all calls. It is designed for *client–server* (*q.v.*) computing, in which a server process encapsulates data and provides operations on it that can be invoked by client processes; that is, it is an "active" version of a monitor or CCR.

Types of Concurrent Programs

Concurrent programs are as diverse as sequential programs, but there are some common patterns of concurrency that arise in operating systems, parallel algorithms, and distributed processing.

Producer–consumer interactions are one very common form of concurrent computation. A resource manager is an example; processes consume resources and then return ("produce") them. In simple producer–consumer interactions, one process produces data and passes it to a consumer process. It is often useful to decouple them so that each can run at its own rate, and this can be done with message passing to a mailbox that stores the data, or with an intermediate process that receives the product and forwards it to the consumer on demand.

Domain decomposition is another common structure for concurrency, often used when there is a computational domain that can be subdivided, with each subdomain assigned to a process. Computation can proceed independently in each subdomain, but some communication is required to maintain consistency at their boundaries. This is typical of many scientific computations, such as finite element methods. When the time required to communicate boundary information is much less than the time to compute a solution in each subdomain, such domain decomposition is efficient.

Computations may be *peer-to-peer*, when any process may initiate an action calling for further actions from others. The multiagent systems used in some artificial intelligence work are typical of these.

Operating systems deal with *resource management* problems, in which processes may be competing for resources and risk deadlock if they are poorly allocated. The same issues arise in distributed databases, a common application of concurrent programming. The *dining philosophers* problem was designed to illustrate some of the issues that arise in resource management (*see* Fig. 1 of COORDINATION LANGUAGES).

Finally, concurrent programming is a tool for structuring even sequential computations by partitioning them into many processes or threads of computation, each of which performs a simple task. The advantage that concurrent programming offers is that the order of execution of the components can be controlled by the availability of data rather than by a single main program that may have to evaluate complex conditions. This is the strategy used in operating systems like Unix in which a *pipeline* (*q.v.*) of processes can be constructed, each performing a task and communicating results to the next in line.

Languages

One of the first languages designed for concurrent programming was Concurrent Pascal in 1975; it used monitors for synchronization. Other languages with support for concurrency have included Modula-2 which provides monitor-like operations; Occam which uses message-passing; Ada; Java, with monitor primitives; and SR, a language used largely for research and teaching, which has a wide variety of synchronization methods. There are also numerous concurrent variants of standard languages like C, C++, and the functional language ML.

Semantics

There are also more general models of concurrency such as Petri nets in which instructions execute in parallel rather than in some interleaved sequence. In either case, the formal description of concurrent programming semantics is more difficult than the formal description of sequential programs, because timing as well as input values must be considered. One approach is to use temporal logic to specify what must *always, never* or *eventually* happen (for example: collision in a critical section must never occur; a waiting process must always eventually resume). There are also axiomatic approaches and those based on process algebras. As in sequential programming, it is important to characterize concurrent programs in terms of invariants: properties that are true of the program state at the beginning, end, and all important intermediate points of the computation.

Bibliography

1965. Dijkstra, E. W. "Cooperating Sequential Processes," in *Programming Languages* (ed. F. Genuys), 43–112. New York: Academic Press.

1988. Gehani, N., and McGettrick, A. D. (eds.) *Concurrent Programming*. Reading, MA: Addison-Wesley.

1990. Ben-Ari, M. *Principles of Concurrent and Distributed Programming*. Upper Saddle River, NJ: Prentice Hall.

1997. Schneider, F. B. *On Concurrent Programming*. New York: Springer-Verlag.

2000. Lea, D. *Concurrent Programming in Java*, 2nd Ed. Reading, MA: Addison-Wesley.

David Hemmendinger

CONTENT-ADDRESSABLE MEMORY

See ASSOCIATIVE MEMORY.

CONTENTION

For articles on related subjects, *see*

+ Bus
+ Channel
+ Concurrent Programming
+ Multiprocessing
+ Multiprogramming
+ Multitasking
+ Mutual Exclusion

Originally, the term *contention* was used to describe a communication system in which the terminals, or lines, were competing for a circuit and the first one to find it free obtained it. This concept can be generalized to the case of multiple users (jobs–*q.v.*, tasks, processes) competing for sharable resources (processors, buses, devices). For example, in a multiprogramming system, two processes may simultaneously require the use of the processor-memory bus. As another example, consider the case of a multiprocessor system where a process can be split into several tasks and the number of tasks ready to be processed in parallel is larger than the number of available processors.

Contention is solved by using priority schemes; the simplest one is first-come-first-served. However, all processes contending for a shared resource must either ask for the resource continuously or must be remembered so that they will, in turn, be able to use it. In addition, access to the shared resource must be synchronized. This implies the presence of either hardware arbiters or of software queues, with adequate synchronization mechanisms and buffers associated with each sharable resource.

Jean-Loup Baer

CONTROL STRUCTURES

For articles on related subjects, *see*

+ Data Structures
+ Guarded Command
+ Procedure-Oriented Languages
+ Structured Programming
+ Subprogram

A *control structure* is a programming language construct that specifies a departure from normal sequential execution. A control structure controls the sequence of statement execution within a given program unit, and encompasses special facilities for selection, repetition, and exception handling. Usually, such facilities are in the form of statements that extend over several lines of the source program—hence, the term *control structure*.

Arbitrary Control

The normal pattern of program execution is sequential control in which statements are executed in the order they appear. If $\langle S1 \rangle$ and $\langle S2 \rangle$ are each program statements (or self-contained sequences of statements) that perform some processing (e.g. assignment, I/O, or procedure call) then,

$\langle S1 \rangle;\langle S2 \rangle$ or $\langle S1 \rangle$
            $\langle S2 \rangle$

represents the execution of $\langle S1 \rangle$, followed immediately by the execution of $\langle S2 \rangle$. A pictorial representation of sequential control is

All nontrivial programs (*q.v.*) involve execution path control other than strictly sequential, and therefore all programming languages provide facilities for specifying such control. A simple and fundamental, yet powerful and "complete" set of execution control facilities consists of the ability (1) to insert a label $\langle L \rangle$ at any point in the program for identification of that location, and (2) to unconditionally or conditionally, depending upon the value of a Boolean expression $\langle B \rangle$, transfer execution control to such points, using goto (branching) statements.

```
goto ⟨L⟩
if ⟨B⟩ goto ⟨L⟩
```

The conditional **goto** involves two possible paths of execution, as shown, one of which continues sequential control (if $\langle B \rangle$ is **false**) and the other ($\langle B \rangle$ **true**) transfers control to the specified label: all computing hardware contains efficient machine-level instructions to perform conditional and unconditional branching, and normally all high-level language control structures are implemented using these instructions. In what follows, control structures are described in terms of **goto** to show how they may be implemented.

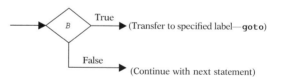

With conditional and unconditional **goto** statements, arbitrary execution control may be achieved. Typically, in programming languages, labels are either numbers (e.g. in Fortran: GO TO 210) or alphanumeric identifiers (e.g. in Ada: **goto MatchFound**).

Reliance on **goto**s for specifying program control tends to be error-prone. This was pointed out by Edsger Dijkstra in a now classic letter (1968). Bohm and Jacopini (1966) showed that essentially, any control flow can be achieved without the **goto** by using appropriately chosen sequential, selection, and repetition control structures. Therefore, high-level general-purpose programming languages include facilities designed expressly for their optimum implementation.

Selection

A very common control pattern is that of selectively executing, or not executing, a sequence of statements, $\langle S \rangle$ depending upon the current value (**true** or **false**) of a Boolean expression $\langle B \rangle$. The control structure for such a pattern is as follows, with the equivalent control using `goto` shown below the pictorial representation.

```
if ⟨B⟩ then ⟨S⟩ endif
```

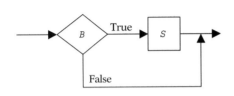

```
if not ⟨B⟩ goto ⟨L⟩;⟨S⟩
⟨L⟩:
```

Another common pattern has one group of statements $\langle S1 \rangle$, being executed if $\langle B \rangle$ is true, and a different group, $\langle S2 \rangle$, if $\langle B \rangle$ is false.

```
if ⟨B⟩ then ⟨S1⟩
        else ⟨S2⟩
endif
```

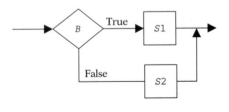

```
if not ⟨B⟩ goto ⟨L2⟩
⟨S1⟩; goto ⟨L1⟩
⟨L2⟩: ⟨S2⟩
⟨L1⟩:
```

This structure is known as the **if-then-else** selection control structure, and is the most commonly found selection control structure in high-level languages.

Another common control pattern is that of selecting one group of statements to be executed from among 3,

4, 5, or more different statement groups. In general, one can think of n groups of statements ($n < 0$), $\langle S1 \rangle, \langle S2 \rangle, \ldots, \langle Sn \rangle$, from which (at most) one group is to be selected for execution. The conditions governing the selection are formulated as a set of Boolean expressions, $\langle B1 \rangle, \langle B2 \rangle, \ldots, \langle Bn \rangle$, as may be appropriate for the needed control, so that if $\langle B1 \rangle$ is true $\langle S1 \rangle$ is selected; otherwise, if $\langle B2 \rangle$ is true $\langle S2 \rangle$ is selected and, in general, for the first $\langle Bi \rangle$ that is true, the corresponding $\langle Si \rangle$ is selected.

```
if ⟨B1⟩ then ⟨S1⟩
   ⟨B2⟩ then ⟨S2⟩
        ⋮
   ⟨Bn⟩ then ⟨Sn⟩
           [else ⟨Sn + 1⟩]
endif
```

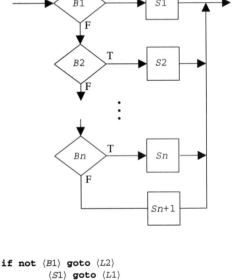

```
if not ⟨B1⟩ goto ⟨L2⟩
        ⟨S1⟩ goto ⟨L1⟩
⟨L1⟩: if not ⟨B2⟩ goto ⟨L3⟩
        ⟨S2⟩ goto ⟨L1⟩
⟨L3⟩:

      ⋮

⟨Ln⟩: if not ⟨Bn⟩ goto ⟨Ln + 1⟩
        ⟨Sn⟩ goto ⟨L1⟩
⟨Ln + 1⟩: ⟨Sn = 1⟩
⟨L1⟩:
```

Since there are no restrictions on the Boolean expressions in this n-way selection control structure, more than one such expression may be true. Still, at most one statement group is executed—the one associated with the first true Boolean expression—and possibly none is executed (when there are no true Boolean expressions and the **else** option is absent).

In none of the selection control structures is there any restriction on the statements that any ⟨S⟩ may contain. And, in particular, any ⟨S⟩ may contain other (nested) selection control structures. For example, *n*-way selection control may be achieved using nested **if-then-else** structures, but the *n*-way structure is much more readable.

The *n*-way selection structure involves an ordered evaluation of a *sequence* of Boolean expressions. Another common selection pattern involves, conceptually, "parallel" selection of one from among several statement groups. The **case** selection structure is often used to express such "parallel" selection. If ⟨X⟩ is an expression, and each ⟨V_i⟩ is a constant value of the same data type as ⟨X⟩, the **case** structure has the form shown below.

```
case ⟨X⟩
    ⟨V1⟩ then ⟨S1⟩
    ⟨V2⟩ then ⟨S2⟩
        ⋮
    ⟨Vn then ⟨Sn⟩
        [else ⟨Sn + 1⟩]
endcase
```

Since the ⟨V⟩s are disjoint, their order in the **case** structure is immaterial. Also, any ⟨V⟩ may consist of a set or range of values, rather than just a single value, so long as all of the ⟨V⟩s remain disjoint. As with the *n*-way if, there may be any number of cases in a **case** structure and the else part is optional.

Repetition Control

An extremely important aspect of programming is the specification of repetitive execution of a statement group ⟨S⟩. The following structure, with its **goto** equivalent at the bottom, will repeat execution of ⟨S⟩ indefinitely:

```
loop
    ⟨S⟩
endloop
```

```
⟨L1⟩
    ⟨S⟩
    goto ⟨L1⟩
⟨L2⟩ :
```

The above loop control results in an *infinite loop* unless execution of one of the statements in ⟨S⟩ causes either program termination (e.g. execution of a **stop** statement) or a branch out of the loop (e.g. **goto** ⟨L2⟩).

Loop structures often have the more general form

```
loop ⟨C⟩
    ⟨S⟩
endloop
```

where ⟨C⟩ specifies the desired control of repetition. With loop control specified in this manner, the need for **exit** statements in ⟨S⟩ is typically much reduced (although exit statements may still be allowed in ⟨S⟩). Two of the more common types of control, ⟨C⟩, are

1. Conditional: **while** ⟨B⟩
2. Indexed: **for** ⟨I⟩ ← ⟨X1⟩ to ⟨X2⟩ [**by** ⟨X3⟩]

where ⟨I⟩ is an integer variable, the ⟨X⟩s are integer expressions, and ⟨B⟩ is a Boolean expression. The effect of each of these control options is as follows (Z is an "internal" integer "hidden" from the programmer):

```
loop while ⟨B⟩
    ⟨S⟩
endloop

loop
    if not ⟨B⟩ exit
    ⟨S⟩
endloop

loop for ⟨I⟩ ← ⟨X1⟩ to ⟨X2⟩ by ⟨X3⟩
    ⟨S⟩
endloop

Z ← ⟨X3⟩/abs(⟨X3⟩)
⟨I⟩ ← ⟨X1⟩ − ⟨X3⟩
loop
    ⟨I⟩ ← ⟨I⟩ + ⟨X3⟩
```

```
    if Z*(I) > Z*(X2) exit
    ⟨S⟩
endloop
```

A number of variations of these loop facilities are implemented in various computer languages. One such class of variations is control at the bottom of the loop rather than at the top, that is, a **repeat-until** loop.

Exception Handling

A number of things can happen during program execution that can prevent execution from successfully continuing. These include division by zero, subscript out of bounds, numeric overflow, **case** value missing, unavailable read-only file, wrong data type on input, insufficient storage available, and referencing an undefined value. Such exceptions, when detected, normally result in program termination without further processing unless provision is made for some other action, and possibly recovery. Such provision is called *exception handling*. The structural nature of an exception handler is essentially that of a **case** selection control structure. One of a predefined set of exception values is presented to the handler, which then selects the routine that performs the action desired in the event that that particular exception occurs. If corrective action is possible, then that routine may include such action, followed by resumption of normal processing. The form of such an exception handler is

```
exception
    ⟨E1⟩ then ⟨S1⟩
    ⟨E2⟩ then ⟨S2⟩
        .
        .
        .
    ⟨En⟩ then ⟨Sn⟩
endexception
```

When an exception occurs, execution control automatically passes to the beginning of the exception handler, along with the identification ⟨E⟩ of the exception that has occurred. Selection is then made of the corresponding routine ⟨S⟩ to be executed. Program execution is terminated after execution of ⟨S⟩, unless ⟨S⟩ specifies recovery and resumption of program execution.

Control structures are major features of high-level programming languages, and a language's control structures play a major role in its effectiveness in software development. Actual syntax used by particular languages will differ somewhat from that used in this article, but the functionality is the same.

Bibliography

1966. Böhm, C., and Jacopini, G. "Flow Diagrams, Turing Machines, and Languages with Only Two Formation Rules," *Communications of the ACM*, **9**(5), (May), 366–371.

1968. Dijkstra, E. W. "Goto Statement Considered Harmful," *Communications of the ACM*, **11**(3), (March), 147–148.

1974. Kernighan, B. W., and Plauger, P. J. *The Elements of Programming Style*. New York: McGraw-Hill.

1999. Sebesta, R. W. *Concepts of Programming Languages*, 4th Ed. Reading, MA: Addison-Wesley.

Jerrold L. Wagener

COOPERATIVE COMPUTING

For articles on related subjects, *see*

+ Client-Server Computing
+ Cluster Computing
+ Cryptography, Computers in
+ Cyberspace
+ Distributed Systems
+ Internet
+ Multitasking
+ Parallel Processing

Cooperative computing (collective computing, or "farming") is a form of highly distributed computing done by several thousand or even, potentially, several million computers. The "cooperators" are the owners of the widely dispersed computers, principally personal computers (PCs), who voluntarily devote machine cycles that would otherwise be wasted to computations "farmed out" to them by some central authority. This sponsoring authority then harvests and combines the partial results. Powerful Beowulf clusters used as supercomputers (*q.v.*) are built from perhaps 10 000 interconnected microprocessors, but however impressive, this number pales in comparison to the millions of processors attached to the Internet.

The magnitude of the world's unused machine cycles is prodigious. Current high-performance PCs are capable of executing 3000 million instructions per second (3000 MIPS, or 3 GIPS), 10.8 billion per hour, or about 85 trillion instructions over a typical "3rd shift" during which its owner typically sleeps. At least another 85 trillion instructions can be appropriated during the day by running the cooperative software in the background while the primary user is running other programs, or pausing to think or eat meals or take a nap (*see* MULTITASKING). So either the PC occasionally "naps" too, or, for the betterment (or at least amusement) of humankind, its user can enroll in a consortium of altruistic users very few of whom are known one to another.

When organized this way, a loosely coupled but coordinated network of some tens of thousands of PCs is more powerful than the world's fastest supercomputer, but only for a restricted class of problems. Consider, for example, the problem of bandwidth (*q.v.*). Two computers sufficiently near one another to be joined by a local area network (LAN–*q.v.*) can exchange data at the rate of several megabits per second or more. But the data transfer rate to a PC equipped with a 56 KB/s modem (*q.v.*) is just a small fraction of that. (The situation is fast improving, however, since satellite dish reception and access to fiber optic (*q.v.*) channels through TV cable companies will ultimately be ubiquitous.) As a result, it makes no sense for the central coordinating computer to take more time to tell a remote assistant what to do than it would to do it itself. The best candidates, then, for cooperative computing are problems whose algorithm is conducive to parallel processing and whose initial data is compact and sufficient to keep the client busy for a long time.

Number theory has proved a fertile source of such problems. Typical are the attempts to find previously unknown prime numbers, or to find the factors, if any, of a number thought likely to be composite. Large composite numbers are a staple of public key cryptosystems where the supposed difficulty of factoring 100-digit or larger numbers (in order to recover the decryption key) is the basis for the security of the system (*see* CRYPTOGRAPHY, COMPUTERS IN). Hayes (1998) gives some interesting anecdotes regarding cooperative computing contest successes in this area.

The search for ever-larger prime numbers has centered on finding more so-called Mersenne primes, primes that have the form $2^n - 1$ (and which therefore consist of a sequence of n consecutive 1s in binary) where n itself is prime. Since not all numbers of this form are prime (the lowest prime n for which $2^n - 1$ is not prime is 11), number theorists value the discovery of new Mersenne primes. On 14 November 2001, after a two and one-half year search involving tens of thousands of networked volunteers, 20-year-old Michael Cameron found that the 39th Mersenne Prime is $2^{13,466,917} - 1$, which has more than four million digits. Then, on 17 November 2003, Michael Shafer's computer found the 40th known Mersenne prime, $2^{20,996,011} - 1$, which contains 6 320 430 decimal digits (*see* http://www.mersenne.org/prime.htm). It is also the largest known prime of any kind, surpassing GIMPS' last discovery by more than 2 million digits. It is projected that the first billion-digit Mersenne prime will be discovered in 2009.

The largest currently running cooperative computing project is the Search for Extra-Terrestrial Intelligence (SETI) run by the University of California at Berkeley (*see* www.seti.org). Almost two million users, about half active at any one time, use a special Web browser that processes radio astronomy data from SETI in the background, forming the world's most powerful computer. Once cooperative computing becomes common across, say, 200 million PCs whose cost has dropped to $500 each, the resulting megacomputer will have a replacement value of 100 billion dollars. And, like the Internet, no one will own it!

Bibliography

1988. Litzkow, M. J., Livny, M., and Mutka, M. W. "Condor—A Hunter of Idle Workstations," *Eighth*

International Conference on Distributed Computing Systems, San Jose, CA, 13–17 June, 104–111.

1989. Lenstra, A. K., and Manasse, M. S. "Factoring by Electronic Mail," *Advances in Cryptology*, Eurocrypt '89, 355–371. New York: Springer-Verlag.

1998. Hayes, B. "Collective Wisdom," *American Scientist*, **86**(2), (March–April), 118–121.

Edwin D. Reilly

COORDINATION LANGUAGES

For articles on related topics, *see*

+ Client-Server Computing
+ Concurrent Programming
+ Distributed Systems

Introduction

When humans collaborate to achieve a shared objective, it is usual for one of the collaborators to be appointed as a coordinator. Increasingly, we see an analogous situation in computing. *Coordination languages* are a new class of programming languages that offer a solution to the problem of managing the interaction among concurrent programs. Among other things, they have been applied to electronic commerce (*q.v.*), game playing (chess), Internet services (distributed knowledge base search engines), and workflow management problems. Gelernter and Carriero were the first to use the term *Coordination* in the sense of this article through their slogan: "Concurrent programming = Computation + Coordination."

Basic Principles

In defining coordination languages we must address what is being coordinated, the media for coordination, and the protocols (*q.v.*) used for coordination. Coordination languages are not general-purpose programming languages; rather, they are often defined as language extensions or scripting languages (*q.v.*). They have much

in common with object-based approaches. Their entities must be *encapsulated* (*see* ENCAPSULATION) and they should persist beyond a single transaction.

Coordinated Entites

The coordinated entities are usually active, that is, *agents* or *processes*. Coordination of agents should not require reprogramming of the agents; the coordination mechanism is a wrapper around the existing, independent agents. The agents may have been programmed in a variety of different programming languages.

Coordination Media

In many coordination languages, coordination is accomplished via a shared data space. In such models, communication is *generative*: agents communicate by "generating" data in the shared space; this data is then available to any other agent that has access to the space. This contrasts with the message-passing paradigm of concurrency where communication is usually a private act between the participating agents. In a heterogeneous system, in which the agents are written in different languages, the data must be stored in a common format.

Coordination Rules

The Linda proposal identifies a set of coordination primitives that may be used to access a shared data space. The primitives are normally implemented as library routines that are called from some host language such as C (*q.v.*) or Prolog. In contrast to Linda, many recent proposals have been for rule-based languages; one consequence of this shift to a more declarative view of coordination is increased reasoning power. In either case, the coordination "rules" provide a level of abstraction that hides much of the complexity of coordination from the programmer.

Examples
Linda

The central feature of Linda (Carriero and Gelernter, 1990) is the *tuple space*. This is the coordination

Figure 1. The Dining Philosophers Problem.

medium—it is a shared data structure that contains *tuples* (records—*q.v.*). Tuples may be passive (data) or active (processes). Tuples are created and manipulated by processes using a small set of operations. Only passive tuples can be accessed; tuple selection involves pattern matching. The operations include the following:

in(t): looks for a tuple matching t; if found, the tuple is deleted; otherwise the process waits until matching succeeds.

out(t): creates a new passive tuple whose contents are specified by t.

eval(t): creates an active tuple whose contents are specified by t. An active tuple must have at least one field that is a function to be computed.

Both of the last two operations are guaranteed to succeed; the issuing process continues immediately. The full set of operations includes a nondestructive read and predicates for testing the state. We give a solution to the classic Dining Philosophers problem with five philosophers in a language dialect called C-Linda. The philosophers sit around a circular table with a bowl of spaghetti in

the middle and five forks. Each philosopher alternately thinks and then eats. In order to eat spaghetti, the philosopher requires two forks (*see* Fig. 1). The situation is modeled by the program in Fig. 2 (based on a solution suggested by Paolo Ciancarini). The philosophers are numbered from 0 to 4, and so are the forks. The program (real_main()) generates five passive tuples representing forks and five active tuples representing the philosophers. The program also generates four meal tickets; a philosopher must have a meal ticket before attempting to eat. The fact that there are only four tickets means that at least one philosopher has access to two forks and the system does not deadlock. When a philosopher is ready to eat he or she must pick up the fork with the same number and an adjacent fork (% is the modulus operation in C).

Gamma

The coordination medium in Gamma is a *multiset*—a set-like collection that may contain many copies of the same element. In the basic model, the multiset is

```
#define TRUE 1
philosopher(int i)
{
    while(TRUE)      {
        think();
        in ("meal ticket"); in ("fork",i);
                            in ("fork",(i+1)%5);
        eat();
        out("fork",i);out("fork",(i+1)%5);
                        out("meal ticket");
}}

real_main()
{
    int i;
    for (i=0,i<5,i++){
     out("fork",i);
     eval(philosopher(i));
     if (i<4) out ("meal ticket");
    }
}
```

Figure 2.   The Dining Philosophers in C-Linda.

untyped, so it is rather similar to the Linda tuple space but, in contrast to Linda, all of the elements of the multiset are passive. Simple agents are represented as pairs consisting of a reaction condition and an action, written: action ⇐ reaction. An action is a rewrite rule: lhs → rhs. The action selects some elements (which match the left-hand side of the rule and satisfy the reaction condition) from the multiset and rewrites them according to the rule (replacing them by the elements listed on the right-hand side of the rule).

Future Directions

Both Linda and Gamma were first proposed in the mid-1980s. However, the real need for coordination languages has become apparent only recently, with the emergence of the Internet and distributed computing. With the exception of Linda, many of the languages that we have discussed are still research prototypes. We need to develop theories and logics of coordination languages so that we can construct programming support tools. A good theory would enable us to provide deeper comparisons among various proposals and provide a solid basis for the design of the next generation of coordination languages.

Bibliography

1990. Carriero, N., and Gelernter, D. *How to Write Parallel Programs: A First Course*. Cambridge, MA: MIT Press.

1996. Andreoli, J. -M., Hankin, C., and Le Métayer, D. (eds.) *Coordination Programming: Mechanisms, Models and Semantics*. London: Imperial College Press.

1996. Ciancarini, P., and Hankin, C. (eds.) *Coordination Languages and Models*. Berlin: Springer-Verlag.

Chris Hankin

COROUTINE

For articles on related subjects, *see*

+ Activation Record
+ Concurrent Programming
+ Subprogram

A *coroutine* resembles the more familiar *subprogram* or *function* of most programming languages. However, coroutines differ from subroutines in that their lifetimes are not tied to the flow of control. When a subroutine is called, a new instance of its activation record is created, which is destroyed when control is relinquished. But when a coroutine returns control, its execution is not finished and so its activation record is preserved. Each time control reenters the coroutine, it resumes execution where it left off with its local control and data state retained. Coroutines are generally used in cooperating pairs, hence the prefix "co."

Since a new activation record is not created on every call, coroutines can be more efficient than subroutines. Furthermore, because coroutines can be entered directly at the appropriate point to continue some computation, their use can simplify the implementation of some algorithms. This is especially true when the processing to be done on a given call depends in a complex fashion upon previous calls. For example, a program that needs to determine whether two trees (*q.v.*) of quite different structure contain the same terminal (leaf) elements in the same order might use a separate coroutine to traverse each tree. The first would find its next leaf, pass it to the second coroutine, and then pause. The second would find *its* next leaf and compare it with the one passed to it. If they differed, that coroutine could immediately report the difference and terminate; otherwise it would resume the first coroutine and wait for another value to be passed to it.

Coroutines are often used to implement logically concurrent processes (*threads* or *lightweight processes*) on a uniprocessor. These coroutine threads do not pass control to each other directly; instead, the transfer is indirect and is done as a side effect (*q.v.*) of a call on a library routine. For example, the programming language Modula-2 provides a *processes* library module with procedures that support synchronization, scheduling, and mutual exclusion for coroutine-based threads (Wirth, 1985). These threads are called "coroutines" to distinguish them from truly parallel threads.

Applications of coroutines include operating systems, compilers, and discrete event simulation programs (*see* SIMULATION). For example, the language Simula 67 supports discrete event simulation with flexible coroutine mechanisms (Dahl, 1972). Coroutines are also used in text manipulation, artificial intelligence (*q.v.*), and sorting (*q.v.*) programs. Many programming languages now provide threads (Java—*q.v.*), or a coroutine library, as does C++ (*q.v.*). Others, such as concurrent logic languages, provide a coroutine-like transfer of control among routines by means of "freeze" and "thaw" operations or guarded-command

(*q.v.*) control structures (*q.v.*) that suspend and resume routines. Functional programming (*q.v.*) languages that use *lazy evaluation* (i.e. compute values only as needed) also employ coroutine-like control.

Bibliography

1972. Dahl, O. -J., and Hoare, C. A. R. "Hierarchical Program Structures," in *Structured Programming* (eds. O. J. Dahl, E. W. Dijkstra, and C. A. R. Hoare), 175–220. New York: Academic Press.
1980. Martin, C. *Coroutines: A Programming Methodology, a Language Design, and an Implementation*. New York: Springer-Verlag.
1985. Wirth, N. *Programming in Modula-2*, 3rd Ed. New York: Springer-Verlag.
1996. Finkel, R. A. *Advanced Programming Language Design*. Reading, MA: Addison-Wesley.

Brian T. Lewis

CPU

See CENTRAL PROCESSING UNIT (CPU).

CRIME, COMPUTER

See COMPUTER CRIME; and VIRUS, COMPUTER.

CRT

See MONITOR, DISPLAY.

CRYPTOGRAPHY, COMPUTERS IN

For articles on related subjects, *see*

+ Authentication
+ Colossus

Cryptography is the science of transforming messages for the purpose of making the message unintelligible to all but its intended receiver. The term *data encryption* refers to the use of cryptographic methods in computer communications for the same reason, and also implies the additional goals of providing assurance to the both the receiver and, if necessary, a third party that the message is not a forgery. These various aims are called, respectively, the goals of *communication security*, *authentication*, and *digital signatures.*

The transformation used to encipher a message involves both a general method, or algorithm, and a *key*. While the algorithm may be public knowledge, some or all of the key information must be kept secret. The process of transforming (enciphering) a message is to apply the enciphering algorithm to the message using the key as auxiliary input. The reverse operation (deciphering) is performed similarly.

Classical encryption techniques involve such operations as substituting for each message letter a substitute letter; in this case, the key is the correspondence between message (plaintext) letters and the enciphered message (ciphertext) letters. Such *substitution ciphers* can also be based on substituting for two or more letters at a time. Another common technique is to use a *transposition cipher* that permutes the order of the message letters using an algorithm whose steps are determined by a *key*. Many complicated hand or mechanical ciphers have been developed in the last few centuries. These techniques are insecure in general; the breaking of the German Enigma cipher during the Second World War attests to the vulnerability of even complicated rotor-machine ciphers (*see* COLOSSUS).

The *one-time pad* is a technique that provides the ultimate in security: it is provably unbreakable. To encipher a 1000-bit message, however, requires the use of a 1000-bit key that will not be used for any other message. Each ciphertext bit is the exclusive-or of the corresponding message and key bits. The one-time pad is used only in very important applications because of the expense in creating and distributing the large amount of key information required.

Cryptosystems that use an amount of key information that is independent of message length are breakable in theory. What makes them usable in practice is that the person trying to break the cipher (the *cryptanalyst*) must use an impractical or infeasible amount of computational resources to do so.

The major application of cryptography today is for data transmitted between computers in computer communication networks and for computer data encrypted for storage. Secure transmission of credit card information over the Internet is a particularly important problem.

The most widely used cipher in the USA for the encryption of stored or transmitted computer data is the Data Encryption Standard (DES), which was designed at IBM and approved by the National Bureau of Standards in 1976. The DES enciphers a 64-bit message block under control of a 56-bit key to produce a 64-bit ciphertext. The enciphering operations consist of roughly 16 iterations of the following two steps:

1. Exchange the left half of the 64-bit message with the right half.
2. Replace the right half of the message with the bit-wise exclusive-or of the right half and 32-bit word, which is a complicated function *f* of the left half, the key, and the iteration number.

Conventional cryptosystems (including DES) use the same key at both the enciphering and deciphering stations. In 1976, Diffie and Hellman proposed *public-key cryptosystems* in which the deciphering key was different from, and not computable from, the enciphering key (and vice versa). A person might create a matched pair of such keys and distribute copies of the enciphering key to friends, while keeping the deciphering key secret. The friends can send enciphered mail to the creator of the enciphering key that only the creator can read. (Even if a cryptanalyst obtains a copy of the enciphering key, it does no good.) This demonstrates the flexibility of a public-key cryptosystem for *key distribution*, an area where conventional cryptosystems are awkward because all keys must be kept secret. Public-key cryptosystems can also be used to provide *digital signatures* (*q.v.*).

The first proposal for a function to implement public-key cryptosystems was by Rivest, Shamir, and Adleman (1978). Their cryptosystem (the *RSA cipher*) enciphers a message M (first coded into numeric form by, for example, setting $A = 01$, $B = 02$, etc.) using a public key (e, n) to obtain a ciphertext C through the relation $C = M^e$ (mod n). Here, all quantities are large numbers (several hundred bits long), and n is the product of two very large prime numbers p and q. The security of the cipher rests mainly on the practical impossibility of factoring the number n into its parts p and q. The deciphering operation is similar, except that the exponent is different: $M = C^d$ (mod n). Since d depends on p and q, it is provably as hard to compute d from e and n as it is to factor n. When n is more than roughly 400 bits long, this becomes a prohibitively time-consuming task. Although the enciphering operation itself is quite complicated, enciphering rates of 1–10 Kb/second are possible with a special-purpose VLSI chip.

Two firms that specialize in cryptographic security are RSA Data Security of San Mateo, CA (http://www.rsa.com) and Counterpane Systems of Minneapolis, MN (http://www.counterpane.com). RSA has often stressed the vulnerability of "short" 56-bit DES keys and has sponsored contests to factor long decimal numbers, RSA-129 and RSA-130, for example, each containing the number of decimal digits implied by their names. Brian Hayes (1998) has described the successful attacks on these problems through the use of *cooperative computing* (*q.v.*), the Internet coordination of thousands of PC users who put what otherwise would be hours of unused machine cycles to work on different pieces of the same problem. Counterpane Systems has emphasized that cryptographic systems are vulnerable to attacks other than exhaustive key search (*see* Schneier, 1998).

Bibliography

1976. Diffie, W., and Hellman, M. "New Directions in Cryptography," *IEEE Transactions on Information Theory*, **IT-22**, 644–654.

1978. Rivest, R., Shamir, A., and Adleman, L. "A Method for Obtaining **D**igital **S**ignatures and Public-key **C**ryptosystems," *Communications of the ACM*, **21**(2), 120–126.

1996. Kahn, D. *The Codebreakers*. New York: Scribner's. The third update of the 1967 classic.

1996. Schneier, B. *Applied Cryptography*, 2nd Ed. New York: John Wiley.

1998, Hayes, B. "Collective Wisdom," *American Scientist*, **86**(2), 118–122.

1998. Schneier, B. "Cryptographic Design Vulnerabilities," *Computer (IEEE)*, **31**(9), 29–33.

Ronald L. Rivest

CYBERNETICS

For articles on related subjects, *see*

+ Analog Computer
+ Artificial Life
+ Automation
+ Genetic Algorithms
+ Information Theory
+ Robotics
+ Wiener, Norbert

The term *cybernetics* was coined by Norbert Wiener (1948). Derived from the Greek "kybernetes," or "steersman," it was defined as "the study of control and communication in the animal and machine." Over time, its meaning has broadened to cover the abstract principles of organization in any complex system. Thus, cybernetics stands as a crucial component of those systems sciences that are best manifested in the schools of *evolutionary systems, complex adaptive systems*, and *artificial life*.

Historical Roots

Inspired by work done before and during the Second World War on mechanical control systems based on servomechanisms, Wiener set out to develop a general theory of organization and control. Of course, *control theory* and *control systems engineering* have since developed into full disciplines in their own right. What distinguishes cybernetics is its emphasis on control and communication not only in engineered artificial systems but also in evolved natural systems such as organisms and societies.

Cybernetics grew out of a series of interdisciplinary meetings held from 1946 to 1953 that brought together a number of noted intellectuals, including Wiener, John von Neumann (*q.v.*), Warren McCulloch, Claude Shannon, Heinz von Förster, Gregory Bateson, Ludwig von Bertalanffy, and Margaret Mead. Hosted by the Josiah Macy Jr. Foundation, these became known as the Macy Conferences on Cybernetics. Through the 1950s, cybernetics became a crucial influence on the development of computer science, in particular information theory, automata theory, artificial intelligence and neural networks, computer modeling and simulation, robotics, and artificial life.

Relational Concepts and Information Theory

Concepts such as order, organization, structure, variety, constraint, randomness, freedom, complexity, development, self-organization, growth, emergence, learning, adaptation, and evolution are called *relational* because they let us pose abstract questions about systems organization, for example whether complexity increases naturally over evolutionary time. The development of relational concepts began with Shannon's mathematical theory of communication (Shannon and Weaver, 1964), in which he introduced statistical *entropy* as a measure of the variety in a probability distribution, and the *bit* (binary digit) as the unit of measure of that capacity. This theory came to be known as *information theory* and has many important applications in coding theory, cryptography, and dynamical systems. Statistical entropy can be related to the thermodynamic entropy of a physical system, which measures its distance from equilibrium. A high degree of disequilibrium is necessary for a physical system to be highly organized, and there are thermodynamic approaches to evolution and thermodynamic interpretations of relational concepts.

Entropy, related concepts, and correlates to such important results as Shannon's 10th Theorem and the Second Law of Thermodynamics were also sought in nonthermodynamic contexts such as biology, ecology, psychology, sociology, and economics. One important result is (W. Ross) Ashby's Law of Requisite Variety, which states that in a control system, the amount of information kept within the system places an upper bound on the amount of variety in the environment, which the control system is able to counteract. Another is von Förster's analysis of self-organization as a decrease in internal entropy, and his Order from Noise Principle, according to which self-organization can be accelerated by random perturbations (von Förster, 1960).

Biological and Mechanistic Isomorphisms

After the Second World War, early cyberneticists were eager to explore the similarities between technological and biological systems and the limits of mechanism as an explanatory paradigm. Newly armed with a theory of information, early digital circuits, Boolean logic, and automata theory, it was natural that they would propose digital systems as models of brains, and treat information as the "mind" to the machine's "body." Cybernetics thus contributed to early developments in computer science and artificial intelligence. Concepts that are central to these fields, such as complexity, self-organization, self-reproduction, selection, autonomy, connectionism, and adaptation, were proposed and explored by cyberneticists during the 1940s and 1950s. Examples include von Neumann's computer architecture (*q.v.*), game theory, and cellular automata (*q.v.*), and the work of Warren McCulloch (1965), who introduced artificial neural models, neural nets, and *perceptrons*.

A central contribution of cybernetics is its explanation of *purposiveness*, or *goal-directed* behavior in terms of control relations and relational concepts. A simple example of a control system is the thermostat, for which achieving and maintaining a specific temperature can be seen as its *goal*. The thermostat *regulates* or *controls* the room temperature by compensating for any perturbation that may push it away from its ideal range of values. This process, by which a system returns to equilibrium after a perturbation, is known as *homeostasis*.

The ultimate problem of biological and mechanistic isomorphism is whether there is any method to distinguish the living from the nonliving in principle, and if so, whether this can this be understood in terms of relational concepts. It follows that the origin of life, as a scientific problem, is a central concern for cybernetics and all of the systems sciences.

Cybernetics Today

Cybernetics played an important historical role in the origins of computer science, but it and the other interdisciplinary systems sciences have not generally become recognized as independent disciplines. The core ideas of cybernetics have largely been incorporated into other disciplines, however, in which they continue to influence scientific developments. Perhaps the most significant of these is the explosive growth of interest in complex adaptive systems, which has largely taken up the cybernetics banner in its use of mathematical models of relational concepts for interdisciplinary systems studies. "Artificial life" has also become a computational approach to simulation of biological systems and to the problem of the origin of life.

Bibliography

1948. Wiener, N. *Cybernetics or Control and Communication in the Animal and the Machine.* New York: John Wiley, MIT Technology Press, 1948; 2nd Ed., 1965.

1960. von Förster, H. "On Self-Organizing Systems and their Environments," in *Self-Organizing Systems* (ed. M. C. Yovits and S. Cameron), 31–50. Oxford: Pergamon.

1964. Shannon, C. E., and Weaver, W. *Mathematical Theory of Communication.* Urbana, IL: University of Illinois Press.

1965. McCulloch, W. (ed.) *Embodiments of Mind.* Cambridge, MA: MIT Press.

1966. von Neumann, J. *Theory of Self-Reproducing Automata.* Urbana, IL: University of Illinois Press.

Cliff Joslyn and Francis Heylighen

CYBERSPACE

For articles on related subjects, *see*

+ Cooperative Computing
+ Electronic Commerce
+ Electronic Mail (Email)
+ Internet
+ Multimedia
+ Online Conversation
+ Pretty Good Privacy (PGP)
+ Privacy, Computers and
+ Virtual Reality
+ World Wide Web

The term *cyberspace* was the invention of the novelist William Gibson. As described in *Neuromancer* (Gibson, 1984) and later novels, cyberspace was an artificial environment created by and maintained by computers. Transcending 2D audio-visual movies, Gibson's 3D cyberspace conveyed realistic detail to all five senses, a technologically simulated experience that has come to be known as *virtual reality*.

Cyberspace is now associated primarily with interaction over computer networks, most particularly the combination of the Internet and the World Wide Web. In this sense, "cyberspace" has become a synonym for "information superhighway," a term popularized in 1978 by then-Congressman Albert Gore, Jr to refer to a unified, interactive system of electronic communication analogous to the US Interstate Highway System. The prospect of such a system, with the capacity to deliver an unprecedented range of informational services to the home, school, or office, has been the driving force behind the creation of a multitude of commercial ventures, many of them Internet startup companies such as

Amazon, Ebay, and Yahoo! Traditional brick and mortar retail sales outlets, those unequipped to handle "click and order" electronic commerce (*q.v.*), are now under great strain and, other than supermarkets, may not survive.

Cyberspace encourages the formation of "virtual communities" that share a common interest. Such communities operate without regard to national boundaries, spreading the concept of free speech to many areas of the world to which that idea had been utterly foreign. On the Internet, every user is a potential publisher, liberating public discourse from the control of the privately controlled print and broadcast media.

Widespread global interconnection was envisioned, surprisingly early, in the 1946 short story "A Logic Named Joe," by Murray Leinster. And although he envisioned mental, quasi-spiritual interconnections rather than electronic, the Jesuit paleontologist and philosopher Pierre Teilhard de Chardin postulated that human evolution would ultimately produce a "noösphere" of knowledge that would envelop the earth just as palpably as does the current atmosphere and ionosphere.

There is great danger in the potential for violations of civil and privacy rights through the use of computer networks. As ever more social and commercial transactions are conducted in cyberspace, it becomes easier to track user spending habits, private interests, and political beliefs. Advocacy groups such as the Electronic Frontier Foundation (`www.eff.org`) have called for vigorous protection of privacy rights in cyberspace.

Cyberspace also places at risk the traditional concept of copyright. If an online document is downloaded to a diskette (*q.v.*) or hard drive (*q.v.*), an unscrupulous viewer, or perhaps only an uninformed careless one, can alter the document and republish it without credit or payment to its author, a practice of great concern to defenders of intellectual property rights. But the very notion of copyright—unknown before the invention of printing—may prove untenable in cyberspace.

Bibliography

1984. Gibson, W. *Neuromancer*. New York: Ace Books.

1992. Landow, G. P. *Vannevar Bush and the Memex*. Baltimore, MD: Johns Hopkins University Press.

1995. Negroponte, N. *Being Digital*. New York: Alfred E. Knopf.

1996. Slatalla, M., and Quittner, J. *Masters of Deception: The Gang That Ruled Cyberspace*. New York: Harper-Perennial Library.

1999. Lessig, L. *CODE and other Laws of Cyberspace*. New York: Basic Books.

Edwin D. Reilly

CYCLE TIME

For articles on related subjects, see

+ Access Time
+ Central Processing Unit (CPU)
+ Reduced Instruction Set Computer (RISC)
+ Register

The *cycle time* of a computer is the time required to change the information in a set of registers. This is also sometimes called the *state transition time*. The register cycle time of a processor is sometimes referred to as the *internal cycle time, clock time*, or simply *cycle time*. Main memory cycle time is usually several times the internal cycle time.

The internal cycle time may not be of constant value. There are basically three different types of cycle-timing organization:

1. *Synchronous (fixed)*. In this scheme, all operations are composed of one or more cycles, with the fundamental time quantum being fixed by the design. Such systems are also referred to as *clocked*, since a master oscillator (or clock) is used to distribute and define these cycles.

2. *Synchronous (variable)*. This is a slight variation of the first scheme; certain long operations are allowed to take multiple cycles without causing a register state transition. In such systems, there may be several different cycle lengths.

For example, a register-to-register transfer of information cycle might take one cycle, while a register-to-adder and return-to-register cycle would perhaps be two or three cycles.

3. *Asynchronous operation*. In a completely asynchronous machine, there is no clock or external mechanism that determines a state transition. Rather, the logic of the system is arranged in stages; when the output value of one stage has been stabilized, the logic signals the input at that stage to admit new operands.

In current practice, almost all processors use a fixed synchronous cycle as this is required to support a pipelined implementation (*see* PIPELINE). Access to main memory is sometimes implemented as an asynchronous operation.

Michael J. Flynn

a
b
c
d
e
f
g
h
i
j
k
l
m
n
o
p
q
r
s
t
u
v,w
x,y
z

D

DATA COMMUNICATIONS

PRINCIPLES

For articles on related subjects, *see*

+ Bandwidth
+ Baud
+ Channel
+ Codes
+ Communications and Computers
+ Error Correcting and Detecting Code
+ Ethernet
+ Gateway
+ Internet
+ Mobile Computing
+ Modem
+ Multimedia
+ Multiplexing
+ Network Protocols
+ Open Systems Interconnection
+ Packet Switching
+ Protocol
+ TCP/IP

Introduction

Data communications is the most rapidly expanding communication area, with Public Switched Telephone Network (PSTN) market penetration approaching saturation. Over the last decade, public data communication services have evolved from terminal and mainframe computer communications to real-time networked multimedia (*q.v.*), Web access (*see* WORLD WIDE WEB) and electronic mail (*q.v.*), as well as the more traditional computer traffic. The network infrastructure and the communications techniques themselves have also undergone a major revolution, allowing today's public data networks to deliver gigabits per second to the user.

Network technology usually relies on synchronous high-speed digital transmission over a range of different media, such as fiber optics (*q.v.*), twisted pairs, and mobile radio channels. Even over the local loop, which consists of one twisted pair per line, techniques such as the Asymmetric Digital Subscriber Loop (ADSL) have been developed that can deliver up to 6 Mbps from the local exchange to the home.

Massive increases in the speed of the underlying transmission medium, together with much lower error rates, have been reflected in the communications protocol stack. For most wired networks, error and flow control are no longer achieved on a hop-by-hop basis between network nodes, but rather by application software at the sending and receiving ends. Similarly, radical changes in switching and multiplexing technology have meant that circuit switching, which is very inefficient for data, has been replaced by packet switching, which is much more suitable. These changes throughout data communications technology have led to the ability to build and deploy *global* public data communications networks such as the Internet.

Information Transmission Over Computer Networks

Data transfer within a computer is in finite-sized chunks—bits, bytes, or words. Network communications must often be only one bit at a time, and the data must be serialized and deserialized again in the serial–parallel converter upon arrival at the remote computer. Data can usually flow in both directions simultaneously (*full duplex*). Sometimes, information can flow only in one direction (*simplex*), or data transmission in the two directions may not proceed simultaneously (*half duplex*).

Public data communication networks are made up of nodes (switches or routers) with interconnecting links. These links may carry either analog or digital representations of the digital data. A diverse range of traffic needs to be sent between one node and the next, and multiplexing enables a single link to carry multiple flows of data. The network accepts data in, *blocks, frames,* or *packets.* A set of messages is passed between the computer and the switch or router or between the source computer and the destination computer to facilitate this. The set of messages is called a *Network Protocol (q.v.—see also* PROTOCOL).

Transmission Techniques

Digital communication is most simply transmitted using square wave signals, consisting of on-and-off pulses (*see* Halsall, 1996). An example is shown in Fig. 1. These are commonly referred to as *baseband signals.* The range of frequencies from 0 Hz to the highest frequency present is the "electrical" *bandwidth (q.v.)* of the signal. The data link also has an electrical bandwidth that limits the frequencies that can propagate along it without excessive attenuation or distortion. The electrical bandwidth of the link limits the capacity of the network. The theoretical limit to the information transfer rate or link *capacity, C,* is given by the Hartley–Shannon law as $C = B \log_2(1 + S/N)$, where B is the electrical bandwidth and S/N is the ratio of signal strength power to noise level power—the *signal-to-noise ratio.* The maximum transmission rate of a communication link with usable electrical bandwidth B is $2B$ (Nyquist's law). The rate at which symbols are sent is called the *baud rate.* When only two levels are used, the baud rate

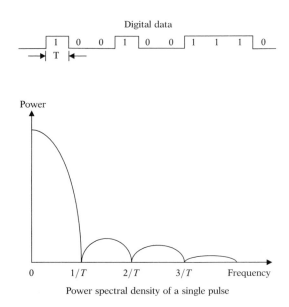

Figure 1. Baseband digital transmission uses square pulses. The graph shows the spectrum of this signal. T = pulse duration.

is also equal to the rate of information transfer in bits per second (bps). If multiple-levels are used, as shown in Fig. 2 for four-level coding, then the bit rate is higher than the baud rate.

The characteristics of the physical link can lead to degradation of the baseband signal's received pulse shapes. There are three main factors here: attenuation, dispersion, and noise. Attenuation leads to a reduction in the received signal strength, thereby making the signal more susceptible to the effect of noise, which can, for example, lead to a 1 being mistaken for a 0. Attenuation is also usually frequency dependent, and increases with frequency. This effective band limiting leads to a smearing of the received pulses, which can

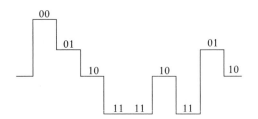

Figure 2. Multilevel signaling.

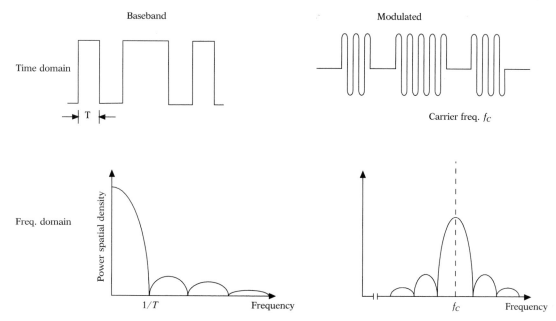

Figure 3. Signals and frequency spectra of direct transmission of the digital signal (baseband) and the result of modulating carrier signal of frequency f_c with the digital data (modulated). The diagram shows amplitude modulation.

cause a pulse to interfere with an adjacent pulse. This is called inter-symbol interference (ISI).

Dispersion is the phenomenon in which different frequency components of the pulse travel at different velocities down the link. This again causes spreading of the pulses, leading to ISI. Uncertainty in the position of the pulse edges caused by the above effects, and by imperfect clock stability at the transmitter, causes telegraph distortion (TD). The impact of distortion can be reduced by a combination of the use of line codes and pulse shaping. Pulse shaping tailors the temporal profile of the pulses, to minimize the interference between adjacent pulses (ISI).

Baseband signals can be transmitted as digital signals over the link if the usable part of the frequency spectrum of the link lies in the baseband region; this is true for twisted pair copper and coaxial cables, but not true for fiber optic cables and radio transmission. These cases require the use of analog techniques: the digital data is used to modulate the amplitude, frequency, or phase of a carrier sine wave (analog transmission—Fig. 3), using a modem.

While the trunk portion of the telephone network in most countries is based on digital transmission, the local network is still mainly analog. Relatively recently, the introduction of Integrated Services Digital Network (ISDN) to the home has allowed small businesses and home computer users to transmit digital data directly at 128 Kbps but this now being overshadowed by the introduction of Digital Subscriber Loop technology. Using multilevel, multiphase modulation, xDSL modems achieve effective data transmission rates of well over 10 Mbps.

Sharing a Single Transmission Medium

Some communication systems need to send data down a link only at irregular intervals. Such systems are termed *asynchronous*. In an asynchronous system the transmission rate is predetermined, but it is necessary to delimit information by sending a *start-of-frame* sequence before and an *end-of-frame* sequence after transmission of the data. The frame is preceded by a preamble to synchronize the receiver for the duration of the frame.

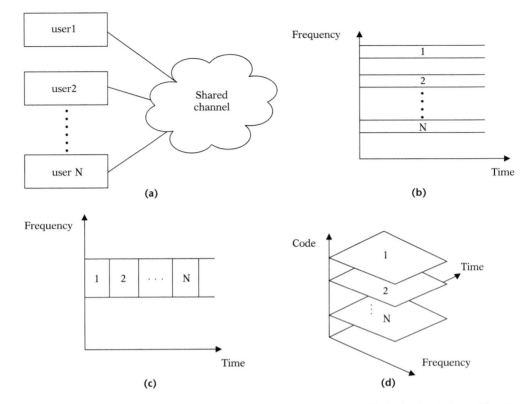

Figure 4. Sharing the capacity of the communications link using a multiplexing technique. The diagram shows (b) FDM; (c) TDM; (d) CDM.

The sender can send (or receive) data along the channel connecting it to the other hosts, and by the appropriate use of addressing information in a frame header, it is possible to ensure that the data is received at its correct destination. This mode of communication is called *broadcast*, which is commonly used over local area networks (LANs).

Systems that need to send data down a link all the time are called *synchronous*. Data is sent in frames, and the transmission of frames is continuous and back-to-back, as is the case for high-speed digital carriers that interconnect switches. In Fig. 4, the transmission medium is carrying a multiplexed data stream. Multiplexing may be achieved in a variety of ways such as by using a different carrier frequency for each channel (*frequency division multiplexing, FDM*), or by using a different slot in a high-speed synchronous digital transmission system (*time division multiplexing, TDM*). Mobile transmission systems use a third kind of

multiplexing, called code division multiplexing (CDM), where digital data pulses are used to modulate a high-speed pseudo-random sequence that is known only by the intended receiver.

Multiplexing techniques are not mutually exclusive, and often two of the techniques can be used together. An example of joint use of TDM and FDM is in the synchronous high-speed carriers in the Synchronous Digital Hierarchy (SDH, or SONET in the USA). TDM is used to multiplex data from a number of users into a single data stream, and an optical variant of FDM (*wavelength division multiplexing, WDM*) is used to transmit multiple composite streams down the fiber optic cable. CDM is more commonly used in mobile systems, where it is also called *spread spectrum*.

Multiplexing at the Switch or Router

The ability to multiplex data from multiple users down a single transmission link implies multiplexing at the switch or router in terms of packets (packet switching) or cells (cell relay). There is a limit to the number of simultaneous calls that can be handled by a switch, or the number of packets by a router. If packet switching is used, this limit on the number of packets may be a by-product of the processing required for each packet header (e.g. defined by the IP protocol), or the capacity of the output links. If circuit switching (or even virtual circuit switching) is used, the limit is determined by the number of simultaneous buffers required for each call that can be supported (e.g. as in an Asynchronous Transfer Mode (ATM) switch).

Public Data Networks

Public data transmission facilities used to be offered solely as leased telephone lines, over which modems could be used to transmit digital data. Public data transmission facilities are now offered either by an Internet Service Provider (ISP) over a dial-up link (telephone line) into the Internet, by telephone carriers as a switched line (N-ISDN), or via high-speed leased lines (frame relay and Switched Multimegabit Data Service—SMDS). The ISDN uses digital transmission to provide two information channels (at 64 Kbps each) and one signaling channel (at 16 Kbps), simultaneously in both directions (full duplex) over one two-wire line to the nearest switch. From this point, data is switched and multiplexed onto the standard digital data hierarchy for inter-exchange transmission, and the data is sent to the nearest packet switch. In totally leased facilities, the user has a dedicated transmission link to the packet switch, and bypasses the PSTN switch.

Frame relay is a new frame level best-effort service (i.e. generally reliable but not guaranteed) that relays individual frames across multiple virtual circuits, which have been set up previously using the D channel. Enhanced reliability can be provided at the frame level using the frame switching service. Frame relay is multiplexed and routed at the link level, and throughput can be much greater for frame relay than for packet switching. SMDS is offered over a frame relay network, which typically interconnects local area networks.

ATM simplifies this still further, by multiplexing and switching at the physical layer. ATM promises to offer many megabits per second to the user, and may be the basis for the new range of broadband ISDN public data services. ATM may form the backbone of new very high-speed public data networks.

The Internet differs from the previous networks discussed because it consists of many disparate networks. Internetworking is achieved at the network layer, using the IP protocol. The underlying networks in the Internet may be frame relay (SMDS), ATM, or a dial-up local telephone link from a user's home, but the details are hidden from the Internet user by the IP protocol. IP routers process *datagrams* (independent packets), which have a globally unique address in the header of the packet. IP provides a connectionless datagram or "best-effort" service, so any applications that require extra facilities, such as guaranteed delivery of data, must do so on an end-to-end basis. Over the Internet, this is commonly achieved by using the Transmission Control Protocol (TCP), which provides a reliable bit-pipe service to the layer above. Other applications, (such as real-time voice and video) would not require this level of reliability, and so would use the other transport layer protocol, the Universal Datagram Protocol (UDP), which provides very little extra to the service provided by IP.

Public Data Services

Public data networks are now mature enough to support public data services for the home as well as the office user. To date, the services over the global Internet are mainly the World Wide Web (WWW) and email, although others such as multimedia conferencing are now becoming more widely used. The most popular public data service is the Web, which is an unregulated service, free at the point of use. Home users commonly gain access to the Internet via a dial-up link to an ISP site, and from there to anywhere else. At any location on the Internet, hosts that are acting as Web servers allow users to access multimedia information using a client browser, such as Netscape Navigator or Microsoft Internet Explorer. The real power of the Internet lies in the ability to embed paths (Uniform Resource Locators—URLs) to other documents, perhaps held on other servers within normal documents. These hyperlinks protect the user from having to know about the actual network topology, and allow access to vast amounts of information.

Bibliography

1995. Fluckiger, F. *Understanding Networked Multimedia, Applications and Technology.* Upper Saddle River, NJ: Prentice Hall.

1996. Halsall, F. *Data Communications, Computer Networks, and OSI*, 4th Ed. Reading, MA: Addison-Wesley.

1999. Bateman, A. *Digital Communications.* Reading, MA: Addison-Wesley.

Vicky J. Hardman, Phil M. Lane, and Peter T. Kirstein

STANDARDS

The Need for Standards

Most computer manufacturers have their own network architectures, but there is increasing emphasis on the use of internationally agreed standards for communication. The ability of machines of different types to communicate has become progressively more important as the focus has shifted from the dedicated networks within an organization to the public networks that link separate organizations.

The Organizations Involved

Two major bodies are involved in the creation of standards. These are the International Organization for Standardization (ISO), representing primarily the computer industry and its customers, and the Telecommunication Standardization Sector of the International Telecommunication Union (ITU-T, formerly CCITT), representing the communication carriers via their national post and telecommunications authorities (the PTTs). Many standards are now produced jointly by ISO and ITU-T, with the two organizations agreeing to publish technically identical texts. Preliminary standards are also produced by the European Computer Manufacturers' Association (ECMA) and the Committee of European Posts and Telegraphs (CEPT). In the USA, the IEEE has played a major role in drafting standards proposals, particularly in the field of local area networks (LANs—*q.v.*) Standards of general interest from ECMA and IEEE are often fed into the ISO for wider discussion and support with the option of rapid publication as an ISO standard. Outside the formal standardization process, a number of large organizations issue their own specifications; of particular note are the Internet specifications from the Internet Engineering Task Force (IETF) and the middleware specifications from the Object Management Group (OMG).

Major Areas of Standardization

The wide range of data communications standards is organized within the framework of the Open Systems Interconnection (OSI—*q.v.*) Reference Model. Within the structure created by the reference model, individual service and protocol standards are defined for each of the layers except the application layer. In many layers, provision is made for choice of either a connection-oriented mode of operation, in which streams of information are sent between the communicating systems in the period during which a connection exists, or a connectionless mode of operation in which individual items of data are transmitted independently. The mode chosen depends on the application and the economics of the situation, and, in the lower layers, different families of standards have been created to meet the requirements of local and wide area networks.

The seven layers of the reference model can be considered in two groups. The three layers below the network service deal with the problems of the various network technologies, and with the use of networks in combination and the routing of information between different networks. The transport layer and the layers above it are concerned with the organization of the communication from end to end between the participating systems. Thus, the lower layers are primarily concerned with the process of data communication itself, while the upper layers address the incompatibilities of data formats or representations (in the presentation layer) and of operating system control of communication (in the session layer) between systems.

Distributed Systems

The development of data communications standards is ongoing. Standardization of applications involves considerations outside pure communication, and aspects such as system configuration, management, and the relation of communication to other system interfaces become important. These considerations have led to the formulation of a new reference model within ISO, providing a framework for Open Distributed Processing (ODP), and standards resulting from it open the way to the construction of more flexible and powerful distributed systems. This work has been carried out in close liaison with the OMG, and their Common Object Request Broker Architecture (CORBA) has provided a number of important components within the ODP framework.

Bibliography

1987. Knowles, T., Larmouth, J., and Knightson, K. G. *Standards for Open Systems Interconnection*. Oxford: BSP Professional Books.

1996. Tanenbaum, A. S. *Computer Networks*, 3rd Ed. Upper Saddle River, NJ: Prentice Hall.

Peter F. Linington

DATA COMPRESSION

For articles on related subjects, *see*

+ Codes
+ Cryptography, Computers in
+ File
+ Image Compression

Data compression is the process of reducing the amount of space used to store data by changing its representation. It is used to squeeze more files onto disks, to decrease the time to send files over the Internet, to send faxes quickly over telephone lines, and to increase the apparent speed of modems (*q.v.*).

A compression method is either *lossless* or *lossy*. Lossless methods enable the original data to be reconstructed exactly from its compressed form, which is important for general-purpose compression systems. Lossy methods make small changes to the data to make it more compressible—for example, they might reduce the amount of detail in an image or decrease the quality of an audio recording. Often these changes are imperceptible to a human, but they can result in a significantly more compact representation. Other than a brief discussion of MP3 sound compression, this article focuses on *lossless* compression. Other lossy compression methods are discussed in IMAGE COMPRESSION.

The compression performance of a method is often measured in *bits per character* (bpc), the number of bits in the compressed file divided by the number of characters (bytes) in the input file. For English text it is not difficult to achieve 4 bpc compression (i.e. reduce a file to about a half of its size), and some of the better compression methods can achieve closer to 2 bpc.

One of the earliest compression methods (1952) is *Huffman coding*. It works on a similar principle to Morse code: the more common characters are represented by shorter codes. In the 1970s, there were several important advances that have had a significant impact on the field of data compression. One was the discovery of *arithmetic coding*, which has become the basis of some of the best performing compression methods. Another is the development of *Ziv–Lempel coding*, currently the most widely-used commercial approach.

A number of *ad hoc* systems also exist, such as run-length coding (in which repetitions of the same character are replaced with a code for the number of repetitions), and diagram coding (where unused character codes are used to represent common pairs of characters), but, these generally give poor compression.

Compression may be divided into two parts: *modeling and coding*. Modeling is concerned with capturing the structures and regularities in a document, while coding is concerned with choosing exactly which bits should be used to represent the document, based on the information captured in the model. For example, a simple model might count the relative frequency of characters in a text, and a coder would use this relative frequency to assign a code for each character. If the model somehow determines that the letter "e" accounts for 9% of the characters, the coder could assign it a short code, such as the sequence of bits "100." The problem of coding is well understood, and efficient algorithms for finding optimum codes exist. Modeling is more difficult because it involves capturing the structure and rules of natural languages.

Coding

Coding is the task of representing the data to be compressed based on probabilities provided by some model. Shannon's *Noiseless Source Coding Theorem* has established that a character with an estimated probability p is best represented by—$\log_2 p$ bits (this value relates to the *entropy* of the probability distribution). For example, suppose we wish to send the character "h" to represent that a coin toss came up "heads." The probability of this character occurring is 1/2, and according to Shannon's theorem, it should be transmitted using exactly one bit.

The *Huffman coding* algorithm generates a code tree such as the one shown in Fig. 1. The example tree is for inputs that contain only five different symbols, with the probabilities shown provided by some model. The path from the root of the tree to the symbol gives the code for that symbol; for example, the code for "a" is 000, and the code for "d" is 10. Because each symbol is a leaf of the tree, no code for a symbol will be a prefix of any other code. This property makes decoding easy, because each bit-string that is the code of a symbol can be found without ambiguity. The tree is constructed by linking the two least probable symbols (in the example, "a" and "b"), and treating the linked pair as a new symbol with a probability equal to the sum of the two original probabilities ($0.25 = 0.13 + 0.12$). This step of linking the two least probable symbols is then repeated; the next two to be linked will be "d" and "e", then the $a + b$ subtree will be linked to "c". This continues until a complete tree has been constructed, when there will be just one "symbol" left, with a probability of one.

An alternative to Huffman coding is *arithmetic coding*. Arithmetic coding is able to encode symbols arbitrarily close to the optimum size of $-\log_2 p$ bits, even if this value is not an integer! For example, if a symbol has a probability of 0.9, ideally it should be represented in $-\log_2(0.9) \approx 0.15$ bits. An arithmetic coder achieves this by having one coded bit representing more than one input symbol. This makes arithmetic coding particularly suitable for models in which symbols have high probabilities. Each symbol coded typically requires two integer multiplications and a similar number of additions, so it is relatively fast, although not as fast as using a pre-calculated Huffman code.

Huffman coding is preferred where speed is important. It is particularly suitable for *static* coding, in which the probabilities are determined beforehand, and do not change during coding. However, it is not so suitable for *adaptive* coding, in which the probabilities can change frequently. In an adaptive model, the probability of a symbol is generally increased a little immediately after that symbol is coded, to reflect its being more likely to occur again.

Modeling

The coding methods described represent the "back end" to most compression methods. The "front end" is the modeling technique used to generate the probabilities. There are two main classes of models: *symbolwise* and *dictionary*. Symbolwise models provide a probability estimate for each symbol as it is coded. In contrast, dictionary methods have some sort of table, or dictionary, which contains words (or more generally, strings) that can be replaced in the input data with a code.

Dictionary Methods

A dictionary compression model goes through the input looking for strings of characters that are in the dictionary, and replacing them with a code. Static dictionaries are only effective if the dictionary has been generated explicitly for the text being compressed. Adaptive dictionary models are most common in general-purpose systems, and the most widely-used forms of these are known as *Ziv–Lempel* coding (often abbreviated as LZ), which is based on the intriguing idea of using the text as its own dictionary. Variants of LZ are widely used in general-purpose compression systems and archivers with names such as ZIP, GZIP, and PKZIP. These systems are very fast and give good compression.

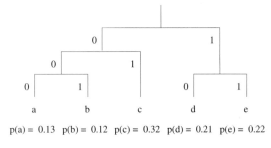

$p(a) = 0.13$ $p(b) = 0.12$ $p(c) = 0.32$ $p(d) = 0.21$ $p(e) = 0.22$

Figure 1. A Huffman encoding tree.

Symbolwise Methods

In contrast to dictionary methods, symbolwise methods encode individual characters. Such methods generally offer better compression performance although they can be slower and require more memory to perform encoding and decoding. A simple symbolwise method uses a model that keeps count of how many times each different character has been observed in the input, and uses the character's relative frequency as a probability to drive a Huffman or arithmetic coder. However, this model generally gives mediocre compression performance, and a significant improvement can be achieved by taking into account the context in which a character occurs. As the size of the context used in the model increases, the compression is likely to improve for a while. The solution to deciding whether to use large or small contexts is to use both, an idea captured in a method called *Prediction by Partial Matching* (PPM), one of the best techniques available.

MP3 Sound Compression

MP3 (Moving Picture Experts Group Audio Layer 3) is a data compression format that shrinks audio files to about one-tenth their size with only a small degradation from CD sound quality. A 4-megabyte MP3 file contains about three minutes of music. MP3 can be used to compress voice to an even greater degree than music. The MP3 compression algorithm was invented in the mid 1980s at the Fraunhofer Institut in Erlangen, Germany, with the help of Dieter Seitzer, a professor at the University of Erlangen. MP3 has made the downloading of music files from the Internet extremely popular, to the point at which the Recording Industry Association of America took legal action to shut down the popular *Napster* website that facilitated distribution of copyrighted music. However, similar websites continue to foster the sharing of such music and the attendant legal proceedings continue.

Performance Evaluation

The most important performance characteristics are the amount of compression, the speed at which it is performed, and the amount of primary memory (RAM) required to perform compression (and decompression). The relative compression performance of different

methods can vary depending on the type of file being compressed. For English text, the better methods give compression between two and three bits per character. A black and white bitmap image can typically be compressed to a tenth of its original size, while a full color image is difficult to compress losslessly.

Bibliography

1990. Bell, T. C., Cleary, J. G., and Witten, I. H. *Text Compression*. Upper Saddle River, NJ: Prentice Hall.

1991. Nelson, M. *The Data Compression Book: Featuring Fast, Efficient Data Compression Techniques in C*. Redwood City, CA: M&T Books.

1994. Witten, I. H., Moffat, A., and Bell, T. C. *Managing Gigabytes: Compressing and Indexing Documents and Images*. New York: Van Nostrand Reinhold.

1997. Jayant, N. *Signal Compression: Coding of Speech, Audio, Text, Image and Video*. Singapore: World Scientific.

Tim Bell

DATA ENCRYPTION

See CRYPTOGRAPHY, COMPUTERS IN; and PRETTY GOOD PRIVACY (PGP).

DATA MINING

For articles on related subjects, see

+ Data Warehousing
+ Database Management System (DBMS)
+ Electronic Commerce
+ Fuzzy Logic
+ Information Retrieval
+ Pattern Recognition
+ Relational Database

Introduction

Data mining is the process of finding previously unsuspected patterns in information contained in large databases. It is a research area at the intersection of several disciplines, including statistics, databases, pattern recognition and AI, visualization, optimization, and high-performance and parallel computing. With the success of database systems, and their widespread use, the role of the database expanded from being a reliable data store to being a decision support system (DSS). This has been manifested in the growth of *data warehouses* that consolidate transactional and distributed databases. Examples of applications of data mining include fraud detection in banking and telecommunications; marketing; science data analysis involving cataloging objects of interest in large data sets (e.g. sky objects in a survey, volcanoes on Venus); and problem diagnosis in manufacturing, medicine, or networking. The techniques are particularly relevant in settings where data is plentiful, but the processes generating it are poorly understood.

Definitions

Adopting the definition of the author

> *Knowledge discovery in databases* (KDD) is the process of identifying valid, novel, potentially useful, and ultimately understandable structure in data.

Here *data* is a set of facts and *structure* refers to either patterns or models. A *pattern* is an expression representing a parsimonious description of a subset of the data. A *model* is a representation of the source generating the data. The term *process* is used to indicate that KDD is composed of many steps. *Data mining* is a step in the KDD process which, under acceptable computational efficiency limitations, enumerates structures (patterns or models) over the data.

There are many more patterns or models that can be derived from a finite data set than there are data records. To be deemed *knowledge*, the derived structure must pass certain criteria. Notions of utility (e.g. gain, dollars saved by improved predictions) and *validity* (e.g. estimated prediction accuracy) have classical definitions in decision analysis and statistics. However, notions of *novelty, understandability,* and *interestingness* are much more difficult to define. The overall KDD process includes the *evaluation* and possible *interpretation* of

the "mined" structures to determine what may be considered new "knowledge."

Data Mining Methods
Predictive Modeling

This method predicts some field or fields in a database based on other fields. *Regression* refers to prediction of numeric (continuous) variables. *Classification* refers to prediction of categorical fields. The problem is to determine the most likely value of the variable being predicted given the other fields (inputs), the training data, and assumptions representing prior knowledge. Linear regression combined with nonlinear transformation on inputs may be used to solve a wide range of problems.

Data Segmentation

Also known as *clustering*, data segmentation groups the data items into subsets that are similar to each other. A two-stage search is employed: an outer loop over possible numbers of clusters and an inner loop to fit the best possible clustering for a given number of clusters.

Data Summarization

Extracting compact descriptions of subsets of the data can be done by taking horizontal (cases) or vertical (fields) slices of the data. The former provide summaries of subsets (e.g. sufficient statistics, or logical conditions that hold for subsets), the latter find relations between fields as opposed to predicting a specified field (classification) or grouping cases (clustering).

Dependency Modeling

Insight into data is often gained by deriving causal structure: *probabilistic* (statement about the probability distribution governing the data) or *deterministic* (functional dependencies between fields). In addition to density estimation there are methods for explicit causal modeling (e.g. belief network representations of density functions). The latter class provides an intuitive and more easily interpretable representation of causal influences in the model.

Change and Deviation Detection

These methods account for sequence information: time series or some other ordering (e.g. protein sequencing in genome mapping). Unlike methods above, ordering of observations is important and must be accounted for. Scalable methods for finding frequent sequences in databases, while in the worst-case exponential in complexity, do appear to execute efficiently given sparseness in real-world transactional databases. For example, in transactions representing users visiting Web pages on an Internet site, such techniques can find paths frequently traversed by site visitors, thus helping to understand how a Website is used.

Bibliography

1998. Fayyad, U. Editorial in *Data Mining and Knowledge Discovery*, **2**, 2.
1999. *IEEE Computer*. Special issue on Data Mining, **32**(8), (August).

Usama Fayyad

DATA PROCESSING

For an article on a related subjects, see

+ Computer Science

In a broad sense, *data processing* is what computers *do*. In this context it should be compared to *information processing*, a term some prefer because "information" does not carry the connotation of "number," as "data" usually does. But, the "data" in data processing really connotes any kind of information in symbolic form. Thus, information may be viewed as "knowledge," while data are the physical symbols used to represent the information.

Until the 1960s, it was common to divide the world of computer applications into two realms—business data processing and scientific computing—with the latter encompassing all engineering, scientific, or other technical applications of computers where the emphasis was on extensive numerical calculations rather than on the manipulation of data (sorting, etc.), which was the province of business data processing.

Another distinct contrast between the two areas was their relative dependence on the central processing unit facilities of the computer on the one hand and on the input–output facilities on the other. Most scientific calculations seemed to require little input data and produced relatively few numbers as results, but relied heavily on the arithmetic and logical capabilities of the central processing unit (CPU—*q.v.*) Indeed, computers that handle large scientific calculations are still often called "number crunchers." By contrast, business data processing tasks usually involve large amounts of input data—hence the name "data" processing—perform relatively few calculations, and then produce large amounts of output (e.g. payroll checks).

Increasingly, scientific calculations (e.g. meteorological and high-energy physics applications) process large amounts of input data and produce copious results. Also increasingly, business applications involve sophisticated mathematical techniques involving considerable calculation (e.g. various statistical and related forecasting applications). Thus, while there remain many applications that conform to their original stereotypes, it is more reasonable to use the terms "business data processing" and "scientific data processing" to distinguish between applications areas but not between the characteristics of the applications themselves.

The development of PL/I in the mid-1960s had, among its motivations, the desire to develop a language that could be used for both scientific and business problems because of increasing cognizance of common properties in these two areas. PL/I's failure to achieve wide popularity cannot be ascribed to any deficiency in this viewpoint. Rather, it was due to the inertia among Fortran and Cobol users that prevented them from switching to a new language because of extensive investment in so-called *legacy* programs. Undoubtedly the distinctions between the scientific and business applications areas will become further blurred as the widespread use of data communications and the increasing use of large databases further pervade all applications areas.

Bibliography

1990. Senn, J. A. *Information Systems in Management*, 4th Ed. San Rafael, CA: Wadsworth.

Anthony Ralston

DATA SECURITY

For articles on related subjects, *see*

+ Authentication
+ Computer Crime
+ Cryptography, Computers in
+ Digital Signature
+ Error Correcting and Detecting Code
+ Hacker
+ Password
+ Pretty Good Privacy (PGP)
+ Virus, Computer

Preserving the security of data necessarily requires consideration of the security of the entire computing system—its hardware, software (*q.v.*), firmware (*q.v.*), and internal data. It is impossible to protect just data if the programs that access and potentially modify that data have been corrupted. In the Internet age, data security has become of paramount importance because of the literally millions of users in cyberspace (*q.v.*) who might, accidentally or otherwise, invade and compromise the integrity of data on the computer calling into the Net.

Properties of Data Security

Data security is typically defined in terms of three properties

- *Confidentiality*—Assurance that data, programs, and other system resources are protected against disclosure to unauthorized persons, programs, or systems.

- *Integrity*—Assurance that data, programs, and other system resources are protected against malicious or inadvertent modification or destruction by unauthorized persons, programs, or systems.
- *Availability*—Assurance that use of data, programs, and other system resources will not be denied to authorized persons, programs, or systems.

Additionally, one might add authentication (*q.v.*—the property that persons, programs, or systems are accurately identified by a computing system) and nonrepudiation (the property that communications received from persons, programs, or systems can be assured to have indeed been sent by their purported senders).

A security flaw results from the lack, breach, or failure of confidentiality, integrity, or availability. The flaw can arise from a variety of causes, including human, mechanical, and environmental faults, as well as problems internal to the computing system. A *risk analysis* is a study to determine the susceptibility of a computing system to various kinds of security failure. Risk analysis is performed by analyzing general threats to the security of the system (such as loss of electrical power or sabotage), and then determining whether the threats could affect the system. A threat that could conceivably affect a system adversely is called a *vulnerability*.

Computer security embraces many aspects of a computing system, including hardware design, operating systems (*q.v.*), networks, database management systems (*q.v.*), compilers (*q.v.*), and user applications programs and systems. Vulnerabilities of computer systems range from the possibility of a trusted employee's selling (or being forced to reveal) secrets to a competitor, disk failures that render data unreadable, unauthorized operating system penetration (*see* HACKER), inferences about confidential data through carefully chosen queries posed to a database, loss of data because of floods or fires, acquisition of data through wiretapping or sensing the radiation from electronic equipment, or denying access to computing resources by flooding the system with other requests for service.

Cryptography

Cryptography is one important tool by which to preserve confidentiality and integrity. Confidential materials are encrypted to prevent their disclosure to unauthorized individuals. Furthermore, encryption usually prevents unauthorized, undetected modification: someone may be able to corrupt an encrypted text so that its bits decrypt to nothing meaningful, but, without breaking the encryption, no one can change a specific field of the underlying plaintext data.

Access Control

Confidentiality, integrity, and availability have been defined in terms of "authorized access." Two things are necessary in order to enforce such access: first, a reliable structure is needed under which authorizations to use resources are conferred (or revoked), and second, a reliable mechanism must exist to verify the authorization each time an access is attempted. Part of the authorization process is procedural and external to the computing system. For example, an employee may be authorized to access certain files because of his or her job responsibilities, an individual may be authorized to access classified data through a personal security clearance, a file's creator may confer access rights to a selected set of trustworthy users; or the administrator of a system may determine that data on that system may be shared with other specified systems. These permissions must be established in a reliable manner.

Once the list of authorized accesses is reliably established, individuals (human users, programs, or systems acting as representatives for the individuals) will request access. All such individuals are called *subjects*; the resources, called the *objects* of a computing system, consist of files, programs, devices, and other items to which subjects' accesses are to be controlled. For each subject and each object, the system must be able to determine whether access by the subject to the object is allowable and, if so, what type of access (e.g. read, write, delete). The access control system must have a reliable mechanism for verifying the requestor's identity. For example, operating systems often use passwords (*q.v.*) to ensure the authenticity of a user attempting to log in.

Program Security

Computers make access requests only under control of programs. Every program operates under the control of or in the name of a particular user. However, programs are also modifiable, that is, its bits can be read, written, modified, and deleted as any data can be (*see* STORED PROGRAM CONCEPT). While a user program may be designed to read a file, the program, with minor modification to its executable code, could instead write or delete the file. Those modifications can be the result of hardware errors and failures, a flaw in the logic of the program, or a change induced by some other program in the system. Hardware errors are uncommon, and checking circuitry is built into computers to detect them.

The first line of defense against program errors is *memory protection* (*q.v.*), which is designed to prevent one user from deliberately or accidentally accessing files and memory assigned to another. A second protection is careful and thorough *software engineering* (*q.v.*), including structured design, program reviews, and use of *chief programmer teams*. Such programming practices will help protect a user from unintentional errors. The third form of protection is *software testing*. Unfortunately, however, a well-known maxim states that testing can confirm the presence of errors, but not their absence.

Malicious Program Code

Computer data is vulnerable to attacks by malicious programs. Such programs range from overt attempts at accessing unauthorized data to more covert ones that attempt to subvert a benign program. While the overt, blatant attempts are typically precluded by the methods just described, the more subtle attempts may succeed (*see* VIRUS, COMPUTER).

Bibliography

1996. Pfleeger, C. P. *Security in Computing*, 2nd Ed. Upper Saddle River, NJ: Prentice Hall.
1998. Tipton, H. F. (ed.) *Handbook of Information Security Management*. Boca Raton, FL: CRC Press.

Charles P. Pfleeger

DATA STRUCTURES

For articles on related subjects, *see*

+ Abstract Data Type
+ File
+ Graph Theory
+ List Processing
+ Record
+ Stack
+ String Processing
+ Tree

Basic Terminology

A *data structure* is a collection of data values, the relationships among them, and the functions or operations that can be applied to the data. If any one of these three characteristics is missing or not stated precisely, the structure being examined does not qualify as a data structure.

Example The arithmetic expression $3 + 4 * 5$ is constructed in a systematic way from data components that are integers, 3, 4, and 5, and operators, $+$ and $*$. The structure of this expression may be thought of as either a string or a tree structure in which each operator is the root of a subtree whose descendants are operands (Fig. 1). As a string, the operations to be performed on it might include *evaluation* to obtain an arithmetic result or *concatenation* with other strings to form still longer expressions. As a tree, relevant operations would include insertion and deletion of objects in the tree or various kinds of tree traversal that yield prefix, infix, or postfix equivalents of the original expression (*see* TREE).

When the data for this data structure is stored in a computer, it must be stored so that components are readily accessible. This may be done by storing the expression $3 + 4 * 5$ as a character string A so that the ith character is retrieved by referring to the element $A[i]$. Alternatively, the string may be stored as a list structure in which the vertex associated with $+$ has a left child 3 and a right child $*$, which in turn has left and right children 4 and 5 (Fig. 2).

Figures 1 and 2 illustrate the relation between data structures, which specify *logical* relations between data components, and *storage structures*, which specify how such relations may be realized in a digital computer. The storage structure of Fig. 2 could be represented in a digital computer by five three-component storage cells, where each cell has one component containing an operator or integer and two components respectively containing a *pointer* (*q.v.*) to the left and right children. The three cells that have no successors contain special markers in their pointer fields, here indicated by the word "nil."

In order to define a class of data objects having a common data structure, it is usual to start with a class of primitive data elements called *atoms*, or elementary objects, and to specify *construction operators* by means of which *composite objects* may be constructed from the atoms. In the preceding arithmetic expression example, the atoms are operands (integers) and arithmetic operators. The construction operators specify how expressions are built up from operators and operands. A prescribed set of construction operators is called a *grammar*.

In order to access and manipulate composite objects specified by a given set of atoms and construction rules, *selectors* must be defined that allow the components of a data object to be accessed, and *creation* and *deletion* operators must be defined that allow the components of data structures to be created and deleted. Data structures may be characterized by how they are accessed and their creation and deletion operators.

Arrays

An *array* is a data structure whose elements may be selected by integer selectors called "indexes." If A is a one-dimensional array whose indexes start at 1, then

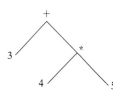

Figure 1. A tree structure.

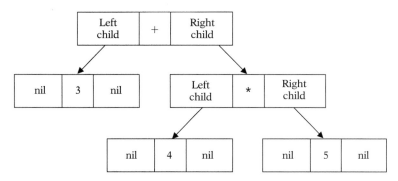

Figure 2.   Storage structure of the tree structure of Figure 1.

$A[3]$ (or $A(3)$ in some languages) refers to the third element of A. If B is a three-dimensional array, then $B[I, J, K]$ or $B(I, J, K)$ refers to the I, J, K element (B_{ijk}) of the array B. The set of all elements of an array is generally created at the same time by means of *declarations* (*q.v.*) such as

```
REAL A(100)          Fortran array declaration
Integer array        Algol 60 array declaration
   A[1:N];
A:array [1..N]        Pascal array declaration
   of real;
Int A[100];          C++ array declaration
```

The arrays introduced are *homogeneous* because all elements of an array have the same data type, and are *Cartesian* (rectangular) because all vectors in a given dimension have the same size. Most modern programming languages permit nonhomogeneous data aggregates called *records* or *structures* to be declared. The following is a PL/I declaration of a PAYROLL record with a 50-character name field, fields of mode FIXED for the number of regular and overtime hours worked, and a field of mode FLOAT for the rate of pay

```
DECLARE  1 PAYROLL
            2 NAME CHARACTER (50),
            2 HOURS
               3 REGULAR FIXED,
               3 OVERTIME FIXED,
            2 RATE FLOAT;
```

If it is desired to refer to the number of overtime hours in the record PAYROLL, then this is given by PAYROLL HOURS OVERTIME.

Sets

Sets are a convenient form of data structure when the order of elements is irrelevant, as in (for x ∈ S do sum := sum + x;). Sets and operations upon sets are supported in their full generality by the very high-level language SETL, which allows the user to make mathematical assertions using mathematical set theoretic notation. Pascal also has a data type "set" that allows us to talk about subsets and test for set membership.

Lists

List structures, just as array structures, may be characterized by their accessing creation and deletion operators. Elements of a list structure are generally accessed by "walking" along pointer chains, starting at the head of the list. In a single-linked linear list (SLLL), each list element has a unique successor and the last element has an "empty" successor field, usually denoted by the symbol "nil." In general, list elements may have more than one successor, and lists may be circular in the sense that pointer chains may form cycles. Knuth (1997) describes doubly linked lists that have forward and backward pointer chains passing through each element, and a number of other kinds of lists. Figure 3 illustrates a doubly linked circular list (DLCL) named L, whose head element H is linked both to the next element A and to the last element B.

If the forward pointer is referred to by RLINK (for right link) and the backward pointer is referred to by LLINK (left link), then the second list element

Figure 3.   Doubly linked circular list L.

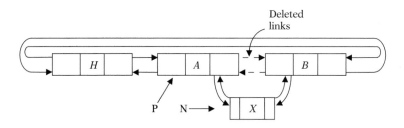

Figure 4.   Insertion of *X* into list in Figure 3.

(labeled a) may be accessed in either of the two following ways:

```
RLINK(L)              Forward chaining
LLINK(LLINK(L))       Backward chaining
```

Insertion of an element into a list is accomplished by creation of a new list cell and by updating pointers of existing list elements and the newly created list element (*see* Fig. 4). Lisp, which was developed by John McCarthy in the late 1950s, is the most important list processing language.

Trees and Graphs

A *tree* is a list in which there is one element called the *root* with no predecessor and in which every other element has a unique predecessor. That is, a tree is a list that contains no circular lists, and in which no two-list elements may have a common sublist as a successor. Elements of a tree that have no successor are called *leaves* of the tree. In Fig. 1, the symbol "+" is the root of the tree and the digits 3, 4, and 5 are leaves. Tree elements, just as list elements, are generally accessed by walking along a pointer chain. However, the guarantee that there are no cycles or common sublists makes it possible to define orderly procedures for the insertion and deletion of subtrees.

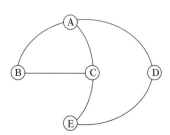

Figure 5.   A graph of five nodes and six edges.

A collection of data objects (nodes) so interconnected that their network may contain cyclic paths is called a *graph*. A typical graph is shown in Fig. 5. Such a structure can be represented by an adjacency list, a "list of lists," each of which tells which nodes are connected to the node at the head of the list (*see* Fig. 6). Alternatively, the same information can be represented as a generalized list (list with sublists) for processing by algorithms written in Lisp

$$((A \ (B \ C \ D)) (B(A \ C)) (C(A \ B \ E)) (D(A \ E)) (E(C \ D)))$$

Stacks

A *stack* is a linear list in which elements are accessed, created, and deleted in a last in, first out (LIFO) order. In order to access an element in a stack, it is necessary to delete all more recently entered elements from the stack.

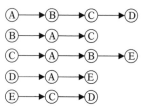

Figure 6. An adjacency list for graph of Figure 5.

Thus, only the top of the stack is immediately accessible. The two principal stack operations are *popping* and *pushing*. If S is a stack, then pop(S, x) causes the top element of the stack to be removed and stored at x and push (S, x) causes x to be placed on top of the stack.

Queues and Deques

A *queue* is a linear list in which elements are created and deleted in a first in, first out (FIFO) order. A line of people waiting to be served in a cafeteria is a queue, since the person having waited longest is always the first to be served (deleted from the queue). However, the trays in the cafeteria self-leveling dispenser form a stack, since additions and removals take place at the top (LIFO). A queue in which deletions are made only at the front, but in which items are usually inserted into the interior, is called a *priority queue*.

A generalization of queues and stacks in which elements may be added and deleted at either end of a linear list is called a *deque*. ("Deque," a shortened form of "double-ended queue," is pronounced "deck.")

Abstraction

An important programming language concept is that of an *abstract data type*, which has an interface of named operators accessible to the user and which operates on a hidden internal data representation. For example, an abstract "stack" data type would provide the user with "push," "pop," and "test empty" operators, but hide from the user the stack data representation (as an array or list). The language Ada (*q.v.*) has a concept called *packages* (*q.v.*) that provide collections of resources with hidden implementation to the user, but are not actually

abstract data types. Object-oriented languages such as C++ (*q.v.*) and Eiffel provide full abstract data type mechanisms.

Classification of Data Structures

Any imaginable data structure can be placed into one of three categories

1. A *static data structure* consists of a fixed number of contiguous cells arranged in a geometric pattern. That pattern usually, but not always, has a certain symmetry, such as that of a rectangular or hexagonal array.
2. An *elastic data structure* consists of a variable number of contiguous cells arranged in a geometric pattern.
3. A *dynamic data structure* consists of a dynamically changeable number of nodes, some or all of which have a stated logical connection to one another or to several others. Examples are trees, graphs and linked lists.

Static and elastic data structures are sometimes called *geometric data structures*, in contrast to dynamic ones, which are also called *topological data structures*.

Representative data structures are classified in the three categories in Table 1. In each of the three categories in Table 1, structures are arranged from simplest at the bottom to most complex at the top. This is easiest to see in the dynamic category. The nodes of a graph may be arbitrarily interconnected, either partially, as in Fig. 5, or completely. The smallest degree of interconnection among nodes in a dynamic structure is none at all, as is exemplified by the set, the last entry in the dynamic category of Table 1.

Using a language such as C (*q.v.*) or Pascal, dynamic data structures have to be synthesized by using records for nodes and pointers (*q.v.*) for interconnections. Alternatively, another programming language that supports the given structure could be used. If a language does a particularly good job of supporting a certain structure, it is cited in Table 1.

Data structures represent an appropriate and practicable level of abstraction for characterizing computational structure, and it is for this reason that their study is so important in computer science.

Table 1. Classification of representative data structures.

Static data structures (fixed number of contiguous cells)	Elastic data structures (variable number of contiguous cells)	Dynamic data structures (variable number of noncontiguous nodes)
Noncartesian array	File	Graph:
		n-ary tree
		binary tree
Cartesian array:	*n*-dimensional	
n-dimensional array	elastic array (APL)	
Three-dimensional array		List with sublists (Lisp)
Two-dimensional array	Matrix (APL)	
One-dimensional array	Deque	Simple linked lists:
	Queue (Simula)	DLCL, DLLL,
	Stack (Forth)	SLCL, SLLL
Fixed-length record	Variable-length	
(Pascal)	record (Cobol)	
	Variable-length string	
	(Snobol, Icon, APL)	
		Set (SETL)

Notes: DLCL—Doubly Linked Circular List; DLLL—Doubly linked Linear List; SLCL—Singly Linked Circular List; SLLL—Singly Linked Linear List.

Bibliography

1996. Weiss, M. A. *Algorithms, Data Structures, and Problem Solving with C++*. Reading, MA: Addison-Wesley.

1997. Knuth, D. E. *The Art of Computer Programming 1*, 3rd Ed. Reading, MA: Addison-Wesley.

1997. Main, M., and Savitch, W. *Data Structures and Other Objects Using C++*. Reading, MA: Addison-Wesley.

Peter Wegner and Edwin D. Reilly

DATA TYPE

For articles on related subjects, *see*

+ Abstract Data Type
+ Arithmetic, Computer
+ Character Codes
+ Coercion
+ Data Structures
+ Declaration
+ Expression
+ Extensible Language
+ Procedure-Oriented Languages

A *data type* is an interpretation applied to a string of bits. Data types may be classified as *structured* or *scalar*. Scalar data types include integer, real, double precision, complex, logical ("Boolean"), character, pointer, and label. Structured data types are collections of individual data items of the same or different data types.

Most programming languages provide a *declaration facility* or standard convention to indicate the data type of the variable used. This is necessary, since a string of bits may have several meanings depending on context. The *integer* (or *cardinal*) data type is used to represent whole numbers, that is, values without fractional parts. The *real* data type is used to represent floating-point data, which contains a normalized fraction (mantissa) and an exponent (characteristic). *Double precision* is a generalization of the real data type that provides greater precision and sometimes a greater range of exponents. *Complex* data contains two real fields representing the real and imaginary components of a complex number $a + bi$ (where i is the square root of -1). *Logical*, or *Boolean*, data has only two possible values, *true* or *false*. *Character* or *string* data is the internal representation of printable characters. Some coding schemes permit 64 characters and use six bits; others (EBCDIC and extended ASCII) permit up to 256 characters and use eight bits. *Label* data refers to locations in the program and *pointer* data refers to locations of other pieces of data.

The commonly used operators for addition (+), subtraction (−), multiplication (∗), division (/), and exponentiation (∗∗ or ↑ or ˆ) may be applied to real, integer, double precision, or complex data in high-level language programs, with a few restrictions. The actual operation that takes place depends on the data type of the operands. Although some language processors permit "mixed mode" expressions (i.e. expressions involving operands of differing data types), this is accomplished by converting ("coercing") the operands to a common data type before the operation is performed (*see* COERCION).

The logical operators *and, or, not, implies*, and *equivalence* may be applied to logical data having true or false values only. Character operations include concatenation and selection of substrings. For all data types, the assignment operator (typically, ← or := or =) may be used to copy the contents of one location into another, and relational operators may be used to compare values.

Many programming languages, such as Snobol, Pascal (*q.v.*), Modula-2, Ada (*q.v.*), C++ (*q.v.*), and Haskell, are *extensible* in the sense that users may define new data types to suit the needs of a particular problem (*see* EXTENSIBLE LANGUAGE). Such user-defined data types have become important for program clarity. User programs may contain declarations of new data

types, such as color, which might have a limited number of values such as *red, orange, yellow, green, blue*, and *violet*. Variable names could be declared to be of type *color* and could take on only the stated values. A Pascal example is

```
type COLOR = (RED, ORANGE, YELLOW, GREEN,
                            BLUE, VIOLET);
var CRAYON, PAINT: COLOR;
```

A user-defined data type might also be a subrange of a standard data type. For example, an age data type might be restricted to range from 1 to 120. A Pascal example is

```
type AGE = 1..120;
var TREEAGE, CITIZENAGE: AGE;
```

The data type concept can also include sequential or random access files and structured data types such as records (*q.v.*), arrays, or trees, that are formed from scalar data types.

Bibliography

1976. Wirth, N. *Algorithms+Data Structures = Programs*. Upper Saddle River, NJ: Prentice Hall.

1983. Aho, A. V. Hopcroft, J. E., and Ullman, J. *Data Structures and Algorithms*. Reading, MA: Addison-Wesley.

1995. Carrano, F. *Data Abstraction and Problem Solving with C++*. Reading, MA: Addison-Wesley.

Ben Shneiderman

DATA WAREHOUSING

For articles on related subjects, *see*

+ Data Mining
+ Database Management System (DBMS)
+ Relational Database

Introduction

Systems that use a large database management system as a central component for decision support are referred to as *data warehouses*. The evolution of databases from transactional to repositories of information to be

Figure 1. The evolution of the view of a database system.

analyzed by *decision support* tools is illustrated in Fig. 1. Some of the decision support tools are either natively supported in databases or are external client/middleware applications.

Data Warehouses

A data warehouse represents a collection of data together with a suite of data retrieval functions to facilitate data analysis. The data is typically stored in a back-end relational server or in specialized stores. The first step in creating a useful warehouse is to insure that data quality is sufficiently high for subsequent analysis to be meaningful. This *data cleaning* is responsible for the integration of multiple sources of data in multiple formats, thus providing a unified logical view of the data collection. Once the data has been cleansed, it needs to be *loaded* efficiently in the warehouse. In order to achieve scalability, a relational database is typically used as the backend warehouse. Once the warehouse has been populated, it needs to be *refreshed* by propagating the updates on source data to the warehouse.

Two key aspects of the refresh step are its periodicity and the propagation technique. These vary depending on the source and the target databases as well as the data analysis requirements. Incremental refresh can often be supported using the replication capabilities of commercial database management systems. *Data cleaning, load, and refresh* together provide the mechanisms for populating the data warehouse and updating it.

Online Analytical Processing (OLAP)

The principal reason to build a warehouse is to enable data analysis. The functionality of the standard database language SQL as a retrieval and data manipulation interface provides some elements of data analysis that are augmented by client query tools or application-specific analysis programs. Traditional data analysis over warehouses consists of predefined queries that are used to generate reports. A new class of analysis capabilities, called *Online Analytical Processing* (OLAP) has been advocated as a natural way to view and operate business data stored in warehouses. E. F. Codd (1993) coined and used the term OLAP in 1993 when he set forth some of the requirements of *ad hoc* data analysis.

OLAP emphasizes a *multidimensional* view of data. A simple way of appreciating the multidimensional view is to think of databases as spreadsheets (*q.v.*). In this view, a database consists of a set of *facts*. Each fact represents one or more numerical *measures* in the context of one or more variables (referred to as *dimensions*). The dimensions form the multidimensional coordinate system often referred to as a *data cube*. The facts may be viewed as a set of sparse points in the cube. The number of dimensions reflects the degree of complexity of the data. Figure 2, from Chaudhuri and Dayal (1997), illustrates some of the key concepts of the model. The figure shows a multidimensional database consisting of three dimensions: product, place of sale, and date. Each of these dimensions is organized as a hierarchy or a lattice. Querying of OLAP data is driven by navigation through the cube using *data-centric* operations augmented by powerful visualization primitives. For example, *slicing and dicing* enables selecting a partial cube consisting of a subset of all the dimensions for selected values of other dimensions.

The primary aim of OLAP is to achieve fast response times to aggregate queries that may otherwise require a long time on a traditional relational database. Furthermore, optimization of data layout, managing trade-offs between in-memory vs relational store use, and supporting efficient caching between the server and clients are major challenges in OLAP. *Data mining* represents a step towards automating some of the tedious aspects involved in enumeration and searching for patterns of interest in large data stores.

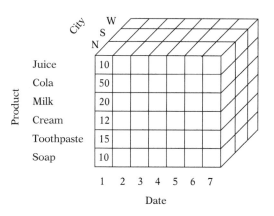
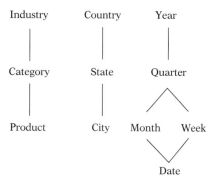

Figure 2.   An example of a multidimensional view of data.

Bibliography

1996. Kimball, R. *The Data Warehouse Toolkit*. New York: John Wiley.

1997. Chaudhuri, S., and Dayal, U. "An Overview of Data Warehousing and OLAP Technology," *ACM SIGMOD Newsletter* (March), 65–74.

                    Surajit Chaudhuri and Usama Fayyad

DATABASE MANAGEMENT SYSTEM (DBMS)

For articles on related subjects, see

+ File
+ Management Information Systems (MIS)
+ Record
+ Relational Database

Database

A *database* is a collection of interrelated data of different types. The difference between a database and a file is analogous to the difference between a thoroughly cross-referenced set of files in cabinets in a library or an office and a single file in one cabinet that is not cross-referenced with any other file. An important feature of a good database is that unnecessary redundancy of stored data is avoided along with the consistency problems that redundancy creates. The most widely used database management approach is called *relational*, and a more recent one is referred to as *object-oriented database management*. Furthermore, some of the ideas that stem from the object-oriented approach have been included in relational systems, giving rise to the term *object–relational databases*.

Tables, Columns, and Constraints

A conventional file, definable in Cobol since the early 1960s, is regarded as a collection of records of the same or possibly different types. In the relational approach, a file is referred to as a *table* containing *columns* and *tuples* (rows). A row in a table is essentially the same as a record in a file. A column in a table corresponds to a Cobol *item*.

Constraints

The difference between the database and Cobol approach is the use of *constraints*. Data values that are to be stored in computerized databases are often subjected to a validation condition. For example, the condition might be expressed as a range of values within which a tentative data value must lie in order to be accepted as correct at the time it is stored. In relational terms, such a condition is called a *constraint*. Two typical kinds of constraint will be described.

Uniqueness constraints

The simplest kind of constraint is that a value which is stored in a column of a table must be different from the values already stored in the same column on other rows in the same table. This is called a *uniqueness constraint*. While it is quite common to apply a uniqueness constraint to a single column in a table, it is also possible to impose a constraint between or among two or more columns in the same table. The term *key* is sometimes used to convey the concept similar to that associated with uniqueness constraint, but *key* has a specifically different meaning when used in conjunction with a relational database (*q.v.*).

Referential constraints

The other important kind of constraint is called a *referential constraint*. To illustrate this concept, consider Tables 1 and 2.

In Table 1, the column headed "Supplier number" and in Table 2, the column headed "Purchase order number" should each be the subject of a uniqueness constraint. In fact, it is a fundamental rule in a relational database that each table should have at least one uniqueness constraint and it is possible for a table to have two or more.

The concept of a referential constraint can be illustrated using the column in the Purchase order table that is headed "Supplier number." Narratively, the referential constraint reads: *The value stored in the Supplier Number column of the Purchase Order Table must match a value which has already been stored in the Supplier Number column of the Supplier Table.* More simply, the constraint is: *When the purchasing department sends a purchase order to a supplier, the supplier must already be known.*

The effect of expressing the constraint on the Supplier Number in the Purchase Order table is that the database management system then carries out a check each time

Table 2. Purchase order table.

Purchase order number	Date	Supplier number
4321	990406	12
74322	990406	32
74323	990408	13
74324	990408	12
74325	990410	32
74326	990411	32

a new row is added to the Purchase Order table. If the check fails, then typically the table is not updated.

The Database Language SQL

SQL is an international standard language used for defining the structure of a relational database in terms of tables, columns, and various kinds of constraints. SQL originally meant "structured query language," but since SQL is also used for many other purposes, the decoded form of the acronym is no longer accurate. The latest version of the ISO SQL standard [9075: 1992] contains the definition of concrete language syntax and associated semantics that can be used for many purposes associated with database management.

Database Management System

The handling of the various kinds of constraints is the capability that distinguishes a database from a file. In order to build a database, it is the normal practice to use a piece of generalized software called a *database management system* (DBMS). A DBMS that is based on the SQL database language requires the database

Table 1. Supplier table.

Supplier number	Supplier name	Supplier address	Phone
43	Smith	23 South Street Walton	234567
32	Jones	12 High Street Weybridge	678912
12	Brown	17 First Street London	1234566
13	Black	23 West Street Putney	245456

structure to be defined in terms of tables of columns and rows, and constraints. The resulting definition is often referred to as a *schema* or database schema. This schema is referred to when defining the processes to be performed on the data. The statements that a DBMS uses to perform the processes on the data in the tables are called *data manipulation statements* and are typically specified as part of a database language.

Data Structure Diagrams

Diagrammatic techniques are widely used among analysts and designers to present an overall picture of the major data concepts and how they are interrelated. It is important to distinguish in this context between analysis and design. *Data analysis* is an activity carried out to discover the major data concepts in a given business area and how one or more subject experts in that business area consider these concepts to be interrelated. One of the major techniques used as a means of communication between analyst and subject expert is *data structure diagramming*.

During analysis, each major data concept is often referred to as an *entity type*. For example, one would refer to the entity type "Supplier" and the entity type "Purchase Order" (*see* Fig. 1). During the dialog between analyst and subject area expert, it might be agreed that there is a *relationship* between these two entity types. The precise nature of the relationship could

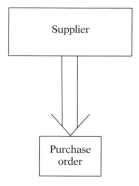

Figure 1. Data structure diagram showing two entity types and the relationship between them. The double stem arrow indicates a one-to-many relationship: a particular supplier may have been sent several purchase orders.

Table 3. Cross-reference between suppliers and purchase orders.

Purchase order	Smith	Jones	Brown	Black
21			×	
22		×		
23				×
24			×	
25		×		
26		×		

be analyzed by looking at some specific suppliers and specific purchase orders and preparing a cross-reference table, such as Table 3.

Note that in Table 3 there is one cross in each row. This indicates that each purchase order is related to one supplier. No purchase order has been sent to Smith; Black has one; Brown has two; and Jones has three. Thus, each column contains zero, one, two or three crosses, which is evidence that there may be zero, one or more purchase orders for each supplier. This is an example of the most common kind of relationship permissible between two entity types, namely, one to many, where the word "many" should be taken as meaning "zero, one or more."

Data Analysis and Database Design

There is a close tie between data analysis and database design. Some experts choose not to recognize the two as separate activities, but others prefer a distinctly different way of modeling data for analysis from that used for design. For example, some analysis techniques permit relationships among three or more entity types, but this capability is not allowed in database languages such as SQL.

Bibliography

1998. Darwen, H., and Date, C. J. *Foundations for Object/Relational Databases: The Third Manifesto.* Reading, MA: Addison-Wesley.

2003. Date, C. J. *An Introduction to Database Systems*, 8th Ed. Reading, MA: Pearson Addison-Wesley.

T. William Olle

DEBUGGING

For articles on related subjects, *see*

Types of Errors

Mistakes (bugs) find their way into a computer program for many reasons, but they may generally be classified as follows:

1. An otherwise logically correct program contains one or more isolated statements or instructions that are syntactically incorrect in the programming language being used.
2. A potentially correct algorithm may be coded in a logically incorrect way.
3. The algorithm implemented may function correctly for some but not all data values, or, more insidiously, it may fail for just some few combinations of input values.

These three types of error create debugging problems of increasing severity and typically require substantially different approaches to debugging (finding and correcting errors).

Syntactic Errors

The more flexible the syntax of a programming language, the easier it is to make syntactic errors. Thus, the simplicity and rigidity of machine language makes syntactic errors (such as illegal operation codes) relatively rare. From assembly language up through high-level language, however, it becomes increasingly easy to write a statement that is not grammatically acceptable to the language processor. Whether such statements occur because of typographical errors, imperfect understanding of language syntax, or just plain lack of concentration, such statements

will prove to be only a minor annoyance, since they will produce diagnostic messages (diagnostics) when the errant program is assembled, compiled, or interpreted.

Logical Errors

Logical errors are sometimes called semantic errors because they cause the program to have a meaning which, though syntactically valid, is other than what is needed for consistency with the algorithm being implemented. No translator will object to $C = A + B$ even if $C = A - B$ is what is needed, but such an error is certain to cause an incorrect result (unless B is always 0). Of course, most logical errors are more subtle. Typical errors cause programmed loops to run one time too few, one time too many, indefinitely ("infinite" loops), or not at all; cause misallocation of memory relative to actual space needed; cause input data to be read with improper formats; or cause weird program behavior in any number of ways. Those errors that cause program termination with run-time diagnostics are easier to isolate than those that lead to infinite loops or to "normal" termination with incorrect answers.

When program execution does not lead to an easily localized error, the programmer has recourse to several debugging tools. One of the more efficient is to embed some temporary print statements at strategic places in the program flow in order to monitor the progress of intermediate results, the objective being to pinpoint the exact transition from successful progress to the point at which the logic goes awry. (The information printed comprises what is sometimes called a snapshot dump, since, after capturing a record of conditions at a particular checkpoint, the computation continues. At two other extremes, the programmer may ask for extensive printout only at (normal or abnormal) program termination—a so-called post-mortem dump—or (a last resort because of its gross inefficiency) a printout of key registers or variables after every statement (or perhaps every nth statement) or instruction executed; that is, a trace of program flow. Narrowing the source of the error to a small section of code by one of these means or another is the necessary prelude to final identification of the error being pursued.

Algorithmic Error

When all known syntactic and semantic errors have been removed from a program, there is still a question as to whether the implemented algorithm actually solves the desired problem for all legal combinations of input values. Such algorithmic error can be very difficult to detect. If a program has been running satisfactorily for a sustained period, its users may place undue confidence in its output to the point where they would not detect answers that are nearly, but not quite, correct. Extensively tested programs that compute reliable results for a wide range of input values and that carefully check and reject illegal input are said to be robust.

A program that gives correct answers for some or even many input cases may nonetheless contain huge stretches of code that have never been executed. A significant component of programming talent is the ability to devise a sufficiently comprehensive set of test cases that, at a minimum, exercise all program branches not only serially but also in such sequential combinations as to give reasonable assurance that the program will indeed be robust.

Symbolic Debuggers

Most modern assemblers and compilers are now supported by a software tool known as a symbolic debugger. The word "debugger," however, connotes an intelligence that does not exist. Such a debugger does not and almost certainly could not automate the debugging process. A symbolic debugger is no more than an information gatherer, one that helps the user gather evidence much more easily than having to splice gratuitous output statements into source code.

The fact that a debugger is "symbolic," however, is very valuable. When an executing program halts prematurely or emits wrong answers, it is object code that is doing so, and, at this stage, the symbolic content of the source code from which the object code was produced is not ordinarily available. But, when we assemble or compile the source code we tell the language system being used that we intend to debug with a symbolic debugger, a mapping of symbols to numeric locations will be created and made available in the event that something bad happens at run time. If and when it

does, we may then ask to see, for example, the current value of some variable such as Radius or Volume by those very names rather than their memory cell locations.

A second prime attribute of a symbolic debugger is that it allows us to run a program incrementally, a step at a time, rather than allowing execution to proceed as far as it can without aborting. One may take either small or large steps, whichever one chooses, by moving either from statement to statement or from one checkpoint to another, pausing as needed to examine key variables or machine registers.

Correction of Errors

The correction of a serious algorithmic error might necessitate the rewriting of all or a substantial portion of a program, using essentially the same tools used to create it in the first place, but the correction of a syntactic or simple logical error is usually a trivial mechanical operation on a modern time-shared computer or even on a personal microcomputer. The principal tool is either a general text editor running under control of the computer's operating system or, in some cases, a special-purpose editor embedded in a specific language processor such as those that are typically part of Lisp, APL, Visual Basic, and C++ implementations.

Bibliography

1978. Van Tassel, D. *Program Style, Design, Efficiency, Debugging, and Testing.* Upper Saddle River, NJ: Prentice Hall.

1996. Rosenberg, J. B. *How Debuggers Work: Algorithms, Data Structure and Architecture.* New York: John Wiley.

1999. Kernighan, B. W., and Pike, R. *The Practice of Programming.* Reading, MA: Addison-Wesley.

Edwin D. Reilly

DECLARATION

For articles on related subjects, *see*

+ Executable Statement
+ Procedure-Oriented Languages

+ **Programming Languages**
+ **Statement**

A *declaration* (*declarative statement*) is a high-level programming language statement that provides descriptive information (contrasted with an *imperative*, or *executable, statement*, which specifies explicit processing operations). Besides specifying the actual computations, decision rules, and input–output operations involved in the implementation of a particular algorithm, a high-level language program must also provide the compiler (*q.v.*) with descriptive information that allows it to perform a variety of organizational tasks directly connected with the production of an executable object program. For example, the description of a variable (its name, together with the type of data to be stored in it) enables the compiler to allocate the proper amount of storage, associate its location with the variable's name, and set up any necessary data conversion mechanisms (coercion-*q.v.*) prior to the assignment of a value to that variable. Such information is supplied through special statements characterized as being *nonexecutable* (or more properly, *declarative*). Once defined, simple variables, arrays, files, and other items can be used throughout the program simply by alluding to their properties via use of their names.

Consider the following Pascal program, which reads a number N and uses it to compute

$$Y = \sum_{X=1}^{N} X(1 + X^{1/2}).$$

N and Y are displayed with appropriate identification.

```
program sumup;
    var i, n : integer;
        x, y : real;
    begin
        read(n);
        y := 0;
        for i := 1 to n do begin
            x := i;
            y := y + x*(1.0 + sqrt(x))
            end;
        writeln('n = ',n,' y = ',y)
    end.
```

The first statement is a declaration that defines the program's name. The two statements subsumed by the **var** declaration direct the compiler to allocate storage for two integers and two real values. A subsequent reference to any of the names specified there will be automatically associated with the appropriate storage location.

Seymour V. Pollack

DELIMITER

For an article on a related subject, *see*

+ **Procedure-Oriented Languages**

A *delimiter* is an item of lexical information whose form or position in a source program denotes the boundary between adjacent syntactic components. As with natural language, the meaning and clarity of statements in programming languages often depend on the inclusion of explicit indicators that "punctuate" the statement; such signals are termed *delimiters*. The most common of these are the blank space and the comma used as a *separator* between language elements.

Parentheses represent a commonly used type of delimiter. One of their primary purposes in computer languages parallels traditional mathematical usage, that is, to define the extent of a component in a computational expression. For example, the use of parentheses in the ordinary arithmetic expression $A + B(C - 2D)$ is clearly paralleled by the equivalent in many high-level languages: $A + B * (C - 2 * D)$.

Most contemporary programming languages provide a relatively free physical format in which there is no intrinsic association with a specific input medium, such as the terminal's keyboard. Consequently, in the absence of an implicit correspondence in such languages between the end of a statement and the physical boundary of the medium, it is necessary to impose explicit delimiters. The semicolon serves that purpose in C (*q.v.*), and the period in Cobol (*q.v.*).

Another type of delimiter is used to bracket a sequence of statements when the intent is to consider it to be a single *compound statement*. For instance, the Pascal structure

```
for i := 1 to 18 do
  begin
    read(x,y);
    sum1 := sum1 + x;
    sum2 := sum2 + 2.7*y
  end;
```

specifies a loop in which the sequence enclosed by the **begin**...**end** delimiters is to be executed during each of the 18 trips through the loop.

Pascal terminology distinguishes *separators*, such as colon (:), semicolon (;), and comma (,), which separate one language token from another, and *delimiters*, which occur in pairs in order to bracket a sequence of statements or tokens. Example Pascal delimiter pairs are (), [], **begin**...**end**, **repeat**...**until**, and the keyword **program**, which begins a program, and the final period (.), which ends it. Other languages have similar separators and delimiters, though in many of them, such as C and C++, the semicolon is an unpaired delimiter that terminates a statement.

Seymour V. Pollack and Ron K. Cytron

DESK CALCULATOR

See CALCULATING MACHINES; and CALCULATORS, ELECTRONIC AND PROGRAMMABLE.

DESKTOP PUBLISHING

For articles on related subjects, *see*

+ Computer Graphics
+ Markup Languages
+ PostScript
+ T$_E$X
+ Text Editing Systems
+ Typefont
+ Word Processing

Desktop publishing is the creation and printing of high-quality documents using software that supports complex page design and allows users to view and edit page images before printing. This form of publishing became widespread during the late 1980s when three essential ingredients became small enough to fit on a desk

- Interactive software for document design and editing.
- A printer capable of printing diagrams and multiple typefonts.
- A personal computer or workstation (*q.v.*) with a graphics screen and pointing device (typically a mouse–*q.v.*).

Instant Publishing

Desktop publishing provided major advantages over traditional methods of document production and typesetting. The interactive software provided a what-you-see-is-what-you-get (WYSIWYG) interface so that users could see the current state of the document on the screen and manipulate it directly via the keyboard and pointing device. This allowed them to experiment with the page layout and edit the content until they were satisfied with the result.

Early desktop publishing systems produced documents containing graphics as well as text, but the quality of the printed documents was poor compared with those typeset by traditional methods. This was due partly to the relatively crude formatting methods used by the software and partly to the quality of the printers available at the time (often laser printers with a resolution limited to 240 or 300 dots per inch). Current desktop publishing software now offers sophisticated formatting methods (letter spacing, kerning, etc.), and provides high-resolution color and graphical capabilities.

Desktop Publishing and Word Processing

There are two types of software for producing documents. *Desktop publishing* or *page-layout* systems are intended primarily for short documents with complex page designs, such as newspapers, catalogs, posters, and leaflets. They provide sophisticated facilities for page design and manipulation, but may have limited facilities for editing text or for creating other types of content. Users may often prefer to import document content from word processors, spreadsheets (*q.v.*), or graphics packages. *Word processors* or *document layout* systems are intended primarily for producing longer documents, such as technical manuals, journals, and books. They provide better built-in facilities for handling continuous text, for making systematic changes throughout long documents, and for dealing with cross-references, indexes, and tables of contents. They are, however, relatively inflexible for page layout.

Page Design

Users typically design a page by defining rectangular areas within it to contain text or graphics. These areas are known as *frames* or *boxes* or *grids*. Once users have defined a frame, they can fill it with text or graphics, edit its contents, move it around on the page, or change its size. Different page designs can be created by placing frames corresponding to single or multiple-column layout and setting aside different areas of the pages for illustrations.

In order to simplify the overall document design, a facility for defining *master pages* is usually provided. A master page contains the frames that are to appear in the same place on several pages in the document. Items such as company logos, page numbers, and page headers and footers are typically dealt with in this way. Individual pages can be designed by adding extra frames to one of the master pages.

Accurate positioning of frames is essential in page design. Examples of positioning tools are *rulers* that are shown across the top and down the sides of pages, *grids* that are shown across the whole page area, and *guidelines* or *crosshairs*—one horizontal and one vertical line that may be positioned across the page area. Users draw and position frames approximately by hand, and can then have them positioned and sized accurately by asking for their edges to be "snapped" to the nearest appropriate grid line or ruler marking.

Text Handling

Desktop publishing software provides all the control capabilities needed for text formatting: hyphenation, justification, kerning, and avoiding *widows* and *orphans* (single lines of a paragraph at the beginning or end of a page). It also gives access to a wide range of character fonts and sizes and allows fine control of spacing. Several typefonts are generally available, in sizes ranging from 4-point to over 100-point at intervals of half a point or less.

Simple text editing facilities for inserting and deleting text are provided, together with some form of cut-and-paste for moving blocks of text to different positions in the document. These may be supplemented by a variety of more complex features, such as search-and-replace or a spelling checker (*q.v.*). Text may be typed in directly or may be imported from a wide variety of other software.

Styles

Most desktop publishing systems provide *styles* or *style sheets*. Different document constituents can be named and have particular styles attached to them. Thus, there may be different styles to cover headings, several levels of sections, and a variety of paragraph types. The styles define details of font, type style, size, spacing, hyphenation, justification, and margins, and may also include information on automatic numbering of the constituents.

Graphics and Images

All desktop publishing systems provide simple built-in drawing facilities for lines, rectangles, and circles. Further facilities for curves, patterns, and borders may also be provided, and text can be wrapped around the graphics. There may also be ways of "anchoring" graphics, either to a particular piece of text or to a position on a page. Graphics and images created by a selection of other software tools can be imported, and facilities are available for scaling, rotating, and cropping these to fit frames. A wide variety of digitized pictures, called *clip art*, is available for importation into desktop publishing software.

Printing Facilities

High-quality output demands, as a minimum, the availability of a laser printer operating at 1200 dots per inch. For top quality output, an imagesetter operating at 3000 dots per inch or more is required. Desktop publishing relies heavily on the use of the PostScript page description language that is used to drive a variety of laser printers and imagesetters.

Future Developments

Desktop publishing is now firmly established as an effective method of producing both simple and complex documents. The early problems with quality have been overcome as advances in digital typography and image handling techniques have been incorporated into the software. Although desktop publishing is geared primarily towards the production of high-quality paper output, developments in word processing and the use of structured documents are also appearing in desktop publishing systems—as are some elements of hypertext (*q.v.*), particularly HTML-like links (*see* MARKUP LANGUAGES). Further developments are likely to include more use of "active documents," where document elements have processing methods attached to them.

Bibliography

1985. Adobe Systems Incorporated. *PostScript Language Reference Manual.* Reading, MA: Addison-Wesley.

1996. Shushan, R., and Wright, D., with Lewis, L. *Desktop Publishing by Design: Everyone's Guide to PageMaker 6,* 4th Ed. Redmond, WA: Microsoft Press.

1998. Blattner, D., and Davis, N. (eds.) *The QuarkXPress Book: For Macintosh and Windows.* Berkeley, CA: Peachpit Press.

Heather Brown

DEVICE DRIVER

See DRIVER.

DIAGNOSTIC

For an article on a related subject, *see*
+ Debugging

A *diagnostic* (short for *diagnostic program*) helps determine whether there are hardware faults in a computer or errors in software. Hardware diagnostics are programs designed to determine whether the components of a computer are operating properly. Circuit components are electronically exercised individually and in groups to try to induce failures. When a failure is detected, the location of the faulty equipment is printed and a technician can repair or replace the element.

Diagnostic messages emitted by software are the error messages produced by compilers (*q.v.*), utilities, and operating system software. These messages are designed to indicate to programmers where their programs are, or may be, at fault. Diagnostic messages at compile time may only be warnings to the programmer, or they may indicate invalid syntax that prohibits execution. A severity level indicator is often included in the diagnostic message. Run-time diagnostic messages are produced by the operating system. These messages indicate attempts to perform illegal operations, such as dividing by zero, taking the square root of a negative number, illegal operation codes, illegal address references, page faults, and so on.

Diagnostic messages should avoid a negative tone and be nonthreatening, specific, and constructive. Instead of just pointing out what is wrong, they should, whenever possible, tell the user what to do to set things right.

Ben Shneiderman

DIFFERENCE ENGINE

For articles on related subjects, *see*
+ Analytical Engine

+ Babbage, Charles
+ Digital Computers, History of: Origins

A *difference engine* is a machine that automates the calculation of mathematical tables. Any short section of a mathematical function, such as a sine, can be approximated by a polynomial, the degree or complexity of which is determined by the accuracy required in the tables. Using the method of finite differences, the tabulation of these polynomials can be reduced to the operation of repeated addition of differences only. The most famous attempt to mechanize this process was made in the 1820s by Charles Babbage, who produced a small demonstration model of a difference engine by mid-1822. Unfortunately, nothing of this model has survived, but it appears to have included six digits and to have tabulated the polynomial $x^2 + x + 41$ (whose values for integer values of x from 1 to 39 happen to be prime numbers).

With the aid of intermittent support from the British government, Babbage then embarked on the construction of a much more extensive machine, intended to provide six orders of differences, each of 18 digits. Babbage realized that the printing of tables using movable type was as great a source of error as the calculations themselves. He therefore included in the difference engine a mechanism for automatic preparation of stereotype printing plates. The Difference Engine was never built; work on Difference Engine No. 1 ceased in 1833. In 1847, Babbage designed the simpler Difference Engine No. 2, based on ideas evolved for his Analytical Engine (*q.v.*).

In the 1850s, Georg and Edvard Scheutz of Sweden built a difference engine inspired by Babbage's work, but it never worked reliably. Later nineteenth century designs by Wiberg in Sweden and Grant in the USA fared little better. In the 1930s, L. J. Comrie of the British Nautical Almanac Office adopted Burroughs and National Cash Register accounting machines for use as difference engines. These were used mainly for checking proofs of tables by applying the difference method in reverse.

In 1991, the Science Museum in London completed the construction of a working Difference Engine No. 2

Figure 1.   A working difference engine.

based on Babbage's drawings (Fig. 1). The machine is 10 feet long, 6 feet high, 18 inches deep and has 4000 parts machined using modern tools but to an accuracy no greater than Babbage could have achieved had he persevered.

Bibliography

1990. Bromley, A. G. "Difference and Analytical Engines," in *Computing Before Computers* (ed. W. Aspray), 59–98. Ames, IA: Iowa State University Press.

1998. Collier, B., MacLachlan, J. H., and Gingerich, O. *Charles Babbage and the Engines of Perfection*. Oxford: Oxford University Press.

2000. Swade, D. *The Difference Engine: Charles Babbage and the Quest to Build the First Computer*. New York: Viking.

Allan G. Bromley

DIGITAL CAMERA

See DIGITAL PHOTOGRAPHY.

DIGITAL COMPUTER

For articles on related subjects, *see*

+ Arithmetic-Logic Unit (ALU)
+ Central Processing Unit (CPU)

A *digital computer* is a machine that will accept data and information presented to it in a discrete form, carry out arithmetic and logical operations on this data, and then supply required results in acceptable form. The resulting information (output) produced by these operations depends on the accepted information (input). Thus, correct and complete answers cannot be obtained until correct and sufficient input data has been provided. This is a necessary but not sufficient condition; additionally, the correctness of output answers also depends critically on the logical procedures called *algorithms* (*q.v.*) used to compute them.

Computer Characteristics

The main characteristics of the digital computer are that it is automatic, general purpose, electronic, and, of course, digital. We discuss each in turn.

Automatic

A machine is *automatic* if it works without human intervention. But computers are machines with no will of their own; they have to be instructed. They are, however, automatic, in that once started on a job, they will carry on until it is finished. A computer works from a *program* (*q.v.*) of coded instructions that specify exactly how a particular job is to be done. While the job is in progress, the program is stored in what is called the computer's *memory*, and its instructions are interpreted and executed. The fact that programs are stored in the same physical memory as data is called the *stored-program concept* (*q.v.*) and computers that embody the

concept (early ones did not) are called *von Neumann machines* (*q.v.*) after the scientist who first emphasized the importance of doing so. Except for computers capable of *parallel processing* (*q.v.*), instructions are executed sequentially; as soon as one is completed, the next one in logical (not necessarily physical) sequence is executed automatically.

General Purpose

Digital computers are *general-purpose* machines—a computer can do any job that its programmer can express in suitable basic operations. Put a payroll program into a computer and it becomes a payroll machine. Replace the program by one for inverting a matrix, and the computer temporarily becomes a special-purpose mathematical machine.

Electronic

The word *electronic* refers to the *information-processing* components of the machine. It is the nature of the electronic components that make possible the very high speeds of modern computers. The history of electronic digital computers distinguishes a number of "generations" defined by the nature of the electronic components most prevalent in each. Thus, the first generation made extensive use of vacuum tubes, the second generation used discrete transistors, and the third used integrated circuits.

Digital

A computer may be either *digital* or *analog*. The two types have some principles in common, but they employ different types of data representations and are, in general, suited to different kinds of work. Digital computers are so called because they work with *numbers* in the form of separate discrete digits. The numbers stored in a digital computer are represented in our traditional positional number system. Early computers were decimal, or rather, the engineers who designed them made them appear to be decimal to the programmers who wrote procedures for them. But virtually all digital computers now use the *binary number system*, a system that uses only the binary digits (bits) 0 and 1 (*see* NUMBERS AND NUMBER SYSTEMS). The most common unit of memory storage is a sequence of eight bits called a *byte*.

Main Elements

Only very rarely does a computer have a unique, fixed specification. Normally, it is better described as a *computer system*, consisting of a selection from a wide variety of units appropriate to meet a defined need. The particular selection made is called a *configuration* of the system. Differences in configuration can adversely affect the *compatibility* (*q.v.*) of programs. For example, given two installations that use the same basic model computer, the one with the larger memory may be able to run certain programs that the other cannot. Even if two installations are using the same configuration of the same model computer, they may be incompatible to a large degree if they adopt different *operating systems* (*q.v.*), the highest level of installed *software* (*q.v.*) "under" which all other software programs operate. The combination of a particular model computer and its operating system is called a *platform*. Thus we speak of an Intel 80×86 microcomputer that runs the Microsoft Windows operating system as being a "Wintel" platform, which would be substantially incompatible with, say, a platform consisting of a Sun workstation controlled by *Unix* (*q.v.*)

The principal groupings of computer units are shown in Fig.1 and are defined as follows:

1. *Input units*: An input unit accepts the data, the raw material that a computer uses, communicated from outside. Input units convert data into electronic pulses, which are then fed into the machine's memory.

2. *Central Processing Unit (CPU)*: The "heart and brain" of the computer that performs its arithmetic and executes its logical decisions.

3. *Main memory unit*: All information stored in the main memory unit is "remembered" and made available to other units as required, under the direction of the control unit.

4. *Auxiliary storage units*: These units store the massive information required for reference as needed during a computation. The information may and often is updated during the course of the computation (*see* DATABASE MANAGEMENT SYSTEM (DBMS)).

5. *Output units*: After information is processed, an output unit communicates it to the outside world. When needed, the results are recalled from memory under the direction of the control unit and presented by the output units in an appropriate form. Input and output units are often called *peripheral units*, or just *peripherals*.

Input

Interactive input devices (*q.v.*) accept data from the world outside the computer and transfer it in suitably coded form into the memory, a process frequently described as *data capture*. A high proportion of input data is prepared by using the keyboard of a personal computer or *workstation*. Alternatively, there may be some intermediate carrier of the data, such as magnetic tape, or more frequently now, magnetic *diskettes* (*q.v.*). Data may also be scanned from hard copies and processed using *optical character recognition* (OCR–*q.v.*). In each case, the data preparation device produces a coded representation of the data, which is recorded on a storage medium in some appropriate form, for example, magnetized blips on the surface of a magnetic storage device or pits etched into the surface of an optical storage (*q.v.*) device such as a compact disc.

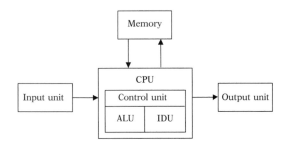

Figure 1. The principle components of a stored-program digital computer.

Central Processing Unit (CPU)

The CPU is the focal point of the computer system. It receives data from input units and auxiliary storage, carries out a variety of arithmetic and logical operations on this data, and transmits results to output units or back to auxiliary storage. It is the CPU that determines the intrinsic processing power of a digital computer. There are now so many brands and models of digital computer that they span a virtually continuous range of processing power, but it is convenient to recognize at least six categories, from least to most powerful: *portable computers* (*q.v.*), desktop *personal computers* (PCs) (*see* PERSONAL COMPUTING), *workstations* (*q.v.*), *minicomputers* (*q.v.*), *mainframes* (*q.v.*), and *supercomputers* (*q.v.*). A CPU consists of three parts: (1) a control unit; (2) an arithmetic-logic unit (ALU); and (3) an instruction decoding unit (IDU).

The control unit functions so as to cause the whole machine to operate according to the instructions in the program. Instructions are normally transferred sequentially from the memory to the control unit, where each instruction is interpreted and the appropriate circuits are activated to "execute" the instruction. This strict sequence is broken, for example, when a "test and jump" (or *branch*) instruction occurs. There is then a transfer of control to a program step in a different part of the program, from which the sequential pattern continues until again broken. It is this facility that provides the decision-making and repetition capabilities that give digital computers their power.

Examined in isolation, the data and instructions stored in memory are indistinguishable. No one looking at the pattern of bits (1s and 0s) can possibly tell, without being given more information, whether the bit pattern is intended to be an instruction to be obeyed or data to be processed. The task of making that decision is assigned to the CPU's *control unit*. The control unit decides whether a given bit pattern is an instruction, in which case it is sent to the IDU for decoding, or data, in which case it is sent to the ALU. The control unit does this by maintaining, at all times, a pointer to (i.e. the address of) the next instruction to be executed. That pointer, called the *program counter* (*q.v.*) or *instruction counter*, keeps track of the flow of control of a running program. At the moment when the program counter points to a bit pattern, that pattern is considered to be an instruction. At some different point in program flow,

it may be treated merely as a data value. If that value is modified and later becomes targeted by the program counter, a different instruction will be executed than the one originally stored at the same address.

When a linear sequence of instructions concludes with a test that causes control to be transferred back to the first instruction of the sequence, that sequence is said to constitute a program *loop*. A faulty test can cause what is called an *infinite loop*, which is a serious *bug* (*q.v.*) in the program, but a well-behaved loop will terminate after a finite number of *iterations* (*q.v.*), that is, loop traversals. (*See* MACHINE- AND ASSEMBLY-LANGUAGE PROGRAMMING.)

The ALU carries out arithmetic operations. It also has one or more *registers* (*q.v.*), sometimes called *accumulators*, which are fast one-word storage elements. To add a number stored in address 113 of the memory to that stored in address 207, first the contents of address 113 are read into a register and then the contents of address 207 are added to that register. The answer could then be stored in another address in memory, or used in another arithmetic operation.

Memory

Memory (or *main memory*, to distinguish it from auxiliary memory) is able to hold, for as long as desired, coded representations of numbers and letters in convenient groupings; each group is held in a uniquely addressable part of the memory from which it can be transferred on demand. The memory may be figuratively described as a large number of pigeonholes, each identifiable by a serial number called its *address*. One purpose of the memory is to hold data. The second use of the memory is to hold the instructions of the program required to carry out a job.

Auxiliary Memory

There are relatively few computer applications in which the only input is fresh, raw data. For example, in inventory control, the new data consists of stock issues and receipts, but data in file storage indicates the number of items left in stock calculated at the last inventory and the average value of that stock. These files also include more static information about each item, such as its name, dimensions, batch order quantity, and supplier. Thus, the computer must also have its "filing cabinets" (albeit electronic ones) if it is to be used in business applications. Such file storage units must act as input and output units to the computer (*see* ARITHMETIC-LOGIC UNIT (ALU)).

Output

Output devices enable a computer to communicate results to the outside world. They fall into two main categories, those that produce output that is readily handled and understood by human beings, for example, printers and display monitors (*see* MONITOR, DISPLAY), and auxiliary storage devices that hold data intended for further processing by machine (e.g. magnetic disks).

The most obvious members of the first group are printers. Where the volume of printing is large, it is usual to use a *line printer*, one capable of producing a whole line of print at a time (usually from 120 to 160 characters). Such printers are capable of quite high speeds, typically up to 30 or more lines per second on a continuously fed roll of stationery. Such line printers are ideal for applications requiring voluminous end-results, such as payrolls, invoices, or inventory listings. The output device of choice when high print quality and graphics are important is the *laser printer*. The high resolution of such printers is based on xerographic principles similar to those used with photocopy machines. Less expensive but slower *ink-jet printers* can also provide good quality color printouts.

A related device is the video display monitor, a cathode ray tube (CRT) on which letters or digits can be projected, or a flat-panel monitor based on solid-state picture elements. Compared with the typewriter, monitors have the advantage of displaying a large amount of information at once, and a fresh display of additional information can be generated very rapidly. On the other hand, since they cannot produce "hard copy" (i.e. a permanent record), they are best used in circumstances in which an operator needs to examine a small quantity of transient output information that

does not have to be printed, or to view that information before directing it to a printer.

Some display monitors called "dumb terminals" have no processing power of their own. Increasingly, *personal computers* (PCs) have replaced free-standing video display monitors. PCs have their own display monitor plus the added advantage of processing power and the capability of saving data, which supplements that of the *host computer* with which it communicates through a network (*see* NETWORKS, COMPUTER).

Microprocessors and Microcomputers

From the inception of digital computing, there has been a continual decrease in the physical size of *computer circuitry* (*q.v.*) due to ever more compact integration of circuit components. Millions of minute components and the printed wiring to interconnect them can now be formed on a single "chip"—a thin slice of silicon about 0.7 cm square (*see* MICROCOMPUTER CHIP). The components include transistors, resistors, and capacitors, which are the raw material from which the computer's registers, arithmetic unit, control unit, and memory can be made. CPUs based on these chips and the small computers that house them are called, respectively, *microprocessors and microcomputers* (*q.v.*).

Graham J. Morris

DIGITAL COMPUTERS, HISTORY OF

ORIGINS

For articles on related subjects, *see*

+ Aiken, Howard Hathaway
+ Analytical Engine
+ Babbage, Charles
+ Calculating Machines
+ Colossus
+ EDVAC
+ ENIAC

Mechanical aids to calculation and mechanical sequence-control devices were the earliest and most important achievements in the development of computer technology. The first adding machines date from the early seventeenth century, the most famous of which was invented by the French scientist and philosopher Blaise Pascal. A number of Pascal's machines still exist. During the subsequent two centuries, numerous attempts to develop practical calculating machines were made by Morland, Leibniz, Mahon, Hahn, and Müller, among others. However, it was not until the mid-nineteenth century that a commercially successful machine was produced. This was the 1820 "arithmometer" of Thomas de Colmar, a machine that used Leibniz's stepped-wheel mechanism.

In 1834, Charles Babbage became dissatisfied with the accuracy of printed mathematical tables. Earlier, in 1822, Babbage had built a small machine that would automatically generate successive values of simple algebraic functions using the method of finite differences (*see* DIFFERENCE ENGINE). His attempt at making a full-scale model was abandoned in 1834, and he then started to design a more versatile machine. The machine, which he called the *Analytical Engine (q.v.)*, was to have been controlled by programs represented by sets of cards, with conditional jumps and iteration loops being provided for by devices that skipped forward or backward over the required number of cards.

The Jacquard loom was the probable source of Herman Hollerith's idea of using punched cards to represent logical and numerical data. Developed for use in the 1890 US National Census, his system,

incorporating hand-operated tabulating machines and sorters, was highly successful. Following a dispute with Hollerith, the Bureau of the Census, in time for the 1910 Census, developed a new tabulating system involving mechanical sensing of card perforations, as opposed to Hollerith's system of electrical sensing. James Powers, the engineer in charge of this work, eventually left the Bureau to form his own company, which later became part of Remington Rand.

In 1937, Howard Aiken of Harvard University approached IBM with a proposal for a large-scale calculator to be built from the electromechanical devices that were used for punched-card machines. The result, the Automatic Sequence Controlled Calculator, or Harvard Mark I, was built at the IBM Development Laboratories at Endicott, NY. The machine, which was completed in 1944, was a huge affair with 72 decimal accumulators and capable of multiplying two 23-digit numbers in six seconds. It was controlled by a sequence of instructions specified by a perforated paper tape.

After completion of the Mark I, Aiken and IBM pursued separate paths. Several more machines were designed at Harvard, the first being another tape-controlled calculator, built this time from electromagnetic relays. IBM produced various machines, including several plugboard-controlled relay calculators and the partly electronic Selective Sequence Electronic Calculator (SSEC). Not until well after the Second World War was it found that in Germany there had been an operational program-controlled calculator built earlier than the Mark I, namely, Konrad Zuse's Z3 machine, which first worked in 1941.

The earliest known electronic digital calculating device was a machine for solving simultaneous linear equations, initiated in 1938 at Iowa State College by John Atanasoff and Clifford Berry (*see* ATANASOFF–BERRY COMPUTER). The earliest known efforts at applying electronics to a general-purpose, program-controlled computer were those undertaken by Schreyer and Zuse in 1939, but their plans for a 1500-vacuum tube machine were later rejected by the German government. In Britain, a series of large special-purpose electronic computers, intended for code-breaking purposes, was developed by a team at

Bletchley Park led by Tommy Flowers. The first of these "Colossus" machines, which incorporated about 2000 tubes, was operating in December 1943. By the end of the war 10 Colossi were in use.

The most influential line of development was that carried out at the Moore School of Electrical Engineering at the University of Pennsylvania by John Mauchly, J. Presper Eckert, and their colleagues, starting in 1943. This work, derived at least as directly from Vannevar Bush's mechanical *differential analyzer*, led to the development of the ENIAC, which was officially inaugurated in February 1946. This machine was intended primarily for ballistics calculations, but by the time it was completed it was really a general-purpose device, programmed by means of pluggable interconnections. It could perform 5000 10-digit arithmetic operations per second, which was approximately 1000 times faster than the Harvard Mark I.

Even before the ENIAC was complete, the designers, joined by John von Neumann, started to plan a radically different successor, the EDVAC. The EDVAC was a serial binary machine, far more economical on electronic tubes than ENIAC, which was a decimal machine in which each decimal digit was represented by a ring of 10 flip-flops. The EDVAC was to have a much larger internal memory than ENIAC, based on mercury delay lines. The EDVAC included only one-tenth of the equipment used in ENIAC, yet provided a hundred times the internal memory capacity.

With EDVAC, the invention of the modern digital computer was basically complete. The plans for its design were widely published and extremely influential, so that, even though it was not the first operational stored-program electronic digital computer, it was the major inspiration that started the vast number of computer projects during the late 1940s.

Bibliography

1972. Goldstine, H. H. *The Computer from Pascal to von Neumann*. Princeton: Princeton University Press.

1982. Randell, B. (ed.) *The Origins of Digital Computers*, 3rd Ed. Berlin: Springer-Verlag.

1983. Ceruzzi, P. E. *Reckoners: The Prehistory of the Digital Computer from Relays to the Stored Program Concept, 1935–1945*. Westport, CT: Greenwood Press.

1990. Aspray, W. (ed.) *Computing Before Computers*. Ames, IA: Iowa State University Press.

2003. Reilly, E. D. *Milestones of Computer Science and Information Technology*. Westport, CT: Greenwood Press.

Brian Randell

EARLY

After the ASCC (Harvard Mark I), no other large machines using rotating shafts were built, but there were a number of successful magnetic relay machines. Bell Telephone Laboratories had been working in this area since 1938. Their first fully automatic computer was the one now referred to as the Bell Model V, of which two examples were constructed. A relay computer constructed in Sweden (BARK) was operational early in 1950. Independent work on relay computers had also been done by Konrad Zuse in Germany, and a Zuse Z4 was running in Zurich in 1950. All of these machines had floating-point arithmetic operations, a feature that did not appear in electronic computers until much later.

J. Presper Eckert and John W. Mauchly were already building the ENIAC when the Harvard Mark I was commissioned. While the ENIAC was still under construction, Eckert and Mauchly began to plan a machine not only much more powerful than the ENIAC but also much smaller. They were joined by John von Neumann on a part-time basis, and it was from the group so formed that the ideas of the modern *stored-program* computer emerged. They were summarized in a document entitled "First draft of a report on the EDVAC," prepared by von Neumann and dated 30 June 1945. Because this report bore von Neumann's name only, the term *von Neumann computer* is often used as a synonym for "stored-program computer," giving the impression that the ideas were all von Neumann's own. I prefer the term *Eckert–von Neumann computer*.

Eckert and Mauchly did not stay at the Moore School to work on the EDVAC. Instead, they founded the Eckert–Mauchly Corporation, with the

Figure 1. The BINAC computer. (Courtesy of the Hagley Museum & Library.)

Figure 2. Tom Kilburn with the Ferranti Mark I computer at Manchester University. (Courtesy of the National Archive on the History of Computing, University of Manchester.)

object of designing and marketing the UNIVAC. The Corporation had demonstrated a smaller machine, the BINAC (Fig. 1), in August 1949, but this was not very successful and they decided to concentrate their efforts on the UNIVAC. In March 1951, the first UNIVAC was delivered to the US Census Bureau.

When the Moore School group broke up, von Neumann established a project for the construction of a computer at the Institute for Advanced Study, Princeton. von Neumann himself, assisted by Herman H. Goldstine, laid down the logical structure of this computer, and the engineering development and design was in the hands of Julian H. Bigelow. It was the first bit-parallel computer to be designed.

The experimental computers that came into action first were those that were least ambitious, both in specification and in performance. One of these was the EDSAC, a computer directly inspired by the EDVAC, designed and constructed by William Renwick and myself in Cambridge, UK. This computer did its first calculation on 6 May 1949, and was used for much early work on programming techniques. Activity at Manchester University arose out of work by Fred Williams on what became known as the Williams tube memory. In order to test this system, Williams and Tom Kilburn built a small model computer with a memory of 32 words and only five instructions in its instruction

set. The Ferranti Mark I computer (Fig. 2), inaugurated at Manchester University in July 1951, was based on this work.

A third center of activity in England was at the National Physical Laboratory (NPL), where the inspiration came from Alan Turing. Turing did not stay there long, leaving for Manchester University in 1948, but the Pilot ACE, which was running by December 1950, reflected very strongly his rather personal view of computer design.

The first of the American machines was the SEAC, dedicated on 20 June 1950. This was built under the direction of Samuel N. Alexander at the National Bureau of Standards in Washington. The SEAC was elegant in design and construction, and pioneered the use of small plug-in packages; each package contained a number of germanium diodes and a single vacuum tube. The SEAC used an ultrasonic memory, but a Williams tube memory was added later. Meanwhile, Harry D. Huskey, who had formerly been a member of the team at NPL in England and had worked on ENIAC, was completing the SWAC at the NBS Institute for Numerical Analysis at UCLA. This was a parallel machine with a Williams tube memory and was very fast by the standards of the day.

Whirlwind I was a computer with a short word length, aiming at very high speed and intended ultimately for air traffic control and similar applications. It was designed and built under the direction of Jay W. Forrester at MIT and was operating in December 1950. From its specification, one would take it to be the first minicomputer, but in fact it occupied the largest floor area of all the early computers, including the ENIAC. The memory was electrostatic, but the cathode ray tubes were of special design and operated on a different principle from that used by Williams.

Bibliography

1985. Wilkes, M. V. *Memoirs of a Computer Pioneer.* Cambridge, MA: MIT Press.

1993. Cortada, J. W. *Before the Computer: IBM, NCR, Burroughs, and Remington Rand and the Industry they Created, 1865–1956.* Princeton NJ: Princeton University Press.

Maurice V. Wilkes

SINCE 1950

For articles on related subjects, *see*

+ Apple
+ Atlas
+ IBM
+ IBM PC
+ Microsoft
+ Minicomputer
+ Supercomputers
+ UNIVAC I
+ Whirlwind

The notion that there were three major generations of computers, based on device technology (vacuum tubes, discrete transistors, and integrated circuits), served well to characterize machines for the beginning of the electronic era. But, nearly all computers have used silicon integrated circuitry (*q.v.*) since the 1970s. IC technology has advanced in those years, and the microprocessor was a significant milestone, but computers still use a descendant of the IC technology invented by Robert Noyce and Jack Kilby around 1959. Computing has

thus been in the "third generation" for at least as long as it took to progress from the ENIAC to the PDP-11, an early minicomputer.

The von Neumann Architecture

The von Neumann machine (*q.v.*) computer architecture has persisted through successive waves of hardware and software advances. That model, originally conceived in the mid-1940s, emerged in response to the need for a practical design for the EDVAC, a machine proposed as a follow-on to the ENIAC, then under construction. But the von Neumann model's influence was to be much greater. The term "von Neumann Architecture" implies a rigid division between memory and processing units, with a single channel between the two. Instructions as well as data are stored in the primary memory, which is configured to be large, random-access, and as fast as practical. The basic cycle of a computer is to transfer an instruction from memory to the processor, decode that instruction, and execute it with respect to data that is also retrieved from memory. Despite all that has happened, these patterns remain.

Classes of Computers

One may classify a computer as being either super-, mainframe, mini-, workstation, or personal. These terms did not come into common use until the 1970s and 1980s, but today they have fairly precise meanings. At any given moment, the classes are distinct and represent a descending order of computing power, but over the years each category ratchets upward. Thus, today's PC has the power of yesterday's mini (and the day before yesterday's mainframe), but is still called a personal computer.

Software-Compatible Families of Computers

A third pattern has emerged, and it, too, is likely to persist: families of general-purpose upwardly compatible computers. A major portion of the costs of any computing system is the software developed for it. With a family of products, a vendor can amortize these costs over a longer period of time. Philco marketed a series of upward-compatible Transac S-2000, models 210, 211, and 212, between 1958 and 1964. Philco sold out to Ford, who subsequently left the computer business. IBM System/360, introduced in April 1964, was the first commercial system based on a family of upward compatible processors all of which were announced on the same day. Other notable families include the UNIVAC 1100 series, the Burroughs B5000 and its successors, the CDC Cyber series, and the Digital Equipment Corporation VAX series. Since about 1980, Intel has maintained software compatibility with its 80×86 line of microprocessors.

The First Generation, 1950-1960

The first generation began around 1950 with the introduction of commercial computers manufactured and sold in quantity. Computers of the first generation stored their programs internally and used vacuum tubes as their switching technology. Beyond that they had little else in common. The reports describing the IAS computer, written by Arthur Burks, Herman Goldstine, and John von Neumann, emphasized the advantages of a parallel-memory device that could read and write a full word at a time. The device they favored, the RCA Selectron tube, took longer than expected to appear, and only the Rand Corporation's Johnniac used it. America's first commercial machine, the UNIVAC I, used a mercury delay line, which accessed data one bit at a time. The only parallel devices available at the time were cathode ray tubes that were notoriously unreliable. The most popular memory device for first-generation machines was the rotating magnetic drum. It was slow, but its reliability and low cost made it suitable for small-scale machines such as the IBM 650, Bendix G-15, Alwac III-E, and Librascope LGP-30. By the end of this period, machines were introduced that used magnetic core memory. With the advent of ferrite cores, the memory problem endemic to the first generation was effectively solved.

UNIVAC

The UNIVAC (*see* Fig. 1), designed by J. Presper Eckert and John Mauchly, was first delivered in 1951 by Remington–Rand. It was the first American computer to be produced as a series and sold to commercial customers. Over 40 were built. Most customers used

Figure 1. UNIVAC I. (Courtesy of the Hagley Museum & Library.)

the UNIVAC for accounting, statistical, and other applications that would later be known as *data processing* (*q.v.*).

IBM 701, 650

In 1952, IBM announced the 701 computer, originally called the Defense Calculator after its perceived market. Most of the 19 models installed went to US Defense Department or aerospace customers. Initial rental fees were $15 000 a month; IBM did not sell the machines outright. For primary memory, the machine used Williams tubes that could store up to 4096 36-bit words. Oxide-coated plastic tape was used for backup memory, and a magnetic drum provided intermediate storage. It could perform about 2000 multiplications/second, but, unlike the UNIVAC, the 701's central processor handled control of the slow input–output facilities directly. IBM also developed a similar-sized, but character-oriented machine, the 702, for business customers.

IBM also initiated development of a smaller machine, whose origins lay in proposals for extensions of punched card equipment. In the course of its development, its nature shifted to that of a general-purpose, drum-based, stored-program computer. The machine, the IBM 650, first delivered in 1954, proved to be very successful. Eventually, there were over a thousand 650 installations at a rental of about $3500 per month.

ERA 1103

Another important first-generation computer was the ERA 1103, developed by Engineering Research Associates, the Minnesota firm that Remington Rand bought in 1952. This machine was geared toward scientific and engineering customers. The 1103 used binary arithmetic, a 36-bit word length, and parallel arithmetic operation. Internal memory (1 K words) was supplied by Williams tubes, with an ERA-designed drum for backup. It employed a two-address instruction scheme, with the first six bits of a word used to encode a repertoire of 45 instructions. Arithmetic was performed in an internal 72-bit accumulator. In late 1954, the company delivered to the National Security Agency and to the National Advisory Committee for Aeronautics an 1103 with magnetic core in place of the Williams Tube memory.

IBM 704, 709

In late 1955, IBM began deliveries of the 704, its successor to the 701. The 704's most notable features were core memory (initially 4 K words, up to 32 K by 1957) and a rich instruction repertoire. The 704's processor had hardware floating-point arithmetic and three addressable index registers (*q.v.*)—both major advances over the 701. Partly to facilitate the use of floating point, an IBM team led by John Backus developed the programming language Fortran (*q.v.*). Fortran became and has remained, with Cobol (*q.v.*), one of the two most successful programming languages of all time. IBM installed over a hundred 704 s between 1955 and 1960.

In January 1957, IBM announced the 709 as a compatible upgrade to the 704 just as it became clear that transistors were finally becoming a practical replacement for vacuum tubes. Indeed, when the transistorized Philco Transac S-2000 and Control Data 1604 were announced, IBM quickly withdrew the 709 from the market and replaced it with the transistorized 7090. The first delivery of the 7090 in late 1959 marked the beginning of IBM's entry into the solid-state era.

The Second Generation, 1960–1965

The second generation, 1960 to 1965, was characterized by discrete transistors for switching elements and ferrite magnetic core for main memory. In software, this era saw the acceptance of high-level programming languages such as Fortran and Cobol, although assembly language programming remained common.

From the perspective of the early twenty-first century, the second generation appears more like a transitional period than a major discrete era. The term "revolution," as applied to the invention of the integrated circuit, obscures the fact that the IC's inventors saw their work as an evolutionary outgrowth of their work in materials, circuits, and packaging pioneered in the discrete transistor era. It was during the second, not third, generation, that some of the toughest challenges were faced, especially regarding the serial production of reliable devices with consistent performance. It took from 1949 to 1959 to bring transistors from the laboratory to commercial production in computers, but the IC went from invention to commercial use in half that time.

IBM 1401

One of the most important transistorized computers was the IBM 1401, introduced in 1960. This machine employed a character-oriented, variable-length data field, with one bit of each character code reserved to delimit the end of a field. As with the 650, the 1401's design evolved from a plug-wired, punched card calculator to a stored-program, general-purpose computer that used magnetic tape and punched cards for its input–output. Magnetic cores provided a central memory of from 1400 to 4000 characters, while transistorized circuits supported a multiplication speed of about 500 numbers/second. With the 1401, IBM also introduced the Type 1403 printer, a rugged and fast printer that carried type on a moving chain. This printer played an equally important role in effecting the transition from tabulators to computers for data processing.

Concurrently with the 1401, IBM also offered the 1620, a small machine intended for scientific applications. And in 1962 the company introduced the 7094, a version of the 7090 that added additional index registers (*q.v.*) to its CPU. It, too, sold well and became the standard large-scale scientific computer of the time.

By the mid-1960s, the IBM Corporation had seized and was vigorously defending a dominant share of the US computer market. UNIVAC, Burroughs, NCR, RCA, Control Data, Philco/Ford, General Electric, and Honeywell were its chief competitors.

LARC, Stretch, Atlas, B5000

Several architectural innovations first appeared in second-generation computers, but they were premature. That is, the features saw only limited use until the next generation, when they became commonplace.

In 1955, Remington Rand UNIVAC contracted with the Lawrence Livermore Laboratory to produce a high-performance computer for weapons design. Design and development of the LARC were beset with problems, but in 1960 the first model was completed and accepted by Livermore Laboratory, with a second model delivered to the Navy's David Taylor Model Basin. IBM undertook a similar project called "Stretch," implying that it would dramatically extend the state of the art. Work began in 1956, with the first delivery (to Los Alamos Laboratory) in 1961. Like the LARC, the Stretch (IBM 7030) introduced a number of innovations in architecture and device technology. It used a pipelined processor, very fast transistors, and Emitter-Coupled Logic (ECL). A total of seven were delivered.

The Atlas computer, introduced in 1962 by the British firm Ferranti, employed virtual memory (*q.v.*) with paging and provision for multiprogramming (*q.v.*). Ferranti provided the Atlas with a "supervisor" program that foreshadowed the operating systems (*q.v.*) common after 1965. In 1962, Burroughs introduced the B5000 series of computers that incorporated some of these innovations. This series was further designed for optimal execution of programs written in a high-level language (Algol—*q.v.*). Its processor architecture was also novel in using a stack-oriented addressing scheme. Neither of these features prevailed in the market-place, but multiprogramming and virtual memory became common a generation later.

The Third Generation, 1965–1970

The IBM System/360 (Fig. 2), announced on 7 April 1964, inaugurated the third generation of computers.

Figure 2. IBM System/360 Model 44. (Reproduced by the permission of IBM Archives.)

This series did not use true integrated circuits, but rather small modules consisting of discrete devices laid onto a ceramic substrate. IBM had considered using the newly invented IC for the 360, but went instead with what they called *Solid Logic Technology* (SLT), in part because they had a better grasp of its manufacture in large quantities than they had with ICs. The success of the S/360 spawned competitors. In 1965, RCA began delivering four computers, the Spectra Series, which were software compatible with the equivalent S/360 models. These had the distinction of being built with true integrated circuits, but RCA was unable to sustain the line and sold its computer business to UNIVAC in 1971.

Because semiconductor memory, unlike core, loses its information when power is switched off, the S/370 needed a way to store its microprogrammed instructions in a nonvolatile fashion. IBM engineers invented the floppy disk (*see* DISKETTE) for this purpose. The floppy became the pivotal technology for establishing the personal computer class later in that decade.

Minicomputers

The term "minicomputer" was coined in the mid-1960s by a DEC salesman to describe the PDP-8. Informally, a minicomputer was low in cost, small in size, and intended for use by a single individual, small department, or for a dedicated application. That concept was expressed as early as 1952, when several companies introduced computers aimed at such a market. Producing such a machine with adequate performance was another matter. First-generation computers like the Bendix G-15, Alwac III-E, or Librascope LGP-30 achieved low cost by using a drum memory, which was incapable of high-speed random access to data.

The MIT Whirlwind, completed in the early 1950s, used a 16-bit word length, and was envisioned for real-time simulation and control applications. It was housed in several rooms of a building on the MIT campus, and in its initial configuration used fragile and sensitive electrostatic tubes for memory. It was hardly a *mini*computer, but it was used like one.

In 1960, Control Data Corporation introduced a transistorized, 12-bit machine called the CDC 160. The 160 was intended as an input–output controller for the 48-bit CDC 1604. The 160 could also be used as a computer on its own, and as such, was one of the first machines to fit the definition of a mini. Both the 160 and the 1604 sold well and helped establish CDC as a major computer manufacturer.

The DEC's PDP-8, a 12-bit computer announced in 1965, made the breakthrough. Up to that time, DEC had produced and sold a variety of machines with varying word lengths, including the 36-bit PDP-6, and its PDP-10 successor, a full-size mainframe widely used in a time-sharing environment. The success of the PDP-8 established the minicomputer class of machines, with DEC being the leading supplier.

Data General, formed by ex-DEC employees, brought out the 16-bit Nova in early 1969. The Nova had a simple but powerful instruction set and was the first to use medium-scale integrated (MSI) circuits. Its word length set a standard for minis from then on. DEC countered the Nova with its 16-bit PDP-11 in 1970, which kept DEC competitive with Data General. These two computers, along with the HP-2000 series offered by Hewlett-Packard, may be said to define the minicomputer's "second generation."

Supercomputers

In 1954, IBM built a fast computer called NORC for the US Naval Proving Ground in Dahlgren, Virginia. At its dedication, John von Neumann (*q.v.*) expressed his hope that computer companies would continue from time to time "...to write specifications simply calling for the most advanced machine which is possible in the present state of the art." IBM's Stretch and UNIVAC's LARC fit that category. In the late 1960s, Burroughs built the ILLIAC-IV, a parallel processing machine based on a design by Daniel Slotnick of the University of Illinois. These were well regarded by the customers who used them, but they usually incurred financial losses for the companies that manufactured them, even with the government subsidies each of these machines enjoyed. It remained for Control Data Corporation to find a way not only to make reliable and practical supercomputers, but to sell them profitably as well. The machine that brought the term "supercomputer" into common use was the 6600 (*see* Fig. 3.), designed by Seymour Cray and delivered in 1964.

The CDC's architecture employed a 60-bit word central processor, around which were arranged 10 logical 12-bit peripheral processors, each having a memory of 4 K words. Within the central processor were 10 "functional units" which contained specialized circuitry that performed the operations of fixed- or floating-point arithmetic and logic. Logic circuits, taking advantage of the high-speed silicon transistors then becoming available, were densely packed into modules called "cordwood" from the way they looked. The 6600

Figure 3.   CDC 6600. (Courtesy of Control Data Corporation.)

had two floating multiply units, each of which could perform a multiplication in 1 microsecond. Seymour Cray believed in a very sparse instruction repertoire, and his ideas presaged in many ways the current trend toward reduced instruction set computers (RISCs—*q.v.*).

CRAY-1

Control Data upgraded the CDC 6600 with the 7600 in 1969 and produced an incompatible supercomputer called the STAR in 1972. The latter machine was capable of parallel operations on vector data—a feature also used in the design of the Texas Instruments Advanced Scientific Computer (1972). Around that time, Seymour Cray left CDC and formed Cray Research, whose goal was to produce an even faster machine. In 1976, Cray Research announced the CRAY-1 (*see* Fig. 4), with the first delivery in March

Figure 4. CRAY-1. (Courtesy of Cray Research, Inc.)

to the Los Alamos National Laboratory. Preliminary benchmarks showed it to be ten times faster than the 6600. The CRAY-1 had 12 functional units and extensive buffering between the instruction stream and the central processor. Memory options ranged from 250 K to 1 million 64-bit words. The chief difference between the 6600 and the CRAY was the latter's ability to process vector as well as scalar data. In contrast to Cray's approach, Thinking Machines, Inc. of Cambridge, Massachusetts introduced a computer in the mid-1980s called the Connection Machine, which was characterized by a massively parallel architecture. Meanwhile, Seymour Cray left Cray Research and founded Cray Computer Corporation in 1989, where he continued to pursue fast performance using innovative packaging and materials.

Personal Computers

With the hindsight of two decades of furious growth that saw computers become faster, smaller, and less expensive, the advent of the *personal computer* (PC) does not seem surprising. However, the PC's invention was not inevitable; if anything its viability was unforeseen by those in the best position to market one. The PC was the result of a conscious effort by individuals whose vision of the industry was quite different from that of the established companies. Some of the first electronic computers of the late 1940s were operated as personal computers, in that all control and operation of a machine was turned over to one user at a time. Prospective users took their place in line with others waiting to use it, but there were no supervisory personnel or computer operators between them and the machine. This mode of operation is one of the defining characteristics of what constitutes a PC (*see* PERSONAL COMPUTING).

Throughout the late 1960s, the semiconductor manufacturers were continuing to place even more circuits on single chips of silicon. Around 1970, these developments led to the first consumer products: digital watches, games, and calculators. Four-function pocket calculators, priced near $100, appeared around 1971, and the following year Hewlett-Packard introduced the HP-35, which offered floating-point arithmetic and a full range of scientific functions. The HP-35 sold for $395 and was an immediate success for Hewlett-Packard, a company that had not been part of the consumer electronics business.

In late 1971, Intel introduced the 4004 microprocessor, a "chip" on which much of the architecture of a minicomputer was implemented, and whose functions could be modified by programming a *read-only memory* (ROM–*q.v.*). Intel designed this chip set for a customer, Busicom, who wanted to build calculators. When Busicom dropped the project, Intel sought another market for what was a set of chips that provided general-purpose computing functions.

Some individuals within DEC, Xerox, HP, and IBM proposed to build and market an inexpensive, general-purpose PC around this time, but their proposals were either turned down or only weakly supported. Meanwhile, Intel designed developer's kits that it sold or even gave away to potential customers to familiarize them with the nuances of designing with a microprocessor. Rockwell, Texas Instruments, and others all announced microprocessors by 1973. Intel followed the 4-bit 4004 with an 8-bit 8008 in 1972, followed by a more powerful 8080 in April 1974. The price was set at $360.

In January 1975, *Popular Electronics* published a cover story on a computer kit called Altair that sold for less that $400. The Altair was designed for the magazine by MITS, a company consisting of about 10 employees located in Albuquerque, NM. Despite its many shortcomings, this kit filled the space of "personal computer" that had been empty. It cost less than an HP-35 calculator. It was designed around the Intel 8080 microprocessor, with a rich instruction set, flexible addressing, and a 64-KB addressing space. Ed Roberts, the head of MITS, designed the Altair along the lines of the best minicomputers, with a bus architecture and plenty of slots for expansion. There were many things the Altair lacked, however, including decent mass storage and I/O. As delivered, it represented the minimum configuration of circuits that one could legitimately call a "computer." Between the time of the Altair's announcement and the end of 1977 the PC field witnessed an unprecedented burst of creativity and talent that transformed the device into something

truly practical. This drama was played out in three arenas: hardware, software, and in the social community of users.

The social community was perhaps most important. On the west coast of the USA, the now legendary Homebrew Computer Club was founded in March 1975, with the early meetings devoted to getting Altairs and comparable kits working. Newsletters and magazines sprouted, the most famous survivor of which was *Byte*, founded in September 1975. *Byte* was a fairly "normal" magazine, while *Doctor Dobb's Journal of Computer Calisthenics and Orthodontia* [sic] was typically filled with hexadecimal machine–language code. There were over a hundred such periodicals that sprouted up in the decade following the Altair's announcement.

Some critical design decisions made by Ed Roberts and his small group at MITS set the course for the early hardware evolution of PCs. The first was his choice of the Intel 8080, a decision that would reverberate through the computer industry for the next 25 years. The second was to design the machine along the lines of the Data General Nova and advanced DEC minicomputers, with their open architectures. That allowed entrepreneurs to come out with circuit boards that added capabilities such as better memory and I/O to the original Altair, which sorely needed those features.

Not long after seeing the *Popular Electronics* article describing the Altair, William Gates III contacted Ed Roberts and told him that he could have a version of Basic (*q.v.*) for the Altair by July 1975. Gates, with Paul Allen and Monte Davidoff, wrote and delivered the language as promised. Gates never became a MITS employee, but instead retained the rights to the language for his company "Micro Soft" (later "Microsoft"). After MITS got into financial troubles, Microsoft marketed the language to all the others who were making 8080-based machines.

Another critical piece of software was an operating system that allowed the newly invented floppy disk to serve as the PC's mass storage device. The system was called CP/M, for "Control Program (for) Microcomputers"; it was written by Gary Kildall almost as an afterthought. CP/M, like Microsoft Basic, was strongly influenced by work done at DEC and even used many of DEC's cryptic acronyms such as "PIP," "TECO," and "DDT." Like the DEC minicomputer systems, it took up very little memory of its own and had none of the bloat that was characteristic of mainframe OSs. Kildall sold it for under $100, and it made the floppy an integral part of the PC.

By 1977 PCs were being packaged and sold as appliances, with three models introduced that year from Apple, Radio Shack, and Commodore setting the trend. None of those three used the Altair bus or architecture, but the Apple II used Microsoft Basic, and one could plug a card into it that let it run CP/M. The Apple II, though more expensive, was by far the superior machine, with very good color graphics, tight integration with floppy disk storage, and attractive packaging.

The field matured in 1981, when IBM introduced a machine called simply the IBM PC, which combined the best of the features described above with the respectability of the IBM name. This was not IBM's first attempt in this market, but it quickly set a new standard. In many ways it was a descendant of the Altair. Its microprocessor was the Intel 8088, a 16-bit version of the 8080. It had a bus architecture that invited others to provide cards to expand its abilities. It used Microsoft Basic, supplied in a ROM. Like the Apple II it could be configured with a color monitor to play games. Early versions had a cassette port, but most came with at least one floppy drive. Customers were given the option of one of three disk-operating systems; but the cheapest, simplest, and first to market was PC-DOS, supplied by Microsoft and based in part on CP/M.

Apple, by 1981 one of the industry's fastest-growing companies, did not feel threatened by IBM's entry into the field. The company considered its Apple II a superior machine, and it thought that IBM's entry would make its own products more accepted by business customers. When IBM quickly took the lead in sales, Apple responded with an Apple III, which suffered from reliability flaws, and then, in 1984, with the Macintosh. The "Mac" was a closed machine and a philosophical opposite of the Altair/IBM approach, but its graphical user interface (GUI) was, once again, revolutionary. Sales were slow at first, but Apple had set a new standard.

Microsoft grew on the sales of its DOS, which, like Microsoft Basic, it was free to sell to others besides the company for which it developed the software. As with the Altair, a vigorous clone market for IBM-compatible PCs emerged, led by the Texas firms Compaq and Dell. Compaq grew even faster than Apple, from the delivery of its first clone in 1983 to become one of the top 100 computer firms by 1985.

Workstations

In the mid 1980s, a number of companies introduced personal workstations, and since the late 1980s, their architecture has reversed the trend set by the 360, VAX, and 80×86 series. Instead of using a complex, microcoded instruction set, these workstations use RISC processors, which have small instruction sets applied to many fast registers. These computers are intended for use by a single individual, and provide high-resolution graphics, fast numerical processing, and networking capability. As such, they combine the attributes of the personal computer with those of the higher classes. Their performance reaches into the low end of the supercomputer range, but prices for simpler models touch the high end of the PC class. At present, the more advanced PCs, using the latest Intel microprocessor and running Microsoft's Windows 95, 98, 2000 or NT, overlap the cheapest workstations, which typically use a Sun Sparc or other RISC microprocessor and run under a version of Unix (*q.v.*).

Networking

The biggest change in computing since 1990 has been the emergence of networking as an integral part of what it means to have "a computer." Not only workstations but also PCs are linked into local area networks. Typically some form of Ethernet is used, although for PCs in offices, the leader has been a proprietary network offered by Novell. On the national and even global level, access to the Internet moved rapidly from something available to only a few to a necessary feature bundled into every installation.

Conclusion

It is hard to avoid the impression that whatever happened in computing from 1950 to 1999 was "mere" prolog to the present culture of the World Wide Web. Although computers continue to be designed, manufactured, and sold as discrete entities, it seems no longer appropriate to discuss the history of computing without focusing as much on the way the machines are networked. That implies that the patterns of stability that have guided the history just told may no longer apply.

The von Neumann architecture still reigns, but it seems no longer to be as central an organizing principle. Supercomputers with massively parallel designs are now the norm, while the Internet has blurred the distinction between computing that goes on inside a local box and what goes on "out there." New programming languages like Java (*q.v.*) point to a future where such a distinction may become meaningless.

A new class of pocket-sized machines known as personal digital assistants (PDAs) has now emerged. These use a stylus and handwriting recognition for input, but they are not displacing the more standard configuration based on the keyboard and the mouse. As for output, LCD screens can be made smaller and lighter, but users often prefer CRTs, which, though not as good as the printed page, have crisp, easy to read screens. Other I/O methods such as voice are being developed and may soon become commonplace. Researchers at Xerox PARC and elsewhere are working on a concept of *wearable computers*—devices embedded into eyeglasses, credit cards, ID badges, and clothing. The idea holds great promise, although it will more likely supplement, not replace the general-purpose machine on one's desk.

Bibliography

1986. Bashe, C. J., Johnson, L. R., Palmer, J. H., and Pugh, E. W. *IBM's Early Computers*. Cambridge, MA: MIT Press.

1991. Pugh, E. W., Johnson, L. R., and Palmer, J. H. *IBM's 360 and Early 370 Systems*. Cambridge, MA: MIT Press.

1996. Campbell-Kelly, M., and Aspray, W. *Computer: A History of the Information Machine*. New York: Basic Books.

1998. Ceruzzi, P. E. *A History of Modern Computing*. Cambridge, MA: MIT Press.

2003. Reilly, E. D. *Milestones of Computer Science and Information Technology*. Westport, CT: Greenwood Press.

Paul E. Ceruzzi

PRINCIPAL CURRENT US COMPUTER COMPANIES

For articles on related subjects, *see*

+ Apple
+ IBM
+ Microsoft

Cisco

Leonard Bosack and Sandra Lerner founded Cisco Systems in 1984, in response to the frustrations they experienced as graduate students at Stanford University. University mainframes were often unable to handle simple messages passed between incompatible hardware systems. Bosack and Lerner developed an electronic box called a *router* that was capable of simultaneous translation (*see* GATEWAY). Their router enabled IBM computers to talk to Digital Equipment Corporation (DEC) computers, and identical computers running different operating systems to intercommunicate. A router can cost upwards of $50 000, but they are indispensable to Internet infrastructure. In 1990, Cisco sold 5000 routers, and by 1998 sales were running close to a million units. Cisco is now the third most valuable NASDAQ computer company after Microsoft and Intel with 2002 revenues of $19 billion.

Dell

Dell was founded in Austin, TX in 1984 by Michael Dell while still a college student. His vision was to assemble and sell IBM-compatible personal computers directly to end users via mail or phone order. The Internet has opened a third avenue and now accounts for $50 million per day in orders for "Wintel machines" (platforms consisting of Microsoft Windows and "Intel inside"). Dell offers a complete line of servers, desktops, notebook and laptop computers, and their accessories. The company holds almost a quarter of the US market and 13% of the world market for PCs, first in both categories.

Hewlett-Packard (*hp*)

Hewlett-Packard (*hp*) was founded in 1938 by William Hewlett and David Packard to make electronic analytical instruments. After selling electronic calculators such as the HP-35 in the 1960s and the HP-65 programmable calculator a few years later, *hp* developed a successful minicomputer, the HP 3000, in 1972. In the 1980s, *hp* began to sell its still highly profitable line of *LaserJet* printers. In 1989, *hp* acquired Apollo, which had once been the leading manufacturer of workstations but had lost most of its market share to Sun Microsystems. In the mid-1990s through the present, *hp* has offered a successful line of IBM-compatible personal computers. On 19 March 2002, *hp* stockholders approved a proposal that the company purchase Compaq, which had absorbed the historic DEC in 1998. Passage of the proposal was seen as a major victory for *hp* CEO Carleton S. Fiorina, who strongly advocated approval. The new company is the largest ever to be led by a female CEO. Michael Capellas, former CEO of Compaq, was appointed President on 7 May 2002.

Intel

Intel (INTegrated ELectronics) was founded in 1968 by Robert Noyce, coinventor of the integrated circuit (IC) while at Fairchild Semiconductor, and Gordon Moore, the expositor of Moore's law (*see* LAWS, COMPUTER), in order to produce and market semiconductor products. In 1970, Intel made two significant advances a month apart, the *Erasable Programmable Read-Only Memory* (EPROM), and the first DRAM memory chip. In 1971, Intel scientists developed the Intel 4004, the first microprocessor, and in 1974, the Intel 8080, the first microprocessor to be used in a personal computer. The 8088 and 8086 followed in 1978, the latter being the first of a long line of Intel 80×86 products that extends through the current Pentium IV. Intel also produces an extensive line of specialized chips for *embedded systems* (*q.v.*). Through the longest stretch of it history, 1968 to 1998, Intel was led by Andrew Grove, who served first

as Director of Operations and then later as President and Chief Operations Officer in 1979, CEO in 1987, and Chairman of the Board in 1997. Intel continues to hold the major share of the market for 80×86 chips, its only serious competitor being Advanced Micro Systems (AMD).

National Cash Register (NCR)

National Cash Register (NCR) was founded by John Patterson in 1884 in order to market the product for which the company is named. Patterson adopted the motto "Think" that one of his managers, Thomas J. Watson Sr., brought to the Computing-Tabulating-Recording Company (C-T-R, later IBM) in 1914. In 1952, NCR entered the computer business through purchase of the Computer Research Corporation (CRC), which made special-purpose digital computers for aviation. In 1953, NCR and General Electric jointly produced the NCR 304, the first fully transistorized large-scale computer. In 1968, the NCR Century 100 and the CDC 7600 became the first computers built entirely with integrated circuit logic. By 1979, NCR was second only to IBM in revenue derived from computer products. Over the last seven years, NCR has divested its computer manufacturing division but acquired several specialized companies that support the company's new focus on full-service electronic commerce (*q.v.*). The NCR marketing division is credited with introducing two widely-used computer terms, "online," and "tower," the latter describing a personal computer whose disk access apertures are arranged vertically rather than horizontally.

Oracle Corporation

The *Oracle Corporation* was founded as *Software Development Laboratories* (SDL) in June 1977 by Bob Miner, Ed Oates, and Larry Ellison, the latter as president. The corporation soon changed its name to *Oracle* to conform to that of its major product, a relational database software system whose queries are expressed in SQL. *Oracle*, a name boldly borrowed from a CIA project of that name, was originally a mainframe product but now runs on workstations and personal computers as well. The company's rapid ascent to over ten billion in sales was due partially to how quickly it converted *Oracle* for use on the IBM-PC, and to the fact that IBM also chose SQL as the language to support its own System R database software. That decision boosted *Oracle* over it major competitor, *Ingress*, which used a proprietary query language.

Sun Microsystems

Sun Microsystems was founded in 1982 by Stanford MBAs Scott McNealy and Vinod Khosla, with McNealy as CEO. Their business plan was to market a powerful workstation designed by Stanford engineering Andreas Bechtolsheim. Their school's influence is reflected in the company's name, since SUN originally meant *Stanford University Network*. McNealy recruited Bill Joy, an operating system expert from the University of California at Berkeley, to design a version of Unix for the first Sun workstation. Production began in 1984. The machines used the MIPS integrated circuit chip, a RISC microprocessor made by MIPS Computer Systems, Inc. MIPS had been incorporated as the outgrowth of another Stanford project named for the customary unit of processing speed, Millions of Instructions Per Second (MIPS). Sun emphasized the ease with which multiple workstations could be networked through use of Ethernet interconnections. By 1987, Sun held 29% of U.S. workstation revenue, edging out the former leader Apollo at 21%. McNealy had hoped that his company's version of Unix would become an industry standard, but that plan was thwarted when his competitors formed the *Open Software Foundation*. Sun now derives revenue from Bill Joy's invention of the popular Internet language Java (*q.v.*).

Texas Instruments (TI)

Texas Instruments (TI) is the current name of the Texas firm founded in 1930 as *Geophysical Service, Inc.* (GSI) by physicists John C. Karchner and Eugene B. McDermott. The company's original product line was equipment for seismic oil exploration. In 1951, GSI was renamed Texas Instruments, with Erik Jonsson as president and later Chairman of the Board through 1966. In 1952, TI entered the semiconductor business by purchasing a license to build transistors from Western

Electric. In 1954, TI marketed the first commercial silicon transistor, and in 1958, TI engineer Jack St. Clair Kilby invented the integrated circuit (IC), for which he received the Nobel Prize in physics in 2000. In 1967, Kilby coinvented the first electronic handheld calculator with Jerry Merryman and Jim Van Tassel. In 1971, TI developed the first single-chip microprocessor. Beginning in the late 1970s, TI began to concentrate on special-purpose integrated circuitry. In 1978, TI developed the first single-chip microprocessor for speech synthesis, and a year later both TI and Bell Labs developed a single-chip *digital signal processor* (DSP–*q.v.*). TI and Motorola are the current leaders in sales of high-performance DSPs.

Unisys

Remington Rand, founded in 1927, entered the digital computer business in 1950 through acquisition of the short-lived Eckert-Mauchly Computer Corporation (EMCC), and then grew through acquisition of Engineering Research Associates (ERA) in 1952. Sperry Rand was formed in 1955 through merger of the Sperry Corporation and Remington Rand. *Unisys* was formed in 1986 through the merger of Burroughs Corporation and Sperry Rand. Unisys is now concentrating on support for electronic commerce. Its major hardware product, introduced in 2000, is the Cellular Multi-Processing (CMP) server.

Edwin D. Reilly

DIGITAL PHOTOGRAPHY

For an article on a related subject, see

+ Image Processing

Digital photography is to personal computers (PCs) what image processing is to larger ones, that is, it brings to home and office users the capability to store, modify, and transmit photographs over the Internet. Digital photography grew out of the perfection of the optical scanner in the 1970s. Even before most PCs had their own scanner, amateur photographers were able to ask photo developers to scan their prints and deliver them on diskettes (*q.v.*) or post them on an accessible website. The development of reasonably priced digital cameras in 1995 provided a still more direct way to produce digital images that can be transferred to a PC.

A *digital camera* captures images on what is essentially a solid-state retina instead of film. The artificial retina uses either a charge-coupled device (CCD) or a CMOS (complementary metal oxide semiconductor) array. Images may be stored on removable and reusable flash memory cards or may be transferred to computer memory over a cable attached to a Universal Serial Bus (USB) port. The digital camera dates to the mid-1970s when Kodak invented several solid-state image sensors that converted light to digital pictures. In 1986, Kodak scientists invented the first megapixel sensor, one capable of recording 1.4 million pixels that could produce a $5'' \times 7''$ print of photographic quality. As of 2003, digital cameras offered 2 to 5 megapixels at prices proportional to these resolutions.

Once created by either a scanner or digital camera, images may be edited with image-processing software and sent to friends and relatives via electronic mail (*q.v.*). These programs allow such operations as modifying contrast, color hue and intensity, sharpening an image, and changing its size and orientation. One of the first popular packages that allowed these operations was *Adobe Photoshop*. A very versatile image editor called *IrfanView* is available free over the Internet. There are now ink-jet printers that use six colors (instead of the usual four) and that may be used to make $19'' \times 13''$ prints of high-resolution images on special photo paper. The resulting prints are virtually indistinguishable from those made by a professional photo finisher.

Bibliography

2003. Long, B. *Complete Digital Photography*, 2nd Ed. Hingham, MA: Charles River Media.

Edwin D. Reilly

DIGITAL SIGNAL PROCESSOR (DSP)

For articles on related subjects, *see*

+ Embedded System
+ Microprocessors and Microcomputers
+ Real-Time Systems

A *Digital Signal Processor* (DSP) is a special-purpose integrated circuit microprocessor that is optimized to convert incoming analog signals to digital form and to process them in real time. A DSP does its specialized computations about 10 times faster than a general-purpose microprocessor made with the same technology. DSPs are now essential to the operation of any real-time system, for which noise suppression or clarification of images is important.

DSPs are embedded in every automobile, cellular telephone, digital camera, and personal computer sound card (*see* EMBEDDED SYSTEM). Digital signal processing can restore vintage music recordings to their original clarity, erase static from long-distance phone lines, and enable satellites to resolve terrestrial objects as small as a baseball (*see* GLOBAL POSITIONING SYSTEM (GPS)). In automobiles, DSPs monitor suspension systems that adjust automatically to road conditions. In cell phones, DSPs squeeze more information into limited bandwidth (*q.v.*) and scramble signals to thwart eavesdropping. The leading producers of DSPs are Motorola and Texas Instruments.

Bibliography

2003. El Ali, T. S. *Discrete Systems and Digital Signal Processing with MATLAB*. Boca Raton, FL: CRC Press.

Edwin D. Reilly

DIGITAL SIGNATURE

For articles on related topics, *see*

+ Authentication
+ Cryptography, Computers in

✦ Electronic Commerce

✦ Pretty Good Privacy (PGP)

Digital signatures establish the origin of a message in order to settle disputes as to what message (if any) was sent. They typically involve two keys—a *signing key*, which is private to a user, and a *signature verification key* that is made public. A user can operate on a message with the private signing key to generate a signature, a short string that depends on all the bits in the message and the signing key in such a way that it cannot economically be forged; yet it can be verified by anyone with the public verification key.

A digital signature thus combines two protection primitives—message integrity and nonrepudiation of origin. The most common technique is RSA, named after its inventors Rivest, Shamir, and Adleman (1978). This was the first system to be used to control access to the zero-power plutonium reactor at Idaho Falls; more recently, it has been adopted as the European standard for healthcare signatures, and as the mechanism used in the SET protocol to protect credit card payments over the Internet.

RSA is based on the assumption that calculating cube (and other) roots modulo a large number is hard unless we know its prime factors. The simplest form of RSA signature S on a message M is just

$$S \equiv \sqrt[3]{M} \pmod{N}$$

The public signature verification key is the modulus N, while the secret signing key consists of its factors—two large randomly chosen prime numbers p and q.

Two further mechanisms are commonly found in digital signature systems: *hashing* and *certification*. Modern practice is to pass messages through a cryptographic hash function before signing. The idea is that the hash function reduces each message to an essentially unique digest, which we can sign in its stead; the hashing process saves us from having to sign each block of a long message individually.

The second aspect is certification. How do we know that a given public key actually corresponds to a given individual? Users who meet in person prior to initiating electronic communications can manually verify each others' public keys and certify them by applying their own signatures. Direct certification can be effective in closed communities, such as the banking industry, where the principals are in regular contact or at least trust a small number of organizations such as central banks to make introductions. But, how can such arrangements be scaled worldwide so as to enable people who have never met to verify each others' signatures? This aspect is highly controversial. The approach favored by governments is to establish a hierarchy of "trusted third parties"—nationally licensed certification services that will simultaneously sign users' public keys and enforce certain regulatory functions, such as ensuring that copies of users' encryption keys are archived for access by law enforcement and national intelligence agencies. In this model, a user's key certificate is somewhat like a passport or identity card. An alternative approach is for users to sign each others' keys, thereby creating a "web of trust." The idea is that two people who wish to sign or encrypt electronic mail to each other can search the publicly available key certificates to find a path of introductions between them. (*See* PRETTY GOOD PRIVACY (PGP).)

The evidential status of digital signatures may be uncertain. In the UK, some legal experts say that signature is a matter of intent, so a digital signature should be as good as a manuscript one. In other jurisdictions (such as Utah), specific laws have been passed giving digital signatures equal force. In most places, however, their exact status remains to be clarified.

Bibliography

1978. Rivest, R. L., Shamir, A., and Adleman, L. "A Method for Obtaining Digital Signatures and Public-key Cryptosystems," *Communications of the ACM*, **21**(2), (February), 120–126.

1995. Anderson, R. J., and Needham, R. M. "Robustness Principles for Public Key Protocols," in *Advances in Cryptology—Crypto 95* (ed. D. Coppersmith), 236–247. New York: Springer-Verlag.

1995. Schneier, B. *Applied Cryptography*, 2nd Ed. New York: John Wiley.

Ross Anderson

DIGITAL SUBSCRIBER LINE

See INTEGRATED SERVICES DIGITAL
NETWORK (ISDN).

DISABLED, COMPUTERS AND THE

For an article on a related subject, *see*

✦ Speech Recognition and Synthesis

Introduction

A *disability* is any condition that has a severe impact upon any major life function, such as seeing, hearing, or walking. In computing, a disability is usually the result of an interface problem. If someone cannot read a monitor screen, then the computer must be adapted to provide speech output. If the user cannot hear, then alternative text messages can be displayed in place of audio output. If typing is a problem, then one needs a speech recognition system that can process oral commands.

Suitably equipped portable computers (*q.v.*) can function as communication devices for individuals who cannot speak. Desktop and notebook computers are flexible programmable machines that can be easily modified using hardware or software to suit the special needs of the end user.

Traditionally, computer designers developed software interfaces to fit able-bodied users but not users with disabilities. For example, graphical user interfaces (GUIs) still present great difficulty for blind computer users, but Microsoft (*q.v.*) and the disability community are working on new technology to make such software more accessible.

Visual Impairments

There are numerous adaptive technologies designed to assist people who are visually impaired. Screen readers and speech synthesizers can be used to verbalize information displayed on a computer screen, and are useful for word processing, database management,
bookkeeping, and Internet access. Screen magnification software can enlarge the size of text and graphics on the screen, allowing people with limited vision to read in a type size that is comfortable. Optical character recognition (OCR–*q.v.*) systems can scan books, magazines, and other printed text into the computer. That scanned material can then be spoken aloud using a screen reader and speech synthesizer. Scanned documents may also be converted to Braille with the use of a Braille embosser and translator.

Physical Impairments

Physical impairment refers to those with limited or no use of their hands. Some impairments result in the inability to use a standard keyboard, mouse, or writing tools, or to handle disks and printouts. Lesser difficulties include the inability to write, hold books or papers, or turn pages. Adaptive technologies designed to assist people with these disabilities involve providing an input device more suited to the user's abilities. For example, a miniature keyboard is well suited to an individual with limited hand or finger movement, while a larger keyboard would be more appropriate for an individual lacking fine motor control. Some other options include on-screen keyboards that can be controlled using a head-mounted pointing device, or with a sip-and-puff switch operated by breath control (*see* Fig. 1). Voice recognition systems allow the computer to be operated by spoken command sequences (*see* SPEECH RECOGNITION AND SYNTHESIS).

Hearing Impairments

Hearing impairments range from mild hearing loss to total deafness. Most computer operating systems can signal a deaf user visually when the computer's speaker beeps. There are also utilities that can add captions to sounds, allowing for a text representation in parallel with the spoken material. The TTY (Teletype) and TDD (Telecommunications Device for the Deaf) have long permitted persons who are deaf to send and receive telephone messages using a portable keyboard and visual display, and now the computer is being adapted to fill the same function.

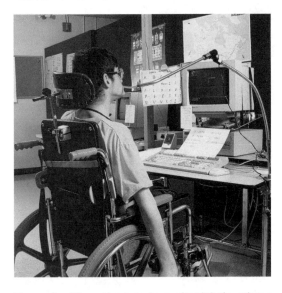

Figure 1. View of a man in a wheelchair using a computer by manipulating a mouthpiece. The man uses the mouthpiece at upper center because he does not have the use of his hands and arms. (Courtesy of De Repentigny, Publiphoto Diffusion/Science Library.)

Speech Impairments

People whose speech is impaired frequently use laptop computers with augmented communication speech software to communicate with others. The user may enter messages to be spoken directly from the keyboard, or use a prestored message to communicate.

Bibliography

1997. Coombs, N., and Cunningham, C. *Information Access and Adaptive Technology.* Phoenix, AZ: Oryx Press.

Joseph J. Lazzaro and Norman Coombs

DISCRETE MATHEMATICS

For articles on related subjects, *see*

+ Algorithms, Analysis of
+ Automata Theory
+ Boolean Algebra
+ Codes
+ Computational Complexity
+ Computer Algebra
+ Formal Languages
+ Graph Theory
+ Logic Design
+ Program Specification
+ Program Verification
+ Searching
+ Sorting

Discrete mathematics encompasses those branches of mathematics that deal with discrete objects, in contrast to other branches, such as calculus and analysis, whose main concern is with continuous functions. Some branches of mathematics, such as numerical analysis and linear algebra, have both continuous and discrete components. Because problems in discrete mathematics often involve the integers, which form an infinite set, discrete mathematics is not necessarily *finite* mathematics. Digital computers are discrete engines, since all calculations done on them are effectively based on the integers. Even floating-point numbers form a discrete system because the floating-point numbers representable in any computer are a discrete, finite set of points on the real line, an abstraction of the mathematical real number line, which is continuous and infinite in extent.

Discrete Mathematics and Algorithms

Although algorithms play an important role in continuous as well as discrete mathematics, they are much more a part of the warp and woof of discrete mathematics, mainly because algorithms are so closely related to computer programs. Moreover, *algorithmics*, the systematic study of algorithms, which is concerned with the development, analysis, and verification of algorithms, is a much more important subject in discrete mathematics than in continuous mathematics.

Proof in Discrete Mathematics

While many different methods of proof are applicable in discrete mathematics, one method—mathematical induction—is quintessentially the most important. In its most basic form, mathematical induction proves the truth of a proposition $P(n)$, which depends on some integer parameter n, for all $n \geq n_0$ by first proving the *basis case* $P(n_0)$ by any available proof method. Then, assuming the truth of $P(n)$ for any unspecified value of n and again using any available method, $P(n+1)$ is proven to be true. These two things together suffice to prove the truth of $P(n)$ for all $n \geq n_0$.

The Content of Discrete Mathematics

There is no universally agreed upon set of topics included under the rubric of discrete mathematics, but certain branches of mathematics are clearly part of the field.

Graph Theory

The "graph" in graph theory is not the familiar graph of secondary school mathematics, which is a "picture" of a continuous function, but rather a collection of *vertices* (or nodes) and *edges* (or branches) joining pairs of vertices. Figure 1 displays a *weighted digraph*: weighted because of the weights associated with each edge, and a digraph (directed graph) because each edge has a direction. The problem is to find the path (i.e. sequence of edges) from v_0 to v_7 that is shortest (i.e. for which the sum of the edge weights is smallest). Figure 2 displays a pseudocode sketch of *Dijkstra's algorithm* for the solution of this problem for a graph of $n+1$ vertices,

where we want the shortest path from v_0 to v_n. The distance function $d(v)$ is the length of the shortest path from v_0 to vertex v of the graph that passes through only vertices in the set U. Thus, initially, all distances are ∞ except for $d(v_0)$, which is 0. Figure 3 shows how the computation proceeds for the graph of Fig. 1, with the first row giving the initial values and each subsequent row giving the results after the kth passage through the loop of Fig. 2. The shortest path is $(v_0, v_1, v_3, v_5, v_6, v_7)$, whose length is 8.

Combinatorics

Combinatorics is about counting the number of objects of some type or about how many ways there are to do something. Applications of combinatorics play a major role in the analysis of algorithms. For example, it is often necessary in such analyses to count the number of times that a particular portion of an algorithm is executed averaged over all possible input data sets.

Difference Equations

Another name sometimes used for this subject is *recurrence relations*. Two main sources of these equations are the *discretization* of differential equations for solution on a computer and the analysis of algorithms. In general, a difference equation of *order k* has the form

$$y_n = f(y_{n-1}, y_{n-2}, \ldots, y_{n-k}) \qquad (1)$$

$$y_i = b_i, \quad i = 1, \ldots, k$$

where (1) is the difference equation itself and below it are the *initial conditions*. By far the most important difference equations are *linear* in which

$$y_n + a_1(n)y_{n-1} + a_2(n)y_{n-2} + \cdots + a_k(n)y_{n-k} = g(n)$$

where each $a_i(n)$ can be any function of n. When $g(n) = 0$, we call the equation *homogeneous*, otherwise, it is *nonhomogeneous*. When each $a_i(n)$ is a constant a_i, we speak of *linear, constant coefficient difference equations*, which are the easiest to solve. The solution of

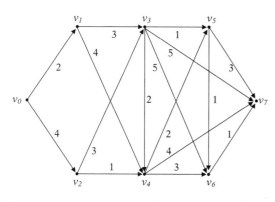

Figure 1. The shortest path problem. Object: find the shortest path from v_0 to v_7.

```
Initialize d(v0) and d(vi) to  ∞, i = 1,…,n
U ← {v0}
repeat
        Update the current distance function.
        Find the vertex u not in U for which d(u) is a minimum;
               if there is a tie choose u arbitrarily.
        U ← U{u}
endrepeat when    u = vn
```

Figure 2. A sketch of Dijkstra's algorithm.

k	$d(v_1)$	$d(v_2)$	$d(v_3)$	$d(v_4)$	$d(v_5)$	$d(v_6)$	$d(v_7)$	Vertex Added to U
0	∞	∞	∞	∞	∞	∞	∞	v_0
1	2	4	∞	∞	∞	∞	∞	V_1
2	2	4	5	6	∞	∞	∞	V_2
3	2	4	5	5	∞	∞	∞	V_3
4	2	4	5	5	6	10	10	V_4
5	2	4	5	5	6	8	9	V_5
6	2	4	5	5	6	7	8	V_6
7	2	4	5	5	6	7	8	V_7

Figure 3. Application of Dijkstra's Algorithm to the graph of Figure 1. *k* represents the count of the passages through the loop with $k = 0$ the initial state.

a homogeneous, linear, constant coefficient difference equation of order k has the form

$$y_n = \sum_{i=1}^{k} c_i r_i^n \qquad (2)$$

where the r_i in (2) are the roots of the polynomial equation

$$r^k - \sum_{i=1}^{k} a_i r^{k-1} = 0$$

and the c_i are found using the initial conditions.

Mathematical Logic

Mathematical logic has always played an important role in the design of computers and is playing an increasingly important role in various branches of computer science, particularly artificial intelligence (*q.v.*). The basis of much of mathematical logic is the *propositional calculus*, which is concerned with the analysis of propositions that can be stated in natural language (e.g. traditional

```
Input  x                          [Integer≥0]
       Y                          [Integer]
Algorithm Mult
   {x≤0}                          [Input specification]
   prod←0 ; u←0
   {prod=uy}                      [Loop invariant]
repeat until  u=x
   prod←prod+y
   u←u+1
   {prod=uy}
endrepeat
{prod=uy∧u=x}   [Loop termination condition]
{prod=xy}                         [Output specification]
Output prod                       [=xy]
```

Figure 4. A multiplication algorithm with assertions.

syllogisms), as well as those that arise in the verification of algorithms (e.g. the assertion of a *loop invariant* in an algorithm). As an example of the latter, Fig. 4 displays an algorithm to multiply two integers by repeated addition together with the *assertions* to be used in the proof of the algorithm. Focusing on the one labeled *loop invariant*, we note that the proposition *prod = uy* can be proved to be true when the loop is first entered and after each execution of the loop. The proof is essentially by mathematical induction. Since $u = x$ when the loop is finally exited, the final value of *prod* is xy as desired.

Propositional logic is used in the design of computers in its form as Boolean algebra (*q.v.*), wherein it is used to design logical circuits that realize particular Boolean functions (*see* LOGIC DESIGN). Such logical circuits can then be fabricated on chips.

In more sophisticated attempts at the verification of algorithms, it is not the propositional calculus but its more sophisticated cousin, the *predicate calculus*, that must be used. The predicate calculus deals with *predicates*, which are propositions containing variables so that whether a predicate is true or false depends upon the values of its variables. Thus, "x is a tennis player" is a predicate that would be true if x is Steffi Graf and false if x is Michael Jordan. The crucial concept in the predicate calculus is that of a *quantifier*. The *universal quantifier* is written ∀ and read "for all" so that

$$(\forall n)P(n)$$

is true if $P(n)$ is true for *all* values of n and false otherwise. The domain of n is normally the positive integers or the nonnegative integers. Using the universal quantifier, we may express formally the idea of proof by (weak) mathematical induction. That is, to prove

$$(\forall n : n \geq n_0)P(n)$$

it suffices to prove

$$P(n_0) \wedge (\forall n : n \geq n_0)[P(n) \Rightarrow P(n+1)]$$

The other significant quantifier is the *existential quantifier*, which is written ∃ and read "there exists" so that $(\exists n)P(n)$ is true if $P(n)$ is true for *any* n and false otherwise.

Other Branches of Discrete Mathematics

Here are brief descriptions of areas of mathematics that are sometimes but not always covered in discrete mathematics courses.

Discrete probability This deals with the familiar notions of probability where the *sample space* (i.e. the space of possible *events*) is finite or countably infinite. The probability distributions of discrete probability include the familiar binomial and Poisson distributions. Discrete probability is an important tool in the analysis of algorithms because generally average case analyses require that you consider all possible input data and the probability that each occurs.

Sequences and series Although a standard part of college and university calculus courses, sequences in their entirety and series, except for power series, are bona fide discrete mathematics. Some aspects of sequences and series are particularly pertinent to computers and computer science. For example, whereas mathematicians are usually most interested in convergent sequences, computer scientists are more interested in divergent sequences, in particular those that represent the *execution sequences* of algorithms and programs. For example, the sequence $\{n^2/4\}$ is the average case execution sequence of insertion sort (*see* SORTING), which means that, on average, $n^2/4$ comparisons of elements on a list of length n will be needed in order to sort it into lexical order. Thus, we say that insertion sort is an $O(n^2)$ (read "order n^2") algorithm. By determining the execution sequences of various algorithms for the same task, you can judge when one algorithm is to be preferred over another.

A powerful idea in discrete mathematics (and in continuous mathematics, as well) that arises from the study of series is that of *generating functions*. If $\{a_k\}$ is a sequence, its generating function $G(s)$ is defined to be

$$G(s) = \sum_{k=0}^{\infty} a_k s^k.$$

Using this *formal power series*, many problems in discrete mathematics, including many kinds of difference equations, can be solved. So can a variety of combinatorial problems. For example, the number of combinations a_{nmk} of n distinct objects, k at a time with up to m repetitions of each object can be found by determining that the generating function of the sequence

d

$\{a_{nmk}\}$ is $(1 + s + s^2 + \ldots s^m)^n$ with a_{nmk} the coefficient of s^k. For example, with $n = 3$, $m = 2$, $k = 3$, a_{323} is given by the coefficient of s^3 in $(1 + s + s^2)^3$, which is easily determined to be 7. If we denote the three objects by a, b, and c, the seven combinations are *aab*, *aac*, *abb*, *abc*, *acc*, *bbc*, and *bcc*.

Abstract and linear algebra

Algebras generally deal with discrete objects and are, therefore, a natural part of discrete mathematics. Abstract algebra has many applications in computer science. For example, semigroups have application to formal languages and automata theory, and groups have important applications in coding theory. A particularly important application is the use of finite-state machines in compiler construction for the *recognition* of syntactically correct language structures (*see* COMPILER and AUTOMATA THEORY).

Linear algebra (and linear programming) are uncommon topics in discrete mathematics, but are also quite natural, since, although the variables in linear algebra are normally real variables, the structures (e.g. matrices) and manipulations are generally discrete.

Bibliography

1995. Rosen, K. H. *Discrete Mathematics and its Applications*, 3rd Ed. New York: McGraw-Hill.

2001. Dossey, J. A., Otto, A. D., Spence, L. E., and Van Den Eynden, C. *Discrete Mathematics*, 3rd Ed. Reading, MA: Addison-Wesley.

1998. Maurer, S. B., and Ralston, A. *Discrete Algorithmic Mathematics*, 2nd Ed. Natick, MA: A. K. Peters.

Anthony Ralston

DISKETTE

For articles on related subjects, *see*

+ Hard Disk
+ Memory: Auxiliary
+ Optical Storage

The *diskette* is the primary removable storage medium for a PC. Diskettes were originally called *floppy disks* in distinction to the *hard disk* (*q.v.*) because the earliest such disks were intrinsically flexible and remained so when encased in their square cardboard protective envelopes. Diskettes are made by depositing a metallic oxide material on a mylar substrate. The oxide coating is ferromagnetic and responds to the magnetic fields generated by the heads in the disk drive. Diskettes come in a variety of sizes. The 8″ disks used with early CP/M personal computers are now obsolete, as are the 5.25″ diskettes used with the earliest MS-DOS and Apple (*q.v.*) systems. Currently, the most popular variant is a 3.5″ diskette encased in hard plastic (and hence no longer "floppy"). Diskettes are easy to mail and carry, and cost as little as 20 cents each. A 3.5″ diskette (Fig. 1) fits easily into a pocket.

Information is recorded on both sides of the diskette in what is known as double-sided format. Therefore, each disk drive must have two read–write heads.

Figure 1. The front and back of a 3.5″ diskette. The drive into which it is inserted moves the metal slide (to the left with respect to the front of the diskette) in order to access the magnetic surface of the disk through a rectangular window as the disk spins within its protective plastic case. A small plastic tab at the bottom right of the back of the diskette has two positions: "up" for normal read-write capability and "down" to make the diskette read-only in order to protect recorded information against accidental modification.

Information is organized in concentric *tracks* that are either prerecorded when the diskette is manufactured or magnetically encoded by a formatting program that comes with the operating system. Each track is subdivided into *sectors* and each sector into bytes. On the IBM PC (*q.v.*) and PC compatibles, each side of a double density (DSDD) 5.25″ floppy held 40 tracks of nine 512-byte sectors. The smaller 3.5″ diskettes use 80 tracks per side, 18 sectors per track, and 512 bytes per sector, yielding a capacity of 1.44 MB.

Floppy disks first appeared in the late 1960s when IBM used them in an early minicomputer. These 8″ floppies could hold almost a megabyte, but the physical size of the disk drive became a consideration as computers got smaller. Even 3.5″ drives are rather heavy (and power hungry) relative to the weight of the lightest portable computers (*q.v.*). A 2″ diskette was introduced in the late 1980s, but did not catch on.

The future of the 3.5″ diskette is unclear. The original Apple iMac series did not include a 3.5″ drive as standard equipment, but the leading manufacturers of Pentium-based machines continue to package a 3.5″ drive as standard equipment and offer internal 100 MB or 250 MB drives as an option.

Stephen J. Rogowski

DISPLAY MONITOR

See MONITOR, DISPLAY.

DISTRIBUTED SYSTEMS

For articles on related topics, *see*

+ Client-Server Computing
+ Communications and Computers
+ Cooperative Computing
+ Electronic Commerce
+ Ethernet
+ Internet
+ Local Area Network (LAN)
+ Networks, Computer
+ Sensor Network
+ World Wide Web

Nearly all large software systems are necessarily distributed over computers at geographic locations remote from one another. For example, enterprise business systems must support multiple users running common applications across different sites. A *distributed system* encompasses these applications, their underlying support software, the hardware they run on, and the communication links that connect the distributed hardware. The largest and best-known distributed system is the Internet. The most common distributed systems are networked client–server systems.

Properties

Distributed systems have these defining properties

- *Multiple computers* (nodes) Software for the system and its applications executes on multiple independent computers (not merely multiple processors on the same computer, which is the realm of *parallel computing-q.v.*). Each node may primarily take the role of a *client* that requests services by others, a *server* that provides computation or resource access to others, or a *peer* that does both (Fig. 1).
- *Resource sharing* The most common reason for connecting a set of computers to operate distributively is to allow them to share physical and computational resources; for example, printers, files, databases, mail services, stock quotes, or collaborative applications. Distributed system components that support resource sharing play a role similar

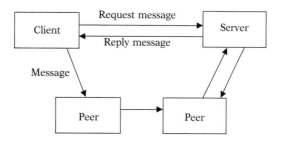

Figure 1.   A small distributed system.

to operating systems (*q.v.*) and are increasingly indistinguishable from them.

- *Concurrency* Each of the nodes in a distributed system provides independent functionality, and operates concurrently with all of the others (*see* CONCURRENT PROGRAMMING). More than one *process* (executing program) per node, and more than one *thread* (concurrently executing task) per process may participate as components in a system. Most components are *reactive*, continuously responding to commands from users and messages from other components.
- *Message passing* Software communicates via structured message passing disciplines built upon any of a number of networking protocols (for example TCP/IP–*q.v.*) in turn running on any of a number of connection technologies such as Ethernet (*q.v.*) and modems (*q.v.*). The nodes in most distributed systems are *completely connected*–any node may send a message to any other node.

Distributed systems also possess, to varying degrees, the following characteristic properties:

- *Heterogeneity* The nodes participating in a system may consist of diverse computing and communication hardware. Some heterogeneity issues are addressed by agreeing upon common message formats and low-level protocols that can be readily implemented across different platforms. Others may require construction of *bridges* (*see* GATEWAY) that translate one set of formats and protocols to another.
- *Multiple protocols* The most basic form of distributed communication is inherently *asynchronous*; similar to mailed letters in a postal system. Senders issue messages without relying on receipt or reply by their recipients. Distributed messages usually take much longer to reach recipients than do local invocations, sometimes reach recipients in a different order than they are sent, and may fail to reach them at all.
- *Openness* Most sequential programs are *closed*: their configurations never change after execution commences. Most distributed systems are to some degree *open*: an unbounded number of nodes,

components, and applications may be added or changed even while the system is running. Openness requires that each component obey a certain minimal set of policies, conventions, and protocols to insure *interoperability* among updated or added components.

- *Fault tolerance* A program running on a single computer is, at best, only as reliable as that computer. But most distributed systems remain at least partially available and functional even if some of their nodes, applications, or communication links fail or misbehave.
- *Persistence* At least some data and programs are maintained on persistent media that outlast the execution of any given application.
- *Security* Only authorized users may access sensitive data or perform critical operations. Security in distributed systems is intrinsically a multilevel issue, ranging from the basic safety guarantees provided by the hardware and operating systems residing on each node, to message encryption and authentication (*q.v.*) protocols, to mechanisms supporting larger social policy issues concerning privacy, appropriateness of content, and individual responsibility.
- *Isolation* Each component is logically or physically autonomous, and communicates with others only via structured message protocols. In addition, groups of components may be segregated for purposes of functionality, performance, or security. For example, while the connectivity of a corporate distributed system may extend to the entire Internet, its essential functionality could be segregated (often by a *firewall*) to an *intranet* operating only within the company.
- *Decentralized control* No single computer is necessarily responsible for configuration, management, or policy control for the system as a whole. Distributed systems are instead *federations* (domains joined by protocols) of autonomous agents.

Theoretical Foundations
Computational Models

Distributed systems cannot be modeled adequately as Turing Machines (*q.v.*). Unlike Turing Machines, distributed systems may be *open*, arbitrarily extensible by adding new nodes or functionality, and *reactive*, continuously responding to changing environments. One overarching framework that encompasses most current approaches to modeling distributed systems is Wegner's 1997 notion of an *interaction machine*, an abstract characterization that encompasses any object with state and the ability to send and receive messages. Active objects are in turn structured using sets of *passive* objects that conform to a given sequential model of object-oriented computation.

Specification

Distributed systems do not merely compute a single function or perform a single action. Instead, they perform a never-ending stream of diverse operations. Specification of the functionality of distributed systems cannot rely solely on the use of techniques that describe inputs and outputs of sequential programs. Specifications must additionally describe ongoing properties of the system as a whole.

Fundamental Limitations

The implementation of several desired properties of distributed systems runs up against inherent limitations that have been uncovered in theoretical studies. These mainly surround the ability of a set of independent nodes to reach some global property based on the notion of *consensus*: that a set of nodes all agree about a given predicate. Consensus plays a central role for example in fault tolerance, where some nodes must agree that another node has failed.

Distributed Algorithms

Many distributed systems rely on a common set of basic algorithms and protocols that are employed to solve problems including the detection of termination of a distributed computation, election of a leader of a group of nodes, synchronization of redundant computations performed for the sake of fault tolerance, coordination of database transactions, and mutually exclusive access to shared resources. More specialized algorithmic problem domains include distributed *simulation* (*q.v.*), *electronic*

commerce (*q.v.*), digital libraries, distributed *multimedia* (*q.v.*), and collaborative "groupware."

System Engineering

The earliest but still common form of distributed system is a *client–server* design, in which one or more independent servers perform centralized tasks such as database maintenance (Fig. 2). Clients each execute programs that provide user interface and computational capabilities, but communicate via database queries with servers whenever accessing or updating shared data. An examination of the limitations of the simplest, most fragile client–server systems reveals the main problems that are addressed in contemporary scalable, structured, distributed programming frameworks.

- *Fixed addresses* When there are only a few fixed nodes in a system, and each performs a single dedicated task, all communication might be performed by issuing packets to fixed Ethernet addresses or by broadcasting them on a local network. But these tactics do not scale; they are the distributed analogs of using raw memory addresses to locate data and instructions.

- *Ad hoc messaging* A small, fixed set of nodes with dedicated functionality can communicate by sending handcrafted messages that are known to be of a form acceptable by recipients. This practice does not scale to systems providing possibly many services on possibly many nodes.

- *Monolithic components* In the most fragile systems, each node runs a single very large program. Such monolithic software components are difficult to design, implement, and test, and even more difficult to reuse, extend, and update.

- *Fixed architecture* The communication patterns, protocols, and policies seen in pure client-server designs

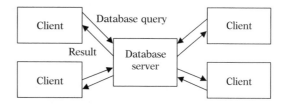

Figure 2.   Client-server interactions.

are sometimes sensible choices for database-centric applications, but they are by no means universally appropriate. For example, a fixed architecture could not support the sorts of applications deploying mobile agents.

Solutions to these problems and limitations mainly reflect experience-driven design knowledge accrued during the historical progression from custom small-scale systems, to specialized systems such as network file systems (for example, NFS; *see* FILE SERVER), to enterprise-level business systems.

Names and Identifiers

Contemporary distributed systems rely on *naming services* that maintain sets of logical names and map them to physical addresses and associated low-level protocols. The most common and familiar naming service is DNS (Domain Naming Service), which provides a basis for the Web page naming scheme used on the World Wide Web. DNS maps Internet names (for example, www.sun.com) to Internet addresses, which are then further translated to hardware-level addresses and connection protocols.

Interfaces and Implementations

Interfaces are formal declarations of operations (methods) supported by implementation objects. Most distributed systems rely on a standard means for defining interfaces that describe sets of services, enforced with an Interface Definition Language (IDL). Systems maintain interface descriptions, along with bindings to available implementations, in repositories that are tied to naming services in order to provide lookup capabilities. Object interfaces are very similar to *classes* (*q.v.*) in object-oriented programming (*q.v.*) languages. Each interface consists of a set of service declarations. Each service is declared in a fashion similar to an object-oriented *method*, a named operation that may carry arguments, results, and exceptions.

Component Management

Systems composed of many small-granularity interfaces, classes, and objects are generally more reusable, reliable, and economical than those built using only a few custom monolithic programs. For example, a Bank object may be composed mainly of sets of Account objects. In some systems, just about any software object may be a candidate for independent use as a distributed component. Such practices lead to the existence of many more components than there are computers in a system. Object components are managed by *life cycle* services that are somewhat analogous to, but extend, virtual memory (*q.v.*) techniques that allow computers to act as if they have more memory than they really do.

The Grid

Recent interest in distributed computing has centered on a next-generation Internet called *The Grid*. The Grid evolved from the desire to connect supercomputers (*q.v.*) into *metacomputers* that could be remotely controlled. The word *grid* was borrowed from the electricity grid, implying that any compatible device should be able to be plugged in at any point on The Grid and be guaranteed a certain level of resources, regardless of where those resources might originate. Though distributed computing evokes associations with initiatives like *cooperative computing* (*q.v.*) in which individuals donate their spare computing power to worthy projects, The Grid will link PCs to each other to serve the scientific community in a much more cohesive way. The Grid will not only enable sharing of documents and MP3 files but also connect PCs with such things as telescopes, tidal-wave simulators, and widely distributed sensors (*see* SENSOR NETWORK). The objective is to make computing a utility similar to traditional utilities. The Grid is intended to distribute storage and processing power in the same way that the World Wide Web distributes content. Grid organizers are intent on building a new kind of Internet about which its creators have a better knowledge of where bottlenecks are likely to arise and hence how to avoid them. The thorniest issues will involve social and political dimensions, for example, how to facilitate sharing between strangers among whom there is no history of trust.

Bibliography

1994. Coulouris, G., Dollimore, J., and Kindberg, T. *Distributed Systems: Concepts and Design*, 2nd Ed. Reading, MA: Addison-Wesley.

1996. Barbosa, V. *An Introduction to Distributed Algorithms.* Cambridge, MA: MIT Press.

1997. Wegner, P. "Why Interaction is More Powerful Than Algorithms," *Communications of the ACM*, **40**(5), (May), 80–91.

2003. Berman, F., Fox, G., and Hey, T. (eds). *Grid Computing: Making The Global Infrastructure a Reality.* New York: John Wiley.

Jos Marlowe, Doug Lea, and Malcolm Atkinson

DNA COMPUTING

See MOLECULAR COMPUTING.

DRIVER

A *driver* is a program or subprogram that is written to control either a particular hardware device or another software routine. The term originates both from the concept of harness race drivers or automobile drivers putting their steeds or cars through their paces to see what they can do, and from the fact that machinery components that apply motive force are called *drivers*. The most common examples of drivers that control hardware are those that pertain to particular brands and models of printers attached to personal computers.

One speaks of having or needing, for example, a printer driver that allows a word processor to communicate with a particular model printer.

In another context, we may have written a procedure that is to play an important role in conjunction with some large main program that is not yet written. To test the procedure while we wait, we might write a simple main program that calls the procedure with sufficiently realistic parameters to test it. The temporary main program whose only role is to provide a test bed for the new procedure may also be called a driver.

Bibliography

1996. Mittag, L. "Device Drivers for Nonexistent Devices," *Embedded Systems Programming*, **9**(8), 30–40.

Edwin D. Reilly

DSL

See INTEGRATED SERVICES DIGITAL NETWORK (ISDN).

DVD

See OPTICAL STORAGE.

ECKERT, J. PRESPER

For articles on related subjects, see

+ Digital Computers, History of
+ ENIAC
+ UNIVAC I

J(ohn) Presper Eckert, coinventor of ENIAC, was born in 1919 in Philadelphia (see Fig. 1). He received a BS degree from the University of Pennsylvania's Moore School of Electrical Engineering in 1941, and his Master's degree under a graduate fellowship from the Moore School in 1943. Eckert collaborated with John W. Mauchly of the Moore School's staff on developing ENIAC for US Army Ordnance between 1943 and 1946. This was the world's first all-electronic general-purpose digital computer, and could perform 5000 additions or subtractions per second. Its development launched the computer industry as we know it today.

In 1947, Eckert and Mauchly incorporated their venture as the Eckert–Mauchly Computer Corporation. They developed BINAC, the first electronic and fully self-checking computer, in 1949. Their next project, UNIVAC, was well under way when Remington Rand acquired the Eckert–Mauchly firm in 1950. Eckert became director of engineering for Remington Rand's Eckert–Mauchly Division that completed UNIVAC I. He became vice-president and director of research in 1955, vice-president and director of commercial engineering in 1957, vice-president and executive

Figure 1. J. Presper Eckert (courtesy of the Collections of Archives and Records Center, The University of Pennsylvania).

assistant to the general manager in 1959, and vice-president and technical advisor to the president of Sperry-Rand, Univac division, in 1963. He retired in 1989.

Eckert received an honorary degree of Doctor of Science in Engineering from the University of Pennsylvania in 1964. In 1969, he was awarded the National Medal of Science, the US's highest award for distinguished achievement in science, mathematics, and engineering. He died in his home town in 1995.

Bibliography

1996. Eckstein, P. "J. Presper Eckert," *Annals of the History of Computing*, **18**(1), 25–44.

Michael M. Maynard

E-COMMERCE

See ELECTRONIC COMMERCE.

EDITOR

See TEXT EDITING SYSTEMS; and WORD PROCESSING.

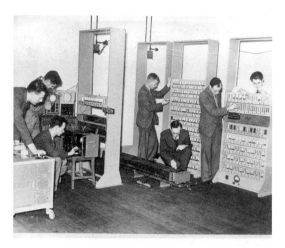

Figure 1. The EDSAC being constructed by Wilkes and his team. (Courtesy of the National Archive on the History of Computing, University of Manchester.)

EDSAC

For articles on related subjects, *see*

+ Digital Computers, History of: Early and Origins
+ EDVAC
+ ENIAC
+ Wilkes, Sir Maurice V.

The EDSAC (Electronic Delay Storage Automatic Calculator) was built in England during the late 1940s at the Mathematical Laboratory of the University of Cambridge. It was designed according to the principles expounded by J. Presper Eckert, John W. Mauchly, and others at the summer school held in 1946 at the Moore School of Electrical Engineering in Philadelphia.

The EDSAC (Fig. 1) was a serial binary computer with an ultrasonic memory. The mercury tanks used for the main memory were about 1.5 m long and were built in batteries of 16 tanks. Two batteries were provided. A battery, with the associated circuits, could store 256 numbers of 35 binary digits each, one being a sign digit. An instruction occupied a half-word of 17 bits, and it was also possible to use half-words for short

numbers. Numbering of the storage locations was in terms of half-words, not full words. The instruction set (*q.v.*) was of the single-address variety, and there were 17 instructions. Multiplication was included, but not division. Input and output were by means of five-channel punched-paper tape. The input and output orders provided for the transfer of five binary digits from the tape to the memory, and vice versa.

Operation of the machine could not start until a short standard sequence, known as the *initial orders*, had been transferred into the ultrasonic memory from a mechanical read-only memory (*q.v.*) formed from a set of rotary telephone switches. The initial orders determined the way in which the instructions were punched on the paper tape, and this was quite an advance for the period.

The EDSAC did its first calculation on 6 May 1949 and ran until 1958, when it was finally switched off.

Bibliography

1950. Wilkes, M. V. "The EDSAC (Electronic Delay Storage Automatic Calculator)," *MTAC*, **4**, 61.

1956. Wilkes, M. V. *Automatic Digital Computers*. London: Methuen; New York: John Wiley.

1980. Lavington, S. *Early British Computers*. Manchester: Manchester University Press.

Maurice V. Wilkes

EDUCATION IN COMPUTER SCIENCE

For an article on a related subject, see

+ Computer Science

UNITED STATES

Academic programs in computing at institutions of higher education began in the mid-1950s under pressure from early users of computing equipment, or from computing center staff deluged with questions about the use of these new devices. Initially, the "educational program" might have consisted only of a short noncredit course given by the computing center staff. Such a course mainly emphasized hardware characteristics, binary arithmetic, and machine or assembly language programming (*q.v*). At times, some of the instructional material was absorbed into an existing course in mathematics or engineering, generally in three or four lectures. However, with the rapid growth of broadly based university computing installations during the 1960–1965 period, and with the growth of an organized body of knowledge, it became necessary to establish more formal educational programs.

One of the most influential early efforts took place at the University of Michigan, and subsequently at the University of Houston, during the period 1959–1962. These efforts, conducted jointly by the Computing Center and the College of Engineering, were aimed less at establishing computer science as a distinct academic discipline than at the "Use of Computers in Engineering Education." At approximately the same time, Stanford University was establishing the discipline of computer science as an optional field of study in the department of mathematics.

In 1962, Stanford University established a Department of Computer Science in the School of Humanities and Sciences, and in the same year, Purdue University created a Department of Computer Science in its Division of Mathematical Sciences. In each case, the bond between the service and academic functions of computing was evident from the fact that one person was both director of the computing center and chairman of the department (George Forsythe at Stanford, Sam Conte at Purdue); this pattern was followed subsequently by other universities. Another pattern established by Stanford and Purdue was that of initially offering only graduate programs in computer science. The thinking at the time was that there could be no well-defined undergraduate program in computer science, and that specialization in computing should start only at the graduate level.

By the mid-1960s, developments in computer science education were proceeding apace. The National Academy of Sciences report on "Digital Computer Needs in Universities and Colleges" (Rosser *et al.*, 1966) recommended that campuses should "increase as rapidly as possible the number of persons trained annually as computer specialists and the support of pioneering research into computer systems, computer languages, and specialized equipment." The President's Science Advisory Committee report on "Computers in Higher Education" (Pierce *et al.*, 1967) recommended that "the Federal Government expand its support of both research and education in computer sciences." These reports helped obtain government and university support for the new discipline.

During the same period, university-sponsored conferences produced reports and books, such as "University Education in Computing Science" (Finerman, 1968), indicating that computer science was truly emerging as an academic discipline and not a short-lived curiosity. Reports of the Mathematical Association of America (Committee on the Undergraduate Program in Mathematics) and the Commission on Engineering Education (Cosine Committee) recommended changes in existing academic programs to ensure that students in mathematics and engineering received adequate preparation in computing. The studies of the Association for Computing Machinery (ACM–*q.v.*) had the most widespread effect. ACM chartered a Curriculum Committee on Computer Science to recommend necessary academic programs. The subsequent influential report of the Committee, "Curriculum 68" (Atchison *et al.*, 1968), defined for the first time the scope and content of a recommended undergraduate program. Subsequently, the Committee considerably revised and updated the recommended undergraduate program in its report, "Curriculum 78" (Austing *et al.*, 1979).

Separately, the Institute of Electrical and Electronic Engineers Computer Society (IEEE-CS–*q.v.*) chartered a Model Curricula Subcommittee of the Education Committee, which published guidelines and curricula for programs of computer science and engineering in 1977 and 1983 (Cain, 1977; *IEEE Computer Society Reports*, 1983). The ACM and IEEE also cooperated in a joint curricula task force that presented its first report in 1989 (Denning *et al.*, 1989) and its final recommendations in 1991 (Tucker *et al.*, 1991).

The two societies joined to publish accreditation guidelines in 1983 and to form a Computer Science Accreditation Commission (CSAC) of the Computing Sciences Accreditation Board (CSAB) in 1984. CSAC was later absorbed by the Accreditation Board for Engineering and Technology (ABET). As of late 1999, 155 programs in computer science had been accredited; for more information, contact CSAC at 111 Market Place, Suite 1050, Baltimore, MD 21202-4012 (email: csac@abet.org).

ACM also chartered Curriculum Committees for master's level programs in computer science, undergraduate and graduate degree programs in information systems, and related computer science programs in vocational–technical schools, community and junior colleges, and health computing. The effect of all these studies, conferences, and reports was a proliferation of academic programs in computer science and engineering. From the early graduate programs have come myriad graduate and undergraduate programs at two-year colleges (associate's degree), four-year colleges (bachelor's), five-year colleges (bachelor's and master's), and universities (bachelor's, master's, and doctoral); these programs are in addition to the numerous computing service courses available to students majoring in other disciplines.

University Educational Programs

Higher education programs in computing go by different names, such as computer science, computer engineering, computer science and engineering, information science, data processing, and information systems. Each name has also come to denote a particular emphasis and origin. Thus, *computer science* usually indicates a mathematical and scientific emphasis generally found at universities; *information systems* usually indicates computing applied to organizational systems generally related to business administration programs; and *data processing* usually indicates computing applied to administrative and commercial applications generally taught at two-year colleges. The programs may be housed in a department of computer science, computer engineering, computer science and engineering, computer and information science, or data processing, or given as an option in mathematics, engineering, or business administration.

From 1970 to 1997, the number of master's and doctor's degrees continually increased. The number of bachelor's degrees peaked in 1985–1986 at almost 42 000 and then declined rapidly to just over 24 000 in 1992–1996 but increased to almost 27 000 in 1997 and is rapidly increasing once again. The growth of computer science students at institutions of higher education generally parallels corresponding growth in demand in industry. In the late 1990s, demand surged to an all-time high, largely spurred by the growth of the Internet (*q.v.*).

Community college programs

Two-year community (or junior) colleges have grown rapidly in recent years, both in quantity and in scope of offerings. Forty years ago, the community college was rather rare, usually specializing in such areas as agriculture, forestry, and mining. Today, the community college has become as broadly based and diversified as is a university. More often than not, the career paths open to community college graduates are technician-oriented. On the other hand, graduates wishing to continue toward a bachelor's degree sometimes find the transition quite difficult. Community college standards are not always the same as university standards; community college courses are not always identical or even similar to corresponding courses at the university.

Some of these difficulties are being addressed; for example, community colleges and universities have been cooperating in facilitating the transfer process by making courses more compatible. Transfer still remains a problem, however. Increasingly, as the "computer profession" evolves and becomes better defined, the broader educational scope of a bachelor's degree becomes a prerequisite for a professional career.

The Undergraduate Curriculum

The program prescribed in *ACM Curriculum 68* reflected the viewpoint of those advocating a strong specialization in computing at the undergraduate level. As such, it follows the traditional pattern of most scientific and engineering undergraduate programs. The large component of computer and mathematics courses recommended, plus technical electives in computer-related disciplines, leaves little room for nontechnical subjects in the humanities and the social sciences within a normal four-year program.

Curriculum 78 revised the recommendations for the undergraduate program, reflecting the significant developments that had occurred within computer science education during the intervening decade. *Curriculum 78* provides somewhat greater flexibility than *Curriculum 68* in the content of courses, emphasizing the objectives of the undergraduate program and the subject matter to be covered. Aside from the proposed curriculum itself, the report discusses such topics as service courses, continuing education, computing facilities, and staff.

As requirements for computer science majors, *Curriculum 78* proposed a core of eight computer courses that would be taken by all majors, four elective courses chosen from a group of ten advanced courses described in the report, and five mathematics courses (calculus, mathematical analysis 1 and 2, linear algebra, discrete structures, probability, and statistics). *Curriculum 78* has been criticized because of its reduced number of mathematics courses and the fact that the required mathematics courses are not prerequisite to the computer courses—and therefore are not as integral a part of the prerequisite structure as in *Curriculum 68*.

Joint Curriculum Task Force (ACM and IEEE)

In the spring of 1988, ACM and the IEEE Computer Society formed a joint curriculum task force whose charter was to present recommendations for the design and implementation of undergraduate curricula in computing. The motivation was the recognition that despite strong and fundamental differences among institutions that house the departments offering undergraduate programs, these departments share a substantial curriculum in common. Any curriculum recommendations that attempt to speak for the entire discipline must not only identify the shared subject matter but also suggest ways in which it can serve as the basis for building undergraduate programs in differing kinds of institutions.

Graduate Curricula in Computer Science

Graduate programs in computer science preceded the introduction of undergraduate programs, the earliest programs appearing in the early 1960s. Although concentrating on undergraduate computer science, *Curriculum 68* also provided recommendations for master's programs. In 1981, the ACM Curriculum Committee on Computer Science published recommendations for master's programs (Magel *et al.*, 1981). This report recognizes the emergence of two kinds of programs with different goals: academic programs designed to prepare students for Ph.D. study, and professional programs designed to prepare students for business and industry. The committee rejected the idea of a purely terminal program, believing that all programs should make it possible for students to study beyond the master's level.

Although early master's programs in computer science did not require a bachelor's degree in computer science or even substantial prior study in the field, students entering a master's program now should have a B.S. in computer science or at least the equivalent of the material included in CS 1 through CS 8 of *Curriculum 78*, and mathematics through calculus, linear algebra, discrete structures, and one course in probability and statistics. Maturity in both abstract reasoning and the use of models, as well as one or more years of practical experience in computer science, are desirable.

According to this report, the master's program should provide both breadth in several areas and depth in a few. In addition, it should allow a degree of flexibility to address individual needs. The typical program will consist of 30 to 36 semester hours of courses in programming languages, operating systems and computer architecture, theoretical computer science, and data and file structures. The report lists 30 courses in these four areas, as well as in other areas, with brief descriptions.

Doctoral programs in computer science are intended for students with theoretical or research interests, and most such programs reflect the research interests of the faculty members. The doctoral dissertation, the heart of the doctoral program, is the means by which the student demonstrates the capability for making an original contribution to knowledge and is the fundamental requirement for the doctorate.

Bibliography

1966. Rosser, J. B. *et al. Digital Computer Needs in Universities and Colleges*. Washington, DC: National Academy of Sciences/National Research Council.

1967. Pierce, J. *et al. Computers in Higher Education*. The President's Science Advisory Committee, The White House. Washington, DC: U.S. Government Printing Office.

1968. Atchison, W. *et al.* "Curriculum '68," *Communications of the ACM*, **11**, 151–197.

1968. Finerman, A. (ed.) *University Education in Computing Science* (ACM Monograph). New York: Academic Press.

1968. Atchison, W. *et al.* "Curriculum '68," *Communications of the ACM*, **11**, 151–197.

1970. Finerman, A., and Ralston, A. "Undergraduate Programs in Computing Science in the Tradition of Liberal Education," *IFIP World Conference on Computer Education 2*, 195–199.

1977. Cain, J. T. (ed.) *A Curriculum in Computer Science and Engineering*. IEEE Publication EHO 119-8.

1979. Austing, R., Barnes, B., Bonnette, D., Engel, G., and Stokes, G. "Curriculum '78," *Communications of the ACM*, **22**, 147–165.

1981. Ralston, A. "Computer Science, Mathematics, and the Undergraduate Curricula in Both," *American Mathematical Monthly*, **88**, 472–485.

1981. Magel, K. *et al.* "Recommendations for Master's Level Programs in Computer Science," *Communications of the ACM*, **24**, 115–123.

1983. IEEE Computer Society. *The 1983 Model Program in Computer Science and Engineering*. IEEE Publication EHO 212-1.

1983. ACM. *ACM Curricula Recommendations for Computer Science*, Volume I. ACM Order #201831, and *for Information Systems*, Volume II. ACM Order #201832.

1984. Ralston, A. "The First Course in Computer Science Needs a Mathematical Corequisite," *Communications of the ACM*, **27**, 1002–1005.

1989. Denning, P. *et al.* "Computing as a Discipline," *Communications of the ACM*, **32**, 9–23.

1991. Tucker, A. (ed.) *Computing Curricula 1991—Report of the Joint (ACM/IEEE) Curriculum Task Force*. New York: ACM Press; Los Alamitos, CA: IEEE Computer Society Press.

Elliott B. Koffman and Aaron Finerman

EUROPE

The teaching of computer science and technology has developed in Europe along more or less the same lines as in the United States, and for the same reasons. Some of the first computers in Europe were installed or built in universities: Cambridge and Manchester in the United Kingdom; Göttingen, Munich, and Darmstadt in Germany; Zurich in Switzerland; and Paris, Grenoble, and Toulouse in France. They were used mainly for research purposes in departments of applied mathematics and sometimes in electrical engineering, but these research projects led to the development of academic programs. By the mid-1950s, optional courses had started at the universities that had their own computers or could afford to rent a computer mainly for students in mathematics or physics. At that time, a curriculum in computer science was usually divided into three parts—numerical analysis, hardware, and programming.

In 1965, there was one university in England offering a B.Sc. degree in computer science, but in Germany, there were no similar degrees before 1970, despite an extensive teaching program at a number of Hochschulen (schools of engineering). In France, degrees in computer science were given by the Institut de Programmation starting in 1964, although the teaching of computer science started much earlier at the Universities of Grenoble (1956), Toulouse (1957), and Paris (1957). It was also in France that computer science and technology acquired the status of an autonomous scientific discipline very early because of the definition of the word "informatique" by the Académie Française in 1966. Except in English-speaking countries where "computer science" is still the normal designation, *informatique* or its variants in other languages is the standard name for the discipline in Europe. As of 2003, the teaching of computer science in Europe is not very different from that in the United States.

Bernard Levrat

ASIA

Universities in Japan and India started installing computers in the 1950s; in Thailand, Singapore, and Malaysia in the 1960s; and in the remaining countries later than this. Indeed, in 1964, only two computers were installed in Thailand, one in Singapore, and none in all the other countries in Southeast Asia. By the 1990s, all universities in all the countries in Southeast Asia had significant numbers of computers as well as access to the Internet (*q.v.*). Early Southeast Asian educators in computer-related areas were educated mainly in the United States, the United Kingdom, Canada, and, later,

in Japan before being educated in their own countries. As in the United States, most of the early computer science programs featured numerical analysis, both theoretical and applied.

ACM Curriculum 68 (Atchison *et al.*, 1968) was the model for most early undergraduate programs at universities in Asia. Mathematically oriented students prospered in this curriculum, but other students did not. The latter claimed that they needed more applied courses to be able to find jobs. Thus, many universities in Southeast Asia modified Curriculum 68 by adding business administration courses and applied courses such as *Computer Applications in Banking* or *Computer Applications in Hotel Administration*. Such programs were often then renamed *Business Computing* or something similar.

Masters and Doctoral level computer science curricula in Southeast Asia are generally patterned after those in the United States, United Kingdom, or Japan. Some Japanese-like programs concentrate mainly on research in laboratories where a variety of equipment is readily available. Several Ph.D. programs in Southeast Asia require the student to publish in a refereed journal in the United Stated or the United Kingdom before graduation.

Srisakdi Charmonman

EDVAC

For articles on related subjects, see

+ Digital Computers, History of: Early
+ Eckert, J. Presper
+ ENIAC
+ Stored Program Concept
+ von Neumann, John
+ von Neumann Machine

The EDVAC (Electronic Discrete Variable Automatic Computer), *see* Fig. 1, was a direct outgrowth of work on the ENIAC. During the design and construction of the

Figure 1. The EDVAC (John W. Mauchly Papers. Rare book and manuscript library, University of Pennsylvania).

ENIAC in 1944 and 1945, the need for more storage than its twenty 10-decimal-digit numbers was realized. Experience with acoustic delay lines led to the concept of recirculating storage of digital information. The group at the Moore School of Electrical Engineering at the University of Pennsylvania started development work on mercury delay lines for such storage, and initiated the design of the EDVAC. As the first stored program computer, EDVAC instructions were stored in the same way as data. The basic logical idea is described by von Neumann (1945), and computers based on such designs have come to be known as von Neumann machines (*q.v.*).

The EDVAC had about 4000 tubes and 10 000 crystal diodes. It used a 1024-word recirculating mercury delay-line memory, consisting of 23 lines, each 384 μs long. The words were 44 bits long, and instructions consisted of a 4-bit operation code and four 10-bit addresses. The arithmetic unit did both fixed and floating-point operations at a clock frequency of 1 MHz. Input and output were via punched paper tape and IBM cards.

Although the conceptual design of the EDVAC was complete in 1946 and was delivered to the Ballistic Research Laboratories at Aberdeen, Maryland, by 1950 the entire computer had not yet worked as a unit and was still undergoing extensive tests. The delay was primarily due to the exodus of computer people from the Moore School in 1946. Eckert and Mauchly resigned and launched a commercial venture (UNIVAC). Herman Goldstine and Arthur Burks went to Princeton to work with von Neumann, and the author left to work with Turing in England. The EDVAC finally became operational as a unit in 1951.

Bibliography

1945. von Neumann, J. *First Draft of a Report on the EDVAC*, Contract No. W-670-ORD-4926, U.S. Army Ordnance Department, Philadelphia, PA: University of Pennsylvania, Moore School of Electrical Engineering (30 June).

1972. Goldstine, H. H. *The Computer from Pascal to von Neumann.* Princeton, NJ: Princeton University Press.

1981. Stern, N. *From ENIAC to UNIVAC.* Bedford, MA: Digital Press.

Harry D. Huskey

EFT

See ELECTRONIC FUNDS TRANSFER (EFT).

ELECTRONIC CALCULATOR

See CALCULATORS, ELECTRONIC AND PROGRAMMABLE.

ELECTRONIC COMMERCE

For articles on related subjects, *see*

+ Distributed Systems
+ Electronic Funds Transfer (EFT)
+ Electronic Mail (Email)
+ Smart Card
+ Internet
+ World Wide Web

Electronic commerce (e-commerce) enables the execution of transactions between two or more parties using interconnected networks. These networks can be a combination of POTS (plain old telephone service), cable TV, leased lines, or wireless. Information-based transactions are creating new ways of doing business and even new types of businesses. Improvements from implementing e-commerce may result in more effective performance, lower costs, and more rapid exchange of information.

A Brief History of E-Commerce

During the late 1970s and early 1980s, e-commerce became widespread within companies in the form of electronic messaging technologies: electronic data interchange (EDI) and electronic mail. Electronic messaging technologies streamline business processes by reducing paperwork and increasing automation. Electronic data interchange allows companies to send and receive business documents in a standardized electronic form to and from their suppliers. For example, combined with just-in-time (JIT) manufacturing, EDI enables suppliers to deliver parts directly to the factory floor, resulting in savings in inventory, warehousing, and handling costs. Electronic mail does much the same for unstructured organizational communications.

During the 1970s, the introduction of electronic funds transfer (EFT) between banks over secure private networks changed financial markets. EFT optimizes electronic payments with electronically provided remittance information. Today there are many EFT variants, including the debit card used at points of sale (POS) in retail outlets and direct deposits to employee bank accounts.

In the mid-1980s, a completely different type of e-commerce technology began to spread among consumers in the form of online services that provided a new form of social interaction (such as chat rooms and Internet Relay Chat (IRC)—*see* ONLINE CONVERSATION) and knowledge sharing (such as newsgroups and file transfer programs). Social interaction created a sense of virtual community in cyberspace (*q.v.*) and gave rise to the concept of a "global village." At the same time, information access and exchange have become more affordable.

In the 1990s, the advent of the World Wide Web on the Internet represented a turning point in e-commerce by providing an easy-to-use technological solution to the problem of information publishing and dissemination. The Web made e-commerce a cheaper way of doing business (economies of scale) and enabled more diverse business activities (economies of scope).

Forces Fueling the Growth of E-Commerce

Interest in e-commerce is being fueled by economic forces, customer interaction forces, and technology-driven digital convergence (Kalakota and Robinson, 1999).

Economic Forces

Under pressure to reduce costs and stay competitive, firms are attracted to the economic efficiencies offered by e-commerce. These efficiencies include low-cost technological infrastructures, accurate electronic transactions with suppliers, global information sharing and advertising, and low-cost customer service alternatives to expensive retail bank branches and telephone call centers. The economic forces motivating the shift to e-commerce are internal as well as external. The immediate application of e-commerce is in the internal integration of a firm's operations. External integration molds the vast network of suppliers, government agencies, large corporations, and independent contractors into a single community with the ability to communicate across any computer platform.

Marketing and Customer Interaction Forces

Companies also employ e-commerce to provide marketing channels, to target microsegments or small audiences, and to improve post-sales customer satisfaction. Companies want to supply target consumers with product and service information in greater detail than that provided in a TV or newspaper advertisement. Target marketing is becoming an increasingly important tool of differentiation. Not only are new types of products emerging but so are new players in old product categories, new spins on traditional plans, new pricing strategies, new target markets, new market research methods, and more.

Technology and Digital Convergence

Digital technology has made it possible to convert characters, sounds, pictures, and motion video into a bit stream that can be combined, stored, manipulated, and transmitted quickly, efficiently, and in large volumes without loss of quality. As a result, e-commerce and the multimedia (*q.v.*) revolution are driving previously disparate industries, such as communications, entertainment, publishing, and computing, into ever-closer contact, forcing industries with traditionally different histories and cultures to compete and cooperate.

The E-Commerce Technology Framework

E-commerce not only affects transactions between parties but also influences the way markets are structured. Traditionally, market ties were created through the exchange of goods, services, and money. E-commerce adds a new element: information. Market ties, such as those forming around online payments, are now based on information goods, information services, and electronic money.

The Network Infrastructure

The networking infrastructure (popularly called the *information superhighway*) has many different types of transport system and does not function as a monolithic entity. Instead, the architecture is a mixture of many forms of high-speed network transport, whether it be land-based telephone, air-based wireless, cable-based PC, or satellite-based. The players in this industry segment can be called *information transport providers*. They include telecommunication companies that provide phone lines; cable TV systems that provide coaxial cables and direct broadcast satellite (DBS) networks; wireless companies that provide mobile

radio and satellite networks; and computer networks, including private networks like America Online (AOL) and public data networks like the Internet.

The Component Infrastructure

When a technology system acts as an intermediary to deliver e-commerce results, it is called a *component* or *middleware* platform. There are two popular forms of middleware: Component Object Model (COM) and Common Object Request Broker Architecture (CORBA). The Component Object Model (COM) from Microsoft is a general software architecture for component software. Although COM addresses specific areas such as controls, compound documents, automation, data transfer, storage and naming, and others, any developer can take advantage of the structure and foundation that COM provides for cross-platform e-commerce applications. CORBA is the Object Management Group's answer to the need for interoperability among the rapidly proliferating number of hardware and software products available today. Simply stated, CORBA allows applications to communicate with one another no matter where they are located or who has designed them.

Messaging and Information Distribution

Messaging vehicles provide ways for communicating nonformatted (unstructured) as well as formatted (structured) data. Unstructured messaging vehicles include fax, email, and form-based systems like Lotus Notes. Structured documents messaging consists of the automated interchange of standardized and approved messages between computer applications via telecommunications lines. Purchase orders, shipping notices, and invoices are examples of structured document messaging.

Common Business Services Infrastructure

Doing business online has received attention for its potential, as well as for such shortcomings as inadequate directories, inadequate online payment instruments, and inadequate information security. The common business services infrastructure includes the different methods for facilitating online buying and selling. In e-commerce, the buyer sends an electronic payment (a form of electronic check or digital cash) as well as remittance information to the seller. Settlement occurs when the payment and remittance information are authenticated by the seller.

Client/Browser Infrastructure

The first publicly available browser, Lynx, was character-based. The modern browser, such as Internet Explorer or Netscape, is a full infrastructure on which a variety of programs interoperate. The browser is also evolving into a thin version—mobile phone browsers—to support the wireless medium. For instance, the next generation of browsers such as Spyglass's Wireless Device Mosaic is a small microbrowser designed to display WML (Wireless Markup Language), the WAP-specified wireless content language that is similar to HTML.

E-Commerce Applications

There are three distinct classes of e-commerce applications: interorganizational (business-to-business—B2B), intraorganizational (within a business), and customer-to-business (C2B).

Interorganizational

Interorganizational e-commerce applications include the following:

- *Supplier management* Electronic applications help companies reduce the number of suppliers and facilitate business partnerships by reducing purchase order (PO) processing costs and cycle times, and by increasing the number of POs processed with fewer people.
- *Inventory management* Electronic applications shorten the order-ship-bill cycle. If the majority of a business's partners are electronically linked, information once sent by fax or mail can now be instantly transmitted.

- *Distribution management* Electronic applications facilitate the transmission of shipping documents such as bills of lading, purchase orders, advanced ship notices, and manifest claims, and enable better resource management by ensuring that the documents themselves contain more accurate data.
- *Channel management* Electronic applications quickly disseminate information about changing operational conditions to trading partners. Technical, product, and pricing information that once required repeated telephone calls and countless hours can now be posted to electronic bulletin boards.

Intraorganizational

Intraorganizational e-commerce applications include the following:

- *Workgroup communications* These applications enable managers to communicate with employees using electronic mail, videoconferencing, and bulletin boards. The goal is to use technology to increase the dissemination of information, resulting in better informed employees.
- *Collaborative publishing* These applications enable companies to organize, publish, and disseminate human resources manuals, product specifications, and meeting minutes using tools such as the World Wide Web.
- *Sales force productivity* These applications improve the flow of information between the production and sales forces, and between firms and customers. The goal is to allow firms to collect market intelligence quickly and to analyze it more thoroughly.

Within intraorganizational electronic commerce, the largest area of growth can be seen in the development of "Corporate Intranets," which are primarily set up to publish and access vital corporate information.

Customer to business

Customer to business e-commerce applications include the following:

- *Social portals* Electronic applications enable consumers to find online information about existing and new products and services. This also includes applications that enable consumers to communicate through electronic mail, videoconferencing, and newsgroups.

- *Transaction portals* These include applications that enable and facilitate the completion of transactions between buyers and sellers.

The objective of this class of e-commerce is to provide consumers with greater convenience and lower prices. E-commerce provides consumers with convenient shopping methods, from online catalog ordering to phone banking, both of which eliminate the costs of expensive retail branches ("bricks and mortar"). E-commerce facilitates factory orders by eliminating many intermediary steps, thereby lowering a manufacturer's inventory and distribution costs and indirectly providing consumers with lower prices.

Bibliography

1996. Kalakota, R., and Whinston, A. *Electronic Commerce: A Manager's Guide*. Reading, MA: Addison-Wesley.

1999. Kalakota, R., and Robinson, M. *E-Business: Roadmap for Success*. Reading, MA: Addison-Wesley.

Ravi Kalakota and Marcia Robinson

ELECTRONIC FUNDS TRANSFER (EFT)

For articles on related subjects, *see*

+ Data Security
+ Distributed Systems
+ Electronic Commerce
+ Electronic Mail (Email)
+ Networks, Computer
+ Privacy, Computers and
+ Smart Card

An *Electronic Funds Transfer* (EFT) system is one that involves the electronic movement of funds between financial institutions. There are two major worldwide EFT networks: the Clearinghouse Interbank Payments System (CHIPS) and FedWire (the oldest EFT system in the USA). In 2003, these networks moved $3 billion (US) each banking day. A third major network, the Society for Worldwide Interbank Financial Telecommunications (SWIFT), is capable of handling over two million messages per day.

The Evolving Forms and Extensions of EFT

The original expansion of EFT was stimulated by the standardization of magnetic ink character recognition (MICR) technology in the mid-1950s. EFT systems were anticipated to be a lower-cost alternative to paper transactions. EFT has progressed through four various forms: automated teller machines (ATMs), automated clearing houses (ACH), electronic funds transfer point of sale systems (EFTPOS) and debit cards, and electronic funds transfer electronic data interchange systems (EFT-EDI).

Automated Teller Machines (ATMs) provide the basis for the most familiar EFT system in current use. These target the consumer market. ATMs are installed by financial institutions and retail stores to provide unattended, online computerized banking "teller" services. ATMs are user-activated through a magnetic strip on a plastic card. ATMs read account information, verify a user's personal identification number (PIN), and then allow cash withdrawals, deposits, transfer of funds between accounts, and balance inquiry. In 1990, it was estimated that, for some users, EFT saved more than $1 per transaction. More recently, however, some financial institutions have come to believe that ATM transactions are more costly to them than teller transactions and have begun to charge their customers a fee for initiating them. Despite this threat of escalating cost, ATMs have become ubiquitous and extremely popular.

The *automated clearing house* (ACH) network is a nationwide system that processes preauthorized electronic payments on behalf of depository financial institutions. ACH networks in the United States resulted from a joint effort by the Federal Reserve System and the banking industry in the mid-1960s.

The National Automated Clearing House Association (NACHA) is a US trade association representing 42 regional ACH associations whose members comprise over 20 000 depository financial institutions. Expanding direct deposits of payroll and similar services increased the volume of transactions substantially in the late 1960s.

Electronic funds transfer at point of sale (EFTPOS) is the blending of electronic point of sale technology with EFT, usually accomplished with a "debit" card that is similar to those used for ATMs. Electronic point-of-sale advantages such as better pricing and inventory planning and control are thus enhanced by the characteristics of EFT such as the convenience of cash and the security of a credit card. EFTPOS systems involve a network of retail-based terminals linked online to a financial institution's computer. Payments rendered at retail operations can then be debited from a customer's account and credited to the retailer's automatically.

Electronic funds transfer and electronic data interchange (EFT-EDI) is the direct, rapid, computer-to-computer transmission and translation of business information (e.g. invoices, purchase orders, claims forms) in a standard format. No human intervention is necessary. For example, EDI-transmitted invoices can update inventory orders and generate exception reports for back orders.

Architectural Requirements

A successful EFT system relies on fault-tolerant computing (*q.v.*). Message authentication (*q.v.*) entails a watchdog generator and controller, a security card, and a mainframe peripheral security module. The US Data Encryption Standard (DES) has traditionally been the encryption algorithm used to secure EFTPOS systems (*see* CRYPTOGRAPHY, COMPUTERS IN). As transaction volumes increase, however, the algorithm's effectiveness tends to decrease.

EFT Trends and Issues

Electronic benefits transfer (EBT) is the US government's use of EFTS technology to automate programs such as Social Security, child support, Medicaid, and food-stamp distribution. The Internal Revenue Service (IRS) is seeking to use EFT-EDI for refunds. Off-site mainframe computers can now deliver EFT advances automatically through facsimile transmission (fax). Security and interface/interconnection issues are becoming more important as the industry matures. *Smart cards* (invented in 1974 by Roland Moreno) are beginning to be used to identify users. Smart cards (*q.v.*) have embedded integrated chips with up to 64 KB of indelible memory. A microcomputer on the chip executes unalterable programs, thus making such cards more secure than the plastic, magnetic-striped cards currently in use.

Banks and other financial institutions face legal risks that are partially protected if the EFT system used is part of CHIPS or the FedWire system (since these are underwritten by the Federal Reserve System). However, liability issues are still somewhat unsettled, with many different acts and regulations coming into play. Legal documents generally require paper forms and proofs of signature in order to be binding, which tends to lessen the attractiveness of the technology to an organization considering an investment in EFT-EDI.

Bibliography

1996. Ice, T., and Demy, T. J. *The Coming Cashless Society*. Eugene, OR: Harvest House Publishers, Inc.

1996. Furche, A., and Wrightson, G. *Computer Money: A Systematic Overview of Electronic Payment Systems*. Heidelberg: Dpunkt Verlag.

1999. Welch, B. *Electronic Banking and Treasury Security*, 2nd Ed. Boca Raton, FL: CRC Press.

Janice F. Cerveny

ELECTRONIC MAIL (EMAIL)

For articles on related subjects, see

+ Internet
+ Online Conversation
+ World Wide Web

Introduction

Electronic mail (email) is the transfer of a message in electronic form from one computer user to another

From Dave Nakayama Mon Feb 8 01:00:53 1999

X-Apparently-To:	geoff@yahoo.com via mdd601.mail.yahoo.com
Received:	from web1.rocketmail.com (205.180.57.67)
	by mta107.yahoomail.com with SMTP; 8 Feb 1999 01:15:53 -0800
Received:	from [207.181.208.205] by web1; Mon, 08 Feb 1999 01:00:53 PST
Message-ID:	< 19990208090053.13315.rocketmail@web1.rocketmail.com >
Date:	Mon, 8 Feb 1999 01:00:53 -0800 (PST)
From:	Dave Nakayama < dave@rocketmail.com > Add to Address Book
Reply-To:	dave@yahoo.com
Subject:	Re: breakfast meeting
To:	geoff@yahoo.com
MIME-Version:	1.0
Content-Type:	text/plain; charset = us-ascii
Content-Length:	134

} Header

Hi Geoff,

It was good to finally get a chance to talk in person.
I look forward to getting together again soon.

} Body

Best Regards,
Dave

Figure 1. The header shows the recipient, the intermediate systems that transferred the message, specified by Internet domain name or IP address, the date, sender, and return address. It also identifies the message as conforming to the MIME protocol, with simple ASCII text. The actual message is in the body. Add to Address Book gives the recipient the option of entering the sender's name and address in the mail agent's list of correspondents.

over a network. Email is now the world's most common form of written communication, supplanting traditional mail and fax, and has begun to replace much telephone conversation. The number of email "boxes" has grown from several hundred thousand to tens of millions in a few short years.

An email message is typically composed on a personal computer using an email program such as Microsoft *Outlook*. The completed message comprises two parts, the main message content or *body*, and subject and addressing information contained in the *header*. The body can be anything from a simple text document to a collection of various files such as pictures or other documents. The email message is transferred from one computer to another on its way to a final destination (*see* Fig. 1).

Email Architecture and Protocols
Store and Forward

The Internet email delivery system uses the principle of *store and forward*, a series of exchanges between message submission and delivery end-points across the network.

A user composes a message with the assistance of an email program known as a *User Agent* (UA), addressing it to one or more intended recipients. The composed message is handed off from the client program to a mail server program known as a *Message Transfer Agent* or MTA, which *stores* the message on local storage. Subsequently, on a periodic basis, the server program attempts to *forward* the queued message to another MTA running on a remote computer in the network that is presumably closer to the destination mail server. The message continues to be routed on a "hop-by-hop" basis through the network from one MTA to another until it reaches the recipient's mail server, which accepts it and stores it in a location accessible to the recipient—a process known as *final delivery*. Should final delivery fail, a *bounce* message is generated to the message sender. The most common reason for a bounce is "unknown recipient" (e.g. when the sender mistypes the recipient's address). Automatically generated bounce messages may be identified by the message header, in which the "from" address is usually "MAILER-DAEMON."

The Email Address

Recipients of an email message are specified via their email address. The most common format is quite simple: ⟨user name⟩@⟨domain name⟩. A *user name* is a restricted set of characters (e.g. geoff or anand_tolani), which is locally unique. The *domain name* (*q.v.*) is unique throughout the Internet and indicates where the final delivery of this message is to take place, for example, yahoo.com. The combination of the user name and the domain name creates a globally unique address for this email box. Examples are joe_smith@yahoo.com, sue@southcampus.iu.edu, edr@acm.org, and pierre@societe.co.fr.

Role of the User Agent

Email client programs allow users to read delivered messages as well as to compose and send replies or new messages. Modern user agents provide mail folders that allow messages to be moved out of the main *inbox* into specific folders where they can be grouped with other related messages. Likewise, recent standards such as the Interactive Mail Access Protocol (IMAP) can manipulate remote messages within and between folders. Advanced features such as mail filters allow arriving mail to be sorted automatically into target folders or even discarded, using properties of the arriving message such as the message sender or the presence of specified keywords in the message.

Role of the Message Transfer Agent

The MTA is responsible for the hop-to-hop forwarding of messages through the network. It also accepts outbound messages from user agents at the message submission end-point, as well as inbound messages from forwarding MTAs at the final delivery endpoint. In all cases, client programs communicate with receiving MTAs using SMTP, the Simple Mail Transfer Protocol. SMTP provides simple commands with which a client specifies the sender's email address and one or more recipient email addresses. ESMTP or *Extended* SMTP is a new superset of the protocol, which lets clients test servers for specific feature support and negotiate parameters such as allowable message size and transmission time-outs.

Remote Access Protocols

Computers that are not directly connected to the Internet use a remote access protocol rather than SMTP. For example, suppose a home user connected to the Internet by an Internet Service Provider (ISP) wishes to read new mail using an email program. The physical location of the email is on a mail server machine at the ISP's operations center. A common remote access protocol is the simple POP3 (Post Office Protocol, version 3), which allows the user agent program running on the home computer to retrieve messages from a remote mail server, as long as adequate user authorization is provided. Various authorization mechanisms are possible, such as simple plain-text passwords (*q.v.*) or more sophisticated encrypted key authentication (*q.v.*).

Anatomy of an Email Message

Every email message consists of two parts: a set of consecutive header fields collectively referred to as the message *header*, and the actual message content itself, that is, the message body. Each *header field* consists of a field name followed by a colon and a value. Example header fields are *To:, From:, Subject:, Date:*. Header fields are mainly of interest to user agents, who fill them in during composition and parse them for display during message viewing. For example, the route of a message may be traced backwards by examining the Received: headers, each having been appended by an MTA indicating a hop in the message route.

Several email standards, the most important being SMTP, require that email message headers and bodies contain only 7-bit ASCII (*see* CHARACTER CODES) text. This restriction allows messages to pass through the various flavors of MTAs on the network without being corrupted or altered. Encoding mechanisms have been devised to include other forms of data in an email message. One of the earliest is *uuencoding* (Unix-to-Unix encoding), which allows arbitrary binary data to be encoded as 7-bit ASCII text, which can then be decoded back into binary form by the receiving user agent or by a separate standalone program. This allows small binary files to be appended to messages. While simple, uuencoding does not provide a mechanism with which to add structure to an email message body, nor does it allow the type of the binary data (e.g. sound clip or word processing document) to be specified except through conventions for file naming. MIME (Multipurpose Internet Mail Extensions) was introduced to address these shortcomings, and has since been adopted into other Internet technologies such as HTTP (*see* WORLD WIDE WEB). MIME specifies a set of standardized *type* and *subtype* pairings for messages and data, as well as structure for dividing a message into multiple sections, ghoulishly referred to as *body parts*. Each part is itself typed and subtyped on the basis of its data content. Standard encoding schemes, *base64* and *quoted-printable* for binary and 8-bit ASCII text, respectively, can be used on a per part basis, allowing an arbitrary number and mixture of data types to be encoded and added to a single message within organized boundaries in the message structure.

A Brief History of Email

Electronic mail began as a simple messaging scheme in the first time-sharing systems (CTSS at MIT, DTSS at Dartmouth) in the 1960s. A message sender would use a very simple interface to place messages in a file accessible by another user. That user could then read the messages directly from the file. It was not until after key elements of the Arpanet were created at Bolt, Beranek, and Newman (BBN) in 1969 that email messages were sent between different computers. This seminal event took place in 1971 during an experiment by Ray Tomlinson in a BBN lab.

That very simple experiment began an explosion that soon dominated the use of the Arpanet and its successor, the Internet. By 1973, three-quarters of all traffic on the Arpanet was email and Ray Tomlinson had gained both fame and notoriety as the inventor of today's standard *at sign* (@)-based email address. (The notoriety was due to early systems such as *Tenex*, which had difficulty with the @.) Other early networks such as UUCPnet and Bitnet quickly adopted email systems. Proprietary mail systems were developed mainly to work within a local area network (*q.v.*) for a university or company. The mid-1980s saw a period of competition between standards from the Internet community such as SMTP and OSI (*q.v.*) standards developed and backed by the International Organization for Standardization (ISO). The best example of such a standard is the *Message Handling System* (MHS), also known as *X.400*. Plagued by poor implementations, the OSI systems have all but disappeared. Today, MHS's legacy is perhaps best found in the influence of its better ideas in current Internet standards such as LDAP, the Lightweight Directory Access Protocol.

In the late 1990s, certain providers, such as *RocketMail* (`http://www.rocketmail.com`), began offering free email accounts used exclusively via the World Wide Web. These services, which provided new users with simple-to-use email and current users with additional accounts, allowed worldwide access to email for the price of a local phone call.

Bibliography

1994. Angell, D., and Heslop, B. *The Elements of Email Style: Communicate Effectively Via Electronic Mail.* Reading, MA: Addison-Wesley.
1995. Schneier, B. *Email Security: How to Keep Your Electronic Messages Private.* New York: John Wiley.
1997. Rhoton, J. *X.400 and SMTP: Battle of the Email Protocols.* Bedford, MA: Digital Press.
1998. Schwartz, A., and Garfinkel, S. *Stopping Spam.* Sebastopol, CA: O'Reilly & Associates.

Geoff Ralston, Katie Burke, David Nakayama, and Anand Tolani

E-MAIL OR EMAIL

See ELECTRONIC MAIL (EMAIL).

EMBEDDED SYSTEM

For articles on related subjects, see

+ Ada
+ Microcomputer Chip
+ Microprocessors and Microcomputers
+ Real-Time Systems

In computer science and engineering, an *embedded system* is one that is physically embedded within a larger system in order to achieve an overall objective. Embedded computers are now used in a wide variety of systems, such as aircraft, automobiles, appliances, weapons, medical devices, and toys. The vision of widespread use of embedded systems, or "computers in everything," is called *pervasive computing*. The related prediction of "computers everywhere" is called *ubiquitous computing* (*see* MOBILE COMPUTING).

The embedded computer reads data from sensors and provides commands to actuators in order to ensure that the goals of the overall system are achieved. It accomplishes this by maintaining some property or relationship among the components of the larger system at some specified value over time or by effecting some sequence of state changes over time.

Embedded systems have certain characteristics that complicate the process of constructing software:

Real-time–The correctness of the outputs is dependent not only on their value but also on their timing.
Reactive–The embedded computer interacts and responds to its environment.
Process control–The computer is responsible for monitoring and partially or completely controlling mechanical devices and physical processes.
Critical–There is usually a high-cost computer failure.

Embedded software requires a different type of development strategy than software in which the computer is at the center of the application. In the computer-centered system, peripheral equipment such as input, storage, and output devices are there to serve the needs of the computer. In the embedded system, the computer is used to service the needs of the other components; thus, its behavior and design is usually severely constrained by the external process being controlled.

In most computer systems, detecting that an error has occurred and aborting the affected transaction is usually satisfactory. The transaction can be rerun later. But in embedded systems, errors and failures must be dealt with immediately, and often the detection and recovery from errors must be automated. The computer must be *robust* even though other components of the system may fail. The Year 2000 (Y2K) problem was a particular threat to embedded systems since devices that failed at the onset of the millennium had to be recalled and replaced. Fortunately, there were very few instances of this.

Bibliography

1992. Ganssle, J. G. *The Art of Programming Embedded Systems*. New York: Academic Press.
1997. Heath, S. *Embedded Systems Design*. Oxford: Butterworth–Heinemann.
1997. Baron, C., Geffroy, J.-C., and Motet, G. (eds.) *Embedded System Applications*. New York: Kluwer Academic Press.

Nancy G. Leveson

EMULATION

For articles on related subjects, see

+ Firmware
+ Microprogramming
+ Read-Only Memory (ROM)
+ Simulation

Emulation is the ability of one digital computer to interpret and execute the instruction set of another. To see how, note first that the control unit of a computer contains sequences of *microinstructions*, one sequence for each operation code (op-code) in the machine's instruction set. These sequences are called *microprograms* or sometimes *macroinstructions*, the same term used at the assembly language level (*see* MACRO). The difference is that in the latter case, the instructions that comprise a macro are native machine-language instructions and in the former, they are microinstruction sequences. The control unit can consist of either *hard-wired logic* (i.e. special-purpose digital logic circuitry for each op-code) or *microprogrammed* control. On a machine with hard-wired logic, emulation in the sense of this article cannot be done. On a machine with microprogrammed control, macroinstructions are stored in read-only memory (ROM—*q.v.*) and thus can be modified through use of an alternative ROM.

Each microprogram in the control unit may simply be the macroinstruction that will perform one of the operations belonging to the instruction set normally associated with the particular model computer that hosts the microinstructions. Another possibility, however—and this is the essence of emulation—is to place a set of macroinstructions for a *different* computer into the hardware of the host computer, that is, one encodes the macroinstruction set of one computer by micro-programming those instructions in the hardware of another.

Emulation was common until the advent of operating systems and application programs written in portable high-level languages like C and C++ (*q.v.*). Once these were available, together with efficient compilers for them, software could be moved to new systems by recompilation, so emulation is now less important as a means of running old programs on new hardware.

Bibliography

1988. Habib, S. (ed.) *Microprogramming and Firmware Engineering*. New York: Van Nostrand Reinhold.

1989. Milutinovic, V. (ed.) *Introduction to Microprogramming*. Upper Saddle River, NJ: Prentice Hall.

Stanley Habib

ENCAPSULATION

For articles on related subjects, *see*

+ Abstract Data Type
+ Concurrent Programming
+ Information Hiding
+ Modular Programming
+ Object-Oriented Programming
+ Software Reusability

Encapsulation is a technique used to isolate some of the design decisions made in writing a program. To encapsulate decisions, a program is organized into an interface, such as a set of procedures, and an internal part. All access to the program's services is available only through the interface. As a result, programs that use those services cannot reference variables internal to the program or arbitrarily transfer control to its internal part.

Decisions that are typically encapsulated are the representation of data, the way that hardware facilities are accessed, and the way in which algorithms are implemented. A typical entity suitable for encapsulation is an abstract data type, such as a stack (*q.v.*). The program that manages physical changes to the stack provides the interface to it. Programs that merely use the stack (through execution of the familiar *push* and *pop* operations) cannot access the mechanisms and data structures used within the encapsulated stack manager and need have no knowledge of those data structures and their associated algorithms.

One reason for encapsulation is to provide a mechanism for information hiding. If, for example, the storage structure used to implement the abstract concept of a stack is changed to provide greater efficiency, the programs that use the stack have no need to know that the hidden structure was changed. The programs would, presumably, run more efficiently without their creators having to change a single line of source code.

Another reason to encapsulate is to enforce a particular access discipline—for example, using monitors to enforce access to critical sections of a program so that only one user program can gain access to such a section at the same time (*see* MONITOR, SYNCHRONIZATION). Encapsulation also provides compatibility among programs that are intended to be used together but which do not share resources, perhaps because they reside in different parts of a distributed system (*q.v.*). Standards for component programming require strict adherence to encapsulation rules for the sake of compatibility.

Bibliography

1988. Liskov, B. "Data Abstraction and Hierarchy," *Sigplan Notices*, **23**(5), 17–23.
1994. Booch, G. *Object-Oriented Analysis and Design with Applications*, 2nd Ed. Reading, MA: Addison-Wesley.

David Weiss

ENCRYPTION, DATA

See CRYPTOGRAPHY, COMPUTERS IN; and PRETTY GOOD PRIVACY (PGP).

ENIAC

For articles on related subjects, see

+ Digital Computers, History of
+ Eckert, J. Presper

The ENIAC (Electronic Numerical Integrator and Computer) was developed at the Moore School of the University of Pennsylvania in Philadelphia between 1943 and 1946 (*see* Fig. 1). It was the first electronic general-purpose automatic computer, and was a landmark leading to the development of many automatic computer designs. The logical design of the system was based on the ideas of John Mauchly and J. Presper Eckert who were granted a patent on the ENIAC in 1964. After a lengthy trial (Honeywell vs Sperry Rand), this patent

Figure 1. The ENIAC (courtesy of the Hagley Museum & Library).

was declared invalid on the grounds of public use and publication more than one year prior to the application date. (The ENIAC was demonstrated to the public in February 1946 and the patent application was filed in June 1947.)

The court also ruled that Eckert and Mauchly derived the subject matter of the patent from John V. Atanasoff. Whatever the provenance of ideas between Mauchly and Atanasoff, it seems clear that Charles Babbage (*q.v.*) invented the programmed mechanical general-purpose computer, that Atanasoff invented the automatic electronic computer (though his work was little known and made no contribution to the mainstream of computer development), and that the ENIAC was the first programmable general-purpose electronic computer.

The ENIAC contained more than 18 000 vacuum tubes, weighed 30 tons, and occupied a room 30 ft by 50 ft. The computer consisted of 20 electronic accumulators, multiplier control, divider and square root control, input, output, two function tables, and a master program control. Each accumulator could store, add, and subtract 10-decimal digit numbers. Two accumulators could be interconnected to perform 20-digit operations. Addition and subtraction took 200 μs. Multiplication involved six accumulators and took 2600 μs. Decimal digits were stored in 10-stage ring counters, and signed decimal numbers were transmitted in parallel over 11 lines. Each digit was represented during transmission by a train of 0 to 9 pulses. The clock rate was 100 KHz and pulse widths about 2 μs. All logic was accomplished with direct-coupled vacuum-tube circuitry.

As initially designed, programming was by patch panel interconnection, with a wire required for each event at each unit. The ENIAC was later converted to a card-programmed computer. In this scheme, certain standard operations were set up in the patch-panel wiring, and sequences of these macro (*q.v.*) operations were initiated from the card reader.

ENIAC was formally accepted a few months after its dedication by the US Army Ordnance Corps, but was still operated at the Moore School until late 1946, when it was dismantled and shipped to the Aberdeen Proving Ground in Maryland. It became operational again in 1947, and was operated until 2 October 1955. Portions of the ENIAC are now in the Smithsonian Institution in Washington, DC.

Bibliography

1981. Burks, A. W., and Burks, A. R. "The ENIAC: First General-purpose Electronic Computer," *Annals of the History of Computing*, **3**(4), (October), 310–399.

1981. Stern, N. *From ENIAC to UNIVAC*. Bedford, MA: Digital Press.

1996. *Annals of the History of Computing*, **18**(1), (January). Special issue devoted to ENIAC.

1999. McCartney, S. *ENIAC: The Triumphs and Tragedies of the World's First Computer*. New York: Walker.

Harry D. Huskey

ENTERTAINMENT INDUSTRY, COMPUTERS IN THE

For articles on related topics, *see*

+ Computer Animation
+ Computer Art
+ Computer Games
+ Computer Graphics
+ Image Processing
+ Multimedia
+ Videogames
+ Virtual Reality

Introduction

Computer technology has transformed entertainment. Television has grown more powerful because of computer assistance, providing multiple windows, programmed recording, digitally enhanced images, and even Internet (*q.v.*) access. Computer technology has also introduced digital audio and video technologies that provide higher quality recordings. Video cassette recorders have been replaced by laser disc players and digital video discs (DVDs), which allow real-time random access of data (*see* OPTICAL STORAGE). There are also any number of computer-controlled home videogames.

Computers in Feature Films

The design of any movie begins with previsualization and set design. By creating portions of the set on a computer, the director is able to look at it before it is built, test some possible stagings, and make changes. Matte paintings, which were historically hand-painted on huge canvases, are now created on computers and recorded directly onto film where they are integrated into the movie during compositing (combining several images into one). One of the best-known applications of computer technology in film is the creation of computer graphic imagery for special effects. In 1968, Stanley Kubrick's *2001: A Space Odyssey* reintroduced special visual effects to the motion picture industry, and in 1977 and again in 1999, George Lucas's *Star Wars* made such special effects a box office hit.

The design of visual effects begins with the *storyboard*. The storyboard is a visual reference of a proposed shot used by the filmmaking team. It is created from written descriptions in the script and conversations between the effects supervisor and the film's producer or director. It was traditionally hand-drawn by an artist and included background and effects elements. Storyboards often use elements that are scanned into a computer and combined digitally.

The production of visual effects has always used a few core techniques including *motion control, model building, animation*, and *compositing*. However, all these techniques have advanced dramatically since the introduction of computer technology. Motion control enables the filmmaker to move the camera in a precise, repeatable manner. Camera controls are computerized in order to record and playback complicated camera moves (Fig. 1). Using this repeatability, the filmmaker can record several distinct passes that can be combined during compositing to create one final image.

Traditional character and effects animation, such as the creation of lightning bolts, are usually drawn on animation cells (transparent plastic sheets) and filmed on an animation stand. Computer control of the animation stand provides the same advantages, repeatability and refinement of moves, as does motion control of stage cameras.

Puppet animation or *creature creation*, the building and animation of miniature synthetic characters, has also benefited from the introduction of computers. One of the great advances in creature work was the development of *go-motion photography* by Industrial Light and Magic, Inc. Go-motion is a refinement of

Figure 1. The Mark Roberts Motion Control "Milo" is a fast and highly portable motion control rig for both studio and location work. (Courtesy of Mark Roberts Motion Control.)

Figure 2. An example of stop-motion photography. A Close Shave © Aardman/Wallace & Gromit Ltd. 1995.

stop-motion photography (*see* Fig. 2), the process by which a model, puppet, or any object is filmed one frame at a time and moved slightly between frames by an animator. Go-motion differs from stop-motion in that the motion of the puppets is computer-controlled. However, it is still the artistic skill of the animator that creates the illusion of life.

Digital creature animation begins with the design of the character. This process has three parts: *modeling, enveloping*, and *texturing*. Modeling is the process of creating the shell, or shape, of the character. This shape might be simple (like a snowman) or complicated (like a human figure). Once the model is completed, it is handed off to an *enveloper* who ensures that it bends and moves in an expected way. For example, when the human arm bends, one expects that the skin will not crease or break apart but rather will gently stretch around the joint. This is accomplished by creating an inner skeleton for the model and attaching the two using varying weights and mathematical rules, or dynamics. The skeleton is never seen in the final images, but rather is used by the animator to control the motion of the creature. When the skeleton is completed and the model is moving logically, it is given to a texturer to create the look of the surface. For example, if the model is a spaceship, it may need several layers of texture, including the metal, painted decals, rust, dirt, and soot.

Computers in Television and Video

Computers are used in virtually all television content including flying logos, commercials, music videos, and television series production. Other uses of computer technology in television include weather presentation, digitally-assisted slow motion, interactive chalkboards, and news graphics. One of the most important uses of computers in video is the restoration and enhancement of classic movies. Unfortunately, film breaks down over time, leading to the loss of much of our film history. In response to this threat, several of the major studios in Hollywood have developed techniques to scan their classic movies onto digital media where they can be repaired, enhanced, and stored indefinitely without fear of erosion.

Computer Graphics

Computer graphics has revolutionized the entertainment industry (*see* Fig. 3). Examples range from the first video games like Pong, to Academy Award–winning animation like *Tin Toy* or *Toy Story* and Academy Award–winning visual effects as in *The Abyss* or *Jurassic Park*. Videogame graphics have increased in complexity and animation quality since their introduction. They were initially 2D and used the system

Figure 3. Cinesite (Europe) Ltd. modeled, animated, and tracked a "talking" muzzle onto a live action dog for *Animal Farm*. The modeling and animation were completed using Alias/Wavefront's Maya and the compositing of the new muzzle was completed using Kodak's Cineon Software. (© Hallmark Entertainment/Cinesite. Reproduced by permission of Hallmark Entertainment.)

to draw small prestored images on the screen. As the technology developed, modern computer games became interactive stories, allowing the player to see, hear, and interact in real time with a synthetic 3D world.

Traditional film animation has also been revolutionized by computer graphics. The drawing, in-betweening, inking, and opaquing of 2D drawings, previously done entirely by hand, used to be very expensive because of the large number of people required. Almost all inking, opaquing, compositing, and special animation effects are now done on computers.

3D computer animation is similar to 2D animation in the creation of keyframes or keyshapes that are "in-betweened" by the computer, but it is different in that computer models are built and animated, and a *synthetic digital camera* generates the resulting images. The computer models used range from simple spheres and logos to complex models of working machinery, animals, and even people.

Computer graphics in television runs the gamut from high-end effects and commercials through corporate logos and station identifications to low-end "visuals." Developing technology is continually revolutionizing the look of what we see. The development of workstations and more powerful PCs has assisted the development of more realistic imagery.

Current uses of computer graphics range from the hidden, such as with some digital compositing, reduction of film grain, and removal of dirt, scratches, and unwanted objects from a scene to the generation of digital creatures (*see* ARTIFICIAL LIFE), environments, and even entirely computer-generated feature films.

Bibliography

1989. Bernard, W. *The Technique of Special Effects in Television*, 2nd Ed. New York: Focal Press/Hastings House.

1997. De Leeuw, B. *Digital Cinematography*. New York: Academic Press/Morgan Kaufmann.

Scott E. Anderson and Lindy L. Wilson

ERROR CORRECTING AND DETECTING CODE

For articles on related subjects, *see*

+ Codes
+ Parity

Error-detecting and *error-correcting codes* are essential parts of most forms of digital communication and storage. Proper operation of the Internet (*q.v.*), modems (*q.v.*), compact discs (*see* OPTICAL STORAGE), and computers would be impossible without them. Codes introduce redundant bits into a data stream so that transmission errors in the original data bits can be detected and sometimes corrected.

The best-known error code is the simple parity check that uses a single redundant bit and can detect an odd number of errors in a group of bits. In interactive communication, such as the Internet, it is often sufficient to detect errors, and then to request retransmission of the data. In other situations, such as data storage on a compact disc, rereading erroneous data from the disc frequently results in the same error, so the errors must be corrected before use even though the disc itself cannot be.

A simplified coding scheme is shown in Fig. 1. In this type of coding (called *block coding*) a group of k data bits are read into the encoder, which then produces a corresponding n-bit code word with $n > k$. There are 2^k possible k-bit patterns at the input, and 2^k corresponding n-bit code words. This collection of possible code words is called a *code*. Since it can produce only 2^k out of the 2^n possible n-bit patterns, the encoder introduces redundancy into the data stream. The *code rate*, defined as the ratio of k to n, is a measure of this redundancy. As an example, consider a "repetition" code that simply repeats each input bit 3 times. A 1 is encoded as 111, and a zero is encoded as 000. For this code, $n = 3$ and $k = 1$. Only 2 out of the 8 possible 3-bit patterns are used as code words. The code rate of 1/3 indicates that only one-third of the bits contain data; the other 2/3 of

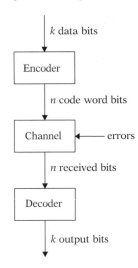

Figure 1.   Encoding/decoding.

the bits are redundant in that they can be constructed using the data.

After the n bits are transmitted and received, they may contain one or more errors. If the bit pattern received by the decoder matches a code word, then with high probability there were no errors. If the received bit pattern does not match a code word, then the decoder determines that one or more bits are in error. It may request retransmission (if only error detection is being used) or try to decide which code word was actually sent (if error-correction is being used).

For the above repetition code, if 111 is received, the decoder would decide that no errors have occurred, and output data bit 1. It is possible, although unlikely, that three errors were present and the transmitted code word was 000. Such an error event would escape detection. If the received bit pattern were 010, the decoder would signal an error. It could also try to correct this error by noting that, since two of the three received bits are 0, it is more likely that the code word was 000 than 111.

The ability of a decoder to detect errors depends upon the number of bit positions in which code words differ. In the repetition code, the code words 000 and 111 differ in three bit positions. This is called the *Hamming distance* between the code words and indicates that it would take three errors to change 000 into 111. The minimum distance, d, for a code is the minimum Hamming distance between all pairs of code words in the code, and gives the smallest number of errors that can change one code word into another. For the above repetition code there are only two code words, so the minimum distance, d, is three. In general, a code with minimum distance d that uses n-bit code words is capable of detecting up to $d - 1$ errors and correcting up to $\lfloor (d - 1)/2 \rfloor$ errors in each n bits received.

Powerful error detection or correction involves finding codes with large minimum distance, which implies a large code word size, n. Similarly, for any given minimum distance, d, using long code words can increase the code rate. For example, a single-bit parity-check code has a minimum distance of 2 so that it can detect one error. The code rate for a parity check code can be made closer to 1 by increasing the code word size.

A family of codes developed by Richard Hamming has a particularly elegant choice of parity checks that simplifies error correction. A parity check is assigned to those positions in the code that have a 1 in the rightmost position of their binary representation, a second parity check for those positions that have a 1 in their second to right position, and so on. Thus, when a single error does occur, exactly those parity checks will fail for which the binary expansion of the position of the error has 1s. Thus, the pattern of the parity-check failures points directly to the position of the error. In a binary system of signaling, it is easy to change that bit to its opposite value and thus correct the error. When there are no errors, all the parity checks will succeed.

Codes used in practice often add even more structure to simplify encoding and decoding. Linear codes have the property that the bitwise mod 2 sum of any two code words is also a code word. Cyclic codes have the property that any cyclic shift of a code word is also a code word. These properties allow encoding and decoding using high-speed shift register circuits. Shortened versions of cyclic codes are used to form the *cyclic redundancy check* (CRC) codes that are commonly used in data transmission hardware. Other important classes of cyclic codes include the Golay, Reed–Solomon, and BCH (Bose–Ray-Chaudhuri–Hocquenghem) codes. Computer protocols such as TCP/IP (*q.v.*) use a different approach to generate redundant checkbits (called the Internet checksum) based upon 1s complement addition. This method is not as powerful as CRC codes, but is easier to implement in software.

Reed–Solomon codes are among the most powerful codes known, and can be efficiently decoded. They have been used in applications as diverse as compact discs and deep space communication. In applications such as the compact disc, where burst errors are especially important to detect and correct, interleavers are used to disperse the bits from one code word over a long portion of the data stream. When the data stream is deinterleaved, the burst of errors will appear as a large number of code words each with one correctable error. The combination of interleaving and two Reed–Solomon codes used in compact discs can correct bursts of over 4000 errors.

Bibliography

1968. Berlekamp, E., Jr. *Algebraic Coding Theory*. New York: McGraw-Hill.

1977. MacWilliams, F., and Sloane, N. J. A. *The Theory of Error Correcting Codes*. Amsterdam: Elsevier.

1977. McEliece, R. J. *The Theory of Information and Coding*. Reading, MA: Addison-Wesley.

Richard Hamming and John M. Spinelli

ETHERNET

For articles on related subjects, *see*

+ Cable Modem
+ Communications and Computers
+ Fiber Optics
+ Internet
+ Local Area Network (LAN)
+ Networks, Computer
+ Network Protocols
+ TCP/IP

Ethernet is the most widely used local area network (LAN) technology and is likely to remain so for the foreseeable future. Since its invention in the mid-1970s, it has evolved to the point that now it supports data transmission rates of 10, 100, and even 1000 million bits per second (Mbps); bus or star topologies; and multiple transmission media such as coaxial cable, unshielded twisted pairs, and single or multimode optical fibers.

History

Ethernet was developed by Robert Metcalfe and David Boggs at Xerox PARC to interconnect a number of desktop computers and laser printers at a data transmission rate of 2.94 Mbps. It was so successful that in 1980, Xerox, Digital Equipment Corporation, and Intel published the specifications for a 10-Mbps Ethernet. These specifications formed the basis for the IEEE 802.3 standard released in 1983. There now exist a number of 802.3 standards defining Ethernets that support different network topologies operating at various transmission rates over a variety of physical transmission media. Despite these differences, all Ethernet standards share several important characteristics, including a common frame or packet structure and a common multiple access protocol called *Carrier Sense Multiple Access/Collision Detect* (CSMA/CD).

Ethernet Frame Format

The format of an Ethernet frame or packet is as follows:

Preamble (7 bytes)
Start frame delimiter (1 byte)
Destination address (6 bytes)
Source address (6 bytes)
Length/type (2 bytes)
Client data (0–1500 bytes)
Optional pad characters (0–46 bytes)
Check sequence (4 bytes)

A frame consists of a preamble of 7 bytes (56 bits) having alternating 1 and 0 values that are used for synchronization among distributed computers on a LAN. The frame delimiter is a special character with a 10101011 bit configuration that indicates the start of the frame, and is followed by the destination and source addresses, a length or type field, the data itself, optional pad characters, and a check sequence (cyclic redundancy check–*q.v.*) for the detection of errors during transmission. If the value of the length/type field is 1500 or less, it indicates the number of bytes in the data field. If it is equal to or greater than 1536, then this field indicates the protocol type being used, which allows Ethernet to support multiple protocols such as TCP/IP or IPX for Novell networks. If necessary, optional pad characters are added to the data field to ensure that the shortest Ethernet frame length is 64 bytes. Originally, the largest frame size was 1518 bytes. In 1998, the IEEE 802.3ac standard increased the maximum frame size to 1522 bytes to allow a VLAN tag to be inserted into the frame between the source address and length fields to support the concept of Virtual Local Area Networks (VLANs) that help ease network administration, enhance network security, and limit the size of broadcast domains.

Ethernet Physical Transmission Media Specifications

The original version of Ethernet operated at 2.94 Mbps and used a thick coaxial cable (about 0.5 inches in diameter) as the physical transmission medium to which all devices were attached. Since that time, it has evolved to include speeds of 10, 100, and 1000 Mbps, as well as a variety of transmission media including thin coaxial cable, twisted copper pairs, and optical fibers, with the latter two supporting star topologies, rather than the linear bus topologies used for coaxial cables. To keep better track of the possible combinations, the IEEE classifies Ethernet using a code of the form ⟨speed⟩ ⟨basebandorbroadband⟩ ⟨physicalmedium⟩. The first part indicates the speed in million bits per second, while the second part indicates whether baseband or broadband transmission is used. In baseband transmission, only one device can transmit at a time and the entire bandwidth (*q.v.*) of the medium is available for transmission. In broadband transmission, the bandwidth of the medium is divided into two or more different channels, each with its unique frequency band, to allow the support of multiple simultaneous transmissions over a single cable. Cable modems, for

example, use broadband transmission. The third part, physical medium, is either a number, in which case it refers to the longest allowable Ethernet segment length in hundreds of meters, or a letter used to denote a particular transmission medium. For example, 10Base5 refers to 10-Mbps baseband transmission using a thick coaxial cable whose maximum segment length is 500 m, 100BaseT refers to 100-Mbps baseband transmission using unshielded twisted pairs, while 1000BaseSX refers to 1000-Mbps baseband transmission (Gigabit Ethernet) using a short wavelength laser over two multinode fibers.

Bibliography

1976. Metcalfe, R. M., and Boggs, D. R. "Ethernet: Distributed Packet Switching for Local Computer Networks," *Communications of the ACM*, **19**(7), 395–404.

1997. Keshav, S. *An Engineering Approach to Computer Networking.* Reading, MA: Addison-Wesley.

John S. Sobolewski

EXCEPTION HANDLING

For articles on related subjects, see

✛ Control Structures
✛ Interrupt
✛ Software Engineering

Exception handling deals with mechanisms and techniques for detecting, recovering from, and dealing with errors that arise during program execution. Exception handling techniques are used by programmers to make programs *robust*. Exceptions arise when illegal operations are requested or operation operands are inappropriate. For example, dividing by zero will cause an error in almost all systems. Robust programs deal gracefully with exceptions, whereas fragile programs stop or produce erroneous results when exceptions are encountered.

All exception systems have certain concepts in common. An exceptional condition must first be *detected* or *recognized*. Once an exception is known, it must be *thrown*, or *raised*. Throwing or raising an exception involves gathering information about the exception and searching for an exception handler, which may be a standard of the language or user-defined. If an exception handler is found, it is invoked with the exception information. When invoked, the exception handler can execute some programmatic action to recover from or ameliorate the exception. The exception at this point is said to have been *caught* or *handled*. By their nature, exception handlers must be associated with the exceptional condition before an exception occurs and are typically found by searching in the dynamic context of the execution control stack (*see* ACTIVATION RECORD and STACK). If no handler is found, the language run-time system takes some default action, usually terminating the program and posting some diagnostic in a standard location.

Bibliography

1996. Gosling, J., Joy, B., and Steele, G. L. *The Java Language Specification*. Reading, MA: Addison-Wesley.
1999. Sebesta, R. W. *Concepts of Programming Languages*, 4th Ed. Reading, MA: Addison-Wesley.

James C. Spohrer and Ken Dickey

EXECUTABLE STATEMENT

For articles on related subjects, see

+ Declaration
+ Procedure-Oriented Languages

An *executable statement* is a procedural step in a high-level imperative programming language that calls for processing action by the computer, such as performing arithmetic, reading data, making a decision, and so on. It is convenient to distinguish between executable and nonexecutable language statements (*declarations*) that provide information about the nature of the data or about the way the processing is to be done without themselves causing any processing action. Executable statements are sometimes called *imperative* statements because their form closely resembles that of an imperative sentence in a natural language. For example, the formula $y = a + bx + cx^2$ follows an imperative form that persists in corresponding structures in programming language statements:

```
Pascal    y := a + b * x + c * x * x
Fortran   Y = A + B * X + C * X ** 2
C++       y = a + b * x + c * pow(x,2);
```

Specifications for data transmission between internal storage and an external medium are constructed along similar lines:

```
Fortran   READ (5,12) HERE
          WRITE (6,21) HERE
Cobol     READ INFILE INTO HERE.
          WRITE OUTFILE FROM HERE.
C++       cin >> here;
          cout << here;
```

The numerical specifications in the Fortran example are coded references to additional information about the source (for input), destination (for output), and format of the data to be transmitted. The "c" in the cin and cout of C++ stands for "console."

Sometimes, executable statements are subdivided into imperative and conditional statements because the latter, such as the "if" statement in C++, specify alternative imperative actions linked through a decision mechanism. A language implementation may have rules about the relative placement of executable and nonexecutable statements. Older languages require all declarations to appear before a program's first executable statement, but newer languages require only that they appear before their first use. Cobol requires total separation of executable statements (in the *Procedure* division) from nonexecutable statements (in the *Environment* and *Data* divisions).

In C and C++, function and method declarations and global variables are usually placed in a *header file*, so that they can be imported into any compilation unit requiring them. In this manner, C and C++ distinguish between a function or method's declaration (the number and type of its parameters) and its definition, which contains executable statements.

Seymour V. Pollack and Ron K. Cytron

EXECUTION TIME

See COMPILE AND RUN TIME.

EXECUTIVE

See OPERATING SYSTEMS.

EXPERT SYSTEMS

For articles on related subjects, *see*

+ Artificial Intelligence (AI)
+ Knowledge Representation

An *expert system* (ES) is a computer program that *reasons*, using *knowledge*, to solve complex problems. Traditionally, computers have solved complex problems by arithmetic calculation (not logical reasoning), and the knowledge needed to solve the problem is known only by the human programmer and is used to cast the solution in terms of an algorithm (*q.v.*). With expert systems, such human knowledge is captured and embedded explicitly within the program.

Principles and Technology

One approach to understanding the principles of expert systems is to trace the history of the emergence of ES within Artificial Intelligence (AI). Perhaps AI's most widely shared early goal had been the construction of extremely intelligent computers. That

is, in addition to other goals (such as learning and language understanding), most researchers shared a goal to produce programs that performed at or beyond human levels of competence. For example, an early (late 1950s) program took the New York State Regents Examination in plane geometry to validate its human-level abilities in this domain. In the late 1950s, leading AI researchers also predicted that an AI program would be the chess champion of the world within 10 years. (If one accepts Deep Blue's victory over Garry Kasparov as significant, it took about 40; *see* COMPUTER CHESS.)

In the early 1960s, the focus of AI shifted from performance to generality—how one problem-solving mechanism can solve a wide variety of problems. The best-known AI efforts of the time were the *general problem solvers*, both heuristic programs and theorem provers, but the actual problems they were able to solve were very simple "toy" problems; that is, the programs had high generality but low power.

In 1965, Feigenbaum, Lederberg, and Buchanan at Stanford initiated a project in modeling scientific reasoning for which the goal of high performance was once again given prominence. The task of this program, called *DENDRAL*, was to interpret the mass spectrum of an organic molecule in terms of a hypothesis as to its structure. The intent was that the program be able to perform the difficult mass spectral analysis task at the level of competence of specialists in that area. As it turned out, AI problem-solving methods were useful, but not sufficient. More important was knowledge of chemistry and mass spectroscopy.

The knowledge that DENDRAL needed was provided by scientists of the Stanford Mass Spectrometry Laboratory in an intense collaboration with the AI scientists. Such efforts at codifying the knowledge of specialists for use in expert systems later came to be called *knowledge engineering*. The first use of the term *expert* in connection with such programs was made in an article analyzing the generality vs power issue in light of the results of DENDRAL experiments. Thus, DENDRAL was the progenitor of the class of programs subsequently called *expert systems*.

Transfer of ES Technology into Practice

In the late 1970s, the two best-known industrial applications were XCON from Digital Equipment Corporation (DEC) and the Dipmeter Adviser from Schlumberger Ltd. XCON's task was the configuration under constraints of a DEC minicomputer (*q.v.*) from a large number of component subassemblies. The configuration task was done so fast and so accurately by XCON that DEC saved millions of dollars per year in manufacturing and sales operations. XCON configured minicomputers about 300 times faster than human engineers.

Schlumberger's Dipmeter Adviser (DA) is typical of programs that analyze streams of data and propose hypotheses to account for and explain the data. DA interprets the data taken from instruments lowered into bore holes during the search for oil and gas. It offers hypotheses about the tilt, or "dip," of the rock layers far beneath the earth's surface. Knowing the dip of each of the hundreds of rock layers in a bore hole is valuable in oil exploration.

The use of an ES to improve the quality of human decisions was the motive behind the Authorizer's Assistant (AA) of American Express. To assist a human authorizer with the decision to allow or disallow a particular charge, the AA analyzes a large amount of customer data from the company's database files. AA then issues a recommendation, offers the rationale for it, and gives the human authorizer a screen of data that supports the recommendation. The payoff in avoiding bad debt and fraud amounts to millions of dollars per year, a result of the high quality and consistency of the AA decisions.

Expert System Technology

Every expert system consists of two principal parts: the *knowledge base* and the *reasoning* or *inference engine*. The knowledge base contains both factual and heuristic knowledge. The factual knowledge is that knowledge widely shared in the domain and commonly agreed upon by experts. The heuristic knowledge is the nonrigorous experiential knowledge, the rules-of-thumb, the knowledge of good judgment. Heuristics constitutes the "art of good guessing." *Knowledge representation* formalizes and organizes the knowledge for use by the inference engine. One widely used representational form is the *production rule*, or simply the *rule*. A rule consists of an IF part and a THEN part (also called a *condition* and an *action*). The IF part lists a set of conditions in some logical combination. The piece of knowledge represented by the rule is relevant to the line of reasoning being developed. Expert systems whose knowledge is represented in rule form are called *rule-based systems*, and representations of this kind are said to be *action-oriented*.

Another widely used representational form, called the *unit*, or *frame*, or *schema*, is based on a more passive object-oriented view of knowledge. Systems of units (sometimes called *frame-based systems*) are siblings of the object-oriented systems common in computer science (*see* OBJECT-ORIENTED PROGRAMMING). Typically, a unit consists of a symbolic name, a list of attributes of some entity, and the values associated with the attributes. That is, the unit is a complex symbolic description of an entity that the ES needs to know about. There is a *knowledge base management system*, akin to a database management system (DBMS–*q.v.*), associated with the units. One of its important functions is to handle automatically some routine inference functions for knowledge updating and knowledge propagation. The automatic handling is called *inheritance* (i.e. changes to attributes of a unit are automatically applied to all subunits and instances of that unit).

In every expert system, the *inference engine* (embodying the problem-solving method or procedure) uses the knowledge base to construct the line of reasoning leading to the solution of the problem. The most common method involves chaining of IF–THEN rules. If the chaining starts from a set of conditions and moves toward some (possibly remote) conclusion, the method is called *forward chaining*. If the conclusion is known (e.g. it is a goal to be achieved) but the path to that conclusion is not known, then *backward chaining* with rules is employed, seeking conditions under which a particular line of reasoning will be true.

Bibliography

1986. Waterman, D. A. *A Guide to Expert Systems*. Reading, MA: Addison-Wesley.

1988. Feigenbaum, E., McCorduck, P., and Nii, H. P. *The Rise of the Expert Company*. New York: Times Books.

1995. Stefik, M. *Introduction to Knowledge Systems*. San Francisco: Morgan Kaufmann.

Edward A. Feigenbaum and Philip Klahr

EXPRESSION

For articles on related subjects, *see*

+ Backus–Naur Form (BNF)
+ Coercion
+ Functional Programming
+ Operator Precedence
+ Procedure-Oriented Languages: programming
+ Statement

An *expression*, in high-level language syntax, is a character sequence that specifies a rule for calculating a value. That value may be either numeric, as in the C++ (*q.v.*) expression a+6, or alphanumeric, as in the Basic (*q.v.*) expression LEFT$(A$,5) (whose value is the leftmost 5 characters of string A$). An expression may appear to the right of the replacement symbol (usually = or := or ←) in statement-oriented languages such as Pascal (*q.v.*) or Fortran (*q.v.*), or may stand alone and be evaluated immediately to yield a particular value in expression-oriented languages such as Lisp (*q.v.*) or APL (*q.v.*).

A *statement-oriented language* is one in which sentence-like statements calculate and save intermediate values but (except for specific I/O statements) do not print them. In Pascal, for example, the statement p := a*b+c is composed of an *identifier* (variable name) p, a *replacement symbol*, :=, and the *expression* a*b+c. Such an expression makes sense to the Pascal compiler if all of its identifiers have been previously declared as to type (real, integer, etc.) and if it is *well-formed* according to the grammatical rules of the language.

An *expression-oriented language* is one in which expressions may stand alone such that when encountered during program flow, their values are calculated and printed immediately. Thus, if the expression 3+4 is presented to APL at an interactive terminal session, APL will respond immediately by outputting 7.

An expression that is valid in one high-level language might be invalid in another or, even if valid, produce a different result. Thus, a**b is a valid Fortran expression, but is not valid in Pascal, which does not have an exponentiation operator. The uppercase equivalent of the expression A*B+C would be acceptable to APL, but would have an entirely different meaning in APL because of different interpretations of the * operator (multiplication in Pascal, exponentiation in APL) and different operator precedence. To obtain the same meaning, the APL programmer would write $(A \times B)+C$ or $C+A \times B$ and the Lisp programmer would write (PLUS (TIMES A B) C) because that language uses a fully-parenthesized prefix notation.

Expressions may also be classified as being either *homogeneous* (all constituents of the same type) or *mixed-mode*. An example of the latter is A+J*Z where, perhaps, A has been declared as being real (floating-point), J as being integer, and Z as being complex. What should be done? Early dialects of Fortran declared such expressions syntactically illegal and refused to process them. Almost all current languages accept mixed-mode expressions whenever reasonable type conversions can be inferred (e.g. automatic conversion of A and J to complex prior to evaluation of the cited expression), which allow calculation to proceed (*see* COERCION).

An expression may be very simple as well as complicated. In most languages, the single digit 7 or the single-letter variable Q are valid expressions. Thus, the Pascal statement

k := 3*a + b[round(j + sqrt(x))], contains 10 recognizable expressions:

1-4. `3`, `a`, `j`, and `x` are expressions.

5. `3*a` is an expression.

6. The function `sqrt(x)` is an expression.

7. `j + sqrt(x)` is an expression.

8. The subscript `round(j + sqrt(x))` is an expression.

9. The subscripted variable

```
b[round(j + sqrt(x))]
```

is an expression.

10. The entire right-hand side is an expression.

Since complex expressions may be built up recursively from simpler ones, the rules for recognizing a well-formed (syntactically valid) expression in any given language may be stated quite rigorously in a notation such as Backus–Naur Form (BNF–*q.v.*).

Bibliography

1973. Wirth, N. *Systematic Programming: An Introduction.* Upper Saddle River, NJ: Prentice Hall.

1996. Pratt, T. W., and Zelkowitz, M. V. *Programming Languages: Design and Implementation*, 3rd Ed, 123–136. Upper Saddle River, NJ: Prentice Hall.

Edwin D. Reilly

EXTENSIBLE LANGUAGE

For articles on related subjects, *see*

+ Ada
+ Data Type
+ Macro
+ Operator Overloading
+ Object-Oriented Programming
+ Procedure-Oriented Languages
+ Programming Languages

An *extensible* (programming) *language* allows the user to enrich the language by introducing new features or by modifying existing ones. A language is called *extensible* if the new features can be made to resemble the built-in language constructs. Extensible languages should be distinguished from the *ad hoc* extensions made to many programming languages by introducing features not present in the language standard.

In one respect, any programming language that has subprograms (*q.v.*) is extensible, since the programmer can define new operations as functions or procedures. Subprograms generally do not resemble built-in operations; however, a call to a vector-addition subprogram might be `vec_sum(v1, v2, vsum)`, rather than `vsum := v1 + v2`. Normally extensibility refers to the ability to introduce new language elements that are used like existing ones.

Assembly language macros (*q.v.*) were the first language extensions. Introduced in 1960, they permitted a programmer to define a new instruction by giving a name to a sequence of assembly-language instructions. Among high-level languages, Algol 68 gave programmers the ability to give names to data types and to use them in subsequent variable declarations, as in this definition, and use of a data type *point* to specify an ordered pair of reals:

```
mode point = struct(real x, y);
real a, point u, v;
```

Algol 68 also allowed a programmer to declare new operators so that, for example, one might define `--` to be a *distance* operator that would take two points and return the Euclidean distance between them. The programmer could then write `a := u -- v` rather than `a := distance(u,v)`. Ada (*q.v.*), C++ (*q.v.*), and other object-oriented languages also provide this capability. To benefit fully from it, a language must allow *operator overloading* (*q.v.*), giving new meanings to old ones, as Ada and C++ do. Then one can define, say, vector addition as a new meaning of the + operator, rather than invent a new notation.

Several programming languages in the early 1970s were designed to support extensibility: EL1 (Extensible Language 1), GPL (General Purpose Language), and

PPL (Polymorphic Programming Language) were three of them. Forth is now the most commonly used extensible language.

Bibliography

1975. Standish, T. A. "Extensibility in Programming Language Design," *Sigplan Notices*, **10**(7), (July), 18–21.

1976. Melkanoff, M. A. "Extensible Programming Languages," in *Formal Languages and Programming* (ed. R. Aguilar), Amsterdam: North-Holland, 31–41.

1999. Harold, E. R. *XML Bible*. Foster City, CA: IDG Books.

David Hemmendinger

FAULT-TOLERANT COMPUTING

For articles on related subjects, *see*

+ Cluster Computing
+ Distributed Systems
+ Error Correcting and Detecting Code
+ Redundant Array of Inexpensive Disks (RAID)

Fault-tolerant computing relates to computing systems that continue to operate satisfactorily in the presence of faults. A fault-tolerant system may be able to tolerate one or more fault types, including (1) transient, intermittent, or permanent hardware faults, (2) software and hardware design errors, (3) operator errors, or (4) externally induced upsets or physical damage.

Basic Concepts

Hardware Fault Tolerance

The majority of fault-tolerant designs have been directed toward building computers that automatically recover from random faults occurring in hardware components. The techniques employed generally involve partitioning a computing system into modules that act as fault-containment regions. Each module is backed up with protective redundancy so that, if the module fails, others can assume its function. Special mechanisms are added to detect errors and implement recovery. Two general approaches to hardware fault recovery have been used, fault masking and dynamic recovery.

Fault masking uses structural redundancy to completely masks faults within a set of redundant modules. A number of identical modules execute the same functions, and their outputs are voted to remove errors created by a faulty module. With triple modular redundancy (TMR), circuitry is triplicated and voted. A TMR system fails whenever two modules in a redundant triplet create errors so that the vote is no longer valid. Hybrid redundancy is an extension of TMR in which the triplicated modules are backed up with additional spares that are used to replace faulty modules. Voted systems require more than three times as much hardware as nonredundant systems, but they have the advantage that computations can continue without interruption when a fault occurs.

Dynamic recovery is required when only one copy of a computation is running at a time, and it involves automated self-repair. As in fault masking, the computing system is partitioned into modules backed up by spares as protective redundancy. In the case of dynamic recovery, however, special mechanisms are required to detect faults in the modules, switch out a faulty module, switch in a spare, and instigate those software actions (rollback, initialization, retry, restart) necessary to restore and continue the computation. Dynamic recovery is generally more hardware-efficient than voted systems, and it is therefore the approach of choice in resource-constrained (e.g. low-power) systems, and especially in high-performance scalable systems in which the amount of hardware resources devoted to active computing must be maximized.

Software Fault Tolerance

Efforts to attain software that can tolerate software design faults (programming errors) have made use of static and dynamic redundancy approaches similar to those used for hardware faults. One such approach, *N*-version programming, uses static redundancy in the form of independently written programs (versions) that perform the same functions, and their outputs are voted at special checkpoints. An approach called *design diversity* combines hardware and software fault-tolerance by implementing a fault-tolerant computer system using different hardware *and* software in redundant channels. This is a very expensive technique, but it is used in very critical aircraft control applications.

History

The SAPO relay computer, built in Prague, the Czech Republic in 1950–1954 under the supervision of A. Svoboda, was the first fault-tolerant computer. The processor used triplication and voting (TMR), and the drum memory implemented error detection with automatic retries when an error was detected. A second machine developed by the same group (EPOS) also contained comprehensive fault tolerance features.

Long-Life, Unmaintainable Computers

Applications such as spacecraft require computers to operate for long periods of time without external repair. Typical requirements are a probability of 95% that the computer will operate correctly for 5–10 years. Machines of this type are typically constrained to low power, weight, and volume. NASA was an early sponsor of fault-tolerant computing. In the 1960s, the first fault-tolerant machine to be developed and flown was the on-board computer for the Orbiting Astronomical Observatory (OAO), which used fault masking at the component (transistor) level.

The JPL Self-Testing-and-Repairing (STAR) computer was NASA's next fault-tolerant computer, developed in the late 1960s for a 10-year mission to the outer planets. The STAR computer, designed under the leadership of A. Avizienis, was the first computer to employ dynamic recovery throughout its design. Various modules of the computer were instrumented to detect internal faults and signal fault conditions to a special test and repair processor that effected reconfiguration and recovery.

Ultradependable Real-Time Computers

These are computers for which an error or delay can prove to be catastrophic. They are designed for applications such as control of aircraft, mass transportation systems, and nuclear power plants. The applications justify massive investments in redundant hardware, software, and testing. One of the first operational machines of this type was the Saturn V guidance computer, developed in the 1960s. It contained a TMR processor and duplicated memories. Processor errors were masked by voting, and a memory error was circumvented by reading from the other memory.

High-Availability Computers

The most widely used fault-tolerant computer systems developed during the 1960s were in electronic switching systems (ESS) that are used in telephone switching offices. The first of these AT&T machines, No. 1 ESS, had a goal of no more than two hours downtime in 40 years. The computers are duplicated to detect errors, with some dedicated hardware and extensive software used to identify faults and effect replacement.

The largest commercial success in fault-tolerant computing has been in the area of transaction processing for banks, airline reservations, and so on. The design approach is a distributed system using a sophisticated form of duplication. For each running process, there is a backup process running on a different computer. The primary process is responsible for checkpointing its state to duplex disks. If it should fail, the backup process can restart from the last checkpoint.

The *server* market represents a new and rapidly growing market for fault-tolerant machines driven by the growth of the Internet and local networks and their needs for uninterrupted service. Many major server manufacturers offer systems that contain redundant processors, disks, and power supplies, and automatically switch to backups if a failure is detected. Examples are Sun's ft-Sparc and the HP/Stratus Continuum 400. Other vendors are working on fault-tolerant cluster technology where other machines in a network can take over the tasks of a failed machine. An example is the Microsoft MSCS technology.

Bibliography

1990. *Computer* (Special Issue on Fault-Tolerant Computing), **23**(7), (July).

1998. Kropp, N. P., Koopman, P. J., and Siewiorek, D. P. "Automated Robustness Testing of Off-The-Shelf Software Components," *Proc. 28th International Symposium on Fault-Tolerant Computing, FTCS 28*, Munich.

1998. Spainhower, L., and Gregg, T. A. "G4: A Fault-Tolerant CMOS Mainframe," *Proc. 28th International Symposium on Fault-Tolerant Computing, FTCS 28*, Munich.

David A. Rennels

FIBER OPTICS

For articles on related subjects, *see*

+ Bandwidth
+ Multiplexing
+ Networks, Computer

Optical fibers are thin, flexible strands of clear glass or plastic that can serve as a transmission medium capable of carrying up to several gigabits per second over short or long distances. They perform the same basic functions as copper wires or coaxial cables, but they transmit light instead of electrical signals. An optical fiber transmitter uses a light-emitting or laser diode to convert electrical information signals to light signals while the receiver uses a photodiode to convert the light back into electrical signals. Optical repeaters are needed to regenerate light signals for links that exceed their distance limitations.

Optical fibers offer so many distinct advantages that they are rapidly replacing older transmission media in applications ranging from telephony to computers and automated factories. These advantages include large bandwidth, low attenuation loss, immunity to electromagnetic interference, and small size and weight. The major disadvantages of fibers are that they are more difficult to work with than the more conventional twisted pairs or coaxial cables.

Types of Fibers

Optical fibers are made of plastic, glass, or silica. Plastic fibers are the least efficient, but tend to be cheaper and more rugged. Glass or silica fibers are much smaller, and their lower attenuation makes them more suited for very high capacity channels. The basic optical fiber consists of two concentric layers—the inner core and the outer cladding, which has a refractive index smaller than that of the core. The characteristics of light propagation depend primarily on the fiber size, its construction, the refractive index profile, and the nature of the light source.

The two main types of refractive index profiles are *step* and *graded*. In a step index fiber, the core has a uniform refractive index n_1 with a distinct change to a lower index, n_2, for the cladding. Multimode step index fibers usually have a core diameter of 0.05 to 1.0 mm. With a light source such that the light injected always strikes the core-to-cladding interface at an angle greater than the critical angle, the light is reflected back into the core. Since the angles of incidence and reflection are equal, the light continues to propagate down the core of the fiber in a zigzag fashion by total internal reflection, as shown in Fig. 1(a). In effect, the light is trapped in the core and the cladding not only provides protection to the core, but may be thought of as the "insulation" that prevents the light from escaping. A narrow pulse of light has a tendency to spread as it travels down the fiber, an effect known as *modal dispersion*. Fibers with high modal dispersions tend to be used over short to medium distances. Modal dispersion can be reduced by using graded index fibers, as shown in Fig. 1(c).

As in the case of electrical conductors, optical fibers are usually cabled by enclosing many fibers in a protective sheath made of some material such as polyvinyl chloride or polyurethane. The cable is strengthened by adding steel wire or Kevlar aramid yarn to give the cable assembly greater tensile strength.

Light Sources and Detectors

In fiber optics communication systems, the light source must efficiently convert electrical energy (current and voltage) into optical energy in the form of light. The

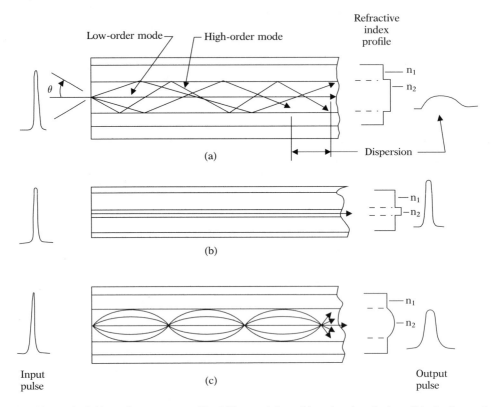

Low-order mode   High-order mode

Refractive
index
profile

θ

n_1
n_2

(a)

Dispersion

(b)

n_1
n_2

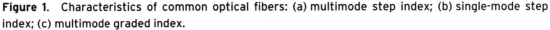

(c)

n_1
n_2

Input
pulse

Output
pulse

Figure 1.   Characteristics of common optical fibers: (a) multimode step index; (b) single-mode step index; (c) multimode graded index.

most commonly used light sources are gallium arsenide light-emitting diodes (LEDs) and injection laser diodes (ILDs). Both devices come in sizes compatible with the cores of fibers and emit light wavelengths in the range of 800 to 900 nm, where fibers have relatively low loss and dispersion. LEDs are not monochromatic, which limits their upper bit-rate capacity to about 1000 Mbps. ILDs produce light that is almost monochromatic and can transfer almost 100 times more light energy into the core than LEDs, allowing fibers to be driven at multi-Gbps rates.

Applications of Optical Fibers

As the world moves towards an *integrated services digital network* (ISDN—*q.v.*) in which voice, video, and data can be seamlessly transmitted over public and private networks, the need for more and higher bandwidth communication channels will continue to grow. Optical fibers offer capacities well beyond those of copper cables or microwave radio at lower cost and will play a major role in the implementation of new information highways.

Bibliography

1998. Palais, J. C. *Fiber Optic Communications*. Upper Saddle River, NJ: Prentice Hall.
1999. Hecht, J. *City of Light: The Story of Fiber Optics*. Oxford: Oxford University Press.

John S. Sobolewski

FICTION, COMPUTERS IN

For articles on related subjects, see

+ Automation
+ Robotics

Fictional computers comprise a broad range of imagined and feigned devices in literature, exhibits, and film. Overlapping with fictional automata and robots, they play a significant role in the cultural matrix of actual computers.

Prehistory

Jonathan Swift's *Gulliver's Travels*, published in 1726, presents an inventor who has constructed a gigantic machine designed to allow "the most ignorant Person" to "write Books in Philosophy, Poetry, Politicks, Law, Mathematicks, and Theology." This "Engine" contains myriad "Bits" crammed with all the words of a language, "all linked together by slender Wires" that can be turned by cranks, thus generating all possible linguistic combinations. Squads of scribes produce hard copy by recording any sequence of words that seems to make sense. The kooky inventor and his society value the random text produced by this marvelous machine more than human thoughts.

The most famous eighteenth-century automaton was the chess player constructed by Wolfgang von Kempelen in 1770 and which toured Europe and the United States through the 1830s, beating many skilled chess players, including Napoleon. In 1820, British inventor Robert Willis demonstrated that a human chess player was concealed inside the machine. In 1836, Edgar Allan Poe published his own version of Willis's proof. Ironically, part of Poe's argument reiterated the widespread belief in the infallibility of machines: "The Automaton does not invariably win the game. Were the machine a pure machine, this would not be the case—it would always win." Ambrose Bierce's 1909 story "Moxon's Master" more accurately anticipated the chess-playing capabilities of modern computers.

The most influential fictional automaton of the early nineteenth century was Olympia, who dances perfectly, always focuses her gaze adoringly on her lover, and exclaims "Oh, Oh!" in response to his every utterance in E. T. A. Hoffman's "The Sandman" (1816), later immortalized in Offenbach's "The Tales of Hoffman." There is a direct line from Olympia through the metal woman built by the evil scientist in Fritz Lang's film *Metropolis* (1926). Also in the lineage of female automaton is one that may claim

to be the first fictional stored-program computer, the title character of M. L. Campbell's "The Automatic Maid-of-All-Work" (1893).

The tendency to conceive of thinking machines as humanoid in appearance was dominant until the advent of those first huge digital computers of the 1940s. For example, even though American author Edward Page Mitchell was aware of the substantial dimensions of Babbage's Difference Engine (*q.v.*), his 1879 story "The Ablest Man in the World" envisions a tiny computer explicitly superior to Babbage's being inserted into the head of a man.

George Parsons Lathrop in his 1879 story "In the Deep of Time" imagines vast automated factories of the twenty-second century run by a single person at a keyboard. Jules Verne prophesied in his 1863 manuscript, *Paris in the Twentieth Century* (published in 1996), giant "calculating machines" resembling "huge pianos" operated by a "keyboard" and hooked to "facsimile" machines. Fears of machines evolving until they replace people appeared as early as "The Book of the Machines" in Samuel Butler's 1872 novel *Erewhon* and soon became commonplace. Early twentieth-century examples include Michael Williams's "The Mind Machine" (1919), in which living computers take over the cities but eventually disintegrate, and Edmond Hamilton's "The Metal Giants" (1926) featuring an atom-powered metal brain that constructs a rampaging army of 300-foot-tall robots.

By the 1930s, fiction about human overdependence on computers or the replacement of humans by intelligent machines was quite commonplace. Influential science fiction editor John W. Campbell wrote several stories on this theme, including "The Last Evolution" (1932), "Twilight" (1934), and "The Machine" (1935). A classic story in this vein is Jack Williamson's "With Folded Hands" (1947).

Computers as Robots

Although the word "robot" was coined by Karel Čapek in *R.U.R.* (*Rossum's Universal Robots*), the robots in this 1920 play are organic androids, not computerized mechanical people. Popular culture, however, soon appropriated the term robot to identify those hordes of walking, talking machines that would became a staple of science fiction in print, film, and exhibits—such as

Voder, the talking mechanical man at the 1939 New York World's Fair. For example, in Harl Vincent's "Rex" (1934) the title character uses his "marvelous mechanical brain" to create a robot dictatorship. The most influential shaper of this fiction was Isaac Asimov, who conceived of all-purpose mechanical robots with "positronic brains" governed by his Three Laws of Robotics, first articulated in his 1942 story "Runabout." According to these "Laws," all robots' brains were preprogrammed to guarantee that they would never harm humans, would obey orders, and would protect themselves, in that order.

The first memorable movie robots appeared in the 1950s, and the two highlights were both products of extraterrestrial civilizations: the all-powerful Gort in *The Day the Earth Stood Still* (1951) and Robby the Robot in *Forbidden Planet* (1956). Robby is the ancestor of all those lovable robots through R2D2 and C-3PO of *Star Wars*.

Dawn of the Computer Age

One early fiction that accurately anticipated how computers would look and function in the society of the 1990s is Murray Leinster's 1946 short story "A Logic Named Joe." Each home has at least one "logic," a personal computer complete with a screen and keyboard, networked to centralized supercomputers containing all knowledge and recorded telecasts. People access information, solve problems, view entertainment programs, communicate with each other, run their charge accounts, and so on from their personal computer through the network. There are even built-in censors that prevent children from seeing inappropriate material (thus anticipating the V-chip).

Fiction that projected computer-based catastrophe flourished in the 1960s. A good example is D. F. Jones's 1966 novel *Colossus*, whose vision of a computer gaining mastery reached a wide audience when it was made into the 1970 film *Colossus—The Forbin Project*. But the masterpiece of this genre is Harlan Ellison's 1967 short story "I Have No Mouth, and I Must Scream," in which the American, Russian, and Chinese supercomputers waging thermonuclear war merge into a single conscious entity that destroys the entire human race except for five people it saves to torture.

More imminent social effects of computers are projected in the bleak *Player Piano* (1952), Kurt Vonnegut Jr.'s first novel. Meaningful work is available only to a small group of technocrats, while other people can join either the huge standing army needed to control the world or the "Reeks and Wrecks," a mob of dissolute idlers pretending to do useless jobs. Real political power resides in the central computer, EPICAC XIV.

Perhaps the most sympathetic role played by a fictional computer in this period appears in Robert A. Heinlein's 1966 novel *The Moon Is a Harsh Mistress*. Mike, the central computer of the lunar colony, helps lead a libertarian lunar replay of the 1776 American Revolution against an authoritarian Earth while raising existential questions about its own identity.

Meanwhile, in Poland, Stanislaw Lem was creating a profound exploration of the significance of computers. In the framing narrative of *Memoirs Found in a Bathtub* (1961), historian computers attempt to comprehend the human civilization that has destroyed itself. *The Invincible* (1964) contemplates the evolution of a nonorganic form of devastating intelligence. A number of Lem's cybernetic fables are collected in *Cyberiad* (1965).

What Next?

Fiction about normal existence in industrial and post-industrial societies could no more exclude computers than telephones, airplanes, and TV. During the 1980s, computers became a central icon in the science fiction known as *cyberpunk*, especially in the work of William Gibson. Gibson's *Burning Chrome* (1986), an influential collection of his stories from 1977 on, included several in which characters "jack" into the Web. In his Neuromancer trilogy—*Neuromancer* (1984), *Count Zero* (1986), and *Mona Lisa Overdrive* (1988)—cyberspace (*q.v.*) becomes the central locale.

Conceptions of computers in science fiction during the last 15 years of the twentieth century reached far beyond what might have been imaginable even in the 1940s. Illustrative are the bold extrapolations in the speculative fiction of Greg Bear, such as *Eon* (1985), *Blood Music* (1985), and *Queen of Angels* (1990). In *Blood Music*, for example, "Medically Applicable Biochips" inadvertently convert DNA molecules into living computers that transmute the human species into the progenitor of "an intelligent plague" designed to reshape some of the fundamental principles of the universe.

Bibliography

1954. Conklin, G. (ed.) *Science-Fiction Thinking Machines.* New York: Vanguard Press.

1977. Mowshowitz, A. *Inside Information: Computers in Fiction.* Reading, MA: Addison-Wesley.

1982. Dunn, T. P., and Erlich, R. D. (eds.) *The Mechanical God: Machines in Science Fiction.* Westport, CT: Greenwood Press.

1982. Warrick, P. S. *The Cybernetic Imagination in Science Fiction.* Cambridge, MA: MIT Press.

1983. Dunn, T. P., and Erlich, R. D. *Clockwork Worlds: Mechanized Environments in SF.* Westport, CT: Greenwood Press.

1985. Porush, D. *The Soft Machine: Cybernetic Fiction.* New York: Methuen.

H. Bruce Franklin

FILE

For articles on related subjects, *see*

+ **Database Management System (DBMS)**
+ **File Server**
+ **Record**

A *file* is a collection of data representing a set of entities with certain aspects in common and which are organized for some specific purpose. An *entity* is any data object, such as *employee* or *part*, and is represented in a file by a *record occurrence*. A card deck containing information on automobile parts and a cabinet drawer filled with manila folders containing data sheets on employees are examples of (noncomputer) files. In computing, a file is an organized collection of data records, possibly of different types, stored on some external storage device, such as magnetic tape or disk. The usual distinction between a *file* and a *database* is that an individual file is typically accessed

Employee number	Employee name	Salary	Department	Sex
10836	B. Cohen	36,000	Hardware	Male
20111	C. Gonzales	28,000	Shoe	Female
20177	R. Jackson	32,000	Houseware	Female
⋮	⋮	⋮		
31112	B. Verdetti	34,000	Hardware	Male

(a) Raw data

EMPLOYEE

(b) Logical structure

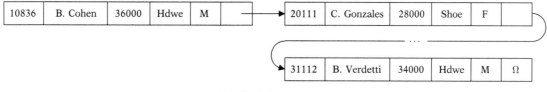

(c) A physical structure

Figure 1. Raw data to logical file structure to physical file structure.

by only a small number of persons at a single location, whereas a database consists of an integrated collection of multiple files accessed by many people, often over a network.

Storage Devices

The variety of external storage devices on which files can be stored is continually increasing. Storage technologies like recordable (CD-R) or rewritable (CD-RW) optical storage (*q.v.*) and flash-programmable read-only memory (*q.v.*) are being used to replace the magnetic disk in certain situations. The former serves for backup and archival storage; the latter is used with digital cameras and audio recording devices. While these new memories are appealing, magnetic disk remains the most popular device for storing large files online. Magnetic tape, because of its high access time, its portability and compactness characteristics, and its relatively low cost, has been relegated to serving as a storage medium for archival and backup files.

File Structure

A file has a structure that is both logical and physical. The *logical structure* of a file is essentially the application program's (i.e. the user's) view of the file (*see* Fig. 1). A file declaration that appears in a high-level language such as Cobol (*q.v.*) or C++ (*q.v.*) is basically a logical structure specification and usually involves defining the attribute(s) of the record type(s) and possibly specifying an ordering relationship on the record occurrences. *Physical structure* is associated with how a file is actually organized on the storage medium on which it resides.

Files can be structured and accessed in various ways. The earliest and most common type of file organization was sequential because computer files were first stored on inherently sequential storage media such as magnetic tape. To access a record in a sequential file, the preceding records must be passed over. Among the various other access methods that have been developed are the indexed-sequential and direct-access methods.

Billy G. Claybrook

FILE SERVER

For articles on related subjects, *see*

+ Cache Memory
+ Client-Server Computing
+ Distributed Systems
+ Local Area Network (LAN)
+ Workstation

One approach to handling file transfer among multiple machines is to connect the machines to a local area network. A second approach is to place shared data on a *file server* and have individual machines access data files located on the remote file server rather than on a local disk. The file server approach is an example of *client–server* interaction. Clients executing on the local machine forward all file requests (e.g. open, close, read, write, and seek) to the remote file server. The server accepts a client's request, performs its associated operation, and returns a response to the client. When client software is structured *transparently*, the client need not even be aware that files being accessed physically reside on machines located elsewhere on the network (*see* TRANSPARENCY).

The file server approach has several benefits. First, multiple machines can access shared files concurrently. Thus, a user can run the same programs on the same data files regardless of which client machine is being used. Second, the cost of supporting and maintaining a small number of large file servers is less than the cost of maintaining file systems on individual machines. Indeed, client machines need not even have disk drives. As disks have become cheaper, diskless clients are less common than they were in the 1980s, but it is still less expensive to implement fault-tolerant systems (*q.v.*) that use redundant or swappable components (*see* REDUNDANT ARRAY OF INEXPENSIVE DISKS (RAID)) on fewer machines.

A server can either be a *disk server* or a *file server*. A disk server presents a raw disk interface through which client machines read and write disk sectors. Disk servers are primarily useful as a backing store for swapping or paging. In contrast, a file server provides access to files. A *mail server* is a particular kind of file server. Clients open files, read and write file contents, and so on. All details about how the file system is represented on the physical device are hidden within the server. When a client opens a file, the client's operating system forwards the open request across the network to the file server and waits for its response.

File servers must address the problem of *authentication* (*q.v.*). That is, if a client requests file pages, how can the server be sure that clients really are who they claim to be? In a networked environment, an unauthorized client may pose as another in an attempt to access sensitive data. Authentication is handled by using cryptographic techniques.

Another aspect of file server design is whether the server should be *stateful* or *stateless*. Upon machine reboots, a stateless server retains no knowledge about the files client machines are using. When a client makes a request, each request contains complete information needed to service it. For example, when reading a file sequentially, each request contains the starting and ending byte offsets of the desired information rather than requesting "the next 1024 bytes." In contrast, stateful servers keep track of which clients are using files and in what ways. Such information is important for maintaining cache consistency and for providing such services as exclusive file locks.

Bibliography

1996. Tanenbaum, A. *Computer Networks*, 3rd Ed. Upper Saddle River, NJ: Prentice Hall.

1998. Silberschatz, A., and Galvin, P. *Operating System Concepts*, 5th Ed. Reading, MA: Addison-Wesley.

Thomas Narten and James D. Teresco

FINITE-STATE MACHINE

See CHOMSKY HIERARCHY.

FIREWALL

For articles on related subjects, *see*

+ Data Security
+ Networks, Computer
+ Gateway

A *firewall* is a system that prevents unauthorized access to a proprietary network by a personal computer (PC) or workstation connected to it, or inversely, access by a networked PC to another PC connected to the same network. Firewalls are frequently used to prevent unauthorized Internet (*q.v.*) users from accessing *intranets*—private networks connected to the Internet. All messages entering or leaving the intranet pass through the firewall, which examines each message and blocks those that do not meet the specified security criteria. See `http://csrc.nist.gov/publications/nistpubs/800-10/node30.html`

Firewalls can be implemented in hardware or software or a combination of both. The *packet filter* examines each data packet entering or leaving the network and accepts or rejects it based on user-defined rules. These rules may specify which computers may have access to the network and which services are allowed. An *application gateway* is a computer that applies security measures to specific applications, such as File Transfer Protocol (FTP) and Telnet servers. It provides *proxy services* that intercept all FTP or Telnet communications entering and leaving the network, forwarding them to internal nodes while hiding their true network addresses. A firewall is merely the first line of defense in protecting private information and must be carefully planned to allow all appropriate activities while blocking all others. For greater security, data encryption is also essential.

Bibliography

2002. Strassberg, K., Rollie, G., and Gondek, R. *Firewalls: The Complete Reference*. New York: McGraw-Hill Osborne Media.

Edwin D. Reilly

FIRMWARE

For articles on related subjects, *see*

+ Embedded System
+ Emulation
+ Microprogramming

+ Read-Only Memory (ROM)
+ Software

Early in the history of digital computation, the useful distinction was made between *hardware*, the tangible componentry of a computing system, and *software*, the collection of instructions that directed what was to be computed. While it was true that software had to be recorded on some tangible medium, such as punched cards or paper or magnetic tape (early), or later, hard or floppy disks (*see* DISKETTE), the software itself was considered to be pure information and hence intangible. Supporting the "softness" of this interpretation was the fact that when recorded on a magnetic medium, software could be modified with ease.

The question soon arose as to what to call programs recorded indelibly on a medium such as read-only memory (ROM) or embodied in hard-wired computer circuitry. The result, no longer "soft" enough to be modified, was still functionally "software," but had it become, though still executable, "hardware." The term coined to solve this dilemma was *firmware*.

Given adequate memory, any general purpose digital computer can execute programs written for any other through use of a *simulator*, a program that interprets each target machine instruction and executes whatever sequence of host machine instructions is needed to do the same thing, bit for bit. Interpretation is naturally slow, but implementation of key parts of the simulator as firmware provides a significant increase in speed of execution (*see* EMULATION).

Bibliography

1992. Marge, D. *Microprogrammed Systems: An Introduction to Firmware Theory.* London: Chapman & Hall.

Edwin D. Reilly

FLOATING-POINT ARITHMETIC

See ARITHMETIC, COMPUTER.

FLOPPY DISK

See DISKETTE.

FLOWCHART

For an article on a related subject, *see*

+ Structured Programming

Definition

A *flowchart* is a graphic means of documenting a sequence of operations. Flowcharts serve as a pictorial means of documenting the time-ordering of events or actions. Flowcharts have been the subject of both an International and an American National Standard.

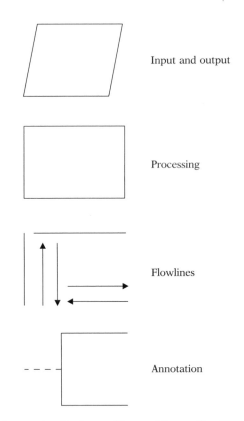

Input and output

Processing

Flowlines

Annotation

Figure 1. Basic outlines. (From N. Chapin, *Flowcharts*. New York: Petrocelli Books, 1971.)

Format

The two main varieties of flowchart are the *flow diagram* and the *system chart*. A flow diagram gives a detailed view of what is shown as a single process in a system chart. Flow diagrams and system charts use different pictorial conventions, but also share certain conventions. The basic outlines shown in Fig. 1 are common to both. The additional outlines of Fig. 2 are all used in flow diagrams. System charts are pictorially richer. While analysts can prepare system charts using only the basic outlines of Fig. 1, they often selectively substitute some of the specialized outlines for media, equipment, and processes shown in Fig. 3.

System Chart

Analysts most commonly prepare system charts to show graphically the interactions in execution among the

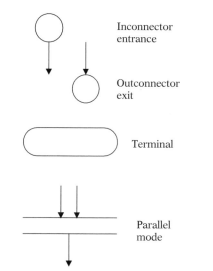

Figure 2. Additional outlines. (From N. Chapin, *Flowcharts*. New York: Petrocelli Books, 1971.)

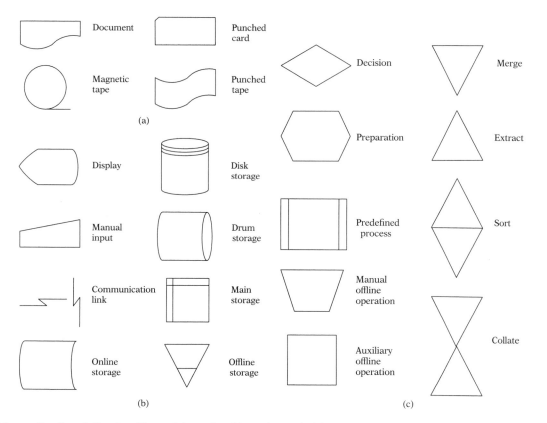

Figure 3. Specialized outlines: (a) media; (b) equipment; (c) processes. (From N. Chapin, *Flowcharts*. New York: Petrocelli Books, 1971.)

programs of a system. The inputs and outputs of each program are shown, either in a generalized form using the basic outlines, or in a particularized form using the specialized outlines. Analysts may prepare system charts at a logical level (using the basic outlines) or at a physical level (using the specialized outlines). Analysts may also prepare system charts for other situations that are characterized by an alternation of data and action. Some general examples are the situations in which a dataflow diagram could be used, or in which an integrated data engineering facility diagram (IDEF) or state transition diagram could be used.

Program Flowchart

Analysts most commonly prepare flowcharts or flow diagrams to describe the time-sequence of functions, actions, or events. Such sequences usually comprise a process that takes in input data and produces output data. A flow diagram begins and ends with a labeled terminal outline (Fig. 2) to mark each entrance and exit. Then successive outlines connected by flow arrows depict the acceptance of data as input, the processing steps taken, and the disposition of data as output. Decisions are shown explicitly (*see* Fig. 4).

Alternatives

Historically, analysts drew flowcharts by hand. Currently, some popular Computer-Aided Software Engineering (CASE) software tools facilitate drawing and revising flowcharts. Flowcharts have been declining in favor as alternatives have appeared, such as the dataflow diagram. The term *structured flowchart* usually refers to either Chapin charts (Chapin, 1974) or to Nassi–Shneiderman iteration diagrams (Nassi 1973). Warnier–Orr diagrams provide a way of depicting both data and software structures hierarchically (Warnier, 1974).

Bibliography

1973. Nassi, I., and Shneiderman, B. "Flowchart Techniques for Structured Programming," *SIGPLAN Notices*, **8**(8), 12–26.

1974. Chapin, N. "New Format for Flowcharts," *Software—Practice and Experience*, **4**(4), 341–357.

1974. Warnier, J. D. *Logical Construction of Programs*. New York: Van Nostrand Reinhold.

1995. Boillot, M. H., Gleason, G. M., and Horn, L. W. *Essentials of Flowcharting*. New York: WCB/McGraw-Hill.

Ned Chapin

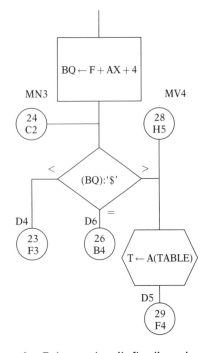

Figure 4. Entry and exit flowlines in a flow diagram. (From N. Chapin, *Flowcharts*. New York: Petrocelli Books, 1971.)

FORMAL LANGUAGES

For articles on related subjects, *see*

+ Automata Theory
+ Backus-Naur Form (BNF)
+ Chomsky Hierarchy
+ Language Processors
+ Machine Translation

+ Metalanguage
+ Turing Machine

Languages and Grammars

Formal languages are abstract mathematical objects used to model the syntax of programming languages or natural languages. For example, consider a simple English sentence, such as THE MAN ATE THE APPLE. The study of English syntax attempts to answer the question: when is a string of words a grammatically correct English sentence? And when it is a sentence, how can it be parsed?

To model this situation, we let V be a finite set of symbols called a *vocabulary*. In the previous example, V contains the four words APPLE, ATE, MAN, and THE. More generally, V might contain all English words and punctuation marks. Let V^* denote all finite-length strings of symbols from V. Then a *formal language* L is simply a set of strings from V^*. For example, if V^* is the set of all finite sequences of English words, then L could be the subset of V^* consisting of all grammatically correct sentences. Although V is always finite, in most cases L will be infinite, and we will wish to have a finitely specified way of generating, or recognizing, or *parsing* the strings in L.

The sample sentence given earlier can be parsed by the treelike diagram in Fig. 1, where $\langle S \rangle$, $\langle NP \rangle$, $\langle VP \rangle$, $\langle A \rangle$, $\langle N \rangle$, and $\langle V \rangle$ are six variables ranging over all *sentences, noun phrases, verb phrases, articles, nouns,* and *verbs*, respectively. Using the *rewriting* rules in Fig. 2, it is possible to generate our sample sentence from the variable $\langle S \rangle$. The generation proceeds as follows:

$$\langle S \rangle \Rightarrow \langle NP \rangle \langle VP \rangle$$
$$\Rightarrow \langle A \rangle \langle N \rangle \langle VP \rangle$$
$$\Rightarrow \langle A \rangle \langle N \rangle \langle V \rangle \langle NP \rangle$$
$$\Rightarrow \langle A \rangle \langle N \rangle \langle V \rangle \langle A \rangle \langle N \rangle$$
$$\Rightarrow \text{THE } \langle N \rangle \langle V \rangle \langle A \rangle \langle N \rangle$$
$$\Rightarrow \text{THE MAN } \langle V \rangle \langle A \rangle \langle N \rangle$$
$$\Rightarrow \text{THE MAN ATE } \langle A \rangle \langle N \rangle$$

$$\Rightarrow \text{THE MAN ATE THE } \langle N \rangle$$
$$\Rightarrow \text{THE MAN ATE THE APPLE}$$

With these rules, we can also generate various improbable but grammatically correct sentences such as THE APPLE ATE THE MAN, and with more rules we could generate more sentences. Rewriting schemes of this sort were introduced by the linguist Noam Chomsky, who called them *context-free grammars*.

To see a simple example of context-free rewriting rules that give rise to an infinite language, suppose that the vocabulary consists of two abstract symbols a and b, and let S be a variable. Then, using the rules $S \to aSb$ and $S \to ab$, we can generate the infinite language $L = \{a^n b^n | n \geq 1\} = \{ab, aabb, aaabbb, \ldots\}$. Rewriting rules of this type are called "context free" because they permit any occurrence of a variable within a string to be rewritten without regard to the context in which

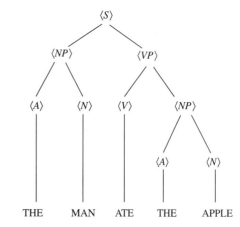

Figure 1.   Tree for parsing sentence.

$$\langle S \rangle \to \langle NP \rangle \langle VP \rangle$$
$$\langle NP \rangle \to \langle A \rangle \langle N \rangle$$
$$\langle VP \rangle \to \langle V \rangle \langle NP \rangle$$
$$\langle A \rangle \to \text{THE}$$
$$\langle V \rangle \to \text{ATE}$$
$$\langle N \rangle \to \text{MAN}$$
$$\langle N \rangle \to \text{APPLE}$$

Figure 2.   Rewriting rules.

that variable occurs. By contrast, a rewriting rule like $aXab \rightarrow aYZcab$ is not context-free. It is called *context-sensitive*, since it allows X to be rewritten as YZc only when X occurs in strings of the form s_1aXabs_2, where s_1 and s_2 are arbitrary strings.

To describe different kinds of grammars more precisely, let us define a *phrase-structure* grammar to be a quadruple $G = (V_N, V_T, P, S)$, where

1. V_N is a finite vocabulary of nonterminal symbols or variables.
2. V_T is a finite vocabulary of terminal symbols.
3. P is a finite set of rewriting rules (also called *productions*) of the form $\alpha \rightarrow \beta$, where α is a nonempty string of variables and β is an arbitrary string of variables and terminal symbols.
4. S is a particular variable called the *start* variable.

For all strings s_1 and s_2, we may write $s_1\alpha s_2 \Rightarrow s_1\beta_2 s_2$ if $\alpha \rightarrow \beta$ is a production of the grammar G. Then the language generated by G is the set of all strings t of terminal symbols such that $S \Rightarrow s_1 \Rightarrow s_2 \Rightarrow 0 \cdots \Rightarrow s_n \Rightarrow t$ for some choice of intermediate strings s_1, $s_2, \ldots, s_n$. The intermediate strings may consist of both variables and terminal symbols. Let α, α_1, and α_2 denote arbitrary strings of variables and terminal symbols, and let A and B denote variables. If the productions in G have the specialized form $\alpha_1 A\alpha_2 \rightarrow \alpha_1 \beta\alpha_2$, where β represents any nonempty string, then G is a *context-sensitive* grammar. If the productions in the grammar G have the form $A \rightarrow \alpha$, then G is context-free. If productions have the form $A \rightarrow w_1 B$ or $A \rightarrow w_2$, where w_1 and w_2 are strings of terminal symbols, then G is *right-linear*. A language is called a *phrase-structure* language, or a *context-sensitive, context-free*, or *right-linear* language, if it can be generated by a phrase-structure grammar, or a context-sensitive, context-free, or right-linear grammar, respectively.

The four types of grammars (phrase-structure, context-sensitive, context-free, and right-linear) are also known as type 0, type 1, type 2, and type 3 grammars, respectively. They form a grammatical hierarchy, called the *Chomsky hierarchy*. Among the four corresponding families of languages, the smallest family, the right-linear languages, is important because it consists precisely of those languages that can be recognized by finite-state automata. These languages are very easy to parse.

The family of context-free languages is important because context-free languages are good approximations to the syntax of programming languages. For example, the syntax of an assignment statement in a programming language can be described in a context-free grammar, as: $\langle$assn-stmt$\rangle \rightarrow \langle$variable$\rangle := \langle$expression$\rangle$.

Context-sensitive languages are powerful enough to encompass any complications in syntax that may have been missed by the context-free model, but they are so general that they are difficult to work with.

The family of phrase-structure languages is important because it represents the largest class with which one is likely to be concerned when modeling natural or artificial languages. This is so because the family of phrase-structure languages is in fact the same as the family of all recursively enumerable languages—that is, of all languages L such that membership of a string w in L can be verified by some algorithm (or, more precisely, by some Turing machine).

Programming Languages

Context-free languages are good approximations to the syntax of many programming languages. Consider the following very simple example of syntax specifications in *Backus–Naur form*, or *BNF* (the :: = is an alternative to $\rightarrow$):

```
⟨digit⟩ ::= 0|1|2|3|4|5|6|7|8|9
⟨unsigned integer⟩ ::= ⟨digit⟩
        | ⟨unsigned integer⟩ ⟨digit⟩
```

This means that $\langle$unsigned integer$\rangle$ and $\langle$digit$\rangle$ together define the set of strings satisfying the following conditions: 0, 1, ..., 9 are digits (i.e. they are in the set $\langle$digit$\rangle$); any digit is an unsigned integer; and any unsigned integer followed by a digit is an unsigned integer. Any programming language whose syntax can be specified in BNF is context-free. Generally, most but not all of the syntax of a programming language can be specified in BNF. So languages such as Pascal (*q.v.*) and C++ (*q.v.*) are not quite context-free, but they are close to being so, and context-free languages are useful approximations to their syntax.

Languages and Automata

The four families of languages in the Chomsky hierarchy can be obtained from automata as well as from grammars (*see* AUTOMATA THEORY). The phrase-structure languages are the languages accepted by linear-bounded automata or *lba*; the context-free languages are the languages accepted by pushdown automata; and the right-linear languages are the languages accepted by finite-state automata. For this reason, right-linear languages are sometimes called *finite-state* languages. Usually, however, right-linear languages are known as *regular languages* or *regular sets*.

Bibliography

1996. Linz, P. *Introduction to Formal Languages and Automata.* Sudbury, MA: Jones and Bartlett.

Jonathan Goldstine

FORTRAN

For articles on related subjects, *see*

+ Procedure-Oriented Languages
+ Programming Languages

Fortran was the first popular *high-level language*. A program by J. H. Laning and N. Zierler that translated mathematical equations into machine language seems to have been the first operational compiler (*q.v.*), but Fortran was the first widely used programming language. The proposal that led to the development of Fortran was made in late 1953 by John Backus of IBM to his boss, Cuthbert Hurd. The team that Backus put together in 1954 to design the language that became Fortran included, among others, Sheldon Best, Harlan Herrick, Robert Nelson, Roy Nutt, Peter Sheridan, and Irving Ziller. They published a preliminary report in 1954, which differed little from the Programmer's Reference Manual published in 1956. The first Fortran compiler (called then a *translator*) was distributed in April 1957 and within a year was widely used on IBM computers.

Fortran was developed with the aim of decreasing programming and debugging costs. Great effort was expended on generating efficient object code; the first Fortran compiler had an efficiency not matched until optimizing compilers appeared a decade later.

As Fortran became widely used, various deficiencies of the original design became clear. Fortran II, first distributed in the spring of 1958, corrected some of these. The two main additions were much-improved diagnostics and a subroutine facility. Fortran III was essentially stillborn. It added a few additional facilities and was used at some IBM installations, but was never distributed widely.

Fortran IV, whose first compilers became available in 1963, added the now familiar features of COMMON storage, double-precision and logical data types, relational expressions, and a DATA statement that provided a simple facility to initialize variables. Fortran IV became the standard dialect of Fortran for many years and became the basis of the first Fortran standard, ANSI Standard X3.9 in 1966 and the later ISO Standard 1539 in 1972.

By the mid-1970s, even Fortran IV was showing its age. Although the investment in legacy Fortran programs was by this time immense, developments in high-level language programming, particularly the advent of *structured programming* (*q.v.*), meant that Fortran was no longer considered a modern language. Technical work on what became Fortran 77 (F77) began in 1967 and was completed in 1977. F77 became the official Fortran standard in April 1978.

Long before F77's fate became clear, technical work on its successor began in earnest in 1978. F77 had, at the last minute, added an if-then-else control structure, and this limited venture into modern control structures prompted a 5-year plan to produce a truly "modern" successor. A case selection construct was designed, and the original Fortran DO-loop was augmented with several flavors of a modern iteration (do-enddo) structure. Numerous other modernizations were completed, but not until 1990.

F90 was developed by the US Fortran standards committee, but during this period ISO became increasingly important and active in developing language standards; it was this new ISO muscle that ultimately resolved the controversy. As a consequence, ISO established a 5-year schedule for subsequent revisions of the Fortran standard. Thus, soon after F90 became official, Fortran 95 (F95) and Fortran 2000 (F2000) were scheduled.

F95 succeeded F90 on schedule, without controversy. It is a minor extension of F90, refining many of the features introduced in F90 and adding a few array features for increased performance in massively parallel environments. The major enhancements planned for F2000 are numerical exception handling, modest facilities for object-oriented programming (*q.v.*), and interoperability with C (*q.v.*) and C++ (*q.v.*).

Bibliography

1981. Backus, J. W. "The History of Fortran I, II and III," in *History of Programming Languages* (ed. R. L. Wexelblat), 25–74, New York: Academic Press.

1996. Adams, J., and Brainerd, W. "A Little History and a Fortran 90 Summary," *Computer Standards and Interfaces*, Special Issue: Fortran 90, **18**(4), 277–380.

1998. http://www.ionet.net/~jwagener/j3. The Fortran Standards Web Page.

Jerrold L. Wagener and Anthony Ralston

FRACTALS

For articles on related subjects, *see*

+ Computer Art
+ Computer Graphics
+ Image Processing
+ Pattern Recognition
+ Scientific Applications

Introduction

Natural shapes such as mountains, clouds or trees cannot easily be modeled in Euclidean geometry, but *fractal geometry*, as conceived by Mandelbrot, provides a mathematical model for many of the seemingly complex forms found in nature. One of his key observations has been that these forms possess a remarkable statistical invariance under magnification. This may be quantified by a *fractal dimension*, a number that agrees with our intuitive understanding of dimension but need not be an integer.

Even in very simple nonlinear dynamical systems, such as the double pendulum, long-term predictions are not possible despite exact knowledge of the underlying governing equations. Such systems exhibit behavioral patterns that we can conceive only as erratic or chaotic despite their very simple and deterministic generating mechanisms. Arbitrarily small perturbations of solutions are blown up by such systems until the perturbed solutions have lost all correlation with the original solution. This phenomenon has been termed *sensitive dependence on initial condition* and is the trademark of what became known as *chaos theory*. There is a strong connection between chaos and fractal geometry, that is, as one follows the evolution of the states of a chaotic nonlinear system, it typically leaves a trace in its embedding space, which has a very complex geometric structure: this trace is a fractal.

Random Fractals

Fractal geometric structures exhibit a self-similarity when the distance at which they are viewed is changed. This self-similarity may be either exact or statistical. An exact self-similar fractal is the snowflake curve devised by Helge von Koch in 1904 (*see* Fig. 1). The curve is self-similar: magnify one-quarter of the snowflake curve by a factor of 3 to obtain another complete snowflake curve. When a self-similar object is given as N copies of itself, each one scaled down by a factor of r, the *self-similarity dimension* of the object is defined as

$$D = \frac{\log N}{\log 1/r}.$$

This definition assigns the dimension 1 to straight lines and 2 to squares, as expected. Fractals typically have a non-integer dimension. The snowflake curve has a dimension $D = \log 4/\log 3 \approx 1.262$.

The notion of self-similarity dimension is extended to sets that do not have *exact* self-similarity. Let A be a set in n-dimensional Euclidean space R^n, and define

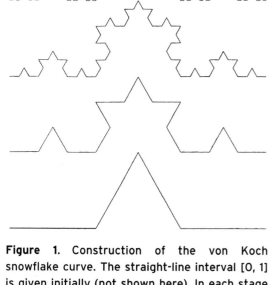

Figure 1. Construction of the von Koch snowflake curve. The straight-line interval [0, 1] is given initially (not shown here). In each stage (going from bottom to top), each straight-line segment is replaced by the four line segments that result from expanding the center of the original line segment into the point of a star. As stages are added, the total length of the curve tends to infinity although the curve is confined to a finite region.

$N(r)$ as the minimal number of n-dimensional cubes necessary to cover the set A. Then the (box-counting) *fractal dimension* is

$$D_f(A) = \lim_{r \to 0} \frac{\log N(r)}{\log 1/r}.$$

This quantity can be estimated from a given data set by drawing a graph of the function $N(r)$ on doubly logarithmic paper. The negative slope of the resulting line fit to this data is an estimate for D_f. Such a model describes *uniform fractals*, that is, the fractal dimension does not vary with direction as we move through its graphical representation. In nonuniform fractals, the fractal dimension does vary with direction,

either randomly or deterministically. We examine only the latter.

Deterministic Fractals

Random fractals involve an element of chance. In contrast, deterministic fractals are given by means of exact formulas. In this section, we consider those deterministic fractals that arise from *discrete dynamical systems*, that is, the iteration of mappings. These may be derived, for example, from *population dynamics* in biology and yield maps that describe growth of population from one generation to the next. Iteration of the maps simulates the dynamics over longer time periods. Other mappings are motivated by time-variant processes described by differential equations and associated *Poincaré sections*.

The first system of differential equations discovered for which a fractal structure is central consists of the Lorenz equations

$$x = \sigma\,(y - x),$$
$$y = Rx - y - xz,$$
$$z = xy - bz.$$

These equations, named after the meteorologist E. Lorenz, were motivated by the problem of weather forecasting and represent a much simplified model of Rayleigh–Bénard convection in fluids. As solutions are followed, they tend to a set in 3-space with a complicated fractal structure, a *strange attractor* (*see* Fig. 2).

One way to study the dynamics given by a system of three differential equations such as the Lorenz equations consists in reducing the description to a two-dimensional map, called the *Poincaré section*. A model for the Lorenz system suggested by Hénon and Pomeau in 1976 is

$$x_{k+1} = 1 + yk - ax_k^2, \, a = 1.4,$$
$$y_{k+1} = bx_k, \, b = 0.3.$$

Given an initial point (x_0, y_0), the formula defines a successor point (x_1, y_1) and all following points iteratively. Again, there is a strange attractor with

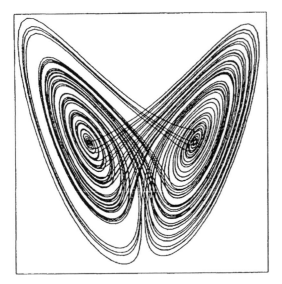

Figure 2. The Lorenz attractor for parameters $R = 28$, $\sigma = 10$, $b = 8/3$.

self-similar fractal structure. It is remarkable that important aspects of complex dynamical behavior found in nature can be captured in such simple discrete maps.

A related discrete model is the quadratic mapping

$$z_{k+1} = R_c(z_k) = z_k^2 + c,$$

where z_k, $k = 0, 1, \ldots$ are complex numbers, and c is a complex parameter. This iteration has found widespread interest not only in the scientific community but also among amateur scientists due to its computer graphics potential. It is the iteration procedure that yields the Mandelbrot set

$$M = \{c \in |\lim_{k \to \infty} z_k \neq \infty \text{ with } z_0 = c\}$$

and the Julia set J_c, which is the minimal completely invariant closed subset of C (i.e. we have that $z \in j_c$ if and only if $z^2 + c \in j_c$ except in the special case $c = 0$ where the Julia set is the unit circle). As in the case of other exact self-similar fractals, any small neighborhood of a point in the Julia set can be mapped onto the complete Julia set. However, the necessary similarity mapping is not affine, but *nonlinear*. The fractal dimension of J is typically a noninteger value between 0 and 2.

Most phenomena that occur with rational maps already appear in the quadratic map $R(z) = z^2 + c$. The Mandelbrot set reflects qualitative aspects for all parameters c of this map, that is, it collects all parameters c whose Julia set J_c is a connected set. Outside of the Mandelbrot set, corresponding Julia sets are not connected, but are just clouds of points. The Mandelbrot set (Fig. 3) itself is also a fractal with a certain self-similarity: any small neighborhood of a boundary point of M contains a complete copy of M. The conjecture that the boundary of M has a dimension equal to 2 has now been proved.

Applications

Fractals are found almost everywhere in nature, from the very large scales of clusters of galaxies down to the microcosmos of molecular particles. Wherever nature is to be *simulated*, fractals are of value. Landscapes and clouds were two of the first natural phenomena discussed in the computer graphics community. Research now studies effects such as erosion of a fractal landscape, allowing rivers and river networks to be included in the long list of simulated phenomena.

There are numerous applications of fractal geometry in image processing and pattern recognition. Two of

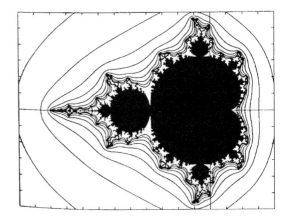

Figure 3. The Mandelbrot set with some equipotential lines.

them are: automatic segmentation of images based on fractal dimension, lacunarity, and so on, which is useful in differentiating objects in an image, such as artificial structures, forest and sky, and optimization of camouflage methods based on fractal analysis of the surroundings.

A method to generate fractal shapes that grow in space is based on *Lindenmayer systems*. Objects are represented as strings of symbols that are generated from an *axiom* (initial short string) and a set of *production rules* that are applied recursively to the symbols of the axiom and the resulting strings. The geometric representation of these strings is obtained through *turtle graphics* (*see* LOGO). Classic fractal curves such as the snowflake curve, Hilbert's space filling curve, the Sierpinski gasket, and so on, are easily and compactly formulated as L-systems. The main application is the modeling of growth and form of trees, bushes, and plants.

Because of their beauty, Julia sets and the Mandelbrot set have provided inspiration for computer art (*q.v.*) and serve as a pleasing demonstration object in computer trade shows. Another unforeseen, but perhaps relevant, side effect of the colorful Mandelbrot set images is that they convey a hint of the beauty that lies within mathematics. They thus supply motivation to regain the widely lost assertion that mathematics is a worthwhile and important part of the human culture.

Bibliography

1976. Hénon, M., and Pomeau, I. *Two Strange Attractors with a Simple Structure.* Lecture Notes in Mathematics **505**. New York: Springer-Verlag.

1982. Mandelbrot, B. *The Fractal Geometry of Nature.* New York: W. H. Freeman.

1986. Peitgen, H.-O., and Richter, P. H. *The Beauty of Fractals.* Heidelberg: Springer-Verlag.

1999. Dekking, M., Lutton, E., and Tricot, C. *Fractals: Theory and Applications in Engineering.* New York: Springer-Verlag.

Dietmar Saupe

FREE SOFTWARE FOUNDATION (FSF)

For articles on related subjects, *see*

+ Freeware and Shareware
+ Linux
+ Unix

The Free Software Foundation is sponsor of the GNU project. GNU is a recursive acronym that stands for "GNU's Not Unix." The GNU Project was founded in 1984 to develop a complete free Unix-compatible operating system, also called GNU. "Complete" means covering the full range of components of Unix—kernel (*q.v.*), libraries, shells, editors, compilers, development tools, mailer, and the rest. "Free," here, means that users have certain freedoms, including the freedom to use the system for any purpose, and to redistribute copies, either verbatim or modified, either gratis or for a fee. The freedom to modify implies availability of source code.

When the GNU project was launched, all the operating systems available for computers of the day were proprietary (non-free). Since source code was usually not available, users could not adapt the software to their needs, or even fix problems. They were also legally prohibited from helping their neighbors by sharing software with them. The GNU project strove to liberate users from these restrictions.

The Free Software Foundation is a tax-exempt charity, formed in 1985 to raise funds for developing free software. It pays programmers to write and upgrade GNU software, and technical writers to write and upgrade manuals, but most work on GNU software is done by volunteers. It receives most of its funds from selling copies of otherwise free software source code and manuals. This is not a contradiction, because "free" refers to the freedom that users have in using their copies. FSF also makes the software and manual source code available on the Internet without fee. The most notable GNU software packages include

GNU Emacs, a programmable text editor, and GCC (GNU C compiler), a portable optimizing compiler that now supports several languages and several dozen target machines.

The term *copyleft* was coined to describe the use of copyright law to protect users' freedom. The GNU GPL is one implementation of copyleft. Certain GNU software packages use alternative copyleft licenses. Some libraries use the GNU Library General Public License, which permits using these libraries in nonfree software applications.

In 1992, when GNU was almost complete, the Unix-compatible kernel, Linux, was developed by Linus Torvalds, and released under the GNU GPL. This filled the last major gap; soon after, complete operating systems were produced by combining Linux with the GNU system. These Linux-based GNU systems are most often called just "Linux," but Linux is actually the kernel, not the whole operating system. Estimates are that GNU/Linux systems had over twenty million users by 2002.

Richard Stallman

Copyright Richard Stallman 2004.
Verbatim copying and distribution of this article is permitted provided this notice is preserved.

FREEWARE AND SHAREWARE

For an articles on a related subject, *see*

+ Free Software Foundation (FSF)

Internet Websites contain many programs available for downloading. In most cases, these programs are being distributed either as *shareware* or *freeware*, or as a hybrid of the two. These programs appear to be distributed "for free," but the real story is more complicated. The first use of the terms freeware and shareware is uncertain, but in 1982, Andrew Fluegelman and Jim Knopf called some PC programs that they had written freeware.

With shareware, the program owner makes the program available for a free trial, hoping that consumers will like the product enough to buy it. Any software can be marketed as shareware, although the method is most popular among small, independent software developers. The volume of the shareware industry in 2003 was estimated to have been as high as US$450 million.

Freeware

Freeware is free and may be redistributed freely. However, there may be certain limitations on its use. For example, the author may request that you do not alter the program, or do not charge money for its distribution. Or the author may make it free to individuals, but ask companies to pay a fee. Popular browsers available from Netscape and Microsoft are free in that anyone may download and use the full version, but the owners prohibit people from altering it. Adobe Acrobat Reader, which reads Portable Document Format (PDF) files, is free because its widespread availability encourages document authors to buy Adobe's software to produce PDF documents.

Public Domain and Open Source

Public domain software is software for which the author has relinquished all rights to it; anyone may alter it. Software in the public domain should be distinguished from *open source* software, for which the author retains copyright but grants the free use of the software, including the right to modify it, though generally not the right to impose restrictions on the use of the modified product. The Linux operating system is one of the best-known examples of open source software.

Shareware

A program that is "true shareware" is distributed in its full version to anyone who wants to try it. The author requests that you send payment if you continue to use it after a certain time period. One might be doubtful of such an honor system, but several companies have made money with shareware, suggesting that people will pay for a product that they like if asked to do so. One of the best-known examples is PKZip, developed by the late Phil Katz (hence the "PK" in the name). PKZip is a utility program that compresses files for storage or transfer; a companion program PKUnzip decompresses the compressed files. PKZip can also be purchased in a boxed version in stores, but it remains widely distributed as shareware. Other examples of shareware include Paint Shop Pro and WinZip.

Demoware is like shareware except that the distributed version is not the same as the full program. *Crippleware* is a cousin to demoware. Instead of developing a demo version of the software, the company simply disables certain crucial features of the product and distributes the crippled version as a demo. For example, a drawing program may be fully functional except that it doesn't save or doesn't print.

Light or "lite" software is free, fully functional software that lacks some of the capabilities of its commercial counterpart. One well-known example is Qualcomm's Eudora Light email program for personal computers. Its features are quite adequate for personal and even professional use, but its Eudora Pro counterpart offers additional features appropriate for commercial use.

Bibliography

1994. Reichard, K. *Unix Shareware and Freeware.* Foster City, CA: IDG Books Worldwide.

1997. Cnet. *C/net Guide to Shareware.com.* New York: Ziff-Davis Publishing Company.

1999. Ford, N. "The History of Shareware," Public Software Library. http://www.digibuy.com/cgi-bin/history.html

Faithe Wempen

FUNCTIONAL PROGRAMMING

For articles on related subjects, *see*

+ Binding
+ List Processing
+ Recursion

Functional programming (applicative programming) is a style that uses function application as the only control structure (*q.v.*). Rather than conditional statements, one uses conditional expressions to yield alternative results; rather than an assignment statement, one uses binding of parameter to argument to give a name to a value; rather than explicit sequencing or looping of control flow, one uses patterns of nested invocations to direct the generation of a result.

Consider a program that reads a list of triples and returns a list of pairs; a triple contains the coefficients of a quadratic equation with real roots and the pair is its computed roots, so that if an input triple is (1,3, 2), the output pair would be (2, 1). In the functional language Haskell, the algorithm could be rendered as shown in Fig. 1. The functional language Scheme (similar to Lisp—*q.v.*) could have been used in a similar way.

This style makes the nesting of function calls, argument binding, and the conditional expression very important. For instance, a search can be specified as follows. The parameters here are a pair of linear lists that contain, respectively, keys and their associated information, as well as a targetKey. The lists hold homogeneously typed elements, and elements of the key type must be capable of being tested for equality. Then a sequential search (*see* SEARCHING) can be programmed in Haskell as shown in Fig. 2.

Haskell provides an infix list constructor function (:) and uses it in a serial pattern-match to decompose both lists. The last two lines specify that if the first element in the list of keys matches the target key, then search returns the corresponding info, and if not, then it returns what it finds by searching deeper into the two lists.

There are various approaches to a pure applicative (functional) style. Some restrict user-defined functions to receive only elementary data objects as arguments and return them as results. Examples of this class include primitive recursion, pure expressions in Iverson's APL (*q.v.*), and Backus's FP. More contemporary examples demand that functions themselves be data objects, to be passed freely throughout the system. Examples include very pure versions of McCarthy's Lisp (and of Scheme), Clean, Id, Miranda, ML, and Haskell.

```
solveQuads :: Floating n => [(n, n, n)] -> [(n, n)]
solveQuads = map quad where
    quad (a,b,c) = ( (- b + rtDiscriminant)/denominator,
                     (-b- rtDiscriminant) / denominator) where
        rtDiscriminant = sqrt (b*b - 4*a*c)
        denominator = a+a
```

Figure 1. A Haskell program that returns a list of quadratic-equation roots. The first line declares `solveQuads` to be a function that takes a list of real number triples and returns a list of pairs (the brackets denote "list of"). In the next line, the definition is `map quad`, a function that applies the `quad` function to all elements of a list (quad takes a coefficient-triple and returns the pair of roots).

```
search:: (Eq keyType) =>[keyType]->[infoType]->keyType->infoType
search (key:moreKeys) (info:moreInfo) targetKey
    |key==targetkey = info
    |otherwise      = search moreKeys moreInfo targetKey
```

Figure 2. A Haskell program to search a list for a value associated with a given search key.

```
buildTable:: (Eq keyType) =>[keyType]->[infoType]->keyType->infoType
buildTable lisKeys lisInfo targetKey = search liskeys lisInfo where
    search (key:moreKeys) (info:moreInfo)
        |key==targetkey = info
        |otherwise      = search moreKeys moreInfo
```

Figure 3. A Haskell program that returns a search function that encapsulates a lookup table.

A more interesting formulation of the search function is `translate`, which demands only a key as its parameter, and returns only the associated information as its result. The assembly of key–information pairings is internal to it. Such a function can be used freely and repeatedly once that "table" is built. So we show how to build such a function from the `lisKeys` and the `lisInfo` incrementally in Fig. 3. Of course,

```
buildTable [1, 5, 2, 4, 3] ["one", "five",
                "two", "four", "three"] 5
```

just reduces to "five" but the result of

```
buildTable [1, 5, 2, 4, 3] ["one", "five",
                "two", "four", "three"]
```

(the same thing without the final argument 5) is the `translate` function that translates one of these numbers into the string that names it. More interestingly,

```
buildTable [1, 5, 2, 4, 3]
```

yields the skeleton of a search builder already seeded with these five keys, later to be augmented with alternative information lists to be associated with them; another might be `["odd", "odd", "even", "even", "odd"]`.

Many applicative languages, including Haskell, default to *lazy evaluation*, whereby no computation need occur until it becomes essential to the next visible (output) behavior of the program. For instance, suppose that the list `Lisinfo` in the examples above is being read very slowly from the Internet. Since the content of the list is not directly necessary to build the `translate` function, Haskell can construct it before that list is completed. It does so by planting a *suspension* (or a "promise") of some suffix of that list inside the closed function, which will happily search and find information that has been read—and, of course, wait for any that has not. Laziness makes input and output streams themselves into lists of which only the first element need be explicit; the rest becomes manifest only as it is accessed. A typical use for such a *stream* is to print it, and the traversal during printing forces more of it to become explicit. But not all functional languages provide lazy evaluation.

The feature of functional languages that enables lazy evaluation is the same one that makes them so attractive for parallel processing (*q.v.*): nothing in the program can require specification of, or a change to, the state of the machine. In procedure-oriented languages (*q.v.*), assignment statements or input–output commands allow the programmer to affect state, but without such control, the implementation is freer to alter the sequence of computation to suit the demand for results or to balance resources available to the program.

Functional programming offers expressiveness for machine architectures that goes beyond that used by conventional procedure-oriented languages. Since results are defined without sequential imperatives, much of a functional program can be adapted to use available parallelism (e.g. multiple or pipelined processors—*see* PIPELINE) without tailoring it to a particular machine.

Bibliography

1996. Thompson, S. *Haskell: The Craft of Functional Programming*, 2nd Ed. Reading, MA: Addison-Wesley.
1998. Bird, R. *Introduction to Functional Programming using Haskell*, 2nd Ed. London: Prentice Hall.

David S. Wise

FUZZY LOGIC

For article on a related subject, see

✛ Discrete Mathematics

The concept of a *fuzzy set*, introduced by Lofti Zadeh in 1965, deals with the representation of classes whose boundaries are not sharp. It uses a characteristic function taking values in the interval [0, 1]. In a fuzzy set, transition between membership and nonmembership is gradual rather than abrupt; some elements that are considered as "marginal" or "less acceptable" are given a degree of membership that is intermediate between 0 (nonmembership) and 1 (full membership).

Fuzzy set–based methods, often referred to as *fuzzy logic*, have been used in a variety of applications, including process and quality control, fault detection, production scheduling, robotics (*q.v.*), chemistry, civil engineering, ergonomics, project planning, management, and finance. Examples of popular applications can be encountered in transportation systems and process control, as well as in domestic appliances where rules with fuzzy descriptors provide the model of the control strategy.

Historically, fuzzy sets have been noted for their ability to model linguistic categories. This is because many natural language concepts have *degrees of* applicability. Fuzzy sets provide an interface between the numerical data observed in the physical world and the linguistic categories that people apply to it. Thus, fuzzy sets naturally arise when a finite set of terms has to be mapped to a linguistic scale. For instance, if the scale of human heights is chosen to be the real interval [0, 250] in centimeters, to which a set of terms {short, medium-sized, tall} corresponds, then it is difficult to find exact thresholds a and b, such that, for instance short $= [0, a)$, medium-sized $= [a, b]$, and tall $= (b, 250]$. Indeed, the predicates *short, medium-sized, tall* are imprecise rather than clear-cut.

Semantics

Different semantics (interpretations) can be associated with the use of fuzzy sets. One is the expression of closeness, proximity, similarity, indiscernibility, indistinguishability, and so on. Under this semantics, elements with membership 1 are viewed as prototypical elements of the fuzzy set, while the other membership values estimate the closeness of elements to the prototypical ones. This view is most commonly used in pattern classification, where objects that are judged to be sufficiently similar are gathered in the same (fuzzy) class.

A second semantics for fuzzy sets, introduced by Zadeh in 1978, is related to the representation of incomplete or vague states of information as *possibility distributions*, for example, we know only that "John is tall" without knowing his height more precisely. Such a view of fuzzy sets enables imperfect, imprecise, or uncertain information to be modeled. This gives rise to a new theory of uncertainty. *Possibility theory* can be related to probability theory, but whereas probability theory is additive, possibility theory is "maxitive": the possibility of a disjunction of events is the maximum of the possibilities of each event. The possibility of an event is an estimate of its degree of "unsurprisingness," while its necessity evaluates its degree of acceptance. Numerical possibility theory is the simplest theory of imprecise probabilities.

Application Domains

Fuzzy sets offer a methodology for devising hierarchical models of complex linguistic categories that embody high-level objectives. For example, assessing the degree to which a seat is comfortable or a bank customer is creditworthy are examples of complex categories for which fuzzy set-based models have been proposed.

Fuzzy arithmetic is also well suited to engineering design. Poorly specified parameters can be represented by fuzzy numbers, and since the parameters are controllable by the designer, membership functions represent preference profiles. Indeed, performing operations on fuzzy numbers comes down to a constraint propagation problem including preference propagation. Moreover, knowing the overall performance level enables design parameters to be chosen accordingly.

Bibliography

1996. Zadeh, L. A. *Selected Papers on Fuzzy Sets, Fuzzy Logic and Fuzzy Systems* (eds. G. J. Klir and B. Yuan). Singapore: World Scientific.

1996. Zimmermann, H. J. *Fuzzy Set Theory and its Applications*, 3rd Ed. Boston: Kluwer Academic.

Didier Dubois and Henri Prade

GAMES

See COMPUTER GAMES.

GATE, LOGIC

See COMPUTER CIRCUITRY; and LOGIC DESIGN.

GATEWAY

For articles on related subjects, *see*

+ Data Communications
+ Local Area Network (LAN)
+ Network Protocols
+ Networks, Computer
+ Open Systems Interconnection
+ Packet Switching

A *gateway* is a communications device that interconnects networks. There are two common ways to do this, and the term gateway is used to describe both.

1. A gateway can interconnect two or more network services. Figure 1 shows a simple device that takes packets from one network and forwards

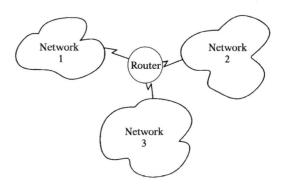

Figure 1. Gateway: internetwork router.

them to another. The underlying technology and formats of packets may be different, but the essential service/protocol is the same. Alternative terms for this device are *router*, *switch*, and network or internetwork level relay. A gateway that verifies user identity and refuses network access to unauthorized users is called a *firewall*.

2. A gateway can convert between two different ways of providing a particular communications application (see Fig. 2). Alternative terms for such a gateway are *application level relay*, *application protocol converter*, and *application protocol translator*. An example of this is a device that takes electronic mail (*q.v.*) from one system and converts and forwards it to another.

Both these devices are distinct from *repeaters* and *bridges*. However, it has become common

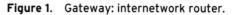

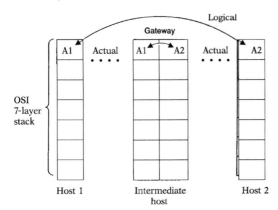

Figure 2.   Application level gateway.

to combine the distinct logical functionality of a bridge and a router into a single physical unit, commonly known as a *bridging router*, bridge-router, or *brouter*.

In the OSI layered service model, a gateway operates either in layer 3 or layer 7. A repeater operates at layer 1, while a bridge operates at level 2. Any of the interconnection devices can be built around a standard microcomputer and its bus (*q.v.*), connecting the latter to a number of communications-link port-controller devices. Alternatively, the system may be built around a special-purpose *switch fabric* with autonomous input and output port controller devices communicating directly with one another. A router of the latter design is called a *switched router*.

Networks that employ different network services cannot be connected using network level relay type gateways. Instead, they must employ application level gateways, or else use some *ad hoc* means such as a Transport Service Bridge (Rose, 1990).

Bibliography

1990. Rose, M. T. *The Open Book*. Upper Saddle River, NJ: Prentice Hall.

1997. Stevens, W. R. *Unix Network Programming*, 2nd Ed., Vol. 1. Upper Saddle River, NJ: Prentice Hall.

Jon Crowcroft

GENETIC ALGORITHMS

For articles on related subjects, *see*

+ Algorithms, Design and Classification of
+ Artificial Life
+ Molecular Computing

Genetic algorithms (GAs) are computational search, learning, optimization, and modeling methods, loosely inspired by biological evolution. Very roughly, evolution can be viewed as searching in parallel among an enormous number of possibilities for "solutions" to the problem of survival in an environment where the solutions are particular designs for organisms. The "rules" of evolution are remarkably simple: species evolve by means of *heritable variation* (via mutation, recombination, and other operators), followed by *natural selection* in which the fittest tend to survive and reproduce, thus propagating their genetic material to future generations. Yet these simple rules are thought to be responsible, in large part, for the extraordinary variety and complexity we see in the biosphere. Seen in this light, the mechanisms of evolution can inspire computational search methods for finding solutions to hard problems in large search spaces or for designing complex systems automatically.

GAs were originally formulated by Holland (1975), not to solve specific problems, but rather as a means to study formally the phenomenon of adaptation in nature and to develop ways in which the mechanisms of natural adaptation might be imported into computer systems. Only after Holland's original work were GAs adapted to solving optimization problems.

Genetic algorithms begin with a population of randomly generated candidate solutions ("individuals"), and perform fitness-based selection and random variation to create a new population. Some number of the individuals of highest fitness are chosen under selection to create offspring for the next generation. Often, an offspring will be produced via a crossover between two or more parents, in which the offspring receives "genetic material" (different parts of candidate solutions) from different parents. Typically the offspring is also mutated randomly. Offspring are created in this way until a new generation is complete. This process iterates for many generations, often ending up with one or more optimal or high-quality individuals in the population.

Genetic algorithms are one of several evolution-inspired search methods. Two other well-known methods are *evolution strategies* (ESs) and *evolutionary programming* (EP). These three methods were developed independently in the 1960s: GAs by Holland, ESs by Rechenberg and Schwefel, and EP by Fogel, Owens, and Walsh (1966). Genetic programming, a variant of genetic algorithms, was developed in the 1980s by Koza (1992, 1999). Such methods were part of a general movement for using biological ideas in computer science that started with pioneers such as von Neumann (*q.v.*), Turing (*q.v.*), and Wiener (*q.v.*), and continues today with evolutionary methods, neural networks, and methods based on the immune system, insect colonies, and other biological systems.

Setting the parameters for the evolutionary process is often a matter of guesswork and trial and error, though some theoretical and heuristic guidelines have been discovered. An alternative is to have the parameters "self-adapt"—by changing their values automatically over the course of evolution in response to selective pressures. Self-adapting parameters are an intrinsic part of ESs and EP, and are the subject of much research in GAs.

Bibliography

1966. Fogel, L. J., Owens, A. J., and Walsh, M. J. *Artificial Intelligence through Simulated Evolution.* New York: John Wiley.

1975. Holland, J. H. *Adaptation in Natural and Artificial Systems.* Ann Arbor, MI: University of Michigan Press. (2nd edition, MIT Press, 1992).

1992. Koza, J. R. *Genetic Programming: On the Programming of Computers by Means of Natural Selection.* Cambridge, MA: MIT Press.

1996. Mitchell, M. *An Introduction to Genetic Algorithms.* Cambridge, MA: MIT Press.

1999. Koza, J. R., Forrest, H. B., Martin, A. K., and David, A. *Genetic Programming III: Darwinian Invention and Problem Solving.* San Francisco: Morgan Kaufmann.

Melanie Mitchell

GEOGRAPHIC INFORMATION SYSTEM (GIS)

For articles on related subjects, *see*

+ Computer Graphics
+ Database Management System (DBMS)
+ Relational Database

Geographic information describes the locations, characteristics, and shapes of features and phenomena on the surface of planets such as Earth. Traditionally, such information has been produced, disseminated, and used in the form of paper maps and atlases. Increasingly, however, it has been possible to produce such information in digital form, and the advent of instruments capable of sensing Earth's surface from space accelerated this process. A system that handles, processes, edits, manipulates, analyzes, and displays geographic data is called a *geographic information system* (GIS).

History and Applications

GIS began in the mid-1960s; the Canada GIS is often credited with being the first major project. It applied computer technology to the analysis of vast amounts of map data collected by the Canada Land Inventory (Foresman, 1998). GIS requires specialized input and output devices, including map-sized *digitizers*, high-resolution *scanners*, and pen *plotters*, and the development of these peripherals in the 1960s was a major impetus. However, the major growth period of GIS began only in the early 1980s, following the development of *database management systems* (DBMS) that support a *relational database* and super-minicomputers such as the VAX. Today a GIS is most often encountered as a networked application running under Unix (*q.v.*) or Microsoft Windows.

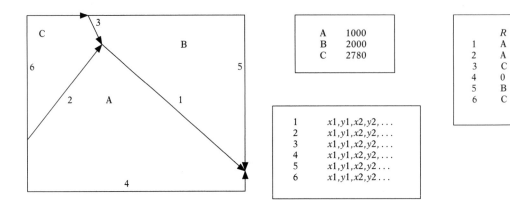

Figure 1. A simple map of counties (left) and the three structures used to represent it in a vector-based GIS: a relational table of county names and attributes (upper middle); a relational table of county adjacencies that indicates the area to the right and left of each directed edge with 0 representing the outside (upper right); and a file of ordered coordinates for each common boundary.

GIS databases make use of both *raster* and *vector* representations—application domains tend to be dominated by one or the other. Raster-based representations are most common where remote sensing is a major source of raw data, and where spatial resolution is limited, and are thus most likely to be found applied to natural resource management, agriculture, forestry, or environmental science. In vector-based representations, geographic phenomena are represented as discrete points, lines, areas, or volumes, with associated attributes. A vector-based GIS is most likely to be found in transportation, assessment and management of land ownership records, infrastructure and utility maintenance, vehicle routing and scheduling, and related applications.

An important concept in GIS is the *layer*, defined as a representation of some specific variable, class of objects, or phenomenon over the geographic area of the database. The ability to combine information from different layers, and thus to analyze the relationships between facts about the same geographic location that may be separated on different paper maps, is an important characteristic of a GIS.

Architecture

Most GIS products are built on a standard relational DBMS. Because of the difficulty of handling variable-length strings of coordinates efficiently in a relational DBMS, the early products of the 1980s adopted a *hybrid* architecture in which the attributes of objects and the topological relationships between them are represented in relational tables. For example, a map of population by county could be represented by three structures: a relational table identifying the name of each county and its associated population; a relational table identifying each common boundary between two counties with the names of the adjacent counties; and a file of variable-length records, each containing the ordered pairs of coordinates needed to describe one common boundary. Figure 1 shows a simple example of this basic GIS concept (note the use of 0 to denote the unmapped area, and the use of the order of coordinates to determine the right and left sides of each common boundary). More recently, the improved performance of computer platforms has allowed integration of all three data structures within a relational DBMS, leading to a new architecture in which the DBMS is the sole repository of the GIS database.

Bibliography

1997. Demers, M. N. *Fundamentals of Geographic Information Systems.* New York: John Wiley.

1998. Foresman, T. W. (ed.) *The History of Geographic Information Systems: Perspectives from the Pioneers.* Upper Saddle River, NJ: Prentice Hall.

1998. Longley, P. A., Goodchild, M. F., Maguire, D. J., and Rhind, D. W. (eds.) *Geographical Information Systems: Principles, Techniques, Management and Applications.* New York: John Wiley.

Michael Goodchild

GLOBAL AND LOCAL VARIABLES

For articles on related subjects, *see*

✛ Block Structure
✛ Procedure-Oriented Languages
✛ Side Effect

The entity denoted by a variable name in a computer program can generally be accessed (i.e. examined or changed) only in certain parts of the program. The domain of the program within which a variable name can be used is called the *scope* of the variable. In a *block-structured* language, the scope of a variable is the block in which it is declared, but excludes any subblocks that are internal to the defining block *and* in which the same variable name is declared. This is illustrated in Fig. 1, which shows the schematic of an Algol program with an outer block L1 and an inner subblock L2, which in turn contains two further subblocks L3 and L4. Also shown in Fig. 1 is the scope of each variable. Note in particular that a variable such as C, defined in the outer block, has a scope L1 exclusive of L4 because a C is declared again in L4.

A variable in a block in which it is defined, such as G in block L4 in the example, is said to be *local* to that block, and is therefore a *local variable*. Correspondingly, variable A is *global* to block L4, since it is defined outside this block, although it may be referred to in the block. The variable C defined in the outer block is also global to block L4, but it cannot be referred to in L4 because of the declaration of C

```
L1: begin
      real A, C, D; real array B[1:10];
    L2: begin
          real D, E; real array F[4:12];
        L3: begin
              real F, G;
                .
                .
              end L3;
        L4; begin
              real B, C, G;
                .
                .
              end L4;
        end L2;
    end L1;
```

Variable name	Label of defining block	Scope of name
A	L1	L1
B	L1	L1,~L4
C	L1	L1,~L4
D	L1	L1,~L2
D	L2	L2
E	L2	L2
F	L2	L2,~L3
F	L3	L3
G	L3	L3
B	L4	L4
C	L4	L4
G	L4	L4

Note: L1,~L4 means, for example, that the variable's scope holds throughout block L1 except for block L4.

Figure 1. Scope of variable names.

in block L4, the latter (but different) C being local to L4.

Variables that are global to many blocks may conveniently be used by all of them, but the operations in one block may then interfere with those of another by changing a global variable. It is good programming practice to avoid such *side effects* by using global variables sparingly, if at all, and to share information between blocks by parameter passing (*q.v.*) in subprograms.

Bibliography

1993. Louden, K. C. *Programming Languages: Principles and Practice.* Boston: PWS-Kent Publishing Company.

J. A. N. Lee and Anthony Ralston

GLOBAL POSITIONING SYSTEM (GPS)

For articles on related subjects, *see*

+ Embedded System
+ Geographic Information System (GIS)

The *Global Positioning System* (GPS) is a satellite-based digital information system that enables the location of objects on the surface of the Earth, precise within a few feet. GPS is funded and controlled by the U.S. Department of Defense (DoD). GPS provides specially coded satellite signals that can be processed by a ground receiver that contains an embedded digital signal processor (DSP–*q.v.*). Because incoming data must be corrected for relativistic effects, the associated satellite must contain a very high precision atomic clock. Four GPS satellite signals are used to compute positions in three dimensions and a time offset with respect to the clock.

The spatial segment of the system consists of GPS satellites whose *transponders* emit radio signals. The GPS *Operational Constellation* consists of 24 satellites that orbit the earth at an altitude of 10 900 nautical miles every 12 hours. As the earth turns underneath, the satellites repeat the same track and configuration over any point every 24 hours, but four minutes earlier each day. There are six orbital planes with four satellites in each, equally spaced at 60° apart and inclined at about 55° with respect to the equatorial plane. This constellation provides the user with between five and eight satellites visible from any point on the earth.

The GPS concept was conceived by Ivan Getting (1912–2003) in the 1960s while he was president of the Aerospace Corporation. Bradford Parkinson led the engineering team that developed the first experimental system in 1978. The system, as we now know it, was deployed in 1988.

GPS systems are now available as optional equipment in some luxury automobiles that use them to gather the information needed for display of a map of current position and heading on a dashboard screen. Handheld GPS receivers are popular with hikers and boaters. Additionally, GPS systems are used in archeology, oceanography, geographic information systems (*q.v.*), mining, space exploration, and many other fields.

Bibliography

1998. Farrell, J. A., and Barth, M. *The Global Positioning System and Inertial Navigation.* New York: McGraw-Hill.
2002. Ashby, N. "Relativity and the Global Positioning System," *Physics Today*, **55**(5), (May) 41–47.

Edwin D. Reilly

GNU SOFTWARE

See FREE SOFTWARE FOUNDATION (FSF); and LINUX.

GRAPH THEORY

For articles on related subjects, *see*

+ Algorithms, Analysis of
+ Computational Complexity
+ Data Structures
+ Discrete Mathematics
+ NP-Complete Problems
+ Tree

Terminology

A *graph* is a set of points (commonly called *vertices* or *nodes*) in space that are interconnected by a set of lines (called *edges*). For a graph G, the edge set is denoted by E and the vertex set by V, so that $G = (V, E)$. Common nomenclature denotes the number of vertices $|V|$ by n and the number of edges $|E|$ by m. Figure 1 shows a graph G with $V = \{v_1, v_2, v_3, v_4, v_5\}$, $E = \{e_1, e_2, e_3, e_4, e_5, e_6, e_7\}$, $n = 5$, and $m = 7$.

If the values of both n and m are finite, G is said to be a *finite* graph. The *degree* of a vertex v (denoted by

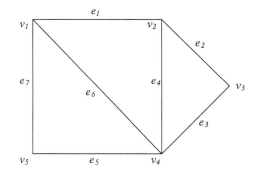

Figure 1. A graph with 5 vertices and 7 edges.

$d(v)$) is the number of edges that have v as an endpoint. An elementary theorem is that within a finite graph there are always an even number of vertices with odd degree. For example, in the graph of Fig. 1 there are two vertices (v_1 and v_2) of odd degree (both have degree 3). A *self-loop* is an edge (v_i, v_j) where $v_i = v_j$. Two edges (v_i, v_j) and (v_r, v_s) are *parallel edges* if $v_i = v_r$ and $v_j = v_s$. A *simple graph* is a graph without self-loops and without parallel edges. A *multigraph* contains parallel edges but no self-loops. A *path* between vertices v_1 and v_s is a sequence of vertices (v_1, v_2, v_3, ..., v_s) such that (v_i, v_{i+1}) $\in E$ for $1 \leq i \leq s - 1$. If $v_1 = v_s$, the path is a *circuit* (or cycle). If no vertex appears more than once on a path, then the path is a *simple path* (similarly, a *simple circuit* passes through any vertex at most once). A *component* of a graph is defined by stating that a path exists between any pair of vertices if and only if the two vertices belong to the same component of the graph. A graph consisting of a single component is said to be a *connected graph*. A *tree* is a connected graph containing no circuits. For any tree T with n vertices and m edges, $m = n - 1$ and there exists precisely one path between any pair of vertices of T.

In many applications, it is natural to associate a direction with each edge of the graph. The graph is then said to be a *directed graph* or *digraph*. In specifying any edge of a digraph by its endpoints, by convention the edge is understood to be directed from the first vertex towards the second. The *indegree*, $d^-(v)$, of any vertex v is the number of edges directed towards v. Similarly, the *outdegree*, $d^+(v)$, of v is the number of edges directed from v. A digraph G is *strongly connected* if, for any pair

of vertices u and v of G, there exists a path from u to v and a path from v to u.

Many applications require a number to be associated with each edge of a graph. Such a graph with associated *edge weights* is said to be a *weighted graph*. For any edge (u, v), $w(u, v)$ denotes the edge weight, which is also sometimes called the *length* of (u, v).

In a *complete graph*, there is an edge between every pair of vertices. The complete graph with n vertices is denoted by K_n. Figure 2 shows K_3 and K_4. In a *regular* undirected graph, every vertex has the same degree; if this is k, the graph is *k-regular*. Note that K_n is $(n - 1)$-regular.

If, for a graph G, it is possible to partition the vertex set v into two disjoint subsets, V_1 and V_2 ($V_1 \cup V_2 = V$), such that every edge of G connects a vertex in V_1 to a vertex in V_2, then G is a *bipartite graph*. If there is an edge between every vertex of V_1 and every vertex of V_2, then G is said to be a *complete bipartite graph*, which is denoted by $K_{i,j}$, where $|V_1| = i$ and $|V_2| = j$. Figure 3 shows two representations of $K_{3,3}$. In this figure, dots distinguish vertices from edge crossings. The graphs

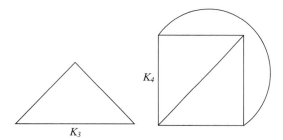

Figure 2. The complete graphs with 3 and 4 vertices.

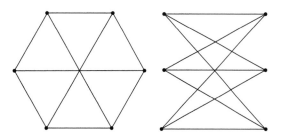

Figure 3. The complete bipartite graph $K_{3,3}$.

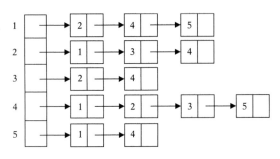

Figure 4. An adjacency list representation of the graph of Figure.1.

of this figure are said to be *isomorphic*. Two graphs are isomorphic if there is a one-to-one correspondence between the vertices of one and the vertices of the other such that the number of edges between any two vertices of one is equal to the number of edges between the corresponding vertices in the other.

Computations involving graphs require that the graph be represented within computer storage. The choice of data structure may have important implications for the complexity of the algorithm. A natural form of representation is provided by a so-called *adjacency matrix*. An adjacency matrix A is an $n \times n$ matrix where $A(i, j) = 1$ if $(v_i, v_j) \in E$ and is 0 otherwise. Such a representation requires $O(n^2)$ storage space and consequently requires $O(n^2)$ time to initialize. Adjacency matrices are very useful for algorithmic questions concerning paths in graphs.

Another common data structure for graphs is the so-called *adjacency list* representation. In this representation, for every $v \in V$, $L(v)$ is a pointer to a list of vertices adjacent to v. Figure 4 shows the adjacency list representation of the graph of Fig. 1. The adjacency list representation of a graph requires $O(n + m)$ space and thus $O(n + m)$ time to initialize. This is usually an improvement compared with adjacency matrices.

Graph Algorithms

Many graph algorithms are structured by systematically searching (or *traversing*) the graph. Consider the following technique for traversing a (connected) graph. Initially, mark all vertices as being "unvisited." Now

start the search at some arbitrarily chosen vertex and, when visiting any vertex v, proceed as follows. If v has not been previously visited, mark v as "visited." Next, visit an "unvisited" vertex in the adjacency list for v. If no such vertex exists, return to the vertex visited just before v was visited for the first time. The visit terminates when all vertices adjacent to the initial vertex have been visited and the search has returned to the initial vertex. Such a search is called a *depth-first search* (DFS), which can be done in $O(n + m)$ time.

Another frequently employed traversal method is *breadth-first search* (BFS). In a BFS for a connected graph, some arbitrary vertex is visited first, and this vertex is placed on an initially empty queue Q. At any point in the traversal, remove the head element in the queue and then mark all vertices adjacent to the element removed "visited" and place them on the queue. Repeat this until the queue becomes empty.

An *Eulerian circuit* of a graph is a circuit that contains every edge of the graph precisely once. Of course, not every graph contains an Eulerian circuit. A necessary and sufficient condition for a connected, undirected graph to contain an Eulerian circuit is that every vertex of the graph is of even degree.

A *Hamiltonian circuit* of a connected graph is a circuit that passes through each vertex precisely once. Such a circuit can be defined for both directed and undirected graphs (of course, in the case of digraphs, edges are traversed in the same sense as they are directed). Not every graph contains a Hamiltonian circuit and there seems to be no polynomial time test for whether such a circuit exists for a given graph. The problem of determining whether a graph contains a Hamiltonian circuit is a classic NP-complete problem. If the graph is weighted, the problem of finding a shortest Hamiltonian circuit is one variation of the well-known *traveling salesman* problem.

Planar graphs are an important subclass of graphs. A graph is planar if it can be arranged on a planar surface (the arrangement is called an *embedding*) so that, at most, one vertex occupies or, at most, one edge passes through any point of the plane. There exist algorithms that can test whether a graph is planar (such algorithms normally generate an embedding) in $O(n)$ time.

Scheduling and timetabling problems, among others, generate problems equivalent to coloring graphs. A *vertex coloring* of a graph is the assignment of a color to each vertex of the graph in such a way that no two adjacent vertices have the same color. Normally, the interest is to find a vertex coloring that employs a minimum number of colors; this number is called the *vertex-chromatic index*. Similarly, an *edge coloring* is an assignment of colors to the edges in such a way that no two edges sharing an endpoint have the same color. The minimum number of colors required to do this is the *edge-chromatic index*.

A *spanning tree* of a connected graph G is a connected circuitless subgraph of G that contains every vertex of G. The *connector problem*, a classic problem of graph theory, is to find a spanning tree of a weighted connected graph such that the sum of the edge weights of the tree is a minimum. Such a solution is also called a *minimum weight spanning tree*. Spanning trees can be found in $O(m + n)$ time (e.g. a depth-first search tree). Prim's or Kruskal's algorithms provide classic solutions to the connector problem at low-order polynomial-time cost.

Given the intractability of many problems in graph theory, it is natural that this area has given rise to the development of many approximation algorithms. An *approximation algorithm* is an algorithm that runs in polynomial-time but that provides an approximation (within known bounds) to the problem in hand. A classic example is provided by *Christofides' algorithm*, which finds a solution to the traveling salesman problem that guarantees that the solution found is no more than a factor of 3/2 longer than an optimum solution.

Bibliography

1976. Biggs, N. L., Lloyd, E. K., and Wilson, R. J. *Graph Theory 1736–1936*. Oxford: Oxford University Press.
1979. Even, S. *Graph Algorithms*. Potomac, MD: Computer Science Press.
1995. Harary, F. *Graph Theory*. Cambridge, MA: Perseus Press.
1997. Wilson, R. J. *Introduction to Graph Theory*. Reading, MA: Addison-Wesley.

Alan M. Gibbons

GRAPHICAL USER INTERFACE (GUI)

See USER INTERFACE; and WINDOW ENVIRONMENTS.

GRAPHICS

See COMPUTER GRAPHICS.

GRID COMPUTING

See DISTRIBUTED SYSTEMS.

GUARDED COMMAND

For articles on related subjects, *see*

+ Concurrent Programming
+ Control Structures
+ Program Verification

A *guarded command* (Dijkstra, 1975) is synonymous with a conditionally executed statement. More precisely, a guarded command is the combination of a Boolean expression B and the statement S whose execution is controlled by B. In a sense, B "guards" the execution of S. In Dijkstra's notation, a guarded command is represented as $B \rightarrow S$. In more common notation, the meaning of a guarded command is very much like that of the simple selection structure (**if** statement): if B

then S. Unlike the **if** statement, however, a guarded command, by itself, is not a complete statement in a programming language. Rather, it is one component of a more extensive control structure containing one or more guarded commands.

The most interesting applications of guarded commands are those involving a set of n of them, for $n > 1$.

$$
\begin{array}{ccc}
B_1 & \rightarrow & S_1 \\
B_2 & \rightarrow & S_2 \\
& \vdots & \\
B_n & \rightarrow & S_n
\end{array}
$$

When a structure containing a set of guarded commands is executed, the order in which the guards are evaluated is immaterial. Upon evaluation of all n, a (possibly empty) subset of the guards will have the value *true*. Of this subset, one is chosen at random and its corresponding S is selected for execution. If all of the guards in a given guarded command set are disjoint, then the selection of S is well defined despite the randomness of guard evaluation and selection. Otherwise, selection of S is not well defined (and indeed may be different from one execution of the program to the next). Thus, guarded command sets are fundamentally *nondeterministic*.

Guarded command sets may be incorporated into control structures in a number of ways. The following examples were first described by Dijkstra.

A *selection* control structure has the syntax

```
if
    B₁  →  S₁
    B₂  →  S₂
         ⋮
    Bₙ  →  Sₙ
fi
```

The semantics of this structure are that after execution of an S, execution of the **if-fi** terminates. Only one execution of an S is performed, the selection of which is as described above. If no B is true in an execution of an **if-fi** structure, then execution of the **if-fi** does not terminate, causing the program to abort. In a multitasking (*q.v.*) environment, an alternative might be to wait for a guard to become true.

This **if-fi** structure is very much like the classical case control structure (*see* CONTROL STRUCTURES), in that only one statement group is executed and the order of the statement groups is immaterial. Unlike the usual case structure, however, the guards in the **if-fi** structure may be nondisjoint arbitrary conditions. In the case structure, the "guards" are disjoint sets of constants. Thus, the case structure is completely deterministic, whereas the **if-fi** is in general nondeterministic.

The following program is a simple application of the **if-fi** structure:

```
            [determine max(P,Q)]
    if
        P ≥ Q  →  MAX  ←  P
        Q ≥ P  →  MAX  ←  Q
    fi
        [MAX  =  max(P, Q)]
```

In this example, one of the two guards must be true, so that execution of this **if-fi** is guaranteed to terminate. Note also that both guards may be true (when $P = Q$), and that in this case execution of either statement gives the same result. Thus, at termination of execution of the **if-fi**, MAX = *max*(P, Q).

A *repetition* control structure involving guarded commands has the form

```
do
    B₁  →  S₁
    B₂  →  S₂
         ⋮
    Bₙ  →  Sₙ
od
```

The semantics are that a statement S is selected in the manner described above, and, after execution of S, this entire process is repeated. Execution of the do-od structure terminates only when all guards evaluate to false. By constructing the appropriate guards, any desired repetitive control can be achieved.

The following program for calculating the greatest common divisor of two positive integers illustrates the use of do-od for specifying repetition control.

```
                   [determine gcd(P,Q)]
X ← P, Y ← Q
do
    X > Y → X ← X − Y
    Y > X → Y ← Y − X
od
                   [X = Y = gcd(P,Q)]
```

Note that the two guards in this program for *gcd* are disjoint, so that this example is completely deterministic.

The `if-fi` and `do-od` are quite versatile control structures. The inefficiencies of guard evaluation, however, currently discourage their use as practical control structures in sequential programming languages. However, since `if-fi` and `do-od` are inherently "parallel," concurrent guard evaluation resolves this problem in parallel execution environments. Languages used in such environments, and which support versions of guarded commands, are Ada (*q.v.*) and Occam.

Bibliography

1975. Dijkstra, E. J. "Guarded Commands, Nondeterminancy and Formal Derivations of Programs," *Communications of the ACM*, **18**(August), 453–457.

1976. Dijkstra, E. J. *A Discipline of Programming.* Upper Saddle River, NJ: Prentice Hall.

1995. Barnes, J. G. P. *Programming in Ada 95.* Reading, MA: Addison-Wesley.

Jerrold L. Wagener

GURU

For articles on related subjects, *see*

+ Power User
+ Wizard

The term *guru*, a Hindi word, is used in computing with its conventional meaning: a wise person—a teacher, perhaps—who knows a great deal about a particular subject and who is readily available and anxious to share knowledge with others. Some early computer gurus were Jackson Granholm, who held forth in *Datamation*, and H. R. J. Grosch, who promulgated, among other percepts, Grosch's Law (*see* LAWS, COMPUTER). The era of the personal computer has spawned more gurus than mainframe computers ever did, current exemplars being John Dvorak of *PC Magazine*, Esther Dyson of EDventure Holdings, and Stewart Alsop of *InfoWorld*.

Gurus, who *know* much, are not necessarily programmers and hence not usually *wizards*, who can *do* much, though they may very well be *power users* of particular operating systems (*q.v.*), user interfaces (*q.v.*), or applications software.

Edwin D. Reilly

HACKER

For articles on related subjects, *see*

+ Computer Crime
+ Guru
+ Power User
+ Privacy, Computers and
+ Virus, Computer
+ Wizard

Hackers are obsessed with computers; they strive to master them. The classic hacker of the early decades of computing was simply a compulsive programmer; the term carried no pejorative connotation (Levy, 1984). It is only since the era of heavily networked computers that the term *hacker* has become associated with computerized vandalism. Those who seek to preserve and promote the honor of the original meaning call the vandals "Black Hat hackers" or "crackers" rather than helpful "White Hat" hackers.

Early hacker communities developed around accessible interactive computer systems at places such as MIT. Today, hacker communities are linked via the World Wide Web (*q.v.*), Usenet, and electronic mail (*q.v.*), and their members may never have met or even know each other's real names. A hacker gains status by demonstrating mastery of the system. This was traditionally done by writing clever programs ("hacks") but there is a growing temptation to attract attention by penetrating ("cracking") a system's security, crashing it, infecting it

with a computer virus, or accessing supposedly secure information.

Most early hackers were programmers. Hacking, as a programming style, is distinguished by its lack of apparent method. Hackers are impatient with structured programming (*q.v.*), object-oriented programming (*q.v.*), documentation, and any kind of systematic development. Instead, the hacker spends long hours at the terminal interactively developing and debugging intuitively. Hackers believe that programs should be built "straight from your mind" (Turkle, 1984). They prize concise, efficient, elegant, and even tricky code. Although this programming style is usually frowned upon, many hacker-developed projects such as the text editor (*q.v.*) Emacs, the operating system Linux (*q.v.*), and the Apache server software are premier examples of the programming craft.

The cyberpunk movement in science fiction has had a powerful influence on hackers. The seminal work in this genre is that of William Gibson. The genre popularizes the notion of cyberspace (*q.v.*) as a virtual reality (*q.v.*) with cyberpunks or network cowboys "jacking in" (connecting) and penetrating *ice* (computer security) to obtain information from corporate databases. Crackers seek to penetrate computer systems. They see computer system security as a challenge and a puzzle to solve. The hackers who have caused the greatest concern are the vandals who turn their skills toward damaging computer systems. Websites have been frequent targets. Crashers demonstrate their mastery of computer systems by causing them to fail precipitously or behave so erratically that they meet the legal threshold of "denial of service."

The public has become fascinated by hackers. Depictions in Gibson's books, movies such as *War Games* and *Sneakers*, and television series such as *Max Headroom* show the hacker in a sympathetic light. System break-ins by crackers, the activities of crashers, and even such disruptive activities as the Internet Worm have been excused as harmless pranks or even praised as valuable lessons in the need for system security. This tolerance is fading rapidly as more and more people become dependent on the Internet.

Bibliography

1984. Levy, S. *Hackers: Heroes of the Computer Revolution.* New York: Anchor Press/Doubleday.

1984. Turkle, S. *The Second Self: Computers and the Human Spirit.* New York: Simon & Schuster.

2000. Johnson, S. *The Hacker Ethic.* New York: Random House.

Robert G. Rittenhouse

HANDSHAKING

For articles on related subjects, *see*

+ Bus
+ Network Protocols
+ Protocol
+ TCP/IP

The exchange of predetermined sequences of control signals or control characters between two devices or systems to establish a connection, to break a connection, or to exchange data and status information, is called *handshaking.* Consider Fig. 1, which shows the sequence of signals on the input–output bus (*q.v.*) of a small computer when writing a single character. The computer first places the device address on the DATA OUT lines and raises the ADDRESS control line to tell the device that the data on the DATA OUT lines is an address. The device recognizes its address and raises the control line OK. This causes the computer to drop ADDRESS and DATA OUT. The device responds by dropping OK, upon which the computer places the character on the DATA OUT lines and raises the control line WRITE. The device then accepts the character and raises OK, signifying that it has accepted it. The computer then drops DATA OUT and WRITE, which causes OK to go down. This completes the handshaking sequence for transferring a character from the computer to the device.

Handshaking also occurs when two remote computers communicate over a network. Here, instead of electrical signals, predetermined sequences of packets containing address, data, and control information are interchanged to establish a connection, transfer

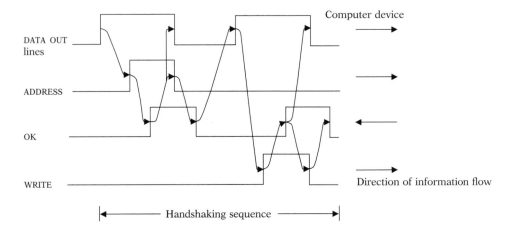

Figure 1. Example of a handshaking sequence. The arrows are used to indicate which control signal causes which response during the sequence.

data or control information, recover from any error conditions, and terminate the connection. Such handshaking sequences between devices over a network obey a set of rules defined by a *communication protocol*, or simply a *protocol*. Such a predominant protocol is the Transmission Control Protocol/Internet Protocol (TCP/IP).

John S. Sobolewski

HARD DISK

For articles on related subjects, *see*

+ Access Time
+ Bus
+ Diskette
+ Memory: Auxiliary

A *hard disk* is a high-capacity, high-speed rotational storage device. They are also called *Winchester drives*, a name derived from a 1969 IBM drive that stored 30 MB of information on each of two spindles, a 30–30 arrangement reminiscent of the famed Winchester 30–30 rifle.

A hard disk consists of a rigid aluminum alloy disk that is coated with a magnetic oxide material, much like a diskette. Because the disks are rigid, they can be spun much faster than a floppy—up to 10 800 rpm. The drive itself may contain a number of platters mounted on a rotating spindle (*see* MEMORY: AUXILIARY). Each platter surface has its own read–write head. The head actually floats above the surface of the disk on a cushion of air. The heads float very close to the disk surface, the gap being about 1/100 000 of an inch. Because the platters are rigid, magnetic material can be densely packed so that hard disks have very high capacities. With a large number of platters, some mainframe hard disks can hold up to a terabyte—a trillion characters. Hard disks used with microcomputers range in storage capacity from 2 to 80 GB or more.

The disk stores data in *tracks* of magnetically oriented particles. There may be over 10 000 tracks on a high-capacity hard disk. The collection of tracks with the same number arranged vertically on all platters is called a *cylinder*. Tracks are divided into sectors. The sectors are laid down when the disk undergoes a low-level software format. The format also establishes the *interleave factor* for the disk. Because a disk is capable of feeding information to an operating system before it is ready to accept it, the controller card may not be ready to read the second sector of a file right after the first. If consecutively numbered sectors are interleaved according to the average time it takes to read data, the disk can operate more efficiently.

On hard disks used with the IBM PC (*q.v.*) and compatibles, track zero is dedicated to system files. To prepare for use of the hard disk and probable later installation of Windows, a high-level format must first be performed using a DOS FORMAT command. This copies some code into the boot sector and starts to expand the file allocation table (FAT). The FAT contains information about which sectors are assigned to which files. When a file is written to a hard disk, it is not written in consecutive sectors. Sectors are scattered all over the disk, organized as a linked list. The disk *directory* knows how big a file is and when it was created.

A SCSI (pronounced "scuzzy") bus has controller hardware that can manage multiple disks or other peripherals. The SCSI subsystem can queue and issue multiple disk-access requests to one or more drives (*command tag queuing*), sort and reorder multiple commands for efficient physical disk access (*elevator seeking*), and permit disconnection and reconnection of drives from the SCSI bus for better bus utilization in multidrive environments.

EIDE devices move much of the controller electronics onto the circuitry of the drive itself. In recent tests with comparable devices, SCSI and EIDE drives performed about the same. The newest EIDE devices use a *bus-mastering* controller with its own CPU to relieve the host processor of burdensome I/O calculations.

Bibliography

1999. Rosch, W. L. *Winn L. Rosch Hardware Bible*, 5th Ed. Indianapolis, IN: Que Publications.

Stephen J. Rogowski

HARDWARE DESCRIPTION LANGUAGES

For articles on related subjects, *see*

+ Instruction Set
+ Logic Design
+ Nonprocedural Languages
+ Procedure-Oriented Languages

Motivation

Hardware description languages (HDLs) are languages that facilitate the conception, design, analysis, simulation, documentation, and manufacturing of digital computer systems. A digital system can be described at many different levels: requirements, system, behavioral, and structural.

A system can be described from the system level to the logic gate level as a network of elements of varying degrees of complexity, including timing diagrams, behavior, and structure. Figure 1 shows examples of

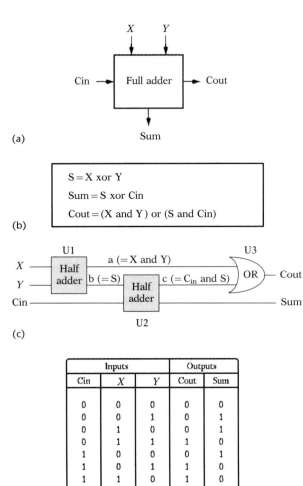

Figure 1. A one-bit full adder and three descriptions of its operation. (a) The full adder component, with inputs and outputs. (b) Logic equations for the full adder. (c) Construction of a full adder from simpler components. (d) Truth table for a full adder.

different descriptions of a 1-bit adder circuit. While a complete digital computer can be described at any level, the amount of low-level information would be too extensive for a human designer to comprehend, and higher-level languages are used to abstract or hide details, resulting in a system-level description of the design. HDLs must provide the ability to include information to support both human-readable and machine-readable functional specifications and design documentation; a mechanism to manage design data; human–computer interaction in the design process; and test analysis for a designed part.

Languages–A Historical Perspective

Languages that may be used for a design description include Ada, C++, Esterel, Hardware C, Verilog, and VHDL. An HDL must be applicable to more than just hardware, so a System Level Description Language (SLDL) is also being developed to permit description of both software and hardware designs at the most abstract levels of design work.

In high-level descriptions, software functions are often included in the system models. Hardware/software systems may be decomposed into a data part and a control part, operating in discrete steps, and some of the lower-level details, such as gate interconnection, placement, and individual gate delays, may be suppressed at the early stages of the design process. Above the gate level, standard or predefined networks of gates and flip-flops are often used as building blocks at the register transfer level. Typical components are registers, multiplexers, and arithmetic-logic units (ALUs—*q.v.*). At the gate level, the elements of design are primitive blocks—the basic logic gates.

Structure is normally depicted by block diagrams. Historically, special-purpose programming languages (called *register transfer* (RT) languages) were used to create simulation models, and a number of such RT-languages were proposed. The existence of digital components capable of interpreting instructions stored in memory (i.e. instruction set processors) motivates the use of a programming level of description. At the programming level, the basic components are the interpretation cycle, the machine instructions, and operations (all of which are defined as register transfer level operations). The programming level describes the behavior

rather than the structure of processors. The proliferation of HDLs in the 1960s and 1970s led to the definition of CONLAN. CONLAN (CONsensus LANguage) was an attempt to design a language construction mechanism rather than a specific hardware description language. The effort thus centered on the definition of a primitive notation and a powerful extension mechanism.

Complexity of the Design Environment

Product Life Cycle

Figure 2 depicts the life cycle of an electronics product. A design starts with the requirements that are to be met. Requirements generate abstract descriptions that evolve into specifications that include the environment and the function of the design. Then comes implementation. The designer iterates between the specification and the implementation to ensure that the implementation captures the intent of the specification. Testing is performed on the product in several stages. The chips are tested, mounted chips are tested, an entire subsystem is tested, and so on. The product then moves to the end user. While the product is being used, new requirements are often generated and the cycle begins again.

Current Languages

Several industry-supported efforts have sought to establish means to represent product data in a standard format. Three of these efforts are the Very high-speed

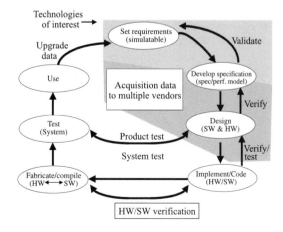

Figure 2.   The product life cycle.

integrated circuits Hardware Description Language (VHDL), Verilog, and the Electronic Design Interchange Format (EDIF).

In VHDL, the hardware entities are modeled as abstractions of the real hardware, called *design entities*. Each design entity has an *interface* and a *body* or *architecture*. The interface description allows one to describe input and output ports and various attributes associated with the interface, such as pin names or timing constraints. The body description allows one to describe the function or the structure of the design. The body may be written as an abstract algorithm, or as a less abstract architectural description made up of algorithms and real hardware representations (e.g. gates, arithmetic-logic units), or made up totally as a structure of real hardware representations.

Verilog functions are similar to VHDL at the lower levels of abstraction, but VHDL's modeling capability extends also to the higher end of abstraction. VHDL 200x is now being considered for extension beyond the recently accepted VHDL 1999 standard. Both VHDL and Verilog also address the analog and mixed-signal environments. SLDL is an industry project to provide a language beyond VHDL and Verilog to describe systems composed of hardware and software even more effectively.

EDIF, which is a format, not a language, provides a hierarchical syntax for data necessary for chip and printed circuit board fabrication. EDIF's primary application is as a means of transferring design data from the design environment to the fabrication environment. In EDIF, there are several "view types": the *behavior* view (compiled simulation model), the *document view* (supports text documentation), the *graphic* view (supports portions of artwork repeatedly used), the *logic model* view (definition of primitive simulation logic models), the *mask layout* view (artwork and fabrication data), the netlist view (netlist data), the PCB *layout* view (similar to the mask layout view, but for printed circuit boards), the *schematic* view (netlist plus graphics providing a graphic schematic), the *stranger* view (an escape hatch for two-party special agreements), the *symbolic* view (a virtual grid somewhere between a schematic and a mask layout), and a test view.

The many industry standards attempt to answer the needs of the various product life cycle activities. However, the development of some of these standards has not been well coordinated with others, although there are efforts being made to do so. Users need a thorough understanding of the objectives and uses of each standard. The technology of HDLs has not matured to the point that one standard language or format can satisfy the wide diversity of product description requirements, at least for the immediate future.

Bibliography

1983. Piloty, R., Barbacci, M. R., Borrione, D., Dietmeyer, D., Hill, F., and Skelly, P. *CONLAN Report*. Berlin: Springer-Verlag.

1989. Waxman, R., and Saunders, L. "The Evolution of VHDL," *Proceedings of the IFIP Congress*, San Francisco, CA, August.

1996. Ashenden, P. J. *The Designer's Guide to VHDL*. San Francisco, CA: Morgan Kaufmann.

1997. Institute for Electrical and Electronic Engineers. *Verilog Language Reference Manual*, Standard 1364–1998. New York: IEEE Press.

Ronald Waxman and Michel Israel

HIERARCHY OF OPERATORS

See OPERATOR PRECEDENCE.

HIGH-LEVEL LANGUAGE

See PROBLEM-ORIENTED LANGUAGES; and PROCEDURE-ORIENTED LANGUAGES.

HISTORY OF DIGITAL COMPUTERS

See DIGITAL COMPUTERS, HISTORY OF; and SOFTWARE HISTORY.

HOLLERITH, HERMAN

For an article on a related subject, *see*

+ Digital Computers, History of: Early

Herman Hollerith (b. Buffalo, NY, 1860; d. Washington, DC, 1929), *see* Figure 1, was the inventor of the punched-card data processing machine. His systems and the applications he developed for them laid the foundations for the data processing industry. He held the foundation patents in the field and nearly 50 other US and foreign patents on basic techniques and equipment. He developed applications of punched-card data

463-465 PENNA. AVENUE
WASHINGTON, D. C.

Figure 1. Herman Hollerith (courtesy of IBM Archives).

processing for the US Census, medical and public health statistics, railroad and public utility accounting, stock and inventory control, and factory cost accounting.

Upon graduation from the Columbia College School of Mines in 1879, Hollerith took a job as special agent with the US Census. At that time, Dr. John Shaw Billings, a member of the Surgeon General's Office, was also serving as director of the division of vital statistics for the Census Bureau. Billings suggested to Hollerith that a good machine for tabulating population and similar statistics was badly needed and that using cards with the description of each individual punched into them was a good approach to the problem. Intrigued, Hollerith decided to his own satisfaction that this was indeed feasible.

In 1882, Hollerith became an instructor in mechanical engineering at MIT. While there, he worked hard on his "Census machine," concentrating initially upon a variant of an earlier machine developed by Colonel Charles W. Seaton, chief clerk for the 1870 Census. This prototype had used a player-piano roll type of feed mechanism rather than individual cards. At the end of his first year at MIT, Hollerith returned to Washington and secured a position with the US Patent Office to learn the arts of invention and patent protection. He obtained his first patents for electrically actuated railroad brakes, and soon applied for several other patents, which included the foundation patents on punched-card data processing.

In 1889, his punched card system was installed in the Army Surgeon General's office to handle medical statistics. Also in 1889, a comparative test made of the Hollerith and two competitive systems resulted in the choice of the Hollerith system for use in the 1890 Census. A description of this system and his plans for the Census was accepted by Columbia as a doctoral dissertation, and he was awarded a Ph.D. in 1890.

About 1905, the management in the Census Bureau began to object to the profits that Hollerith derived from his machines and decided to back a talented inventor named James Powers. Powers eventually sold out to the company that evolved into Univac. In poor health, Hollerith sold his patent and proprietary rights to a holding company in 1911.

Bibliography

1971. Hollerith, V. "Biographical Sketch of Herman Hollerith," *ISIS*, **62**(210), 69–78.

1982. Austrian, G. D. *Herman Hollerith: Forgotten Giant of Information Processing.* New York: Columbia University Press.

1989. Reid-Green, K. S. "The History of Census Tabulation," *Scientific American*, **260**, 78–83.

1991. Kistermann, F. W. "The Invention and Development of the Hollerith Punched Card," *Annals of the History of Computing*, **13**, 245–259.

William F. Luebbert and Geoffrey Austrian

HOPPER, GRACE MURRAY

For articles on related subjects, *see*

+ Aiken, Howard Hathaway
+ Cobol
+ Digital Computers, History of: Early
+ Mark I, Harvard

Figure 1.   Grace Murray Hopper.

Grace Brewster Murray Hopper (Fig. 1) was born in New York City on 9 December 1906. She received her B.A. in Mathematics and Physics from Vassar College in 1928, where she was elected to Phi Beta Kappa. She continued her graduate studies in mathematics at Yale University, where she was awarded her M.A. (1930) and Ph.D. (1934). From 1931 to 1943, she was a member of the mathematics faculty at Vassar College. In December 1943, she joined the United States Naval Reserve and attended Midshipman's School at Northampton, Massachusetts.

She graduated in 1944 with a commission in the US Navy (Lt. J.G.) and was assigned to the Bureau of Ordnance's Computation Project under the direction of Howard Aiken at Harvard University. It was at Harvard that Hopper was first exposed to the world of automatic digital processing. There she joined Robert Campbell and Richard Bloch as a "coder." At the end of the Second World War, Hopper resigned from Vassar and was appointed to the Harvard faculty as a Research Fellow in the newly founded Computation Laboratory.

In 1949, she joined, as senior mathematician, the fledgling Eckert–Mauchly Corporation, where BINAC and UNIVAC I (*q.v.*) were under construction. She remained with the organization after its acquisition by Remington Rand, through the merger with Sperry Rand, and until her retirement from the Univac division in 1971. Throughout this period, she maintained her activity in the US Naval Reserve and was promoted successively through the ranks up to Rear Admiral in 1985. She continued on active duty until her forced retirement in 1986.

For more than three decades, Captain Hopper was an innovator and major contributor to the development of programming languages. She developed the first compiler, A-0 (1952); the first compiler to handle mathematical computations, A-2 (1953); and the first English language data processing compiler, B-0 (Flow-Matic), which was in use as early as 1957. In April 1959, Hopper and others met to plan a formal meeting whose object would be to develop the specifications for a common business language for automatic digital computers. This meeting triggered a sequence of events that culminated in the development of Cobol.

Hopper received almost every major award in her profession. These include DPMA's "Man(!)-of-the-Year" (1969); AFIPS' Harry Goode Memorial Award (1970); and Yale University's Wilbur Lucius Cross Medal (1972). In 1971, the Univac Division of Sperry Rand Corporation created the Grace Murray Hopper Award, which is awarded annually by ACM to a distinguished young computer professional. In 1991, she was awarded the National Medal of Technology.

Grace Hopper retired with the rank of Rear Admiral on 14 August 1986. Befitting the oldest serving officer in the US Navy, her retirement ceremony was held on the USS Constitution ("Old Ironsides"). Admiral Hopper died on 1 January 1992 and was buried at Arlington Cemetery in a full naval ceremony. On 6 January 1996, the US Navy launched an Arleigh Burke Class Aegis Destroyer named the USS Hopper in her honor.

Bibliography

1984. Tropp, H. "Grace Hopper: The Youthful Teacher of Us All," *Abacus*, **2**, 6–18.

1988. Hopper, G. M. "The Education of a Computer," *Annals of the History of Computing*, **9**(3/4), 271–281. Reprint of a 1952 ACM Publication. Introduction by David Gries.

1989. Billings, C. W. *Grace Hopper, Navy Admiral and Computer Pioneer*. Hillfield, NJ: Enslow Publishers.

1995. Lee, J. A. N. "Grace Brewster Murray Hopper," *Computer Pioneers*, 380–387. Los Alamitos, CA: IEEE Computer Society Press.

Henry S. Tropp

HTML

See MARKUP LANGUAGES.

HYPERMEDIA

See MULTIMEDIA.

HYPERTEXT

For articles on related subjects, *see*

+ Information Retrieval
+ Markup Languages
+ Multimedia
+ User Interface
+ World Wide Web

Hypertext is both the concept of interrelating (linking) information elements and the name used to describe a collection or *web* of interrelated or linked nodes. A hypertext system allows an author to create the nodes and the links among them, and allows a reader to *traverse* these links, that is, to *navigate* from one node to another using these links. Typically, hypertext systems mark link access points or *link anchors* in some manner when they are displayed on a computer screen (e.g. underlined colored text). When the user selects the link marker, for example, by clicking on it with a mouse (*q.v.*), the hypertext system traverses to and displays the node at the other end of the link. Hypertext systems include many *navigation*, *annotation*, and *structural features* that take advantage of the node and link structure to support authors and readers.

Hypertext enables people to read, comprehend, and write information more effectively than traditional documents. People typically read documents from start to end, that is, *linearly*. Paper constrains (and encourages) authors to present information in this format. Hypertext frees readers and authors from this constraint. Hypertext links and structural features enable authors to provide a rich context of related information around elements. As a side effect, through the process of crafting an information structure of nodes and links, authors often come to understand the information better. For readers, freedom of access within a web enhanced with contextual information provides a richer environment for understanding the information they find. Hypertext also enhances comprehension because it mimics the associative networks that people use cognitively to store and retrieve information.

Historical Perspective

Hypertext is not a new concept. In 1945, Vannevar Bush proposed the Memex system, which would maintain links and annotations over printed materials (Bush, 1945). In the 1960s, Theodor Holmes Nelson coined the terms *hypertext* and *hypermedia*. Nelson envisioned a worldwide integrated document base of hypertext-linked information that all people would be able to access and work within. He also laid out the specifications for his Xanadu hypermedia system in the 1960s, although its first working prototypes came 30 years later. Douglas Engelbart demonstrated NLS/Augment, the first distributed, shared-screen, collaborative hypertext system at the 1968 Fall Joint Computer Conference. Several commercial hypertext systems appeared in the 1970s and 1980s.

Until the 1990s, the vast majority of hypertext systems were standalone nondistributed systems. In the early 1990s, HyperG (now called HyperWave) and the World Wide Web (WWW) appeared—the first distributed hypertext systems since NLS/Augment to take full advantage of the Internet.

Hypertext Components

Nodes and Composites

Hypertext components include nodes, links, link anchors, link markers, and composites. Hypertext nodes contain the content and attributes of information elements. Approximately half of the hypertext systems before the 1990s used fixed-size windows without scroll bars. Their designers believed that hypertext nodes should contain a single *chunk* of information, that is, a single idea. The others supported entire documents as individual nodes. Many models of hypertext support *composite nodes*, that is, a distinct set of nodes, perhaps with interrelating links. An example would be a book of separate chapters or a car of many components. The

entire composite can be treated as a single high-level node. Links can be made to the composite or to any of its component nodes.

Link Anchors and Link Markers

Links connect entire nodes, but they focus on a particular aspect of each node endpoint. *Link anchors* specify a particular target area within each node corresponding to this aspect. Users typically do not see the *link anchor*, which is embedded in the node's internal code (e.g. HTML). Instead, the hypertext system displays a *link marker* that users can select to activate the anchor and traverse its link. In WWW browsers, a link marker is often blue underlined text, denoting a link anchor. For example, a link might connect two newspaper articles if they both mention the same person. The person's name is associated with an anchor in each of the two nodes' internal code. On the computer screen, the hypertext system highlights the person. Many hypertext systems will highlight the *destination link marker* or target area in some special way (e.g. displaying it in a different text style or flashing a box around it several times or shading its background).

Links

Links represent relationships among nodes. As with nodes, links may have *semantic link types* (e.g. "supporting evidence for" or "criticism of") and associated *keywords*. Many hypertext systems display *semantic link types* as labels near the link's marker in nodes, and within maps and overviews. This can orient users by showing how nodes are interrelated, and can help them decide whether to traverse particular links. Users may also specify link types and keywords within *structural search* queries for nodes with specific relationships.

Transclusions, warm links, and hot links all connect two instances of the same information. *Transclusions* (or inclusions) enable the exact same node or anchor to appear in multiple places. Whereas copying and pasting creates an identical copy, transclusions essentially are pointers that connect the original to places that use it. Through transclusion, readers always have access to the original element, and therefore, to its original context, which can facilitate *deep intercomparison*. *Warm links* and *hot links* are not pointers, but connect actual copies of their anchor content. With hot links, when the content of one anchor changes, the hypertext system automatically updates all other copies immediately. With warm links, the system asks the users whether to update the other copies.

Some models of hypertext do not contain explicit links. Instead, they handle links implicitly. *Set-based hypertext* could also support the teacher and chemical bond examples, treating a class or molecule as a set of elements. *Spatial hypertext* uses pattern matching to interrelate nodes positioned near each other or sharing the same virtual composite and attribute structure. Both support other hypertext functionality using these *implicit links*.

Hypertext Features

The hypertext navigation, annotation, and structural features build upon the hypertext constructs of nodes, links, anchors, and composites. Hypertext *navigation* features transport the user among information elements. They include *browsing* (link traversal), backtracking, standard *content-based query*, and structural query based on interrelationships. An example of a structural query is "find all nodes of semantic type 'product information' within a two-link distance of any node of semantic type 'legal advice' where one of the connecting links has the semantic type 'prohibited by' or the keyword 'urgent.'"

Backtracking serves four purposes: to return to a prior position in a web (which allows users to take "detours" from their main task safely), to review the content of a previously visited node, to recover from a link chosen in error, and as part of undoing. Backtracking differs from *undoing*, however, in that backtracking returns the reader to a previously visited node in its current state. *Parametric backtracking*, written as "go-back(X)," allows the user to specify a value for a node attribute in parameter X, which causes the system to backtrack to the most recently departed node with that attribute value.

Annotation features include bookmarks, landmarks, and comments. *Bookmarks* are one-way links from the reader's desktop to nodes they wish to access easily. Landmarks are one-way links from everywhere to a specific place, such as a home page. *Landmarks* typically remain permanently in view. Authors create landmarks; readers create bookmarks. Bookmarks are essentially personal landmarks.

Trails or *paths* connect a chain of links through an information space. They provide a context for viewing and understanding a series of nodes. They can record a path of information to remember or share. They can suggest a subset or ordering of nodes within a hypertext web, which can reduce cognitive overhead. Authors can prepare multiple "recommended" trails, each focusing on a different aspect of a web or tailored to different readers (a novice, an expert, etc.) *Guided tours* are restricted trails with link anchors that lead away from the trail dimmed or hidden. Users have to suspend or exit the tour to access these. Trails can contain *branches* allowing the reader to choose among subpaths. Hypertext systems often display and highlight trails in an overview diagram, so readers can maintain their orientation.

Hypertext Standards

Four major *standards* efforts exist in the hypertext community. HyTime is an extension of SGML for specifying common hypertext concepts that sets of multimedia SGML documents can share. Because of its complexity, HyTime has never been widely used for hypertext. The *Dexter* reference model provides a detailed model of hypertext components. Several hypertext systems are based on Dexter. The Open Hypertext Systems group is developing an Open Hypertext Protocol for passing messages and sharing hypertext services among interoperating hypertext systems. Several hypertext systems have been made OHP-compliant. Many hypertext researchers are active in the World Wide Web Consortium's various standards efforts. The WWW's XML, XLink, and XPointer standards are being designed to support more sophisticated hypertext constructs and features on the World Wide Web.

Bibliography

1945. Bush, V. "As We May Think," *Atlantic Monthly*, **176**, 101–108.

1974. Nelson, T. *Computer Lib/Dream Machines*. Chicago, IL: Hugo's Books. Revised edition (1987). Redmond, WA: Microsoft Press.

1987. Conklin, E. J. "Hypertext: A Survey and Introduction," *IEEE Computer*, **20**(9), 17–41.

1997. Snyder, I. *Hypertext: The Electronic Labyrinth*. New York: New York University Press.

Michael Bieber

I

I/O BUS

See BUS.

I/O CHANNEL

See CHANNEL.

I/O PORT

See PORT, I/O.

IBM

For articles on related subjects, *see*

+ Aiken, Howard Hathaway
+ Digital Computers, History of
+ Fortran
+ Hollerith, Herman
+ IBM PC
+ Mark I, Harvard
+ Punched Card

Introduction

For much of the twentieth century, IBM (previously the International Business Machines Corporation) was the preeminent name in data processing (*q.v.*) and digital computation. IBM was incorporated in the state of New York on 15 June 1911 as the Computing-Tabulating-Recording Company, but its origins can be traced back to 1890 when the US Census Bureau solicited competitive proposals to find a more efficient way to tabulate census data. The winner was Herman Hollerith (*q.v.*) whose Tabulating Machine used an electric current to sense holes in punched cards and kept a running total of processed data. To capitalize on his success, Hollerith formed the Tabulating Machine Company in 1896.

In 1911, Charles R. Flint brokered the merger of Hollerith's company with two others, the Computing Scale Company of America and the International Time Recording Company, to form the Computing-Tabulating-Recording Company (C-T-R). C-T-R manufactured and sold machinery ranging from commercial scales and industrial time recorders to meat and cheese slicers, and of course, tabulators and punched cards. In 1914, Flint recruited as General Manager a former executive of the National Cash Register Company, the 40-year-old Thomas J. Watson (Fig. 1). The next year, Watson became President. In 1924, C-T-R changed its name to the International Business Machines Corporation. In 1937, Thomas Watson Jr. joined his father at IBM as General Manager. Ten years later, a second Watson son, Arthur K. "Dick" Watson, was hired and became a vice president of the IBM World Trade Corporation in 1949.

Figure 1.   Thomas J. Watson THINKing (courtesy of IBM).

Figure 2.   An IBM Selectric typewriter (reproduced by permission of IBM Archives).

Data Processing
The IBM Card

IBM's earliest rival was the Powers Accounting Machine Company founded by James Powers in 1911. The Powers punched cards were 45-column cards with round holes that were sensed mechanically. In 1928, IBM introduced the higher-capacity 80-column card, which used rectangular or "slotted" punched holes that were sensed electromechanically. Watson began touting the new medium as not *just* punched cards, but as "IBM cards." The regard for card format pertained not only to competition over the sale of card processing machines, but also to the sale of the card stock. As of 1956, IBM still derived 20% of its revenue and 30% of its profits from the sale of cards of its own manufacture.

Other Business Machines

In 1933, IBM acquired the Electromatic Typewriter Corporation and manufactured electric typewriters for

57 years. By 1958, IBM was deriving 8% of its revenue from the sales of electric typewriters. In 1961, IBM announced the Selectric typewriter (Fig. 2), developed by H. S. ("Bud") Beattie. Sales of the Selectric remained strong for 25 years, but by 1990 word processing on personal computers had so depressed the market for electric typewriters that IBM sold its typewriter division to Lexmark of Lexington, KY.

The Card Programmed Calculator (CPC)

In 1946, IBM began to sell its IBM 603 Multiplying Card Punch, an electronic version of a machine that had been offered since 1934. About 100 were sold before an upgrade to the IBM 604, of which a remarkable 5600 were sold over the next 10 years. But in 1947, an enterprising customer, Northrop Aircraft, hooked up a 603 to a specially developed storage unit and other punched card equipment. The result, the Card Programmed Calculator (CPC), with the later 604 rather than the 603, was capable of 1000 operations per second. It was not a stored program computer, but it could add, subtract, multiply, divide, and even extract square roots with a special prewired plugboard. By 1955, over 700 CPCs had been placed in service over a period during which only 14 Univac Is (*q.v.*) were installed, and IBM's CPC revenue of $21 million in that year was almost double that of its stored program computers. A year later, the ratio would be reversed.

The Harvard Mark I

In 1936, Howard Hathaway Aiken (*q.v.*) was a graduate student in applied physics at Harvard who perceived the need for an electromechanical device to solve some nonlinear equations relating to his research. Thomas Watson agreed to grant funds to Aiken, $15 000 initially, but much more as design progressed. The result was an enormous machine, 51 ft (15.5 m) wide but only 2 ft (0.6 m) deep (Fig. 3). Its capacity was only 72 numbers, and it could perform only three additions or subtractions per second, with multiplication taking as long as six seconds. Its IBM name was *Automatic Sequence Controlled Calculator*, but it was more commonly known as the Mark I (*q.v.*).

The EDP to Computer Transition

The Selective Sequence Electronic Calculator (SSEC)

In 1945, IBM employees Frank Hamilton and Rex Seeber began design of a "super calculator" to be called the Selective Sequence Electronic Calculator (SSEC). The machine was completed in the summer of 1947 and shipped to the company's headquarters at 590 Madison Avenue in New York City (Fig. 4). Displayed

Figure 3.   The Harvard/IBM Mark I (reproduced by permission of IBM Archives).

Figure 4.   The SSEC (reproduced by permission of IBM Archives).

in the window and dedicated in January 1948, the machine had 12 500 vacuum tubes and could do 14 by 14 digit decimal multiplication in 20 ms, division in 33 ms, and addition or subtraction of 19-digit numbers in just 300 μs. The machine was 250 times faster than the Harvard Mark I, which took 6 s for multiplication and 11.4 s for division. Only one SSEC was ever built.

SAGE and the IBM AN/FSQ-7

In 1949, the US government solicited bids from a number of private contractors to expand the Whirlwind (*q.v.*) project at MIT to form SAGE (Semi-Automatic Ground Environment), whose development work was to be done at the newly formed MIT Lincoln Laboratory. IBM won the contract over Remington Rand, which had just acquired Engineering Research Associates (ERA), and Raytheon. Each new SAGE machine, which carried the military designation AN/FSQ-7, was actually two identical computers that operated in duplex mode. The AN/FSQ-7 was a single address machine with 8 K 32-bit words that ran at about 75 KHz. Each CPU was capable of supporting 100 display consoles while sending and receiving data from 12 remote sites. From 1952 to 1955, SAGE contributed only 4% to IBM's total revenue, but more significantly, it accounted for 80% of its earnings from stored program digital computers.

The SABRE Airline Reservation System

In 1953, Blair Smith, a top IBM salesman, found that his seatmate on a flight from Los Angeles to New York was the president of American Airlines, C. R. Smith. The talk of the (unrelated) Smiths quickly turned to AA's need for a wholesale replacement of its antiquated airline reservation system. Thomas Watson Jr. placed SAGE engineer Perry Crawford in charge of developing a system to meet the needs of the airline. In 1960, system design was far enough along to warrant the acronym SABRE, for Semi-Automatic Business Research Environment. The system was fully implemented by 1963, the culmination of the largest commercial data processing operation undertaken as of that time.

Early IBM Commercial Computers

As of 1950, IBM had under development the Magnetic Drum Calculator (MDC), the forerunner of the IBM 650; the decimal Tape Processing Machine (TPM), which would later become the IBM 702; the binary Defense Calculator, which would become its scientific machine, the IBM 701; and the IBM 7030 (Stretch), one of the first supercomputers (q.v.). Seven IBM 7030s were delivered, mostly to government laboratories, and the effort produced many innovations used on later machines.

In 1950, the Korean War began, and Tom Watson diverted IBM resources to development of the Defense Calculator and to the Naval Ordnance Research Calculator (NORC), a machine that IBM delivered in 1954 for a fee of cost plus one dollar. But now he worried that while doing so, Remington Rand's Univac would capture the lion's share of the market for commercial computers. In response, IBM announced the binary IBM 701 (Fig. 5) for scientific

Figure 5.   The IBM 701 (courtesy of IBM).

and engineering users and the decimal IBM 702 for business users. It was claimed that the 702, a renamed TPM, would outperform the Univac and cost less.

In November 1952, IBM was stunned by the magnitude of the publicity the Univac received when CBS used it to predict, on the basis of very early returns, that Eisenhower would defeat Adlai Stevenson by a much wider margin than polls had predicted. Watson was able to stimulate sales of the 700 series, but could not accelerate its production schedule. By June 1954, IBM had 50 orders for the 702, but its first delivery in 1955 came four full years after the first Univac.

By 1956, Univac held only a slight edge in the number of installed machines, 30 vs 24. But by a year later, the score stood at 66 702s and 46 Univacs, and the order position was even better: 193 for IBM and 65 for Sperry Rand, formed in 1955 through merger of Remington Rand and Sperry Gyroscope. And in that same year, IBM was able to announce higher performance replacements for its two leading machines, the 704 (Fig. 6) for the 701 and the 705 for the 702, the principal advance being use of magnetic core memory. In May 1956, with an important anti-trust suit settled and at the height of IBM's power and influence, Thomas J. Watson Sr. passed the title of CEO to his son, Thomas J. Watson Jr. One month later, the senior Watson died.

Figure 6. A typical IBM 704 layout (courtesy of IBM).

The IBM 305 RAMAC

Over 1000 copies of the IBM 305 RAMAC (Random Access Memory Accounting Machine; Fig. 7) were sold over the period 1956 to 1961. Still a vacuum tube computer, the machine is historically significant for its use of the model 350 Disk Storage Unit. Its capacity of five megabytes seems quaint by today's gigabyte standards, but was nonetheless a breakthrough innovation.

The 1400 Series

The IBM 1400 series, introduced in 1959, began with the IBM 1401 and eventually consisted of models 1401, 1410, 1440, 1460, and 7010. The 1401, whose rental began at $2500 per month, was a fully transistorized second-generation machine having original memory

Figure 7. The IBM 305 RAMAC (courtesy of IBM).

capacity options ranging from 1.4 K to 16 K 6-bit characters. As with the 702, arithmetic was decimal.

The Competition

By the late 1950s, the only major US corporations other than IBM that were able to commit sufficient resources to make computers and stay the course for at least a few years were RCA, GE, Philco, Burroughs, NCR, Sperry Rand, and Honeywell, which had enjoyed the modest success described above. But eventually, RCA left the computer business and was later absorbed by GE; GE sold its computer division to Honeywell; Philco sold its division to Ford, which left the business shortly thereafter; and Burroughs was absorbed by Sperry Rand, renamed Unisys. Of the many computer start-up companies of that era, only the Control Data Corporation survived to the end of the century, but as a "solutions company" that no longer sells computers of its own manufacture. The Digital Equipment Corporation (DEC) almost made it, but that company was bought by Compaq in 1998, and Compaq, in turn, was absorbed by Hewlett-Packard in 2002.

The IBM 1620

In 1962, IBM began delivery of a remarkable little machine called the IBM 1620. Up to that time, computers were sufficiently complex that they were tended by professional operators; not even a programmer was allowed to touch one. The operators mounted relevant tapes, fed card decks to the machine, ran the program that caused the machine to devour them, and then collected all input and output media for return to the program sponsor. It was the age of *batch processing*. Programmers were lucky to get four vicarious cracks a day at the machine, and the slightest error of a comma or decimal point would cause them great consternation. But the 1620, an $85 000 decimal computer whose Fortran compiler made excellent use of a meager 20 000 digit memory, was a programmer's delight. The machine's already relatively low cost was deeply discounted to universities, where it became a great favorite with students, providing their first "hands-on" computer experience. Their allegiance lasted for decades.

System/360

By the early 1960s, IBM was writing and maintaining software for seven incompatible computer systems. Something had to be done. IBM began planning its New Product Line (NPL) in 1962. The idea of introducing a compatible family of the same *computer architecture* (*q.v.*), a term coined at IBM in that year, was neither new nor unique. Philco and GE had done it first and Univac, CDC, and Burroughs did so at about the same time, but none of these competitive families included models that spanned a factor of 50 in performance.

The "architects" of the NPL (later S/360) were Gene Amdahl, one of the technical leaders of the IBM 704 project, and Fred Brooks, each reporting to Data Systems Division manager Bob Evans. When it became clear that concomitant development of a complex *operating system* (*q.v.*) was crucial to the success of NPL, Brooks was assigned the task of directing the efforts of almost 2000 programmers to produce what was initially introduced as OS/360. The initially delivered OS/360 was disappointingly sluggish and prone to crash, but the product eventually matured into the more successful OS/MFT (Multiprogramming with a Fixed number of Tasks) and OS/MVT (Multiprogramming with a Variable number of Tasks).

The System/360 machines (Fig. 8) used what IBM called *Solid Logic Technology* (SLT), a conservative choice midway between discrete components and true integrated circuitry (*q.v.*). To a good approximation, each model offered twice the performance of the one below it at a cost of only 40% more, either in validation of Grosch's Law (*see* LAWS, COMPUTER) or because IBM used the "law" as a guide to setting prices.

In 1970, IBM moved to a fully transistorized System/370 product line. Its extended S/360 architecture included *dynamic address modification*, which supported efficient time sharing. The series began with models 155 and 165 (quickly upgraded to models 158 and 168), each rated at 3 to 5 times faster than the corresponding S/360 models 50 and 65. Over the next six years, additional models were introduced in the order 145, 195, 135, 125, and 115. A new but still upward-compatible S/390 line was brought out in the late 1980s.

Unbundling Creates a New Industry

In 1969, IBM made a fateful decision to "unbundle" its software and hardware. Up to that time, those who leased or purchased an IBM system were entitled to receive, upon request and at no additional charge, any software package that IBM had created in support of the system; *all* software was "freeware" (*q.v.*). Customers who complained that they now had to buy their software were told that the added expense would be more than recovered because unbundling would allow hardware costs to be reduced in the future. Though difficult to prove or refute, the effect was to create a whole new industry. Until this decision, there was little or no point in any software company developing products for IBM

Figure 8.   Five S/360 models (courtesy of IBM).

equipment, but suddenly there was. And although the next 30 years saw the establishment and rapid growth of many software companies, none of this has hurt IBM, since it still claims to be the largest software company in the world. Microsoft certainly sells more units, but the price of mainframe and minicomputer software greatly exceeds that of PC software.

Small Business Systems

In July 1969, rather than bringing out a System/360 Model 10, IBM introduced its System/3, a small business system that could be rented for less than $1000 per month, half the cost of a typical S/360 model 20. The S/3 used a unique architecture and small 96-column punched cards. Sales of S/3 models 32, 34, and 36 were strong for nine years, but as the series began to show its age in 1978, IBM announced a successor, the S/38. Strangely and surprisingly, the S/38 was not compatible with the S/3 series, but it nonetheless sold very well. After another ten years, when sales of the S/38 began to sag, some elements of IBM wanted to discontinue it, but it was saved by a project called *Silverlake*. As the 1990s began, sales of the resulting upwardly compatible AS/400 exceeded the total annual revenue of the Digital Equipment Corporation, which had the second highest revenue in the industry, and sales remained strong through 2000.

The PC Era

In 1975, IBM attempted to sell its 50-pound (23 kg) IBM 5100 computer as being "portable," but, due to weight and price—$9000 to $20 000 depending on configuration—there were few takers for this early "luggable" computer (*see* PORTABLE COMPUTERS). Burned by the failure of the 5100, IBM shied away from designing small computers until it felt it could not ignore the success of the "personal computers" brought out by Radio Shack (later Tandy), Commodore, and Apple in the period 1978–1980. So as to be able to compete quickly, IBM decided not to introduce a native design for which it would have to write new software, but instead opted for the *open architecture* (*q.v.*) that would result from mating the Intel 8088 microprocessor to the PC-DOS (later MS-DOS)

operating system contracted to Bill Gates and Paul Allen of Microsoft (*see* PERSONAL COMPUTING).

The resulting IBM PC was easily cloned by any number of other vendors (*see* IBM PC). Since neither Intel nor Microsoft was constrained not to sell 80×86 chips or MS-DOS, respectively, to anyone they chose, all that was necessary was to reverse engineer the only part of the IBM PC that was proprietary, the BIOS (*q.v.*) (Basic Input–Output System), which was stored in read-only memory (ROM—*q.v.*). "IBM" PCs are now sold in great numbers by, among many others, Dell, Gateway, Tandy, Hewlett-Packard, SONY, and Packard-Bell. IBM still markets PCs, the latest version being the *Aptiva*, but as of 1998 that machine had captured only a minor share of the overall market. IBM's excellent line of laptops, the *ThinkPad*, did somewhat better.

But the principal fallout from the PC phenomenon is not that IBM is not selling enough small machines, but rather that these small machines have become so capable that the market for its formerly high-profit mainframes (*q.v.*) is rapidly disappearing. After a record-setting paper loss of $8 billion in 1993, IBM has restored profitability by emphasizing that it is a "solutions company," specializing in electronic commerce (*q.v.*), networked database management systems (*q.v.*), and "enterprise computing."

University Relations

IBM has always been cordial to colleges and universities, both because they were a potential source of customers for equipment, but, more important, because they were the best source of good young talent. Beginning with the IBM 650 in 1954, IBM offered a 60% discount to colleges and universities who would use it in support of courses in computing. No other vendor could come close to matching this, so the 650 soon became the most widely used computer in the academic domain. The policy was continued with the IBM 1620, which had even greater penetration of that market. Thus, IBM deserves credit for fostering the early growth of university computing and the acceptance of *computer science* (*q.v.*) as a respected academic discipline.

User Groups

Customers using the same computer often bond in order to obtain and share information about their complex product as well as to apply group pressure on the vendor. The principal IBM-oriented user groups were SHARE (formed in 1955 and originally attuned to the 700 series) and GUIDE (organized in 1956 for the 1400 series). From the mid-1950s and continuing for about 15 years, the members of each user group had considerable clout, with the ability to call IBM officers to their meetings and extract promises about improving maintenance or delivering successor products with certain desirable features.

Anti-Trust and Other Litigation

In 1932, the US Justice Department filed an anti-trust suit against IBM, alleging that the company and Remington Rand together controlled virtually the entire market for punched card machinery and were also illegally requiring buyers of their machines to buy their punched cards. In 1936, the Supreme Court ruled in favor of the Justice Department, and IBM (and Remington Rand) then had to agree that its customers could purchase cards from competitors.

In 1952, the Justice Department charged that IBM had grown so large that it was unrestrained by competition. In 1956, IBM signed a consent decree that required the company to create a competing market of used tabulators by selling, as well as leasing, its machines. Previously, the machines were available only through lease. But IBM coped well with this enforced and seemingly drastic change in established policy. By setting the ratios of price to monthly rentals in the range of 40 to 60 to 1 depending on the product and prevailing rates of inflation, IBM's revenue stream averaged over all accounts remained robust.

In 1968, just as sales of the CDC 6600 were strong, IBM announced that it was adding supercomputers to the top of its S/360 product line. As orders for the 6600 began to fall off, CDC President William Norris denounced the new machines as "paper tigers" and sued IBM for allegedly engaging in predatory sales practices. In the ensuing settlement, IBM ceded its Service Bureau Corporation and $100 million to CDC.

Research and Development

IBM has always placed great emphasis on research and development. In 1945, the senior Watson recruited Wallace Eckert to establish and direct its Watson Scientific Computing Laboratory at 612 West 116th Street in New York City. Since the establishment of its Zurich Research Laboratory in 1956 and the relocation of the Watson Research Center to Yorktown Heights in 1961, it has commendably supported basic as well as applied research. Six additional research laboratories have been commissioned since 1982. Five IBM employees have received the Nobel Prize in physics: Leo Esaki in 1973 for his work on electron tunneling; Gerd K. Binnig and Heinrich Rohrer in 1986 for their work in scanning tunneling microscopy; and J. Georg Bednorz and K. Alex Muller in 1987 for their discovery of (relatively) high-temperature superconductivity.

For his leadership of the Fortran project and other contributions, John Backus received the McDowell Award in 1967 and the Turing Award in 1977. Other IBM employees who have earned McDowell Awards are Fred Brooks, the project manager of OS/360, and Gene Amdahl, who was a leading architect of that system. Other IBM Turing Award winners were Kenneth Iverson for invention of the language APL (q.v.), and Edgar Codd for his creation of the relational database (q.v.) model. In 1977, the US government adopted the cryptographic system developed by Walter Tuchman and Carl Meyer of IBM as the national Data Encryption Standard (DES).

Financial Prowess and Employment Levels

Revenue and Earnings

Over the 34-year period 1934 to 1968, IBM revenue grew exponentially at 18.9% per year, phenomenal growth over such a long period, and over the next 20 years, at the reduced but still remarkable rate of at least 11.4% per year. For the last 10 years, growth has been much more modest and closer to linear. IBM e-commerce revenue has now reached $20 billion, 25% of overall revenue, figures likely to grow substantially

Table 1. Estimated number of model units installed.

Machine	Approximate life span	Estimated number installed
IBM 604	1946-1956	5600
CPC	1947-1964	6000
Mark I	1944-1959	1
SSEC	1948-1952	1
AN/FSQ-7 (SAGE)	1952-1962	46
NORC	1954-1968	1
IBM 7030 Stretch	1961-1971	7
IBM 350 RAMAC	1956-1961	1100
IBM 650	1954-1964	1800
IBM 701	1952-1954	19
IBM 702	1955-1957	14
IBM 704	1955-1957	267
IBM 705	1955-1960	305
IBM 709	1957-1958	38
IBM 7080	1960-1965	160
IBM 7090/7094	1959-1965	250
IBM 1400 series	1959-1965	14000
IBM 1620	1962-1967	5000
IBM 1130	1965-1968	800
IBM 5100	1975-1977	2000
S/360 series models 20, 22, 30	1965-1971	13000
S/360 series models 40, 44, 50, 65, 75	1965-1971	5000
S/360 model 67	1966-1971	10
S/360 model 85	1969-	30
S/360 model 91	1967-	15
S/360 model 95	1968-	2
S/360 model 195	1971-1972	1
S/370 series	1971-1988	80000
S/390 series through 1998	1988-1998	50000
S/3, S/32, S/34, S/36	1969-1988	300000
S/38 (incompatible with above)	1986-1988	20000
AS/400	1988-	NA
Enterprise G-series	1999-	NA
RS/6000	1990-	NA

over the coming years. IBM's only period of sustained "losses" occurred in the early 1990s, when the company began to experience the effect of a significant decrease in orders for new mainframes. In 1980, IBM had set a goal of reaching revenues of $100 billion by 1990, but actual revenue by that date was $30 billion less. The losses of 1991–1993 were not actual monetary losses but rather "restructuring charges" stemming from downsizing, an accounting practice authorized by the US tax code. In fact, IBM had operational earnings of about $3 billion in each of 1991 and 1992 and $300 million in 1993.

After the disastrous record-setting loss of almost $8 billion in 1993, the very year in which Thomas J.

Watson Jr. died, profits returned to the $3 billion level in 1994 and then doubled to $6.3 billion in 1998, not quite back to the $6.6 billion earned in the peak year of 1984. On 21 April 1999, IBM announced that its earnings for the prior quarter were 42% higher than the corresponding quarter of the prior year, the 12th consecutive quarter that earnings exceeded the expectations of financial analysts. The next day, IBM stock advanced by 13%, $23 per share, the largest one-day gain in the company's history. Services and software accounted for 60% of the quarter's gross profit and hardware sales only 40%; the disparity in the two categories is likely to increase into the indefinite future.

Acquisitions

In recent years, IBM employment has grown more through acquisition of other companies than it has through individual recruitment to businesses in which it was already engaged. The addition of the Lotus Corporation in 1995 and Tivoli a year later raised IBM's software revenue by 15%, making it, by IBM's own claim as analyzed earlier, the world's largest software company.

Employment Levels

Worldwide IBM employment levels rose steadily from 1346 in 1914 to a peak of almost 406 000 in 1985, the year following its greatest earnings, but was then downsized to 220 000 in 1994, the year following its greatest loss. As profitability returned, employment began to rise again, reaching 291 000 in 1998, 72% of its peak value.

Machine Sales

Since the prices of the various IBM machines varied widely, the number of each model installed is not the sole indicator of sales importance to the company, but it is nonetheless historically interesting to cite this data as best it can be reconstructed. The more recent the figure, the more IBM is reluctant to reveal it, so the later the entry in Table 1, the rougher are the estimates of units sold.

Bibliography

1963. Watson, T. J. Jr. *A Business and its Beliefs: The Ideas that Helped Build IBM*. New York: McGraw-Hill.

1984. Pugh, E. W. *Memories that Shaped an Industry*. Cambridge, MA: MIT Press.

1986. Bashe, C. J., Johnson, L. R., Palmer, J. H., and Pugh, E. W. *IBM's Early Computers*. Cambridge, MA: MIT Press.

1991. Pugh, E. W., Johnson, L. R., and Palmer, J. H. *IBM's 360 and Early 370 Systems*. Cambridge, MA: MIT Press.

1995. Pugh, E. W. *Building IBM: Shaping an Industry and its Technology*. Cambridge, MA: MIT Press.

2003. Tedlow, R. S. *The Watson Dynasty: The Fiery Reign and Troubled Legacy of IBM's Founding Father and Son*. New York: HarperCollins.

Edwin D. Reilly

IBM CARD

See PUNCHED CARD.

IBM PC

For articles on related subjects, *see*

+ Apple
+ Digital Computers, History of
+ IBM
+ Microsoft
+ Personal Computing

The foundation for the personal computer (PC) was developed at MIT, the Stanford Research Institute, and the Xerox Palo Alto Research Center, beginning in the 1940s. However, the PC industry did not begin until 8-bit microprocessors with at least 32 KB of memory became available. In 1975, the Intel 8080, MOS Technology 6502, and Motorola 6800 microprocessors were incorporated into dozens of commercial PCs beginning with Altair from Micro Instrumentation and Telemetry Systems (MITS). The first of these 8-bit machines were generally sold in kit form. Soon, several companies began to recognize the demand for preassembled computers. These systems broadened the market from electronic hobbyists to some schools, homes, and small businesses.

In 1977, Digital Microsystems introduced a computer designed for the business and professional market. It was preassembled with an Intel 8080 CPU, 64 KB memory, two floppy disk drives, and built-in I/O ports (*see* PORT, I/O). Most importantly, it used a disk operating system called CP/M, which had been developed by Gary Kildall, a consultant to Intel. The CP/M operating system and the bus structure of the MITS Altair, later called the S-100 Bus, became *de facto* standards for high-end business and professional personal computers during the late 1970s.

The PC-1

IBM waited for the next generation machine, made possible by 16-bit microprocessors. A group headed by Phillip "Don" Estridge was chartered to develop a PC and bring it to market within a year. The short time limit meant that the PC would be IBM's first product built from off-the-shelf components and third-party software.

Nearly all of the hardware—the disk drives, monitors, memory, CPU, printer, and so on—was purchased from outside vendors, as was system software. IBM turned to Microsoft for consultation on the system architecture and a Basic (*q.v.*) interpreter, as well as to three vendors for operating systems (*q.v.*). An Intel CPU was chosen because its architecture was close to that of the Intel 8080 used in CP/M-based machines. Intel had two compatible CPUs, the 8086 and 8088, and IBM chose to use the lower cost (and performance) 8088. The minimum configuration had only 16 KB memory. Memory could be expanded to 64 K by plugging 16 KB memory chips into sockets on the system board. Further expansion entailed plugging add-in boards into the five-bus expansion slots on the system motherboard (*q.v.*). This PC bus soon became the industry standard.

Disk drives were optional on the first PCs, which came standard with an audio cassette interface. The original floppy disk drives used only one side of a 5.25-in. disk and had a capacity of 160 KB. IBM did not initially offer a hard disk. There were two display adapters, the monochrome display adapter (MDA) and a color graphics adapter (CGA). The MDA was a character display with a monochrome monitor (*see* MONITOR, DISPLAY). Resolution and character quality were excellent by the standards of the time, and the MDA was targeted to character-oriented applications like word processing (*q.v.*), spreadsheets (*q.v.*), and software development. The CGA delivered color and graphics on a more expensive RGB monitor.

The operating system was more problematic than the hardware. CP/M could not be used directly because the 8088 architecture was not identical to that of the 8080. Digital Research was working on an operating system for the new Intel CPUs (CP/M-86), but so were other companies. One such was Softech Microsystems, which had acquired the P-System, an operating system and software development environment developed by Ken Bowles at the University of California at San Diego (*see* PASCAL). Another was the Seattle Computer Products DOS, a CP/M-like operating system for use on early 8086 systems. IBM eventually decided to offer three operating systems: DOS, CP/M-86, and the P-System. However, DOS was priced much lower than the others, and eventually became the standard.

The IBM PC was announced in April 1981, with forecast sales of 250 000 units over five years. By the end of 1983, the IBM PC had become a *de facto* standard and had an installed base of a million machines. IBM eventually recognized the strategic importance of workstations (*q.v.*) and defined a system application architecture (SAA) to integrate distributed systems (*q.v.*) and workstations.

Evolution

After its introduction, the PC underwent three major upgrades. The first was the PC-XT. The XT was a response to the needs of business and professional customers, who had clearly emerged as the major market. With the XT, IBM added a hard disk and expanded the amount of memory on the system board. Even before the introduction of the XT, they had upgraded the floppy disk drives to 360 KB by using both sides of the disk and writing in a higher-density (9-sector) format.

The next major upgrade was the PC-AT. The AT used Intel's 80286 CPU, as had Tandy in marketing the excellent but short-lived Tandy 2000. The 80286 was faster than the 8088, and had a 16-bit data bus; therefore, the PC bus was extended by adding additional data lines. The AT bus was upward compatible with the PC bus, so PC and XT add-in cards worked in the AT.

The AT was followed by the PS/2 line in 1987. The original line consisted of six models, using the 8086, 80286, and 80386 CPUs. Models using the 80386 SX and the 80486 CPU were announced subsequently. The PS/2s introduced 3.5-in. floppy disk drives with 1.44 MB capacity on all but the low-end model, which used 720 KB drives. The minimum hard disk for the PS/2 was 20 MB.

IBM also announced OS/2, a new operating system, with the PS/2. OS/2 was not compatible with DOS, but added features including multitasking (*q.v.*), multiple threads, a graphical user interface (GUI), and extended file and communication management. But then Microsoft began to market a competitive product, Windows, a DOS extension that included a GUI and limited multitasking. The product was only moderately successful until the Windows 3.1 (and its 95, 98, and 2000 successors) became very popular in the 1990s.

The Early Competition

IBM was able to bring the PC to market quickly because it used commercially available components, rather than building its own. By 1982, several companies were marketing PC-compatible computers. One of these, Compaq, combined PC compatibility with transportability (along the lines of the Osborne CP/M-based computers), a high-resolution display, and quality workmanship. Compaq, Zenith, and Tandy emerged as major challengers to IBM in the personal computer market but Zenith has withdrawn from that market.

Figure 1. A typically configured IBM Aptiva. (Courtesy of IBM.)

Current Situation

There has ceased to be an "IBM PC" as such; there are merely PCs made by IBM. By performance, IBM's latest PC series, the Aptiva (Fig. 1), is quite competitive with PCs made by other manufacturers, but IBM has dropped to third in US sales, behind Dell and Hewlett Packard/Compaq, each with about 20% of the market. At best, IBM is tied with Gateway at about 10% each. Sony and Tandy account for another 5% each, and the remaining 30% of the market is spread among another ten or so companies.

It is not just the loss in sales share that has diminished the concept of an "IBM PC." It is no longer IBM that defines advances in PC architecture, it is the combination of chip manufacturer Intel and software colossus Microsoft that does so. Popular computer magazines no longer discuss a generic "IBM PC." The term in vogue is "Wintel" machine, implying that the combination of *Win*dows running on an In*tel* chip is what matters, not the company that assembles the hardware and installs the operating system.

One niche in which IBM has been relatively more successful is that of the laptop computer (*see* PORTABLE COMPUTERS). The IBM Thinkpad, though not a sales leader, has earned a reputation as being a technically superior laptop.

Bibliography

1990. Bradley, D. J. "The Creation of the IBM-PC," *Byte*, **15**(9), (September), 414–420.

1991. Sheldon, K. M. "You've Come a Long Way, PC: The 10th Anniversary of the IBM-PC," *Byte*, **16**(8), (August), 336.

Larry Press and Edwin D. Reilly

ICON

See USER INTERFACE; and WINDOW ENVIRONMENTS.

IDENTIFIER

For articles on related subjects, *see*

+ Expression
+ Procedure-Oriented Languages
+ Programming Languages
+ Statement

In a programming language, an *identifier* is a string of characters used as a name for some element of the program. This element may be a statement label, a procedure or function, a data element (such as a scalar variable or an array), or the program itself. Most commonly, the word *identifier* is used almost synonymously with variable name. In a system where the location of a program's data remains fixed throughout program execution, the identifier associated with a scalar variable is related to a memory address, which in turn references a physical location within the memory of the machine, which in turn contains a value representation. In most programming languages, identifiers may be formed from any alphanumeric string, often of some restricted length, provided the leftmost character is alphabetic. Some languages also permit the use of special characters, the dollar sign and underscore being typical.

In Ada (*q.v.*), letter-case does not matter, so TAXRATE, taxrate, and TaxRate are all the same identifier, but in other languages, such as C (*q.v.*) and C++ (*q.v.*), these identifiers would be distinct.

J. A. N. Lee

IEEE COMPUTER SOCIETY

See INSTITUTE OF ELECTRICAL AND ELECTRONIC ENGINEERS—COMPUTER SOCIETY (IEEE-CS).

IMAGE COMPRESSION

For articles on related subjects, *see*

+ Computer Graphics
+ Data Compression
+ Image Processing
+ Medical Imaging

Image compression methods reduce the space necessary to encode, store, or transmit digital images by changing the way they are represented. Consider an 8×10 in. color picture, digitized using a resolution of 600 pixels per inch and a byte for each of three color planes. Then the number of bytes required to represent each image is

$$8 \times 10 \times 600 \times 600 \times 3 \text{ bytes} \approx 85 \text{ MB}.$$

On PCs with only a few gigabytes of hard disk (*q.v.*) space, 85 MB is too much for storage of all but a small number of pictures. Even with larger stores, the ability to compress images by a factor of 25 or more is highly desirable.

Digital Image Representation

The simplest images are bilevel. This format is often used to encode sharp documents and faxes, where a pixel can assume only one of two values, black or white. Pixel encoding is usually one bit ("0" or "1"). But when several gray midtones are present, as in black and white photos, two values are no longer sufficient to encode all possible gray intensities. Thus, each pixel must be assigned a numerical value, proportional to the brightness of that point. Typical choices for these values fall in the ranges 0–15 or 0–255 (requiring respectively 4 and 8 bits for each pixel). This kind of image is referred to as a *gray-level* picture.

Color images take advantage of the fact that each color can be expressed as a combination of three primary colors (red, green, and blue; or yellow, magenta, and cyan, for example). Therefore, a color picture can be considered as the superimposition of three "simpler" pictures (called *color planes*), with each of them encoding the brightness of a primary color. In other words, each color plane of an image can be treated much like a gray-level picture with a range of values based on the *luminosity* of that particular color. This type of representation, called RGB or YMC according to the color planes, is "hardware-oriented" and is used when dealing with synthetic (computer-generated) images.

Lossless vs Lossy Methods

When it is possible to recover the original data from the compressed data precisely, the algorithm is called *lossless*. When part of the original information is irremediably lost, the algorithm is called *lossy*. Lossy compressors, since they can discard part of the information, achieve a more compact representation than lossless systems. We focus on lossy methods because lossless methods are covered in the article DATA COMPRESSION.

Lossy Image Compression
Transform Coding

Transform coding uses a transformation that exploits peculiar characteristics of the signal, increasing the performance of a scheme such as Huffman or arithmetic coding (e.g. *see* DATA COMPRESSION). For natural sources (audio, images, and video), relevant information is best described in the frequency domain.

When a pictorial scene is decomposed into its frequency components, the low frequencies (gradual luminosity changes) correspond to the scene illumination, and the high frequencies (rapid changes) characterize object contours.

Several time-domain to frequency-domain transformations have been proposed for digital image signals. The Discrete Cosine Transform (DCT) has the advantage of good decorrelation of the signal (which reduces redundancy), requiring only an acceptable computational effort. Transformations are not compression methods in the literal sense, but when used properly they provide a powerful enhancement of entropy-based compression methods.

Wavelet Compression

Another transform compression scheme is based on *wavelet* functions. The basic idea is to process data at different scales of resolution. If we look at a painting from a distance, we notice its macrostructure (i.e. its *subject*). If we move close to it, we notice the microstructures (e.g. brush strokes). Using wavelets allows us to see both the subject and the microstructure. This is achieved using two versions of the picture at a different scaling of the same prototype function called the *mother wavelet* or *wavelet basis*. A contracted version of the basis function is used for the analysis in the time domain, while a stretched one is used for the frequency domain.

Localization (in both time and frequency) means that it is always possible to find a particular scale at which a specific detail of the signal may be discerned. Wavelet analysis enables the amplitude of the input signal to be drastically reduced. This is particularly appealing for image compression, since it means that half of the data is almost zero and thus easily compressible.

Vector Quantization

A *dictionary* (or *codebook*) is a collection of a small number of statistically relevant patterns (codewords). Every image is encoded by dividing it into blocks and assigning to each block the index of the closest codeword in the dictionary. Matching can be exact or approximate, thereby achieving, respectively, lossless or lossy compression. The best known dictionary method is *vector quantization*, a lossy compression scheme that uses a static dictionary. A set of images (the *training set*) statistically representative of the source's behavior is carefully selected, each image is divided into blocks, and a small set of dictionary codewords is determined. The codewords are selected to minimize the coding error on the training set. The mean square error is usually used as the error metric and is used to guide both the design and the encoding process. The compression rate depends both on the size of each block and on the size of the dictionary. A dictionary with N codewords of $n \times n$ pixels each compresses an image digitized with b bits per pixel with a ratio:

$$R = \frac{n \times n \log_2 b}{\log_2 N}.$$

Once the dictionary is determined, encoding is performed by assigning to each block of the image the index of the closest codeword in the dictionary (i.e. the one with the minimum mean error). The decoder, which also knows the dictionary, simply expands the indices of the codewords into their appropriate blocks. Vector quantization may be proved to be asymptotically optimal when the size of the block increases; unfortunately, the size of the codebook also grows exponentially with the block size.

Fractal Compression

Algorithms based on fractals (*q.v.*) have very good performance and high compression ratios (32 to 1 is not unusual), but their use can be limited by the extensive computation required. The basic idea can be described as a "self-vector quantization," where an image block is encoded by applying a simple transformation to one of the blocks previously encoded. Transformations frequently used are combinations of scaling, reflections, and rotations of another block.

Data Compression Standards
JPEG

The Joint Photographic Experts Group (JPEG) developed a standard for color image compression that was issued in 1990. The standard was mainly targeted for compressing natural black and white and color images. JPEG, like almost every other transform coding image compression algorithm, defines two steps. The first is lossy and involves transformation and quantization; it is used to remove information that is perceptively irrelevant for a human user. The second step is a lossless encoding that eliminates statistical redundancies still present in the compressed representation. JPEG assumes a color image divided into color planes and compresses each of them independently. Run-length encoding is applied to compress the sequences of consecutive zeros. The result is then further compressed using a Huffman or an arithmetic coder.

Performance Evaluation

The performance of an image compression algorithm is mainly determined by two characteristics: the *compression ratio* and the *magnitude of the error* introduced by the encoding. In a lossless compressor, the size of the image is minimized while retaining the quality of the original. But a lossy algorithm must compromise between these two qualities. A fundamental problem in lossy compression is controlling the error introduced by the encoding process. Among several quality metrics that are commonly used, the mean square error (MSE) criterion is much the most important. The MSE between a given image $i(x, y)$ and its encoded version $\hat{i}(x, y)$ is the square root of the sum of the squares of the differences between the corresponding values of the samples in the two signals:

$$\mathrm{MSE} = \sqrt{\sum_{x,y} (i(x, y) - \hat{i}(x, y))^2}.$$

The MSE gives a good measure of the random error introduced in the compression; this is enough for many applications, but when encoded images are mainly used by humans, the use of distortion measures based on the MSE may give misleading results.

Bibliography

1995. Fisher, Y. (ed.) *Fractal Image Compression: Theory and Application*. New York: Springer-Verlag.

1996. Sayood, K. *Introduction to Data Compression*. San Francisco, CA: Morgan Kaufmann.

1997. Mitchell, J., Pennebaker, W., Fogg, C., and Le-Gall, D. *MPEG Video Compression Standard*. New York: Chapman & Hall.

1997. Salomon, D. *Data Compression: The Complete Reference*. New York: Springer-Verlag.

Giovanni Motta, Francesco Rizzo, and James A. Storer

IMAGE PROCESSING

For articles on related subjects, see

+ Computer Graphics
+ Computer Vision
+ Image Compression
+ Medical Imaging
+ Pattern Recognition

Introduction

Digital *image processing* deals with the systematic manipulation of an input image to produce an output image that is better suited for viewing or analysis. The processed images are either examined by a human, such as a radiologist viewing an X-ray, or they form input to an automatic machine vision system. A digital image is represented as a discrete two-dimensional (2D) array of numbers. Each element in the array is known as a *pixel* (for picture element). These pixels are assigned values called *gray levels* that correspond to the relative brightness of the tiny portions of the image that they depict. Image processing deals with the systematic manipulation of these pixel gray levels.

Image processing depends on the use of the *digital signal processor* (DSP–*q.v.*). The advent of digital computers and development of efficient algorithms for processing and analyzing one-dimensional signals provided insights and a general framework for the development of early image processing algorithms. DSP algorithms and approaches make possible efficient implementation of many image processing and machine vision systems.

Image Processing Approaches

Image processing methods can be classified in two groups: *spatial domain approaches* and *transform* (or *frequency*) *domain approaches*. The spatial domain techniques work directly on 2D digital images. The spatial domain approaches have intuitive appeal and are relatively easy to develop and implement. The transform domain techniques require an image to be transformed mathematically into another domain. Some of the more commonly used algorithms include Fourier, cosine, Hadamard, Haar, Hough, Walsh, wavelet, and Gabor transforms.

Image Quantization and Sampling

Quantization and sampling deal with the formation of a digital image that can be processed by a computer. Digital images are 2D discrete representations. This digitization of the signals is performed to allow subsequent processing of these signals. Conversion of continuous analog signals into digital form involves digitization of the amplitude of the signals, a process called *quantization*, and *sampling*, the formation of the spatial grid associated with an image.

Image Registration

Many image-processing tasks involve extraction of information from multiple copies of the same scene. These copies might have been acquired at different wavelengths, different times, or slightly different perspectives or resolutions. In order to perform a systematic analysis of such a data set, one requires an ability to match these copies accurately to a standardized grid so that the images are in perfect spatial registration. This involves corrections for rotational, translational, and scale differences present in the images, a process called *image registration*.

Image Compression

Compression techniques are divided into two categories: (1) *reversible* (or *lossless*) *techniques*, and (2) *irreversible* (or *lossy*) *techniques*. One can achieve a much larger compression ratio by using lossy methods. Two types of compression, *predictive* and *transform coding*, use the high correlation between the gray levels associated with neighboring pixels to achieve compression. Typically, predictive coding schemes are relatively simple to implement but are not robust, that is, they suffer from high sensitivity to various statistical parameters. Transform coding schemes achieve higher compression ratios but are harder to implement. Hybrid coding schemes combine the best features of both approaches.

Image Enhancement

The goal of *image enhancement* is to highlight or enhance a particular type of image feature. Suppression of unwanted image detail is also a part of the enhancement process. These techniques encompass the following:

1. Object/background contrast stretching.
2. Modification of the dynamic range of an image.
3. Removal of false contours introduced through inadequate quantization levels.
4. Reduction of "salt-and-pepper" noise.
5. Edge sharpening.
6. Image smoothing ("blurring").
7. "False color" enhancement of detail.

Figure 1 deals with the enhancement of a neutron radiographic image of a nuclear fuel rod. The original image is corrupted by a nonuniform intensity pattern imposed by the flux of neutrons from the cylindrical fuel rod. This nonuniformity is independent of the vertical position, so that a simple column-by-column gray-level averaging operation allows us to isolate the intensity pattern, which is then subtracted from the original image.

Image Restoration

Image restoration techniques use an image-formation model. When it is assumed that the image formation is spatially invariant and linear, it is possible to describe image formation by an integral equation involving

Figure 1. Enhancement of a neutron radiograph of a nuclear fuel rod. A two-step enhancement procedure was used to eliminate the nonuniform illumination variations and to enhance the contrast highlighting fuel pellets and casing. (Courtesy of Dr. G. Mastin, Sandia National Laboratory.)

the original image convolved with the point spread function (PSF) of the imaging system, a model for the electro-optical sensor, and a random noise term. The "inverse filter" approach involves use of the noise model and knowledge of the PSF to estimate the original image from the recorded image. For many practical problems, the PSF may not be known. In such cases, it may be possible to analyze the power spectrum of the recorded image to deduce the parameters of the PSF. This can be explained with the help of the examples shown in Fig. 2. Parts (a) and (b) of this figure show recorded images that are corrupted by defocus and uniform motion blur, respectively. Part (c) shows the Fourier domain signature of the image of Fig. 2a. The diameter of the visible ring is equal to the circular aperture PSF used to describe the lens defocus. Similarly, part (d) shows the uniform motion blur signature. The strong intensity spikes located in a horizontal plane indicate the blur direction. An example

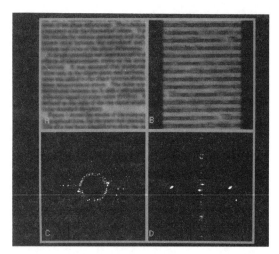

Figure 2. Part (a) shows an image blurred due to defocus. Part (b) shows an image with uniform motion blur. Parts (c) and (d) show their respective Fourier domain blur signatures. (Courtesy of Dr. G. Mastin, Sandia National Laboratory.)

of the restoration of an image affected by motion blur is presented in Fig. 3. Figure 3a shows one of the seven images recorded with motion blur. Figure 3b shows the restored image.

Image Reconstruction

This topic deals with the problem of reconstructing a digital image, given a set of image projections. There are several important application areas in which the only practical way to acquire two-dimensional or three-dimensional images of an object is by using a set

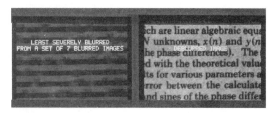

Figure 3. Example of restoration of a motion blurred image. Part (a) shows one of the seven images affected by motion blur. Part (b) shows the restored image. (Courtesy of Drs. D. Ghiglia and G. Mastin, Sandia National Laboratory.)

of image projections. For example, image reconstruction is an important requirement in medical imaging, geophysical exploration, underwater exploration, and radio astronomy.

Image Segmentation

Segmentation deals with the partitioning of an image into parts for further processing. There are basically two types of approach: edge-based and region-based. Edge-based segmentation uses properties of dissimilarity between adjacent pixels to identify all edge pixels in an image. While developing such operators, issues such as accuracy in detection and localization are considered. For each edge pixel, the *strength* of the edge (magnitude of the discontinuity value) and the *direction* of the edge are evaluated. Once edge pixels in an image are identified, the task is to form boundaries that segment the image into distinct regions. Such boundary formation can also involve complex computations. In situations where the boundaries are linear or of a specified parametric form, techniques such as Hough transforms have proved to be quite useful.

An example of image segmentation is presented in Fig. 4. Figure 4a shows a high-resolution aerial image of the Pentagon. Figure 4b shows the results of applying a region-growing segmentation algorithm (Levine, 1985). The basic premise is to merge pixels belonging to the same statistical distribution in a region. From a perceptual psychology viewpoint, region growing is based upon two important criteria of perceptual grouping. The criterion of *proximity* is observed by evaluating each pixel with pixels in its neighborhood, and the *similarity* criterion is observed through comparison of a specified pixel property with that of its neighbors. If the pixels are judged to be similar, they are merged; otherwise they are assigned to different regions. In Fig. 4c, results of applying an edge operator are shown. A 5×5 kernel was used in the edge operator, and a threshold was used to reject weak edges.

Image-Processing Hardware

Advances in image-processing hardware result from dramatic advances made in fields such as electro-optics, electronics, VLSI, material science, semiconductor

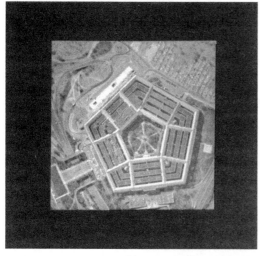

(a)

(b)

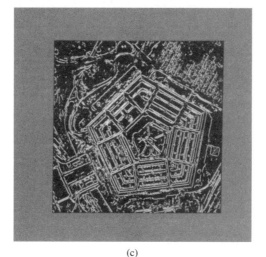

(c)

Figure 4.   Image segmentation: Part (a) shows a high-resolution aerial image of the Pentagon. Part (b) shows the result of applying a region-growing algorithm to identify homogeneous regions. Part (c) shows the result of applying an edge operator to identify the intensity discontinuities.

processing, digital signal processing (*q.v.*), and computer architecture (*q.v.*). As these technologies advance, image-processing hardware is able to acquire higher resolution images at faster rates, to do complex manipulations of images faster, to store and to access large amounts of image data quickly, and to display images with more dynamic range and resolution.

Bibliography

1985. Levine, M. D. *Vision in Man and Machine.* New York: McGraw-Hill.

1989. Jain, A. K. *Fundamentals of Digital Image Processing.* Upper Saddle River, NJ: Prentice Hall.

1995. Sanz, J. L. C. *Image Technology: Advances in Image Processing, Multimedia, and Machine Vision.* Berlin, Germany: Springer-Verlag.

2003. Laplante, P. A. *Software Engineering for Image Processing Systems*. Boca Raton, FL: CRC Press.

Mohan M. Trivedi

INDEX REGISTER

For articles on related subjects, see

+ Addressing
+ Computer Architecture
+ Instruction Set
+ Register

An *index register* is a CPU (*q.v.*) register most often used in the determination of an operand address, but which may be used for other purposes, mainly as a counter. In constructing the address of an operand, one can distinguish three basic parts. Consider, for example, the ADD instruction in an assembly language program that sums the elements of an array. The operand address of the ADD instruction is formed from the following:

1. The address of the base of the array (its first element) relative to the beginning of the program module. This relative address is known when the program is being written.
2. The memory address into which the program module is loaded, known at load time.
3. The offset from the base of the array, which depends on the element that is currently being added and which is known only at execution time.

Index registers are normally involved with only the last of these.

The address computed with an index register is referred to as the *effective address*. Either the address is formed from a constant in the address field of an instruction plus a changing offset in the index register, or the address as a whole is contained in the index register. In the former case, shown in Fig. 1, the index register is used as a *pointer* (*q.v.*) into a *data structure* (*q.v.*), typically an array or *record* (*q.v.*).

Index registers were introduced in the Mark I Manchester University computer (*q.v.*) in 1949. Without such registers, a program must modify its own instructions in order to loop through an array, changing the address contained in the instructions on each iteration. Although

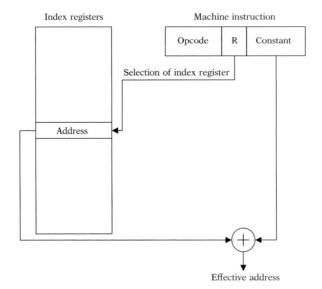

Figure 1. Example of the formation of an effective address.

once a common practice, self-modifying code is very error-prone, can be difficult to debug, and inhibits creation of *reentrant programs* (*q.v.*).

Bibliography

2000. Murdocca, M. *Principles of Computer Architecture.* Upper Saddle River, NJ: Prentice Hall.

Gideon Frieder

INFORMATION HIDING

For articles on related subjects, see

+ Abstract Data Type
+ Class
+ Data Structures
+ Encapsulation
+ Modular Programming
+ Object-Oriented Programming
+ Software Reusability
+ Transparency

Information hiding is a principle used to organize software into modules that are intended to be independently implementable, changeable, and understandable. The objectives are to produce software that accommodates change and to manage complexity during both development and maintenance.

The information hiding principle states that independently changeable information should be hidden through *encapsulation*. Information that is hidden in a module, known as the *secret* of the module, typically includes decisions such as data structures, hardware characteristics, and behavioral requirements. A decision has been hidden successfully if it can be revised without requiring a change to other work assignments. For example, in one formulation of a stack (*q.v.*), as an information-hiding module, the stack's secret is the data structure used to represent its state and details of the algorithms used to manipulate the data structure. The data structure chosen might be an array or a linear list. If properly designed, the stack module conceals the decision, and changing its implementation from array to list can be done independently of changes in any of the programs that use the stack.

An information-hiding module provides its services through an interface that provides sole access to the module, analogous to a black box that has a set of switches that the user may operate and a set of dials that the user may observe. The device can be used without knowing how it operates internally. Designers who use information hiding need to make explicit what is hidden and what is not when designing their modular structure and the interface to each module.

A number of programming languages provide support for information hiding. Examples include classes in languages such as Java (*q.v*) and C++ (*q.v.*), packages in Ada (*q.v.*), modules in Modula, signatures and structures in ML, and type classes in Haskell.

Bibliography

1972. Parnas, D. L. "On the Criteria to be Used in Decomposing a System into Modules," *CACM*, **15**(12), 1053–1058.

1997. Anderton, R. (ed.) *Information Hiding: 1st International Workshop*, Cambridge, UK, May 30–June 1, 1996; *Proceedings (Lecture Notes in Computer Science 1174).* New York: Springer-Verlag.

David M. Weiss

INFORMATION RETRIEVAL

For articles on related subjects, see

+ Database Management System (DBMS)
+ Data Security
+ Data Structures
+ Hypertext
+ Internet
+ Management Information Systems (MIS)
+ Natural Language Processing
+ Optical Storage
+ Searching
+ World Wide Web

Information retrieval (IR) is concerned with the structure, analysis, organization, storage, searching, and dissemination of information. At one time, that information consisted of stored bibliographic items, such as online catalogs of books in a library or abstracts of scientific articles. Now, however, the information is more likely to be full-length documents, either stored in a single location, such as newspaper archives, or available in a widely distributed form, such as the World Wide Web (WWW).

In this article, the term *document* is used broadly to include any type of text in machine-readable format; but by extension, an IR system may also be used to access collections of drawings, audio and video files, photographs of museum artifacts, patents, and so on.

Document Indexing and Content Analysis

In some operational retrieval situations, information analysis is carried out manually by using subject experts or trained indexers to assign content identifiers to information items and search requests. Such information identifiers are known variously as *keywords, index terms, subject indicators*, or *concepts*, and the search operation usually consists of matching sets of keywords assigned to stored information items with keywords representing the search requests. The matching is followed by the retrieval of those items whose content indicators exhibit a sufficiently high degree of similarity to the query indicators. In most retrieval systems, the manual assignment of keywords and content identifiers is avoided by assuming that the words that occur in the document texts can serve adequately for content representation. The use of the content of articles as their index is called *automatic indexing*.

Instead of using ordinary index terms for the representation of document content, it is also possible to use other features of the document. For example, bibliographic items could be described by using lists of citations related to the particular item to be described. The citations may consist of the reference lists that normally appear at the end of a given article or book, or a *citation index* can be used to identify lists of external documents, all of which refer to a given document. The representation of document content through the use of citations is indirect; a document dealing with toxicity, for example, is described by citing other toxicity-related documents from the literature.

A second example of indirect representation is via the creation of links for browsing within or across documents. These *hypertext* (*q.v.*) links can be generated manually or automatically, and usually point to similar or related documents. Using hypertext links allows multiple ways of accessing a document, such as by following "preselected" paths through instruction manuals or by linking to auxiliary information including dictionary definitions of unusual words, cross-references within the document, or audio/video files. The Web can be viewed as a multidocument/multilocation manually generated hypertext net. A very active area of both academic and commercial research is the use of new types of links, such as interactive Java *applets*, to enhance the user's searching and browsing capabilities (*see* JAVA).

File Organization and Search Strategies

Several classes of file organizations are commonly used, the simplest of which is the *serial file*. A search is performed by a sequential comparison of the query with the identifiers of all stored items. Such a serial file organization is most economical in storage space; however, a sequential search operation is time-consuming and is thus unusable if reasonable response time is expected from large amounts of data (*see* SEARCHING).

The best known and most universally used file organization in information retrieval is the *inverted file*, where a large inverted directory or file is used to store a set of document pointers for each applicable keyword. The file is thus partitioned into sets of items with common keywords, and a search of the document file is replaced by the directory search. Inverted file organizations are advantageous in a static environment in which the set of terms usable for content identification is not subject to frequent change. In a dynamic situation in which changes are frequent, a clustered file organization may be preferable. In a *clustered file*, items that exhibit similar sets of content identifiers are automatically grouped into common classes, or clusters, and a search is performed by looking only at those clusters that exhibit a high similarity with the corresponding query identifiers.

Retrieval Operations

In many older retrieval situations, a search request is constructed by choosing appropriate keywords and content terms and appropriately interconnecting them by Boolean operations (*and, or, not*) to express the intent of the requestor. For example, a request covering "tissue culture studies of human breast cancer" may then be transformed into the more specific statement of Fig. 1.

Newer retrieval systems allow users to express their searches in natural language, without the need for specific syntax. The returned documents are ordered in decreasing query–document similarity, allowing graceful transition between strict matching of query terms and partial matching of these terms. Figure 2 shows a screen from one such search system. The upper left corner shows a selection of appropriate databases to search, a window to enter a query, and the ability to require specific phrases or to search specific fields. The lower left corner shows the titles of the retrieved documents

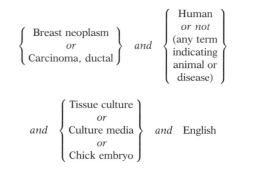

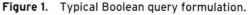

Figure 1. Typical Boolean query formulation.

displayed in order of decreasing query–document similarity. Users can select documents to view (right side of screen), or can ask the system to suggest additional terms for enhancing their query (overlay on right side of screen).

Retrieval Applications

The most common type of retrieval situation is exemplified by a retrieval system performing "on demand" searches submitted by a given user population. One example would be searches using online catalogs where

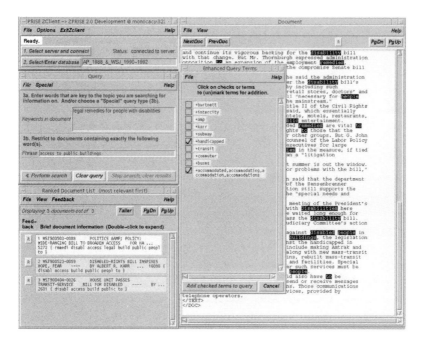

Figure 2. A screen in the ZPRISE information retrieval system (courtesy of NIST).

the text being searched is bibliographic information for each item, including authors' names, titles, journals, places of publication, dates, and applicable keywords and content identifiers. Another example would be searches against the full text of documents, where these documents may be current or back issues of newspapers, complete sets of Supreme Court cases, or electronically available versions of encyclopedias. Some of the operational systems for such a *selective dissemination of information* (SDI) use responses submitted by the user population following receipt of a retrieved document to update automatically the stored user profiles. Thus, as users become more or less interested in some areas, the positive or negative responses of the recipients are used to add to or upgrade (or, correspondingly, to delete or downgrade) the respective terms from the profiles. The principles and techniques behind SDI systems are also used in the so-called "push" technology of the Web.

A final class of language processing applications of interest in retrieval is the language-understanding or *question-answering* systems, wherein a direct rather than indirect answer (document citations) is expected in response to a submitted query. The depth and complexity of the document-and-query analysis must be much greater in question answering than in standard reference retrieval, since a precise and detailed understanding of a query is needed before an answer can be supplied.

Related Legal and Social Issues

The use of information resources such as the Web raises complicated legal and social problems. These are connected in part with the possibility of unlimited duplication and transmission of information that may be subject to legal restrictions (e.g. patented and copyrighted information), and in part with the preservation of information privacy. The question of *information privacy*, involving the right of individuals to obtain access to a given piece of information under specified conditions, is most complex, and no solution acceptable to all user classes is likely to emerge soon. On the other hand, it is relatively easy, at least conceptually, to provide *file security* by implementing any given set of privacy decisions. Elaborate systems of

user *authentication* (*q.v.*) by means of special *passwords* (*q.v.*) and of monitoring devices designed to detect unauthorized access are now widely used. Encryption of proprietary data will play an increasingly larger role in the future as more and more information is made available only to those who subscribe to a particular service.

Bibliography

1992.   Frakes W. B., and Baeza-Yates, R. *Information Retrieval: Data Structures and Algorithms.* Upper Saddle River, NJ: Prentice Hall.

1997.   Korfhage, R. *Information Storage and Retrieval.* New York: John Wiley.

1997.   Sparck Jones, K., and Willett, P. (eds.) *Readings in Information Retrieval.* San Francisco, CA: Morgan Kaufmann.

Gerard Salton and Donna Harman

INFORMATION TECHNOLOGY

For an article on a related subject, *see*

+ Computer Science

Information technology (IT) is a term frequently applied to a broad area of activities and technologies associated with the use of computers and communication, but generally implying the application of computers to storage, retrieval, processing, and dissemination of data, particularly in the field of commerce. But the term is sufficiently amorphous to encompass the activities of those who design or even use *any* form of device used to gather, transmit, or process digital information: digital satellite and cable television, DVDs, digital telephony, digital photography (*q.v.*)—even photocopiers.

According to the *Oxford English Dictionary*, the first recorded use of the term *information technology* was in 1958 when Leavitt and Whisler wrote in the *Harvard Business Review* (XXXVI 41/1): "The new technology does not have a single established name. We shall call it *information technology*." By 1984, the term had, according to the *National Westminster Bank Quarterly Review* of 13 August, become established in Britain, but by then seemed to have taken on a new meaning: "The development of cable television was made possible by the convergence of telecommunications and computing technology (...generally known in Britain as information technology)."

By the end of the twentieth century, the use of IT had burgeoned. Large accounting firms have IT departments, there are specialist IT lawyers, some governments have ministries of IT, universities have established IT faculties, IT journalists are legion, and IT professionals abound.

Bibliography

1997. Cortada, J. W. *Best Practices in Information Technology: How Corporations Get the Most Value from Exploiting their Digital Investments.* Upper Saddle River, NJ: Prentice Hall.

1998. Senn, J. A. *Information Technology in Business: Principles, Practices, and Opportunities.* Upper Saddle River, NJ: Prentice Hall.

1999. Thorp, J. *The Information Paradox: Realizing the Business Benefits of Information Technology.* New York: McGraw-Hill.

Major Keary

INFORMATION THEORY

For articles on related subjects, *see*

+ Bandwidth
+ Error Correcting and Detecting Code

Information theory began with the paper "A Mathematical Theory of Communication" published by Claude Elwood Shannon in the *Bell System Technical Journal* in 1948, and, together with material by Warren Weaver, was republished in a book of the same name by the University of Illinois Press in 1949.

According to Shannon, communication resolves uncertainty. If we toss an honest coin, communicating

the outcome takes one bit (binary digit) of information: a *heads* or *tails*, a *yes* or *no*, a *1* or a *0*. But with a biased coin for which heads comes up more often than tails, the sequence of *heads* and *tails* is *redundant* and can be encoded in less than one bit per toss. A message source may produce text, speech, or other messages. Shannon models a message source as *stochastic* or *probabilistic* in nature. He defines a quantity called *entropy*, which is a measure of the unpredictability of messages from the source. Entropy can be expressed in terms of bits per symbol or bits per message.

Shannon deals with continuous signals through use of the *sampling theorem*. A signal of bandwidth B can be *exactly* and *recoverably* represented by 2B numbers per second, each giving an instantaneous amplitude of the signal. Information from a *message source* is transmitted over a *communication channel*. For actual channels, there is always some noise or uncertainty, some random difference between what goes into and what comes out. Despite errors in transmission, communication channels have a *channel capacity* measured in bits per character or bits per second. Shannon gives formulas for the capacities of various channels in terms of either probabilities of errors in transmitting characters, or in terms of signal power, noise, and bandwidth. The Shannon formula for the channel capacity C of a channel of bandwidth B with a signal power P and added Gaussian noise power N is $C = B \log_2(1 + P/N)$ bits per second. Shannon's crucial theorem is that if the rate of transmission of a message source is less than the channel capacity of a noisy channel, messages from the source can be transmitted over the channel with less than any assignable error rate through the use of *error-correcting codes*.

The equation for channel capacity can be used to find the absolute minimum power needed to send one bit of information. The noise power N is considered to be the unavoidable thermal noise power kTB associated with a source of temperature T degrees Kelvin (degrees above absolute zero); k is Boltzmann's constant; and the bandwidth B is made very large. Then the minimum energy needed for transmission is $kT/\ln 2 = 0.95 \times 10^{-23} T$ joules per bit. The communication links used with today's superbly engineered research spacecraft come very close to this.

Bibliography

1949. Shannon, C., and Weaver, W. *The Mathematical Theory of Communication.* Urbana, IL: University of Illinois Press.

1977. McEliece, R. J. *The Theory of Information and Coding.* Reading, MA: Addison-Wesley.

1993. Sloane, N. J. A., and Wyner, A. D. (eds.) *Claude Elwood Shannon: Collected Papers.* New York: IEEE Press.

John R. Pierce

INPUT-OUTPUT OPERATIONS

For articles on related topics, *see*

+ Bus
+ Central Processing Unit (CPU)
+ Channel
+ Driver
+ Instruction Set
+ Interrupt
+ Mass Storage
+ Memory-Mapped I/O
+ Port, I/O
+ Redundant Array of Inexpensive Disks (RAID)

I/O Operations and Addressing

Input–output (I/O) systems transfer information between computer main memory and the outside world. An I/O system is composed of I/O devices (peripherals), I/O control units, and software to carry out I/O transaction(s) through a sequence of operations. I/O devices can be classified as *serial*, that is, able to transfer bit streams one bit at a time, or *parallel*. Parallel devices have a wider data bus and can therefore transfer data in words of one or more bytes.

I/O is a concerted work of both hardware and software. The software that is executed to carry out an I/O transaction for a specific I/O device is called a *device driver*. In a simple system, with a minimal I/O

control unit, the CPU must perform all I/O operations. This includes initiating the transaction, checking device status, transferring data between the devices and main memory, and terminating the I/O transaction. In this case, the system is said to be using *programmed I/O*. At the other extreme, the CPU may only initiate the I/O transaction, which is then carried out through completion by an intelligent control unit, such as an I/O coprocessor.

To distinguish among the different I/O devices in the system, two I/O addressing methods are used: *memory-mapped I/O* and *I/O-mapped I/O*. In memory-mapped I/O, a part of the memory address space is used for I/O ports, where a typical I/O device may have a data port for buffering data to be transferred and a control/status port that allows the CPU to control the I/O device and read its status. In this case, each of these I/O ports will be assigned a memory address and the CPU can use all instructions that load or store data to exchange information with these ports. Thus, a *load* instruction can be used by the CPU to read the device status or read data from the device, while a *store* instruction can be used to write data to the device or write a new control word to its control port. The Motorola 680×0 processors, for example, use memory-mapped I/O.

In the I/O-mapped I/O, there are two distinct address spaces for main memory and I/O ports. An I/O port could have the same address as a memory location; however, the CPU uses separate control lines for I/O so that only I/O devices are enabled in I/O operations. The CPU also uses separate control lines to address only the memory chip(s) during memory transfers. Processors that support I/O-mapped I/O have distinguished I/O instructions (such as IN or OUT). The use of an I/O or memory transfer instruction determines whether the I/O or the memory control lines will be activated. The Intel 80×86 processor family, for example, uses I/O-mapped I/O.

CPU Managed I/O

Input–output architectures can be classified into two major categories. In the first category, the CPU has the burden of carrying out the transfers between the I/O device and the main memory. As the size of the system grows, this becomes a burden on the CPU and can slow down the whole system. Therefore, in the second category, which includes more sophisticated systems, I/O functions are largely delegated to other "smart" modules that can carry out I/O on their own.

Programmed I/O

Programmed I/O is the simplest possible control scheme and requires very minimal hardware support. In this case, the CPU does not only carry out the I/O transaction, but also waits for the device to be ready for a transfer. In the I/O structure of Fig. 1, the I/O device interface provides a data register for exchange of data, and a control and status register to select the mode of operation and to determine whether the device is busy or ready for a transfer. The process starts with the CPU placing a control word into the control register through a store instruction. The CPU also uses a counter to keep track of the number of words transferred. The CPU uses a *pointer* (*q.v.*) to keep track of where the incoming data is to be placed. Once the counter and the pointer are initialized, the CPU reads the status register to determine whether the device is ready. If not ready, the CPU goes into a *busy–wait* loop, repeating the status check until the device becomes ready. When the device is ready, one word is read from the data register, the counter and the pointer are both updated accordingly, and the word counter is checked to determine whether the block transfer is complete. Programmed I/O is so named because the entire I/O process is managed by a software program.

Interrupt-Driven I/O

External interrupts are separate inputs to processors that are used to inform the processor of a system event that requires processor intervention. Processors typically sample their interrupt inputs towards the end of each instruction cycle. When an interrupt is detected, the processor starts identifying the interrupting device and performing the service requested. In one case, called the *vectored interrupt* method, the I/O device identifies itself to the CPU, for example, through an ID called the *device number*. In another method, called the *polled interrupt*, the CPU checks all the devices to find out which one is requesting the interrupt.

Interrupts free a processor from the need to check devices repeatedly. I/O devices are connected to the external interrupt inputs of the CPU (Fig. 2). Once one or more of these devices are ready for an I/O transfer, the device can activate its interrupt request output. At the end of each instruction cycle, the CPU checks its interrupt request input and if it finds an outstanding interrupt, it enters the so-called *interrupt acknowledge cycle*. In Fig. 2, the CPU has no way of telling which device has requested the service. Therefore, it uses the interrupt acknowledge cycle to poll the I/O devices and determine which one of them is requesting the interrupt; hence the name *polled interrupt*.

While polled interrupt eliminates the busy–waits that have to be performed by the CPU to know whether a device needs service, it still requires the CPU to go through all I/O devices to find out which one is

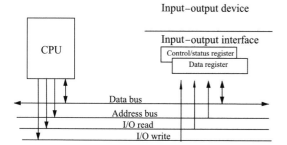

Figure 1. A typical programmed I/O configuration.

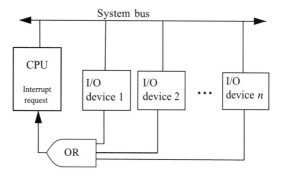

Figure 2. A hardware configuration for polled-interrupt I/O.

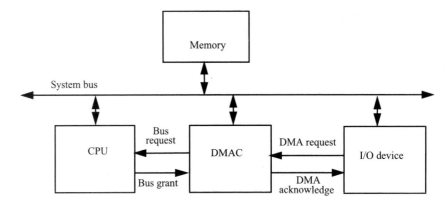

Figure 3. A DMA I/O system configuration.

requesting the interrupt. In vectored interrupt systems, the interrupting device identifies itself to the CPU either by supplying a unique device number or by supplying a memory location that holds the address of its interrupt service routine. In all interrupt-driven I/O transactions, the processor state (program counter, special status registers) must be saved, typically on the system stack prior to transferring the control to the interrupt service routine. This allows a successful resumption of normal execution after returning from the I/O service.

Direct Memory Access Systems

To minimize reliance on the CPU, devices like disks, which need to transfer large volumes of data at high rates, generally use *direct memory access* (*DMA*) controllers, which can act like simple processors for the purpose of I/O operations. DMA controllers are capable of resolving device priorities, can read data from I/O devices and write them to memory and vice versa without the intervention of the CPU, and can generate address sequences to access blocks of data.

A DMA controller can seize control of the system bus and use bus cycles to transfer data between devices and memory without CPU involvement. To do so, a DMA controller has a memory address register to put the relevant memory address on the address bus, a data register to buffer the data being transferred, and a word counter to keep track of the remaining data to be transferred. When a peripheral device, such as a disk controller, requests a transfer by issuing a DMA

request as in Fig. 3, the DMA controller (DMAC) issues a bus request to the CPU. As soon as the CPU finishes the execution of its current instruction, it disconnects itself from the bus and issues a bus grant signal to the DMA controller. Upon receiving a bus grant, the DMA controller starts administering the I/O operation. The I/O transfer is much faster in this case since the full bus bandwidth becomes available solely for memory transfers.

DMA controllers have two modes of operations, *burst mode* and *cycle-stealing*. In the burst mode, the transfer continues without interruption. If the peripheral is not able to handle the speed of the transfers, the DMA controller must keep the bus idle between the transfers. In cycle-stealing, a DMA request is generated for each transfer. In the case of slow devices, this allows the CPU to use the bus and perform useful activities while the device is getting ready for the next transfer. In higher-performance systems, dual-ported memory systems (*see* PORT, MEMORY) can be used where both the DMA controller and CPU operate concurrently.

Input-Output Coprocessors and Channels

I/O *coprocessors* can execute specialized I/O instructions in addition to many other standard instructions, such as arithmetic and branching. An I/O coprocessor is called a *channel* (*q.v.*). One may think of an I/O coprocessor as a "smart" communication channel—one capable of arbitration functions and full I/O control.

Bibliography

1998. Hayes, J. P. *Computer Architecture and Organization*, 3rd Ed. New York: WCB/McGraw-Hill.

Tarek El-Ghazawi and Gideon Frieder

INSTANT MESSAGING

See ONLINE CONVERSATION.

INSTITUTE OF ELECTRICAL AND ELECTRONIC ENGINEERS– COMPUTER SOCIETY (IEEE-CS)

For articles on related subjects, *see*

+ Association for Computing Machinery (ACM)
+ British Computer Society (BCS)
+ International Federation for Information Processing (IFIP)

The *IEEE Computer Society* traces its beginnings to the formation in 1946 of the Committee on Large-Scale Computing Devices of the American Institute of Electrical Engineers (AIEE), which was followed in 1951 by the formation of the Computer Group of the Institute of Radio Engineers (IRE). In 1963, the IRE merged with the AIEE to create the Institute of Electrical and Electronics Engineers (IEEE), with Computer Group as the name of the merged computer subgroups. IEEE-CS assumed its current name in 1972 and is the largest of the many societies that comprise the IEEE.

IEEE-CS, with a current membership of 100 000, was formed to advance the theory and practice of computer and information processing technology and promote cooperation and exchange of technical information among its members. It annually sponsors over 110 conferences, meetings, workshops, and symposia, and is one of the world's leading publishers of technical material on computing. Its publications include periodicals, books, monographs, tutorials, conference proceedings, executive briefings, and CD-ROMs, one of which contains the 14 000 pages of each year's IEEE-CS periodical content. More than 300 titles bear the imprint of the Computer Society Press. The leading IEEE-CS periodicals are its monthly, *Computer*; the monthly *Transactions on Computers*, a research journal; and the quarterly *Annals of the History of Computing*, one of a small number of scholarly journals devoted to the history of a single scientific or engineering discipline.

Technical activities are carried out by 32 semiautonomous technical committees (TCs). The TCs act like little societies, holding meetings and conferences, and publishing newsletters and conference proceedings. IEEE-CS itself publishes 10 special-interest periodicals, 12 transactions on various subjects, and cooperates with the Association for Computing Machinery (ACM) in the publication of *Transactions on Networking*, with the American Institute of Physics in publishing *Computing in Science and Engineering*, and with several IEEE societies in the publication of *Transactions on Multimedia*.

IEEE-CS has 12 committees charged with the development of IEEE standards. It conducts an active awards program honoring technical achievements and service to the profession, society, and itself. It has more than 200 regular and student chapters, about half outside the USA.

On 1 January 1999, IEEE-CS became a full member of the International Federation for Information Processing (IFIP–*q.v.*). Along with ACM, IEEE-CS had been one of the two members of FOCUS that had represented the United States in IFIP up through 31 December 1998. It has a joint membership arrangement with ACM, is affiliated with 12 other US societies and 25 societies in other countries, and is an executive member of the Internet Society. In addition to its headquarters at 1730 Massachusetts Ave. NW, Washington, DC 20036-1992, it maintains a publications office on the west coast, the original base of the Computer Group (P.O. Box 3014, Los Alamitos, CA 90720-1264), a European office (13, Avenue de l'Aquilon, B-1200 Brussels, Belgium), an Asia/Pacific office (Ooshima Building,

2-19-1 Minami Aoyama, Minato-ku, Tokyo 107-0062, Japan), and a Website http://computer.org.

Eric A. Weiss

INSTRUCTION

See INSTRUCTION DECODING; INSTRUCTION-LEVEL PARALLELISM; and INSTRUCTION SET.

INSTRUCTION COUNTER

See PROGRAM COUNTER.

INSTRUCTION DECODING

For articles on related topics, *see*

+ Arithmetic-Logic Unit (ALU)
+ Central Processing Unit (CPU)
+ Computer Architecture
+ Instruction Set
+ Microprogramming
+ Reduced Instruction Set Computer (RISC)

The execution of an instruction in a digital computer occurs in three or four phases.

1. Fetching the instruction from main or cache memory into the instruction register in the CPU.
2. Decoding the instruction and generation of its operand addresses, if any.
3. Fetching (or storing) the operands.
4. Final execution of the operation.

In many modern instruction sets, steps 3 and 4 are mutually exclusive (e.g. Sun Sparc or DEC Alpha). In these processors, any one instruction can either do a memory-based operation (e.g. LOAD register from memory) or an ALU operation (e.g. ADD registers with result in a register), but not both (e.g. ADD a register to a value in memory). In older instruction sets (e.g. IBM S360/370/390 or Intel 80×86), instructions are available that use all four phases. Each phase is partitioned into one or more steps or "cycles." A cycle is the time required to reconfigure (change the contents of) a data register in the processor. Several cycles may be required to complete the execution of the instruction. Simple processors of the early 1990s (e.g. MIPS 2000) used 4 cycles to complete most instructions. More modern processors (DEC Alpha or Intel Pentium Pro) use 8 to 10 or more cycles to complete instruction execution. In both cases, the instruction execution is pipelined or overlapped so that the number of cycles required for instruction execution does not degrade performance (*see* PIPELINE).

The decoding phase of instruction execution initiates the specific control process specified by the instruction. When an instruction is transferred to the instruction register, its op code is decoded into a sequence of control steps that configure the flow of data between registers and activate the ALU and other execution resources specified by the instruction. The unit that responds to the op code, called the *instruction decoder*, is responsible for the interpretation of the instruction. The decoder can be implemented in combinational logic ("hardwired") or through microprogrammed control storage (*see* MICROPROGRAMMING).

Bibliography

1996. Stallings, W. *Computer Organization and Architecture*, 4th Ed. Upper Saddle River, NJ: Prentice Hall.

Michael J. Flynn

INSTRUCTION-LEVEL PARALLELISM

For articles on related subjects, *see*

+ Compiler
+ Computer Architecture

Instruction-level parallelism (ILP) is a set of processor and compiler design techniques that speed up program execution via the parallel execution of individual RISC-style operations, such as memory loads and stores, integer additions, and floating-point multiplications. Although operations are executed in parallel, there is only a single thread of execution. The processor–compiler system is handed a single program, written for a sequential processor, from which it extracts the parallelism automatically. An important feature of these techniques is that they are largely transparent to users.

If ILP is to be achieved, the compiler and the run-time hardware must perform the following functions:

- Determine which operations can be legally executed in a given cycle. (Sometimes an operation must wait for the completion of an earlier operation, in which case the later operation is said to have a *dependence* on the earlier one.)
- From among the ready-to-execute operations, select certain ones for execution. These must be assigned to some specific functional unit, and must be assigned a register into which the result may be deposited. This task is called *scheduling*.

What all ILP processors have in common is multiple functional units that can execute multiple operations in parallel, as shown in Fig. 1. The two most important types of ILP processors differ in how and when they decide what to schedule:

- *Superscalar* processors are given sequential programs, just as they might run on a processor containing no ILP. Since the program contains no explicit information regarding the dependences between the instructions, the dependences that exist must be determined by the hardware, which must then make the scheduling decisions as well. All of this is carried out by the processor as the program runs.

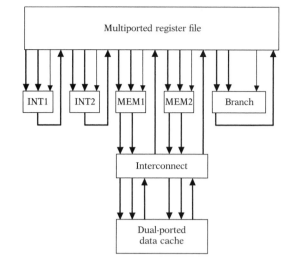

Figure 1. Execution hardware of a sample processor for executing programs with instruction-level parallelism. This consists of two identical integer units and two identical memory ports. INT1 and INT2 perform integer addition, subtraction, and multiplication. MEM1 and MEM2 represent the hardware that prepares and presents load and store operations to the dual-ported data cache. BRANCH performs conditional and unconditional branches. It is able to read a pair of registers, compare them, and branch on the Boolean result. It is also able to store the Boolean result of a comparison into the register file for use as a predicate. Every operation has a third input, a Boolean value, shown as the thin arrow into each functional unit. It this value is true, the operation executes normally. If not, it is not executed at all.

- *Very long instruction word* (*VLIW*) processors are given programs in which the compiler has already identified the parallelism in the program and has embodied that information in the program itself—in each machine-level program statement, several operations may be packaged as a single VLIW instruction.

Superscalar Processors

In a fully sequential processor, each instruction is issued after the previous one has been completed. Such a processor falls short of achieving an issue rate of even a single instruction per cycle except in the unlikely circumstance that every instruction completes execution in a single cycle. Superscalar processors take a number of measures to improve upon this.

Run-Time Scheduling

The first step in increasing the issue rate is to attempt to issue an instruction every cycle, even if prior instructions have not been completed, using the related techniques of pipelining and overlapped execution. If the semantics of the program are to be preserved, instruction issue must pause if the instruction that is about to be issued depends on a previous uncompleted one. To accomplish this, the processor must check whether the instruction's operands coincide with the operands of any other instruction that has been issued but has not yet completed. If this is the case, instruction issue must be delayed.

The next step toward achieving the goal of an instruction per cycle is out-of-order execution. Instead of stalling instruction issue as soon as an instruction that depends on one that is still being executed is encountered, the dependent instruction is set aside. In the meantime, the processor may issue and begin the out-of-order execution of subsequent instructions that prove to be independent of all sequentially preceding instructions. The CDC 6600 and the IBM System 360/91 were among the earliest processors to do this.

Run-Time Speculative Execution

Conditional branches pose a major obstacle to ILP since operations that would be issued after the branch must wait for the branch to resolve which way the program flow will go. Speculative execution is a special form of out-of-order execution, in which the instructions following a conditional branch are allowed to execute before the branch has been completed and before it is certain that the program's flow of control will actually mandate the execution of those operations. Using speculative execution, the potential ILP is increased, often dramatically. When an operation is executed speculatively, it may happen that the flow of the program is such that that instruction ought not to have been executed. In that case, the speculative operation is wasted and a time penalty is incurred to restore the processor state before going down the correct path. It is important, therefore, that an extremely accurate *branch prediction* scheme be used.

Superscalar Execution

Superscalar execution has the goal of issuing multiple, independent instructions in parallel in each cycle even though the hardware is handed a sequential program. To do so, the processor must determine the dependences between the instructions that it wishes to issue simultaneously. Specifically, it may issue each instruction only if it is independent of all the other instructions that are being issued concurrently but which would have been executed earlier in a sequential execution of the program. The first superscalar processor built commercially was the Astronautics ZS–1. Since then, a number of superscalar microprocessor products have been introduced, including the Motorola 68060, the MIPS R1000, the IBM PowerPC, the Sun UltraSparc, and the Intel Pentium Pro.

VLIW Processors

VLIW processors evolved in an attempt to achieve high levels of ILP with reduced hardware complexity. The archetypal VLIW processor is defined by two features:

- *MultiOp* instructions, each of which specifies the concurrent issue of multiple operations per instruction, and
- *Nonunit assumed latencies*, that is, where part of the architectural contract between the hardware and the compiler is that precisely a specified number of instructions will be issued between the issuance and the completion of any given operation.

With VLIW processors, it is important to distinguish between an instruction and an operation. An *operation* is a unit of computation, such as an addition, memory load, or branch that would be referred to as an instruction in the context of a sequential architecture. A (parallel) VLIW *instruction* is the set of operations that are supposed to be issued simultaneously.

Compile-Time Scheduling

With a VLIW processor, most of the measures that were taken by the superscalar processor at run time to achieve ILP are performed by the compiler. Conceptually, the compiler emulates what a superscalar processor with the same execution hardware would do at run time. The compiler takes the sequential internal representation of the program and analyzes the dependences among the operations. If needed, it eliminates spurious dependences that are due to writing unrelated values to the same variable, by performing *register renaming*, that is, writing each distinct value to its own compiler-generated variable. The compiler then performs *scheduling*, which involves delaying the scheduled initiation time of operations that depend upon others to a time when they will have completed scheduling the out-of-order execution of other operations that are independent, and performing the allocation of the requisite functional units, buses, and registers.

Compile-Time Speculative Execution

Run-time speculation is expensive in the hardware needed to support it. The alternative is to perform speculative code motion (reordering of instructions) at compile time. The compiler for a VLIW machine specifies that an operation be executed speculatively merely by scheduling it before the branch that determines whether it should, in fact, be executed. During execution, the VLIW processor executes these speculative operations in the exact order specified by the program just as it does for nonspeculative operations. As a result, these operations end up being executed before the branches that they were originally supposed to follow; hence they are executed speculatively in relation to the original sequential code that the scheduler received.

Speculations and Predictions

Traditionally, the lack of object code compatibility has been viewed as an important shortcoming of VLIW processors, and as a significant reason for preferring superscalar over VLIW. An improved understanding of the issues involved makes this position invalid.

First, the run-time mechanisms for performing dynamic scheduling, and thereby achieving object code compatibility, are now understood for VLIW processors as they have been for superscalar processors, but are almost as expensive for VLIW processors as they are for superscalar processors. The complexity of dynamic scheduling is primarily a function of the number of operations that the processor attempts to issue per cycle, and less a function of the nature of the ILP processor.

Bibliography

1985. Ellis, J. R. *Bulldog: A Compiler for VLIW Architectures.* Cambridge, MA: MIT Press.

1991. Fisher, J. A., and Rau, B. R. "Instruction-level Parallel Processing," *Science*, **253**(5025), (September), 1233–1241.

1991. Johnson, M. *Superscalar Microprocessor Design.* Upper Saddle River, NJ: Prentice Hall.

1993. Rau, B. R., and Fisher, J. A. "Instruction-Level Parallel Processing: History, Overview and Perspective," *The Journal of Supercomputing*, **7**(1/2), (May), 9–50.

1999. Silc, J., Robic, B., and Ungerer, T. *Processor Architecture: From Dataflow to Superscalar and Beyond.* New York: Springer-Verlag.

B. Ramakrishna Rau and Joseph A. Fisher

INSTRUCTION SET

For articles on related subjects, *see*

+ Addressing
+ Central Processing Unit (CPU)
+ Computer Architecture
+ Input-Output Operations
+ Instruction Decoding
+ Instruction-Level Parallelism
+ Machine- and Assembly-language Programming
+ Microprogramming
+ Reduced Instruction Set Computer (RISC)

The *instruction set* (or *instruction repertoire* or *command set*) of a computer is the set of all possible operations that the computer can perform. A machine *instruction*, in turn, is a string of digits in the number base in which the machine operates, which when interpreted by the hardware, causes a unique and well-defined change in the state of the computer. Most computers are based on the binary system. For almost all cases, therefore, the "string of digits" will be a string of bits, each having the value 0 or 1. The "change in state of the computer" is, in fact, a change in the content of various registers or memory locations. The changed registers may be those explicitly or implicitly referred to by the instruction, or they may be some internal registers not directly known to the user. For example: the 16-bit string 0000010000001001 (hexadecimal 0409), when interpreted by the hardware of an Intel Pentium computer, causes the value 9 to be added to the special AL register, the result replacing the previous contents of that register. In this case, the change of state is apparent to the user of the machine.

Each computer model possesses its own instruction set. The same bit string may mean completely different things on two different computers, even if the number of bits needed for expressing an instruction is the same on the two machines. For example, the bit string 0409 (hexadecimal), which we used previously, invoked an addition in the Pentium computer. But when interpreted by a PowerPC computer, whose instructions are 32 bits long, the same bit string can be only part of an instruction, and the first 8 bits (hexadecimal 04) is not a legal combination in that machine—that is, there is no instruction with the op code 04. Thus, bit strings are not a good basis for classification of machine instructions.

Classification of Machine Instructions

There is usually a simple relation between the length of the computer word or addressable unit and the instruction length. In old machines with limited address space, the addressing was by words, and the instructions were of different sizes and packed into the words—typically two to four in one word. In more modern machines, the addressing is by bytes, with various data structures and instructions consisting of multiple bytes. Some architectures—in particular the Intel 80×86—have varying lengths for the instructions. Others, such as PowerPC (IBM and Motorola) and Alpha (DEC), have a single-length instruction with various formats. Instructions, therefore, can be initially classified by length and structure.

The bit string representing a machine instruction is generally divided into two major field groups: the operation (or "op code") field and operand fields (address fields). The op code is usually first, followed by the address fields, analogous to the prefix notation used with mathematical functions; that is, $g(x, y, z)$ means the function (operation) g applied to variables (operands) x, y, z. Basic operations are roughly divided into arithmetic, logical, data alignment, data move, and control operations.

Arithmetic Operations

Arithmetic operations are usually confined to the four basic ones (add, subtract, multiply, and divide) and to the "compare" operation, which records status information about the relative magnitude of the operands compared. The different operand types are typically integers and floating-point numbers with different precision (half-, single-, double-, or quad-), or strings of differing length used in more complex instruction combinations. The operands may be signed or unsigned, and the most common mode is binary.

Logical Operations

Logical operations are Boolean operations on the bit values of the operands. Although there are 16 possible Boolean operations on two operands, usually only a subset of these (e.g. AND, OR, and NOT) is available. Although this subset is sufficient to reproduce all other Boolean operations, some machines include other operations, such as XOR, NOR, or NAND. Boolean operations are used for the manipulation of parts of words, for decision processes, and for nonnumerical processing. Data alignment operations are sometimes lumped with logical operations, and include the various possible shift instructions, although in some classifications these form a category of their own. Shifting operations, as their names implies, shift the bits in a word to the left or right.

Data Move Operations

Data move instructions include moves (copying) of data between memory locations and registers, and the input–output instructions necessary for communication between the CPU and peripheral devices. Examples of the former are instructions to load and store registers and to move data from one location in memory to another.

Control Operations

Control instructions include conditional and unconditional branches, test instructions, and status-changing instructions. For example, there may be instructions like BRANCH (or JUMP) to a given address (to begin a new sequence of instructions) when the result of the last operation is negative, or if there is an arithmetic overflow. Program flow can be affected not only by explicit control instructions issued by the programmer but also by interrupts (*q.v.*). Some computers—the Intel Pentium is an example—also contain *repeat* instructions that cause a specific number of instructions following the *repeat* to be executed a specific number of times or until some condition is met, thus affecting the sequencing of the program.

Different instruction types usually possess different numbers of operands. Whereas arithmetic operations usually refer to three operands (two for the data locations and one for the result location), either

explicitly or implicitly, certain control instructions may have one or no operands at all. For example, an unconditional BRANCH has one operand, but a CLEAR ACCUMULATOR instruction has none.

Machine Language and Instruction Formats

As defined earlier, a computer's instruction set (or repertoire) is the set of all of its defined op codes and their variants. There are, however, other types of computer design possible, such as *tagged architecture* machines, in which the operation performed is defined by the type of the operand. For example, there is only one ADD operation, and this is done in floating-point or integer mode depending on the type of the operand, which is stored with the operand and not in the instruction stream. The instruction repertoire of such a computer is still the set of all possible operations. However, it is now defined not just by the set of all op codes, but by both op codes and operand tags. The Sparc processor, for example, has some tagged arithmetic instructions.

Historically, instruction sets were divided into *vertical* and *horizontal*. Vertical instructions are those of the type where a single operation (or a time-ordered series of a fixed number and type of operations) is performed on a single set of operands. Vertical instructions are usually highly encoded.

Horizontal instructions, later called very long instruction words (VLIW) are those in which operations packed into single very long words (up to 128 bits) are independent or mildly interdependent and are performed on the respective operands in parallel or in a well-defined time sequence.

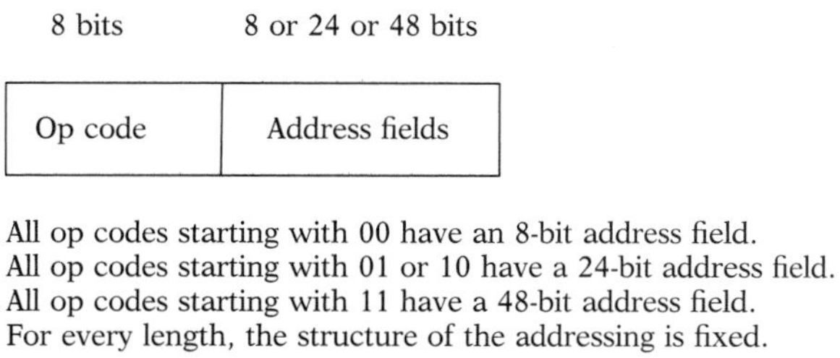

8 bits   8 or 24 or 48 bits

Op code	Address fields

All op codes starting with 00 have an 8-bit address field.
All op codes starting with 01 or 10 have a 24-bit address field.
All op codes starting with 11 have a 48-bit address field.
For every length, the structure of the addressing is fixed.

Figure 1. Typical structure of a vertical instruction set.

The instruction set of a computer such as the Intel Pentium or the PowerPC is an example of a vertical instruction set (*see* Fig. 1). Vertical instructions are found in most machines today. Horizontal instructions are mainly found in microprogrammed machines and are rare outside them. In a highly coded arrangement, the number of possible instructions is equal to the total information contents of the field. In a field of n bits, this means a total of 2^n possible instructions. On the other hand, one can envision a completely different situation in which each part of the instruction code conveys some information about the type of the operation. In this case, we speak about a *low level of encoding*. The number of instructions expressible in this case is smaller than the total information content of the op code field, since some of the combinations may be unused.

Bibliography

1994. May, C., and Warren, H. (eds.) *The PowerPC Architecture*, 2nd Ed. San Francisco, CA: Morgan Kaufmann.

1996. Kain, R. Y. *Advanced Computer Architecture*. New York: Simon & Schuster.

1996. Stallings, W. *Computer Organization and Architecture*, 4th Ed. Upper Saddle River, NJ: Prentice Hall.

Gideon Frieder

INTEGRATED CIRCUITRY

For articles on related subjects, *see*

+ Computer Circuitry
+ Laws, Computer
+ Logic Design
+ Microcomputer Chip
+ Microprocessors and Microcomputers

Introduction

Integrated Circuit (IC) history began with John Bardeen, Walter Brattain, and William Shockley of AT&T Bell Laboratories, who did the pioneering work in 1947 that led to the invention of the point-contact transistor, the basic building block of the IC. The team was awarded the Nobel Prize in Physics in 1956. What made the first transistor possible was a semiconductor material, the element germanium. Unlike metals, which conduct electricity with relative ease, and insulators, which almost always block any motion of electrons, semiconductors can conduct or insulate; and there are a variety of ways in which these conductive properties can be controlled and exploited. But the developments that truly launched the IC age did not come until 1958 and 1959. Within a few months of each other, Jack Kilby of Texas Instruments and Robert Noyce of Fairchild Semiconductor invented different versions of the IC. Both inventors filed for patents in 1959, and Texas Instruments and Fairchild were each offering ICs commercially by 1961.

Kilby sought to make resistors, capacitors, and diodes—all the elements of electronic circuits—out of germanium. At that time, germanium was easier to work with than silicon, the semiconductor that is now the material of choice for ICs. Kilby's invention was cumbersome and costly to produce in large quantities. Four months after Kilby built his germanium IC, Noyce found a way to join the circuits by printing on the circuit board, using lithography and a silicon substrate. The commercial devices that followed showed the advantages of silicon over germanium for integrating multiple components on a single chip. The fabrication techniques developed by Noyce are the forerunner of current IC fabrication technologies. In 2000, ten years after Noyce died, Kilby was awarded the Nobel Prize in physics. Almost certainly, Noyce would have been cohonored had he been alive.

Integrated Circuits
Basic Principles

An integrated circuit is a functioning assembly of various elements or "devices"—transistors, resistors, capacitors, diodes, and so on—all electrically connected and packaged to form a predefined fully functioning circuit. ICs fall into two major categories: hybrid circuits and monolithic circuits.

In a hybrid circuit, all the IC elements are wired together on a ceramic substrate, somewhat similar to a printed circuit board (PCB), and are packaged and sold as a single functioning unit with input–output (I/O) leads. In essence, a hybrid circuit is a miniaturized version of the PCB. However, the elements used in PCB assemblies are encapsulated for protection from moisture and atmospheric impurities. For example, an individual transistor used on a PCB actually consists of a protective capsule containing the transistor proper, with its leads connected to leads on the capsule. Hybrid ICs, on the other hand, use bare elements; the whole package is assembled first and then the entire unit is encapsulated in a protective polymeric material.

In a monolithic circuit, the major IC in a modern computer, the circuit elements are formed on a single silicon substrate using advanced materials and sophisticated processes and equipment. In this case, the silicon substrate serves not only as a support for the circuit elements but also as one of the materials that form the components of the circuit. The nature of processing allows the arranging of circuit elements in close proximity, thereby reducing the wiring lengths by orders of magnitude as compared to a hybrid IC. As a result, monolithic ICs offer higher signal speeds than hybrid or PCB assemblies.

Monolithic ICs

Monolithic ICs are silicon-based because silicon can be grown to high perfection in large crystal diameters, currently up to 500 mm. The key to IC fabrication is the proper treatment of silicon in such a way as to form the desired circuit components. The basic notion is that selected impurities, when introduced into a pure crystalline silicon matrix in a precisely controlled manner in a process called *doping*, can appreciably alter its electrical properties, and therefore, control the flow of electricity in a solid (hence the name *solid-state device*). These impurities actually settle in the silicon matrix and for some elements, such as arsenic or phosphorus, produce an excess of electrons within the matrix, thus yielding what is known as *n-type* silicon (n for negative). Introduction of elements such as boron, on the other hand, causes a deficit of electrons, and produces p-type silicon (p for positive).

Diodes

Important physical phenomena occur when n- and p-type semiconductors are placed in contact to form a p–n junction, the simplest semiconductor structure. In this case, the completed junction is formed of three distinct semiconductor regions, as shown in Fig. 1a: a p-type region, a depletion region, and an n-type region. The depletion region arises when the two regions are placed in contact with each other and the holes diffuse to the n-side (electron-rich) of the junction while electrons diffuse to the p-side (electron-deficient) of the junction. The region, extending a few microns on both sides of the junction is called the *depletion region* because it is depleted of mobile charge carriers, namely, electrons and

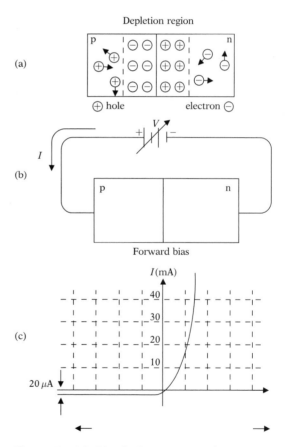

Figure 1. (a) Physical arrangement of a p–n junction. (b) A diode (p–n junction) under forward bias. (c) The characteristic current curve for a real diode.

holes. The region forms a potential barrier that prevents the further diffusion of holes and electrons across the junction and insures zero current flow when no external voltage is applied.

The most notable feature of this p–n junction is its ability to pass current in only one direction. Such behavior, called the *diode action*, is due to the fact that when a positive external voltage from a battery is applied to the p-side junction, as shown in Fig. 1b, the overall barrier is reduced, resulting in a current that increases rapidly with increasing forward voltage or bias, as displayed in Fig. 1c. For reverse bias (a positive voltage from a battery applied to the n-side junction), the potential barrier is increased, resulting in a very small reverse current that quickly reaches a saturation value.

Transistors

A transistor is a structure of silicon, dielectric (insulator), metal, and impurities precisely located to create the millions of minuscule on–off switches that make the brains of a microprocessor or the memory of a computer. Every IC chip has a base layer of transistors, with layers of metal wires stacked above to interconnect the transistors. ICs currently use two important device technologies: the Bipolar Transistor, whose function results from the physical phenomena at the p–n junctions, and the Field Effect Transistor (FET), particularly the Metal Oxide Semiconductor FET (MOSFET), which depends on the physical phenomena occurring close to the surfaces.

Bipolar transistor

The bipolar transistor is basically an n–p–n (or p–n–p) junction. Its operation exploits the voltage of the base (the p-type region) to control the flow of current between the collector and the emitter (the two n-type regions). For instance, if the collector is made more positive than the emitter, no current will flow because of the diode effect between the base and the collector unless the base is also made more positive than the emitter, in which case current will flow from the base to the emitter and, subsequently, from the collector to the base. The device is called *bipolar* because both electrons and holes, and consequently two polarities (positive and negative), are involved in the flow of current.

FET transistor

The operation of an FET transistor also exploits the voltage of the gate with respect to the source. For instance, if the drain is made more positive than the source, no current will flow because of the diode effect between the drain and the source due to the existence of the p-type region, unless a positive voltage is applied to the gate. In this case, the insulator region (gate oxide) blocks the flow of current and forms a capacitor that has its negative charge, or electrons, in the p-type region just below the insulator, and its positive charge, or holes, in the gate. At sufficiently high gate voltages, the electrons in the p-type region form a thin n-type channel beneath the gate oxide, which connects with the n-type regions of the source and drain, thus allowing current to flow easily through this channel. The FET is also known as a unipolar transistor, because only one type of charge, namely, electrons, is involved in the flow of current. Since the gate is normally fabricated of metal and the insulator of silicon dioxide, the FET is also commonly referred to as a metal oxide semiconductor (MOS) transistor. A prefix is frequently employed to indicate the type of charge carrier in the FET. For example, an n–p–n device is referred to as an NMOS transistor (electrons are the charge carriers), while a p–n–p-based FET would be known as a PMOS transistor (holes are the charge carriers). Historically, PMOS transistors were used initially because of ease of manufacturing and control of dopant. However, current ICs employ NMOS transistors because of their inherently higher speed than PMOS devices. The two types of transistors are coupled in CMOS (Complementary MOS) devices, the technology of choice for memories and logic ICs. A CMOS device cross section is shown in Fig. 2.

Evolution of IC Devices and Families

There are two main categories of ICs: memory and logic (including microprocessors). There is a variety of memory ICs available: DRAM, SDRAM, SRAM, EEPROM, and so on. The logic ICs include bipolar, CMOS, BiCMOS (bipolar CMOS), and other ASICs (application-specific ICs). For the first 20 years of ICs, the bipolar transistor was the preferred device because of its speed. It continued to dominate the scene in

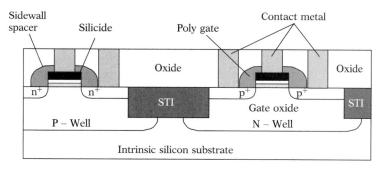

Figure 2. Cross section of a Twin Well CMOS device.

Table 1. Prevalent device and circuit technologies.

Bipolar devices	FET devices	Bipolar logic circuits	FET memory circuits
NPN	NMOS	ECL–Emitter coupled logic	RAM–Random access memory
PNP	PMOS	TTL–Transistor-transistor logic	ROM–Read-only memory
BiCMOS	CMOS	IIL–Integrated injection logic	SRAM–Static RAM
	BiCMOS	STL–Schottky transistor logic	DRAM–Dynamic RAM
			SDRAM–Synchronous dynamic RAM
			EEPROM–Electrically erasable programmable ROM

Note: BiCMOS: Bipolar CMOS.

the areas of high-speed switching, logic, and memory until about 1990; since then it has gradually been replaced by complementary MOSFETs (CMOSFET or simply CMOS) because they consume less power than bipolar ICs. CMOS devices integrate NMOS and PMOS transistors on a single chip, connected in series in such a way that when one is on, the other is off, so that it draws power only during switching. This results in a very low standby power consumption in static CMOS circuits.

Common device and circuit technologies are summarized in Table 1. MOSFET devices are the pacesetter and a barometer for technological innovations and development. The number of circuit elements on a chip and their minimum dimensions are often employed as an indicator of progress in technological evolution. Figure 3 shows the evolution of IC density for MOSFET/DRAM memory (number of bits), and CMOS and bipolar logic (circuits/chip),

starting from 1970. The various generations of circuits shown in the figure are classified according to the degree of integration. The nomenclature for six successively greater chip storage densities is given in Table 2.

IC Fabrication Processes

Because of the high complexity and level of integration of integrated circuits, quality control of incoming materials, process control, and equipment cleanliness are critical if acceptable levels of product yield and reliability are to be realized.

The requirements for the emerging sub-quarter-micron technologies and the larger 300-mm diameter wafer size in the early 2000s are dramatically redefining the materials and reshaping the processes that constitute the building blocks of electronic devices, and the necessary equipment.

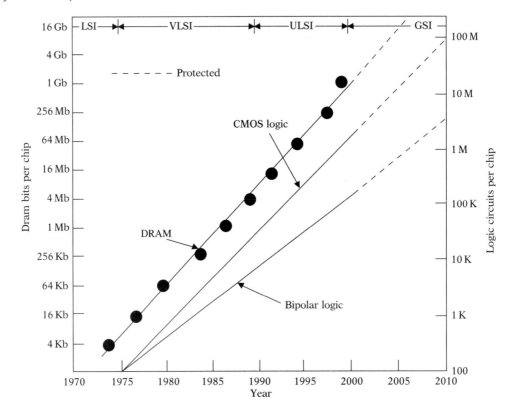

Figure 3.   Evolution of IC density.

Table 2.   Generations of IC families.

IC generation	Size (bits/chip)
SSI—Small-scale integration	$1-10^2$
MSI—Medium-scale integration	10^2-10^3
LSI—Large-scale integration	10^3-10^5
VLSI—Very large scale integration	10^5-10^6
ULSI—Ultra-large scale integration	10^6-10^9
GSI—Giga-scale integration	$>10^9$

Lithography

Lithography is the process of placing an image of a circuit pattern onto a radiation-sensitive polymer (resist mask). Successful lithography requires optimal performance of several elements simultaneously: photo-resist materials (resistant to etching), exposure tools, and lithographic processes (e.g. resist coating, photo exposure, image development, baking) to form the desired pattern. The most common imaging methods employ optical light sources in combination with conventional optical projection methods using specially designed high numerical aperture (NA) lenses.

Ion Implantation

Ion implantation is the process by which dopant impurities (e.g. As^+, B^+) can be introduced by energetic beams in a controlled manner into selected areas of the silicon wafer in order to alter their electronic (conduction) properties. Implantation is ordinarily performed with voltages in the range of 1 to 500 KeV (thousand electron volts), with new shallow junction devices using even lower energies, less than 500 eV.

Basic requirements for implantation systems are the ion sources and processes to generate, purify, and accelerate the ions. Impurity incorporation is achieved through a bombardment process that implants the ions of desirable elements into the silicon lattice.

Reactive Ion Etching

Reactive ion etching (RIE) is a high-fidelity transfer process in which a lithographically developed circuit pattern in resist is transferred to an underlying film (e.g. SiO_2) by the removal of unwanted areas from the film through the use of low-temperature weakly ionized gaseous processes. The material is removed from the unmasked areas of the film by converting it to a volatile gaseous state through chemical reactions with one or more energetic reactive ions and neutral elements, produced within the gaseous plasma in what are known as plasma reactors. These RIE processes make possible the development and manufacture of today's high-density, high-resolution ICs.

Thin Film Deposition

Deposited metal and dielectric thin films are widely used in the fabrication of ICs. These films provide conducting paths, like a wire; electrical insulators between electrically active areas of the device, like a dielectric; and protection from the ambient, like a passivation layer that prevents corrosion.

Metallization

Metallization connects the IC components (e.g. transistors, resistors) on a wafer to form circuits, using low-resistance wiring and contacts to n^+ and p^+ silicon junctions. The process involves the deposition of both metal and isolation dielectric films in several interconnection layers, each metallized layer electrically connected through metal vias or plugs. AlCu alloy, the most commonly used metal today, is deposited using sputtering, a plasma process. Tungsten, another metal used to make contact with the transistors and as first-level wiring, is deposited with chemical vapor deposition (CVD) techniques using WF_6 (tungsten hexafluoride) as the source gas. Interlevel dielectric films

like TEOS (tetrathylorthosilicate) oxides are generally deposited using plasma-enhanced deposition methods in high-density plasma reactors.

Copper metallization uses electroplated copper deposition or CVD in oxide trenches and vias, followed by polishing or planarization with a process known as *dual damascene*. Figure 4 is an electron microscope view of the surface of IBM's PowerPC CMOS logic chip with multiple levels of copper wiring. Figure 5 shows a typical end product of the wafer manufacturing process, namely, a 256-Mb DRAM chip fabricated on a 200-mm wafer. Once the processing is complete, the wafer is tested for functionality. The lines between the various chips are then marked and the wafer diced along these lines, called *kerfs*. The resulting IC chips are then packaged, tested again as a module, and shipped to the customer.

Circuit Yields, Reliability, and Cost

In an ideally produced wafer, 100% of the circuits will work. In reality, however, the number of good circuits

Figure 4. Scanning electron microscope view of PowerPC chip with copper metallization (courtesy of IBM Microelectronics USA).

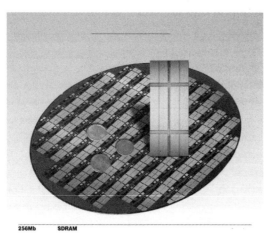

256Mb   SDRAM

Figure 5. A 200-mm silicon wafer containing a 256 Mb memory chip.

(or the yield) depends upon process maturity, circuit design, and random defects in the circuit. Achieving high process yields requires robust processes and equipment (e.g. high uptime, stability, and online diagnostics). Many innovative designs have been implemented to achieve these goals, such as computer control of process parameters, vacuum processing, vacuum load locks, and inline diagnostic measurements. Proper design of circuits requires recognizing the tool/process interactions and assessing circuit sensitivities to process parameters.

Despite proper design of circuits and robust processes, the yields will be less than 100% due to random point defects (areas that are small compared with the chip size) generated by imperfect processing, particles, stacking faults, mask defects, and so on. The effect of these defects on yield increases as the minimum feature size continues to shrink. At present, the fabrication facilities for the production of ULSI (Ultra-large scale integration) circuits (e.g. 64 Mb DRAM) cost about $1.5 billion for a 300-mm fab. This cost is projected to exceed $2 billion for a 500-mm wafer fab producing 0.18-μm, 1 Gb DRAMs. In spite of such capital investments, the ever-increasing applications and the demand for faster, more cost-effective computers are likely to keep the IC factories humming for years to come.

Bibliography

1998. Ross, I. M. "The Invention of the Transistor," *Proceedings of the IEEE*, **86**(1), 7–28.

2003. Rabaey, J. M., Chandrakasan, A., and Nikolic, B. *Digital Integrated Circuits*, 2nd Ed. Upper Saddle River, NJ: Prentice Hall.

G. Swami Mathad and Alain E. Kaloyeros

INTEGRATED SERVICES DIGITAL NETWORK (ISDN)

For articles on related subjects, *see*

+ Communications and Computers
+ Multiplexing
+ Network Protocols
+ Networks, Computer
+ Open Systems Interconnection

History

The *Integrated Services Digital Network* (ISDN) is a telephonic system that can support a variety of digital services through a limited set of standard interfaces. ISDN comes in two flavors: "Narrowband" and "Broadband" (B-ISDN). N-ISDN emerged from preexisting telephone network technologies and covers bit-rates of up to 2 Mbps. B-ISDN is a completely new technology covering much higher bit-rates. This article addresses only N-ISDN.

The development of N-ISDN followed from the adoption of digital transmission by many public telephone systems. This was due both to the ease with which digital signals could be regenerated without deterioration and the availability of VLSI-based technologies for the processing of digital streams. Voice traffic in such Integrated Digital Networks (IDNs) is encoded using pulse-code modulation at 64 Kbps.

Although an IDN integrated many different kinds of traffic internally, the services it supported were accessed through unrelated interfaces. For example, data services might be accessed via the X.25 interface, while telephony was accessed via normal analog lines ("local loops") between the customer's premises and the telephone exchange. *Local loops* are mainly copper and of variable quality, but one requirement of N-ISDN was that it should operate over the existing local loops.

Signaling

IDNs use "common channel signaling" (CCS). This means that the messages that pass between exchanges are carried in dedicated signaling channels. This contrasts with earlier analog systems, in which signaling was carried along with the speech channel to which it related. The principal advantage of CCS is a great reduction in the number of signaling terminations at an exchange. ISDN also employs CCS at the user–network interface. A very much wider range of signaling messages is available than was possible with the old analog systems.

Transmission Technology

N-ISDN uses the transmission and switching capabilities of the existing IDN. This is based on 64 Kbps bit-streams that are combined into higher-capacity "trunks" using time division multiplexing. In Europe, the first multiplex combines 32 64 Kbps channels into one 2 Mbps channel, while in the United States, 23 64 Kbps channels form one 1.544 Mbps channel.

User Interfaces

The user interfaces reflect the 64 Kbps and 2 Mbps infrastructure and CCS. The basic rate interface (BRI) offers two 64 Kbps "B-Channels" for data or voice and one 16 Kbps "D-Channel" for signaling. In principle, this is available to all subscribers through the existing local loops. The presence of two B-Channels means that it is possible to offer subscribers two telephone connections where previously they had only one. The primary rate interface (PRI) offers 30 (23 in the USA) 64 Kbps B-channels and one 64 Kbps D-Channel. Data channels at higher rates (H-channels) are also defined. This interface is intended for the connection of PABXs and large computer installations. Industry standards such as "Asymmetric Digital Subscriber Loop" (ADSL) and "High-speed Digital Subscriber Loop" (HDSL) provide much higher bit-rates and are capable of carrying high-definition digital TV.

Applications

The circuit-switched service provides an unstructured 64 Kbps bit-stream (a physical layer service in OSI terms), which may be switched in a manner analogous to an ordinary telephone call. Once established, such circuits may carry voice (via CODECs), fax, or data. The service is well-suited to fax and provides high-quality, high-speed transmission. The signaling also allows proper call identification allowing incoming calls to be routed directly to a fax machine. N-ISDN is quite widely used as an Internet (*q.v.*) access technology. In this case, a frame structure is imposed on the circuit—normally through the use of the Internet *Point-to-Point Protocol* (PPP). Internet datagrams are then carried in PPP frames.

Transition to Broadband ISDN

The newest and fastest growing traffic types often require high and variable bit-rates. N-ISDN's internal structure is strongly biased towards fixed 64 Kbps circuits and is not well suited to this kind of traffic. A completely new infrastructure is now being deployed on the basis of optical fibers and using Asynchronous Transfer Mode (ATM) as a multiplexing technology. ATM fragments all traffic types into a series of fixed-length "cells" of 48 bytes. Cells are allocated to traffic streams in a flexible way allowing a wide range of network services.

Digital Subscriber Line Variants

The following acronyms are used to describe some of the many Digital Subscriber Line (DSL) variants:

ADSL	Asymmetric DSL
BDSL	Broadband DSL
CDSL	Consumer DSL
FDSL	Fixed Directory Subscriber List
HDSL	High-Data-Rate DSL
IDSL	Integrated Services Digital Network DSL
RDSL	Rate-Adaptive DSL
SDSL	Single-Line DSL or Symmetric DSL
VDSL	Very-High-Bit-Rate DSL
VADSL	Very-High-Rate Asymmetric DSL
VDSL	Very-High-Data-Rate DSL

Bibliography

1988. CCITT. *Integrated Services Digital Network: Overall Aspects and Functions*, Melbourne, Australia: ISDN User–Network Interfaces. Blue-book Vol. III, Fascicle III.8. November.

1990. Griffiths, J. M. (ed.) *ISDN Explained.* New York: John Wiley.

1998. Kessler, G. C., and Southwick, P. V. *ISDN: Concepts, Facilities, and Services.* New York: McGraw-Hill.

Graham Knight

INTERACTIVE INPUT DEVICES

For articles on related subjects, *see*

+ Computer Graphics
+ Disabled, Computers and the
+ Mouse
+ Speech Recognition and Synthesis
+ User Interface
+ Videogames
+ Virtual Reality
+ Workstation

Input devices allow the user to enter data or interact with running programs, and are used for activities ranging from editing programs to playing videogames (*q.v.*). Input devices can be separated into five classes: *keyboards, locators, picks, valuators,* and *buttons.* The classification is determined by the distinct functions performed. In many cases, these divisions are blurred because a device of one class can simulate the functions of another.

Keyboards

A *keyboard* is used for entering textual data into a computer file (*see* Fig. 1). Keyboard keys are usually arranged similarly to those of a standard typewriter, the so-called QWERTY keyboard (named for the sequence of keys in the top row). This is a historical artifact, since early typewriter keys had to be arranged to allow

Figure 1. A computer keyboard with attached function keys. The function keys to the left and right have specific functions. The function keys on the top row labeled F1 through F12 are programmable, and their function will vary with the application.

typists to work quickly without the keys jamming. To do this, frequently used keys were placed far apart. Other keyboard designs that group frequently used keys together have been explored. An example is the Dvorak keyboard (*see* Fig. 2).

Locator Devices

Locators are used for indicating a position for placing objects on the screen or quickly moving the cursor in a text editor. Visual feedback of the current position is provided with an arrow or a crosshair. A digitizing tablet, mouse, trackball, and joystick are examples of location devices.

Figure 2. The Dvorak keyboard that has the potential for higher typing speeds than the QWERTY keyboard.

The *digitizing tablet* is a flat surface that has a fine grid of horizontal and vertical wires embedded in it. There is an attached stylus or *puck* that produces a magnetic field and is centered at the location to which it points. The magnetic field will induce a current in the wires of the tablet. By sensing the strength of the current on a set of neighboring wires, the tablet can determine where the stylus or puck is and whether it is touching the tablet or being held above it.

A *mouse* is a small hand-held device that is used to indicate a position or movement. Typical uses for a mouse include quickly repositioning the cursor in a word processor and moving an object by *dragging* it to a new location. A mouse can be either physical or optical. A *physical mouse* has a ball that protrudes from its bottom. When the mouse is moved, friction will cause the ball to move an amount proportional to the movement of the mouse. An *optical mouse* uses a light-emitting diode (LED), a light sensor, and a special ruled mouse pad instead of the ball and potentiometers. As the mouse is moved, light from the LED is reflected by the pad to the sensor. In 1999, Microsoft introduced an improved optical mouse that works on any surface other than glass and which does not depend on detection of a ruled mouse pad. A related device is the *trackball*, which is essentially a physical mouse turned upside down so that the ball can be directly manipulated by the palm of the hand.

A *joystick* (*see* Fig. 3), popular among those who play videogames, is also used to indicate position. The joystick has a rod that protrudes from a base. Inside the base is a set of potentiometers that can sense when the rod is deflected from a vertical position. These joysticks indicate a change of position by the direction of the push and a change of speed by the amount of deflection. Like a mouse, a joystick is good for gross movement, but not for precision work.

Pick Devices

A *pick device* is used to choose an object that appears on the screen, whether it be graphical, like a line in an architectural drawing, or textual, like

Figure 3.   A joystick (photo used with permission of Microsoft Corporation).

a word or sentence. *Lightpens* and *touch screens* are examples of pick devices. The name *lightpen* is a misnomer, since the pen does not produce light, but rather senses light produced by an object on the screen.

The basic idea of a *touch screen* is that one need only point at an object on the screen with a finger to choose it; there is no special device that the user must hold. Touch screens are based on either beams of light or electrical currents. In the first case, a series of LEDs are placed along a vertical and horizontal edge of the screen and a series of light sensors are lined up on the two opposite edges. When the user touches the screen, one or more lights are blocked in the vertical and horizontal directions. By checking which lights have been blocked, the computer can determine an approximate position. In the second case, when the user makes contact with the screen, two films placed over the screen are pushed together. The first has a conductive surface and the second has a resistive surface, and when they make contact, there is a change in voltage that determines where the touch was made.

Valuator Devices

Valuators are used to indicate a real (nonintegral) numeric value over a specific range. These are implemented as slide and dial potentiometers that work in the same way as a rheostatic light dimmer. When the valuator is all the way to the left, it produces high resistance; when it is all the way to the right, it produces low resistance. The resistance is then converted to a real value over some specified range.

Button Devices

Buttons are special-purpose function keys that are frequently attached to a keyboard. For use with word processors, for example, some of these are marked with arrows (*arrow keys*) and are used to move the cursor. Others can be used to delete or insert a character, word, sentence, or paragraph. Because the design of computer keyboards typically includes arrow keys and a set of function keys, users usually consider them to be an integral part of the keyboard device, but there is a conceptual difference. Whereas the conventional keys of the keyboard produce one ASCII character each time one is pressed, function keys produce a group of two- or three-character codes per stroke. Function buttons are used to choose options with one keystroke that perform a function specific to the application program that is running. For this reason, they are also referred to as *programmable function keys*.

Other Devices

Software is available that allows a user to give spoken commands to a computer over a small microphone or to conduct an Internet (*q.v.*) telephone conversation. Personal Digital Assistants (PDAs) allow input of a constrained set of handprinted characters (*see* PORTABLE COMPUTERS) and data tablets are available for personal computers, which are essentially "electronic yellow pads" on which the user may make sketches and handwritten notes.

Small video cameras allow two similarly equipped network users to conduct a "picture phone" conversation. At the communications speeds now available to most users, successive picture frames cannot be transmitted quickly enough to provide smooth motion, but visual quality will steadily improve as more and more users gain access to fiber optic (*q.v.*) or satellite communications channels.

Bibliography

1989. Brown, J., and Cunningham, S. *Programming the User Interface*. New York: John Wiley.
1990. Foley, J. D., Van Dam, A., Feiner, S. K., and Hughes, J. F. *Computer Graphics: Principles and Practice*. Reading, MA: Addison-Wesley.
1998. Bernsen, N. O., Dybkjaer, H., Dybkjaer, L., and Bernsen, N. *Designing Interactive Speech Systems: From First Ideas to User Testing*. New York: Springer-Verlag.

Jeffrey J. McConnell

INTERLEAVING

For articles on related subjects, *see*

+ Access Time
+ Memory: Main

In systems with more than one autonomous memory module, considerable advantage in system speed may be acquired by an arrangement such that logically sequential memory addresses occur in different physical modules. By this means, the total time taken to access a sequence of memory locations can be much reduced, since several memory accesses may be overlapped by a high-speed central processing unit (CPU—*q.v.*). Two-way and four-way *interleaving* is commonly encountered (*see* Fig. 1).

Assume, for example, a memory with 60-ns access time (i.e. the time to get a word from memory to the processor) and a 120-ns cycle (i.e. the time after the initiation of an access before the memory can be

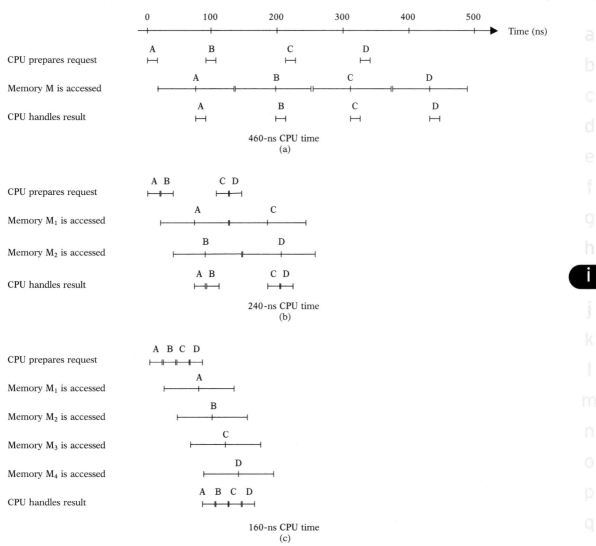

Figure 1. Timing diagram, showing a sequence of four memory accesses (A, B, C, D) in a speed-limited memory system with (a) no interleaving, (b) two-way interleaving, and (c) four-way interleaving.

accessed again), and a processor requiring 20 ns to prepare a memory request and a further 20 ns to handle the result. Also assume processor and memory overlap. Under these conditions, a sequence of four memory accesses would take 460 ns with no interleaving, 240 ns with two-way interleaving, and 160 ns with four-way interleaving. For very high-speed CPUs (particularly those involving *instruction lookahead*), for multiple CPUs, and for block transfers to cache memory (*q.v.*), it is possible to keep many modules busy simultaneously. Up to 32 interleaved modules have been reported.

Bibliography

1996. Hamacher, V. C., Vranesic, Z. G., and Zaky, S. G. *Computer Organization*, 4th Ed., 243–245. New York: McGraw-Hill.

Kenneth C. Smith and Adel S. Sedra

INTERMEDIATE LANGUAGE

For articles on related topics, *see*

+ Compiler
+ Language Processors
+ PostScript

Definition

Many computer application programs can be regarded as *language translators*, in the sense that they accept an input source language and produce an output *target* language. Compilers are among the most important examples of such programs, as are text processors such as PostScript, which accept text and formatting specifications and produce an image to be viewed or printed. Some language processors proceed from source to target by way of an *intermediate language* (IL). For example, early C++ (*q.v.*) compilers did not produce machine code directly; they translated a C++ program into a C (*q.v.*) program, which could then be compiled by a standard C compiler (*see* Fig. 1). The LATEX text-processing system in which this article was written does not produce print images directly; instead, LATEX is translated into a more basic representation called TEX (*q.v.*), which is then translated into a device-independent representation called *dvi*, which is then printed.

Advantages of Intermediate Languages

A system that uses an IL may not perform as well as a rival product that takes a more direct approach. But consider the compiler vendor who produces a suite of compilers for s source languages (C++, Pascal, Java, etc.) and currently supports these compilers for t target architectures (IBM PC, Sun Sparc, Dec Alpha, etc.). If a different product is needed for each situation, then this company must develop and support $s \times t$ compilers (*see* top part of Fig. 2). However, this work can be reduced to $s + t$ if an IL can be introduced between the source and target specifications, as shown at the bottom of that Figure: the company need only develop s front ends that translate a given

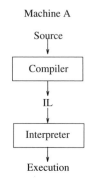

Figure 1. Overview of the functionality of a compiler/interpreter pair running on the same computer.

Table 1. Some source languages and their intermediate languages.

Source language	Intermediate language
Pascal	PCODE
Java	Java VM
Ada	Diana

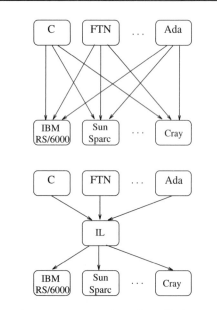

Figure 2. An IL can reduce the effort needed to resource or retarget a compiler.

source language to the IL along with t back-ends that translate from the IL to a given target architecture.

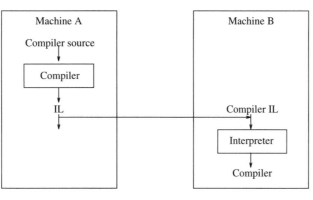

Figure 3. Porting a compiler using its intermediate language.

Thus, an IL makes the compiler more *portable*. Table 1 shows the ILs of some well-known languages.

Origin of Intermediate Languages

There are primarily three methods by which ILs are born:

- *Extension*: The early C++ compiler and the LATEX system are examples of layering a new software system on top of an existing one. Thus, while TEX is a text-processing language in its own right, it is viewed as an intermediate language from the LATEX perspective (Lamport, 1995).
- *Between*: In this approach, an IL interface is extracted from an existing system by dividing the system into components that create and use the IL.
- *New design*: When an IL can be designed without a legacy of constraints from existing systems, there is typically much greater flexibility in defining it.

Case Studies: PCODE and the Java Virtual Machine

Pascal PCODE is designed so that writing a PCODE interpreter is vastly simpler than writing a Pascal compiler, and the compiler and interpreter components can be written in Pascal. These two design considerations were instrumental to the success of Pascal because they significantly reduced the cost of porting the compiler. A PCODE-generating Pascal compiler is ported between platforms as shown in Fig. 3. If machine A already has a PCODE-generating Pascal compiler, then PCODE generated on *A* can be executed on machine *B* once *B*

has a PCODE interpreter. The compiler itself is compiled into PCODE on *A*, and when that PCODE is moved to *B* and interpreted by its PCODE interpreter, the result is a Pascal compiler that runs on *B*. Because of its portability, the UCSD Pascal compiler quickly became available on a great number of microcomputers and thus fostered a broad Pascal user community.

Like PCODE, Java VM uses a "stack machine" model to evaluate expressions, with instructions to place values on a stack and to perform arithmetic operations on them (*see* STACK). Since Java is object-oriented, Java VM has instructions to invoke methods (operations belonging to an object), to refer to data encapsulated within class instances, and to check object instances with respect to a class hierarchy (*see* ENCAPSULATION and OBJECT-ORIENTED PROGRAMMING). Java objects can be compiled independently. This is important, since the objects, which may be defined at physically separated locations, can still interoperate correctly without recompilation.

Bibliography

1983-4. Chow, F. C., and Ganapathi G. "Intermediate Languages in Compiler Construction—A Bibliography," *Sigplan Notices*, **18**(11), 21–23; **19**(7), 25–27.

1985. Brinch Hansen, P. *Brinch Hansen on Pascal Compilers*. Upper Saddle River, NJ: Prentice Hall.

1995. Lamport, L. *LATEX: A Document Preparation System*. Reading, MA: Addison-Wesley.

Ron Cytron

INTERNATIONAL FEDERATION FOR INFORMATION PROCESSING (IFIP)

For articles on related subjects, *see*

+ Association for Computing Machinery (ACM)
+ British Computer Society (BCS)
+ Institute of Electrical and Electronic Engineers–Computer Society (IEEE-CS)

The *International Federation for Information Processing* (IFIP), founded in 1960 as a result of the Herculean efforts of Isaac L. Auerbach, is a multinational federation of societies and groups of societies concerned with information processing. At the end of 1999, it had 45 national members as well as 15 affiliate, associate, and corresponding members. IFIP was founded under the auspices of UNESCO and retains an official relationship with UNESCO.

IFIP aims to foster international cooperation, to stimulate research, development, and applications, and to encourage education and the dissemination and exchange of information on all aspects of computing and communication. To these ends, it organizes symposia, workshops, and conferences, which result in the publication of 30 to 40 IFIP books annually. Its major international conferences are its biannual World Computer Congresses, which take the form of a half-dozen parallel independent conferences plus a trade-show-like exhibition. The Congresses attract as many as 5000 participants and are rotated through the member nations. Table 1 lists the dates and locales of the World Computer Congresses.

The technical work of IFIP is carried out by 12 Technical Committees (TCs), and, under these committees, 81 Working Groups (WGs). The Committee and Working Group subjects change from time to time but represent the current areas of interest to the academic world. IFIP's address is IFIP Secretariat, Hofstrasse 3, A-2361 Laxenburg, Austria; email: `ifip@ifip.or.at`; Website: `http://www.ifip.or.at`.

Eric A. Weiss

Table 1.   IFIP congresses.

Date	Location
1962	Munich
1965	New York
1968	Edinburgh
1971	Ljubljana
1974	Stockholm
1977	Toronto
1980	Tokyo and Melbourne
1983	Paris
1986	Dublin
1989	San Francisco
1992	Madrid
1994	Hamburg
1996	Canberra
1998	Vienna and Budapest
2000	Beijing
2002	Montreal
2004	Toulouse

INTERNET

For articles on related subjects, *see*

+ Cyberspace
+ Distributed Systems
+ Electronic Commerce
+ Electronic Mail (Email)
+ Ethernet
+ Firewall
+ Network Protocols
+ Networks, Computer
+ Online Conversation
+ Packet Switching
+ TCP/IP
+ World Wide Web

Introduction

In the 1970s, Arpanet, the forerunner of the Internet, was used by a small number of researchers doing work for the US Department of Defense (DoD). In the 1980s, Internet use spread among universities, and in the 1990s, its use surged among people and organizations worldwide. It is likely that the entire communications infrastructure of the twenty-first century will be organized around the Internet or its successor.

The *Internet*, or just *Net* for short, is a network of networks linked by several layers of protocols. It uses the Internet Protocol (IP) to route digital packets of information across a multiplicity of networks and communications media in an efficient and generally reliable manner (*see* PACKET SWITCHING). Transmission and receipt of entire messages between two points on the network is managed by the Transmission Control Protocol (TCP), which uses IP packets and guarantees orderly delivery of the bits in the message (*see* TCP/IP). Above TCP are the *application protocols*, such as those used for email, file transfer, and the World Wide Web.

The physical layer of the Internet connects users on telephone, satellite, and cable TV networks; local area networks (LAN–*q.v.*); and wide area networks. The Internet is like a pipeline, with wide (high-speed) main segments and branches that narrow as they reach single nodes. Internet applications trade for reliability. The trade-off is imposed by the TCP/IP-based application protocols that may exploit the speed and the reliability of the propagation channel.

History

Internet history can be traced to a military research network established in 1968 called the Arpanet. The Arpanet was sponsored by the Advanced Research Projects Agency (ARPA) of the US Department of Defense (DoD) and was based on a simple packet-switching protocol. Early switching nodes were at Bolt, Beranek, and Newman (generally acknowledged as the architects of the Arpanet), Carnegie Mellon University, UCLA, Stanford Research Institute (SRI International), and the University of California at Berkeley. When other research networks such as the National Science Foundation Network (NSFnet) were connected to the Arpanet, the network gradually came to be known as the connected Internet and then, simply, the Internet.

Indeed, modern usage of the word includes networks that do not conform to Internet standards or that use proprietary standards, such as private bulletin board services and certain Internet Service Providers (ISPs) such as America Online (AOL). In the late 1990s, a new high-speed network initiative, Internet 2, started (*see* www.internet2.org). It is intended to support high-performance computing at major universities and other research centers (*see* SUPERCOMPUTING CENTERS and CLUSTER COMPUTING). As with the Arpanet, its use is likely to broaden and eventually become the new Internet infrastructure.

Applications of the Internet
Early Applications
Email

Email accounts for more than 90% of all Net traffic. SMTP, the Simple Mail Transport Protocol, which runs over TCP/IP, is extremely reliable. Because the information is transferred asynchronously in a store-and-forward manner between mail servers, if a server is down, the message will be queued for later transmission, and the user is almost guaranteed that an email message will be received at its destination.

FTP

FTP (File Transfer Protocol) provides the ability to transfer files between machines over the Internet. FTP is defined in Request for Comment 959 (RFC–see below), published in 1985, and is still responsible for considerable Internet traffic. FTP deals with protocol issues unique to the transmission of long files and that are likely to be associated with large databases or computer programs. It also allows concurrent access to the same Internet server by multiple users. FTP was once *the* Internet standard for file transfer, but is now almost entirely supplanted by the Web http protocol.

Telnet

Telnet is a standard Internet application that gives the user the ability to log in to a remote machine over TCP/IP. With such a connection, users may execute standard programs remotely. Such programs might include reading email, although today it is more common to use an email program on a personal computer. Such remote login creates security issues, and services like Telnet and FTP may be restricted by *firewalls*, programs that investigate each packet and, pursuant to preestablished rules, decide whether to pass or reject it.

Usenet

Usenet (Unix User Network) is the common name of a distributed client–server computer bulletin board system. News readers are used to access *newsgroups*, of which there are tens of thousands. Some examples are `rec.food.cooking`, `alt.sources.wanted`, which posts anonymous FTP sites, `news.announce.newsusers`, `comp.sys.linux`, and the like.

Contemporary Applications
World Wide Web

The World Wide Web, or just *Web*, resides on top of the Internet as an enormous client–server (*q.v.*) layer. The Web is likely to prove the future multimedia (*q.v.*) integrator of Internet applications and may replace applications that operate at lower levels of the Internet, such as Lotus Notes. The principal Web tool is the *browser*, a program that uses the HyperText Transfer Protocol (http) to retrieve information provided by http servers worldwide—an activity known as *surfing*, that is, searching for and accessing different Websites that contain *Web pages* linked as *hypertext* (*q.v.*). The first page of what may be a sequence of linked pages at that site is called a *home page*. Browsers provide a graphical *user interface* (*q.v.*), or GUI, for receiving or sending multimedia information. The most commonly employed browsers are Netscape Navigator and Microsoft Internet Explorer, which offer similar capabilities. Other browsers, such as Opera, are smaller and faster, but account for only a few percent of all browser use.

Search engines

With millions of Websites and Web pages and an astonishing growth rate, a major issue for many users is finding the correct information at the correct Website. For this purpose, several *search engines* have evolved, such as Google, AltaVista, Yahoo, Lycos, Webcrawler, Northern Light, Infoseek, Hotbot, Snap, Excite, and many others. Users may query search engines using keywords or key phrases and a variety of classical search query syntax. Most engines support complex searches with Boolean and other operators. There are also search engine sites that specialize in searches for a host of applications in such areas as law, medicine, and health.

Push

Push is the automatic delivery of information to multiple sites on the Internet. It is useful for the delivery of news or software updates to a known distribution list. Push is a one-to-many distribution system, and as such, occasionally causes congestion at a particular server. Some of the push systems deliver their content via email, while others, like Pointcast, deliver their information directly to an application such as a screen saver. Programs called *channels* use push by automatically updating their own content and code. For security purposes, they are restricted to the delivery of information to areas in the target server or terminal called *sandboxes*.

Intranets and extranets

An *intranet* is a local or wide area network that uses the TCP/IP protocol for restricted use within a particular corporation. Intranets connect to the external Internet through a firewall. Intranet users are generally employees of a single company. An *extranet* is a wide area network based on public TCP/IP protocols and can be thought of as an Intranet with external interfaces. An extranet frequently exchanges information with other corporate extranets for electronic commerce (*q.v.*) and collaboration. Extranet users are generally employees of companies related through a common supplier relationship.

Electronic commerce

Electronic commerce (*e-commerce–q.v.*) uses the Web and other Internet resources to let vendors and service providers do business online. E-commerce requires a support infrastructure for customers (users) to browse items offered for sale, peruse or search digital catalogs, visit virtual shopping malls, and use *shopping carts* (applications that provide for depositing selections in a single place for subsequent payment).

CyberCash

CyberCash offers consumers and vendors services for making secure and authenticated transactions on the Internet. With a digital "wallet" that functions as a secure credit card, consumers can execute cash or debit transactions, receive electronic invoices, and encrypt a credit card number that gets sent to a merchant. The merchant then appends an encrypted confirmation code to a transaction and forwards it to a CyberCash server, which then routes the information to a bank. A competing idea is the DigiCash system that allows a user to send cash via a credit card or ATM to a bank that issues a certificate known as *ecash*.

Telephony

Another new application drawing the attention of regulatory agencies is Internet telephony. In this application, the Internet provides the same functionality as the telephone network for carrying voice traffic. Analog voice signals are digitized, split into packets, and then sent over the Internet. In this manner, one can place the equivalent of free long distance (in the USA) and international calls. For example, one can now use conventional telephone services on the Internet with companies like IDT that offer very low cost long distance service. Similarly, Time-Warner *RoadRunner* and competitive services offer high-speed Internet access over cable TV networks.

Internet Communications

The Evolution of TCP/IP and the Internet Suite

As the Arpanet evolved, it became more important to connect disparate networks with different propagation, reliability, and throughput (*q.v.*) characteristics. While one could use TCP as a transport service for use on contiguous homogeneous networks in which hosts and servers are directly connected before initiating data transmission, it was necessary to find some other method for dealing with traffic that had to leave the homogeneous network and transit one or more other networks. For that, the connectionless *packet switching* (*q.v.*) Internet Protocol (IP) was developed. Early work on AlohaNet, a wireless 10 Kbps FM radio network at the University of Hawaii, and Ethernet (*q.v.*), a 3 Mbps LAN technology at Xerox PARC, had encouraged ARPA to look towards the deployment of similar technologies and protocols in a self-organizing radio network for military research purposes. This network, known as Packet Radio, provided 100 Kbps access to terminals and 400 Kbps connections between network repeaters. On the basis of *spread spectrum modulation*, the system was secure and reliable. But because of substantial differences in delay and reliability between a radio network and a land-based network, it became necessary to design a *gateway* (*q.v.*) to serve as a buffer and traffic manager between the two networks. The original work was first reported as the Kahn/Cerf Protocol in 1973, named after Robert Kahn and Vinton Cerf but now called TCP/IP. The birth of the TCP/IP gateway is widely considered to be the defining moment of the Internet.

Managing Network Operations
Protocol suites

As the Internet developed, a competing suite of protocol layers was established under the Open Systems Interconnection (OSI—*q.v.*) Standard. OSI represented international standards interests outside the United States. It offered a seven-layer protocol implementation to correspond to the ARPA levels. Under OSI, the layers (from lowest to highest) are: (1) Physical; (2) Data link; (3) Network; (4) Transport; (5) Session; (6) Presentation; and (7) Application. The TCP/IP model omits OSI levels 5 and 6.

Network management

Network management encompasses five functions: (1) security management, (2) fault management, (3) performance management, (4) configuration control, and (5) accounting and financial reporting. Both the Simple Network Management Protocol (SNMP) and the Common Management Information Protocol

(CMIP) have gained substantial popularity on the Internet. Both CMIP and CMOT (CMIP Over TCP/IP) have been supported by the Internet Activities Board and both use agent/manager operational models. In these systems, *objects* are managed. Most entities in the network connection can be represented by objects, such as servers, routers, or hosts. Objects are organized in eight groups, three of which, for example, are *system, interface,* and *IP.* Each object must be essential for either error or configuration measurement, and each has four characteristics that are monitored: its attributes, relationship to other objects, how it operates, and its output. These characteristics are deposited in a Management Information Base (MIB). The *agent* operates inside the object and reports behavior to the manager. The manager contains the interface to the user world, and manages the database and the communications.

Security

Internet system security is provided through physical routers that serve as *firewalls.* Firewalls isolate a server from unauthorized intruders on the Internet. In addition, *proxy servers* are used as additional barriers to control traffic entering or leaving the Internet. Some proxy servers are used to sit between the population of users and the Internet so that no traffic may enter or leave the Net without passing through the proxy. Proxies can be nested and provide additional layers of insulation. There also is an increasing use of virtual private networks (VPNs) in which the Internet is used to communicate information from one private secure network to another.

Addressing

Internet addressing has been an increasingly demanding problem. As the number of addresses has exploded, it became necessary to revamp addressing schemes, and in 2000, a major new protocol, IP Version 6, vastly increased the address space from 32 bits to 128. According to Vinton Cerf, the extension to 128 bits should permit "every light bulb, light switch, power socket, and appliance ... on the net in addition to personal computing and communication devices, on-line information services, radio and television

transmitters and receivers ... telephones and sensors of all kinds ... [to be connected to the Internet]."

Domain names

Internet address names are managed by the Domain Name System (DNS). The DNS arranges names hierarchically and uses a standard ordering system. Specific sites are then identified relative to higher-level domains. In the educational domain, a specific site might be cs.umd.edu, indicating the computer science department at the University of Maryland in the "edu" Internet domain. A (fictitious) email address might be jvn@cs.umd.edu. Each DNS name is composed of one or more labels separated by dots. There are two kinds of top-level domain names: generic and geographical. The top-level generic domain names widely used in the United States include "com" (commercial), "edu" (educational), "gov" (US government), "mil" (US military organization), "net" (network provider), "org" (not-for-profit organization), and "int" (international organizations established by treaties). The top-level geographical domain generally used in other countries is the two-letter ISO 3166 code (an exception is the UK, which uses the code "uk" instead of the ISO code "gb").

The DNS supports a uniform naming service, maintains distributed databases around the net with a replication model, and sets naming standards for fields. Throughout the Internet, these DNS *name servers* resolve IP addresses from domain names and execute complex protocols to find names that are not on the local name servers. In the most common case, users will encounter DNS errors when sending email to nonexistent servers or when searching the Web for a nonexistent URL (Universal Resource Locator—a Website address).

For companies and organizations, the domain name serves as their identity on the Internet. For example, www.ibm.com, www.gm.com, www.acm.org, and www.stanford.edu serve as Website URLs for IBM, General Motors, ACM, and Stanford University respectively. To be effective, domain names must be unique, and to ensure uniqueness they must be registered with some authority. In the United States, this can be done through Network Solutions, Inc., or a number of other companies that ensure that a name has not been used and that routing tables in the Internet are set to the correspondingly correct IP address. A good, easily remembered domain name is a valuable commodity that, once duly registered, can be sold for whatever the traffic will bear. Speculators register names that have no corresponding Website and often auction them through Websites such as www.ebay.com or www.amazon.com.

Standardization

The Internet Activity Board (IAB), a volunteer organization founded in 1983, has served as the codifying organization for the Internet. The IAB manages all of the standards developments around TCP/IP and sets official policies and standards, manages the RFC process, provides planning on a long term basis, and serves as the liaison to international bodies. There are two major suborganizations under the IAB: the Internet Engineering Task Force (IETF) and the Internet Research Task Force. Both these organizations have working subgroups that are composed of a community of network designers, operators, vendors, and researchers who coordinate the operation, management, and evolution of the Internet and resolve protocol issues.

RFCs (Request For Comments) were originally established as a means for communicating between research groups developing the Internet. These groups, originally known as ARPA Working Groups and now as Working Groups of the IETF, issue papers of work-in-progress. While edited, these are not refereed archival technical journal papers but rather represent technical engineering ideas or proposals as well as accepted standards. Over time, the collection of RFCs has come to represent the collective design of the Internet and the standards accepted by the IAB and the participating community on the Internet.

Network Access Points (NAPs)

In order to avoid large numbers of hops from Internet node to Internet node, connection interchanges have been established in the United States and in several other countries, most notably Japan. These connections allow participating carriers or ISPs to exchange traffic directly between their backbones (main high-speed paths through the network). Evolving after NSF acquired management of the Internet from the DoD in 1990, four connection points were established in the United States in 1993. These points provided an ability for any backbone connecting LANs to connect to other service providers thus providing unrestricted access to all Internet users.

Propagation and Infrastructure

Carriers such as MCI and Sprint provide Internet backbones with transfer rates ranging up to OC-12 (622.08 Mbps). OC stands for Optical Carrier and is a Synchronous Optical Network (SONET) standard for fiber optic communications channels. Sonet provides for communications between different networks that require complicated multiplexing and demultiplexing and complex coding and decoding to exchange traffic. The most elementary Synchronous Transport Speed (STS) is OC-1, which is 51.84 Mbps. The fastest routers operate at speeds such as OC-3 (155.52 Mbps) so the full speed of the backbones still cannot be exploited. Nevertheless, the trend is clearly toward OC-12 as soon as faster routers are available.

Because the US Telecommunications Act of 1996 frees AT&T to turn to local markets and the Baby Bells to enter the long distance markets, AT&T, the Baby Bells and many companies are creating technology that enables them to offer high speed Internet connections (DSLs—Digital Subscriber Lines) over conventional phone lines. AT&T hopes to offer complete packages that include local, long distance, wireless, cable and Internet access in one integrated service.

Internet Service Providers (ISPs)

Each user of the Internet requires a connection (*connectivity*) to the Internet. The most common method of use for the consumer is dial-up to a local ISP. Each ISP offers a large range of services from simple connectivity to email services to news and Internet Relay Chat, a service that facilitates person-to-person line-by-line communications. The local dial-up telephone number is usually referred to as a *Point of Presence* (POP). ISPs offer anywhere from small numbers of local POPs to hundreds of national and international POPs. For the typical consumer who requires local access, the smaller ISPs provide adequate connectivity through local POPs. For travelers, remote access is necessary to control long distance and international toll and hotel charges. This requires one or more international ISPs with local POPs in many cities. The user dials a local POP and makes an Internet TCP/IP connection often using *Point-to-Point Protocol* (PPP), which allows TCP/IP to run over a serial communication line. Once connected, an email application or a Web browser may be invoked over the TCP/IP layer to provide access. Some users now subscribe to Integrated Services Digital Network (ISDN—*q.v.*) services that operate at substantially higher speeds but which require special modems and software to provide connectivity.

As of 2003, there were over 10 000 ISPs in the United States offering connectivity to both consumers (dial-up) and corporate customers (leased lines). About 20% of the ISPs have connections to long haul backbone providers WorldCom UUNET and Compuserve (bought by AOL in 1997), 31% were connected to MCI, and 24% used Sprint. In the United States, the largest ISP by far is America Online (AOL), with over 35 million subscribers. AOL operates a proprietary service but also offers Internet connectivity and supports standard browser operations. AOL originally used a proprietary browser, but now uses a slightly modified version of Microsoft's Internet Explorer, even though AOL now owns Netscape.

Limits to Growth?

By the end of the twentieth century, Internet use had become global, but the extent of access from country to country still varies widely. Fig. 1 shows the situation as of 1994, plotting Internet nodes against gross national product (GNP). It is dangerous to make Internet predictions since the Internet has

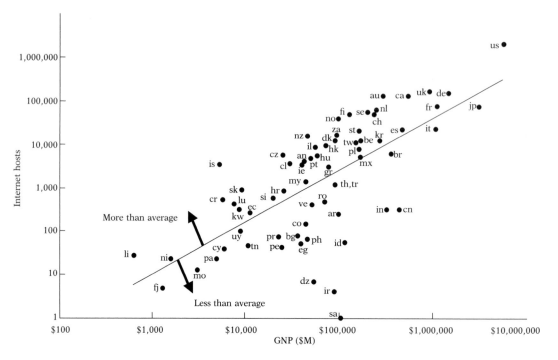

Figure 1. Internet hosts plotted against gross national product (GNP), 1994 data. For country codes, see http://www.webmaster.bham.ac.uk/country_codes.html. (Sources: Mark Lottor, Encyclopaedia Britannica, Eric Arnum. Copyright © 1994 A. M. Rutkowski and the Internet Society).

proven so adept at evolution despite its complex problems. Still, those factors that could impede the growth of the Internet include the possibility of an ultimate traffic jam creating a requirement to stop and redesign subsystems of the Internet. The US government has declared the Internet a duty-free zone for at least three years, but one can anticipate that various governments will ultimately try to tax its traffic and transactions. This will undoubtedly have a chilling effect on the growth of commercial applications on the Internet.

Privacy will continue to be a thorny problem. It is common practice for Websites to collect information from clients surfing their Website through the use of *cookies*, small swatches of data and program code planted in computer memory while its user surfs a particular Website. Cookies collect information and report back on terminal behavior. Most browsers give the user control over whether cookies are accepted, and many cookies are useful. For example, they are used by Internet retailers to greet a returning user by name and to allow additional purchases without reentering credit card and shipping information. On the other hand, cookies aggravate the problem of protecting privacy, as do large online consumer databases that lead to spamming and telemarketing abuse.

Bibliography

1996. Hafner, K., and Lyon, M. *Where Wizards Stay Up Late: The Origins of the Internet*. New York: Simon & Schuster.

1997. Reid, R. H. *Architects of the Web*. New York: John Wiley.

1998. Tapscott, D. *Growing Up Digital: The Rise of the Net Generation*. New York: McGraw-Hill.

1998. Segaller, S. *Nerds 2.0.1: A Brief History of the Internet*. New York: TV Books.

1999. Clark, D. "The Internet of Tomorrow," *Science*, **285**(5426), (16 July), 353.

David H. Brandin and Daniel C. Lynch

INTERPRETER

See LANGUAGE PROCESSORS.

INTERRUPT

For articles on related subjects, *see*

+ Channel
+ Input-Output Operations
+ Interval Timer
+ Operating Systems
+ Real-Time Systems
+ Supervisor Call
+ Time Sharing

The capability to *interrupt* a program permits systems to respond quickly to external or exceptional events that occur at unpredictable times. Some external events of this type are input arriving from a keyboard, modem (*q.v.*), or network; a signal that an output device like a printer is ready for data; or a signal generated by an instrument or sensor monitoring some industrial or laboratory process. Exceptional events include invalid memory references during program execution, division by zero, or an attempt to execute an illegal instruction.

The response to an interrupt is the invocation of a responding subprogram (*q.v.*), and in this respect, an interrupt resembles a subprogram call, but one that is initiated by a hardware device rather than by the main program. An interrupt facility enables a computer to communicate with a rich variety of external devices, but is also helpful to the system in managing its own resources. Although basically implemented by hardware, the logical power of interrupts is also provided by programming languages that permit an event-driven style of programming, such as Java (*q.v.*) and other object-oriented languages.

An external event causes an interrupt by an "interrupt request"—a signal on a physical line connected to the CPU (*q.v.*) or to a special interrupt-chip that is connected to the CPU. To respond to an interrupt request, the CPU signals "interrupt granted," the current program is stopped gracefully (i.e. *interrupted*), and the CPU switches to a subprogram called the *interrupt service routine* (ISR). Interrupts are thus a mechanism that enables several logically unrelated subprograms to time-share a single CPU.

A Particular Example

The PowerPC, a microprocessor developed jointly by IBM and Motorola, has a relatively simple interrupt structure. All external devices share a single interrupt request line. The processor has a 64-bit *machine state register* (MSR) with an *external interrupt enable* (EE) bit that is set to 1 to allow interrupts. When an interrupt request is issued, the following steps occur.

1. The current PC value (the address of the next program instruction) is saved in a *save/restore register*, SSR0.
2. The MSR, which contains other program status information, is saved in part of a second register, SSR1. The low order bits of the MSR are unused, and so the CPU places information about the interrupting device in the part of SSR1 not occupied by the MSR bits.
3. The EE bit in the MSR is set to 0 to prevent another interrupt from occurring.
4. The CPU gets the address of the ISR from address 500 of main memory.
5. Control is transferred to the ISR. It must have a table of all devices capable of interruption, together with the routine to execute for each. The ISR uses the high-order bits of the SSR1 to identify the routine to execute.
6. The ISR ends with a return-from-interrupt (RFI) instruction. Its execution reloads the PC and the MSR from the saved values in SSR0 and SSR1, thereby resuming normal program execution at the point of interruption.

The table of devices and routines to handle their interrupts is called a table of *device vectors*. Some processors, such as the Intel Pentium, have a fixed set of memory addresses for device vectors. When a device interrupts, it sends the bits that specify its

vector, and control can be transferred directly to the routine specified. Other variations are to have multiple priority levels of interrupts (perhaps eight). When an ISR is active, only devices with higher priorities than the one being serviced can interrupt. The resulting nested interrupts use a stack (*q.v.*) for last in, first out completion order.

Interrupt Request Classes

Interrupt requests may be roughly categorized as follows:

1. Processor operations.
2. Privileged operations.
3. Software call instruction.
4. Machine malfunction.
5. Timer.
6. Input-output.

Class 1 includes arithmetic overflow, divide checks, illegal operation codes, and address-out-of-bounds. A class 2 interrupt occurs if execution of a *privileged instruction* is attempted while the machine is not in privileged mode. Class 3 refers to the ability to initiate an interrupt explicitly by software to invoke a particular operating system routine. Class 4 is rather obvious. Class 5 refers to an interval timer that can be set to a positive value by a machine instruction. Circuitry is provided to decrement this value automatically at regular time intervals and generate an interrupt request when the value reaches zero. Class 6 includes a wide variety of input and output devices: keyboard, printer, disk drive, and communication line, and also specialized devices in control applications—sensors monitoring a real-time process and actuators that need to signal when they are ready for another step.

The term *synchronous interrupt* is sometimes used for one whose cause is associated with the currently executing instruction, while other interrupts are called asynchronous. Thus, classes 1, 2, and 3 are synchronous and the remaining ones asynchronous. Another term for synchronous interrupt is *trap*.

The complete problem of interrupt-handling is always solved by a combination of hardware and software. In general, the more done in hardware, such as having a fixed set of device vectors, the greater can be the speed of response, but the higher the cost and the less the flexibility to accommodate changes in interrupt logic. Because of these economy–speed relationships, systems differ greatly in the choice of which interrupt functions to implement in hardware. Much of the complexity of interrupt handling is in the software servicing of the interrupt. The software is usually a part of the operating system program that manages the assignment of all hardware/software resources to workload demands. In fact, most operating systems are *interrupt-driven*, that is, the interrupt system is the mechanism for reporting all changes in resource states; and such changes are the events that induce new assignments. This fact makes interrupt handling an excellent way to monitor resource-use for performance analysis and billing. The combination of a processor and external devices is a system with concurrent activities. Since ISRs may be regarded as device-initiated programs, perhaps the best way to understand interrupt handling is as an instance of concurrent programming (*q.v.*).

Bibliography

1995. Shanley, T. *PowerPC System Architecture*, 2nd Ed. Reading, MA: Addison-Wesley.

1996. Hamacher, V. C., Vranesic, Z. G., and Zaky, S. G. *Computer Organization*, 4th Ed. New York: McGraw-Hill.

1999. Brey, B. *The Intel Microprocessors: 8086/8088, 80186/80188, 80286, 80386, 80486, Pentium, Pentium Pro, Pentium II Processors*, 5th Ed. Upper Saddle River, NJ: Prentice Hall.

Herbert Hellerman and David Hemmendinger

INTERVAL TIMER

For articles on related subjects, *see*

+ Interrupt
+ Multiprogramming
+ Operating Systems

An *interval timer* (or *real-time clock*) is a mechanism whereby elapsed time can be monitored by a computer system. In most systems, a word in memory is used as the interval timer and is incremented automatically by one interval unit every millisecond, microsecond, or other fixed period. The timer is useful for reporting the date and time of execution of various parts of a job or for checking the timing for segments of a routine. An interval timer is also essential for timing components of multiprogrammed systems, since time may be allocated to jobs in increments of only a few microseconds.

Chester L. Meek

ISDN

See INTEGRATED SERVICES DIGITAL NETWORK (ISDN).

ITERATION

For articles on related subjects, *see*

+ Control Structures
+ Procedure-Oriented Languages
+ Recursion
+ Structured Programming

To *iterate* means to do repeatedly. In computer programming, iteration is the repeated execution of lines of code or statements until some condition is satisfied. For example, 10 numbers $A(1)$, $A(2)$, $A(3)$, ..., $A(10)$ can be summed using the following Basic program:

```
10 L = 10
20 I = 1
30 S = 0
40 S = S + A(I)
50 I = I + 1
60 IF I <= L THEN 40        (1)
```

The statements 40–60 are executed repeatedly until I becomes 11.

In contrast, the sum could be computed by

$$S = A(1) + A(2) + A(3) + A(4) + A(5)$$
$$+ A(6) + A(7) + A(8) + A(9) + A(10) \quad (2)$$

which does not involve iteration. This last statement is more efficient in the example given, since the sum is obtained with fewer program steps. However, if more elements are to be summed, then statement (2) must be changed by adding more terms. In the first program, however, only the value of L need be changed in order to do so.

Control of Iteration

Programming languages generally have both definite iteration (*for* loops) and indefinite iteration (*while, do, repeat* loops). The former specifies a number of times to iterate; the latter iterate until some condition holds or fails to hold. This Pascal code uses definite iteration to do the same as program (1).

```
Sum := 0;
for i := 1 to 10 do
    Sum := Sum + a[i];
```

In APL, the same summation can be written as just +/A. Here, at the source language level, no iteration appears to be involved. However, at the level of the interpretive program that evaluates the APL statement, iteration will certainly occur.

Iteration in Numerical Methods

Many numerical problems can be solved by iterative techniques. Here, a succession of values for one or more variables are computed. It is hoped that the successive values approach the true values. The iterative process is terminated when some error criterion is satisfied. Computing a square root by the Newton–Raphson method is an example of an iterative numerical procedure. Numerical iteration is usually characterized by the use of successive approximations and termination depending upon error bounds.

Iteration vs Recursion

A program is recursive if at least one of its executable statements refers to the program itself. For example, in Pascal one may write

```
function ABC(X:integer):integer;
    ...
    Z := ABC(Y);
    ...
end;
```

That is, the function calls itself. This requires a so-called *stack* (*q.v.*) mechanism to keep track of parameters and to provide locations for the returned values at each level of call (*see* ACTIVATION RECORD). Needless to say, other statements in the program must in some way limit the levels of calling. A frequently used example is the factorial function. In pseudocode:

```
function factorial(n)
    if n < 2 then
        return 1
    else
        return (n*factorial(n-1))
    endif
endfunc;
```

Although portions of the code are executed repetitively, the control is by reference to the named procedure. Therefore, this example is said to be *recursive*, not iterative.

The factorial of *N* can, of course, be computed iteratively:

```
function factorial(n)
    f ← 1;
    for I ← n downto 2
        f ← f*I
        endfor;
    return f
endfunc
```

In this iterative example, the function does not call itself and, therefore, does not have to save the parameter n each time it is called, as the recursive function must do.

In general, a straightforward iterative algorithm may both be faster and use less memory than a corresponding recursive algorithm. These savings are often slight, however, and there are many algorithms for which recursion is more natural than iteration (*see*, for example, Quicksort in the article STRUCTURED PROGRAMMING, and tree-traversal algorithms in TREE). In such cases it is better to use recursion than to write a more complex iterative program.

Bibliography

1997. Chan, R. H., Chan, T. F., and Golub, G. H. (eds.) *Iterative Methods in Scientific Computing*. New York: Springer-Verlag.

1999. Sebesta, R. W. *Concepts of Programming Language*. Reading, MA: Addison-Wesley.

Harry D. Huskey

JAVA

For articles on related subjects, see

+ C
+ C++
+ Class
+ Concurrent Programming
+ Exception Handling
+ Object-Oriented Programming
+ World Wide Web

Java is a high-level programming language developed by James Gosling and others at Sun Microsystems. All Java data attributes and functions *must* be in classes, which define *types* of objects, so the language is truly object-oriented. Java resembles C and C++, but it omits many unwieldy features. It has no pointers (*q.v.*). Memory management (*q.v.*) is automatic; this, combined with static (i.e. compile time) and run-time type and array bounds checking, makes Java programs more reliable than programs written in most other languages.

Java has gained popularity because of its appropriateness for programming on the Internet, particularly using *applets*, small Java program components that run within a Web browser to provide animation and other features. Java programs are usually compiled to an interpreted *byte code* that is run on the *Java Virtual Machine* (*see* INTERMEDIATE LANGUAGE). The virtual machine can be run on any adequate computer,

making Java very portable. Java uses the Unicode character set (*see* CHARACTER CODES), so almost all of the world's alphabets are supported. For security, the Java virtual machine includes a verifier that performs various checks on Java code as it is loaded, insuring that such code is unlikely to break the systems it runs on. This makes Java ideal for running programs downloaded from possibly untrustworthy sources.

Basic Types

There are three main types of data in Java: objects, arrays, and basic values. Although arrays are themselves objects, basic values—like characters and integers—are not objects and are handled conventionally for efficiency reasons. Basic values can, however, be converted (*wrapped*) into objects when required. Objects are declared in classes, combining data fields, polymorphic functions (*methods*), and in various ways inheriting from (*extending*) other class definitions. (*Polymorphism* means that the same method can have various implementations that differ in the number and types of their parameters—*see* OPERATOR OVERLOADING.)

Arrays, a special class, can be constructed out of basic values or objects and, like objects, they respond to some standard methods, but the programmer cannot introduce more.

Java has rules for converting between data types. For example, an integer can be assigned to a floating-point number, and an object that is a subclass of some type can be assigned to a variable of that type. This insures concise programs. However, some conversions are obscure, and combined with polymorphism, inheritance and run-time typing of objects can result in unanticipated behavior.

Exceptions

Java provides explicit exception handling. Some errors, such as array subscript errors, automatically give rise to *throw* exceptions; others can be explicitly *thrown* by the programmer. Both can be *caught* by an *exception handler* routine written by the programmer to take appropriate action when an error occurs.

Java as a Programming Technology

Java is a programming technology, not just a programming language. It would be hard to write Java programs without drawing heavily on *application programming interfaces* (APIs), which provide huge libraries, including interfaces to databases, portable user interfaces (e.g. the *Abstract Windows Toolkit*, AWT), networking, and specialist applications. The behavior of important classes like `String` are defined in standard APIs.

Java's inheritance capability allows programmers to modify or extend APIs rather than start from scratch; thus many applications require little detailed coding. Rapid application development (RAD) environments can be used to manage what coding remains.

Unlike C++, Java has single inheritance: it permits a class to be a subclass of only one class. However, a class can implement any number of *interfaces*. Interfaces provide many advantages of multiple inheritance without its complexities. Software vendors can sell code that conforms to interface standards, and which need not reveal details of implementation.

Summary

Although there is now a Java standard, specialized forms are evolving such as *JavaCard* (a version of smart cards–*q.v.*), and *EmbeddedJava* (for embedded systems–*q.v.*). Other languages (e.g. Ada–*q.v.*) can be compiled into Java's byte code, thereby reaping Java's implementation benefits for themselves.

Because of licensing restrictions imposed by Sun, Microsoft announced its own Java-like language called C# ("C sharp") in June 2000. The language, designed and implemented by Anders Hejlsberg and Scott Wiltamuth, is intended for use with a new Microsoft distributed application framework called .Net. Like Java, C# looks much like C++ and compiles to an intermediate language.

Bibliography

1996. Gosling, J., Joy, B., and Steele, G. *The Java Language Specification*. Reading, MA: Addison-Wesley.

1996. Lindholm, T., and Yellin, F. *The Java Virtual Machine Specification*. Reading, MA: Addison-Wesley.

1997. Arnold, K., and Gosling, J. *The Java Programming Language*. Reading, MA: Addison-Wesley.

2000. Lea, D. *Concurrent Programming in Java: Design Principles and Patterns*, 2nd Ed. Reading, MA: Addison-Wesley.

Harold W. Thimbleby

JOB

For articles on related subjects, *see*

+ Multiprogramming
+ Multitasking
+ Operating Systems
+ Time Sharing

A *job* is a task or group of tasks to be performed by a computer. A job may be classed as an *interactive job* if an operator, usually at a terminal or networked PC or workstation (*q.v.*), provides some of the input and/or receives some of the output as the job is running. A job may be classed as a *batch job* if the inputs are all presented to the computer with the job instructions, and the output will be routed to disk, printer, or other noninteractive devices.

The number of tasks (or steps) per job is usually a preference of the programmer, but is also subject to the conventions of the operating system. For example, many temporary files supplied by the operating system are automatically closed and released at the end of a job. If a programmer wishes to use one of these temporary files to store some intermediate information between two steps, then the two steps must be contained within the same job. However, in a multiprogrammed environment, where several jobs are run concurrently, there is a need to ensure that the jobs are executed in sequence. To accomplish this automatically, many multiprogramming operating systems allow job sequencing, which allows the programmer to specify that a job cannot be selected for execution until its predecessor has been completed.

Chester L. Meek

K

KERNEL

For articles on related subjects, *see*

+ Linux
+ Memory Management
+ Operating Systems
+ Virtual Memory

The term *kernel* is applied to the set of operating system programs that implement the most primitive of that system's functions. Typical kernels contain programs for five classes of functions.

1. *Process management.* Routines for switching processors among processes; for scheduling; for sending messages or timing signals among processes; for creating and removing processes; and for controlling entry to supervisor state.
2. *Memory management.* Routines for transferring pages or segments between main memory and secondary memory; for controlling multiprogramming load; for mapping virtual to real addresses; and for handling protection violations.
3. *Interprocess communication.* Routines for opening and closing connections between processes; for transferring data over open connections; and for network protocols and routing.
4. *File and device management.* Routines for creating and deleting; for opening and closing; for keeping track of a file's records; for allocating and releasing buffers; for starting I/O requests on particular devices; for handling device completion interrupts; and for managing directories.
5. *Security.* Routines for enforcing the access and information-flow control policies of the system; for changing protection domains; and for encapsulating programs.

Each of the classes of kernel programs contains routines for handling interrupts pertaining to its class.

The system kernel should not be confused with the portion of the operating system that is continuously resident in main memory. Two criteria determine whether a particular system module should be resident—frequency of use, and whether the system can operate at all without it. Very small continuously resident kernels are sometimes called *microkernels*.

Bibliography

1992. Tanenbaum, A. S. *Modern Operating Systems.* Upper Saddle River, NJ: Prentice Hall.

Peter J. Denning

KNOWLEDGE REPRESENTATION

For articles on related subjects, *see*

+ Artificial Intelligence (AI)
+ Cognitive Science
+ Computer Vision

+ Expert Systems
+ Logic Programming
+ Machine Learning
+ Natural Language Processing
+ Robotics

The term *knowledge representation* was originally used in artificial intelligence (AI) to refer to the encoding of knowledge that an intelligent program needs in order to plan, observe, or draw conclusions. It is now used more broadly to refer to any organized body of general knowledge, including large-scale repositories of information intended largely for human use. The distinction between "knowledge" and "data" (as in "database") is not precise, but knowledge representation (KR) is usually taken to refer to the representation of general knowledge that can support some nontrivial reasoning. To represent knowledge, one must choose a *notation*, a suitable collection of *concepts*, and a *system of inference rules* or processes that use the notation. We consider them in inverse order.

Notations

A wide variety of KR notations have been invented, including labeled networks, lists of logical sentences, object-oriented hierarchies, and various programming languages. We will treat all of the notations as divergent forms of syntax for first-order predicate calculus (FOPC). The basic units of FOPC are atomic assertions that *relations* hold between *individuals*, [e.g. Loves (Harry, Sally) or HasMeeting(Joe, DepartmentOf (Mathematics), ThreePM(May 14))]. These can be combined by connectives such as and, or, not, and implies, and general facts can be expressed by replacing some names by variables bound by the quantifiers Forall and Exists. This recursive syntax can produce complex expressions, such as

```
(Forall x)( IsBabyOf(x, me) implies
   (Forall y) (Loves(y,x) and
              (Forall z)(not Equal(z,me)
              implies not Loves(x,z))))
```

Many equivalences hold between FOPC expressions, allowing the use of certain standard forms of which the most common is a conjunction of *clauses*, that is, implications of the form (atom and atom and...) implies (atom or atom or...) where all the variables are assumed to be universally quantified. The above expression becomes two clauses

```
IsBabyOf(x,me) implies Loves(y,x)
(IsBabyOf(x,me) and Loves(x,z) ) implies
      Equal(z,me)
```

An alternative notational style organizes the knowledge around individuals rather than propositions. The resulting structures, called *frames* or *units*, represent either an individual or a certain type of individual (e.g. *Chris* or *Human*). Each unit has associated with it a number of slots that encode all its relationships to other individuals. The slots may consist of simply the name of a relationship and a list of units to which this individual bears the relation (i.e. an atomic assertion) or it may be associated with a more elaborate piece of code. Units form a hierarchy of individuals and types, so that we might have *Chris* being an instance of *Man*, which is itself a subtype of *Human*, of *Mammal*, and also of *Agent*, and so on, forming a directed acyclic graph. Each unit is understood to inherit the slot values of units above it, so that the fact that all mammals have warm blood can be expressed by attaching the relevant information about warmbloodedness to the unit *Mammal*. This "frame" style of notation has been very influential and is the basis of several *expert system shell* languages.

Another notation is based on *semantic networks* in which the edges of a directed graph represent two-place relations holding between individuals labeling the nodes. Semantic networks usually come with a particular set of conventions on how certain kinds of nodes or arcs are to be used, amounting to syntax for a network language. A common device is the use of *is-a* links to express general statements of a type hierarchy, a concept first developed in network languages. Any link attached to a type represents something true of all instances of that type, and can be inherited back along an *is-a* link. These instantiation links can form hierarchies of more general types, allowing a limited form of universal quantification.

Inference Rules and Semantics

What do the various notations mean? This is not a trivial question, since "obvious" axioms can have unintuitive consequences. For example, the two clauses shown earlier have the rather surprising consequence

```
IsBabyOf(x,me) implies Equal(x,me)
```

which follows from the assertion that *everybody* loves my baby: in particular, therefore, she loves herself; but since she doesn't love anybody but me, she must *be* me. Clearly, the universal quantifier made a stronger statement than intended. Such phenomena are quite common and illustrate the importance of avoiding the *gensym fallacy* (named after a Lisp (*q.v.*) function that generates meaningless names) of assuming that symbols in a KR notation must have a meaning that is inherited from their English meaning.

Not all KR systems are intended to support a complete inference process (e.g. some are considered to be more like organized repositories of information or as data models for databases), but in AI applications, the function of the KR formalism is usually to support inferences. Designers of such knowledge representation systems have tried to find a workable compromise between the very intractable nature of full FOPC and the impoverished expressive power of many *ad hoc* schemes. For example, the two clauses shown earlier are examples of *Horn clauses* in which the disjunctive consequent has at most one element. Horn clauses are the basis of *logic programming* (*q.v.*).

Concepts

The most important aspect of knowledge representation is the choice of concepts to be used to express the intended content. A suitably organized system of concepts is called an *ontology*; a current active area of research attempts to develop useful "standard" ontologies for various topics. Notations such as Ontolingua are designed to record and systematize collections of ontologies.

Time and Change

One basic idea is the use of states to describe change in a dynamic world. Relations that are subject to change are thought of as functions on states, often called *fluents*, so that in a logical notation we might write `IsWearing(Susan,PinkDress3,ThursdayEvening)`. The results of events or actions can be described by a function from these things and states to new states

```
IsDressing(x,s) implies
    IsWearing (x,y,result(x,putOn(y),s))
```

where the term `result(x,putOn(y),s)` describes the state after `x` performs the action `putOn(y)` in state `s`. This style of writing axioms is called the *situation calculus*, and supports a form of planning by inference. States are typically thought of as essentially static, but other approaches to describing change focus instead on time intervals during which some process is happening. The situational calculus has been extended into an elaborate ontology, which can describe ongoing processes taking place during intervals, parallel events, and other complexities.

Beliefs and Other Mental States

In order to lie successfully, cheat or steal, it is necessary to reason about other agents' beliefs, while knowing them to be false. The most common technique is to assume a relationship between the agent and some fragment of one's own representational notation, so that one might write

```
Believes(Joan, (Forall x)(Friend(x,Harry)
        implies Fool(x)))
```

where one argument of the `Believes` relation is a whole logical assertion. In general, it is rather tricky to describe a state of belief that is very different from one's own. In particular, there are problems in properly interpreting *de re* expressions where a quantifier includes a belief assertion. For example,

```
(Forall{a}x)(Friend(x,Harry) implies
        Believes(Joan, Fool(x)))
```

could be true even while the earlier sentence is false, if Joan didn't realize that she knew all of Harry's friends.

Space and Shape

Linguistic analyses of spatial prepositions such as *on*, *through*, *over*, and *in* suggest complex systems of concepts, not always purely spatial. For example, a person in a room in a building is in the building, but an apple in a bowl in water is not in the water. It is not easy to formalize these in consistent ways, and some have argued that these systems are essentially metaphorical, so that some kind of best-fit structural matching is the most appropriate way to use this kind of information.

Bibliography

1975. Minsky, M. "A Framework for Representing Knowledge," *Memo 36*. MIT Artificial Intelligence Laboratory; Reprinted in 1985. Brachman, R. J., and Levesque, H. J. (eds), *Readings in Knowledge Representation*. San Mateo, CA: Morgan-Raufman, 245–262.

1992. Hayes, P. J., and Ford, K. (eds.) *Reasoning Agents in a Dynamic World: The Frame Problem*. Boston, MA: JAI Press.

Patrick J. Hayes

a
b
c
d
e
f
g
h
i
j
k
l
m
n
o
p
q
r
s
t
u
v,w
x,y
z

LANGUAGE PROCESSORS

Before a program written in a high-level language can be executed, it must be translated into the machine language of the computer that will perform the execution. There are two primary mechanisms for accomplishing this: *compilation* (followed by later execution), and *interpretation*.

Compilation

In compilation, a program called a *compiler* takes as input a *source program* written in one programming language and produces as output an equivalent *target* or *object program* in another programming language. The language of the source program is usually relatively high level, and the language of the target program is usually relatively low level, such as assembly language or machine language. In pure compilation (*see* Fig. 1a), the compiler produces a machine language program; this program may be linked with whatever library and other external modules are necessary (*see* LINKERS AND LOADERS) to create an *executable* program. The compilation process has several stages: *lexical analysis*, in which the character sequences in the source program are grouped into logical tokens; *syntax analysis*, or *parsing*, in which the tokens are cast into an intermediate representation in accord with the syntactic rules of the language; *semantic analysis*, in which this intermediate representation is examined for semantic errors; *optimization*, in which the intermediate representation is further transformed to allow more efficient code to be generated; and *code generation*, in which the target program is actually produced.

Interpretation

In interpretation, a program called an *interpreter* maintains control over both translation and execution. It takes as input the source program and interleaves translation and execution of that program so that the generated code corresponding to a portion of the source program is executed as it is produced. In an imperative (procedural) language, this means that each statement is translated and executed before the next statement is translated. The translated code is not saved, so if the same source statement is executed many times, as in a loop,

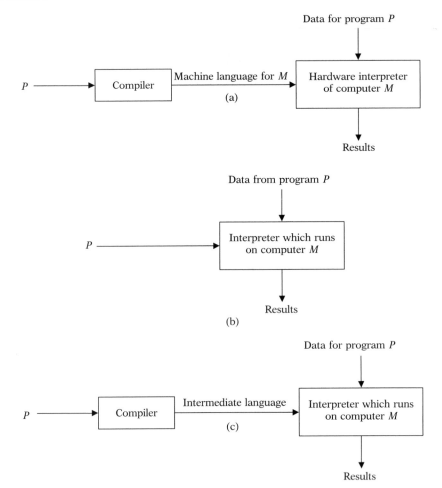

Figure 1. Three possibilities in compilation and interpretation: (a) pure compilation (hardware interpreter); (b) pure interpretation (interpretation of source language); (c) mixed compilation and interpretation (interpretation of intermediate language).

it will be retranslated each time. Pure interpretation is illustrated in Fig. 1b.

Hybrid Systems

In practice, compilation and interpretation are often combined. Many systems translate the source code into an *intermediate language* (*q.v.*) that is then interpreted by a software interpreter. This strategy is illustrated in Fig. 1c. Whether this is considered a compiler or interpretive system depends largely on the level of the intermediate code, that is, how much of the translation process is done in the first step and how much is left

to the software interpreter. Two examples of hybrid systems are UCSD Pascal and Java (*q.v.*). Each was designed for portability in response to the many and rapidly changing hardware platforms being developed; the compiler generates an intermediate form for a virtual machine that is realized by a software interpreter.

Compilation vs Interpretation

Compilation followed by later execution results in faster execution than interpretation, but interpreters usually provide better run-time error information because the source code is still available at run time. Some of the advantages of interpreters over compilers have diminished as compiler technology has matured. Compilers can give informative error messages, and they are often coupled with symbolic debuggers (*see* DEBUGGING) that give access to the source code associated with a run-time error, just as an interpreter does. There are also *incremental* compilers that can compile or recompile a part of a program "on the fly." The ML functional programming (*q.v.*) language, for example, has an interactive run-time system whose compiler translates each function as it is written, so that it behaves like an interpreter from the user's standpoint.

Bibliography

1986. Aho, A. V., Sethi, R., and Ullman, J. D. *Compilers—Principles, Techniques, and Tools.* Reading, MA: Addison-Wesley.

1990. Kamin, S. N. *Programming Languages: An Interpreter-Based Approach.* Reading, MA: Addison-Wesley.

1998. Ghezzi, C., and Jazayeri, M. *Programming Language Concepts,* 3rd Ed. New York: John Wiley.

Adrienne Bloss

LANGUAGE TRANSLATION

See MACHINE TRANSLATION.

LANGUAGES, NATURAL

See NATURAL LANGUAGE PROCESSING.

LANGUAGES, PROGRAMMING

See PROCEDURE-ORIENTED LANGUAGES; PROGRAMMING LANGUAGES; FUNCTIONAL PROGRAMMING; LOGIC PROGRAMMING; LIST PROCESSING; and STRING PROCESSING. See also names of particular languages.

LAPTOP COMPUTER

See PORTABLE COMPUTERS.

LAWS, COMPUTER

For articles on related subjects, *see*

+ Integrated Circuitry
+ Networks, Computer
+ Parallel Processing

Introduction

From time to time, individual computer scientists have noted that some aspect of computer technology or performance seems to conform to a pattern that (1) can be quantified, and (2) is likely to hold into the indefinite future. When and if their colleagues gather evidence that supports the observation, the prediction is deemed a "law" that is thereafter associated with the name of its proposer. This article defines and discusses the implications of four widely known computer laws.

Moore's Law

In 1965, Gordon Moore prepared an article for the 35th anniversary of *Electronics* magazine (Moore, 1965). Plotting the growth in the number of components on a chip over time, he discovered that over the period 1959–1965, the number of components (e.g. transistors) per chip increased at roughly a factor of 2 every year. This trend suggested that processing power would rise at an exponentially fast rate, leading to a computing revolution. At the 1975 IEEE International Electron Devices meeting, Moore revised his prediction to the number of transistors on a chip doubling every two years (*see* Moore, 1995), a prediction that has become known as *Moore's Law.* In 1973, Intel microchips contained about 8000 transistors, by 2000 they contained 42 million, and one planned for 2007 will contain a billion per chip—1.25×10^5 more than in 1973. There are 17 two-year periods from 1973 to 2007, and 2^{17} is almost exactly 1.25×10^5. Thus,

Moore's 1975 prediction is very consistent with the empirical evidence.

Metcalfe's Law

In a network with N nodes, there are $\frac{1}{2}N(N-1)$ possible two-way interconnections. If each interconnection has the same intrinsic value, then, for large N, the overall value of the network is proportional to N^2. Thus, each additional user adds more than a proportionate value to the network, because just by being there, all other users then have the ability to interact with the new one. The precept that the value of a network increases as the square of the number of its interconnections is known as *Metcalfe's Law*. The law is named after network pioneer Robert M. Metcalfe, who proposed the Ethernet (*q.v.*) in his Ph.D. dissertation at Harvard University and continued his research at the Xerox Palo Alto Research Center and Stanford University.

In 1979, Metcalfe cofounded 3Com Corporation, which sold Ethernet adapter cards and became a major communications products company. 3Com stands for *Com*puter, *Com*munication, *Com*patibility—reflecting the idea that the Ethernet standard facilitates the addition of more computer users to the network, which increases its value according to Metcalfe's Law. The law was not named by Metcalfe himself but rather by George Gilder, who praised the power of interconnection as reflected by the philosophies of both Ethernet and the Internet (*q.v.*).

Grosch's Law

While with IBM, Herbert Grosch formulated *Grosch's Law*, which states that the total cost $C(P)$ of a computer system with overall performance P is proportional to the square root of P: $C(P) = KP^{1/2}$, where K is a "constant" characteristic of a given technological era. The law is often stated in the opposite sense, namely, that if one spends twice as much on a replacement computer, one may expect that its performance will be four times greater. Grosch's Law used to be cited by large system vendors and data-processing managers who argued that hardware economies of scale provided an economic justification for large-scale centralized computing.

The empirical evidence shows that Grosch's Law provided an approximate description of the relationship between cost and system performance in the 1960s and 1970s. Mendelson (1987) showed that Grosch's Law ceased to hold in the 1980s: across a large variety of data-processing computers, cost was merely *proportional* to overall machine performance, that is, the average cost per unit of performance was independent of system size.

Amdahl's Law

Amdahl's Law places a theoretical limit on the ability to speed up program execution using parallel computation. The law was formulated by Gene Amdahl of IBM and, later, the corporation that bears his name. Amdahl (1967) noted that the performance gain that can be achieved from parallelizing a program is limited by that part of the program that runs sequentially. Specifically, if s is the fraction of a program that runs *sequentially*, p is the fraction that runs in parallel (i.e. $s + p = 1$), and there are N processors that speed up the parallel part by a factor of N, then the overall speedup is given by $(s+p)/(s+p/N) = [s + (1-s)/N]^{-1}$, which is bounded from above by $1/s$. Thus, even with an infinite number of parallel processors, the overall speedup is bounded by the reciprocal of the program fraction that runs sequentially. For example, if 5% of the program runs sequentially, speedup cannot exceed a factor of 20.

In 1987, the Sandia National Laboratories achieved a 1000-fold speedup on its massively parallel 1024-processor hypercube system. This result was surprising in light of the predictions of Amdahl's "Law." Gustafson (1988) explains the apparent contradiction by noting that for many practical problems, it is the parallelizable part of the program that scales with problem size. If the parallelizable part of the program scales linearly while the sequential part remains constant, speedup becomes a linear function (rather than being bounded). This result, sometimes called *Gustafson's Law*, vindicates the use of massively parallel processing.

Bibliography

1953. Grosch, H. R. J. "High Speed Arithmetic: The Digital Computer As a Research Tool," *Journal of the Optical Society of America*, **43**, 306–310.

1965. Moore, G. E. "Cramming More Components Onto Integrated Circuits," *Electronics*, **38**(8), (19 April), 114–117.

1967. Amdahl, G. M. "Validity of the Single Processor Approach to Achieving Large-scale Computing Capabilities," *Proceedings of the American Federation of Information Processing Societies*, Vol. 30. Washington, DC, 483–485.

1987. Mendelson, H. "Economics of Scale in Computing: Grosch's Law Revisited," *Communications of the ACM* **30**(12), 1066–1072.

1988. Gustafson, J. L. "Reevaluating Amdahl's Law," *Communications of the ACM*, **31**, 532–533.

1993. Gilder, G. "George Gilder's Telecosm: Metcalfe's Law and Legacy," *Forbes ASAP*, **152**, Supplement 13 (September), 158–166.

Haim Mendelson

LEARNING

See COMPUTER-ASSISTED LEARNING AND TEACHING; and MACHINE LEARNING.

LEGAL PROTECTION OF SOFTWARE

For articles on related subjects, *see*

+ Free Software Foundation (FSF)
+ Freeware and Shareware

Computer software is expensive to develop and maintain. It has high monetary value because it can be sold to or licensed for use by others. Software, however, is very easy to copy and thus susceptible to pirating. Legally, software is categorized as *intellectual property*. Intellectual property is a form of intangible personal property comprised of ideas, processes, information, or symbols. Such property contrasts with tangible personal property, such as hardware or supplies, and real property, such as office buildings and other structures. Intellectual property is protected in one of five principal ways: by patent, copyright, trade secret, trademark, or contract.

Patent

In the United States, patent protection is a federal statutory right that gives an inventor or his or her assignee exclusive rights to deny others the right to make, use, or sell the patented invention throughout the USA or to import the invention into the USA beginning on the date the patent is issued for a period of 20 years from the date of filing of the application for patent. To be patentable, inventions must be of statutory subject matter—physical methods, apparatus, compositions of matter, devices, and improvements—but not mere ideas. Further, they must be new, useful, and not obvious. They must be described in a properly filed and prosecuted patent application.

The courts have held that a mathematical algorithm is like a law of nature (which is not patentable subject matter) and has evolved a two-step process for determining whether a computer program is patentable subject matter. First, does the claim recite such an algorithm, and, if so, does it in its entirety wholly preempt that algorithm? Claims that do both of the above are deemed to be unpatentable subject matter. A negative response to either test permits the claim to be evaluated on the basis of the other tests of patentability.

Copyright

Copyright is one of the powers granted to Congress under the US Constitution. Under the Copyright Act of 1976, as amended, the protection extends to original works of authorship including computer programs. Exclusive rights are granted to the owner of the copyright to reproduce the copyrighted work; prepare derivative works based on the work; distribute copies of the work by sale, rental, lease, or lending; perform the work publicly if it is literary, musical, dramatic or choreographic, pantomime, or a motion picture and other audio-visual works; and display each of those works and pictorial, graphic, or sculptural works publicly. An infringement comes either from direct copying or by copying the "structure, sequence and organization" (the "look and feel") of a program. In 1996, the US Supreme Court held that a computer *user interface* (*q.v.*) is a "method of operation" and not eligible for copyright protection; *Lotus Development Corp. v. Borland International*, No. 94–2003 (US).

To be eligible for copyright protection, a work must be original and must be fixed in a tangible means of expression, such as a book, tape, or disk. Protection arises automatically for protected works upon fixation and covers the expression in the work (but not the underlying ideas). As of 27 January 1999, protection lasts for the life of the author plus 70 years and, in the case of works made for hire, for 95 years from first publication or 120 years from creation.

The US Copyright Law covers work made for hire. A work made for hire is a work prepared by an employee within the scope of his or her employment, or a work specially ordered or commissioned for use. Computer programs as such do not qualify for work made for hire if written by nonemployees.

Trade Secret

A *trade secret* is a right that is protected state by state rather than by a federal law and is defined in the Uniform Trade Secrets Act, adopted in many states, including a formula, pattern, compilation, program, device, method, technique, or process that derives independent economic value, actual or potential, from not being generally known to the public, and is the subject of efforts that are reasonable under the circumstances to maintain its secrecy. In a number of court cases, computer programs have qualified as trade secrets.

Trademark

Trademark embodies the exclusive use of a symbol to identify goods and services. As distinguished from a patent, which does not exist until issued by the Patent Office, or a copyright, which exists as soon as the work is fixed in a tangible form, a trademark arises upon use, or, if one has a *bona fide* intent to use the mark, one may acquire rights by filing a federal application to register the mark. The symbol protected can be both a name and a logo, such as *17 Mile Drive*.

However, one cannot trademark an entire program, only its identifying symbol(s).

Contract

Because copies of software are ordinarily transferred to others in the course of business, provision of the software is frequently made under an agreement to keep its source code confidential. Patented and copyrighted software can be transferred via contracts that may have other restrictions than the law requires simply by the status accorded by the patent or copyright. One may, for example, contract with another not to disclose a copyrighted piece of software. One may also agree to remedies for disclosure or unauthorized copying, set up complex formulas for royalty payment for legitimate use, and agree to the ownership of enhancements and changes to the software.

Bibliography

1982. Nycum, S. H. *Protection of Proprietary Interests in Software*. Reston, VA: Reston Publishing Company.
1992. Carr, H., and Arnold, R. *Computer Software—Legal Protection in the UK*, 2nd Ed. London: Sweet & Maxwell.

Susan H. Nycum

LEIBNIZ, GOTTFRIED WILHELM

For articles on related subjects, *see*

+ Calculating Machines
+ Digital Computers, History of: Origins
+ Pascal, Blaise

Gottfried Wilhelm Leibniz (b. Leipzig, 1646; d. Hanover, 1716) (Fig. 1) had obtained an excellent education in his father's library before entering the University of Leipzig at age 15 and receiving a bachelor's degree at 17. At 20 he received a doctorate in jurisprudence from Altdorf, and for six years thereafter pursued a career of law and diplomacy, working to create an effective defense for the German states against

Figure 1.   Gottfried Wilhelm Leibniz. (Courtesy of the Mary Evans Picture Library.)

Louis XIV. These diplomatic intrigues took him to Paris (1672), where he spent the four most fecund years of his mathematical career. Under the tutelage of Huygens, Leibniz systematically studied mathematics, especially the work of Descartes and Pascal. His 1666 dissertation, *De Arte Combinatorica* (*On Combinatorics*) developed the mathematics of permutations and combinations, and he is frequently credited with having developed binary arithmetic. In 1673, Leibniz made discoveries in differential calculus, and in 1675, he observed that the summation process of integration was equivalent to reversing the operation of differentiation, the fundamental theorem of calculus.

Pascal's calculating machine stimulated Leibniz's interest. By adding a movable carriage operating on wheels using an active-and-inactive pin principle and a delayed carry mechanism, Leibniz modified Pascal's machine so that it would multiply and divide directly (i.e. without the operator having to use an algorithm).

In 1676 Leibniz left Paris for Hanover, where for the next 40 years he was a historian and librarian actively pursuing philosophy, theology, diplomatic missions, and scientific correspondence, and only intermittently working on his calculating machines. In 1700, he organized the Berlin Academy of Science and at his death was carrying on the now-famous correspondence with Clarke about the theological implications of Newton's *Principia* and *Opticks*.

Bibliography

1665. Leibniz, G. "On his Calculating Machine," in *A Source Book in Mathematics* (ed. D. E. Smith), Vol. 1, 173–181. New York: Dover, 1959.

1994. Jolley, N. (ed.) *The Cambridge Companion to Leibniz*. London: Cambridge University Press.

1997. Rutherford, D. *Leibniz and the Rational Order of Nature*. London: Cambridge University Press.

Charles V. Jones

LIBRARY PROGRAM

See PROGRAM LIBRARY.

LINKED LIST

See LIST PROCESSING.

LINKERS AND LOADERS

For articles on related subjects, *see*

+ Binding
+ Bootstrap
+ Compiler
+ Global and Local Variables
+ Object Program

In early operating systems, processing of a program between compiling and execution took place in two distinct stages. The function of a *linker* (or *linkage editor*) was to combine a number of independently compiled or assembled *object files* into a single *load module*, resolving cross-references and incorporating routines from libraries as required. The *loader* then prepared this module for execution, physically loaded it into memory, and started execution. The loader was required because in the multitasking (*q.v.*) systems of the day the exact address in memory at which the program would be loaded was not known in advance of loading. Later systems were able to dispense with an explicit loader since relocation was not required; virtual memory systems provided each program (process) with a large flat virtual address space that starts at address zero. However, the introduction of dynamic link libraries has brought back the need for a loader, since in systems employing dynamic linking some symbols cannot be resolved until the executable module is actually loaded.

The Link Editor

A complete program typically comprises a number of files that are compiled separately, which include references to functions stored in one or more *libraries*. In a C (*q.v.*) program, for example, each file will contain a number of functions, together with *header files* that provide templates describing the functions used within the file but defined somewhere else—external functions. Likewise, a C++ (*q.v.*) program includes header files that provide definitions of classes whose member functions are defined elsewhere—another example of an *external reference*.

We describe first the process of "static linking." The link editor operates in two passes; the function of the first pass being to resolve the references between separately compiled modules. Figure 1 shows two such modules. The external reference tables are merged into a single table, as are the global definition tables. External references are resolved initially from the merged global definition table. Any remaining unresolved references are either errors or references to a library. The link editor scans the symbol table for each library specified, attempting to resolve unmatched external references. When a match is found,

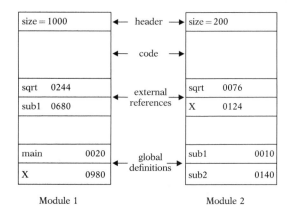

Figure 1. Two program modules, each with external references to names defined in other modules and global definitions of names referred to in other modules. Module 1, for example, has a globally declared variable named X at address 0980, and it refers to an external subroutine, sub1 at address 0244 of its code.

the relevant object module is extracted from the library and added to the program. Figure 2 shows the merged tables.

The function of pass 2 is to adjust relative addresses in all modules after the first so as to produce a contiguous program with all addresses relative to the start of the first module. During this pass the appropriate relocation counter value for a module is added to all relative addresses in the module, and the entries in the global definition tables are also relocated relative to the origin of the first module. The result is a loadable or *executable* module.

Dynamic Linking

If a library function is widely used, a separate copy of its code will be incorporated in the executable file of every program that uses it. Dynamic linking ensures that only one copy of the code is loaded into memory, being shared by all programs that are currently using it. We describe here the dynamic link library (DLL) structure used in Microsoft Windows.

A DLL is a relocatable module containing the executable code for a number of functions each of which is identified by a numerical entry point. Functions

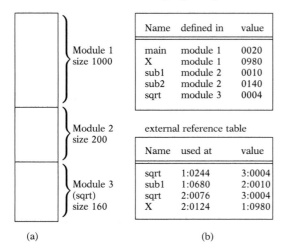

merged global symbol table

Name	defined in	value
main	module 1	0020
X	module 1	0980
sub1	module 2	0010
sub2	module 2	0140
sqrt	module 3	0004

external reference table

Name	used at	value
sqrt	1:0244	3:0004
sub1	1:0680	2:0010
sqrt	2:0076	3:0004
X	2:0124	1:0980

(a)   (b)

Figure 2. (a) The code blocks of the two program modules and a third module, the sqrt function, extracted from a library archive, are assembled into one block of code; (b) The global symbol table lists all global symbols with their values and the module in which they are defined. This external references table uses this information to give a value to each external symbol, relative to the start of its module, written here as a module-number address.

defined in DLLs are referenced via import libraries that map function names onto unique DLL/entry point pairs. These *import libraries* are scanned by the link editor, and so an external reference to a DLL function will appear in the final load module as a DLL name/entry point pair, which is then resolved by the loader.

Remote Booting

Diskless workstations have to boot off a network, and even if workstations have local disks, management may prefer booting over the network in order to ensure that every workstation has the latest version of the system. Remote booting requires the existence of a "boot server" somewhere on the network from which a binary image of the system can be loaded by code stored in ROM on the workstation.

Bibliography

1972. Presser, I., and White, J. R. "Linkers and Loaders," *Computing Surveys,* **4**, 149–168.

1978. Barron, D. W. *Assemblers and Loaders*, 3rd Ed. New York: American Elsevier.

1992. Salomon, D. *Assemblers and Loaders*. Chichester: Ellis Horwood.

David W. Barron

LINUX

For articles on related subjects, *see*

+ Free Software Foundation (FSF)
+ Freeware and Shareware
+ Unix

Linux, pronounced "Lynn-ucks," is one of three major free software versions of Unix, the others being *GNU Unix* and *FreeBSD*. Strictly speaking, Linux is just a version of the Unix *kernel (q.v.)*; the complete equivalent to Unix should be called GNU Linux.

Linux is named for the Finnish programmer Linus Torvalds who created it in 1994 while still a student at Helsinki University. Linux, along with the Apache program for Web servers, is one of the two most widely used open software products. GNU Linux brought Unix, originally a mainframe operating system, to the personal computer (PC) and is now available for all commonly used PCs. Its source code and a host of related ancillary programs, all written in C or C++, may be downloaded from the Internet without charge, or may be purchased for a nominal fee from companies such as Red Hat and Caldera who ship it on CD-ROM bundled with a choice of graphical user interface (GUI) programs and supporting manuals. Linux is now second only to Microsoft Windows as an operating system for Intel 80×86-compatible PCs, and at least one handheld computer, the Sharp Zaurus, uses Linux.

Bibliography

2001. Torvalds, L., and Diamond, D. *Just for Fun: The Story of an Accidental Revolutionary*. New York: HarperCollins.

2003. Siever, E., and Weber, A. *Linux in a Nutshell*, 4th Ed. Sebastopol, CA: O'Reilly.

Edwin D. Reilly

LISP

For articles on related subjects, *see*

+ Artificial Intelligence (AI)
+ Functional Programming
+ List Processing
+ Programming Languages

Why has Lisp Lasted So Long?

Fortran (*q.v.*) is the only language in widespread use that is older than Lisp (LISt Processor). Lisp owes its longevity to two facts. First, its core elements occupy a kind of local optimum in the "space" of programming languages, given the resistance to purely notational changes. Recursive use of conditional expressions, representation of symbolic information externally by lists and internally by list data structures (*q.v.*), and the representation of programs in the same way as data will probably have a very long life. Second, Lisp still has operational features unmatched by other languages that make it a convenient vehicle for higher-level systems for symbolic computation and for artificial intelligence (AI).

Lisp Prehistory

In late 1958 John McCarthy and Marvin Minsky, assistant professors of EE and mathematics respectively at MIT, began the MIT Artificial Intelligence Project and initiated the implementation of Lisp. To simplify the task of programming the substantive computations, for example, logical deduction, algebraic simplification, differentiation or integration, the design gave up the familiar infix notation in favor of parenthesized prefix *Polish notation* (*q.v.*). The core of Lisp is a functional programming (*q.v.*) language, though Lisp also has the imperative features common to procedure-oriented languages (*q.v.*). Early Lisp was interpretive; Lisp 1.5 was stable and well documented. Now most implementations rely heavily on compilation into assembly language for fast execution as well as for compile-time debugging. Compilers for Lisp can be written in Lisp, and examples of this as far back as 1959 provide early examples of language bootstrapping (*q.v.*).

The Growth of Lisp Dialects

Attempts to correct the inefficiencies of Lisp 1.5 led to several projects, ultimately dominated by one machine architecture, the Digital Equipment Corporation (*q.v.*) PDP-6 and DEC-10. Major systems came from MIT and Stanford, and from Bolt, Beranek, and Newman (BBN) and Xerox PARC's Interlisp.

Lisp systems began to outgrow the DEC-10 in which only 2^{18} 36-bit words (about one MB) could be conveniently addressed. AI funding from government agencies (ARPA in particular) was abundant, and efforts to solve this address-space problem led to a version of MIT's MACLisp on the GE-645 Multics timesharing system and then to special single-user "Lisp machines." In the early 1970s, designs at MIT were sold to two companies, LMI, later acquired by Texas Instruments, and Symbolics Inc. Special hardware/software systems for InterLisp were also produced at Xerox and Carnegie Mellon University. None of these special-purpose hardware systems has survived.

The Scheme dialect, a small and semantically clean reaction to the alarming complexity of Lisps, also appeared in the 1970s and subsequently became an IEEE standard. It is a popular pedagogical language, and has several serious implementations.

Reunification

In 1984, a grassroots effort sought to produce a unified new language called Common Lisp. Vendors and academics produced implementations that were testbeds for the resulting ANSI Common Lisp, a standards effort that reached fruition in 1994 (standard X3J13). Guy Steele Jr's *Common Lisp: the Language* is an approachable reference and a definitive description of the ANSI language is most easily available on the Web.

Bibliography

1981. McCarthy, J. "History of Lisp," in *History of Programming Languages* (ed. R. L. Wexelblat), 173–185. New York: Academic Press.

1990. Steele, G. Jr. *Common Lisp: The Language*, 2nd Ed. Bedford, MA: Digital Press.

1996. Abelson, H., and Sussman, G. J. *Structure and Interpretation of Computer Programs*, 2nd Ed. Cambridge, MA: MIT Press.

1996. Steele, G. L., Jr., and Gabriel, R. P. "The Evolution of Lisp," in *History of Programming Languages II* (ed. T. J. Bergin Jr., and R. J. Gibson Jr.), 233–308. New York: Addison-Wesley.

Richard Fateman and John McCarthy

LIST PROCESSING

For articles on related subjects, *see*

+ Abstract Data Type
+ Artificial Intelligence (AI)
+ Computer Algebra
+ Data Structures
+ Data Type
+ Functional Programming
+ Graph Theory
+ Lisp
+ Pointer
+ Storage Allocation
+ String Processing
+ Symbol Manipulation
+ Tree

PRINCIPLES

List Concepts

Any data object that contains other objects is a *compound data object*. On one end of the spectrum is the *homogeneous array*, a collection of objects, all of the same type, with an implicit relationship defined by the indices of the elements of the array. Further along the spectrum in complexity is the *record*, a collection of data objects, not necessarily all of the same type, into a single unit whose representation is hidden (a Pascal *record* or C *struct*, for example). The complexity of a *list* is somewhere between the array and the structure: it is a collection of anonymous, frequently heterogeneous elements, whose elements cannot be directly accessed. Instead, elements of lists must be reached through two primitive operations.

Each element of a list other than the last has a next element. At any given moment, one can look at the current element or *sublist* that follows it. The basic operations are typically called *first* and *rest*—the first element of the list is the current element, and the rest of the list is everything but the first element. All other elements are reached by repeating those two operations: the second element is the first of the rest, the third is the first of the rest of the rest, and so on.

Lists are a good example of an *abstract data type* (*q.v.*). They are characterized in terms of the elements that they may hold—for example, simple object like numbers, compound objects such as structures, or other lists—and in terms of these basic operations. A list has a simple recursive definition: a list is either empty or consists of a first element of some type, followed by a list (the rest).

List Implementation

Lists are commonly implemented as *linked lists*, in which each element has a link (a *pointer–q.v.*) to its successor. A list element can be considered to be a data object that also has a "next" field (the link), or as a primitive *node* with a data field and a "next" field. The former approach is often taken for objects that are designed from the start to be combined into lists: a structure or abstract data type is given an additional field, which will contain a pointer to another such object. The latter view is taken by Lisp and related languages: the *cons* operation makes a node with two fields (called a *cons cell* or *dotted pair*) that can contain any other object (or a pointer to the object). Lists are built out of these nodes, with the *first* field holding the data object and the rest field pointing to the next node. New nodes are taken from *free storage*, (also called the *heap*, or the *list of available space*) and deleted nodes must be returned to free storage lest it run out. The process of making new nodes is part of *storage allocation*, and the process of reclaiming unused nodes is called *garbage collection*.

It is very easy to insert new elements into and delete current elements from a linked list. Given a list of 5, 8, and 9, it is simple to insert the number 6 in order: make an element containing 6 with its link pointing to the element containing 8, and then change the first element's link to point to the new one (Fig. 1). Similarly, deleting an element from a list simply involves changing one element's link to the deleted element to point to the next one, and splicing out the deleted node. Lists are inherently variable-sized, in contrast to arrays and structures that usually have a fixed number of elements.

Doubly linked lists have two links per element: one pointing to the next element, and one to the previous one. The benefit of the second link is that it makes insertion and deletion easier. In the example above, to insert the 6 between the 5 and the 8, we needed to reach both the 5 and 8 list elements, because they were on either side of the insertion point. With a singly linked list, we have to keep track of both of them ourselves. If we knew we wanted to insert the 6 before the 8, but didn't already have a handle on the 5, we would have to start at the beginning of the list and work down to the insertion point. With a doubly linked list, all we need

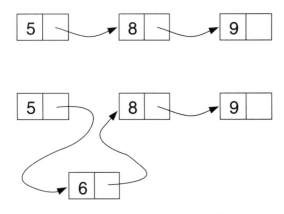

Figure 1. Inserting an element into a list.

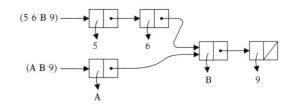

Figure 2. Sharing parts of a list.

is one list element, and it will allow us to look both forward and backward.

Since list elements point to other list elements, it is possible for more than one to point to the same object. When this happens, multiple lists can share parts of themselves, with the obvious consequences: identical data is not duplicated, and if part of the shared data is changed as part of operating on one list, all the sharing lists see the changes (*see* Fig. 2). A list may even be *circular*, sharing structure with itself: an element somewhere in the list may point to an element elsewhere in the list.

Applications of Lists

Lists can also be used to implement trees and other graph structures (*see* GRAPH THEORY). Pair nodes can be linked into simple binary trees, and larger nodes into trees of greater degree or with data at the nodes of the tree. Larger nodes can even be simulated by lists built from pair nodes. Since list nodes can contain pointers to arbitrary data objects—even other nodes in the same list—graph structures of all complexities can be built by connecting nodes.

Two other structures easily built with lists are the *stack* (*q.v.*) and the *queue*. A stack is just a list that is used in a certain way. To *push* an object onto the stack, make a new node containing the object, link it to the stack, and then use that new node as the new top of the stack. To *pop* an object off, change the stack pointer to point to the next element and discard or process the old top. Since, by the definition of "stack," only the first element of a stack may be accessed, the basic linked structure of a list suffices to implement a stack. Similarly, queues can be built as lists of elements, with insertion defined as attaching a new node to the end of the list and deletion the same as is done with a stack.

Bibliography

1996. Abelson, H., and Sussman, G. *Structure and Interpretation of Computer Programs*, 2nd Ed. Cambridge, MA: MIT Press.

1997. Carrano, F. *Data Abstraction and Problem Solving With C++: Walls and Mirrors*. Reading, MA: Addison-Wesley.

Paul Fuqua

LANGUAGES

A list-processing language is a computer language that facilitates the processing of data organized in the form of lists. Lisp and Scheme are typical list-processing languages. Other languages, such as Prolog, have extensive support for list processing.

External List Representation

We begin with some simple examples to show what kinds of problems are solved by list processing and also how the lists look as they are used for input and output.

Traditional notation	*List notation*

French to English translation

Oùest le Métro?   (OU EST LE METRO?)

Arithmetic expression

$2 + (3 * 5 - 1)$ (+2 (- (*35) 1))

Note use of Polish prefix notation in the above.

Logic

$(\forall x)(Q(x) \vee \neg P(x))$ (ALL X ((Q X) OR
                              (NOT (P X))))

Some of the terms used in connection with list processing are used in slightly different ways by different writers. Some rough definitions are as follows:

The basic data type is the *atom*. Atoms can be numbers or symbols. A symbol corresponds to a word in English. In the examples above, EST, 5, X, and NOT are symbols. A *list* is a sequence of zero or more elements enclosed in parentheses. An *element* is an atom or a list.

A list is represented externally to the computer in terms of characters, and internally in terms of memory cells. The external representation is designed for the convenience of the user and is used by the computer for input and output operations. The preceding examples use the notation of Lisp.

The internal representation of a list is the way the computer stores it in memory. In Lisp a list is represented by means of pointers. A *pointer* is the address of a memory word. Other terms sometimes used for pointer are *link* and *reference*. Each element in a list is represented by a pair of pointers: the first a pointer to the first element of the list, the second a pointer to the rest of the list.

The Lisp Language

Lisp is the most popular list-processing language. Lisp was developed by John McCarthy and his associates at MIT during the late 1950s and early 1960s. During its long history, Lisp has undergone numerous changes until a formal American National Standard for Common Lisp was produced in 1994.

Data

First we define the Lisp data language. An S-expression (symbolic expression), the general name for legal input data, is either an atom or a list structure. An *atom* is a sequence of characters other than blanks or parentheses. The start and finish of each atom is indicated by parentheses or blanks. A list structure consists of a left parenthesis followed by any number of atoms or list structures, followed by a right parenthesis. For example, each of the items below is an S-expression.

```
DOG
1984
(WHERE IS TURING NOW)
((MCCARTHY) IS MASTER OF (THE DARK TOWER))
(A LIST ((((CAN))) BE (((VERY)))
                  ((((((DEEP)))))))))
```

Numbers may be integers, fixed-point numbers, or floating-point numbers. All Lisp functions that operate on numbers automatically test the number type and perform needed conversions. In Lisp, the objects have a type but not the variables, so the same variable can be used as a name for different types of objects. The symbol NIL is a special atom in Lisp and is used to indicate an empty list or to indicate the truth value "false."

Programs

The language for writing programs in Lisp is actually a subset of the data language. Therefore, it is easy to write Lisp programs that operate on other Lisp programs. Lisp has few special rules and exceptions. It has the virtues of mathematical elegance and simplicity. The semantics of Lisp is also straightforward. The Lisp system contains a program called the *interpreter*. The interpreter reads a Lisp expression, computes its value, and then prints it out.

Lisp programs are organized as forms and functions. *Forms* are expressions that are evaluated and produce values as a result of the evaluation. *Functions* are objects that can be invoked as procedures. They may take arguments and return values. A form may be a self-evaluating form (a number, a character, a string, etc.), a variable, or a list.

Numbers, T, and NIL are examples of self-evaluating forms. T means "true," NIL means "false" and also "empty list." The empty list can also be indicated by ( ).

Symbols are used as names of variables. When a symbol is evaluated, it returns the value of the variable it names. The value is stored in the computer as a pointer to some expression. For example, a variable X may have as value a list of three elements (A B C).

Lisp includes a set of built-in primitive functions. The primitive function CONS (short for `construct`) is used to build lists. CONS takes two arguments. If the second argument is a list, it returns a new list with the first argument added to the front. For example, if X has the value of (A B C) and Y has the value A, then (CONS Y X) has the value (A A B C). (CONS A NIL) forms the one-element list (A). The second element of CONS is not necessarily a list; it could be any other Lisp object. In this case CONS constructs an S-expression that is called a *dotted list*, since it is not terminated by NIL as regular lists are.

CAR is a primitive function that returns the first element of a list. If X has the value (A B C), then

(CAR X) has the value A. A companion to CAR is CDR, which returns the rest of the list. The value of (CDR X) is (B C). One can use nested CARs and CDRs to isolate any component of an S-expression. The names CAR and CDR are historical fossils. They relate to assembly language on the IBM 704 computer, the first machine on which Lisp was implemented.

Among the Lisp primitives there are *predicates*, that is, functions that return either true or false (T or NIL). For instance, ATOM is a predicate of one argument. (ATOM X) has the value T if X is an atom and NIL ("false") otherwise. Predicates are particularly useful in *conditional forms*, the Lisp equivalent of a branch instruction. The following is a typical conditional form:

```
(COND ((ATOM X) X) (T (CAR X)))
```

The arguments of a conditional form come in pairs. In each pair, the first is the predicate part and the second is the value part. The interpreter evaluates conditional pairs from left to right. If the predicate has the value T, the interpreter then evaluates the second portion of the conditional pair and returns this as the value of the entire conditional form. If the value of the predicate is NIL, the interpreter starts to work on the next pair. If X is (A B C), the value of the sample conditional form above is A, since (ATOM X) is NIL and (CAR X) is A.

A function can be given a name by using the special form DEFUN. DEFUN requires as arguments a name, a list of variables, and one or more forms. The forms comprise the body of the function. The list of variables is like the list of variables used in the LAMBDA expression. Below is an example of a simple function being defined and then used. In this example, * means multiply.

```
(DEFUN SQUARE (X) (* X X))
(SQUARE 9)
```

The DEFUN special form in this example will assign to the atom SQUARE a function of one argument (X). When evaluating (SQUARE 9), the Lisp interpreter will first look up the definition of the function attached to the atom SQUARE, and then evaluate the form (* X X) in it, using 9 as the value for X. Thus, the value of (SQUARE 9) is 81.

Recursive Functions

A useful property of Lisp is the ability to evaluate a recursively defined function, that is, a function that uses its own name as part of its definition. For example,

```
(DEFUN LAST (X)
    (COND ((ATOM (CDR X)) (CAR X))
          (T (LAST (CDR X)))
        ))
```

where LAST searches a list of one or more elements and returns the last element of that list. (ATOM (CDR X)) is true only if X is a list of just one element since then its CDR is NIL, an atom. If X is a list of two or more elements, LAST calls itself and shortens the list by removing the first element. Eventually, the list is shortened to just one element. Then (CAR X) is returned, which is the only element of a one-element list.

The Garbage Collector

The garbage collector, or *reclaimer*, aids the dynamic storage allocation in Lisp. It periodically searches memory to locate list structures that are no longer needed. The memory cells in this garbage are then added to the list of available space to be used in making new list structures.

Other List-Processing Languages

IPL-V is the grandparent of all list-processing languages. It was developed by Allen Newell and his associates at the Rand Corporation and later at Carnegie Mellon University. IPL is an acronym for Information Processing Language. IPL-V, the fifth member of the IPL family, was the first language to use lists made of memory cells linked with pointers, but garbage collection was the programmer's responsibility.

Scheme is very similar to Lisp. Scheme is a much smaller language, with a simpler and cleaner semantics. It treats lists the same way Lisp does.

The language Pop-2 is a descendant of Lisp and Algol. It was developed by R. J. Popplestone in the Department of Machine Intelligence and Perception at the University of Edinburgh. Programs written in Pop-2 look very much like Algol. Pop-2 is a very general

language with many ingenious features. It might be described as a combination of Algol and Lisp.

Other languages provide extensive support for list processing, including functional programming (*q.v.*) languages such as ML, Miranda, and Haskell. Prolog (*see* LOGIC PROGRAMMING) has lists among its primitive data types.

Bibliography

1961. Newell, A. (ed.) *Information Processing Language-V Manual.* Upper Saddle River, NJ: Prentice Hall.
1990. Steele, G. L. *Common LISP*, 2nd Ed. Bedford, MA: Digital Press.
1996. Abelson, H., and Sussman, G. J. *Structure and Interpretation of Computer Programs*, 2nd Ed. Cambridge, MA: MIT Press. (Uses Scheme.)
1998. Grillmeyer, O. *Explaining Computer Science with Scheme.* New York: Springer-Verlag.

James R. Slagle and Maria L. Gini

LOADER

See LINKERS AND LOADERS.

LOCAL AREA NETWORK (LAN)

For articles on related subjects, see

+ Ethernet
+ Fiber Optics
+ File Server
+ Gateway
+ Network Architecture
+ Network Protocols
+ Networks, Computer
+ Open Systems Interconnection
+ Packet Switching
+ Workstation

Historical Overview

Development of the first-generation *local area network*, or LAN, took place during the 1970s. The goal was an inexpensive network suitable for use in a classroom, laboratory, office suite, or an entire building to enable PCs to share more expensive peripherals such as printers and large disk drives. Standardization in the early 1980s was followed by worldwide deployment of 10 Mb/s LANs. By the end of the decade, LANs were common.

Second-generation LAN development began with the 100 Mb/s FDDI (fiber distributed data interface) in the late 1980s. At the same time, MAC (media access control)-level bridges were developed as a means of interconnecting LANs, primarily within a site, both to extend the range of coverage and to constrain traffic local to a single LAN to prevent flooding a whole site.

The 1990s saw a number of advances in LAN technology: use of copper twisted-pairs and the introduction of structured cabling; deployment of hubs and switches; and the development of other 100 Mb/s LAN technologies, most notably 100 Mb/s Ethernet. Gigabit Ethernet products are also available.

Basic Principles

The key feature of a LAN is use of a shared medium. In its most basic form, a LAN is realized by attaching all devices directly to the transmission medium. Each data packet (or *frame*) transmitted by any station is seen by all the others, each of which examines the destination address field of the packet to determine whether it should receive it (*see* PACKET SWITCHING). As a consequence, such a network does not have to perform any routing. Moreover, this basic LAN is intrinsically capable of supporting broadcast communication by any station to all others. Since there are no switching elements or buffer (*q.v.*) in the network, the only resource for which stations have to contend is the transmission medium itself. All such contention (*q.v.*) and associated buffering takes place in the stations, not the network.

Two of the most common LAN topologies are the *bus* (*q.v.*) and the *ring* (Fig. 1). The two principal designs associated with these topologies, Ethernet and token ring, are described here.

Ethernet

Ethernet was invented by Robert Metcalfe at the Xerox Palo Alto Research Center in 1973. In its simplest form, it uses a single length of coaxial cable, terminated at the ends to prevent signal reflections, to which stations are attached by passive taps that provide multiple access to the medium. A station wishing to transmit a packet first senses the transmission medium to see if another station is transmitting; if not, it begins its own transmission. This is referred to as carrier sense and the terms *carrier*

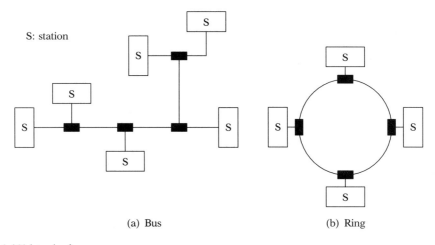

(a) Bus   (b) Ring

Figure 1.   LAN topologies.

sense multiple access (CSMA) and CSMA with *collision detection* (CSMA/CD) are used to describe a class of basic LAN designs that use it. For CSMA/CD to work, packets must be sufficiently long that a station cannot finish transmitting before a collision has been detected. This fundamental design is the basis of the CSMA/CD LAN standardized by IEEE in the 802.3 family of standards.

Token Ring

An alternative scheme for allocating access to the transmission medium is based on the use of a *token*. A station can transmit only while it holds the token. When it finishes transmitting, it passes it to the next station, typically the next (active) station in a physical ring (Fig. 1b). By restricting the maximum amount of data that can be transmitted by a station before the token must be relinquished, it is possible to specify the maximum time that a station may have to wait before being able to transmit. This single fact constitutes the main advantage that token-passing schemes have over Ethernet.

Slotted Techniques

Another way in which access to the transmission medium may be organized is by arranging to have a continuous stream of small frames or *slots* available for use by nodes. Such slots are typically a few tens or hundreds of bits long. Each slot may be marked *full* or *empty*. Any station at which an empty slot arrives may fill it with data, set the source and destination addresses, and mark it *full*. As with frame stripping in the token ring, two schemes are possible for emptying the slot, and the trade-off is between superior ring capacity (slot emptied by receiver), and having low-level acknowledgment (slot emptied by sender). A feature of slotted techniques is the potential for frequent, rapid, and regular access with small variation ("jitter") in these parameters. This makes

the scheme attractive for carrying continuous media traffic. Slotted techniques, which are synchronous, have seen limited exploitation in commercial ring products, but a slotted ring in which the receiver empties the slot has been proposed as an ATM ring standard. A slotted, dual bus technique called *distributed queue dual bus* (DQDB) has been standardized by IEEE in 802.6 for use with a *metropolitan area network* (MAN).

Packet Format

The general format of the packet (frame) used for LANs is shown in Fig. 2. The first item is typically a *preamble*, which indicates the start of the frame; it may also be used to enable the receiver to synchronize. The preamble varies in length from as few as two bits for empty-slot rings, to 64 bits for 10 Mb/s Ethernets. The preamble is followed by destination and source addresses. These may be as short as eight bits, but are more typically 48 bits long. The data carried by the frame may be of fixed length, as for empty-slot rings, or of variable length. In the latter case, the length of the data can be indicated by terminating the frame with a delimiter (*q.v.*) (token bus and ring), by including a length field, or by detecting the end of a frame by the absence of signal (the Ethernet, in effect, uses a combination of the last two). For Ethernet, padding is added at the end of the data field, if necessary, to ensure that the frame size (excluding the preamble) always exceeds the minimum.

Protocols and Standards

LAN standardization has been pursued primarily under the auspices of the IEEE 802 committees and has resulted in a series of standards covering Ethernet, token ring, and token bus LANs, and also the DQDB MAN standard. Owing to the fundamentally different ways in which LANs operate at the link and physical levels of the seven-layer reference model for OSI, an additional sublayer was introduced, known as the *media*

Preamble	Destination	Source	Data	Check

Figure 2.   General format of a LAN frame.

access control (MAC) layer, which forms the lower of two sublayers in the OSI data link layer. It essentially encapsulates the principles of operation for the various forms of LAN described above.

The upper sublayer is called the *logical link control* (LLC) layer. It provides essentially two modes of service: connectionless and connection-oriented. The former just allows stations to exchange single packets, with as much indication about the success or otherwise of the operation as the MAC layer may provide. In connection-oriented mode, its purpose is to set up, maintain, and close down an orderly, flow-controlled, error-free logical link between two stations on a LAN. For synchronous rings, frame synchronization typically relies upon phase-locked loop techniques and requires careful design to achieve stability. The token bus uses coaxial cable and is based on single- or dual-cable broadband cable TV technology.

FDDI uses independent clocks of specified tolerance in each station, defines a maximum frame size, and uses small elastic buffers in each station to compensate for the small differences of clock rate in each station.

High-speed LANs

As LAN transmission speed is increased, the size of a packet relative to the size of the medium decreases. In general, the size of a packet is outside the control of the LAN designer, being determined instead by application requirements and the design and implementation of higher-level protocols. Were it not for this, LAN operating speed could be increased 10 or 100 times by increasing the transmission speed by this factor and using packets 10 or 100 times as large.

100 Mb/s Ethernet (referred to as 100Base-T) is an upgraded form of 10Base-T, the 10 Mb/s 802.3 standard for use with twisted-pair and fiber optic cable, and uses the same minimum packet size, but essentially reduces the maximum size of the network by a factor of 10. Gigabit (1 Gb/s) Ethernet uses not only reduced physical size but also an increased minimum packet size of 512 bytes. To accommodate packets originating from stations operating to 10 or 100 Mb/s standards, packets

shorter than this are extended by carrier signal to the equivalent of 512 bytes.

The token ring design for a LAN does not contain any restriction similar to that of Ethernet. The FDDI LAN, standardized by ANSI, is a 100 Mb/s token ring. By using early token release, it is possible to achieve high utilization even in rings of the order of 100 km in length.

LAN Interconnection

LAN interconnection can take place at a number of levels of the ISO OSI model. Physical layer interconnections are peculiar to each type of LAN and do not exist in every case. Repeaters have been in use for Ethernet or CSMA/CD networks almost since their inception, and provide two basic functions: media conversion among thick coax, thin coax, fiber, and twisted pair cables; and branching to support the (rootless) tree topology used by CSMA/CD networks. *Multiport repeaters*, also known as *hubs*, can have ports to support any combination of media. Such hubs are now common in wiring closets to support twisted-pair connections to offices. A repeater works by retransmitting whatever it receives on one port to all other ports. There is no buffering in a repeater, but extra delay is introduced in the process. Collision indication is also forwarded, since all Ethernet segments connected via repeaters form a single Ethernet or CSMA/CD *collision domain*. Repeaters or hubs commonly detect malfunctions on particular Ethernet segments and isolate that segment to preserve the integrity of the rest of the LAN.

Switched LANs

A *multiport bridge* is also known as a *LAN switch*. Although a switch is substantially more expensive than a basic hub, it has the additional advantages of filtering and interconnecting LANs of different types and speed. In the case of an Ethernet installation, the filtering also separates collision domains. In a switched Ethernet installation using only twisted-pair or optical fiber cables, each host-switch or inter-switch link between two LANs forms a single collision domain. Since such links are point-to-point, it is also possible to operate them in full-duplex mode using fiber optic links.

Logical LANs

The basic LAN is characterized by use of a single, shared medium without routing. For CSMA/CD LANs, this is extended by use of the repeater or hub to several media forming a single LAN having a single collision domain and also a single broadcast or multicast domain: that is, stations may send to all or a selected group of stations by means of a single frame addressed to the broadcast or multicast group address. By introducing bridges or switches, Ethernet collision domains are contained, but the property of a network without conventional routing and having a single broadcast (and multicast) domain is retained; this is sometimes referred to as an extended LAN.

Virtual LANs

VLAN (Virtual LAN) enables stations on the same extended LAN to be partitioned into a number of distinct virtual LANs, each with its own broadcast domain. It is implemented on switches by extending the filtering function already present. A station may be defined to belong to a particular VLAN by its port identifier, by its MAC address, by its level-3 address such as an IP (Internet Protocol) or IPX (Internet Packet eXchange) address, or by protocol, or a combination of these. Apart from broadcast containment, it is also possible to maintain VLAN membership for a system regardless of where it is situated on the extended physical LAN.

Bibliography

1976. Metcalfe, R. M., and Boggs, D. R. "Ethernet: Distributed Packet-switching for Local Computer Networks," *Communications of the ACM*, **19**(7), 395–403.

1996. Peterson, L. L., and Davie, B. S. *Computer Networks: A Systems Approach*. San Francisco: Morgan Kaufmann.

1997. Stallings, W. *Local and Metropolitan Area Networks*, 5th Ed. Upper Saddle River, NJ: Prentice Hall.

Christopher S. Cooper

LOCAL VARIABLE

See GLOBAL AND LOCAL VARIABLES.

LOGIC DESIGN

For articles on related subjects, *see*

+ Arithmetic-Logic Unit (ALU)
+ Boolean Algebra
+ Codes
+ Computer Architecture
+ Computer Circuitry
+ Integrated Circuitry

The term *logic design* refers to the process of specifying an interconnection of logic elements in digital computer hardware. Examples are the design of a circuit that accepts data representing numbers in a Gray code and converts this data into a binary-coded decimal (BCD) representation, and the specification of the gates and interconnections required to implement the arithmetic-logic unit of a computer.

Digital logic networks operate on signals that are restricted to two possible values only, and are thus called *binary* values. For some binary networks, it is possible to specify the desired performance by means of a *table of combinations* (also called a *truth table*), as shown in Table 1, which lists each possible combination of binary signals on the inputs to the network and the corresponding combination of desired output signals.

In Table 1, (a) shows the table of combinations for a network having one input and one output. The output of this network will have a signal representing the zero value on it whenever the input signal represents a 1, and will have an output signal representing a 1 value whenever the input signal has a zero. Such a network is called an *inverter*, and the symbol used to represent it is shown in Fig. 1a. An inverter is one of the basic building blocks from which more complex logic networks are constructed. Other basic building blocks, or *elementary*

Table 1.   Tables of combinations for elementary gates.

(a) Inverter		(b) AND gate		
Input	Out put	Inputs		Out put
A	A′	A	B	AB
0	1	0	0	0
1	0	0	1	0
		1	0	0
		1	1	1

(c) OR gate			(d) XOR (exclusive OR) gate		
Inputs		Output	Inputs		Output
A	B	A+B	A	B	A⊕B
0	0	0	0	0	0
0	1	1	0	1	1
1	0	1	1	0	1
1	1	1	1	1	0

(e) NAND (not AND) gate			(f)NOR (not OR) gate		
Inputs		Output	Inputs		Output
A	B	$\overline{AB}$	A	B	$\overline{A+B}$
0	0	1	0	0	1
0	1	1	0	1	0
1	0	1	1	0	0
1	1	0	1	1	0

Note: See Figure 1.

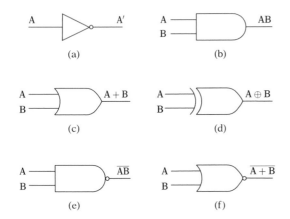

Figure 1.   Elementary gate symbols: (a) inverter; (b) AND gate; (c) OR gate; (d) XOR gate; (e) NAND gate; (f) NOR gate.

gates, are shown in Table 1 as (b), (c), (d), (e), and (f), with the corresponding logic symbols shown in Figs. 1b, 1c, 1d, 1e, and 1f.

The table of combinations for a more complex logic network is shown in Table 2. This network has four input signals and four output signals. If the four input signals appearing on the network inputs represent one decimal digit encoded in the 8-4-2-1 code (i.e. BCD—*see* CODES), the four output signals will represent the encoding of the 9s complement of the input digit. In addition to entries of 1 and 0, there are also entries in this table represented by "d," which stands for "don't care." A table of combinations that contains "don't care" entries is an *incompletely specified table of combinations*.

Table 2.   Table of combinations for generating the 9s complement of a BCD(8421) digit.

	Inputs				Outputs			
	b_8	B_4	b_2	b_1	c_8	c_4	c_2	c_1
(0)	0	0	0	0	1	0	0	1
(1)	0	0	0	1	1	0	0	0
(2)	0	0	1	0	0	1	1	1
(3)	0	0	1	1	0	1	1	0
(4)	0	1	0	0	0	1	0	1
(5)	0	1	0	1	0	1	0	0
(6)	0	1	1	0	0	0	1	1
(7)	0	1	1	1	0	0	1	0
(8)	1	0	0	0	0	0	0	1
(9)	1	0	0	1	0	0	0	0
	1	0	1	0	d	d	d	d
	1	0	1	1	d	d	d	d
	1	1	0	0	d	d	d	d
	1	1	0	1	d	d	d	d
	1	1	1	0	d	d	d	d
	1	1	1	1	d	d	d	d

Note: See Fig. 2.

An incompletely specified table of combinations is actually a representation for a whole family of completely specified tables of combinations that would satisfy the given design requirements. Techniques exist that effectively choose a completely specified table of combinations that leads to the most efficient network design. An efficient network to realize the specifications of Table 2 is shown in Fig. 2.

Networks such that output values at any given instant are dependent solely upon the input values present at the same time are called *combinational logic networks.* The other type of logic network is called a *sequential logic network* or a *sequential circuit.* These networks have the property that their outputs are dependent not only on their present inputs but also on the inputs that may have been present previously.

An example of a sequential circuit is a network whose input is a series of pulses on a single lead and whose outputs display the count modulo n of the number of input pulses. Such a circuit is called a *counter.* Since

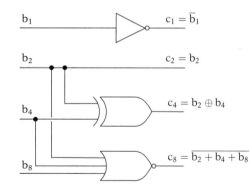

Figure 2.   Network for Table 2.

the output of a sequential circuit at any particular time may depend on previous inputs, there must be contained in the circuit some mechanism for recording some information about these previous inputs. This function is achieved by providing feedback loops in the circuit that are capable of storing information. The most commonly used type of feedback loop consists of

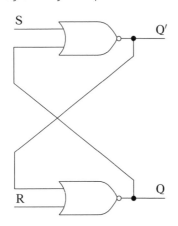

Figure 3. Interconnected NOR gates forming an S-R latch.

two gate elements interconnected as shown in Fig. 3. This type of circuit is called a *set–reset* (S–R) *latch* and operates as follows. The input combination S = R = 1 is not permitted. When input S = 1 and input R = 0, it follows from Table 1(f) that Q′ = 0 and, therefore, Q = 1. Conversely, when S = 0 and R = 1, Q = 0 and Q′ = 1. When the input that was 1 is changed to 0 so that both inputs are zero, the output remains equal to the value it had for the last nonzero input. Thus, when the inputs are both zero, the circuit "remembers" the last nonzero input.

Figure 3 is an example of a whole class of memory elements in which information is stored in interconnected gates. Such elements are known as *latches* or *flip-flops*. *Flow tables* or *state diagrams* or *regular expressions* are used as formal specifications for the action of a sequential circuit.

Classical *switching theory* is concerned with the problem of designing optimum networks that correspond to given formal specifications. Algorithms have been developed for designing networks that contain a minimum number of gates under certain constraints; for example, the condition that there be no more than two gates connected in series between any input and any output. While a great deal of attention has been devoted to the *minimization problem*—that of obtaining minimum element networks—this problem has been solved only for networks having very specific constraints.

General design algorithms with flexible constraints have proved to be very difficult to discover, but it is now possible to use switching theory synthesis techniques to carry out a major portion of the design of new computer systems. The current trend is to specify a system design using a high-level hardware description language (*q.v.*) such as Verilog or VHDL to confirm the correctness of the design by simulation and then to use synthesis programs to derive the gate or transistor level implementations.

Bibliography

1970. Kohavi, Z. *Switching and Finite Automata Theory.* New York: McGraw-Hill.
1986. McCluskey, E. J. *Logic Design Principles.* Upper Saddle River, NJ: Prentice Hall.
1997. Gajski, D. *Principles of Digital Design.* Upper Saddle River, NJ: Prentice Hall.

Edward J. McCluskey

LOGIC PROGRAMMING

For articles on related subjects, see

+ Expert Systems
+ Functional Programming
+ Knowledge Representation
+ Program Verification

PRINCIPLES

Origins

Logic programming emerged in the early 1970s from a convergence of work in the fields of automated theorem proving, artificial intelligence (*q.v.*), and formal languages (*q.v.*). In its simplest form, logic programming may be characterized as the *procedural interpretation* of Horn clauses: a sentence of the form A if B_1 and $B_2 \ldots$ and B_n, $n \geq 0$ can be interpreted as a procedure "to solve problem A, solve subproblems B_1 and $B_2 \ldots$ and B_n. The theorem-proving method that treats such sentences as procedures is called SLD (*SL-resolution for definite clauses*, that is, Horn clauses with exactly one conclusion, "*A*"). Clark (1978) extended the procedural interpretation to allow negative conditions. The resulting theorem-proving method is called SLDNF (*SLD with negation by failure*). SLDNF is the basis for most work in logic programming today. SLDNF is the foundation, not only for Prolog, but for deductive databases, for concurrent logic programming (including such languages as Parlog, concurrent Prolog, and GHC), and for constraint logic programming (including such languages as Prolog 2 and 3, CLP(X), and Chip).

Declarative vs Procedural Knowledge Representation

Arguments over the relative merits of declarative vs procedural knowledge representation were a major theme in artificial intelligence in the 1970s. Logic programming combines declarative and procedural knowledge in the same representation. For example, logic programming automatically converts the declarative statement

> *X* is a potential customer for product *Y*
> > if   *Y* is useful for activity of type *Z*
> > and   *X* has work of type *Z*

into both the procedure

> to   find a potential customer *X* for a given product *Y*,
> find a type of activity *Z* for which *Y* is useful, and
> find an *X* that has work of type *Z*

and the procedure

> to   find a product *Y* for a given potential customer *X*,
> find a type of work *Z* for which *X* has, and
> find a *Y* which is useful for activity of type *Z*.

Depending upon which of *X* and *Y* are given as input and which are to be found as output, one or the other of the two procedures is more appropriate.

The Syntax and Declarative Interpretation of Logic Problems

A *Horn clause logic program* is a collection of statements

> A if B_1 and ... and B_n $n \geq 0$

Each such statement is called a *definite clause*. In the case where $n = 0$, the statement is usually written as a *fact*: A without the implication sign "if." The *conclusion*, A, and the *conditions*, B_i, are *atomic formulas*, which are usually written in the form $p(t_1, \ldots, t_m)$ $m \geq 0$ where p is a *predicate symbol* and the t_i are *terms*, consisting of *variables, constants*, or *function symbols* applied to other terms. In this article, as in most Prolog implementations, variables, for example, X, Y, Fred are distinguished from constants by an initial uppercase letter. This syntax reflects the *declarative interpretation*. A definite clause is understood as a universal statement:

> for all X_1 and ... and X_k
> A if B and ... and B_n

where $X_1, \ldots, X_k$ is a list of all the variables occurring in the statement. Predicate symbols are understood as names of relations, and variable-free terms are understood as names of individuals. Problems to be solved or queries to be answered are posed in the form of a conjunction of conditions

> B_1 and ... and B_n? $n \geq 1$

In the declarative interpretation, such a problem or query is understood as an existential statement

> there exists X_1 and ... and X_k such that
> B_1 and ... and B_n

where $X_1, \ldots, X_k$ is a list of all the variables occurring in the problem. The statement is a *candidate theorem*, to be proved from the collection of statements constituting the program. A proof of the theorem constructs a substitution

> $X_1 = t_1, \ldots, X_k = t_k$

of terms for variables, which constitutes a solution to the problem or an answer to the query.

The Sorting Problem

The sorting problem illustrates some of the subtleties of the relationship between declarative and procedural knowledge representation in logic programming. At the topmost level, the statement

```
sort(X, Y) if permutation(X, Y) and ordered(Y)
```

defines the sorting predicate. The statement has the declarative reading:

```
for all X and Y,
  Y is the result of sorting X if Y is a
    permutation of X and Y is ordered.
```

As a simple case, the variables X and Y can range over all terms that can be constructed from a constant symbol "nil" as the name of the empty list and a two-place function symbol "cons." As in Lisp, the term $cons(s, t)$ names a list whose first element is s followed by the list t. Thus, for example, the term $cons(2, cons(1, nil))$ names the list of numbers 2,1.

Given appropriate definitions of the lower-level predicates, "permutation" and "ordered," the definition of sort can be used to solve such problems as

```
sort(cons(2, cons(1,nil)),Y)?
sort(X, cons(1, cons(2, nil)))?
sort(X, Y) ?
```

The first problem is to find a list Y, which is the result of sorting the list 2,1. It has the unique solution

```
Y = cons(1, cons(2, nil))
```

The second problem is to find a list X which, when sorted, results in the list 1,2. It has two answers

```
X = cons(1, cons(2, nil))
X = cons(2, cons(1, nil)).
```

The third problem is to find all pairs, X, Y, where Y is the result of sorting X. It has infinitely many solutions. Problems of the third kind, where all terms are variables, are especially useful for validating logic programs because they generate all instances of the defined relations.

The Procedural Interpretation

The SLD theorem-proving method treats definite clauses of the form

```
A if B₁ and ... and Bₙ
```

as *procedures*

```
to solve A, solve B₁ and ... and Bn
```

Facts of the form A are treated as procedures that solve problems of the form A without introducing further subproblems. Conditions B_i, whether in queries or in definite clauses, are treated as procedure calls. In theory, procedure calls can be executed in any order and even in parallel. In practice, the order in which they are executed is important for efficiency, and should depend upon the input–output pattern of variables.

Given an initial problem to be solved, the SLD theorem prover searches a tree of possible derivations (or computations) having that problem as root. Every node in the tree has the form

$$B_1 \text{ and } ... \text{ and } B_n? \quad n \geq 0.$$

If $n = 0$, then the branch from the root to the node successfully terminates, solving the problem at the root. If $n \neq 0$, then one of the conditions is selected to be executed as a procedure call. Without loss of generality, by reordering conditions if necessary, we may assume that the selected condition is the first condition B_1. The condition is executed by unifying it with the conclusion of some program clause of the form

$$B \text{ if } C_1 \text{ and } ... \text{ and } C_m$$

A successor node is derived having the form

$$(C_1 \text{ and } ... \text{ and } C_m \text{ and } B_2 \text{ and } ... \text{ and } B_n) \, \theta$$

where θ is the unifying substitution, which is the most general substitution that makes B_1 and B identical.

If no conclusion of a program clause unifies with the selected condition, then there are no successor nodes, and the branch to the node with no successors is said to terminate in failure. If more than one conclusion unifies with the selected condition, then there is a successor node for each such conclusion. In the latter case, the selected condition (or procedure call) is said to be *nondeterministic*. The different procedures whose conclusions unify with the procedure call can be executed in any order and even concurrently or in parallel.

The Procedural Style of Logic Programming

Although the specification of the sorting problem as the problem of finding an ordered permutation is not an efficient program, the following representation of quicksort is:

```
quick(nil, nil)
quick(cons(X,Y),Z ) if
        partition (X,Y,Y₁,Y₂)
        and quick(Y₁,Z₁)
        and quick(Y₂,Z₂)
        and append (Z₁,cons(X,Z₂),Z).
```

Arguably the most natural way to understand the second statement is to interpret it as a procedure:

```
to quicksort a nonempty list, with first
            element X followed by list Y,
                    obtaining result Z,
    partition the list Y
        into the list Y₁ of all elements < X
        and the list Y₂ of all elements ≥ X,
    quicksort Y₁ obtaining result Z₁,
    quicksort Y₂ obtaining result Z₂,
    append Z₁ followed by X, followed by Z₂,
        to obtain Z.
```

This example shows that, although the declarative syntax of logic programs encourages their declarative reading, a programmer is best advised to think first and then and only then program procedurally.

Unification and the Logical Variable

Viewed procedurally, nondeterminism, unification, and the logical variable are possibly the most characteristic features of logic programming. Given a problem of the form

$$B_1 \text{ and } \ldots \text{ and } B_n?$$

with selected procedure call B_1 and a procedure of the form

$$B \text{ if } C_1 \text{ and } \ldots \text{ and } C_m,$$

unification generates a most general substitution θ of terms for variables, such that

$$B_1 \, \theta \; = \; B \, \theta.$$

The unifying substitution θ passes input from the procedure call B_1 to the new procedure calls $C_1, \ldots, C_m$. It simultaneously passes output from the conclusion B to the old procedure calls B_2 and $\ldots$ and B_n. The output may contain (logical) variables. Consider, for example, the recursive program

```
member (X, cons(X, Y))
member (X, cons(Z, Y)) if member (X, Y)
```

which defines the membership relation between elements and lists.

Given the procedure call

```
member (2, cons(1, cons(2, nil)))?
```

SLD uses the second procedure to replace the call by the new call

```
member (2, cons (2, nil))?
```

and uses the first procedure to solve the new call, without introducing further subproblems. All unifying substitutions in this example pass input from procedure calls to procedures.

Given, on the other hand, the procedure call

```
member (X, cons(1, cons (2, nil)))?
```

the first procedure solves the call with output X = 1 and the second procedure, followed by the first, solves the call with output X = 2.

Negation by Failure

An important example of procedural knowledge representation in logic programming is the interpretation of negative, variable-free conditions, *not* A, as holding when the attempt to show the corresponding positive condition, A, finitely fails. In general, a problem A *finitely fails* if (and only if) every branch of an SLDNF search tree having A as its root terminates in failure. Otherwise, *not* A finitely fails if A succeeds. Much research in logic programming has been devoted to finding an appropriate, declarative meaning for such *negation by failure*. The earliest and simplest of these, due to Clark, is to interpret each program statement as expressing one clause of the if-half of an implicit if-and-only-if definition of the predicate symbol of the conclusion of the statement.

Deductive Databases

For certain applications a purely declarative representation can be both natural and efficient. Relational databases are a special case. A relational database (*q.v.*) can be regarded as the special case of a logic program where all statements have the form of conclusions without any conditions, variables, or function symbols. For example:

```
father(john, fred)
mother(mary, fred).
```

A *deductive database* can be regarded as a logic program that does not contain function symbols. A typical application of deductive databases is to represent rules and regulations. The following rules, for example, are typical of those that might be used to represent part of a simplified citizenship law:

```
citizen(X, usa)  if     born(X, usa)
citizen(X, usa)  if     not born(X, usa)
                 and    parent(Y, X)
                 and    citizen(Y, usa).
```

Because deductive databases contain no function symbols, their domain of discourse is finite. As a consequence, the problem of determining whether or not a query has an answer is *decidable*.

Integrity Constraints

One of the attractions of logic programming for database applications is that it provides a single uniform language for data, queries, transactions, and integrity constraints. Integrity constraints can be viewed as persistent queries or goals that must always be satisfied, no matter how the database changes over time. As in relational databases, queries and integrity constraints can be arbitrary formulas of first-order logic. In the simplest case, a database update is rejected if it violates an integrity constraint. Consider, for example, a database that contains the fact father (john, fred) together with the integrity constraint

if father$(X_1,$Y$)$ and father$(X_2,$Y$)$ then $X_1 = X_2$.

The update, father (peter, fred), violates the integrity constraint, under the assumption that john $\neq$ peter.

Abductive Logic Programming (ALP)

Whereas ordinary logic programming uses deduction to derive consequences C from programs P, abduction generates hypotheses H such that $P \cup H$ imply C. For example, given the program

```
grass is wet if rain
grass is wet if sprinkler
```

and the consequence

```
grass is wet
```

abduction generates the two alternative hypotheses

```
    rain
or  sprinkler.
```

The hypotheses generated by abduction can be used to update the current state of the logic program. Like external updates, such internally generated updates may be constrained by integrity constraints.

Default Reasoning and Extended Logic Programming

Negation by failure is commonly used to implement default reasoning. For example, the following statements express that, by default, all birds fly, but ostriches and penguins do not:

```
fly(X) if bird(X) and not nofly(X)
nofly(X) if ostrich(X)
nofly(X) if penguin(X).
```

Here the predicate nofly(X) represents the negation of the predicate fly(X).

In *extended logic programming*, nofly(X) can be expressed directly as the negation of the positive predicate fly(X) using an explicit negation, ¬ different from negation by failure:

```
fly(X) if bird(X) and not ¬fly(X)
¬fly(X) if ostrich(X)
¬fly(X) if penguin(X).
```

The combination of the two negations provides a natural way of expressing the English phrase "unless the contrary can be shown."

Constraint Logic Programming (CLP)

Constraint logic programming (CLP) shares with abduction and negation by failure the property that certain conditions are not solved by backward problem-reduction, but are treated as hypotheses that need to satisfy certain constraints. In CLP, these constraints are "built-in" and implemented by means of specialized algorithms. A typical example of such a constraint predicate and associated algorithm is the inequality predicate and the simplex algorithm. Some CLP languages allow the programmer to specify integrity constraints, as "constraint handling rules."

Metalogic Programming

Metalogic is the use of logic to reason about linguistic and logical entities. Metalogic programming is the use of logic programming for this purpose. A common example of such reasoning is the implementation of metainterpreters, which define (and implement) some "object level" language. The so-called "vanilla metainterpreter," which implements Horn clause logic programming in itself, is one of the simplest examples:

```
demo(P,X) if clause(P,X if Y) and demo(P,Y)
demo(P,X and Y) if demo(P,X) and demo(P,Y).
```

Here demo(P, X) expresses that X can be derived (or demonstrated) from the program P, and clause(P, X if Y) expresses that X if Y is a clause in the program P.

Bibliography

1978. Clark, K. L. "Negation as Failure," in *Logic and Data Bases* (eds. H. Gallaire, and J. Minker), 293–322. New York: Plenum Press.

1994. Doets, K. *From Logic to Logic Programming.* Cambridge, MA: MIT Press.

1998. Marriott, K., and Stuckey, P. J. *Programming with Constraints: An Introduction.* Cambridge, MA: MIT Press.

Robert Kowalski

LANGUAGES

Overview

The SLD and SLDNF schemes described in the companion article are abstract evaluators for Horn clause logic programs. Logic programming languages, such as Prolog, are restricted implementations of such abstract evaluators, augmented with a wide range of primitive predicates. The changes made in moving from the abstract SLDNF evaluator to Prolog are analogous to those made in moving from the lambda calculus to Lisp (*q.v.*). The primitives invoke routines written in machine code or C (*q.v.*). Some of them are just efficient implementations of relations that could be defined using Horn clauses.

Some Logic Programming Languages
Prolog

The name "Prolog," the backtracking search, and strict left to right evaluation of calls, are all inherited from the first interpreted implementation of Prolog by Colmerauer's research group at the University of Aix-Marseille in 1972. The syntax and most of the standard set of primitives of current commercial Prologs derive from the 1977 Edinburgh University compiler re-implementation by David H. Warren and colleagues. Clocksin and Mellish (1994) was the first of many text-books on Prolog.

Syntax

Everything in Prolog is a *term*. A term is a number, an atom, a variable or a compound term of the form f(t1,..,tn), $n > 0$, where f is an atom and t1,..,tn are terms. The f is the functor of the term. Atoms are alphanumeric, symbolic, or quoted. Alphanumeric atoms begin with a lower-case letter.

```
Apple   tom   bill_gates      are alphanumeric atoms
+    *     ^^     ++    :    -    !   are symbolic atoms
'X'   'Tom'   'hello there'       are quoted atoms
```

Variable names are alphanumeric character sequences beginning with an *uppercase letter* or with _.

    Tom   _2 Man_in_Charge   are variable names

Operators

Prolog has an operator precedence (*q.v.*) syntax. Atoms can be declared as associative or nonassociative, prefix, postfix or infix operators. Atoms such as > < * + :-, are predefined infix operators. With operators, compound terms such as > (X,Y) can be written as X>Y, and normal arithmetic expressions such as 2*X+6 can be used instead of +(*(2,X),6).

Clauses

In Prolog, a clause is an atom or a compound term. (When written in a program it must be followed by a full stop immediately followed by a white space character—space, tab or newline.) If the compound term has :- as outermost functor, it is a clause with preconditions. The :- is read as "if," and commas separating the preconditions are read as "and."

Program 1

```
Parent of (mary,fred).        Is male (john).
parent_of(john,fred).
father_of(F,C) :- parent_of(F,C),
                              is_male(F).
grand_parent_of(Gp,Gc):- parent_of(Gp,P),
                          parent_of(P,Gc).
sibling_of(C1,C2):-  parent_of(P,C1),
                  parent_of(P,C2),not C1=C2.
```

The first three clauses are facts. The last three are rules defining the father_of/2, grand_parent_of/2 and sibling_of/2 relations. (The p/n notation is used to indicate the number of arguments n.) The facts about father_of/2 and is_male/1 can be viewed as the tuples of a relational database (*q.v.*). Usually, we would have many more such facts in the program, and more rules for other relations such as mother_of/2, ancestor_of/2, grand_father_of/2 etc.

Because :- and, are predefined infix operators, the rule for father_of/2 is the compound term

```
':-'(father_of(F,C),
    ','(parent_of(F,C),is_male(F))).
```

(Operators such as ':-' and ',' need to be quoted when used as prefix functors.) The fact that clauses are just terms of a certain form is important for *meta-level* programming.

Lists

There is a special syntax for list terms.

[2,3,4]	instead of cons(2,cons(3,cons(4,nil)))
[X]	pattern of a list with *exactly* one member X
[X|T]	pattern of a list with *at least* one member X—will match [2] with T=[]
[2,V|T]	pattern of a list starting with 2, followed by another element V, followed by tail list T

In list patterns, the | is read as "followed by."

Prolog query evaluation

Prolog's backtracking search and left to right evaluation of calls means that the query

    father_of(X,fred)

to Program 1 will be evaluated as follows. First it will be reduced using the only clause for father_of/2 to the conjunction

    parent_of(X,fred),is_male(X).

The first call will now be selected and the clauses for parent_of/2 will be unified with the call in turn, in the order in which they are written in the program. The call will unify with the first clause, making X = mary. As the clause has no preconditions, this solves the call. Prolog now tries to solve

    is_male(mary)

which fails to unify with the single is_male/1 clause. This causes Prolog to backtrack to try the next clause for father_of/2 in order to find an alternative solution for father_of(X,fred). This gives the binding X =john. The second call is now is_male(john) which does unify with the is_male/1 clause. X =john is the solution to the query.

Other logical features of prolog

In addition to negation of calls, implemented as negation as failure, Prolog has disjunction, a `forall` construct, and primitives for wrapping up all the solutions to a query as a list.

Program 2

```
person(P) :-   male(P) ; female(P)
          % ; is the disjunction operator
ordered(L) :-
   forall(adjacent_on(X,Y,L),X=<Y)
           % alternative defn of ordered
children_of(P,L) :-
   setof(C,parent_of(P,C),L)
          % L is a list of all children of P.
```

The `children_of/2` definition of Program 2 is very powerful, for it can be used even if P is not given. A query `children_of(P,L)` will find each parent P in the database, and for each such P bind L to a lexically ordered list of names of their recorded children. The term `setof/3` even removes duplicates if there are any.

Prolog II

Colmerauer's team modified their original Prolog into a variant language, Prolog II. There are minor syntactic differences between it and standard Prolog. The user cannot declare operators, `->` is used instead of `:-`, clauses are terminated with a semicolon rather than a period (full stop), and the variable/nonvariable convention is reversed. However, the major differences are in the operational and logical semantics.

Prolog III

Prolog III (Colmerauer 1990) extends Prolog II in having a far richer set of constraint primitives. In addition to =, the inequalities >, <, =<, >=, will automatically delay if either argument is unbound. The delayed call is added to the set of delayed constraint calls. Linear arithmetic equations such as $2X+ 5Y = 45$, are also handled as constraints rather than as normal calls. If neither side of the equation contains unbound variables, each side will be evaluated and compared, and the call will succeed or fail. If there is only one unbound variable, the equation will be algebraically solved to find

its value. Otherwise the call is delayed and added to the set of delayed linear equations. Each time a constraint is added to a set of delayed constraints, and each time a variable appearing in any of them is bound by the normal evaluation, the delayed constraints are checked for consistency or partial solvability.

Eclipse

This is a primarily a finite domain constraint logic programming (CLP) language. Program 3 is an example Eclipse program. It is a program to find a three-color coloring for a map of four countries represented by the variables C1, C2, C3, and C4. Adjacent countries cannot have the same color.

The `::` condition specifies that C1, C2, C3, and C4 each have the same finite domain and that they can have as value only one of the symbols blue, red, and yellow. The topology is specified by the `##` conditions. `C##C'` means that the assigned values for C and C' must be disjoint. So, country C1 borders countries C2, C3 and C4, C2 borders C3, and C3 borders C4. A `##` call automatically suspends until either variable is assigned a value. As soon as one of them has a value, this value is removed from the domain of the other variable and the call succeeds. Finally, a variable can only be given a value, by an `assign_color/1` call, if that value is in its current domain. Thus, as the evaluation moves through the sequence of `assign_color/1` calls, the domains for C2, C3 and C4 are progressively narrowed, eliminating a lot of backtracking search.

Program 3

```
color_map(C1,C2,C3,C4) :-
   [C1,C2,C3,C4] :: [blue,red,yellow],
   C1##C2, C1##C3, C1##C4, C2##C3, C3##C4,
   assign_color(C1),assign_color(C2),
   assign_color(C3),assign_color(C4).

assign_color(C) :-  C=blue; C=red; C=yellow.
```

Bibliography

1986. Giannesini, F., Kanoui, H., Pasero, P., and van Caneghem, M. *Prolog*. Reading, MA: Addison-Wesley.

1990. Colmerauer, A. "An Introduction to Prolog III," *Communications of the ACM*, **33**(7), 69–90.

1994. Clocksin, W. F., and Mellish, C. S. *Programming in Prolog*, 4th Ed. New York: Springer-Verlag.

Keith L. Clark

LOGIC, COMPUTER

See LOGIC DESIGN.

LOGO

For articles on related subjects, *see*

+ Computer-Assisted Learning and Teaching
+ Functional Programming
+ Lisp
+ List Processing: Languages

Logo, a name derived from the Greek word $\lambda o \gamma o \varsigma$, meaning "word," is a dialect of Lisp designed for educational use. Logo is a general-purpose programming language with special emphasis on symbolic computing and functional programming. Three things give Logo its special educational focus: a simplified syntax, detailed attention to the programmer's metaphors for computational processes in the naming of primitive procedures and the wording of error messages, and a collection of application areas that combine inherent interest with open-ended intellectual content.

The first version of Logo was developed in 1967 at Bolt, Beranek, and Newman, Inc., by Wallace Feurzeig, Seymour Papert, and others. The project grew out of their experience teaching junior high school students with a more conventional algebraic programming language. Many students were uninspired by the numeric emphasis, so a language was designed with tools to manipulate English words and sentences. Papert later established a Logo research group at MIT, where the language was redesigned.

Educational Goals

The goal of the Logo developers was to provide an environment for mathematical thinking in the context of concrete projects. Developmental psychologist Jean Piaget argued that people learn mainly by *construction*—fitting new ideas with already understood ideas. Much of traditional school mathematics is abstract and disconnected from a child's ordinary experience, so this incremental learning process is difficult. Writing a computer program gives the learner practice in formal, mathematical reasoning, but each Logo application area is connected with things children do outside the context of computers or mathematics.

For example, consider the difference between Logo's turtle graphics and the Cartesian graphics traditionally used in other languages. In the latter, a fixed pair of coordinate axes is associated with the display screen; a line segment is drawn by specifying the coordinates of its end points. In Logo, the metaphor is that segments are drawn by a pen controlled by a robot turtle. At any moment this turtle is in some position and facing in some direction; a segment is drawn by moving or turning relative to this position and heading. Since absolute coordinates are not used, a single procedure can draw a given shape anywhere and in any orientation. The way the turtle moves in drawing some shape is the same way that a person would move in walking over that shape on the floor. The ability to draw a picture at any position and heading is particularly convenient for the exploration of fractals (*q.v.*), in which an overall picture is made by including several smaller versions of the same picture (*see* Fig. 1).

Logo Syntax

Each Lisp expression represents the application of a procedure to arguments; the notation is a list in parentheses, in which the first element is the procedure and the other elements are the arguments, which are themselves Lisp expressions in the same form. Logo expressions have the same logical structure, but the notation is more relaxed. Parentheses are not required for every procedure call, and

```
TO TREE :SIZE :LEVEL
IF :LEVEL=0 [STOP]
FORWARD :SIZE/3
LEFT 20
TREE 2*:SIZE/3 :LEVEL-1
RIGHT 20
FORWARD :SIZE/6
RIGHT 15
TREE :SIZE/2 :LEVEL-1
LEFT 15
FORWARD :SIZE/4
LEFT 15
TREE 2*:SIZE/3 :LEVEL-1
RIGHT 15
FORWARD :SIZE/8
RIGHT 10
TREE :SIZE/3 :LEVEL-1
LEFT 10
FORWARD :SIZE/8
BACK :SIZE
END
```

Figure 1. An example of a Logo program for a fractal tree and its output.

conventional infix notation is allowed for arithmetic operators:

```
TO FACTORIAL :N
IF :N = 0 [OUTPUT 1]
OUTPUT :N * FACTORIAL (:N-1)
END
```

Despite the difference in notation, Logo maintains the Lisp idea that everything is done by procedure calls. For example, the word IF in the procedure above is not a special syntactic keyword as it would be in most languages. It is an invocation of the IF procedure with two arguments. The first argument must have the value TRUE or the value FALSE. The second argument is a list (indicated by the square brackets) containing instructions that will be carried out if the first argument is TRUE. The colon in :N above (pronounced "dots N") indicates that the value of a variable is wanted. A name without the colon requests calling the procedure with that name. Logo makes this distinction because certain names, such as LIST, are both popular variable names and primitive procedure names. OUTPUT does not mean "print"; it specifies the procedure's return value and ends the procedure call, like return in C (*q.v.*).

In Lisp, every procedure is a function that returns a value. The use of procedures that make permanent changes in the environment (such as assigning a value to a variable) is possible but discouraged. Logo does support this functional programming style (the FACTORIAL procedure above is an example), but a distinction is made between *operations* (procedures that return a value) and *commands* (procedures called for effect), like the distinction between functions and procedures in Pascal (*q.v.*). In most other respects Logo follows traditional Lisp ideas.

Attention to Computational Metaphors

Logo teachers use the metaphor of "teaching the computer" to describe procedure definition. The keyword that announces a definition is TO, rather than Lisp's DEFINE, to suggest the sentence "I'm going to teach you how TO SORT" (or TO DIFFERENTIATE, or TO AVERAGE). The keyword TO suggests that the procedure name is a verb, as befits an action we are teaching the computer.

The attention to metaphor extends beyond the choice of names. One application of Logo is in natural-language processing; an English sentence is represented as a list of words. As in Lisp, the underlying selection operations that can be applied to a list are to select the first element of a list or all but the first element. (Lisp calls these CAR and CDR; Logo calls them FIRST and BUTFIRST.) In Logo, however, the same operations can also be used to extract the first letter, or all but the first letter, of a word. It is natural to use the same tools to manipulate words and sentences, even though the representations inside the computer are different. The rules for forming the plural of an English word depend on its last letter or letters. Here is a partial implementation:

```
TO PLURAL :WORD
IF MEMBERP LAST :WORD [O S X]
                [OUTPUT WORD :WORD "ES]
IF EQUALP LAST :WORD "Y
   [IF NOT MEMBERP LAST BUTLAST :WORD
                             [A E I O U]
      [OUTPUT WORD BUTLAST :WORD "IES]]
OUTPUT WORD :WORD "S
END
```

This says that a word ending in O, S, or X forms its plural by adding ES; a word ending in Y forms its plural by changing the Y to IES unless the letter before the Y is a vowel; otherwise, the plural is formed by adding S.

Bibliography

1980. Papert, S. *Mindstorms: Computers, Children, and Powerful Ideas.* New York: Basic Books.

On technical details:

1997. Harvey, B. *Computer Science Logo Style, Volume 1: Symbolic Computing*, 2nd Ed. Cambridge, MA: MIT Press.

Brian Harvey

Figure 1. Augusta Ada Byron. (Courtesy of the Mary Evans Picture Library.)

LOVELACE, COUNTESS OF

For articles on related subjects, *see*

+ Analytical Engine
+ Babbage, Charles
+ Difference Engine
+ Digital Computers, History of: Origins

Augusta Ada Byron was born in London on 10 December 1815 (*see* Fig. 1). She was the daughter of Lord Byron and Annabella Milbanke Byron. She married William, Eighth Lord King, in 1835, and three years later, on his elevation to an Earldom, became the Countess of Lovelace, and hence Lady Lovelace.

Ada was educated by governesses and tutors, and later by much self-study. Augustus De Morgan, professor at the University of London, helped her in her advanced studies, and formed a very high opinion of her abilities. Her correspondence with contemporary scientists, such as Michael Faraday, Mary Somerville, and Sir John Herschel, reveals her deep interest in varied scientific topics. She was also an accomplished musician.

Lady Lovelace, fascinated by Babbage's machines after first viewing his Difference Engine in 1833, translated L. F. Menabrea's paper on Babbage's Analytical Engine from French into English. Babbage suggested that she add some notes to the translation, which she did with great enthusiasm. Of particular interest is her description of the repeated use of a set of cards with a purpose similar to that of subroutines in today's computer programs. With the help of Babbage, she worked out a nearly complete program to compute Bernoulli numbers. Because of this, she has been called the first female computer programmer and, in 1979, a new language was named Ada (*q.v.*) in her honor.

All her life, Lady Lovelace was plagued by ill health. She died on 27 November 1852, just before her 37th birthday.

Bibliography

1843. Taylor, R. (ed.) "Lovelace, Ada, Countess of. Sketch of the Analytical Engine Invented by Charles Babbage, Esq. by L. F. Menabrea, of Turin, Officer of the Military Engineers: With Copious Notes by the Translator," *Scientific Memoirs*, Vol. III, 666–731. London: R. & J. E. Taylor; (Reprinted in 1953. Bowden, B. V. *Faster Than Thought*. London: Sir Isaac Pitman & Sons).

1980. Huskey, V. and Huskey, H. "Lady Lovelace and Charles Babbage," *Annals of the History of Computing*, **2**(4), (October), 299–329.

1999. Woolley, B. *The Bride of Science: Romance, Reason and Byron's Daughter*. London: Macmillan.

Velma R. Huskey

M

MACHINE- AND ASSEMBLY-LANGUAGE PROGRAMMING

For articles on related subjects, *see*

Machine Language

Machine language (ML) has traditionally meant that particular representation of instructions and data that is directly usable by the central processing unit (*q.v.*) of the machine in question. It is a *low-level* language—indeed, the lowest possible—since it reflects the machine's internal structure. ML is that programming language that is directly executable by the CPU of some specified machine, and whose typical statement consists of a single operator/operand(s) pair. Each operand of such a statement (instruction) is typically an address—that is, a binary integer designating one of the storage elements called either *words* or *bytes*. *Byte* is the usual term for a segment designed to hold one 8-bit alphanumeric character; *word* is usually reserved for the addressable segments of machines specialized for numerical computation, and hence is anywhere from 8 to 64 bits long, with 32 being common. For convenience, we will use the term "word" hereafter when referring to an addressable memory segment.

The operator part of an ML statement will typically call for (1) a dyadic arithmetic or logical operation upon the contents of the addressed word and any of the CPU registers in which these operations can be carried out; or (2) the movement of contents between one of these registers and a word; or (3) the movement of contents between a register, or word, and one of the machine's I/O devices. The bit pattern in an addressed word will, if the operator is an ordinary arithmetic one, be treated as the representation of a scalar quantity in base 2 (or an integral power of 2, such as octal or hexadecimal).

Some machines offer *multiple-address* instructions—that is, instructions that include the addresses of two or more operands, such as the augend and addend of an addition operation. Also, many machines offer some instructions whose operands are *immediate*—that is, they are themselves the data to be operated on, not the address of that data. Other instructions interpret their address fields in just the opposite way: practicing *indirect addressing*, they take the value in that field not as the address of the data, but as the address of the address of the data. Many instructions can be *indexed*; that is, they contain a field that can be used to designate some *index register* whose contents are to modify the value initially specified in the address field (the "apparent address") into a value that is actually to be used at execution (the "effective address").

Finally, all machines include instructions, variously called *jumps*, *transfers*, or *branches*, whose purpose is to cause the machine executing them to depart from a strictly sequential order of execution. Some jumps are absolute (unconditional): when executed, they always force program execution to continue at the programmer-specified point in the program, rather than at the normal point, the next instruction following the jump itself. Other jumps are conditional: they change the order of instruction execution only if the result of some test satisfies a specified condition.

Assembly Language

ML is not a convenient language for human use. During the 1950s, more congenial notations arose along with programs for translating them into ML. In doing so, they created not only assembly language (AL), but also founded that large branch of computer science and software development that is devoted to improving the *user interface* (q.v.).

The earliest assemblers were little more than routines for translating some more convenient representation of ML instructions into ML proper, with none of the additional features now expected in AL as a matter of course. The primitive assembler offered the programmer at most a symbolic representation of operators—"ADD" instead of 000101000000, for example, with decimal or octal representation of operand addresses—or just octal representation of the entire instruction—05050000003770 instead of 36 bits. But a modern AL is a fully symbolic language: one in which all operators and virtually all operands are normally represented by names chosen for their explanatory and mnemonic power. Some of these names, particularly those for the operators, will have been chosen by the AL designer; operands are left for the user to name, and the names chosen are typically restricted as to their length in characters.

Example of AL

Here is a tiny AL program:

```
CLA  AUGEND ; (AC)  <- (AUGEND)
ADD  ADDEND ; (AC)  <- (AC) + (ADDEND)
STO  SUM    ; (SUM) <- (AC)
```

in which AC stands for Accumulator, (..) means "contents of" the enclosed operand address, and comments follow the semicolons.

Among the substantive new features offered by an assembler are those that allow data to be introduced in octal, decimal, hexadecimal, character-string, and other "natural" forms; that reserve execution-time storage space; that produce a printed, cross-indexed listing of the program.

The way in which the operand names used in the example would be defined is through the use of one or another assembler feature. These features are usually called *pseudo-operations*, since they look, in their AL representation, like the AL representation of actual operation codes (or instructions), but are really artifacts introduced by the assembler. They are directives to the assembler as to how it is to do its job. The distinction between pseudo-ops and real instructions is analogous to that between an author's marginal notes to a typist ("double-space the next paragraph"), and the content of the manuscript to be typed. The *symbolic addresses* AUGEND, ADDEND, and SUM, for example, would have been assigned their respective values by means of pseudo-ops like these:

```
AUGEND   PZE   0
ADDEND   DEC 173
SUM      PZE   0
```

where "PZE" is a pseudo-op standing for "Plus ZEro," meaning that the word in question is to contain the machine's representation of plus zero, and that any symbol to its left is to be recorded as the symbolic name of that word. The pseudo-op "DEC" directs the assembler to interpret the number that follows it as a decimal number, and to put the binary representation of that number in the word being reserved.

Each of the names so assigned to a word, or memory location, is entered into a *symbol table* created by the assembler as it does its job, along with the numeric address of the location to which it has been assigned. Whenever the assembler encounters a symbolic address in the program, it substitutes the numeric equivalent of that symbol. By doing so, it frees programmers to use a symbol (e.g. AUGEND) that is meaningful to them (and to others who may read the program) and leaves it to the assembler to see that AUGEND is replaced by its binary equivalent throughout the ML program that the assembler will produce.

The most important advantage of programming symbolically rather than in bit patterns is the control it gives the programmer over *binding*: the act of reducing a variable or expression in the program to an explicit, fixed value. Symbolic programming allows the programmer to defer such binding and leave appropriate parts of the program on a generalized, somewhat abstract level until it is convenient to make them specific.

If the program computes a payroll, for example, the fact that AL will encourage the programmer to represent a tax rate throughout it as TAXRATE rather than as 17.25%, and allow it to be numerically defined just once, by use of a DEC pseudo-op, will not only make the program easier to write, but will also allow it to survive a change in the tax rate at no greater cost than a reassembly with a new definition of TAXRATE.

The final assignment of a computable value to a program is called *binding*, and the moment of its occurrence, *binding time*. The degree of control over binding offered by a multipass assembler working in conjunction with a linking loader (*see* LINKERS AND LOADERS) and an operating system (*q.v.*) is substantial. Symbols can be defined in terms not only of final numeric values, but of elaborate expressions containing other symbols that may themselves be as yet undefined, to form an indefinitely deep regression, with the resolution of the most primitive layer of symbols deferred until the end of the source program, or even, in the limit, to load or execution time.

A linking loader prepared to handle object programs (*q.v.*) in which so much binding remains to be done is misnamed, in fact, since its loading function is by this point incidental. It is actually the last (and sometimes the longest) pass of the assembler it works with, and its use amounts to a "load-and-go" concept in which final assembly is followed immediately by loading and execution, rather than simply the production of an object program that is to be executed only when the programmer so orders.

Subroutines and Macroinstructions

The occasion for creating a *subroutine* arises when a programmer notices that essentially the same routine (e.g. one that converts external representation numerals to an internal computable form) has been written over and over, possibly with minor variations. Creating a subroutine for the function in question will obviate the need ever to do it again. Once created, a subroutine need only be assembled along with a calling AL program (or loaded with its object program) to be available as often as needed throughout that program. At whatever points in the program the function performed by the subroutine is required, a *calling sequence* (*q.v.*) to the subroutine is inserted by the programmer, and a transfer to it will be made when that point is reached in program execution. After the subroutine has been executed, a return jump from it is made to a point some fixed number of words from the most recent call, and the calling program resumes.

Like the subroutine, the *macro* is a way of packaging common routines for later use, but the conventions governing both its creation and its use differ greatly from those of the subroutine. The root of the difference is that the macro facility is usually embedded within an assembler (yielding a macroassembler). The macroassembler is given as input a source program consisting of a mixture of macros and AL statements, transforms the macros into AL, and assembles the extended source code. The consequent differences between programming with macros and with subroutines may be summarized under three heads: locus of creation, form of call, and code-generating economy.

Locus of Creation

A new macro can be created, or defined, at any point in any program that will be processed by a macroassembler or macroprocessor. Since the macro assembler is put into a special macro-defining mode when it encounters a macro definition, the creation of a macro generates no instructions in the program; only an explicit invocation of the macro does that.

A subroutinized version of the miniature program given earlier, for example, would take a form like this:

```
TRISUM    CLA*    1,4
          ADD*    2,4
          STO*    3,4
          TRA     4,4
```

In this (trivial) subroutine, to which we have given the name TRISUM, some new programming features are used. The addresses of the four instructions refer respectively to the first, second, third, and fourth words following the instruction that will be used to call TRISUM. The 4 following the comma in each of these instructions is the designation of an *index register* (*q.v.*), a specialized register, one of whose principal uses is to record the location of an instruction calling on a subroutine. Its action is such that an address within the subroutine of the form "$n, 4$" will refer to the nth location following that calling instruction.

Another item of notation new to this example is the * following each of the first three instructions, denoting *indirect* use of the address that follows in each case. This means that the assembler is being directed to interpret the address (first modified if necessary by any index register used) as the location not of the data, but of the address of the data. Accordingly, the interpretation of CLA* 1,4 is "Bring to the accumulator the quantity whose address is located one word below that in which the instruction calling on this subroutine is located." Using the calling sequence in (2) as an example, the quantity specified would be that whose address was in LOCA.

An equivalent macro would take a form like this:

```
TRISUM    MACRO   A,B,C
          CLA     A
          ADD     B                          (1)
          STO     C
```

The first line of this macro definition declares that TRISUM is its name, and that this name, when used to call the macro, will be accompanied by three values—*parameters*—that are to replace A, B, and C—the dummy parameters, or just *dummies*—respectively, wherever those dummies occur in the definition.

Form of Call

The subroutine is traditionally called by a stereotyped series of AL instructions—see (2)—known as a *calling*

sequence. This consists of (1) an instruction that jumps to the subroutine while recording its own location (in index register 4, in our example machine) so that the subroutine will know how to reach back for parameters, and where to return to the calling program when it is done; (2) a number of words reserved for the parameters that are to be passed to the subroutine with each call; and (3) one or more locations for the subroutine to transfer back to when it has completed execution, depending on the number of exit conditions that its author has decided to distinguish and handle separately. This is the general form; each subroutine will have its own specific calling sequence requirements, and it is the responsibility of the subroutine user to construct a correct calling sequence for each call upon a subroutine. An example of a simple calling sequence:

```
TSX    TRISUM, 4
PZE    LOCA
PZE    LOCB                                   (2)
PZE    LOCC
(return location)
```

The first of these instructions, TSX (Transfer and Set indeX), is the special transfer instruction referred to earlier that transfers control to TRISUM while marking its own location in an index register (4, in this case). The three PZE pseudo-ops that follow are simply placeholders whose function is to hold in their address fields the addresses at which parameters A, B, and C can be found by the subroutine. Each call upon the subroutine would then cost the execution time of the TSX and the return transfer at the end of the subroutine, plus the storage space for these two instructions and the three PZEs.

To call the functionally equivalent TRISUM macroinstruction, the programmer simply uses its name as if it were an ordinary AL operation code. A simple call on TRISUM would take the form:

```
TRISUM ALPHA, BETA, GAMMA
```

where ALPHA, BETA, and GAMMA are the values the user wants inserted into the code wherever A, B, and C appears in the macro's definition. The macroprocessor would make these substitutions, and generate into the program, at the point where the user called the macro, the instructions:

```
CLA  ALPHA
ADD  BETA
STO  GAMMA
```

Code-generating Economy

The macroinstruction and the subroutine differ most obviously in that each use of a macro causes a fresh copy of its defining instructions to be inserted into the text of the program being generated, while a subroutine appears in the program using it just once, no matter how often called.

The economics of programming is such that the advantage sometimes lies with generating the substantive code as many times as it is to be executed, sometimes with generating only multiple calling sequences to a single copy of that code. The decision will hinge on such considerations as the length of the calling sequence vs that of the routine to be executed, and the relative importance of memory and time during execution.

Applications of AL

Beyond the general grounds for the survival and flourishing of AL/ML lie several specific roles for which it seems uniquely well-suited. Among these, four are worth noting: fine tuning, machine exploitation, pioneering, and craftsmanship.

Fine Tuning

Because only AL/ML programmers directly choose the machine-language instructions that are to be executed and the bit-by-bit internal representation of the data upon which they are to operate, they alone can guarantee that a program will fit within a given chunk of memory, or execute within a given period of time. They are the only programmers who can plausibly claim that a program has been so written as to occupy the least possible space, or execute as fast as possible.

Machine Exploitation

Machine exploitation refers to its unique ability to permit full access to all features built into a machine, whether ever available through a high-level language or not. Providing such access may be virtually impossible

for these languages, which—again, because of their need to remain machine-independent—cannot refer to any machine facility not common to all on which they are to run. If some, but not all, of the machines on which a compiler is to run include, say, a program-testable clock, then the language cannot offer statements that let users refer to that clock without affecting program portability.

Pioneering

AL is almost always involved when a wholly new computer application is being pioneered, even though it may later turn out not to be needed. When it is uncertain what the demands of a new species of program are going to be, the safest course is to use the language that imposes no constraints.

Craftsmanship

Another reason for the continued use of AL is that programming in that language is widely felt to be the most professional and demanding kind, and many career programmers will seek to use it even when none of the reasons discussed above applies. To a considerable extent, the programmer's private wish to use AL can coincide with the best interests of the installation. No matter how adamant management may be about running a pure Ada (*q.v.*) or C++ (*q.v.*) shop, there must always be a few programmers behind the scenes who can read dumps, help the application programmers with special debugging problems, understand the operating system (*q.v.*), and deal as equals with the computer manufacturer's systems engineers.

CISC, RISC, and ML's Newest Role

The traditional reason for using ML/AL is saving memory space and execution time by minimizing the amount of code to be executed. But something new has entered the picture with RISC (reduced instruction set computing) architecture. Assembly-language operation codes were traditionally chosen with at least one eye on the convenience of programmers; they were designed to accommodate the limitations of programmers, and this indulgence of human weakness made them less amenable to computer interpretation and execution.

RISC architecture represents a refusal to make that compromise, and a decision to adopt instead a set of assembly-language instructions optimized for generation by compilers, and efficient execution by the computer. A computer with a more traditional rich instruction set such as the DEC VAX is called a complex instruction set computer (CISC).

Bibliography

1972. Barron, D. W. *Assemblers and Loaders*, 2nd Ed. New York: American Elsevier.

1991. Halpern, M. "On the Heels of the Pioneers: A Memoir of the Not-quite-earliest Days of Programming," *Annals of the History of Computing*, **13**(1), 101–111.

1992. Halpern, M. "Turning Into Silicon: Further Episodes from Programming's Early Days," *Annals of the History of Computing*, **14**(1), 61–69.

Mark Halpern

MACHINE LANGUAGE

See MACHINE- AND ASSEMBLY-LANGUAGE PROGRAMMING.

MACHINE LEARNING

For articles on related subjects, see

+ Artificial Life
+ Expert Systems
+ Genetic Algorithms
+ Pattern Recognition

Machine learning is the study of methods for constructing and improving software systems by analyzing examples of their desired behavior. Machine learning methods are appropriate in application settings where people are unable to provide precise specifications for desired program behavior, but where examples of this behavior are available. Such situations include optical character recognition (OCR–*q.v.*), handwriting recognition, speech recognition (*q.v.*), and automated steering of automobiles. People can perform these tasks quite easily, but cannot articulate exactly *how* they perform them in the detail needed to model them algorithmically.

Machine learning methods are also appropriate for situations where the task changes with time and different users. For example, machine learning methods have been used to assess credit card risk, to filter news articles, to refine information retrieval (*q.v.*) queries, and to predict user behavior in browsing the World Wide Web (*q.v.*). Yet another area of application for machine learning algorithms is to the problem of finding interesting patterns in databases, sometimes called *data mining* (*q.v.*).

Supervised Learning

In *supervised learning*, the goal is to learn the form of a function $y = f(x)$ by analyzing examples of the form (x_i, y_i), where $y_i = f(x_i)$. Each input value x_i is usually an n-dimensional vector, where each dimension and output value is either discrete or real-valued. For example, in optical character recognition, each input value x_i might be a 256-bit vector giving 4-bit pixel values of an 8×8 input image, and each output value y_i might be one of the 95 printable ASCII characters. When, as in this case, the output values are discrete, f is called a *classifier* and the discrete output values are called *classes*.

Alternatively, in credit card risk assessment, each input might be a vector of properties describing the age, income, and credit history of an applicant, and the output might be a real value predicting the expected profit (or loss) of giving a credit card to the applicant. In cases where the output is continuous, f is called a *predictor*.

To design a supervised learning algorithm, one must choose a set of possible functions H that is likely to contain the unknown function f. It is also important to keep H small, because the larger it becomes, the more training examples are needed to learn successfully. Given a training set of examples $\{(x_1, y_1), (x_2, y_2), \ldots, (x_m, y_m)\}$, a learning algorithm will implicitly search H to find a hypothesis $h \in$ H that is estimated to be accurate for predicting the y_j values of new data points x_j. A good way to estimate the predictive accuracy of a hypothesis h is to see how accurately it classifies examples from the training set of known examples. Hence, most learning algorithms attempt to find an h that minimizes prediction error on the training set.

Reinforced Learning

Reinforced learning problems arise when a computer program must make a sequence of decisions before receiving a reward signal. Imagine a computer playing chess. The computer must make a long sequence of moves before it finds out whether it wins or loses the game. Similarly, in robot navigation, the robot must choose a sequence of actions in order to get from a starting location to some desired goal. We could train computers to play chess or control robots by telling them which move to make at each step. But this is difficult, tedious, and time-consuming. It would be much nicer if computers could learn these tasks from only the final outcome—the win or loss in chess, the success or failure in robot navigation. Reinforced learning algorithms are designed to solve this kind of *learning from delayed reward.*

Reinforced learning algorithms learn a task by performing. Before each move, the algorithm examines the current state, s, of the world (e.g. the current board position in a chess game) and then chooses an action (e.g. a particular move). The action causes the world to change to a new state s'. After each state transition, the computer receives a reward, $R(s')$. In chess, the reward is zero until the end of the game, where it is 1 (win), 0 (draw), or -1 (loss). The goal of reinforced learning is to construct an optimal policy for choosing actions. A policy is a function, π, which maps from states to actions: $a = \pi\ (s)$. An optimal policy is the policy that receives the highest total reward.

Unsupervised Learning

Unsupervised learning algorithms attempt to find structure in a set of data points. Consider, for example, an astronomy project in which the spectra of thousands of stars have been gathered. Each spectrum is a vector of numbers giving the intensity of a star's light at various wavelengths. Can we find patterns in this data? Could we use this data to identify different classes of stars and group the stars into those classes? Unsupervised learning often involves clustering data in this fashion.

One way to do this is to adopt a *generative model* for how the data is generated. For example, the model might say that each spectrum is generated by first choosing a star class at random and then taking the "standard spectrum" for that star class and adding random noise to the light intensities. An unsupervised learning algorithm can then be applied to compute the "standard spectrum" for each class and to estimate the amount of random noise that is being added to generate the data points. Since the goal is to construct a probability distribution that is most likely to have generated the data, unsupervised learning in this instance is a form of probability density estimation.

Bibliography

1994. Kearns, M. J., and Vazirani, U. V. *An Introduction to Computational Learning Theory.* Cambridge, MA: MIT Press.

1996. Bishop, C. M. *Neural Networks for Pattern Recognition.* Oxford: Oxford University Press.

1997. Mitchell, T. *Machine Learning.* New York: McGraw-Hill.

Thomas G. Dietterich

MACHINE TRANSLATION

For articles on related subjects, *see*

+ Artificial Intelligence (AI)
+ Knowledge Representation
+ Natural Language Processing

History

Within a few years of the first appearance of "electronic calculators," research had begun on using computers as aids for translating one natural language into another. The major stimulus was a memorandum of July 1949 by Warren Weaver, who, after mentioning tentative efforts in the United Kingdom (by Andrew Booth and Richard Richens) and in the United States (by Harry Huskey and others), put forward possible lines of research. His optimism stemmed from the wartime success in code-breaking, from developments by Clande Elwood Shannon in *information theory* (*q.v.*), and from speculations about universal principles underlying natural languages. Within a few years, research had begun at many US universities, and in 1954 there was the first public demonstration of the feasibility of machine translation (MT), a collaboration of IBM and Georgetown University. Although using a very restricted vocabulary and grammar, it was sufficiently impressive to stimulate massive funding of machine translation in the United States and to inspire the establishment of MT projects throughout the world.

Optimism remained at a high level for the first decade of research, but disillusion grew as researchers encountered "semantic barriers" for which they saw no straightforward solutions. There were some operational systems—the Mark II system (developed by IBM and Washington University) installed at the USAF Foreign Technology Division, and the Georgetown University system at the US Atomic Energy Authority and at Euratom in Italy—but the quality of output was disappointing. By 1964, the US government sponsors had become increasingly concerned at the lack of progress, and set up the Automatic Language Processing Advisory Committee (ALPAC). It concluded in its 1966 report that MT was slower, less accurate, and twice as expensive as human translation and that "there is no immediate or predictable prospect of useful machine translation."

The ALPAC report was widely condemned as narrow, biased, and shortsighted, but the damage had been done. It brought a virtual end of MT research in the United States for over a decade and it had great impact elsewhere in the Soviet Union and in Europe.

However, MT research did continue in Canada, France, and Germany. In the 1960s, in the United States and the Soviet Union, MT activity had concentrated on Russian–English and English–Russian translation of scientific and technical documents for a relatively small number of potential users, most of whom were prepared to overlook mistakes of terminology, grammar, and style in order to be able to read something that they would have otherwise not known about. Since the mid-1970s, the administrative and commercial demands of multilingual communities and multinational trade have stimulated the demand for translation in Europe, Canada, and Japan beyond the capacity of the traditional translation services.

The 1980s witnessed the emergence of a variety of system types from a widening number of countries. First, there were a number of mainframe systems, whose use continues to the present day. Best known is Systran, now installed worldwide and operating in many pairs of languages. Others are: Logos for German–English translation and for English–French in Canada; the internally developed systems for Spanish–English and English–Spanish translation at the Pan American Health Organization; the systems developed by the Smart Corporation for many large organizations in North America; and the Metal system from Siemens, initially for German–English translation and later for other languages.

The end of the decade was a major turning point. First, a group from IBM published the results of experiments on a system based purely on statistical methods. Second, at the same time, certain Japanese groups began to use methods based on a corpus (collection) of translation examples, that is, using the approach now called *example-based* translation. In both approaches, the distinctive feature is that no syntactic or semantic rules are used in the analysis of texts or in the selection of lexical equivalents to multiple-word phrases that occur in those texts.

A third innovation has been research on speech recognition and synthesis (*q.v.*) and translation modules, the latter mixing traditional rule-based methods and newer corpus-based approaches. Inevitably, the subject domains have been highly restricted. The major projects have been at ATR (Nara, Japan) on a system for telephone translation of conference inquiries and hotel bookings; a collaborative project (JANUS) involving ATR, Carnegie-Mellon University, and the University of Karlsruhe; and in Germany, the government-funded Verbmobil project for a system to aid Germans and Japanese to conduct business negotiations in English.

Linguistic Problems of MT

The basic processes of translation are the analysis of the source language (SL) text, the conversion (or *transfer*) of the *meaning* of the text into another language, and the generation (or *synthesis*) of the target language (TL) text. There are basically three overall strategies. In the direct-translation approach, systems are designed in all details specifically for one particular pair of languages. Vocabulary and syntax are not analyzed any more than strictly necessary for the resolution of ambiguities, the identification of TL equivalents, and output in correct TL word order. Analysis and synthesis are combined in single programs, sometimes of monolithic intractability (e.g. the Georgetown system).

The second strategy is the *interlingua* approach that assumes the possibility of converting SL texts into (semantic) representations common to a number of languages, from which texts can be generated in one or more TLs. In interlingua systems, SL analysis and TL synthesis are monolingual processes independent of any other languages, and the interlingua is designed to be language-independent or "universal."

The third strategy is the *transfer* approach, which operates in three stages: from the SL text into an abstract "intermediary" representation that is not language-independent but oriented to the characteristics of the SL (analysis); from such an SL-oriented representation to an equivalent TL-oriented representation (transfer); and from the latter to the final TL text (synthesis). Major examples of the transfer approach are the GETA, SUSY, Mu, and Eurotra systems.

The main linguistic problems encountered in MT systems are fourfold: lexical, structural, contextual, and pragmatic or situational. In each case, the problems are primarily caused by the inherent ambiguities of natural languages and by the lack of direct equivalences of vocabulary and structure between one language and another. Some English examples are:

- *Lexical*: homonyms (*fly* as "insect" or "move through air," *bank* as "edge of river" or "financial institution") require different translations (*mouche, voler; rive, banque*).
- *Structural*: nouns can function as verbs (*control, plant, face*) and are hence "ambiguous," since the TL may well have different forms (*contrôle: diriger; plante: planter; face: affronter*).
- *Contextual*: other languages make distinctions which are absent in English: river can be French *rivière* or *fleuve*, German *Fluß* or *Strom*; blue can be Russian *sinii* or *goluboi*.

Often all of these combine, as illustrated by a simple example, the word *light*. In English, *light* can be a noun meaning "luminescence," an adjective meaning "not dark," another adjective meaning "not heavy," or a verb meaning "to start burning." In French, the meanings are conveyed by four different words *lumière, léger, clair*, and *allumer*.

Various aspects of syntactic relations can be analyzed. There is the need to (1) identify valid sequences of grammatical categories; (2) identify functional relations: subjects and objects of verbs, dependencies of adjectives on "head" nouns, and so on; and (3) identify the constituents of sentences: noun phrases, verb groups, prepositional phrases, subordinate clauses, and so on. Each aspect has given rise to different types of parsers: the *predictive syntactic analyzer* of the 1960s concentrated on sequences of categories; the *dependency grammar* has concentrated on functional relationships; and the *phrase structure grammars* have been the models for parsers of constituency structure. All have their strengths and weaknesses, and modern MT systems often adopt an eclectic mixture of parsing techniques within the framework of a "unification grammar" formalism.

MT in Practice

Many researchers have been persuaded that for the foreseeable future, it is unrealistic to attempt to build fully automatic systems capable of the translation quality achieved by human translators. The most obvious recourse, which has been adopted since the first MT systems, is to employ human translators to revise and improve the crude and inaccurate texts produced by MT systems. Initially, "postediting" was undertaken manually; later systems incorporate online revision and in some cases special facilities for dealing with the most common types of error (e.g. transposition of words, insertion of articles). Revision for MT differs from the revision of traditionally produced translations; the computer program is regular and consistent with terminology, unlike the human translator, but typically it contains grammatical and stylistic errors that no human translator would commit. The development of powerful microcomputer text editing facilities has led to the introduction of interactive MT systems. During the translation process, a human operator (normally a translator) may be asked to help the computer resolve ambiguities of vocabulary or structure.

Another possibility is to constrain the variety of language in the input texts. There are two approaches: either the system is designed to deal with one particular subject matter or the input texts are written in a vocabulary and style which it is known that the MT system can deal with. The former approach is illustrated by the METEO system, introduced in 1976, which translates weather forecasts from English into French for public broadcasts in Canada. The latter approach has been taken by the Xerox Corporation in its use of the Systran system; manuals are written in controlled English (unambiguous vocabulary and restricted syntactic patterns), which can be translated with minimal revision into five languages. Other examples are the Smart systems installed at a number of large US and Canadian institutions that combine online editing to ensure clear documentation in English and "restricted language" MT to produce translations for subsequent editing.

Bibliography

1992. Hutchins, W. J., and Somers, H. L. *An Introduction to Machine Translation*. London: Academic Press.
1992. Newton, J. (ed.) *Computers in Translation: a Practical Appraisal*. London, New York: Routledge.
1995. Mason, J., and Rinsche, A. *Translation Technology Products*. London: Ovum Ltd.

W. John Hutchins

MACRO

For articles on related subjects, *see*

+ Machine- and Assembly-language Programming
+ Preprocessor
+ Programming Languages
+ Software Portability
+ Subprogram

A *macro* is a single statement that stands for an arbitrarily long sequence of operations. Historically, macros grew out of assembly language. Assume, for instance, that at several points in a program, a programmer needs to increment a variable whose name is COUNT by 1. Assume further that this takes three assembly language instructions:

```
LOAD    COUNT
ADD     ONE
STORE   COUNT
```

It would be wasteful of a programmer's time to keep writing out these three instructions in full. It would be much better to choose a single name (BUMPCOUNT, say) to stand for these instructions, and then to write the name each time it was necessary to specify them. A *macro definition* defines BUMPCOUNT and the instructions that are to replace it. The macro processor then scans the program, replacing each occurrence of BUMPCOUNT by its expanded form. It would similarly process any other macros that had been defined. As a result of this, the program is then in pure assembly language and can be passed on to the assembler, which processes it in the normal way.

To implement macros, there must exist a *preprocessor* (*q.v.*) to the underlying software, in this case, the assembler. The preprocessor processes the macros and passes the result to the language processor, which is completely unaware of the macros. Macros are therefore a way to allow users to define small extensions to a base language. Macros are used in a variety of environments. They find uses in high-level programming languages; for example, in Lisp (*q.v.*) they can be used to define new control structures (*q.v.*). They also find uses in such software as spreadsheets (*q.v.*) and word processors (*q.v.*); here the "language" is the set of commands that the word processor or spreadsheet accepts, and a macro is a way of defining a new command that is a combination of the existing ones. Sometimes macros are defined by a single user for a particular application; sometimes a group of macros is put into a library that is accessible to any user.

Macros can have arguments. To return to the BUMPCOUNT example, its defect as it stands is that it works only for one variable, COUNT. In practice, it would be much more useful to have a general macro (called, say, BUMP) that could be used to increment *any* variable by 1. This can, in fact, be done. The name of the variable to be incremented is written immediately after BUMP, and is called the *argument* of the macro. The macro processor can be told to insert the argument at various points in the replacement of the macro. Thus, BUMP name would be replaced by

```
LOAD    name
ADD     ONE
STORE   name
```

where any name of a variable could occur as name.

A macro may have more than one argument. For example, one could specify a macro of the form PRODUCT X, Y, Z, which, for any X, Y, and Z, would compute Z to be the product of X and Y. A macro processor may also support conditional statements and iteration, so that when a macro is expanded, the macro processor inspects the arguments and generates the consequent replacement. For example, the replacement of the macro might be different depending on whether the argument was FAST or CONCISE. Portable software written in high-level languages such as C or C++ often uses conditional macros to specify which subprogram

libraries to use when they vary from one operating system to another.

Bibliography

1960. McIlroy, M. D. "Macro Instruction Extensions of Compiler Languages," *Communications of the ACM*, **3**(4), 214–220.

1974. Brown, P. J. *Macro Processors and Techniques for Portable Software*. New York: John Wiley. Manuals for macros incorporated in various software products.

Peter J. Brown

MAGNETIC CORE

See MEMORY: MAIN.

MAGNETIC DISK

See DISKETTE; HARD DISK; and MEMORY: AUXILIARY.

MAGNETIC DRUM

See MEMORY: AUXILIARY.

MAIN MEMORY

See MEMORY: MAIN.

MAINFRAME

For articles on related subjects, *see*

+ Central Processing Unit (CPU)
+ Memory: Main

+ Minicomputer
+ Supercomputers

The term *mainframe* as a single word has come to be used as a designation of medium- and large-scale computers that contain a "main frame" as defined in this article; thus, we speak of a *mainframe* computer in contrast to a *microcomputer, minicomputer, personal computer*, or *workstation* (*q.v.*). Originally, the *mainframe* of a computer system was the cabinet that housed its central processor and main memory. It is, therefore, separate from the peripheral devices (disks, printers, tape drives, etc.) and device controllers. Typically, it was the largest component in size and cost, but modern electronics has allowed great reductions in both. The central processor and main memory were housed together as an aid in increasing processing speeds and improving reliability (e.g. both will be at a similar temperature and humidity). The term *mainframe* comes from the use of "frame" as a device to hold electronics (rack is also frequently used), and the frame holding the electronics that does the computing might reasonably be called the *main frame*.

Chester L. Meek

MANAGEMENT INFORMATION SYSTEMS (MIS)

For articles on related subjects, *see*

+ Data Processing
+ Database Management System (DBMS)
+ Information Retrieval
+ Relational Database

Historical Development of Management Information Systems

When computers were first used in the mid-1950s, the applications were primarily the simple processing of transaction records and preparation of business documents and standard reports. This use was termed *data processing* (DP) or *electronic data processing* (EDP). By the mid-1960s, many users and builders of information processing systems developed a more comprehensive vision of what computers could do for organizations. This vision was termed a *management information system* (MIS). It enlarged the scope of data processing to add systems for supporting management and administrative activities including planning, scheduling, analysis, and decision making.

In the 1980s and 1990s, there was a merging of computer and communications technologies. The organizational use of *information technology* (*q.v.*) was extended to internal networks (*intranets*), *local area networks* (*q.v.*), external networks that connect an organization to its suppliers and customers, and communications systems that enable employees to work alone or in groups. Innovative applications of information technology created value by providing customized services at any time and at any location, and information systems began to prompt changes in organizational structures and processes.

Although the scope of systems providing information technology services has increased dramatically, the broad concept of MIS as a system that combines transaction and operational requirements with administrative and management support remains valid. The term *MIS* is still in common use despite a recent tendency to use the simpler term *information system*.

The Purposes of an Organizational Information System

To achieve its purpose, an organization must (1) define the characteristics of goods and services to be provided, (2) deliver those goods and services to customers, and (3) manage, direct, coordinate, and control the organization and its resources. The objectives for an information system follow naturally from these organizational purposes:

1. Add functionality and information value to products and services.
2. Support transaction and operational processes.
3. Support administrative and management activities.

Conceptual Structure of an Information System

An MIS consists of the following:

1. *Technical infrastructure.* This consists of computer and communications hardware, system software, and the repository management software.
2. *Databases and other repositories.* The repositories store data required for transactions, operations, analysis, decision making, explanations and justifications, and government/legal requirements.
3. *Transaction processing systems.* Transaction processing systems record and process business transactions such as accepting a customer order, placing an order with a vendor, making a payment, and so forth.
4. *Operations systems.* These applications schedule and direct the operations of the organization as products are produced and distributed and services are scheduled and performed.
5. *Administrative and management support systems.* These applications support knowledge workers (including managers) in performing tasks individually and collaboratively.

MIS Applications to Support Levels of Management Activities

As illustrated in Fig. 1, the information system support for management activities is often defined as a pyramid with more structure and programmed decisions at the lower levels and less structure and nonprogrammed decisions at the higher levels.

Operational Control

Operational control is the management process of insuring that operational activities associated with delivery of goods and services and internal administrative procedures are carried out effectively and efficiently. Operational control makes use of fairly stable preestablished procedures, communication, and decision rules. The decisions, communications, and actions cover relatively short time periods (a day, a week, or a month depending on the cycle of activities being controlled). The information system support for operational control

Figure 1. Management information system support for management. (Reprinted by permission from Davis and Olson, 1985.)

consists of access to transaction records, operational reports, communications, and inquiry processing in support of operational analysis and decision making. Data used in reports and analyses is primarily from internal transactions.

Management Control

Management control information is needed by managers of organizational units such as divisions, factories, departments, profit centers, and so on. The information is needed to measure performance, decide on control actions, formulate new decision rules, and allocate resources. Management actions based on control information have a time horizon longer than operational control: a month, quarter, or year. Management control reports typically compare results to some standard of performance in order to calculate variances from expected results and to analyze the causes. Analyses and reports use transaction data and plans/budgets from the organization and also some external data relative to the environment, competitive products and services, competitor costs and pricing, and so forth.

Strategic Planning

Strategic planning develops the strategy an organization will follow to achieve its objectives of profitability, quality, and service. Strategic planning assists decisions about fundamental issues of what business to be in and how to conduct it. Strategic planning is part of the responsibility of the management of the business functions as well as top management, and often involves specialists who organize and interpret competitive intelligence and market trends.

MIS Support for Knowledge Work

One of the well-developed areas of information system support for knowledge work is decision making. In planning and designing decision support applications, MIS developers have applied the *Simon framework* for decision making. This consists of three phases: intelligence, design, and choice. The intelligence phase is discovering problems and opportunities. The MIS support for this phase requires access to external data in order to scan the external environment plus database access to search internal data. The search processes can be both structured using predefined search and analysis processes or unstructured scanning and unique analyses. Adaptive analysis through use of neural networks (*q.v.*) may aid in identifying shifts in demands and other key factors affecting an organization. The decision design phase—for generation of alternatives—involves inventing, developing, and analyzing possible courses of action. MIS support for decision design consists of statistical, analytical, and model-building software. The final step in the Simon model is choice. MIS support for choice consists of various decision models, sensitivity analysis, and choice procedures. *Expert systems* (*q.v.*) may be useful in some applications.

The Organization Function for MIS

The management information systems or information management function is a specialized organization function with responsibility to plan, design, build, maintain, operate, and manage the information infrastructure and applications. This includes acquisition and management of both internal staff and external resources. It also includes technical, advisory, and educational support to aid users in applying appropriate technology to their tasks.

The major activities of the MIS function are as follows:

- Provide input to development of organizational strategy and plans for use of information technology to achieve competitive goals and to support organization objectives.
- Development and maintenance of the MIS plan and budget for the organization.
- Design, development, operation, and maintenance of infrastructures and support systems that enable organizational use of information technology.
- Set standards and quality control for desktop information technology and end-user systems acquisition, operation, and use.
- Development and operation of organizational databases.
- Acquisition or development and operation of a portfolio of applications for the organization.
- Provide information technology expertise and education for users in the organization.

The information management function may include both a separate organization function and personnel assigned to organization functions that use the technology.

Bibliography

1997. Davis, G. B., and Naumann, J. D. *Personal Productivity with Information Technology*. New York: McGraw-Hill.

1999. Groth, L. *Building Organizations with Information Technology*. London: John Wiley.

1999. Turban, E., McLean, E., and Wetherbe, J. *Information Technology for Management: Improving Quality and Productivity*. New York: John Wiley.

Gordon B. Davis

MANCHESTER UNIVERSITY COMPUTERS

For articles on related subjects, see

✛ Atlas

+ Turing, Alan Mathison
+ Wilkes, Sir Maurice V.

Manchester University has played an important role in the development of computer science. As early as the 1930s, Douglas R. Hartree had constructed a differential analyzer, a mechanical calculating machine based upon the theoretical ideas of Lord Kelvin and the designs of the American engineer, Vannevar Bush. This was an analog device. After the Second World War, these machines were overtaken by electronic stored-program digital computers.

In 1946, Professor F. C. Williams and Professor Tom Kilburn began work at Manchester with the intention of developing a novel form of computer storage using cathode ray tubes. The system, which involved the use of the "Williams tube memory" to store binary digits of information, was perfected during 1947. Kilburn reported the results, together with the outline design for a hypothetical computer, in December of that year. The team was then joined by G. C. Tootill and a prototype—the "Baby Machine," the forerunner of the Manchester Mark I—was built, and on 21 June 1948, became the world's first operational stored-program digital computer (*see* Fig. 1).

In 1948, the attention of Sir Ben Lockspeiser, then Government Chief Scientist, was drawn to the Mark I.

The result was a government contract with Ferranti Ltd to make a production version of the machine. The first Ferranti Mark I was installed at Manchester University in February 1951, thereby becoming the world's first commercially available computer to be delivered. Besides building the world's first stored-program computer, as well as the world's first commercially available computer, Kilburn and his group can be credited with building the first proper transistorized computer in 1953. The Metropolitan Vickers Company later built a commercial version of the design, the MV950, which was completed in 1956.

The University's involvement with Ferranti continued through the 1950s when the design team was working on a Mark II computer nicknamed MEG (megacycle engine). The production version of MEG was known as the Ferranti Mercury, and the first machine was delivered in August 1957. Collaboration in these years eventually resulted in Atlas, an ambitious project that pioneered many concepts in storage and addressing that are still in common use today.

Bibliography

1975. Lavington, S. H. *A History of Manchester Computers*. Manchester: National Computer Centre.

1980. Lavington, S. H. *Early British Computers*. Manchester: Manchester University Press.

1993. *IEEE Annals of the History of Computing*, **15**(3), (Special Issue on Computing at the University of Manchester).

Geoffrey Tweedale

Figure 1. Part of the Manchester Mark 1 (1949). (Courtesy National Archive for the History of Computing, University of Manchester.)

MARK I, HARVARD

For articles on related subjects, *see*

+ Aiken, Howard Hathaway
+ Digital Computers, History of: Early
+ Hopper, Grace Murray
+ IBM

The Harvard Mark I, originally named the IBM Automatic Sequence Controlled Calculator (ASCC), was the first large-scale automatic computer in the United States. Its unveiling in August 1944 demonstrated the practicality of computing machines that could function automatically according to a programmed sequence. The machine was the brainchild of Howard Hathaway Aiken, who, in 1936, while a graduate student in physics engaged in research for his dissertation, encountered computational problems beyond the capacity of desk calculators. He thereupon wrote a proposal explaining the operations the automatic calculator was to perform, showing the kinds of mathematical problems the machine was to solve. In April 1937, the Monroe Calculating Machine Company decided not to build Aiken's machine but suggested that Aiken try IBM. At IBM, Aiken received strong support from its chief engineer, James Wares Bryce, and the project gained the approval of IBM President Thomas J. Watson, Sr.

The overall direction of the project was assigned to Clair D. Lake, but the actual day-to-day planning and construction was done by Francis (Frank) Hamilton and Benjamin Durfee, at IBM's Endicott, NY, facility. During the early years of the work, Aiken made regular visits to Endicott. He gave detailed specifications to the IBM engineers and showed them the kinds of calculations the machine would be called upon to make. In the spring of 1942, Aiken, an officer in the Naval Reserve, was called to active duty and his part of the assignment was turned over to his deputy, Robert V. D. Campbell, a graduate student in physics at Harvard.

Although Aiken first approached IBM in 1937, the calculator was not completed and tested until late in 1943, some six years later. Soon after the machine had been moved to Harvard, the operation was taken over by the US Navy Bureau of Ships. The unit was under the command of Aiken, now with the rank of Commander (USNR). Among the members of his staff of programmers was Lt. (jg) Grace Hopper, USNR, later celebrated for her own contributions to computing.

Mark I was gigantic, standing 8 ft high and 51 ft long (*see* Fig. 1). The operation of its separate parts was powered by a long horizontal rotating shaft. The machine used 530 miles of wire and was composed of

Figure 1.   Harvard Mark I. (Courtesy of IBM.)

760 000 individual parts. It weighed approximately 5 tons. In later language, Mark I would be described as a parallel synchronous calculator. It had a word length of 23 decimal digits, with a 24th place reserved for the algebraic sign. There were 60 registers for the input of constant numerical data, each one containing 24 dial switches corresponding to 24 digits. For any problem, these had to be set by hand and could then be used by the program.

The operative portion of the machine was composed of 72 registers (*q.v.*), each of which was a signed 23-digit "accumulator." This unit comprised both the store (memory) and the processing unit. There were separate devices for multiplication and division and four tape readers. Programs were fed into the machine by punched paper tape. Basic cycle time, slow by the standard of the later ENIAC (*q.v.*), was 300 ms. Simple addition and subtraction required a single step or cycle, but multiplication took 20 cycles (6 s) and division took 38 cycles (11.4 s).

Mark I continued to function for 14 years after the war, until it was finally retired in 1959. During these years, Mark I served generations of students at Harvard, where Aiken had established a pioneering program in what was later to be called *computer science*.

Bibliography

1946. Aiken, H. H., and Hopper, G. M. "The Automatic Sequence Controlled Calculator," *Electrical Engineering (IEEE)*, **65**, 384–391, 449–454, 522–528.

1964. Aiken, H. H. "Proposed Automatic Calculating Machine," *IEEE Spectrum*, **1**, (August), 62–69.

1999. Cohen, I. B., Welch, G. W., and Campbell, R. V. *Makin' Numbers: Howard Aiken and the Computer.* Cambridge, MA: MIT Press.

I. Bernard Cohen

MARKUP LANGUAGES

For articles on related subjects, see

+ Desktop Publishing
+ Hypertext
+ T$_E$X
+ Text Editing Systems
+ World Wide Web

Markup information is embedded in document text but is not intended for printing or display. It may consist of instructions to a printer, commands for a Web browser, or comments to a coauthor. The most powerful language for markup is the Standard Generalized Markup Language (SGML). SGML has been an international standard since 1986 and has been used to define various specialized markup languages. The most widely used of these is Hyper-Text Markup Language (HTML). HTML, originally created by Tim Berners-Lee, is the markup language used in documents distributed on the World Wide Web.

Types of Markup

There are three main types of markup. Specific markup, often called *procedural markup*, is used to give display or printing instructions to a text processing system. These are most often visual indicators such as text color or font size (*see* TYPEFONT). Generalized markup, also called *descriptive markup*, is used to inform the text processing system about the components of the document. These are items such as section headings and paragraphs. *Content markup* is the use of generalized markup to identify the meaning of portions of a document. For example, in a transcription of a radio show, a section of text could be identified as "speaker," "music," or "commercial."

Procedural markup directs the text formatting performed by a particular document processor. Word-processing systems typically embed invisible (nonprintable) codes within document to record specific styles and visual characteristics of text. These codes are interpreted by the text processor for specific layout functions such as adjusting the size or style of a font, text alignment, and other visual characteristics of the document. Document processing systems commonly used in writing scientific literature, such as T$_E$X or the Unix (*q.v.*) text formatter *troff*, require the author to enter procedural markup codes within the text.

Content markup is used to identify meaning. For example, in a transcription, specific speakers or the type of speech might be explicitly identified with markup. The Text Encoding Initiative (TEI 1999), another SGML application, was created to help in the scholarly analysis of humanities texts and to facilitate interchange of documents marked for analysis. A large set of Document Type Definitions (DTDs) and guidelines has been created by the TEI and is used by over 50 significant projects to aid in the analysis of archival information, dictionaries, language corpora, and literary and religious texts.

Creating Markup

Specific markup can be created simply by using a particular word processor. The markup codes are embedded in the document text and are not visible when the document is displayed by a browser. SGML and HTML markup consists of *tags*. Markup tags, usually denoted by the angle brackets surrounding them, denote the beginning and end of a portion of text. The tags marking the beginning and end, respectively, of an HTML document are ⟨HTML⟩ and ⟨/HTML⟩. In general, the end of a section is marked by the same keyword as began it, prefixed by '/'. Since HTML markup is in plain ASCII, any text editor or word processor can be used to create marked-up HTML text.

Without special editors, markup creation is a tedious and error-prone process. One complicating factor is that

```
<HTML>  <!-- Comments begin and end as this one does.-->

<HEAD>  <!-- Nothing in the scope of the Head will be displayed.-->
<!-- List nonprinting keywords for the use by search engines:-->
  <META NAME= "Keywords" CONTENTS= "Platonic solid, tetrahedron,
     cube, octahedron, icosahedron, dodecahedron, Euler, polyhedron">
<!-- Choose a title for the Web page:--> <TITLE>Platonic Solids</TITLE>
</HEAD>

<!-- Start Body and choose colors for the text, background, and links:-->
<BODY TEXT ="#000000" BGCOLOR= "#33CCFF"
     LINK="#000EE" VLINK="#551A8B" ALINK= "#FF0000">

<!-- Choose style, color, and size for 1ˢᵗ line displayed; B=Bold:-->
<CENTER>
  <B><FONT COLOR= "#990000"><FONT SIZE=+3>PLATONIC SOLIDS, INC.
     </FONT></FONT></B></CENTER>

<!-- Break to next line to create a blank line:--><BR>

<P>    <!-- Start first paragraph, which leaves another blank line.-->
<B><FONT SIZE=+1>Our polished aluminum polyhedra are precision
   made in a wide variety of sizes. The vertices(V), faces (F),
   and edges (E) of each solid are guaranteed to confirm to
   Euler's relation V+F-E=2.</FONT></B>

<P>    <!-- Insert two images, side by side, with 160 pixels to left
          and right of the first:-->
     <IMG SRC= "icosa.gif" HSPACE=160 HEIGHT=100WIDTH=133>
     <IMG SRC= "dodeca.gif"          HEIGHT=100WIDTH=133>

<p>  <B> <FONT SIZE=+1>For complete specification on any of our
          five products, choose an item from the list.</FONT></B>

<UL>      <!-- Start an Unordered(unnumbered) List of Links;
              items begin and end with bracketed LI and /LI-->
  <LI><B><A HREF= "tetra.htm">tetrahedron        </A></B></LI>
  <LI><B><A HREF= "octa.htm">octahedron          </A></B></LI>
  <LI><B><A HREF= "icos.htm">icosahedron         </A></B></LI>
  <LI><B><A HREF= "cube.htm">cube                </A></B></LI>
  <LI><B><A HREF= "dodec.htm">dodecahedron        </A></B></LI>
</UL>

<!-- Set up a link to an email form:-->
<CENTER>
   <B>Dirtct inquires to
   <A HREF= "mailto:info@platonicsolids.com">
   info@platonicsolids.com</A></B>
</CENTER>

</BODY>
</HTML>
```

(a)

Figure 1. (a) The program illustrates just a few of the many features of the markup language HTML.

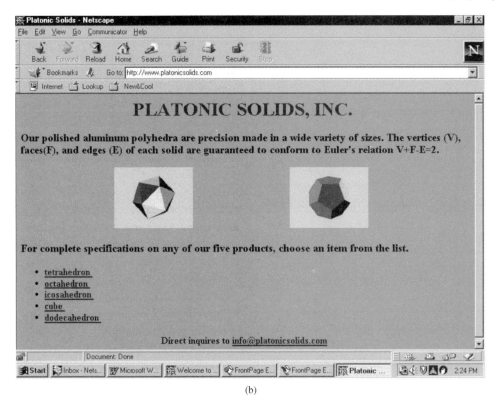

Figure 1. (b) When interpreted by a browser, the code produces a color version of the screen image as shown.

all whitespace (excess consecutive blanks) in an HTML document is ignored when the document is displayed; displayed whitespace must be forced by embedding just the right codes into the marked document to achieve the effect desired. This property of markup languages was chosen to make documents independent of the particular type of device used to display them.

Embedding tags into a document manually is analogous to machine- and assembly-language programming (*q.v.*). Fortunately, there now exist the counterparts of high-level languages, WYSIWYG editors that let users edit a displayed document and perfect it to their satisfaction. Each change made that affects the appearance of the "page" being viewed causes a background change in markup codes in its base document, exactly the reverse of what will happen when the HTML document is processed by a browser. An HTML document being viewed using Netscape Communicator can be toggled between Browser Mode (what a remote viewer will see once the page is "published" on the Web) and Edit Mode. Microsoft markets a product called *Front Page* that does the same thing, as does Adobe, whose software is called *PageMill*.

Specialized HTML editors help ensure that starting tags always have the required end tag, and that required attributes are created. Some of the more complicated tags, such as those specifying images in a Web document have over a dozen possible attributes relating to, for example, the placement of an image, the way text is or is not wrapped around it, and whether or not the image itself is to serve as a link to a larger version of the picture. An image can also serve as a link to a MIDI file that will play music or to a menu that invites the user to write an email message. Specialized editors can take care of the syntactic tedium involved in choosing these attributes. Figure 1 shows the correspondence between a particular

HTML document and the appearance it produces when viewed with a browser.

Extending HTML

An effort to bring the extensibility of SGML to the Web has resulted in the Extensible Markup Language (XML). XML, a simplified form of SGML, is a project sanctioned by the World Wide Web Consortium, the official developers of HTML and the Web. XML provides more robust linking facilities than HTML; its links can be unidirectional, bidirectional, and multidirectional. The XML XPointer is derived from the TEI Extended Pointer syntax. XPointers allow specification of absolute or relative textual targets. For example, the Xpointer: `CHILD(3,DIV1)(29,P)` selects the 29th paragraph of the third major division of the target text.

Bibliography

1998. Korpela, J. "Lurching Toward Babel: HTML, CSS, and XML," *Computer*, **31**(7), (July), 103–106.

1999. Lee, H. W., and Saarela, J. "Multipurpose Web Publishing Using HTML, XML, and CSS," *Communications of the ACM*, **42**(10), (October), 95–101.

Sandy Ressler

MASS STORAGE

For articles on related subjects, *see*

+ Channel
+ Data Mining
+ Data Warehousing
+ Database Management System (DBMS)
+ Fiber Optics
+ File Server
+ Hard Disk
+ Memory: Auxiliary
+ Redundant Array of Inexpensive Disks (RAID)
+ Virtual Memory

A *mass storage system* or MSS is a collection of software, computing elements, input–output, and data storage components that jointly automate the archiving, storage, management, and retrieval of very large quantities of digital information. A typical high-end mass storage system may store from hundreds of *terabytes* (10^{12} bytes) to *petabytes* (10^{15} bytes) of data contained in millions of files. The MSS provides access to those files to client computer systems ranging from desktop workstations (*q.v.*) to supercomputers (*q.v.*) at speeds from megabits per second over a local area network (LAN-*q.v.*) to gigabits per second over high-speed I/O channels. Examples of early mass storage systems are the Common File System or CFS developed at Los Alamos National Labs, Unitree from Lawrence Livermore National Labs, and the National Center for Atmospheric Research (NCAR) MSS, each of which was developed in the mid-1980s.

There are many examples of the need for mass storage systems. A medium-size metropolitan medical institution generates two terabytes a year of multimedia (*q.v.*) patient information, the bulk of which consists of digitized X-ray images. The NASA Earth Observing Satellite launched in 1998 is expected to generate seven petabytes of data by the year 2007, at a peak rate of three terabytes a day, or the equivalent of six 660 MB CD-ROMs every minute. The US Department of Energy Accelerated Strategic Computing Initiative (ASCI), responsible for computer simulations of the nuclear stockpile, will require hundreds of petabytes of storage. In each case, the prodigious amount of data being generated must be archived for as long as decades, must be made easily available for computer processing, and must be stored as economically as possible.

Architecture and Operation of an MSS

Mass storage systems place no interpretation on data; they store *bitfiles*—uninterpreted strings of bits. To achieve a balance of performance and economy, a mass storage system uses a *multilevel storage hierarchy*. For this reason, mass storage systems are sometimes referred to as *hierarchical storage managers* (HSMs). Bitfiles that are active are cached on disks. The total capacity of an MSS disk farm may be hundreds of gigabytes in size, and aggregate transfer rates for disk arrays can be hundreds of megabits per second. The expense of direct access storage calls for the bulk of the data archive to be stored on a more economical medium, such as magnetic tape cartridges or optical discs. Larger or less frequently accessed bitfiles are cached in robotic libraries, each of which may contain thousands of tape cartridges or optical discs, and hold a total of hundreds of terabytes (*see* Fig. 1).

A LAN may be used to move data between an MSS and its clients. Commercial mass storage systems such as Unitree use Internet protocols such as File Transfer Protocol (FTP) or Network File System (NFS), allowing the MSS to appear to be a terabyte-size file server. However, LAN bandwidth (*q.v.*) is inadequate for high-performance MSS clients such as supercomputers or massively parallel processors (*q.v.*). Also, Internet protocols are typically inefficient for moving large amounts of data quickly because most are limited by response time rather than by network capacity.

MSS data moves directly between the client system and the storage device, both of which are attached to a common *data fabric* or *storage area network* (SAN). The term *fabric* is used to distinguish it from a more typical local area network and to reflect the fact that data fabrics are frequently woven from optical fiber. Data fabrics usually employ switch-based I/O channel interconnection technologies such as High Performance Parallel Interface or HIPPI (at 800 Mb/sec), or Fibre Channel Standard (at 1 Gb/sec). Either may be implemented with optical fiber or copper.

Associated with each bitfile in the mass storage system is *metadata*, for example, the name of the file, who owns it, when it was created and last used, who is allowed to access it, and where it is located in the storage hierarchy. Losing metadata is as catastrophic as losing the data itself, since data without context is of little value. Database and data mining tools are often provided with the MSS for users to manage and manipulate data and metadata efficiently.

The longevity of all digital information, both data and metadata, is a critical issue in the selection of storage technology for a mass storage system. Of concern is not only the physical lifetime of the media, for example, how long a tape cartridge or optical disc will remain readable, but also the lifetime of the hardware and software technology used to create and access them. A digital magnetic tape may still be readable 10 or more years after it is written, but the technology used to read it may not be commercially available for anywhere near as long.

Figure 1. This robotic tape library contains about 6000 tape cartridges each holding 50 GB (or more with data compression), for a total capacity of 300 TB. The Storage Tek Automated Cartridge System or "silo" is about 7 ft (2.35 m) high and 11 ft (3.25 m) in diameter. Tape drives and integrated controllers can be seen surrounding the silo (Storage Technology Corporation).

Bibliography

1990. Levy, E., and Silberschatz, A., "Distributed File Systems: Concepts and Examples," *ACM Computing Surveys*, **22**(4), (December), 321–374.

1995. Rothenberg, J. "Ensuring the Longevity of Digital Documents," *Scientific American*, **272**(1), 42–47.

1995. Watson, R., and Coyne, R. "The Parallel I/O Architecture of the High Performance Storage System (HPSS)," *Proceedings of 14th IEEE Symposium on Mass Storage Systems*. Monterey, CA: IEEE Comp. Soc. Press.

J. L. Sloan

MEDICAL IMAGING

For articles on related subjects, see

+ Biocomputing
+ Image Processing

Medical imaging, is the study of human functions and anatomy through pictorial information. It encompasses the methods and procedures of converting a conventional medical image, or synthesizing biological, anatomical or physiological information, to a digital image; analyzing the digital image; and extracting parameters suitable for presentation and decision making.

Some successful medical imaging applications in the early 1970s were the blood cell analyzer and the gamma camera in nuclear medicine (NM) and the development of computerized tomography (CT or CAT for computer-assisted tomography). Major developments in the 1980s and 1990s were electron microscopy (EM) and laser microscopy (LM), digital subtraction angiography (DSA), magnetic resonance imaging (MRI), positron emission tomography (PET), computed radiography (CR), direct digital radiography (DR), Doppler ultrasound, picture archiving and communication systems (PACS), and medical image informatics (MII). EM can reveal minute details in biological infrastructures as small as a few angstroms in size. LM yields thin serial images providing three-dimensional (3D) morphology of living cells. Digital subtraction angiography (DSA) allows real-time subtraction to enhance the vascularities in angiograms. MRI reveals high-contrast images of 3D anatomical structures without the use of ionizing radiation. MRI is the method of choice for neuroradiological, vascular, and musculoskeletal examinations. The American Paul C. Lauterbur of the University of Illinois and Sir Peter Mansfield of the University of Nottingham in England received the 2003 Nobel Prize in Medicine for its invention, 30 years after its initial conception and many years after its widespread use.

PET provides chemical and physiological images of the human body that complement anatomical images obtained by using MRI and CT. The registration of MRI or CT with PET head images provides an insight into the specific function of various parts of the brain. CR and DR allow an X-ray image to be recorded directly as a digital image.

PACS is a concept for medical image management and communication. When fully implemented, the system can revolutionize medical practice to improve health care delivery. PACS storage technology includes parallel transfer disks and optical disc/tape libraries. In the former, a conventional X-ray chest examination composed of posterior- and lateral-view images of 20 MB can be stored or retrieved from the parallel transfer disks within one second. In the latter, an optical disc/tape library allows the storage of five TB of information, equivalent to about five years' worth of all MR and CT examinations conducted in a large 600-bed teaching hospital.

Medical Image Detectors and Recorders

Medical image detection and recording methods are either photochemical or photoelectronic. An example of a photochemical method is the phosphorous screen and silver halide film combination system used for X-ray detection. The television camera and display monitor used in fluorography is photoelectronic. The photochemical method has the advantage of combining image detection and image recording in a single step. With DSA, an image intensifier tube is used as the X-ray detector instead of a screen/film combination. The detected X-rays are converted first into light photons and then into electronic signals that are recorded by a video camera. The photoelectronic system has the advantage that its output can be converted from light or electrons to digital format for image processing.

Sources of Medical Images

In radiology, about 70% of the examinations, including those that involve skull, chest, abdomen, and bone,

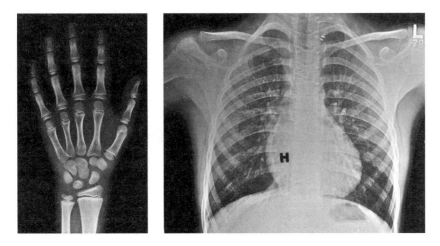

Figure 1. Examples of medical images obtained from various energy sources.

produce images that are acquired and stored on X-ray film. These images have a spatial resolution of about 5 line pairs per millimeter (lp/mm), a measure of spatial resolution; one line pair represents two pixels. In clinical practice, X-ray films are digitized to 2000 × 2500 pixels. Computed radiography (CR), which uses a laser stimulable luminescence phosphor imaging plate as a detector, is gradually replacing the screen/film as the image detector. In this case, a laser is used to scan the imaging plate that contains the latent X-ray image. The latent image is excited and emits light photons that are detected and converted to digitized electronic signals forming a digital X-ray image. Direct digital radiography (DR) does not require an intermediate step; after the detector system receives the attenuated X-rays, it converts the signal directly to a digital image. The other 30% of radiological examinations—those that involve CT, US, MRI, PET, and DSA—produce images that are already in digital format.

Other medical image sources used in anatomy, biology, and pathology are from light and electron microscopes. Images from these sources are collected with a video or a CCD camera and then digitized to a 512 × 512 × 8 image (or 24 bits for true color) with a frame grabber (an areal A/D converter). Light microscopy produces true color images, using red, green, and blue filters for color separation. Thus, a color

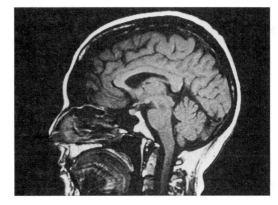

Figure 2. An MR image of the head.

image after digitization yields three digital images, the combination of which produces a true-color digital image encoded at 24 bits/pixel. Figures 1 and 2 show some black and white examples of these images. Table 1 describes the dimensions and storage requirements of some common medical images.

Image-Processing Systems

After a medical image is formed, it is analyzed by an image-processing system. The architecture of an image-processing system (IP) consists of three major components: image-processor(s), image memories, and video processor(s). They are connected by internal computer buses to form an integrated system. An

Table 1. Size of some common medical images.

	One image (bits)	No. of images/exam	One examination (MB)
Nuclear medicine (NM)	128 × 128 × 12	30-60	1-2
Magnetic resonance imaging (MRI)	256 × 256 × 12	60	8
Ultrasound (US)[1]	512 × 256 × 8 (24)	20-230	5-60
Digital subtraction angiography (DSA)	512 × 512 × 8	15-40	4-10
Digitized electronic microscopy	512 × 512 × 8	1	0.26
Digitized color microscopy	512 × 512 × 24	1	0.79
Computed tomography (CT)	512 × 512 × 12	40	20
Computed radiography (CR)	2048 × 2048 × 12	2	16
Digitized X-rays	2048 × 2048 × 12	2	16
Digitized mammography	4000 × 5000 × 12	4	160

[1] Doppler US with 24 bit color images.

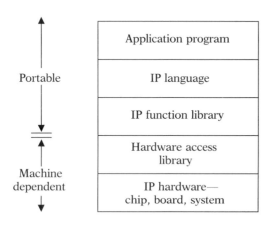

Figure 3. Organization of image processing software. The three higher levels should be portable for future hardware architecture.

IP system requires extensive software support. The trend in IP development is *software portability (q.v.)*. Figure 3 shows the general organization of IP software. Portability is preferred in the three higher levels so that they can be used again when system hardware is upgraded. The two lower levels are machine-dependent and have to be rewritten for each new hardware architecture. In most IP software development, the preferred language is C (*q.v.*) running under Unix (*q.v.*) or Microsoft Windows.

TeleImaging

Recent health care reforms have prompted the use of telemedicine as an efficient healthcare delivery system. In teleimaging, teleconferencing and teleconsultation are two important clinical protocols, both requiring the transmission of large medical image files (*see* Table 1) through some wide and local area networks (LANs–*q.v.*). When these image files are transmitted through a public network with limited bandwidth (*q.v.*), they will create a bottleneck. A major research effort is to design the Next Generation Internet (NGI) to prevent this.

Bibliography

1990. Huang, H. K., Aberle, D. R., Lufkin, R., Grant, E. G., Hanafee, W. N., and Kangarloo, H. "Advances in Medical Imaging," *Annals of Internal Medicine*, **112**, 203–220.

1996. Huang, H. K., Wong, A. W. K., Lou, S. L., Bazzill, T. M., Andriole, K., Zhang, J., Wang, J., and Lee, J. K. "Clinical Experience with a Second Generation PACS," *Journal of Digital Imaging*, **9**(4), 151–166.

1997. Huang, H. K., Wong, S. T. C., and Pietka, E. "Medical Image Informatics Infrastructure Design and Applications," *Medical Informatics*, **22**(4), 279–289.

H. K. Huang

MEMORY

MAIN

For articles on related subjects, *see*

Different levels of memory (or *storage*) are employed in a computer system. At one extreme are very fast and relatively small storage units used as fast access *registers* by the central processing unit (CPU–*q.v.*). At the other extreme are relatively slow, large-capacity units of *auxiliary storage*. The auxiliary storage devices may be magnetic disks, tapes, or optical discs. The characteristics of *main memory* lie between these two extremes. In general, the main memory will contain instructions and data that are accessed by a program while it is executing.

Definitions and Terminology

Digital computers store data as a representation of binary digits. Each digit is called a *bit*, the minimum storage element. A bit may assume the value 1 or 0; nothing else. Data may be both read from and written to any location in main memory. This type of memory is known as *random access memory* (RAM). To access the data in main memory, some element of the computer system must first provide the memory system with an address that describes the location of the data in memory (*see* ADDRESSING). The address may come from the CPU, from a cache memory, or from a memory mapped I/O device. This address is a binary representation placed on the *address bus* of the memory system (*see* BUS). After an *access time*, the memory system will return the selected data on its *data bus* where it can be captured by the computer system. Alternatively, the computer system can write data into the memory by signaling a write operation to the memory system and placing data on the data bus and addresses on the address bus. New data can be read from or written to the memory system every *cycle time*. The access and cycle times are a function of both the technology and organization of the memory system.

The minimum uniquely addressable unit of data in main memory is typically eight bits, or a *byte*, but data is also usually accessible in 4- or 8-byte chunks called *words*. The length of a word depends upon the computer system, the memory unit, and the access mode. The choice of a *data path*, the number of bytes simultaneously transferred per memory access, is governed by the trade-off between performance and cost. A wider data path will allow a greater rate of transfer of data in and out of the memory, but is accompanied by additional expense, power consumption, and system complexity.

An alternative technique for increasing the memory system data rate is the use of *interleaving* (*q.v.*). An interleaved memory system is physically implemented using a number of independent memory subsystems, or banks, of identical size and performance. Adjacent memory addresses are assigned to different physical subsystems. Hence, if the processor accesses sequential memory locations, each memory subsystem can be activated concurrently.

Even small computer systems now have relatively large memories. Since memory addresses are binary numbers, the memory size is typically related to a power of two and described in units of kilobytes (KB), megabytes (MB), gigabytes (GB), or (for mass storage—*q.v.*) terabytes (TB). A kilobyte is 2^{10} or 1024 bytes (i.e. approximately 10^3 bytes, which explains the use of the prefix "kilo"). A megabyte is 2^{20} or 1 048 576 bytes, a gigabyte is 2^{30} or 1.074×10^9 bytes, and a terabyte is 2^{40} or 1.10×10^{12} bytes. Main memory sizes range from 64 MB on an inexpensive personal computer to several gigabytes on a mainframe (*q.v.*).

Memory Technologies

Main memory may be realized through a number of technologies and designs that are distinguished by their unique characteristics of density, performance (access and cycle time), power dissipation, and volatility. Density is important to the system through its impact on cost, size, and performance. A significant part of the delay in modern, high-speed computers comes from the delay along signal lines. Smaller, denser components allow the use of shorter signal lines and therefore improve performance.

Memory *volatility* refers to the inability of the memory to retain its data after power is removed from the system. Most main memories are volatile, that is, information is lost when power is removed. However, in some applications that require rapid restart after power failure or maintenance of data for intervals of power-off, nonvolatile memories are available at greater cost. In general, nonvolatile magnetic medium auxiliary storage devices are used to hold programs and data in the absence of system power. Table 1 describes the relative characteristics of popular main memory technologies. The "D" and "S" in "DRAM" and "SRAM" respectively stand for *dynamic* and *static*, properties defined in the next section.

Semiconductor Technologies

Main memory systems are most often realized using semiconductor technologies. To achieve high density and low cost, semiconductor memories use very large-scale integration (VLSI) to integrate many memory cells as well as decoder and detector circuits on the same chips. Typically, each chip receives an address as input, and outputs 1 to 32 bits corresponding to this address.

Several memory chips will be activated at the same time to access an entire byte or memory word.

MOSFET Dynamic RAM

Metal Oxide Semiconductor Field Effect Transistor Dynamic Random Access Memory (MOSFET DRAM) is the dominant main memory technology. MOSFET DRAMs are chosen primarily for their characteristics of low cost, low power, and moderate performance that make them an ideal choice for large main memories. DRAMs achieve their low cost through use of a relatively simple semiconductor technology (CMOS) and a small memory cell consisting of a single transistor and a single capacitor. The CMOS technology provides both n-channel and p-channel field effect transistors (*see* INTEGRATED CIRCUITRY). The equivalent circuit of a DRAM memory cell, called the *one-device cell*, is shown in Fig. 1. The value of the memory bit is represented by voltage stored on the cell's capacitor. This voltage is written into the storage capacitor by asserting

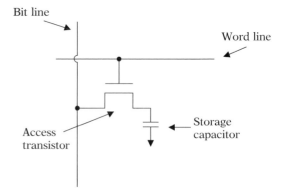

Figure 1. Equivalent circuit of a one-device DRAM memory cell.

Table 1. Relative characteristics of technologies used in main memories.

Technology	Density	Performance	Power	Cost per bit	Volatile
Semiconductor MOSFET DRAM	1	3	2	1	yes
Semiconductor MOSFET DRAM	2	2	3	2	yes
Semiconductor bipolar SRAM	3	1	4	3	yes
Magnetic core (obsolete)	4	4	1	4	no

Note: 1 (best) → 4 (worst).

the *word line* such that the transistor is turned "on." The desired data state is then imposed on the *bit line*. Since the transistor is on, this voltage will be transferred onto the capacitor. Next, the word line voltage is returned to a low voltage, which turns the transistor off, isolating the charge on the capacitor.

To read the information from the cell, the word line is again asserted after the bit line has been connected to the input of a sense amplifier circuit. The charge from the capacitor is then transferred to the amplifier, where it can be detected as a 1 or a 0. Since the procedure is destructive, the read operation must be followed by a subsequent write operation. This *refresh* requirement distinguishes the "dynamic" RAM (DRAM) from a "static" RAM (SRAM).

A large number of one-device memory cells can be fabricated on a single integrated circuit chip (*see* MICROCOMPUTER CHIP). Chips containing 64 megabits (Mb) are commonly available in large quantities. Chips containing a gigabit (Gb) have been demonstrated in the laboratory. DRAM density (bits per chip) has historically grown 60% per year for over 20 years. To provide the high packing density of the cells and to allow hierarchical addressing, the memory cells are physically configured in a square or rectangular array on the integrated circuit chip. A single bit line is shared by many memory cells.

The important elements of a DRAM subarray are shown in Fig. 2. The *row decoder* accepts as input a portion of the data address presented to the chip. From this address, the row decoder activates one of the word lines. When this word line is activated, all of the memory cells located on this line are selected and the charge from their capacitors will be placed on the bit lines. Since this is a destructive read-out, each bit line must be equipped with *sensing write-back* circuitry. Once the signal on each of the bit lines is sensed and amplified, the *column decoder* uses as input a separate portion of the data address to select which sense amplifier output to connect to the *data bus*. Typically, several memory chips will be activated at the same time to access an entire byte or memory word.

The sense amplifier and write-back circuitry are typically merged into one cross-coupled sense amplifier

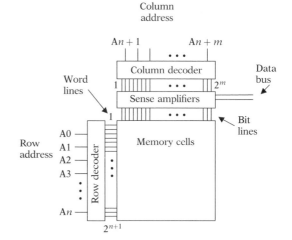

Figure 2. Important elements of a DRAM subarray.

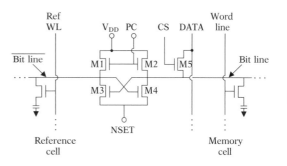

Figure 3. Cross-coupled sense amplifier circuit.

circuit, as shown in Fig. 3. Successful operation of this circuit requires the use of a *reference cell*, which is often implemented as an extra row of cells that store a voltage between a 1 and a 0. Whenever a memory cell is accessed, a reference cell on a separate bit line is also selected. The sense amplifier compares the voltage on the reference bit line with the voltage on the memory cell bit line in order to determine the logical state of the memory cell.

Several classes of DRAM chips exist. Three popular types of DRAMs are Fast-Page-Mode DRAM (FP DRAM), Extended Data-Out DRAM (EDO DRAM), and Synchronous DRAM (SDRAM). The latter modes of operation have evolved in response to a need for ever-increasing data transfer rate from the main memory. FP DRAM and EDO DRAM have very similar characteristics. They operate asynchronously, independent of the system clock. The number of bits per DRAM chip has quadrupled every generation, with a new generation of DRAMs becoming available approximately every three years.

MOSFET Static RAM

To reduce the cycle time of the main memory, some computer designs choose to use static memory technologies that can be read nondestructively. Since the memory cell need not be rewritten after every read, the memory cycle time can be reduced. The static RAM cell consists of cross-coupled inverter circuits (also known as *flip-flops*), as shown in Fig. 4, as well as two access transistors. The cross-coupled inverters possess two stable states. In one state, the right transistor (M2) is on and the left transistor (M1) is off. The second stable state has M1 on and M2 off. Each stable state represents a binary value. The memory cell's state is probed by raising the word line, turning on the access transistors. This transfers the state of the cross-coupled inverters onto the bit lines. Data is written into the cell by simply forcing a voltage onto the bit lines.

Since each static memory cell requires either 4 FETs and 2 resistors or 6 FETs, the size of a static RAM cell is large compared to a dynamic RAM cell. For comparable technologies, SRAM chip densities tend to be approximately a factor of 4

less than that of DRAMs. Recently, the performance of static RAMs has been enhanced by using a hybrid technology base called BiCMOS that integrates bipolar devices and CMOS devices on the same chip.

Bipolar Static RAM

The first integrated semiconductor memory to be used in computer systems was the bipolar static RAM. Early IBM System 360 computers employed 64-bit bipolar static RAM chips. While this cell affords the fastest speed when compared to the previously discussed technologies, its high power dissipation makes it unusable for large main memory systems. The bipolar static RAM cell, shown in Fig. 5, is configured as cross-coupled inverter circuits. The load devices for the inverters include a resistor as well as a diode to improve speed.

Ferrite Core Memory

Ferrite core memory was the first widely used technology for computer main memory. The idea of using magnetic loop toroids was first discussed by Jay Forrester in 1950. His concept of using Permaloy tape-wound cores was quickly extended to the use of mass-produced ferrite material. Figure 6 shows a schematic representation of a single ferrite core memory cell. For several decades,

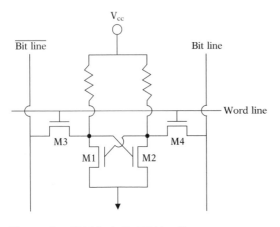

Figure 4. CMOS static RAM cell.

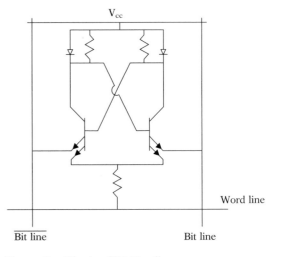

Figure 5. Bipolar SRAM cell.

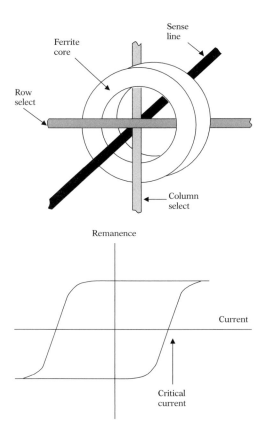

Figure 6.   Ferrite core memory: (a) schematic of a single memory cell; (b) remanence curve of a single ferrite core.

core memory was the dominant main memory, but main memories are now based almost entirely on semiconductor technology.

Bibliography

1986. Chuang, G., Tang, D. D., Li, G. P., Hackbarth, E., and Boedecker, R. R. "A 1.0 ns 5-kbit ECL RAM," *IEEE Journal of Solid-State Circuits*, **SC-21**, (October), 670–675.

1990. Itoh, K. "Trends in Megabit DRAM Circuit Design," *IEEE Journal of Solid-State Circuits*, **SC-25**, 778–789.

1998. Various authors. "Special issue on the 1997 ISSCC: Digital, Memory and Signal Processing," *IEEE Journal of Solid-State Circuits*, **SC-32**, 1712–1765.

Matthew R. Wordeman

AUXILIARY

For articles on related subjects, *see*

+ Diskette
+ Hard Disk
+ Mass Storage
+ Optical Storage
+ Read-Only Memory (ROM)
+ Redundant Array of Inexpensive Disks (RAID)
+ Smart Card

Auxiliary memory is distinguished from main memory in that only from the latter are instructions taken for execution. The central processing unit (CPU—*q.v.*) and main memory are carefully designed components, matched for speed and the width of the data path. Auxiliary memory comprises all other memories whose contents must be fetched into main memory before processing by the CPU. It is used for backup storage to safeguard against loss, and for programs and data not in current use that will be needed again. Most auxiliary memory is rewritable. Certain types of optical auxiliary memory are read-only. Auxiliary memory generally uses electromagnetic or optical digital technology for storing data.

There are at least seven different types of auxiliary memory: magnetic tape, cassette tape, magnetic drum, diskette (floppy disk), fixed- and moving-head hard disks (*see* HARD DISK), and optical discs (*see* OPTICAL STORAGE).

Magnetic Tapes

The use of magnetic tape, once the dominant form of auxiliary memory, has diminished greatly as the availability of inexpensive random-access disks of large capacity has risen. Magnetic tapes are long narrow ribbons (typically 2400 ft long and 0.5 in. wide) of plastic film coated with iron oxide and wound on hard plastic reels approximately 1 ft (30 cm) in diameter. Information is stored transversely on tape, once at 7 bits per *frame* (character of data recorded on tape), later at 9

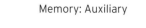

bits per frame (one 8-bit byte plus a parity bit). Several frames are consecutively recorded as a block of data; blocks are separated by *inter-record gaps* (IRGs), and files of such blocks by *inter-file gaps* or "tape marks."

Longitudinally, data is typically stored at a density of 200, 556, 800, 1600, 6250, or 38 000 bits per inch (although the first two densities cited apply only to very early magnetic tapes). For example, a fully written reel of tape, recorded at 38 000 frames per inch (or, on each track, bits per inch, normally abbreviated as *bpi*), contains about one gigabyte computed as follows: 2400 feet by 12 inches/foot by 38 000 bytes/inch = 1 094 400 000 bytes. Still later technology doubled this capacity to 2 GB, but, depending on the blocking factor used, interrecord gaps would reduce either number by about one-third.

Cassette Tapes

The preceding section described magnetic tapes created and used primarily *within* large computing centers. Cassette tapes are typically used for data originating outside them, as follows:

Acquisition of data from laboratory instruments

Analog voltages are digitized and written onto a cassette. Paper tape punches had performed data acquisition for decades; cassettes and diskettes have generally displaced paper tape for these functions, though direct instrument—computer connections are now commonplace as well.

Cash register, gasoline, credit card, and other retailing applications

Some cassette-oriented devices are small and light enough to be hand-held. Typically, these cassette tapes are either 4 mm, 1/4 in. (~6 mm), or 8 mm wide and store several megabytes, in contrast to full-sized tapes, which are 1/2 in. wide and store up to a gigabyte. For minicomputers (*q.v.*) used in data acquisition environments, cassette tapes were sometimes used both to load programs into main memory and to capture data. Cassette drives are also often installed on terminals, serving as a local data-capture auxiliary memory.

Direct Access Devices

Drums, hard disks, diskettes, video-recorded cartridges, and optical/laser discs are collectively termed *direct access* or *random access* devices for their ability to access blocks of data without sequentially passing over a major portion of their contents. Direct access devices cannot access individual bytes as fast as main memory devices, the former having access times of several milliseconds and the latter access times of as little as a few nanoseconds up to, at most, a tenth of a microsecond.

Magnetic Drums

The earliest direct access devices were magnetic drums (Fig. 1), used in the 1950s and 1960s. A cobalt–nickel substrate was coated with iron oxide, which was magnetized and sensed, much as in magnetic-tape operations. Drums were typically 8 to 20 in. (20 to 50 cm) in diameter, 2 to 4 ft (0.6 to 1.2 m) in length, and revolved at 1800 to 3600 rpm. Each character was stored on one or more tracks circumferentially, blocks of characters being separated by inter-record gaps of several thousandths of an inch. Densities of 4000 bpi were commonplace, yielding R/W rates of 1 to 3 MB/sec.

Drums hold considerably less data than disks, magnetic tapes, and so on. However, they can access blocks of data at random more quickly than other direct access devices, 5 to 8 ms on average because each track had its own read–write head. Since a drum is a narrow cylinder, its typical rotational speed of 3600 rpm was considerably higher than that of disk drives of the same era, typically 2400 rpm. A speed of 3600 rpm means

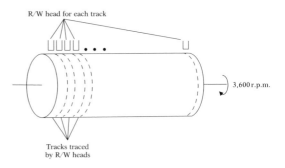

Figure 1.   Magnetic drum.

an average rotational time of 16.7 ms. This compares to 12 to 80 ms for disk drives because of the time required to move the read–write head to the proper track. Despite these advantages, drums are now rarely used, their functions having been taken over by some form of disk storage.

Disks

There are two major varieties of disk drives:

Fixed head, multiple platter

Although their geometry is considerably different from that of drums, fixed-head (FH) disks have comparable access times and transfer rates and greater storage capacity—up to a gigabyte. Each FH drive contains several steel platters coated with iron oxide aligned vertically on a common spindle. R/W heads extend between the platters, facing up and down from the *comb* suspending the heads and containing signal cables. Since there is a head for each track, the only delay in accessing a data block is due to rotational *latency* (0 to 15 ms required for the block to revolve beneath the corresponding R/W head). Although track lengths vary linearly with distance from the spindle, R/W heads are calibrated in such a way that track capacities are all identical. Therefore, there is a universal transfer rate for data, whether read from inner or outer tracks. The average delay for reading a random block is half the maximum rotational latency, although *rotational position sensing* (RPS) considerably reduces inefficiencies caused by I/O, as follows.

Moving head

Since only two heads and associated electronics are required per platter, moving head (MH) drives are considerably cheaper to build than FH drives, although the former require sophisticated servomechanisms to move their R/W heads over the platters. Per-character cost for MH storage is typically 10 to 15% of the cost for FH storage. Some MH drives permit removal of their disk-and-spindle socket assemblies: a *disk cartridge* in the case of a single platter, and a disk pack in the case of multiple platters. An installation can store an indefinite

number of cartridges/packs offline to be mounted as required by various applications programs.

The *Winchester architecture* for disk packs superseded disk-and-spindle socket assemblies by the mid-1980s (*see* HARD DISK). Winchester drives (derived from IBM's pre-announcement product name) do not themselves contain R/W heads, the latter being manufactured together with the platters they access. Winchester drives with high storage capacities (30 GB or more) do not have removable modules.

Moving-head drives may be either single-platter or multiple-platter.

- *Moving-Head Single Platter (MHSP)* Typically, a fork (two-tined comb) that contains two R/W heads is used to enable reading from or writing to either surface; the fork is inserted/withdrawn radially according to the track address furnished with each I/O request.
- *Moving-Head Multiple Platter (MHMP)* The MHMP (Fig. 2) drives generalize the MHSP type, with combs containing $2P-2$ heads, P being the number of platters. (The top surface of the top platter and bottom surface of the bottom platter are not used on MHMP packs, since they are much more exposed to scratches and dust contamination than are interior surfaces.) Widely used drives have 3 to 12 platters, with capacities of 4 to 80 GB.

Soft-Surface Direct Access Devices

Diskettes ("floppy disks"), video-recorded cartridges, and similar devices compete against moving-head disk

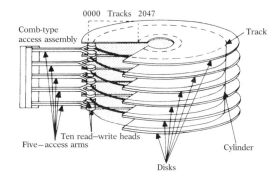

Figure 2. Moving head, multiple platter drive.

drives for selected application areas. Diskettes are structurally similar to MHSP hard-surface disk drives, except that their recording medium is a flexible plastic substrate—8, 5.25, or 3.5 inches in diameter—coated with iron oxide. The 3.5-in. size has now become the *de facto* standard, but is no longer called "floppy" since the recording medium is enclosed in a hard plastic case. Information is recorded and read back just as for an MHSP hard-surface drive. Unlike the latter, a diskette can be easily pocketed and even sent through the mail without extraordinary protective wrapping. They are very inexpensive, about 20¢ for a diskette preformatted to hold 1.44 megabytes. Very high capacity Iomega Corporation Zip drives are now available whose diskettes hold 250 megabytes and cost about $20 each, about 8¢ per megabyte. A newer version, the Jaz drive, uses $100 diskettes that hold two gigabytes (5¢ per megabyte) and hence are attractive for backing up hard drives.

Mass Storage

During the 1970s, several manufacturers developed mass storage systems (*q.v.*): trillion-bit (terabit) storage devices based on reels, cartridges, or cassettes of videotape or wide magnetic tape. In late 1974, marketing of such devices to commercial users began with the IBM 3850 Mass Storage System, whose online capacity was 50 to 500 billion bytes, or *gigabytes* (0.4 to 4×10^{12} bits). A tape-based mass storage system typically had a large magazine of cartridges or cassettes from which a transport mechanism extracted requested units. Each cartridge or cassette contained approximately 50 Mb, comparable to a fully packed reel of conventional magnetic tape. A full mass storage system of this type comprised 500 to 5000 cartridges or cassettes, together with transports and read–write stations. Often, the transports and R/W stations were duplexed or triplexed to assure continuity of operation should one of these devices malfunction. With modern disk technology, it has become easier to assemble terabyte mass storage systems with much better access time and transfer rate (*see* REDUNDANT ARRAY OF INEXPENSIVE DISKS (RAID) and

MASS STORAGE). Dell, for example, markets a 2-terabyte (2 TB) disk system for $18 000—less than 1¢ per megabyte.

Optical Storage

CD-ROM, DVD, and laserdisc memories are discussed in the article OPTICAL STORAGE. These are read-only auxiliary memories, prerecorded by the vendor. A variant called a CD-R (Compact Disc-Recordable) or WORM drive (Write Once, Read Many times) allows the user (once) rather than the vendor to do the recording. Yet other variants, generally called Erasable Optical (EO) or WMRM drives (Write Many, Read Many) devices are rewritable and hence are true auxiliary memory rather than just secondary storage. Among them are: CD-RW (CD-ReWritable); Magneto-Optical (MO) drives of 5.25-in. CD-size, which hold 500 MB; 3.5-in. floppy optical drives ("flopticals") that hold 20 MB; and DVD-RAM. No two of these use exactly the same technology, but some type of laser is fundamental to all four.

Summary

Table 1 provides comparative data for the various memory types, giving cost/benefit comparisons of using various types of memory for both mainframes and smaller computers. Not surprisingly, the general trend is that the greater the storage capacity, the lower the cost per megabyte and the slower the transfer rate. Decade by decade, older forms of data storage obsolesce as ever-newer technology of greater capacity but lower cost per megabyte is developed. The only downside is the very worrisome problem of how important data recorded in earlier eras can be read and transferred to the newer devices. Is there a surviving drive, even if only in a museum, that can still read data from the old storage medium? Are the data bits still *there*, or have they crumbled to bits of another kind? For a fascinating discussion of this topic, *see* Rothenberg (1995).

Table 1.   Typical characteristics of various types of memory.

Memory	Access time	Transfer rate	Capacity	Device cost	Media capacity	Media cost	Cost/MB
Mainframes							
Main	20 ns	100 MB/sec	2 GB	$500k	–	–	$250
Drum	5 ms	2 MB/sec	4 MB	$20k	–	–	$5000
FH Disk	10 ms	10 MB/sec	100 MB	$10k	–	–	$100
MHMP disk	20 ms	1 MB/sec	–	$20k	4 GB	$200	5¢
Magnetic tape	minutes	1 MB/sec	–	$10k	2 GB	$26	1.3¢
Mass storage	50 ms	1 MB/sec	2 TB	$18k	–	–	0.9¢
Personal computers and workstations							
Main	60 ns	40 MB/sec	128 MB	$320	–	–	250¢
Diskette	100 ms	0.2 MB/sec	–	$35	1.44 MB	20¢	14¢
Zip drive	29 ms	0.2 MB/sec	–	$200	250 MB	$20	8¢
Jaz drive	16 ms	7 MB/sec	–	$350	2 GB	$100	5¢
MO-RW	60 ms	4 MB/sec	–	$1800	2.6 GB	$130	5¢
Hard disk	15 ms	5 MB/sec	80 GB	$300	–	–	3¢
CD-RW	80 ms	1 MB/sec	–	$200	650 MB	$1	0.15¢
CD-ROM (32X)	10 ms	4.8 MB/sec	–	$150	650 MB	20¢	0.03¢
DVD-RAM	20 ms	1.3–2.4 MB/sec	–	$300	2.6 GB/side	$6	0.1¢
DVD (16X)	20 ms	2.4 MB/sec	–	$100	8.5 GB	$8	0.1¢
Cassette tape	minutes	1 MB/sec	–	$400	4 GB	$4	0.1¢

Note: TB = Terabyte = 1000 GB. X = 150 KB/sec = 0.15 MB/sec, the transfer rate of first-generation CD-ROM drives.

Bibliography

1995. Rothenberg, J. "Ensuring the Longevity of Digital Documents," *Scientific American*, **272**(1), 42–47.

1998. Stone, M. D. "Removable Storage," *PC Magazine*, **17**(8), (21 April), 153–179.

1998. White, R. *How Computers Work*, 4th Ed. Indianapolis, IN: QUE. Contains excellent color-illustrated descriptions of many of the devices discussed in this article.

David N. Freeman

MEMORY ADDRESSING

See ADDRESSING.

MEMORY ALLOCATION

See STORAGE ALLOCATION.

MEMORY HIERARCHY

For articles on related subjects, *see*

+ Addressing
+ Cache Memory
+ Memory
+ Register
+ Virtual Memory

Introduction

Memory in a conventional digital computer is organized hierarchically (*see* Fig. 1). At the top are *registers* that

Table 1. Properties of the memory hierarchy.

Memory type	Access time	Cost/MB	Typical amount used	Typical cost
Registers	1 ns	High	1 KB	–
Cache	5–20 ns	$100	1 MB	$100
Main memory	60–80 ns	$1.10	64 MB	$70
Disk memory	10 ms	$0.05	30 GB	$200

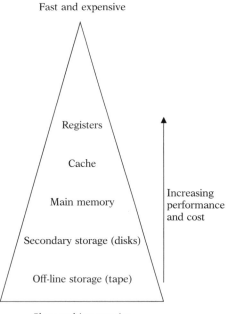

Fast and expensive

Registers

Cache

Main memory

Secondary storage (disks)

Off-line storage (tape)

Increasing performance and cost

Slow and inexpensive

Figure 1. The memory hierarchy.

are matched in speed to the *central processing unit* (CPU—*q.v.*), but tend to use a large chip area and consume significant power. At the bottom are auxiliary and offline storage memories, such as hard disks (*q.v.*) and magnetic tapes, in which the cost per stored bit is small but *access time* (*q.v.*) is long compared to registers. Between these extremes are a number of other forms of memory.

As hierarchical level increases, greater performance is realized but at greater cost. Table 1 shows some of the properties of the components of the memory hierarchy. Typical Cost, computed by multiplying Cost/MB ×

Typical Amount Used, is approximately the same at each level of the hierarchy. But access times vary by approximately factors of 10 except for disks, which have access times 100 000 times slower than main memory.

Computer Memory

Main memory consists of a collection of consecutively numbered locations, each of which stores exactly one binary value. Each of the numbered locations corresponds to a specific stored byte. The unique number that identifies each byte is referred to as its *address* (*see* ADDRESSING). Since addresses are counted in sequence, beginning with 0, the highest address is one less than the size of the memory. The highest address for a 2^{32} byte memory is $2^{32} - 1$.

The example memory architecture shown in Fig. 2 has a 32-bit *address space*, which means that a program can access a byte of memory anywhere in the range from 0 to $2^{32} - 1$. The address space for this example architecture is divided into distinct regions that are used for the operating system, input and output (I/O), user programs, and the system *stack* (*q.v.*), which comprise the *memory map* at the left side of Fig. 2. The portion of the address space between 2^{31} and $2^{32} - 1$ is reserved for I/O devices. The memory map thus does not necessarily represent real memory; there may be large gaps where neither real memory nor I/O devices exist. Treating I/O device space like memory locations is called *memory mapped* I/O.

Locality

Typically, 90% of the execution time of a program is spent in just 10% of its code and data, a small portion of the total memory allocated to the program. This

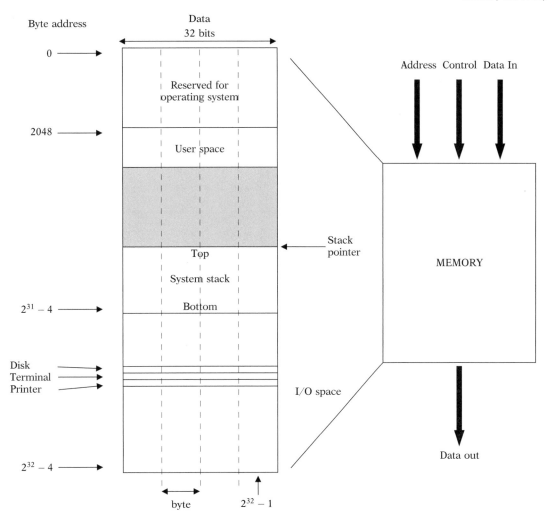

Byte address

Data
32 bits

0

Reserved for
operating system

2048

User space

Stack
pointer

Top

System stack

$2^{31} - 4$

Bottom

Disk
Terminal
Printer

I/O space

$2^{32} - 4$

byte $2^{32} - 1$

Address Control Data In

MEMORY

Data out

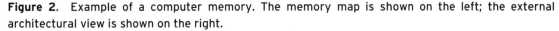

Figure 2. Example of a computer memory. The memory map is shown on the left; the external architectural view is shown on the right.

property is known as *locality of reference*. Memory access is generally slow in comparison with the speed of the CPU and thus poses a significant bottleneck. Locality of reference can be exploited to improve performance. A small but fast *cache memory* in which the contents of the most commonly accessed memory locations are maintained, can be placed between the main memory and the CPU. When a program executes, needed data is fetched from the cache if present or copied to it if not. Although needed copying takes longer than accessing main memory directly, the overall performance can be improved if a high proportion of memory accesses are thereafter satisfied by the cache.

Virtual Memory
Overlays

One method of extending the apparent size of the main memory is to augment it with disk space. An early approach made use of *overlays*, in which an executing program overwrites its own code with other code as needed. In this scenario, the programmer must manage memory usage. An alternative method that can be managed by the operating system is *paging*.

Paging

Paging is a form of automatic overlaying in which the address space is partitioned into equal sized blocks, called *pages*. Pages are normally an integral power of two in size, such as $2^{10} = 1024$ bytes. Paging makes the physical memory appear larger than it truly is by mapping the physical memory address space onto some portion of the virtual memory address space, which is stored on a disk. Paging requires that every memory reference must be looked up in the page table before it is accessed. This means there must be two memory references to access a data item: one to look in the page table and another to access the data. Performance can be improved by keeping track of the most recent page table lookups inside the CPU, in what is known as a *translation lookaside buffer* (TLB). In the ideal case, the TLB contains the address of the data, and the cache itself contains the data.

Segmentation

Paging is one-dimensional in the sense that addresses grow either up or down. *Segmentation* is a different form of virtual memory that allows several one-dimensional address spaces to exist simultaneously. This allows tables, stacks, and other data structures (*q.v.*) to be maintained as logical entities that grow independently. Segmentation allows for *protection*, so that a segment may be specified as "read only" to prevent changes, or "execute only" to prevent unauthorized copying.

Bibliography

1990. Hamacher, V. C., Vranesic, Z. G., and Zaky, S. G. *Computer Organization*, 3rd Ed. New York: McGraw-Hill.

1999. Tanenbaum, A. *Structured Computer Organization*, 4th Ed. Upper Saddle River, NJ: Prentice Hall.

2000. Murdocca, M. J., and Heuring, V. P. *Principles of Computer Architecture*. Reading, MA: Addison-Wesley Longman.

Miles J. Murdocca and Vincent P. Heuring

MEMORY MANAGEMENT

For articles on related subjects, *see*

+ Cache Memory
+ Data Type
+ Database Management System (DBMS)
+ Distributed Systems
+ List Processing
+ Memory Hierarchy
+ Operating Systems
+ Pointer
+ Stack
+ Storage Allocation
+ Virtual Memory
+ Working Set

Memory management is concerned with the organization of data for periods up to the duration of a program's execution. In contrast, database management is concerned with shared data of much longer persistence. The term *memory management* is also used to cover address transformation and data movement between levels of the memory hierarchy.

Disk Memory Management

Long-lived data is normally held on disk in files and databases. In this context, memory management is implemented both in operating systems and in database management systems. Application programmers use databases and file systems as a matter of course and hence rely on automated memory management for disk storage and long-lived data.

Main Memory Management

Two regimes are available for main memory management, *automatic* and *explicit*.

Explicit Memory Management

Many programmers, using languages such as C (*q.v.*) and C++ (*q.v.*), use an explicit regime and much legacy code depends on such regimes. That is, programs explicitly request or allocate space, and explicitly decide when space can be returned for reuse.

Automatic vs Explicit Memory Management

With an automatic regime, only the language implementers have to understand how to implement main memory management correctly and efficiently. With the explicit regime, many more programmers have to tackle this laborious and error-prone task. Historically, languages such as C (*q.v.*) did not provide reliable information for automatic memory management. But the balance has tipped in favor of automated memory management. The advent and popularity of Java (*q.v.*) is both a consequence of these changes and a catalyst for the trend towards the increased use of improved automatic regimes.

Garbage Collection

In some computations, it is relatively easy to determine when space is no longer needed. For example, when *independent* processes (threads) terminate, their space may be returned. Similarly, return of space is straightforward when a GUI window is closed. But in many computations, references to stored data are stored in multiple locations, so the application program cannot easily determine when it is safe to return space for fear of generating dangling references.

Fragmentation

Memory can be viewed as a continuous range of allocatable cells, for example, words or bytes. In an ideal system none would be wasted. However, it is hard to allocate space so that there are no gaps between useful cells. The occurrence of these unused gaps is called *fragmentation*. It can both increase the requirement for memory and slow down computation due to less efficient use of the storage hierarchy. Memory managers therefore invest a certain amount of background computation to reduce fragmentation.

Requirements for Storage Regimes

Programming languages have supported the automatic management of storage space by using one of two policies. *Static allocation* is a policy in which the provision of space is determined at compilation time. *Dynamic allocation* is a policy in which the requirements for space are determined by the computation. Dynamic allocation now predominates.

A Stack Regime for Space Allocation

With uniform size memory cells, space allocation is straightforward. The total area of space available for

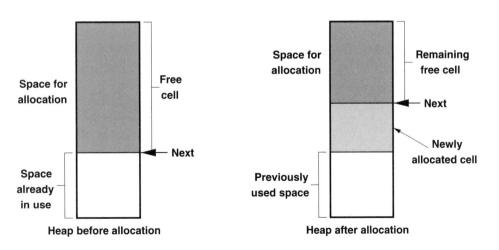

Figure 1. The operation of a stack regime.

allocation is viewed as a sequence of cells. A *pointer* (*q.v.*) records a position in this space indicating the start of the next free cell. On making an allocation, the value of the pointer is returned as the address of the new cell, and the pointer is moved on, by the length of the space allocated, to the remaining cells (*see* Fig. 1). Such a regime is simple to implement and reasonably fast to operate. As space is relinquished in the reverse order from which it is claimed, the return of space is recorded by decreasing *next*. An allocated block may hold the previous value of *next*. When the block is returned, *next* is reset to that recorded value. This is the normal way of allocating *frames* holding local variables in block-structured languages.

Handling Random Sequences of Requests and Deallocations

When demand is interspersed with return in some random sequence, different strategies are appropriate depending on whether or not all the cells are of the same size. The range of memory from which cells are allocated and deallocated randomly is called a *heap*. A list is kept of all the cells available for issue. When a cell is returned, it is added to this *list of available space*. If all cells are of the same size, the first one on the list is allocated when a cell is requested.

Cell Allocation Strategies

When the cells vary in size, the first cell in the list may not be large enough, or will not be the optimum one to allocate. When choosing an algorithm to perform cell allocation, it is necessary to compromise between the computational cost of finding the cell and the optimality of the cell found. The optimality depends on the rate of *fragmentation*; that is, on the proportion of small cells generated that are not contiguous and therefore cannot be coalesced and that are too small to be useful. Two extremes of this compromise are presented.

The best-fit strategy

The *best-fit* algorithm requires a search of all cells available for allocation until one is found that is the correct size or is the smallest that is sufficiently large. In the example (Fig. 2), *A*, *B*, *C*, and *D* form the free list. If a cell of size 3 were requested, cell *D* would be allocated after a search of the entire free list. A structure such as several lists corresponding to defined ranges of cell size would accelerate the search for the optimum cell, but would also increase the cost of returning a cell. Suppose that a cell is now returned consisting of the four words (memory locations) between *B* and *C*. Then, as shown in Fig. 2, the system could coalesce *B*, *E*, and *C* into a single cell.

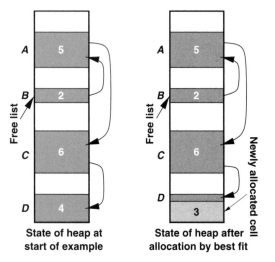
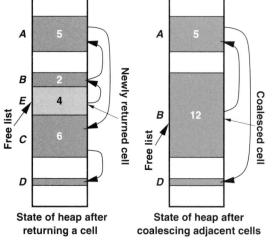

Figure 2.   The operation of a best-fit strategy.

The first-fit strategy

The *first-fit* algorithm scans the list and allocates the first cell that is large enough, retaining the fragment left over. The operations involved in allocating a cell are shown in Fig. 3. Return of cells is similar to best fit.

Advances in Memory Management

A few examples of the recent advances in memory management are presented to illustrate its growing sophistication.

The Storage Hierarchy

It is now common for processors to have on-chip memory caches and other nearby caches that are between 100 and 1000 times faster to access than the large volume RAM. Modern memory management algorithms attempt to exploit this. Most cells are allocated, used for a very short time, and then freed for reallocation. If these short-lived cells are kept in the fast cache, a significant acceleration is achieved. But when multithreaded programs are running on multiprocessor architectures, it is necessary to ensure that these allocation spaces are in the appropriate processor. Although RAM may now be very large, it is invariably underpinned by a virtual memory (*q.v.*) mapping to disk. This introduces a factor of 1000 in access time. To avoid incurring this penalty too often, it is necessary to ensure that large heaps fit in the *working set* (*q.v.*), or that allocation and garbage collection minimize page faults.

Distributed Systems

With distributed systems, it is possible to construct references from data in one processor to cells in another. This implies that the memory-management system now has to preserve the meaning of incoming references; it may not reallocate their referenced cells nor move cells so that the reference is lost. A *protocol* (*q.v.*) is therefore needed to ensure that processors inform others that their local memory manager has discovered it no longer needs a reference. Distributed memory management algorithms are difficult to make safe, resilient to local failures, and efficient.

Large-scale Memories

The volume of RAM on computers has increased rapidly; 256 MB is not unusual, and servers may have tens of gigabytes. The time taken to read or write this much memory is significant. This has led to the development of incremental and concurrent techniques for memory management that avoid overly long pauses for garbage collection. The basic principle is to divide the space into separately administered partitions. Allocation and computation is then supported in the majority of these partitions, while housekeeping tasks such as garbage collection and archival dumping (saving data in long-term storage) are performed on the others.

Persistent Systems

Long-lived data held on disk requires all of the techniques just introduced. Localizing space management on disk using a two-level system is essential to handle the typically concurrent load and to avoid disk-head movement for every allocation. Incremental algorithms are the only way to avoid inordinate delays and to offer a continuous service. It is common to introduce a localized indirect addressing mechanism to avoid the need to update data all over the disks when space has to be rearranged. Typically, the transfers between disk and main memory also include translations. The object

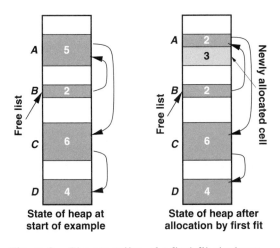

State of heap at start of example   **State of heap after allocation by first fit**

Figure 3.   The operation of a first-fit strategy.

cache and the remainder of the main memory management interact. For example, they compete for space and space can be recovered either by garbage collection or cache eviction. Both of these have to handle references between transient and persistent space correctly.

Trends in Memory Management

While safe and automatic memory management has been possible with research and academic languages for many years, it has now become significant commercially. This trend will undoubtedly have an impact on hardware. Support for memory management activities is appearing. Architectures will appear that reflect partitioned memory management. In these, each memory component will support the local administration of its memory.

Bibliography

1995. Wilson, P. R., Johnstone, M. S., Neely, M., and Boles, D. "Dynamic Storage Allocation: A Survey and Critical Review," *Proceedings of the International Workshop on Memory Management*, 1–116. New York: Springer-Verlag.

1996. Jones, R. E., and Lins, R. D. *Garbage Collection Algorithms for Automatic Dynamic Memory Management*. New York: John Wiley.

Malcolm P. Atkinson and Tony Printezis

MEMORY-MAPPED I/O

For articles on related subjects, *see*

+ Input–Output Operations
+ Memory: Main
+ Microprocessors and Microcomputers
+ Monitor, Display
+ Personal Computing
+ Port, Memory

In some large computers equipped with a display monitor, a programmer must direct characters to the monitor in much the same way as output is directed to a tape, disk, or other online I/O device; that is, the program must execute an I/O statement that (typically) names the channel (*q.v.*) to which the display device is attached, the number of characters to be transmitted, the screen location where they are to be displayed, and the starting address in memory where the data to be transmitted may be found. Some mini- and microcomputers, however, now use a simpler and more flexible system known as *memory-mapped I/O*, whereby characters are transferred to the display monitor with the same move or store instructions that are part of the processor instruction set (*q.v.*).

With memory-mapped I/O, individual character positions on the screen are mapped one-to-one to bytes in the computer's main memory. For example, suppose that a certain (hypothetical) 64 × 128 character display screen is mapped onto the 8192-byte memory segment starting at hexadecimal address A000. This has a twofold advantage. First, to display, say, Hello in the middle of the screen, one would merely store the five-byte ASCII equivalent of HELLO at hexadecimal memory locations A83E to A842, which correspond to the desired portion of the screen. Instantaneously and automatically, the desired message will appear without need for any further instructions. Second, unlike the programmer of a system without memory-mapped I/O, whose programs cannot detect what is currently on the screen, the programmer of a memory-mapped system need only check the current contents of the memory map area to ascertain what is being displayed. If a user at the console changes it through keyboard action, the storage map will change to conform.

When a display is in graphics mode, individual pixels are memory-mapped. This will, of course, take considerably more memory—a megabyte for a 1024 × 1024 array of pixels—but that is no longer a serious overhead storage penalty relative to the amount of main memory typically available on current computers.

A keyboard may also be memory-mapped in a similar way, with individual keys associated with memory addresses. This allows the software to use simple memory accesses to be able to sense at any given time which keys (or combination of keys) are being depressed and to take appropriate action.

The alternative to memory-mapped I/O is called *port-mapped* I/O (*see* PORT, MEMORY).

Edwin D. Reilly

MEMORY ORGANIZATION

See MEMORY HIERARCHY.

MEMORY PORT

See PORT, MEMORY.

MEMORY PROTECTION

For articles on related subjects, see

+ Addressing
+ Memory Management
+ Multiprogramming
+ Multitasking
+ Operating Systems
+ Storage Allocation
+ Virtual Memory

Memory protection is a hardware mechanism that limits or prevents access to specified areas in the main memory of a computer. It first became important when systems became capable of permitting more than one program to be resident in memory at the same time. The possibility then existed that while one program was running, it might inadvertently write over part of another and thus invalidate that program.

In *uniprogramming* operating systems, there were typically two programs resident in memory—an executive program and a user program. The earliest memory protection mechanism provided a switch register that could be set to a memory address that marked the upper limit of a protected area. The lower limit was zero. No program running outside the protected area could write into any location inside the protected area. The executive routine, presumably debugged, would reside in the protected area. The user program would run outside of it and thus could hurt only itself.

With the development of *multiprogramming* and *multitasking*, more elaborate memory protection mechanisms were needed. In such systems, supervisory programs and a number of user programs may reside in memory simultaneously. While a user program is running, it is important to be able to designate the areas that belong to that program and to limit its access to other areas.

The first effective memory protection mechanism for a multiprogramming system used a *base register*, now commonly called a *relocation register*, and a *limit register*. A program would reside in a contiguous area of memory; when that program was to run, the executive placed the program's origin (i.e. its lowest address) in the base register and its length in the limit register. Any attempt by a program to access a memory location outside its own area would cause control to switch to the executive routine.

It is now common for a program to have several *segments*—one for the program code, one for its data, and perhaps one for its run-time stack (*see* ACTIVATION RECORD). Segments are disjoint regions of memory, and processors frequently have several relocation registers, one to hold the base address of each segment. The Intel Pentium II has six such "segment" registers. Together with memory-management (*q.v.*) hardware, they provide rapid access to and protection for each segment (a code segment would be read-only; a data segment read–write). Since modern systems are multitasking, there can be many segments of memory. The combination of access-right protection for segments and protection against access outside a program's segments is now common in virtual memory systems.

Saul Rosen

MERGING

See SORTING.

METALANGUAGE

For an article on a related subject, *see*

+ Backus–Naur Form (BNF)

A *metalanguage* is a set of symbols and words used to describe another language in which these symbols do not appear. The most common application is in the definition of programming languages. The first- and best-known example was the definition of Algol 60 (*q.v.*). The metalanguage used in this case, Backus–Naur Form, consists of the symbols ⟨, ⟩, |, : : =, together with a number of metalinguistic variables that are used to define the elements of Algol. The brackets ⟨ ⟩ are used as delimiters for the metalinguistic variables, the vertical stroke | has the meaning "or," and the symbol ::= means "is defined as." The following extract from the report on Algol 60 gives the definition of an integer and illustrates the use of the symbols:

```
⟨digit⟩ ::= 0|1|2|3|4|5|6|7|8|9
⟨unsigned integer⟩ ::= ⟨digit⟩
         |⟨unsigned integer⟩ ⟨digit⟩
⟨integer⟩ ::= ⟨unsigned integer⟩
         |+ ⟨unsigned integer⟩
         |- ⟨unsigned integer⟩
```

The example uses three metalinguistic variables: ⟨digit⟩, ⟨unsigned integer⟩, and ⟨integer⟩. In defining a complete language, there will normally be one metalinguistic variable that is never used in the definition of any other variable; this is known as the *starting type*. In programming languages, this would normally be ⟨program⟩, and in natural languages it might be ⟨sentence⟩. The digits 0, 1, . . . , 9 and the signs + and − are *terminal symbols* of the language; that is, they will appear in statements written in the language. For this reason, they are sometimes printed in bold-face to distinguish them from the *nonterminal symbols*

(digit, integer, etc.), sometimes called *defined types or metavariables*.

Bibliography

1993. Fisher, A. E., and Grodzinsky, F. S. *The Anatomy of Programming Languages.* Upper Saddle River, NJ: Prentice Hall.

1999. Sebesta, R. W. *Concepts of Programming Languages*, 4th Ed. Reading, MA: Addison-Wesley.

Kathleen H. V. Booth

MICROCOMPUTER CHIP

For articles on related subjects, *see*

+ Integrated Circuitry
+ Microprocessors and Microcomputers
+ Minicomputer
+ Personal Computing

A *microcomputer chip*, or *microchip* or just *chip*, is an integrated circuit component that is the building block of a computer system. Typically, microcomputer chips are very large-scale integrated circuit components (VLSI) containing millions to tens of millions of transistors. By 2000, the largest such components contained over one hundred million transistors. A typical PC contains about 40 chips of different varieties.

Physical Description

Silicon wafers are typically 8 in. in diameter and thinner than cardboard. During semiconductor manufacturing, a single such wafer contains tens and possibly hundreds of individual microcomputer chips. The wafers are cut or diced into individual chips that are the size of a thumbnail (*see* Fig. 1). The surface of each chip is covered with transistors that are etched into the surface of the silicon through a complex sequence of superimposed photographically developed layers. The photographic

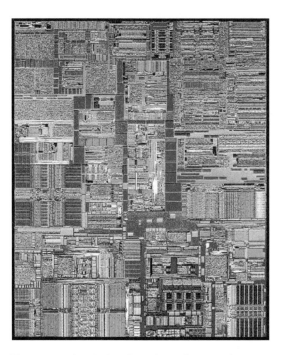

Figure 1. Die photo of Intel Pentium II micropro-cessor. (Copyright (©) 2004, Intel Corporation.)

layers provide a stencil for sequences of carefully controlled chemical procedures that create metal lines for signal flow, transistors, and their interconnections. Some chip packages have pins that allow them to be connected to a circuit board that subsequently allows interconnection to other components. The individual signals of the chip are connected to the package with gold wires that are finer than hair. Packages contain 50 to 500 pins (*see* Fig. 2).

Over three decades, the number of transistors that can be fabricated as a single integrated circuit has more than doubled every two years (*see* LAWS, COMPUTER). The largest microprocessor of 1990 had over one million transistors. Chips containing 50 to 100 million transistors are now in volume production, and Intel is planning a chip that will contain a billion transistors in 2007.

History

The precursor to the first microcomputer chip was the integrated circuit invented almost simultaneously by Jack Kilby of Texas Instruments and Robert Noyce, then of Fairchild Semiconductor, in 1959. Noyce is deceased, but Kilby received the year 2000 Nobel Prize in physics for his contribution. The microcomputer chip traces its origin to the microprocessor, invented in the early 1970s (*see* MICROPROCESSORS AND MICROCOMPUTERS). Prior to the microprocessor, integrated circuits were rather simple, performing a single function on an individual chip. The breakthrough of the microprocessor was the combination of several different computing elements or functional units of a computer into a single integrated circuit. The first such microprocessor was the Intel 4004 invented by Marcian (Ted) Hoff in 1972. In the case of the microprocessor, the functions combined on a

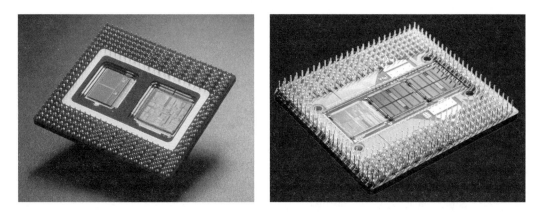

Figure 2. Packaged Intel Pentium Pro microprocessor. (Copyright (©) 2004, Intel Corporation.)

single chip were those that constitute most of a computer's CPU.

The memory typically contains the program or sequence of instructions that the microprocessor is to execute. In this way, the microcontroller can be embedded into a host system and perform a function repetitively, as needed, for extended periods of time. One example might be a traffic light controller whose memory is loaded with a program indicating what sequence of lights should be used for each conceivable configuration (*see* EMBEDDED SYSTEM). Other examples include the microcontrollers that govern modern automobile engines and antilock braking systems.

Types of Microchip
Microprocessors

Microprocessors combine all the capabilities of a CPU on a single chip and perform up to billions of instructions per second. Microprocessors have typically integrated new functions as required to remove bottlenecks that inhibit the performance of a microcomputer system. Some examples are the integration of memory management (*q.v.*), cache memory (*q.v.*), floating-point operations, and recently, provisions for a single instruction to process multiple pieces of data simultaneously (*see* INSTRUCTION-LEVEL PARALLELISM and PARALLEL PROCESSING).

Microcontrollers

A single modern car may have as many as 25 microcontrollers that perform tasks ranging from audio systems to global positioning systems, ignition control, engine control, and suspension balancing. As microcontrollers have become very powerful (hundreds of millions of instructions per second) at very low costs (about US$20), they have begun to replace many special-purpose hard-wired chips.

Graphics

Another microcomputer chip of interest is the *graphics accelerator*, whose function is to perform some of the specialized display processing needed to put two- and three-dimensional graphics upon the screen. As the graphics chip combines more functions and runs faster, it is able to update more pixels, draw lines more quickly, or display more information. Over the next decade, displays will increase in resolution to the point of photographic realism—resolution that exceeds what the human eye can detect—and that such displays will allow photographs and motion video to be played in real time.

Computer Architecture

The chief characteristic that distinguishes microprocessors and microcontrollers from "hard-wired" devices is their programmability. Most software written for microprocessors is realized in a high-level language such as C (*q.v.*) or Java (*q.v.*). A compiler (*q.v.*) converts a high-level language program into the machine instructions of the target processor. Those machine instructions, along with certain other aspects of a processor, are collectively known as the processor's instruction set (*q.v.*) architecture. Microcontrollers also have instruction set architectures, but it is generally less important that they be strictly compatible, because they are programmed permanently and do not have to run older software.

Bibliography

1990. Hennessy, J., and Patterson, D. *Computer Architecture—A Quantitative Approach*. San Francisco, CA: Morgan Kaufmann.
1995. Malone, M. S. *The Microprocessor: A Biography*. New York: Springer-Verlag.
1998. Yu, A. *Creating The Digital Future*. New York: Free Press.

Patrick P. Gelsinger and Robert P. Colwell

MICROPROCESSORS AND MICROCOMPUTERS

For articles on related subjects, *see*

+ Computer Circuitry
+ Embedded System
+ Integrated Circuitry

+ Instruction-Level Parallelism
+ Microcomputer Chip
+ Reduced Instruction Set Computer (RISC)

A *microprocessor* is a single-chip integrated circuit (IC) implementation of a general-purpose central processing unit (CPU—*q.v.*). It contains a controller to direct the execution of program instructions, registers to store control and data values temporarily, and an arithmetic logic unit (ALU—*q.v.*) to calculate results. A microprocessor chip is a very large-scale integrated (VLSI) circuit fabricated on a sliver of silicon less than $7\,mm^2$ (about 1/4 in) and 0.5 mm (1/50 in) thick.

There are many different kinds of microprocessors. In 1990, there were about 50 different microprocessor families, including 995 varieties of CPU chips; by 2000, there were 35 000 CPU and controller chip types sold by 250 vendors. Each CPU chip contains the equivalent of 4000 to 20 000 000 transistors; and in accordance with Moore's Law, chip complexity increases roughly by a factor of 32 every decade (*see* LAWS, COMPUTER). A transistor-equivalent is able to make one simple logic decision or store one bit (a 0 or a 1). A popular CPU categorization is based on the width of its internal data path, commonly 16-bit, 32-bit, or 64-bit.

A *microcomputer* is a more complete system than a microprocessor, containing not only the CPU logic, but also memory for storing programs and data plus I/O interfaces for exchanging data with peripheral devices. In 1990, most microcomputers combined a CPU chip with 1 to 200 support chips on a single circuit board no larger than a double book page. Most extra chips contained from 262 144 (2^{18}) to 4 194 304 (2^{22}) bits of memory. A 100-chip microcomputer usually controlled a workstation (*q.v.*) with I/O interfaces for a graphics display, mouse (*q.v.*) input keyboard, storage disk, loudspeaker, and network communications; it executed from 64 to 300 different instructions at rates from 1 million to 80 million instructions per second (MIPS) and contained 9 to 36 MB of memory.

By 2000, the circuitry for a personal computer had shrunk to a module the size of a deck of playing cards and containing about 10 chips: CPU, memory bus, memory controller, I/O bus, I/O controller,

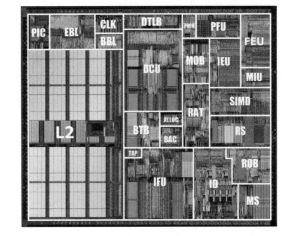

Figure 1. Photomicrograph of an Intel Pentium III processor introduced in 1999. It is a VLSI circuit with 28.1 million transistors. Among the major parts of the chip, marked with an overlay, are: left side: the cache memory (L2), and interface to the external bus (EBL); top center: data allocation units, including the data cache (DCU); bottom center: the instruction fetch unit and front-end of the instruction pipeline (IFU); top right: arithmetic execution units (IEU: integer execution), (FEU:floating-point execution), (SIMD: MMX technology instructions); bottom right: instruction decoder (ID) and associated logic for instruction scheduling. (© 2004, Intel Corporation.)

and 2 to 8 memory chips of 67 108 864 (2^{26}) to 1 073 741 824 (2^{30}) bits each, giving 64 MB to 1024 MB of memory. Common execution rates were 100 to 1000 MIPS.

The ever-increasing number of transistors that a single integrated circuit can hold has made possible *single-chip microcomputers* (Fig. 1), small systems with large application markets. They range in processing speeds from slow, tiny appliance controllers to low-end supercomputers (*q.v.*). A *digital signal processor* (DSP–*q.v.*) is a microcomputer designed for high-speed numerical processing ("number crunching"). DSP chips are very useful for speech recognition and synthesis (*q.v.*). A *coprocessor* is an older, optional function unit on a separate chip that can rapidly

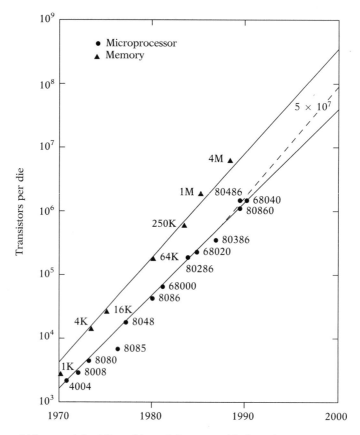

Figure 2. The almost bi-annual doubling of transistors per chip for microprocessors and memories (*see* Moore's Law in LAWS, COMPUTER). The graph shows the densest memory chips and microprocessors from Intel (4044, 80xx, 80xxx) and Motorola (680xx). As microprocessors are built with more on-chip memory for fast access, the two lines will merge, as indicated by the dashed line. (© 2004, Intel Corporation.)

execute complex floating-point arithmetic instructions (*see* ARITHMETIC, COMPUTER).

In the 1990s, a new technology became popular for making fast processor prototypes: *programmable gate arrays* (PGAs—*see* COMPUTER CIRCUITRY). Each chip holds regular arrays of hundreds of thousands of AND and OR gates with memory-selectable interconnections. Some arrays, called *complex programmable logic devices* (CPLDs), also contain small fast RAMs for data and may have specialized DSP logic.

A *microcontroller* is a single-chip microcomputer built to control embedded systems, such as appliances and traffic lights. It typically has on-chip permanent program memory, a small amount of data memory for temporary values, and an assorted selection of interfaces and peripheral units such as serial and parallel ports, timers, and analog-to-digital converters.

Organization

A microcomputer comprises three major subsystems: processor, memory, and I/O.

The *central processing unit* (CPU) contains the control units, execution units, and data registers that perform the instructions of a computer program. It can fetch instructions and data from the memory system, store results back into memory, and can exchange data with the input–output subsystem.

The *control unit* is in charge of decoding instructions and sequencing the actions of various functional units. A *bus interface unit* controls instruction and data transfers to and from the CPU (*see* BUS).

A *register* (*q.v.*) is a storage location within an execution unit capable of holding one number. Because reading a value from a register is much faster than reading from memory, keeping needed values in registers greatly improves execution speed. High-performance architectures have dozens or hundreds of *general registers*. For fast execution, optimizing compilers (*q.v.*) must carefully allocate registers to values.

Dedicated registers play specific roles during execution of some instructions. For instance, the stack pointer in the Motorola 68000 is one of the general-purpose registers, but is implicitly modified by instructions that access the stack.

Floating-point registers are general-purpose registers accessible only by floating-point and data transfer instructions. They provide storage space for lengthy floating-point numbers, freeing the integer registers. Having them as separate registers simplifies control of instruction pipelines (*q.v.*).

To the CPU, the *memory* subsystem appears to be a large array of locations that can hold data values or program instructions. *Random access memory* (RAM) has become synonymous with "computer main memory." (*see* MEMORY).

Read-only memory (ROM) is a simple type of memory with contents that cannot be changed, even by loss of electrical power.

PROMs, EPROMs, EEPROMs, and flash memory are erasable nonvolatile memories. A programmable read-only memory (PROM) can be written only once via an irreversible process. Data in erasable PROM (EPROM) are reset by exposure to intense ultraviolet light. Both electrically erasable PROM (EEPROM) and flash memory are alterable by a high voltage input. Nonvolatile memories are very useful because they can survive power losses, but they can be rewritten only very slowly and for a limited number of times. Flash memory needs only 12 volts for erasure and writes much faster than EEPROM; it can directly replace RAM for some applications.

Cache memories are very fast SRAMs accessed directly by the processor and filled with copies of data from slower but cheaper DRAMs.

The input–output (I/O—*see* INPUT–OUTPUT OPERATIONS) subsystem includes all interfaces that connect the CPU to external peripherals, usually via device controllers that translate general commands from the CPU into specific details. The most common I/O units are serial and parallel interfaces, or ports (*see* PORT, I/O). *Serial interfaces* accept data, such as 8-bit bytes, convert them into one-bit-at-a-time serial form, and send them over an optical fiber or a wire pair. The I/O interfaces must generate light or voltage signals corresponding to the data bits. *Parallel interfaces* are similar, but send or receive eight or more bits of data simultaneously on multistranded wire cables. *Network interfaces*, such as those for Ethernet (*q.v.*), allow computers to exchange data over communication links.

Direct memory access (DMA) controllers can autonomously and rapidly transfer large blocks of data.

Disk controllers are common peripheral interface units and one of the earliest produced in single-chip form. They convert I/O read and write requests into the right sequence of seeks, delays, and data transfer operations.

Video controllers put the electronics for a video display into one chip. Typically, they repeatedly read image data from memory, convert the data to pixels and colors, and send it to the screen. They calculate data addresses, look up colors, position pixels, and generate timing.

Special controller circuits for speech synthesis, speech recognition, and three-dimensional (3D) graphics imaging were added to I/O chips and some CPUs in the late 1990s. The Intel Pentium/MMX processor of 1997 and many later chips included special parallel floating-point instructions to speed calculations for 3D graphics images.

History

Microelectronics began at Bell Laboratories in 1947 with the development of small transistor amplifiers on the surface of semiconductor materials, such as pure germanium and silicon. A transistor is hundreds of times smaller than a vacuum tube, which it replaced for building computers by the late 1950s.

In late 1958, Texas Instruments created an integrated circuit of five connected transistors. In 1959, Fairchild produced a planar transistor, the first device using integrated circuit (IC) technology on silicon with layers of silicon dioxide for insulation and thin films of evaporated aluminum for connectors. In 1961, Fairchild marketed the first commercially available IC, a flip-flop (1-bit) memory circuit with four transistors and two resistors.

In 1967, eight ex-Fairchild executives led by Robert Noyce founded Intel. In 1969, Intel began developing a general-purpose chip set for handheld calculators. They abstracted the control mechanism into a programmable unit—the Intel 4004 chip. The idea of a controller on a chip originated with Gilbert Hyatt, who had the first microprocessor prototype running in 1968.

The Intel 80×86 Family

The microcomputer revolution started in 1971, when Intel sold the first microprocessor chip, its 4004 controller. It contained 2124 transistors, addressed 256 8-bit instructions, and operated on 4-bit data, each enough for a decimal digit (0–9). It was followed soon by the 4040 and several processors for 8-bit data: 8008 and 8080. The 8008 (1972) was designed to control video display terminals and keyboards. The 8080 and faster 8080A (1974) provided more registers, a stack ($q.v.$) for calling subroutines, and rudimentary 16-bit arithmetic. They executed 8-bit instructions, operated on 8-bit and 16-bit data, and had eight limited-use registers: a stack pointer (SP), three pairs of 8-bit registers (B, C, D, E, H, L), and an arithmetic accumulator (A). The 8080 and 8080A were the first widely used microprocessors. Their descendants are the 80×86 chips in many millions of PCs.

Improvements continued in 1978 with the 8086 and 8088, internally identical chips for 16-bit operations. The 8088 retained a narrow 8-bit external data bus for compatibility. Both used segmentation to extend the memory address range to 1 MB (2^{20} bytes). The 80186 (1981) was an 8086 with on-chip peripheral circuits for embedded applications. Subsequent improvements to 8086 performance were made through the 80286 (1982), 80386 (1985), 80486 (1989), 80586 (1993),

80686 (1995), 80786 (2001), 80886 (2004), and a projected one-billion transistor 80986 in 2007. The packing densities of the first three membres of this family extension are shown in Fig. 2.

Starting with the 80386, the architecture was radically upgraded to form a 32-bit microprocessor supporting a nonsegmented 4 GB (2^{32} bytes) address space, virtual memory, and many new instructions. Compatibility with previous versions was provided by retaining the same register structure and supporting a virtual 8086 mode. The 80486 had the same instructions as the 80386, but added an on-chip memory cache, instruction pipelines, and a floating-point unit to improve performance greatly.

Intel retained the 80×86 architecture throughout the 1990s. The 80586 P5 Pentium (1993) had more on-chip cache and was superscalar: it could start two instructions per cycle to use both integer ALUs, or its single FPU plus one ALU (*see* INSTRUCTION-LEVEL PARA-LLELISM). The MMX CPU (1995) added "Matrix Math eXtension" instructions to perform two to eight, 32- to 8-bit vector integer operations at once in its 64-bit FPU, speeding calculations for 3D graphic images. The 80686 P6 Pentium Pro (1995) added level-2 (L2) cache on-chip and lessened pipeline delays after conditional branch instructions by speculative execution: guessing which instruction will follow a branch and starting to execute it immediately but not changing registers until the branch direction is known.

The Pentium II (1997) was a Pentium Pro with MMX instructions and an off-chip L2 cache, sold together on a heatsink module. Celeron (1998), a Pentium II with no L2, sold cheaply for under-$1000 PCs. It was too slow; a small on-chip L2 was added late in 1998. The Pentium III (1999) added a large on-chip L2 cache. The Pentium IV and first 64-bit Intel processor (Itanium) were released in 2001.

Other Early Microprocessor Families

Eight-bit microprocessors were important because they were the first to address enough memory and to be powerful enough for general-purpose computing. Zilog was founded by designers of the Intel 8080A. The Z80 (1976) was upwardly compatible with the 8080A, but faster. It had more instructions, more addressing modes, and an alternate register set for fast interrupt responses. Its support chips were less expensive. It was used for most personal computers before IBM adopted the 8088 for the PC. The Z80 and its successors are still used in embedded applications.

The Motorola 6800 (1974) had two accumulators, a stack pointer, and an index register (*q.v.*), but no data registers. The 6802 added a small, fast, on-chip RAM. The 6809 was the last 8-bit architecture from Motorola. The Motorola MC68000 (1980) was significantly different. It used a 16-bit data bus to access 32-bit values and had eight data registers, eight index registers, two security levels, an orthogonal instruction set (with operand addressing modes chosen independently of the instruction), and a nonsegmented 16 MB (2^{24}) address space. It was adopted for many PCs and embedded applications. The 68010 (1982) restarted instructions after page fault interrupts to support virtual memory. The full 32-bit 68020 (1984) had a 4-GB address range, an on-chip memory cache, and many powerful new instructions and addressing modes. It became the standard CPU for high-performance Unix workstations. The 68030 (1989) added an on-chip MMU to map virtual addresses. The 68040 (1990) used large on-chip caches, integrated floating-point, and aggressive pipelining to run four times faster than the 68030, but was the last of its family.

Fast Reduced Instruction Set Computer Chips

The late 1980s saw the rise of a new style of high performance CPUs, the single-chip reduced instruction set computer (RISC) processors: the MIPS, Sparc, and PowerPC families. The key feature of these processors is efficient use of instruction pipelines (*q.v.*) made possible by easy-to-decode uniform code formats, large sets of registers for all arithmetic operands and results, and memory accesses limited to load and store operations.

The 1981 Berkeley "Reduced Instruction Set Computer" (RISC) and 1982 Stanford "Microprocessor without Interlocked Pipe Stages" (MIPS) projects popularized simple instructions, pipelines, and code

reordering. Limited to 100 000 transistors each in 1982, fast one-chip CPUs had circuit space for only the most useful instructions and hardware features. Early RISC chips had small, regular, hard-wired instruction sets, very different from the prevailing microcoded, complex instruction set computers (CISCs).

In 1983, Hewlett-Packard began work on a high-performance precision architecture (HPPA). Stanford engineers founded MIPS Computer Systems in 1984 and released the MIPS R2000 in 1986. In 1985, Sun Microsystems began designing its SPARC processor family based directly on the Berkeley RISC-II chip, and had CPUs by 1987. Many commercial RISC processors followed: Advanced Micro Devices (AMD) 29000 (1986), Motorola 88000 (1988), Intel 80960 controller (1988), MIPS R3000 (1988), Intel 80860 graphics accelerator (1989), and the powerful "post-RISC" IBM Power-1 for the RS/6000 in 1989.

In 1992, IBM, Motorola, and Apple joined forces to design a series of PowerPC CPUs to replace the 68040 and 80486 processors in Apple and IBM PCs: 601 (1993), 603 (1994), 604 (1995), and 750, marketed by Apple as G3, the third-generation PowerPC (1998).

In 1992, Digital Equipment (DEC) released its pioneering fast superscalar 64-bit RISC chip, the Alpha 21064 running at 150 MHz, then the 366 MHz 21164 (1995)—rated at 1000 MIPS—and the 525 MHz 21264 (1998). In 1998, Compaq bought DEC in order to own Alpha, but decided to phase it out in 2001.

MIPS had a 64-bit R4000 chip in 1991, but its superscalar R10000 (1996) with on-chip FPUs was much faster. Sun Microsystems (design) and Texas Instruments (fabrication) released their 64-bit RISC SuperSPARC chip prematurely in 1992; it was slower even than Intel 80×86 CPUs. Their Russian-designed 64-bit UltraSPARC chip (1995) was much faster.

Applications

Almost all computers, even highly parallel and expensive supercomputers, use commercial microprocessor CPUs because of their unmatched performance to cost ratio. Only the very highest performance computers have architectures too complex or use implementation technologies too sparse to fit the CPU on one chip. The great majority of microcomputers are dedicated to controlling everything from consumer appliances to cars to space probes. In embedded applications, microprocessors serve as cheap replacements for otherwise very complicated control circuitry and often offer functionality not feasible any other way. Personal electronics is a ready match for microprocessors. Many household electrical appliances such as washers and dryers have replaced complex electromechanical systems with simpler and more reliable electronic ones. Digital keypads on microwave ovens allow programmed cooking sequences; an unattended video cassette recorder (VCR) can tape several programs at different times on different channels; a digital chess game can provide a challenging opponent; digital wrist watches can calculate and play music; and telephones can store frequently dialed numbers.

Bibliography

1989. Slater, M. *Microprocessor-Based Design: A Comprehensive Guide to Effective Hardware Design.* Upper Saddle River, NJ: Prentice Hall.

1996. Hennessy, J. L., and Patterson, D. A. *Computer Architecture: A Quantitative Approach*, 2nd Ed. San Francisco, CA: Morgan Kaufmann.

Larry D. Wittie

MICROPROGRAMMING

For articles on related subjects, see

Microprogramming, as originally conceived by Maurice Wilkes in 1951, is a specific technique "to provide a systematic approach to designing the control section of any computing system." In Wilkes' context, the term *control* is taken to mean the interpretation and execution of a machine instruction.

Microprogramming was widely used throughout the 1970s and 1980s as the preferred implementation of the instruction *decoder*. The IBM System/360/370 series and the DEC VAX systems are typical examples of microprogrammed control. The opcode of an instruction contained in the instruction register was used as an address to a read-only control store. The contents of this address would define the first of a sequence of microinstructions that implemented the register-to-register data movements and arithmetic logic unit (ALU–*q.v.*) operations required for instruction execution. The regular implementation of the decoder through the use of storage provided a convenient way to change an instruction set by changing control store. The availability of an extendible control memory also allowed for the execution of multiple separate instruction sets in a process called *emulation*. The IBM System/360/370 provided emulation of older instruction sets including the IBM 7090 and IBM 1401.

The second generation of microprogrammed systems was distinguished by its small number of internal machine cycles per main memory cycle. By the late 1960s, main memory access time had dropped below 1 μs, yet the technology for control store had not noticeably improved, and the best access for read-only store varied between 200 and 400 ns. In addition, the read-only storage technologies tended to be exotic.

The third generation of microprogramming dates from about 1970, with the advent of fast read–write control stores. The development of bipolar monolithic technology created a storage medium with the same access time as combinational decisions. The *writable control store* (WCS) represented an important transition and became a true member of the *memory hierarchy* (*q.v.*).

After the mid-1980s, the density of control store implementations became a problem for single-chip processors. The area occupied by a control store or microprogrammed implementation of a decoder exceeded that of a hardwired implementation. Additionally, the area budgets for processor implementations were tight. Still, the Motorola 68000 family of processors used microprogrammed control in the late 1980s as logic density on chips improved.

In the 1990s, the Intel Pentium processors had a vestigial form of microcode. Their instructions were composed of microoperations, but typical instructions had three or four microoperations that were generated directly by the instruction decoder. In general, however, current processors use hardwired control circuits.

Bibliography

1988. Habib, S. *Microprogramming and Firmware Engineering Methods.* New York: Van Nostrand Reinhold.
1996. Carter, J. W. *Microprocessor Architecture and Microprogramming: A State Machine Approach.* Upper Saddle River, NJ: Prentice Hall.

Michael J. Flynn

MICROSOFT

For an article on a related subject, see

+ Digital Computers, History of: Since 1950

Microsoft was founded by Bill Gates and his partner Paul Allen in 1975. The company initially developed an interpreter for the Basic (*q.v.*) programming language for the then nascent PC. By the start of the 1980s, Microsoft was still a small company with just 25 employees and sales of $2.5 million. In July 1980, however, Microsoft secured a contract with IBM to develop the operating system PC-DOS for the IBM PC (*q.v.*). Microsoft retained the right to market that system independently as MS-DOS. When the company made its initial public offering in 1986, it had over a thousand employees and its market value exceeded $600 million. The following year, Gates was lauded as America's youngest billionaire.

Revenue from the sales of MS-DOS enabled Microsoft to develop PC applications software, such as a word processor and a spreadsheet (*q.v.*). In November 1985, Microsoft released the first version of Windows, its graphical user interface (GUI) and operating system for the IBM-compatible PC. Microsoft was one of a number of software companies attempting to produce a Macintosh-like interface for the PC in the mid-1980s, but none was highly successful until the release of Windows version 3.1 in 1990. By this time, Microsoft had become a major company with over 5000 employees and revenues of $1 billion. In 1993, Microsoft released Windows NT, a robust networked operating system, with the aim of competing with Unix (*q.v.*) and other products in the corporate operating system market.

In August 1995, Microsoft was at the peak of its powers with the launch of Windows 95, for which the publicity alone was said to have cost of the order of $200 million. By the end of the 1995–1996 financial year, Microsoft had over 20 000 employees and revenues exceeding $8 billion, and its market valuation exceeded that of IBM.

Microsoft's dominance of the PC software market has attracted antitrust concern since 1989. In 1994, Microsoft entered a consent degree with the US Department of Justice (DoJ), by which it revised its charging policies for operating systems bundled with newly manufactured PCs.

The emergence of the Internet as a new computing paradigm around 1993, and the success of Netscape Communications Corporation in capturing the market for browser software, was seen as a long overdue counterbalance to Microsoft's hegemony of desktop software. However, Netscape's browser monopoly did not last long, and even Microsoft's most ardent critics have had to admire the speed and urgency with which the company came to terms with the Internet, first producing its own browser, Explorer, and then reshaping many of its software products to accommodate the new mode of computing.

In 1997, Microsoft "bundled" Explorer into all versions of its Windows operating system so that anyone who installed Windows automatically received an installed ready-to-use Explorer. The antitrust division of DoJ quickly filed suit against Microsoft claiming, among other things, that its purpose in combining Windows with Explorer was to undermine Netscape and attempt to put it out of business. In the subsequent trial, which began in 1998, the government's case, based in important measure on internal Microsoft email, was strenuously opposed by Microsoft. On 5 November 1999, Judge Thomas Penfield Jackson issued "findings of fact" that constituted a severe and wide-ranging denunciation of Microsoft's business practices. Breakup of the company into several smaller ones was then conceivable, but in March 2001 an appellate court severely criticized Judge Jackson's handling of the case. On 12 November 2002, the US District Court for the District of Columbia issued a "final order" that merely restrains Microsoft from interfering with companies that make software that runs under Windows, or with hardware vendors that choose to ship PCs with dual operating systems such as, for example, Windows and Linux (*q.v.*).

Bibliography

1992. Ichbiah, D., and Knepper, S. L. *The Making of Microsoft*. Rocklin, CA: Prima Publishing.

1996. Stross, R. E. *The Microsoft Way: The Real Story of How the Company Outsmarts Its Competition*. Reading, MA: Addison-Wesley.

1998. Selby, R. W. *Microsoft Secrets: How the World's Most Powerful Software Company Creates Technology, Shapes Markets, and Manages People*. New York: Simon and Schuster.

Martin Campbell-Kelly

MINICOMPUTER

For articles on related subjects, see

+ Addressing
+ Digital Computers, History of: Since 1950
+ Instruction Set
+ Microprocessors and Microcomputers
+ Microprogramming
+ Personal Computing
+ Workstation

With the exception of the IBM AS400 series, the *minicomputer* has been largely replaced by workstations and PCs. The minicomputer was developed at a time when expensive, large mainframes (*q.v.*) could be replaced by smaller computers whose price and functionality were sufficient for smaller applications. The developmental history of minicomputers is paralleled by the later development of PCs. Both types of computer eventually evolved to include high-resolution graphics display devices and fast network connections, along with increasingly larger main memories and *hard disks* (*q.v.*). The minicomputer was different in that it was often relegated to the task of either providing time-sharing (*q.v.*) services to a large number of users, or was used as a standalone real-time processor. The PC has largely remained a single-user system.

Minicomputers could be broadly classified as having 12-, 16-, 18-, 24-, or 32-bit word lengths with memory sizes of 128 MB to one gigabyte provided in modules of 256 KB or 1 MB. Nearly all minicomputers employed a parallel internal processor structure with a high-speed bus and a clock rate of 4 to 40 MHz. The basic configuration ranged in price

Figure 1. An HP 3000 minicomputer system. (Courtesy of Hewlett-Packard.)

from $4000 to $500 000, with the cost of peripheral devices usually far outstripping the cost of the machine.

A *turnkey* minicomputer system had a complete operating system capable of supporting one or many users simultaneously. Indeed, when 32-bit machines were introduced, they looked increasingly like their mainframe counterparts. The languages available on these machines usually included Fortran, Basic, APL, Cobol, C, and Pascal (*see* each).

Applications

The greatest use of minicomputers was in areas other than general-purpose computing. These included industrial applications, biomedical control for experiment monitoring, supplements to larger computer systems, intelligent graphics terminals, and microprogrammable systems capable of being tailored to specific applications and environments.

One important aspect of minicomputer design was the large-scale use of microprogramming (*q.v.*). The value of the microprogrammable machine could be found in its compatibility with other different machines by emulation (*q.v.*) of the same instruction set, in its ability to allow the user to tailor a machine at the most primitive level to accommodate particular requirements, or in its ability to allow the user the flexibility of experimenting with new ideas and designs. These same features are found in today's microcomputers and microcontrollers.

Bibliography

1979. Eckhouse, R., and Morris, R. *Minicomputer Systems: Organization, Programming and Applications (PDP-11)*. Upper Saddle River, NJ: Prentice Hall.

1989. Levy, H., and Eckhouse, R. *Computer Programming and Architecture: the VAX*, 2nd Ed. Bedford, MA: Digital Press.

1999. Tanenbaum, A. *Structured Computer Organization*, 4th Ed. Upper Saddle River, NJ: Prentice Hall.

Richard H. Eckhouse

MOBILE COMPUTING

For articles on related subjects, *see*

+ Communications and Computers
+ Global Positioning System (GPS)
+ Networks, Computer
+ Portable Computers

Mobile computing uses a device that communicates through a wireless channel. The field is as broad as traditional computing. Consumers expect the same convenience and computing power in the mobile device as in a desk computer. Furthermore, mobility opens up new venues for interesting and unique products and services. Freedom from geographic constraints can allow a more effective, convenient, and timely use of computing and communication. Examples include the executive working on a laptop while traveling and the field engineer having remote electronic access to technical documentation and diagnostics.

The combination of the rapid reduction in computing device sizes, small portable displays, and wireless networking capabilities has fostered the growing interest in *wearable computers*. Emerging experimental systems are small enough to be mounted on belts or helmets and often provide as much processing and networking power as their desktop counterparts. Besides the obvious capabilities for browsing the World Wide Web (*q.v.*) while performing mundane tasks, these "wearables" foster the creation of computer-mediated reality. Applications such as technicians having field manuals projected through glasses while they are working on a device, and computer-assisted facial recognition for instantly matching contact information with faces are just two examples. Similar applications have been proposed as computer resources for the disabled (*see* DISABLED, COMPUTERS AND THE).

Some cellular phones already allow Web browsing and email reception; palmtop computers come with scaled-down versions of desktop operating systems and applications; and radio-frequency identification devices (RFID) provide intelligent communication and computing power with nearly any type of object. A fundamental requirement of today's computer is network connectivity. This generally calls for radio-frequency (RF) wireless communications for mobile devices. Although infrared mobile computer communications can also be used, interference from the Sun as well as the difficulty of non-line-of-sight communications make RF the preferred method for location-independent mobile communications.

Mobility requires use of a battery as a portable power source. Since battery power depends on size and weight, it is essential that all the parts of the mobile device are power-efficient. Since battery capacities are not expected to increase by more than 30% in the near future, while computing capabilities and features have ever-increasing expectations, power efficiency has become a fundamental technology.

Mobile Networking

From the emergence of network-oriented languages such as Java (*q.v.*) to the legislatively encouraged convergence of communication technologies, communications has become an essential requirement of computing. Mobile computing is no exception, with the additional challenge of using the radio-frequency (RF) bandwidth (*q.v.*) effectively. All of the three basic ways to connect a wireless computer to the world assume the existence of a wired base station infrastructure. Satellite communication would also be possible, but would be extremely power-intensive. The first method is to use a modem (*q.v.*) over a voice-grade cellular phone. Second, Mobitex and ARDIS are two examples of dedicated packet data networks that are emerging to meet the demand for higher efficiency and data rates than analog modems over radio can provide. Lastly, a hybrid of these two approaches uses the cellular networks designed for voice for transmitting packet data (*see* PACKET SWITCHING). Cellular Digit Packet Data (CDPD) is a system that uses idle voice channels on the analog Advanced Mobile Phone Service (AMPS) voice cellular system

to transmit data. Additionally, the newest digital cellular systems such as Global System for Mobile Communications (GSM) also include provisions for multiplexing packet data for transmission with digitized speech.

The part of the RF spectrum usable for communications is limited and must be shared with television, radio, military, satellite communications, and many other services. Therefore, the frequency band available for mobile computer communication is extremely small when compared with that of a wire connected to a desktop computer. The challenge to mobile computing is to maintain high data rates in the presence of high errors while still maintaining fair access to a multitude of subscribers.

Wireless connectivity to the Internet via Internet service providers (ISPs) using Wi-Fi (wireless fidelity) products, cell phones, and laptops, is being called the "next big thing." Wi-Fi growth seems to be exponential, and major hotels and businesses such as Starbucks are already creating "hot spots" where customers can sit comfortably within range of wireless Internet service.

Ubiquitous computing, a term coined by Mark Weiser of Xerox PARC in 1988, implies the pervasive use of wireless handheld computers so small, perhaps even wearable, that their users are never out of range of the Internet. Ubiquitous computing is sometimes summarized as "computers everywhere," in contrast to pervasive computing, which implies "computers *in* everything" (*see* EMBEDDED SYSTEM).

Bibliography

1995. Pahlavan, K., and Levesque, A. *Wireless Information Networks*. New York: John Wiley.

1997. Mann, S. "Wearable Computing: A First Step Toward Personal Imaging," *IEEE Computer*, **30**(2), (February), 25–32.

1998. Perkins, C. *Mobile IP: Design Principles and Practice*. Reading, MA: Addison-Wesley.

Imre Chlamtac and Jason Redi

MODEM

For articles on related subjects, see

+ Bandwidth
+ Baud
+ Cable Modem
+ Error Correcting and Detecting Code
+ Networks, Computer

A *modem* is a device used to transmit data between computers and other peripheral devices interconnected by conventional telephone communication lines supporting analog transmission. Modems transform (modulate) data from a digital device to analog form suitable for transmission over such lines. Since, in general, data flows in both directions, modems are also able to receive an analog signal from some remote device and restore (demodulate) it back to its original digital form. The word "modem" stems from *mo*dulation–*dem*odulation.

Modem Types

Many different types of modem are available, depending on their transmission speed, whether they are installed internally or connected externally to their computer, and whether they are used for serial or parallel transmission; synchronous or asynchronous transmission; simplex, duplex, or full duplex operation; long distance (long-haul) or limited distance (short-haul) operation; operation over dedicated or dial-up lines; and transmission of data only or faxes and data (fax modem). *Internal* modems are built into computing equipment such as PCs. *External* modems have their own separate case with independent power supply and are connected to the computer by cable.

Most modems transmit characters serially, bit by bit, but others are designed to transmit a character in one-bit time by receiving or transmitting its bits in parallel over several lines in order to increase the effective transmission rate. In synchronous transmission, the characters are transmitted at a fixed rate, usually at or in excess of 2400 bits per second (bps). This mode of transmission was used primarily for high-speed communication between buffered systems. Synchronization between receiver and transmitter is achieved by using special SYNCH characters at the beginning of each block or message. In asynchronous transmission, the characters are sent one at a time and the interval between them can vary arbitrarily. Synchronization is accomplished by adding *start* and *stop* bits to each character to allow delineation of adjacent characters. Synchronous transmission is more difficult to implement but is more efficient, since no start and stop bits are needed.

Most modern modems can operate in simplex, half duplex, and full duplex modes. *Simplex* refers to one-way transmission only and hence is rarely used. *Full duplex* refers to simultaneous transmission in both directions, while in *half-duplex* systems the data may flow in both directions but not at the same time.

Modulation Techniques

Conventional telephone lines have a bandwidth of about 3000 Hz (cycles per second). Data transmission over such lines was once limited to 2400 band or line state changes per second. To modulate a digital signal over such a communication channel, a modem may use amplitude modulation (AM), frequency modulation (FM), or phase modulation (PM). The type of modulation used depends upon the transmission speed. FM, in the form of *frequency-shift keying* (FSK), is used almost exclusively for asynchronous communication up to 1800 bps. A form of PM is used for synchronous communication at 2000 to 2400 bps. A combination of AM and PM, called *Quadrature Amplitude Modulation* (QAM), is used for speeds between 2400 and 9600 bps. Much more sophisticated modulation techniques, such as *Trellis Code Modulation* (TCM), are commonly used to achieve transmission rates up to 56 000 bps over conventional telephone lines.

Bibliography

1988. McNamara, J. E. *Technical Aspects of Data Communication*, 3rd Ed. Bedford, MA: Digital Press.

John S. Sobolewski

MODULAR PROGRAMMING

For articles on related subjects, *see*

+ Abstract Data Type
+ Encapsulation
+ Information Hiding
+ Object-Oriented Programming
+ Package
+ Program Verification
+ Software Engineering
+ Structured Programming

A program *module* is a logically self-contained and discrete part of a larger program. A complete program is thus a collection of modules. A properly constructed module accepts input that is well defined as to content and structure, carries out a well-defined set of processing actions, and produces output that is well defined as to content and structure.

In the context of structured programming, a module packages a stage of processing. In this sense, a properly constructed module has only one entry point and only one exit point. If it is a subroutine, it always returns only to the statement following the one that invoked it. Breaking a task into modules is a kind of functional decomposition called *procedural abstraction*. In many languages, a subroutine (procedure) can serve as a module, although some languages permit violations of the guidelines just stated, such as allowing multiple entry and exit points.

In another—now more common—view, a module is a "responsibility center," which packages a set of operations on data that they share and to which only they have access. This notion of modularization characterizes *object-oriented programming* in which a module provides data *encapsulation* and *information hiding*. A module in this sense provides *data abstraction* as well as procedural abstraction.

The purpose of *modular programming* is to break a complex task into smaller and simpler subtasks, which, among other things, facilitates writing correct programs. A program consisting of modules of properly designed scope is much simpler to design, write,

and test than the same program when it is not so modularized.

Bibliography

1972. Parnas, D. L. "On the Criteria to be Used in Decomposing Systems into Modules," *Communications of the ACM*, **15**(12), (December), 1053–1058.
1997. Meyer, B. *Object-Oriented Software Construction*, 2nd Ed. Upper Saddle River, NJ: Prentice Hall.

Daniel D. McCracken

MOLECULAR COMPUTING

For articles on related topics, *see*

+ Computational Complexity
+ NP-Complete Problems
+ Parallel Processing
+ Quantum Computing

Molecular computing (DNA computing) is founded on the idea that, given enough strands of DNA, and using certain biological operations, one can use DNA molecules to solve some classic computations efficiently. The original insight is due to Leonard Adleman (1994) who showed how DNA can be used to solve the Directed Hamiltonian Path (DHP) graph problem (*see* GRAPH THEORY).

A DNA strand is essentially a sequence (polymer) of four types of nucleotide distinguished by the bases they contain, bases denoted A, C, G, T (adenine, cytosine, guanine, and thymine). We will be dealing with short strands containing at most 10 000 nucleotides. Two strands of DNA are said to be Watson–Crick complements if their respective bases are complements—A matches T and C matches G. Under appropriate conditions, two complementary DNA strands form a double strand that has the shape of the famous double helix. For our purposes, we regard a single strand of DNA containing n nucleotides as a character string of length n over the alphabet {A, C, G, T}.

DNA sequencing enables the biologist to "read" the sequence of nucleotides on a short DNA strand given a solution containing many copies of that strand. This is one way to read the output of a DNA computation. The basic computational step of a DNA computer is the separation of a solution of DNA strands into two solutions: one that contain a certain sequence and one that does not.

One can think of a DNA computer as a massively parallel machine where each DNA strand serves as a separate processor. Assuming each strand contains fewer than 10 000 nucleotides, it is possible to dissolve 10^{18} strands in a liter of water. Unfortunately, these processors are extremely slow, requiring several hours to complete the simplest Boolean operations. Still, a parallel computer that can perform 10^{18} Boolean operations every several hours seems promising.

Comparison of Several DNA Computing Results

Table 1 summarizes a few of the DNA computing models proposed thus far. The results listed there are compared according to two parameters. The first is the number of biological steps used by the algorithm. This roughly corresponds to the running time. The second is the number of DNA strands used. This corresponds to the volume of DNA needed to run the algorithm. If either parameter is too large, the algorithm cannot be implemented.

The six problems in Table 1 are described below.

1. This is Adleman's famous result (1994). A Hamiltonian path in a graph is a path that visits all nodes in the graph exactly once. Testing whether a graph has a Hamiltonian path is an NP-complete problem. Here, n is the number of vertices in the graph. Adleman showed how to embed the graph in DNA such that the resulting DNA strands encode paths in the graph. He then described a procedure for filtering out all strands except the one representing a Hamiltonian path, if it exists. The actual Hamiltonian path in the graph can then be found by sequencing any of the remaining strands (i.e. reading the DNA sequence).

2. This is the result of Lipton (1995) that SAT (satisfiability for formulas in conjunctive normal form) can be done in time linear in the size of the formula s. The number of strands needed is 2^n, where n is the number of variables in the formula.

3. This result, due to Boneh et al. (1996) shows how, given a function $F(x)$ taking n-bit binary inputs, one can construct a library of DNA strands representing all pairs $(x, F(x))$. In a sense, the entire lookup table for the function $F(x)$ is encoded in DNA. If the function F is computable by a Boolean circuit of size s, the construction requires $O(s)$ biological operations and produces a library of size 2^n.

4. Several research groups discovered how to simulate a Nondeterministic Turing Machine (NTM) using DNA (Boneh et al., 1996). The n in Table 1 is the number of nondeterministic branches taken during a computation.

5. This is a construction due to Erik Winfree that shows how complicated DNA patterns can be used to simulate cellular automata (q.v.). The number

Table 1. DNA computing models.

Problem	Biological steps	Number of strands
1. Directed Hamiltonian path	$O(n)$	$n!$
2. Formula satisfiability	$O(s)$	2^n
3. Boolean circuit simulation	$O(s)$	2^n
4. 1-tape NTM	$O(t)$	2^N
5. Cellular automata	1	$t \cdot s$
6. PSPACE	$O(s)$	2^{2s}

of nucleotides used by the DNA pattern is proportional to the product of the space used by the automata (s) and the number of generations for which it is run (t).

6. This result, independently discovered by Beaver, Reif, and Papadimitriou, shows how to simulate computations requiring polynomial space (PSPACE) with DNA operations; s denotes the space needed.

Application to Cryptology

The first "real-world" application is due to Boneh *et al.* (1996) showing how to break the Data Encryption Standard (DES)—a widely deployed symmetric cipher. The problem is this: given a plaintext M and a ciphertext C find a key K such that C = DES(M,K). That is, find a key mapping the given plaintext to the given ciphertext. The massive parallelism of a DNA computer is used to test all possible keys until the correct one is found. Testing a single key is a simple operation that can be performed by a single strand. A DNA computer would take several months to discover any one key, but subsequent DES keys could then be broken in just a single day each by reusing the library of DNA strands produced in the initial break.

Bibliography

1994. Adleman, L. "Molecular Computation of Solutions to Combinatorial Problems," *Science*, **266**(11 November), 1021–1024.

1995. Lipton, R. "Using DNA to Solve NP-complete Problems," *Science*, **268**(28 April), 542–545.

1996. Boneh, D., Dunworth, C., Lipton, R., and Sgall, J. "On the Computational Power of DNA," *Discrete Applied Mathematics, Special issue on Computational Molecular Biology*, **71**, 79–94.

1997. Setubal, J. C., and Meidanis, J. *Introduction to Computational Molecular Biology*, Ch. 9. Boston, MA: PWS Publishing Company.

Dan Boneh

MONITOR, DISPLAY

For articles on related subjects, *see*

+ **Computer Graphics**
+ **Multimedia**
+ **Personal Computing**
+ **User Interface**
+ **Window Environments**

Display monitors produce real-time dynamic graphic images from computer output. They were originally used to monitor the state of the machine—hence the name. In the early days of computer graphics, displays were vector-based (i.e. they drew lines on the screen), but virtually all displays are now *bitmapped* (*see* TYPEFONT).

The image on the screen is made up of individual dots known as *pixels* (short for *picture elements*). Each dot represents a location in the computer memory in an area known as the *frame buffer*. The frame buffer can be a designated part of main memory, or more often, a separate type of memory designed specifically for the purpose. At each memory location, a value is stored representing the color of the pixel. The number of colors can vary, typically from 256 (8 bits per pixel) to 16.7 million (24 bits per pixel) or more depending on the size and arrangement of the buffer memory. The number of pixels held in the frame buffer defines the *resolution*. The number of colors is known as the *color depth*. The color value can either represent the direct color value (e.g. 8 bits for red, 8 bits for blue, and 8 bits for green in a 24-bit system) or can represent an entry in a look-up table that stores the actual color values. The look-up table is known as the *color palette*.

Table 1 gives some typical resolutions and corresponding memory requirements. The display is usually serially addressed, with pixels being sent to the display one at a time, from top left of the first row to bottom right of the last row on the screen. Most displays are analog, so the frame buffer color values are translated from binary data to a voltage for each color by a Digital-to-Analog Converter (DAC) or by a "Look-up Table DAC" (LUTDAC) when a palette is used.

Table 1. Typical monitor resolutions and memory requirements.

Resolution	Colors	Minimum 2D memory	Typical board memory
640 × 480	16 (4 bit)	150 KB	256 KB
800 × 600	256 (8 bit)	469 KB	512 KB
1024 × 768	256 (8 bit)	768 KB	1 MB
1024 × 768	16.7 M (24 bit)	2.25 MB	4 MB
1152 × 864	256 (8 bit)	972 KB	1 MB
1280 × 1024	256 (8 bit)	1.25 MB	2 MB
1600 × 1200	256 (8 bit)	1.83 MB	2 MB
1600 × 1200	64 K (16 bit)	3.66 MB	4 MB
1600 × 1200	16.7 M (24 bit)	5.49 MB	8 MB

Note: K = 1024; M = 1024 K.

Over time, the analog interface will be replaced by a digital one and the D/A stage is likely to disappear from the architecture. The use of digital interfaces eliminates the errors involved in digital–analog conversion, losses due to analog transmission, and the conversion back to digital. Most computers contain a special graphics processor chip that acts as a memory controller, but which is also likely to include special circuitry to accelerate both 2D and 3D graphics functions to process motion video for multimedia applications.

Cathode Ray Tubes

The cathode ray tube (CRT) is the major display component used in computer monitors. The CRT, which was invented in 1897 by Karl Ferdinand Braun, is a type of thermionic tube and uses a beam of electrons from a heated cathode to excite phosphors that emit light. An assembly called a *gun* focuses and shapes the beam of electrons (Fig. 1). The CRT uses horizontal and vertical magnetic deflection coils to bend and control the position of the beam and to scan the face of the CRT

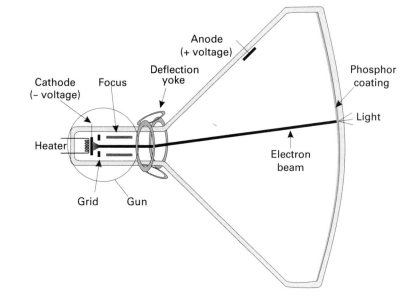

Figure 1. Cross-sectional view of a monochrome CRT.

from side to side and from top to bottom to synchronize with the stream of pixels being sent from the graphics controller. By careful choice of phosphors, the image on the CRT can be made to seem flicker-free to the human eye when the full screen is scanned at 70 to 80 Hz or above (the *refresh rate*).

In a monochrome CRT, a single beam is used to create the image on the phosphor, with the display color controlled by the formulation of the phosphor. In a color CRT, three separate guns are used to excite three different kinds of phosphors that emit red, green, and blue (RGB) light. The distance between the RGB dots is known as the "dot pitch," which, on most current CRT monitors, is 0.25 mm. The lower the number, the better the resolution.

LCDs

For portable applications, the liquid crystal display (LCD) is the most common display device and LCDs are also being used in desktop monitors as price and performance improves. Such "flat screen" monitors (Fig. 2) have a much smaller desk "footprint" than CRT monitors. The LCD uses the special properties of a group of chemicals that are able to twist the polarization of

Figure 2. A Mitsubishi LCD-80 flat screen monitor. (Courtesy of Mitsubishi Corp.)

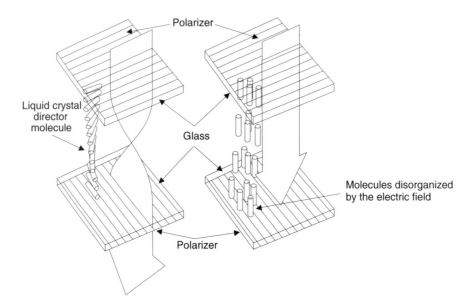

Figure 3. LCD structure: (a) the liquid crystal rotates the plane of polarization to transmit light; (b) without rotation, the second polarizer blocks the transmission.

light that is passed through them. In most types of LCD, the degree of the twist is controllable by the application of an electric field along the length of the crystal. When a field is applied across the crystal, it "untwists" and less light passes out of the display allowing for different brightness levels (gray scales) for each pixel. In a color display, the front of the display is fitted with a color filter so that each pixel is red, green, or blue.

In a *passive matrix display*, the field for each pixel is applied serially. In order to avoid visible flicker, an LC formulation with a slow response time is needed. Unfortunately, materials with a longer persistence are also relatively slow to turn on, so the monitor cannot respond to fast-changing screen items such as a rapidly moving cursor or motion video. This means that there is some smearing of the image on the screen where there is motion. The solution is to put a switch under each pixel to maintain the field across the crystal for the whole of the frame period. The array of switches is known as an *active matrix* (AM). In AM-LCDs, a transistor (usually a thin film transistor—TFT) is fabricated under each pixel to maintain the field. The performance improves significantly with no crosstalk and much reduced smearing, but at greater cost. In order to make the matrix of transistors on the glass substrate, semiconductor processes must be used, making active LCDs cost about twice as much as passive LCDs.

Bibliography

1993. Peddie, J. *High-Resolution Graphic Display Systems*. New York: McGraw-Hill.

Robert Raikes

MONITOR, SYNCHRONIZATION

For articles on related subjects, see

+ Abstract Data Type
+ Class
+ Concurrent Programming
+ Operating Systems

A *synchronization monitor* is a control program that oversees the allocation of resources among a set of user programs. The term *monitor* was, along with *supervisor* and *executive*, an early synonym for *operating system*. An old example is the Fortran Monitor System (FMS), which appeared on the IBM 709 series beginning in the late 1950s to provide run-time support for Fortran programs. A more recent example was the Conversational Monitor System (CMS), a single-user interactive system that ran on a virtual machine (VM) implemented by the control program (CP) of the IBM VM/370 operating system.

In the early 1970s, the term *monitor* was applied to a formal program construct used to simplify operating systems by providing a separate scheduler for each class of resources. This kind of monitor has a syntactic form that generalizes the idea of an *abstract data type* (ADT) or *class*; it defines a set of procedures for manipulating a set of objects concurrently. As with ADTs, the monitor's procedures enable the caller to perform high-level operations on the monitor's resources; the details of resource status and structure are hidden inside the monitor (*see* INFORMATION HIDING). But unlike ADTs, monitors have internal locks that permit only one process at a time to execute monitor instructions. Synchronization monitors in their modern sense have been used as tools for structuring operating systems and are provided by some languages for concurrent programming. They are used to implement synchronization in Java (*q.v.*).

Bibliography

1974. Hoare, C. A. R. "Monitors: An Operating System Structuring Concept," *Communications of the ACM*, **17**(10), 549–557.

1977. Brinch Hansen, P. *The Architecture of Concurrent Programs*. Upper Saddle River, NJ: Prentice Hall.

1991. Andrews, G. R. *Concurrent Programming: Principles and Practice*. Reading, MA: Addison-Wesley.

Peter J. Denning and Walter F. Tichy

MONTE CARLO METHOD

For articles on related subjects, see

✛ Scientific Applications
✛ Simulation

The name *Monte Carlo* is given to the method of solving problems by means of experiments with random numbers. This name (after the casino at Monaco) was first applied by John von Neumann (*q.v.*) and Stanislaw Ulam around 1944 to the method of solving deterministic problems by reformulating them in terms of a problem with random elements that could then be solved by large-scale sampling. But, by extension, the term has come to mean any simulation that uses random numbers.

A classical example is that of Buffon, who in 1733 pointed out that π could be determined experimentally by repeatedly throwing a needle onto a ruled surface and counting the number of times the needle crossed a line (*see* Fig. 1). The idea is more remarkable for its sophistication in geometric probability than for its practicality, and the technique remained little more than a curiosity until the advent of large-scale computers.

The Monte Carlo Method has become one of the most important tools of applied mathematics. A significant proportion of articles in technical journals in such fields as physics, chemistry, and statistics contain articles reporting results of Monte Carlo simulations or suggestions on how they might be applied. Some journals are devoted almost entirely to Monte Carlo problems in their fields. Studies in the formation of the universe or of stars and their planetary systems use Monte Carlo techniques, as do studies in genetics, the biochemistry of DNA, and the random configuration and knotting of biological molecules. In number theory, Monte Carlo methods play an important role in determining primality or factoring of very large integers far beyond the range of deterministic methods.

Bibliography

1986. Kalos, M. H., and Whitlock, P. A. *Monte Carlo Methods.* New York: John Wiley.
1998. Gentle, J. E. *Random Number Generation and Monte Carlo Methods.* New York: Springer-Verlag.

George Marsaglia

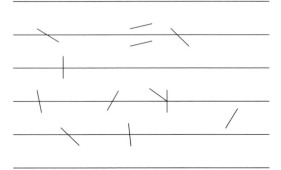

Figure 1. Buffon's needle problem. If a needle of length L (≤ 1) is dropped on a ruled surface of parallel lines spaced one unit apart, the probability that the needle will cross a line is $2L/\pi$. If the needle is dropped N times, the number of line crossings (say, X) should be about $2NL/\pi$, and hence $2NL/X$ is a Monte Carlo estimate of π. The estimate will have low precision (q.v.) unless millions of needles are dropped.

MOTHERBOARD

For articles on related subjects, see

✛ Bus
✛ Integrated Circuitry
✛ Open Architecture

The *motherboard* of a PC is its main logic board containing its central processing unit (CPU—*q.v.*) and memory chips. The term antedates personal computing since it was used by electronic hobbyists who often connected small ancillary "breadboard" circuits to a larger, principal circuit board that was dubbed "motherboard" to the smaller ones. On computers that employ an *open architecture*, the motherboard has attached *slots* into which specialized supplemental logic cards can be inserted to augment the primitive functions supported by the minimum configuration of the computer system.

Edwin D. Reilly

MOUSE

For articles on related subjects, *see*

+ Interactive Input Devices
+ Personal Computing

A *mouse* is a small hand-held interactive input device which, when rolled over a flat surface, controls placement of the cursor on a display monitor. The oval-shaped palm-sized device is usually connected to the computer by a wire that is suggestive of a tail, hence the affectionate name "mouse." A mouse that deliberately exploits comparison to a live mouse is shown in Fig. 1.

The mouse was invented by Douglas Englebart at the Stanford Research Institute in 1965, but mouse technology has changed considerably since then. The mouse used with the Apple Macintosh was a one-button device. After positioning the cursor by moving the mouse, single or multiple clicks of its only button select a course of action from a menu or, in word processing

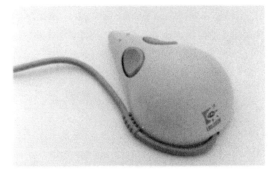

Figure 1. The Logitech Kidz Mouse. (Courtesy of Logitech.)

Figure 2. The Microsoft IntelliMouse Explorer. (Courtesy of Microsoft Corporation.)

(*q.v.*), affect whether a word is to be highlighted for additional processing. Screen icons can be "dragged" across the screen by moving the cursor over it, holding the mouse button down, and moving it to a new position by moving the mouse and then releasing the button. The mouse used with the IBM and other PCs and with workstations (*q.v.*) is usually a two- or three-button device.

The most common mouse is electromechanical. As the mouse is moved over a flat surface, the rolling motion of a rubber-coated steel ball that protrudes from its bottom is detected by two orthogonal rollers that touch the surface of the ball. These rollers act as transducers that are able to convert the speed and direction of the rolling ball to electrical signals that are fed to a software driver that moves a screen cursor accordingly. To provide good traction, an electromechanical mouse is generally used with a flat soft-cushioned *mouse pad*. In late 1999, Microsoft introduced an electro-optical mouse, the *IntelliMouse Explorer*, that has no moving parts and may be used on any surface other than glass; no mouse pad is needed (*see* Fig. 2). In 2001, Logitech introduced its MouseMan wireless optical mouse.

Bibliography

1998. White, R. "The Mechanical Mouse," in *How Computers Work*, 4th Ed., 160–161. Indianapolis, IN: Que/Macmillan.

2001. Fischetti, M., "Mice and Men: Evolution of the Desktop Mouse," *Scientific American*, **285**(4), (October) 86–87.

Edwin D. Reilly

MP3

See DATA COMPRESSION.

MULTIMEDIA

For articles on related topics, *see*

+ Computer-Assisted Learning and Teaching
+ Computer Games
+ Data Compression
+ Entertainment Industry, Computers in the
+ Hypertext
+ Image Compression
+ Speech Recognition and Synthesis
+ Videogames
+ Virtual Reality
+ Workstation
+ World Wide Web

The term *multimedia* implies the integration of audio, video, and images with more traditional types of data such as text and numerics. It is an application-oriented technology that caters to the multisensory nature of humans and is based on the evolving ability of computers to store, transmit, and convey diverse types of information. *Multimedia computing* is defined as the manipulation and presentation of such media in a computer system.

Representative Applications

The following four areas exemplify multimedia applications.

Online News

Online news is the multimedia analog of the printed newspaper. Through a Web browser, a reader can browse through pages of a newspaper, read articles, and view pictures or audio/video presentations. In addition, the user can perform index or *relational database* (*q.v.*) searches or queries to locate specific articles or advertisements. The user may also participate in chat groups and provide feedback to the editors.

Distance Education

Distance education enables students at remote locations to participate in live instruction via video conferencing; to collaborate on projects through shared "whiteboards"; or to replay instructional material that has been prerecorded or preorchestrated. Through multimedia distance learning using the Web, a student can browse through a database consisting of course material in various formats. Alternatively, the student can issue queries to the database while reading text or viewing illustrations and audio/video presentations.

Interactive, Gaming

Interactive games present a great demand on the multimedia delivery system due to the requirement for real-time, 3D imaging coupled with interactions among multiple players. SwineOnline is an example of a Web-enabled game involving the raising of pigs by participants in a virtual state fair. Each participant is responsible for interacting with and nurturing the virtual pet as its weight increases. A characteristic of this application is the need for low-latency interactions and support for a large number of interacting players.

Video-on-Demand

Video-on-demand (VOD) refers to networked multimedia applications that use full-screen video. Examples include movies delivered to a home from a central video server.

General Requirements for Multimedia Applications

The examples in the previous section belong to the class of distributed multimedia information system (DMIS) applications that together define multimedia technology. The major system-wide requirement for a DMIS is the ability to integrate real-time multimedia data retrieved from *distributed databases*. This mode of integration differs drastically from the important problem of computer systems integration that is concerned with unifying heterogeneous operating systems, networks, instruction sets (*q.v.*), and data formats. *Data integration, composition, or fusion* describes the assembly of multimedia data elements for presentation depending on the temporal and spatial characteristics of the data. This requirement establishes the need for system components capable of performing real-time data retrieval, delivery, and presentation.

Workstation, Technology

Multimedia applications need appropriate multisensory I/O devices. High-resolution display monitors and audio output can be used as presentation devices. The output device must allow presentation of both visual (text, graphics, video) and aural (voice, music) components. For data capture, additional specialized devices are required depending on the type of data. For example, still images can be captured using a scanner, voice can be captured with a microphone and digitizer, text can be input via a keyboard, and video can be handled with a camera and digitizer. Early multimedia systems showed that conventional devices for user interaction, such as the mouse (*q.v.*) and keyboard, are not suitable for many multimedia applications because they provide poor control of the spatial manipulations required. Multiple axis joysticks, foot pedals, "data gloves," and eye-motion tracking systems represent the next generation of multimedia I/O devices.

Communication Protocols

Interactive multimedia traffic places stringent real-time service demands on a communication system.

Existing protocols, such as TCP/IP (*q.v.*) for data communication, are not ideal for such traffic since they were not designed for error-free service rather than time-critical delivery of data. Many multimedia application traffic types, such as some interactive voice and video applications, can tolerate errors in transmission due to corruption or packet loss without retransmission or correction since dropped packets do not seriously degrade the service. Multimedia applications also require high performance in terms of predictable end-to-end delays, a feature not provided by most of the existing protocols or operating systems.

Asynchronous Transfer Mode (ATM) promises to provide a flexible communication mechanism for a variable Quality of Service (QoS) using variable-bandwidth channels in a form of packet switching (*q.v.*). This technique achieves a single network interface to communication channels for each media type, adaptability of the application's bandwidth requirements, flexibility for handling different data types, and a common signaling structure.

Communication Bandwidth

A summary of the data storage and communication requirements for various multimedia applications is shown in Table 1. A single audio/video videoconference connection pair requires 150 Mb/s without compression. Compression can reduce this bandwidth

Table 1. Bandwidth requirements of high-end media delivery.

Medium	Nominal bandwidth
Text file	60 Kb/s
Image file	400 Kb/s
MPEG 1 compressed video/audio	1.5 Mb/s
MPEG 2 compressed video/audio	7 Mb/s
Internet streaming compressed video	28 Kb/s
Uncompressed video/audio	150 Mb/s

requirement with acceptable signal degradation. For the enormous bandwidth necessary to support multiple sessions, high-speed networks are needed. Bandwidth (*q.v.*) availability is currently the most significant restriction on the ubiquitous deployment of multimedia applications and is the source of frequent complaints about the usability of the Web. Bandwidth availability is also the key to the viability of interactive TV or VOD consumption in the home. For residential networks, proposed solutions include Hybrid Fiber-Coaxial (HFC) (via cable TV) and Asymmetric Digital Subscriber Line (ADSL) (via the telephone network) to provide the aggregate bandwidth.

Internetworking

In order to gain access to the thousands of public and private databases currently available, a DMIS must extend beyond the simple LAN environment. High-speed networks can link such geographically dispersed data stores and users requiring broadband services. Both LAN and Metropolitan Area Network (MAN) technologies are well-suited for such interconnections.

Data Storage

Like communication bandwidth, the data storage requirement for multimedia data types is very large. For example, the storage of 10 000 full-screen color still images (3 colors/pixel × 8 bits/color × 1200 × 1200 pixels = 35 Mb) requires 350 Gb, or 43 GB of storage. Similarly, for digital video storage applications, a video archive of 500 movies of 120 min duration each requires 531 Tb, or 66 TB of storage (3 colors/pixel × 8 bits/color × 512 × 400 pixels × 30/ s = 147 Mbps). With a compression of 20 : 1, this can be reduced to a "mere" 3.3 TB. This volume is particularly problematic when the multimedia applications require random access storage, for which streaming drives, such as magnetic tape, are not suitable. For example, MPEG-2 compressed video requires a transfer rate of 6.2 Mbps. Although this rate is readily achievable from a magnetic disk drive or large database server, it is not typical of a CD-ROM. The recent Digital Versatile Disc (DVD)

standard addresses both the capacity and bandwidth limitations of CD-ROM; however, it is intended to support only a single video data stream (*see* OPTICAL STORAGE).

Applications Interfaces and Authoring Tools

Additional important problems faced by multimedia application developers are the design of user interfaces (*q.v.*) and the authoring of content for the applications. Tools for developing such interfaces include window systems and application programming interfaces (APIs) which permit the developer a full range of access to the utilities available in a DMIS. Substantial improvement in window-based interface models and toolkits has been achieved, particularly in the domain of the Web.

Multimedia content uses diverse data types. Construction of a multimedia application requires that there be instructions, or scripts, on how the content should be interpreted by the workstation. Authoring tools provide a means for technical and nontechnical content developers to produce multimedia works dealing with spatial layout and temporal presentation. Most of these tools produce proprietary data representations that are playable only with their own components. Increasingly, however, tools are being developed that yield standards-based output such as HyTime, SGML, or some other scripting language (*q.v.*) that is supported on a wider scale through open Web-based systems.

Executable content refers to scripting information that can be coupled directly with the content to be delivered. Most of the early Web-based content delivery approaches relied on both the workstation and server participating in interactions with the content. Executable content (e.g. programs written in Java—*q.v.*) allows for a tighter coupling of the content with the program that is required for its presentation.

Information Retrieval

New approaches to accessing information have also been developed that facilitate operation in novel ways. For example, high-end workstations can provide access to 3D information via the use of large display devices and oscillating-aperture glasses. For database applications, the trend is to move away from traditional relational query-type interfaces that require substantial knowledge of the content and structure of the stored information. Object-oriented and hypermedia models (nonsequential access by reference) are increasingly popular for managing very large multimedia data items such as digital libraries. On the Web, the hypermedia or hypertext (*q.v.*) paradigm is fundamental, but is often coupled with conventional relational database components.

Bibliography

1995. Streinmetz, R., and Nahrstedt, K. *Multimedia: Computing, Communications and Applications.* Upper Saddle River, NJ: Prentice Hall.

1996. Furht, B. (ed.) *Multimedia Tools and Applications.* Norwood. MA: Kluwer Academic.

Thomas Little

MULTIPLEXING

For articles on related subjects, *see*

+ Bandwidth
+ Channel
+ Contention
+ Local Area Network (LAN)
+ Modem
+ Networks, Computer
+ Packet Switching
+ Polling
+ TCP/IP
+ Time Sharing

Multiplexing is a technique that allows a number of lower bandwidth communication channels to be combined and transmitted over a higher bandwidth channel. At the receiving end, *demultiplexing* recovers the original lower bandwidth channels. The three basic multiplexing methods in use are *space division multiplexing* (SDM), *frequency division multiplexing* (FDM), and *time division multiplexing* (TDM).

Space Division Multiplexing

Space division multiplexing (SDM) refers to the physical grouping of many individual transmission channels to form a channel with a much higher total aggregate bandwidth. Hundreds of twisted wire pairs, coaxial cables, and/or optical fibers can be grouped to form a larger diameter cable. Each wire pair, coaxial cable, or fiber in the main cable is an individual communication channel capable of being frequency or time division multiplexed. Such cables have enough total bandwidth to carry hundreds of thousands of two-way voice channels of 4000 Hz each in a cable diameter under 3 inches.

Frequency Division Multiplexing

Frequency division multiplexing (FDM) divides a higher bandwidth channel into many individual smaller bandwidth channels (*see* Fig. 1). Signals (data, voice, or video) on these channels are transmitted at the same time but at different carrier frequencies. *Guard bands* are needed between the channels to help reduce interchannel interference. A

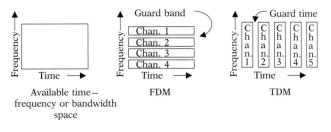

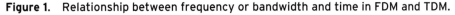

Figure 1.   Relationship between frequency or bandwidth and time in FDM and TDM.

familiar example of FDM is television broadcasting. Stations broadcast programs continuously, each at a different frequency.

Time Division Multiplexing

In time division multiplexing (TDM), the entire bandwidth of the channel is dedicated to one low-speed channel for a short period of time, and then to the other low-speed channels in round-robin fashion or some other predetermined sequence. In effect, the low-bandwidth channels are accommodated on the high bandwidth channel by time-domain *interleaving* (*q.v.*). Guard times are used to separate *time slices* (*q.v.*), and the transmitting and receiving ends must be synchronized. A familiar example of TDM is the bus (*q.v.*) of a computer servicing many peripherals, one at a time, for short periods of time.

Circuit and Packet Switching

A circuit switch refers to equipment that can transfer any one of m input lines to any one of n output lines or trunks ($m > n$), as shown in Fig. 2. Once established, the connection is typically held for the duration of the transaction. At the end of transmission, the trunk is freed and is available for assignment to the next input line needing a connection. This technique is mainly used in telephone networks to establish an end-to-end circuit for the entire duration of a call and,

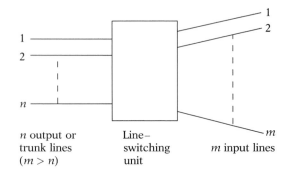

n output or trunk lines ($m > n$)   Line–switching unit m input lines

Figure 2.   Line or circuit-switching unit connects any one of m input lines to any one of n trunk lines. This is widely used where the probability of all input lines being used at a given time is small, resulting in more efficient usage of the trunk lines.

although it has sometimes been called space division multiplexing, it is more appropriate to call it circuit or line switching. This should be contrasted with packet switching, in which the trunk is used only for the duration of transmission of a single packet. By limiting the length of packets, wait times for other users are limited. Packet switching is, therefore, very effective for transmitting data for interactive computing over a wide area network (WAN) such as the Internet. Packet switching is a form of message switching multiplexing (MSM) and, therefore, TDM.

Multiplexer Hierarchies

As networks become more complex, hierarchies of multiplexing are required in which low-bandwidth channels are multiplexed onto higher bandwidth channels, which in turn are multiplexed onto even higher bandwidth channels, and so on. In the FDM hierarchy, multiplex levels correspond to increasingly higher frequency bands. In the TDM hierarchy, they correspond to increasingly higher pulse rates.

Bibliography

1996. Tanenbaum, A. S. *Computer Networks*, 3rd Ed. Upper Saddle River, NJ: Prentice Hall.
1997. Keshav, S. *An Engineering Approach to Computer Networking: ATM Networks, the Internet, and the Telephone Network*. Reading, MA: Addison-Wesley.

John S. Sobolewski

MULTIPROCESSING

For articles on related subjects, *see*

+ Cache Memory
+ Cluster Computing
+ Concurrent Programming
+ Contention
+ Mutual Exclusion
+ Multiprogramming
+ Multitasking

+ Parallel Processing
+ Supercomputers

Multiprocessing is the simultaneous processing of two or more computational portions of the same program by two or more processing units. Multiprocessing involves a departure from the classical von Neumann machine (*q.v.*) organization in which there is a single instruction stream (single program counter) and a single data stream (unique communication channel between CPU and memory). From an architectural viewpoint, extensions to this Single Instruction Single Data (SISD) organization will yield Single Instruction Multiple Data (SIMD) architectures and Multiple Instruction Multiple Data (MIMD) architectures. This classification is due to Flynn (1966). Here we restrict ourselves to MIMD systems.

MIMD architectures are differentiated according to whether they are shared-memory machines, that is, communication occurs as the result of load–store instructions, or operate according to a message-passing paradigm. In shared-memory MIMD systems, further differentiation arises when one considers the switching structure between processors and memory modules. Typical switching structures in *tightly coupled* systems, where all processors operate under the control of a single operating system, are a common single shared bus, a multistage interconnection network, meshes or tori, or a crossbar (a switch that connects any processor to any memory module). A fundamental difference between tightly coupled systems and networks of workstations (NOW) is the unit of communication, namely a few bytes (word or cache line) for the former and a few kilobytes (a *page*) in the latter.

Single-Bus Systems

In the shared-bus architecture called *symmetric multiprocessors*, (*SMP*), processors have access to a common *bus* (*q.v.*) via their off-chip caches (Fig. 1). Global memory is also attached to the bus. Since all processors access memory with the same latency, this architecture is called *Uniform Memory Access* (UMA). Cache coherence is solved using *snoopy protocols* whereby each cache controller listens to all bus transactions. The single bus

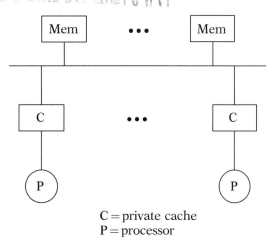

C = private cache
P = processor

Figure 1.   Multi: multiprocessor with a shared bus.

is therefore a major source of *contention* (*q.v.*). Early systems with (relatively) slow processors and fast buses contained up to 30 processors (Sequent Balance and Symmetry, SGI Challenge). Recent offerings of SMPs are limited to four.

NonUniform Memory Access (NUMA) Systems

Larger multiprocessors (e.g. on the order of tens to a few hundred processing elements) require another switching structure. Multistage interconnection networks such as those in Fig. 2—$O(\log n)$ stages for n processor and memory modules—as well as 2D and 3D meshes and tori, have been used to connect *nodes*: processors and associated memory modules. The number of switches, and stages, can be reduced by using 4×4 or 8×8 crossbars rather than 2×2 switches. Moreover, each node of the multiprocessor can itself be an SMP, as in Stanford's DASH experimental machine, or a small number (two to eight) of processors connected by a crossbar as in the SGI Origin and HP/Convex Exemplar. These more powerful nodes are often referred to as *clusters*. In these larger systems, access to memory is *nonuniform* since the latency to reference memory within a node (home memory) is much smaller than access to the memory of a remote node; hence the name *distributed shared memory* for these systems.

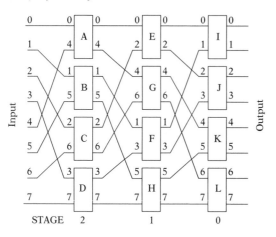

Figure 2. Example of a multistage interconnection network: the Omega network.

Programming Shared Memory Systems

In multiprocessing systems, the increase in performance resides mainly in path parallelism, that is, the concurrent execution of several different parts of the program, or of the same part with different data. The basic form of parallelism is via a FORK–JOIN pair where FORK indicates the creation of several paths that JOIN at a given point. A higher-level construct for FORK is the creation of concurrent threads that share common memory and have their own private stacks. A *create* procedure with parameters for the number of threads is a common way to achieve this. A *wait* construct implements the JOIN with an argument for the number of threads that must be ending before the flow of control can proceed with the statement following the wait. A *barrier* statement, a global synchronization primitive with an argument indicating the number of instances of a parallel loop, is used to start (fork) and finish (join) the instances of the loop.

In MIMD architectures, the most common type of control is a decentralized mode whereby each processor can have access to the operating system and schedule itself. In this case, it can happen that two concurrent processes will wish to access and modify the same data structures. This has been referred to as the *mutual exclusion* problem. In any given path, the portion of

code that accesses the shared data is called the *critical section* of that path.

Bibliography

1966. Flynn, M. J. "Very High-speed Computing Systems," *Proceedings IEEE* 54, 12 (December), 1901–1909.

1998. Hwang, K., and Xu, Z. *Scalable Parallel Computing.* New York: McGraw-Hill.

1999. Culler, D., Singh, J. P., and Gupta, A. *Parallel Computer Architecture. A Hardware/Software Approach.* San Francisco: Morgan Kaufmann.

Jean-Loup Baer

MULTIPROGRAMMING

For articles on related subjects, *see*

+ Concurrent Programming
+ Data Security
+ Interleaving
+ Multitasking
+ Operating Systems
+ Parallel Processing
+ Time Sharing
+ Virtual Memory

Multiprogramming—overlapping and interleaving the executions of more than one program—achieves several goals. It achieves higher resource utilization by keeping the resources of the computer system working simultaneously. It permits two or more programs to operate in parallel, so their effects are observed simultaneously, rather than sequentially. The concept of multiprogramming was conceived in 1962 at the University of Manchester and first implemented on Atlas (*q.v.*) by a team led by Tom Kilburn.

Early computer systems executed only one program (or *job*) at a time. Certain programs were *input–output* (I/O) *bound*; that is, their rate of progress was limited by the speed of I/O units. In mainframe (*q.v.*) computers, devices such as tape drives or card readers slowed execution; in desktop systems it is typically serial modems (*q.v.*) or printers that consume significant amounts of real-time. In contrast, CPU- bound programs performed mostly numerical calculations, with little input–output. Neither of these types of program can fully use the resources of the computer system.

Once a computer has begun to read data from a disk or modem, the processor can execute instructions while data is being transferred into an area of memory used as a *buffer* (*q.v.*). Each program requires allocated address space to hold the data and instructions being, or ready to be, executed. If sufficient memory and other resources exist and can be allocated to multiple programs, then the computer can be multiprogrammed.

Figure 1 is an example of how two programs can be interleaved and overlapped by multiprogramming. The first program (shown in Fig. 1a) is heavily I/O-bound, and uses the CPU only 10% of the time. The second

program, shown in Fig. 1c, has the opposite nature, and would like to use the CPU 90% of the time. If these programs were executing alone, each would behave as shown in Figs. 1a and 1c, respectively, but Fig. 1b shows how often the demands of the first program and those of the second conflict because each wants to use the same resource. Notice that this happens about 20% of the time.

Multiprogramming does not require a large operating system in order to coordinate the demands of each program. On a small computer, it is common to provide a *background/foreground* system that permits two programs to execute. The foreground, or real-time, program may consist of a job to monitor periodically a number of instruments and perform some corrective adjustment. In between measurements, the system may have sufficient resources to permit a background program to execute, doing compilations or calculations. In order to control resources effectively such as space for

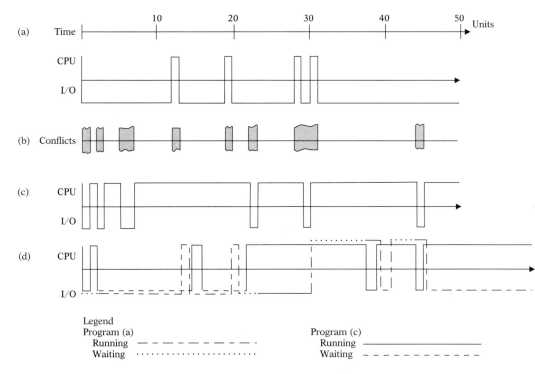

Figure 1. An example of the advantages of multiprogramming. The area of overlap between the I/O-bound program (a) and CPU-bound program (c) is shown in (b). In (d), one way of multiprogramming these two programs is shown.

data or file storage, modern systems centralize all I/O operations in an *operating system* that performs services on behalf of the user programs. In this manner, the users of the system cannot corrupt each other's data or invade the privacy of secure information.

Multiprogramming may also take place within a single job. For example, the system may be able to overlap the computational needs of a single program with its I/O needs. The capability of a program to spawn (or create) additional tasks (user processes) that are to be executed as if they were jobs, but which possess a filial relationship to the parent task, is referred to as *multitasking* or *multithreading*.

Bibliography

1972. Lorin, H. *Parallelism in Hardware and Software: Real and Apparent Concurrency*. Upper Saddle River, NJ: Prentice Hall.

1997. Silberschatz, A., and Galvin, P. B. *Operating Systems Concepts*, 5th Ed. Reading, MA: Addison-Wesley.

Harry J. Saal

MULTITASKING

For articles on related subjects, *see*

+ Concurrent Programming
+ Multiplexing
+ Multiprocessing
+ Multiprogramming
+ Operating Systems
+ Parallel Processing
+ Real-Time Systems
+ Time Sharing

Multitasking refers to an operating system's ability to support multiple processes simultaneously. The term is sometimes used as a synonym for multiprocessing, but is more often used when the processes in question all emanate from the same user.

A *process* is a program in execution. Support for multiple processes is necessary in applications where several computations must proceed in parallel. On a PC, a user may edit a file while another file is being printed and electronic mail (*q.v.*) is received. These three activities are best supported by three processes running simultaneously. Real-time systems that control multiple devices also need to support multiple processes.

Modern operating systems distinguish between two types of processes. *Lightweight processes* or *threads* are described by their *stateword* or *statevector*, that is, the contents of the processor registers such as the program counter, stack pointer, general purpose registers, condition codes, and so on. A *user process*, also called a *task*, is a significant extension. It includes at least one thread, a virtual memory (*q.v.*) containing a program (instructions and data), and context information such as descriptors for open files and communication channels.

Thread-Level Support for Multitasking

The simplest way to execute multiple threads simultaneously is to assign each thread to its own processor in a multiprocessor system. If the number of threads exceeds the number of processors, then processors must be multiplexed among the threads. *Processor multiplexing* implements quasi-parallelism: by switching a processor rapidly from one thread to the next, it appears to the observer as though all threads are making progress, even though the processor can execute instructions of only one process at a time.

Processor multiplexing works as follows. Time is divided into disjoint intervals called *time slices*, and the processor is assigned to at most one thread during each interval. At the end of a time slice, the operating system performs a *context switch*: it switches the running thread off its processor by first saving the processor registers into memory, and then loads the stateword of the next thread into the processor registers.

Task-Level Support for Multitasking

At the task level, memory management (*q.v.*) is an important issue. A simple approach is *swapping*: the operating system keeps only a single task's program in the main memory at a time; the programs of other tasks are stored in secondary storage (usually disk). As part of a context switch, the operating system must first unload its memory to disk and then reload it with the program of the next task. In order to reduce I/O traffic, a multiprogrammed operating system keeps programs or program segments of several tasks in main memory simultaneously. Multiprogramming reduces the number of reads and writes to secondary storage, provided main memory is large enough to hold the working sets (*q.v.*) of several tasks. Multiprogramming and hence multitasking are facilitated by virtual memory (*q.v.*), a mechanism that simulates an address space much larger than the physical memory available to each task.

Bibliography

1997. Tanenbaum, A. S. *Operating Systems—Design and Implementation*, 2nd Ed. Upper Saddle River, NJ: Prentice Hall.

Walter F. Tichy

MUSEUMS, COMPUTER

For articles on related subjects, *see*

+ Computer Art
+ World Wide Web

Computer museums are places, both real and virtual, that seek to preserve, celebrate, and explain humankind's most profound technical achievement of the mid- to late twentieth century, the digital computer. There are broad differences among computer museums in emphasis, funding, size, and intended audience. Computer museums of any type share the same challenges and opportunities as do traditional museums. To some extent, all such institutions exist to place objects in a context which no longer exists outside museums and to foster the scholarly study and preservation of such objects as a means of reconstructing the original context. Much as Goethe noted that "architecture is frozen music,"

so are the objects in a computer museum congealed embodiments of the technical constraints, economic possibilities, and expressive power of the human mind at particular instants.

Some of the more popular museum collection guidelines include:

1. *The first of something.* This comprises the "successes" of the industry, for example, representative instances of an IBM System/360 or the first Fortran (*q.v.*) compiler (*q.v.*). "Firsts," however, are frequently matters of controversy or interpretation and may change over time (e.g. the Atanasoff (*q.v.*)/Mauchly case) so care needs to be exercised with respect to both object selection and the claims made on behalf of such objects.
2. *Mass-produced.* Driven by market success, the object becomes collectible precisely because it once was so common. The first IBM PC (*q.v.*) is the classic example.
3. *Special provenance.* Something owned or used by an important inventor, for example, John von Neumann's (*q.v.*) slide-rule. These objects appeal

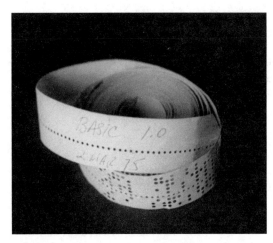

Figure 1. Bill Gates' original BASIC paper tape. The Altair microcomputer inspired Bill Gates, then at Harvard University, to write a BASIC assembler so that users could easily program the machine. This was the start of Microsoft, then known as "Micro Soft." From the collection of The Computer Museum History Center (×507.84).

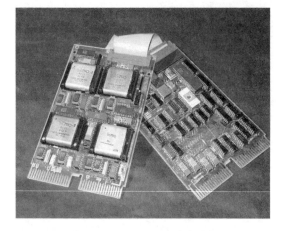

Figure 2. A 4-MB Intel bubble memory module. Magnetic bubble memory, a technology whose introduction seemed imminent for over a decade, was finally abandoned in the early 1980s as inexpensive DRAMs made it uneconomical. Although bubble memory had the advantage of being nonvolatile, that advantage was also eclipsed by advances in semiconductor technology, specifically the EPROM and battery backed-up DRAM. From the collection of the Computer Museum History Center (×8.81 A-B).

to people's fascination with anything a famous person may have touched or used (see Fig. 1).

4. *Failures*. Many curators find "failures" to be more instructive of invention than successes (see Fig. 2).

5. *Seminal inventors*. Certain people contribute a disproportionate amount of disciplinary knowledge (e.g. Seymour Cray or Donald Knuth) and, as such, objects they have created or supervised are always of interest.

Types of Collected Objects

Parallel to these taxonomies are "object types" related to the central item being collected. What, for example, will a specific museum collect about an Altair microcomputer? Types of objects a computer museum might consider collecting fall into five broad categories: hardware, software, ephemera, documentation, and media. Let us briefly examine these five object types.

Hardware

Collecting and displaying hardware is the most expensive means of preserving computer history, but it is also the means with the greatest visitor impact. From a research perspective, having a physical object also establishes an epistemic datum one cannot obtain from books, Websites, or other simulacra of an object (see Fig. 3). The issue of whether hardware needs to be operational to be valid for display is a matter of some debate. Generally, an inverse relationship exists between a machine's age and its likelihood of ever operating again.

Software

Software seems particularly evanescent as a museum object. Particularly in large institutions, this impermanence is exacerbated by the uncertainty concerning under whose professional jurisdiction its preservation should fall: curators (who generally collect physical objects) or archivists (who collect records). As a result of this uncertainty, many museums have forestalled resolution of this debate with the regrettable outcome that

Figure 3. The Enigma enciphering machine used by Nazi forces in the Second World War, for secure communications. Breaking Enigma transmissions, undertaken in part by Alan Turing and others at Bletchely Park outside of London, UK had a dramatic impact on the outcome and conduct of the war. From the collection of The Computer Museum History Center (B197.81).

software is not being preserved at all or is being collected only very haphazardly. Many critical programs have already been lost. The earliest versions of Unix (*q.v.*), for example, in either source or executable form, appear to have disappeared.

Emulators mimic machine architectures to the functional level; simulators, being a subset of emulators, do so to the register-transfer, gate, or behavioral level. Both allow the running of historical software on present-day (i.e. nonnative) hardware. In some cases, the fidelity of these emulators is remarkable—even unpublished machine features are emulated—resulting in extremely accurate portrayals of a machine's operation.

Ephemera

Ephemera refers to the cultural objects accreting around a physical item, including software. Items in this category include T-shirts, coffee mugs, lucite-encased mementos, marketing literature, buttons, posters, lab notebooks—in essence, any item directly or peripherally related to a machine or program that, while not required for such items to function, yield information about the intended purpose and function of such objects. Ephemera allow a cultural decoding of the time and context in which such products were introduced.

Documentation

This category includes items such as technical manuals, quick reference cards, schematics, memoranda, and books. For either type of computer museum, there is great research utility in converting at least the more significant documentary holdings into electronic format. A popular method is to make these documents available in Portable Document Format (PDF), a format that maintains the original "look" of a document while permitting searching and indexing.

Media

Media refers to film, videotape, photographs, and their digital equivalents. Museums often maintain at least a minimal archive for exhibit support but such archives can also be a significant source of revenue.

Like ephemera, the various media types can be useful in elucidating context for a particular machine. An inexpensive, simple, and historically useful activity is to make video recordings of operating machines just prior to their decommissioning. The sights and sounds of such machines can be highly evocative and can provide insights that no amount of text, code, or mute hardware can provide.

Bibliography

The Computer Museum History Center (USA). `http://www.computerhistory.org`.

The Heinz Nixdorf Museum Forum (Germany). `http://www.hnf.de/index_en.html`.

Charles Babbage Institute (USA). `http://www.cbi.umn.edu`.

The National Museum of Science and Industry (UK). `http://www.nmsi.ac.uk`.

The Smithsonian Institution (USA). `http://www.si.edu`.

Computer Conservation Society (UK). `http://www.cs.man.ac.uk/CCS/`.

Dag Spicer

MUSIC, COMPUTER

See COMPUTER MUSIC.

MUTUAL EXCLUSION

For articles on related subjects, *see*

+ Concurrent Programming
+ Contention
+ Monitor, Synchronization
+ Multiprocessing
+ Multiprogramming
+ Multitasking

When several processes are executing simultaneously, it may happen that two or more of them want to access and modify the same data. For example, in a multiprogramming system a WRITE process (producer) and a READ process (consumer) might share the same buffer area, so that the consumer has to be protected from having its data garbled by the producer before the READ is completed. As a second example, in a system with multiple CPUs two processors can be idle and request a new task at the same time. If no precaution is taken, both will access the table where the list of waiting tasks is stored, and both may initiate the same task. To circumvent this problem, means must be provided to protect the shared data from disorderly changes. Such means are usually called *mutual exclusion*, or *lockout*. The portion of code in a process that accesses a shared area is called a *critical section* of that process.

At the hardware level, the implementation of mutual exclusion is based on the atomic (indivisible) exchange of a value in a register with a value in memory. Similar schemes have been proposed for high-level languages. In order to allow programs to be independent of specific implementations of mutual exclusion, Dijkstra (1968) defined a new type of variable, called a *semaphore*, which can assume only nonnegative integer values. Dijkstra's elegant solution is based on two primitive and indivisible operations on semaphores, namely:

$V (S)$ defined as: $S \leftarrow S + 1$.

$P (S)$ defined as:

if $S = 0$, **then** block process, **else** $S \leftarrow S{-}1$.

Initially, the semaphore is set to 1. Before entering a critical section, the process performs a P operation. If S is 1, the process decrements S and enters its critical section. Since S is now 0, no other process may enter its critical section. If S were 0, the process would be blocked and would remain so as long as another process was executing in a critical section. When a process terminates its critical section, it performs a V operation, setting S to 1 and thus allowing another process to enter its critical section.

The semaphore concept has become ubiquitous as an efficient means of protection between *cooperating sequential processes* and has been implemented in various forms in most operating systems (*q.v.*). Because reasoning about semaphores might be tricky, some high-level language constructs such as *monitors* and associated *condition variables*, whose underlying structures rely on the semaphore concept, have been introduced to facilitate writing correct interprocess communication programs.

Bibliography

1968. Dijkstra, E. W. "Cooperating Sequential Processes," *In Programming Languages* (ed. F Genuys). New York: Academic Press.

1996. Hennessy, J., and Patterson, D. *Computer Architecture: A Quantitative Approach*, 2nd Ed. San Francisco: Morgan Kaufmann.

1997. Tanenbaum, A., and Woodhull, A. *Operating Systems Design and Implementation*, 2nd Ed. Upper Saddle River, NJ: Prentice Hall.

Jean-Loup Baer

N

NANOTECHNOLOGY

For an article on a related subject, *see*

+ Integrated Circuitry

In 1959, the Nobel physicist Richard Feynman predicted that it would one day be possible to synthesize any chemical substance atom by atom. Twenty years later, MIT engineer Eric Drexler advocated beginning work on *nanoelectronics*, building electronic logic elements from individual molecules. Doing so is called *nanotechnology*.

The prefix "nano-" means "one-billionth." Light travels only about a foot in a nanosecond. Nanotechnology implies the harnessing of electronic action at scales of a nanometer, one one-hundred-thousandth of the thickness of a human hair and about the size of the sugar molecule. An integrated circuit (IC) with a thousand carbon nanotubes acting like transistors was devised by Phaedon Avouris of IBM in early 2001. *Nanotubes*, discovered by Sumio Iijima of the Nippon Electric Corporation (NEC) in 1991, are cylinders of nanometer radius made of hexagonal arrangements of carbon atoms that, magnified, look like rolled-up chicken wire. "Nanoxisters" are nanotubes that can sustain current densities hundreds of times greater than that of common metals and can be made in either metallic or semiconductor form. Bundled nanotube cables are so strong and light that it is being seriously suggested that they be used

to form the structure of a directly connected temporary "elevator" to hoist supplies to satellites in orbit.

Conventional microcomputer chip (*q.v.*) manufacture is a "top-down" process whereby increasingly higher transistor densities are achieved by deposition of ever smaller clumps of molecules in a race to keep up with Moore's Law that is destined to be lost (*see* LAWS, COMPUTER). Nanoelectronics, in contrast, proceeds from the bottom up: first build individual molecular logic gates and then interconnect them to form a complete computer. The first step—construction of molecular logic gates—was announced in back-to-back papers in the 9 November 2001 issue of *Science* magazine. In the first, Yu Huang and his colleagues describe how a group at Harvard used nanowire building blocks to configure AND, OR, and NOR logic gates and used them for simple computations. In the second, Adrian Bachtold and his coauthors announced that a group at the Delft University of Technology in the Netherlands had created field-effect transistors (FETs) made of single carbon molecules called *nanotubes* and assembled them into inverters, NOR gates, and a static random-access memory (RAM) cell. The first *nanocomputer* may be only a decade or two away.

Bibliography

1992. Drexler, K. E. *Nanosystems: Molecular Machinery, Manufacturing, and Computation*. New York: John Wiley.
2003. Poole, C. P., and Owens, F. J. *Introduction to Nanotechnology*. New York: Wiley-Interscience.

Edwin D. Reilly

NATURAL LANGUAGE PROCESSING

For articles on related subjects, *see*

+ Artificial Intelligence (AI)
+ Database Management System (DBMS)
+ Information Retrieval
+ Knowledge Representation
+ Logic Programming
+ Machine Translation
+ Relational Database
+ Speech Recognition and Synthesis

Natural language processing (NLP) refers to computer systems that analyze, attempt to understand, or produce one or more human languages, such as English, Japanese, or Russian. The input might be text, spoken language, or keyboard input. The task might be to translate to another language, to comprehend and represent the content of text, to build a database or generate summaries, or to maintain a dialogue with a user as part of database information retrieval.

It is extremely difficult to define how we would ever know that a system actually "understands" language. All we can actually test is whether a system appears to understand language by successfully performing its task. The Turing test (*q.v.*), proposed by Alan Turing in 1950, has been the classical model. In this test, the system must be indistinguishable from a human when both answer arbitrary interrogation by a human over a terminal.

The principal difficulty in processing natural language is the pervasive ambiguity found at all levels of the problem. For example, all natural languages involve the following:

- Simple lexical ambiguity (e.g. "duck" can be a noun (the animal) or a verb (to avoid something thrown)).
- Structural or syntactic ambiguity (e.g. "I saw the man with a telescope.").
- Semantic ambiguity (e.g. "go" as a verb has well over 10 distinct meanings in any dictionary).
- Pragmatic ambiguity (e.g. "Can you lift that rock?" may be a yes/no question or a request to lift the rock).
- Referential ambiguity (e.g. in "Jack met Sam at the station. He was feeling ill . . .").

It is the prevalence of ambiguity that distinguishes natural languages from precisely defined artificial languages, such as logic and programming languages. It also makes most of the techniques developed in programming language grammars, parsing, and semantics ineffective for NLP unless significantly modified.

Natural Language Database Query Systems: Syntax and Semantics

The most successful NLP systems to date have been front ends to databases. These systems can understand isolated questions dealing with the content of the database (*see* Fig. 1). The LUNAR system was the first system to develop this technology and serves as the prototype for many current-day commercial systems. The core of LUNAR was a syntactic grammar in a formalism called an *Augmented Transition Network* (ATN) Grammar. An ATN is a graphical notation that can be shown to be equivalent to context-free grammars.

New grammatical formalisms that slightly extend context-free grammars are an active area of research. These theories require finer distinctions than found in the traditional Chomsky Hierarchy (*q.v.*). Semantic processing is at a considerably less developed stage, and most work is still being done within research prototypes of limited scope; there are very few commercial applications. Most current NLP systems use a knowledge

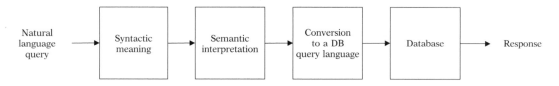

Figure 1.   The architecture of an NL database query system.

representation expressively equivalent to or weaker than the first-order predicate calculus (FOPC). A comparison of how a simple English sentence is expressed both as a parse tree and in FOPC is shown in Fig. 2. But significant aspects of language appear to remain outside the range of first-order logic, and considerable basic research into more expressive formalisms is needed.

Text Understanding: Pragmatics and World Knowledge

Understanding extended text, such as newspaper articles, paper abstracts, or books, requires significant additions to the capabilities required for question-answering systems. There is a strong pragmatic component as well—namely, the use of common everyday knowledge about the world in order to determine the relationships between the sentences in the text. There is a need for significant world knowledge even within single sentences. For example, the sentence *Jack couldn't drive to work because he lost his keys* requires knowledge about cars and keys. Without this basic knowledge, a system will not be able to determine why Jack couldn't drive to work, and wouldn't know that car jacking is not the same as jacking up a car.

Machine Translation

Machine translation (language translation) was one of the first applications that led to AI work on natural language processing. Machine translation is a very active area of research, especially in Europe and Japan, and is now undergoing a resurgence in the

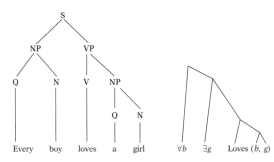

Figure 2. The structure of natural language compared with FOPC quantification. [S: Sentence; NP: Noun Phrase; VP: Verb Phrase; N: Noun; V: Verb; A: quantifier].

USA. There are two primary approaches. The first is based on defining corresponding lexical, syntactic, and semantic correspondences between a pair of languages, and defining a transducer based on these rules. The second is based on a notion of a language-independent representation or *interlingua*. To translate, one would parse one language into the interlingua and then from that generate text in the second language. While the second is the more general approach, the most successful systems to date are based on the former techniques. It is commonly accepted that high-quality machine translation of general text is either impossible or a very long way off in the future. What is feasible currently, however, is the development of machine translation tools to aid human translators, and the development of translation systems that then require postediting by a human. A rudimentary system currently in place is part of the AltaVista search engine on the World Wide Web (*q.v.*). A user who obtains a "hit"—a short possibly relevant text passage received in a "foreign" language—can request automatic translation into the user's native language.

Prospects

Natural language processing should make considerable strides early in this millennium. Large-scale grammars of natural languages are being written, and there is considerable effort in building large English lexicons using automatic techniques. We can expect to see the emergence of quite sophisticated question-answering systems. In the area of text skimming and summarizing, substantial progress should be made in identifying and capturing a specific set of predetermined topics (e.g. a brief summary of the major financial transactions described in the *Wall Street Journal*). Such a system could automatically read the newspaper and build a database of the transactions described, which could then be searched and used to generate short paragraph summaries of the information extracted.

Bibliography

1986. Grosz, B., Sparck-Jones, K., and Webber, B. *Readings in Natural Language Processing*. San Francisco, CA: Morgan Kaufmann.

1995. Allen, J. *Natural Language Understanding*, 2nd Ed. Reading, MA: Addison-Wesley.

1997. Suereth, R. *Developing Natural Language Interfaces: Processing Human Conversations*. New York: McGraw-Hill.

James F. Allen

NET

See INTERNET.

NETWORK ARCHITECTURE

For articles on related topics, *see*

+ Local Area Network (LAN)
+ Networks, Computer
+ Network Protocols
+ Open Systems Interconnection
+ TCP/IP

Computer networks may consist of thousands of computing devices of various kinds, often made by different vendors and interconnected by many types of transmission media, including standard telephone lines, satellites, digital microwave radio, optical fibers, or digital data lines. For such heterogeneous devices to be linked, either the hardware and software need to be compatible or else complex interfaces need to be built to allow meaningful communication. *Network architecture* helps achieve this compatibility.

Objectives

A *network architecture* defines the message and data formats as well as the protocols and standards to which hardware and software must conform. Such architectures are designed to achieve the following objectives:

1. *Connectivity* to permit diverse hardware and software built in conformance with the architecture to communicate over the network.

2. *Flexibility* to permit easy modification as user needs change.

3. *Modularity* to permit mass production of hardware and software modules that can be used in a wide variety of devices.

4. *Reliability* to permit error-free communication by providing appropriate error detection and correction capabilities.

5. *Simplicity* to permit easy implementation, installation, and reconfiguration of the network.

6. *Diversity* of network services that can be easily used and yet isolate users from the details of network structure or implementation.

Implementation

Designing a network architecture to achieve these objectives is a difficult task. Consequently, the common set of rules for generating and interpreting messages sent and received by the communicating devices to implement these functions can be large and complex. For this reason, the entire set of rules is often partitioned into groups or layers of manageable size, with each layer containing only those rules needed to perform some specific subset of functions. By making the functions in each layer independent of those in other layers, new functions or enhancement of existing functions can be implemented with little or no disruption to other layers.

The Reference Model for Open Systems Interconnection (the OSI model) shown in Fig. 1 is a layered network architecture. The term *open* denotes the ability to transfer information between any two systems that conform to the model and its associated standards. The actual transfer of data occurs through the physical medium (telephone line, coaxial cable, or some other transmission medium) located just below layer 1 of the model. The seven layers collectively provide all the functions necessary for communication between two systems, with each layer providing a service to the layer above and enhancing the service provided by the layer below. With this approach, a process initiated at the highest layer has the full set of services at its disposal (*see* OPEN SYSTEMS INTERCONNECTION).

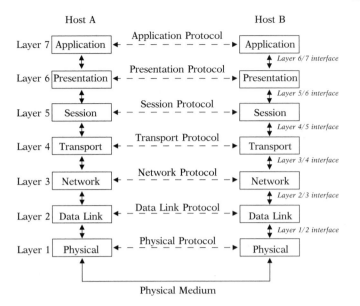

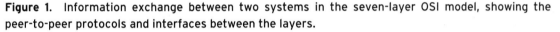

Figure 1. Information exchange between two systems in the seven-layer OSI model, showing the peer-to-peer protocols and interfaces between the layers.

Virtual and Physical Data Transmission in the OSI Model

For two machines to communicate, the same set of layered functions must exist on each machine. Each layer, n, on one machine can be thought of as communicating with the corresponding layer on the other machine as a peer process using the appropriate layer n protocol. This is illustrated by the dotted horizontal lines in Fig. 1. An application on machine A requiring a file transfer from machine B, for example, will invoke a file transfer process on machine A that will communicate with its peer process on machine B, using a file-transfer protocol designed to communicate the name of the file and other needed details of the request. If compression/decompression is used for data transmission, the application layer on machine B will pass the file to its presentation layer to perform the data compression, while the peer process on machine A will perform the corresponding decompression and pass the decompressed data through its application layer to the application that made the original request. Again, the compression/decompression can be thought of as being performed by communication between peer processes, using the appropriate presentation layer protocols.

The TCP/IP suite of protocols, used by the Internet, supports many different protocols at the application level. Using the HyperText Transfer Protocol (HTTP) for the World Wide Web as an example of an application level protocol, Table 1 shows the Internet protocol stack in relation to the OSI model. Sockets/streams are used to provide the session layer services while the network and transport layer services are provided by the Internet Protocol (IP) and the Transmission Control Protocol (TCP)/User Datagram Protocol (UDP) respectively.

Table 1. OSI layers and the Internet protocols.

OSI layer	IP protocol stack
7. Application	Many, for example, HTTP, FTP, Telnet, NFS
6. Presentation	Not specified
5. Session	Not specified—sockets/ streams commonly used
4. Transport	TCP/UDP
3. Network	IP
2. Datalink	Many—network-dependent
1. Physical	Many—network-dependent

Since the Internet does not specify a physical or datalink layer standard, the IP can be layered over many types of networks, including Ethernet, Token Ring, FDDI, and ATM networks.

Bibliography

1989. Keiser, G. E. *Local Area Networks*. New York: McGraw-Hill.

1993. Spohn, D. *Data Network Design*. New York: McGraw-Hill.

1996. Tanenbaum, A. S. *Computer Networks*, 3rd Ed. Upper Saddle River, NJ: Prentice Hall.

John S. Sobolewski

NETWORK PROTOCOLS

For articles on related subjects, see

+ Handshaking
+ Internet
+ Network Architecture
+ Networks, Computer
+ Open Systems Interconnection
+ Protocol
+ TCP/IP

A *protocol* is the set of formal operating rules, procedures, or conventions that govern a given process. A *communication* or *network protocol*, therefore, describes the rules that govern the transmission of data over communication networks. These rules are designed to help provide needed network services or to solve operating problems, including the following:

1. *Formatting*, or *framing*, which defines which group of bits or characters within a frame or a packet constitutes data, control, addressing, or other information.
2. *Error control*, which refers to the acceptance of correct messages, the detection of errors, and the retransmission of errant messages.
3. *Sequence control*, which defines the method of numbering messages to detect loss or duplication.
4. *Flow control*, which defines the mechanisms used to ensure effective use of network resources without causing traffic congestion.
5. *Initiation and termination control*, which define how connections are established, maintained, and terminated across the network.
6. *Routing control*, which provides sufficient information to allow data to be routed from source to destination.
7. *Recovery control*, which defines mechanisms used for graceful recovery in case of abnormal conditions.

Types of Protocols

Protocols may be divided into three general categories:

1. *Bit-oriented protocols*, in which a unique flag character delimits individual message frames. An example is IBM's Synchronous Data Link Control (SDLC) protocol in which the beginning and ending characters of a frame must be 01111110.
2. *Character-oriented protocols*, which use special characters to delineate the various fields within a message and to provide needed control functions.
3. *Byte count-oriented protocols*, which keep track of the number of bytes transmitted. An example is the Internet's Transmission Control Protocol/Internet Protocol (TCP/IP).

TCP/IP

TCP/IP is a widely used set of byte count–oriented routing protocols that evolved from the implementation of the ARPA network (Arpanet), an early packet switching network. The IP allows data packets to be sent and received across networks, while the Transmission Control Protocol (TCP) provides flow control and reliable transmission using cyclic redundancy checking. TCP/IP is supported by the Unix (*q.v.*) operating system, as well as by personal computer operating systems.

Figure 1 shows the header format added by the TCP (Transport Layer). The source and destination port addresses identify the applications associated with this message. The sequence number identifies the position of the sender's byte stream, and the acknowledgment number identifies the next byte expected by the receiver.

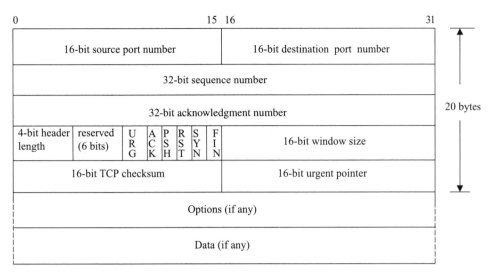

Figure 1.   Transmission Control Protocol (TCP) header format.

The header length is needed because the TCP header can be of variable length, since it may include one or more optional fields. The six flag bits (URG, ACK, RST, etc.) determine the use of the segment—the RST bit, for example, resets the receiver during a TCP three-way handshake (Keshaw, 1997, section 12.4.4). The window size defines the amount of data the application is willing to accept, the TCP checksum is for error control, the *urgent pointer* points to the last byte in the frame that has "urgent" data, and the option field is application-specific.

Protocol Implementation

Network protocols specify the type of control messages needed for establishing and terminating connections, transmitting data, and recovering from various error conditions. This "handshaking" can be quite complex and is outside the scope of this article. The seven-layer model for network architecture helps reduce this complexity and simplifies protocol design at each layer of the model (*see* OPEN SYSTEMS INTERCONNECTION).

Bibliography

1988. McNamara, J. E. *Technical Aspects of Data Communication*, 3rd Ed. Maynard, MA: Digital Press.

1997. Keshaw, S. *An Engineering Approach to Computer Networking: ATM Networks, the Internet, and the Telephone Network*. Reading, MA: Addison-Wesley.

John S. Sobolewski

NETWORKS, COMPUTER

For articles on related topics, *see*

+ Distributed Systems
+ Ethernet
+ Gateway
+ Internet
+ Local Area Network (LAN)
+ Network Architecture
+ Network Protocols
+ Open Systems Interconnection
+ Sensor Network
+ TCP/IP
+ World Wide Web

A *computer network* consists of a set of channels interconnecting a set of computing devices or *nodes* that can communicate with each other. The nodes may be computers, terminals, workstations (*q.v.*), or communication units of various kinds distributed over different locations. They communicate over communication channels that can be leased from telephone companies or are provided by the network owners. These channels may use a variety of transmission media, including fiber optics (*q.v.*), coaxial cable, twisted copper pairs, satellite links, digital microwave radio, or one of the new emerging wireless technologies. The nodes may be distributed over a wide area (distances of hundreds or thousands of miles) or over a local area (distances of a hundred feet to several miles), in which case the networks are called *wide area networks* (WANs) or *local area networks* (LANs) respectively. A *metropolitan area network* (MAN) is a network that spans distances between those of a LAN and a WAN. The Internet is a public WAN. A MAN or WAN that is accessible only to those who belong to the same organization is called an *intranet*.

Network Applications

The basic reasons for the rapid growth in computer networks are that networks can provide users with convenient access to special computing resources regardless of the physical location of the resources; can provide local and remote users with access to unique databases; allow users to exchange data, graphs, or documents; and to communicate using electronic mail (*q.v.*), bulletin boards, or teleconference, irrespective of the time or their location.

Network Objectives

Networks share a common set of objectives. They include the following:

- *Connectivity* to permit various hardware and software products to be connected and communicate seamlessly.
- *Simplicity* to permit easy installation and operation of all network components.
- *Modularity* to enable building of a wide variety of network devices from a relatively small set of mass-produced building blocks.
- *Scalability* to allow the network to grow in all dimensions when needed.

- *Reliability* to permit error-free transmission by providing appropriate error correcting and detecting (*q.v.*) capabilities.
- *Flexibility* to permit the network to evolve.
- *Diversity* of network services.
- *Manageability* to detect and isolate problems, and to take appropriate corrective action.

Network Architecture

A *network architecture* defines the protocols, message formats, and other standards to which communication hardware and software must conform. Communication between devices that conform to different network architectures is possible only through routers and complex gateways (*q.v.*) designed to translate the protocols between them. Some early implementations of network architectures include the Xerox Network Systems (XNS) architecture, IBM's System Network Architecture (SNA), and DEC's Digital Network Architecture (DNA). By far, the most widely used network architecture is that of the Internet, which is based on the suite of protocols (notably TCP/IP) developed by the Department of Defense for the Arpanet.

Network Topology

Two important network parameters are its topology and the transmission media used. The basic topologies are illustrated in Fig. 1 and include the following:

- *Point-to-point connection*. This has the disadvantage that the reliability of the network depends on the reliability of the weakest link.
- *Linear bus*, in which all network nodes have unique addresses and are connected to a common transmission medium. When a device transmits data onto the bus, it is received by all devices and is ignored, except by the one that is addressed. Local area networks based on the *Ethernet* use this topology.
- *Ring connection*. Information is passed from node to node around a closed path (ring) until it arrives at the node that is addressed. *Token ring networks* use this topology.
- *Star connection*, in which all nodes are connected to a node called the *central node* or *hub*. The central node can be active or passive. If it is active, it

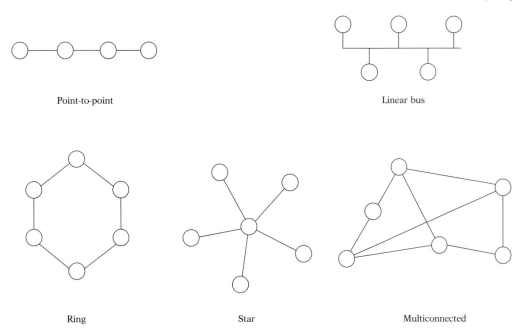

Point-to-point

Linear bus

Ring

Star

Multiconnected

Figure 1. Basic methods of interconnecting nodes in a network. The circles represent computing devices or network nodes.

is usually used to control the entire network and performs all the routing. This topology is used in applications where a central computer communicates with remote terminals or workstations.

• *Multiconnected networks,* in which nodes are connected by point-to-point links in an arbitrary fashion, with each node connected to at least two others. This improves reliability and reduces the likelihood of congestion, but makes routing much more complex.

Transmission Media

Data transmission media provide the physical communication channel to interconnect nodes in a network over which the data is actually transmitted. Commonly used media for computer networks include unshielded twisted wire pairs, shielded twisted pairs, coaxial cable, optical fibers, microwave radio, satellite links, and wireless radio. Networks usually use a combination of the above media.

Computer Network Hardware

Communication adapters of various kinds provide the interface between the computer or workstation and the physical transmission medium over which data is actually transmitted. They vary in function from simple Ethernet cards to more complex adapters that support 620 Mbps data rates using Asynchronous Transfer Mode (ATM) networks to connect a supercomputer to network-attached storage. Networks may also include a variety of other devices, such as routers, switches, and gateways.

Types of Networks

Networks can be characterized as LANs, MANs, or WANs. As their names imply, the first two are usually limited to a geographical area that extends no more than a few miles between the extremities. Because of the smaller distances involved, LANs usually operate at relatively high speeds of between 10 and 1000 Mbps. The Ethernet, the token ring, FDDI (fiber distributed data interface), and ATM are examples of commonly used LAN technologies operating at speeds up to 10, 100, 155, and 622 Mbps respectively. WANs can cover distances of hundreds or thousands of miles and, in general, use a variety of transmission media leased from common carriers.

Internets

Despite the growing acceptance of the OSI reference model for network architectures, the current abundance of incompatible network types will not go away very soon. The need arises, therefore, to interconnect two or more compatible or incompatible networks to form an *internet* or a network of networks. This is usually done by using communication control units called *routers* or *gateways* whose complexity depends mostly on the similarity of the networks connected in terms of frames, messages, protocols, and services supported.

Examples of Networks

The sections that follow describe some well-known networks that have played, or will play, an important role in modern networking.

The Arpanet

In the late 1960s, the Advanced Research Projects Agency of the US Department of Defense (DoD) began funding research in computer networks. This research led to an experimental four-node network in late 1969, which expanded to include almost 1000 computers by the early 1980s. Although the Arpanet, as it was called, spanned half the globe from Hawaii to Sweden, most of these systems were located at US universities and research laboratories that had DoD research contracts.

When the Arpanet technology had proven itself by years of reliable operation, Milnet (Military Network) was implemented, using the same technology, and extended to Europe. Since many user organizations connected their own local area networks to Arpanet and Milnet, the resulting ARPA internet included thousands of interconnected computing devices and a total of about 100 000 users by 1985. After 1985, ARPA continued to support Milnet, but began phasing out support of the Arpanet.

BITNET

BITNET (Because It's Time NETwork) was started in 1981 by the City University of New York and Yale University. The goal was to create an inexpensive mechanism for universities to communicate by using electronic mail (*q.v.*) and exchange information using file transfer. It used an old IBM protocol, and at its peak, it connected about 3000 mainframes at universities in the USA, Canada, Europe, South America, Asia, and Australia. By 1990, it had been largely replaced by NSFNET.

NSFNET

In the early 1980s, the importance of the Arpanet for sharing resources and information among academic researchers had become obvious. But Arpanet was funded by the Department of Defense, and its use was therefore restricted to those with DoD research contracts. As the DoD began phasing out its support for Arpanet after 1985, the National Science Foundation (NSF) began funding a number of network initiatives to ensure that university researchers could access the national supercomputing centers (*q.v.*) established to help support NSF funded research.

The network that emerged from these initiatives in the late 1980s became known as NSFNET. It was based on the TCP/IP suite of protocols and consisted of a high-speed multiconnected backbone network designed to handle expected traffic patterns and provide reliability through redundant data paths. Initially, this backbone consisted of 56 Kbps leased lines, but these were upgraded to 1.54 Mbps (T1 lines) in 1990 and to 45 Mbps (T3 lines) three years later because of the exponential growth in data traffic. In the early to mid-1990s, as commercial and private use of the Internet kept growing, the Internet was increasingly becoming a commodity and NSF started phasing out the funding for university connections. By 1995, the US Internet traffic was carried exclusively by commercial Internet providers.

Advanced Networks

The current Internet delivers traffic on a "best effort" basis. While this may be adequate for applications such as electronic mail and Web browsing, it is inadequate for new generations of applications such as scientific visualization (*q.v.*), teleimmersion (i.e. virtual reality—*q.v.*) and advanced computer-based education systems that include audio and video clips. This new breed of applications requires guaranteed Quality of Service (QoS), which cannot be provided by the current Internet. Consequently, there are a number of initiatives to build the next generations of networks to support new emerging applications. Some of these include vBNS (very high Bandwidth Network Service), Internet2, and NGI (*Next Generation Internet*). These initiatives are likely to result in new generations of commercial networks that support not only current applications, but also new applications that will further change the way we play, teach, learn, work, and communicate.

Bibliography

1990. Robertazzi, T. G. *Computer Networks and Systems*. New York: Springer-Verlag.

1996. Tanenbaum, A. S. *Computer Networks*, 3rd Ed. Upper Saddle River, NJ: Prentice Hall.

John S. Sobolewski

NONPROCEDURAL LANGUAGES

For articles on related subjects, see

+ Functional Programming
+ Logic Programming
+ Problem-Oriented Languages
+ Procedure-Oriented Languages
+ Programming Languages
+ Relational Database

Introduction

This article describes some of the basic characteristics of the class of programming languages commonly referred to as *nonprocedural* or *very high level* (see Leavenworth and Sammet, 1974). The term *nonprocedural* connotes emphasis on the goals to be achieved (i.e. *what*), rather

than the specific methods used to achieve them (i.e. *how*). No programming language is nonprocedural in any absolute sense; we can only say that a language possesses certain nonprocedural features. In general, a *program* is a prescription for solving a particular problem. A *procedure* is a series of steps followed in a regular, orderly, definite way. Procedural programming is based to a great extent on the necessity to conform to the inherent sequential organization of the conventional digital computer. A nonprocedural program is a prescription for solving a problem without regard to the details of *how* it is solved. That is, the solution should be specified in terms of structures or abstractions that are relevant to the problem rather than those operations, data, and control structures (*q.v.*) that are based on some particular machine organization.

History

Early in the history of programming, *automatic programming* meant the process of writing a program in some high-level language. In that context, "high-level" was by comparison with machine code. Once it became clear that the coding was only a portion of the entire problem-solving task, the phrase *automatic coding* came to mean use of a language such as Fortran. Thus, even quite early, the proper distinction was made between detailed coding and the larger activity of specification and design. One of the first significant accomplishments was the work of the Codasyl Language Structure Group in the development of its *Information Algebra* of 1962. This was essentially a mathematically oriented way of describing a data processing application in terms of its input–output relationships; these were actually defined by means of transformations on sets of entities called *areas* (analogous to files). As another example, we note that a string- and pattern-directed language such as Snobol or Icon (*see* STRING PROCESSING: LANGUAGES) is much less procedural for those features than a language such as Fortran (*q.v.*) or Cobol (*q.v.*).

Features of Nonprocedural Languages

We discuss three features that are considered of major importance for inclusion in a programming language that claims to be nonprocedural. Some examples of languages possessing some of these features are included.

Associative Referencing

We will use the term *associative referencing* to denote the accessing of data according to some intrinsic property of the data (rather than by its location). Associative referencing is usually provided in languages such as SETL that contain *sets* as a data structure (*q.v.*). The operation of selecting elements from previously defined sets, and of defining new sets from the old on the basis of some property of the members, is sometimes called the *set former*. An example of the power of SETL can be seen by the following expression, which specifies the prime numbers between 2 and 100.

```
{P,2 <= P <= 100↑(∀2 <= N < P↑(P//N) NE.0)}
```

This can be read as "the set of Ps between 2 and 100 such that for every N greater than or equal to 2 and less than P, the remainder of P/N is not equal to zero." The importance of associative referencing is that the programmer does not have to specify access paths explicitly or program an algorithm to conduct a search for a specific data structure. Associative referencing is also used in database management languages.

Relational databases (*q.v.*) provide the traditional set operations of Cartesian product, union, and intersection. They also have relational operations: projection, join, division, and restriction (*see* Codd, 1972). These operators effectively provide associative referencing.

Aggregate Operators

It is possible to avoid writing loops in some programming languages that provide aggregate operators. The + operator in APL is the simplest example of an operator that applies equally to scalars and aggregates. For example, the addition of two vectors **x**, **y** is obtained merely by writing **x** + **y**, whereas in most programming languages, the elements of the result vector would have to be obtained one at a time under the control of a loop. Another example of an aggregate operator in APL is the

use of the reduction operator to sum the elements of a vector **x**, as shown in the following expression: +/**x**.

Elimination of Arbitrary Sequencing

We will define *arbitrary sequencing* as any sequencing that is not dictated by the data dependencies of the application. A pure functional programming language is one that does not contain any assignment, iteration, or goto statements. "Functional" thus appears to be a synonym for "nonprocedural," since it means that a program specifies the outcome desired as a function of the inputs, rather than indicating a step-by-step sequence of program steps. A program in a functional language such as pure Lisp (*q.v.*) or Haskell avoids side effects (*q.v.*), which are a concomitant of procedural programming. A side effect may be caused in procedural languages during expression evaluation by the modification of memory by an assignment statement (e.g. during repeated iterations of a loop). Pure functional languages produce no side effects, since they have no assignment operation and cannot modify memory during expression evaluation.

APL "one-liners" (without assignments or function calls with side effects) exemplify functional programming. The following APL one-line function will delete leading elements from a vector X up to but not including the first element of X, which is not in Q, where Q represents a quoted character string or a numeric vector that contains examples to be deleted. Thus, 'BAR' DELETE 'ABRACADABRA' returns 'CADABRA'.

```
∇R ← Q DELETE X
[1] R ← (~Λ \ X ∈ Q)/X
∇
```

Prolog possesses some of the attributes we have been describing (*see* LOGIC PROGRAMMING: LANGUAGES). Prolog allows one to describe known facts and relationships about a problem, rather than prescribing a sequence of steps. Prolog uses pattern matching and "backtracking" to infer new facts from given facts. It therefore satisfies the associative referencing and lack of arbitrary sequencing criteria for nonprocedurality.

The ultimate expression of lack of arbitrary sequencing is a pure *dataflow*-programming language. In this formalism, a program is composed of a set of modules that produce data or consume it, organized so that consumers wait for their data to be produced (*see* CONCURRENT PROGRAMMING). An example of a dataflow language is GPSS (General-Purpose Systems Simulator), in which sequencing of a simulation program is controlled by transactions (data) moving through the model.

Database Languages

Database languages have many nonprocedural characteristics. Relational algebra, developed by Codd (1972), consists of the operators SELECT, PROJECT, and JOIN, among others. Each operation of the relational algebra takes either one or two relations as its operand(s) and produces a new relation as a result. A relation has a precise mathematical definition, but can be considered to be a *table* for our purpose. An example of a relation (table) called S is shown below:

S	S#	SNAME	STATUS	CITY
	S1	Smith	20	London
	S2	Jones	10	Paris
	S3	Blake	30	Paris

The heading SNAME stands for supplier name, and the first row can be interpreted as the supplier Smith who has supplier number (S#) S1, has status 20, and is in London. The SELECT operator constructs a new relation by taking a horizontal subset of the argument table (i.e. all rows that satisfy some condition) and the PROJECT operator constructs a new relation by taking a vertical subset of the argument table. As an example, consider the query to find S# and STATUS for suppliers in Paris. This can be determined in two stages:

```
TEMP ← SELECT S WHERE CITY = 'PARIS'
```

This returns the table:

TEMP	S#	SNAME	STATUS	CITY
	S2	Jones	10	Paris
	S3	Blake	30	Paris

We then do a projection:

```
RESULT ← PROJECT TEMP OVER S#, STATUS
```

The result is the relation:

RESULT	S#	STATUS
	S2	10
	S3	30

Note that the SELECT operator uses associative referencing and is an aggregate operator. PROJECT is an aggregate operator, too.

It is not necessary to break up the retrievals into two distinct steps as indicated above. We could combine the query into one operation using the following syntax.

```
SELECT S#, STATUS
FROM S
WHERE CITY = 'PARIS'
```

Many of the newer database languages, such as SQL (Date, 2003), have extensive data manipulation capabilities in addition to their retrieval function.

Other Nonprocedural Systems

A spreadsheet (*q.v.*) is a two-dimensional grid of cells, where a cell may contain a datum (number or string) or a formula for computing a number based on values computed in other cells. There is no notion of sequencing other than dependencies that are implicit in the cell formulas, so that a spreadsheet is a form of dataflow language, with the user as the ultimate producer of data.

RPGs (report program generators) are nonprocedural to a degree. The output format of an RPG is specified by stating what is wanted rather than how it should be produced, but its calculation section is decidedly low-level. This confirms our statement that no language is nonprocedural in any absolute sense.

Fourth-generation languages (4GLs) are rather poorly named and not clearly defined; most tend to have both procedural and nonprocedural components. It is only the latter that are of concern here. The major nonprocedural elements of a 4GL are generally similar to database languages and report writers, and thus do *not* represent a new nonprocedural concept. Some of the 4GL systems actually generate code for procedural languages such as Cobol, or link to them.

Bibliography

1972. Codd, E. F. "Relational Completeness of Data Base Sublanguages," in *Data Base Systems* (ed. R. Rustin), 65–98. Upper Saddle River, NJ: Prentice Hall.

1974. Leavenworth, B. M., and Sammet, J. E. "An Overview of Nonprocedural Languages," *Proceedings of ACM SIGPLAN Symposium on Very High Level Languages, ACM SIGPLAN Notices*, **9**(4), (April), 1–12.

2003. Date, C. J. *An Introduction to Database Systems*, 8th Ed. Reading, MA: Pearson Addison-Wesley.

Burton M. Leavenworth and Jean E. Sammet

NOTEBOOK COMPUTER

See PORTABLE COMPUTERS.

NP-COMPLETE PROBLEMS

For articles on related subjects, *see*

+ Algorithms, Analysis of
+ Algorithms, Theory of
+ Computational Complexity
+ Discrete Mathematics

Many seemingly intractable problems belong to a class known as *NP-complete problems*. NP stands for *nondeterministic polynomial*. The only known algorithms for these problems require an amount of time that is an exponential function of the problem size (measured by some parameter, n, on which the problem depends). Such algorithms are called *exponential time algorithms*. For problems of size n, exponential time algorithms may take time 2^n, $2^{n^{1/2}}$, 3^{n^2}, and so on. In contrast, many problems can be solved by algorithms that require an amount of time that is a polynomial function of the problem size. These algorithms are called *polynomial time algorithms*. For problems of size n, they may take time n, $n \log n$, n^2, n^3, and so on. Because polynomials grow more slowly than exponentials, polynomial time algorithms are regarded as "efficient," and exponential time algorithms as "inefficient."

Computer scientists have proved that if one efficient (i.e. polynomial time) algorithm can be found for *any* of the NP-complete problems, then efficient algorithms can be devised for *all* of them. Conversely, if any requires exponential time, they all do. Most computer scientists are pessimistic about the possibility that nonexponential algorithms for these problems will ever be found, so proving a problem to be NP-complete is now regarded as strong evidence that the problem is intrinsically intractable.

We illustrate these concepts with three NP-complete problems—one from graph theory (*q.v.*), one involving summing numbers, and one involving sets.

Clique Problem

A *graph* is a set of nodes with edges connecting certain pairs of nodes (such as the graph in Fig. 1). A clique is a set of nodes from a graph where every pair of nodes in the set is connected by an edge. In the figure, {1, 3, 7} is a clique set. Set {2, 4, 5, 6} is not because nodes 5 and 6 in this set are not connected by an edge.

Problem. Given a graph and a "clique size" k, decide if the graph has a clique of that size. For the problem given in Fig. 1 and $k = 4$, the answer is "YES" because {1, 2, 4, 5} is a clique of size 4. If, instead, the clique size in the problem were 5, the answer would be "NO."

Knapsack Problem

Given a list of numbers and a "knapsack size," determine if some subset of the listed numbers adds up to the

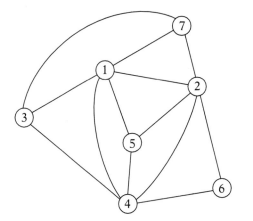

Figure 1. Example of a clique problem. Is there a clique of size 4?.

knapsack size. For the problem given in Fig. 2, the answer is "YES" because

$$4 + 18 + 25 + 42 = 89.$$

If, instead, the knapsack size were 90, the answer would be "NO."

Set Covering Problem

For a given set, a collection of subsets is said to cover the set if each member of the set belongs to at least one set in the collection.

Problem. Given a set to be covered, a list of available subsets, and a "cover size" k, determine whether k of the available subsets can be chosen so that the collection of chosen subsets covers the given set. For the problem given in Fig. 3, the answer is "YES" because the three subsets S_3, S_6, and S_7 can be chosen. If, instead, the cover size were 2, the answer would be "NO."

The three problems illustrated have the common property that if the answer is "YES," there is a short, easily verified demonstration of this fact. For the clique problem, the demonstration is a list of nodes, equal in number to the clique size, that form a clique. For

List of numbers: 47 13 18 25 32 42 49
Knapsack size: 89

Figure 2. Example of a knapsack problem.

Set to be covered: $\{a, b, c, d, e, f, g, h\}$
Available subsets: $S_1 = \{d\}$, $S_2 = \{a\}$, $S_3 = \{a, b, c\}$
$S_4 = \{f\}$, $S_5 = \{b, e, g\}$, $S_6 = \{c, d, e, h\}$, $S_7 = \{f, g, h\}$
Cover size: 3

Figure 3. Example of a set covering problem.

the knapsack problem, the demonstration is a subset of the listed numbers whose sum equals the knapsack size. For the set covering problem, the demonstration is a collection of the available subsets that contain every element of the set to be covered. This common property suggests a common approach to solving these problems; namely, enumerate the potential demonstrations and check each potential one to see if it is an actual demonstration. For the knapsack problem, this means enumerating the subsets of the given numbers and adding the numbers in each subset to see if their sum is the knapsack value. Unfortunately, these enumerate-and-check algorithms require exponential time due to the number of things to be enumerated. In the knapsack case, with n numbers, there are 2^n subsets to be checked.

The preceding problems are called *recognition problems* because the answer for a given problem example is "YES" or "NO." A recognition problem is called *nondeterministic polynomial* (or NP) if, whenever the answer is "YES," there is a "polynomial" demonstration of this fact. A problem is considered to have polynomial demonstrations if there are constants c and k such that, for all n, a problem example of size n with answer "YES" has a potential demonstration that can be verified correct in at most cn^k steps. Thus, if the answer is "YES," a lucky person might guess a correct demonstration and verify the guess, all in polynomial time. However, *nondeterministic* is not meant to imply randomness or any use of probability; it signifies only that no *rule* is given for determining what the guess should be.

The key concept in comparing problems is *polynomial-time reducibility*. Problem A is said to be *reducible* to problem B if problem A can be solved using as a subroutine an algorithm that solves problem B. In particular, problem A is polynomial-time reducible to problem B if there is a polynomial bound on the number of steps taken by a main program to solve problem A, where the main program can call a subroutine for problem B. Note that the number of steps taken by the subroutine is not counted. If there is an efficient (i.e. polynomial-time) algorithm for solving problem B, then using that algorithm as the subroutine produces an efficient algorithm for problem A. Conversely, if problem A is intrinsically hard, then no efficient subroutine for B can exist, and so problem B is also intrinsically hard. To show that a new problem is NP-complete, it suffices to show that it is an NP-problem, and that any one problem already known to be NP-complete is polynomial-time reducible to it.

In 1971, Cook formulated the concept of NP-completeness and showed that the problem of testing a logical formula for satisfiability is NP-complete. Shortly thereafter, Karp extended the set of known NP-problems to include about 20 other problems of practical interest, and thousands are now known. It is now routine for a computer scientist confronting an apparently hard problem to investigate whether the problem is NP-complete.

Showing that a problem is NP-complete effectively eliminates the possibility of developing a completely satisfactory algorithm for its solution. However, the situation is not necessarily hopeless for the following reasons:

1. Even an exponential algorithm can be satisfactory for small cases.
2. There may be fast approximation algorithms with satisfactory accuracy.
3. The problems of most interest may be special cases for which a fast algorithm is available.
4. Although an algorithm may be bad "in the worst case," it may solve most cases in a satisfactory amount of time.

Bibliography

1971. Cook, S. A. "The Complexity of Theorem-Proving Procedures," *Proceedings of the Third ACM Symposium on Theory of Computing*, 151–158. New York: ACM.

1979. Garey, M. R., and Johnson, D. S. *Computers and Intractability: A Guide to the Theory of NP-Completeness*. San Francisco, CA: W. H. Freeman and Co.

1992. Harel, D. *Algorithmics: The Spirit of Computing*, 2nd Ed. Reading, MA: Addison-Wesley.

Daniel J. Rosenkrantz and Richard E. Stearns

NUMBERS AND NUMBER SYSTEMS

For articles on related systems, see

+ Arithmetic, Computer
+ Complement
+ Precision

The representation in which we normally write decimal numbers, for example,

$$276.1069 \tag{1}$$

is nothing more than shorthand symbolic representation for the precise mathematical equivalent

$$2 \times 100 + 7 \times 10 + 6 \times 1 + 1 \times 0.1 + 0 \times 0.01$$
$$+ 6 \times 0.001 + 9 \times 0.0001 \tag{2}$$

or

$$2 \times 10^2 + 7 \times 10^1 + 6 \times 10^0 + 1 \times 10^{-1}$$
$$+ 0 \times 10^{-2} + 6 \times 10^{-3} + 9 \times 10^{-4} \tag{3}$$

Equations (2) and (3) express clearly that the decimal system we use has a *base*, or *radix*, $R = 10$. By analogy, therefore, the *binary*, or *base 2* (i.e. $R = 2$), system so commonly used with computers can become immediately understandable. Notation (1)—often called *positional notation* because the position of a digit specifies the power of 10 in (3) that is associated with it—effectively hides the real mathematical content of a number.

Radix Representation

The notation in (2) or (3) above is called the *radix representation* of a number. The general form of any decimal number may be written

$$\sum_{i=-m}^{n} d^i \cdot 10^i \quad 0 \le d_i \le 9 \quad (d_i \text{ is an integer})$$

The two other number systems most important in computing are binary and *hexadecimal* ($R = 16$). In binary, numbers are represented as

$$\sum_{i=-m}^{n} b_i \cdot 2^i \quad b_i = 0 \text{ or } 1 \tag{4}$$

In the hexadecimal, or base 16, system, numbers are represented by

$$\sum_{i=-m}^{n} h_i \cdot 16^i \quad 0 \le h_i \le 15 \quad (h_i \text{ is an integer}).$$

An important task in any number system is to be able to *count*. The rule for counting in a number system of radix R, whose digits range from 0 to $R - 1$, is as follows:

1. When the rightmost digit of the number whose successor is desired is less than $R - 1$, increase that digit to its successor digit.
2. When the rightmost digit of the number whose successor is desired is equal to $R - 1$, replace $R - 1$ by 0, "carry" a 1 to the second radix position from

the right, and repeat this two-step process until carries no longer need to be propagated to the left.

If $R = 10$, this algorithm will successfully generate the familiar sequence of decimal numbers. But when $R = 2$, we get the sequence of binary numbers, the first 18 of which are

0	1	10	11	100	101
110	111	1000	1001	1010	1011
1100	1101	1110	1111	10000	10001

Binary

The addition and multiplication tables for binary numbers are particularly simple (Table 1) and, once learned, so is binary arithmetic using these tables. Figure 1 gives examples of all four arithmetic operations in binary, with the corresponding decimal arithmetic also given. Finding the decimal integer equivalent to a given binary integer is very simple using Eq. (4). Thus,

Table 1. Binary addition and multiplication tables.

+	0	1		×	0	1
0	0	1		0	0	0
1	0	10		1	0	1

Addition

```
            10011
            11001        25
   Carries +10011       +19
           ──────       ───
           101100        44
```

Subtraction

```
Borrows    10   1   1
         0   1̶0̶  1̶0̶  10 10
         1̶    0   0    0  0      24
        -0    1   0    1  1     -13
             ───────────────    ───
              1   0    1  1      11
```

Multiplication

```
      1  1  0  1      1  3
    × 1  1  1  0    × 1  4
    ──────────      ──────
      1 1 0 1 0       5 2
      1 1 0 1        13
    1 1 0 1         ───
    ──────────      18 2
    10110110
```

Division

```
          11                 3 1/9
    ┌──────────         9) ─────
1001│1 1 1 0 0             28
    │1 0 0 1
    ──────────
      1 0 1 0
      1 0 0 1
      ─────────
            1
```

Figure 1. Binary arithmetic.

for example,

$$1011010 = 1 \times 2^6 + 0 \times 2^5 + 1 \times 2^4 + 1 \times 2^3$$
$$+ 0 \times 2^2 + 1 \times 2^1 + 0 \times 2^0$$
$$= 64 + 16 + 8 + 2 = 90.$$

Hexadecimal

This system became especially important with the advent of the IBM 360 system, which, while binary internally, from the user's point of view used hexadecimal arithmetic for descriptive purposes and as the base of the exponent in floating-point numbers. Because hexadecimal requires 16 distinct characters, 6 characters in addition to $0, 1, \ldots, 9$ are needed to represent $10, 11, \ldots, 15$. These are usually taken to be A, B, C, D, E, F.

A binary number is easily converted to a hexadecimal number by dividing the bits of the binary number into groups of four bits, starting from the binary point and working in both directions. Thus, $111|1010|0001|.0010|0001|110$ becomes $7A1.21C$ in hexadecimal with the 7 corresponding to 111 with an implicit leading zero and the C corresponding to 1100 with the final 0 implicit.

At one time, *octal* (base 8) representation was quite widely used in computing because binary numbers are easily converted to octal by using groups of 3 bits. However, since the preponderance of computers in current use—mainframes and all popular personal computers—have word lengths that are divisible by four but not by three (16, 32, or 64 bits), octal is seldom used now.

Radix Conversion

To convert a number in a system with base p to a number in base q, we consider the integer and fractional parts of the number separately. Let $(I)p$ and $(F)p$, respectively, be the integer and fractional parts of the number in base p, which we wish to convert to base q; let $(q)_p$ be the expression of q in the p system.

Example 1 Convert 6753.31 in decimal to binary. Then $p = 10$, $q = 2$, $(I)_p = 6753$, $(F)_p = 0.31$, and $(q)_p = 2$.

To convert $(I)_p$ to binary, divide it and successively isolated quotients by 2, save the remainders, and list them in inverse order,

	Quotient	Remainder	
6753/2	3376	1	↑
3376/2	1688	0	
1688/2	844	0	
844/2	422	0	
422/2	211	0	
211/2	105	1	
105/2	52	1	
52/2	26	0	
26/2	13	0	
13/2	6	1	
6/2	3	0	
3/2	1	1	
1/2	0	1	

Thus, $(I)_p = 1\,1\,0\,1\,0\,0\,1\,1\,0\,0\,0\,0\,1$.

To convert $(F)_p$ to binary, multiply by 2 and save the integral part of the result, 0, and the fractional part, .62, separately. Repeat the process until a fractional part of 0 is obtained, or until the desired number of bits are isolated. Thus $0.31_{10} = .010011\ldots$

	Fractional part	Integral part	
0.31×2	0.62	0	
0.62×2	0.24	1	
0.24×2	0.48	0	
0.48×2	0.96	0	
0.96×2	0.92	1	
0.92×2	0.84	1	↓

Thus, combining the results, we find that 6753.31 in decimal is equivalent to $1101001100001.010011\ldots$ in binary. Note that the binary fraction is nonterminating (i.e. not expressible in a finite number of bits), even though the decimal fraction terminates.

Example 2 Convert 1001100.011 in binary to decimal. Here, $p = 2$, $q = 10$, $(I)_p = 1001100$, $(F)_p = 0.011$, and $(q)_p = 1010$, which is the binary representation of 10 in decimal.

	Quotient	Remainder
1001100/1010	111	110 → 6 in decimal
111/1010	0	111 → 7 in decimal

Thus, the integral part of the decimal number is 76.

	Fractional part	Integral part
0.011 × 1010	0.110	11 → 3 in decimal
0.110 × 1010	0.100	111 → 7 in decimal
0.100 × 1010	0.000	101 → 5 in decimal

Thus, the decimal equivalent of 1001100.011 is 76.375. In this instance, a finite binary fraction became a finite decimal fraction. This is always the case because all the negative powers of 2 have finite fractional expansions in the decimal system.

Because of our natural facility with decimal arithmetic, an easier way to do Example 2 is to apply expression (4) directly,

$$1001100.011 = 1 \times 2^6 + 1 \times 2^3 + 1 \times 2^2$$
$$+ 1 \times 2^{-2} + 1 \times 2^{-3}$$
$$= 64 + 8 + 4 + 0.25 + 0.125$$
$$= 76.375$$

The conversions illustrated in Examples 1 and 2 are indeed precisely those performed when a program written in a high-level language in decimal notation is compiled into the machine language of a binary computer, and the results computed in that computer are printed out as decimal numbers.

Bibliography

1994. Omondi, A. R. *Computer Arithmetic Systems: Algorithms, Architecture, and Implementation.* Upper Saddle River, NJ: Prentice Hall.

1997. Knuth, D. E. *The Art of Computer Programming*, Vol. 2, 3rd Ed. Reading, MA: Addison-Wesley.

Anthony Ralston

OBJECT-ORIENTED PROGRAMMING

Introduction

A programming language is said to be *object-based* if it supports objects as a language feature, and is said to be *object-oriented* if, additionally, objects are required to belong to *classes* that can be incrementally modified through *inheritance* (whereby a class may *inherit* the capabilities of a base class and also extend or modify these capabilities). Among the object-oriented languages (OOPs) are Simula, Smalltalk, C++, Eiffel, Ada, and Java, but not Fortran, C, or Pascal.

Functional, logic-based, and procedure-oriented paradigms execute algorithms whose semantics are described by computable functions, while objects provide persistent services to clients over time, which cannot be entirely described by computable functions.

Objects can better model embedded systems, graphical user interfaces (GUIs), and distributed systems (*q.v.*) than procedures and algorithms, supporting more powerful forms of problem solving.

Objects

Objects are collections of operations that share a state. The operations determine the messages (calls) to which the object can respond, while the shared state is hidden from the outside world (*see* Fig. 1). Variables representing the internal state of an object are called *instance variables* and its operations are called *methods*. The collection of methods of an object determines its *interface* and its behavior in accord with the structure

```
name:object
    local instance variables (shared state)
    operations or methods (interface of
        message patterns to which the
        object may respond)
```

For example, the particular object named `point` with instance variables x, y and methods for reading and changing them may be defined as

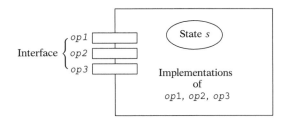

Figure 1. Object modules.

```
point:object
    x:=0; y:= 0;
    read-x: ↑x; -return value of x
    read-y: ↑y; -return value of y
    change-x(dx):x:=x + dx;
    change-y(dy):y:=y + dy;
```

The object `point` protects its instance variables *x, y* against arbitrary access, allowing access only through messages to `read` and `change` operations. The object's behavior is entirely determined by its responses to acceptable messages and is independent of the data representation of its instance variables. Moreover, the object's knowledge of its callers is entirely determined by its messages. Object-oriented message-passing facilitates two-way abstraction: senders have an abstract view of receivers and receivers have an abstract view of senders.

An object's interface of operations (methods) can be represented by a record

```
untyped object interface: (op1,op2,..,opN)
```

Objects whose operations `opi` have type `Ti` have an interface that is like a typed record, but differs from records in that fields of object records may be interdependent because of the shared state. Typed record interfaces are called *signatures*.

```
Typed Object Interface (Signature):
            (op1:T1,op2:T2,..,opN:TN)
```

The `point` object has the following signature:

```
Point-interface =
    (read-x: Real,
    (read-y: Real,
    change-x: Real → Real,
    change-y: Real → Real
```

The parameterless operations `read-x` and `read-y` both return a Real number as their value, while `change-x` and `change-y` expect a Real number as their argument and return a Real result.

Nonlocal references in functions and procedures are generally considered harmful, but they are essential for operations within objects, since they are the only mechanism by which an object's operations can access its internal state. Sharing unprotected data within an object is combined with strong protection (encapsulation) against external access.

Classes

In object-oriented languages, the behavior of objects is specified by classes, which are like the data types of traditional languages, but serve additionally to classify objects into hierarchies through the inheritance mechanism. Classes serve as record-structured templates from which objects can be created. The class `point` has precisely the same instance variables and operations as the object `point`, but their interpretation is different. Whereas the instance variables of a point object represent actual variables, class instance variables are potential, being instantiated only when an object is created. We may think of a class as specifying a behavior common to all objects of the class. The instance variables specify a data structure for realizing the behavior. The public operations of a class determine its behavior, while private instance variables determine its structure.

Inheritance

Inheritance is a mechanism for sharing code and behavior. It allows reuse of the behavior of a class in the definition of new classes. Subclasses of a class inherit the operations of their parent class and may add new operations and new instance variables. Figure 2 describes mammals by an inheritance hierarchy. The class of mammals has persons and elephants as its subclasses. The class of persons has mammals as its superclass and students and females as subclasses. The instances John, Joan, Bill, Mary, and Dumbo each have a unique base class. In *single inheritance*, illustrated here, membership of an instance in more than one base class,

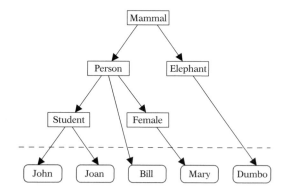

Figure 2. Example of an inheritance hierarchy.

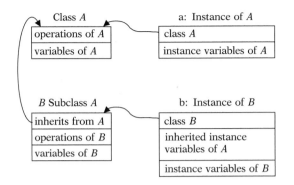

Figure 3. Implementation of inheritance.

such as Joan being both a student and a female, cannot be expressed.

Multiple inheritance, which supports subclasses that share the behavior of one or more superclasses (*see* Fig. 3), gives rise to more complex structures, such as directed graphs (*see* GRAPH THEORY), since a subclass can inherit from several parents. C++ and Eiffel have multiple inheritance; Simula and Smalltalk have single inheritance.

Virtual classes are incomplete behavior specifications that require subclasses to complete their behavior specification before they can be instantiated. The class of mammals in Fig. 2 is a virtual class. It specifies behavioral attributes common to all mammals and must be supplemented by behavioral attributes of specific mammals (persons or elephants) before instances like Joan and Dumbo can be created.

Evolution of Object-Oriented Programming

Simula 67 was the first object-oriented language. Its language primitives included objects, classes, and inheritance, and it was used extensively for simulation and other applications, primarily in Europe. Smalltalk, developed by the software concepts group at Xerox PARC in the 1970s and embodied in a stable implementation in Smalltalk 80, caught public imagination because of its implementation on personal computers and its interactive graphical interface that permitted browsing and the display of objects in multiple windows.

The language Ada (*q.v.*) included the notion of *packages*, which are like objects, but did not have a notion of classes or inheritance in its 1983 version.

Starting in the mid-1980s, OOP became a popular term, and object-oriented dialects of existing programming languages began to appear, such as Object-Pascal, Objective C, and C++. The preeminence of C++ as the dominant OOP language is now being challenged by Java, which has a cleaner design, built-in threads that support *concurrent programming* (*q.v.*), class libraries for graphical user interfaces and system software, and excellent documentation.

In the software engineering community, attention is shifting from object-oriented languages to object-oriented design, epitomized by design methods such as OMT (object modeling technique), UML (universal modeling language), and OOAD (object-oriented analysis and design); and component software systems such as CORBA/OpenDoc, COM/OLE/ActiveX, and Java/JavaBeans. There is also much work on CASE (computer-aided software engineering) tools for OOP.

Bibliography

1991. Rumbaugh, J., Blaha, M., Premerlani, W., Eddy, F., and Lorensen, W. *Object-Oriented Modeling and Design.* Upper Saddle River, NJ: Prentice Hall.

                                Peter Wegner

OBJECT PROGRAM

For articles on related subjects, *see*

+ Language Processors
+ Linkers and Loaders
+ Procedure-Oriented Languages
+ Source Program

An *object program* is the output of a translator program, such as an assembler or a compiler (*q.v.*), which converts a *source program* written in one language into another language, such as machine language, capable of being executed on a given computer. This output may be an *intermediate language* (*q.v.*), needing further translation; it may be *relocatable*, in which data and program references are still expressed relative to a base address; or it may be *absolute*, in which all linkages between program elements have been made and absolute address assignments established so that the program is ready to be loaded and executed. Usage varies as to which of these may be called the object program. In some sense, any output of a translating program is the object of that step, and hence is an object program, but the term is most often used to denote a binary file which, after *linking* to other binary files, is ready for direct execution (*see* LINKERS AND LOADERS).

Charles H. Davidson

OCR

See OPTICAL CHARACTER RECOGNITION (OCR).

ONLINE CONVERSATION

For articles on related subjects, see

+ Electronic Mail (Email)
+ Internet
+ World Wide Web

Online conversation is communication in which there is little or no delay between sending a message and it being received and read. Whereas electronic mail may be compared to sending or receiving a letter by post, online communications are very much like face-to-face or telephone conversations.

Two popular online conversation methods are Instant Messaging (IM) and Chat. IM extends a service which had been available on many time-shared computer systems for years, to the Internet. This service would typically allow a user to determine whether another user was logged in and, if so, to send a message directly to his or her terminal, or to open up a two-way "talk" session with split screens for the two sides of the conversation. IM services make this possible on the Internet via a

"Buddy List" of the set of online users with whom a user may exchange instant messages. Specialized servers keep track of everyone currently running the IM program as well as which of these users have "buddied" with which others. When a user on a list comes online (and runs a copy of IM), the first user's list will indicate that this user is online (and vice versa) and will allow instant messaging. When a message is sent, it pops up in a window on the recipient's computer screen. If the recipient chooses to reply, a conversation begins.

IM was first popularized by America Online (AOL) and brought to the Internet largely by Mirabalis' ICQ (pronounced "I seek you") product. Other entrants to the IM market include Yahoo! with Yahoo! Messenger and Microsoft with Microsoft Messenger. As of this writing, these online communities are isolated from one another; users in one cannot send IMs to users in the others. However, standards organizations are building bridges between the communities and it seems likely that at some point IM will become as universal to the Internet as the phone system is to the outside world.

Chat, on the other hand, may be thought of as an interactive version of the online bulletin board. A *chat* is an electronic conversation between several participants, centered in a virtual place called a *chat room*. The participants rendezvous there and, using specialized software, send messages that are seen by all the users currently "in" that room. Chat, like IM, evolved from early time-shared programs that allowed users to communicate in real time. In the late 1970s, MUDs or Multi-User Dungeons appeared. An MUD is a fantasy-based game in which multiple participants play (and chat) with one another. In 1988, Jarkko Oikarinen wrote a program called the *Internet Relay Chat* (IRC), which brought multiperson conversations to the Internet. It was designed to replace "talk" and soon became an institution on the net. MUDs were quickly adapted to use IRC and to open the games to users throughout the Internet.

Bibliography

1993. Oikarinen, J., and Reed, D. "Internet Relay Chat Protocol," Request for Comments 1459 (May). http://www.ietf.org/rfc/rfc1459.txt.

1999. Day, M., and Rosenberg, J. "A Model for Presence and Instant Messaging," Internet Draft, Internet Engineering Task Force (June). http://www.ietf.org/ids.by.wg/impp.html.

1999. http://www.apocalypse.org/pub/u/lpb/muddex/. The MUDdex (History of MUDs).

Geoff Ralston

OPEN ARCHITECTURE

For articles on related subjects, see

+ BIOS
+ Bus
+ Digital Computers, History of
+ Motherboard
+ Personal Computing

An *open architecture* is one that allows insertion of additional logic cards to the interior of a personal computer chassis beyond those used with the most primitive configuration of the system. This is done by inserting the cards into *slots* in the computer's *motherboard*, the main logic board that holds its central processing unit (CPU—*q.v.*) and memory chips. A computer vendor that adopts such a design knows full well that, since the electronic characteristics of the motherboard slots will be public knowledge, other vendors who wish to do so can design and market customized logic cards. The rationale is that the greater the variety of cards marketed, the greater will be the sales of the host computer itself. The logic cards provide a host of services, such as one form of hard disk (*q.v.*), greater degrees of color graphics resolution, supplemental memory, sound, and Ethernet (*q.v.*) boards that enhance network capability.

Interestingly, a reversal of position with regard to the merits of an open architecture has played a significant role in the commercial history of Apple (*q.v.*). Its initial, highly successful products, the Apple I and II used an open architecture, whereas its Macintosh line used a closed architecture. Just as significantly, about the time of introduction of the Macintosh, IBM brought out its PC, which was based on an open architecture. The combination of open architecture and a bus and BIOS system that were easy to reverse-engineer led to the marketing of a plethora of IBM–PC (*q.v.*) compatibles which, perhaps more than any other factor, led to the rapid growth of personal computing.

Edwin D. Reilly

OPEN SYSTEMS INTERCONNECTION (OSI)

For articles on related subjects, see

+ Communications and Computers
+ Data Communications
+ Gateway
+ Network Protocols
+ Protocol

Two computer systems can communicate successfully only if they are prepared to use the same set of *protocols*. Each machine could, in principle, be provided with facilities for translating foreign protocols, but if their range is large, this becomes a burdensome task. The objective of the *open systems interconnection* (OSI) is to create a single set of standard protocols, drawing on the best features of existing practice. The term *open* is used here in the sense of freedom from technical barriers to communication. The decision as to what should be communicated and when communication should take place must be taken by the owner of each system. The OSI standards define only the protocols themselves; they do not constrain the internal structure of the systems that use them.

Work to create the OSI standards was begun by the International Organization for Standardization in 1978.

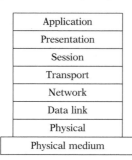

| Application |
| Presentation |
| Session |
| Transport |
| Network |
| Data link |
| Physical |
| Physical medium |

Figure 1.   The seven OSI protocol layers.

The first step was the creation of the OSI Reference Model, the communication architecture that provides a framework for the various component standards of the OSI family of protocols. Individual members of the family were published one by one throughout the 1980s.

The OSI Reference Model defines seven layers (Fig. 1). Starting from the most abstract, these provide the following functions:

Level 7   The *application layer* performs the functions that are the reason for the communication.

Level 6   The *presentation layer* manages the problems of format and encoding between the two systems.

Level 5   The *session layer* provides tools for structuring the dialogue between applications.

Level 4   The *transport layer* handles end-to-end reliability and quality of service (QoS).

Level 3   The *network layer* handles problems of routing and switching.

Level 2   The *data link layer* provides an orderly error-free path between adjacent systems.

Level 1   The *physical layer* is concerned with electrical compatibility.

Bibliography

1988. Henshall, J., and Shaw, S. *OSI Explained: End-to-End Computer Communication Standards.* New York: Ellis Horwood.

1993. Hebrawi, B. *Open Systems Interconnection: Upper Layer Standards and Practices.* New York: McGraw-Hill.

Peter F. Linington

OPERATING SYSTEMS

For articles on related subjects, *see*

+ Bootstrap
+ Cache Memory
+ Client-Server Computing
+ Concurrent Programming
+ Distributed Systems
+ File Server
+ Interrupt
+ Kernel
+ Linux
+ Memory Management
+ Memory Protection
+ Monitor, Synchronization
+ Multiplexing
+ Multiprocessing
+ Multiprogramming
+ Multitasking
+ Mutual Exclusion
+ Parallel Processing
+ Shell
+ Supervisor Call
+ TCP/IP
+ Throughput
+ Time Sharing
+ Unix
+ User Interface
+ Virtual Memory
+ Window Environments
+ Working Set

GENERAL PRINCIPLES

Introduction

Early *operating systems* were small control programs of a few thousand bytes that scheduled jobs, drove peripheral devices, and kept track of system usage for billing purposes. Current operating systems are much larger, ranging from hundreds of kilobytes for early personal computers (e.g. MS-DOS) to tens of megabytes for mainframes (e.g. Honeywell's Multics,

IBM's MVS, Unix) and hundreds of megabytes for recent PCs (Microsoft Windows). In addition to managing processors, memory, and dozens of I/O devices, operating systems also provide services such as Internet communications, Web communications, interprocess communications, file and directory systems, data transfer over local networks, and command languages and graphical user interfaces (GUIs) for invoking and controlling programs.

Historical Development

Most operating systems for mainframes and servers are descendants of third-generation systems, such as Honeywell Multics, IBM VMS, VM/370, and CDC Scope. These systems introduced important concepts such as time-sharing, multiprogramming, virtual memory, sequential processes cooperating via semaphores, hierarchical file systems, and device-independent I/O.

During the 1960s, projects were established to construct time-sharing systems and test many new operating system concepts. These included MIT's Compatible Time-Sharing System (CTSS), the University of Manchester ATLAS (*q.v.*), the University of Cambridge Multiple Access System, IBM TSS/360, and RCA Spectra/70. The most ambitious project was Multics (Multiplexed Information and Computing Service) for the General Electric 645 processor. Multics embraced every important system concept of the day: processes, interprocess communication, segmented virtual memory, page replacement, linking new libraries to a computation on demand, automatic multiprogrammed load control, access control, protection rings, security kernel, hierarchical file system, device independence, I/O redirection, and a high-level language shell.

Perhaps the most influential current operating system is Unix. Originally developed at AT&T Bell Laboratories for DEC PDP computers, Unix distilled the most useful features of Multics into a kernel that fits into the small memory of a minicomputer (*q.v.*). Unix retained its predecessor's processes, hierarchical file system, device independence, I/O redirection, and a high-level language shell. Though the first version of

Unix did not have virtual memory, most of the later versions did. It introduced an innovation, the *pipe*, which enables programs to be sequenced by directing (piping) the output of one program for use as input of the next. Unix offered a large library of utility programs that were well integrated with the command language.

In the 1980s, a new genre of operating systems was developed for PCs, including MS-DOS, PC-DOS, Apple-DOS, CP/M, Coherent, and Xenix. All these systems were of limited function, being initially designed for 8- and 16-bit microprocessor chips with small memories. Multiprogrammed operating systems for microcomputers appeared late in the 1980s in the forms of multiple background tasks (multitasking). Multiprocessing operating systems soon followed, for example, Windows and OS/2. Established, single-machine operating systems such as Unix and DEC's VMS evolved to accommodate networks of computers. Such operating systems typically support standards for accessing files on remote servers from any machine in a network. Locus and Apollo DomainOS are early examples of operating systems providing a directory hierarchy that spans an entire network. Sun's Network File System (NFS) was one of the first open, and hence widely available, systems. Network management functions can be found in server operating systems such as Sun Microsystem's Solaris, Microsoft's NT, and Linux.

A Model Operating System
Overview

Over the years, operating system designers have tended to use just two strategies for organizing the software: the monolith and the kernel architectures. The monolith results from a design strategy based on defining modules for operating system functions; any module can call any other provided it follows the interface specifications. All the modules must be linked to create the operating system executable file, and that file must be completely loaded into the computer's memory. Every module operates in supervisor mode so that it can have access to the hardware resources of the computer. Application programs must make a supervisor call to invoke a module to perform such access on its behalf.

Table 1. Microkernel layers.

Level	Name	Objects	Example operations
5	Processes	Process	Fork, suspend, resume, join, signal, exit, kill
4	Interprocess communication	Message, port	Send, receive, transmit
3	Memory management	Address, segment	Create, destroy, map
2	Threads	Thread, ready list, semaphore	Fork, suspend, resume, wait, signal, kill
1	Low-level I/O	Device, device driver	Read, write

Monolithic operating systems can become extremely large and unwieldy. The monolith accumulates all the software that might ever be needed on all platforms, while the computer on which it is actually running needs only a fraction of it. The operating system becomes difficult to adapt to different hardware configurations, and difficult to extend and contract. Microsoft Windows and Apple MacOS, both illustrate this trend.

The kernel architecture avoids these problems by careful design of the modules. The kernel is designed as a small set of modules that must run in supervisor mode; every other operating system function (and application) is designed as an extension that can be invoked as needed, does not have to be memory resident, and does not have to operate in supervisor mode. A typical kernel implements interrupts, low-level I/O, processes, semaphores, virtual memory, and interprocess communication. Everything else is treated as an extension—files, directories, network services, and user interfaces. Since the number of kernel functions is small, these systems tend to be more stable than their monolithic counterparts. The term *microkernel* is now frequently used to call attention to compact kernels.

The principle of levels can be used to structure either a monolithic or kernelized system. The first operating system constructed as a hierarchy of levels was Dijkstra's THE of 1968 (Dijkstra, 1968). The idea has been extended to generate families of operating systems for related machines and to increase the portability of an operating system kernel. The Provably Secure Operating System (PSOS) is the first complete level-structured system reported and formally proved correct in the open literature.

The Microkernel

Table 1 shows the minimal set of abstractions in a microkernel. The microkernel contains no file or directory system, offers no remote procedure call, and may even require some of the memory management to be performed in user mode. The functions in the microkernel are included there because they are difficult or inefficient to provide elsewhere.

Level 1 dispatches interrupts and manages access to peripheral devices. Device driver programs manage operations such as positioning the head of a disk drive and transferring blocks of data.

Level 2 implements threads. A *thread* is a single flow of control in some address space. It is an abstraction for the instruction trace of a CPU executing program code. Each thread operates in a context that includes a program stack (*q.v.*), the CPU register contents, interrupt masks, and any other flags or state information needed by the CPU to continue running the thread.

Level 3 manages the computer's main memory, or RAM (random access memory).

Level 4 implements interprocess communication (IPC). Threads that do not share the same address space and threads running on different computers in a network exchange messages via *ports*, buffers that retain messages in transit.

Level 5 supplies the full-blown process, a program in execution on a virtual computer. A process consists of one or more threads, an address space, one or more

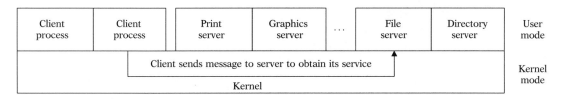

Figure 1.   The client-server model on a single machine.

input ports for incoming messages, and output ports for outgoing messages. The threads of a process share access to the address space and the ports. A process can create offspring (child) processes.

User-Level Servers

The remaining levels of the operating system are structured according to the client–server (*q.v.*) model. In this model certain processes are designated as servers because they perform functions for other processes, called clients, on request. Clients and servers use IPC to exchange requests and responses. Figure 1 shows how clients send messages through the kernel to servers on the same machine; Fig. 2 illustrates the distributed case.

When a server process is the only server on a machine, the machine itself is often called the server; a common example is a *file server* (*q.v.*). Some servers, such as printer servers, directory servers, mail servers, authentication servers, and Web servers, can run alone on a machine or can be part of a group of services offered from a single machine. Although clients and servers communicate with messages, most systems allow programs to invoke services as procedure calls. The mechanism for this, called remote procedure call (RPC), is implemented completely by compilers and does not have to be a component of the IPC level.

Level 6 (*see* Table 2) implements a common interface to *information objects*. Info-objects produce, consume, store, or transmit streams (sequences) of bytes. There

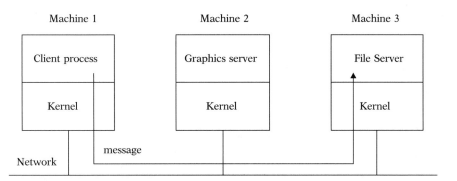

Figure 2.   The client-server model in a distributed system.

Table 2.   Layers in the user services.

Level	Name	Objects	Example operations
9	Graphics server	Window, input event	Resize, move, draw, receive, send
8	Shell	Application program	Statements in shell language
7	Directories	Directory	Create, delete, enter, remove, search, get
6	Streams	File, device, pipe	Create, delete, open, close, read, write

are three types of info-objects: devices, files, and pipes. Devices are external equipment that either produce or consume streams of bytes; a keyboard is an example of an input (stream-producing) device and a display is an example of an output (stream-consuming) device. A file stores a stream of bytes for an indefinite time. A pipe conveys a stream of bytes from a sender process to a receiver.

Level 7 manages a hierarchy of directories that catalogs the hardware and software objects to which access must be controlled throughout the network: files, devices, pipes, ports, processes, and other directories. A *directory* is a table that matches *external names* of objects to *internal names*. An *external name* is a string of characters chosen by a user; an internal name is a binary code, chosen by the system, which can be guaranteed to be unique.

Level 8 provides command language interfaces called *shells*. The shell is the layer of software that separates the user from the rest of the machine. The user expresses a command to the shell, which in turn, invokes low-level and kernel services as appropriate to implement the command. The shell is in essence a parser that interprets commands in the syntax of the command language. It creates processes and pipes and connects them with files and devices as needed to carry out the command. A graphical user interface uses point-and-click facilities (windows, icons, mouse, menus) to accomplish the same objective.

At level 9, a graphics server provides user programs with the ability to present pictorial information to the user and coordinate that information with input from user devices such as a keyboard, a mouse (*q.v.*), or a joystick.

Operating System Architecture
Level Structure

In a functional hierarchy, a program at one level may directly call any visible operation of a lower level; input is communicated directly to the lower-level operation without any intermediate level's involvement; and output is returned directly to the caller. The level structure can be completely enforced by a compiler

(*q.v.*), which inserts procedure calls or expands functions inline.

It is important to distinguish the operating system level structure from the layer structure of the ISO model of long-haul network protocols (*see* OPEN SYSTEMS INTERCONNECTION). In the ISO model, data input to a remote operation is passed down through all the layers on the sending machine and back up through all the layers on the receiving machine; return data follow the reverse path. A significant advantage of functional levels over information-transferring layers is efficiency: a program that does not use a given function will experience no overhead from that function's presence in the system.

Names

Naming of objects is a very important design problem in operating systems. The system of object names has two principal requirements: (1) it must allow individual users to choose local names as character strings that make sense to them, and (2) it must also allow any two users to share an object even though they have no prior agreement on the name that each will use for the object. These requirements can be met by allowing objects to have two names: the user-assigned (external) name and a system-assigned (internal) name. Although users can reuse external names at will, internal names must be unique. The simplest internal names are bit-strings, called *handles*, generated by the operating system when an object is created. In its simplest form, a handle is a pointer (*q.v.*) to the object or an index into a table of objects managed by a particular level.

Simple handles are good for object sharing but inadequate for access control. Nothing prevents anyone from passing a handle for an object to the wrong type manager, or from attempting to overwrite a read-only object. To overcome these limitations, some systems rely on *capabilities* rather than handles. A *capability* is a handle augmented with type and access codes. These codes can be checked by an object manager to make sure that it performs only the operations allowed by the access code only on its type of object.

System Initialization

An operating system startup procedure called a *bootstrap* sequence begins with a very short program copied into memory from a permanent read-only memory (ROM). This program loads a longer program from disk, which then takes control and loads the operating system itself. Finally, the operating system creates a special login process connected to each terminal of the system. When a user correctly types an identifier and a password (*q.v.*), the login process will create a shell process connected to the same terminal. When the user types a logout command, the shell process exits and the login process resumes.

Bibliography

1968. Dijkstra, E. W. "The Structure of the THE-Multiprogramming System," *Communications of the ACM*, **11**(5), (May), 341–346.

1972. Organick, E. I. *The Multics System: An Examination of its Structure*. Cambridge, MA: MIT Press.

1973. Brinch Hansen, P. *Operating System Principles*. Upper Saddle River, NJ: Prentice Hall.

1995. Tanenbaum, A. S. *Distributed Operating Systems*. Upper Saddle River, NJ: Prentice Hall.

Peter J. Denning and Walter F. Tichy

CONTEMPORARY ISSUES

The Role of an Operating System

From a functional viewpoint, an operating system is a collection of programs that acts as an intermediary between the hardware and its users, providing a high-level interface to low-level hardware resources such as the CPU, memory, and I/O devices. From a structural viewpoint, an operating system offers services to clients. The fundamental task is to control interaction among users and also between users and system services. Wide variations are encountered both in the demands that are placed upon operating systems, and in the operating system structures that are adopted in response to those demands.

A Historical Perspective

The earliest computer systems were employed by a single user at a time to run a single program at a time. By operating toggles on the front panel of the system, the user would cause a machine language program to be loaded at a specific memory address from a simple device, such as a paper tape reader. Execution of the program would be commenced manually by specifying an address to which control should be transferred. During execution, the program might read input or produce output; low-level machine instructions to operate I/O devices would be embedded in the program. Execution would terminate when the program branched to a "halt" instruction.

Among the drawbacks to this style of operation were that every user had to know the computer system at a detailed level. Some of the requirements for detailed knowledge of the computer system were ameliorated by the simple expedient of sharing partial programs: a single individual would write routines to control the I/O devices and would make these routines available to others. In some sense, these were the first operating system routines. The idea of a *resident monitor* was a further improvement: these routines would be permanently loaded in a region of memory, and user programs (loaded elsewhere in memory) would call them (*see* MONITOR, SYNCHRONIZATION).

The inefficiencies that resulted from the sequential nature of system operation were ameliorated by overlapping I/O with computation within a single job. The program would initiate a physical input operation before the data was actually required; the I/O device would read the data into a buffer other than the one the program was currently accessing. Output also used multiple buffers. *Time-sharing* (multiuser interactive computing) was possible, even on computer systems that ran one program at a time. MIT's Compatible Time-Sharing System (CTSS) was a very simple landmark time-sharing system. The memory of the computer system on which CTSS ran was only large enough to accommodate a single user. At the end of a time slice, *swapping* was used to suspend, temporarily, the execution of one user program and allow another to execute.

Multiprogramming was a significant advance, for it allowed multiple users to share a computer system simultaneously, rather than sequentially. In early multiprogramming systems, the memory of the computer system was partitioned into a fixed set of regions of various sizes (*see* Fig. 1). The *long-term scheduling* algorithm determined which of the waiting jobs would be allocated the next available region of memory. The *short-term scheduling* algorithm determined which of the memory-resident jobs would be allocated the CPU. More sophisticated multiprogramming systems divided memory into a variable number of regions of sizes tailored to the specific requirements of jobs. *Memory fragmentation* was a problem with either fixed-partition or variable-partition multiprogramming systems: *internal* fragmentation if a program was allocated a larger region than it required; *external* fragmentation if regions went unused because of a mismatch with the actual demands of the available jobs.

A drawback of all of the operating system designs discussed thus far is that each user program was required to be fully resident in a contiguous region of memory. *Paging* and *segmentation* are two approaches to removing the requirement for contiguity by using an indirection table. *Virtual memory* systems remove the requirement for full residency. A *page fault* occurs when a reference is made to a portion of a program's address space that is not memory-resident, and this page is fetched from secondary storage and the program resumed.

Concurrency

Concurrency is a prevalent theme in operating systems. There is physical concurrency: multiple I/O devices simultaneously active. There is logical concurrency: multiple users sharing the system, even though only one can actually be using the CPU at a particular instant (on a uniprocessor system). In early operating systems, this concurrency was managed using *ad hoc* techniques. A user program would *trap* to the operating system, requesting some service. The program's state would be saved as part of the trap procedure. The operating system would initiate the requested activity, typically by sending a *start I/O* command to a device. The operating system would then *resume* some other program, restoring its previously saved state. When the I/O completed, the device would *interrupt* whatever program happened to be running at the time, saving the program's state and transferring control to an *interrupt handling routine* in the operating system. The operating system would resume the program that had been waiting for the I/O to complete.

Sequential Processes

The most important of these techniques was the idea, due to Dijkstra, of structuring the system as a collection of *cooperating sequential processes*. A *process* is the execution of a program by a (virtual) CPU. A *sequential* process does not deal with asynchronous events, although it does communicate with other processes through a well-defined synchronous interface. An individual process may be in one of three states: *running* (i.e. actively computing), *ready* (i.e. ready to run, but not currently allocated the CPU), or *blocked* (awaiting some event, such as a message or an interrupt) (*see* Fig. 2). These multiple processes, *cooperating* through the communication interface, can be used to implement an operating system.

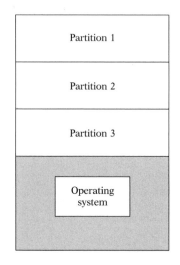

Figure 1.   Multiprogramming with a fixed number of partitions.

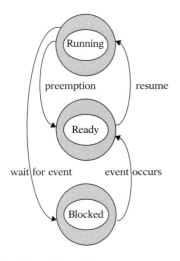

Figure 2. The states of a process.

Microkernels

A system design based upon the idea of cooperating sequential processes would involve a small kernel, a *microkernel*, whose main responsibilities are to support processes and interprocess communication. Separate processes are used to manage each I/O device, to implement spooling, to represent each user, to manage virtual memory, and so on. These processes interact by means of mechanisms such as synchronization monitors or message passing. A user's I/O request is communicated through the kernel to the manager process for the appropriate device. The user's process is then blocked. The device manager process, which was blocked waiting for a request message, is unblocked. The role of the kernel is to translate asynchronous interrupts into synchronous signals that awaken device manager processes and, more broadly, to implement interprocess communication and process scheduling.

Concurrent Programming Using Monitors

Monitors, attributed to Hoare, are one key approach to programming operating systems. As a first example, consider the *critical section problem*, which arises frequently in operating systems. A *critical section* is any piece of code that must be accessed by only one process at a time. For instance, suppose that several processes are counting occurrences of some type of event, such as I/O operations on various disks. When an I/O operation takes place at the disk being managed by a particular process, the process loads the value of a shared counter, adds one, and stores back the result. The code to increment the counter is a critical section. Suppose, for example, the increment sequences happen to interleave as follows:

Time	Process A	Process B
1	load	
2		load
3	add 1	
4		add 1
5	store	
6		store

Two events occur, but the value of the shared counter increases by only one.

Clearly, the incrementation sequences are interacting sequential processes: they loop, working largely independently but sharing the counter. However, some discipline must be imposed on accesses to the shared counter to turn the interaction into cooperation and avoid erroneous results. A *monitor* is one way to discipline this interaction. A monitor is somewhat like an *abstract data type* (*q.v.*) that encapsulates a data structures, but each monitor has the key property that at most one process may be executing its procedure at any time (*see* MUTUAL EXCLUSION).

Deadlock

Deadlock is a problem that can arise in concurrent systems when one process is waiting for a resource that is held by a second process, which in turn is waiting for a resource that is held by the first process (*see* Fig. 3). For example, suppose that the system's input spooler fills the disk with jobs waiting to run, with the result that there is no space in which to put the output of jobs that are trying to complete. One algorithm to prevent deadlock is to have each process claim every resource it will need at the outset, aborting if this is not possible. This is clearly safe, but may dramatically restrict the set of jobs that can execute concurrently. A second algorithm is to number resources and require that resources always be

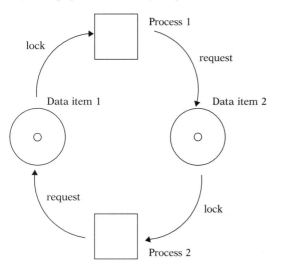

Figure 3.   Two-process deadlock.

acquired in ascending order. This algorithm is also safe (less obviously so) and is less restrictive.

Virtual Address Spaces

In a traditional multiprogramming system and in many small personal computers, there is a single *address space* with a size equal to the size of physical memory. Different programs are allocated different parts of this address space, with protection typically achieved by hardware tags associated with fixed-size pieces of memory. This organization is simple, but has several drawbacks. A program must be fully resident in a contiguous region of memory, with provision made for relocating the program once its region is determined.

Most computer systems, even PCs, employ some form of paged virtual memory. In a paged virtual memory system, each program has its own address space, which begins at address 0 and runs to some hardware-defined maximum. All address references in the program are within this address space. All address spaces are logically divided into *pages* of some fixed size. The physical memory is physically divided into *page frames* of the same fixed size. Any logical page can be stored in any physical page frame, which greatly simplifies memory allocation for the operating system and eliminates external fragmentation.

Many contemporary computer systems also support some rudimentary form of *segmentation*. In a fully flexible segmentation system, each program element is assigned to a variable-sized segment, and dynamic linking between segments is supported. More common is to have just a few segments in each address space, for example, an operating system segment, a user code segment, and a user data or stack segment.

Demand Paging

A page table entry may be marked as *invalid*, meaning that the correct page of data is not resident in memory. Should a reference to such a page occur, the dynamic address translation unit generates a *page fault* interrupt. The operating system gets control, brings the desired page from secondary storage to a page frame in primary memory, updates the page table entry, and then restarts the user program. This allows a program's physical memory allocation to be less than the size of its address space—sometimes by a very large factor. Most systems rely on *demand paging*: they do not attempt to anticipate the pages that a program will need, but rather wait for a fault to occur and then fetch the page. A variety of *page replacement algorithms* is used to determine which page frame should be allocated to a page that has faulted. Some variation of *least recently used* (LRU) is common in practice.

File Systems

Typical file-system operations are `Create`, `Destroy`, `Open`, `Close`, `Read`, `Write`, and `Seek`. Four key issues in the design of a file system are *allocation*, *organization*, *naming*, and *protection*. *Allocation* concerns the way in which a file is mapped onto the physical disk. Two extreme allocation strategies are *contiguous* and *linked*. Under contiguous allocation, the file is allocated in a contiguous area on disk. This makes access rapid, but makes creation and expansion difficult and may result in considerable wasted space. Under linked allocation, the file is allocated in fixed-size linked blocks. This makes creation and expansion easy and reduces wasted space, but access is slow. A compromise is indexed allocation: the file is allocated in fixed-size blocks that are accessed through a set of index blocks, making random access efficient. Some cleverness is required to insure that the index itself remains of manageable size. Unix (*q.v.*) uses an indexed allocation scheme in which each file is headed by an *i-node* containing a small number of pointers some of which point to a block of pointers and so on, cascaded to considerable depth (*see* Fig. 4).

Organization concerns the "file model" available to the programmer. In Unix, all files adhere to a single model: files are sequential *streams* of bytes. This has the advantage of simplicity, and integrates well with other fundamental abstractions of Unix (e.g. pipes). Most operating systems support several file models and *access methods*. The organization and the allocation strategy interact closely. Certain allocation strategies are most efficient for particular organizations.

Nearly all modern operating systems employ a hierarchical directory structure for naming. A *directory* maps names to files; files can be either data or other directories. A hierarchical directory structure allows the user to organize files in a structured and intelligent manner with due regard for file protection.

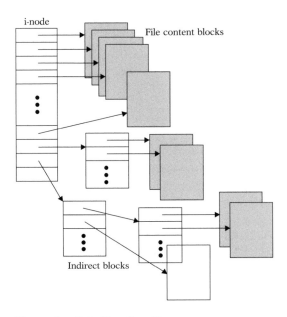

Figure 4. Unix file allocation.

Processor Scheduling

Processor scheduling is another aspect of process management that has been thoroughly studied and is well understood. The most important theoretical result is that *shortest remaining processing time first* (SRPT) is the optimum strategy to minimize response time when jobs' service times are deterministic and known at the instant the job arrives. Unfortunately, neither of these things is typically true in time-sharing systems, but most actual schedulers attempt in some way to mimic the behavior of SRPT.

Round-robin is a practical policy that preemptively rotates the CPU among the ready jobs, giving each job some *quantum* of service before moving on to the next. Its advantage over *first come, first served* is that a short job cannot get "stuck" behind a long job.

Real-Time Systems

A *hard real-time* system must always, under every circumstance, meet its deadlines. A *soft real-time* system may sometimes (very seldom) miss a deadline. Soft real-time is, for example, sufficient for a video system that may sometimes, perhaps once per hour, deliver a frame too late. Clearly, that is unacceptable for an aircraft control system, which must meet real-time constraints. Real-time operating systems therefore focus on how to guarantee *predictability*, not on optimizing average behavior. Only predictable worst-case behavior matters.

Personal Workstations

The idea of dedicating the power of a traditional multiuser computer to a single user, of coupling this computing power to a high-resolution bitmap display, and of viewing these workstations (*q.v.*) as participants in a distributed system (*q.v.*) rather than as isolated computers, was pioneered by Xerox in the 1970s and became commercially successful in the 1980s. The basic operating system requirements for a single-user workstation differ little from those for a more traditional multiuser computer. Unix, developed in the early 1970s as a time-sharing system, has become widely accepted as a workstation operating system, with the key addition of a *window system* to provide multiple logical displays on the single physical bitmap display. Menu-oriented *window environments* (*q.v.*) are largely replacing more traditional command language interpreters as the user interface (*q.v.*) of choice.

Clients and Servers

In the context of a distributed system, the terms client and server are used to differentiate between types of host nodes (*see* CLIENT-SERVER COMPUTING). The same terms are, however, used to denote different processes in an operating system. In both cases, clients request services from servers, for example, file access from a file server, printing from a print server, and so on. The concept of client–server processes can be applied on a single machine as well as on a cluster. Client process and server processes may reside on different machines or on the same machine. The communication principles are similar, although timing and security might be quite different.

Distributed Systems

Distributed systems involve multiple computer systems (*hosts*) connected by networks. The hosts are often high-performance single-user workstations or PCs. Key issues that arise are *communication, file systems, authentication and security*, and *distributed programming support*. File sharing in a distributed system can be achieved by a mechanism as crude as the explicit transfer of files using, for example, the Internet's File Transfer Protocol (FTP). Much greater integration, though, is provided by file systems such as the Network File System (NFS) and the Andrew File System (AFS).

Authentication (*q.v.*) is more difficult in a distributed system than in a centralized system because one entity cannot necessarily trust another. In a centralized system, once the user is authenticated all parts of the system accept the identity of the user. Not so in a distributed system. *Kerberos* is an example of an authentication service that offers considerable promise in the distributed environment. Kerberos is a scalable system that employs a secret key cryptographic protocol for initial authentication, and then grants "tickets" of finite lifetime, enabling the use of specific services. Data security is more difficult in a distributed system than in a centralized one because there are many opportunities for eavesdropping.

Multiprocessor Systems

Symmetric multiprocessing (SMP) processors operate independently on a shared memory. The single shared memory inherently limits SMP scalability. Even with very large per-processor caches, more than four or eight processors cannot be served without the memory substantially degrading processor performance. *Nonuniform memory access* (NUMA) systems are much more scalable. Systems with tens of thousands of processors can be built. Typically, they consist of multiple SMP nodes with fast interconnect hardware. Memory access to local memory is then much faster than accessing memory that belongs to a different node.

It is possible, although not trivial, to take a uniprocessor operating system (e.g. Unix) and make it run on a multiprocessor. The difficulty arises because the way in which shared kernel data structures are protected from corruption in uniprocessor operating systems usually relies on the existence of only a single processor. In particular, when the kernel is active, hardware-level mutual exclusion is achieved by disabling interrupts. This does not work correctly on a multiprocessor because a second processor can execute in the kernel even in the absence of interrupts. Thus, the mechanism for achieving hardware-level mutual exclusion must be changed, for example to one involving *busy-waiting* (*spin-locks*) to make a processor idle while another is (briefly) executing in the kernel.

A multiprocessor operating system must provide a facility for running parallel programs. The process mechanism is conceptually suitable, but such large overheads may be incurred for creating and synchronizing processes that only parallel computations with very coarse *granularity* (the relative size of a parallel unit of work) can be run with reasonable efficiency. Much effort in the design of multiprocessor operating systems has been devoted to the design of *lightweight threads*—threads of control that can be created and synchronized more efficiently than traditional processes, and thus can be used in programming fine-grained applications.

Bibliography

1989. Leffler, S. J., McKusick, M. K., Karels, M. J., and Quarterman, J. S. *The Design and Implementation of the 4.3BSD UNIX Operating System.* Reading, MA: Addison-Wesley.

1993. Stankovic, J. A., and Ramamritham, K. (eds.) *Advances in Real-Time Systems.* Los Alamitos, CA: IEEE Computer Society Press.

1998. Stallings, W. *Operating Systems: Internals and Design Principles*, 3rd Ed. Upper Saddle River, NJ: Prentice Hall.

Edward D. Lazowska and Jochen Liedtke

OPERATOR OVERLOADING

For articles on related subjects, see

+ Extensible Language
+ Object-Oriented Programming
+ Procedure-Oriented Languages
+ Subprogram

Programming language operators generally take two arguments, frequently but not always of the same type, and return a value of the type of one (or both) of the arguments. When binary, they are written in *infix* form, between the arguments, so that one can write x:= y + z, for example. An operator symbol is *overloaded* when it is used to denote multiple operations on variables of different types. Most programming languages overload common arithmetic operators like + and *, which are operations both on integers and on real numbers (and perhaps also on strings or sets). The term *operator overloading* is commonly used to characterize the property of some programming languages that permits a programmer to assign new meanings to operator symbols, in addition to the predefined ones.

Operator overloading provides a convenient notation for user-defined functions when they represent mathematical operations that go by familiar names. If a program has vectors (one-dimensional arrays) or matrices (two-dimensional arrays), overloading lets us define vector or matrix addition or multiplication with the same notation that one would use in mathematics: for example, v1 + v2, or M * N, rather than the more cumbersome notation required by a programming language that requires that these operations be written as subprogram (*q.v.*) calls.

Good notation is important in programming as well as in mathematics. In object-oriented programming, in which we define abstract data types (*q.v.*) that package data and operations, it is desirable if the vector type, the matrix type, and the complex number type can all use + as their addition operator, rather than arbitrarily assigning, say, ++ to one, +++ to a second and ++++ to the third. Subprogram names can also be overloaded when a language processor (*q.v.*) can use information about the number or types of the subprogram parameters to recognize which subprogram is being called. Ada (*q.v.*) allows such overloading, as does Prolog (*see* LOGIC PROGRAMMING).

Overloading should be distinguished from *coercion* (*q.v.*). Many languages allow expressions like n + r in which n is an integer and r a real number. This is not because there is an addition operator tailored to such a pair; rather, one argument is *coerced* to the type of the other, in which coercion means that a new value of the required type is formed and that value is used in the operation.

Operator overloading is a valuable tool for expressing similar concepts in similar notation, and thus a means of achieving program clarity. It can also be misused to suggest such similarity where there is none, and it is the programmer's responsibility to take care to use it wisely.

Bibliography

1985. Cardelli, L., and Wegner, P. "On Understanding Types, Data Abstraction, and Polymorphism," *Computing Surveys*, **17**(4), (December), 471–522.

1993. Louden, K. C. *Programming Languages: Principles and Practice.* Boston: PWS-Kent.

David Hemmendinger

OPERATOR PRECEDENCE

For articles on related subjects, *see*

✛ Compiler
✛ Expression
✛ Language Processors
✛ Operator Overloading
✛ Polish Notation

Operator precedence refers to the hierarchy of priority that determines the order in which operators are applied to their operands. For example, is the expression A+B*C to be interpreted as A+B*C or (A+B)*C? One way to solve this problem would be to enforce a strict left-to-right or (as in APL–*q.v.*) a right-to-left order of evaluation. However, most programming languages resolve possible ambiguities by establishing precedence relations that determine the order in which operators are applied. A major purpose of such relations is to assure that as many expressions as possible have their "natural" interpretation (e.g. most people would regard A+(B*C) as the natural interpretation of A + B * C).

The operator hierarchy includes not only arithmetic operators but also relational operators ($<$, $>$, $\leq$, $\geq$, $=$, $\neq$), logical operators (**and**, **or**, **not**), concatenation, and other operators (such as those that apply to bit strings). Table 1 gives the arithmetic, relational, and logical operator hierarchy in Fortran, Pascal, and C. It is to be interpreted as follows: in an expression containing more than one operator, the operator to be applied first is the one that is highest in the hierarchy. Thus,

Expression	Interpretation
3+4*5-6	3+(4*5)-6=17
16/4+8	(16/4)+8=12
3<4+5	3<(4+5)=true

Table 1.   The arithmetic, relational, and logical operator hierarchy in three popular procedure-oriented languages.

	Fortran	Pascal	C
High	**		
		not	!
	−(unary)		−(unary)
	*, /	*, /, **div, mod, and**	*, /, %
	+, −	+, −, **or**	+, −
	.LT., .LE., .EQ., .NE., .GE., .GT.	<, <=, =, <>, >=, >, **in**	<, <=, >=, >
			==, !=
	.NOT		
	.AND.		&&
	.OR.		||
	.EQV .NEQV.		
Low			

Notes:

**	Exponentiation
in	set membership
div	Integer quotient of integer division
==	Equality
mod and %	Integer remainder of integer division
<> and !=	Inequality

Note that the position of the relational operators relative to the arithmetic operators is forced if expressions containing a combination of these operators are to be meaningful. Thus, the Pascal (*q.v.*) or Ada (*q.v.*) expression `3<4+5` makes sense only if interpreted as `3<(4+5)`.

When an expression contains two operators of equal precedence, the usual rule is to evaluate them from left to right (although successive exponentiations are usually evaluated right to left). Thus, `A/B*C` is to be interpreted as `(A/B)*C`. In all languages, parentheses may be used to override the precedence rules.

The operator precedence rules together with the parentheses rule are used to enable the compilation of a program written in a high-level language into machine executable code. This procedure is referred to as the *arithmetic scan*, in which the first step is a transformation that converts normal infix form to reverse Polish notation (RPN). Such a transformation is required because of the difficulty of associating operands with operators in infix notation. As an example, consider the expression

$$(A * X + B)/(C * X - D) \qquad (1)$$

which, because of the precedence relations discussed above, is to be interpreted as

$$(((A * X) + B)/((C * X) - D)). \qquad (2)$$

By use of a classical algorithm that scans across the string in expression (1) from left to right just once, this string can be converted to the Polish postfix string

$$AX * B + CX * D - / \qquad (3)$$

Which, when evaluated in accord with RPN rules, has the unique interpretation of expression (2).

Anthony Ralston

OPTICAL CHARACTER RECOGNITION (OCR)

For articles on related subjects, see

+ Image Processing
+ Pattern Recognition
+ Typefont
+ Universal Product Code

Optical character recognition (OCR) is performed by optical character readers—machines that scan textual material and invoke software to interpret it. OCR may be defined as the process of converting images of machine printed or handwritten numerals, letters, and symbols into a computer-processable format.

Two types of automated reading equipment, distinct from optical character readers, are optical mark readers (OMRs) and magnetic ink character readers (MICRs). OMRs characteristically read nontextual input such as bar codes. Examples of OMRs are grocery store bar code readers that read the Universal Product Code (UPC) and the United States Postal Service's wide-area bar code reader that reads ZIP codes encoded in the PostNet code. One common MICR is a bank check reader that reads account numbers on the bottom of checks.

Commercial OCR predominantly handles machine-printed text. Although neatly printed handwriting is accepted by OCR systems, the technology for handwriting recognition is generally distinct from OCR technology for machine-printed text. Handwriting recognition systems can be divided into two types: online and offline. Online systems allow recognition of characters and words as they are written on a surface. The interactive nature of these systems enables recognition algorithms to use information about how characters are written. Many online systems allow interactive correction of misrecognized characters. Examples of applications using online recognition include the Apple Newton, the 3Com PalmPilot and Cross's Crosspad. Offline systems recognize characters that have been previously written on a document. Therefore, no information is available on the writing style or the implement path used to create the character strokes. Examples include address reading machines used by post offices and check amount reading machines.

OCR Systems

A typical OCR system contains three logical components, an image scanner, OCR software and hardware, and an output interface. The image scanner optically captures text images to be recognized. Text images are processed with OCR software and hardware. The process involves three operations: document analysis (extracting individual character images), recognizing these images (based on shape), and contextual processing (either to correct misclassifications made by the recognition algorithm or to limit recognition choices). The output interface is responsible for communication of OCR system results to the outside world.

Image Scanner

Four basic building blocks form functional image scanners: a detector, an illumination source, a scan lens, and a document transport. The document transport places the document in the scanning field, the light source floods the object with illumination, and the lens forms the object's image on the detector. The detector consists of an array of elements each of which converts incident light into a charge, or analog signal. These analog signals are then converted into an image. Scanning is performed by the detector and the motion of the text object with respect to the detector.

Recent advances in scanner technology have made available resolution in the range of 600 pixels per inch (ppi) to 1200 ppi. Recognition methods that use features (as opposed to template matching) use resolutions in the range of 200 ppi to 400 ppi, and careful consideration of gray scale. Lower resolutions and simple thresholding tend to break thin lines or fill gaps, thus invalidating features.

OCR Software and Hardware

Document analysis. Text is extracted from the document image in a process known as *document analysis*. Reliable character segmentation and recognition depend upon both original document quality and registered image quality. Processes that attempt to compensate for poor quality originals or poor quality scanning include image enhancement, underline removal, and noise removal. Image enhancement methods emphasize character vs noncharacter discrimination. Underline removal erases printed guidelines and

other lines, which may touch characters and interfere with character recognition, and noise removal erases portions of the image that are not part of the characters.

Character recognition. Two essential components in a character recognition algorithm are the *feature extractor* and the *classifier*. Feature analysis determines the descriptors, or feature set, used to describe all characters. Given a character image, the feature extractor derives the features that the character possesses. The derived features are then used as input to the character classifier.

Template matching or *matrix matching*, is one of the most common classification methods. In template matching, individual image pixels are used as features. Classification is performed by comparing an input character image with a set of templates (or prototypes) from each character class. Each comparison results in a similarity measure between the input character and the template. One measure increases the amount of similarity when a pixel in the observed character is identical to the same pixel in the template image. If the pixels differ, the measure of similarity may be decreased. After all templates have been compared with the observed character image, the character's identity is assigned as the identity of the most similar template.

Template matching is a trainable process because template characters may be changed. In many commercial systems, PROMs (programmable read-only memory) store templates containing single fonts. To retrain the algorithm, the current PROMs are replaced with PROMs that contain images of a new font. Thus, if a suitable PROM exists for a font, template matching can be trained to recognize that font.

Structural classification methods use structural features and decision rules to classify characters. Structural features may be defined in terms of character strokes, character holes, or other character attributes such as concavities. For instance, the letter "P" may be described as a vertical stroke with a loop attached to the upper right side.

Character misclassifications stem from two main sources: poor-quality character images and poor discriminatory ability. Poor document quality, image scanning, and preprocessing can all degrade performance by yielding poor-quality characters. Recognition rates for machine-printed characters can reach well over 99%, but handwritten character recognition rates are typically lower because each person writes differently. Figure 1 shows several examples of machine printed and handwritten capital "O"s. Each capital O can be easily confused with the numeral 0 and the number of different styles of capital "O"s demonstrates the difficulties recognizers must cope with.

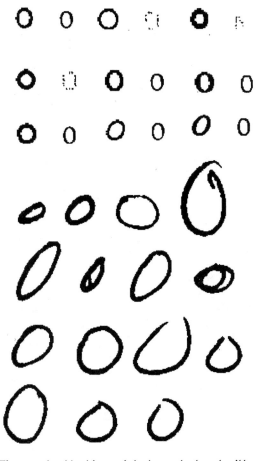

Figure 1. Machine-printed and handwritten capital "O"s.

ICR. *Intelligent character recognition* refers to the reading of handwritten characters. The term "ICR" was first coined by Kurzweil Computer Products, Inc. in the late 1970s to highlight its own "omni-font" OCR system, which was trainable and could learn new fonts. In the late 1980s, this term was usurped to describe the systems developed to read handwritten characters. By its very nature, the variations in handwriting are limitless, so any algorithm that attempts to read handwritten characters will have to be more intelligent than, say, an OCR algorithm that reads only a limited set of fonts. Hence the term "ICR."

The next step is size-normalizing the input image. Handwritten characters in general are much bigger than machine-printed characters, as can be seen in Fig. 2. In this step, the input image is reduced (or in the unlikely event that it is smaller than the target size, it is enlarged) to fit a target size, usually something on the order of 32 × 32 pixels. This entire process is called "preprocessing."

Contextual processing. Contextual information can be used in recognition. The number of word choices for a given field can be limited by knowing the content of another field, for example, to recognize the street name in an address, first recognize the ZIP code, and then the street name choices can be limited to a lexicon. Alternatively, the result of recognition can be post-processed to correct at least some of the recognition errors. For example, a spelling checker

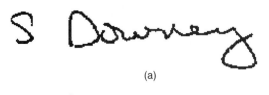

(a)

(b)

Figure 2. Two cursive words.

(*q.v.*) can be applied to detect obviously misspelled words.

Output Interface

Commercial OCR systems allow direction of results to spreadsheets (*q.v.*), databases, and word processors. The output interface is vital to the commercial success of a recognition system because it communicates results to the world outside of the OCR system.

Historical Perspective

An ideal model OCR system uses the human eye as the scanner and the human brain as the character recognizer. Accordingly, many of the early developments in OCR technology stemmed from attempts to help visually impaired people to read (*see* DISABLED, COMPUTERS AND THE). The first patents for reading devices to aid the blind were awarded in 1809. The first retinal scanner was developed by C. R. Carey in 1870 by using a mosaic of photocells to scan characters. In 1890, P. Nipkow developed a scanning disk that many consider a forerunner of modern television cameras, and in 1912, E. Goldberg converted scanned text into Morse code to be sent over a telegraph line.

Modern OCR technology was born in 1951 with David Sheppard's invention, GISMO—A Robot Reader–Writer. In 1954, Jacob Rabinow developed a prototype machine that was able to read upper case type-written output at the "fantastic" speed of one character per minute. Several companies, including IBM, Recognition Equipment, Inc., Farrington, Control Data, and Optical Scanning Corporation, marketed OCR systems by 1967. But as of that date, OCR systems were still considered exotic and futuristic, being used only by government agencies or large corporations. Systems that cost one million dollars were not uncommon. Current OCR systems are cheaper, faster, and more reliable. It is not uncommon to find PC-based OCR packages for under $100 capable of recognizing several hundred characters per second. The two ANSI-standard machine-printed fonts and the standard hand-printed character font are pictured in Fig. 3.

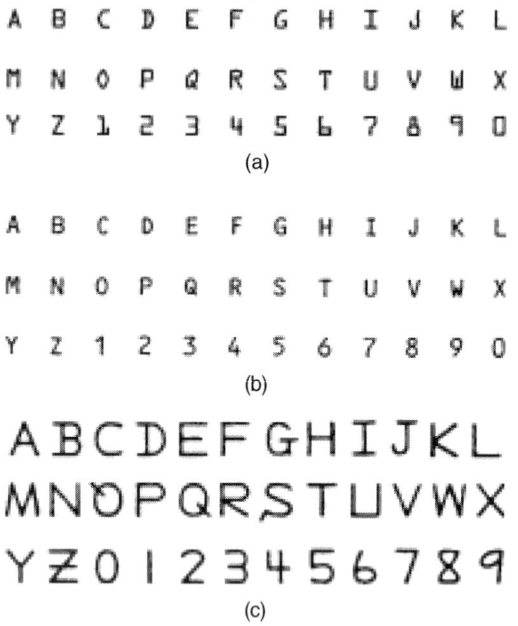

Figure 3. Standardized fonts: (a) OCR-A font; (b) OCR-B font; and (c) handwritten font.

Commercial Applications

Commercial OCR systems can be grouped into two categories: *task-specific readers* and *general-purpose page readers*. A task-specific reader handles only specific document types. Some of the most common task-specific readers read bank checks, letter mail, or credit card slips. These readers usually use custom-made image lift-hardware that captures only a few predefined document regions. For example, a bank check reader may just scan the courtesy amount field and a postal OCR system may just scan the address block on a mail piece. Such systems emphasize high throughput rates and low error rates. Applications such as letter mail reading have throughput (*q.v.*) rates of 12 letters per second with error rates less than 2%.

General-purpose page readers are designed to handle a broader range of documents such as business letters, technical writings, and newspapers. These systems capture an image of a document page and separate the page into text regions and nontext regions. Nontext regions such as graphics and line drawings are often saved separately from the text and associated recognition results. Text regions are segmented into lines, words, and characters and the characters are passed to the recognizer. Most of these page readers can read machine-written text, but only a few can read hand-printed alphanumerics.

Bibliography

1985. Smith, J. W., and Merali, Z. *Optical Character Recognition: The Technology and its Application in Information Units and Libraries*, Repart 33. London: The British Library.

1999. Rice, S. V., Nagy, G., and Nartker, T. A. *Optical Character Recognition: An Illustrated Guide to the Frontier.* Boston: Kluwer.

**Sargur N. Srihari, Ajay Shekhawat,
and Stephen W. Lam**

OPTICAL COMPUTING

For articles on related subjects, see

+ Fiber Optics
+ Optical Character Recognition (OCR)
+ Optical Storage
+ Universal Product Code

Digital computing using optical components was considered at least as early as the 1940s by John von Neumann (*q.v.*). If lasers had been available at the time, the first digital computers might well have used optics. Historically, optical technology has found a few special-purpose uses as an adjunct technology to electronics for analog and digital computing. Starting in the early 1960s, optical technology has been used for computing Fast Fourier Transforms (FFTs) of military images in matched filtering operations. Synthetic aperture radar (SAR) signal processing is an optical pattern recognition application that matches images in stored photographic form with input images. Spectrum analysis is another application that is performed with acoustoöptic signal processing. These applications are performed optically when the need for high bandwidth (*q.v.*) exceeds electronic capability.

The fastest transistors switch on the order of 5 picoseconds (ps), but the fastest computers have cycle times of the order of 1 nanosecond (ns), 1/200th as fast. This disparity arises from a number of problems related to conventional electronics which include electromagnetic interference at high speed; distorted edge transitions; complexity of metal connections; drive requirements for pins; large peak power levels; and impedance matching effects. The contrasting advantages of optics include high connectivity through imaging; no physical contact for interconnects; non-interference of signals; high spatial and temporal bandwidth; no inherent feedback to the power source; and inherently low signal dispersion.

The success of digital optics depends heavily on advances in optical hardware. The development of suitable optical logic gates has historically been one of the most critical obstacles to achieving an all-optical digital computer. The properties expected of optical logic gates are that they support a fan-in and fan-out of at least two; comprise a logically complete set such as {AND, OR, NOT}, {NAND}, or {NOR}; support indefinite cascadability; operate at low switching powers; and switch at higher rates than electronic devices. Devices that meet these goals are typically fabricated from semiconductor materials such as gallium arsenide (GaAs).

There are a number of ways that optics can supplement or replace electronics in computing. Optical fibers typically transport information over long distances, of the order of several tens of kilometers, without a need for signal restoration. Fiber optics is a preferred medium for long-haul transmission because of low losses and high information-carrying capacity. Fibers are also used for distances on the order of a few tens of centimeters in connecting circuit boards. Both of these applications address transmission problems, but optics can be used for computation as well as transmission of information.

The SEED (Self-Electroöptic Effect Device— Miller *et al.*, 1985) has been used in optical processor testbeds at Lucent Technologies. The SEED is based on an

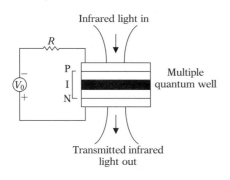

Figure 1. Schematic of the self-electroöptic effect bistable device. (Miller *et al.*, 1985).

electrically coupled optical modulator and detector pair. The basic device is made up of approximately 1200 alternating layers of GaAs and GaAlAs in an 8 μm-thick quantum well structure placed inside a PIN photodiode detector, as shown in Fig. 1. When light is applied to the detector, a current is generated that reduces the potential across the quantum well. When a strong enough current is created, the positive feedback allows the device to retain its state after the light source is removed. The electrical properties of the device make it relatively easy to use in experimental setups, and the speed of a computer made of these devices is limited only by the device speed. Operating rates for the FET-SEED, an improved SEED that uses Field Effect Transistors (FETs), are several hundred megahertz, and the devices can be monolithically integrated with digital electronics.

Although optical digital computing has the potential to achieve a greater level of performance than electronic digital computing, this superiority has yet to be demonstrated. The outlook for all-optical computing is one in which the impact of optics is far greater for communication bandwidth than for computational logic.

Bibliography

1985. Miller, D. A. B., Chemla, D. S., Damen, T. C., Wood, T. H., Burrus, C. A., Gossard, A. C., and Wiegmann, W. "The Quantum Well Self-electro-optic Effect Device: Optoelectronic Bistability and Oscillation and Self-linearized Modulation," *IEEE Journal of Quantum Electronics*, **QE-21**, 1462.

1991. McAulay, A. D. *Optical Computer Architectures.* New York: John Wiley.
1990. Murdocca, M. J. *A Digital Design Methodology for Optical Computing.* Cambridge, MA: MIT Press.

Miles J. Murdocca

OPTICAL STORAGE

For articles on related subjects, *see*

+ Memory: Auxiliary
+ Read-Only Memory (ROM)

In contrast to memory that functions magnetically, an *optical storage* device uses a laser to etch and later detect microscopic pits in the surface of its recording medium. There are three principal kinds used as auxiliary computer memory, two of which had their origin as audio or audiovisual entertainment media.

CD-ROM

CD-ROM (compact disc read-only memory) is an optical storage medium used primarily with PCs (*see* Fig. 1). Information is recorded on a 12-cm disc by

Figure 1. CD-ROM.

using a laser to etch billions of tiny pits into a thin metallic layer on its surface. In contrast to the concentric tracks used with hard disks (*q.v.*) or diskettes (*q.v.*), the pits are arranged in a 3-mile long spiral that is read from the center of the disc to the edge. The unetched space between any two pits is called a *land*. Both pits and lands convey information. During production, pits are burned into the disc from the top, but the pits are later read from the bottom, so from that perspective, the laser which does so considers the pits to be *bumps*. The laser, called the *detector*, is the CD counterpart of the read head used with a magnetic disk. Information on audio CDs is encoded using a Cross Interleave Reed–Solomon code in which data and multiple parity bits are combined into uniform-length code words. (*See* ERROR CORRECTING AND DETECTING CODE.)

Magnetic disks rotate at constant speed (constant angular velocity, or CAV), but CD rotational speed varies, decreasing toward the periphery, in order to provide constant linear (tangential) velocity. This allows use of the same pit density throughout the CD's single spiral track.

CD-ROM storage was adapted from audio CD, developed in the mid-1970s by Sony and Philips, and CD-ROM units have been available for PCs since the mid-1980s. The capacity of a CD-ROM is 650 MB, enough to hold roughly 250 copies of this Concise Encyclopedia, exclusive of space for digitized photographs and figures.

There are now CD-R (Compact Disc Recordable) drives available that record information on a conventional blank CD, but only once, and hence are a type of WORM device (Write Once, Read Many). However, even better, there are also CD-RW (Compact Disc ReWritable) drives available at somewhat higher cost that provide true auxiliary memory that can be recorded (up to about a million times) and read back and are thus a type of WMRM (Write Many, Read Many) drive.

Laserdisc

Most of today's motion video applications involve the presentation of analog video under computer control. The *laserdisc*, originally called *videodisc*, is the most

common source of *analog* video material for interactive applications because it allows random access, and the economies of scale derived from the extensive home and entertainment market have reduced player prices. Laserdiscs are either 8 or 12 inches in diameter, with 12-in. discs being most common. As with CD-ROM, information is recorded by pressing a spiral of microscopic pits into a polished surface. There are about 14 billion pits on one side of a 12-in. disc. Information may be recorded at either constant linear velocity (CLV) or CAV. Each side of a 12-in. laserdisc holds a half-hour of video when recorded in CAV format, and an hour when recorded with CLV. The drive speed of a CLV disc varies from 600 to 1800 rpm as a function of head position. The innermost "track" (rotation) of a 12-in., CLV disc holds one frame, the outermost track holds three frames. With the CAV format, the disc rotates at a constant 1800 rpm and there is always one frame per track. CAV discs are most commonly used in computer-based systems because they allow random access to any track, freeze frame, step frame, and multi-speed playback.

DVD

A DVD (Digital Versatile Disc, formerly Digital Video Disc) has the same 12 cm ($4\frac{3}{4}$-in.) size as a CD but is called "versatile" because it appears destined to replace

Figure 2. The Hitachi GD-2500BX DVD ROM drive.

Figure 3.   The Hitachi GF-1000 DVD RAM drive.

not only the laserdisc and the audio CD for entertainment but also the CD-ROM for use as auxiliary computer memory (*see* Fig. 2). DVD technology uses a higher frequency (shorter wavelength) laser to etch pits than is used to make a CD, so the pits are much smaller. Furthermore, the DVD's spiral tracks are more dense than those of a CD, both circumferentially—0.4 μm rather than 0.83 μm—and radially—0.74 μm rather than 1.6 μm. These attributes and other compression techniques allow a DVD to contain up to 8.5 GB, 13 times as much as a 650-MB CD (and as much twice again—17 GB—when recorded on both sides). In keeping with the claim of versatility, a DVD drive can read CDs.

Like CD-ROM and LD-ROM, an ordinary DVD is DVD-ROM, that is, its prerecorded pit-encoded information can be read but not rewritten. But DVD-RAM drives are now available which, through use of technology similar to that described earlier for use with CD-RW, are WMRM devices (*see* Fig. 3). These are likely to become the optical storage medium of choice for use with personal computers (*see* MEMORY: AUXILIARY).

Bibliography

1992. Pohlmann, K. C. *The Compact Disc Handbook.* Madison, WI: A-R Editions Inc.

1998. White, R. *How Computers Work*, 4th Ed. Indianapolis, IN: QUE.

1999. Goodwin, M. "Taking DVD for a Spin," *PC World*, **2**(2), (February), 143–154.

Larry Press

PACKAGE

For articles on related subjects, see

+ Block Structure
+ Encapsulation
+ Global and Local Variables
+ Information Hiding
+ Modular Programming
+ Object-Oriented Programming

A *package* is that part of a programming language that supports multiple name spaces, a *name space* being the collection of names that have meaning within a particular package. Name space collisions occur when different programmers accidentally use the same variable or function name with different meaning within the same name space. Package systems were developed to prevent these. Many early programming languages had only one name space.

Conceptually, a package is a data structure (*q.v.*) used to maintain a mapping between names and their values, the variables or functions denoted by those names. Variables and functions that are not explicitly shared are safely hidden in the package. Named values visible outside their package are said to be *exported*. Named values from outside a package that are visible inside a package are said to be *imported*. Every name belongs to some package. Packages help manage large software systems because the public interface to package services is usually much smaller and more comprehensible than the total number of names used within the package. Many modern programming languages have a package mechanism; C++ (*q.v.*) calls them *namespaces*, Java (*q.v.*) and Common Lisp (*see* LISP) have *packages*.

Kenneth A. Dickey

PACKET SWITCHING

For articles on related subjects, see

+ Communications and Computers
+ Distributed Systems
+ Network Protocols
+ Networks, Computer
+ Internet
+ Integrated Services Digital Network (ISDN)
+ TCP/IP

Packet switching describes the internal operations of a particular type of data communications network. A packet-switched data communication network is composed of a number of geographically separate nodes connected by dedicated high-speed data links. The nodes are computers that have internal data link connections to the other nodes and external data links connected to local terminals and computers (*see* Fig. 1). A unit of information, called a *packet* (usually 128 bytes or less), is routed from one *packet-switching*

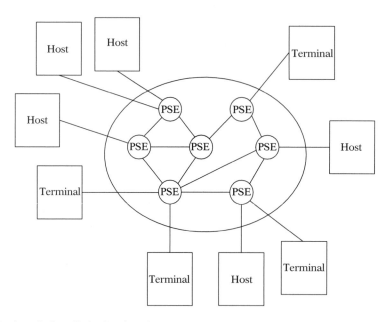

Figure 1. Typical packet-switched network.

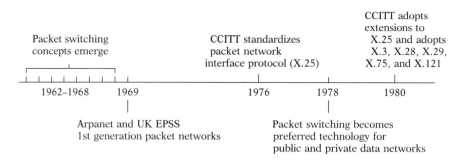

Figure 2. Evolution of packet switching. CCITT is now the International Telecommunications Union (ITU).

exchange (PSE) to another via transmission lines until it reaches its destination. The destination address is contained in the packet header. Each packet of a group that comprises an overall message may go by a different route, but all packets are eventually collected in order to reassemble the message. A variant of packet switching called *cell switching*, used in broadband ISDN services, is based on fixed size 48-byte packets. Figure 2 shows the evolution of packet switching. In 1976, the international standards body responsible for worldwide telecommunications standards (ITU-T) recommended the first interface protocol, called X.25, for attaching terminal equipment to a packet network.

When a packet arrives at a PSE, the exchange determines whether it is a transit node or a destination node. If the former, it chooses a transmission line to forward the packet. This is called *store-and-forward* transmission, a term created in message-switching systems. In packet-switching systems, the store-and-forward operations generally occur in tens of milliseconds. Source to destination transmission delay is typically about 100 ms for transcontinental packets, though it can be a second or more on slower portions of the Internet.

Two alternative strategies have evolved in the implementation of packet-switching systems—*datagrams* and *virtual circuits*. In the *datagram* (also called *connectionless*) strategy, each packet is totally independent of all others. They are independently routed and have the properties that they can be lost or duplicated with some probability, and transmission order between packets is not preserved. Proponents of the datagram approach argue that a simpler network interface can be achieved and that transmission of datagrams can easily be routed around failed links and nodes. The Internet uses datagrams and the Internet Protocol (IP–*see* TCP/IP) for controlling routing and transmission. In the *virtual circuit* (VC) approach, a logical path is created between source and destination. The virtual circuit allows the network to maintain order, discard duplicates, and detect missing packets.

An important issue in packet switching is *Quality of Service* (QoS). The IP protocol provides "best effort" service, which routes packets without any guarantee of minimum throughput (*q.v.*). This is appropriate for "traditional" Internet services like file transfer and email, but not for real-time audio or video.

Bibliography

1996. Metcalfe, R., Salus, P. H., and Cerf, V. G. *Packet Communications*. Menlo Park, CA: Peer-to-Peer.
1996. Peterson, L. L., and Davie, B. S. *Computer Networks: A Systems Approach*. San Francisco: Morgan Kaufmann.

Barry D. Wessler

PAGED MEMORY

See VIRTUAL MEMORY.

PALMTOP COMPUTER

See PORTABLE COMPUTERS.

PARALLEL I/O

See INPUT–OUTPUT OPERATIONS; and PORT, I/O.

PARALLEL PROCESSING

For articles on related subjects, *see*

+ Cellular Automata
+ Cluster Computing
+ Computer Architecture
+ Concurrent Programming
+ Cooperative Computing
+ Multiprocessing
+ Pipeline
+ Supercomputers

PRINCIPLES

Parallel processing is the use of concurrency in the operation of a computer system to increase throughput (*q.v.*) and fault-tolerance, or reduce the time needed to solve a problem. Parallel processing is the only route to the highest levels of computer performance.

Pipelining and Parallelism

To reduce the time needed for a mechanism to perform a task, we must either increase the speed of the mechanism or introduce concurrency. Two traditional methods have been used to increase concurrency: pipelining and parallelism. If an operation can be divided into a number of stages, *pipelining* allows different tasks to be in different stages of completion. An automobile assembly line is an example of pipelining. *Parallelism* is the use of multiple resources to increase concurrency, such as a group of combines working together to harvest a wheat field.

To illustrate and contrast these two methods, consider the following pizza-baking example. Suppose a pizza requires 10 min to bake, and the baking time cannot be reduced without ruining the quality of the pizza. An oven that holds a single pizza can yield six baked pizzas an hour. To increase productivity, a way must be found to have more than one pizza baking at once. If 5 ovens are used, the ovens yield 5 pizzas every 10 min and 30 pizzas an hour. Note that the 5 ovens are used most efficiently if the number of pizzas needed is a multiple of 5. For example, the ovens require the same amount of time, 20 min, to produce 6, 7, 8, 9, or 10 pizzas.

Another way to increase production is through the use of pipelining. Imagine a conveyer belt running through a long pizza oven. A pizza placed at one end of the conveyer belt spends 10 min in the oven before it reaches the other end. If the conveyer belt has room for 5 pizzas, a cook can place an unbaked pizza at one end of the belt every 2 min. Ten minutes after the first pizza has been put into one end of the oven, it appears as a baked pizza at the other end. From that time on, another baked pizza will appear every 2 min, and the production of the oven will be 30 pizzas an hour. The pizza-baking speeds of the single-oven, parallel-oven, and pipelined-oven methods are compared in Table 1, and the relative speedups attainable are shown in Fig. 1.

Table 1. Contrasting the pizza-baking times of a single oven, five ovens, and a conveyor-belt oven.

Pizzas baked	Single oven (min)	Five ovens (min)	Conveyor oven (min)
1	10	10	10
2	20	10	12
3	30	10	14
4	40	10	16
5	50	10	18
6	60	20	20
7	70	20	22
8	80	20	24
9	90	20	26
10	100	20	28
11	110	30	30
12	120	30	32

Parallelism in Hardware

Virtually all modern computer systems take advantage of at least some low-level hardware parallelism in order to improve performance. A *bit-parallel memory* allows all the bits in a word to be accessed in parallel. A *bit-parallel*

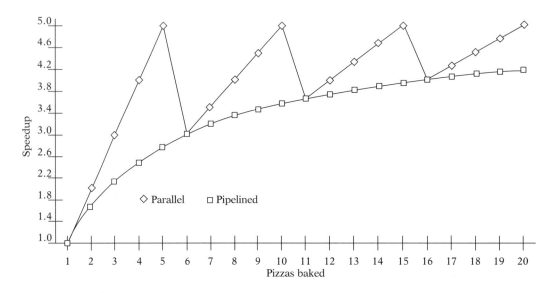

Figure 1. Contrasting the speedup achieved through pipelining and parallelism.

arithmetic unit performs an arithmetic operation on all bits of a pair of operands in parallel. An *I/O processor*, or channel (*q.v.*), receives I/O instructions from the CPU but then works independently, freeing the CPU to resume arithmetic processing. An *interleaved memory* is divided into a number of memory banks that can be accessed concurrently (*see* INTERLEAVING). Computers with *instruction lookahead*, or *instruction buffering*, prefetch instructions from memory, which reduces the amount of waiting done by the instruction unit. More than one instruction in some stage of execution at the same time is called *instruction pipelining*.

In the fastest computers, parallelism appears at the highest levels in the architecture. Two important categories of high-speed computers are vector computers and multiple-CPU computers.

A *vector computer* has an instruction set that includes operations on vectors as well as scalars. Processor arrays and pipelined vector processors are two examples of vector computers. A *processor array* is a set of identical synchronized processing elements (PEs) managed by a single control unit, which are capable of performing the same operation on different data elements in parallel. By associating each PE with a vector element, operations such as element-wise vector addition can be performed in a single step. A pipelined vector processor pipelines the flow of data from memory through pipelined functional units and back to memory, eliminating the overhead involved in fetching, manipulating, and storing the individual scalar elements of a vector.

Each CPU of a multiple-CPU computer is capable of independently executing its own instruction stream. A *multiprocessor* is a multiple-CPU computer with a single address space. Every processor can read from and write to every memory location. The globally accessible memory may be centralized, but more commonly it is distributed among the processors, so that a processor will have faster access to some memory locations than to others. A *multicomputer* is a multiple-CPU computer in which each CPU has its own local address space. Since a processor cannot directly access nonlocal memory locations, communication and synchronization between processors is accomplished solely through message passing.

Frequently, parallel computers are hybrid designs. For example, a collection of multiprocessors can be connected by a fast switching network to form a multicomputer (*see* CLUSTER COMPUTING).

Flynn's Taxonomy

The taxonomy proposed by Flynn (1966) is still the best-known classification scheme for parallel architectures. The taxonomy is based on the amount of concurrency present in the instruction and data streams. The hardware may support only a single instruction stream, or it may have multiple program counters and other control hardware needed to support the simultaneous execution of multiple instruction streams. Likewise, the hardware may allow arithmetic operations to be performed on only a single pair of operands at a time, or it may support the simultaneous application of an operation to multiple data items. These combinations result in four classes of computers:

- *Single Instruction Stream, Single Data Stream (SISD)*: Uniprocessors fall into this category.
- *Single Instruction Stream, Multiple Data Stream (SIMD)*: Processor arrays fall into this category. A processor array executes a single stream of instructions, but contains a number of arithmetic processing units, each capable of fetching and manipulating its own data. Hence, in any time unit, a single operation is in the same state of execution on multiple processing units.
- *Multiple Instruction Stream, Single Data Stream (MISD)*: No current architectures fit naturally into this category.
- *Multiple Instruction Stream, Multiple Data Stream (MIMD)*: Multiprocessors and multicomputers fall into this category. These systems contain multiple CPUs, each capable of executing its own instruction stream and performing operations on its own data stream.

Many early parallel computers used SIMD architecture, but most contemporary parallel computers are MIMD systems. MIMD architectures have two important advantages over SIMD machines. First, because they have multiple CPUs, MIMD computers may accommodate more than one user at a time, making them more general purpose. Second, MIMD computers can take advantage of the price/performance advantages associated with off-the-shelf microprocessors. In 1996, Intel built a multicomputer out of more than 9000 Pentium Pro microprocessors, the first general-purpose computer to exceed one teraflops (one trillion floating-point operations per second) on a real application.

Parallelism in Software

In order to use parallel hardware, there must be some way to express parallelism in, or extract parallelism from, a user's program. In the case of a vector computer, which executes a single instruction stream containing vector as well as scalar operations, all that is needed is some mechanism to express or extract vector operations. In the case of a multiple-CPU computer that supports the concurrent execution of multiple instruction streams, there must be some way to express or extract the generation and cooperation of parallel processes. This aspect of parallel processing has been heavily influenced by what has been learned about managing cooperating processes for multiprogrammed operating systems (*q.v.*).

Bibliography

1966. Flynn, M. J. "Very High-speed Computing Systems," *Proceedings of the IEEE*, **54**(12), (December), 1901–1909.

1994. Quinn, M. J. *Parallel Computing: Theory and Practice*, 2nd Ed. New York: McGraw-Hill.

1998. Culler, D. E., Singh, J. P., and Gupta, A. *Parallel Computer Architecture: A Hardware/Software Approach*. San Francisco: Morgan Kaufmann.

Michael J. Quinn

ARCHITECTURES

Introduction

Since serial computers are now within 2 orders of magnitude of the limit imposed by the speed of light, alternative solutions must be considered for problems that require orders of magnitude more computing power than today's fastest uniprocessor machines. Such problems include weather prediction, molecular modeling, and flow dynamics. An alternative to the traditional single-processor machine is the *multiprocessor*, often called a *parallel computer* or *multicomputer*. By the late 1990s, almost all supercomputers contained multiple processors, and PCs containing multiple processors became commonplace.

In 1952, John von Neumann (*q.v.*) designed a hypothetical machine that consisted of a two-dimensional (2D) array of simple processors (*see* CELLULAR AUTOMATA). In the late 1950s, another parallel computer was designed by Stephen Unger, who proposed a 2D array of processors targeted at problems in image processing (*q.v.*) and pattern recognition (*q.v.*). Eventually, such theoretical designs led to the production of what was then called "the first highly parallel supercomputer," the 64-processor ILLIAC IV, which was designed in 1967 and became operational in 1975. The 64 processors were connected as an 8 × 8 two-dimensional grid. The ILLIAC IV, originally designed to have four 8 × 8 arrays of powerful processors, was targeted at matrix computations and partial differential equations. Unfortunately, due to technological limitations and inadequate software, many of the early parallel machines were destined to fail. However, due to advances in computer chip (VLSI), compiler (*q.v.*), language, and operating system (*q.v.*) technology, commercially available parallel computers have become the computing systems of choice in computationally intensive settings and are currently being used to solve significant scientific and industrial problems (*see* SCIENTIFIC APPLICATIONS).

Terminology

Parallel computing terminology has not become standardized, but in this section we present some fundamental terms and concepts that are fairly well accepted.

Shared Memory vs Distributed Memory

In a *shared memory* machine, there is a single global set of memory that is available to all processors (*see* Fig. 1). The processors in a shared-memory system are connected to the common global memory by a bus (*q.v.*) or switch. Care must be taken when two processors try to write to the same memory location

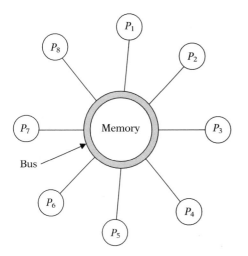

Figure 1. A shared-memory system in which the processors (P_i) are connected to a common global memory via a bus.

simultaneously. Each processor in a *distributed memory* machine has access only to its own private (local) memory (*see* Fig. 2). Distributed memory machines avoid the memory contention problem. Access to nonlocal data in a distributed memory system is provided by passing messages between the processors through the interconnection network. In a distributed memory system, contention (*q.v.*) for message-passing channels is a major concern.

Granularity

Granularity refers to the relative number and complexity of multiple processors. A *fine-grained machine* consists of a relatively large number of small, simple processors, while a *coarse-grained machine* consists of a few large, powerful processors. Fine-grained machines have of the order of 1 000 000 simple processors, while coarse-grained machines have on the order of 100 powerful processors. *Medium-grained* machines having the order of 1000 processors represent a compromise in performance and size between the two.

Fine-grained machines typically fall into the SIMD category, where all processors operate in lockstep fashion (i.e. synchronously) on the content of their own small local memory. Coarse-grained machines typically fall into the shared-memory MIMD category, where processors operate asynchronously on the large shared memory. Medium-grained machines typically fall into the distributed memory MIMD category, where the programming style is often that of *single program, multiple data* (*SPMD*). In SPMD, all processors store an identical copy of the same program, which consists of computations on local data interspersed with communication steps for retrieving necessary data from nonlocal memory. At any given time, different processors could be executing different sections of the code.

The vast majority of parallel machines fall into one of three categories:

1. Many manufacturers are creating coarse-grained servers that appear as a shared-memory machine to the user. Typically, these machines fall into the *NonUniform Memory Access* (*NUMA*) model.
2. The observation that enormous numbers of workstation cycles are not being used, and the

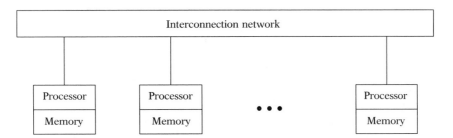

Figure 2. A distributed memory system. Every processing element consists of a processor and memory module.

deployment of packages of communication standards that can work efficiently in heterogeneous platforms, has led to the emergence of *Networks of Workstations (NOWs)*, sometimes referred to as *Clusters of Workstations (COWs)* (see CLUSTER COMPUTING).

3. A few "massively parallel" machines are being constructed using PCs as processors.

Interconnection Networks

Interconnection networks are used for processor-to-processor and processor-to-memory communication. In this section, we briefly discuss a small subset of these networks.

Processor-to-Processor Interconnections

The *degree of a processor P* is defined to be the number of other processors that P is directly connected to via bidirectional communication links. The *degree of the network* is defined to be the maximum degree of any processor in the network. The *communication diameter* of the network is defined to be the maximum of the minimum distance between any two processors.

Ring

In a *ring* network, as shown in Fig. 3a, the n processors are connected in a circular fashion so that processor P_i is directly connected to processors P_{i-1} and P_{i+1}. While the degree of the network is only 2, the communication diameter is $[n/2]$, which is quite high.

Mesh

The n processors of a two-dimensional square mesh network, as shown in Fig. 3b, are typically configured so that an interior processor $P_{i,j}$ is connected to its four neighbors, processors $P_{i-1,j}$, $P_{i+1,j}$, $P_{i,j-1}$, and $P_{i,j+1}$. The four corner processors are each connected to their two neighbors, while the remaining processors that are on the edge of the mesh are each connected to three neighbors. So, by increasing the degree of the network

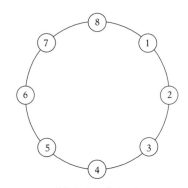

(a) A ring of size 8

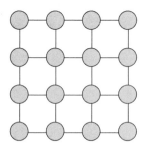

(b) A mesh of size 16

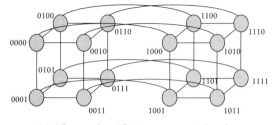
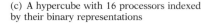

(c) A hypercube with 16 processors indexed by their binary representations

Figure 3. Processor-to-processor interconnection networks.

to 4, the communication diameter of the network is reduced to $2 (n^{1/2} - 1)$.

Hypercube

A hypercube with n processors, where n is an integral power of 2, has the processors indexed by the integers $\{0, \ldots, n - 1\}$. Viewing each integer in the index range as a $(\log_2 n)$-bit string, two processors are directly connected if and only if their indices differ by exactly one bit, as illustrated in Fig. 3c. Unlike the fixed degree ring and mesh networks, the number of links that are needed by each processor in a hypercube grows as $\log_2 n$. This makes it difficult to manufacture reasonably generic hypercube processors. The advantage of a hypercube is that the communication diameter is only $\log_2 n$, for example, 4 in Fig. 3c.

Processor-to-Memory Interconnections

Bus

In a *single bus–based system*, the processors, memory modules, and *I/O* devices are connected by a single high-speed *bus* (*q.v.*). This is the least complicated interconnection network, but it has the disadvantage that only one processor can access the shared memory at a time. An alternative to using a single bus is to use *multiple buses*, where each processor and memory module, whether regular or cache, is connected to multiple buses.

Crossbar Switch

A *crossbar switch* provides every one of the n processors with a logical connection to each of the m memory modules. This allows every processor to communicate simultaneously with a distinct memory module without contention, but requires nm switches, as shown in Fig. 4.

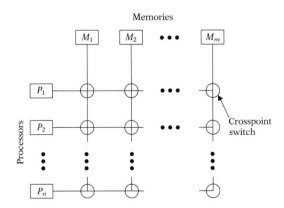

Figure 4. A crossbar switch with *n* processors and *m* memory modules.

Multistage Interconnection Networks

A *multistage interconnection network* (*MIN*) connects processors and memory modules through a specialized switching network. Typical MINs include the Omega network, the Benes network, and the butterfly network. These networks typically have logarithmic depth. MINs permit multiple paths between processors and memory modules and require fewer components than a crossbar switch, while still allowing good connectivity between the processors and memory.

Bibliography

1992. Leighton, F. T. *Introduction to Parallel Algorithms and Architectures: Arrays, Trees, Hypercubes.* San Francisco: Morgan Kaufmann.

1998. Hwang, K., and Xu, Z. *Scalable Parallel Computing: Technology, Architecture, and Programming.* New York: McGraw-Hill.

Russ Miller

ALGORITHMS

Introduction

There are a number of basic approaches that can be used in developing efficient parallel algorithms. One approach is to port existing sequential algorithms to these new machines, but many such algorithms do not run efficiently on parallel computers. Another approach is to design a new intrinsically parallel algorithm.

Examples and Discussion

Sum

Suppose that we need to sum n values, initially distributed one per processor on a fine-grained machine with n processors. Consider an algorithm for a square mesh ($n^{1/2} \times n^{1/2}$) of processors. First, sum the values in each row simultaneously and independently so that the leftmost processor in each row knows the sum of its row. Then, in the first column, sum these partial sums to the topmost processor. Finally, the sum of these n values, which is stored in the top-left processor of the mesh, can be distributed to all processors by reversing the previous data movement, as follows. Send the solution from the top-left processor to all processors in the first column, and then in a similar fashion distribute the solution in parallel within each row. So, if processor $P_{i,j}$ starts with value $v_{i,j}$, then the following code shows how to compute the sum of these values:

```
for j:= n^{1/2} downto 2 do
    v_{i,j-1} ← v_{i,j-1} + v_{i,j}
              (simultaneously for all rows i)
    for i:= n^{1/2} downto 2 do
        v_{i-1,1} ← v_{i-1,1} + v_{i,1}
```

Notice that while summing n values on a serial machine takes $O(n)$ time, this mesh algorithm requires only $O(n^{1/2})$ time. While this is asymptotically optimal for the mesh, since the communication diameter of the mesh is $O(n^{1/2})$, other architectures can compute the sum even faster. For example, a hypercube with n processors can compute the sum in $O(\log n)$ time.

Matrix Transpose

Consider computing the transpose of a matrix on a mesh computer. Given an $n \times n$ matrix A stored so that processor $P_{i,j}$ contains element $a_{i,j}$, it is possible to compute the transpose of A in $O(n)$ time, where the transpose of A, denoted A^T, is given by $a_{i,j}^T = a_{j,i}$. The algorithm consists of two complementary phases that are each completed in $O(n)$ time, as follows. Denote diagonal processors $P_{i,i}$, $1 \le i \le n$, as *routers*. For all above-diagonal processors $P_{i,j}$, $I < j$, send the value of $a_{i,j}$ down to diagonal processor $P_{j,j}$ in lockstep fashion. Each value $a_{i,j}$, $i < j$, reaches diagonal processor $P_{j,j}$ in $k = j - i$ steps. As each router $P_{j,j}$ receives an $a_{i,j}$, it sends the data to the left where it will move for $k = j - i$ steps, until it reaches below-diagonal processor $P_{j,i}$. Next, in a similar fashion, all below-diagonal processors $P_{i,j}$, $i > j$, send their data to the right, where diagonal processor $P_{i,i}$ routes the data upwards. Finally, in $O(n)$ time every processor $P_{i,j}$ contains $a_{j,i}$.

Matrix Multiplication

Given two $n \times n$ matrices, A and B, the matrix product $C = AB$ is given by $c_{i,j} = \sum_{k=1}^{n} a_{i,k} b_{k,j}$. The product

can be computed in $O(n)$ time on a mesh with $4n^2$ processors; the complete algorithm for doing so is contained in the full Encyclopedia.

Bibliography

1992. Leighton, F. T. *Introduction to Parallel Algorithms and Architectures: Arrays, Trees, Hypercubes*. San Francisco: Morgan Kaufmann.

1996. Miller, R., and Stout, Q. F. *Parallel Algorithms for Regular Architectures*. Cambridge, MA: MIT Press.

1997. Akl, S. G. *Parallel Computation: Models and Methods*. Upper Saddle River, NJ: Prentice Hall.

Russ Miller

LANGUAGES

Parallel programming languages can be categorized according to whether the parallelism inherent in a program must be specified explicitly by the programmer or may be left implicit. Languages in which potential parallelism is implicit include common imperative programming languages such as Fortran (*q.v.*) and C (*q.v.*), functional programming (*q.v.*) languages such as Haskell and VAL, and logic programming (*q.v.*) languages such as Prolog. In order for a program written in such a language to take advantage of the power of parallel hardware, a *parallelizing compiler* must determine which operations may be executed in parallel.

Languages with Explicit Parallelism

By citing parallel operations explicitly, the programmer makes it easier for the compiler to generate code suitable for execution on parallel computers. The simplest kind of parallelism to introduce into a programming language is *data parallelism*. Data parallelism is the simultaneous application of a single operation across an entire data set. Data-parallel extensions to Fortran, C, Modula-2, and other languages have been proposed. For example, Fortran 90 supports data parallelism by allowing operations to be performed on arrays as well as scalar values. Thus, the statement A = B + C may express either scalar addition if B and C are real numbers or integers, or array addition if B and C are arrays. *High*

Performance Fortran (HPF) is an extension of Fortran 90 that supports additional parallel constructs and directives designed to make it easier for compilers to translate HPF programs into efficient code for parallel computers.

Despite the advances being made in compiler technology for data-parallel languages such as Fortran 90 and HPF, the best performance is still achieved by writing parallel programs using a low-level approach based on message passing. This approach is called *SPMD* (*single program, multiple data*). The programmer writes a single program in a language such as Fortran or C. A set of processes executes the program concurrently. Each process manipulates a subset of the data structures. The processes may be mapped to processors of a single parallel computer, or they may be distributed across a network. Processes coordinate their actions and communicate with each other through calls to a message-passing library.

In 1993, a group of parallel-computer vendors, researchers, and applications developers met to develop a standard portable message-passing library definition called *MPI* (*Message-Passing Interface*). The MPI specification describes a library of 129 functions that can be called from C and Fortran programs. These functions initiate and terminate MPI computations, allow processes to determine the total number of parallel processes and their unique identifier number, enable processes to send and receive messages, and support collective communication operations.

Another communication-oriented system is based on the *Bulk Synchronous Parallel* (BSP) model, proposed by Leslie Valiant. Central to BSP programming is the idea of a superstep. A step is a basic operation performed by a process on its local data. A *superstep* is a sequence of steps followed by a *barrier synchronization* among the processes at which point nonlocal data accesses take effect. When a process reaches a barrier, it waits until all processes have also reached that point. Because requests for nonlocal data may be made at any point during a superstep but are not guaranteed to be completed until the end of the superstep, the compiler and run-time system may perform various optimizations, such as combining communications or overlapping communications with computations.

Bibliography

1996. Wolfe, M. J. *High Performance Compilers for Parallel Computing*. Reading, MA: Addison-Wesley.

1999. Gropp W., Lusk, E., and Skjellum, A. *Using MPI: Portable Parallel Programming with the Message-Passing Interface*, 2nd Ed. Cambridge, MA: MIT Press.

Michael J. Quinn

PARAMETER PASSING

For articles on related subjects, *see*

+ Calling Sequence
+ Expression
+ Side Effect
+ Subprogram

When a subprogram is called, information may be passed to it by means of a *parameter*, or *argument*. The placeholder for this information in the subprogram's header is called the *formal parameter*; the information that is actually passed on a given invocation is called the *actual parameter*. This article is concerned with the means by which the actual parameters supplied to a procedure or function are transferred to the formal parameters. The three basic techniques are *call by value, call by reference*, and *call by name*.

Call by Value

In *call by value*, the actual parameter is evaluated at the time of the subprogram call and its value is copied into the formal parameter. The actual parameter is evaluated whether or not the formal parameter is ever used inside the subprogram. For this reason, *call by value* is sometimes called *eager evaluation*. Since the formal parameter receives a copy of the actual parameter, modifications to the formal parameter have no effect on the actual one. *Call by value* is illustrated using Pascal syntax in Fig. 1a.

(a) Call by value (Pascal). X holds the *value* of Y * Z and operations on X cannot affect Y or Z.

Calling program   Procedure

    P(Y*Z)   **procedure** P(X: integer);

    Y 2   Z 3   X 6

(b) Call by reference (Pascal). Since W and X hold the *locations* of Y and Z, whatever P does to the variables W and X is stored in Y and Z.

Calling program   Procedure

    P(Y,Z)   **procedure** P(var W,X: integer);

    Y 2   Z 3   W   X

(c) Call by name (Algol). Within P, X will hold the value of Y * Z, which is evaluated whenever the value of X is needed.

Calling program   Procedure

    P(Y*Z)   **procedure** P(X: integer);

    Y 2   Z 3   X

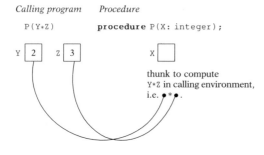

                          thunk to compute
                          Y*Z in calling environment,
                          i.e. •*•.

Figure 1.   Passing arguments to procedures.

Call by Reference

In *call by reference*, the calling routine does not provide the value of the actual parameter to the subprogram but instead provides the address of the memory location at which that value can be found. From the programmer's standpoint, the subroutine and the routine that invokes it share memory (Fig. 1b).

When an actual parameter is an expression rather than a variable name, like Y*Z in Fig. 1a, there is no automatically corresponding address in the calling program. Therefore, if Y*Z were passed by reference, the calling routine would have to create a location for the value of Y*Z, evaluate Y*Z, put it in this location, and then transfer the address of this location to the subprogram, having essentially the same effect as passing by value. Some languages, such as Fortran (*q.v.*), do exactly this; most others, such as Pascal

(*q.v.*), do not allow expressions to be passed by reference.

The difference between call by reference and call by value is important in two ways:

1. In *call by value*, modification of a formal parameter cannot and does not affect the value of the corresponding actual parameter. But in call by reference, the formal and actual parameters share memory, so any modification of a formal parameter modifies the actual parameter as well (a possibly harmful *side effect* of invoking the relevant subprogram). This means that in *call by value*, information can be passed only *into* the subprogram, while in *call by reference* information can be passed both into the subprogram and back to the calling routine. For this reason, value parameters are sometimes called *input parameters* and reference parameters are sometimes called *output parameters* or *input-output parameters*.

2. In *call by value*, a copy of the entire actual parameter is passed to the subprogram, while in *call by reference* only an address is passed. This means that when a large data structure (*q.v.*) is passed, significant space savings can be realized using *call by reference* instead of *call by value*.

An alternative to *call by reference* is *call by value/result*, in which the value of the actual parameter is copied into the formal parameter as for *call by value*, but when the subprogram terminates the value of the formal parameter is copied back into the actual one. This provides an input–output parameter without having the formal and actual parameters share memory as in *call by reference*.

Call by Name

In *call by name*, the entire actual parameter expression is passed to the subprogram (so that a better name would have been *call by expression*). What is passed is not the symbolic string that defines the expression, but a machine language subprogram created by the compiler, sometimes called a *closure or thunk*. The use of the latter term is due to Peter Ingerman (1961) and refers to the fact that in such a closure, the environment in which an expression is to be evaluated has already been "thought out" by the compiler, hence "thunk." In addition to the code to be evaluated, the closure contains the referencing environment for variables in that code, since it may be different from the referencing environment (i.e. the association of names with objects) in the called subprogram. This is illustrated in Fig. 1c using Algol syntax.

Call by name was used in Algol (*q.v.*), but has not been common. It is a form of *late binding* (*see* BINDING), which offers flexibility but can be difficult to use. Some functional programming (*q.v.*) languages use call *by need*, or *lazy evaluation* (in contrast to *eager evaluation*), a variation on *call by name* in which the expression that is passed is evaluated exactly once, the first time its value is demanded in the subprogram.

Parameter Passing in Common Languages

Call by value is the most widely used parameter-passing mechanism, but many languages offer alternatives. In Fortran, all parameters are passed by reference. In Pascal and C++, the programmer may choose between *call by value* and *call by reference*. In C, all parameters are passed by value, but the programmer can explicitly pass the address of any variable, so the effect of *call by reference* can be achieved as well. In Algol, all parameters are passed by name unless *call by value* is specified. Functional programming languages are either *lazy* or *nonstrict* languages, such as Haskell, which use *call by need*, and *strict* languages, such as Scheme (a dialect of Lisp—*q.v.*), which use *call by value*.

Bibliography

1961. Ingerman, P. Z. "Thunks," *Communications of the ACM*, **4**, 1.

1964. Randell, B., and Russell, L. J. *Algol 60 Implementation*. New York: Academic Press.

1997. Stroustrup, B. *The C++ Programming Language*, 3rd Ed. Reading, MA: Addison-Wesley.

1999. Thompson, S. *Haskell: The Craft of Functional Programming*, 2nd Ed. Reading, MA: Addison-Wesley.

Adrienne Bloss and J. A. N. Lee

PARITY

For articles on related subjects, *see*

+ Codes
+ Error Correcting and Detecting Code
+ Universal Product Code

A bit sequence has even *parity* if it contains an even number of 1 bits; otherwise it has odd parity. The parity of a set of bits, such as data recorded on a disk or transferred over a network, may be used for a simple form of error detection. A *parity bit* is a check bit whose value (0 or 1) depends upon whether the sum of bits with value 1 in the unit of data being checked is to be odd or even. Checking methods may use either even or odd parity. An error caused by the detection of incorrect parity is called a *parity error*. The unit of data to which a parity check is applied may be a character, a byte, a word, and so on, the character parity check being most common. Since two or any even number of errors in the unit of data cannot be detected by a single parity bit, the smaller the unit of data to which the check is applied, the higher the probability that multiple errors will not occur.

Jiri Necas

PASCAL

For articles on related subjects, *see*

+ Control Structures
+ Data Structures
+ Data Type
+ Procedure-Oriented Languages
+ Programming Languages
+ Structured Programming

Pascal was developed by Niklaus Wirth (1971) in the late 1960s following some earlier work by Wirth and

Hoare to improve upon Algol (*q.v.*) in the area of data types. While Pascal was designed in part to serve as a language for teaching computer programming as a systematic discipline, Wirth also showed that a reliable and efficient implementation of a large procedure-oriented language was possible on real computers then available. Pascal was the first widely adopted programming language to embrace the principles of structured programming.

One of the distinguishing characteristics of Pascal is the small size of its definition, both syntactic and semantic. Wirth achieved this by carefully choosing a set of orthogonal control structures (statements) and data structures (declarations-*q.v.*). Every structured type in Pascal has a corresponding control structure;

array;	**for-do**
record;	**if-then-else**
set;	**case-of**
file;	**while-do**
pointer;	(recursive procedures)

Pascal was designed to be compiled efficiently in a single pass through the source code (*see* COMPILER). This property made its compilers relatively small and fast, a practical advantage for their use in teaching. It also contributed to some aspects of the design of the language. For example, every procedure or function had to be declared before it was used, with the main program body at the end of the program. Such declare before-use also helps with error-checking.

Pascal supports both data and procedural abstraction, which allows the definition of data structures and program statements to model their corresponding physical entities closely. By holding the concept of "type" paramount, Pascal compilers are able to detect many errors at compile time by checking assignment statements and procedure parameter lists for mixed types and out-of-range operations. The sample program in Fig. 1 is adapted from Wirth (1973).

The spread of Pascal was greatly accelerated in the 1970s by Wirth's research group. They wrote and distributed a portable "Pascal-P" compiler that

```
program GeneratePrimes(Output);
  const n = 25;                              {number of primes to compute}
  type Index = 1..n;                         {scalar data type is subrange of Integer}
  var x: integer;
      i, k, limit: Index;                    {variables i, k, limit are of type Index}
      Prime: boolean;                        {prime is either True or False}
      p: array[Index] of integer;            {p[i] is ith prime}
begin
  p[1] := 2;                                 {first prime}
  writeln(2);                                {output this prime on one line}
  x := 1; limit := 1;                        {initialize method}
  for i := 2 to n do                         {compute next n − 1 prime numbers}
    begin
    repeat
      x := x + 2;                            {only odd numbers need to be considered}
      if sqr(p[limit]) <= x then limit := limit + 1;
                                             {to determine greatest prime needed as a divisor}
      k := 2; Prime := True;
      while Prime and (k < limit) do
          begin
          Prime := (x div p[k]) * p[k] <> x;
                                             {div results in integer part of quotient}
          k := k + 1
          end
    until Prime;                             {if Prime is True, no prime divisor of x exists}
    p[i] := x;
    writeln(x)                               {output the prime}
    end                                      {of for loop}
end.                                         {GeneratePrimes}
```

Figure 1. A Pascal program to print prime numbers.

produced an intermediate language (*q.v.*) called P-code for a hypothetical stack computer and could be used to bootstrap (*q.v.*) itself on a real computer with a modest programming effort. Several languages can trace their origins to Pascal, including Concurrent Pascal, Modula-2, Object-Pascal, Ada, and Oberon. Following an evolution from structured, to modular, to extensible programming, Wirth designed Modula-2 and Oberon as Pascal successors for machine-independent systems programming (*q.v.*). Modula-2 (late 1970s) extended Pascal to support the modularity concepts of information hiding (*q.v.*) and separate compilation while maintaining type consistency checks (*see* MODULAR PROGRAMMING). Oberon (late 1980s) is a small, powerful language that adds support for *object-oriented programming* (*q.v.*) to a minimal Pascal-like core.

Bibliography

1971. Wirth, N. "The Programming Language Pascal," *Acta Informatica*, **1**(1), 35–63.

1973. Wirth, N. *Systematic Programming: An Introduction*. Upper Saddle River, NJ: Prentice Hall.

1996. Wirth, N. "Recollections About the Development of Pascal" and Mickel, A. "Pascal Users Group and the Rise of Pascal," in *History of Programming Languages—II* (eds. T. J. Bergin Jr., and R. G. Gibson Jr.), 97–120. Reading, MA: Addison-Wesley.

Andrew B. Mickel

PASCAL, BLAISE

For articles on related subjects, *see*

+ Calculating Machines
+ Digital Computers, History of: Origins
+ Leibniz, Gottfried Wilhelm

Blaise Pascal (b. Clermont, France, 1623; d. Paris, 1662) (*see* Fig. 1) discovered a proof of Euclid's Proposition

Figure 1. Blaise Pascal. (Courtesy of the Mary Evans Picture Library.)

32 at age 12, and four years later he proved a now-famous theorem in projective geometry. In 1640, the 17-year-old began to develop a calculating machine to help in his father's tax work in Rouen. He completed the first operating model in 1642 and built 50 more during the next ten years. The machine, called Pascaline, was a small box with eight dials, each geared to a drum that displayed the digits in a register window. Pascal's fundamental innovation was a ratchet linkage (*sautier*) between the rotating drums, which transferred rotating motion from one drum to the next higher-position drum only during carryover. This kept the digit of each drum aligned with its display window. The machine added and subtracted directly, and multiplied and divided by using repeated addition and subtraction.

Pascal moved to Paris in 1647, where he associated with Roberval, met Descartes, published treatises on the vacuum and on conics, and prepared the Puy-de-Dômes (barometer) experiment. In 1654, he produced two papers establishing the foundations of the integral calculus and of probability theory. In 1658, using the pseudonym Amos Dettonville, he challenged mathematicians to a mathematical contest and created a controversy by awarding himself the prize. No further significant research followed.

Bibliography

1995. Adamson, D. *Blaise Pascal: Mathematician, Physicist, and Thinker About God.* New York: St Martin's Press.

Charles V. Jones

PASSWORD

For articles on related subjects, *see*

+ Authentication
+ Computer Crime
+ Cryptography, Computers in
+ Data Security
+ Hacker
+ Pretty Good Privacy (PGP)
+ Privacy, Computers and

Multiuser computer systems generally have an account for each user, which gives the user access to his or her own files and to public files and programs. An account is protected by a *password*, a word or phrase that must be supplied in order to authenticate a user and permit access to information. Password-protected accounts typically reside on time-shared computers such as those run by an Internet Service Provider (ISP) or by an employer, on workstations (*q.v.*) with a networked *file server* (*q.v.*), or even on a single-user computer that may be used by several people. Specific services such as email (*q.v.*) may also require password authentication to gain access to their data.

Since the purpose of requiring a password is to protect against unauthorized access, it would be most unwise to store actual passwords in the same memory as holds user files. In fact, the best practice is that passwords are not only encrypted, but that the encryption is done in such a way that even a system operator with access to all information in the computer cannot recover the original password. Commonly, the user's password is used as a key to encrypt a known common character string through an algorithm similar to that of the Data Encryption Standard (DES—*see* CRYPTOGRAPHY, COMPUTERS IN). Once encrypted, the original password is discarded. When a user logs on and enters the password, the same encryption is performed and the result is compared to the stored string. Since the password itself cannot be recovered from the encrypted form with such a system, the user who forgets a password must endure the nuisance of having to ask for a new one, but the dividend is a much more secure system.

Of course, there are always malicious hackers ("crackers") who try to break into computing systems, and the more allegedly secure the system, the greater the challenge. Some hackers automate password guessing, using their own local computer to test, one by one, words from a dictionary as possible passwords. Because of this, users are advised not to use short passwords, not to use names or phrases connected to themselves, and not to use a dictionary word, whether forward or reversed.

Bibliography

1994. Cheswick, W. R., and Bellovin, S. M. *Firewalls and Internet Security: Repelling the Wily Hacker.* Reading, MA: Addison-Wesley.
1995. Cohen, F. B. *Protection and Security on the Information Superhighway.* New York: John Wiley.
1995. Kaufman, C., Perlman, R., and Speciner, M. *Network Security: Private Communication in a Public World.* Upper Saddle River, NJ: Prentice Hall.
1996. Schneier, B. *Applied Cryptography: Protocols, Algorithms, and Source Code in C*, 2nd Ed. New York: John Wiley.

Edwin D. Reilly

PATTERN RECOGNITION

For articles on related subjects, *see*

+ Artificial Intelligence (AI)
+ Computer Vision
+ Data Mining
+ Image Processing
+ Optical Character Recognition (OCR)

As an area of computer science, *pattern recognition* is the study of concepts, algorithms, and implementations that provide artificial systems with a perceptual capability to categorize abstract objects, or *patterns*, in a simple and reliable way. As a human experience, pattern recognition refers to a perceptual process in which patterns in any sensory modality (vision, hearing, touch, taste, or smell) or patterns in conceptual or logical thought processes are analyzed and recognized as being familiar either in the sense of having been previously experienced or of being similar to a previous experience.

The major applications of pattern recognition fall into three categories: (1) patterns in images (spatial patterns); (2) patterns in time (temporal patterns); and (3) patterns in more abstract data environments. The most important image processing applications are optical character recognition (OCR) for systems ranging from bank check processing to reading machines for the blind, industrial robot vision, and unmanned planetary exploration systems; biomedical analyses, such as automated cytology and computerized tomography; and remote sensing applied to earth resources, meteorology, and military applications. Signal processing applications include speech recognition (*q.v.*), radar and sonar signal analysis, seismological monitoring, and medical waveform analysis, as in electrocardiography (EKG) and electroencephalography (EEG).

Terminology

The process of a general pattern recognition system is shown in Fig. 1. In observing a pattern, *measurements* of an object are made that directly or indirectly reflect attributes of the object that distinguish it from other objects. *Features* are functions of the measurements intended to recover the defining attributes. The extracted features are used by a *classification procedure* to give a class assignment to the object.

As an example, let us consider the recognition of hand-printed characters on a page. The measurement process consists of optically scanning a region of the paper where the character (i.e. pattern) is written so as to represent the pattern as a two-dimensional array whose values represent shades of gray from white to black. A second stage of the measurement process is concerned with enhancing the data prior to analysis and includes operations such as smoothing to reduce noise (irrelevant variations), sharpening to enhance edges, segmentation of the image into separate characters, and transformations to allow for variations in size, position, and orientation of the characters to be recognized.

The feature extraction stage searches for features in the input—*global* features such as the number of holes in the character, the number of concavities in its outer contour, the relative protrusion of character extremities, or *local* features such as the relative positions of line-endings, line crossovers, and corners. The final classification stage identifies each character by considering the detected features. In practice, it is difficult to choose a set of features that reliably distinguishes handwritten characters (e.g. *see* Fig. 2, in which the letters H and A are represented almost

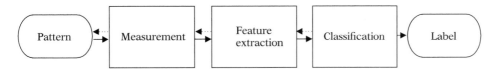

Figure 1.   Stages in a pattern recognition system.

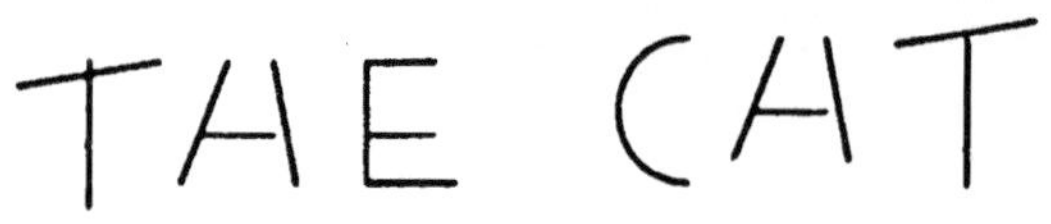

THE CAT

Figure 2. Identical patterns in different contexts have different meanings; most people read the same patterns as "H" in the first word and "A" in the second.

identically). Thus, the later phases may need to reinvoke earlier phases to reexamine contextual evidence to help with interpretation. The *top–down* flow of control information necessary to use *context* (as opposed to the *bottom-up* flow of pattern information) is represented by the dotted left arrows of Fig. 1.

Class Definitions

A *class* is a group or set of patterns that are similar or equivalent in some sense. Class definitions are based on the intuitive notion that members of a class share some common attributes. To represent a class, either a prototype or a set of samples must be known. A philosophical distinction may be made between *canonical*, or natural, pattern classes, such as animal species and diseases, and *conventional*, or symbolic, pattern classes, such as letters and musical notes. The feature selection process attempts to recover the pattern attributes characteristic of each class. For canonical classes, appropriate features may be inferred from an understanding of the natural phenomenon. For conventional classes, the features may be specified by the class definition, although, as in the case of hand-printed characters, they may not be explicit.

Approaches to Pattern Classification

Ultimately, the process of pattern recognition consists of assigning a pattern to a class. The assignment is made by a classification algorithm (or *classifier*), based on the features extracted and the relationships among the features. Since members of a class are equivalent or similar inasmuch as they share defining attributes, the measurement of similarity, either explicitly or implicitly, is central to any classifier. Depending on the features extracted—which, in turn, depend on

the data environment, variability within classes, and defined attributes—classifiers are derived by using either statistical or structural approaches.

Statistical Pattern Recognition

In statistical pattern recognition, a pattern that is represented by a set of m measurements is thought of as a point p in an m-dimensional measurement space. Feature extraction is expressed as a transformation that maps p into a point x in an n-dimensional feature space; it may be viewed pragmatically as a process that reduces pattern space dimensionally and consequently simplifies the classification task. The classifier then assigns x to a class by means of a decision function $d(x)$, which in effect is a method of partitioning the feature space into territories corresponding to different classes. The performance of the classifier is measured by an objective function, which is usually the probability of error (misclassification). The techniques for handling such problems may be grouped into three categories: feature extraction methods, classification methods, and clustering methods.

Feature Extraction

On a conceptual level, feature extraction is concerned with recovering the defining attributes obscured by imperfect measurements. Ideally, the feature extraction transformation would be derived according to a misclassification criterion, but in most practical situations this approach is not possible. Consequently, feature extraction schemes generally attempt to choose features that minimize within-class variability; that is, find a feature space in which the samples within each class are as close together as possible while insuring that the different class sets are well separated. Other feature selection criteria include measures of correlation between features (different features should be uncorrelated, to minimize redundancy in the representation object) and information theoretic measures relating features to classes.

Classification

On the basis of their implementations, statistical pattern classifiers may be distinguished as being *probabilistic, geometric, discriminant-based,* or *conceptual.* Other elaborations also exist. The first uses *context* in making decisions. A second is based on *sequential decision theory,* which applies to a situation in which successive features are measured only as necessary to achieve a desired expected probability of error. Finally, the theory of *fuzzy logic* (*q.v.*) has been applied when a nonexclusive assignment of patterns to classes is desired. If the classes do not have precisely defined membership criteria (e.g. tall people, beautiful women, numbers much greater than one), the concept of a membership function with value between 0 and 1 is useful. A fuzzy classifier then provides the degree of membership of a pattern to each of the classes.

Probabilistic classifiers are based on the principle that a pattern should be assigned to the class that is most probable, given the observed features; that is, a point x of feature space is assigned to the class that maximizes the *a posteriori* probability $P(C_i|\mathbf{x})$ over the set of classes $\{C_i\}$. From the Bayesian theory of conditional probabilities, this is mathematically equivalent to assigning $\mathbf{x}$ to the class C_i that maximizes $p(\mathbf{x}|C_i) * P(C_i)$, where $p(\mathbf{x}|C_i)$ is called the *class-conditional probability density function* (it gives the probability that the pattern has value x, given that it is in the class C_i) and $P(C_i)$ is the probability of class C_i before the pattern is observed (the *a priori* probability). Labeled samples representative of each class are used to determine the $p(\mathbf{x}|C_i)$ and $P(C_i)$ values necessary to implement such a classifier.

Geometric classifiers are based on matching in which the observed pattern is compared to *templates* (or *prototypes*) that represent each class and are classified according to the best match (or minimum mismatch). The distance between pattern $\mathbf{x}$ and the prototype of class C_i is computed by a *metric function* $d(\mathbf{x}, C_i)$ and $\mathbf{x}$ is assigned to the class that minimizes this function. $d(\mathbf{x}, C_i) = (\mathbf{x} - \mathbf{m}_i)^{\mathsf{T}} S_i^{-1} (\mathbf{x} - \mathbf{m}_i)$, where $\mathbf{m}_i$ and S_i are the mean and covariance matrix of class C_i. A metric that is useful for patterns having binary valued features is the *Hamming distance*—the number of features in which the observed pattern differs from the prototype of class C_i. A character-recognition example using three

Templates

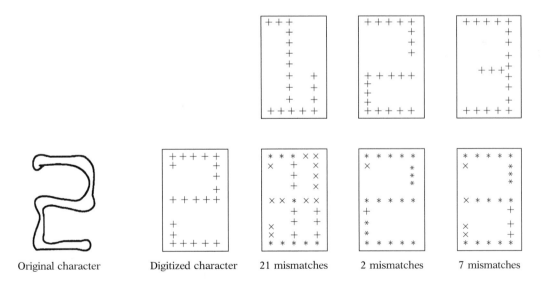

Original character   Digitized character   21 mismatches   2 mismatches   7 mismatches

Figure 3. Template matching using the Hamming distance. All points of the digitized character (i.e. features) are compared with corresponding points in each template. If the two are not the same (i.e. both 0 or both 1), a mismatch, or distance 1, is counted. Here, the second template is selected as a result of minimum (x: mismatch; *: match).

prototypes and the Hamming distance measure is shown in Fig. 3.

Discriminant function classifiers associate a function $f_i(\mathbf{x})$ with class C_i and assign $\mathbf{x}$ to the class that has the maximum discriminant function value. In the case where the classes are *linearly separable* (i.e. there is a linear decision function that is greater than zero for all samples in one class and less than zero for all samples in the other class) in the chosen feature space, an iterative algorithm known as the *perceptron* finitely converges to discriminant functions that correctly classify all given samples. For linearly nonseparable classes, various criterion functions can be used in gradient descent procedures to obtain discriminant functions. As with geometric classifiers, some of the discriminant function classifiers are equivalent to probabilistic classifiers.

Conceptual processing With reference to character recognition, contextual processing techniques use knowledge at the word level to correct errors in character recognition. These methods use information about other characters that have been recognized in a word, as well as knowledge about the text in which the word occurs. Typically, the knowledge about the text takes the form of a dictionary (a list of words that occur in the text). For example, character recognition may not be able to distinguish reliably between a *u* and *v* in the second position of *qXote*. A contextual postprocessing technique would determine that *u* is correct, since it is very unlikely that *qvote* would be in an English language dictionary.

Clustering

Simple clustering algorithms establish clusters on the basis of the similarity of (distance between) individual samples, while more complex schemes employ formal criteria, such as measures of *within* and *between* cluster scatter (variability) in iterative optimization algorithms. In the first category are the hierarchical clustering algorithms, such as the *nearest neighbor algorithm*, in which clusters are merged (or split) in a hierarchical fashion according to the proximity of the nearest neighbors, and graph-theoretic algorithms that relate clusters with connected subgraphs, patterns with nodes, and similarities (distances) with edges.

Structural Pattern Recognition

Interpreting a list of characteristic attributes of a pattern as the coordinates of a point in feature space reduces the classification problem to one of partitioning the feature space. In problems such as computer vision, the patterns are quite complex and the number of features required is often very large. Thus, the idea of using the structural information that describes each pattern to simplify its representation is attractive. The basic idea of the structural approach is to describe complex patterns in terms of a composition of simpler patterns. Another approach is to extract structural features and represent them as a feature vector and use statistically determined discriminant functions. When asked to describe an alphanumeric character, people are most likely to use structural features (Fig. 4). For example, an upper case "A" has two straight lines (strokes) meeting with a sharp point (end point) at the top, and a third line crossing the two at approximately their midpoint (cross points), creating a gap in the upper part (hole). The basis of any structural technique is the representation of the pattern with a set of feature primitives that are able to describe all encountered patterns and to discriminate between them.

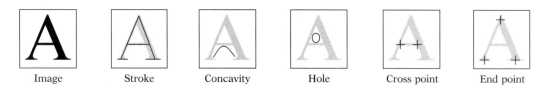

| Image | Stroke | Concavity | Hole | Cross point | End point |

Figure 4. Structural features of stroke, concavity, hole, cross points, and end points can be used as the dimensions of a feature space to classify characters; the locations of these features for "A" are illustrated.

Bibliography

1986. Devijver, P. A., and Kittler, J. *Pattern Recognition Theory and Applications.* Berlin: Springer-Verlag.

1993. Rabiner, L., and Juang, B. -H. *Fundamentals of Speech Recognition.* Upper Saddle River, NJ: Prentice Hall.

1996. Theodoridis, S., and Koutroumbas, K. *Pattern Recognition.* New York: Academic Press.

S. N. Srihari and V. Govindaraju

PDA (PERSONAL DIGITAL ASSISTANT)

See PORTABLE COMPUTERS.

PERSONAL COMPUTING

For articles on related subjects, see

+ Apple
+ Cache Memory
+ Diskette
+ Electronic Mail (Email)
+ Freeware and Shareware
+ Hard Disk
+ IBM PC
+ Internet
+ Microsoft
+ Modem
+ Monitor, Display
+ Motherboard
+ Multimedia
+ Optical Storage
+ Portable Computers
+ Power User
+ Spelling Checker
+ User Interface
+ Window Environments
+ Word Processing
+ Workstation
+ World Wide Web

Introduction

Personal computing, simply enough, is computing done on a personal computer. And a *personal computer* (PC) is, in turn, a digital computer sufficiently inexpensive that it can be purchased and used as a home appliance. Prior to the late 1970s, even the least expensive small computers—minicomputers—cost at least a few tens of thousands of dollars, well beyond affordable levels to almost all individuals. The PC has been in existence only since 1974 and did not gain widespread popularity until the 1980s. Yet in this very short time span, it has radically changed the way society does business, learns, plays, and gathers information.

History

In Albuquerque, New Mexico, in 1974, a small manufacturer named MITS developed a kit to build a microcomputer. Named the *Altair* by reviewer Leslie Solomon, the system was built around an Intel 8080 microprocessor. When Solomon's story about the kit appeared as a cover feature in the January 1975 issue of *Popular Electronics* magazine, MITS was deluged with orders and the age of personal computing began.

Soon other companies began offering add-on parts or peripherals for the Altair, and teenagers Bill Gates and Paul Allen founded Microsoft to develop a Basic *interpreter*, a program to allow programmers to use that language on the Altair. Other firms began to develop commercial software for the computer, and competitive manufacturers began to appear. One of the earliest, Processor Technology, marketed the Sol, designed by industry pioneer Lee Felsenstein and named after Leslie Solomon. Computer retail stores arose to market the new computers and in September 1975, *Byte* magazine became the first of the half dozen periodicals that would spring up within a year to address the new market.

Early PCs, however, had little overall impact on society. The majority were built from kits and attracted only a group of hobbyists and electronics tinkerers. These early users formed computer clubs where people could gather and exchange information about these novel machines. Shortly thereafter, two existing companies, Commodore and Radio Shack, entered the marketplace with their Pet and TRS-80 systems (*see*

Figure 1. A Radio Shack TRS-80 Microcomputer system.

Fig. 1). These systems differed from those that had come before in that they were preassembled and were intended to attract not just hobbyists, but also people who saw the new device as a tool to do things, rather than as an end in itself.

While the Pet and TRS-80 made PCs available to the nonhobbyist, it was the rise of Apple Computer and the development of a software product called VisiCalc that fostered the proliferation of PCs throughout corporate America. Apple Computer had its genesis at the California Homebrew Computer Club, where Steve Wozniak, a young Hewlett-Packard engineer, frequently brought in computers that he had designed. Another member, Steve Jobs, persuaded Wozniak to leave Hewlett-Packard and join with him in founding Apple Computer, Inc. Although the company began operations in Jobs's garage and living room, where the moderately successful Apple I was created and marketed, the firm grew rapidly when Jobs was able to entice retired millionaire A. C. "Mike" Markkula to join the firm as a partner. Markkula was able to bring establishment venture capital into the firm to provide the funding necessary for Apple's development. Apple's second venture, the Apple II, built around the Mostek 6502 processor and the floppy disk drive was extremely successful.

As the Apple II was gaining in popularity, a graduate student at the Harvard School of Business, Daniel Bricklin, was groping with the case-method system used in business school that required students to redo continually large financial workpapers or *spreadsheets* (*q.v.*) to show the effect of such normal business occurrences as interest rate changes, tax increases or decreases, inflation, and so on. The process was extremely tedious and often required recalculating a large number of formulas and totals dependent in some way on the changed variable. Bricklin, a former programmer at Digital Equipment Corporation, reasoned that there must be something that could be done with the new PCs to reduce the effort involved. He and a friend, Bob Frankston, designed what became the first electronic spreadsheet, VisiCalc.

Since each of the existing computers of that time used a different microprocessor, it was necessary for Bricklin and Frankston to decide which of the existing microcomputers to choose as a host for VisiCalc. They chose the Apple II and completed the product for that system. Upon product completion, they took out a small ad in *Byte* magazine and began to sell the product through a software publisher, Personal Software.

With the subsequent success of VisiCalc, entrepreneurs tended to choose the Apple II as their platform. One, Mitchell Kapor, a graduate school student at Yale, produced a graphics and statistics program, Tiny Troll, which he sold from his home for $100. Another, John Draper, developed a word processing program called EasyWriter. A third, Dennis Hayes, developed a microprocessor, the Hayes Micromodem II, which allowed the Apple II to communicate over telephone lines and obtain information from the many large databases such as Dow Jones, CompuServe, the Source, and Dialog. Each of these products generated additional sales for the Apple II.

IBM had remained on the sidelines for most of the early PC development. Its desktop offerings, the 5100 series, had been overly expensive for most and had fallen far short of the Apple II in user-friendliness. In an effort to develop a system that could properly compete in this marketplace, IBM set up a business component under the direction of Philip D. "Don" Estridge in Boca Raton, FL, and gave it the charter to do whatever was necessary to enter the market successfully. When the IBM PC was introduced in August 1981, there were versions of VisiCalc, EasyWriter, the PeachTree Accounting System, and Microsoft Adventure ready to run on the brand new equipment. As its operating system, IBM chose MS-DOS, a system adapted by Microsoft from a product developed by a small West Coast firm. They called their version PC-DOS. From the moment of its introduction, the IBM PC was dramatically successful. Data processing managers, weary of confrontations with accountants, analysts, engineers, portfolio managers, and so on, who wanted to buy and use strange sounding computers named Apple and Pet, could now recommend a firm that they knew well and that had decades of experience in data processing.

VisiCalc actually ran faster and used less memory on the Apple II than on the newer system. The Apple technical advantage, however, lasted only until the development of the rival spreadsheet program Lotus 1-2-3 by Mitch Kapor. Lotus 1-2-3 soon became the VisiCalc of the IBM PC, causing sales of the new system to skyrocket. The success of the system caused other manufacturers to come into the marketplace with compatible computers that ran like the IBM PC. While the Apple II contained proprietary hardware that was illegal to copy, the IBM, based on *open architecture* (*q.v.*), did not, and other firms brought compatible machines to market. Initially, the most successful of these, Compaq Computer Corporation, started with a portable system, a 22-lb computer with a handle and built-in monitor and disk drives. Computers that competed with IBM on the basis of power or features were called *compatibles*, while products whose prime attraction was low price were called *clones*. Soon, the description of these machines evolved from "IBM-compatible" to simply "MS-DOS machine," that is, a system that ran under the Microsoft MS-DOS operating system.

While the majority of IBM's competitors in the PC market, such as Tandy, Zenith, Hewlett-Packard, Digital, Data General, Texas Instruments, and AT&T, eventually marketed MS-DOS systems, Apple Computer chose to go in its own direction and building on technology originally pioneered by Xerox with its Star microcomputer, developed a system, the Lisa, which made use of an operating environment in which all programs worked in generally the same

fashion and which used a pointing device called a mouse (*q.v.*) to perform routine activities. Although the Lisa failed commercially, its graphical user interface (GUI) became the basis of Apple's highly successful Macintosh computer and following that success, of Microsoft's Windows operating environment. The Commodore Amiga also used a GUI and earned a modest share of the PC market into the early 1990s, based on the offering of features similar to the Macintosh at a much lower price. Both the Macintosh and the Amiga used the Motorola 68000 processor.

The increased penetration of the Macintosh into businesses and the expanded exposure of the graphical user interface gave impetus to Microsoft's Windows environment, which provided for MS-DOS machines many of the same features as the Macintosh. It also resulted in the development of GUIs for the Unix (*q.v.*) operating system, one that had been developed in a highly technical environment at Bell Laboratories and had not originally been considered an operating system for nontechnical users.

While the software and operating systems were developing, PC hardware itself was growing rapidly in speed and capacity. The Intel 8088 processor on which the IBM PC and other compatible systems were based has had many compatible descendants: the 8086, the 80286, the 80386, the 80486, and several increasingly powerful versions of the 80586 (Pentium) with each chip having greater speed and the ability to address more memory than its predecessor (*see* MICROCOMPUTER CHIP). As of 2003, Pentium-based machines were capable of 3 GHz, about 1400 times faster than the 8088. IBM PC compatibles that use an Intel or Intel-compatible 80×86 chip and the Microsoft Windows operating system are called "Wintel" machines. In addition to IBM, Wintel machines are marketed by Compaq (now absorbed by Hewlett-Packard), Dell, Gateway, Micron, and many other firms. An image of a PC made by Compaq is shown in Fig. 2.

On the Macintosh and Amiga side, the original Motorola 68000 processor soon fostered the 68020, 68030, and 68040 processors. The Amiga is no longer marketed, but Apple now markets the popular iMac and other products. The top of Apple's line, the PowerPC, is

Figure 2. The Compaq Deskpro system (courtesy of Compaq).

Figure 3. The Apple G5 computer (courtesy of the Apple Picture Library).

now based on the G5 chip developed for Apple by IBM and Motorola (*see* Fig. 3). The G5, a dual-processor pipeline (*q.v.*) machine, has a 64-bit data path rather than the 16-bit (early) or 32-bit (most recently) data paths used with IBM PC compatibles, and is capable of a sustained speed of several gigaflops (billions of floating-point operations per second), once considered supercomputer speed.

Bibliography

1999. Rittner, D., and Kawasaki, G. *The iMac Book*, Scottsdale, AZ: The Coriolis Group.

2000. Freiberger, P., and Swaine, M. *Fire in the Valley: The Making of the Personal Computer*, 2nd Ed. New York: McGraw-Hill.

Barbara E. and John F. McMullen

PERSONAL DIGITAL ASSISTANT (PDA)

See PORTABLE COMPUTERS.

PERVASIVE COMPUTING

See EMBEDDED SYSTEM.

PICTURE PROCESSING

See IMAGE PROCESSING.

PIPELINE

For articles on related topics, *see*

+ Central Processing Unit (CPU)
+ Computer Architecture
+ Instruction Decoding

+ Instruction-Level Parallelism
+ Parallel Processing
+ Supercomputers

Pipelines have been used for many years by designers of high-performance computers in order to improve the performance of their machines. Similar to assembly lines in manufacturing, pipelines partition the processing of an instruction into a set of steps. The pipeline then allows multiple instructions to be at different stages of processing simultaneously.

The performance of a computer is usually measured by the amount of work (or number of instructions) it completes in a fixed amount of time, or alternatively, the amount of time it takes to complete a fixed amount of work. This can be described by the equation:

Time to execute program =

Number of instructions in program

$\times$ Clock cycles needed per instruction (CPI)

$\times$ Time of one clock cycle.

If we assume that the number of instructions is held constant, then improving performance will require a reduction in the second term (the CPI) and/or the third term (the cycle time).

Most computers employ an internal signal called a *clock* that alternates between a high state and a low state. This clock is used to synchronize operations within the computer and between the computer and external devices. The number of times this signal oscillates per second is referred to as the *clock frequency*, and is measured in hertz (Hz). The amount of time between successive high (or low) points is called the *clock cycle time*. Therefore, a clock with a frequency of 500 MHz oscillates 500 million times per second and the time for one oscillation is 2 ns. Since a higher clock speed corresponds to a decrease in the time per cycle, the third term in the equation above will be reduced and execution time will be shortened. Increasing the clock speed is primarily a function of technology and the size of the physical devices used. Higher clock speed has been

a major driving force behind the tremendous increase in computer performance over several decades.

Another approach to improving processor performance is to overlap the execution of multiple instructions, reducing the average number of clock cycles needed per instruction. Increasing the clock rate and overlapping instruction execution are not mutually exclusive—it is entirely possible, and in fact quite common, for a designer to do both. In the realm of computer design, the latter technique is referred to as *instruction-level parallelism*. Pipelining is the oldest and best-understood technique for achieving this.

A typical general-purpose processor must perform a sequence of well-defined steps in order to execute an instruction. First, the instruction must be fetched from its location in memory. Once it has been retrieved, the processor must "decode" the instruction to determine the operation that it specifies, and to identify its operands. Finally, the specified operation is performed (executed). This sequence of steps must be repeated for every instruction that is to be executed, and is commonly called the *Fetch–Decode–Execute* (FDE) cycle.

Performing all of these steps in a single clock cycle will reduce the CPI term to 1, but that requires that the cycle time term be big enough to allow all three steps to complete. The cycle time term can be reduced by making each step take one cycle, but doing this will mean that each instruction will take three cycles to complete (the CPI will go to 3).

Fortunately, as long the operations of each step (also known as a stage) can be kept independent of the subsequent stages, it is possible to have instructions in each stage simultaneously. For example, while one instruction is being fetched from storage, another instruction can be in the decode stage and a third instruction can be in the process of being executed. Such pipelining works as follows:

```
                 Time
Inst    1    2    3    4    5    6    7
 1     IF   ID   EX
 2          IF   ID   EX
 3               IF   ID   EX
 4                    IF   ID   EX
 5                         IF   ID   EX
```

```
IF=Instruction Fetch
ID=Instruction Decode
EX=Instruction Execution
```

A processor pipeline works in much the same way as an actual pipeline. In an oil pipeline, for example, oil is pumped in one end and flows out the other. If the pipeline is empty, then it will take some time before the oil starts appearing at the output, but if the pipeline is full then the oil flows out as fast as it is put in. A given oil molecule will take a fixed amount of time to get from one end of the pipeline to the other, but rate of flow at the output end should be the same as at the input end. As seen above, the first instruction enters the pipeline at time 1, but does not leave until time 3. After this initial delay, the following instructions finish at a rate of one per cycle. So, while each instruction requires three clock cycles to be processed, on average, instructions complete execution at a rate of one per cycle. Pipelining thus produces a factor of three speed-up over processing the instructions in a nonoverlapped fashion.

Most pipelined machines have more stages than those described above. Consider that an instruction operates on data items (operands) and produces a result. The execute stage must perform three steps—fetch the operands, operate on them, and return the result to its destination. The execute stage can thus be divided into three stages: OF, EX, and WB, one for each of these steps (respectively). In this way, the three-stage FDE pipeline is turned into a five-stage pipeline, and the previous diagram is modified to look as follows:

```
                         Time
Inst   1    2    3    4    5    6    7    8    9
  1    IF   ID   OF   EX   WB
  2         IF   ID   OF   EX   WB
  3              IF   ID   OF   EX   WB
  4                   IF   ID   OF   EX   WB
  5                        IF   ID   OF   EX   WB

IF=Instruction Fetch
ID=Instruction Decode
EX=Instruction Execution
OF=Operand Fetch
WB=Write (result) Back
```

Here, there is a longer latency (five cycles) than in the simpler pipeline—however, once the pipeline is full, instructions still finish at a rate of one per cycle.

It might appear that it would be advantageous to continue to divide a pipeline into more and more stages indefinitely, but there are several practical reasons for limiting the number of pipeline stages (the *pipeline depth*) that have to do with how the pipeline is implemented in hardware and the interactions among instructions in the pipeline.

Bibliography

1996. Heuring, V. P., and Jordan, H. F. *Computer Systems Design and Architecture* Reading, MA: Addison-Wesley.

1997. Patterson, D. A., and Hennessy, J. L. *Computer Organization and Design: The Hardware/Software Interface*, 2nd Ed. San Francisco: Morgan Kaufmann.

1999. Omandi, A. *The Microarchitecture of Pipelined and Superscalar Architectures*. Norwell, MA: Kluwer Academic Publishers.

Matthew K. Farrens and Andrew R. Pleszkun

POINTER

For articles on related subjects, *see*

+ Addressing
+ Data Structures
+ List Processing
+ Tree

A digital computer memory contains *cells*, which may be referred to by *addresses*. The address of a memory cell is sometimes called a *pointer*, since it may be thought of as pointing to the memory cell to which it refers. A memory cell that contains the address of another cell is also called a *pointer*. Thus, pointers may occur at the level of machine language both as direct addresses and as indirect addresses. In general, a pointer p_1 may point to a cell containing a pointer p_2, and the pointer p_2 may in turn contain a pointer to a cell containing a pointer p_3. A sequence of pointers $p_1, p_2, p_3, \ldots$ such that p_i points to a cell containing p_{i+1} for $i = 1, 2, \ldots$ is called a *pointer chain*.

Pointers also occur in high-level languages such as C (*q.v.*) and C++ (*q.v.*). In those languages, the declaration `int *p` defines `p` to be of type "pointer to integer." If A is a variable of type integer, then the address of A can be assigned to p by writing `p=&A`. Some languages, such as Pascal (*q.v.*) and Ada (*q.v.*), do not have an "address-of" operator, but assign a value to a pointer variable by a call to an operation that allocates storage for a data structure and puts its address in the pointer variable. If p is a variable that can point to a structure of type *data*, then `p:=new(data)` would place the address of an anonymous variable of type *data* in p.

Dynamic data structures may be implemented as directed graphs in which vertices represent memory cells and directed edges represent pointers between memory cells. For example, the tree structure in Fig. 1 contains five memory cells a, b, c, d, and e, with a pointer from a to b and pointer chains from a through c to d and e.

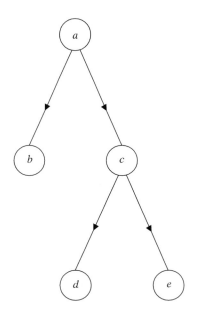

Figure 1. A binary tree formed from five nodes and four pointers.

In general, pointers may be used to connect individual memory cells and also to point from one composite data structure to another.

Pointers are essential in any composite data structure for linking components of the data structure. Nevertheless, they must be used with care because their indiscriminate use leads to undesirable complexity in data structures in much the same way that indiscriminate use of `gotos` leads to control structure (*q.v.*) complexity.

Bibliography

1998. Liberty, J. "A Few Pointers," *C++ Report*, **10**(10), (November–December), 57–62.

Peter Wegner

POLISH NOTATION

For articles on related subjects, see

+ Compiler
+ Expression
+ Language Processors
+ Procedure-Oriented Languages
+ Stack

In the 1920s, the Polish logician Jan Łukasiewicz devised a *parenthesis-free* notation, for use in algebra and other operator–operand systems, which has become known as *Polish notation*. Basically, by consistently placing operators before (or after) their operands, the need for parentheses is eliminated, provided each operator has a fixed number of operands.

Polish notation was originally developed in *prefix* form, in which the operators precede the operands. The *postfix* or *suffix* form, also known as *reverse Polish notation* or *RPN*, which is logically equivalent, has been widely used in computing. Many compilers first transform an arithmetic expression from its ordinary or *infix* form into RPN, so that its evaluation can

Table 1. Polish notation.

Expression	Prefix	Postfix
$a + (-b)$	$+a - b$	$ab-+$
$(-a) + b$	$+-ab$	$a - b+$
$a * (b + c)$	$*a + bc$	$abc+*$
$(a * b) + c$	$+*abc$	$ab * c+$
$(p \Rightarrow q) \equiv (\sim p \vee q)$	$\equiv \Rightarrow pq\vee \sim pq$	$pq \Rightarrow p \sim qv \equiv$

be done in a single left-to-right scan. RPN is also used as the basis of operation for some pocket calculators, such as those produced by Hewlett-Packard.

Parenthesis elimination is made possible by the fixed number of operands for each operator. Thus if + denotes ordinary addition, we expect two operands. Hence +ab (prefix) and ab+ (postfix) are as clearly understandable as $a + b$. Table 1 gives several examples of Polish notation.

If a postfix expression is evaluated from left to right, then whenever an operand is encountered it is fetched to a stack (conceptual or actual), and whenever an operator is encountered, it is applied to the operands at the top of the stack. Hence, the operator can be immediately processed. For example, the expression $ab * c+$ is evaluated in the order fetch a, fetch b, multiply to form the product of a and b, fetch c, and, finally, add c to that product so as to leave at the top of the stack the equivalent of the infix expression $(a * b) + c$. Evaluated subexpressions placed on a stack are naturally "popped" from the stack in the order of their use. These two properties—ease of evaluation and unique representation of an expression without use of parentheses or other punctuation—justify Polish notation for use high-level language processors.

Bibliography

1979. Copi, I. *Symbolic Logic*, 5th Ed. Upper Saddle River, NJ: Prentice Hall.

Robert R. Korfhage

POLLING

For articles on related subjects, *see*

✛ Contention
✛ Local Area Network (LAN)
✛ Multiplexing
✛ Networks, Computer

When a number of processes or devices compete for shared resources, *polling* is used to resolve such problems and enforce discipline. In polling, the order of accessing the shared resource is managed so that competition is avoided and each process or device can use the shared resource for a limited time only. *Centralized polling* requires a master process or device to control access by devices subservient to the shared resource (*slaves*). The master simply addresses or polls each slave to provide access when it is needed. If access is not needed, the addressed slave sends a *negative acknowledgement*, which causes the master to poll the next slave. A centralized system has the advantage that either all slaves can receive equal access, or else priority can be given by polling some slaves more often than others. Furthermore, the system can function effectively over long distances. For this reason, it can be used to connect a large number of widely separated slave stations to a host computer over a single communication line. The disadvantage is that there is a single point of failure. When the host goes down, so does the entire system.

Distributed polling is implemented by passing a *token* in a predetermined order amongst devices connected by a bus (*q.v.*) or a ring. The owner of the token, which is a special bit pattern, has the exclusive use of the bus or ring if it has data to transfer. If not, it passes the token to the next device. Token systems provide the fairness and distance insensitivity of the centralized polling system, but they depend on the reliability of the nodes, and provision must be made to recover gracefully from failures that cause the token to disappear.

John S. Sobolewski

PORT, I/O

For articles on related subjects, *see*

+ Bus
+ Driver
+ Ethernet
+ Hard Disk
+ Modem

I/O ports are the interfaces through which computers communicate with external devices such as printers and scanners. They are superficially distinguished by their connectors, which have different shapes and numbers of contact pins, and by the varieties of devices that may be connected to them. A more significant difference is the variety of their protocols (*q.v.*), which specify what control and data signals the port uses and how they are to be interpreted.

Parallel Ports

A *parallel port* transmits the bits of a byte of data in parallel, so it has eight data lines as well as more for control of devices. It is a simple and widely used way to connect a printer to a computer. The original 36-pin parallel port was designed by Centronics, while IBM developed 25-pin parallel ports. In neither case did all the pins need to be used—some carried control signals appropriate for high-speed line printers but not needed for slower ones. Although parallel ports can use simple protocols, their cables must be relatively thick, encompassing 18 to 25 or more wires. Interference

among the multiple signals limits the cables to short distances, roughly 10 ft.

Serial Ports

Serial ports are designed for relatively low-speed communication, such as with a keyboard or mouse (*q.v.*). They transmit the bits of a byte one at a time. The serial port interface is a Universal Asynchronous Receiver–Transmitter (UART), containing a shift register that loads a byte in parallel from the computer and shifts its bits serially through the port. At the other end, the bits are reassembled into the byte. A serial-line cable can be simple, with as few as two signal lines (for transmitting and receiving) and ground. Although serial communication can use as few as three wires, serial ports frequently use one or more additional ones to synchronize data transmission, and the RS-232C standard for serial lines defines 10. The original connectors had 25 pins, and the newer IBM PC/AT connector has nine. Serial cables can be 25 ft or longer, though a long cable will limit the maximum possible bit-rate.

USB

The *Universal Serial Bus* port was introduced in 1996 to simplify connection of serial devices. Multiple devices may be connected to a USB port (through a simple *hub*). The USB protocol allows devices to identify themselves to the computer, and to exchange data with it at their own rates, not all the same. The USB port controller interrogates the devices to determine their characteristics and assigns each a 7-bit address (with one bit-pattern reserved, there can be up to 127 devices connected to a USB port). The devices all share in the total bandwidth (*q.v.*) of the bus, 12 Mbps for shielded-wire cables, and 1.5 Mbps for unshielded. The USB cable has four wires, two for data and two for power to the devices. The cable is limited to 16 ft between hubs, which serve as *repeaters* to restore signal strength. USB ports can be used for external disk drives.

Firewire

Firewire is a new IEEE standard (1394) for a high-speed serial port. As of 2001, it could operate at speeds of

100 to 400 Mbps, fast enough to carry video signals between a video camera and computer with no loss of image quality or size. It is intended for high-bandwidth multimedia (*q.v.*) data, but is fast enough to be used as a disk-drive connection. Multiple devices can be connected to a Firewire port, and they take turns transmitting packets of data. The Firewire connector has six wires; four for data. Like USB, Firewire uses differential signaling for high bandwidth. Firewire uses two pairs of data lines to maintain synchronization at its high speeds, and the cables can be about 15 ft long.

Other Ports

Two other kinds of ports are Ethernet, which is the subject of a separate article, and SCSI ("skuzzy"). The parallel SCSI port is used for internal and external disk drives on Apple computers and workstations, among others, and for other high-speed devices like tape and CD-ROM drives. Like USB, it is a bus protocol, and multiple devices can be connected to a SCSI port in a serial "daisy-chained" fashion. It can currently operate at up to 40 Mbps.

Bibliography

1999. Rosch, W. L. *The Winn L. Rosch Hardware Bible*, 5th Ed. Indianapolis, IN: Que Corporation.

David Hemmendinger

PORT, MEMORY

For articles on related subjects, see

+ Bus
+ Channel
+ Input–Output Operations
+ Memory: Auxiliary

In some early computers, the main memory had a single *port* (Fig. 1a) or logical connection through which to transfer data under CPU control. In current systems, a single memory port is connected to a *bus* through

which several CPUs and I/O devices have memory access (Fig. 1b). On the more powerful systems, bus traffic can become so intense that, with only a single memory port, the speed of some important high-speed activity may be sacrificed. Thus, a second port may be added to the memory to serve the CPU separately from the bus (Fig. 1c).

Dual-port memory has several other uses. Some Non-Uniform Memory Access (NUMA) multiprocessing (*q.v.*) systems use dual-port memory to give each processor rapid access directly to its own memory through one port, while connecting the system bus to the

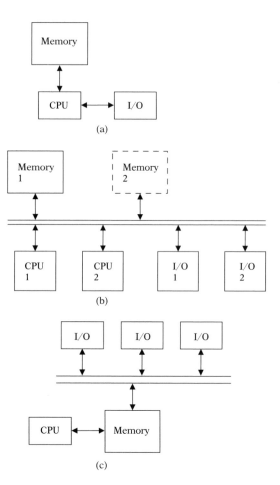

Figure 1. Memory port connections: (a) single-port, simply connected; (b) single-port, bus-connected; (c) dual-port memory serving a CPU and a bus.

other port, thereby allowing any other processor slower access to that memory via the bus. Dual-port memory can be used to accelerate digital signal processing (DSP), which uses the Fast Fourier transform, making repeated calculations of arithmetic expressions of related variables. A multiport memory must have some form of interlock (*q.v.*) to arbitrate conflict between port requests when both attempt to write to the same memory cell (*see* MUTUAL EXCLUSION). Because of the complexity of arbitration, multiport memory generally has two ports; four ports are feasible, but not common.

Bibliography

1998. Baumann, M. *The Most Commonly Asked Questions about Dual-Ports*. AN-91. Santa Clara, CA: Integrated.

David Hemmendinger

PORTABILITY

See SOFTWARE PORTABILITY.

PORTABLE COMPUTERS

For articles on related subjects, see

+ Mobile Computing
+ Personal Computing

A *portable computer* is small, light enough to be carried, and can operate on an internal battery or external electrical power. In terms of decreasing weight and the order in which they were developed, portable computers can be classified as luggable, laptop, notebook, or palmtop (or hand-held, or PDA—*Personal Digital Assistants*). Hand-held computers resemble pocket calculators but possess many of the capabilities of a PC. *Laptops* and *notebook* computers offer complete PC functionality in a size convenient for holding on the lap. Luggable

computers, no longer competitive because of weight, furnished fully functional machines in a small-suitcase-sized package.

The enabling technologies for the laptop computer, the most prevalent type of portable computer, include flat-panel displays; electronic components and disk drives that use very little power; long-life, rechargeable batteries; and a compact keyboard that provides some way to move the display cursor other than through an (optional) external mouse. A telecommunications capability can be added through use of a miniaturized modem having the form of a PCMCIA card or by an Ethernet (*q.v.*) connection.

Evolution of Portable Computers

The first portable computers weighed 28 to 33 lb and were packaged in a ruggedized case very similar to the housings used for their desktop counterparts. The Osborne 1 Portable, introduced in 1981, was the first such "luggable." It used a standard CRT screen that measured a scant 5 diagonal inches—a screen very similar to that of an oscilloscope and very difficult to read. The machine, which required AC power, came with dual built-in floppy disk drives, a detachable keyboard, and the CP/M operating system.

In that same year, Epson America introduced the first laptop computer. Its HX-20 used a 20 character by 4 line liquid crystal matrix flat-panel display (LCD), ran on standard lead-acid batteries, and sported a built-in printer very similar to a cash register tape printer. But the limited built-in software and small display made the machine only marginally useful.

In 1983, Radio Shack proved the usefulness of the laptop computer concept with the introduction of the TRS-80 Model 100. This 4 lb, battery-operated computer used a 40-character by 6-line LCD screen and provided useful built-in text editing and communications software. The machine soon became a favorite of journalists who found the computer to be an ideal writing tool to take on the road. A later version, the Model 200, provided a built-in disk drive, a larger screen, and the now common "clamshell" design in which the screen folds onto the keyboard when the computer is not in use.

In 1985, laptops began to use diskette (*q.v.*) and hard disk (*q.v.*) storage. In 1988, the NEC UltraLite machine heralded the arrival of the "notebook" computer, a laptop that weighed under 5 lb, and provided all the functionality of an IBM PC-AT class computer. Other vendors began calling their laptops "notebooks" even when by weight—8 to 10 lb—they did not qualify.

The state of the art in notebook computers provides a fast Intel Pentium, Sparc, or PowerPC microprocessor; CD-ROM, diskette, and hard-disk storage; a high-resolution flat-panel color screen; built-in networking capability; and the ability to run almost all desktop computer applications consistent with its processor. One of the lightest and thinnest is the Toshiba Portégé 3010CT whose screen has a 10.4-in. diagonal, is only 3/4 in. thick and weighs less than 3 lb (*see* Fig. 1).

Figure 2. The 3Com Palm Pilot V palmtop computer.

Hand-held computers

Innovative technologies, such as stylus and pen-based input devices coupled with character-recognition software have created a whole new generation of very small computers variously called hand-held PCs (HPCs), pen computers, palmtops, or Personal Digital Assistants (PDAs). The typical palm computer with dimensions of about $5 \times 3 \times 1/2$ in. and weight less than a pound fits easily into the pocket. In lieu of a physical keyboard, input is entered by writing on a touchscreen display or by entering words letter-by-letter by touching a displayed keyboard. One of the first of these, the Apple Newton, was not a commercial success. But the 3Com Corporation has sold several million of its popular Palm Pilot PDAs (*see* Fig. 2).

Bibliography

1997. Sweeney, D. "Is Bigger Always Better?" *Mobile Computing and Communications*, **8**(3), 66–72.

1997. Bassak, G. "Running On Empty," *Mobile Computing and Communications*, **8**(6), 76–85.

1999. Bassak, G. *PC Novice Guide to Computing: Portables and Windows CE*, **6**(11), (January); Lincoln, NE: Sandhills Publishing.

Figure 1. The Toshiba Portégé 3010CT notebook computer.

G. Michael Vose

POSTSCRIPT

For articles on related subjects, see

+ Desktop Publishing
+ Markup Languages
+ Problem-Oriented Languages
+ Programming Languages
+ T$_E$X
+ Typefont
+ Word Processing

PostScript is a device-independent page description language. Page description languages are programming languages that are optimized to render document images on display devices such as workstation (*q.v.*) screens, laser printers, film recorders, fax machines, or phototypesetters. PostScript programming is especially applicable to situations in which a user has a mathematical description of an image and wants to know what it looks like.

The PostScript Language

The public-domain language specification for PostScript is derived from work that was done at Xerox PARC in the late 1970s. When Xerox declined to market a PostScript product, the Adobe Systems Corporation was formed and developed an implementation that has become the *de facto* standard page description language. Adobe Systems licensed the technology to printer manufacturers, most notably to Apple (*q.v.*) for its LaserWriter introduced in January 1985. Barely three years later, publishing products had to support PostScript output in order to be commercially viable. PostScript and Adobe PageMaker are essentially responsible for creating the increasing popularity of desktop publishing. Ghostscript is a freely available PostScript interpreter that runs on PCs and workstations.

PostScript source code is characterized not only by device independence, but also by an ASCII representation and a postfix syntax (*see* POLISH NOTATION) that makes it easy to generate from programs. Like Forth, its stack-oriented operations are interpreted and

not compiled. PostScript is designed to be portable; its ASCII representation allows PostScript files to be transmitted across electronic networks easily and reliably. The descriptions of objects and paths are separated from their imaging for any particular display technology

```
%
%Define a procedure to print the words
%"Heather and Courtney" on the three sides
%of an imaginary box centered at the origin.
/hcprint
{
gsave
  90 rotate
  -45 90 move to (Heather) show
  -90 rotate
  -21 90 moveto (and) show
  -90 rotate
  -54 90 move to (Courtney) show
  grestore
}
def
%Make the current font 30 point Times
%Roman
/Times-Roman findfont 30 scalefont setfont
%Move the coordinate system origin 3
%inches up and right
216 216 translate
%Draw a 240 degree circular arc centered
%near the origin
9 9 72-30 210 arc stroke
%Print "Heather and Courtney" 20 times at
20 increasingly dark gray levels, each
%time moving the origin slightly up and
%to the right
.95-.05 0{set gray hcprint 11 translate}
for
%Print "Heather and Courtney" one more
%time in white.
1 setgray hcprint
%Produce the printed page.
showpage
```

Figure 1.   A short PostScript Program.

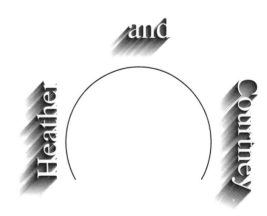

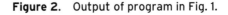
Figure 2.   Output of program in Fig. 1.

or device. Objects can be stroked or filled. *Stroking* a path produces an image on the page consisting of a line of specified thickness. Filling a path paints areas inside the path with a specified gray level. Paths and outlines can be specified as sequences of lines, circular arcs, and Bezier cubic *splines*. PostScript also supports embedded bitmap images. A typical small PostScript program is shown in Fig. 1. Lines that begin with the percent sign (%) are comments. The printed output generated by the program is shown in Fig. 2.

Bibliography

1985. Adobe Systems, Inc. *PostScript Language Tutorial and Cookbook*. Reading, MA: Addison-Wesley.

1990. Smith, R. *Learning PostScript: A Visual Approach*. Reading, MA: Addison-Wesley.

1997. Adobe Systems, Inc. *PostScript Language Reference*, 3rd Ed. Reading, MA: Addison-Wesley.

1999. The Source of Ghostscript and Related Programs and Documentation. `http://www.cs.wisc.edu/~ghost/`.

David L. Rodgers

POWER USER

For articles on related subjects, *see*

+ Guru
+ Wizard

A *power user* is a person who knows and uses a particular piece of software to its maximum extent. The term is always qualified by the name of the applicable software; we speak of a Unix (*q.v.*) power user, a WordPerfect power user, an Excel power user, and so on. Such a person is not usually a programmer who can modify the system, but rather one who knows its cited capabilities inside out and who can apply not only that knowledge, but also additional "lore" that he or she constantly gleans from trade magazines, Internet surfing, conferences, user groups, and email caucuses

with others who share a similar desire to master use of a particular item of software.

Edwin D. Reilly

PRECEDENCE

See OPERATOR PRECEDENCE.

PRECISION

For articles on related subjects, *see*

+ Arithmetic, Computer
+ Numbers and Number Systems

For a numeric representation that employs strings of symbols from a finite alphabet to represent numbers, the *precision attribute* of a number is expressed in terms of the *finite precision numbers* of that representation. For the fixed-point radix representation $d_m d_{m-1} \ldots d_1 d_0 \cdot d_{-1} d_{-2} \ldots d_l$, $d_m \neq 0$, the precision attribute is the triple $(m - l + 1, -l, m + 1)$; for example, 310.25 has precision (5, 2, 3) and 0.0024 has precision (2, 4, -2). If $l \leq 0 \leq m$, then $-l$ and $m + 1$ may be interpreted as the number of digits in the fractional and integer parts, respectively, of the $m - l + 1$ digit number. The precision triple $(m - l + 1, -l, m + 1)$; thus provides both the number of digits and base-point normalization information.

The precision attribute is used for numeric formats in input, output, and internal storage allocation in high-level programming languages. Precision, as defined here, is intimately related to the displayed representation of a number, in contrast to *accuracy*, which is concerned with freedom from error. Thus, a highly precise number is not necessarily an accurate one, since its accuracy is limited to the number of its *significant* digits independent of the number of digits displayed.

Bibliography

1976. Matula, D. W. "Radix Arithmetic: Digital Algorithms for Computer Architecture," in *Applied Computation Theory: Analysis, Design and Modeling* (ed. R. Yeh). Upper Saddle River, NJ: Prentice Hall.

David W. Matula

PREPROCESSOR

For articles on related subjects, see

+ Language Processors
+ Macro
+ Object Program
+ Source Program

A *preprocessor* is a language processor that accepts input statements written in one computer language and outputs statements that are acceptable to a similar but less complete language. Suppose, for example, that we have available a standard Pascal compiler but that we would like to be able to write programs that are compatible with extended versions that are richer in string manipulation constructs. Given an input file that contains source code for a program written in the extended language, the preprocessor must read each statement and parse it to see if its syntax pertains to string manipulation. If so, the preprocessor writes a sequence of standard Pascal statements that, when later compiled and executed as part of the artificially created (and longer) source file, produce the same effect as the desired string manipulation statement. The process is shown schematically in Fig. 1.

Preprocessor operation is very similar to macro expansion, but takes place at an early phase of language translation. Software processors that support a macro facility accept macro definitions as an integral part of language translation and then expand instances of the macro when encountered in the source code. To cope with a language that lacks a macro facility, we can write a preprocessor whose macro definitions are

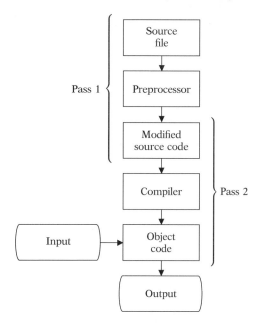

Figure 1. Preprocessing, shown as pass 1, precedes compilation and execution, shown as pass 2.

essentially embedded in its parsing logic. The definitions correspond to the syntactical constructs we wish we had in the host language but do not. The preprocessor then detects incoming statements that correspond to these constructs and expands them before the host language translator has a chance to reject them as being ungrammatical.

Edwin D. Reilly

PRETTY GOOD PRIVACY (PGP)

For articles on related subjects, see

+ Authentication
+ Cryptography, Computers in
+ Digital Signature
+ Electronic Mail (Email)
+ Password
+ Privacy, Computers and

PGP (*Pretty Good Privacy*) is (1) a 1990s program for encrypting electronic mail (*q.v.*); (2) a company founded by the program's author, Phil Zimmerman; and (3) a trademarked brand of encryption products offered by the US firm Network Associates. The PGP program is (partially) based on the RSA data encryption algorithm invented in 1977 by MIT professors Ronald Rivest, Adi Shamir, and Len Adleman. But the algorithm did not find widespread use because computers of the 1970s were too slow to perform the mathematical operations necessary to implement it.

In 1980, Charles Merritt discovered a technique for performing RSA encryption on low-cost micro-computers. Merritt's program, *DEDICATE*/32, could encrypt a small file in 20 to 30 s. He had no success in marketing his program until 1983, when he called Meta-morphic Systems, a small computer vendor in Boulder, CO, and spoke with programmer Phil Zimmermann. Zimmermann and Merritt became friends, and over the next two years Merritt taught Zimmermann the techniques for performing mathematical operations with large numbers on small computers.

In 1986, Merritt and Zimmermann met with Jim Bidzos, the president of RSA Data Security, a small company that had been created by Rivest, Shamir, and Adleman to commercialize their patented algorithm. Earlier that year, Rivest had created for RSA an email encryption program called MailSafe that used the RSA algorithm. After the meeting, Zimmermann decided to write his own email encryption program routine. He finished it during the summer of 1991 and called it *Pretty Good Privacy*. At about that the same time, the US Senate was considering an omnibus anti-crime bill that included language that would outlaw the use of encryption systems within the United States that did not "permit the government to obtain the plaintext contents of voice, data, and other communications when appropriately authorized by law." Fearing that use of his program would soon be illegal, Zimmermann gave copies of PGP 1.0 to a few of his friends. One of them uploaded the program to a few bulletin board systems. In late 1992, a much strengthened version, PGP 2.0, was released on the Internet.

In February 1993, the US Customs Department launched a formal investigation of Zimmermann. Although the investigation was originally based on the exporting of a program that violated RSA's patent, the investigators quickly refocused on the exportation of a program that allegedly violated the US laws prohibiting the export of cryptographic software without a license. The investigation was dropped on 11 January 1996.

In March 1996, Zimmermann founded PGP, Inc., which went on to develop several new products including a telephone encryption system and a disk-drive encryption program called *PGPdisk*. But despite good technology, PGP, Inc. faltered, and in February of 1998, was sold to Network Associates, a company formed just a year earlier through the merger of Network General and the McAfee company known for its virus protection software (*see* VIRUS, COMPUTER). PGP, incorporated into several popular products, continues to thrive.

Bibliography

1995. Garfinkel, S. *PGP: Pretty Good Privacy*. Sebastopol, CA: O'Reilly & Associates.

1995. Zimmermann, P. *The Official PGP User's Guide*. Cambridge, MA: MIT Press.

1996. Schneier, B. "Pretty Good Privacy (PGP)," in *Section 24.12 of Applied Cryptography*, 2nd Ed., 584–587. New York: John Wiley.

Simson Garfinkel

PRIVACY, COMPUTERS AND

For articles on related subjects, see

+ Computer Crime
+ Cryptography, Computers in
+ Electronic Mail (Email)
+ Pretty Good Privacy (PGP)

The Right to Privacy

The generally held feeling that individuals have a right to privacy has very little constitutional support. Privacy is not mentioned in the US Constitution, although courts have at times interpreted its first, fourth, and fifth amendments to include certain limited rights to privacy. The 1948 Universal Declaration of Human Rights specifically advocates protection of privacy in its Article 12, and some recent constitutions (e.g. Hong Kong, Malawi) include a right to privacy in relation to search or intrusion, but are silent on the particular question of data privacy.

Computers and Privacy

Computers allow storage of masses of seemingly small bits of information about individuals over long periods of time. Techniques like *data mining* (*q.v.*) permit the analysis and use of this information in unanticipated ways. Also, previously separate databases of information gathered for unrelated purposes can be combined, creating a more revealing picture of individuals and their habits. Computers permit the use of biometrics, which use biological characteristics such as retinal scans, handprints, and fingerprints. Biometric identification is designed to eliminate identity fraud but may also reduce the number of situations in which a person can act anonymously. These technologies and others can be used to trace an individual's physical location even without that person's knowledge.

Data Privacy

United Nations Resolution 45/95 of 14 December 1990 recommends that each nation develop regulations that require fairness, accuracy, and transparency of data files, as well as a ban on using collected data for discriminatory purposes. Data privacy concerns have increased as computer technology has made it possible to gather, store, and manipulate large amounts of personal data. The US Privacy Act of 1974 places limits on the use of personal data by Federal agencies. Under the Act, individuals must be informed about what data is being gathered and how it will be used. They also have the right to examine this data and obtain corrections to erroneous entries.

Data privacy concerns increase with the development of electronic commerce (*q.v.*) because each transaction creates an audit trail. This information about consumers and their activities becomes a commodity in its own right and active markets exist for the purchase of information about consumers and their buying habits. The European Union's October 1998 Directive on Data Privacy (Directive 95/46/EC) requires each member nation of the EU to conform to privacy guidelines that protect the individual consumer, and prohibits data collection on the part of companies whose country's laws do not provide adequate privacy protection.

Privacy of Communications

The growth of the Internet (*q.v.*) has meant that hundreds of millions of people are using computer technology as a communications system. In 1986, the United States enacted the Electronic Communications Privacy Act (ECPA) to update earlier laws that had specifically addressed wiretapping and telephone communications. ECPA protects digital communications from point-to-point across computer networks. Intrusions into computer systems, however, gave evidence that laws must be combined with strong computer security in order to have an effect. Mistrust of online communications was high and Internet users were advised to treat each email message "as a postcard, not a letter" in terms of expected privacy. While ECPA protects the content of communications, transaction data and "clickstream" records are not protected. Owners of sites on the World Wide Web (*q.v.*) can gather information on who visits their sites, either by tracking requests for information or by placing a small file called a *cookie* on the visitor's computer. User distrust of such technology is often cited as a reason for not engaging in electronic commerce.

Encryption and Public Key Technology

Message encryption has been a privacy technology since ancient times, with special application in the military and diplomatic arenas. The development of encryption techniques was greatly increased by the computational power of computers, and, by the late 1980s, a PC could securely encode messages in a way that would ensure privacy for most communications needs. The development of public key cryptography in the 1980s (*see* CRYPTOGRAPHY, COMPUTERS IN and PRETTY GOOD PRIVACY (PGP)) makes very secure cryptography available to all computer users.

Computer Privacy and Law Enforcement

There is tension between the desire for privacy and the perceived needs of law enforcement. Law enforcement agencies maintain that encrypted communications could be used to hide crimes ranging from money laundering to terrorism. Many governments, including that of the United States, favor the requirement that anyone using encrypted messages be required to place a copy of each key in escrow with a trusted agency that would be authorized to reveal the key under specific circumstances. In 1994, the development of the Clipper Chip, a key-escrowed encryption technology for secure telephone communications that was considered a model for similar computer communications, drew a strong response from the Internet community and the technology never came into wide use. Although electronic communications in the USA are protected by ECPA, law enforcement continues to have wiretap rights with a court order.

Bibliography

1994. Branscomb, A. W. *Who Owns Information? From Privacy to Public Access.* NewYork: Basic Books.

1997. Schneier, B. and Banisar, D. (eds.) *The Electronic Privacy Papers: Documents on the Battle for Privacy in the Age of Surveillance.* New York: John Wiley.

2000. Garfinkel, S. L. *Database Nation: The Death of Privacy in the 21st Century.* Sebastopol, CA: O'Reilly & Associates.

Karen Coyle

PROBLEM-ORIENTED LANGUAGES

For articles on related subjects, *see*

+ Expert Systems
+ Hardware Description Languages
+ Procedure-Oriented Languages
+ Programming Languages
+ Robotics
+ Simulation

Taken literally, the term *problem-oriented language* (POL) includes any programming language that helps solve problems. Thus, Fortran (*q.v.*) is a POL when one solves scientific or numeric problems. Cobol (COmmon Business-Oriented Language—*q.v.*) is a POL, even by title, for business problems. However, accepted usage in computer science literature has imposed a narrower context for POL than one that could encompass Fortran and Cobol. From this more restricted point of view, synonyms for *problem-oriented* are *applications-oriented*, or *special-purpose*, or *specialized-application*, or *domain-specific*.

An Early Problem-Oriented Language–DYANA

Shortly after the successful introduction of Fortran for scientific and engineering calculations, the General Motors Research Laboratories developed a specialized language for describing vibrational and other dynamic systems. DYANA (dynamic analyzer) was developed originally for the IBM 704 in 1958 and was an extension of Fortran. DYANA provided for the definition of variables to specify the elements, excitation, and dependent and independent variables in a dynamic system. The variables define the topology of the mechanical system.

Using a Problem-Oriented Language–APT

One of the most successful and widely implemented POLs was APT, which stands for *automatically programmed tools*. It was first developed at MIT in the early 1950s to assist in the production of punched tapes for numerically controlled machine tools. The early versions of APT were restricted to two-dimensional (2D) objects, using only straight lines and circles. Later developments, which were sponsored by the Aerospace Industries Association, resulted in a system called APT II. APT II used a specialized language to describe geometric surfaces. In the 1960s, the APT Long-Range Program, sponsored by numerous industries and conducted by the Illinois Institute of Technology Research Institute, developed APT III, which eventually became the *de facto* standard for numerical control applications.

The use of numerical control for machine tools is one of the most significant modern developments in manufacturing. Numerical control (N/C) has been applied to milling machines, drilling and boring machines, lathes, machine centers, automatic wiring machines, welding and flame-cutting machines, and so on. The APT system includes a programming language, which provides a vocabulary for describing the geometry, motions, and machine functions necessary to produce a part using N/C, and a group of computer programs, called the *part program*, which translate APT language, perform the required calculations, and produce the control tape. The APT language provides a vocabulary to describe a large variety of 2D and 3D part geometry, to define tool shape, to specify tolerance, to command cutter motion, to indicate machining functions, to perform in-line computations, and to execute program logic and specify geometric transformations. These features, when used individually and in combination, offer the part programmer the possibility of producing simple or complex parts efficiently and economically.

Civil Engineering Applications

The solution of civil engineering problems involves many disciplines. For example, in the design of a highway interchange, the engineer uses surveying, highway engineering, soil mechanics, structural engineering, hydraulic engineering, transportation engineering, and so on. Computer aids to each of these fields have been developed over the past 40 years. Work

was done to combine these separate applications into an integrated package of programs known as ICES (Integrated Civil Engineering System), which was initially developed in the mid-1960s. This section discusses some of the work that led up to the design and implementation of ICES, and then discusses ICES as an example of a unified POL system.

Cogo

Cogo (*coordinate geometry*) is a POL used to perform the geometric calculations required in surveying. It was developed by Professor C. Miller of the MIT Civil Engineering Department around 1960. It is now available on most computers and has also been implemented under several time-sharing systems.

Stress

Structural Engineering Systems Solver (Stress) was developed with the objective of facilitating the use of computers in analyzing structures. The principal objective of Stress was to provide a wide variety of structural analyses with a minimum of programming effort. It can be used to analyze 2D and 3D structures, with either pinned or rigid joints, with prismatic or nonprismatic members, and subjected to concentrated or distributed loads, support motions, or temperature effects. Stress was developed in the early 1960s under the direction of Professor S. J. Fenves at MIT. It was essentially replaced later in the 1960s by STRUDL.

ICES

The POLs discussed to this point have provided the user with language capability to solve very special problems, such as producing tapes for numerically controlled machine tools, solving problems in plane geometry, and performing structural analysis. The ICES, on the other hand, was designed to function as a series of subsystems, each subsystem corresponding to an engineering discipline. Each subsystem in ICES uses its own data structure; nevertheless, it provides for common files of problem data. ICES also provides an engineering programming language, command-definition language, and data-definition language to create subsystems. Thus, ICES is a framework within which engineering programs can be embedded. The engineering programming language is Icetran, which is an extension of Fortran designed to handle civil engineering programming. With Icetran, a programmer can develop problem-oriented subsystems that become part of the ICES package.

Electrical Engineering Applications

Computers are essential aids to the electrical engineer in many applications, circuit analysis being the dominant computation for most electrical engineering applications. The two most commonly used circuit analysis programs are ECAP (Electronic Circuit Analysis Program) and SCEPTRE. ECAP allows the electrical engineer to perform dc, ac, and transient analysis. Under control of ECAP, network equations are formulated and solved after the appropriate topological information and element values of the network have been provided. SCEPTRE also performs dc and transient analysis, but was designed to provide several improvements over ECAP in transient analysis.

Robot Languages

One of the more recent specialized areas is the development of languages to program robots. Various authors represent robot programming on different levels, but the simplest way to consider the issue is to define only three conceptual levels: servo, manipulator, and task. At the servo level, a program consists of a series of endpoints, speeds, and input–output commands; the path between endpoints is generated by calculating a series of intermediate points between the endpoints. At the manipulator level, the program contains motion commands (e.g. move from Point A to Point B), some

Table 1. Illustrations of problem-oriented languages.

Application area	Program name
Statistics	SPSS: Statistical Package for the Social Sciences SAS Statistical Library OMNITAB
Computer-assisted instruction	TUTOR PLANIT COURSEWRITER
Simulation	GPSS: General-Purpose Systems Simulator SIMSCRIPT CSSL: Continuous System Simulation Language
Systems programming	AED: Automated Engineering Design BLISS: Basic Language for Implementing System Software C and C++
Computer design	CDL: Computer Design Language CSL: Computer structure language VHDL: VHSIC Hardware Description Language
Expert systems	KRL: Knowledge Representation Language OPSS
Robotics	AML/2: A Manufacturing Language/2 KAREL VAL: Versatile Assembly Language

sensor capability (e.g. force specification), and branching and looping constructs.

Expert Systems Languages

In the 1980s, the concept of *knowledge-based systems* or *expert systems* (*q.v.*) became significant, with many practical applications developed. An expert system involves (1) a language, (2) an inference engine, and (3) specific rules and data for an individual application. Expert systems are specific software programs intended to operate at, or close to, the level of a human expert in a specific task domain (e.g. auto repair, computer configuration, medical diagnosis), although in a given case the system may be limited to a specific subset of the task domain (e.g. correcting poor auto performance, configuring minicomputers, controlling excessive bleeding). The purpose of the rules is to specify the information and choices to be used as the system is applied. The inference engine represents the methodology used to invoke the rules, and the language expresses the computations to be performed.

Other POLs

Literally hundreds of POLs have been developed over the past 35 years. We have looked at the areas of numerical control, civil engineering, electrical engineering, robotics, and expert systems. Table 1 summarizes some other illustrative languages, by their areas of application.

Bibliography

1964. Fenves, S. J., Logcher, R. D., and Mauch, S. P. *STRESS: A User's Manual.* Cambridge, MA: MIT Press.

1967. IIT Research Institute. *APT Part Programming.* New York: McGraw-Hill.

1968. Jensen, R. W., and Lieberman, M. D. *IBM Electronic Circuit Analysis Program—Techniques and Applications.* Upper Saddle River, NJ: Prentice Hall.

1969. Sammet, J. E. *Programming Languages: History and Fundamentals.* Upper Saddle River, NJ: Prentice Hall.

1991. Sammet, J. E. "Some Approaches to, and Illustrations of, Programming Language History," *Annals of the History of Computing,* **13**(1), 33–50.

Benjamin Mittman and Jean E. Sammet

PROCEDURE

See SUBPROGRAM.

PROCEDURE-ORIENTED LANGUAGES

For articles on related subjects, *see*

+ Abstract Data Type
+ Ada
+ Algol
+ APL
+ Basic
+ Block Structure
+ C
+ C++
+ Calling Sequence
+ Cobol
+ Compiler
+ Control Structures
+ Data Type
+ Debugging
+ Declaration
+ Diagnostic
+ Expression
+ Fortran
+ Functional Programming
+ Iteration
+ Java
+ Language Processors
+ List Processing: Languages
+ Lisp
+ Logo
+ Object-Oriented Programming
+ Operator Precedence
+ Parameter Passing
+ Pascal
+ PostScript
+ Program
+ Programming Languages
+ Recursion
+ Side Effect
+ Statement
+ String Processing

+ **Structured Programming**
+ **Subprogram**

SURVEY

Procedure-oriented language (POL)—an acronym shared with Problem-Oriented Language—(*q.v.*) is an artificial language used to define the actions required by a computer to solve a problem. A POL frees a programmer from the time-consuming chore of expressing algorithms in lower-level languages such as assembly and machine language. Additionally, POLs are more portable. The defining characteristic of a POL is the expression of an algorithm as a series of discrete statements or steps, each of which typically embodies far more logic than any one machine language instruction. Execution proceeds from one statement (*q.v.*) to the next sequentially, embodying a single flow or thread of control. A programmer uses a POL to create a *source program* (*q.v.*) that can be translated by a *compiler* into machine language. Sophisticated compiler technology allows the programmer to use high-level languages that approximate the original mathematical form of the algorithm.

As POLs have developed, they have increased the level of abstraction available to the programmer. A POL combines *expressions* into larger programming units called *procedures* or *subprograms*. This *procedural abstraction* lets the programmer treat a complex sequence of operations as a single unit that can be reused. POLs also allow the grouping of data of homogeneous type into indexed aggregates called *arrays*. They provide *structures* or *records* (*q.v.*) to group complex heterogeneous data such as mixtures of numbers and character strings into single data objects. These structures can be combined, so that there can be arrays of records or records containing arrays or other records. Such data structures let a programmer model features of the problem being solved at a level more or less matching the problem statement.

Together with abstraction capabilities, POLs provide type checking, which prevents many run-time errors by detecting them during compilation. In addition to declaring complex data structures, programmers define the *type* of each structure. A *phone_book*, for example,

may be the name of a type defined as an array of records, each containing a string and a number. POLs generally require that the type of each variable be specified when the variable is first declared. The compiler then uses this type information to insure that the program uses its data structures correctly. A *strongly typed* language is one in which each entity has a precise type that cannot be changed in the program, thus providing considerable protection against programmer error.

One of the most important kinds of abstraction is to have program units that contain both data structures and the procedures that operate on them—that is, *abstract data types*. These units may be compilation units called *modules*, or (in Ada) *packages*, or they may be *classes* (*q.v.*) that have multiple instances *(objects)*. Such data abstractions separate a program into well-defined segments that permit access to the data structures only through their associated procedures. The segments can be reused in other programs, or they can provide a basis for building new segments (*see* MODULAR PROGRAMMING and OBJECT-ORIENTED PROGRAMMING).

This survey lists, in approximate historical order, general-purpose POLs that the author regards as having been either popular or significant during that period cited.

Fortran is in some sense both the oldest and the newest language. Designed for numerical computations, the first versions of Fortran in the late 1950s proved that a higher-level language compiler could produce efficient machine code. Fortran has gone through numerous revisions, the most recent of which is Fortran 95.

Algol was first defined by an international committee in the late 1950s. It introduced block structure (*q.v.*) and the explicit declaration of variable types (*strong typing*). It also introduced recursion (*q.v.*). Algol is the ancestor of many important POLs—Pascal, Ada, and Modula-2, among others—the so-called "Algol family."

APL was originally developed in the 1950s by Kenneth E. Iverson as a concise mathematical notation for expressing computer science concepts. It contains a rich set of operators on vectors and arrays that allow very compact statements. There are no control structures, such as `while`, `if-then-else`, and `for`. These are replaced by recursion, array operations, and a single transfer-of-control operator, $\rightarrow$, which means "go to."

Cobol was developed in 1959 for business data processing applications, and continues to be one of the most widely used languages. Cobol was the first language to place equal importance on data and procedures, providing separate specifications for each.

Simula, introduced in 1967, was a general programming language intended specifically to be used for simulation (*q.v.*). It introduced the important concepts of *class* and *object*, and was thus the first object-oriented language.

Basic, developed in the late 1960s, was intended to be small, portable, and easy to learn. It was interpreted rather than compiled, which gave it the advantage of rapid feedback on syntax and run-time errors. Its early versions lacked many of the resources needed for large programs, such as strong data typing and parameter-passing to subprograms. Later versions added more features including "visual" ones for Microsoft Windows.

Pascal was developed in the early 1970s to refine the programming ideas of Algol into a small, compact, reliable, yet full-featured language suitable for teaching the principles of software design. It became a major language for programming instruction, and provided user-defined data types, though not full data abstraction.

C was developed in the early 1970s at Bell Laboratories as the implementation language for the Unix (*q.v.*) operating system. C and its successor C++ have become the primary languages of discourse in systems programming.

Modula-2, developed in the mid-1970s as a successor to Pascal, introduced data abstraction by means of an elegant module system. It was intended for systems programming as well as for software design, and provided support for coroutines (*q.v.*).

Ada, developed in the early 1980s, was the result of nearly 20 years of effort by the US Department of Defense to develop a single language for all applications–commercial, scientific, and particularly, *embedded systems* (*q.v.*).

C++ dates from the early 1980s. It was intended to preserve the efficiency of C but to add abstraction capabilities—stronger data typing and structuring features,

and the object-oriented features of Simula. By the late 1990s, it had become one of the most popular languages for teaching, as well as for applications programming (*q.v.*) and systems programming (*q.v.*).

Eiffel was designed in the late 1980s as an object-oriented language with a carefully chosen set of features. Although less popular than C++, it is a useful language for teaching programming principles as well as for large-scale programming.

Java, an object-oriented language of the early 1990s, uses much of the syntax of C++ but is intended to be free of the low-level features that C++ inherited from C. It avoids machine-specific operations like address manipulation, and is thus capable of being compiled on one system and run on another—such as in the applets that are part of the World Wide Web (*q.v.*).

Bibliography

1981. Wexelblat, R. L. (ed.) *History of Programming Languages*. New York: Academic Press.

1987. Horowitz, E. *Programming Languages: A Grand Tour*, 3rd Ed. Rockville, MD: Computer Science Press.

1996. Bergin, T. J., and Gibson, R. G. (eds.) *The History of Programming Languages II*. Reading, MA: Addison-Wesley.

1999. MacLennan, B. J. *Principles of Programming Languages*, 3rd Ed. Oxford: Oxford University Press.

Tony L. Cox

PROGRAMMING

Statements

Each of the hundreds of procedure-oriented languages (POLs) is designed to meet a particular set of objectives. Some are intended for use over a wide range of applications; other *domain-specific languages* (problem-oriented languages—*q.v.*) address a more limited spectrum of problem types characteristic of a specific discipline. All but pure functional languages share a common property: the elemental vehicle for expressing the programmer's intention, the *statement*, conveys a level of complexity consistent with the procedure being represented. Thus, the activity that can be described in a single line of code bears no direct resemblance to a single machine-language instruction. Instead, many languages try to provide some similarity between a language statement and its counterpart in the notation appropriate to the application. For example, the following statement in the Fortran language,

$$H = 0.023 * (C/D) * (D * V * R/U) * *0.8$$
$$*(U*P/C)**0.4, \qquad (1)$$

is easily related to the same formula in conventional algebraic form:

$$H = 0.023 \frac{C}{D} \left(\frac{DVR}{U} \right)^{0.8} \left(\frac{UP}{C} \right)^{0.4} \qquad (2)$$

As could be ascertained by examining the corresponding compiled object code, this expression requires a considerable number of machine operations to produce the specified result (i.e. a value for H).

Specifications and Type Systems

A program in any language is eventually translated into elementary machine operations on strings of bits stored in memory. The distinction between low- and high-level languages is that in the former, the programmer must think in terms of storage and operations on what is stored, while in the latter, the programmer may think in terms of variable names. In assembly language, a programmer may introduce names, but only as labels attached to storage locations. In languages like Pascal, Ada, and Java, a programmer declares variables by name and the language translator associates the names with locations. The programmer is thus free to attend to the significance that the program variables have for the problem to be solved.

The association between a name and a location is part of the *binding* (*q.v.*) of the name. Depending on the language and the kind of variable (global to an entire program or local to one part of it, for example), the location may be determined by the translator at translation time, or it may not be fully determined until the program runs.

Procedural languages generally require that every variable be explicitly declared. A *declaration* (*q.v.*) specifies the *type* of the variable as well as its name. The type may be a primitive type of the language—real, integer, character—or it may be a programmer-defined type. The latter sort is particularly important in giving the programmer the ability to organize program data to correspond to the elements of the problem to be solved. A language that provides arrays of data but not heterogeneous records (*q.v.*), for example, would require that the programmer operate in parallel on an array of strings (names) and an array of integers (salaries), while a language with records, such as Pascal, C, or Ada, would let the programmer manipulate personnel records as units in the program, as they are in the problem domain. The following examples illustrate the forms of variable declarations in several languages.

```
Fortran   REAL X, Y, Z
C         double x, y, z, ar[100];
Pascal    var x, y, z : real;
          ar : array[1..100] of real
Ada       x, y, z : integer;
```

Each of these statements reserves storage for three variables x, y, and z to hold numerical values placed there later. Since nothing further is specified, internal language rules (*default conditions*) will determine the amount of reserved storage and the form for the numerical values.

The declarations of the array ar in C and Pascal display a difference of level. In C, the array is declared as 100 real numbers; that is, the [100] directs the compiler to allocate an appropriate amount of storage. The Pascal declaration treats the ar as a distinct type, and specifies how it is to be indexed. (In C, all array indexing starts from 0.) Type declarations allow a compiler to check not only that a variable has been declared but also that it is used correctly. Every type, both primitive and user-defined, has a set of operations that may be done on variables of that type.

Object-oriented languages are procedure-oriented languages in which a type can be defined to be a *data structure* (*q.v.*), together with a set of operations on it, in such a way that the data structure is accessible only through those operations. Such *abstract data types* (*q.v.*), called *classes* (*q.v.*), give the programmer still greater ability to define types that reflect the organization of the program's subject matter. A table such as a telephone book may be defined with operations to look up names, and to add and delete entries. The internal implementation of those operations in terms of lower-level types such as arrays or trees (*q.v.*) remains hidden, so that their details cannot affect the rest of the program.

Assignment and Expressions

The statement in Eqn. (1) exemplifies a primary convenience that a high-level language brings to its users—the ability to specify intricate steps with little loss in correspondence between the conventional description and its representation in a program. This intent is implemented by allowing a statement to be sufficiently large so as not to restrict the programmer's ability to maintain the integrity of a procedural step. Thus, it is usually the programmer, and not the computing system or the language, which determines the amount of activity to be specified in a single program "step" without serious regard to the number of actual machine steps these actions will eventually entail.

In procedure-oriented languages, the type of statement in which much of the actual computation is done is the *assignment statement*. An assignment statement has the form

$$variable \leftarrow expression \qquad (3)$$

The $\leftarrow$ in this construction symbolizes the operation of replacement, so that the general sense of the assignment may be stated as follows: "Evaluate the *expression* on the right-hand side of the $\leftarrow$ by performing the indicated operations; then let the result be the new value for *variable*, replacing its current value." The final step of placing the new value in *variable* may be a simple STORE machine instruction. In many high-level languages, such as Basic, C++, and Java, assignment is denoted (inappropriately) by the symbol "=". Algol, Pascal, and Ada use ": =" and APL uses an actual $\leftarrow$. Assignment must not be confused with mathematical equality. The C statement N = N+1 makes no sense as an equation, but is a simple increment operation as an assignment statement.

In (3), *variable*, the term to the left of $\leftarrow$, is a single variable name, because the effect of an assignment is to store a value at the address of the variable. In some languages, it is restricted to be a simple data type such as an integer or real number; in others, it may be a compound data type such as a record.

An *expression* consists of a combination of *terms* and *operators* in which the rules of construction constitute a restricted version of those applicable in ordinary algebra. As in algebra, a programming language expression like A+B/C*D would be ambiguous without rules of *operator precedence* (*q.v.*) to specify the order in which to apply operators. Most procedural languages adopt rules similar to algebraic ones, and give * and / higher precedence than + or -, and evaluate equal-precedence operators like * and / left-to-right. These languages, such as Pascal, C, and Java, would treat the expression above as equivalent to A+(B/C)*D. Some languages use a strict left-to-right or even right-to-left ordering, making the expression equivalent to ((A+B)/C)*D or A+(B/(C*D)), respectively. In all cases, however, the programmer may use parentheses to enforce a different precedence.

Control Structures

Procedure-oriented languages have three basic control structures: sequences, conditionals, and loops. A simple "straight-line" program is just a sequence of assignment statements, together with input and output operations. The power of digital computers, however, arises from their selecting alternative computations on the basis of the values of program variables (*conditional statements*) and their carrying out repetitive loops (*iterative statements*). In virtually all procedural languages, *recursion* (*q.v.*) is another form of control in which a subprogram can solve a problem by calling itself repeatedly until the problem has been reduced to an elementary one.

Conditional and iteration statements both use Boolean (truth–value) expressions such as (x < y) or (z > 0). They build on simple machine-level comparison instructions, together with branch instructions, which are machine-level goto statements. The latter are also available in high-level languages, but they can make a program difficult to understand and are rarely needed.

Conditionals

Early procedure-oriented languages such as Fortran and Basic had `IF .. THEN ..` conditional statements. Later languages, including the current version of Fortran and Basic, all have the more convenient `if.. then.. else..` conditional that lets the programmer write complex decision-structures without the use of `goto` (*see* STRUCTURED PROGRAMMING). There are minor syntactic variations among conditionals in current programming languages. C, C++, and Java, for example, omit `then`, and Ada and some other languages have an `else if` construct that permits a series of alternatives to be expressed conveniently.

Loops

POLs use iterative statements to specify and control repetitive operations. In general, these enable the programmer to identify the beginning and end of a *loop*, specify the number of repetitions, and define a mechanism for (automatically) keeping track of the number of cycles through the loop.

There are two principal kinds of loop: definite iteration, which repeats a specified number of times, and indefinite, which repeats as long as a specified condition is true (or until one becomes true). Definite iteration is appropriate for processing all elements of a fixed-size data structure like an array. Indefinite iteration is suited to processing all elements of a structure of unknown or varying size such as a file, or for processing parts of a fixed-size structure (e.g. searching an array for a given value).

Indefinite iteration is generally data-controlled. The following is a Pascal example of a loop that sums elements of a 14-element array *a*, stopping when the sum exceeds a specified value, or when the array is exhausted.

```
total :=0; i:=1;
while (total<=LIMIT)and(i<=14) do
  begin
    total :=total + a[i];
    i :=i+1
  end;
```

The indefinite loop is the more general construct, since a `for`-loop can be implemented as a `while`-loop that explicitly increments the loop counter. In addition to the `while-do` loops shown here, languages frequently have a `do-while` loop (also called `repeat-until`) that executes the loop body before making the loop-termination test. It, too, can be implemented with a `while`-loop.

Subprograms

With the assignment statement, expressions, and the basic control structures, a programmer can write programs to solve complex programs. These programs will generally be long and difficult to follow. *Subprograms* help simplify the task of writing a program, and equally important, the tasks of debugging and maintaining it. They are like small programs that can be passed inputs from a larger program, and that can provide it with results. Subprograms are either *procedures* or *functions*. They both take input arguments and produce results; a function does that by returning a value that can be used in an expression, while a procedure produces results by modifying some of its arguments, by giving values to variables through input statements, or by producing program output.

Bibliography

1976. Dijkstra, E. W. *A Discipline of Programming.* Upper Saddle River, NJ: Prentice Hall.

1996. Pratt, T. W., and Zelkowitz, M. V. *Programming Languages: Design and Implementation.* Upper Saddle River, NJ: Prentice Hall.

1999. MacLennan, B. J. *Principles of Programming Languages: Design, Evaluation, and Implementation*, 3rd Ed. New York: Oxford University Press.

David Hemmendinger

PROCESS

See JOB.

PRODUCT CODE

See UNIVERSAL PRODUCT CODE.

PROGRAM

For articles on related subjects, *see*

+ Algorithm
+ Debugging
+ Machine- and Assembly-language Programming
+ Modular Programming
+ Object-Oriented Programming
+ Object Program
+ Problem-Oriented Languages
+ Procedure-Oriented Languages
+ Programming Languages
+ Source Program
+ Stored Program Concept
+ Structured Programming

In order to solve a computational problem, its solution must be specified in terms of a sequence of computational steps, or *algorithm*, each of which may be effectively performed by a human agent or by a digital computer. Systematic notations for the specification of such sequences of computational steps are referred to as *programming languages*. A specification of the sequence of computational steps in a particular

programming language is referred to as a *program*. The task of developing programs for the solution of computational problems is referred to as *programming*. A person engaging in the activity of programming is referred to as a *programmer*.

The programs for the earliest digital computers were written in a *machine language*. Pure machine-language programming required the programmer to write out the sequences of binary or decimal digits by which each instruction was represented in computer memory. By the mid-1950s, it became possible for programmers to specify instruction codes and memory locations by mnemonic symbols that could be translated into machine language by a translator, itself a program, called an *assembler*.

In the late 1950s, *procedure-oriented languages* (POLs) were developed to allow programmers to specify algorithms in a notation natural to the problem being solved. Programs specified in a POL were translated into the internal language of a particular computer by a translation program called a *compiler* (*q.v.*). The flavor of programming in a particular POL can be experienced by following the logic in the Pascal (*q.v.*) function in Fig. 1, which finds the maximum of a list of *n* numbers.

A problem specification is generally given in terms of a desired relation between inputs and outputs that specifies *what* is to be computed. It is the task of the programmer to convert static input–output specifications of *what* is to be computed into dynamic specifications that specify *how* the computation is to

```
function max(x: list; n: integer): real;              {Result is real}

{Given that main program has defined a type list as array [1..n] of real; for constant n
having a particular integer value, this function returns the largest number in the list.}

var i: integer; t: real;                              {Declare two local variables}

begin
  t:=x[1];                          {Initialize t to first number, the largest seen so far}
  for i:=2 to n do                                    {Test all remaining numbers}
    if x[i]>t then t:=x[i];                       {Update t if larger number found}
  max:=t                            {Bind the function's name to the desired result}
end {max}
```

Figure 1. A Pascal function. Comments are delineated by braces.

be performed. A given input–output relation may be realized by a wide variety of different algorithms, and each algorithm may in turn be rendered in a variety of different programming languages. Maintenance of frequently used programs is more expensive than developing them, so reading of program *source code* by humans is as important as writing that code. Thus, documentation and other aids to readability are becoming increasingly important.

Bibliography

1969. Sammet, J. *Programming Languages—History and Fundamentals.* Upper Saddle River, NJ: Prentice Hall.

1997, 1997, 1998. Knuth, D. E. *The Art of Computer Programming*, Vol. 1 (3rd Ed.), 2 (3rd Ed.), 3 (2nd Ed.). Reading, MA: Addison-Wesley.

Peter Wegner

PROGRAM CORRECTNESS

See PROGRAM VERIFICATION.

PROGRAM COUNTER

For articles on related subjects, *see*

+ Instruction Set
+ Machine- and Assembly-language Programming

A computer *instruction* is the specification of an operation to be performed, the address of operands on which it will be performed, the address for the location of the result, and a specification (an address) of the next instruction in the sequence. These address specifications may be explicitly placed in the instruction or implicitly defined. By "implicit," it is meant that a particular instruction will assume that an operand will be in a certain place (e.g. the *accumulator*) rather than being specified in the instruction itself.

Unlike early drum-memory machines, current computers commonly assume that the instructions lie in sequence. That is, the next instruction is contained in the address following the location of the current one. This address is kept in a register called the *program counter* (or, in some systems, the *program address register* or *instruction counter*). During the execution of an instruction, the program counter is advanced by one or more address units. If, in a particular machine architecture, instruction lengths are not uniform, then incrementation of the program counter must take this into account. For example, in the IBM System 360/370/390 series, instructions are of three different sizes: 2 bytes, 4 bytes, or 6 bytes. Since addresses always refer to bytes, the program counter must be incremented by either 2, 4 or 6, depending upon the type of instruction currently being executed.

In all systems that use a program counter, there must be a mechanism for initializing its value (starting the program at a specified place) and for changing its value at certain points in the program. This latter mechanism is a special instruction called a *branch* or *jump*. There are two basic kinds—*unconditional* and *conditional*. A branch instruction either always (unconditional) or conditionally causes a new value to be placed in the program counter and thus, when it does do so, defines the starting location of a new sequence of instructions.

Michael J. Flynn

PROGRAM LIBRARY

For articles on related subjects, *see*

+ Compatibility
+ Software Portability
+ Subprogram

A *program library* is a collection of computer programs for a particular application. To be characterized as a library, such a collection should contain a substantial number of computer program modules designed to solve a wide range of problems in the given area. In addition, the programs in a library should be coherent, both in their external appearance and their internal design.

Program Library Development

The first program libraries for numerical computation were written in machine or assembly language for a particular computer at a given site. The earliest of these was a library written for the EDSAC (*q.v.*) in England by Wilkes (*q.v.*), Wheeler, and Gill in 1951. By the early 1960s, computer manufacturers were working on program libraries to help customers and stimulate sales, and in 1961 IBM released the SSP (Scientific Subroutine Package) library. At the same time, many groups began to feel the need to consolidate programming effort into useful libraries. For example, statisticians in the biomedical group at the University of California put together a group of statistical routines known as the BMDP library, the first edition appearing in 1961. Other statistical libraries originating in the early 1960s were SPSS (Statistical Package for the Social Sciences), originally written at Stanford University and further developed by the National Opinion Research Center at the University of Chicago, and SAS (Statistical Analysis System), developed at North Carolina State. Each of these is now supported commercially.

Libraries for numerical computation were also being built in England during this period. One was developed in 1963 for the IBM Stretch computer at the Harwell Atomic Energy Research Establishment. In 1970, six British computing centers began an effort to develop a library for their ICL 1906A/S computers, and in 1971 Mark 1 of the NAG (Nottingham Algorithms Group) library was released. Implementation for other computer systems followed, and by 1976, Numerical Algorithms Group Ltd. had been formed to continue development and distribution. NAG now markets general-purpose numerical libraries in Fortran (*q.v.*), C (*q.v.*), and Ada (*q.v.*), as well as specialized libraries for parallel computing and other mathematical topics.

The first commercial venture formed exclusively to market a general-purpose mathematical subroutine library was IMSL (International Mathematical and Statistical Libraries), which was incorporated in 1970.

The next year, IMSL released a library for the IBM 360/370 class of computers and sold seven copies. By 1976, when the company showed its first profit, it had 430 customers using its library on seven different computer systems. Today, the IMSL Libraries are developed and marketed by Visual Numerics, Inc., which offers Fortran and C implementations for some 35 computer platforms.

In the early 1970s, the NATS (National Activity to Test Software) group was established at Argonne Laboratory under government and university sponsorship to produce quality software for specific areas of numerical computation. Two packages were produced, EISPACK for eigenvalue–eigenvector computation, (1972) and FUNPACK for special function evaluation (1975). The software produced by the NATS effort was very well received, its high standards for performance, transportability, testing, certification, documentation, and dissemination establishing a paradigm for subsequent numerical software development efforts.

Traditionally, the interface to mathematical and statistical libraries has been the procedure call, typically in Fortran. This requires that users write a calling program (*driver—q.v.*) to make the call(s). But this method of interfacing with library routines is inconvenient for more casual users who are not necessarily programming experts. The ELLPACK system for elliptic boundary value problems, developed in the late 1970s, provided a high-level problem-statement language to describe problems and invoke and compose procedures for solving them. During the same period, Cleve Moler of the University of New Mexico developed an interactive system called MATLAB to ease use of the LINPACK and EISPACK libraries for students. A much enhanced commercial version is now marketed by The MathWorks. In 1988, Wolfram Research released Mathematica, a system that combined numerical, symbolic, and graphical tools in a single product, appealing to sophisticated and neophyte users alike. These events set the stage for the large number of general-purpose mathematical computing systems providing high-level interfaces to rich underlying mathematical and statistical software libraries that are now available.

Issues

We next describe some of the issues that must be addressed in the development and maintenance of large numerical program libraries.

Portability

Although most of the libraries described here are written in common programming languages like Fortran and C, not all are easily portable; libraries are often provided in a different implementation for each type of computer system. Several things inhibit portability: first, the dialect of the programming language in use, and second, the arithmetic differences among computers, both in static hardware and dynamic behavior resulting from differences in compiler-generated code. Considerable progress has been made in overcoming these problems. Libraries are now usually programmed in standard Fortran or C, and their adherence to the standard can be mechanically verified. For systems that provide high-level user interfaces to library routines, there is also the added complication of interaction with services provided by the operating system, as well as windowing and graphics systems.

Performance Portability

Modern computer architectures are complex and varied. Architectural details such as number of processors, their type (e.g. vector), type and size of cache (*q.v.*), page sizes (*see* VIRTUAL MEMORY), and so on, can have profound effects on the efficiency of numerical algorithms. As a result, library developers have also become concerned not only with a library routine's ability to perform correctly, but also with its *efficiency*, measured in terms of elapsed time and memory usage, as one moves the routine from one platform to another.

One promising approach to achieving what has come to be known as *performance portability* has been to encapsulate low-level, but compute-intensive, operations into standardized utilities that have good generic implementations, but which can be optimized for each platform. This was pioneered by the Basic Linear Algebra Subprograms (BLAS), released in 1979, which formed the basis for LINPACK. These low-level vector functions provided a degree of performance portability between scalar systems and early vector processors like the CRAY I and the Cyber 205.

Error Handling

In order to protect users from program failure and from their own programming errors, the best quality program libraries do careful error checking. Both the legality of the input parameters to a subprogram and the validity of the computation process must be scrutinized. Some errors must be signaled as *fatal* whereas others can be designated as less serious. Unfortunately, no standard has been adopted for error handling, and procedures vary from one library to another.

Documentation

Increasingly, library documentation is being kept on-line, permitting users to access the information interactively. In some cases, as with the SLATEC library, documentation is provided only in machine-readable form. Because of this, SLATEC established rigid documentation standards for subprograms accepted into their library. The *SLATEC Prologue*, which is included in each subprogram, includes sections on purpose, problem classification, precision, keywords, authors, description, related routines, references, routines called, and revision history. Such standards greatly ease the integration of online documentation into local systems.

Bibliography

1985. Boisvert, R. F., Howe, S. E., and Kahaner, D. K. "A Framework for the Management of Scientific Software," *ACM Transactions on Mathematical Software*, **11**, 313–355.

1990. Dongarra, J. J., Du Croz, J., Hammarling, S., and Duff, I. "A Set of Level 3 Basic Linear Algebra Subprograms," *ACM Transactions on Mathematical Software*, **16**, 1–17.

R. F. Boisvert

PROGRAM SPECIFICATION

For articles on related subjects, see

+ Abstract Data Type
+ Information Hiding
+ Program Verification
+ Software Engineering
+ Software Prototyping

Program specification may refer to a statement of requirements for a program, an expression of a design for a program, or a formal statement of conditions against which the program can be verified. Whatever the kind of specification, there are concerns as to *consistency* (Is the specification logically satisfiable?), *implementability* (Is the specification practically realizable?), *completeness* (Does the specification capture the *full* intent of the specifier?), and *nonambiguity* (Does the specification capture the *precise* intent of the specifier?).

Uses of Specifications

In the *requirement-analysis* phase, a specification helps crystallize the customer's possibly vague ideas and reveals contradictions, ambiguities, and incompleteness. In *program design*, a specification captures precisely the interfaces between program modules. Each interface specification provides the module's client the information needed to use the module without knowledge of its implementation. *Program verification* is the process of showing the consistency between a program and its specification. In *program validation*, a specification can be used to generate test cases for black-box testing. Together with the program, it can be used for path testing, unit testing, and integration testing. Finally, a specification serves as a kind of program documentation.

Example

Consider the specification of a data abstraction for a *bag* (in the sense of a sack that holds inserted items), as expressed in the specification language Larch. The example is from Guttag *et al.* (1985). The first part of this specification, called a *trait*, specifies state-independent properties of data accessed by programs; the second part, called an *interface*, specifies state-dependent behavior (e.g. side effects—*q.v.*, and exceptional termination of program modules). There is an interface specification for each programming language. For example, a Larch/Pascal interface specification describes the behavior of a Pascal (*q.v.*) program; it would look different from a Larch/C interface specification.

Figure 1 presents a trait that is useful for describing values of multisets and is written in the style of algebraic specifications. A *multiset* is an unordered collection of items that may contain duplicates. A *trait* defines a set of function symbols and a set of equations that define the meaning of the function symbols. The equations determine an equivalence relation on terms written using the function symbols. The generated by clause states that all multiset values can be represented by terms composed solely of the two function symbols, new and insert. This clause defines an inductive rule of inference and is useful for proving properties about all multiset values. The partitioned by clause adds more equivalences between terms. Intuitively, it states that two terms are equal if they cannot be distinguished by any of the functions listed in the clause. In the example, we could use this property to show that order of insertion of elements in a multiset does not matter. The converts clause is a way to state that this algebraic specification is sufficiently complete.

Figure 2 gives a Larch/Pascal interface specification of a bag data abstraction. It introduces a type name, three procedures, and one function. The body of each routine's specification places constraints on proper arguments for calls on the routine and defines the relevant aspects of the routine's behavior when it is properly called. It can be translated into a first-order predicate over two states by combining its three predicates into a single predicate of the form

requires predicate ⇒
 (**modifies** predicate & **ensures** predicate).

An omitted **requires** is interpreted as **true**.

In the body of a Larch/Pascal specification, the name of a function stands for the value returned by that

```
        Multiset: trait
            introduces
                new: -> Mset
                insert : Mset, E -> Mset
                isEmpty: Mset -> Bool
                size : Mset -> Card
                count : Mset, E -> Card
                delete: Mset, E -> Mset
                numElements: Mset -> Card
            constrains Mset -> Card
              MSet generated by [new, insert]
              Mset partitioned by [count] for all [C: Mset, e, e1, e2:E]
                  isEmpty (new)=true
                  isEmpty (insert(c,e1), e2)=False
                  size(new) = 0
                  size (insert(c,e) = 0
                  count (new, e1)=0
                  count(insert(c,e1),e2)=count(c, e2) + (if e1 = e2 then 1 else 0)
                  numElements(new) = 0
                  numElements(insert(c,e))=numElements(c)+(if count c,e)>0 then 0 else 1)
                  delete (new,e1) = new
                  delete(insert(c,e1),e2) = if e1 = e2 then c else insert (delete(c,e2),e1)
                  implies converts [isEmpty, size, count, delete, numElements]
```

Figure 1. Specification of multiset values.

```
        type Bag exports bagInit,bagAdd,bagRemove,bagChoose
            based on sort Mset from Multiset with [integer for E]
            procedure bagInit (var b: Bag)
                modifies at most [b]
                ensures b' = new

            procedure bagAdd (var b: Bag; e: integer
                requires numElements(insert(b,e))< = 100
                modifies at most [b]
                ensures b' = insert (b,e)

            procedure bagRemove (var b: Bag; e: integer)
                modifies at most[b]
                ensures b' =delete (b,e)

            function bagChoose (b: Bag; var e: integer): boolean
                modifies at most [b]
                ensures if ~isEmpty (b) then bagChoose & count (b,e') > 0
                             else ~ bagChoose & modifies nothing
```

Figure 2. Interface specification of a Larch/Pascal bag abstraction.

function. Formal parameters may appear unqualified or qualified. An unqualified formal parameter stands for the value of that parameter when the routine is called. A primed formal parameter such as b' stands for the value of that formal parameter when the routine returns. The values of variables on entry to and return from routines must be distinguished because Pascal statements may alter memory. Since the function symbols in a Larch trait specification represent functions, this complication does not arise there, nor would it in an interface language for a functional programming (q.v.) language.

The **modifies** predicate is also related to the imperative nature of Pascal. The predicate **modifies**

at most $[v_1, \ldots, v_n]$ asserts that the routine changes the value of no variable in the environment of the caller except possibly some subset of the variables denoted by the elements of $\{v_1, \ldots, v_n\}$. Notice that this predicate is really an assertion about all variables that do *not* appear in the list, not about those that do.

The **based on** clause associates the type *Bag* with the sort *MSet* that appears in trait *MultiSet*. This association means that Larch trait terms of algebraic sort *MSet* are used to represent Pascal values of type *Bag*. For example, the term **new** is used to represent the value that *b* is to have when *bagInit* returns. The **requires** clause of *bagAdd* states a precondition that is to be satisfied on each call. It reflects the specifier's concern with how this type can be implemented. By putting a bound on the number of distinct elements in the *Bag*, the specification allows a fixed-size representation.

The most interesting routine is *bagChoose*. Its specification says that it must set *e* to some value in *b* (if *b* is not empty, where ' $\sim$ ' denotes negation), but does not say which value. Moreover, it doesn't even require that different invocations of *bagChoose* with the same value produce the same result; in other words, the implementation may be *nondeterministic*. Our implementation is abstractly nondeterministic, even though it is a deterministic program.

This interface specification has recorded a number of design decisions beyond those contained in the trait *MultiSet*. It says which routines must be implemented, and for each routine, it indicates both the condition that must hold at the point of call and the condition that must hold upon return. Thus, a contract that provides a *logical firewall* has been established between the implementers and the clients of type *Bag*. They can then proceed independently, relying only on the interface specification.

Other specification languages for sequential programming are **VDM** (Vienna Development Method) and **Z** (pronounced "zed"). The latter is based on mathematical set theory and predicate logic, and has been used to specify industrial projects, particularly in Europe. There are also specification languages for concurrent programming (*q.v.*), which are less widely used, but have been applied to some safety-critical problems.

Bibliography

1985. Guttag, J. V., Horning, J. J., and Wing, J. M. "The Larch Family of Specification Languages," *IEEE Software*, **2**(5), (September), 24–36.

1990. Wing, J. M. "A Specifier's Introduction to Formal Methods," *IEEE Computer*, **23**(9), (September), 8–24.

1994. Morgan, C. C. *Programming from Specifications*, 2nd Ed. Upper Saddle River, NJ: Prentice Hall.

Jeannette M. Wing

PROGRAM VERIFICATION

For an article on a related subject, *see*

+ Program Specification

Definition

To *verify* a program means to demonstrate, via a mathematical proof, that the program is consistent with its specifications. It may be quite useful just to prove limited properties, such as that the program terminates or that certain variables remain unchanged. The criterion of success is to construct a sufficiently believable proof.

Basic Technique and Example

The most common technique for verifying a program is based on the association of assertions with various points in the program. *Assertions* are propositions involving the variables of the program usually expressed in a system like the first-order predicate calculus. The intent is that each assertion be true every time the execution of the program passes the point with which that assertion is associated. The proof requirement is to demonstrate that this intent is actually satisfied. Those assertions that appear at the end of a program are called *postconditions*; assuming that the program terminates, these give the result of the program. Assertions that appear at the start of a program are called *preconditions*. Because programs do not accept arbitrary inputs, a precondition is intended to give a sufficient condition for the program to compute its result. For example, a program to compute the inverse of a matrix or the reciprocal of a number requires (at least) nonzero input. The only other requirement on the association of assertions is that every loop must contain at least one point with an assertion. An assertion that is true for every execution of a loop is called a *loop invariant*.

The standard way to achieve the proof requirement is to focus on a particular assertion, say P_1, and to follow the program execution from P_1 along all possible paths, stopping on each path when another assertion, P_2, is reached. One must show, for each such path, that P_1 and the effects of the statements between P_1 and P_2

imply that P_2 holds. Suppose we do this for all assertions, including preconditions, and suppose that for each P_1 we can show that P_2 holds. In particular, the postconditions will be a P_2 for one or more P_1 preconditions. Thus, if the postconditions are actually reached (i.e. the program halts), they will be true. This argument by mathematical induction justifies the method and motivates some of its terminology.

As a simple example, consider the program whose aim is to count the nonnegative elements in the n-element array $A[1..n]$.

```
poscount := 0; i := 1;
while i ≤n do
  begin
    if A[i] ≥ 0
    then poscount := poscount + 1;
    i := i + 1
  end
```

Figure 1 is a flowchart of this program with assertions 1, 2, and 3 added. There, the notation `Positive(A, j, k)` informally denotes the number of nonnegative elements of A in the range j to k inclusive. A formal recursive definition is

```
Positive(A, j, k) = if j > k then 0
                       else if A(k) ≡ 0 then
                             1 + Positive(A, j, k-1)
                       else Positive(A, j, k-1)
```

For convenience, we assume that n is nonnegative. The postconditions 3 express the aim of the program. A very informal proof of this program might be simply that *poscount*, initially zero, is incremented for each nonnegative element encountered as A is inspected, element by element, by the **while** loop.

A more rigorous version of this informal proof uses the loop invariant 2 which appears just prior to the

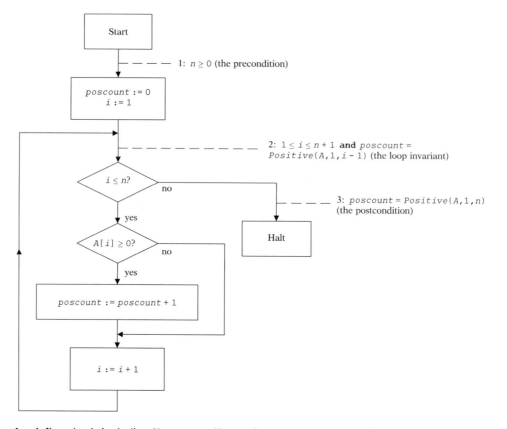

Figure 1. A flowchart, including three assertions, of a program to count the nonnegative elements of array $A[1..n]$.

test to the **while** statement, thereby satisfying the requirement that each loop have at least one assertion point. There are four paths between assertions in this example: (a) 1 to 2, (b) 2 and $A[i] \geq 0$ back to 2, (c) 2 and not $A[i] \geq 0$ back to 2, and (d) 2 to 3. The four propositions to be proved follow:

(a) $n \geq 0$ **and** $poscount = 0$ **and** $i = 1 \Rightarrow$
    $1 \geq i \geq n+1$ **and**
    $poscount$=Positive(A, 1, i-1)
(b) $1 \leq i \leq n+1$ **and** $poscount =$
    Positive(A,1i-1) **and** $i \leq n$ **and**
    $A[i]$ >=0 **and**
    $poscount'$=$poscount$ + 1
    and $i' = i + 1 \Rightarrow$
    $1 \leq i' \leq n+1$ **and**
    $poscount'$=Positive(A, 1, i'-1)

The prime ($'$) has been introduced to denote the "new" value of a variable. The arrow denotes logical implication.

(c) As (b) except $poscount' = poscount$
    and not $(A[i] > 0)$.

(d) $1 \leq i \leq n+1$ **and** $poscount =$
    Positive(A, 1, i-1)
    and not $(i \leq n) \Rightarrow$
    $poscount$=Positive(A,1,n)

Each of these propositions can be easily proved informally, using traditional and elementary mathematical reasoning, or formally, using the techniques of, say, the predicate calculus.

Current Capabilities in Practice

Various program verification systems have been implemented and have been applied to significant examples and applications. Capabilities exist to take annotated programs and produce the required propositions; to prove these propositions; to express mathematical concepts and prove consequences of those concepts; and to combine proofs of parts of programs or mathematical theories into proofs of programs or theories that use these parts. Examples of successful verifications by these systems include computer science algorithms such as sorting (*q.v.*), searching (*q.v.*), pattern matching,

implementations of abstract data types (*q.v.*), numerical calculations, and simple language compilers and interpreters.

Bibliography

1987. Loeckz, J., and Sieber, K. *The Foundations of Program Verification*, 2nd Ed. New York: John Wiley.
1997. Meyer, B. *Object-Oriented Software Construction*, 2nd Ed. Upper Saddle River, NJ: Prentice Hall.

Ralph L. London and Daniel Craigen

PROGRAMMABLE CALCULATOR

See CALCULATORS, ELECTRONIC AND PROGRAMMABLE.

PROGRAMMING LANGUAGES

For articles on related subjects, *see*

+ Ada
+ Algol
+ Basic
+ C
+ C++
+ Cobol
+ Compiler
+ Fortran
+ Functional Programming
+ Java
+ Language Processors
+ Lisp
+ List Processing: Languages
+ Logic Programming
+ Logo
+ Machine- and Assembly-language Programming
+ Nonprocedural Languages

At the lowest level, a programming language is pure binary code. This is so impractical to use that humans almost never use it, even though it is actually the only language that the machine "understands" without further translation. A step above this is what is generally referred to as *machine code or symbolic machine code*. In this case, the user generally writes instruction commands using alphabetic symbols (e.g. SUB for subtract, TRA for transfer control, etc.). Machine addresses are written in normal decimal form (e.g. 1723). At the next higher level is *symbolic assembly language* in which the names of variables as well as commands are written symbolically (e.g. ALPHA, TEMP, X, Y, Z). Thus, a user might write

```
CLA Z      (CLA=clear accumulator and add)
ADD ALPHA
STO TEMP   (STO=store)
```

meaning: "Add the values of variables stored in locations named Z and ALPHA and store the result in a location named TEMP." A program called an *assembler* (*q.v.*) assigns absolute storage locations to the variables and fills in the numeric values for machine addresses in the instructions.

The next level of complexity involves a *macroassembler* in which the user may define new "instructions" as sequences of assembly language statements and use them in a program, with their definitions being given elsewhere in the program; for example, INCR ALPHA might represent the use of a macro (*q.v.*) INCRement which adds 1 to its argument.

The previous levels bring us to what is frequently called *high-level language*, a term used here interchangeably with the term *programming language*.

Definition of Programming Language[1]

A *programming language* is a set of characters, rules for combining them, and rules specifying their effects when executed by a computer, which have the following four characteristics:

1. It requires no knowledge of machine code on the part of the user.
2. A programming language must have some significant amount of machine independence.
3. When a source program is translated into machine language, there is normally more than one machine instruction generated for each high-level language *statement* (*q.v.*).
4. A programming language employs a notation that is closer to that of the specific problem being solved than is machine code.

Benefits of Programming Languages

A major benefit provided by a programming language is that it is easier to learn than a lower-level machine or assembly language. A second benefit is that a problem written in a programming language is generally easier to debug. Third, a program coded in a programming language is generally easier to understand and modify by someone other than the originator. Fourth, the notation of a programming language automatically provides a part of necessary program documentation because its logic is relatively easy to follow. Fifth, a programming language that permits user-defined abstractions as well as those built into the language can be a powerful tool for organizing large programs.

Classifications of Programming Languages

Procedural vs Nonprocedural

Procedure-oriented

In a *procedure-oriented language*, the user specifies a set of executable operations that are to be performed in sequence. These operations can be organized into *procedures* or subprograms (*q.v.*), and a program is constructed as a sequence of procedure calls and other statements. The key property is that these constructs are definitely executable operations, and the sequencing is already specified by the user. Fortran, Cobol, and Ada are examples.

Object-oriented languages such as C++ and Java are procedural languages that allow data to be packaged with the procedures that operate on them and to hide implementation details of the data and of the operations. Such *data abstraction* (*see* ABSTRACT DATA TYPE and INFORMATION HIDING) is an important software engineering tool for the construction of large programs.

Nonprocedural

Nonprocedural language (*q.v.*) is a relative term characterizing the degree to which a user can specify *what* is to be done rather than *how* to do it. The closer the user can come to stating a problem without specifying the sequential steps for solving it, the more nonprocedural is the language. Logic programming languages like Prolog and functional languages like Haskell and pure Lisp are among the best examples of nonprocedural languages. In logic programming, in particular, a problem description can sometimes be a complete program. Other nonprocedural systems (not really languages) are report generators (RPG) and sort generators in which the individual specifies the input and the desired output without any description of the procedures needed to obtain the output.

The so-called "visual languages" are partly nonprocedural. They provide convenient ways of building programs by joining prepared elements like window menus and buttons. As such construction becomes more common, programs may be built without explicit use of programming languages except for the "glue" that combines the parts. However, programming languages are still the means for writing the components themselves.

General- and Special-Purpose Languages

General

Programming languages are designed for application to problem-domains of varying breadth. Fortran is designed to be primarily useful for numerical scientific problems, while Cobol is designed for business data processing. C originated as a systems programming language, and Simula as a language for simulation. Some languages, such as Ada and C++, are useful in multiple application areas. The term *general purpose* is sometimes applied to these languages, but there is no truly general-purpose language in the sense of one that does all jobs equally well.

Domain-specific languages

Several related terms are in use. *Problem-oriented language* (*q.v.*) has been used to characterize a language that is well-adapted to a particular kind of problem, and that is easier to use for it than others are. But any language may be called problem-oriented, being intended to solve problems. Similarly, *application-oriented* is sometimes used to describe languages intended for particular purposes, but any language is application oriented, if only to a broad area like numerical computations. Another term is *special-purpose* language: one that is designed to meet a single objective. The objective might involve the application area, the ease of use for a particular application, or pertain to efficiency of the compiler or the object code. A common and useful term that covers all of these is *domain-specific* language, which indicates that the language has a limited rather than a broad domain. There are many such languages, for computer graphics, simulation, machine-tool control, robotics, expert systems, and architectural design, to name just a few domains.

Specification and Description Languages

A *problem-defining* or *specification* language is one that literally defines the problem and may specifically define the desired input and output, but it *does not* define the method of transformation. There are significant differences between a problem (and its definition), the method (or procedure) used to solve it, and the language in which this method is stated. These languages, such as Z and UML (Unified Modeling Language) play an increasing role in software engineering.

A *reference* language is the definitive character set and form of a language. It usually has a unique character for each concept or character in the language, is one-dimensional, and need not be suitable as computer input.

A *publication* language is some well-defined variation of the reference language that is suitable for publication of programs. It is designed to be suitable for printing or writing; therefore, it will have reasonable rules and characters for such things as subscripts, exponents, Greek letters, and other symbols.

A *hardware* language, sometimes called a *hardware representation*, is a mapping of the reference language into a form suitable for direct input to a computer. The number and types of characters used must be those accepted by the computer involved, and is often determined by those available on input devices.

Parallel-Processing Languages

Languages for parallel processing (*q.v.*) have some distinctive features, intended to handle the need to synchronize access to shared data and to provide communication between parallel activities. In most respects, however, they fall into the classifications already developed. Some, like High Performance Fortran, extend procedural constructs to cover multiple sequential activities, such as computations on many elements of a vector at once.

History and Statistics

A large number of high-level languages have been developed since the first ones in the early 1950s. By 1967, there were more than 115 implemented (Fig. 1) and in use at some time just in the USA. By 1999, there were well over 1000 languages that had been used at one time or another, but many of them are no longer in use. Of this large number of languages developed in a 45-year time span, only a handful have been truly significant, and even fewer have been widely used.

In approximate chronological order, some languages of major significance, and the approximate dates of their earliest public documentation and/or general availability, are shown below.[2] In some instances, earlier

Figure 1. The Tower of Babel, representing the large number of programming languages, is a concept that first appeared in the *Communications of the ACM*. The form shown above was used as the jacket design for *Programming Languages: History and Fundamentals* by J. E. Sammet, ©1969, Prentice-Hall, Inc, Upper Saddle River, NJ.

versions of the language contributed significantly to the ones listed here.

- APT (*Automatically Programmed Tools*); 1957. The first language for a specialized application area.
- Fortran (*FORmula TRANslation*); 1956. The first high-level language to be widely used. It opened the door to practical usage of computers by large numbers of scientific and engineering personnel.
- Flow-Matic; 1958. The first language suitable for business data processing and the first to have heavy emphasis on an "English-like" syntax.
- IPL-V (*Information Processing Language V*); 1958. The first—and also a major—language for doing list processing.

- Cobol (*COmmon Business-Oriented Language*); 1960. One of the most widely used languages on an absolute basis, and the most widely used for business applications. Technical attributes include real attempts at an English-like syntax and at machine independence.
- Algol 60 (*ALGOrithmic Language*); 1960. Developed for specifying algorithms, primarily numerical. Introduced many specific features in an elegant fashion and, combined with its formal syntactic definition, it inspired most of the theoretical work in programming languages and much of the work on implementation techniques. It is more widely used in Europe than in the USA.
- Lisp (*LISt Processing*); 1960. Introduced concepts of functional programming combined with a facility for doing list processing. Used by many of the people working in the field of artificial intelligence (AI–*q.v.*). Its Scheme dialect is used in teaching and research.
- GPSS (*General-Purpose Systems Simulator*); 1961. The first language to make simulation a practical tool for people.
- APL (*A Programming Language*); 1962. Provided many higher-level operators that permitted extremely short algorithms and fostered new ways of looking at some problems. An implementable version was not defined until 1967.
- Formac (*FORmula MAnipulation Compiler*); 1964. The first language to be used fairly widely on a practical basis for mathematical problems needing formal algebraic manipulation.
- Pascal; 1971. Introduced some new ideas about data typing and combined numerous known constructs in a neat and elegant manner in a fairly small language. It was widely used for teaching purposes for many years.
- Prolog; 1971. Developed to provide facilities for logic programming. It has been significantly used in artificial intelligence applications.
- Smalltalk; 1971. This language has undergone numerous distinct versions, the most widely used being that of 1980. Its most significant characteristic is the use of "objects" to permit object-oriented programming in a wide range of applications.

- C; 1974. Originally created to assist in developing the Unix operating system (*q.v.*) but now widely used for systems programming and numerical methods. C++, an object-oriented language, is an extension of C.
- Ada; 1979. A very large, powerful language developed initially for embedded computer systems under the auspices of the US Department of Defense. It has been used for both military and nonmilitary government applications (e.g. FAA, NASA). It has also been used in numerous commercial applications in the private sector and in diverse applications such as artificial intelligence and business data processing.
- Java; 1995. An object-oriented language resembling C++ developed for machine-independent programming and for programs that could be transferred over the World Wide Web for execution on the receiving computer.

Some other languages that have been widely used are Basic, PL/I, Simscript, Snobol, and Icon.

Notes

[1] This section and the next three include material from Sammet (1969).

[2] This list and subsequent text are based on material excerpted with some modifications and additions from "Programming languages: history and future," by J. E. Sammet, *Comm. of the ACM*, **15**, (7) (July, 1972), 603–604, used with permission.

Bibliography

1969. Sammet, J. E. *Programming Languages: History and Fundamentals.* Upper Saddle River, NJ: Prentice Hall.

1996. Pratt, T. W., and Zelkowitz, M. V. *Programming Languages: Design and Implementation*, 3rd Ed. Upper Saddle River, NJ: Prentice Hall.

1999. MacLennan, B. J. *Programming Languages: Design, Evaluation, and Implementation*, 3rd Ed. Oxford: Oxford University Press.

Jean E. Sammet

PROGRAMMING SUPPORT ENVIRONMENTS

For articles on related subjects, see

+ Debugging
+ Software Engineering
+ Software Maintenance
+ Software Reusability

Programming support environments are software tools that improve programmer productivity. All modern programming languages provide some programming support features, such as debugging tools. The Ada (*q.v.*) language project, in particular, has emphasized its *Ada programming support environment* (APSE) from the beginning. Advanced environments can support programmers in designing, coding, debugging, testing, maintaining, browsing, documenting, project tracking, reverse engineering, and customizing software. In addition, online help and embedded instructions assist programmers learning to use programming environments. Some environments support groups of programmers who work collaboratively on large software-development projects. CASE (computer-aided software engineering) tools automate aspects of the software development process and encourage the use of particular programming methodologies.

Design

To improve the process of designing software, programming methodologies have been developed and integrated into some support environments. For instance, tools that support authoring and viewing entity–relationship database diagrams encourage the use of that methodology. Typically, CASE systems provide a user interface (*q.v.*) for authoring models of organizations and systems, specifying complex behaviors and processes, and laying out data structures (*q.v.*).

Coding

Libraries of subroutines and program templates allow the reuse of software and therefore decrease the time and expense of writing new software. Online help systems and menu-based programming systems improve programmer productivity by decreasing the time programmers spend searching through manuals.

Debugging

Programmers use a variety of support tools during the debugging process. A *stepper* allows programmers to monitor execution of code line by line. An *inspector* is used to examine and modify data structures in memory. A *stack backtrace* facility is used to examine the stack (*q.v.*) after an error is detected. A *breakpoint* and *watchpoint* facility is used to help track down side effects (*q.v.*). A *trace* facility is used to monitor function calls and argument values.

Testing

Test-case libraries are used to insure that software meets design specifications. Tools that support developing, maintaining, and executing test cases are required. Bug-tracking facilities are used to inform the development of test cases. An active area of research is concerned with automatic generation of test cases from software design specifications.

Maintenance

To perform software maintenance, programmers require tools that help them understand existing code that they may not have written. Tools exist to generate data flow, control flow, and calling hierarchy diagrams. Since the quality of documentation affects maintenance programmer productivity, an active area of research is concerned with techniques for better capturing the intentions of designers, the strategies of implementers, and the reasoning of maintainers.

Bibliography

1989. McClure, C. "The CASE Experience," *Byte*, 14 April, . 235–236 Highstown, NJ: McGraw-Hill.

1989. Norman, R. J., and Nunamaker, J. F. "CASE Productivity Perceptions of Software Engineering Professionals," *Communications of the ACM*, **32**(9), (September), 1102–1108.

James C. Spohrer

PROGRAMMING

See APPLICATIONS PROGRAMMING;
CONCURRENT PROGRAMMING;
FUNCTIONAL PROGRAMMING; LIST
PROCESSING; LOGIC PROGRAMMING;
MACHINE- AND ASSEMBLY-LANGUAGE
PROGRAMMING; MICROPROGRAMMING;
MODULAR PROGRAMMING;
OBJECT-ORIENTED PROGRAMMING;
STRUCTURED PROGRAMMING; and SYSTEMS
PROGRAMMING.

PROLOG

See LOGIC PROGRAMMING.

PROOF OF CORRECTNESS

See PROGRAM VERIFICATION.

PROPRIETARY PROGRAM

See LEGAL PROTECTION OF SOFTWARE.

PROTECTION, MEMORY

See MEMORY PROTECTION.

PROTOCOL

For articles on related subjects, *see*

+ Bus
+ Gateway
+ Handshaking
+ Internet
+ Network Protocols
+ TCP/IP

A *protocol* is an agreement that two or more communicating entities use to structure their conversations. Like a duet, a protocol is an algorithm whose successful implementation depends on compliance with rules parceled out to two (or more) separate but interacting executors. When the executors are part of a network, their rules of engagement are called a *network protocol*. Protocols may be implemented in hardware, software, or a combination of both.

Because protocols are often highly complex, they are frequently structured in layers and implemented in both hardware and software. The lowest layer is typically concerned with electrical and mechanical aspects. The middle layers deal with grouping bits into well-defined units (frames, packets, messages) and reliably sending them from the originator to the destination, possibly hop-by-hop over several intermediate machines. The upper layers have to do with the meaning of the information sent, such as protocols for file transfer and electronic mail (*q.v.*). The International Organization for Standardization (ISO) has defined a complex set of protocols called the *Open Systems Interconnection* (OSI—*q.v.*) that are intended to cover the entire spectrum of networking applications, from the lowest layer to the highest.

Bibliography

1999. Tanenbaum, A. *Structural Computer Organization*, 4th Ed. Upper Saddle River, NJ: Prentice Hall.

Andrew S. Tanenbaum

PROTOTYPING

See SOFTWARE PROTOTYPING.

PUBLISHING

See DESKTOP PUBLISHING.

PUNCHED CARD

For articles on related subjects, *see*

+ Character Codes
+ Hollerith, Herman

Punched card data processing was invented by Herman Hollerith for the 1890 US population census. In this first application, a single $6\frac{5}{8} \times 3\frac{2}{4}$-inch card was punched for each citizen, recording such nonnumerical data as gender, marital status, and nationality. Following the success of the census, Hollerith incorporated the Tabulating Machine Company (TMC) in 1896 to exploit his machines for statistical and accounting applications in commerce. These applications required data to be recorded in numerical form, so the card was redesigned with a number of vertical columns, each of which could represent a single decimal digit. A numerical value was then represented by a *field* of several adjacent columns. Early forms of the punched

card had 34 and 37 columns, but eventually Hollerith standardized on a $7\frac{3}{8} \times 3\frac{1}{4}$-inch 45-column card with round holes (Fig. 1). The 45 columns were arranged in 12 rows: the top row was known as the "12" or "Y" row; the second row was the "11" or "X" row; and the remaining rows were designated "0" through "9"; rows 0 to 9 were used to record the value of a digit, while the X and Y rows were used to indicate the sign of a number, or other control information. The 45-column format was also adopted by the rival Powers Accounting Machine Company, which was incorporated in 1911.

In 1928 IBM, the successor to TMC, introduced the 80-column card using rectangular "slotted" holes (Fig. 2). The new card enabled nearly twice as much information to be stored on the same size card. In the 48-character Hollerith Code used with the new card, the digits 0 to 9 were represented by a single "digit punch" using the same code as the 45- and 80-column numerical cards. To represent the letters of the alphabet, A to Z, a single-digit punch was supplemented with one of three "zone punches." Special characters were generally coded by means of a zone punch and two-digit punches.

In order to increase the capacity of its own card, Remington Rand, which had absorbed the Powers company, introduced a 90-column card, which consisted of two 45-column tiers. In the 90-column card, each character was represented by a 6-hole code. This code required a relatively complicated decoding

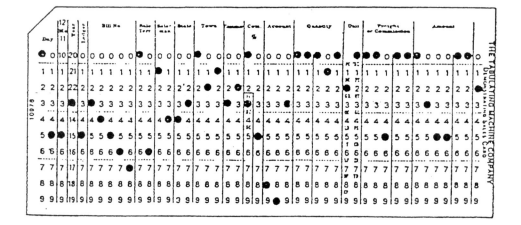

Figure 1. Example of a 45-column card, c.1913.

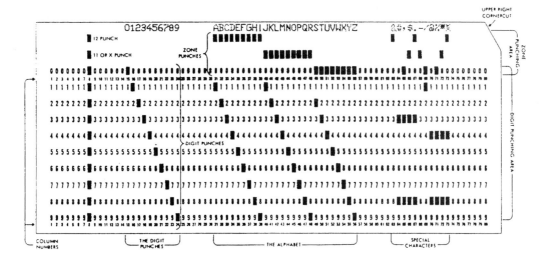

Figure 2.   IBM 80-column card, introduced 1928.

mechanism and was not compatible with the 45-column card. Because of these disadvantages—and Remington Rand's smaller market share—the 90-column card was always much less popular than the 80-column format.

In the 1950s and 1960s, 80-column punched cards became the dominant computer input medium, and the old Hollerith Code was superseded by more generous character sets. These included the 64-character set of the IBM 1400 series, the 128-character ASCII code, and the 256-character EBCDIC code. In 1969, for use with its System/3 computer, IBM introduced a new, small card that measured $3\frac{1}{4} \times 2\frac{11}{16}$ inches and held 96 characters arranged in three tiers of 32 6-bit characters.

As an input medium to computers, punched cards long outlived the electromechanical machines for which they had been designed. However, from the beginning of the 1970s, the advent of interactive terminals caused a rapid falloff in punched card usage, which for all practical purposes, ceased in the mid-1980s.

Martin Campbell-Kelly

PUSHDOWN STACK

See STACK.

QUANTUM COMPUTING

For articles on related subjects, see

+ Cryptography, Computers in
+ Logic Design

In a conventional computer, information is represented by quantities that obey the laws of classical physics, such as the voltage levels in a logic circuit. However, as the size of microelectronics shrinks, underlying quantum physics will eventually become important. In the early 1980s, this observation led Paul Benioff and later Richard Feynman to consider how to compute with information represented by quantum mechanical quantities. For example, an atomic electron has certain quantum states of motion with energies that are discrete or quantized. An electron in one of these states could be used to represent a binary 0 and when it is in a second, to represent a binary 1. A two-state quantum system that is used to store a single bit of information is called a *qubit*.

With two or more qubits, it becomes possible to consider quantum logical "gate" operations in which the state of one qubit changes in a way that is contingent upon the state of another. These gate operations are the building blocks of a *quantum computer* (QC). Quantum computation remained a largely abstract subject until 1994, when Peter Shor showed that a QC could find the prime factors of composite integers much more efficiently than any conventional computer. This is important because integer factorization and related problems that are computationally intractable with

conventional computers are the basis for the security of modern public key cryptosystems. The practical realization of a QC is still in its infancy, but current experiments are producing encouraging results.

The logic gates in a QC are effected through quantum mechanical interactions between the qubits. Because the laws of nature are reversible in time, logic operations themselves must also be reversible. Although many conventional logic operations are not reversible (e.g. neither a nor b can be recovered from the value of $a \vee b$), those required for quantum computation can be performed reversibly, and from them it is possible to perform any Boolean operation (*see* Fig. 1). A computer based on these quantum operations would not necessarily be particularly powerful or fast; the real power of a QC would arise from the ability to perform much more general quantum gate operations that are not limited to the conventional Boolean operations of ordinary computers.

It is one of the most counterintuitive features of quantum physics that, at the atomic scale, material systems can behave with wavelike properties and exhibit the phenomenon of superposition, so that a qubit in a superposition state has aspects of *both* 0 and 1 simultaneously. Of course, once measured, a qubit in a superposition state will always be found to have a definite 0 or 1 value, with only the *probability* of each result being predictable by quantum mechanics, and determined by the amount of each component in the superposition. In 1986, David Deutsch realized that a QC could exploit this distinctly nonclassical phenomenon of quantum

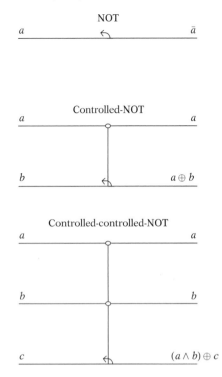

NOT

a $\bar{a}$

Controlled-NOT

a a

b $a \oplus b$

Controlled-controlled-NOT

a a

b b

c $(a \wedge b) \oplus c$

Figure 1. A set of three universal reversible Boolean logic gates, for which the input bit values (*a, b, c*) can be recovered from the output values by a second application of the same logic gate. All of the arithmetic functions for conventional computation can be constructed from this set of gates. The curved arrows represent the qubit in one of its two possible states.

superposition with a sort of continuously-valued (non-Boolean) logic to provide massive computational parallelism. In a QC, a single-qubit operation can be used to prepare a superposition state. Similarly, with only n single-qubit operations, one for each qubit in the register, an n-qubit register could be prepared in a superposition of all possible 2^n values at once, providing a highly parallel memory.

In 1994 Shor showed how non-Boolean qubit operations could be used to perform a quantum Fourier transform (QFT) operation, with exponentially fewer operations than the classical fast Fourier transform (FFT). His QFT could be used to find the period of a function efficiently on a QC, and he related the problem of factoring an integer to a periodicity problem, showing that factoring could be solved efficiently on a quantum computer. To put Shor's algorithm in perspective, during 1994 a 129-digit number known as RSA-129 was factored in eight months, requiring 10^{17} instructions performed on over 1000 networked computers (*see* COOPERATIVE COMPUTING). However, a (still hypothetical) QC with a clock speed of 100 MHz could have factored this number in a few seconds, requiring a memory of about 2000 qubits and 10^9 quantum logic gates. Furthermore, the number of quantum gates required to factor even larger numbers grows as only a polynomial function of the number of digits in the number being factored.

Bibliography

1995. Lloyd, S. "Quantum Mechanical Computers," *Scientific American*, **273**(4), (October), 140–145.

1996. Ekert, A. K., and Josza, R. "Quantum Computation and Shor's Factoring Algorithm," *Reviews of Modern Physics*, **68**, 733–753.

1998. Gershenfeld, N., and Chuang, I. L. "Quantum Computing with Molecules," *Scientific American*, **278**(6), (June), 66–71.

1999. Hey, A. J. G. (ed.) *Feynman and Computation*. Reading, MA: Perseus.

Richard J. Hughes

RAID

See REDUNDANT ARRAY OF INEXPENSIVE DISKS (RAID).

RANDOM-ACCESS MEMORY (RAM)

See MEMORY: MAIN.

RASTER GRAPHICS

See COMPUTER GRAPHICS.

READ-ONLY MEMORY (ROM)

For articles on related subjects, *see*

+ Cycle Time
+ Emulation
+ Firmware
+ Memory: Main
+ Microprogramming
+ Optical Storage
+ Personal Computing

A *Read-Only Memory* (ROM) is a memory that retains its contents in the absence of applied power and which, though readable, cannot be easily written to, if at all (*see* Fig. 1). An example is the use of ROM in early microcomputers to hold an invariant copy of the processor for a high-level language such as Basic (*q.v.*) or Pascal (*q.v.*). Another use of ROM is to hold the *bootstrap* (*q.v.*) loader, a program that is run upon computer startup to load other programs and transfer control to them.

Read-only memory can be factory programmed (and never altered) or Programmable ROM (PROM). In the latter case, the user installs the storage content and may subsequently change it. PROMs are erased by exposing

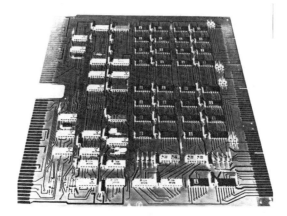

Figure 1. A 24 000-bit read-only storage chip, using field-effect transistor technology packaged in a 1-in square metallized ceramic substrate.

the device to a special light source [E(rasable) PROM] or by using a special voltage line [E(lectrically) EPROM].

Michael J. Flynn

REAL-TIME CLOCK

See INTERVAL TIMER.

REAL-TIME SYSTEMS

For articles on related subjects, *see*

+ Concurrent Programming
+ Distributed Systems
+ Embedded System
+ Fault-Tolerant Computing
+ Interrupt
+ Multiprocessing
+ Multiprogramming
+ Multitasking
+ Time Sharing

Real-time systems are those in which the correctness of the system depends not only on the logical result of computation, but also on the time at which the results are produced. Real-time systems span a broad spectrum of complexity from very simple microcontrollers (such as a microprocessor controlling an automobile engine) to highly sophisticated, complex, and distributed systems (such as air traffic control).

Typically, a real-time system consists of a *controlling system* and a *controlled system*. For example, in an automated factory, the controlled system is the factory floor with its robots, assembling stations, and the assembled parts, while the controlling system is the computers, sensors, actuators, and human interfaces that manage and coordinate activities on the floor. The controlled system can be viewed as the *environment* with which the computer interacts.

Timing correctness requirements in a real-time system arise because of the *physical impact* of the controlling system's activities upon its environment. For example, if the computer controlling a robot does not command it to stop or turn on time, the robot might collide with another object on the factory floor, possibly causing serious damage. In many real-time systems even more severe consequences will result if timing and logical correctness properties of the system are not satisfied, such as would be the case with nuclear power plants or air traffic control systems.

Aspects of Real-Time Systems

A real-time operating system *kernel* (*q.v.*) must provide basic support for predictably satisfying real-time constraints, for fault tolerance and distribution, and for integrating time-constrained resource allocations and scheduling across a spectrum of resource types including sensor processing, communications, CPU, memory, and other forms of I/O. Theoretical results have identified worst case bounds for dynamic online algorithms, and complexity results have been produced for various types of assumed task set characteristics. Queuing theory has been applied to real-time systems covering algorithms based on real-time variations of *first come, first served* (FCFS), earliest deadline, and least laxity. In FCFS, the queue of waiting tasks is ordered by first come, first served, while for earliest deadline it is ordered by the deadlines of the waiting tasks, and for least laxity by deadline minus computation time.

A real-time database is a database system where (at least some) transactions have explicit deadlines and data may have validity intervals. For example, a data item representing pressure in a chemical process may only be valid for 100 ms. In such a system, transaction processing must satisfy not only the database consistency constraints, but also the timing constraints of the transaction and data it uses. Real-time database systems can be found, for instance, in program trading in the stock market, radar tracking systems, battle management systems, and computer-integrated manufacturing systems. Some of these systems (such as program trading in the stock market) are *soft* real-time systems, so designated because missing a deadline is not catastrophic. This is in contrast to *hard* real-time systems (such as controlling a nuclear power plant) where missing a deadline may result in catastrophic consequences. In hard real-time systems, *a priori* guarantees are required for critical tasks.

Bibliography

1994. Stankovic, J., and Ramamritham, K. *Advances in Real-Time Systems*. Tutorial Text, Washington, DC: IEEE Computer Society Press.

1997. Buttazzo, G. C. *Hard Real-Time Computing Systems*. Boston, MA: Kluwer Academic.

1997. Kopetz, H. *Real-Time Systems: Design Principles for Distributed Embedded Applications*. Boston, MA: Kluwer Academic.

John A. Stankovic

REBOOT

See BOOTSTRAP.

RECORD

For articles on related subjects, *see*

+ Data Structures
+ File

A *record* is an organized and identifiable aggregate of related data values transcribed on a computer storage medium. For example, a personnel record usually contains data such as social security number, first name, middle initial, last name, date of birth, and home address. All these data are *attributes* peculiar to an individual. Elements of a record may be of a similar or dissimilar *data type* (*q.v.*): bits, integers, real numbers, character strings, and so on. The contents of punched cards (*q.v.*) and printer lines were often called *unit records*, since these document lengths were predefined for use with associated electromechanical devices. Magnetic tape and disk drives accommodate *variable-length records*.

In theory, a file or even a whole database could comprise a single block containing all its records. In practice, a large file or database may contain hundreds or thousands of blocks, each containing one or more records. The number of records per block, called the *blocking factor*, is an important consideration in determining the efficiency of file processing.

High-level languages permit the creation of record types whose instances become the actual records to be stored in memory. The first widely used language to do so was Cobol (*q.v.*). The corresponding C (*q.v.*) and C++ (*q.v.*) entities are called *structures*. Pascal (*q.v.*) record types are defined through use of the reserved word **record**. An example record type definition and corresponding variable declaration (*q.v.*) in Pascal follows:

```
Type
    payrec = record
                name: array[1..28] of char;
                rate: real;
                hours: array[1..7] of real;
                union: Boolean
             end;
var
    r:payrec; seq: array[1..100] of payrec;
    f: file of payrec;
```

The variable r is now an individual instance of a *payrec*, the variable *seq* is an array of *payrecs* stored in main memory, and the variable f is a sequential file on an external storage medium to which *payrec* records may be written and later read with statements of the form *write(f,r)* and *read(f,r)*. Each record is copied as an aggregate without the programmer having to read or write its components one by one.

With some modification to permit *information hiding* (*q.v.*), records provide a basis for the *objects* of object-oriented programming (*q.v.*). Objects are like records that hold both private data and public routines that operate on the data. Finally, linked data structures such as lists (*q.v.*) and trees (*q.v.*) can be implemented by means of records that hold both data and links to the next part of the structure.

David N. Freeman

RECURSION

For articles on related subjects, see

+ Activation Record
+ Functional Programming
+ Iteration
+ Stack
+ Turing Machine

Recursion refers to several related concepts in computer science and mathematics. We will give examples of increasing complexity.

Recursion Relations

1. The Fibonacci sequence is given by the equations

$$f_0 = 1,$$

$$f_1 = 1,$$

$$f_{n+1} = f_n + f_{n-1} \quad n \geq 1$$

2. When differential equations are to be solved numerically, *recursion relations* such as

$$f(x_0 + nh) = F(f(x_0 + (n-1)h),$$

$$f(x_0 + (n-2)h), \ldots, f(x_0 + (n-k)h))$$

arise where *f* is, in general, a vector of real numbers.

3. When linear differential equations are solved by series, recursion relations for the coefficients of the powers of the independent variables arise.

Recursive Functions

Primitive recursive functions are integer functions of integers built up from addition and multiplication

of integers and previously defined primitive recursive functions by the primitive recursion scheme

$$f(0, x_2, \ldots, x_k) = g(x_2, \ldots, x_k),$$

$$f(x_1 + 1, x_2 \ldots, x_k) = h(f(x_1, \ldots, x_k), x_1, \ldots, x_k).$$

Here, g and h are primitive recursive functions of $k - 1$ and $k + 1$ arguments, respectively. As an example, we define $n!$, where n is a positive integer by $n! = f(n)$ where $f(0) = 1$ and $f(n+1) = (n+1) \cdot f(n)$. So, in this case, g is a function of 0 arguments, namely, the constant 1, and $h(u, v) = (v+1)u$. All the common functions of number theory are primitive recursive.

Primitive recursive functions are included in *general recursive functions*. The definition of general recursive functions is like that given above for primitive recursive functions, except that the relations are replaced by an arbitrary finite collection of equations relating the values of f for different arguments, and the function is considered defined if and only if a unique value of $f(x_1, \ldots, x_k)$ can be deduced from the equations for each k-tuplet $(x_1, \ldots, x_k)$. The set of computable functions is *recursively enumerable* but not recursive. The most famous example of a general recursive function that is not primitive recursive is the *Ackermann function*, defined by the equations

$$A(0, n, p) = n + p, \quad A(1, 0, p) = 0$$

$$A(m + 2, 0, p) = 1$$

and

$$A(m + 1, n + 1, p) = A(m, A(m + 1, n, p), p)$$

An important result for computer science is that the general recursive functions coincide with the functions defined by a Turing machine, which is a simple form of computer. Both programs and general recursion schemata, in general, give *partial functions* because the computation may terminate for some values of the arguments and not for others.

Recursive Procedures

In programming, it is frequently convenient to have a procedure use itself as a subprocedure. If a procedure does this, it is called *recursive*. Recursive procedures are particularly natural in dealing with symbolic expressions because the structure of the programs often matches the structure of the data. Recursive procedures are quite natural; it requires a special statement in the definition of a programming language to forbid them. Recursive programs use a data structure called a *stack* to store the contents of variables that must be saved. This storage can be done by the calling routine before it invokes the subroutine, or by the subroutine before it uses the program variables.

The first languages to use recursive subroutines were the IPL languages of Newell, Shaw, and Simon. Lists were used for the stack and the saving and restoring was done explicitly by the programmer. The first language to provide an automatic mechanism for recursion was Lisp (*q.v.*). Algol 60 and all of its successors, such as Pascal, C++, and Ada, also allow recursion, as do virtually all other programming languages today, including Fortran 95.

Bibliography

1967. Kleene, S. C. *Mathematical Logic*. New York: John Wiley.

1967. Peter, R. *Recursive Functions*. New York: Academic Press.

1986. Roberts, E. S. *Thinking Recursively*. New York: John Wiley.

1993. Dewdney, A. K. *The Turing Omnibus*, 2nd Ed. New York: W. H. Freeman.

John McCarthy

REDUCED INSTRUCTION SET COMPUTER (RISC)

For articles on related subjects, *see*

+ Cache Memory
+ Computer Architecture
+ Instruction-Level Parallelism
+ Instruction Set
+ Microprogramming
+ Pipeline

Until 1975, computer architecture, design, and implementation had grown more complicated with each successive generation. Instruction sets were large and individual instructions were complicated. Some complex instructions had such poor implementations that it was better to program an equivalent sequence than to use them. Prior to the mid-1970s, the only computer architect whose views differed significantly from the foregoing was Seymour Cray, who, while with the Control Data Corporation in the early 1960s, designed the CDC 6600 supercomputer (*q.v.*) to have a small, simple instruction set.

At the beginning of 1975, a group was organized at IBM's T. J. Watson Research Center that had as its goal, the production of a "super mini" computer, one in which the compiler, the operating system, the architecture, and the implementation were done in concert while maintaining a very simple data format and addressing model and uniformity of instruction–execution times. Since the instructions were simple, they were directly implemented in hardware rather than microcode. The impetus for this computer came from IBM Fellow, John Cocke. His basic idea was to make all instructions simple and have a machine organization that could execute one instruction every machine cycle. The basic machine had an instruction fetch and decode stage and a register fetch and execute stage. These stages were organized into a two-deep pipeline; that is, the machine would be executing one instruction while fetching the next sequential instruction. The register write-back of a result was combined with the register fetch of the next instruction. There were two caches, one containing instructions and the other data. As long as the data or instruction needed was in a cache, there was only a one-cycle penalty on loads and a one-cycle instruction fetch penalty if a branch was taken. The instruction cache was viewed as a replacement for microcode memory.

A set of principles emerged from this work that has influenced the work of many others in this field:

1. A small instruction set consisting of simple, fixed length, fixed format instructions that execute in a single machine cycle (see INSTRUCTION DECODING).
2. A large number of registers with all instructions defined to have separate operands for register sources and register targets.
3. Use of an optimizing compiler, where machine performance was directly dependent on the compiler's ability to manage many resources that had previously been managed by hardware, such as storage delays and branch penalties.

These ideas were enhanced and promoted by David Patterson at the University of California at Berkeley and John Hennessy at Stanford University. It was Patterson who first used the term RISC (Reduced Instruction Set Computer) for this philosophy and contrasted it with CISC (Complex Instruction Set Computer). RISC architecture has led to many advances in machine organizations, especially in the areas of pipelining and instruction-level parallelism. It has brought a better understanding of machine organization along with metrics that could be used in evaluating alternative designs. It has given rise to new machine organizations, including superscalar and *very long instruction word* (VLIW) architectures.

Bibliography

1990. Cocke, J., and Markstein, V. "The Evolution of RISC Technology at IBM," *IBM Journal of Research and Development*, **34**(1), 9–38.

1996. Hennessy, J. L., and Patterson, D. A. *Computer Architecture: A Quantitative Approach*, 2nd Ed. San Francisco, CA: Morgan Kaufmann.

Richard R. Oehler

REDUNDANCY

For articles on related subjects, see

+ Error Correcting and Detecting Code
+ Fault-Tolerant Computing
+ Multiprocessing
+ Redundant Array of Inexpensive Disks (RAID)

Redundancy, the incorporation into a system design of more elements than are absolutely necessary, is the principal way to implement fault-tolerance. The redundant elements need not all be hardware components; they might also be additional software (*software redundancy*), additional time (*time redundancy*—e.g. performing a computation more than once and comparing the results), and additional information (*information redundancy*—e.g. the application of error-detection and correction codes).

Redundancies are often interrelated. Additional software requires additional memory and additional time to execute. The term *protective redundancy* is often used to characterize redundancy that has an overall beneficial effect on the system attributes, since redundancy alone without proper application may well become a liability. Protective redundancy is used to realize *fault-tolerant digital systems* and *self-repairing systems* by such means as triple or *N*-tuple modular redundancy (TMR, NMR), quadded redundancy, standby-replacement redundancy, hybrid redundancy, software redundancy, and the application of error-detection and -correction codes.

Bibliography

1998. Siewiorek, D. P., and Swarz, R. S. *Reliable Computer Systems: Design and Evaluation*, 3rd Ed. Natick, MA: A. K. Peters.

Frank P. Mathur

REDUNDANT ARRAY OF INEXPENSIVE DISKS (RAID)

For articles on related subjects, *see*

+ Access Time
+ Error Correcting and Detecting Code
+ Hard Disk
+ Mass Storage
+ Memory: Auxiliary

Introduction

RAID (*Redundant Array of Inexpensive Disks*) is an architectural concept developed to turn relatively slow and inexpensive hard disks into fast, large-capacity, and more reliable storage systems. The RAID concept was introduced by a team from the University of California at Berkeley in 1987. RAID systems derive their speed from "striping" data across multiple disks (placing successive pieces of a file, *stripes*, on different disks), thus allowing parallel data accesses. Reliability is generally achieved through replication ("mirroring") or by using error detection and correction schemes across the disk array.

Raid Levels

RAID-0 (Fig. 1) stripes (splits) the data across the disk array, which achieves speed through parallelism. RAID-0, however, does not improve reliability.

RAID-1 (Fig. 2b) focuses on reliability through redundancy, and does not offer speed. In this configuration, two sets of disks are used, primary and secondary, where the secondary disks maintain an identical image of the primary disk data, which is striped across multiple disks as in RAID-0. Thus, if a disk in one set fails, one in the other set can replace it.

In RAID-2, each block of data is striped across data disks by a stripe unit of either a bit or a byte to allow parallel accesses, as in RAID-0. In RAID-2, all the drive spindles have to be synchronized using a single actuator or multiple coupled actuators, as the data bits must be read in parallel. Error detection and correction is provided using additional disks, whose data is created using a Hamming error-correcting code to allow recovery from a single disk failure (Fig. 2c shows four data disks and three for error correction). RAID-2 performs best for large transfers in which the seek time is rapidly amortized.

RAID 3 (Fig. 2d) is similar to RAID-2, except that a single parity bit is used instead of the Hamming code, thus reducing the number of error detection/correction disks to one. If the parity bit indicates an error, disk controllers can then identify the faulty disk on their own without the need for an error-correcting code to locate the problem. The faulty disk can be then replaced and its data can be reconstructed using the remaining good disks and the parity disk.

RAID-4 (Fig. 2e) is similar in configuration to that of RAID-3, except that the unit used for data striping is the block (sector) rather than the bit or byte.

RAID-5 (Fig. 2f) alleviates the sequential bottleneck of updating the parity disk in RAID-4 by spreading the parity information. Instead of using a single disk

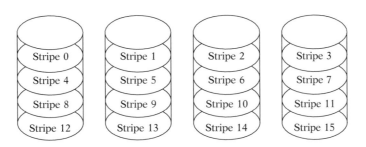

Figure 1. RAID Level 0 configuration showing the data striped across the disks of the array.

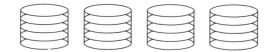

(a) Non redundant (RAID Level 0)

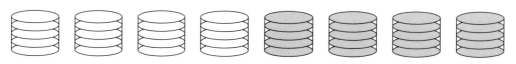

(b) Mirrored (RAID Level 1)

(c) Memory-style error-correcting code (RAID Level 2)

(d) Bit-interleaved parity (RAID Level 3)

(e) Block-interleaved parity (RAID Level 4)

(f) Block-interleaved distributed parity (RAID Level 5)

Figure 2. Redundant array of inexpensive disks. Disks with multiple platters indicate block-level striping while disks without multiple platters indicate bit-level striping. The shaded platters represent redundant information (from Chen *et al.*, 1994, courtesy of ACM).

for parity, each of the data disks contains one of the parity blocks. RAID-5 is therefore the most suitable for transaction processing, as in database applications, and is the last level in the Berkeley-defined RAID architecture.

Modifications introduced by various implementations resulted in the definition of additional RAID levels. RAID-6 is an extension of level 5 in which disks are arranged in a 2D array, and parity is determined in each dimension separately. RAID-7, in addition, uses dynamic mapping where each block of data does not always have to be stored in the same physical sector of a disk. RAID-3 and RAID-5 are the two most popular levels of RAID. Which is better depends upon the application. RAID-5 is more suitable for database applications where small concurrent transactions can be supported efficiently. RAID-3, however, is most suited for large data accesses such as those found in scientific computing applications.

Bibliography

1994. Chen, P. M., Lee, E. K., Gibson, G. A., Katz, R. H., and Patterson, D. A. "RAID: High-performance, Reliable Secondary Storage," *Computing Surveys*, **26**(2), 145–185.

1997. Raid Advisory Board. *The RAIDbook*, 6th Ed., http://www.raid-advisory.com.

Tarek El-Ghazawi and Gideon Frieder

REENTRANT PROGRAM

For articles on related subjects, see

+ Coroutine
+ Multiprogramming
+ Time Sharing

In a multiprogramming environment, a number of user programs may be sharing a common pool of subprograms or processors. Therefore, it is necessary that a shared routine be written so that it can be invoked, interrupted, and later *reentered* at its point of interruption without loss of information, even though multiple higher-level programs have progressed to variously different points in the shared *reentrant program*. Reentrant programs are sometimes called *pure procedures* or *sharable code*.

In order to be reentrant, a program must be written so that it contains no self-modifying code and so that all data required by the reentrant program can be maintained in regions of storage associated with each user program rather than as part of the reentrant program itself. Then the execution of the reentrant program can be interrupted at any point, and—provided that the data it uses is stored together with the contents of the machine registers and the *program counter* (*q.v.*)

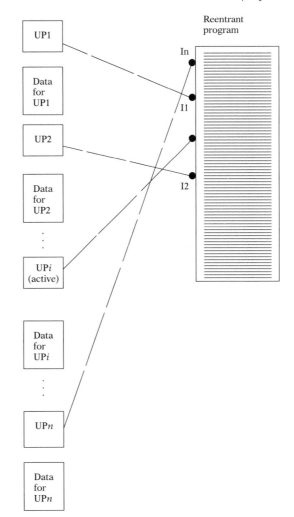

Figure 1. A reentrant program shared by *n* user processes; dashed lines indicate the point in reentrant program at which user process was interrupted; the solid line shows where reentrant program execution is taking place for the currently active user process.

at the point of interruption—the program can be immediately invoked by another user program and can be resumed at a later time by restoring the calling routine's data and program counter. Figure 1 shows a schematic of a reentrant program shared by *n* user processes.

J. A. N. Lee

REGISTER

For articles on related subjects, *see*

+ Arithmetic-Logic Unit (ALU)
+ Central Processing Unit (CPU)
+ Index Register
+ Program Counter

A *register* is a specialized storage element of the CPU consisting of storage elements that respond faster than those typically used to implement main memory. The purpose of a register is to store a string of bits representing related information: the digits of a number, the symbols of an alphanumeric word, the bits representing the status of various parts of a computer, the bits indicating the presence of interrupt requests, and so on. The number of bits that can be stored in a register is its *length*. Registers of several different lengths may be found within the same system, but the most common length is the word length of the computer. The bits X_i that are stored in the n-bit register X are usually numbered right to left and identified by the indices i in the range $0 \leq i \leq n - 1$ (Fig. 1).

All registers within a computer or other digital device are uniquely identified by names or addresses or both. The names (e.g. X, ACC (Accumulator), PC (Program Counter), MSW (machine status word), index register, etc.) often indicate the function of a register. With an addressable register architecture, register addresses are a set of N consecutive integers A $(0 \leq A \leq N - 1)$ which identify registers within a storage array (often called *local memory*).

A *shift register* is a register in which all bits may be displaced by one or more positions to the left or to the right. A *counter* is a register in which the contents progress through a sequence of consecutive binary integers. An *accumulator* is a register to which an *adder* circuit adds a specified number to its prior contents. Shifting, counting, and accumulation are performed upon receipt of appropriate machine-language commands. An *index register* ($q.v.$) keeps track of the current element of an array being processed by a program loop so as to avoid physical modification of array addresses in main memory. A *general register* is a register that can be used either as an index register, a shift register, or an accumulator.

Algirdas Avižienis

RELATIONAL DATABASE

For articles on related subjects, *see*

+ Database Management System (DBMS)
+ Data Mining
+ Data Warehousing

A *relational database* is one constructed in accordance with the *Relational Model of Data* proposed by Codd (1970). This model provides a simple and intuitive method for defining a database, storing and updating its data, and submitting to it queries of arbitrary complexity. More important, it provides a firm, sound, and consistent foundation for all the other topics that database management systems must commonly embrace.

The Relational Model is founded on the mathematics of n-ary relations, which is in turn founded on the disciplines of predicate calculus and set theory. Consider, for example, the proposition: "Brutus killed Caesar." In the context of a discussion about characters in Shakespeare's plays, we can say of this proposition whether it be *true* or *false*. If we were to construct a database of information about Shakespeare's plays, that database might well include a record ($q.v.$) such as (Brutus, Caesar), and that record might be one of a collection of similarly formed records, each

x_7	x_6	x_5	x_4	x_3	x_2	x_1	x_0

Figure 1.   An 8-bit register x.

asserting that the first-named character killed the second-named character.

The mathematical term *relation* as it occurs in predicate logic is most commonly used in connection with predicates of exactly two variables. In the Relational Model, a predicate of any nonnegative number, *n*, of variables is considered as an *n*-ary relation. If we want to say in which play each killing occurs, we might use the ternary (3-ary) relation "*x* killed *y* in *z*." If we want to record those characters who, like Cassius, were ambitious, we might use the unary relation "*x* was ambitious."

Here is how the binary (2-ary) relation "*x* killed *y*" might be represented according to the Relational Model:

KILLED	KILLER	VICTIM
	Brutus	Caeser
	Hamlet	Laertes
	Hamlet	Polonius
	Laertes	Hamlet
	Brutus	Brutus
	Cassius	Caesar

Arising from such a visual representation are several informal terms in common use: *table*, for relation, *heading* for relation schema, *column* (name) for *attribute* (name), *row* for (n-) tuple, and *body* (or *extension*) for the set of tuples "in" the relation.

Note that the verb of the example predicate has become a *relation name*, KILLED, and the variables *x* and *y* have become *attribute names*, KILLER and VICTIM, defined in the *relation schema* of this relation. Associated with each attribute name is an underlying *domain*, the set of permissible values for the attribute in question. In this case, both attributes would draw their values from the domain, "names of Shakespearean characters." A particular instantiation of a predicate in *n* variables is represented by an *n-tuple*. Thus, the 2-tuple (Brutus, Caesar), in combination with the relation schema of KILLED, represents the proposition "Brutus killed Caesar."

Four important principles are illustrated in the above example:

1. At each intersection of a row and column there is exactly one value. This is the principle of *first normal form*, fundamental in the relational model.
2. The order in which the rows are written is unimportant.
3. The order in which the columns are written is also unimportant. It is only important to know, for each value in a row, to which column that value pertains, and we achieve that by writing the value underneath the name of its column.
4. Each row is unique; the Relational Model expressly prohibits duplicate rows.

A *relational database* is a collection of relations. A *relational database schema* is a collection of relation schemas, along with a collection of domain definitions, with the possible addition of integrity rules (*constraints*), access authorizations, and so on. A relational database management system (DBMS) must minimally provide for the definition of domains and relation schemas; the insertion, updating, and deletion of tuples; and a *relational query language* for defining new relations that may be derived from the *base relations* of the database. No commercial product quite matches up to these stated requirements of a relational DBMS. Those based on the standard database language Structured Query Language (SQL) are commonly called *relational DBMSs*, but SQL's concept of "tables," though similar to that of relations, deviates in several important respects from the Relational Model.

Relational query languages are founded on either or both of the *relational algebra* and the *relational calculus* proposed by Codd. The algebra is considered to be the "lower-level" system, but the two systems have been shown to be equivalent. The relational algebra draws on the notion that the body of a relation is a *set* (of tuples), and among its operators are specialized versions of the *union, difference*, and *intersection* operations of set theory. The algebra originally proposed by Codd included those three, two monadic operators—*project* and *restrict* (also known as *select*)—and the dyadic operator *Cartesian product*. Most authorities accept three further monadic operators—*attribute rename, extend*, and *summarize*. The nonprimitive operators *natural join* and *divide* are so useful that they are normally presented as well.

Where the relational algebra draws on set theory, the *relational calculus* draws on the predicate calculus. It is characterized by its adoption of the universal and existential quantifiers ∀ ("for all") and ∃ ("there exists") of the predicate calculus. While the calculus is in a sense "higher level" than the algebra and has more intuitive appeal to logicians, it is the algebra that is more often used as a basis for theoretical discussion of many diverse aspects of database technology.

Relational queries have applications beyond the obvious one of delivering answers to interesting questions. They are used to define *views*, enabling individual users to work with customized database schemas instead of all having to use the same underlying schemas. They are used to define subsets of the database, to which access can be authorized discretely for different users or user groups. And they may be used in the definitions of integrity *constraints*.

Functional Dependence, Keys, and Normalization

The concept of *functional dependence* is completely orthogonal to the principles described above, but is usually included in any discussion of relational databases because of its importance in connection with database design. A *functional dependency* is a truth-valued expression, written as A → B and pronounced "A determines B" or "B depends on A." If A and B are both subsets of the attributes of some relation, *R*, then A → B is said to hold true in *R* if and only if, any two tuples in *R* that agree in value for every attribute in A also agree in value for every attribute in B. For example, suppose that a relation, *R*, includes an attribute, *z*, whose values in *R* are constrained to be the sum of two other attributes in *R*, *x*, and *y* (perhaps *z* is thus computed, in some query). The following functional dependencies hold true in *R*:

$$\{x, y\} \rightarrow \{z\}$$

$$\{x, z\} \rightarrow \{y\}$$

$$\{y, z\} \rightarrow \{x\}$$

The left operand of a functional dependency is the *determinant*, and the members of the right operand are *dependants* of that determinant.

If K is a determinant in *R* such that

- all the attributes of *R* are dependants of K;
- there is no proper subset of K, K′, such that all the attributes of *R* are dependants of K′; and
- this constraint holds true over time in a changing database;

then CK is a *candidate key* of *R*. The Relational Model requires at least one candidate key to be defined for every relation defined by a relation schema in the database schema. The functional dependency implied by such a candidate key is then treated as an integrity rule, prohibiting the insertion of a tuple, *t*, if there already exists some tuple agreeing in value with *t* for every attribute of that candidate key. When more than one candidate key is noted for the same relation, one is arbitrarily nominated as the *primary key*.

The fundamental principle of *first normal form* has been noted. The study of database design involves further normal forms that are recommended to hold true for "base relations" (i.e. relations defined by relation schemas in the database schema) only. The most important of these is *Boyce–Codd normal form* (BCNF). BCNF is defined as holding true in a relation, *R*, if and only if every nontrivial determinant in *R* is a candidate key. It can be shown that a base relation that is not in BCNF can involve redundancy (recording the same data more than once), giving rise to *update anomalies*, such as having to update the same data in several different places where it occurs.

Bibliography

1970. Codd, E. F. "A Relational Model of Data for Large Shared Data Banks," *Communications of the ACM*, **13**(6), (June), 377–387.

1990. Codd, E. F. *The Relational Model for Database Management, Version 2*. Reading, MA: Addison-Wesley.

2003. Date, C. J. *An Introduction to Database Systems*, 8th Ed. Reading, MA: Pearson Addison-Wesley.

Hugh Darwen

RESTART PROCEDURE

See BOOTSTRAP.

REVERSE POLISH NOTATION (RPN)

See POLISH NOTATION.

RISC

See REDUCED INSTRUCTION SET COMPUTER (RISC).

ROBOTICS

For articles on related topics, *see*

+ Artificial Intelligence (AI)
+ Automation
+ Computer Vision
+ Pattern Recognition
+ Telerobotics

Introduction

Robotics is the study of reprogrammable, multifunctional manipulators designed to move materials, parts, tools, or specialized devices through programmed motions for the performance of a variety of tasks. Robots can be said to be programmable machines that either in performance or appearance imitate human activities. In contrast to purely algorithmic computing, which is concerned with the transformation of information from input to output, robotics is concerned with the transformation of the physical world from an input state to an output state. Robotics programs are real-time systems (*q.v.*) that must be able to service commands as close to instantaneously as possible.

Some unusual robotics applications currently being studied or used include: dismantling of nuclear weapons; herding of sheep; searching the sea bed for dumped toxic waste; and robot insects that can fly, crawl, or swim, to be used for battlefield reconnaissance or to spy on terrorists holding hostages. On the domestic front, an unusual robot developed by the University of Western Australia is in use as a sheep shearer, and details of a robotic vacuum cleaner developed by Electrolux have recently been publicized in the UK. A similar device called Dustbot is discussed in Moravec (1998).

History

During the eighteenth century, intricate mechanical puppets and automata were built in Europe. These included accurate models of people with arms, lips, and other body parts driven by linkages and cams controlled by rotating drum selectors. Some could write, some draw, and a famous one, a shepherd designed by Jacques de Vaucanson, could play a repertoire of 12 tunes on a flute.

Until the middle of the twentieth century, mechanically programmed automata were used solely for entertainment. Prior to this, however, considerable advances were made in "programmable" machines for specific industrial processes, starting with the Jacquard loom in 1801. Developments in technology, including the modern electronic computer, feedback control of actuators, and sensor technology, were required before programmable automata were sufficiently flexible to be of any practical use in manufacturing. The forerunners of programmable robots were mechanically fixed manipulators whose motions were set by mechanical cams or stops. These were custom-built to facilitate the manufacture of a specific product, a type of automation still used to make light bulbs.

Robots by that name first appeared in Prague in January 1921, in a play entitled RUR (Rossum's Universal Robots), by the Czech dramatist Karel Čapek. Their first appearance on the New York stage occurred on 9 October 1922. The word *robot* is a derivative of the Czech word *robota*, which can be interpreted as "work," "forced labor," "slave," or "serf." In 1926, the first movie involving robots, *Metropolis*, was released in

Germany. The walking robot Electro and its dog Sparko were displayed at the New York World's Fair in 1939. Robot dogs are still popular; Fig. 1 depicts SONY's "AIBO" Entertainment Robot.

In 1956, more than 30 years after Čapek's play, the firm Unimation was formed whose sole business was robotics. In 1972, 16 years and $12 million later, Unimation turned its first profit through sales of real industrial-grade robots. C. W. Kenward in Britain and George Devol in the United States developed the technology for this work in 1954. The initial device was called a *programmed articulated transfer device*. Joseph Engelberger, often called the father of the industrial robot, bought the rights to the Devol device and developed it further.

In 1968, R. S. Mosher at General Electric built a quadrupedal walking machine, which, because of its size and weight, was called the *walking truck*. During the 1960s, work started on the design of prostheses to replace lost human limbs. The work on *teleoperators* (remote-controlled devices) and prostheses contributed significantly to the development of robots (*see* TELEROBOTICS).

The first robots that could be programmed to respond to external sensory information without direct human intervention were built in artificial intelligence laboratories to test theories in cognition and vision. H. A. Ernst of the MIT Lincoln Laboratory equipped a robot arm with tactile sensors that were used to provide feedback to the control process. In 1962, L. G. Roberts demonstrated that a mathematical description of a three-dimensional scene could be recovered from a corresponding digital image. In 1969, a sophisticated mobile robot called *Shakey* was built at Stanford Research Institute to carry out experiments in using vision to control action. Shakey navigated highly structured indoor environments. In the late 1970s, another device, Hans Moravec's *Stanford Cart* was the first robot to attempt an unstructured environment.

Perception

Most of today's industrial robots are restricted by their lack of sensory capabilities. Many of these robots can measure only joint position, plus a few interlocks and timing signals. In robotics, sensors are classified into two groups: internal and external. Internal sensors measure robot parameters relative to the reference frame of the robot such as joint angle, linkage deflection, and grip force. External sensors measure the environment and the position of the robot relative to the environment. Vision is probably the most important external sense. Computer vision in general is the capability to record, store, and reconstruct a graphic image that matches the original as closely as possible. The use of vision in robotics is more limited. Vision systems usually have a specific assignment, such as checking for proper part orientation, identifying parts, searching for specific defects, or checking alignment for assembly. Tactile sensors serve two purposes, to determine the presence and characteristics of a work piece. Such sensors range from simple mechanically operated ones to those that attempt to simulate the human skin.

Actuation

There are four principal robotic power sources—hydraulic, pneumatic, electric, and mechanical gear and cam. The source has to transmit power from an actuator to the work piece the robot is moving. Typical transmission devices are gears, tendons, and linkages. Robots that can move about are starting to appear in industry, but their motion is still restricted. Before a general-purpose mobile robot can move freely

Figure 1. The "AIBO" Entertainment robot. (Courtesy of the Sony Corporation © 1999.)

in a factory, home, farm, or military environment, an "intelligent" connection between perception (sensing and understanding the environment) and action (control of robot motion within the environment) has to be achieved. Wheeled robots are designed to maintain their wheels in contact with the floor at all times. Consequently, stability is designed into the robot and becomes a problem only when the robot is on a steep slope. A recent example of a wheeled robot application was the Pathfinder mission to Mars.

By contrast, legged robots lift their feet off the ground to walk. The motion of walking dynamically changes the stability of the robot. A robot is statically stable if the center of its gravity always lies within a triangle defined by the contact points between three feet and the ground. If the center of gravity lies outside this triangle, the robot is no longer stable and tends to fall over. For statically stable walking, a robot must have four or more legs in

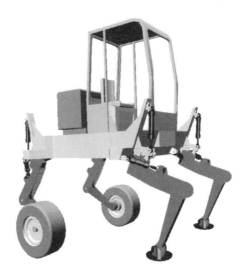

Figure 3. The ALDURO wheeled robot. (Courtesy of Professor Manfred Hiller, Fachgebiet Mechatronik, Gerhard-Mercator-Universität-Duisburg, Germany.)

order to have three feet in contact with the ground at all times.

A number of problems need to be overcome before wheeled or legged robots will match or even approach the sophisticated navigation abilities of people. Such areas include planning in unknown environments, coordination between mobility and manipulability, computation environments for mobile robots, nonlinear control of mobile robots, and environmental modeling using advanced sensing technologies. A particularly interesting walking robot called Honda is shown in Fig. 2. Honda is a self-contained research robot developed over a decade by a group of 30 engineers at Honda Motors of Japan. Two other mobile robots are shown in Figs. 3 and 4.

Programming

Robot programming places special requirements on computer languages and systems. In addition to the data manipulation handled by normal programs, robot programs have to control motion, operate in parallel, communicate with programs, which may be in other computers, synchronize with external events, respond

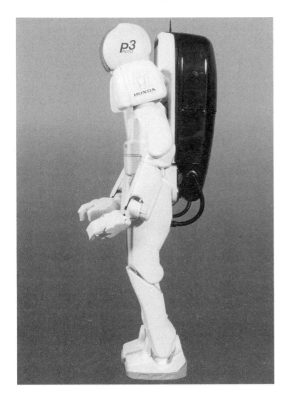

Figure 2. Honda (from Moravec, 1998).

Figure 4. The Walking Gyroscope was the first dynamically stabilized walking toy on the market. It is shown here with the Tonka Hitchhiker robot, which was based on the same idea. (Courtesy of its inventor, John Jameson, San Carlos, CA.)

to interrupts (*q.v.*) in real time, operate on sensor variables, and initialize and terminate in physically safe ways. Reprogramming was a feature missing from the manipulators seen before the advent of the industrial robot in the 1970s. The first robot programming language, WAVE, was developed for research purposes at Stanford Research Institute (SRI) in 1973, followed in 1974 by the AL language. Victor Scheinman and Bruce Simano subsequently combined the two languages into the commercial VAL language for Unimation. Robotics programming languages are often dialectical extensions of popular general-purpose computer languages, such as Basic (*q.v.*). One such dialect is the ARMBASIC robot language, aptly named by Microbot, Inc., its creator and copyright owner. Another language based on Basic is AML, made popular by IBM's version of the SCARA robot.

Artificial Intelligence (AI) must have a central role in robotics if the connection of perception and action is to be intelligent. The application of AI to robotics involves practical problems in a real physical world as opposed to "traditional" applications that involve artificial problems in abstract domains. AI in robotics aims to tackle the problems of knowledge representation (*q.v.*) (particularly sensor data), how to perceive aspects of the world that affect the problems at hand, how to use knowledge in problem solving, and how to act on that knowledge in the robot's current situation. Researchers are working, and trying to copy, the human capabilities of mobility, dexterity, intelligence, and sensory perception.

Bibliography

1998. Fuller, J. L. *Robotics: Introduction, Programming, and Projects*. Upper Saddle River, NJ: Prentice Hall.

1998. Moravec, H. *ROBOT: Mere Machines to Transcendent Minds*. New York: Oxford University Press.

1999. Lee, T. H., Harris, C. J., and Shuzhi, S. G. *Adaptive Neural Network Control of Robotic Manipulators*. Singapore: World Scientific.

1999. Nof, S. Y. *Handbook of Industrial Robotics*. New York: John Wiley.

Raj Bhatti

ROM

See READ-ONLY MEMORY (ROM).

ROUTER

See GATEWAY.

RPN (REVERSE POLISH NOTATION)

See POLISH NOTATION.

RUN TIME

See COMPILE AND RUN TIME.

SCANNER, OPTICAL

See OPTICAL CHARACTER RECOGNITION (OCR); and UNIVERSAL PRODUCT CODE.

SCIENTIFIC APPLICATIONS

For articles on related subjects, *see*

+ Artificial Life
+ Biocomputing
+ Computer Graphics
+ Fractals
+ Genetic Algorithms
+ Global Positioning System (GPS)
+ Image Processing
+ Medical Imaging
+ Molecular Computing
+ Monte Carlo Method
+ Parallel Processing
+ Pattern Recognition
+ Quantum Computing
+ Sensor Network
+ Simulation
+ Supercomputers

Introduction

Truly fundamental physical phenomena are governed by equations that describe what happens to small particles or energy bundles as they move through space and time. In the same way in which the physicist's quest to explore particle phenomena at ever higher ranges of energy leads to the construction of ever larger (and more costly) accelerators, the attempt to solve these equations in increasing detail has led to a continual need for computers of higher speed and greater memory capacity.

The Quest for High-Performance Computation
Direct Calculations
Monte Carlo

It is often of scientific interest to calculate the behavior of aggregates of particles over large regions of space or long time intervals. Scientists facing such a task usually have a choice of two basically different approaches. In the first, one can calculate the flight of an individual particle until it is scattered by a second particle, absorbed, or leaves the region of observation. The exact history of each particle depends on a sequence of random numbers chosen and used in such a way as to constrain the particle to experience one event or another in accord with its correct probability. Tracking and accumulating statistics on thousands of such particles then enable the calculation of quantities of physical interest. Such a technique is called the *Monte Carlo method* (*q.v.*), for obvious reasons, and finds application in such diverse situations as the behavior of neutrons in a reactor, light quanta in stellar atmospheres, and automobiles in heavy traffic. Monte Carlo calculations are inherently time-consuming, even on *supercomputers* (*q.v.*), because of the necessity to follow a sufficiently large number of particles to obtain results that are accurate within statistically acceptable limits of error.

Algebraic, integral, and ordinary differential equations

The second principal line of computational attack is feasible when (1) the behavior of the quantity of interest is known to obey a linear or nonlinear algebraic equation, a differential equation, an integral equation, or an integro-differential equation over some region of space–time of given shape, and when (2) the desired quantity obeys specified boundary conditions in space (and initial conditions in time in time-dependent problems). With regard to differential equations, the simplest situations occur when the dependent variable is a function of only one independent variable, perhaps time or one space dimension. Such differential equations are called *ordinary*. In such cases, either an analytic solution is obtainable or the use of a simple difference equation approximation will allow the production of desired answers in a few seconds of computer time.

Partial differential equations

When the dependent variable is a function of two or more independent variables, the appropriate differential equation is called a *partial differential equation* (PDE) because it involves partial derivatives that indicate the change in the dependent variable as one or another of the independent variables change, while holding all other independent variables fixed. Except under special circumstances, the solution of such equations is computationally formidable.

Reactor design

A scientist will often know that the subject of study is governed by equations whose full complexity places exact solutions beyond the capability of the computer available. A sufficient number of approximations is then made to bring a typical calculation down to an acceptable bound, usually an hour or less. In reactor design, for example, it is known that neutron behavior is governed by a complex integro-differential equation known as Boltzmann's equation. This equation takes into account that, at any given spatial point, the rate of neutron flow depends on the speed and direction of individual neutrons and, to a certain extent, on their past history. The solution of such an equation everywhere throughout the reactor volume for all possible neutron velocities is a task beyond presently available computers. What can be done, however, is to make approximations that replace the Boltzmann equation with a series of coupled partial differential equations, each of which calculates the neutron flux at a particular energy (speed) at a given space point. Each such equation, a so-called *diffusion equation*, is then calculated in either one, two, or three space dimensions, whichever the symmetry of the reactor (or expediency) demands.

Quantum chromodynamics

Although the preceding discussion assumed the use of a 2D slice taken from a full 3D reactor, the technique can be extended to all three space dimensions, or even to four dimensions: three spatial dimensions plus time. An example from another computationally intense field, elementary particle physics, is shown in Fig. 1 (Bitar and Heller, 1992). The three smaller spheres inside the larger one represent quarks that combine to form a single *hadron*, such as a neutron or a proton. The larger sphere represents a "bag" within which the quarks are

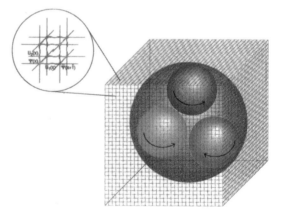

Figure 1. Artist's view of QCD simulation on a lattice used to approximate field interactions between colored quarks that build up a hadron. (From K. M. Bittar and W. M. Heller, Florida State University in Computers in Physics, 6, 1, Jan/Feb 1992, p. 34, permission of AIP.)

forever confined, interacting in accord with the laws of quantum chromodynamics (QCD). To solve the time-dependent equations that describe these interactions, space–time is modeled by a four-dimensional grid, with force fields defined on the sites or links of the lattice. Coping with the nonlinear dynamics of the model has become one of the most demanding computational projects in physics. A typical QCD simulation on a $16^3 \times 32$ lattice (about 100 000 mesh points) requires 10^{16} floating-point operations. Fortunately, the fields at every node of the lattice are treated identically, so that such calculations are highly suitable for both vector supercomputers and massively parallel supercomputers.

Cosmology and astrophysics

At the opposite end of the size scale—the world of the very large rather than the very small—N-body calculations in cosmology and astrophysics are the most computationally intensive in all of science. The first step in understanding how galaxies and stars form is to understand the environment in which this occurs. Thus, scientists use computer simulation to study the shapes and dynamics of "dark matter" halos, which are known to surround observed galaxies. The matter is called "dark" because it does not emit detectable radiation; its presence is inferred by its effect on galaxy rotation. In an astrophysical N-body simulation of dark matter, the phase space density distribution is represented by a large collection of "particles" which evolve in time according to Newtonian laws of motion and universal gravitation. Direct implementation of the system of equations that governs these particles is simply a doubly-nested program loop. In the language of supercomputing, it vectorizes well and it parallelizes easily and efficiently.

In 1995, Junichiro Makino and Makoto Taiji of the University of Tokyo reported an N-body calculation on a GRAPE-4 (GRAvity PipE) massively parallel computer of 1692 pipelines that reached sustained speeds 100 times faster, 529 gigaflops, more than half a teraflop. The calculation simulated the behavior of two massive black holes in the core of a galaxy with 700 000 stars. By 1999, the NEC SX-5 and the Cray T3E were able to reach sustained rates eight times faster, about four teraflops.

Chemical reactions

In some fields, the increasing speed and memory capacity of successive generations of digital computers have transformed the image that the computer conveys to the scientist from that of a tool—albeit a powerful one—to that of a new experimental device in its own right. In chemistry, the basic equation that governs the behavior of molecules, atoms, and (low-velocity) electrons has been known for over 75 years—the Schrödinger equation. Without a computer, only simple systems consisting of two or three particles can be studied in any detail. With the latest computers, however, ions of much larger atomic number can be followed kinetically as they interact with other ions to form molecules. If the chemist is able to watch the progression of such a reaction on a computer monitor, it is just as good or better (and less messy) than mixing the reagents in the laboratory.

Inverse Calculations

All of the examples cited thus far are examples of *direct* calculational situations. We know the characteristics of a target and want to calculate its scattering properties. We know the reactor configuration and desire its lifetime behavior. We know the reagents and want to know their reactivity. As time-consuming as such calculations can be, they are routine in their demand for computer time compared with indirect or *inverse* calculations, where we have access to experimental data but no access at all to details of the source of the phenomena generating the data.

Interstellar dust

An example is the problem of interstellar dust particles. Astrophysicists and cosmologists would like to know the quantity, shape, and composition of these particles, since this knowledge has a bearing on theories of the origin and evolution of the universe. We cannot yet send spaceships to retrieve such matter, but we can observe quantities such as the polarization and absorption of light of various wavelengths passing through it. What kinds of particles produce the scattered light: Spherical? Elongated? Metallic? Anisotropic ferrite needles? Dirty ice? The question is far from settled, and the astrophysicist will need to experiment with many different models to achieve success without being at all sure that the answer is unique.

Planetary systems

A striking recent example of an inverse calculation was the deduction by astronomers that the star Upsilon Andromedae has a planetary system consisting of at least three large planets, each of a specific mass, orbital period, and eccentricity of orbit. Upsilon Andromedae is a bright star, visible to the naked eye, 44 light years away from Earth and roughly three billion years old, two-thirds the age of the Sun. This is the first multiple planet system ever found around a normal star, other than the nine planets in our Solar System. The method used is observation of the Doppler shift of the radial velocity of the star system. Astronomers use a spectrograph to study the light from a star suspected to have planets. Superimposed on the continuous spectrum obtained are many fine dark lines called absorption lines. The positions of these lines are monitored over time to see if they move, an indication that a planet or some other astronomical companion is perturbing the motion of the star. If the star is moving towards the observer, the spectrum is blueshifted; if moving away, it is redshifted. By carefully monitoring a star's spectrum, the star's small wobble indicates what the mass of the planet is and its orbital period. When the data is sufficiently well reduced by intensive computer calculations, the presence of multiple planets of specific mass and orbital characteristics can be deduced.

The innermost of the three planets contains at least three-quarters of the mass of Jupiter and orbits only 0.06 AU from the star. (An astronomical unit (AU) is the distance from the Earth to the Sun.) It traverses a circular orbit every 4.6 days. The middle planet contains at least twice the mass of Jupiter and it takes 242 days to orbit the star. It resides approximately 0.83 AU from the star, similar to the orbital distance of Venus. The outermost planet has a mass of at least four Jupiters and

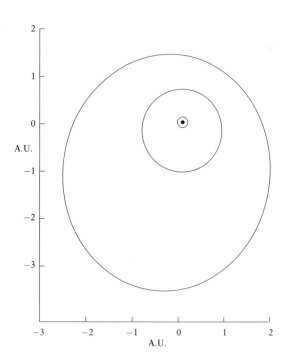

Figure 2. The orbits of the three massive planets of Upsilon Andromedae (the dot at [0,0]).

completes one orbit every 3.5 to 4 years, placing it 2.5 AU from the star (*see* Fig. 2).

Crystallography

It is straightforward to calculate the pattern of X-rays diffracted from a known spatial distribution of atoms, but we cannot get inside crystals or molecules to ascertain those distributions. We can observe the pattern of diffracted X-rays or neutrons impinging on a crystal of unknown structure, but in doing so, important phase information is lost. Using what information is available, however, such as intensity data, suspected symmetries, and chemical formulas learned through destructive testing of portions of the same material, crystallographers are now able to use an organized trial-and-error method to deduce the structure of quite large molecules of up to 500 atoms or so, and the frontier is pushed ahead with each advance in computer technology. Despite their complexity, the structures of several proteins as well as the vitamin B-12 have been determined by computer techniques. Some programs are so sophisticated that they

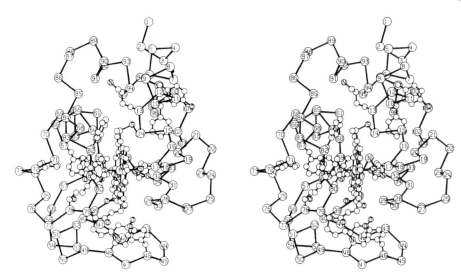

Figure 3. Stereoscopic pair of front view of reduced cytochrome molecule from a tuna. (Source: R. E. Dickerson, California Institute of Technology.)

produce as a final result a stereo pair (Fig. 3) of similar views of the predicted molecular structure; viewing them through an appropriate optical device brings out the spatial arrangement and vibrational characteristics of a crystal's constituent atoms in stunning detail.

DNA sequencing

Traditionally, biologists have not used computers intensively, but that situation is changing rapidly. One of the more important types of inverse calculation is that needed to ascertain DNA sequences in molecular biology. Without high-speed computers, the Human Genome Project, whose goal was to deduce the gene sequences of all human chromosomes, would have been impossible.

Geophysics

Just as the astrophysicist and the crystallographer are barred from entering the domain of the objects of their interest, so is the geophysicist unable to examine more than a tiny fraction of the interior of the Earth. There is data, however, that gives extremely pointed clues as to the internal composition of the Earth—namely that provided through seismological records taken during periods of earthquake, volcanic

eruption, and atomic testing. The Earth, like any (approximate) sphere of given internal composition, has certain characteristic modes of vibration, and allows elastic waves to propagate at certain speeds from point to point on its surface. By using digital computers to vary appropriate parameters in the equations that govern such phenomena, geophysicists have derived a plausible profile of the Earth's interior.

Impact on Hardware Development

One obvious impact of the scientist's perceived need for ever higher performance computers is to create a market climate in which vendors are willing to design and develop supercomputers. Computers capable of 100 million floating-point operations per second (Mflops) are now rather commonplace and speeds in the teraflop (Tflop) range are attainable for certain problems running on massively parallel supercomputers. Scientific users will have no difficulty absorbing additional capacity. The 4D QCD model described earlier used 100 000 mesh points, but only 16 along any one spatial dimension and 32 time-steps. Merely doubling the resolution in each dimension would require a computer 16 times faster in order to do a simulation in the same amount of running time. Simulation of supersonic flow over aircraft typically involves a million or more mesh points, so the scientific and engineering demand for ever larger main memories is also insatiable.

Ancillary Roles

In addition to their obvious value for direct and inverse calculation, digital computers play a role in automating many other aspects of the scientist's personal workload. These will be discussed under the headings of instrumentation, information retrieval, computer algebra, and data reduction and presentation.

Instrumentation

Many of the instruments of modern research science have themselves become so complex that it is often expedient to control their operation automatically with a small computer directly connected to or embedded in the instrument. Nuclear reactors and particle accelerators are often controlled or at least monitored in this way, as are a wide range of other devices, such as radio and optical telescopes, nuclear magnetic resonance equipment, crystallographic apparatus, electron microscopes, and satellites controlled by telemetered signals emanating from computers on the ground below.

Information Retrieval

The profusion of scientific papers being published makes it ever more difficult for working scientists to keep abreast of their fields, even in their own specialties. Some workers subscribe to computerized information retrieval services of one kind or another, or have access to libraries that do. Principal among these is the ability to file an interest profile with such a service center, and then be continually apprised of new papers that match that profile.

Computer Algebra

In an important sense, the digital "computer" has not been named to convey its most significant capability, namely, the ability to manipulate symbols. A digital computer can be programmed to automate the operations of applied mathematics, the very skill that the scientific theorist needs to cast predictions in calculable form (*see* COMPUTER ALGEBRA). The most widely-used commercial computer algebra programs are Derive, Macsyma, Mathematica, Maple, and Reduce.

Data Reduction and Presentation

The data produced by an experimental instrument is seldom directly usable. It usually needs some kind of scaling, noise filtering, time integration, or other treatment that is ideally suited to computer processing. As a byproduct of this data reduction, a properly equipped computer can also display the reduced data, either in hard-copy form on a graph plotter or in a transient visual form on a display screen. Thus, a scientist may monitor an experiment in progress and perhaps even input feedback information that alters the later course of the research.

Pattern recognition

Some of the more interesting applications of data reduction occur in a pattern recognition (*q.v.*) context. The classic example is the widespread use of devices called *bubble chambers* in high-energy physics. Particles passing through such devices leave visible tracks composed of tiny bubbles that can be photographed and scanned for the occurrence of interesting branch-like structures that indicate the presence of a collision or reaction between particles. Although humans can do this quite well, a bubble chamber can snap a new picture every few seconds and easily reach an annual production of over a million frames. Such prodigious output can be coped with only by computerized pattern recognition techniques, and modern accelerators are serviced by large computers devoted almost exclusively to this task.

Image processing

Image processing (*q.v.*) plays a vital role in planetary exploration. NASA space probes that flew by Mars (and Jupiter and Saturn) in recent years transmitted pictures back to Earth in digital form, specifically, as a series of 40 000 six-bit data points, each representing on a scale of 0 to 63 the shade of gray that was observed at the intersection of a 200×200 grid array superimposed on the visual scene. Once read into the memory of a high-speed computer, such a digitized picture was then easily "cleaned up" by removing spurious noise and enhancing its resolution for human viewing, thus producing the sharp and often breathtaking photos presented in news magazines at the time.

Scientific visualization

By *scientific visualization* is meant the ability to present data in simulated 3D form on a high-resolution color graphics display device, rather than as a simple 2D graph or, worse, the raw form that a printed sequence of numbers would provide. The object depicted may or may not be a "real" one that a human of suitable scale could ever see, or, even when it is, "false color" may be used to bring out interrelationships that would otherwise be difficult to ascertain.

Presentation of results

Historically, scientists have presented the results of their work in the specialized journals appropriate to their field. Special care is given to such things as the typography of equations and the choice of photographs, tables, and diagrams used. Until the last few years, any tools that facilitated typesetting were strictly the province of the publisher, and, similarly, any elaborate diagram or figure had to be drawn by a professional graphic artist. Now, many computer-based tools exist which allow scientists to display their equations using elaborate typefonts (*q.v.*) and to construct charts, graphs, and figures of professional quality (*see* COMPUTER GRAPHICS, TEX, TEXT EDITING SYSTEMS, and WORD PROCESSING). Options for graphical output are now routinely provided in spreadsheets, word processors, and computer algebra programs. And the scientist who wishes to take control of the whole process to produce "camera-ready" copy may use any of several powerful programs that automate *desktop publishing* (*q.v.*).

Simulation

There are three major purposes of simulation: for analysis, for design, and for education.

Simulation for Analysis

A principal reason for simulating a complex physical system is analysis sufficiently detailed to enable prediction of its behavior. For example, the physical laws governing the motion of planetary bodies are intrinsically simple for two-body systems, but they are analytically intractable for the complex systems of Earth, Moon, multistage rockets of changing mass, satellites, and so on, whose relative motions must be calculated with great precision in order to ensure the success of the most routine space mission. Of all the technological breakthroughs necessary to support the space programs of the United States, Europe, and Russia, none was more necessary than the development of reliable high-speed digital computers for analysis, prediction, design, and control.

A second and more extensive example of simulation for analysis was given earlier, the N-body calculations of cosmology and astrophysics. A third example of simulation (for both analysis and prediction) is the use of computers for weather forecasting. The equations governing the changes in temperature and pressure with time over even a small region of the Earth's surface require large amounts of computer time. With present speeds and memory capacities, it is difficult to forecast changes in weather patterns for a period of more than a few hours, but as machines improve, longer-range forecasts of reasonable reliability may be possible.

Simulation for Design

Once the analysis of a simulated physical model has advanced to the point where confidence can be placed in its predictions, the model can be used for the design of similar systems with variously different parameters. For example, the calculational problems associated with the behavior of neutrons in a reactor have been discussed previously, but the rationale for studying these problems was not considered. Initially, through the late 1940s and early 1950s, research data was reasonably fundamental, since the properties of neutron propagation in various materials under a variety of operating conditions were imperfectly understood. As in other fields, however, the widespread use of digital computers accelerated the natural progression of a given type of activity, from research to applied science to engineering. The point has now been reached where most reactor calculations are part of a design engineering process whose aim is to simulate performance of tentative reactor designs *in lieu* of constructing an experimental prototype. By this technique, many hundreds of design variations can be tested in theory and only the most promising results need be tested in practice.

Simulation for Education

Computers are invaluable in education. Rather than running laboratory experiments to determine the behavioral characteristics of falling bodies, colliding spheres, pendulums, projectiles, and so on, the event to be studied can be simulated at any desired rate on a display monitor. The student can then interact with the computer to study the effect of changing parameters, such as the mass of a pendulum bob, the angle of elevation of the initial launch of a rocket, or any one or more of the other factors that affect the experiment at hand. Using such techniques, one can even examine phenomena that are closed to easy observation in the laboratory (e.g. the tunneling of a quantum mechanical particle through a potential barrier, the slow-motion fall of water droplets into a pool, or the crashing of water waves upon a beach). These simulations are instructive to watch, and are esthetically pleasing as well. Still photographs of such sequences are often examples of computer art (*q.v.*), just as beautiful as other designs created deliberately.

Bibliography

1990. Nash, S. (ed.) *A History of Scientific Computing.* Reading, MA: ACM Press/Addison-Wesley.

1992. Bitar, K. M., and Heller, U. M. "Lattice Field Simulations Press the Limits of Computational Physics," *Computers in Physics*, **6**(1), (January–February), 33–40.

1997. Heath, M. T. *Scientific Computing: An Introductory Survey.* New York: McGraw-Hill.

1999. Thijssen, J. M. *Computational Physics.* New York: Cambridge University Press.

Edwin D. Reilly

SCRIPTING LANGUAGES

For articles on related subjects, *see*

+ Language Processors
+ Operating Systems
+ Programming Languages
+ Shell
+ Unix
+ User Interface

Through use of a *command language* (CL), computer users can describe to an operating system the requirements of their jobs. Operating systems for mainframes (*q.v.*) and minicomputers provide a CL called *job control language* (JCL) in which the user can identify the job for accounting purposes, specify the resources it requires, and specify the action to be taken in exceptional cases. These languages are typically complex, difficult to learn, unnatural to use, and nonsystematic.

Interactive Command Languages

Since the user of a time-sharing system interacts directly with the computer in real time, typing in a single *command line* at a time and waiting for the system's response, interactive command languages are inherently simpler than batch languages. The command-line interface is implemented by a command interpreter called a *shell*. Many command lines consist of just a command verb followed by one or more arguments to specify files to be operated on, or options to be set; however, the shell provides the user with a convenient syntax for redirecting input or output from the terminal to a file or files, and setting up *pipes* to link a sequence of commands so that the output from one command becomes the input for the next.

The command-line syntax of the Unix shell, with input–output redirection and pipes was also used with MS-DOS, but the use of a CL interface in the PC world is decreasing as graphical user interfaces (GUIs) provided by Microsoft (*q.v.*) and Apple (*q.v.*) become almost universal. Even Linux (*q.v.*), when packaged as GNU/Linux, now contains a choice of GUIs.

Programmable Shells

Unix encourages the user to store complex commands or sequences of commands in an executable file called a *shell script*. The name of such a file can be typed as a command, causing the lines of the script to be processed as if they had been typed at the terminal. The "command" can be followed by up to nine arguments. Almost from the beginning, the Unix shell had a degree of programmability with `goto`s and labels: a powerful `if` command allowed a variety of conditions to be tested, and the `shift` command provided a convenient way of iterating over multiple arguments. The Bourne shell introduced in Unix version 7 added fully programmable capabilities, including conditional branches and looping. This makes shell scripts much more powerful, to the extent that they can be used instead of C (*q.v.*) to define complex new commands and to develop tools for system administration.

Scripting Languages

The limitations of shell scripts, in particular the inconvenient syntax and the lack of string-processing capabilities, led to the development of a number of disparate languages that are commonly called *scripting languages*. Since efficiency is not an issue, they are interpreted not compiled, are easy to use, and have low overhead. Typically, they support powerful string manipulation and associative arrays indexed by strings or other complex values.

We describe here three scripting languages in widespread use.

AWK

AWK was developed to meet the limitations of shell scripts in applications that call for data manipulation and reduction. AWK (Aho, Kernighan and Weinberger, 1988—named after its authors) was originally conceived as a tool for editing and manipulating text files structured as *records* (lines) divided into fields separated by *whitespace*. An AWK script consists of a list of *patterns* and associated *actions*: the target file is read sequentially, and as each record is loaded in turn into the processing buffer, all patterns are checked against the record, and any pattern that is satisfied triggers its corresponding action. The power of AWK derives from the facts that the "pattern" can be specified as matching a regular expression, or as a relationship between values in fields, while the action can be a simple imperative operation like "print," or an arbitrary piece of code in a C-like language. AWK has now been largely superseded by Perl.

Perl

Perl (*Practical Extraction and Report Language*) (Wall, Christiansen and Schwartz, 1996) originated in the late 1980s when its author, Larry Wall, was the system administrator for a project developing secure wide-area networks. Perl rapidly developed from being a fairly simple text-processing language to a fully featured systems programming language, providing system-independent abstractions of files, processes, sockets, and so on. Since Version 5, Perl also provides a full range of object-oriented capabilities. Although the underlying ideas are simple, Perl is an immensely rich language that incorporates the best ideas from many sources, particularly sed (Unix stream editor), AWK, Shell Programming, and C, in pursuit of its aim of keeping easy things easy while making difficult things possible. In less than 10 years, Perl has become one of the world's most popular programming languages. The principal reason for the explosive growth is the World Wide Web (*q.v.*), in which Perl was rapidly adopted as the language of choice for server-side (common gateway interface—CGI) scripting.

TCL/TK

Tool Command Language/Toolkit (Tcl/Tk) (Ousterhout, 1994) is based on the philosophy that application development is best accomplished using a combination of two languages: "... one, such as C or C++ (*q.v.*), for manipulating the complex internal data structures in which performance is key, and another, such as Tcl, for writing smallish scripts that tie together the C pieces and are used for extensions." Thus, Tcl is not so much a language as it is an interpreter that can be embedded in an application to provide a simple command-line interface. Tcl is an enormous success: many large applications are written entirely in Tcl, with no C code at all.

Object-Based Scripting

In recent years the term "scripting" has acquired an entirely new meaning, being applied to the use of specialized languages to manipulate "scriptable objects"—*visual scripting*—and to compose "component-objects" into applications—*component-ware*. Visual Basic, for example, is a tool designed to facilitate the development of Windows applications. The user of Visual Basic is presented with a palette of visual "controls" that can be positioned on the screen to suit the application: each control has a number of "properties" that can be set initially by the designer with a screen dialogue, but can subsequently be changed at run time by code written in a scripting language. Code can be associated with *events* (mouse and keyboard operations) for each control. Thus, a control can be viewed as an object with attributes (properties) and methods, the methods being invoked by external events. This model has extended into Web client software, in which the browser exposes objects (e.g. the current window, the current URL, the history list) that can be controlled by *scripts* attached to events such as page load, mouse click on a link, and so on. Microsoft and Netscape browsers implement an almost common object model so that the objects can be controlled (scripted) by various languages, including JavaScript, Jscript and VBScript. In addition, in Internet Explorer VBScript and Jscript can be used to control Visual Basic-like visual objects, known in this context as ActiveX Controls.

Bibliography

1988. Aho, A. V., Kernighan, B. W., and Weinberger, P. J. *The AWK Programming Language*. Reading, MA: Addison-Wesley.

1994. Ousterhout, J. *Tcl and the Tk Toolkit*. Reading, MA: Addison-Wesley.

1996. Chappell, D. *Understanding ActiveX and OLE*. Redmond, WA: Microsoft Press.

1996. Wall, L., Christiansen, T., and Schwartz, R. L. *Programming Perl*, 2nd Ed. Sebastopol, CA: O'Reilly and Associates Inc.

David W. Barron

SCSI

See BUS; and PORT, MEMORY.

SEARCH ENGINE

See WORLD WIDE WEB.

SEARCHING

For articles on related subjects, *see*

+ Algorithms, Analysis of
+ Data Structures
+ List Processing
+ Sorting
+ Tree

Introduction

For a given searching problem, the particular choice of an algorithm and data structure depends on the nature of the storage medium, the nature of the data being organized and on the requirements of the search. For this article, assume that we are searching a *table* of *n* elements, in which each element has a collection of *fields* associated with it, one field for each of a number of *attributes*. One of these attributes will be the *key* that is used to refer to the element and on which the searching is based.

Lists

In organizing a table as a list, we can vary only two things: the order of the elements in the list and the implementation as either an array or a linked list. The elements may be in no particular order, in an order based on their frequencies as search objects, or in their natural order (alphabetic or numeric). There is a trade-off between arrays and linked lists: the ease with which we can randomly access any element in an array makes it ideal under certain conditions, while under other conditions, the ease of insertion and deletion makes a linked list more appropriate. When both efficient access and ease of modification are needed, dynamic trees should be considered.

Linear Search

Linear search examines each element in turn to see if it is the one sought, continuing until either the element is found or all the elements in the list have been examined. The order of the elements in the list does not affect the correctness of this algorithm, only the amount of time it requires.

The performance of linear search is based on the number of *probes* into the list: a probe is a comparison between the search object and the key of an element in the table. We evaluate all search strategies by the number of probes required to find an object, both in the worst case and on average. The amount of work in searching for an element is not entirely in the probes, but the total work done is usually proportional to the number of probes, since only a constant number of operations are done per probe. The behavior of linear search is summarized as

	Worst case	Best case	Average case
Successful search	n probes	1 probe	$\sum_{i=1}^{n} ip_i$ probes
Unsuccessful search	n probes	n probes	n probes

where p_i is the probability that the ith item on the list is sought. If all the probabilities $p_i = 1/n$, a successful search will use an average of $\sum_{i=1}^{n} ip_i = \sum_{i=1}^{n} i/n = (n+1)/2$ probes; that is, we expect to search half the list. When the probabilities are not all equal, we can

improve linear search by arranging the list so that the value $\sum_{i=1}^{n} ip_i$ is minimized. The minimum value occurs when the items are in decreasing order by frequency, that is, when $p_1 \geq p_2 \geq \cdots \geq p_n$, but it is seldom possible to determine the access probabilities *a priori*.

Ordered Lists

If it is possible to maintain the list in some natural order (such as numeric or alphabetic), it is almost always advantageous to do so. Linear search can then be speeded up somewhat for unsuccessful searches, because in an ordered table the search can stop when it discovers the first element beyond what it is seeking, rather than go all the way to the end of the list. The improvement for unsuccessful search times in tables in the natural order is minor in contrast to the fact that a single probe into the table can now get a good deal more information than when the table is in some other order: by comparing the item sought with the key of the middle element of the table, we can determine which half of the table is of further interest. Continuing this idea recursively yields *binary search* whose behavior is summarized by

	Worst case	Best case	Average case
Successful search	$\lceil \lg(n+1) \rceil$ probes	1 probe	$\left(1 + \frac{1}{n}\right) \times$ $\lg(n+1)$ $+o(1)$ probes
Unsuccessful search	$\lceil \lg(n+1) \rceil$ probes	$\lfloor \lg(n+1) \rfloor$ probes	$\lg(n+1) +$ $o(1)$ probes

The function "lg" is the base-two logarithm, that is, $\log_2$. The symbol $\lfloor x \rfloor$ is the largest integer not larger than x; similarly, $\lceil x \rceil$ is the smallest integer not smaller than x.

Binary Search Trees

A *binary search tree* is a binary tree of the table elements in which every element x has the property that the elements in the left subtree of x are before the key of

x in the natural order and the elements in the right subtree of x are after the key of x in the natural order. This property of the tree makes it easy to search for an element z: compare z with the key of the root element; if the keys are equal, the search ends successfully, and if they are not, search the left or right subtree according to whether z is less than or greater than the key of the root element, respectively. Figure 1 shows a binary search tree of 16 common English words.

Static Trees

The application of binary search trees to static tables is concerned entirely with choosing the tree that minimizes search time; we assume that the table is constructed once and that its contents never change, or change so infrequently that the entire table will be reconstructed to make the change. If we want to minimize the worst-case search time, we simply use the tree corresponding to binary search.

Dynamic Trees

Binary search trees can be used for dynamic tables—tables whose contents change because of insertions and deletions. There is a conflict between efficient search algorithms and efficient modification: fast search requires a rigid structure, while fast modification needs a flexible structure; *balanced trees* provide a compromise between the two requirements. Logarithmic search times can be achieved by keeping the tree nearly perfectly balanced at all times (as is implicit in binary search). Unfortunately, when the tree is thus constrained, it is quite costly to insert or delete an element. Instead, we allow a limited flexibility in the shape of the tree so that insertions and deletions will not be so expensive, yet search times will remain logarithmic. Such techniques keep the trees "balanced" so that they cannot become too skewed (and hence degenerate to linear search times). The height of such trees of n elements will be $O(\log n)$ so that search times are logarithmic. Insertions and deletions will require only local changes along a single path from the root to a leaf, thus requiring only time proportional to the height of the tree, which is logarithmic.

Digital Search Trees

We can use trees to organize tables based on the representation of the elements, rather than on the ordering of the elements as in the previous section. If the alphabet contains c characters, each node in the tree would be a c-way branch—one branch for each possible character. The structure thus obtained is called a *digital search tree* or *trie* (taken from the middle letters of the word "retrieval," but pronounced "try"). This concept is illustrated in Fig. 2 which shows eight mathematical constants. Suppose we are given the number 1.414 as the object of the search. We consider each of the digits 1, 4, 1, and 4 in turn, starting at the root of the tree and proceeding as follows. Follow the branch labeled 1 out

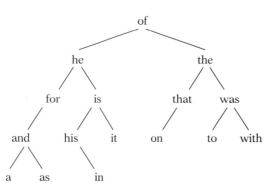

Figure 1. A binary search tree of 16 common English words.

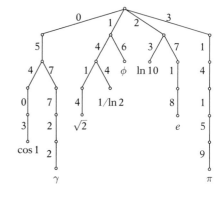

Figure 2. A trie of eight mathematical constants. The implicit decimal point is between the first and second edges of each path.

of the root; at the next node follow the branch labeled 4, then the branch labeled 1, and finally the branch labeled 4. At that point we are at the bottom of the tree and the letters of the search object are exhausted, so we have successfully found 1.414 in the tree. If the search object had been 1.413, we would have followed down branches in the tree corresponding to 1, 4, and 1, but then there would be no branch labeled 3, indicating that 1.413 is not in the tree. The advantage of a digital search tree is that in many circumstances, the multiway branch required at every node of the tree will require little or no more time than a binary decision.

Hashing

In *hashing*, an element is stored in a location computed directly from the key of the element. Suppose that we have an array of m table locations $T[0 \ldots m-1]$ and are given an element z to be inserted; we transform z to a location $h(z)$, $0 \le h(z) < m$, where h is called a *hash function* and $h(z)$ is called the *hash address*. We then examine $T[h(z)]$ to see whether it is empty. If it is empty, we store z there, and we are done. If $T[h(z)]\}$ is not empty, a *collision* has occurred, and we must resolve it somehow. Taken together, the hash function and the collision resolution method are referred to as *hashing* or *scatter storage* schemes.

Hash Functions

The hash function takes an element to be stored in a table and transforms it into a location in the table. If this transformation makes certain table locations more likely to occur than others, it is said to exhibit *primary clustering*. This increases the chance of collisions and decreases the efficiency of searches and insertions. The ideal hash function spreads the elements uniformly throughout the table without primary clustering. There are four basic techniques used for constructing hash functions; while there are no absolute rules, there are several important principles. A hash function should be a function of *all* the bits of the element, not just some of them. A hash function should break up naturally occurring clusters of elements. A hash function should be quick and easy to compute.

Collision Resolution

A *collision* occurs when the location $T[h(z)]$ is already filled at the time we try to insert z. A *collision-resolution scheme* specifies a list of table locations then to be considered for z; these locations are inspected (in order) until an empty one is found. There are two choices: store pointers describing the sequence explicitly (chaining), or specify the sequence implicitly by a fixed relationship with z (linear probing).

Table Look-Up

Suppose that all the items z to be stored in Table $T[0 \ldots m-1]$ have associated with them a unique key k such that $0 \le k < m$. Then the simplest conceivable hash function h is $h(k) - k$, that is, k itself is usable as a naturally occurring index into the table. In such a case, hashing is collision-free and degenerates to simple table look-up. If, for example, each of the 51 geographic units that comprise the USA is numbered 0 to 50 and their respective populations are stored in $T[0 \ldots 50]$, then we can "look up" the population of the kth state by accessing $T[k]$.

Bibliography

1975. Knott, G. D. "Hashing Functions," *Computer Journal*, **18**, 265–278.

1986. Reingold, E. M., and Hansen, W. J. *Data Structures in Pascal*. Boston, MA: Little, Brown and Company.

1997. Knuth, D. E. *The Art of Computer Programming, Vol. III: Sorting and Searching*, 2nd Ed. Reading, MA: Addison-Wesley.

Edward M. Reingold

SENSOR NETWORK

For articles on related subjects, see

+ Distributed Systems
+ Network Architecture
+ Networks, Computer

A *sensor network* is a distributed computing network whose nodes are thousands of very small low-power wireless sensors that relay information about their environment to a host computer for processing. The sensors may be placed throughout an extensive area to measure such things as temperature, vibration, or light levels, or to perform more complicated tasks such as taking pictures or analyzing chemicals. The goal is to develop sensors that are so small and inexpensive that they can be scattered from aircrafts and allowed to settle like "smart dust" over a field of interest. The term was coined in 1997 by Kris Pister, an engineer at the University of California in Berkeley, who proposed that tiny sensors and all their communications gear might some day be squeezed into a package about the size of a grain of sand, one millimeter on a side, that can be produced for a few cents each.

Current sensors are not nearly that small and still cost about $200 each, but are nonetheless finding interesting applications. These range from monitoring the growth of redwood groves, marking the locations of land mines, sensing the need to sprinkle lawns or irrigate fields, detecting impending earthquakes, and recording wear and tear of bridges and buildings. In a project financed by the National Science Foundation, scientists intend to scatter sensors around wildfires to gather information about temperature, humidity and other factors and help firefighters predict and control their spread. In 2001, engineers at the UC-Berkeley installed sensors in a campus building to monitor light and temperature conditions.

There have been four generations of "smart dust" so far, each smaller than the last. The sensors installed in the redwood grove are based on a chip the size of a quarter, but the latest chips are no bigger than the head of a nail. David Culler, Director of the Intel Research Laboratory, predicts that 99% of the Internet will eventually consist of billions of tiny sensors that continuously stream information to those who can make use of it.

Bibliography

2003. Callaway, E. H. Jr. *Wireless Sensor Networks: Architectures and Protocols*. Boca Raton, Fl: CRC Press.

Edwin D. Reilly

SERIAL I/O

See INPUT–OUTPUT OPERATIONS; and PORT, I/O.

SERVER

See FILE SERVER.

SGML

See MARKUP LANGUAGES.

SHAREWARE

See FREEWARE AND SHAREWARE.

SHELL

For articles on related subjects, *see*

+ Kernel
+ Operating Systems
+ Scripting Languages
+ Unix

A *shell* is an interpreter through which the user gives commands to an operating system. The term reflects the principle that an operating system is constructed from a succession of layers, of which the shell is the outermost one. The shell separates the users from the rest of the operating system and provides a *virtual machine* that serves as a high-level programming environment. When a user logs in, the operating system creates a *process* running a copy of the shell program. The shell "listens" to the user's terminal and interprets the inputs as commands to invoke existing programs in specified combinations and with specified inputs.

The Unix operating system has shells in which operations of substantial complexity can be programmed. The following sequence of commands prepares a five-column list of filenames in a directory, saves it as a file, and prints it.

```
ls | pr-5 > filenames
lpr filenames
```

The command `ls` lists the file names in the current directory. The pipe symbol "`|`" connects the output of one command to the input of the next, and `pr -5` produces a five-column format of the filenames. The symbol "`>`" redirects the output to the file named `filenames`, and the printer spooler `lpr` then sends the result to the printer.

If a command line is to be performed often, typing it can become tedious. Unix encourages users to store complicated commands in executable files called *shell scripts*, which become simpler commands. Shell programs can be arbitrarily long and may include assignments to variables, control constructs for alternation and iteration, subroutine calls to commands in other files, and even interrupt (*q.v.*) handling. The Unix shell is a full-fledged, high-level programming language, but not all operating systems have shells, or make them as visible and important as Unix does.

Bibliography

1979. Kernighan, B. W., and Mashey, J. R. "The Unix Programming Environment," *Software: Practice and Experience*, **9**(1), (January), 1–15.
1990. Kochan, S. G., and Wood, P. H. *Unix Shell Programming*. Indianapolis, IN: Hayden Books.

Walter F. Tichy

SIDE EFFECT

For articles on related subjects, see

+ Global and Local Variables
+ Parameter Passing
+ Procedure-Oriented Languages: Programming
+ Structured Programming
+ Subprogram

A *side effect* occurs when a procedure or function changes the value of a global variable. This is the very reason why use of global variables is deplored; they allow the possibility of undesirable side effects. But this is not always so; sometimes, as in database systems, the database itself is global to all procedures, and modifying it is just what many procedures in the system are supposed to do.

Procedures or functions that cause side effects can result in nasty problems. For example, consider the expression A+B*C. It should not matter whether this expression is evaluated by first multiplying B times C and then adding A or by first fetching A, storing it away temporarily, multiplying B*C and then adding A. But what if the expression is instead FCN(A)+B*C where FCN is a function with argument A? Suppose the evaluation of FCN(A) has a side effect that modifies the value of B or C or of both. Then the value of the expression is different if B*C is evaluated before FCN(A) is evaluated or afterward. A related problem can occur in the evaluation of logical expressions such as I<20 **and** FCN(A)=5. If I≥20, then the expression must be false. Some systems will recognize this and not evaluate FCN(A) at all. Others will perform all evaluations of the arguments of **and** and then evaluate the expression. To avoid problems such as these, many languages specify left-to-right evaluation of logical expressions, augmented by precedence relations that specify how arithmetic expressions are to be evaluated.

Bibliography

1980. Wagener, J. *Fortran 77: Principles of Programming*. New York: John Wiley.
1989. Reilly, E. D., and Federighi, F. D. *Pascalgorithms*. Boston, MA: Houghton-Mifflin.

Anthony Ralston

SIMULATION

For articles on related subjects, *see*

+ Analog Computer
+ Artificial Life
+ Computer Games
+ Monte Carlo Method
+ Scientific Applications
+ Virtual Reality

Introduction

Definition

Simulation is the process of designing a model of a real or imagined system and conducting experiments with this model to understand the behavior of the system or to evaluate strategies for its operation. Assumptions are made about this system and algorithms (*q.v.*) and relationships are derived to describe these assumptions. This constitutes a "model" that can reveal how the system works.

History

One of the pioneers of simulation was John von Neumann (*q.v.*). In the mid-1940s, together with physicist Enrico Fermi and mathematician Stanislaw Ulam, he conceived the idea of running multiple repetitions of a model, gathering statistical data, and deriving behaviors of the real system based on these models. This came to be known as the Monte Carlo method because of the use of randomly generated variates to represent behaviors that could not be modeled exactly, but could be characterized statistically.

Purpose

Simulation allows the analysis of a system's capabilities, capacities, and behaviors without requiring the construction of, or experimentation with, the real system. Since it is extremely expensive to experiment with an entire factory to determine its best configuration, a simulation of the system can be extremely valuable. There are also systems, like nuclear reactions and war, which are too dangerous to activate for the sake of analysis, but which can be usefully analyzed through simulation.

Limitations

When conducting a simulation, certain limitations must be acknowledged. Primary among these is the ability to create a model that accurately represents the system to be simulated. Real systems are extremely complex and a determination must be made as to the details that will be abstracted and captured in the model. Some details must be omitted entirely. In both cases, an inaccuracy has been introduced and the ramifications of this must be known and accepted by the model developers.

Uses of Simulation

Simulation is used in some form in nearly all engineering and analysis. Many problems are too complex to solve analytically, but the reward for solving them is so great that a solution must be found—often via simulation. In each case, the expense of constructing a simulation may be significant in itself, but is minuscule compared with the cost of experimenting with an actual or a prototype system. There are several general categories of simulation.

Design

Designers turn to simulation to allow characterization or visualization of a system that does not yet exist. Manufacturing models may describe the capacities of individual machines, the time to prepare material for operation, time to transfer materials from one machine to another, the effects of human operators, and the capacities of waiting queues and storage bins. Simulations of new pieces of equipment may evaluate their performance, stress points, transportability, human interfaces, and potential hazards in the environment. Major airlines use simulation to study complex routing patterns for large numbers of aircraft traveling around the world and to identify routes that serve the most passengers at maximum efficiently. Factors such as aircraft capacity, ground time, flight time, scheduled maintenance, crew availability, weather effects, and unscheduled downtime are all considered in such models.

Analysis

Analysis refers to the process of determining the behavior or capability of a system that is currently in operation. Unlike design, analysis may be supported by the collection of data from the actual system to establish model behaviors. The model can then be modified to determine the optimum configuration or implementation of the real system. A computer network can be described by the volume of traffic carried, capacity of the lines and switches, performance of a router, and the path taken from sender to receiver. On the basis of measured message patterns, the network can be configured to deliver the most information using the shortest or most reliable paths available.

Training

Training simulations recreate situations that people will face on the job and stimulate the subject to react to the situation until the correct responses are learned. These devices prepare personnel without the expense of their making mistakes on the job. Perhaps the best known of these are flight simulators that model dangerous environments where life-threatening situations can be mitigated through learning in nonlethal environments.

Entertainment

The entertainment industry uses simulation to create games that are enjoyable and exciting to play. Arcade games, computer games, board wargames, and role-playing games all require the creation of a consistent model of an imaginary world and devices for interacting with that world.

Computer Technologies

Simulations depend on technologies from other areas of science. The need for a very complex simulation model and the information required to create it has often preceded the ability of computer hardware and software to represent it. However, simulation applications are growing larger and more useful as a result of developments in the computer field that provide tools powerful enough to represent the problems. The most useful technologies are those associated with networks, parallel computing, artificial intelligence, computer graphics, databases, and systems architecture.

Simulation Languages and Packages

A number of simulation languages and packages have been developed specifically to assist developers in constructing models of their systems. These languages are intended to serve a specific problem domain, rather than support general-purpose programming as do Fortran, C, Pascal, and Ada. However, general-purpose languages are still widely used to construct simulations in domains for which simulation-specific languages or packages do not yet exist or where the problem is so unusual that simulation tools cannot be created economically.

Discrete Event Simulation Languages

Discrete event simulation includes a wide array of both problems and commercial tools for solving them. The principal languages used in this realm are Simula (*q.v.*), developed by O. J. Dahl and K. Nygaard in 1967; GPSS/H from Wolverine Software, a block programming language improved from the original GPSS developed at IBM in 1969; SIMSCRIPT II.5 from CACI Products, an event-oriented and process-oriented language that evolved from the original SIMSCRIPT developed at the Rand Corporation in 1962; SIMAN/Cinema from Systems Modeling, a combined simulation language and animation system; SLAM II from Pritsker Associates, predominantly used for process-oriented simulation; and MODSIM from CACI, an object-oriented programming language with graphic extensions to support data input, execution monitoring and control, and output analysis.

Packages

Extend, from Imagine That, Inc., is a visual, interactive simulation package for discrete event and continuous

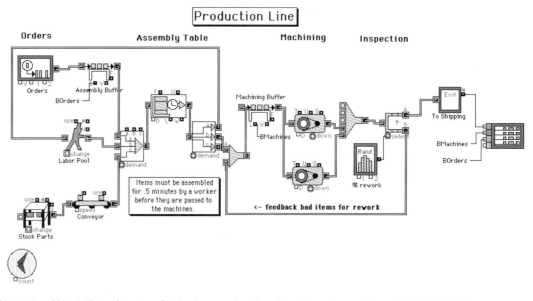

Figure 1.   Simulation of a manufacturing production line. (Courtesy of imagine That, INC.)

modeling that allows users to build models and user interfaces graphically (Fig. 1). Model execution is carried out interactively on the graphic model representation. The package can accept data input through the interfaces or from separate files. Extend provides built-in mathematical and statistical functions and can be customized through the addition of C and Fortran routines. Other packages are Workbench from SES, TAYLOR II from F&H Simulations, COMNET III from CACI Products, BONeS Designer from the Alta Group, CSIM18 from Mesquite Software, SimPack from the University of Florida, and CPSim from BoyanTech.

Continuous Simulation

The Advanced Continuous Simulation Language (ACSL) from MGA Software was developed specifically for modeling time-dependent, nonlinear differential equations and transfer functions. The language allows the user to develop code from block diagrams, mathematical equations, and Fortran statements. There are two distinct groups of user interactions: the first define the model and the structure of the system being represented; the second exercise the model allowing input variation and output analysis.

The Continuous System Modeling Program (CSMP) is constructed from three general types of statements—structural, which define the model; data, which assign numerical values to parameters; and control, which manage the execution of the model.

Interactive Simulation

In the interactive training arena a number of simulation products have emerged, particularly with military domain applications. Among them are VRLink from MAK Technologies, ITEMS from CAE Electronics, FLAMES from Ternion, and MultiGenII from Multigen.

Bibliography

1995. Fishwick, P. *Simulation Model Design and Execution.* Upper Saddle River, NJ: Prentice Hall.
1996. Nance, R. "A History of Discrete Event Simulation Programming Languages," in *The History of Programming Languages—II* (eds. T. J. Bergin, and R. G. Gibson Jr), 369–428. Reading, MA: Addison-Wesley.

Roger D. Smith

SMALLTALK

See OBJECT-ORIENTED PROGRAMMING.

SMART CARD

For articles on related subjects, *see*

+ Authentication
+ Cryptography, Computers in

A *smart card* is a credit or debit card that contains memory and logic in the form of a tiny integrated circuit microcomputer chip (*q.v.*). The idea of incorporating such a chip into an identification card was patented by the German inventors Jurgen Dethloff and Helmut Grotrupp in 1968. In 1974, the French inventor Roland Moreno mounted a chip on a card and devised a system to use it for payment transactions. In 1984, the French Postal and Telecommunications services carried out a successful field trial with telephone cards, and within a few years 60 million such cards were in circulation. Bankcards used with ATM machines are more complex because of their need for data encryption; cryptography is essential to debit cards. By 1994 all French bankcards included IC chips. France Telecom and Carte Bancaire were early adopters of smart cards. VISA, MasterCard, and American Express all issue smart cards.

The current generation of cards has an 8-bit processor, 16 or 32 KB of read-only memory (ROM–*q.v.*), and 1 or 2 KB of random-access memory (RAM)—limits that are certain to increase over time. Smart card readers are typically connected to computers over a universal serial bus (USB). Readers that conform to the standards of the Personal Computer Memory Card International Association are called PCMCIA readers, where the acronym is pronounced by reciting its individual letters.

Smart cards have many applications. There are debit cards that hold monetary values used as retail store gift cards, telephone calling cards that debit their maximum allotment of minutes as they are used, cards that provide secure access to a particular network, and cards that secure cellular phones and set-top TV boxes from fraudulent use. Smart cards make excellent ID cards, especially in the medical field where it is advantageous and possibly life-preserving to include patients' medical history thereon.

Smart cards are also used in conjunction with some touch-screen electronic voting machines, but there is controversy as to the security of the combined system. Master smart cards are inserted into the machine to initialize it and to capture its results at the end of voting. This raises concerns as to who writes its stored program, and whether there is opportunity for the cards to be altered ("hacked") or replaced with fraudulent ones once they are programmed. And since voters are given temporary custody of a personal smart card in order to cast a vote, there is concern that a clever person could arrive with a concealed homemade counterfeit card programmed so as to allow voting multiple times.

Bibliography

2000. Rankl, W., and Effing, W. *Smart Card Handbook*, 2nd Ed. New York: John Wiley.

Edwin D. Reilly

SMART DUST

See SENSOR NETWORK.

SNOBOL

See STRING PROCESSING: LANGUAGES.

SOFTWARE

For articles on related subjects, *see*

+ Object-Oriented Programming
+ Operating Systems

Very early in the development of computers, people referred to the actual physical components—the tubes and relays, the resistors and wires, and chassis—as *hardware*. In 1957, John Tukey coined the word *software* to describe the non-hardware components of the computer, in particular the programs that were needed to make the computers perform their intended tasks. The word caught on rapidly, and was in quite general use by 1960. One speaks of software companies, software maintenance, and, more recently, software engineering. Although *software* can be used to describe any program, it is usually used to denote programs whose use is not limited to one particular job or application. Thus, one speaks of systems software, of software systems, of mathematical software, of software for business applications, etc.

Early computers could run with relatively simple software. A loader (*see* LINKERS AND LOADERS) and a library of subroutines was considered sufficient for most first-generation computers. There were some very significant and sophisticated software developments associated with UNIVAC I (*q.v.*). Grace Hopper (*q.v.*) and her colleagues designed the first, very general, sorting systems, and developed the first high-level languages for business applications. Anatol Holt and William Turanski introduced many software system concepts in their GP (generalized programming) system, such as the *extended machine* or *platform*, the combination of hardware and software that the user sees as the machine for which programs are written.

Still in the first generation, John Backus and his colleagues from IBM and from several IBM user installations developed the Fortran (*q.v.*) compiler for the IBM 704, perhaps the most significant piece of software ever written. Fortran (*q.v.*) became the language of discourse for scientific programmers throughout the world and throughout the computer industry, and once and for all established the importance and usefulness of high-level languages.

The separation of hardware and software, the idea that software was superimposed on hardware in order to enhance its capabilities, persisted throughout the first- and most of the second-generation computers. The distinguishing characteristic of third-generation and subsequent systems is that computer hardware is designed to operate under control of a rather sophisticated software system. Especially in a multiprogrammed time-sharing system, it is essential that there be an *operating system* that maintains control of the allocation of system resources and that avoids problems of conflict, blocking, and interference among simultaneous users of the system. In particular, the I/O functions and the management of central and peripheral storage are software system functions that must be centralized and carefully controlled.

Up until about 1969, it was generally assumed that the acquisition of a computer system entitled the customer to all general-purpose software produced for that system by its manufacturer at no extra cost. Software companies could attempt to produce software systems that were better in some significant ways than those produced by the hardware manufacturers, but this could rarely be done profitably. They urged the *unbundling* of software. In June 1969, IBM announced that it would indeed unbundle. With the exception of essential operating system software, all new software products would henceforth be priced separately. Almost all other computer manufacturers followed suit.

Bibliography

1987. Levy, L. S. *Software Engineering and Software Economics*. New York: Springer-Verlag.

1991. Gelernter, D. H. *Mirror Worlds, or: The Day Software Puts the Universe in a Shoebox*. New York: Oxford University Press.

1998. Szyperski, C. *Component Software: Beyond Object-Oriented Programming.* Reading, MA: Addison-Wesley.

Saul Rosen

SOFTWARE ENGINEERING

For articles on related topics, *see*

+ Debugging
+ Program Verification
+ Software Maintenance
+ Software Prototyping

Software engineering is the disciplined application of theories and techniques from computer science to define, develop, deliver, and maintain, on time and within budget, software products that meet customer needs and expectations. Software products include actual program source code as well as the documents necessary to produce these, and documents and interface programs necessary to use them in the intended environment.

The term *software engineering* was first used in the late 1960s in conjunction with a NATO-sponsored conference of the same name. This and other meetings were held to discuss the problems of large, complex software development projects and to propose strategies to overcome the emerging "software crisis" of cost overruns and reduced functionality in delivered software.

Software Development Activities

There are some fundamental activities that must take place to produce software: requirements specification, design, implementation, and verification/validation.

Specification of requirements involves modeling the system at an abstract level. It may consider just the software system, or may include models of the larger computer-based system of which the software is to be a part. The requirements document *what* the software will do.

The *design* activity defines the structure needed to implement the specified requirements. The design documentation tells *how* the envisioned solution will be implemented by programmers.

Implementation is the translation of the design to source code.

Verification and validation (V&V) involves the exercise of the code to ensure it meets the design and requirements specifications. It includes testing of the individual program units, the integrated units, and the software system as a whole. Testing may consider the code structure within a unit, referred to as *whitebox* testing, or it may disregard internal structure, in which case it is called *blackbox* testing. Generally, individual unit tests are whitebox, while system and integration tests are blackbox.

Prototyping is a technique used within almost every development of large software systems and is essential for certain application areas such as real-time systems (*q.v.*). Prototyping is sometimes confused with simulation (*q.v.*). Often a prototype has only the "look and feel" of what the software product will be like and little or none of the functionality, except perhaps the interface functions. A simulation is not required to look or feel like the product, but rather to match exactly the dynamic behavior of the actual system or some part of it.

The Software-development Process

There are nearly as many distinct software processes as there are development efforts; five of the general software development paradigms are: iterative, transformational, spiral, waterfall, and fourth generation.

The *iterative*, sometimes called *evolutionary*, process paradigm is a flexible scheme consisting of short development "steps" that each results in a software product (Boehm, 1988). The incremental product is developed through specification, design, implementation, and verification. Each of these products is refined until ultimately the final product is achieved through these iterative steps.

The *transformational* process model requires a formal specification of the requirements for the software system under development. A series of transformation steps are then applied to the formal representation to achieve the implementation. These transformations can be reapplied to derive an updated implementation if the specification changes.

The *spiral* paradigm divides the *software life cycle* activities into four repeated stages: planning, risk analysis, development, and evaluation. Progress is made along an outward spiral through these stages (*see* Fig. 1), with the planning stage beginning each spiral loop. The evaluation and risk analysis phases end with a decision to proceed or not with the planned project. The width of the spiral (number of loops) indicates the resources already consumed for the effort. The requirements specification activity takes place during planning, risk analysis, and development. Design and implementation activities are generally in the development stage. V&V activities occur in development and evaluation. Prototyping is often used in early spiral loops to guide decisions for the final implementation.

The traditional *waterfall* life cycle paradigm is the basis for most current practice and has many variations. Its name comes from the progression of activities based on the output of one phase "falling" as input to the following phase (*see* Fig. 2). It is driven by the need to schedule project milestones that are provided by the completion of documents at each level or phase. A strict adherence to this model has the drawback that no product will be available to show to customers until after the implementation phase.

Fourth-generation processes are designed around special languages and tools that automatically generate code from a high-level description. Software development techniques are often viewed historically as belonging to "generations." The first generation saw customized solutions by single developers using low-level programming languages. In the second generation, software was developed for multiple users using procedural languages. The third generation is characterized by high-level, general-purpose languages that were used

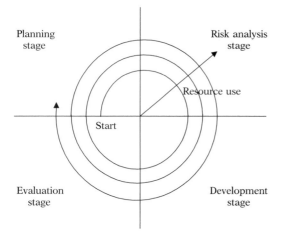

Figure 1. Spiral model.

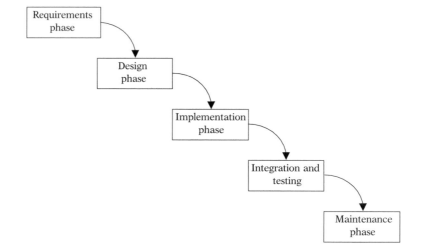

Figure 2. Waterfall model.

to develop software for a multitude of industrial applications. The high-level, nonprocedural languages that followed are hence usually termed *fourth generation.*

An important technique common to all these process models is *abstraction;* it is essential for the development of large systems. Abstraction allows engineers to focus on important aspects of the system under development without becoming overwhelmed by details that will be dealt with later. One type of abstraction for data definition is the abstract data type (ADT—*q.v.*). Here the type of the data and all the operations allowed on that type are encapsulated within one separate compilation unit (*see* ENCAPSULATION). The access to this information by other parts of the program is restricted, as only the names of types and operations are visible across the unit interfaces. This helps considerably when changes are needed, as all the information and operations are located together, and their integrity is assured.

Software Engineering Management

Management of a software engineering project is a challenging task. Management responsibilities include plans and organization, leadership and control, and assessment. The *software project manager* is responsible for scheduling the development process activities. Before activities can be scheduled, the project manager predicts and plans for adequate resources throughout development, including time, personnel, and financial and physical resources. Without good planning, the "on schedule and within budget" goals of software engineering cannot be achieved. An estimate of financial and physical risk of the project must be made and used to make decisions about the obligations and commitments of the organization. The organizing function of management is concerned with assignments of personnel and tasks to teams, individual team structures, and coordination among all teams. Team structures may have central control, for example a chief programmer team, or may have a democratic decentralized control, or some combination of the two.

Software Quality Characteristics

Quality is built into the software; it does not just happen to be there because the developers did a good job. The key to insuring quality is interaction with the customer. No single project can achieve every quality characteristic. Time and financial resources are finite, and some characteristics will be in conflict with others. For example, it is not possible to have a system that is completely portable and still have maximum efficiency for a particular environment. Trade-offs are usually required for the desired quality attributes. The selection of which ones to require in the final product must be based on the value they add for the customer.

Software Engineering Evolution

Software engineering is consumed with the search for the best method to develop software. Industry and government have collaborated to research and develop methods and tools for implementing large, high-quality, software-intensive systems. Among these efforts are the Software Productivity Consortium (SPC) in Herndon, VA, Microelectronics and Computer Technology Corporation (MCC) in Austin, TX, and the Software Engineering Institute (SEI) in Pittsburgh, PA. The contributions of these and other collaborations have led to many new approaches and have had the intention of hastening the transfer of technology from the drawing board into actual industry practice.

In the early 1990s, the SEI established a method for assessing the capability of an organization to develop software. This Capability Maturity Model (CMM) provides a framework for organizations to improve their development process. The five levels of maturity are shown in Fig. 3. The CMM defines key processes associated with the five levels that suggest areas for improvement to advance to that maturity level. Qualification for any level implies that the process embodies all the key processes of the lower numbered levels.

The best evidence for the evolution of software engineering practice is the availability of Computer-Aided Software Engineering (CASE) tools to support process activities. Some tools are for general use, while others support a particular technique or methodology. In fact, some methods would not be practical were it not for tool support. There are tools for management activities, such as configuration management, cost estimation, and

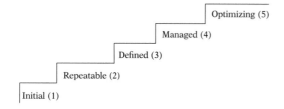

Figure 3. Capability maturity levels.

scheduling; documentation tools, such as editors; design tools, such as rapid prototyping and modeling and simulation tools; programming aids, such as debuggers and code generators; testing tools; and maintenance tools. Some CASE environments have integrated tools for the whole development effort.

Bibliography

1988. Boehm, B. "A Spiral Model of Software Development and Enhancement," *IEEE Computer*, **21**(5), 61–72.

1992. Glass, R. *Building Quality Software*. Upper Saddle River, NJ: Prentice Hall.

1994. IEEE. *Software Engineering Standards Collection*. Los Alamitos, CA: IEEE Press.

1995. Brooks, F. *The Mythical Man Month: Essays on Software Engineering*. Reading, MA: Addison-Wesley.

Bonnie Melhart

SOFTWARE HISTORY

For articles on related subjects, *see*

+ Database Management System (DBMS)
+ Digital Computer
+ Operating Systems
+ Programming Languages
+ Software
+ Software Engineering

From the outset, the development of software has been directed toward the goals of making the computer easier to use and yet insulating users from the innermost details of how the computer operates. The first goal has involved the creation of programming languages and systems to facilitate the development of the applications that make the computer useful. The second has included the operating systems that oversee these applications and manage the hardware and software resources on which they draw. The term *programming language* or *high-level language* refers to the specific form in which the user actually writes a program for input to the computer. The term *operating system* encompasses the general set of tools and techniques that enables both individuals and computer installations to accommodate effectively many jobs with minimum human intervention, allowing for parallel, sequential, interactive, and distributed modes.

Programming Languages

This article pertains to high-level languages; development of assembly language and macroassemblers is not discussed. Language development started as far back as 1945 with the unimplemented "Plankalkül" by Konrad Zuse (*q.v.*) in Germany. Various attempts at developing a language that was closer to the problem expression than was assembly language were made by numerous people and organizations, as described by Knuth and Trabb Pardo (1980) and Sammet (1969). The earliest *operational* compiler (*q.v.*) for a high-level language seems to have been that developed by Laning and Zierler for mathematical computations, which was running on the MIT Whirlwind (*q.v.*) in 1954. However, the first high-level language that received wide usage was Fortran (*q.v.*), developed by John Backus and others at IBM in the mid-1950s.

In 1958, a group of Americans (representing ACM) and Europeans (representing GAMM) collaborated on a language for algorithmic processes known as IAL (*International Algebraic Language*); this language was eventually modified to become Algol 60 (*q.v.*) and the earlier version was renamed Algol 58. Both Algol 58 and Algol 60 led to a major emphasis on and work in the area of programming languages by universities and industry. Several languages based on Algol 58 (e.g. Jovial, Mad, Neliac) and compiler techniques were developed.

In parallel with these developments in scientific languages were the efforts for business data processing; the first of these was Flow-Matic, developed by Grace Hopper (*q.v.*) and her colleagues at Remington Rand Univac in the mid-1950s. As the first programming language oriented toward English, Flow-Matic was one of the major inputs to Cobol (*q.v.*), which was developed by a group of computer manufacturers' representatives and users organized in 1959 under Department of Defense (DoD) sponsorship. Cobol had an effect on the programming of business data processing problems as large as or larger than Fortran had for scientific and engineering problems.

The two years 1958 and 1959 were probably the two most productive years in the history of programming languages. Joining Algol 58 for scientific computation and Cobol for business data processing were Comit and Lisp (*q.v.*), both developed at MIT. Comit was a string processing (*q.v.*) language designed primarily by Victor Yngve for use in translating natural languages. Lisp was a list processing language developed for artificial intelligence (AI) applications by John McCarthy and his students. While Lisp continues to be heavily used by the AI community, Comit was largely supplanted by varying versions of Snobol, which, in turn, has been largely superseded by Icon.

Because the early languages maintained the same dichotomy between scientific and data processing computations that the early computers did, it is not surprising that eventually languages began to be developed that were meant to be more general. Beginning in 1975, the US DoD undertook to develop a single language suitable for *embedded systems* (*q.v.*). The preliminary specifications for this language, called Ada (*q.v.*), were issued in 1979, and the language specifications labeled "final" were issued in July 1980. Ada has been used effectively in almost all types of application, including AI and business data processing.

With the advent of interactive computing systems, languages were developed for effective use in that environment. The earliest was Joss, developed by J. Cliff Shaw at the Rand Corporation in 1963. The most popular, Basic (*q.v.*), originated as part of the Dartmouth (College) Time-Sharing System, developed by John Kemeny and Thomas Kurtz and aimed at making the computer generally accessible to students. The language was first implemented on minicomputers (*q.v.*) and then, most famously, on PCs, and it remains in widespread use, principally in the form of Visual Basic.

A number of languages have been developed to do nonnumeric mathematics (*see* COMPUTER ALGEBRA). The first to receive wide usage was Formac, developed by Jean Sammet and her colleagues at IBM in 1962–1964. It was succeeded by Macsyma, initially developed in the early 1970s at MIT by Joel Moses and others, which gave way in turn by the early 1990s to the powerful Mathematica system developed by Stephen Wolfram.

The ACM Special Interest Group on Programming Languages (SIGPLAN) sponsored a History of Programming Languages (HOPL) Conference in 1978. The languages featured were Algol, APL, APT, Basic, Cobol, Fortran, GPSS, Joss, Jovial, Lisp, PL/I, Simula, and Snobol. Papers on Ada (*q.v.*), C (*q.v.*), Pascal (*q.v.*), Prolog (*see* LOGIC PROGRAMMING), and Smalltalk (*see* OBJECT-ORIENTED PROGRAMMING) were invited for the second ACM SIGPLAN History of Programming Languages in 1993. By the early 1980s, Pascal had become a practical base and spiritual catalyst of language development, just as Algol had been for the 1960s. Initially developed as a systems programming language for Unix (*q.v.*), C's popularity grew with the spread of PCs, especially in its object-oriented version C++ (*q.v.*). Over the course of the 1990s, functional programming (*q.v.*) languages such as ML have gradually moved to the forefront of development.

Operating Systems

Around 1956, a simple operating system was developed jointly by General Motors and North American Aviation for the IBM 704. By the time Fortran became generally available, operating systems had been developed that provided facilities such as sequencing from one job to another, I/O control systems, calling in components (e.g. assembler, compiler), and loading object programs along with library routines. By the early 1960s, batch operating systems such as IBSYS on the IBM 7090 could manage programs requiring differing services.

The programmer specified what functions the operating system was to perform via special *job-control cards*.

Around 1963, Burroughs released its Master Control Program (MCP) written in a high-level language and with facilities for multiprocessing (*q.v.*) and multiprogramming (*q.v.*). OS/360, developed in the middle 1960s for the IBM System/360, typified the very large and powerful batch system, although it was actually designed for a broad range of uses including real-time systems (*q.v.*).

The development of SAGE in the late 1950s demonstrated the feasibility of real-time systems in which the computer responds very rapidly to continuing input. The IBM–American Airlines SABRE system of 1963 (for airline reservations) seems to have been the earliest major system for transaction processing (*see* IBM).

The extension of real-time computing to interactive programming began with the development of the Compatible Time-Sharing System (CTSS) at MIT on the IBM 709/7090 under the direction of Fernando Corbató, starting in 1961 and becoming of significant use by 1963 (*see* TIME SHARING). This was the first significant general system with the following characteristics: (1) numerous typewriter-like terminals were connected to one computer and could be used at the same time; (2) each terminal user seemed to have available the full power and facilities of the computer's hardware and software; and (3) users' tasks were carried out in small *time slices*. CTSS provided various language compilers, file manipulation facilities, and user-developed systems. By the 1970s, the most powerful and flexible of the general interactive systems was Multics, developed in the mid-1960s for the GE (later Honeywell) 645 as a joint effort of General Electric, MIT, and Bell Laboratories; it was heavily influenced by the MIT experience with CTSS.

Toward the late 1960s, the three operating system concepts of interactive, batch, and real time began to merge. It became clear that the design requirement for all three concepts was resource management. Among the resources to be managed was virtual memory (*q.v.*), that is, the facility whereby the user can write a program assuming the memory size is effectively unlimited, a practice started in the late 1950s on the Atlas (*q.v.*) computer at Manchester University (*see* MANCHESTER UNIVERSITY COMPUTERS).

Since the early 1970s, Unix (*q.v.*) has become widely accepted as a model of a small but powerful interactive operating system. Reflecting the experience of Multics and Genie, the initial version was developed by Ken Thompson and Dennis Ritchie of Bell Laboratories between 1969 and 1970 to run on the DEC PDP-7 and PDP-9 computers. Blocked by a consent decree from commercializing Unix, Bell Labs made it and its source code freely available to universities, where it quickly became the system of choice. Written almost entirely in C, Unix invited tinkering and adaptation to local needs and thus spawned a variety of versions, perhaps most famous among them the Berkeley Software Distribution. During the 1980s, it was ported in various flavors to microcomputers, the principal one being Linux (*q.v.*).

At just about the same time, the first PC operating systems, in particular CP/M and various versions of DOS, took shape, adopting in particular the hierarchical file structure, file redirection, and pipes of Unix. With those earlier models came also the notion of a layered system in which applications run on a virtual machine that communicates with the real machine through a kernel (*q.v.*). The rapid expansion of memory and processing speed dedicated to single, standalone use soon led to the commercial introduction by Apple (*q.v.*) of the graphical user interface (GUI) pioneered at Xerox PARC (Palo Alto Research Center) in the mid-1970s and ultimately stemming from the work of Douglas Engelbart in the 1960s. GUIs have separated the user from the computer in a culturally significant sense. Through a "desktop" metaphor, or more recently, that of a browser as a working environment, they have removed the computer itself from the user's view, transforming programming into a set of mediated actions that bear little resemblance to it. In doing so, they have moved beyond high-level programming languages to a point at which programming "languages" are no longer languages.

Data Handling

With the advent of the first Cobol specifications in 1960, the need for file manipulation facilities separate from the actual programs could be eliminated because such facilities were embedded in the support provided by Cobol. But in most data processing environments, installations would create separate files for each set of applications; for example, an employee file was used for payroll purposes and a separate employee file was used for department assignment and transfer purposes. Eventually, it became clear that all of these separate files should be combined into a common framework, and this led to the concept now known as a *database management system* (DBMS—*q.v.*).

There have been three major technical approaches to database management systems. One is based on the Integrated Data Store (IDS), first proposed by Charles Bachman of General Electric in 1964. He proposed a network approach to storing data, and this was used as the basis for the work of the Codasyl Data Base Task Group. A second approach is the hierarchical system in which data is represented as a *tree* (*q.v.*). The earliest manifestation of this approach seems to have been the work at North American Aviation Space Division and IBM in 1965; it is exemplified by IBM's Information Management System issued around 1969. A third approach, now the dominant one, is the *relational database* (*q.v.*) of E. F. Codd of IBM, first introduced around 1970. It involves the concept of linked tables of data where information is not repeated, as it must be in the hierarchical systems.

Software Tools, Techniques, and Methodologies

Compilers are obviously a major class of tools, and initially the emphasis lay on developing techniques that provide rapid compilation and object code that is efficient both in speed of execution and in minimal use of memory. The earliest significant compiler was that for Fortran. The concept of a *syntax-directed compiler* was introduced by E. T. Irons in 1961; in addition to inspiring a great deal of research, it led first to diagnostic compilers that could catch syntactical

errors and mismatches of type as they arose during compilation and then to syntax-driven editors, which guided programming as it progressed.

The concept of a *list* seems to have been introduced by Allen Newell, Herbert Simon, and J. C. Shaw in the mid-1950s as a useful technique in their work on developing programs that would prove theorems in the propositional calculus. Although a sequence of list processing languages (*q.v.*) was also developed (named IPL-I, . . .IPL-V) to do list processing, only the last became significantly used and even it eventually faded from use, while the list *concept* remains as a cornerstone of software techniques.

Debugging (*q.v.*) tools and concepts were created as part of the early development of programming. The tools ranged from very simple to quite sophisticated, and have included static and dynamic traces and cross-references, simulators, measurements, and diagnostic features associated with compilers. Although testing is related to debugging, it was not until a conference in 1972 that *software testing* began to be considered seriously as a distinct subdiscipline.

With interactive time-sharing systems came the development of online tools for file management, editing, and *rapid prototyping* by means of an interpreter, or shell language, operating interactively at the level of the file system and replacing the earlier job-control languages at the user interface (*q.v.*). The concept received full expression in Unix, in which the notion of the *software toolbox* emphasized the utility of "little languages" such as *awk* and *eqn* used as successive filters in the transformation and editing of files. Such languages, which feature powerful pattern-matching engines and associative arrays, are now fundamental to Internet browsers in the form of tools like Perl (a successor to *awk*) and Javascript. As in the case of applications, programming itself has been adapted to the GUI environment in the form of tools for visual programming, in which syntax-directed editors, compilers, and debuggers work interactively, and files, libraries, and other resources are available for selection from menus.

A contribution to the developing discipline of programming has been the creation of ANSI standards.

The main software standards have been the programming languages that started with the first Fortran standard in 1966. Other languages that have had one or more standards, either internationally or in the USA, are Ada, Algol 60, APL, APT, ATLAS, Basic, C, C++, Chill, Cobol, DIBOL, Forth, Mumps, PANCM, Pascal, Extended Pascal, Pilot, PL/I, and Scheme. Standardization has been under way for various other languages.

Bibliography

1969. Sammet, J. E. *Programming Languages: History and Fundamentals.* Upper Saddle River, NJ: Prentice Hall.

1980. Knuth, D. E., and Trabb Pardo, L. "The Early Development of Programming Languages," in *A History of Computing in the Twentieth Century* (eds. N. Metropolis, J. Howlett, and G.-C. Rota), 197–273. New York: Academic Press.

1981. Wexelblat, R. (ed.) *History of Programming Languages. ACM Monograph Series.* New York: Academic Press.

1994. Stroustrup, B. *The Design and Evolution of C++.* Reading, MA: Addison-Wesley.

1996. Bergin, T. M., and Gibson, R. G. (eds.) *History of Programming Languages II.* New York: ACM Press; Reading, MA: Addison-Wesley.

1998. Ceruzzi, P. E. *A History of Modern Computing.* Cambridge, MA: MIT Press.

2003. Reilly, E. D. *Milestones of Computer Science and Information Technology.* Westport, CT: Greenwood Press.

Jean E. Sammet and Michael S. Mahoney

SOFTWARE MAINTENANCE

For articles on related subjects, *see*

+ Compatibility
+ Debugging
+ Object-Oriented Programming
+ Software Engineering

Introduction

The objective of *software maintenance* is to make required changes in software including changes to documentation in such a way that its value to users is increased. Maintenance is not limited to making postdelivery changes. Rather, it starts with user requirements and continues for the life of the software.

Purpose

Maintenance activities are *perfective* (performed to enhance performance, improve maintainability, or improve executing efficiency), *adaptive* (performed to adapt software to changes in the data requirements or processing environments), or *corrective* (performed to identify and correct software failures, performance failures, and implementation failures).

Perfective maintenance restructures code in accordance with structured programming (*q.v.*) principles. Much early software was programmed before the benefits of structured methods were appreciated. Thus, unstructured software ("spaghetti code") is difficult to maintain because the consequences of making a change are not readily apparent. Structured code is much easier to maintain.

Adaptive maintenance changes the format and method of handling data to be compatible with the way data is processed in an application package. This need could arise, for example, when a user decides to process data in spreadsheet (*q.v.*) form. Data in column, row, and cell format is much easier to process accurately than data with little or no structure.

Corrective maintenance changes the code in order to correct a fault or make a correction in a design document.

High Cost of Maintenance

In the early days of information system development, programmer salaries were an almost insignificant percentage of the information system budget and hardware costs were very high. Now that hardware is inexpensive and programmer salaries are high, programmers are often required to maintain efficient but hard to maintain older programs at considerable expense to their organizations. Unfortunately, these *legacy* programs cannot be discarded because so much of this software deals with the business needs of the organization. This software can be reengineered to improve its maintainability or reverse engineered in an attempt to discover its design rules, but it cannot be entirely discarded.

Evolutionary Model of Software

Evolutionary development of software is inevitable. Furthermore, the very act of installing software changes the environment; pressures operate to modify the environment, the problem, and technological solutions. Changes generated by users and the environment and the consequent need for adapting the software to the changes is unpredictable and cannot be accommodated without iteration. Programs must be more alterable and the resultant change process must be planned and controlled. Large programs are never completed, they just continue to evolve.

Relationship between Product and Process Evolution

We can apply this model of maintenance to obtain common measures of product and process evolution. They are desirable because the relationship between product quality and development, and maintenance process capability and maturity has been recognized as a major issue in software engineering, on the premise that improvements in process will lead to higher quality products.

Process Stability

To understand the effect of the maintenance process on product metrics like reliability, one would analyze trends in these metrics (Schneidewind, 1998), looking at two types of trend: across releases and within a release. Either an increasing or a decreasing trend might be favorable. For example, an *increasing* trend in Time to Next Failure and a *decreasing* trend in Failures per KLOC (thousand [K] Lines Of Code) would be favorable. A favorable trend indicates maintenance stability. When the trend in a metric over time is favorable (e.g. increasing reliability), one may conclude that the maintenance process is *stable* with respect to that software metric (reliability). Conversely, when the trends are unfavorable

(e.g. decreasing reliability), one may conclude that that process is *unstable*.

Bibliography

1980. Lientz, B. P., and Swanson, E. B. *Software Maintenance Management*. Reading, MA: Addison-Wesley.

1996. Pigoski, T. M. *Practical Software Maintenance*. New York: John Wiley.

1998. Schneidewind, N. F. "How to Evaluate Legacy System Maintenance," *IEEE Software*, **15**(4), (July–August), 34–42.

Norman F. Schneidewind

SOFTWARE PIRACY

See LEGAL PROTECTION OF SOFTWARE.

SOFTWARE PORTABILITY

For articles on related subjects, *see*

+ Compatibility
+ Software
+ Software Engineering
+ Transparency

Software is said to be *portable* if it can be run on computers other than the one for which it was originally written. Portable software proves its worth when computers are replaced or when the same software is run on many different computers. The simplest aid to portability is the use of standard high-level languages such as C++ (*q.v.*), Fortran (*q.v.*), or Cobol (*q.v.*). Such standard languages do, however, have the following deficiencies: (1) standards change over time; (2) compilers often support nonstandard language extensions; (3) standards are rarely completely precise; (4) programs sometimes require nonstandard parts to interface with the local operating environment. Therefore, extra work is needed to make software properly portable. Useful methods include the use of language subsets common to all compilers; use of verifier programs to ensure adherence to subsets; use of *preprocessors* (*q.v.*) to map a source program into several alternative forms; and separating out machine-dependent aspects of software.

Portability of a language is enhanced if it has a compiler (or interpreter) that is itself portable. This makes it easy to implement the compiler on any desired platform, and thus to run programs written in the language that the compiler supports. Java (*q.v.*), for example, has been designed to be portable over networks. Java programs are converted into a simple and concise intermediate form called *byte-code*, which is machine-independent. This intermediate form can be downloaded and interpreted by any computer on the network.

Bibliography

1996. Sommerville, I. *Software Engineering*, 5th Ed. Wokingham: Addison-Wesley. (Contains useful material on portability within the overall context of software engineering.)

Peter J. Brown

SOFTWARE PROTOTYPING

For articles on related subjects, *see*

+ Software Engineering
+ Software Reusability

A *software prototype* is an executable model of a proposed software system that accurately reflects chosen aspects of the system, such as display formats, the values computed, or response times. Software prototyping is an approach to software development that uses prototypes to help both the developers and their customers visualize the proposed system and predict its properties (Fig. 1). Prototypes are used extensively by designers and engineers working in other disciplines.

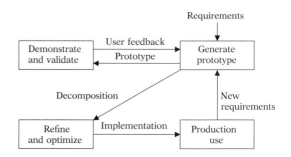

Figure 1.   The software prototyping process.

For example, architects build scale models of buildings to aid visualization of three-dimensional relationships, aeronautical engineers build scale models of airplanes to measure lift and drag in wind tunnel tests, and electrical engineers build breadboard circuits to check the validity of designs based on simplified ideal models of physical components.

Software prototypes may not satisfy all of the constraints on the final version of the system. For example, a prototype may provide only a subset of all the required functions, it may be expressed in a more powerful or more flexible language than the final version, it may run on a machine with more resources than the proposed target architecture, it may be less efficient in both time and space than the final version, it may have limited capacity, and it may not include facilities for error checking and fault tolerance.

New technologies have made computer-aided prototyping feasible. These technologies have reduced the time and cost involved in producing a prototype, thus widening the gap between a software prototype and the cost of the final software system. The new technologies are based on reusable code, computer-aided design, and automatic generation of programs. The most powerful systems are designed for specific problem domains. Some problem domains for which computer-aided prototyping tools have been developed include administrative applications, user interfaces (*q.v.*), programming languages (*q.v.*), and real-time systems (*q.v.*).

Computer-aided prototyping of real-time systems (*q.v.*) is supported by the prototyping language PSDL (Luqi, Berzins and Yeh, 1988) and the associated prototyping system CAPS. CAPS uses a software base of reusable components, a program generator, a static scheduler, and a dynamic scheduler to realize systems containing both functions with hard real-time constraints and non-time-critical functions. PSDL provides a simple representation of system decompositions using dataflow diagrams augmented with nonprocedural control constraints and timing constraints (maximum response times, maximum execution times, minimum inter-stimulus periods, periods, and deadlines). The language models both periodic and data-driven tasks, and both discrete (transaction-oriented) and continuous (sampled) data streams. The CAPS system provides automated tools for generating static schedules to guarantee hard real-time constraints as well as an execution support system that generates code for adapting, interconnecting, and controlling the execution of reusable software components.

Bibliography

1988. Herndon, R., and Berzins, V. "The Realizable Benefits of a Language Prototyping Language," *IEEE Transactions on Software Engineering*, **SE-14**(6), (June), 803–809.

1988. Luqi, Berzins, V., and Yeh, R. "A Prototyping Language for Real-time Software," *IEEE Transactions on Software Engineering*, **14**(10), (October), 1409–1423.

1996. "Special Issue on Computer-aided Prototyping," *Journal of Systems Integration*, **6**(1–2).

Valdis Berzins

SOFTWARE REUSABILITY

For articles on related subjects, *see*

+ Abstract Data Type
+ Class
+ Encapsulation
+ Information Hiding
+ Macro
+ Modular Programming
+ Object-Oriented Programming
+ Program Library
+ Software Portability
+ Subprogram

Software reusability is a software attribute that facilitates its incorporation into new application programs. Reusable software shares many attributes with "good" software (e.g. transportability, maintainability, flexibility, understandability, usability, and reliability). Software reuse was initially proposed by Charles Babbage (*q.v.*) as part of the Analytical Engine (*q.v.*) through a mechanism analogous to a subroutine call.

During the early days of programming, the most successful examples of software reuse were subroutine libraries or system macros. The first practical implementation of a subroutine library, was realized by Maurice Wilkes (*q.v.*) as part of the first stored-program computer, the EDSAC (*q.v.*), in 1951. The modern roots of software reuse can be traced to Doug McIlroy's 1969 paper "Mass Produced Software Components" at the NATO Conference on Software Engineering.

There are several implementation techniques and programming technologies that enhance the reusability of software. These include data encapsulation; information hiding; polymorphism (*see* OPERATOR OVERLOADING); abstract data types, classes, or methods; Unix-like pipes and filters; inheritance (*see* OBJECT-ORIENTED PROGRAMMING); parameterization and genericity (*see* MACRO and PREPROCESSOR); application generators and fourth-generation languages (4GLs); and virtual (abstract) machine interfaces.

Any reusable component needs to be adequately documented before it can be reused. Component documentation must be kept consistent with the current implementation, or else the software developer is faced with the difficult and undesirable task of studying code in order to understand how it can reused. Java has introduced a tool, JavaDoc, to enhance the reusability of a component by supporting the automatic generation of hypertext documentation (i.e. HTML Web pages) from stylized comments embedded in the source code. Special tags inside JavaDoc comments are used to generate standard format Web pages, which also may include HTML text formatting tags. The classes, packages, interfaces, and exceptions found in the Java Library API Package are documented with JavaDoc, making them more readily learned, used, modified, and extended.

If enough well-tested, well-documented, flexible, and reusable components are developed according to these principles and placed in inventory, programmers could easily construct new applications or *applets* simply by assembling and extending selected components. This paradigm shift to "component-based" programming is promoted by the Component Object Model (COM) in Java and Visual Basic and has resulted in the development of a reusable component industry.

Bibliography

1989. Biggerstaff, T. J., and Perlis, A. J. *Software Reusability: Volume I Concepts and Models, Volume II Applications and Experience.* New York: ACM Press.

1996. Tracz, W. *Confessions of a Used Program Salesman: Institutionalizing Software Reuse.* New York: Addison Wesley Longman.

1997. Chan, P., and Lee, R. *Java^{TM} Class Libraries: An Annotated Reference.* New York: Addison Wesley Longman.

Will Tracz

SORTING

For articles on related subjects, *see*

+ Algorithms, Analysis of
+ Searching
+ Tree

Internal Sorting

In computing, *sorting* is the process of rearranging an initially unordered sequence of records until they are ordered with respect to all of or that part of each record designated as its *key*. As used here, a *record* (*q.v.*) may be as small as a single bit, character, integer, or real (floating-point) number—in which case the entire record serves as a key—or it may be an arbitrarily large aggregate of data values of possibly mixed data types, in which case one or more constituent elements are designated as primary key, secondary key, tertiary key, and so on. Multiple keys imply multiple sorting phases in which, for example, the goal might be to sort persons' names so that they are ordered primarily by last name and secondarily by first name.

The most common rationale for sorting a sequence of records is that the time to do so (once) will prove to be insignificant compared to the many times that the sequence will be searched in order to locate a particular record. When such a search is performed on an unordered sequence of n records, then, on average, $(n + 1)/2$ records need to be examined during a successful search (and all n for an unsuccessful search). But an ordered sequence of n records of uniform length can be searched by examining at most $\log_2 n$ records, which, for $n = 1024$ is 51 times faster than the average successful sequential search (*see* SEARCHING).

In choosing or designing a sorting algorithm, the foremost consideration is whether all data records reside in main memory (*q.v.*), or whether some or all are stored on an auxiliary mass storage (*q.v.*) device, such as magnetic tape or disk. In the former case, one of a class of *internal sorting algorithms* may be used, in which, because of the random access property of main memory, records may be freely accessed regardless of their position in what is then essentially an indexable array of records. But when records are stored in an auxiliary mass-storage memory whose latency and additional access time (*q.v.*) imposes a severe penalty on retrieval of single records, one of a class of specialized *external sorting algorithms* must be used. This article emphasizes internal sorting algorithms, with only a brief discussion of external sorting.

For any sorting algorithm, an important consideration is stability. A sorting algorithm is *stable* if, during movement and possible rearrangement of records, no two records having identical keys ever have their original order reversed. For records that are "all key," stability is not a concern, but when a record sequence is to be sorted first on a secondary key and then a primary key (the logically necessary order of use of multiple keys), the desired result cannot be attained if the final sort on primary key permutes the original order of records whose primary keys are the same.

At least four considerations may influence the choice of an internal sorting algorithm:

1. *Running time*–How long does it take to sort n records, and by what factor does this time increase in order to sort $2n$ records?
2. *Memory space*–Do main memory limitations force choice of an algorithm that sorts "in place" (using only the n record spaces needed to hold the data), or are additional n record spaces needed?
3. *Initial order*–Are the records known to be already ordered with just a few exceptions? This is not the usual situation, but when it does occur, the most suitable algorithm (insertion sort) may well be one that is not at all efficient when the initial order of the records is essentially random.
4. *Key range*–Do record keys span a very large range or possibly only a very restricted range (such as integers 0 to 999)? Certain algorithms applicable to keys of narrow range are not feasible for keys that span a large range.

Unless the number of records to be sorted is very small—perhaps 100 or fewer—by far the most important of these considerations is running time.

Sorting algorithms may be classified as being either *comparative or distributive*. A comparative algorithm rearranges record order by comparing record keys. A distributive algorithm moves records to or close to their final correct position based on intrinsic key characteristics.

Comparative Sorting Algorithms

There is an easily derived theoretical upper limit to the rate at which records may be sorted by key comparison. There are $n!$ different sequences of n records, only one of which is the correct ascendingly (or descendingly) ordered sequence. Imagine that these $n!$ permutations form the leaves of a binary decision tree (a binary tree in which each node has 0 or 2 children), each of whose nodes represents a comparison of two record keys. If the tree is reasonably well balanced, it can be shown that its contents can be retrieved in order in $O(n \ln n)$, that is, a constant times $n \ln n$ as $n \to \infty$ (*see* ALGORITHMS,

ANALYSIS OF). Thus, no sorting algorithm *based on key comparisons* can have running time superior to $O(n \log n)$. Since the proof is not constructive, however, algorithms that attain this performance have to be discovered empirically. We will discuss several such algorithms, but only after first examining why the four primitive algorithms that are logically most straightforward fail to achieve $O(n \log n)$ performance.

Selection Sort

The most obvious sorting algorithm is called *selection sort*: look through all n records to find the one with smallest key, then through the remaining $n-1$ records to find the one of next smallest key, and so on. By exchanging each record of successively smaller key with the appropriate record at the top of the unsorted sequence of records, the records can be sorted in place, the length of the sorted sequence at the top growing gradually longer as the length of the unsorted sequence at the bottom shrinks to zero. Selection sort has the undesirable property that when the number of records to be sorted is doubled, the time to do so quadruples, that is, its running time is $O(n^2)$.

Bubblesort

A second reasonably obvious algorithm is based on the simplistic notion that if two adjacent records are out of order they should be exchanged. If this is done to successive (overlapped) record pairs, from the first through the record pair that starts at the $(n-1)$st position, the original list will not necessarily yet be sorted, but one can be sure that the record of largest key will have reached the end of the list. Then, by repeating the process $n-2$ more times, the entire list is certain to be sorted. Successive phases of the sort are called *passes* since each requires that we reexamine (i.e. *pass through*), all remaining unsorted data. The name *bubblesort* stems from the fact that from pass to pass the records of "lighter" (smaller) key gradually rise ("bubble up") to their proper ultimate position. Bubblesort is also known as *exchange sort*.

Both selection sort and bubblesort have $O(n^2)$ average and worst-case running times, but because, on average, each pass of bubblesort needs more exchanges to isolate a new largest key than selection sort needs to identify a new smallest key, bubblesort runs more slowly.

Insertion Sort

The *insertion sort* algorithm is likely to occur to anyone who has sorted cancelled checks or playing cards by simply holding them in the hand and inserting them one by one into the proper position among already sorted items. The computer version, of course, has more difficulty making room for new insertions. Sometimes room must be made for insertion of a record at the top of the list, necessitating movement of all records in the partially ordered list down by one position. But whenever a record is encountered whose key is larger than that of the last one in the partially ordered list, it merely needs to be appended to the list. This implies that in the best case of an already sorted list, or even one that is almost ordered to the point where few insertions need to be made near the beginning of the list, insertion sort is linear, $O(n)$. For the average and worst cases, however, insertion sort is $O(n^2)$.

Enumeration Sort

Selection sort, bubblesort, and insertion sort all involve movement of data records as an integral part of each pass. An alternative is to leave actual data movement to a last pass and concentrate first on key comparisons. By comparing each key to all others, we can count how many keys are smaller than any given key. If, for example, the counting phase shows that there are 17 records whose keys are smaller than the key of the first record of the unsorted list, then that record can be moved into the 18th position of the ordered list being developed. The space needed is n locations of integer length to hold counts and n locations of record length to hold the records.

All four of the primitive sorting algorithms are stable and have worst-case running times that are $O(n^2)$. Thus, none realizes or approaches the theoretically possible $O(n \log n)$ behavior, but three of the four have modifications that do. We will examine them in the same

order: a modified selection sort called *heapsort*, modified exchange sorts called *quicksort* and *radix exchange sort*, and modified insertion sorts called *Shellsort, treesort,* and *mergesort.*

Heapsort – A Better Selection Sort

In 1964, John Williams realized that the principal defect of selection sort was that important information was being developed but then discarded and lost during each pass that isolates the smallest key of the records remaining to be sorted: the value of the next smaller key. How could knowledge of that next smallest key—and the third smallest, and so on—be preserved as the sort progresses? Williams invented an algorithm called *heapsort* based on two observations: (1) information about the relative sizes of keys could be stored in a special kind of binary tree called a *heap* and (2) the nodes of a heap can be mapped one to one to successive cells of an *array*.

A *heap* is a complete binary tree in which the value of every node is less than or equal to the value of either child node. By "complete" it is meant that there are no missing nodes except, perhaps, for one or more leaves at the right of the bottom level. The mapping of a complete binary tree of seven nodes to successive elements of an array is shown in Fig. 1. All that happens throughout is movement of a record from one indexed position in an array to another, so that heapsort might just as well have been called *array sort*. Heapsort running time is $O(n\log n)$, even in the worst case, and the algorithm is stable.

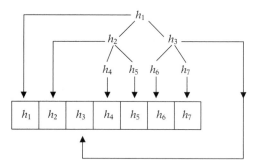

Figure 1. Mapping a binary tree to a one-dimensional array.

Quicksort – A Better Exchange Sort

In 1962, C. A. R. Hoare reasoned that the principal defect of exchange sort (bubblesort) was that the records that were exchanged never moved very far; each exchange moved the records only one record position closer to their ultimate location. What if, he pondered, records were partitioned with respect to a chosen *pivot*, a particular key taken from one of the records in the data set being partitioned. All records having a key less than or equal to the pivot would be placed in a left partition; all other records would be placed in a right partition and the pivot record would lie between them. Neither the left nor right partition would then necessarily be sorted, but the pivot record would be in its final location, never having to be moved again. Next, the left and right partitions are partitioned in the same way, and so on (recursively, in the easiest implementation to program). When all partitions have reached size 1, the sort is complete. Hoare called his algorithm *quicksort*, the name most commonly used, but it is sometimes called *partition exchange sort*.

For a Pascal quicksort procedure, *see* STRUCTURED PROGRAMMING. On average—that is for initial sequences of records whose keys are randomly distributed—quicksort has running time $O(n\log n)$. Running time is sensitive to the choice of pivot, however, and using the first record's key as pivot as that procedure does will yield $O(n^2)$ running time for sequences that are already in order, or are in reverse order. For average data, quicksort is the fastest of all known comparison sorts, but the conventional implementation of quicksort is unstable.

Radix Exchange Sort

Another improved version of exchange sort is the *radix exchange sort* invented in 1959 by Paul Hildebrandt, Harold Isbitz, Hawley Rising, and Jules Schwartz. The basic idea is to look at the binary representation of the keys to be sorted bit by bit, a column (radix position) at a time, starting at the leftmost column that has at least one 1-bit. Then, analogous to a quicksort partition that progresses by moving a pair of pointers from the left and right sides of an array of records until they

meet, pointers (*q.v.*) are moved down from the top and up from the bottom until they meet. The similarity of radix exchange sort to quicksort is striking. The effect is to partition numbers according to a phantom pivot of value 2^j that is not necessarily a member of the set of record keys being examined.

Since radix exchange sort indirectly involves key comparisons, albeit bit by bit, it is subject to the proof that a comparison sort runs, at best, in $O(n \log n)$. Knuth (1998) gives an extensive analysis that this is so, but the $O(n \log n)$ behavior does not set in until very high values of n; for up to at least a million items sorted, radix exchange runs in $O(pn)$, where p (for precision) is the number of bit positions to be examined.

Shellsort – An Improved Insertion Sort

An interesting algorithm that improves the performance of sorting by insertion was published by Donald L. Shell in 1959. In the best case—a list already in order—insertion sort is $O(n)$ because each newly stored item can just be appended to the end of the growing output list. If the data is almost but not quite in order, performance should still be close to $O(n)$ because so few items need to be inserted far up into the output list. So, if only we could do some work taking less than $O(n^2)$, to get the list "almost" sorted prior to a final $O(n)$ insertion pass, we might be able to obtain an overall performance that is less than $O(n^2)$. What Shell proposed was that a certain number of preliminary passes be performed that are also insertion sorts, but of a special kind. Rather than processing all n numbers spaced one storage unit apart (as will be done on the last pass), each earlier pass divides the numbers into groups that are, say, eight index positions apart on the first pass, four apart on the second pass, two apart on the third, and then—finally—one apart on the fourth and last pass. Because of this strategy, Shellsort is also known as a *diminishing increment sort*. Shellsort does not quite attain the theoretical $O(n \log n)$ performance of the best comparison sorts, but empirical evidence is that the algorithm runs as $O(n^{1.2})$, or perhaps $O(n \log^2 n)$. Shellsort endures in the face of better algorithms because it is quite fast for sorting up to several thousand items and because it is iterative rather than recursive. However, it is unstable.

Treesort – Another Improved Insertion Sort

The principal defect of insertion sort is that records occasionally need to be placed high in the list of tentatively sorted records, necessitating downward movement of a large number of records stored as a sequential list in an array. What is needed is an alternative data structure into which new records can be inserted at much less operational cost. A more suitable structure for use with a type of insertion sort is a *binary search tree* (*see* TREE). Suppose that the data to be sorted is the initial sequence of integers 9 2 7 1 4 8 7 6 10. Their corresponding search tree is shown in Fig. 2.

The first unsorted integer becomes the root of the tree. Each successive integer is then inserted recursively into the left subtree if it is strictly less than the root, and into the right subtree if it is equal to (for stability) or greater than the root. If insertions are made according to this rule, then an in-order traversal of the search tree will produce the desired sorted sequence, in this case, 1 2 4 6 7 7 8 9 10. This algorithm, known as *treesort*, was first described by David J. Wheeler in 1957 and Conway M. Berners-Lee in 1958.

With the average case of randomly distributed keys, the search tree formed will be reasonably well balanced and treesort will perform as $O(n\log n)$. But in the worst case of already ordered (or reverse ordered) keys, the search tree will consist of one long linear right (or left) subtree and treesort will degenerate to $O(n^2)$ performance.

Mergesort

An improved insertion sort algorithm based on repetitive merging was discussed as early as 1945 by John von Neumann (*q.v.*). Merging, an information processing technique similar to that of sorting, makes no sense except when applied to two (or more) lists that are already separately in order. To *merge* such lists then means to intersperse their elements to form one overall output list that is entirely in order.

The algorithm for merging two ordered sublists A and B can be stated in pseudocode as

> **while** { still more unmerged items in either list } **do**
> **begin**
>   **if** *A is empty, take the next item from B,* **else**
>   **if** *B is empty, take the next item from A,* **else**
>   *take the smaller of the two items at the heads*
>   *of lists A and B*
> **end**

In the course of being merged, each number in each list is processed only once. This means that the running time needed to merge two lists of size m and n will be proportional to $m + n$: processing time increases only linearly with increasing list sizes. Thus, merging is a far more efficient process than sorting.

As von Neumann observed, repetitive merging can be made the basis of a very efficient sort strategy. Once we are able to form some initially sorted sublists, no matter how short—and that is not difficult if the sublists need only be, say, two numbers long—we can merge two lists of length two to make one of length four, two fours to make eight, and so on, until we have formed one ordered list. Recursion is used in order to make the machine's memory (the stack (*q.v.*) behind the scenes) remember all currently unprocessed lists.

A Pascal *mergesort* procedure is given in ALGORITHMS, DESIGN AND CLASSIFICATION OF. Actual time measurements on one particular computer showed that mergesort was able to sort half a million numbers 500 times faster than bubblesort. The $O(n \log$

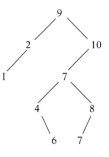

Figure 2.   A binary search tree.

n) behavior of mergesort holds even in the worst case, and mergesort has the added advantage of being stable when properly programmed.

Distributive Sorting Algorithms

Instead of comparing keys, a distributive sorting algorithm moves each record to or close to its final destination based on some intrinsic property of the key itself. The first such sort we will examine is the oldest, one used as the basis for the special-purpose sorting machines that were first developed in the late 1800s by Herman Hollerith (*q.v.*) for processing census data.

Radix Sort

For reasons that will soon become apparent, the algorithm used for sorting on physical card-sorting machines is seldom used on a computer. That algorithm is called *radix sort* because it depends on multiple sort passes, one for each digit (radix) position of the maximum value number to be sorted. On a card-sorting machine, the radix is invariably 10—the digits are decimal digits—but any radix may be used from two upward. The earliest published description of radix sort cited by Knuth (1973) is by Leslie J. Comrie in 1929.

There are two problems in adapting this algorithm for use on a computer:

1. Numbers are stored internally in binary, not in decimal. One might program a binary radix sort, but it is more effective to treat binary keys as if they were octal or hexadecimal by accessing successive groups of three or four bits from right to left.
2. On a physical card sorter, pockets are very deep, relative to the size of the typical card deck being sorted. If pockets are simulated as arrays in a computer, each array has to be prepared to hold all n numbers being sorted (just in case they all have, say, a 7 in the same radix position). If the radix is 16 (hexadecimal), then $16n$ record locations are needed, a storage requirement that is just not competitive with the many algorithms that sort in place, or that use at most an extra n record locations. Linked lists could be used for pockets, but the resulting program is unwieldy.

Since for a given radix r and bit precision p the radix sort makes $\log_2 r$ passes, its running time is expected to be $O([p/\log r]n)$ in the best, average, and worst cases. Thus, for 16-bit integers and radix 16 (hexadecimal), the radix sort should run about four times more slowly than hashsort.

Sorting By Address Calculation (Perfect Hashing)

An $O(n)$ distributive algorithm applicable to data of restricted range was described by Earl Isaac and Richard Singleton in 1956. Suppose that the data to be sorted are integers in the range 1 to *limit* with no duplicates. Then, if there is sufficient memory space to declare an array T of size *limit*, that array is initialized to zero (or any value outside the range 1..*limit*) and unsorted data values are directed, one by one, into the unique space reserved for each: $T[7] \leftarrow 7$; $T[19] \leftarrow 19$, and so on (*see* Fig. 3). After distribution to the temporary array T, the nonzero values from $T[1]$ through $T[limit]$ can be output as the sorted list, or nonzero values can be moved back on top of the original array of unsorted data. When either of these operations is done properly, it takes only $O(limit)$ time, or $O(n)$ time if n is close to *limit*. Since it takes only $O(n)$ time to store the numbers and $O(n)$ time to pack them, the overall performance of the algorithm is $O(n)$.

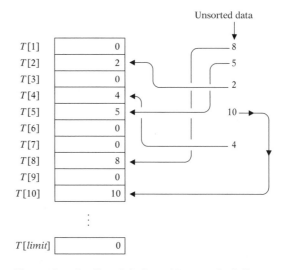

Figure 3. Sorting data by address calculation.

This method was called sorting by *address calculation* in the days of machine language programming—each data value being directed to an address equal to itself—but could now be called sorting by *index calculation* when implemented in a high-level language. It is also called sorting by *perfect hashing* because, since it was postulated that the data set contained no duplicates, each value can be "hashed" to a particular destination address without danger of "collisions."

Hashsort

The condition that a sequence of record keys span the range 1..*limit*, as was required for sorting by address calculation, occurs fairly often, but the restriction that there can be no duplicates is unrealistic. What can be done to salvage sorting by hashing under threat of collisions (two or more records hashed to the same index position)? One way is to build a linked list of collided items at each target destination (*see* LIST PROCESSING). Hashsort is also called *bucket sort* because every record is directed into a particular receptacle, or "bucket." All elements of a target array are initialized to nil pointers (*q.v*), and then all keys that hash to a given index position are entered into a linked list, even if that list never contains more than one item.

When hashsort encounters no collisions, it is clearly an $O(n)$ algorithm. At the other extreme, when the data to be sorted is so skewed that all n items hash to the same index, the sort would be only as good as the $O(n^2)$ running time needed to maintain an ordered singly linked list. But for randomly distributed keys and reasonable pointer table size, we expect collisions to be sufficiently rare that it would be hard to detect any degradation from linear performance.

Ultrasort

When conditions permit, an extremely fast sorting algorithm with a worst-case performance of $O(n)$ can be based on *frequency counting*. Suppose that we want to sort an arbitrarily long sequence of single-digit integers. If we just count the integers, which we can do in $O(n)$

time, the counts of their relative occurrences might conceivably be

$$c[0] = 147 \qquad \text{there are 147 0s}$$
$$c[1] = 89 \qquad \text{there are 89 1s}$$
$$c[2] = 463 \qquad \text{there are 463 2s}$$
$$\vdots$$
$$c[9] = 216 \qquad \text{there are 216 9s}$$

Next, we overwrite the array of unsorted numbers with consecutively, 147 zeros, 89 ones, 463 twos, and so on, up through 216 nines—all in $O(n)$ time. Single-digit numbers were used only as an example; the maximum size of the integers that can be handled with this often overlooked algorithm is limited only by how large a table can be allocated to hold the frequency counts. The algorithm, first described by Harold Seward in 1954, has no standard name. It was called *mathsort* by Wallace Feurzig in 1960 and *ultrasort* by Reilly and Federighi (1989). A Pascal version is given in Fig. 4.

Comparative Performance of Internal Sorting Algorithms

The expected best, average, and worst-case performance of 13 internal sorting algorithms is given in Table 1. Experimentation reveals that Ultrasort sorts a million 6-digit random integers 20 000 times faster than insertion sort, the fastest of the $O(n^2)$ sorting algorithms. Since running times are data dependent, times must be averaged over several data samples. The $O(n^2)$ running time of the four basic polynomial time algorithms was readily apparent. Even on a top-of-the-line 3 MHz Dell PC, insertion sort takes 15 minutes to sort a million random 6-digit integers. Quicksort was three times faster than any other $n \log n$ algorithm, taking only 80 msec to sort a million integers of the same kind on the same computer. The running times of the linear and $n \log n$ routines appeared to be sublinear, but this behavior cannot continue much beyond sorting a million numbers.

```
procedure Ultrasort (var a:data; n:integer);
var
      c:array[0..maxnum] of integer;
      i,j,k : integer;
begin
      for j:=0 to maxnum do c[j] :=0;    {Initialize the counts}
      for i:=1 to n do c[a[i]] :=c[a[i]]+1; {Increment the bin
                                             having the same number}
      k:=1;
      for j :=0 to maxnum do     {Make c[j] copies of each count:}
        for i :=1 to c[j] do
          begin
              a[k] :=j;
              k:=k+1
          end
end {Ultrasort};
```

Figure 4. A Pascal Ultrasort procedure.

Table 1. Comparative performance of internal sorting algorithms.

Algorithm	Best-case performance	Average-case performance	Worst-case performance	Stability
Linear:				
Ultrasort	$O(n)$	$O(n)$	$O(n)$	NA
Hashsort	$O(n)$	$O(n)$	$O(n^2)$	Stable
Radix sort	$O([p/\log r]n)$	$O([p/\log r]n)$	$O([p/\log r]n)$	Stable
Radix exchange sort	$O(pn)$	$O(pn)$	$O(pn)$	Unstable
Logarithmic:				
Quicksort	$O(n \log n)$	$O(n \log n)$	$O(n^2)$	Unstable
Heapsort	$O(n \log n)$	$O(n \log n)$	$O(n \log n)$	Stable
Mergesort	$O(n \log n)$	$O(n \log n)$	$O(n \log n)$	Stable
Treesort	$O(n \log n)$	$O(n \log n)$	$O(n^2)$	Stable
Polynomial:				
Shellsort	$O(n)$	$O(n^{1.2})$	$O(n^2)$	Unstable
Insertion sort	$O(n)$	$O(n^2)$	$O(n^2)$	Stable
Selection sort	$O(n^2)$	$O(n^2)$	$O(n^2)$	Stable
Enumeration sort	$O(n^2)$	$O(n^2)$	$O(n^2)$	Stable
Bubblesort	$O(n)$*	$O(n^2)$	$O(n^2)$	Stable

p = precision in bits.

r = radix.

* $\Rightarrow$ Use of flag to abort when no exchanges made during prior pass.

External Sorting

With the ever-increasing size of main memory, the need for external sorting algorithms diminishes. Suppose, for example, that a file stored on a mass storage device consists of 2 00 000 100-character records. Such a file occupies 20 MB, which does not exceed the scratch main memory storage of most current PCs. To sort such a file, it is feasible to read the entire file into main memory, use an appropriate internal sorting algorithm, and then rewrite the sorted file back onto mass storage.

Bibliography

1989. Reilly, E. D., and Federighi, F. D. *Pascalgorithms.* Boston, MA: Houghton-Mifflin. (Figures 1 and 3 and portions of the text of this article are reprinted with permission.).

1995. Wilt, N. *Classical Algorithms in C++: With New Approaches to Sorting, Searching, and Selection.* New York: John Wiley.

1998. Knuth, D. E. *The Art of Computer Programming,* Vol. 3: *Sorting and Searching,* 2nd Ed. Reading, MA: Addison-Wesley.

Edwin D. Reilly

SOURCE PROGRAM

For articles on related subjects, *see*

+ Compiler
+ Language Processors
+ Machine- and Assembly-language Programming
+ Object Program
+ Procedure-Oriented Languages

A *source program* is a computer program written in a language one or more steps removed from the *machine language* of a given computer. Machine language consists of the very explicit set of instructions and operation codes capable of direct execution by the hardware of the computer. It is, however, extremely tedious and error prone, for it requires that instructions be spelled out in excruciating detail. Accordingly, other languages have been developed to make it easier to express algorithms (*q.v.*). A program written in such a language is called a *source program*, and must be translated into machine language before it can be executed.

If the source program is in assembly language, translation is correspondingly called *assembly*, and the result is an *object program* in machine language. If the source program is in a high-level language like Pascal (*q.v.*) or C++ (*q.v.*), translation is called *compilation.*

Charles H. Davidson

SPECIFICATION

See HARDWARE DESCRIPTION LANGUAGES; and PROGRAM SPECIFICATION.

SPEECH RECOGNITION AND SYNTHESIS

For articles on related subjects, *see*

+ Artificial Intelligence (AI)
+ Computer Vision
+ Disabled, Computers and the
+ Image Processing
+ Pattern Recognition

The use of computers could be greatly expanded if human speech could be reliably used as an input–output medium. Such capability would allow humans to listen to synthetic speech output from a computer rather than read a display. Indeed, commercially acceptable synthetic speech can now be produced as output from a computer, even for unrestricted vocabulary and syntax. The ability of computers to recognize human speech would permit input to the computer without the use of a keyboard. Although commercial units of limited capability are available, *speech recognition* is a far more difficult problem than *speech synthesis.*

Speech Recognition

Assume that all of the information necessary for recognizing spoken words is available in the speech signal itself. The first task is thus to represent the speech signal in a form that contains fewer bits of information, but retains those facets that are thought to be useful for recognition. Most systems base this representation on derived attributes of a model for speech production called the *source-filter model.* The human vocal apparatus is modeled as one or two sources exciting a set of coupled resonators that intensify the sound in the neighborhood of the resonant frequencies. One source is the sequence of puffs of air that can be produced by the vibrating vocal cords, as in "voiced" sounds, such as those in the word "zen" (fricative 'z', vowel 'e', and nasal 'n'). In addition, the vocal tract can produce turbulent airflow at any of a large number of constrictions, leading to noise-like sounds, such as the 's' in "son." Both forms of excitation can be combined, as in 'z'. Whatever the form of excitation, it can be considered to excite a set of resonances (called *formants*) that vary with the shape of the vocal tract. The resulting speech spectrum is thus the result of multiplying the source spectrum by the vocal tract filter spectrum (*see* Fig. 1).

Following parametric representation of the speech, end points of the utterance are detected, and normalization may be performed to compensate for spectral warping due to variation in vocal tract length. Matching against stored templates is then performed, often using abstract mathematical formalisms and sophisticated search procedures to obtain the best match. Many systems use a procedure called *dynamic programming* to warp the time dimension of the input to secure the best match, as computed by a variety of scoring methods. Several commercial systems are available that provide speech recognition based on these procedures. These pattern-matching approaches are based on the assumption that only the information in the speech waveform is necessary for correct recognition.

Neural network classifiers have been proposed for use in speech recognition. These techniques, based on massive parallelism, are also trained automatically and can provide impressive performance in discrimination between classes, such as vowels. Such static classifiers can be useful in many applications, but it is more difficult to use these techniques for sequential constraints and time-varying behavior. Nevertheless, this approach has received far less study than hidden Markov modeling, and new neural network techniques may become increasingly important in the future.

Despite requiring intensive computing power to provide real-time performance, speech recognition systems became viable commercial products in the late 1990s. Dictation systems accepting large vocabularies are available from several firms, notably Dragon Systems, Inc., IBM, and the Kurzweil Educational

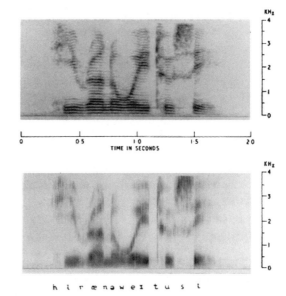

Figure 1. Spectrogram of the sentence "He ran away to sea." The upper record is a narrow-band analysis made with a 30-Hz bandwidth filter. The fine horizontal lines are due to individual harmonics in the buzzing sound produced at the larynx. The lower record is a wideband analysis made with a 240-Hz bandwidth filter. The fine vertical lines are due to the sound of individual pulses of air emitted by the larynx. The dark bands, or formants, are due to resonance peaks in the acoustic response of the vocal tract. Below the bottom figure the spoken phrase is written in phonetic symbols of the international phonetic Association. Each "letter" represents a single sound.

Systems Division of Lernout and Hauspie. They are able to convert speech to text on screens with reasonable accuracy.

Speech Synthesis

The inverse of speech recognition is speech generation (synthesis). Toys and robots that "speak" have been familiar objects for some time. There is also an increasing interest in interactive human–computer dialogue. In these applications, the human speaks to the computer, but the computer must respond using some form of synthetic speech. When the vocabulary is small, recorded or coded speech can readily provide the required voice.

Frequently, however, large vocabularies and unrestricted syntax is needed, or the vocabulary, while possibly small, is changing rapidly enough that recording is impractical. *Text-to-speech* capability has been developed for these needs and is available commercially. The quality of this speech is intelligible, but somewhat unnatural. Among the applications of text-to-speech synthesis are readers for the blind, in which a scanner and a PC combine to provide voice output of books and documents.

Bibliography

1993. Rabiner, L. R., and Juang, B-H. *Fundamentals of Speech Recognition.* Upper Saddle River, NJ: Prentice Hall.

1994. Roe, D. B., and Wilpon, J. G. (eds.) *Voice Communication between Humans and Machines.* Washington, DC: National Academy Press.

1996. Van Santen, J. P. H., Sproat, R. W., Olive, J. P., and Hirschberg, J. (eds.) *Progress in Speech Synthesis.* New York: Springer-Verlag.

1998. Jelinek, F. *Statistical Methods for Speech Recognition.* Cambridge, MA: MIT Press.

Jonathan Allen

SPELLING CHECKER

For articles on related subjects, see

+ Natural Language Processing
+ Word Processing

In addition to supporting conventional word processing, a computer can provide more advanced assistance such as *spelling checking, spelling correction,* and *grammar checking.* The general operation of a spelling checker is simple: it checks each word in a document or file for correct spelling. Allegedly incorrect spellings are reported to the human user, who can then correct the errors. A spelling corrector checks each word (just like a spelling checker) and, in addition, will try to suggest the correct spelling for each misspelled word that is found. Spelling checkers can only guarantee that a word is *some* correctly spelled word, not necessarily the one you meant. If "or" is mistyped as "of" or "affect" is misused for "effect," a spelling checker will not report an error. Trying to detect these kinds of error requires a much more complicated program called a *grammar checker.*

An *interactive* spelling checker reads a document and presents each spelling error to the user as it is found. The user can see each alleged error in context and either change it immediately or leave it alone. A word processor (or email formatter or Web page compositor) may incorporate spelling checking (or correction) directly into its processing, either in response to a menu option or continually as text is entered.

Most checkers use a *word list* to define the set of correctly spelled words. The word list may be the list of all words in a dictionary (without the definitions) or may be accumulated from existing documents. As long as its word list has no incorrectly spelled words, a checker will never "miss" an incorrectly spelled word that is not, coincidentally, some other legal word. On the other hand, spellers often report correctly spelled words as possible errors. These may be proper names, technical terms, or uncommon words that are not in the system word list. Most systems allow a user to augment its main word list with local auxiliary word lists for special subjects, authors, or documents. Doctors and lawyers, for example, generally use extensive auxiliary word lists designed for the specialized vocabularies of their fields.

A spelling corrector is invoked when an incorrectly spelled word is found. Its problem is to produce a list of possible correct spellings for the error. For correction, the set of correctly spelled words is thought of as a set of points in a multidimensional space. The corrector tries to find the nearest neighbor or neighbors of the spelling error in that space. If an error produces one candidate correction that is much closer to the error than other possible corrections, the speller may suggest an automatic correction.

A common typing error is to repeat an entire word, especially at the end of one line and the beginning of the next, creating such obvious errors as "a a" and "the the." Some checkers check for duplicate adjacent words, but would then report spurious errors in those sentences with validly repeated words, such as "I knew that that boy had had the measles."

Grammar checkers try to find errors in sentences or phrases rather than separate words. While it is possible to look for certain simple errors (incorrect use of "a" or "an," capitalization errors, or use of certain incorrect word combinations), the general problem of detecting true errors of grammar is still a research problem. The output of current grammar checkers that attempt to criticize writing style or to assess intrinsic readability are often laughable.

Bibliography

1980. Peterson, J. L. "Computer Programs for Detecting and Correcting Spelling Errors," *Communications of the ACM*, **23**(12), 676–687.

James L. Peterson

SPREADSHEET

For articles on related subjects, *see*

+ Database Management System (DBMS)
+ Nonprocedural Languages

Introduction

A *spreadsheet* is a matrix of data and formulas devised to facilitate financial and business modeling, primarily on microcomputers. First constructed in 1979, spreadsheets rapidly developed into one of the most widely used software products. Their design, in the form of an accountant's spreadsheet of rows and columns, provides a programming environment that has proved to be accessible to managers, accountants, and a vast variety of other end users, as well as to other computer professionals. Originally regarded simply as applications programs, spreadsheets are in fact effective instruments for nonprocedural programming in general.

Brief History

Bob Frankston and Dan Bricklin developed the first spreadsheet program, VisiCalc, in 1979. The program's idea emanated from creating an effective way to use computers to solve business school problems, with the spreadsheet concept patterned after a traditional blackboard production planning layout. Originally written in assembly language for a 32-KB Apple II, VisiCalc was a small spreadsheet with a terse single-line menu. However, its popularity and usefulness led to the rapid development of numerous other spreadsheets.

In 1981, SuperCalc was developed for the Osborne computer, and became the primary spreadsheet for 8-bit CP/M computers. In 1983, Lotus 1-2-3 was created for 16-bit MS-DOS computers. It contained many innovations and advanced features, including online help, sophisticated menus, graphic and database management capabilities, and macros (*q.v.*). It immediately became a best-selling software product. Recent years have seen the development of more powerful spreadsheets with advanced features and presentation-quality graphics. Originally created as small stand-alone programs, spreadsheets now typically are designed as fundamental components of large integrated programs that run under Windows and other operating systems. The list of current leading spreadsheets includes Microsoft Excel, Lotus 1-2-3, and Quattro Pro.

Basic Operation

The spreadsheet format consists of a large rectangular array, a portion of which is shown on the screen. Spreadsheet columns are identified by letters, and rows by positive integers. Individual locations, or cells, are referenced by column and row. For example, E5 refers to the cell in column E of row 5. Figure 1 contains a typical Excel screen display which shows a model for computing compound interest.

One cell is highlighted on the screen by a cursor. The cursor can be moved to other cells by using either arrow keys or a mouse (*q.v.*). After positioning the cursor on a cell, a user can enter into that location a label (or string),

Figure 1. The Excel spreadsheet screen display.

a number, or a formula that references other spreadsheet cells. The program calculates the value of a formula in a cell by using the values of the cells that it references and displays the results on the screen. Generally, the calculation of a spreadsheet is performed in an order that first evaluates any of the cells referenced in another cell, although other options are available. In Fig. 1, the formula in cell E5, =E$2*F4, computes interest as the product of the previous balance (F4) and the interest rate (E2). The initial = sign indicates that the expression is a formula rather than data. A formula may be entered into any cell by highlighting the cell and then typing in the formula.

If the value of any cell is changed, a spreadsheet's formulas are recalculated and the display is updated. This allows a user to interrogate a model by changing its parameters or data and observing the resulting effects. Thus, in financial models it is possible to examine the compound effects of changes of such interrelated components as projected sales, prices, production costs, interest rates, and profit.

Bibliography

1997. Moseley, L., and Boodey, D. *Mastering Microsoft Excel 97, Professional Edition.* San Francisco, CA: Sybex.

1998. Neibauer, A., and Cowpland, M. *Corel WordPerfect Suite 8 Professional: The Official Guide.* Berkeley, CA: Osborne/McGraw-Hill.

Deane Arganbright

SQL

See DATABASE MANAGEMENT SYSTEM (DBMS); and RELATIONAL DATABASE.

STACK

For articles on related subjects, *see*

+ Activation Record
+ Data Structures
+ List Processing
+ Polish Notation
+ Recursion
+ Subprogram
+ Tree

A *stack* is a structure that behaves like a linear list for which all insertions and deletions are made at one end of the list. The properties of a simple stack may be illustrated by a railroad switching network having a track into which railroad cars may be inserted and removed from only one end, as in Fig. 1. At any given time, only the most recently entered railroad car may be removed from the track. Railroad cars are said to enter and leave the track in a *last in, first out* (LIFO) order.

Stack rules can be stated in terms of three operations, commonly called *push*, *pop*, and *top*. Push adds an item to a stack, *pop* deletes the most recently added item, and *top* returns that item, leaving the stack unchanged. We can characterize a stack by means of axioms stating how these operations are related. Here *push* and *pop* are

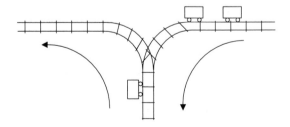

Figure 1. Railroad switching network.

functions that return the stack after modification. The first axiom states that the most recently pushed item is at the top of the stack, and the second that pop removes that item.

$$top(push(item, stack)) = item$$

$$pop(push(item, stack)) = stack$$

Stacks arise in computational processes that deal with structures whose components are nested, as in the following example of arithmetic expression evaluation. The expression $(3 + (4 * 5))$ has a subexpression $(4 * 5)$, which is nested within the complete expression. It is conveniently evaluated by first converting it to the parenthesis-free postfix notation (*see* POLISH NOTATION) 345*+ (in which the operator * immediately follows its operands 4, 5 and the operator + immediately follows its operands 3 and (45*), and then using an operand stack for evaluation. The evaluation of the expression 345*+, using a stack, is illustrated in Fig. 2.

Nested structures may be represented by parentheses, indented outlines, or tree (*q.v.*) structures (*see* Fig. 3). An example of a nested program structure arises in the case of subprograms (*q.v.*). Subroutine calls have the property that a called routine must be completely executed before returning to the higher-level routine

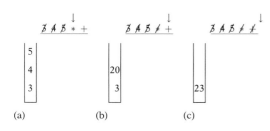

Figure 2.   Evaluation of 345*+.

Figure 3.   Three representations of a nested structure.

that called it. Thus, subroutines are executed in LIFO order (relative to the order in which they are called), and are conveniently implemented by a stack that creates and deletes information about subroutine parameters and the return address in a last in, first out order (*see* ACTIVATION RECORD).

Bibliography

1997. Knuth, D. E. *The Art of Computer Programming*, Vol. 1, 3rd Ed. Reading, MA: Addison-Wesley.

Peter Wegner

STATEMENT

For articles on related subjects, see

+ Concurrent Programming
+ Control Structures
+ Declaration
+ Delimiter
+ Executable Statement
+ Expression
+ Procedure-Oriented Languages
+ Programming Languages
+ Structured Programming

In much the same way that a sentence is the structural unit of expression in natural language discourse, the *statement* is the elemental organizational component of a procedure-oriented language (POL). As such, it embodies a unit of activity in terms of the algorithm being implemented. These units may vary widely; for example, the statements

```
A = 7.82  and  B = (22.4 + (X/Y) **3) * (X * Y - Z)
```

are both legitimate assignment statements in Fortran (*q.v.*), but there is clearly a considerable difference in the amount of computation that each one specifies.

POLs include statement types whose primary purpose is not to convey the intent of an algorithm, but rather to provide supportive information for compilation and other processes auxiliary to the actual execution of the program. Accordingly, they are *nonexecutable,* and usually are treated as a distinct syntactic set of statements called *declarations.*

There are innumerable logical sequences that are linguistically impossible to encode in a single statement. Most high-level languages accommodate these by allowing some type of compound construction. In some cases the construction is formed as a single statement with multiple clauses; in others, a *compound statement* is implemented as a group of single statements enclosed within *delimiters (q.v.)* Such a compound statement may also be the executable body of a *subprogram (q.v.).*

Executable Statements

Executable statements resemble imperative sentences in natural languages. Accordingly, it is often true that the language elements used for specifying activities are verbs. For example, an input activity in Pascal is expressed in the form read(*filename*,*list*) where *filename* and *list* specify the source and destination of the input, respectively. When similarity to natural language is a primary design objective, the correspondence may be more pronounced, as in the Cobol *(q.v.)* statement ADD a TO b GIVING c. The narrative construction persists in an alternative form: COMPUTE c = a + b. The Basic language designates the same operations in a similar manner: LET c = a + b.

Perhaps the most frequently used *compound statement* is the IF-THEN-ELSE construct. A very readable Pascal example is **if** x < y **then** x := x + 3 **else** x := x - 8.2. For other examples of the IF-THEN-ELSE and other compound statement constructs, *see* CONTROL STRUCTURES and STRUCTURED PROGRAMMING.

The ability to treat arbitrarily long sequences as single procedural activities receives formal emphasis in languages whose syntax includes special organizational statements to indicate their bounds. Languages so oriented are termed *block structured (q.v.)* languages. In Pascal, for example, decision alternatives may be extended arbitrarily by bracketing them with **begin** and **end** *delimiters.* C and C++ use {and} for this purpose.

Nonexecutable Statements

Completion of a high-level language program usually requires the inclusion of declarative statements (*declarations*) that do not generate machine code. Rather, they provide the compiler with essential information that governs the allocation of storage and other characteristics of the final program. A primary type of information transmitted by such statements concerns the definition and description of variables to be used in a program. For example, each of the following statements:

(Fortran 90)	REAL *X, Y*
	INTEGER *Z*
(Pascal)	**var** *x,y*:real;
	z :integer

associates the names x and y with certain amounts of storage, indicating further that the contents of these locations are to be treated as numerical values in floating-point form. In addition, the name z is associated with storage whose contents represent an integer value. Definition of entire arrays is no more complicated. For instance, the following declarations:

(Fortran 90)	REAL *X, Y*
	INTEGER *Z*(18)
(Pascal)	**var** *x,y*: real;
	z: **array**[1..18] **of** integer

define variables x, y, and z as they did above, except that z is now an array of 18 elements, each of whose contents accommodates (and expects) an integer value.

Bibliography

1999. MacLennan, B. *Principles of Programming Languages: Design, Evaluation, and Implementation.* Oxford: Oxford University Press.

Seymour V. Pollack and Ron K. Cytron

STORAGE ALLOCATION

For articles on related subjects, *see*

+ Addressing
+ Associative Memory

Storage (memory) in a digital computer system must be *allocated* to programs and data that are being executed. A computer system normally has several levels of storage, usually referred to as "main" (or primary) storage, "secondary" (or auxiliary) storage, and so on. Main storage is implemented using fast but relatively expensive components. Secondary storage is slower and less expensive. A typical system will have more of secondary than of main storage. The lower levels of storage are intended for storing large amounts of information for relatively long periods of time.

Sound resource management dictates that programs and data should be allocated only the amount of main storage that is necessary, but additional amounts are often acquired and released dynamically. Thus, a program may be allocated an initial amount of *static* main storage when it is loaded from secondary storage, which it will use until its execution is completed. During the computation, there may be requests to an operating system (*q.v.*) for additional dynamically allocated main storage which is used only so long as needed.

Another use for dynamically acquired storage is for the introduction of additional segments of programs or data, while parts of the program or data that were used and are no longer needed are released or overwritten. This process is called an *overlay*. One concept introduced at least partly because of the overlay problem is *virtual memory* (*q.v.*). Here, program and data are assigned addresses independent of the amount of physical storage actually available and independent of the location from which the program will actually be executed. Thus, one might use 32 bits to represent an address (thus addressing about four billion items), while the available physical (main) storage might accommodate only about a quarter-million items (needing only 18 bits for the representation of a particular address).

The program and data are thus allocated enough addresses in virtual storage to enable them to be accommodated without explicit need for overlay, but when physical storage is smaller than virtual storage and will be shared with other programs and data, the system will invoke an automatic overlay procedure. This is accomplished by bringing into main storage from secondary storage only those parts of virtual storage that have been referenced. By recording in a table the appropriate mapping, addresses may be translated dynamically. Those references to virtual addresses that are not already mapped into physical storage can be intercepted by special hardware, and that part of virtual storage now needed, called a *page,* can then be brought into main memory. Pages are usually of a fixed size and therefore may be deposited into physical storage wherever a space of that size can be found.

Because the current location is entered into a mapping table whenever a page is introduced into physical storage, *dynamic address translation* can provide up-to-date interpretation of addresses. This allows the effect of dynamic relocation without the overhead of actually modifying the addresses within instructions. The determination of which pages are to be removed from physical storage to make room for the needed incoming pages has itself been the object of research (*see* WORKING SET).

Computers that support virtual storage generally provide a hardware implementation for dynamic address translation. In addition, several computers have introduced an additional concept, *segmentation.* Here, one views virtual storage as having identifiable regions, called *segments,* each containing enough addresses so that programs or data stored in them will not try to assign the same addresses more than once, even if they expand during execution by means of dynamic allocation of additional virtual storage. Segments are thus different from pages in that page boundaries assume a predetermined relationship to blocks of physical storage, whereas segments are viewed as functional subdivisions of virtual storage.

Register 3 (containing base address of segment)

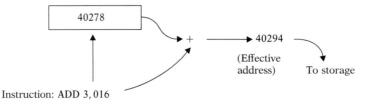

Figure 1.   Relocation within virtual storage.

Segmentation facilitates sharing programs and data. Programs are often written so that all addresses are given as displacements from a *base address,* and this is implemented by maintaining the base address in a hardware register. By establishing a convention that programs and data be *address-free,* relocation within virtual storage can be accomplished (Fig. 1). Now the system may load individual users' programs or data into different segments, but can arrange to share a copy that is actually loaded into physical storage through paging (Fig. 2).

One example of a hardware implementation of dynamic address translation is given in Fig. 3. The virtual address is separated into three parts. The first, the *segment number,* can be viewed as the base address of a segment of virtual storage. In the implementation shown, however, it is used as an index into a segment table maintained for that user to retrieve the appropriate page table; that is, a table showing the virtual-to-physical mapping for those pages of the referenced segment for which the mapping exists. Once the page table–base address has been retrieved from the segment table, the page number obtained as the second part of the original

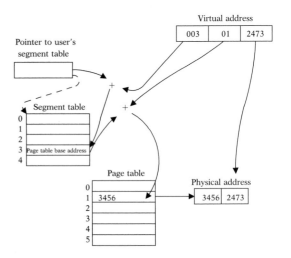

Figure 3.   Mapping from virtual address to physical address.

virtual address is used as an index into the page table to retrieve the base address of that page in virtual storage. The third part of the original virtual address is then appended, and the result is the desired physical address. If the virtual page containing the reference address is not present in physical storage (a *page fault*), an *interrupt* (*q.v.*) is generated, causing a delay in program execution while the desired page is found and loaded.

Bibliography

1997. Tanenbaum, A. S. *Operating Systems: Design and Implementation*, 2nd Ed. Upper Saddle River, NJ: Prentice Hall.

1998. Silberschatz, A., and Galvin, P. B. *Operating System Concepts*, 5th Ed. Reading, MA: Addison-Wesley.

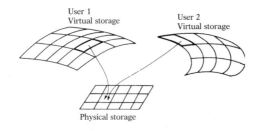

Figure 2.   Sharing in physical storage.

Bernard A. Galler

STORAGE

See MEMORY.

STORED PROGRAM CONCEPT

For articles on related subjects, *see*

+ Addressing
+ Analytical Engine
+ Babbage, Charles
+ Digital Computer
+ EDSAC
+ Machine- and Assembly-language Programming
+ Mark I, Harvard
+ Program Counter
+ von Neumann, John
+ von Neumann Machine

The design feature of modern computers that allows instructions to be held in internal storage on par with data is known as the *stored program concept.* Many computers, beginning with the Analytical Engine of Charles Babbage and including the Harvard Mark I, were designed to perform discrete operations, each specified by a concisely coded instruction. Prior to the use of electronics, however, these instructions were taken by the control unit from a special input device that read a tape or belt. Program loops required a second physical loop of paper tape with provision for control to be passed from one tape to the other to allow some flexibility in the logical structure of the program.

Electronics forced a departure from this arrangement because no tape reader could scan instructions fast enough to keep up with the internal speed of the computer. The first electronic computer, ENIAC (*q.v.*), went back to plugboard programming as used on punched card machines, but this proved extremely clumsy. The stored program concept emerged as an alternative solution from discussions that took place

at the Moore School of Electrical Engineering, where ENIAC was under construction in 1944. Participants included J. Presper Eckert (*q.v.*), John W. Mauchly, John von Neumann, and Herman H. Goldstine, and the concept was first documented in a Moore School report drafted by von Neumann (1945).

Besides solving the speed problem, the concept had two important long-term effects. First, program jumps could be used liberally without incurring the time penalty required to hunt along the program tape. Therefore, much more complex program structures could be contemplated. Second, and more significant, instructions held in internal storage could be accessed and modified during program execution as if they were data. Both these possibilities were quickly explored when the first stored-program computers, EDSAC (*q.v.*) and BINAC, came into service in 1949. Program alteration during execution enormously increased the scope of automatic computing, and was heavily used in the early days. Since then, its use has diminished considerably, for several reasons, the main ones being the introduction of *index registers* and multiprogramming (*q.v.*). The latter requires that shared programs be *pure procedures* (*reentrant programs—q.v.*), that is, code that does not modify itself.

Alan Turing (*q.v.*) had touched on the stored program concept in a paper on mathematical logic in 1936 (*see* TURING MACHINE), though not in a form that anticipated its practicality. The first electronic stored program computer was built by Williams and Kilburn in Manchester, England, and the first to carry out practical calculations was the EDSAC, built by Maurice Wilkes (*q.v.*) at Cambridge, England, which was operating in May 1949.

The stored program concept has characterized the main stream of digital computer development since 1945. This concept, together with the practical development of electronics, made possible the computer revolution as we know it.

Bibliography

1945. von Neumann, J. *First Draft of a Report on the EDVAC*, Contract No. W-670-ORD-4926. US Army Ordnance Department and University of Pennsylvania,

Moore School of Electrical Engineering, University of Pennsylvania, Philadelphia, PA. (30 June). Reprinted in 1981. Stern, N. *From ENIAC to UNIVAC.* Bedford, MA: Digital Press.

Stanley Gill

STRING PROCESSING

For articles on related subjects, *see*

+ List Processing
+ Procedure-Oriented Languages
+ Programming Languages
+ Scripting Languages

PRINCIPLES

A *string* is a sequence of characters, such as QE2. In many cases, computer input is in the form of strings (e.g. commands entered at a terminal). Similarly, computer output is often in the form of strings since printed lines of text are simply strings of characters.

Operations on Strings

There is no general agreement on the kind of operations that should be performed in string processing, nor is there a standard notation. But four operations have achieved reasonably general acceptance: concatenation, identification of substrings, pattern matching, and transformation of strings to replace identified substrings by other strings.

Concatenation (or just "catenation") is the process of appending one string to another to produce a longer string. Thus, the result of concatenating the strings AB and CDE is the string ABCDE.

A *substring* is a string wholly contained within another string. For example, BC and CDE are substrings of ABCDE.

The most important string operation is *pattern matching*, examining a string to locate substrings or to determine if it has certain properties. Examples are the presence of a specific substring, substrings in certain positions, and substrings in a specified relationship to one another. *Transformation* of strings is typically accomplished in conjunction with pattern matching, using the results of pattern matching to effect a replacement of substrings.

LANGUAGES

High-level string-processing languages offer many advantages for solving problems in areas such as machine translation (*q.v.*), computational linguistics, computer algebra (*q.v.*), text editing (*q.v.*), and document formatting. We discuss those that have been historically significant.

Comit

Comit, designed in 1957 to 1958 by Victor Yngve, was the first string-processing language. It was motivated by the need for a tool for mechanical language translation.

Basic Concepts

A Comit string is composed of *constituents* which may consist of more than one character. Thus, a word composed of many characters may be a single constituent in a string. A string is written as a series of constituents separated by + signs—for example,

```
FOURSCORE + AND + SEVEN + YEARS + AGO
```

The hyphen is used to represent a space (blank). Thus, to include spaces between words, the string above becomes

```
FOURSCORE + - + AND - + SEVEN + -
              YEARS + - AGO
```

All characters other than letters have syntactic meaning. A star (asterisk) in front of a character other than a letter indicates that the character is to be taken literally rather than for its syntactic meaning. For example,

```
33 ARE IN THE TOP 1/2.
```

is written

```
*3*3 + - + ARE + - + IN + - + THE + - +
              TOP + - + *1*/*2*.
```

A Comit *workspace* contains the string currently being processed. There are 128 *shelves*, any of which may be exchanged with the current workspace. Thus, there may be at most 129 distinct strings in a program at any one time.

Comit programs are a sequence of rules, each of which has five parts;

```
name left-half = right-half / / routing goto
```

The *name* identifies the rule. The `left-half` is a pattern applied to the workspace, and the `right-half` specifies processing to be performed on the portion of the workspace matched by the `left-half`. The `routing` performs operations other than pattern matching. If a rule has no routing field, the slashes are not required. The `goto` controls program flow.

Pattern Matching

The left-half may specify full constituents as written in a string, a specific number of constituents of unspecified value, an indefinite number of constituents, an earlier constituent referenced by its position in the left-half, and so on. A full constituent is written as it is in a string. Other left-half constituents are represented by special notations. For example: $n matches *n* consecutive constituents, regardless of their value; $ matches any number of constituents. The integer *n* matches the same string that the *n*th constituent of the left-half matched. For example, the left-half

```
THE + $1 + $ + 2
```

has four constituents: the characters THE, followed by any single constituent, followed by any number of constituents until one is encountered that is the same as the one matched by the second constituent, namely, $1. Pattern matching is left to right. Left-half constituents must match consecutive constituents in the workspace.

If the workspace contains

```
THE + FIRST
 └┘   └───┘
  1     2
+ PERSON + IN + LINE + IS + SERVED + FIRST
 └──────────────────────────────┘   └───┘
                3                      4
```

the match for each of the constituents is as shown. The fourth constituent of the left-half matches the same constituents as the second constituent of the left-half. The third constituent of the left-half consequently matches the intervening five constituents. When a match occurs, workspace constituents are associated with the left-half constituents they matched and are subsequently referenced by the number of the corresponding left-half constituent. The right-half may contain full constituents and integers that correspond to the constituents of the left-half. The matched portion of the workspace is replaced by constituents specified in the right-half. Continuing the example above, the rule

```
THE + 1 + $ + 2 = 1 + SECOND + 3 + 4
```

transforms the workspace into

```
THE + SECOND + PERSON + IN + LINE +
                 IS + SERVED + FIRST
```

SNOBOL

The first SNOBOL (StriNg-Oriented symBOlic Language) was designed and implemented in 1962 to 1963 by Ralph Griswold and Ivan Polonsky. Its major motivation was the need for a general-purpose language for string processing. Manipulation of symbolic mathematical expressions was also an important consideration.

Basic Concepts

In SNOBOL, unlike Comit, a string is simply a sequence of characters. Enclosing quotation marks delimit the string, but are not part of the string. An example is

```
'FOURSCORE AND SEVEN YEARS AGO'
```

Such a string is said to be specified *literally*. Strings may be assigned to names for subsequent reference, for example, FIRST =' MORGAN' assigns the string MORGAN to the name FIRST. There is no limit to the number of distinct strings. Storage management is automatic; there are no declarations. Concatenation is denoted by the juxtaposition of strings. Such strings can be given literally or as the value of names, for example

```
FULLNAME = FIRST 'SMITH'
```

assigns to FULLNAME the string 'MORGAN SMITH'. The blank after the 'N' is simply a character like any other.

A SNOBOL program consists of a sequence of statements. There are three kinds of statements: assignment, pattern matching, and replacement. The respective forms are

```
label    subject = object              goto
label    subject pattern               goto
label    subject pattern = object goto
```

An optional *label* identifies the statement. The *subject* provides the focus for the statement and is the name on which operations are performed. The *goto* controls program flow and is optional. An assignment statement assigns a value to a name. A pattern-matching statement examines the value of a name for a *pattern*, and a replacement statement modifies that part of the subject matched by the pattern.

Pattern Matching

Patterns in SNOBOL consist of a sequence of components. There are two types of component: specific strings and *string variables*. A specific string may be given literally or referred to by name. A string variable is indicated by delimiting asterisks that bracket a name. There are several types of string variables. An *arbitrary string variable* can match any string. It is similar to the Comit $ notation, except that whatever the string variable matches is assigned to the name between the asterisks. Pattern matching is left to right, and components of the pattern must match consecutive substrings of the subject. For example, in

```
Z 'T' *FILL* 'N'
```

the value of Z is matched for any string that begins with a T and ends with an N. The substring between the T and N is assigned to the name FILL. If the value of Z is TEEN, the value assigned to FILL is EE.

Replacement is a combination of pattern matching and assignment in which the matched substring is replaced by the object. The statement FULLNAME 'SMITH' = 'JONES' replaces the substring SMITH by JONES and consequently changes the value of FULL-NAME to MORGAN JONES.

Indirect Referencing

A string may be computed and then used as a name. A $ placed in front of a string uses the value of that string as a name. For example, the statements

```
X = 'NUM'
N = '3'
HOLIDAY = X N
$HOLIDAY = 'EASTER'
```

first assign the value NUM3 to HOLIDAY and then assign the value EASTER to NUM3. The indirect referencing operator, similar in concept to indirect addressing in assembly language, provides a way of constructing data names during execution.

SNOBOL4

SNOBOL4 (Griswold, Poage and Polonsky, 1971) is a natural descendant of SNOBOL and is based on many of the same ideas and approaches to string processing. SNOBOL4, however, introduced a number of new concepts. The most important are those dealing with pattern matching.

Patterns

In SNOBOL4, patterns are data objects that are constructed by functions and operations. Consequently, quite complicated patterns can be built piecemeal. There are two basic pattern-construction operations: alternation and concatenation. The alternation of two patterns is a pattern that will match anything that either of its two components will match. The concatenation of two patterns is a pattern that will match anything that its two components will match consecutively. Alternation is represented by a vertical bar and concatenation by a blank; for example,

```
PET = 'CAT' | 'DOG'
PETKIND = PET '-LIKE'
```

The pattern PET matches either of the strings CAT or DOG, and PETKIND matches anything PET matches followed by the string -LIKE (i.e. CAT-LIKE or DOG-LIKE).

Pattern-valued functions generalize the concept of patterns and avoid special notations for each type. For example, the value returned by LEN(n) is a pattern that matches n characters, and the pattern returned by TAB(n) matches a substring through the nth character of the subject string. For example,

```
OPER = TAB(6) 'X'
```

creates a pattern that will match any string containing an X as its seventh character. Other pattern-valued functions create patterns that match any one of a number of specific characters, search for specific characters, and so on. Examples are SPAN('0123456789'), which matches a substring consisting only of digits, and BREAK(';,'), which matches the substring beginning at the current position up to the next comma or semicolon.

As in SNOBOL, pattern matching is left to right, and components must match consecutive substrings of the subject string. Conceptually, the pattern-matching process manipulates a *cursor*, which is an imaginary marker in the subject string indicating the current position of the match. Movement of the cursor is implicit, not under direct control of the programmer, although in some patterns there is a direct correlation. Thus, LEN(3) moves the cursor to the right three characters. The cursor cannot be moved to the left by a successful match.

Names may be attached to components of patterns so that when the component matches a substring, that substring is assigned to the name. Attachment is indicated by the binary $ operator, for example,

```
HEAD = LEN(7) $ LABEL
```

constructs a pattern that matches seven characters. The seven characters, when matched, are assigned to LABEL, so

```
CARD HEAD
```

assigns to LABEL the first seven characters of the string that is the value of CARD. If the match fails (as it will if that string has fewer than seven characters), no assignment is made to LABEL.

Despite its age, SNOBOL4 is still used, and implementations are available for PCs and several workstations.

Icon

Icon (Griswold and Griswold, 1996), developed in the late 1970s, differs from its predecessors in that it uses structured syntax and eliminates patterns, but not pattern matching. The central feature of Icon is a string scanning evaluation mechanism that embodies a search and backtrack algorithm similar to, but simpler than, that used in SNOBOL4 pattern matching. The combination of lexical primitives and the evaluation mechanism yields string-scanning capabilities comparable to those of SNOBOL4. Icon has been implemented for many computers ranging from PCs to mainframes. It is the most widely used and generally available high-level string-processing language.

Bibliography

1971. Griswold, R. E., Poage, J. F., and Polonsky, I. P. *The SNOBOL4 Programming Language*, 2nd Ed. Upper Saddle River, NJ: Prentice Hall.

1996. Griswold, R. E., and Griswold, M. T. *The Icon Programming Language*, 3rd Ed. San Jose, CA: Peer-to-Peer Communications.

Ralph E. Griswold and David R. Hanson

STRUCTURED PROGRAMMING

For articles on related subjects, *see*

Structured programming (SP) is a methodological style whereby a program is constructed by concatenating or coherently nesting logical subunits that either are themselves structured programs or else are of the form of one or another of a small number of particularly well-understood *control structures*. Such a definition is inherently and deliberately recursive. Intense interest in the concept followed the publication of a letter to the editor in *Communications of the ACM* in March 1968 by Edsger Dijkstra. In this letter, Dijkstra reported his observation that the ease of reading and understanding program listings was inversely proportional to the number of unconditional transfers of control ("goto"s) that they contained. This rule of thumb is quite plausible since, when a programmer suddenly writes goto, what he or she is essentially saying to the reader is "However hard you were concentrating on the logical flow of my program, stop and find the continuation of this logic at another (possibly remote) physical point."

Control Structures for Structured Programming

In a 1964 paper, Böhm and Jacopini proved that every "flowchart" (program) however complicated, could be rewritten in an equivalent way using only repeated or nested subunits of no more than three different kinds—a *sequence* of executable statements, a *decision* clause of the if-then-else type described above, and an *iteration* construct, which repeats a sequence of statements while (or until) some condition is satisfied. Using conventional flowchart notation, these so-called *canonical forms* are typically rendered as in Fig. 1. Each control structure has a single entry point and a single exit, a key to their intelligible interconnectibility.

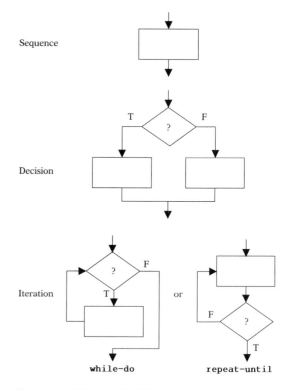

Figure 1. SP canonical forms.

The two forms of iteration differ in this regard: the **repeat-until** variation of iteration does something first and asks a question later (as to whether a termination condition has yet become true), whereas **while-do** cautiously asks a question first, since, if the condition tested is false, the loop under consideration is not executed at all. The Fortran (*q.v.*) DO statement is essentially a weak form of **repeat-until**; for example, the Fortran segment,

```
DO 17 I = 1,L
     .
     .
     .
17 CONTINUE
```

will iterate until I > L becomes true.

Using most compilers for Fortran dialects up through IV, the loop will run once even if L < 1 (and hence I > L) to start with. This can be avoided in Algol through use of the construction

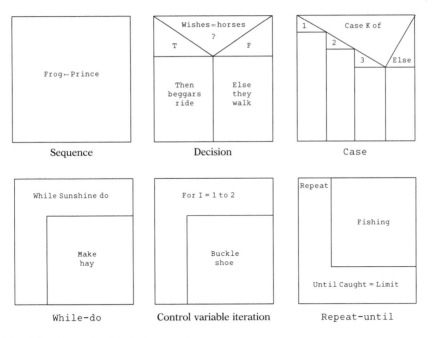

Figure 2.   **Structured flowchart building blocks.**

```
I := 0;
for I := I + 1 while I < L do
(a single, possibly compound, statement);
```

which does not iterate at all if `L < 1`.

Do we need both iteration variants? The Böhm–Jacopini theorem says "no," but that theorem addresses only constructibility and not convenience. For this reason, programmers like to have both variants, as they do in Pascal (*q.v.*). For similar reasons of convenience, three other constructs—**case**, **exit**, and **return**—have proved to be desirable adjuncts to the canonical forms since each eliminates the need for an unconditional branch to a label under some circumstances. The utility of **case** is discussed in CONTROL STRUCTURES **exit** (from a loop) and **return** (from a procedure) are closely related in that it is often contingently desirable to terminate a logic segment abruptly.

Structured Programs

While a fully structured program has no **goto**s (and hence needs no labels), rewriting a program merely to eliminate **goto**s does not necessarily result in a

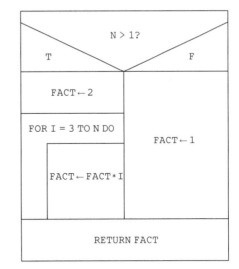

Figure 3.   **Factorial.**

structured program; more is needed. The term SP connotes certain basic principles:

1. *Control structures.* Use of only those canonical control structures of Fig. 1 supported by the host language.

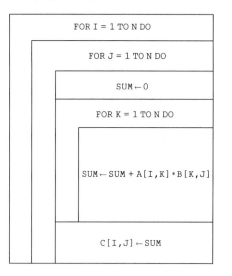

```
FOR I = 1 TO N DO

    FOR J = 1 TO N DO

        SUM ← 0

        FOR K = 1 TO N DO

            SUM ← SUM + A[I,K] * B[K,J]

        C[I,J] ← SUM
```

Figure 4.   Matrix multiplication.

2. *Modular composition.* Subdivision of a program into modules, where a *module* is a program segment that embodies a complete logical thought in about one page of code.

3. *Program format.* Careful organization of each such page into clearly recognizable paragraphs based on appropriate indentation of iteration, decision, and nested structures.

4. *Comments.* Judicious use of embedded comments that describe the function of each variable and the purpose of each module and procedure.

5. *Readability versus efficiency.* A preference for straightforward, easily readable code over slightly more efficient but obtuse code.

6. *Stepwise refinement.* Creation of a program through an evolutionary process of *stepwise refinement* (*top-down design*) whereby the overall logic is first sketched in using a generous admixture of English, which is then gradually replaced in subsequent versions by more detailed logic syntactically acceptable to the intended compiler (*q.v.*) or interpreter.

7. *Program verification (q.v.).* The ability to make assertions about key segments of a structured program to facilitate reasoning about program correctness.

Procedure Quicksort (L, R : integer);
{sorts global array A[L..R] where A[R + 1] > any A[L..R]}

Choose pivot arbitrarily to be element at left end of array A.

[Set pointers to mark positions such that all elements to left of left pointer I are less than or equal to the pivot and all elements to right of right pointer J are greater than the pivot, leaving J − I + 1 elements between I and J (inclusive) to be examined.]

{The initial choices of I and J that satisfy the above are I = L + 1 and J = R.}

Move left pointer to right and right pointer to left until either

    (a) the bracketed condition above is temporarily violated, in which case we exchange elements addressed by the pointers in order to restore that condition, and then continue moving the pointers, or
    (b) the pointers cross.

Replace the first element with the element addressed by right pointer and then replace that right element with the pivot in order to achieve the desired partition.

Now operate similarly on left and right partitions until all subpartitions are of size one.

Figure 5.   First version of Quicksort written primarily in English.

```
procedure Quicksort (L, R : integer);
{sorts global array A[L..R] where the main program has set
A[R + 1] to "infinity"; i.e., a number guaranteed to be larger
than any A[L..R]}

if L < R then
begin
    by initializing a left pointer I := L + 1, which shall move
    to the right, and a right pointer J := R, which shall move
    to the left.

    As an arbitrary pivot element, select PIV := A[L], the first
    element. Now

repeat
    -edly move pointers toward each other in such a way that

    while A[I] <= PIV we increment the left pointer, and then
    while A[J] > PIV we decrement the right pointer.

    After this movement, if I still < J, then pointers haven't
    crossed so

    Exchange A[I] and A[J].
    After this exchange, keep moving pointers

until I > J.

    Now that pointers have crossed, copy A[J] to first position,
    A[L], and replace A[J] with the pivot element. This completes
    a partition. Finally, complete the work by recursively sorting
    the left partition via:

        Quicksort (L, J − 1)

    and the right partition via:

        Quicksort (J + 1, R)

    End logic performed only when L < R.
end procedure Quicksort.
```

Figure 6. Second version of Quicksort using English embedded in Pascal-like control structures.

Nothing in the foregoing referred to the concepts of *algorithm* or *data structure*. The selection of an appropriate algorithm and associated data structure is a strategic concept; the application of SP techniques is a tactical methodology. Neither a structured program that implements an inferior algorithm nor an unstructured program that implements an excellent one is as desirable as the constructive use of good strategy *and* good tactics.

Benefits of SP

Advocates claim at least the following benefits for SP:

1. Structured programs are more readable and hence more intelligible than unstructured ones.

2. This greater readability makes it easier to maintain and modify them.

3. Structured programs are more likely to be correct in the first instance and are more easily shown correct by systematic program verification.

4. This greater likelihood of correctness lessens elapsed time to create a new program because there are fewer bugs (q.v.) to find and fix. The goal is "zero defects"; reasonably complex structured programs have indeed been known to run perfectly on the first attempt.

Structured Flowcharts

Instead of the time-honored *flowchart* (q.v.), which so often contains a spaghetti-like maze of transfers

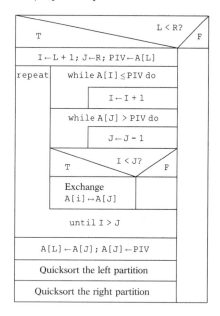

Figure 7.   Procedure Quicksort (L, R).

from box to box—the antithesis of SP—Nassi and Shneiderman (1973) recommend use of certain new diagrams for each principal SP control structure. Among these are a rectangular box for a declarative sequence (or process), "L" or inverted "L" structures for iteration, and other distinctive diagrams for binary (if-then-else) or multiple (case) decisions (Fig. 2). Since each diagram's outer outline is a rectangle and since the subdivision of any structure always leaves rectangles that may be further subdivided, a set of such diagrams can always be sequenced or nested within an outermost rectangle in a manner that models faithfully the recursive definition of a structured program given earlier. Examples of diagram intercombination are given in Figs. 3 and 4, which represent, respectively, procedures for calculating the factorial of N and the product of two $N \times N$ matrices. Such *structured flowcharts* are also called *iteration*

```
program QuickDriver (input, output);
const max = 10001;
var
  A: array [1..max] of integer;
  i: integer;                        {Control variable}
  n: integer;          {number of integers to be sorted}

procedure Quicksort (L, R: integer);
{sorts global array A[L..R] where A[R+1] > any A[L..R]}
var I, J, PIV, T: integer
begin
  if L < R then
    begin
      I := L+1; J := R; PIV := A[L];
      repeat
        {move pointers I and J inwards as far as possible}
          while A[I] <= PIV do I := I+1;
          while A[J] > PIV do J := J-1;
          if I {still} < J then {exchange items pointed to
                                              by I and J}
          begin T := A[I]; A[I] := A[J]; A[J] := T end
      until I > J;
      {now two final replacements finish a partition}
      A[L] := A[J]; A[J] := PIV;
      {finish by recursively sorting the left and
                                      right partitions}
      Quicksort (L, J-1); Quicksort (J+1, R)
    end {logic performed only when L < R}
  end {procedure Quicksort};
```

Figure 8.   Final structured version of Quicksort implemented as a Pascal procedure and embedded in a sample driver (*q.v.*) together with an example of how a particular data set would appear after a single partitioning. The logic of QuickDriver is on the facing page.

```
begin
  write ('Enter number of integers to be sorted: ');
  readln (n);
  for i := 1 to n do read (A[i]);        {Read integer data}
  A[n + 1] := maxint;            {Set "infinite" right guard}
  Quicksort (1,n);
  for i := 1 to n do write (A[i]:5); {Write sorted numbers}
  writeln;
end {QuickDriver}.
```

Example

```
I  J
2  8 | 8  6  12  20   2   5  47  14  Initial array;
3  6 | 8  6   5  20   2  12  47  14  pivot = 8
4  5 | 8  6   5   2  20  12  47  14
5  4 | 2  6   5  [8] 20  12  47  14  Final result
                                     of one partitioning

        Left partition   Right partition
```

To be further processed recursively (by 3rd-last line of the procedure) until partitions of size one result in completely ordered (sorted) data.

Figure 8. (*Continued*).

diagrams or, after their inventors, *Nassi–Shneiderman diagrams.*

A significant feature of iteration diagrams is that the clarity with which nested logic is displayed often facilitates algorithm analysis. Note in particular the three nested loops in Fig. 4, which so vividly emphasize that conventional matrix multiplication of $N \times N$ matrices takes running time proportional to N^3.

An Example

As an example of SP, consider the classic *Quicksort* algorithm for sorting an initially unordered array of (say) integers. One step of this algorithm will partition the array into three parts—a single interior element called the *pivot*, which is guaranteed to have gravitated to its correct final position; a left partition, all of whose elements are less than or equal to the pivot; and a right partition, all of whose elements are greater than the pivot. Recursive application of this process to the left and right partitions and to their subpartitions (until all such subpartitions are reduced to size one) completes the sort.

The program logic is illustrated progressively in four forms, stepwise-refined stages in Figs. 5 and 6,

a structured flowchart in Fig. 7, and, finally, in Fig. 8, the completed structured program. Not only does the program shown work correctly for the data set shown, we can prove that the basic partitioning algorithm works for *any* data set if, according to the precepts of program verification, we can identify two relations say p and c, such that the combined truth of p and $\neg c$ (not c) guarantees a correct partitioning. The relation c is the loop control relation I<=J; that is, an inspection of the program shows that the principal loop runs until $\neg c$ (I>J) is true. A more careful inspection of the program reveals that c switches from true to false in such a way that $\neg c$ is equivalent to the truth of J=I-1. The other relation, p, is the so-called *invariant relation* of the loop, one that was true before the loop began and whose truth is preserved throughout the running of the loop. There may be many such candidate relations for p, most of them irrelevant—we seek the particular one such that p and $\neg c$ proves the desired "theorem." That particular p has been right before us all along; it is precisely the statement in the first pair of square brackets in Fig. 5. When that invariant relation is written with the substitution J=I-1, we obtain

> *Set pointers to mark positions such that all elements to the left of the pointer* I *are*
> > *less than or equal to the pivot and all elements to the right of the right pointer* J
> > *are greater than the pivot, leaving 0 elements between* I *and* J *to be examined.*

This "proves" our theorem to the degree of conviction we achieve that our chosen "invariant" relation really is invariant; that is, no program step destroys the validity it had prior to execution of the primary loop to which it pertains.

Structured Programming Languages

A structured language must have, as a minimum, an **if-then-else** decision statement and at least one form of iteration based on a Boolean decision; that is, either **while-do** or **repeat-until**. The statements **case**, **exit**, and **return** are luxuries. Although classical iteration based on a control variable is not cited as being necessary despite its obvious utility, most SP languages retain such a form in addition to **while-do** and/or **repeat-until**. The first significant SP language was Algol 60 (*q.v.*). Subsequently developed SP languages in current use are Ada, C (*q.v.*), C++ (*q.v.*), Pascal, and Java (*q.v.*).

The major contributions of structured programming have been twofold—the elevation of programming technique to something less of an art and more of a science, and the demonstration that carefully structured programs can be creative works of sufficient literary merit to deserve being read by humans and not just by computers.

Bibliography

1964. Böhm, C., and Jacopini, G. "Flow Diagrams, Turing Machines, and Languages with Only Two Formation Rules," *Communications of the ACM*, **9**(5), 366–371.

1968. Dijkstra, E. "Go to Statement Considered Harmful," *Communications of the ACM*, **11**, 3.

1972. Dahl, O. J., Dijkstra, E., and Hoare, C. A. R. *Structured Programming.* New York: Academic Press.

1973. Nassi, I., and Sneiderman, B. "Flowchart Techniques for Structured Programming," *ACM SIGPLAN Notices*, **12**, (August). See www.geocities.com/SiliconValley/Way/4748/nsd.html.

1995. Fowler, E. C. *Cobol: Structured Programming Techniques for Solving Problems*, 2nd Ed. Boston, MA: Boyd & Fraser.

1997. Forouzan, B., and Gilberg, R. F. *Computer Science: A Structured Programming Approach Using C++.* Minneapolis, MN: West Publishing Group.

Edwin D. Reilly

SUBPROGRAM

For articles on related subjects, *see*

+ Activation Record
+ Block Structure
+ Calling Sequence
+ Coroutine
+ Global and Local Variables
+ Parameter Passing
+ Procedure-Oriented Languages
+ Recursion
+ Side Effect

A *subprogram* (subroutine) is a subordinate portion of a program that performs a specific task. As early as Babbage's era, it was recognized that programs would be written in which the same process is executed at several different points in its flow of control. One example is the evaluation of mathematical functions such as logarithms, exponentials, and trigonometric functions such as sine and cosine. Another example is the printing of output in a particular format, or the updating of a table. To facilitate these tasks, a construct was needed to permit the programmer to write and store the appropriate code once, and then call it (cause it to be executed) as needed. On each call it would be given specific values, the *arguments (parameters)* needed for its operation.

A *procedure* is a subprogram that performs an action but returns no explicit value. For example, it might print a value or update a data structure (*q.v.*). A procedure call is therefore a form of *statement* (*q.v.*). A *function* is a sequence of code that returns a single value, as do mathematical functions. A function that modifies the calling routine's memory in addition to returning a value is said to have a *side effect*. Since it returns a value, a function call is an *expression* (*q.v.*) or part of one. Both functions and procedures are widely used in general-purpose high-level programming languages such as Pascal (*q.v.*), Ada (*q.v.*), and C++ (*q.v.*). Because procedure calls are statements, the fundamental elements of most high-level languages, such languages are called *procedure-oriented languages.* Languages that rely solely on function calls, and in which the fundamental element is the expression, are said to be *functional languages* (*see* FUNCTIONAL PROGRAMMING).

Subprograms in high-level languages may be *intrinsic* (or *built-in* or *library*) or *extrinsic* (programmer-defined). Intrinsic subprograms are those provided with the language so that the programmer need only cite their name to invoke them. For an excerpt from a list of Pascal's numerous built-in functions, *see* Table 1.

Different high-level languages provide different sets of procedures and functions. For example, C provides a large library of subprograms as part of its standard environment. These include subprograms for input and output, mathematical calculations, string manipulation, date and time representation, and so on. C does not distinguish between procedures and functions by name, but treats all subprograms as functions. However, a C "function" may have return type `void`, in which case it returns no value and is thus a procedure. Conversely,

Table 1. Pascal library functions.

Name of function	Mathematical definition	Pascal invocation
Sine	$\sin x$	sin(x)
Cosine	$\cos x$	cos(x)
Natural logarithm	$\ln x$	ln(x)
Absolute value	$|x|$	abs(x)
Square root	$\sqrt{x}$	sqrt(x)

```
program test (input,output);
type array100= array[1..100] of real;
var A,B,C,D: real;
    Q1,Q2,F,G: array100;
function prod(X,Y: array100):real;
var i: integer; sum: real;
begin {prod}
    sum:=0;
    for i:=1 to 100 do
        sum:=sum+X[i]*Y[i];
    p:=sum
end {prod};
begin {test}
    . . .
    C:=A+(B*D)/prod(F,G);
    . . .
    A:=B*prod(Q1,Q2);
    . . .
end{test}.
```

Figure 1. A Pascal function and its driver.

a function may be called as a statement whose return value is discarded.

Figure 1 is an example of a programmer-defined Pascal function to calculate the sum of the products of the corresponding elements of two 100-element arrays. The function is embedded in a *driver* (*q.v.*), a test program containing two invocations of the function. In Pascal, the value returned by a function is the value assigned to its name, and the type of the return value is specified after the types of the parameters. Note that the function is a *declaration* (*q.v.*) placed at the beginning of the *block* that constitutes the driver program.

Pascal procedures are defined in a manner similar to Pascal functions. A procedure, however, returns no value and is expected to perform an action to modify something in its environment, process input, or add to the output stream.

In many languages, subprograms are defined separately from the main program, facilitating separate compilation of each and thus minimizing program development and debugging (*q.v.*).

Bibliography

1999. Sebesta, R. W. *Concepts of Programming Languages,* 4th Ed. Reading, MA: Addison-Wesley.

Adrienne Bloss and J. A. N. Lee

SUPERCOMPUTERS

For articles on related subjects, see

+ Biocomputing
+ Cluster Computing
+ Instruction-Level Parallelism
+ Multiprocessing
+ Parallel Processing
+ Pipeline
+ Scientific Applications
+ Simulation
+ Supercomputing Centers

The most powerful computers of any era have been called high-speed computers, supercomputers, high-performance computers, and high-end computers. The term *supercomputer* is used in this article to encompass all of these. Supercomputers are important tools for modern science. They are routinely used to simulate physical phenomena in an accurate and timely manner. Computer simulation is accepted today as a third mode of scientific research that complements experimentation and theoretical analysis. Supercomputers are also of great importance in engineering because computer simulations can give designers useful feedback on the quality and feasibility of new designs. Supercomputers are an enabling technology, making possible advances that cannot be achieved by any other means.

Some examples of supercomputer applications in science and engineering, mentioned in the 1998 report of the US President's Information Technology Advisory Committee, are:

- designing new cancer-fighting and anti-viral drugs;
- understanding the causes and sources of air, water, and ground pollution, and devising solutions to these problems;
- forecasting local weather and predicting long-range climate changes;
- ensuring the safety and effectiveness of the nuclear stockpile;
- designing new aircraft, such as the Boeing 777.

Supercomputers have also been used for nonnumerical and seminumerical problems. For example, supercomputers are used to compare normal and pathological genetic sequences to help researchers understand the molecular basis of disease. The 1997 victory of IBM's Deep Blue, a supercomputer designed to evaluate chess moves at very high speeds, over world chess champion Garry Kasparov is arguably one of the most important events in the history of computing (*see* COMPUTER CHESS). Supercomputers also have been used to decompose large numbers into prime factors, a seminumerical problem with applications for code breaking (*see* CRYPTOGRAPHY, COMPUTERS IN).

Machine Organization

What distinguishes current supercomputers from ordinary ones is their high degree of parallelism. All modern supercomputers are "multiprocessors" that can cooperate in the execution of a single program. Each processor can execute instructions following a program path independently of the others. Parallelism is achieved by decomposing programs into components, known as *tasks* or *threads*, that can be executed simultaneously on separate processors.

Multiprocessors may or may not have a global address space. In machines without a global address space, known as NORMA machines (for NO Remote Memory Access), processors exchange information and coordinate their work by sending messages to each other (*see* Fig. 1). In multiprocessors with a *global address space* or *shared memory*, there is a region of memory that can be read and written by processors that exchange data by fetching from and storing to that memory (*see* MULTIPROCESSING). Coordination is achieved

P: Processor
M: Private memory

Figure 1. Schematic of a NORMA multiprocessor.

by using software locks and barriers. Locks are typically used to enforce ordering between instructions executed by different processors and to guarantee that a section of code is executed by only one processor at a time (*see* MUTUAL EXCLUSION).

Machines with a global address space date back to the Burroughs B5000 and D-825 of the early 1960s. In that era, multiprocessing was used primarily to increase system reliability and to overlap I/O with computation. But since the Cray X-MP of 1984, multiprocessing has also been used to increase computational speed. Shared-memory machines are now widely available, the largest systems containing hundreds of processors. The presence of a global address space facilitates programming, but shared-memory multiprocessors can be more costly to design and build than NORMA machines.

Cache memories (*q.v.*), or simply *caches*, are an important component of all computer current systems. Copies of data and instructions originally found in main memory are kept in caches which can be accessed much faster than main memory to accelerate program execution.

A popular classification of shared-memory multiprocessors is as follows:

1. *Uniform Memory Access (UMA).* This class of machines, depicted in Fig. 2, has a globally shared memory located remotely from all processors and connected to them by a network such that all data accesses to the global address space take approximately the same time to complete. Typically, UMA systems contain special hardware to maintain cache *coherency* (*q.v.*) across the machine as data is read and written by

the different processors. Current UMA machines typically contain fewer than 64 processors.

2. *Non-uniform Memory Access (NUMA).* Although the typical number of processors in UMA machines may increase significantly in the future, the machines with the largest numbers of processors will most likely be NUMA machines, due to cost and performance advantages. The defining characteristic of NUMA machines is the clustering of processors and memories. A Cache Coherent (CC-NUMA) organization is shown in Fig. 3a, and a Non-Cache Coherent (NC-NUMA) organization is shown in Fig. 3b. Instead of a single memory space equidistant from all processors, NUMA machines cluster processors and memories and a processor can access the memory in its cluster faster than the memory in other clusters.

Processor Organization

The total parallelism of a modern supercomputer is the combination of intraprocessor parallelism and multiprocessing. The processors of today's supercomputers contain two forms of parallelism: multiple functional units and pipelining.

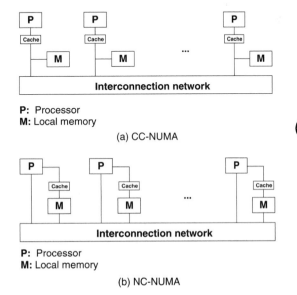

(a) CC-NUMA

(b) NC-NUMA

Figure 3. Schematic of NUMA multiprocessors.

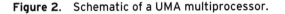

P: Processor
M: Memory module

Figure 2. Schematic of a UMA multiprocessor.

Processors with Multiple Functional Units

A processor may contain two or more functional units to perform arithmetic and logic operations. The functional units can execute in parallel. Usually, the functional units are specialized to perform a subset of the operations that a conventional arithmetic-logic unit (ALU—*q.v.*) can execute. For example, in a certain processor, a functional unit could be devoted exclusively to floating-point multiplication and division while a second functional unit is devoted to floating-point addition and a third to integer and Boolean operations.

Pipelining

In this approach, an operation is divided into stages, each accomplishing a fraction of the work required by the operation (*see* PIPELINE). For example, a floating-point multiplication can be divided into four stages: addition of the exponents, multiplication of the mantissas, rounding, and normalization of the result. The stages are connected in a linear sequence or *pipe*. An operation enters at one end of the pipe and proceeds from one stage to the next until, finally, the result exits at the other end of the pipe. Parallelism is achieved by operating the pipe like an assembly line (i.e. in such a way that several operations, each at a different stage, could be under way at any given time). Usually, pipes are synchronous and, at periodic intervals, the operations on all the stages move simultaneously to the next, and the first stage accepts a new operation. The length of time between such moves is called the *cycle time* of the processor.

Array Processors

An array processor consists of a number of identical arithmetic-logic units usually called *processing elements* (PEs). The processor control unit broadcasts the commands corresponding to each instruction to all the PEs (Fig. 4). In this way, vector instructions could be executed by applying the same operation simultaneously to different (pairs of) array elements. ILLIAC IV, a machine designed at the University of Illinois by Daniel

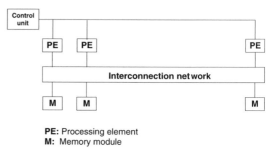

PE: Processing element
M: Memory module

Figure 4.   Schematic of an array processor.

Slotnick in the late 1960s, is an early example of an array processor. Vector supercomputers dominated the late 1980s, but lost popularity in the early 1990s due to the introduction of microprocessor-based multiprocessors.

Commercially Available Machines

During the decade of the 1980s, there was an unprecedented proliferation of supercomputers, as well as a corresponding increase in the number of supercomputer manufacturers. Japan emerged during this decade as an important center of supercomputer design and manufacture. The decade of the 1990s, on the other hand, saw the opposite trend. Many supercomputer companies went out of business, some before even producing a machine. Cray Research and Convex were purchased by Silicon Graphics and Hewlett-Packard, respectively. Nevertheless, supercomputers remain of great commercial importance, and several major manufacturers, such as IBM, SGI, and Sun Microsystems in the USA, and Fujitsu, Hitachi, and NEC in Japan, continue marketing and designing new supercomputers.

Vector supercomputers are measured in terms of their *theoretical peak performance*, which is the maximum number of floating-point operations that a machine can execute per second. Peak performance is measured in *gigaflops* (billions of floating-point operations per second) or *teraflops* (trillions of floating-point operations per second). The fastest vector supercomputer as of 2003 was the NEC *Earth Simulator*, rated at 36 teraflops.

Although parallelism inside the processor in the form of pipelined arithmetic units and multiple functional units is of crucial importance, the dramatic increase in theoretical peak performance for the machines delivered since 1995 is due to an increase in the number of

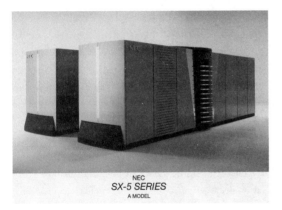

Figure 5.   The NEC SX-5 series supercomputer.

processors rather than an increase in performance of individual processors. In fact, the use of the more cost-effective CMOS technology (*see* COMPUTER CIRCUITRY) since 1995 has meant longer cycle times and slower processors as a result. However, processor performance remains critical. Consider the NEC SX-5 (*see* Fig. 5). Although its cycle time is 4 ns (250 MHz), each of its processor has a peak vector performance of 8 Gigaflops due to its 16 sets of pipelined units. *Cluster computing* (*q.v.*) using relatively inexpensive aggregations of microprocessors called *Beowulf* clusters now come close to matching that performance.

Programming Languages and Compilers

With the advent of Fortran 90, it became possible to express vector operations in a standard language that supports vector expressions and a large number of powerful intrinsic functions for vector manipulation. The vector capabilities of Fortran 90 and its successor, Fortran 95, are the culmination of a long line of vector languages that started in the 1970s when the first vector Fortran extensions were developed for the ILLIAC IV and the Texas Instruments Advanced Scientific Computer (ASC). There are now Fortran 90 or 95 compilers for most vector supercomputers, including those from Cray, Hitachi, Fujitsu, and NEC.

Bibliography

1996. Kuck, D. *High Performance Computing. Challenges for Future Systems.* New York: Oxford University Press.

1997. Murray, C. J. *The Supermen: The Story of Seymour Cray and the Technical Wizards Behind the Supercomputer.* New York: John Wiley.

1998. Pfister, G. F. *In Search of Clusters.* Upper Saddle River, NJ: Prentice Hall.

2000. Pescovitz, D. "Monsters in a Box," *Wired,* **8**(12), (December), 341–347. A well-illustrated survey of supercomputers as of mid-2000.

David A. Padua and Jay P. Hoeflinger

SUPERCOMPUTING CENTERS

For articles on related subjects, *see*

+ Cluster Computing
+ Distributed Systems
+ Multiprocessing
+ Parallel Processing
+ Scientific Applications
+ Supercomputers

In 1985, Congress authorized the National Science Foundation (NSF) to establish a group of super-computing centers—partnerships between academia, industry, and government—to further research in computational science. The goal was to allow researchers access to supercomputers to simulate phenomena that cannot be investigated in a laboratory. From 1985 to 2003, the original four NSF supercomputing centers were joined by several dozen state- and university-sponsored supercomputing centers.

The NSF Supercomputing Centers

The NSF Supercomputing Centers program originally included four centers across the USA: the Cornell Theory Center at Cornell University; the National Center for Supercomputing Applications at the University of Illinois, Urbana-Champaign; the Pittsburgh Supercomputing Center at Carnegie Mellon University; and the San Diego Supercomputer Center at the University of California at San Diego. In addition to high-speed Internet links, the centers were four of the first five sites on the NSF-sponsored very high speed Backbone Network Service (vBNS)—the fifth site being the National Center for Atmospheric Research in Boulder, CO. The vBNS provides researchers with access to a research-only network at speeds many times faster than the typical Internet backbone—it is the initial interconnection network for Internet 2.

Cornell Theory Center

Interdisciplinary research collaborations at the Cornell Theory Center (CTC) among academia, industry, and government have been funded by New York State, the Defense Advanced Research Projects Agency (DARPA), the National Center for Research Resources at the National Institutes of Health, IBM (*q.v.*), and other corporate partners, as well as the NSF. The Advanced Computing Research Institute, a joint effort with Cornell University's Computer Science Department, studied advanced architectures for scientific computation. The Computational Science and Engineering Research Group engaged in research on a variety of problems in computational science and developed new theoretical and computational methods for high-performance computing.

National Center for Supercomputing Applications

In addition to providing high-performance computing resources, the National Center for Supercomputing Applications (NCSA) at UIUC developed software to help users take advantage of computing resources. In 1992, the release of the network browser NCSA Mosaic provided the basis of a technology that generated the World Wide Web "gold rush" on the Internet. NCSA's Virtual Environment Laboratory is one of the world's most advanced virtual reality (VR—*q.v.*) research laboratories available to academic and industrial researchers.

Pittsburgh Supercomputing Center

The Pittsburgh Supercomputing Center (PSC) was established in 1986 as a joint effort of Carnegie Mellon University, the University of Pittsburgh, and Westinghouse Electric Corporation, with additional funding from the National Institutes of Health and the Commonwealth of Pennsylvania. The PSC has been a leader in developing and advancing heterogeneous computing and distributed file systems. A major portion of the center's resources is used for "capability" computing, that is, computationally massive, resource-intensive, and interdisciplinary projects. Many of these enabled significant scientific accomplishments in cosmology, weather modeling, biomedical applications, and materials research.

San Diego Supercomputer Center

The San Diego Supercomputer Center (SDSC) began in 1985 on the UCSD campus, with a consortium of academic and research institutions to provide guidance to the center. Under the PACI program, SDSC became the leading-edge site for the National Partnership for Advanced Computational Infrastructure led by UCSD. SDSC research projects have spanned many disciplines. The Computational Center for Macromolecular Structure, a collaboration started in 1990 between SDSC, UCSD, and The Scripps Research Institute, distributed software to analyze macromolecular structures. The National Biomedical Computation Resource, an NIH-funded collaboration, developed tools for applying high-performance parallel computers to biomedical problems.

The PACI Partnerships

The Partnerships for Advanced Computational Infrastructure (PACI) program builds on the NSF Supercomputing Centers program and focuses on taking advantage of emerging opportunities in high-performance computing and communications. In shifting from centralized facilities to partnerships, the program will provide flexibility to adapt to evolving circumstances and to meet the need for high-end computation. PACI will continue to provide access to high-performance computing systems for the thousands of users of the supercomputing centers. Under the PACI program, which began on 1 October 1997, two of the supercomputing centers became the leading-edge sites for two partnerships that encompass many of the leading research institutions in the country.

National Computational Science Alliance

To realize the PACI mission, the University of Illinois and NCSA joined a broad range of individuals and institutions to create the National Computational Science Alliance, whose purpose is to prototype a National Technology Grid. The Grid built by the Alliance will serve as an early model for a full-scale Advanced Computational Infrastructure, which will be built by the computer, communications, and software vendors to support US computational scientists and engineers in academia, industry, and government.

National Partnership for Advanced Computational Infrastructure

The National Partnership for Advanced Computational Infrastructure (NPACI) led by UCSD and SDSC teams 37 of the nation's leading academic and research institutions to revolutionize the computational infrastructure available to the nation's scientists and engineers. NPACI is developing the software infrastructure to link computers, data servers, and archival storage systems to harness the aggregate computing power. Further, NPACI has teamed applications scientists and computer scientists to support the development and application of new software and hardware techniques for improving the functionality and performance of supercomputers.

Bibliography

1998. Foster, I., and Kesselman, C. (eds.) *The Grid: Blueprint for a New Computing Infrastructure.* San Francisco, CA: Morgan Kaufmann.
1998. Glanz, J. "Beyond 'Big Iron' in Supercomputing," *Science,* **279**(27 March), 2030–2032.

David L. Hart

SUPERVISOR CALL

For articles on related subjects, *see*

+ Interrupt
+ Multiprogramming
+ Operating Systems

A *supervisor call* is a mechanism whereby a program pauses to ask a supervisor (operating system) to perform a service that the program is not permitted to do itself. The most typical supervisor calls have to do with input and output. In a multiprogramming system, it is essential to have system control of I/O devices, especially those devices shared by a number of programs. Most computers that were designed for multiprogramming systems have a supervisory mode of operation and hardware *interlocks* that prevent certain supervisory operations from taking place except when the computer is operating in supervisory mode. This may be handled by means of special *privileged instructions* that can be executed only in supervisory mode.

In the IBM 360/370/390 systems, for example, a supervisor call is made through the execution of an instruction whose effect is to create an *interrupt*. The interrupt proceeds like any other interrupt; it saves the status of the computer (the program status word) and loads a new one that gives control to a supervisor routine whose function is the handling of supervisor calls. Fast response to such calls is an important factor in system performance, and systems that have large amounts of central memory can often improve their responsiveness by increasing the number of memory-resident call routines.

Saul Rosen

SYMBOL MANIPULATION

For articles on related subjects, *see*

+ Automata Theory
+ Computer Algebra
+ List Processing

+ **Stored Program Concept**
+ **String Processing**

The power of a modern computer derives from it being more than an arithmetic calculator. It is, in fact, a *general-purpose symbol-manipulating system.* A symbol token is a pattern that can be compared to some other symbol token and judged equal with it or different from it. The basic test for equality of tokens in an *information processing system* (IPS) determines the fundamental alphabet of symbols it is prepared to recognize and distinguish. The key characteristic of an IPS is its ability to *designate*, that is, to have referents. This means that an IPS can take a symbol token as input and use it to gain access to a referenced object in order to affect it or be affected by it in some way: to read it, modify it, build a new structure with it, and so on. Hence, four concepts are central to understanding symbol manipulation: the IPS itself and its symbol structure, designation, and representation.

Information Processing Systems

An IPS is a system consisting of a memory containing symbol structures, a processor, effectors, and receptors. The characteristics of an IPS are:

1. There is a set of elements, called *symbols.*
2. Symbols may be formed into symbol structures by means of a set of *relations.*
3. There is a *memory*, capable of storing and retaining symbol structures.
4. There is a set of *information processes* that take symbol structures as inputs and produce symbol structure outputs.
5. The IPS has a component, the *processor*, that consists of (1) an ability to execute a set of *elementary information processes* (EIPs); (2) *short-term memory* (STM) that holds the input and output symbol structures of the EIPs; and (3) an *interpreter* that determines the sequence of EIPs to be executed by the IPS as a function of the symbol structures in STM.

Symbol Structures

We say that a symbol structure *designates* an object if there exist information processes that admit the symbol structure as input, and either (1) affect the object, or (2) produce, as output, symbol structures that are affected by the object.

A symbol structure serves as a *program (q.v.)* if the object it designates is an information process, and the interpreter, if given the program, can execute the designated process.

A symbol is *primitive* if its designation is fixed by the elementary information processes or by the external environment of the IPS.

The "objects" that symbols designate may include symbol structures stored in memory (data structures and programs), processes that the IPS is capable of executing, or objects in an external environment of sensible (readable) stimuli. To *read* is to create in memory internal symbol structures (representations) that designate external stimuli; to *write* is to create responses in the external environment that are designated by internal symbol structures.

The relation between a designated symbol and its object may have any degree of directness or indirectness. A structure can point to a structure that points to a structure that points to yet another, and so on. These IPS postulates are entirely abstract, making no assertions about how the structures and processes are realized, whether physically or biologically. Digital computers are physical systems that fit this abstraction; some psychologists, though not all, believe that the human cognitive system is also an IPS in the sense of these postulates.

Designation

It would be more correct to say that symbol *structures* designate than to say that *symbols* designate. For example, if an information process takes as input the symbol structure (color, house A) and produces the symbol "white," then the symbol structure (color, house A) designates *white*, and hence indirectly designates the color of the house in question. Linguistically, one normally takes as prototypic of designation the relation between a proper name and the object named—e.g. "George Washington" and a particular man who was once President of the USA. One then attempts to pass from that relation to others more difficult to envision: for example, the relation between "house" and any of a certain class of sheltering structures, and so on to "truth," "beauty," and "justice."

Representation

IPS symbols must have a well-defined representation. In storing chess information, for example, the pieces can be designated by symbols that have descriptions—defining each piece's type (King, Queen, Rook, etc.), color, and position on the board. A position, in this representation, is a symbol structure that associates with each of 64 squares the symbol of the piece occupying that square, if any, and which identifies the adjacent squares in various directions.

Elementary Information Processes

One of the major foundation stones of computer science is that a relatively small set of elementary processes suffices to produce the full generality of information processing. On the other hand, there is no *unique* basis. However, all alternative schemes do incorporate certain fundamental types of EIPs that constitute a sufficient basic set. Among these types are the following:

1. *Discrimination*. It must be possible for the system to behave in alternative ways, depending on what symbol structures are in its STM.
2. *Tests and comparisons*. It must be possible to determine that two symbol tokens do or do not belong to the same symbol type.
3. *Symbol creation*. It must be possible to create new symbols and set them to designate specified symbol structures.
4. *Writing symbol structures*. It must be possible to create, copy, or modify an existing symbol structure
5. *Reading and writing externally*. It must be possible to designate stimuli received from the external environment by means of internal symbols or symbol structures, and to produce external responses as a function of internal symbol structures that designate these responses.
6. *Designating symbol structures*. It must be possible to designate various parts of any given symbol

structure, and to obtain designations of other parts, as a function of given parts and relations.
7. *Storing symbol structures*. It must be possible to remember a symbol structure for later use.

Interaction with Environment

Progress in scene recognition and language recognition through visual and auditory sense organs has led to a rapid development of robotic (*q.v.*) symbol systems having substantial capabilities for interpretation of sensory information and its coordination with motor capabilities: including steering motor vehicles on highways at high speed, harvesting alfalfa, and playing robot soccer.

Bibliography

1972. Newell, A., and Simon, H. A. *Human Problem Solving.* Upper Saddle River, NJ: Prentice Hall.

Allen Newell and Herbert A. Simon

SYMBOLIC MATHEMATICS

See COMPUTER ALGEBRA.

SYSTEMS PROGRAMMING

For articles on related subjects, *see*

+ Compiler
+ Debugging
+ Distributed Systems
+ Language Processors
+ Linkers and Loaders
+ Machine- and Assembly-language Programming
+ Object Program
+ Operating Systems

Systems programming is concerned with the operating systems, utility programs, and library software needed to keep computer systems running smoothly. By its most general definition, systems programming is practiced by all those who write or maintain systems software, in contradistinction to those who practice applications programming (*q.v.*). Thus, most systems programmers work for large software development companies. But this article focuses on the individual (or small group of) systems programmers who keep the computers at user application sites running.

In traditional large computing centers, systems programming involves three job categories. *System operators* (Sys Ops) are concerned with keeping machines running, rebooting machines that crash, performing file system backups, running special jobs, and so forth. *Systems programmers* focus on such software aspects as installing new releases of application and operating systems software or porting software to a new machine, while *systems analysts* focus on planning and managing growth, finding and eliminating performance bottlenecks, and improving overall throughput (*q.v.*) and response time.

Historically, systems programmers tended to know one system particularly well, reflecting a time when computers were expensive and a site was likely to have only one or two machines. Today, most sites support a range of computers, from PC's and workstations (*q.v.*) to mainframes (*q.v.*) and supercomputers (*q.v.*).

The principal systems programmer's responsibility is that all machines function properly, and that they can communicate with one another across networks.

Systems programming requires basic knowledge of operating system principles, as well as specific information about the local operating system in use. The operating system *kernel* (*q.v.*) controls access to all hardware resources and defines the protection mechanism used to prevent processes created by one user from interfering with another. In addition, the operating system provides access to the file system, defining how files can be created, accessed, and destroyed; how the files of one user are protected from unauthorized access by another; or how a subset of users can share files protected from access by general users.

Bibliography

1990. Beck, L. L. *Systems Software: An Introduction to Systems Programming*. Reading, MA: Addison-Wesley.

1997. Clarke, D. L., and Merusi, D. E. *System Software Programming: The Way Things Work*. Upper Saddle River, NJ: Prentice Hall.

Thomas Narten

T

TASK

See JOB; and MULTITASKING.

TCP/IP

For articles on related subjects, *see*

+ Ethernet
+ Gateway
+ Internet
+ Network Protocols
+ Open Systems Interconnection
+ Packet Switching
+ Protocol

TCP/IP, an abbreviation for two protocols within the Internet Protocol Suite (IPS), stands for "Transmission Control Protocol" and "Internet Protocol." These are protocols developed in the mid-1970s to provide connection between Arpanet and other networks. TCP/IP was provided as the main communications protocol for computers using the Unix (*q.v.*) operating system but is now available on a wide range of computers. The main protocols that comprise IPS are file transfer (FTP), electronic mail (SMTP, including multimedia extensions, MIME), virtual terminal and remote login (TELNET and rlogin), name lookup (DNS), routing (RIP, OSPF, etc.), network management (SNMP), and the Network File System (NFS).

Transmission Control Protocol (RFC 793)

TCP provides a full-duplex link between a socket on the source computer system and a *socket* on the destination one. A socket appears to applications in the host computer as if it were an I/O device. A socket has a globally unique identifier consisting of the IP address of the computer plus a "port" number, assigned by the host computer. A set of port numbers is reserved, each for a different protocol. A connection is made to the "well-known socket" for each required service. TCP implements services such as flow control, sequencing, error checking, acknowledgments and retransmission, and facilities for multiplexing (*q.v.*).

User Datagram Protocol (RFC 768)

This operates at the same level as TCP but is "connectionless," that is, it is used in situations where there is no requirement for a connection-oriented protocol with the attendant overheads of setting up and clearing down. It is used by other protocols such as the Domain Name Server (DNS) and the Simple Network Management Protocol (SNMP) where the reliability of TCP is not required.

Internet Protocol (RFC 791)

IP provides communications over interconnected networks that implement differing technologies; it corresponds to the OSI Network Protocol (ISO/IEC 8473:

1994). It is a *connectionless packet-switched protocol*, which means that its data is broken up into "packets," each of which contains the source and destination addresses. Each system that uses IP has an IP address and a domain name. The original Arpanet used an 8-bit address space, six bits of which defined the IMP (Interface Message Processor) and two specified the host connected to that IMP. This permitted a maximum of 64 IMPs with four hosts per IMP, leading to a maximum of only 256 hosts. As the network grew, this became insufficient and the address space was increased to 16 bits, allowing a maximum of 65 536 hosts. In contrast, the IP-addressing scheme used 32 bits, permitting in theory, about four thousand million addresses. However, Internet addresses were structured into three classes—A, B and C—thus restricting the address space. The structure of the three classes was as follows:

Class A

0	Network (7 bits)	Local address (24 bits)

Class B

10	Network (14 bits)	Local address (16 bits)

Class C

110	Network (21 bits)	Local address (8 bits)

By the mid-1990s, it became clear that this address space would soon be exhausted and a new protocol was needed. *IP version 6* (IPv6—RFC 1833) uses 128-bit addresses and is upward compatible from the current IPv4 so that change to IPv6 will be straightforward. IP addresses are currently 32 bits long and for, simplicity, are normally written as four decimal integers (one per eight bits) separated by *dots* (e.g. "204.101.80.3"). Such an address is not user friendly, so each system also has a textual *domain name* (e.g. "www.acm.org"). The domain name is mapped into the IP address using the DNS protocol.

File Transfer Protocol (FTP; RFC 959)

FTP is a higher-level ("application") protocol, using TCP to transfer whole files from one host to another. It uses two separate (duplex) TCP connections, one for the actual data and one for controlling the transfer. It does not permit parts of files to be accessed and transferred, whereas the corresponding OSI standard (ISO/IEC 8571—File Transfer, Access and Management) does.

Network File Service (RFCs 1813, 1094)

This high-level protocol provides a virtual file store service whereby a host computer can make its file system available to a remote computer as if it were part of the latter's file system. This is often used in local area networks (*q.v.*), permitting PCs to access storage on a *network server*.

Simple Mail Transfer Protocol (SMTP; RFC 821)

SMTP permits the exchange of *electronic mail* (*q.v.*). A major disadvantage of SMTP is that it permits the transfer of only 7-bit characters and so binary (8-bit) files must be encoded by the sender and decoded by the receiver. Various encoding algorithms are used; an early one was UUE (Unix–Unix Encoding). More recently, MIME (Multipurpose Internet Mail Extensions) encoding standards have been developed for a variety of file formats such as video and audio; they provide similar features to the international X.400 standard, including some security services.

Hyptertext Transfer Protocol (HTTP; RFC 2068)

This protocol provides a distributed hypertext (*q.v.*) facility where the various documents are identified by a "Uniform Resource Locator" (URL) of the form "http://www.acm.org" where "http:" specifies the protocol and "www" stands for "World Wide Web," the set of Internet hosts that implement HTTP over the Internet. One of the earliest Web *browsers* (i.e. an HTTP client) was Mosaic; currently the most popular ones are Netscape Navigator and Internet Explorer.

Bibliography

1994–1997.Comer, D. . *Internetworking with TCP/IP.* Vol. 1 *Principles, Protocols, and Architecture;* Vol. 2 *Design, Implementation and Internals;* Vol. 3 *Client/Server*

Programming and Applications for the Windows Sockets Version. Upper Saddle River, NJ: Prentice Hall.

Adrian Stokes

TELECOMMUNICATIONS

See COMMUNICATIONS AND COMPUTERS.

TELEROBOTICS

For articles on related subjects, *see*

+ Automation
+ Computer Animation
+ Robotics
+ Virtual Reality

Introduction

Telerobotics denotes the technology of robotics controlled at a distance by human beings. When a task involving physical exploration, manipulation, and sampling is too dangerous or impractical to be performed directly by a human, it may be suited to a telerobot. The first telerobots, called *teleoperators*, were developed in response to the needs of the Manhattan Project to handle highly radioactive material during the Second World War, and they thus predate the use of electronic computing in robotics. These early electromechanical "master–slave" devices, pioneered by Ray Goertz at the US Argonne National Laboratory, nevertheless broke significant ground through their highly dexterous and precise mechanical design.

The Mars Pathfinder rover, dubbed Sojourner (Matijevic *et al.*, 1997), was the first telerobot to gain the world's attention, as it was guided around the surface of Mars by operators at NASA's Jet Propulsion Laboratory in July of 1997. This 12-kg vehicle was truly a telerobot in that it had on-board laser sensors for obstacle avoidance and the capability to navigate the unknown terrain autonomously under control of a

Figure 1. The Rocky 7 Mars Rover prototype with its sampling arm deployed. (Courtesy of the Jet Propulsion Laboratory, California Institute of Technology, Pasadena, CA. ©1999, California Institute of Technology. All rights reserved. US Government sponsorship acknowledged under NAS7-1407.)

simple microprocessor. Navigation objectives were sent from earth by radio requiring a round-trip time delay of about 20 min. The Rocky 7 Mars Rover, a successor to Sojourner, is shown in Fig. 1.

Engineers are currently developing many new applications of telerobotics. These include remote surgery (*telemedicine*), cleanup of hazardous waste, microassembly, and interactive entertainment.

Technologies

Early telerobotic systems could function only when the master and slave devices were nearly identical. With low-cost computing power, designers are free to modify the basic teleoperator architecture to create more powerful and friendly user interfaces (*q.v.*). Now designers can separately optimize the master side mechanism for effective human interaction and the slave side for the particular class of tasks. Feedback information such as contact force between the slave and the task is sent back to the operator through a set of kinematic transformations.

Control

The dynamics of robot manipulators are nonlinear because they depend strongly on the configuration, or "pose," of the robotic device. Furthermore, robots are frequently called upon to interact with an unmodeled environment and perform unforeseen tasks. As a robot manipulator picks up an object or pushes on something, its dynamic response completely changes. Human operators are also a source of significant model uncertainty. Precise mathematical modeling of the robot and human operator is impossible, so control laws must be robust to substantial variations.

Communication

Telerobotics tends to use bandwidth asymmetrically because the "uplink," relaying commands from the human operator to the robot, requires a much lower data rate (less than 10 kbps) than the returning sensor information (typically requiring megabits per second before compression). For many applications, it is possible to teleoperate robots via the Internet (*q.v.*)—*see* Fig. 2. Through emerging image compression (*q.v.*) technology, higher quality feedback in the form of improved television pictures will be available to the operator.

Advanced Challenges
Haptics (Force Feedback)

A system of "kinesthetic force feedback" creates a loop of information flow between the master and slave sides and thus introduces challenges for stable high performance control. This approach has been successfully implemented in several laboratories but

Figure 2. This telerobotic installation developed at the University of Southern California allows WWW users to view and interact with a remote garden filled with living plants. Members can plant, water, and monitor the progress of seedlings via the intricate movements of an industrial robot arm.

Figure 3. The Force Reflective Endoscopic Grasper (FREG)–Force Feedback Teleoperation Mode, for endoscopic surgery. (Reproduced by the permission of the University of Washington Biorobotics Laboratory.)

is still rare in systems in the field. When round trip time delay of the communication link exceeds about 200 ms, no control approach has yet been developed which achieves a satisfactory balance between stable (safe) operation and force feedback performance. So far, force feedback systems have been limited to those involving only local communication; for example, in the surgical telerobot in Figure 3.

Supervisory Control

When intelligent functions are available in the computer of the remote robot, the system is usually configured for *supervisory control*. In this mode, the operator acts as a supervisor of the robot's autonomous functions, helping it plan high-level strategies, detect task progress or failure, and assisting with error recovery. Low-level functions such as executing a move from one point to another, grasping an object already located within its jaws, or detecting simple visual features, are then performed by the remote robot on its own.

Shared vs Traded Control

Supervisory control can take two forms: "shared" and "traded." In *shared control*, a human operator and remote agent control different aspects of the system at the same time. For example, the human operator may control the position of a robot end-effector (e.g. a grasping arm) while the robot autonomously controls the orientation. In another example, an operator may drive a remote vehicle while the vehicle's control system monitors its sensors for imminent collisions. *Traded control* involves sequentially exchanging control between the operator and the robot's autonomous functions.

Human-Computer Interaction (HCI)

Because the telerobotic system relies so heavily on the intelligence of the human operator, its performance will depend strongly on the quality of the human–computer interface. Although humans are remarkable in their ability to adapt to interfaces of varying quality, extensive training time, fatigue, and errors can be avoided with attention to HCI. Some requirements of telerobotic tasks may require advanced modes of human computer interaction such as stereoscopic vision systems and displays, computer simulation and animation, and force feedback (haptic displays) for better control of contact forces and manipulation at the remote site.

Bibliography

1992. Sheridan, T. B. *Telerobotics, Automation, and Human Supervisory Control*. Cambridge, MA: MIT Press.

1997. Hannaford, B., Hewitt, J., Maneewarn, T., Venema, S., Appleby, M., and Ehresman, R. "Robotic System for Protein Crystal Handling," in *IEEE International Conference on Robotics and Automation*, Albuquerque, NM, April, 1997.

1997. Matijevic, J. R. *et al.* "Characterization of the Martian Surface Deposits by the Mars Pathfinder Rover, Sojourner," *Science*, **278**(5344), (5 December), 1765–1768.

Blake Hannaford

TELNET

See INTERNET; and TCP/IP.

TESTING

See DEBUGGING.

T_EX

For articles on related subjects, *see*

+ Desktop Publishing
+ Typefont
+ Word Processing

T_EX is a computer-controlled typesetting system designed by Donald E. Knuth. The name, pronounced "tech" to rhyme with "blech," is the Greek root for English words such as "technique" and "technology." In 1977, Knuth saw phototypeset proofs for a new edition of a book in his series, *The Art of Computer Programming*. The quality of the typesetting had deteriorated seriously from the previous editions, which had been set with lead type. Knuth had just learned about "digital" devices for typesetting, in which each image on each page is made up of tiny black dots arranged on a grid. He realized that such equipment gave him the power to make his books look good again; all he had to do was write a computer program to put tiny bits of ink in the right places. So he began the TEX project, a nine-year long program of research in digital typography.

From the beginning, Knuth wanted to produce a system capable of high-quality typesetting, one that would incorporate the finest traditions of the printing industry. This meant that TEX users would specify a bit more than was customary with ordinary typewriters. For example, the numeral "1" needs to be distinguished from the letter "l" (lowercase L), and opening quotation marks distinguished from closing ones. TEX is especially adept at mathematical typesetting (see Fig. 1), which involves embedded formulas, subscripts, superscripts, a multitude of symbols, and arrangements of tabular matter.

Portability and stability were also important goals. The system is designed to be device-independent; TEX now runs on hundreds of different computers, from PCs to mainframes ($q.v.$) and high-performance workstations ($q.v.$), producing identical results on each. The finished output can be directed to many devices, including video screens, impact printers, laser printers, and phototypesetters. TEX file prepared today should be able to produce the same output 20 or more years from now, on the machines of the future.

Knuth felt strongly that TEX should be in the public domain, available to everyone without payment

of royalties, and that the algorithms of TEX should be published as a contribution to computer science. These algorithms may be freely incorporated into other systems. However, Knuth requires that the name TEX be restricted to systems that are fully compatible with the program he wrote.

The metaphor of boxes and glue (see Fig. 2) is used to illustrate the way TEX assembles elements on a page. Each letter or character can be thought of as a small box containing an image. These boxes are glued together; a horizontal string of characters forms a bigger box to make up a word. Words, in turn, make sentences, which combine to make paragraphs, and so on. Boxes can be glued together vertically as well as horizontally.

The glue used to assemble groups of boxes has the ability to stretch or shrink. Boxes can be set right next to each other with no glue at all, or they can be spaced far apart with thick glue. The capacity to control the stretching and shrinking of the glue is an important feature of TEX that allows an almost infinite variety of formats to be defined in terms of a small number of basic operations.

The procedure by which TEX hyphenates words, developed by Frank Liang, is constructed in such a way that it can easily be adapted to different languages and to different conventions within a single language. Patterns that appear in a word are used to decide where hyphens are permissible and where they should be forbidden. For example, an English word containing the sequence "onc" normally permits a hyphen after the 'n'; consider "bron-chitis," "discon-certing," and "incon-clusive."

Version 3.0 of TEX, released in 1990, introduced new capabilities for typesetting mixed-language texts with different hyphenation rules for each language. As

Input to TEX:

```
The names of variables in math formulas
such as $e^{x_1^2+\cdots+x_n^2}$ are
usually set in {\it italic type}.
```

Output from TEX:

The names of variables in math formulas such as $e^{x_1^2+\cdots+x_n^2}$ are usually set in *italic type*.

Figure 1. TEX automatically chooses sizes and styles of type for mathematical material that the user has enclosed in dollar signs.

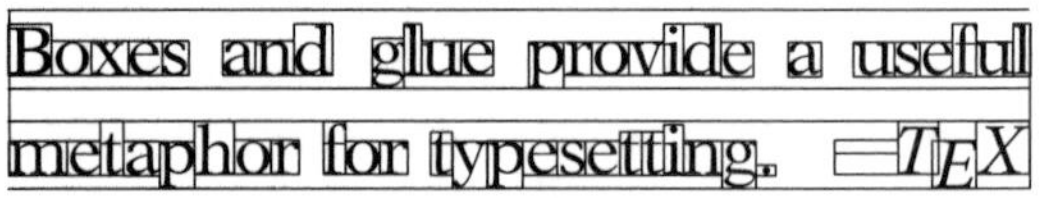

Figure 2. TEX typesets pages by constructing boxes inside of boxes inside of boxes, with flexible glue to hold them in place.

a result, the use of TeX has spread to almost every country in the world, and many facilities have been developed to adapt TeX to the special needs of local users.

When users of TeX find that they are repeating certain groups of instructions over and over, they can create macros (*q.v.*) to remember those sequences.

Several children of TeX have been born, each using its own set of macros. The most prominent of these is LaTeX, by Leslie Lamport, which encourages its users to create documents with nested structure; chapters, sections, subsections, illustrations, equations, and so on. LaTeX has automatic facilities for assigning numbers to itemized lists, and for generating indexes and tables of contents. $A_M \Sigma$-TeX, by Michael Spivak, is designed for technical material that contains advanced mathematics. $\Lambda A_M \Sigma$-TeX is a collection of macros that extends LaTeX by providing the mathematical facilities of $A_M \Sigma$-TeX. The American Mathematical Society uses these systems to typeset most of its journals and books.

The TeX Users Group (TUG), formed in 1979 and numbering about 2000 members in 2003, publishes a quarterly journal called *TUGboat.* TUG holds annual meetings, provides publications, organizes short courses, and hosts a Website at http://www.tug.org.

Bibliography

1979. Knuth, D. E. "Mathematical Typography," *Bulletin of the American Mathematical Society* (new series), **1**, 337–372.

1984. Knuth, D. E. *The TeXbook,* Volume A *of Computers and Typesetting.* Reading, MA: Addison-Wesley.

1986. Knuth, D. E. *TeX: The Program,* Volume B *of Computers and Typesetting.* Reading, MA: Addison-Wesley.

1990. Spivak, M. D. *The Joy of TeX,* 2nd Ed. Providence, RI: American Mathematical Society.

1997. Goossens, M., Rahtz, S. P. Q., and Mittelbach, F. *The LaTeX Graphics Companion.* Reading, MA: Addison-Wesley.

Donald E. and Jill C. Knuth

TEXT EDITING SYSTEMS

For articles on related subjects, *see*

+ Desktop Publishing
+ Hypertext
+ Interactive Input Devices
+ Mouse
+ PostScript
+ Spelling Checker
+ TeX
+ Typefont
+ User Interface
+ Window Environments
+ Word Processing

Introduction

Text editing is the use of a computer to generate and modify written words, usually in order to print out the text. Text editing systems enable the computer and its printer to act as a kind of super typewriter. This use has, as much as any of its many other capabilities, been responsible for the virtually universal acceptance of computing in every kind of office.

Natural Language Applications

Word processing

Using a computer to write and edit text is called *word processing*. The term *word processor* designates both a free-standing special purpose computer for the task and a software program enabling a general purpose PC to do so. The latter meaning now predominates.

Page layout systems

Editors of publications such as newsletters and journals often use programs that provide facilities for page layout and sophisticated print production, an activity referred to as *desktop publishing*. Initially developed for use in the publishing industry, page layout programs have been scaled down for PCs and they are now frequently used as adjuncts or replacements for standard text editors.

Hypertext editing

Hypertext (*q.v.*), a term coined by Ted Nelson, is "the combination of natural language text with the computer's capacities for interactive branching, or dynamic display of . . . a nonlinear text . . . which cannot be printed conveniently on a conventional page." Such texts, which are designed to be read on the computer screen and not on the page, make it possible for the user to jump from the text into other computer sources related to the topic, from there to still other sources, and back to the original place. The jumping-off spots, or *links*, are designated by the author of the text. The hypertext format is familiar to millions of computer users through the home pages of the World Wide Web (*q.v.*).

Text Editing

Text editing programs follow a conceptual model of its user and the computer that guides the design and use of the program. The most common model suggests that the screen is the visible part of a scroll (such as the parchment scrolls used in ancient times), which the user may roll back and forth to make space for the text as it is being created, or to view already existing text. In Apple's Macintosh system, in Microsoft Windows, and in Unix (*q.v.*) with the X Window System, the user can create *windows*, or screen viewing spaces, for several files or documents at one time, which can be viewed side by side, top to bottom, or as alternating screens as the user wishes (*see* WINDOW ENVIRONMENTS). Commonly used commands appear as *icons*, or graphic symbols, along the top of the screen in a *command bar*. These commands, as well as others that appear in a *pull-down menu* the user may view, are issued by the user's click on the mouse or by the use of *function keys*.

Input Devices

The text and the operations that the user wishes to perform upon it (spacing, capitalizing, italicizing, etc.) are entered via various input devices. These include the alphanumeric keyboard, which is made up of keys for numbers, letters, and other commonly used symbols; special function keys on the keyboard used to issue commands, and the Alt and Control keys, used in combination with alphanumeric keys to issue commands to the program; and locator devices such as a *mouse* or a *trackball*.

Handheld or *palmtop* computers (*see* PORTABLE COMPUTERS) offer handwriting recognition as a means of text or command entry. The user writes on a special pad using a stylus and the computer converts these handwritten entries into characters on the screen or commands for formatting or location.

Unlike a typewriter, a text editor makes a whole document available for typing or retyping, and hence needs to show the user where the next typed character will appear. This is done using a *cursor*, usually a character-sized square that flashes in the space to be filled next, or a vertical line that appears directly to the right of the most recently typed character. A mouse or trackball is then used to move the cursor on the screen for text editing.

Output Devices

The screen displays the text input by the user, formatted according to its standard settings or the user's commands. It is the principal output device, far removed from the paper scroll issued by early teletype-like devices. Editing systems now run on either character-based displays or graphics (*bitmap*) displays. Often, the user can see on the screen a display of even a complex document, looking like a photographic image of how it would appear if printed on paper.

Text Editing: A Conceptual Overview
What is Text?

In order to do text editing, we must first have text. Generally, text is provided not only by typing on the keyboard, but also by *scanning*, or *machine-reading* an existing text into a computer file (*see* OPTICAL CHARACTER RECOGNITION (OCR)), or by importing it from some other outside source, such as through email. Text editing then involves adding, deleting, or altering the text. In order to accomplish this, the user must specify exactly where in the existing text the change, addition, or deletion is to take place and what is to be done at that site.

Often, how a text appears on the screen is not how it appears on the printed page. When an editor does show on the screen a faithful image of the text as it will appear on paper, it is referred to as a WYSIWYG (What You See Is What You Get) editor. Non-WYSIWYG editors often have special options allowing the user to preview the text to see how it would look when printed.

Definition of Text Within the Computer

Characters are stored in a computer's memory in code. The most common code is ASCII (*see* CHARACTER CODES), which uses seven bits of information for each character, for a total of 128 different characters. When text is defined as consisting exclusively of the characters included in the ASCII code, it is usually called *plain text* or ASCII text. Extended ASCII Code uses eight bits and thus allows for 256 different characters but this still is not nearly enough to represent multiple fonts with different styles and size such as might be found in this volume, not to mention mathematical symbols or non-Roman alphabets. Hence, such things as umlauts or Greek letters must be represented internally by the editor's own code, usually consisting of several Extended ASCII symbols.

Definition of Text as a Structure

Text may be understood as a simple linear sequence of characters, just as it is represented in a computer. However, to a human, the text has a certain internal structure. If it is a computer program, it may be a sequence of statements, each of which follows a rigid syntax. If it is an essay, it is a sequence of paragraphs separated by a blank line or indentation; each paragraph is a sequence of sentences separated by periods, exclamation marks, or question marks; and each sentence is a sequence of words, each of which is a sequence of alphanumeric characters followed and preceded by a blank. If the text is a hypertext document, then the linear structure is extended into a more complex set of relations that form a web of textual (and perhaps graphical) components. The simplest editors recognize only the linear structure of the characters of the text. More sophisticated editors can recognize the structure of programming languages, hypertext, and, to a limited degree, natural language.

The Editor: A System Viewpoint

Figure 1 gives a simplified view of the organization of a generic editor. The user provides input via a keyboard or mouse that will identify both a *position* and a *portion of an existing text* and some *action* that is to be performed. The action is typically some sort of editing that is to occur at the currently identified position (such as insertion of a character) or on the currently identified portion of text (such as to italicize a selected portion of the text). The actions that can be performed fall generally into the following categories:

1. Highlighting a position or portion of the text that is to be modified.
2. Altering in some way that portion of the text currently identified.
3. Altering the portion of the text that is visible on the screen, or the manner in which the text is displayed.
4. Transferring text to or from the computer's main memory (loading, saving, printing).

The first three affect only the text residing in the main memory of the machine. Only the last one actually affects the text on the disk or on paper.

Screen Updating

Displaying a full screenful of text creates the potential for unacceptably long delays caused by the time required to update the screen. The idea is to exploit the fact that each new screenful of information is most often a variant of the previous screen. Intelligent updating attempts to detect just which portions of the screen have changed, and rewrite only those portions.

File Formats

A text file ultimately consists of a sequence of characters, each most commonly represented in the computer by

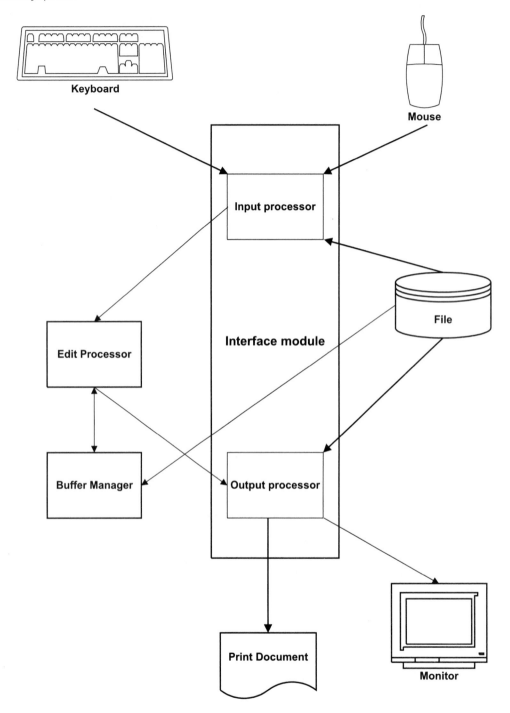

Figure 1. Schematic of a generic text editor.

a sequence of 8-bit Extended ASCII characters. There is now also *Unicode* (*see* CHARACTER CODES), an international standard coding that extends ASCII to 16 bits, but this is not yet in common use because of the additional storage required for each character. Although having 16 bits allows for 65 536 different codes, even that number would be quickly exhausted by the number of different fonts, styles, sizes, and orientations possible for each character to say nothing of the requirements for non-English alphabets. In order to manage all this, word processors insert additional information into the file to describe fonts, sizes, and so on. This extra information must be coded into the file for proper display and printing.

Cutting and Pasting

One of the most common text-editing features involves a reservoir that holds text. When the user deletes a block of text, the text does not disappear entirely, but moves into that reservoir. The text may then be brought from the reservoir into the current document at any place within the document. Similarly, the command to copy a block of text actually copies it into the reservoir. Then it may be pasted into the document. Some computer environments provide a general reservoir for that purpose (called the *clipboard* in Microsoft Windows) that will allow cutting (deletion) and pasting across various applications.

Editing Operations

Creating

Text editors make computer-based typing far more flexible than typing on a typewriter. First, the backspace or delete key can be used to erase the last character typed. Second, typing a carriage return at the end of each line is unnecessary, thanks to automatic *wordwrap*. As the end of each line is reached, it breaks the line at the first blank space before overflowing and automatically pushes the continuing text to the next line.

Deleting

The *delete* command requires that the user select the scope of the operation in order to indicate how much is to be deleted, or *cut*. Some text editors ask for confirmation before actually deleting text; others provide an *undo* command, making the last deletion reversible. For the delete command, as well as for copy and move operations, many systems provide *delete buffers*. The deleted text can be used later as the object of *paste* operations, which put the elements from the delete buffer back into the text, possibly at a different point.

Changing

The simplest change is the replacement of a letter, word, or phrase with another. On mouse-based systems, the user selects the text fragment to be replaced and types its replacement over the old one. Line editors require the user to specify what character(s) to replace. These editors have a change or substitute command that takes as arguments both the scope of the change and the replacement string. *Global* changes are those that take place throughout an entire document, such as from single to double spacing, to a new typeface, or replacing every instance of a particular word with a substitute word.

Moving

To move a block of text, the user specifies the scope of text to be copied and the place where the text is to be pasted. In an editor in which the scope is specified by pointing, the user defines the source by selecting the beginning and end of the text to be moved, and then defines the destination by pointing to the location at which it should be placed.

Historical Development of Editors

Punched cards (*q.v.*) provided the first stage in noninteractive computerized editing. The basic unit of information on punched cards was the 80-column line; corrections of mispunched cards could be made only by typing a replacement card. With the advent of time-sharing environments in the mid-1960s, interactive line editors allowed the user to create and modify disk files from terminals. These editors attached numbers to lines of limited length, initially 80 characters. Simple command languages allowed the user to make corrections within a line or even within a group of contiguous lines. But these and subsequent *context-driven line editors* and *variable-length line editors* did not address three basic problems in manuscript editing: truncation when the line length was exceeded, inability to edit a string crossing line boundaries, and inability to search for a pattern crossing line boundaries. The *stream editor* solved all three problems by eliminating line boundaries altogether: the entire text was considered a single stream or string that was broken into screen lines by display routines. An arbitrary string between any two characters could be defined for searching and editing.

Multiline display screens with cursor addressability and local buffers made possible *full-screen, display*, or *cursor editors*. An early example is Stanford University's TVEDIT. Commands, represented by control character sequences, could be interspersed with the input of normal text. Users could move the cursor to the point of editing, rather than having to describe text arguments using a programming language syntax. The TVEDIT concepts and similar work form the basis of many screen editors in use today.

In 1959, Douglas Engelbart introduced a major conceptual change with his NLS (oNLine System). It was implemented in the 1960s using display terminals, multicontext viewing, flexible file viewing, and a consistent user interface. One of its many important contributions was the mouse, which however, did not achieve popular acceptance until the 1980s. NLS provided support for text *structure* and *hierarchy*: users could manipulate documents in terms of their outline structure, not only their content. NLS and related editors view the editor as an *author's tool*, an interactive means for organizing and browsing through information, rather than simply as a way to alter characters in a single file. In 1970, Hansen's EMILY extended the concept of the structure editor and developed the *syntax-directed editor*, which imposed on the program being edited the structure of the programming language itself, giving users the power to manipulate logical constructs such as do–while loops and their nested contents as single units.

The Unix (*q.v.*) operating system developed in the early 1970s and generally accepted by the middle of the decade, became an important milestone in text editing and text processing. Unix was the first general-purpose

computing environment in which text utilities were given as much weight as programming utilities. Unix's suite of utilities (the *ed, vi*, and *emacs* text editors, the *troff* text formatter, the *eqn* equation formatter, the *tbl* table formatter, the *refer* bibliographic database and formatter, the *spell* spell checker, and the *style* and *diction* text analyzers) became the benchmark for text tools. Interactive drawing techniques from Sutherland's pioneering Sketchpad system were later incorporated into editor interfaces. In the Carnegie Mellon tablet editor, hand-drawn proofreader's symbols were used to edit displayed text. For a *delete* or *substitute* operation, for instance, the user drew a line through the text to be deleted.

The Bravo editor and the Smalltalk environment developed at Xerox's Palo Alto Research Center (Xerox PARC) were the major innovations of the 1970s in text handling and the user interface. These systems blended text and graphics on a high-resolution bitmapped raster graphics screen, using a dynamic graphical interface provided by a dedicated PC and using the mouse as a pointing device. These systems were the first *interactive editor/formatters*.

Throughout the 1980s, the ideas developed at Xerox PARC spread even farther as the WYSIWYG concept influenced the PC industry. These new computers, exemplified by the Apple Macintosh, introduced in 1984, put a priority on ease of use, user interface (*q.v.*) consistency, and interactive editing throughout their operating environment. Content and editing are now so intertwined that very little text processing is distinct from formatting. Several systems now allow the creation of fully editable *composite documents*, which may contain blocks or subdocuments of various types—graphics, text, spreadsheet (*q.v.*)—each of which may be created and edited by a different editor. These systems are exemplified by Quill, an editing system developed at IBM's Almaden Research facility. The developers of this system call it "an extensible system for editing documents of mixed type." Another system with related functions is Hewlett-Packard's NewWave operating environment. In this system, which is overlaid on Microsoft Windows, users create *objects*—documents or part of documents—that can be placed in any document, regardless of their type.

Bibliography

1990. Smith, P. D. *An Introduction to Text Processing.* Cambridge, MA: MIT Press.

1991. Finseth, C. A. *The Craft of Text Editing: Emacs for the Modern World.* New York: Springer-Verlag.

Alton F. and Ruth H. Sanders

THEORY OF ALGORITHMS

See ALGORITHMS, THEORY OF.

THROUGHPUT

For an article on a related subject, *see*

+ Job

The *throughput* of a system is the number of jobs, tasks, or transactions the system completes per unit time. Throughput is often used as a figure of merit, with higher values indicating better performance. System engineers use analytic or simulation models to help determine a system configuration and server capacities that enable the system to meet throughput and response-time targets. Throughput is a central factor in the flow, response-time, and queuing laws of system performance.

A system consists of one or more servers. Two parameters are associated with each server i: (1) the visit ratio V_i is the mean number of visits a job makes to that server before exiting the system; (2) the per-visit service time S_i is the mean time the server processes a job per visit, not including queuing time. The total time demand of a job for the server is denoted D_i and is simply V_iS_i. The response time R_i of the server is the sum of the job's queuing time and its service time.

The mean queue length Q_i of the server is the average number of jobs in the queue. Several important laws can be deduced from these definitions:

1. *Utilization Law* The utilization U_i of a server is the fraction of time the server is busy. Throughput X_i of a server with mean service time S_i per task visit is related to the utilization U_i by the law $U_i = S_iX_i$. The maximum possible throughput $(1/S_i)$ occurs when the queue is full all the time–that is, the server is saturated.

2. *Little's Law* This law states that a server's mean queue length Q_i is related to the per-visit response time R_i and the throughput X_i by the law $Q_i = R_iX_i$.

3. *Forced Flow Law* Let X_0 denote the system's throughput; then $X_i = X_0V_i$. This implies that knowledge of a throughput at any single point in the system is sufficient to know the throughputs everywhere.

4. *System response time laws* The response time of a closed system is $R_0 = N/X_0-Z$, where Z is the average time a user spends thinking before issuing a next request to the system. The response time of an open server is approximately $R_i = S_i/(1-S_iX_i)$. In both cases, higher throughputs imply higher response times.

These simple relationships can be extended to systems with multiple job classes and variable rate servers (Menascé *et al.*, 1994).

Bibliography

1994. Menascé, D., Almeida, V., and Dowdy, L. *Capacity Planning.* Upper Saddle River, NJ: Prentice Hall.

Peter J. Denning

TIME SHARING

For articles on related subjects, see

+ File Server
+ Multiplexing
+ Multiprogramming

+ **Multitasking**
+ **Virtual Memory**

Origins

Time-sharing is a technique of organizing a computer so that several users can interact with it simultaneously. The term also refers to multiuser systems in which arbitrary general-purpose computation is performed and users operate independently, often at locations remote from the computer itself. Time-sharing originated in the late 1950s and early 1960s. In 1959, Christopher Strachey presented a paper at a UNESCO Conference describing the possibility of doing program debugging (*q.v.*) while time-sharing the computer with the normal production-computing load. Independently, that same year, Professor John McCarthy of MIT proposed key hardware modifications to an IBM 709 computer that would allow the possibility of time-shared debugging by multiple users.

Time-sharing is, in a sense, a rediscovery of earlier, more experimental, modes of computer use. In the early 1940s, the Stibitz relay computer at the Bell Telephone Laboratories was operated remotely by a single user a few hundred miles away. In 1955, an Alwac III-E minicomputer at the National Security Agency in Arlington, Virginia, "time-shared" four remote terminals in round-robin fashion, but its 15-min *time slice* did not give the illusion of simultaneity. Also in the mid-1950s, the US Air Defense had the massive SAGE System developed. At each of several sites it had multiple users, each at a terminal interacting independently with information displayed on cathode ray tubes. In the late 1950s, IBM and American Airlines had begun development of the SABRE System, an online airline reservation system with hundreds of terminals distributed geographically. However, these early multiterminal systems were dedicated to single-purpose applications. What was new and striking in the proposals of Strachey and McCarthy was the vision of a computer used independently and virtually simultaneously by different persons for entirely different programs.

By the early 1960s, work on time-shared systems had begun in earnest. Some of the first working prototypes were: at MIT, the Compatible Time-Sharing System (CTSS) of F. J. Corbató, initially on an IBM 709 (1961), and later, the IBM 7090 and 7094 (1963); also at MIT, the DEC PDP-1 System of J. B. Dennis; and at the Bolt, Beranek, and Newman Company in Cambridge a DEC PDP-1-based time-sharing system developed by a team consisting of J. McCarthy, S. Boilen, E. Fredkin, and J. C. R. Licklider. Other early influential prototypes were the Dartmouth College Basic System of J. Kemeny and T. Kurtz, initially implemented on a GE 235; the JOSS System implemented at the Rand Corporation by C. Shaw; and at the System Development Corporation, a time-sharing system developed by J. Schwartz for the AN/FSQ-32 military computer. CTSS was oriented toward a general-purpose service offered by a central computing service; this system was to become the initial research vehicle of Project MAC, an MIT research laboratory organized by R. M. Fano to explore the implications of time-sharing and human–machine interactions. The BBN PDP-1 system was oriented toward an environment for interactive program development that included the use of a high-performance graphics display.

By the mid-1960s, time-sharing systems, especially those of MIT's Project MAC and of Dartmouth College, had attracted considerable attention and development of extensive new time-sharing systems had begun. Among the more notable plans were those for the Multics System (by MIT's Project Mac, the Bell Telephone Laboratories, and the General Electric Company) and the TSS System (by IBM for the IBM 360/67).

How Time-Sharing Works

At any given time, a time-shared computer has, in its main high-speed memory, programs for several users, as well as a master supervisory program (sometimes called an *executive* or *monitor*) under whose control the online system runs. The role of the supervisor is to commute the central processor sequentially through the programs associated with the users, running each for a brief burst of time (often called a *quantum* or *time slice*). One can imagine a simple form of such a system with n terminals and up to n users, each with a program area in the main computer memory that also

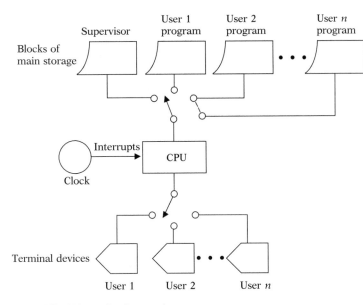

Figure 1. A highly simplified time-sharing system.

contains the supervisor program (*see* Fig. 1). A program that is waiting for input from its associated user terminal does not need processor time, nor does a program that completes its immediate computation in less than a quantum need the remainder of the quantum allotted to it. In the simplest or *round robin* case, where all the user programs are cycled through in order, the programs appear to their users to proceed as if they each had the computer all alone, albeit one that appears to operate slower on extensive requests.

To carry out the above scheme effectively requires three hardware features. The first is a program-settable "alarm clock" (*interval timer—q.v.*), which the supervisor can use to interrupt user programs that are not finished after their time quantum is exhausted. The precise state of these interrupted programs must be preserved for use when the program is next allocated a time slice. The second feature is a privileged operation mode that allows only the supervisor to execute the instructions for initiating I/O operations, setting the interval timer, and so on; the effect is that any user-program misbehavior, intentional or unintentional, causes program control to revert to the supervisor. The third feature is a pair of *bounds registers* set by the supervisor, which can be compared with each memory

access attempted by the processor. As with the user mode, any attempt by a user program to reference a location outside of its area in memory automatically causes program control to revert or *trap* to the supervisor program. Thus, the supervisor can never lose control of the computer, no matter how misprogrammed a user program might be. Furthermore, one user program can be prevented from interfering with, or even reading, the programs or data of another user.

Swapping is the transfer of whole programs or segments thereof between main and secondary memory. The term originated in the systems of the early 1960s. Because there was no memory protection (*q.v.*) hardware to isolate multiple programs, these early systems permitted only one user program to reside in main memory at a time. When a program reached the end of a time slice or stopped for I/O, the operating system exchanged it for another waiting program. But modern operating systems use multiprogrammed virtual memory. In these systems, there are two kinds of information transfer between main and secondary memory: loading a program at the start of an execution period and unloading it at the end of that period (a *warm start*), and fetching new *pages* or segments on demand during the execution period. The first is called *swapping* and the second *demand paging*. The term *roll-in* is sometimes also used for loading a program, and *roll-out* for unloading. Paged virtual memory systems can start a program with an initially empty partition (called *cold start*); demand paging loads the program after the start of execution. This is not an effective use of demand paging. It is much more efficient to load and unload full working sets (*q.v.*) at the start and end of execution periods; demand paging should be used to add pages to the working set during the execution period.

Bibliography

1975.Wilkes, M. V. *Time Sharing Computer Systems*, 3rd Ed. New York: Elsevier.
1997.Tanenbaum, A. W. *Operating Systems: Design and Implementation*, 2nd Ed. (with A. Woodhull). Upper Saddle River, NJ: Prentice Hall.

F. J. Corbató and Peter Denning

TRANSFER RATE

See BANDWIDTH; and MEMORY: AUXILIARY.

TRANSISTOR

See INTEGRATED CIRCUITRY.

TRANSLATION, LANGUAGE

See MACHINE TRANSLATION.

TRANSPARENCY

For articles on related subjects, *see*

+ Compatibility
+ Software Portability

When changes are made to a computer's hardware or software configuration, which do not require any action on a user's part, the changes are said to be *transparent* to the user. This does not mean that the user will see no effect of the change, just that no action is required by the user to experience it. For example, a software vendor might issue a new version of a word processor or operating system, which given exactly the same input in the same form, functions identically to the prior version except for increased speed or stability. In each case, the change would be said to be "transparent to the user."

Edwin D. Reilly

TREE

For articles on related subjects, *see*

+ Computer Games: Traditional
+ Data Structures
+ Graph Theory
+ Polish Notation

A *tree*, or more precisely, a *rooted tree*, is a special form of directed graph with the following properties: (1) either it has no vertices or it has a distinguished vertex called the *root*, which has no predecessors; and (2) every vertex other than the root has a unique predecessor. Vertices (or *nodes*) of a tree that have successors are called *nonterminal vertices*, or *parent nodes*, while vertices that have no successors are called *terminal vertices* or *leaves*. Figure 1 illustrates a tree with root vertex *a*; two nonterminal vertices *a*, *c*; and three leaves *b*, *d*, *e*. Nodes *b* and *c*, since they have the same parent, are said to be *sibling nodes*, as are nodes *d* and *e*. Similarly, all nodes that have a parent (all those other than the root)—*b*, *c*, *d*, and *e* in Fig. 1—are said to be *child nodes*.

Trees in which each nonterminal vertex has at most *n* successors are called *n-ary* trees. Trees in which each nonterminal vertex has at most two successors would then be 2-ary trees, but such structures have little or no application in computer science without the additional

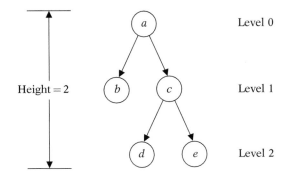

Figure 1. A tree showing terminal and non-terminal vertices.

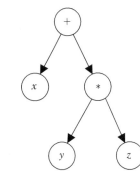

Figure 2. A tree representing an operator-operand structure.

restriction that children are either *left child nodes* or *right child nodes*. Such trees are very useful; they are called *binary* trees. The tree in Fig. 1 is an example of a binary tree.

Each node of a tree determines a subtree whose root is the given node and whose vertices include all descendants of the node. In a binary tree, each nonterminal node has an associated left subtree and right subtree.

A tree is said to be *unordered* if there is no special significance to the order in which the descendants of a given node are listed, and is said to be *ordered* if the order of descendant nodes is significant.

The root of a tree is said to be at level 0, the children of the root at level 1, the grandchildren at level 2, and so on. The highest numbered level is called the *height* (or depth) of the *tree* (*see* Fig. 1).

Binary trees are a natural data structure for expressing the operator–operand structure of arithmetic expressions. The expression $x + (y * z)$ may be represented by the tree structure in Fig. 2, where the operators are represented by nonterminal vertices and the operands of an operator are represented by successor subtrees of the operator vertex. Thus, the operands of $+$ are x and $y * z$, and are represented by successor subtrees of the vertex $+$.

There are four fundamentally different ways to list the nodes of a binary tree. When applied to an expression tree such as that in Fig. 2, the first three yield a recognizable variation of the original expression.

1. *Preorder (or depth-first) traversal* Visit (print) the root. Traverse the left subtree (if any). Traverse the right subtree (if any). When applied recursively, this algorithm yields $+x*yz$ which is the *Polish prefix* form of the original expression (*see* POLISH NOTATION).

2. *Inorder (or symmetric) traversal* Traverse the left subtree. Visit (print) the root. Traverse the right subtree. This yields $x + y * z$, which recaptures the original *infix* form of the expression.

3. *Postorder (or endorder) traversal* Traverse the left subtree. Traverse the right subtree. Visit the root. This yields $xyz*+$, which is the *reverse Polish* or *Polish postfix* form of the expression.

4. *Breadth-first traversal*, that is, level by level. For Fig. 2, the result obtained, $+x*yz$, happens to be the same as obtained via preorder traversal, but for more complex binary trees, this would not usually be the case.

Binary trees play an important role in computer science. Of particular importance are *height-balanced* trees, in which the height (maximum distance from the root to a leaf) of the left subtree of any node differs from that of the right subtree by, at most, one. Such trees are also called AVL trees after their inventors G. M. Adel'son-Vel'skii and E. M. Landis (1962). Keeping a tree balanced in this way provides far superior search time as compared to trees that become highly unbalanced.

The concept of height balancing can also be extended to *n*-ary trees. When data is stored in an external medium, such as a disk file, disk accesses are expensive relative to the reading of the data once an access is completed. Accordingly, it is reasonable to organize the data into a tree structure having a large number of keys per node so that the nodes have a large branching factor. Such trees were called B-trees by R. Bayer and E. McCreight (1972), who were the first to propose use of multiway balanced trees for external searching. For a comprehensive survey of B-trees, *see* Comer (1979).

A special kind of *n*-ary tree called a *trie* (from re*trie*val, but pronounced "try") has a letter at each node, and any path from its root to a leaf represents a valid word in a given dictionary of entries. Imagine that the trie is used with a spelling checker (*q.v.*). If a "word" cannot be found in the trie, it is probably misspelled (though it may merely be missing from that particular dictionary). A trie is a kind of search tree in which, instead of checking whole keys (words) against a target item, constituent letters are checked one by one until either a leaf is reached (success) or no further branch can be taken whose root matches the next letter of the target word (failure). Figure 3 shows a small trie in which leaves, the ends of successful search paths, are represented by squares. The trie shown contains the words THE, THEM, THEN, THEY, THAN, THAT, THAW, TRAM, TRAP, TRAY, and TRUE.

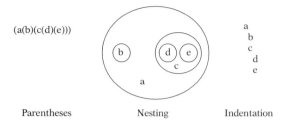

Parentheses   Nesting   Indentation

Figure 4. Alternative representations of the tree of Figure 1.

Tree structures may be indicated by parentheses, nesting, or indentation, as illustrated in Fig. 4, which shows alternative representations of the tree of Fig. 1. The representation (a)(b) (c(d) (e)) may be viewed as a list structure in which the successor nodes of a are represented by the sublists (b) and (c(d) (e)). This representation is used to represent trees in languages such as Lisp (*q.v.*).

Trees are often used in the analysis of strategies for games such as chess and checkers (draughts) (*see* COMPUTER GAMES: TRADITIONAL). In this case, the vertices of the tree represent positions in the game, and a given vertex has as its successors all vertices that can be reached in one move from the given position. The set of all continuations of a game from a given position can be represented by a tree having the given position as its root vertex. The set of all games can be represented by a tree having the initial position as its root vertex. Each path through the tree from the root vertex to a terminal vertex represents a complete game. The complete game tree for checkers has about 10^{40} vertices, while the complete game tree for chess has about 10^{120}. Complete game trees for most nontrivial games are much too large to be exhaustively searched or even stored in a computer. In developing strategies for playing games such as chess and checkers, *tree-pruning strategies* must be used to prune the complete game tree, creating subtrees that explore a limited number of continuations for a limited number of moves. Strategies for playing chess and checkers on a computer are effectively strategies for deciding how the complete game tree should be pruned, and for choosing a move on the basis of information in the pruned game tree.

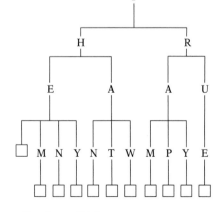

Figure 3.   A small trie.

Bibliography

1962. Adel'son-Vel'skii, G. M., and Landis, E. M. "An Algorithm for the Organization of Information," *Soviet Mathematics Doklady*, **3**, 1259–1263.

1972. Bayer, R., and McCreight, E. M. "Organization and Maintenance of Large Ordered Indexes," *Acta Informatica*, **1**(3), 173–189.

1979. Comer, D. "The Ubiquitous B-tree," *ACM Computing Surveys*, **11**(2), 121–137.

1990. Cormen, T. H., Leiserson, C. E., and Rivest, R. L. *Introduction to Algorithms*. Cambridge, MA: MIT Press, and New York: McGraw-Hill.

Peter Wegner

TROJAN HORSE

See VIRUS, COMPUTER.

TURING AWARD WINNERS

The A. M. Turing Award is made annually by the Association for Computing Machinery (ACM—*q.v.*) "for contributions of a technical nature in the computing community." The award, which currently includes a prize of $25 000, memorializes the extraordinary genius Alan Mathison Turing (*q.v.*). Each recipient gives a lecture that is published in an ACM periodical. The first 22 have been collected into a single volume (Ashenhurst and Graham, 1987). Awards made since its inception in 1966 have been:

1966   Alan J. Perlis (1922–1990) for his work in programming language definition and design and programming techniques, and for his leadership in computer science education.

1967   Maurice V. Wilkes (1913–) (*q.v.*) for his leadership in the early development of stored program computers; his invention of labels, macros and microcode, and for his coinvention of subroutines.

1968   Richard W. Hamming (1915–1998) for his invention of the ERROR CORRECTING AND DETECTING CODE that bears his name.

1969   Marvin M. Minsky (1927–) for his contributions to the theory of computation, programming languages, education, and the beginnings of artificial intelligence (AI—*q.v.*).

1970   James H. Wilkinson (1919–1986) for his contributions to numerical analysis, particularly in the fields of matrix computations and error analysis.

1971   John McCarthy (1927–) for his contributions to AI, particularly the invention of Lisp (*q.v.*).

1972   Edsger W. Dijkstra (1930–2002) for his style and his pervasive influence on programming.

1973   Charles W. Bachman (1924–) for his work in database technology, particularly the creation of the Integrated Data Store (IDS).

1974   Donald Knuth (1938–) for his contributions to the analysis of algorithms, the design of programming languages, and his series of classic texts, *The Art of Computer Programming*.

1975   Allen Newell (1927–1992) and Herbert A. Simon (1916–2001) for their basic contributions to AI, the psychology of human cognition, and their invention of list processing (*q.v.*).

1976   Michael O. Rabin (1931–) and Dana S. Scott (1932–) for their contributions to theoretical computer science.

1977   John W. Backus (1924–) for leading the development of Fortran (*q.v.*) and the creation of the syntax description language Backus–Naur Form (*q.v.*).

1978   R. W. Floyd (1936–) for helping found the theory of parsing, the semantics of programming languages, automatic program verification (*q.v.*), automatic program synthesis, and analysis of algorithms.

1979   Kenneth E. Iverson (1920–) for his pioneering efforts in programming languages and mathematical notation, resulting in the language APL (*q.v.*).

1980   C. A. R. Hoare (1934–) for his fundamental contributions to the definition and design of programming languages, specifically their definitions using axiomatic semantics; his development of ingenious algorithms and advanced data structuring techniques; and his contributions to operating systems (*q.v.*).

1981   Edgar F. Codd (1923–2003) for his contributions to the theory and practice of database management systems (*q.v.*) and the creation of the relational database (*q.v.*) model.

1982   Stephen A. Cook (1939–) for his contributions to the theory of computational complexity (*q.v.*), which laid the foundations for the theory of NP-completeness (*see* NP-COMPLETE PROBLEMS).

1983   Dennis M. Ritchie (1941–) and Kenneth L. Thompson (1943–) for their development and implementation of the Unix operating system (*q.v.*) and the language C (*q.v.*).

1984   Niklaus E. Wirth (1934–) for his development of a sequence of innovative computer languages: Euler, Algol-W, Modula-2, and Pascal (*q.v.*).

1985   Richard M. Karp (1935–) for his fundamental contributions to complexity theory (*see* NP-COMPLETE PROBLEMS), which extended the earlier work of Stephen Cook.

1986   John Hopcroft (1939–) and Robert E. Tarjan (1938–) for their fundamental achievements in the design and analysis of algorithms and data structures.

1987   John Cocke (1925–2002) for his contributions to the design and theory of compilers (*q.v.*) and to the architecture of high-performance computers.

1988   Ivan E. Sutherland (1938–) for his contributions to interactive computer graphics (*q.v.*), exemplified by his invention of Sketchpad.

1989   William M. Kahan (1933–) for his drive and determination to establish and have adopted the current standards for binary and radix-independent floating-point computations (*see* ARITHMETIC, COMPUTER).

1990   Fernando J. Corbató (1926–) for formulating the concepts and leading the development of the Compatible Time-Sharing System (*see* TIME SHARING) (CTSS) and Multics (Multiplexed Information and Computer Service).

1991   A. J. R. G. Milner (1934–) for LCF, the mechanization of Scott's logic of computable functions; ML, the first language to contain polymorphic type-inference; and CCS, a general theory of concurrency (*see* CONCURRENT PROGRAMMING and LOGIC PROGRAMMING).

1992   Butler Lampson (1943–) for his contributions to the development of distributed PC environments and the technology for their implementation.

1993   Juris Hartmanis (1928–) and Richard Stearns (1936–) for their seminal paper that established the foundations for the field of computational complexity (*q.v.*).

1994   Edward A. Feigenbaum (1936–) and Raj Reddy (1937–) for leading in defining the emerging field of applied artificial intelligence and in demonstrating its technological significance.

1995   Manuel Blum (1938–) for his contributions to the foundations of computational complexity (*q.v.*) and its application to cryptography (*q.v.*) and program checking.

1996   Amir Pnueli (1941–) for his seminal work on temporal logic and for outstanding contributions to program verification (*q.v.*).

1997   Douglas Englebart (1925–) for an inspiring vision of the future of interactive computing and the invention of key technologies to help realize this vision.

1998   James Gray (1944–) for seminal contributions to database and transaction processing research and technical leadership in system implementation.

1999   Frederick P. Brooks, Jr. (1931–) for landmark contributions to computer architecture (*q.v.*), operating systems (*q.v.*), and software engineering (*q.v.*).

2000   Andrew Chi-Chih Yao (1947–) for fundamental contributions to the theory of computation, including the complexity-based theory of pseudorandom number generation, cryptography, and communication complexity.

2001   Ole-Johann Dahl (1931–2002) and Kristen Nygaard(1926–2002) for ideas fundamental to object oriented programming (*q.v.*), through their design of the programming languages Simula I and Simula 67.

2002   Ronald L. Rivest (1947–), Adi Shamir (1952–), and Leonard M. Adleman (1947–) for Seminal Contributions to the Theory and Practical Application of Public Key Cryptography.

2003   Alan Kay (1944–) for contributions to object-oriented programming (*q.v.*), personal computing, and development of the Smalltalk language.

Bibliography

1987. Ashenhurst, R. L. and Graham, S. (eds.) *ACM Turing Award Lectures, The First Twenty Years.* New York: ACM Press.

Eric A. Weiss

TURING MACHINE

For articles on related subjects, *see*

+ Algorithms, Theory of
+ Automata Theory
+ Chomsky Hierarchy
+ Formal Languages
+ Turing Test
+ Turing, Alan Mathison

A *Turing machine* is an abstract computing device invented by Alan M. Turing in 1936. A Turing machine consists of (1) a *control unit*, which can assume any one of a finite number of possible states; (2) a *tape*, marked off into discrete squares, each of which can store a single symbol taken from a finite set of possible symbols; and (3) a *read–write* head, which moves along the tape and transmits information to and from the control unit (*see* Fig. 1).

The Basic Model

A Turing machine computes via a sequence of discrete steps. Its behavior at a given time is completely determined by the symbol currently being scanned by the read–write head, and by the internal state of the control unit. On a given step, it will write a symbol on the tape, move along the tape at most one square to the left or right, and enter a new internal state.

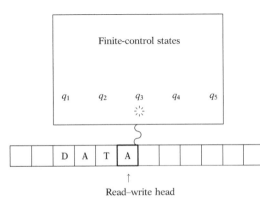

Read–write head

Figure 1. Architecture of a Turing machine.

Table 1.   Program for M.

Present state	B is scanned write/shift/state	O is scanned write/shift/state	1 is scanned write/shift/state	Comment
q_1	1, L, q_7	0, R, q_1	1, R, q_2	Is x 0?
q_2	B, R, q_3	0, R, q_2	1, R, q_2	X $\neq$ 0
q_3	0, L, q_4	0, R, q_3	Error	Write a new 0
q_4	B, L, q_5	0, L, q_4	Error	Go back to x
q_5	Error	1, L, q_5	0, L, q_6	Decrease x
q_6	B, R, q_1	0, L, q_6	1, L, q_6	Go to starting position
q_7	Halt	B, L, q_7	Error	Clean up

The new symbol is permitted to be the same as the current symbol; similarly, it is permissible to stay on the same tape square on a given step and/or to reenter the same state. Certain symbol-state situations may cause the machine to halt. For example, on a single-step the machine in Fig. 1 could begin in state q_3, change the A under scan to an E, move left one square and enter state q_5. It would now be scanning a T; its next action would be uniquely determined by the new state q_5 and the fact that it was scanning a T. It would continue indefinitely in this step-by-step fashion unless it reached a state-symbol combination causing it to halt.

The tape of a Turing machine is often depicted as infinite, but a better approach is to view the tape as finite but indefinitely extendible; that is, new blank squares can be attached to either end of the tape at will to prevent the machine from running off the tape. Thus, there is no uniform bound on either the time or space used by a Turing machine; both are allowed to grow indefinitely.

The *program* of a Turing machine defines its action for the various state-symbol combinations that are possible. This program can be presented in a number of different ways, the two most common being a tabular form and representation as a set of quintuples. In the quintuple convention, the action described above would have been due to the presence of the quintuple $\langle q_3, A, E, L, q_5 \rangle$ where we abbreviate left, right, and no-shift by L, R, and N, respectively.

In tabular form, the state set of a certain machine M corresponds to rows in Table 1 and the symbol set (alphabet) to columns. The blank symbol is denoted by

B. M will compute the function $f(x) = 2^x$ according to the following conventions:

1. x and f(x) are written as binary integers.
2. The tape initially contains x and is blank elsewhere.
3. M begins in state q_1 scanning the leftmost bit of x.
4. When it halts, f(x) will be the only nonblank item on the tape.

The entries in Table 1 labeled *error* cannot occur in a normal computation. By convention, M would halt if started in such state-symbol situations.

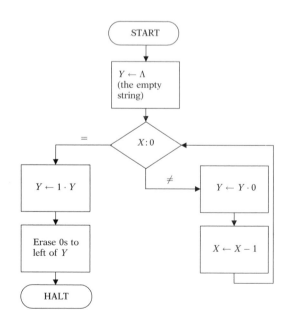

Figure 2.   Flowchart for M.

The algorithm is given by the flowchart in Fig. 2. Essentially, each time the string that initially represents x is changed to represent the next smaller integer, a 0 is written on the tape to the right of x. When x has been decreased to 0, a 1 is written to the left of the generated string of x zeros. The zeros to the left of the 1 are then erased, and M halts. The algorithm is best thought of as an exercise in symbol manipulation rather than as arithmetic.

Modified Turing Machines

Turing's original model has been altered in various ways by a number of different authors. In each case, it has been proved that the altered model and the original model can each compute the same class of functions. This is done by showing that for every machine of a given type, there exists a standard Turing machine that can simulate its behavior, and conversely. Turing machines have also been shown capable of defining exactly the same classes of functions definable by the formal systems of Kleene, Church (*q.v.*), Rosser, Markov, and others. *Church's Thesis* and *Turing's Thesis* assert that their respective models correctly capture the mathematical notion of *effective computability* (i.e. of explicit algorithmic processes). Since the models are equivalent in the sense given above, the two theses are equivalent.

Advantages of Turing's Model

The usefulness of the Turing model of computation lies in its simplicity despite which it has all the fundamental properties that a computing system must possess: a finite program, a large data store, and a deterministic step-by-step mode of computation. In particular, one can show that any computer can be simulated (albeit rather slowly) by a Turing machine. The converse is also true, provided that provisions are made to handle larger amounts of storage as needed. For example, it is true that a minicomputer (*q.v.*) with an accumulator and "sufficiently large" storage can do any computation with only the instructions SUBTRACT, STORE, and TRANSFER ON MINUS, if one assumes the usual conventions of a single-address von Neumann machine (*q.v.*). It is much easier to prove this by showing how to simulate a Turing machine on the minicomputer, rather than by attempting to simulate all of the instructions of a large-scale computer.

Since a Turing machine can simulate any computing device, it follows that anything that cannot be computed on a Turing machine cannot be computed at all. The fact that there are such unsolvable problems motivated Turing to devise his abstract machine.

Turing machines can also simulate each other by interpretive procedures. In particular, it is possible to program a Turing machine to accept the description of the program and input data of any other Turing machine computation, and to simulate that computation. Such a machine is called a *universal Turing machine*.

Bibliography

1956. Shannon, C. E., and McCarthy, J. (eds.) *Automata Studies*. Princeton, NJ: Princeton University Press.

1958. Davis, M. *Computability and Unsolvability*. New York: McGraw-Hill.

1963. Trachtenbrot, B. *Algorithms and Automatic Computing Machines*. Boston: D. C. Heath.

1978. Hartmanis, J. *Feasible Computations and Provable Complexity Properties*. Philadelphia: Society for Industrial and Applied Mathematics.

1997. Lewis, H. R., and Papadimitriou, C. H. *Elements of the Theory of Computation*, 2nd Ed. Upper Saddle River, NJ: Prentice Hall.

Patrick C. Fischer

TURING TEST

For articles on related subjects, *see*

+ Artificial Intelligence (AI)
+ Turing, Alan Mathison
+ Turing Machine

Alan Turing considered the question "Can machines think?" meaningless and suggested that we replace its consideration with a contest that is now called the

Turing Test. In a 1950 article, Turing described an "imitation game": could a human interrogator who uses a teletypewriter to communicate with a human and with a computer determine from the conversation which is the human and which is the computer? The objective of the computer's program is to imitate a human. The computer might say that it had curly hair, liked chocolate ice cream, and preferred skiing to skating. Turing believed that the processes generating intelligent behavior could be understood in terms of the kind of functions that his (abstract) Turing machine could compute. Hence, he believed that an actual computer, if properly programmed, perhaps programmed to learn as a child does, might one day pass the test.

The Turing Test provides an objective, repeatable test that eliminates prejudice based on the appearance of the respondents and focuses on sustained, sophisticated verbal communication that might naturally be taken as a good indicator of intelligence and thinking. Turing did not believe that passing the test constitutes a necessary condition for a computer to think or to be intelligent. He knew that the test requires a certain acting ability upon the part of the computer. For example, Turing suggested that if a computer in the test were asked to add two large numbers, it might pause for thirty seconds and then give an incorrect answer. In principle, a computer might be very "intelligent" and yet incapable of deceiving a human interrogator into believing that it was a conscious, cognitive human.

Many computer programs exist that can maintain limited conversations. ELIZA, a classic conversation program written by Joseph Weizenbaum to appear to emulate a nondirective therapist, is the most famous. ELIZA contains a language analyzer and a script that allows it to carry out conversations in English on a particular theme. The program can take an input from a human and syntactically rephrase it to make it appear to be giving a human response. If a human says to ELIZA, "I'm very excited!" ELIZA may respond, "Is it because you are very excited that you came to me?." When ELIZA cannot produce a syntactical reformulation of the previous sentence entered by a human, it responds with a generic response such as "Please go on."

Turing knew that his test was going to be difficult for a computer to pass, but predicted in 1950 that in about fifty years "an average interrogator will not have more than a 70% chance of making the right identification after five minutes of questioning," but his prediction was too optimistic. But the fifty years has elapsed and no computer has yet come close to passing a Turing Test in which the scope of questioning is unrestricted. Hugh Loebner has offered a $25 000 prize to the creator of any computer program that can pass an unrestricted Turing Test and a $100 000 prize to any computer that can pass a Turing Test using audiovisual input.

The Turing Test has been a controversial test for nearly a half century. Whether a computer will some day pass it is an open question, and the conclusions that should be drawn if a computer does pass it remains a hotly debated philosophical issue.

Bibliography

1950. Turing, A. M. "Computing Machinery and Intelligence," *Mind*, **59**, 433–460.

1976. Weizenbaum, J. *Computer Power and Human Reason.* San Francisco: Freeman.

1999. Krol, M. "Have We Witnessed a Real-life Turing Test?," *IEEE Computer*, **32**, 27–30.

James H. Moor

TURING, ALAN MATHISON

For articles on related subjects, see

+ Algorithms, Theory of
+ Digital Computers, History of: Early
+ Turing Award Winners
+ Turing Machine
+ Turing Test

Alan Mathison Turing (1912–1954) (*see* Fig. 1) was born in London. From an early age, Turing showed an extraordinary aptitude for science and mathematics, and in 1931, entered King's College, Cambridge, as

Figure 1. Alan Mathison Turing (courtesy of the National Archive of the History of Computing, University of Manchester).

a Mathematical Scholar. He was elected a Fellow of King's in 1935 for a dissertation on the Central Limit Theorem of Probability, and the following year was awarded a Smith's prize for his thesis on the same topic.

In 1937, Turing published his now celebrated paper "On Computable Numbers with an Application to the Entscheidungsproblem," in which he introduced the concept of a Turing machine. This paper attracted immediate attention and led to an invitation to Princeton, where he worked with Alonzo Church. After completing a Ph.D. there in 1938, he was offered a post as assistant to John von Neumann (*q.v.*), but he decided to return to Cambridge.

During the Second World War, Turing, being of military age, was required to work on government scientific research. He spent 1939–1945 at Bletchley Park (*see* COLOSSUS), the center of British code-breaking work. For many years, this work was kept confidential by the British government, but it has now

been described by Hodges (1983); Turing's principal role in cracking the codes of the German Enigma cipher machine is now well established. In 1996, the US National Security Agency released Turing's report on his methods. For his work on code-breaking, Turing was awarded the Officer Order of the British Empire (OBE).

In 1945, Turing declined an offer of a Fellowship at King's in favor of joining the newly formed Mathematical Division at the National Physical Laboratory (NPL). His early work on computability, combined with his wartime experience in electronics, had fired him with an enthusiasm for working on the design of an electronic computer. The machine he designed, which was called the *Automatic Computing Engine* (ACE) in recognition of Babbage's pioneering work, was characteristically original. Although Turing knew something of the von Neumann proposals for EDVAC (*q.v.*), he was not unduly influenced by them. The ACE, as Turing conceived it, was too ambitious a project, considering the current state of electronic techniques and he left NPL in 1948, dissatisfied with the rate of progress. But after Turing left NPL, a pilot model embodying Turing's ideas, the Pilot ACE, was completed in 1950. It was a highly successful computer, and some 30 engineered versions of it were subsequently constructed by the English Electric Company under the name DEUCE. The original Pilot ACE is in the Science Museum in Kensington, London.

On leaving NPL, Turing was appointed to a Readership at Manchester University, where he worked in close collaboration with Fred Williams and Tom Kilburn, both pioneers in electronic computers. He was elected a Fellow of the Royal Society in 1951. Papers published while he was at Manchester include work on the Riemann zeta function, a remarkable discussion on computing machinery and intelligence (*see* TURING TEST), and on the chemical basis of morphogenesis.

Turing died tragically in 1954 at the age of 41, a probable suicide. His publications, impressive though some of them are, give only the merest hint of his extraordinary originality and versatility. In recognition of his outstanding pioneering work, the ACM has named its most prestigious award the Turing Award (*q.v.*), awarded annually for outstanding technical contributions to computer science. A definitive biography of Turing has been written by Hodges (1983). *Breaking the Code*, a play based on Hodges' book written by Hugh Whitemore, was performed in London and New York in the late 1980s.

Bibliography

1959. Turing, S. A. M. *Turing*. Cambridge: Heffer & Sons.

1983. Hodges, A. *Alan Turing: The Enigma*. New York: Simon & Schuster. (Reprinted by Walker and Co., New York, 2000).

1992. Turing, A. M. *Collected Works of A. M. Turing. Vol. 1: Machine Intelligence* (ed. D. C. Ince). *Vol. 2: Morphogenesis* (ed. P. T. Saunders). *Vol. 3: Pure Mathematics* (ed. J. L. Britton). Amsterdam: North-Holland.

James H. Wilkinson

TYPEFONT

For articles on related subjects, *see*

+ Monitor, Display
+ PostScript
+ T_EX
+ Word Processing

Introduction

The terms *font* and *typeface* are not quite synonyms. To a professional typesetter, a font is a specific typeface at a specific size. In computing, however, the distinction is often lost because the user can resize any typeface at will. For the purposes of this article, therefore, a *typeface* is a character set having a particular styled appearance, regardless of size or attributes such as italic or bold. A *typefont*, or just *font*, is a typeface of specific size and attribute, such as 12-point italic Helvetica. A *point* is 1/72 of an inch. Common typefonts used with PCs are the italic and bold variants of the *Times Roman, Arial, Chicago*, and *Courier New* typefaces, but there are literally hundreds of specialized fonts that can be added to the menu of those available

for use with word processors, Web browsers, and other software.

Serifs are the tiny picks or tails that, subjectively, make typefonts more readable. Times Roman and the typeface used for the narrative parts of this article are serif fonts. Fonts based on typefaces such as Arial whose letters (like this) do not have serifs are called *sans serif* fonts. Serif fonts are typically used for narrative, and sans serif fonts, because they are arguably more eye-catching at the expense of readability, are typically reserved for headings.

A typefont such as Courier or Courier New in which all characters have the same width is called *monospaced*. A typefont in which each character is allotted a width commensurate to its shape is called *proportional*. Proportional typefonts are more readable, but for printing computer code and numeric output where vertical alignment of data is important, a monospaced format is the usual choice.

Bitmapped vs Outline Fonts

All printers accomplish essentially the same task: they create a pattern of dots on a sheet of paper. The dots may be sized differently or composed of different inks that are transferred to the paper by different means, but all of the images for text and graphics are made up of dots. The smaller the dots, the more attractive the printout. Regardless of how the dots are created, there must be a common method for determining where to place them. The most common schemes are *bitmapped fonts* and *outline fonts*. Bitmapped fonts come in predefined sizes and weights. Outline fonts can, on the fly, be scaled and given special attributes, such as bold, italic, and underlined.

Bitmapped Fonts

Bitmapped images are the computer's equivalent of Gutenberg's type. Bitmaps are generally limited to text and are a fast way to produce a printed page that uses only a few typefonts. Bitmapped fonts are typefaces of a specific size and with specific *attributes* or characteristics, such as bold or italic. The bitmap is a record of the pattern of dots needed

Bitmapped Fonts

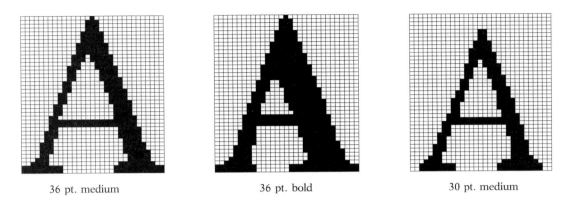

36 pt. medium   36 pt. bold   30 pt. medium

Figure 1. Bitmaps for, respectively, a 36-pt. Times Roman medium capital A, a bold version of the same size letter, and a 30-pt version of the first letter.

to create a specific character in a certain size and with a certain attribute. The bitmaps for a 36-point Times Roman medium capital A, for a 36-point Times Roman bold capital A, and for a 30-point Times Roman medium capital A are all different and specific (*see* Fig. 1). Most printers—whether impact dot matrix, laser, or ink jet—come with a few bitmapped fonts, usually Courier and Times Roman in both normal, italic, and bold varieties as part of their permanent memory (ROM). In addition, many printers have random access memory (RAM) to which the computer can send bitmaps for other fonts.

Outline Fonts

Outline, or *vector* fonts, are used with a *page description language*, such as Adobe *PostScript* or Microsoft *TrueType*, that treats everything on a page—even text—as a graphic. The text and graphics used by the software are converted to a series of commands that the printer's page description language interpreter uses to determine where each dot is to be placed on a page. Page description language interpreters are no longer much slower than matrix printers. Outline fonts are more versatile at producing different sizes of type with different attributes or special effects, and they create more attractive results.

Unlike bitmapped fonts, outline fonts are not limited to specific sizes and attributes of a typeface. Instead, they consist of mathematical descriptions of each character and punctuation mark in a typeface. They are called *outline fonts* because the outline of a Times Roman 36-point capital A is proportionally the same as that of a 24-point Times Roman capital A (*see* Fig. 2). Some printers come with a page description language, most commonly, PostScript or Hewlett-Packard Printer Command Language, in *firmware (q.v.)*—a computer program contained on a microchip. The language can translate outline font commands from the computer's software into the instructions that the printer needs to control where it places dots on a sheet of paper. For printers that do not have a built-in page description language, software can translate the printer language commands into the instructions the printer needs.

Specialized Typefonts

Through use of Knuth's METAFONT or similar techniques, ever newer and more specialized typefonts are being designed and made available. Some may be downloaded free from certain Websites; others are proprietary and licensed for a fee. One of the features that contributed to the early success of the Apple Macintosh was its use of a distinctive sans serif typefont called *Chicago*, **which looks like this** (even

Outline Fonts

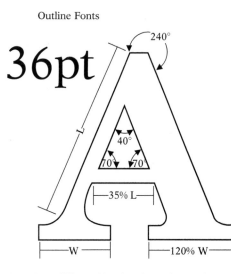

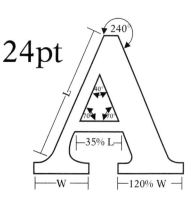

Figure 2. Two differently sized versions of a Times Roman capital A.

when not emboldened). The font is downloadable as freeware for Wintel PCs. And of course, typefonts exist for most of the natural languages of the world, as well as for computer languages such as APL (*q.v.*), which use a specialized typefont. And one can now, for a fee of course, submit samples of one's own handwriting to a company that will return a special typefont that, when used, will mimic that handwriting.

Bibliography

1989. Binns, B. *Better Type*. New York: Watson-Guptill Publications.

1993. Aaron, B. and Aaron, A. *True Type Display Fonts*. San Francisco: Sybex.

1998. White, R. *How Computers Work*, 4th Ed. Indianapolis, IN: Que.

Ron White

UBIQUITOUS COMPUTING

See MOBILE COMPUTING.

UNICODE

See CHARACTER CODES.

UNIVAC I

For articles on related subjects, *see*

+ Digital Computers, History of: Early
+ Eckert, J. Presper

UNIVersal Automatic Computer I (UNIVAC I) was the first commercially available computer in the USA (Fig. 1). Work on the prototype was begun by the Eckert–Mauchly Computer Corporation in 1948 and completed in 1951, when it was delivered to the US Bureau of the Census. During this period, Eckert–Mauchly was acquired by Remington Rand. A total of 46 UNIVAC I computers were delivered during the period 1951–1958.

The UNIVAC I differed from earlier computers in that it handled both numbers and alphabetical characters equally well. One of its innovative features was that it

Figure 1. UNIVAC I.

divorced complex I/O problems from its computational facility. A program, which was stored in ultrasonic memory (*q.v.*), circulated within the delay lines in the form of acoustical pulses that could be read from and written into it. Access time was 40 to 400 μs. Data was transcribed to magnetic tape by a key-to-tape device, or data on punched cards was transcribed to tape with a card-to-tape converter. Input could also be effected from the keyboard of the control console during the processing of a program.

Output was recorded on magnetic tape. Data on output tapes was transcribed to punched cards by a tape-to-card converter or to printed copy by a printer. Alphabetical, numeric, and symbolic characters were accommodated in any combination in reading, writing, and processing operations. Buffered storage registers permitted the central computer to continue processing while other data was being read from or recorded on magnetic tape. Operating characteristics were: circuitry—chiefly serial, 2.25 MHz bit rate; Internal Operating Code—7 bits (four numeric pulses in excess-three notation (*see* CODES), two zone pulses, and one parity pulse); word length—12 characters including sign; block length—60 words; program code—single address, automatic sequencing; internal storage capacity—1000 words or 12 000 characters. Arithmetic speeds were: addition or subtraction, 0.525 ms; multiplication, 2.150 ms; division, 3.890 ms; comparison, 0.365 ms.

Bibliography

1981. Stern, N. *From ENIAC to UNIVAC.* Bedford, MA: Digital Press.

2001. Head, R. V. "Univac: A Philadelphia Story," *IEEE Annals of the History of Computing,* **23**(3), (July–September), 60–63.

Michael M. Maynard

UNIVERSAL PRODUCT CODE

For articles on related subjects, *see*

+ Codes
+ Optical Character Recognition (OCR)
+ Pattern Recognition

Symbols such as that shown in Fig. 1 now appear on almost all retail products for use in electronic checkout procedures. The code is designed to be read by an optical scanner, and is obviously nonsecret, since the numbers used are interpreted just below the code. The five leftmost digits identify the manufacturer through a code assigned by the Uniform Code Council. The five rightmost digits are assigned by the manufacturer to identify various individual products; thus, the price itself is not encoded, but instead a product identification

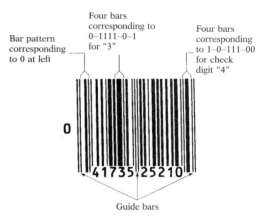

Figure 1. A typical bar code.

number, from which a computer (online to the scanner) can obtain the price by *table lookup* (*see* SEARCHING).

Disregarding the guide bars at the left and right and the two center bars separating the two five-digit groups, all of which are longer than the bars over the interpreted digits, each digit is encoded by a sequence of four alternating light and dark bars of one of four different thicknesses. Each digit will have a unique sequence of bars, or, more precisely, a pair of such sequences, since the pattern of a digit on the right-hand side is the encoded $1s$ complement (*q.v.*) of the pattern it would have had on the left. This is done, so that the program processing the scanner's input can detect whether the product was passed over the reading aperture right-to-left or left-to-right.

In the early 1970s, the first scanners to be widely used by retailers were called *pen* (or *wand*) *scanners.* They used a light-emitting diode (LED) at their tip and a light detector in their barrel and had to actually touch the bar code in order to read it. But laser scanners do not need contact: some can even read a bar code from several feet away rather than the few inches needed for a supermarket scanner, and they are much better able to read a bar code imprinted on a curved surface. The inner workings of a typical supermarket bar code reader are shown in Fig. 2.

Bar code readers have applications other than for retail checkout, inventory control and library circulation being obvious candidates. For this purpose, a pen

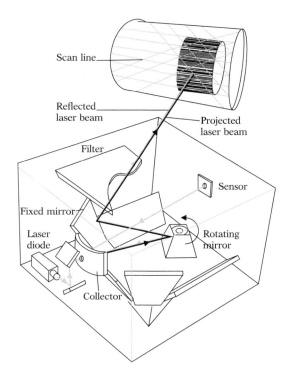

Scan line

Reflected laser beam

Projected laser beam

Filter

Sensor

Fixed mirror

Laser diode

Rotating mirror

Collector

Figure 2. Inside a typical supermarket bar code reader. (Diagram courtesy of *New York Times*).

scanner or a small handheld laser scanner is a very effective tool.

Bibliography

1991. Gallian, J. A. "The Mathematics of Identification Numbers," *The College Mathematics Journal*, **22**(3), (May), 194–202.

1998. Greenman, C. "There's More than One Way to Scan a Bar Code," *New York Times*, **20**, (August), G11.

Edwin D. Reilly

UNIX

For articles on related subjects, *see*

+ C
+ File Server
+ Internet
+ Kernel
+ Linux
+ Multitasking
+ Operating Systems
+ Scripting Languages
+ Shell
+ Time Sharing
+ Virtual Memory
+ Window Environments
+ Workstation

Unix is a time-sharing operating system developed in the early 1970s at Bell Laboratories by Ken Thompson and Dennis Ritchie. Three decades later, Unix stands as one of the most influential systems in computing history. It has been ported to dozens of hardware platforms, and nearly every major vendor supports a product line based on Unix. In 1983, Thompson and Ritchie received the ACM Turing Award (*q.v.*) for their contributions to the computing field.

The roots of Unix can be found in the Multics project of the 1960s in which Thompson and Ritchie were participants. But where Multics was a high-profile collaborative project, Unix was developed quietly by individuals searching for a more hospitable programming environment. The first production version of Unix appeared in 1971 and ran on a PDP-9. In 1973, Unix became the first operating system to be written in a high-level language when all but a small part was rewritten in C, a programming language developed specifically for Unix. The first widely available public release, version 6, was released in 1976 and ran on a PDP-11. Version 7, the first portable Unix system, came two years later and ran on several different hardware platforms, including the PDP-11, Interdata 8/32, and the Digital Equipment VAX.

The most influential of the non-AT&T development sites was the University of California at Berkeley, which produced the Berkeley Software Distributions (BSD) versions of Unix. Berkeley also ported Unix to the VAX architecture and added support for virtual memory, demand paging, and the TCP/IP (*q.v.*) network protocols. Today, many parts of Unix and the C language have been standardized by international standards committees, and Unix has become the operating system of choice for most Internet Service Providers (ISPs).

Structure

Unix is a multitasking, multiuser operating system. Many users can use a single Unix system simultaneously, each of them having in effect a personal machine environment at a networked PC. Any computer running Unix can provide the same services, from small portable computers (*q.v.*) to the largest mainframes (*q.v.*), the only difference being speed and storage capacity.

The Unix Kernel

Unix carefully distinguishes between the operating system *kernel* and user applications. Each user program runs as a separate *process*, making system calls into the kernel to perform such tasks as accessing files or allocating additional memory. The kernel itself was deliberately kept small. By implementing services as processes, users could easily replace an existing implementation of a service with an entirely new one by replacing the utility providing the service. Modern flavors of Unix have adopted symmetric multiprocessor technology with multithreaded kernels that allow any process to run on any CPU in a multiprocessor system. The best-known Unix kernel is called *Linux* (*q.v.*).

Unix Shells

The original user interface (*q.v.*) for Unix was a command interpreter, called a *shell*. A shell processes keyboard input and performs user-requested tasks. The shell is a normal (albeit sophisticated) program executing as its own process. Running the shell as a process has two benefits. First, users can modify it as easily as any other program. Several shells, including the C shell and Korn shell, have become popular in addition to the original Bourne shell. The Bourne shell supports the creation of multiple simultaneous jobs, but provides limited means of controlling them once they have been started. The C shell permits users to suspend and later resume jobs, and

to move jobs from foreground to background. Having shell commands run as regular processes also makes it possible for ordinary users to write *command scripts*, files containing arbitrary commands. The shell can process commands contained in a file as easily as those entered at the keyboard.

Command Names

Unix command names are highly abbreviated (for instance, cp for *copy*, df for *show disk free space*); they arose from the early era in which keyboard entry was slow and painful. Since then, graphical user interfaces (GUIs) have been developed to offer a more user-friendly interface for simple operations. These provide users with mouse and menu control, together with multiple windows, screens, and virtual desktops. The X Window System, developed originally by MIT, solved not only the problem of building GUI systems, but also of how to display windows and data from programs running on hardware at different physical locations. This follows Unix's tradition of remote execution and distributed systems (*q.v.*), based on the client–server (*q.v.*) model.

File System

Unix provides a hierarchical file system in which directories hold files and other (sub) directories. The resulting file tree is shared by all users, making it straightforward to name and find files, including those belonging to other users. A file can be named by its full path name which lists the directories on the path from the root of the tree to the file, or by its short name, in which case, the file is assumed to be in the current directory. A user can lock files so that other users cannot access them; a system of protection bits sets the rights of other users. Other users can be granted selective access to the files on a read-only or a read/write basis.

Unix provides a single, uniform way of accessing file contents. Programs process all files in exactly the same manner; they need not concern themselves with record sizes or differing access methods if they do not wish to. File operations treat the data in files as an uninterpreted bit stream. In addition, Unix uses *device independence* to make such devices as terminals and printers appear the same as files. The shell exploits this abstraction by allowing a program to receive input from any source without prejudice: from the keyboard, a file, or even the output of another program. Redirection operators <, >, and | provide the shell user with powerful tools to control the flow of data between programs and files. For example, the command `sort` reads lines from the terminal (until the user signals end of input) sending the sorted contents back to the terminal. To sort the data in a file, the same utility is invoked, but its input is redirected from the specified file (here called `input`):

```
sort < input
```

Output can then be redirected to an arbitrary file (here called `output`) as follows:

```
sort < input > output
```

Unix provides a service called *pipes* that allows users to connect the output of one program to the input of another without using an intermediary file. For example, entering:

```
Ps -aux | sort
```

invokes the command `ps -aux`, which displays the names of logged in users, and the processes that they are running. It then pipes the output from `ps` into `sort`. The result is a sorted list of user processes. The two commands of a pipeline execute *concurrently*, with each process running just long enough to fill its output or empty its input pipe. Any number of programs can be chained together with pipes. This is one of the most powerful features of the Unix shell.

Tools

Unix is not just an operating system; it is an environment complete with a rich set of powerful tools. The operating system kernel itself runs on a bare machine, controlling access to such resources as memory, devices, and the CPU. Users interact with the shell only indirectly. Instead, they invoke editors, compilers, text processors, and other utility programs that in turn request kernel services when accessing files. Unix introduced many tools now taken for granted in computing, including document formatters and spelling checkers (*q.v.*).

The `make` utility takes a recipe describing the exact steps needed to build one complex system of files from another complex set of files. Typically `make` directs a compiler or text processor to build a program or format a document. If changes occur in the source files, `make` rebuilds only those parts of the system that have changed since the last time the system was built.

The `lex` and `yacc` utilities provide "meta-tools" for the construction of compilers (*q.v.*) and other text translation programs. The `grep` utility searches text files for lines matching a specified *regular expression*. Grep makes it possible to locate quickly all references to a particular variable or keyword in a collection of files. The `awk` utility extends this idea, providing a quick way to extract or modify the information in text files. The Perl language has recently been introduced as a modern replacement for `awk`, providing structured programming (*q.v.*), optimized for text processing.

Evaluation

Unix was the first highly interactive operating system. Unix was written *by* programmers *for* programmers, and interactive systems provide the most productive environment for them. By using the system as it was being developed, its weaknesses quickly became apparent and were corrected before it was too late. Unix's unique ability to change and evolve in response to feedback from its user community and to exploit changes in hardware technology has been a major factor in its success. One of the main goals of the Free Software Foundation (FSF–*q.v.*) is the creation of an improved Unix-like operating system. The GNU Linux operating system, a first step, is a hugely popular PC freeware system. Other popular systems for PCs, not part of the GNU effort, include FreeBSD and Net-BSD based on the BSD 4.4 source code.

Bibliography

1978. Ritchie, D. M., and Thompson, K. "The UNIX Time-sharing System," *The Bell System Technical Journal*, **57**(6), 1905–1930. Special issue devoted to the Unix time-sharing system.

1986. Bach, M. J. *The Design of the UNIX Operating System.* Upper Saddle River, NJ: Prentice Hall.

1999. Cooke, D., Urban, J., and Hamilton, S. "Unix and Beyond: An Interview with Ken Thompson," *Computer,* **32**(5), (May), 58–64.

Thomas Narten and Mark Burgess

USER INTERFACE

For articles on related subjects, see

+ Interactive Input Devices
+ Virtual Reality
+ Window Environments

A *user interface* is that portion of an interactive computer system that communicates with the user. Design of the user interface includes any aspect of the system that is visible to the user. Once, interfaces consisted of jumper wires in patch boards, punched cards prepared offline, and batch printouts. Today, keyboards, mice, and graphical displays are the most common interface hardware. As computers become more powerful, the critical bottleneck in applying computer-based systems to solve problems is more often in the user interface rather than in the computer hardware or software.

Design of a User Interface

The design of a user interface is often divided into conceptual, semantic, syntactic, and lexical levels. The conceptual level describes the basic entities underlying the user's view of the system and the actions possible upon them. The semantic level describes the functions performed by the system. This corresponds to a description of the functional requirements of the system, but it does not address how the user will invoke the functions. The syntactic level describes the sequences of inputs and outputs necessary to invoke the functions described. The lexical level determines how the inputs and outputs are actually formed from primitive hardware operations.

User Interface Management Systems

A user interface management system (UIMS) is a software component that is separate from the application program that performs the underlying task. The UIMS conducts the interaction with the user, implementing the syntactic and lexical levels, while the rest of the system implements the semantic level. Like an operating system or graphics library, a UIMS separates functions used by many applications and moves them to a shared subsystem. It centralizes implementation of the user interface and permits some of the effort of designing tools for user interfaces to be amortized over many applications and shared by them. It also encourages consistent "look and feel" in user interfaces to different systems, since they share the user interface component.

Syntactic Level Design: Interaction Styles

The principal classes of user interfaces currently in use are command languages, menus, forms, natural language, direct manipulation, virtual reality, and combinations of these. Each interaction style has its merits for particular user communities or sets of tasks.

Command Language

Command language interfaces (CLIs) use artificial languages, much like programming languages. They are concise and unambiguous, but they are often difficult to learn and remember. However, since they usually permit a user to combine constructs in new and complex ways, they can be more powerful for advanced users. For them, command languages provide a strong feeling that they are in charge and that they are taking the initiative rather than responding to the computer.

Menu

Menu-based user interfaces explicitly present the options available to a user at each point in a dialogue. Users read a list of items, select the one most appropriate to their task, type or point to indicate their selection, verify that the selection is correct, initiate the action, and observe the effect. If the terminology and meaning of the items are understandable and distinct, users can accomplish their tasks with little learning or memorization and few keystrokes. The greatest benefit may be that there is a clear structure to decision making, since only a few choices are presented at a time.

Form Fill-In

Menu selection usually becomes cumbersome when data entry is required; form fill-in is useful here. Users see a display of related fields, move a cursor among the fields, and enter data where desired, much as they would with a paper form for an invoice, personnel data sheet, or order form.

Natural Language

The principal benefit of natural language-user interfaces is, of course, that the user already knows the language. The hope that computers will respond properly to arbitrary natural language sentences or phrases has engaged many researchers and system developers, but with limited success thus far. Natural language interaction usually provides little context for issuing the next command, frequently requires a "clarification dialogue," and may be slower and more cumbersome than the alternatives. Therefore, given the state of the art, such an interface must be restricted to some subset of natural language, and the subset must be chosen carefully—both in vocabulary and range of syntactic constructs.

Graphical User Interfaces

In a graphical user interface (GUI), a set of objects called *icons* is presented on a screen, and the user has a repertoire of manipulations that can be performed on any of them. This means that the user has no command language to remember beyond the standard set of manipulations, few cognitive changes of mode, and a reminder of the available objects and their states

shown continuously on the display. Examples of this approach include painting programs, spreadsheets (*q.v.*), manufacturing or process control systems that show a schematic diagram of the plant, air traffic control systems, some educational and flight simulations, videogames (*q.v.*), and the Xerox Star desktop and its descendants (Macintosh, Windows, and various X Window file managers).

Virtual Reality

Virtual reality (*q.v.*) environments carry the user's illusion of manipulating real objects and the benefit of natural interaction still further. By coupling the motion of the user's head to changes in the images presented on a head-mounted display, the illusion of being surrounded by a world of computer-generated images, or a virtual environment, is created. Hand-mounted sensors allow the user to interact with these images as if they were real objects located in the surrounding space. Augmented reality interfaces blend the virtual world with a view of the real world through a half-silvered mirror or a TV camera, allowing virtual images to be superimposed on real objects and annotations or other computer data to be attached to real objects. The state of the art in virtual reality requires expensive and cumbersome equipment and provides very low-resolution display, so such interfaces are currently used mainly where a feeling of "presence" in the virtual world is of paramount importance, such as training of firefighters or treatment of phobias.

Other Issues

Although interfaces using modern techniques such as direct manipulation are often easier to learn and use than conventional ones, they are considerably more difficult to build. Appropriate higher-level software engineering (*q.v.*) concepts and abstractions for dealing with these new interaction techniques are still needed. Specialized techniques for the actual design and building of direct manipulation interfaces are one solution. Specifying the graphical appearance of the user interface (the "look") via direct manipulation is relatively straightforward and provided by many current tools, such as Visual Basic, but describing the behavior of the dialogue (the "feel") is more difficult and not yet well supported; predefined or "canned" controls and widgets represent the current state of the art.

Input Devices

Input operations range from open-ended word processing or painting programs to simple repeated Page Up or Page Down key presses for page turning in an electronic document. While keyboards and mice have been the standard computer input devices, there are increasingly attractive alternatives for many tasks. High-precision touchscreens have made this durable device more attractive for public access, home control, process control, and other applications. Joysticks, trackballs, and data tablets with styluses with numerous variations are also useful for various pointing and manipulation tasks. Speech input for voice mail and speech recognition (*q.v.*) for commands are effective, especially over the telephone and for the physically disabled (*see* DISABLED, COMPUTERS AND THE). Other techniques for input include keys that can be dynamically labeled, speech, 3D pointing, hand gesture,

whole body motion, and visual line of gaze. Figure 1 shows a glove input device.

Output Devices

Output mechanisms must be successful in conveying to the user the current state of the system and what actions are currently available. The cathode ray tube display has been the standard approach, but flat panel displays and hard copy devices are alternatives. Current high-resolution screens provide in excess of 1000×1000 pixels; but their resolution (in dots per inch) is still far cruder than a typical paper printout or photograph, and their size is far smaller than a typical user's desk or other work surface. High-resolution displays can improve the readability of textual displays so that performance can match that of typewritten documents. Synthesized or digitized voice output is effective and economical, especially in telephone applications and for the physically disabled. Voice mail systems that store and forward digitized voice messages continue to grow in popularity. Other output media include animated graphics, audio, windows, icons, active value displays, manipulatable objects, hypertext (*q.v.*), multimedia

Figure 2. A head-mounted virtual reality display combined with an eye tracker. The 3D tracker attached above the user's left eye reports the position and orientation of the head. The computer uses this information to update the viewpoint of the display constantly. This unit also measures the position of the user's eye, by monitoring it through the mirror located in front of the left eye. (Courtesy Tuffs University.)

Figure 1. A Cyberglove (® Virtual Technologies, Inc., Palo Alto, CA).

(*q.v.*), and head-coupled displays. Figure 2 shows a head-mounted virtual reality display.

Bibliography

1992. Shneiderman, B. *Designing the User Interface: Strategies for Effective Human–Computer Interaction*, 2nd Ed. Reading, MA: Addison-Wesley.

1995. Myers, B. A. "User Interface Software Tools," *ACM Transactions on Computer–Human Interaction*, **2**(1), 64–103.

1999. Stephenson, N. *In the Beginning Was the Command Line.* New York: Avon Books.

Robert J. K. Jacob

a
b
c
d
e
f
g
h
i
j
k
l
m
n
o
p
q
r
s
t
u
v, w
x, y
z

VW

VARIABLE

See GLOBAL AND LOCAL VARIABLES.

VECTOR COMPUTER

See PARALLEL PROCESSING; and
SUPERCOMPUTERS.

VECTOR GRAPHICS

See COMPUTER GRAPHICS.

VERIFICATION

See PROGRAM VERIFICATION.

VIDEODISC

See OPTICAL STORAGE.

VIDEOGAMES

For articles on related subjects, see
+ Computer Games

+ Personal Computing
+ Virtual Reality

Before the advent of personal computers, the only way to play a "computer game" was to buy a videogame console and attach it to a television set. The first console of this kind was Odyssey, invented by Ralph Baer and marketed by Magnavox. The game allowed one to play ping-pong, hockey, and similar games. Odyssey sold 100 000 units in 1972, and in the same year, Nolan Bushnell's company, Atari, released Pong as an arcade game.

Early Standalone Games

In 1974, Atari developed Pong for the home market. Because the game had not yet been patented, over a dozen competing versions of Pong were released. In 1976, Fairchild Instruments released Channel F, a two-player console with multipurpose controllers and, for the first time, the ability to play different games by inserting game cartridges.

In 1977, Milton Bradley developed a game called CompIV, which was very similar to the "Mastermind" board game. It was played as a standalone game; it did not require a TV set. During the same year, the Atari Video Control System (VCS) was released. Many Atari cartridges played the same games as Atari's arcade games. During Christmas 1977, sales of handheld games cut deeply into video game sales, and at the same time, programmable consoles using the Z80 chip were beginning to spell the end of the dedicated console.

V,W

In 1978, Magnavox released Odyssey2, which was similar to the VCS except that it also had a keyboard. Bally introduced Basic (*q.v.*) on its Professional Arcade, allowing owners to write their own game programs. The VCS became popular when Atari released the home version of Space Invaders, but VCS faced serious competition when Mattel released its Intellivision console. It featured better graphics and more sports titles than the existing systems.

In 1981, Activision released four games to run on the VCS. By 1982, manufacturers had developed more ambitious videogame consoles, with new versions of game controllers and more storage. Milton Bradley's Vectrex had a built-in black and white monitor, 64 KB RAM and an 8-bit processor. Emerson's Arcadia 2001 had 28 KB RAM. Coleco's Colecovision had 32 KB for code, 48 KB RAM, and 48 moving objects. Atari released its 5200 Super Game System to compete with the Colecovision. Voice modules became available for the Intellivision and Odyssey2 consoles. Strategy games increased in popularity.

Modern Videogames

Seven million consoles and 75 000 000 game cartridges were sold in 1983, prior to a big shakeout in which many manufacturers left the videogame market or went out of business. At the same time Nintendo developed its Famicom (Family Computer) for the Japanese market. And at about this time the first interesting games for PCs began appearing.

In 1984, Mattel sold Intellivision to a new company called Intellivision, Inc. Atari was sold to Jack Tramiel, the founder of Commodore. Nintendo sold 2 500 000 Famicoms and 15 000 000 cartridges in Japan and released an American version called the *Nintendo Entertainment System* (NES) in 1985. Nintendo had a huge success with "Super Mario Brothers," an expanded version of their "Mario Bros." arcade game, which itself was an indirect sequel to "Donkey Kong." Intellivision later became INTV Corp.

In 1986, Atari reentered the videogame market by introducing the 7800 console along with "Pole Position II," "Joust," "Ms. Pacman," and "Deluxe Asteroids." Sega introduced its Master System. In 1988, NEC in Japan released the PC Engine, the first machine to support a CD-ROM drive. In 1989, NEC began selling a version of the PC Engine called TurboGrafx-16 in the USA. Sega introduced Genesis, the first 16-bit machine. Nintendo began to sell its monochrome, 8-bit handheld game machine, Gameboy. Packaged with "Tetris," the Gameboy became a worldwide success. Atari's 16-bit color Lynx quickly followed.

By 1991, Sega controlled a large share of the videogame market, thanks largely to a game called *Sonic the Hedgehog*. Nintendo released its 16-bit Super Nintendo Entertainment System (SNES) to compete with the Genesis. Sega retaliated by releasing a CD-ROM add-on to the Genesis, but it was not popular. Nintendo sold more than 1 000 000 copies of "Starfox" in 1993. Acclaim released "Mortal Kombat" for the home but reduced the violence found in the arcade equivalent. Multimedia consoles proliferated.

During 1994, Nintendo's Gateway system was installed in 5000 airplane seats and 10 000 hotel rooms. Sega introduced the 32-X, which in effect turned the 16-bit Genesis into a 32-bit machine. One week later, Sega announced its forthcoming 32-bit CD-ROM-based Saturn, and most customers elected to wait for it rather than switch to the Genesis. Sony announced its 32-bit Playstation. Acclaim's "Mortal Kombat II" and Nintendo's "Donkey Kong Country" for SNES were very popular introductions. Nintendo announced Project Reality, a joint project with Silicon Graphics to develop a 64-bit system.

In 1995, Sega and Sony both released new systems. Sega was first by four months, but the Sony Playstation proved more popular. Nintendo released its Virtual Boy system, which displayed games in 3D, but it did not sell well. Project Reality was renamed Ultra 64 and was delayed until 1996.

The advent of multimedia brought with it the possibility of attractive games for PCs and Macintoshes, but the cost of a PC is roughly 10 times that of a dedicated game machine, so it is not likely that the PC will take over. Instead, the trend is toward faster, better game consoles. Future game consoles will continue to stretch the state of the art, which is 64-bit bandwidth (*q.v.*), multiprocessors (*q.v.*), 3D graphics, DVD, and high-quality sound and picture. Iraq bought thousands of the Sony Playstation 2 in late 2000 just for the sake of the powerful chip that it contains. Microsoft announced its entry into the market in January 2001, sending a strong signal that the demand for videogames will continue to increase.

Keith S. Reid-Green and Leonard Herman

VIRTUAL MEMORY

For articles on related subjects, see

+ Associative Memory
+ Cache Memory
+ Distributed Systems
+ Internet
+ Memory Hierarchy
+ Memory Management
+ Memory Protection
+ Multiprogramming
+ Object-Oriented Programming
+ Operating Systems
+ Working Set
+ World Wide Web

Virtual memory is the simulation of a storage space so large that programmers do not need to reprogram or recompile their works when the capacity of a local memory or the configuration of a network changes. The concept was devised by the designers of Atlas (*q.v.*) at the University of Manchester in the 1950s. Virtual memory is even more useful in modern computers, which have more things to hide—on-chip caches, separate RAM chips, local disk storage, network file servers (*q.v.*), large numbers of separately compiled program modules, and other computers on the local network or the Internet.

Virtual memory designers have three major concerns: (1) address mapping, the process of translating virtual addresses to memory addresses, should easily accommodate the kinds of program objects that programmers are working with; (2) address mapping should cost no

more than a few per cent of memory access time; and (3) overall system throughput (*q.v.*) and response time should be within a few per cent of the best possible performance attainable for a given workload.

Mapping

There are many ways to translate virtual addresses to memory addresses. They depend on whether program and data objects are stored as fixed-size pages or variable-size segments, whether segments are subdivided into pages, and whether objects are individually protectable and sharable. Although virtual memory was invented before object-oriented programming, its designers anticipated the structure and benefits of objects. All mapping varieties depend on a two-level table structure of the kind shown in Fig. 1.

The mapping from a two-dimensional processor address (object s, byte-within-object b) to a one-dimensional memory location address operates in two stages. The objects table maps an object number s to a *handle* (t, a, x) signifying that the object is of type t, the accessing process is allowed accesses only of kind a, and the object's system-wide unique name is x. The descriptor table maps a unique name x to a descriptor for the object. The descriptor contains a presence bit with $P = 1$, meaning that the object is in main memory, a usage bit with $U = 1$, meaning that the object has been recently used, a base address c, and length k of the main memory region holding the object.

There is one object table for each protection domain, and the domain's object table defines the privileges of any process operating within it. A *d*omain *id*entifier register (*did*) in the processor tells the mapper which object table is to be used. There is only one descriptor for every object; a single system-wide descriptor table holds them all. A shared object can be listed in several domains, each with its own local object number; all those handles point to the same descriptor. When an object is relocated—by removing it from main memory or by moving it to a new region of main memory—only its descriptor is updated to show the change. A *translation lookaside buffer* (TLB) accelerates mapping by bypassing the tables on repeat accesses to the same object location path. If the TLB already contains

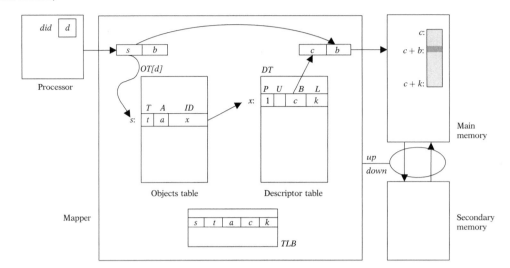

Figure 1. Object-oriented virtual memory.

the path being attempted, the mapper bypasses the lookups in the object and descriptor tables. In practice, small TLBs (e.g. 64 or 128 cells) give high enough hit ratios that address translation efficiency goals that are easy to meet.

Sooner or later the processor will generate an unmapped object address. The mapping unit will detect this and halt, issuing a signal *address fault*. In response, the operating system interrupts the running program and invokes an *address fault handler* that (1) locates the needed object in the secondary memory, (2) selects a region of main memory to put that object in, (3) empties that region if need be, (4) copies the needed object into that region, and then (5) restarts the interrupted program, allowing it to complete its reference. The processor will encounter a *bounds fault* if it attempts an offset larger than the length of a segment. It will encounter a *protection fault* if it attempts an access type not enabled by the access code—for example, attempting to write into a read-only page. Since they signify major unrecoverable errors, these faults invoke fault-handlers that normally abort the running process.

A *page replacement policy* frees memory by removing objects. The objective is to minimize "mistakes"— replacements that are quickly undone when the process recalls the object replaced. This objective is met ideally when the object selected for replacement will not be used again for the longest time among all the loaded objects. When the memory space allocated to a process is fixed in size, the usual strategy is LRU (least recently used); when space can vary, it is WS (working set–*q.v.*).

This structure provides the memory partitioning needed for multiprogramming. A process can refer *only* to the objects listed in its object table. The operating system can adjust the size of the main memory region allocated to a process so that the rate of address faults stays within acceptable limits. If too many processes are active at once, the average space available to any one of them will fall below the limit, the average fault rate will overload the queue at the secondary memory device, and the system throughput will drop sharply—the condition known as *thrashing*. System throughput will be near-optimal when the virtual memory guarantees each active process just enough space to hold its working set.

Bibliography

1995. Tanenbaum, A. S. *Distributed Operating Systems.* Upper Saddle River, NJ: Prentice Hall.

1996. Denning, P. J. "Virtual Memory," *Computing Surveys,* **28**(4), (December), 213–216.

Peter J. Denning

VIRTUAL REALITY

For articles on related topics, *see*

The Beginning

The term *virtual reality* (VR) stems from the work of Jaron Lanier and his coworkers at VPL Research in the late 1980s. Steve Bryson, another early VR researcher, defined VR as "The creation of the *effect of immersion* in a computer-generated *three-dimensional environment* in which objects have *spatial presence*." Bryson simplifies this strict definition to mean "things as opposed to pictures of things." The implementation of this new experience uses advanced computer graphics hardware, interactive software worlds, and immersive interface devices. The interface devices made famous by VPL Research are the head-mounted display (HMD) and an electronic glove (DataGlove). The HMD and gloves are the views of VR that has captured the public's imagination through their use in TV commercials, movies, and magazines.

History

During the 1960s, 1970s, and 1980s, the military was a major sponsor and adopter of computer-based simulators. Some of this early work was funded by the Defense Advanced Research Projects Agency (DARPA). In the late 1990s, the price of the technology required to build VR systems came down rapidly. Desktop workstations, HMDs for less than $200, joysticks that let a user feel parts of the environment (force-feedback), and low-cost or free VR software led to a dramatic increase in the number of universities, students, and companies working in the field. VR research from the

early 1990s has also been a spur for advancements in other fields. An example is the Nintendo 64 game system developed by Silicon Graphics, Inc. (SGI), an early producer of VR computer systems and supporter of VR research. The Nintendo 64 graphics are a combination of hardware and software that was only available to the best-funded researchers in 1994. By 1997, this system could be purchased at toy stores for $150, and even better systems are now available for a comparable price.

Technology
Graphics and Hardware

Some of the most important work in VR centers around three-dimensional (3D) real-time systems (*q.v.*). Computer users in the 1990s were accustomed to computers that display only two-dimensional (2D) graphics. The 2D systems are best exemplified by the desktop metaphors of the Apple Macintosh or Microsoft Windows operating systems. These systems display 2D windows on a standard display monitor (*q.v.*). Three-dimensional graphics are based on object prototypes that are created using 3D data in true 3D space. The ability to build and display complex 3D graphics was beyond the ability of all PCs until the mid-1990s. The first generation of VR computers were advanced computers with specialized graphics hardware. One of the early suppliers was Silicon Graphics (SGI), which began to develop graphics hardware boards for its workstations (*q.v.*) that excelled at 3D mathematics, texturing, and display. By the 1990s, as the market began to expand, SGI encountered competition from a variety of companies such as Microsoft, Sun Microsystems, Intergraph, and a plethora of video-board manufacturers.

Interface Devices

With the creation of 3D worlds, it was quickly realized that the tools that they normally used to interact with PCs, namely keyboards and mice, did not work well in these new worlds. VPL Research was one of the pioneers in the creation of new interface devices with their data glove. Figure 1 shows a haptic feedback device that interacts with the user's sense of touch. The interface

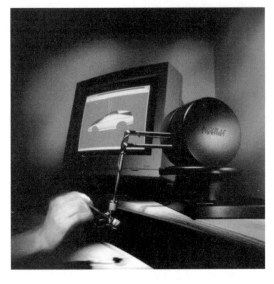

Figure 1. Using the PHANTOM 1.5 haptic device, users can "touch" and manipulate objects that exist within the computer. Applications include surgical stimulation, "digital clay" modeling and seismic data analysis. (Photo courtesy of Sens-Able Technologies, Inc.)

between the user and the computer remains one of most poorly researched areas in VR even as of 2003.

Networking

The early military simulator, SIMNET, did not do much as a standalone unit. But when two or more of these units are connected to form a network, the ability of users to interact with each other and with the virtual world around them makes the simulation much more interesting. Figure 2 shows an application of a networked virtual environment. By the mid-1990s, there existed a small number of research projects, mostly at universities, interested in studying and advancing the use of networked virtual environments. Despite this academic research, large-scale implementation was still dominated by the military. This began to change as the Internet (*q.v.*) became more accessible to the public and the costs of VR systems decreased. With the proliferation of low-cost VR systems, more users began to develop simple worlds.

Figure 2. The Virtual Space Devices Omni Directional Treadmill, which uses the NPSNET-IV networked virtual environment, and the Boston Dynamics BDI-Guy human. (Image courtesy of Michael Zyda, Naval Postgraduate School.)

Areas of Study
Interactivity

The creation of VR worlds was driven by the desire to let users interact with real and imagined environments in new and interesting ways. In the real world, people can interact with anything that they see, hear, touch, or smell. They can interact using a variety of methods and senses. Picking up a glass, smelling a rose, talking to a friend are all common ways by which people interact with the real world. In attempting to duplicate the real world or, more simply, the experience of that world, the need for this level of interaction comes into focus.

Presence and Immersion

People in the real world implicitly know that they are there. For example, you know that when you want to reach out and pick up a glass, your hand will be at the end of your arm, and that your arm is attached to your shoulder. You also know that this arrangement can reach objects within a certain distance from your body. People generally understand their bodies and the presence of those bodies in the environment they inhabit. This issue has been addressed by VR practitioners who build their systems to "remove" the user from the real world. If a user is going to experience a discontinuity in perception when both the real world and the virtual environment can be seen at the same time, one solution is to restrict the user from seeing any of the real world. One advantage to HMDs, in addition to bringing an image close to the user and moving with the user, is that the HMD often limits the user's ability to see the real world.

Latency

Latency is the delay that exists between the issuance of a command and initiation of the desired action. People have a well-developed ability to notice time discrepancies. Talking on the phone to another person halfway around the world is an obvious example—people at both ends notice a lag between the end of a sentence and the start of the other person's response. The time between these two events is the latency. Anyone who has experienced this delay knows how unsettling it can be. This is an issue that pervades VR systems and hinders the user's feeling of immersion. When a user turns his or her head in a VR world, the world should respond. If the world takes half a second to begin turning, the user will notice. Those acquainted with the theater know that inaccuracies in an actor's timing will decrease the user's suspension-of-belief, a property that is thus strongly related to the VR world's issue of presence.

Bibliography

1995. Durlach, N., and Mavor, A. (eds.) *Virtual Reality: Scientific and Technological Challenges.* Washington, DC: National Academy Press.

1999. Singhal, S., and Zyda, M. *Networked Virtual Environments: Design and Implementation.* Reading, MA: Addison-Wesley.

William R. Cockayne

VIRUS, COMPUTER

For articles on related subjects, see

+ Computer Crime
+ Data Security
+ Firewall
+ Hacker

A *virus* is a piece of program code that attaches copies of itself to other programs, incorporating itself into them so that the modified programs, while possibly still performing their intended functions, surreptitiously do other things. Programs so corrupted seek others to which it can attach the virus, and so the "infection" spreads. Successful viruses lie low until they have thoroughly infiltrated the system, and reveal their presence only when they cause damage. Viruses work by altering disk files that contain otherwise harmless programs. When an infected program is invoked, it tries to modify other program files to include a copy of the virus code and inserting an instruction to branch to that code at each program's starting point. A virus can spread when information is shared: on a multiuser system with shared disk facilities, or in a PC environment in which users download programs from the Internet (*q.v.*) or if they share diskettes (*q.v.*), CDs, or other exchangeable media.

Other Malicious Programs

The term "virus" is a popular catchall for other kinds of malicious software. A *logic bomb* or *time bomb* is a destructive program activated by a certain combination of circumstances, or on a certain date. A *Trojan horse* is any bug (*q.v.*) inserted into a computer program that takes advantage of the trusted status of its host by surreptitiously performing unintended functions. A *worm* is a distributed program that invades computers on a network. Like viruses, worms spread by replication; unlike them, they may run as independent processes rather than as a part of a host program, and can occupy volatile memory rather than disk storage. To escape detection, viruses normally reside in binary rather than source code and thus do not survive recompilation or reinstallation of a backup. Just as worms are destroyed by shutting down and then rebooting all affected machines, viruses are eradicated by simultaneously recompiling all affected programs.

V,W

History and Examples

The idea of a maliciously self-propagating computer program originated in Gerrold's 1972 novel *When Harlie Was One*, in which a computer program called telephone numbers at random until it found another computer into which it could spread. Worms were also presaged in science fiction by Brunner's 1975 novel *The Shockwave Rider*. The first actual virus program was created in 1983 as the result of a discussion in a computer security seminar and described at the AFIPS Computer Security Conference the following year.

At 9 P.M. on 2 November 1988, a worm program was inserted into the Internet by Cornell graduate student Robert T. Morris. It exploited several security flaws in systems running Unix (*q.v.*) to spread itself from system to system. Although discovered within hours, it required a huge effort by programmers at affected sites to counteract and eliminate the worm over a period of weeks. Again, it was unmasked by a bug: under some circumstances it replicated itself so fast that it seriously slowed down the infected host. In 1990, Morris was convicted and sentenced to three years probation, fined $10 000, and ordered to perform 400 hours of community service.

On 6 March 1992, the Michelangelo virus, although widely heralded as a worldwide threat to computer systems, actually did little damage. More recent viruses "mutate" each time they copy themselves to other files. This, combined with various cryptographic techniques, makes modern viruses difficult to detect. Some viruses use "stealth" code, and behave differently when a user attempts to detect them. In 2003, a teenager was apprehended and prosecuted for unleashing a variant of the so-called Blaster worm that infected at least a half-million computers that used the latest versions of Microsoft Windows. But the creator of the original Blaster was still being sought.

Defenses

The obvious but impractical defense against viruses is never to use anyone else's software and never to connect with another computer or with the Internet. Given a particular virus, one can write an *antibody program* that spreads itself in the same way, removing the original virus from infected programs, and ultimately removing itself too. But the most practical defense is to run programs that recognize known viruses and that try to eliminate them before they do damage. Because new viruses are being devised almost every day, it is important to keep detection programs up-to-date by regular subscription from a reputable company. Equally important is installation of a software or hardware *firewall* that keeps unauthorized persons at remote locations from taking control of your computer. All approaches are tradeoffs. The only real hope is eternal vigilance on the part of users, and, above all, education of users to the possible consequences of their actions.

Bibliography

1972. Gerrold, D. *When Harlie Was One.* Mattituck, NY: Æonian Press.
1975. Brunner, J. *The Shockwave Rider.* New York: Harper & Row.
1994. Cohen, F. B. *A Short Course on Computer Viruses*, 2nd Ed. New York: John Wiley.

Ian H. Witten and Harold Thimbleby

VISION, COMPUTER

See COMPUTER VISION.

VISUALIZATION

See SCIENTIFIC APPLICATIONS.

VLIW (VERY LONG INSTRUCTION WORD)

See INSTRUCTION-LEVEL PARALLELISM.

VLSI (VERY LARGE SCALE INTEGRATION)

See COMPUTER CIRCUITRY; and INTEGRATED CIRCUITRY.

VOICE RECOGNITION AND SYNTHESIS

See SPEECH RECOGNITION AND SYNTHESIS.

VON NEUMANN MACHINE

For articles on related subjects, *see*

+ Instruction Set
+ Machine- and Assembly-language Programming
+ Program Counter
+ Stored Program Concept
+ von Neumann, John

The most influential paper in the history of computer science was written in 1946 by John von Neumann, then on the staff of the Institute for Advanced Study at Princeton University, in collaboration with Arthur W. Burks and Herman H. Goldstine. Its title is *Preliminary Discussion of the Logical Design of an Electronic Computing Instrument*, and the ideas it contains, collectively known as the *von Neumann machine*, has provided the foundation for essentially all computer system developments since that date. The prototypical von Neumann machine was the IAS computer, named for and installed at the Institute for Advanced Study in Princeton, NJ in 1952, for which von Neumann designed an instruction set. At least 15 subsequent computers were essentially clones of the IAS machine.

Central to the von Neumann machine is the concept of the stored program—the principle that instructions and data are to be stored together in a single, uniform storage medium rather than separately, as was previously the case. Not only can computations proceed at electronic speeds but instructions as well as data can also be read and written under program control. From this basic idea it follows that an arithmetic result placed in storage can be fetched and executed as an instruction. Iteration (*q.v.*) is realized by refetching the instruction as data, modifying it by operating on its address field, and then storing it, refetching, and reexecuting it as an instruction.

Contemporary programming practice, particularly in a multiprogramming (*q.v.*) environment, precludes the physical modification of instructions in storage. However, the basic idea of logical instruction modification is still central in computer science, but is supported by more recent developments such as index registers, base registers, and indirect addressing, which provide similar effects, but leave instructions unchanged.

An essential element of a von Neumann machine is its *program counter*, a register that is used to indicate the location of the next instruction to be executed and that is automatically incremented by each instruction fetch. Branching is, then, easily effectuated by updating the contents of the program counter with an address from some other source, often, but not always, a field in the current instruction.

Bibliography

1963. Taub, A. H. (ed.) *The Collected Works of John von Neumann*, Vol. 5, 34–79. New York: Macmillan.
1981. Stern, N. *From ENIAC to UNIVAC*. Bedford, MA: Digital Press.

Robert F. Rosin

VON NEUMANN, JOHN

For articles on related subjects, *see*

+ Digital Computers, History of: Early
+ EDVAC
+ ENIAC

+ Stored Program Concept
+ von Neumann Machine

John von Neumann (b. 28 December 1903, Budapest, Hungary; d. 8 February 1957, Washington, DC) (Fig. 1) is one of the legendary figures of twentieth-century mathematics. The stories of his quickness of mind, power of absolute recall, linguistic range, and sense of humor abound in the literature and among his former associates. During his career, he made significant contributions to logic, to quantum physics, to the theory of high-speed computing machines, and to economics through the mathematical theory of games and strategy.

Von Neumann received his early education at the Lutheran gymnasium in Budapest from 1911 through 1921. He published his first mathematics paper before he reached the age of 18. In 1926, he received a Budapest Ph.D. in mathematics with a dissertation concerning the axiomatization of set theory. During the late 1920s, he was Privatdozent at Berlin and Hamburg. He quickly established a reputation with publications in set theory, algebra, and quantum mechanics. In 1928, he proved the minimax theorem of game theory. This was later elaborated and applied in his work (with Oskar Morganstern), *The Theory of Games and Economic Behavior* (1944). In 1930, he was invited to be a visiting

Figure 1. John von Neumann with the IAS computer (courtesy of the archives of the Institute for Advanced Study, Princeton, NJ).

lecturer at Princeton University. When the Institute for Advanced Study was founded in 1933, he was appointed one of the original professors of its School of Mathematics. He kept this position for the rest of his life.

Von Neumann's work in the 1930s firmly established his already high reputation as a mathematician. In 1931, he published a book on the mathematical foundation of quantum mechanics, and in that same decade, he formulated and proved the mean ergodic theorem for unitary operators.

The Second World War was a watershed in von Neumann's career. Prior to 1940, his work fell primarily into the area of theoretical mathematics and physics, but for the remainder of his career he was essentially an applied mathematician. Although von Neumann had the ability to perform incredible mental calculations, his research led him to examine the possibility of machine assistance. His work on H-bomb implosion in 1944 led him to make use of Howard Aiken's Automatic Sequence Control Calculator (Mark I, Harvard—*q.v.*).

During the late summer of 1944, a chance encounter with Herman Goldstine made him aware of the world's first electronic computer being built under the direction of John Mauchly and J. Presper Eckert (*q.v.*) at the Moore School of Electrical Engineering of the University of Pennsylvania. His first visit to the ENIAC project in August of that year marked the beginning of his role in the theory of electronic computers and automata. Shortly before that visit, the ENIAC group was already committed to the construction of a successor. While von Neumann's authorship of the first EDVAC proposal in mid-1945 may not entitle his admirers to claim for him stored program conceptual priority, it is indicative of the great impact of his presence as a consultant to the group, his probing questions, and his ability to synthesize critical ideas. With the EDVAC paper, the modern era of electronic computers began.

By late 1945, von Neumann had decided to build a high-speed, general-purpose electronic computer at the Institute for Advanced Study (IAS). The impact of the IAS computer and its progeny (such as Illiac, Maniac, and Johnniac) is well known. The basic organization of most current uniprocessors is so close to that of the IAS that they are still called *von Neumann machines (q.v.).* Von Neumann was clearly one of the major scientific figures of this century.

Bibliography

1972. Goldstine, H. H. *The Computer from Pascal to von Neumann,* 167–183. Princeton, NJ: Princeton University Press.

1980. Heims, S. J. *John von Neumann and Norbert Wiener: From Mathematics to the Technologies of Life and Death.* Cambridge, MA: MIT Press.

1990. Aspray, W. *John von Neumann and the Origins of Modern Computing.* Cambridge, MA: MIT Press.

1992. Macrae, N. *John von Neumann.* New York: Pantheon Books.

Henry S. Tropp

WEB

See WORLD WIDE WEB.

WHIRLWIND

For an article on a related subject, *see*

+ Digital Computers, History of: Early

Project *Whirlwind* was sponsored at MIT by the US Navy. It was originally started in 1944 to investigate the solution of aircraft stability and control problems by analog methods. By 1946, it had become apparent that analog methods would be excessively complex. Thus a proposal was made for a 16-bit binary general-purpose computer using electrostatic storage and a 1 MHz pulse rate. The design goal was 20 000 multiplications per second.

Whirlwind was constructed under the leadership of Jay W. Forrester. When first put in service in 1949, the computer had 3300 tubes and 8900 crystal diodes. By June 1950, one hour of error-free operation with 256 words of electrostatic storage had been achieved. In March 1951, it was operational on a routine basis on a 35-hour-per-week schedule. During 1953, a magnetic tape system and a magnetic drum system were installed, and electrostatic storage was replaced by two banks of magnetic core memory consisting of 1024 words of 16 bits each. By December 1954, the computer had grown to 12 500 vacuum tubes and 23 800 diodes.

Whirlwind occupied a two-story building with its CPU, control console, and CRT displays on the second floor. One bit of the arithmetic-logic unit (ALU-*q.v.*) was a bay of equipment 2 ft wide and 12 ft high. The drum storage system and data communications interface occupied the ground floor. The basement was filled with power supplies, and the roof of the building was covered with 150 KW of air-conditioning equipment.

Whirlwind was a 16-bit parallel, single-address, binary computer (Fig. 1). Instructions as well as data occupied 16-bit memory words. An instruction consisted of an 11-bit address field and a 5-bit opcode that allowed an instruction set of 32 operations. The initial program–load problem was solved by the use of a bank of 32 registers of toggle switches from which bootstrap programs were loaded. Whirlwind operated until 1959. Parts of it are now in the Smithsonian Institution in Washington, DC, and the Computer Museum History Center in Mountain View, CA.

Figure 1. The Whirlwind Computer (courtesy MIT Museum, Cambridge, MA).

Bibliography

1980. Redmond, K. C., and Smith, T. A. *Project Whirlwind: The History of a Pioneer Computer*. Bedford, MA: Digital Press.

John N. Ackley

WIENER, NORBERT

For articles on related subjects, *see*

+ Analog Computer
+ Cybernetics

Norbert Wiener (b. Columbia, Missouri, 26 November 1894; d. Stockholm, Sweden, 18 March 1964) was one of America's most important mathematicians, and a controversial scientist who left a rich heritage of accomplishments (Fig.1). He received his A.B. degree from Tufts College in 1909 and his Ph.D. from Harvard in 1913 for a thesis in mathematical logic. From 1913 to 1915, he traveled and worked under Alfred North Whitehead, Bertrand Russell, G. H. Hardy, and J. E. Littlewood in Cambridge, and David Hilbert and Edmund Landau at Göttingen.

Figure 1.   Norbert Wiener (courtesy of American Mathematical Society).

After America's entry into the First World War, Wiener joined the facility at Aberdeen Proving Ground, where he worked on designing artillery range tables. In 1919, he secured an appointment as an instructor at MIT, an association he maintained until his retirement in 1960. At MIT, he formed a close friendship with Harold Hazen, who introduced him to the theory of feedback and servomechanisms, and met Arturo Rosenblueth, who was engaged in neurophysiological research.

Wiener's wartime work on prediction theory and his research in radar and fire control were all to have a major impact by the end of the 1940s. In his writings on cybernetics (Wiener, 1948), he laid the foundation for the philosophical relations between mechanistic and mathematical scientific theories. This work did much to stimulate research in automata theory (*q.v.*) and in attempts to simulate human thought processes. He was very conscious of the long-range impact of the computer on humans and society (Wiener, 1950).

Norbert Wiener received many honors, such as the Bôcher Prize of the American Mathematical Society (1933). His major publications, in addition to the above, include works on the Fourier integral and its application, Brownian motion, time series, relativity and quantum theory, vector and differential spaces, and potential theory.

Bibliography

1948. Wiener, N. *Cybernetics, or Control and Communication in the Animal and Machine*. Cambridge, MA: MIT Press.

1950. Wiener, N. *The Human Use of Human Beings; Cybernetics and Society*. Boston, MA: Houghton Mifflin.

1956. Wiener, N. *I Am A Mathematician*. Cambridge, MA: MIT Press.

1990. Masari, P. R. *Norbert Wiener, 1894–1964*. Boston, MA: Birkhauser.

Henry S. Tropp

WILKES, SIR MAURICE V.

For articles on related subjects, see

+ Digital Computers, History of: Early
+ EDSAC
+ Microprogramming

Maurice Vincent Wilkes (b. 1913) studied mathematics and physics at Cambridge and conducted research on the ionosphere (*see* Fig. 1). He worked on radar during the Second World War, and then directed the Mathematical Laboratory of the University of Cambridge from 1945 onward throughout the development of stored-program computers. The first of these to go into service, the EDSAC, built by Wilkes and his team, began operating in May 1949. Wilkes led the first practical development of programming for stored-program machines, including the first program library (*q.v.*). He originated labels (which he called "floating addresses"), an early form of macros (which he called "synthetic orders"), and microprogramming (which was used in EDSAC II). He later became interested in machine-independent computing, and in this connection developed a simple list-processing (*q.v.*) language

Figure 1.   Sir Maurice Vincent Wilkes.

known as *Wisp*. He contributed to the development of time-sharing (*q.v.*) systems, both as a visiting member of Project MAC at MIT and through a system developed in his own laboratory during 1965 to 1970.

Maurice Wilkes became a Fellow of the Royal Society in 1956, was the first president of the British Computer Society (*q.v.*) from 1957 to 1960, and the first UK member of the Council of IFIP from 1960 to 1963. He was the ACM Turing Lecturer in 1967 and received the Harry Goode Award from AFIPS in 1968. He was made a Distinguished Fellow of the British Computer Society in 1973, a foreign Honorary Member of the American Academy of Arts and Sciences in 1974, and in 1976 was elected to the Fellowship of Engineering, London. He became a Foreign Associate of both the US National Academy of Engineering (1977) and the National Academy of Sciences (1980).

In 1980, he retired from Cambridge as Emeritus Professor of Computer Technology and became Senior Consulting Engineer at Digital Equipment Corporation (DEC). He received the Eckert–Mauchly Award of ACM and the IEEE Computer Society in 1980, and the IEEE Computer Society's McDowell Award and the IEE Faraday medal in 1981. From 1981 to 1985, he was an Adjunct Professor of Electrical Engineering and Computer Science at MIT; in 1986, he returned to the UK and became Member for Research Strategy of the Olivetti Research Board where he remained until February 1999, when he became a Staff Consultant for AT&T. He was knighted later that year.

Bibliography

1985. Wilkes, M. V. *Memoirs of a Computer Pioneer.* Cambridge, MA: MIT Press.

Stanley Gill

WINDOW ENVIRONMENTS

For articles on related subjects, see

+ Desktop Publishing
+ Interactive Input Devices

+ Software Engineering
+ User Interface
+ Workstation

A *window environment* is an interactive system that supports a graphical user interface (GUI) in which multiple centers of user activity are presented visually as rectangular areas (*windows*) on a graphical display device (Fig. 1). The *window system* in such an environment manages details of user interaction and provides functionality that is shared among application programs. For most computer users today, it is the window environment that defines the computing platform.

Historical Trends

Users of early computers dealt intimately with the internal details and idiosyncrasies of each system. As computing power has grown, an increased focus on human factors has replaced machine details in the interface with more abstract notions that are more closely related to users' work. The window-based approach to GUI design grew out of laboratory research and was enabled by the development of affordable bitmapped *computer graphics* (*q.v.*). Broad commercial exposure to windows came first in 1981 as part of the pioneering Xerox Star (Johnson *et al.*, 1989) and in 1984 with the Apple Macintosh. The network-based X-Window

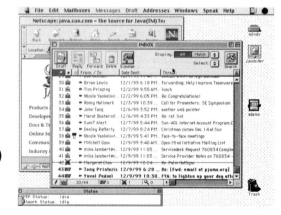

Figure 1. Snapshot of a display with several open windows.

System (Scheifler and Gettys, 1992) eventually became standard with Unix (*q.v.*), as did Microsoft Windows on IBM PC (*q.v.*) and compatible computers (Microsoft, 1995).

Advantages

Window environments have dramatically improved the usability of computers. Users alternate among multiple work tasks conveniently by switching attention between windows; windows typically display documents being read and written, electronic mail (*q.v.*) messages being received and written, World Wide Web (*q.v.*) pages being browsed, and interfaces to other task-related programs. Users organize work through direct manipulation: simple mouse (*q.v.*) or trackball actions move, reshape, expose, and hide windows. Window-management functions are supported by a single underlying window system, leading to consistent behavior that enhances usability.

Window Systems

Window systems typically have a number of attributes that allow them to manage resources and provide shared functionality.

Graphical Display

The most obvious resource is the display device, whose viewing area must be shared among multiple applications programs. In the X-Window system, this is managed using a *window tree*, a hierarchical data structure (*see* TREE) that represents nested rectangles of screen real estate. In Fig. 2, for example, toolbar C and scrollbar E are nested within window A. Figure 3 represents the corresponding window tree. A window tree also contains geometric information so that applications can specify graphical commands independent of their window locations, stacking order (which window should appear in case of overlap), and references to parts of the application program and widgets responsible for painting each rectangle. Efficient algorithms coordinate repainting of the screen in response to user actions such as uncovering or opening windows, determining what is actually visible (*clipping*) and

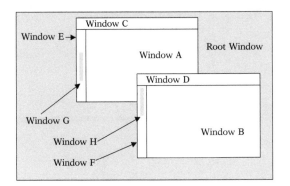

Figure 2. A typical X-Window System hierarchy.

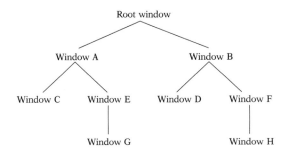

Figure 3. Window tree for Figure 3.

translating painting coordinates into absolute display locations.

Interactive Input Devices

Equally important are the devices with which users control window-based applications, which are, most often, a keyboard and mouse. A typical base window system supplies an abstract interface to these devices that captures user actions and translates them into easily managed *events*. A typical event records the kind of action (keyboard press or release, mouse button press or release, mouse motion), the state (up or down) of modifier keys such as Shift and Control, and mouse location.

Event Management

Window-based software is typically event-driven: an application consists of a collection of program fragments, each of which responds to a particular kind of event and

then stops so that the next event can be handled. Arriving events wait in a system-managed FIFO queue for dispatch to the appropriate program fragment. The dispatch decision is uniform across all applications; it is based on the geometry of the window tree, toolkit policy (does a particular widget react to this kind of event?), specifications from the application (should a widget implement a particular behavior?), and *keyboard focus* (to which window is the window manager currently routing keystrokes?).

Shared Services

Window environments also support shared services in which applications collaborate. For example, both a system-wide *clipboard* (where application data can be "copied to" and "pasted from") and global *drag and drop* (where application data can be "moved" from source to destination) enable data supplied by one application to be incorporated into another. The window system coordinates the activity so that applications need not negotiate directly with one another and so that the user sees uniform behavior.

Remote Services

Although most window environments are closely tied to computation on the underlying (local) computer, the X-Window system (Scheifler and Gettys, 1992) embodies a fundamental architectural separation between computation and interaction. This permits users to run applications interchangeably and simultaneously, independent of their location or platform. Limited forms of remote interaction have been added to other window environments, but without the smooth integration and full functionality made possible by the architectural approach.

Bibliography

1989. Johnson, J., Roberts, T. L., Verplank, W., Smith, D. C., Irby, C. H., Beard, M., and Mackey, K. "The Xerox Star: A Retrospective," *IEEE Computer*, **22**(9), (September), 11–29.

1992. Scheifler, R. W., and Gettys, J. *X Window Systems*, 3rd Ed. Bedford, MA: Digital Press.

1995. Microsoft Corporation. *The Windows Interface Guidelines for Software Design*. Redmond, WA: Microsoft Press.

Michael L. Van De Vanter

WIRELESS CONNECTIVITY

See MOBILE COMPUTING.

WIZARD

For articles on related subjects, *see*

+ Guru
+ Hacker
+ Power User

As first used in computing, a wizard was a programmer who knew a particular piece of software—a compiler (*q.v.*), operating system (*q.v.*), or text editor (*q.v.*), perhaps—so well that he or she could modify or enhance its code on short notice to accomplish an important objective. The term still applies, and a wizard is now accorded the admiration and respect that the *hacker* (*q.v.*) once enjoyed. But unlike the latter term, which now has mixed and opposing connotations, a wizard has no pejorative overtone. Wizards are generally quiet, competent people who operate with surgical precision in a restricted local environment. Wizards seldom aspire to the world stage of the *guru* (*q.v.*). Gurus know things; wizards do things.

The term *wizard* has now been appropriated for use by software developers to refer to what is effectively an automaton rather than a human; namely, that portion of a setup program that guides the user through the decisions needed to complete installation of new software. More generally, any program that tries to automate mundane tasks that would otherwise have to be done tediously—properly formatting a business letter, perhaps—is called a "wizard."

Edwin D. Reilly

WOMEN AND COMPUTING

For articles on related subjects, *see*

+ Lovelace, Countess of
+ Hopper, Grace Murray

Women have played a primary role in computer programming since its origins in the mid-1800s. Augusta Ada Byron, Countess of Lovelace introduced many programming concepts in the context of Babbage's Analytical Engine (*q.v.*). She and many of the world's first programmers in the 1940s were women. Six women programmed the ENIAC (*q.v.*): Kathleen Mauchly Antonelli, Frances Bilas (Fig. 1), Betty Jean Bartik, Frances E. ("Betty") Holberton, Ruth Teitelbaum, and Marlyn Meltzer. In addition, Grace Murray Hopper (*q.v.*) was the first programmer of the Harvard Mark I, Ethel Marden (Fig. 2) wrote the first program on

Figure 1. Betty Jennings (left) inserting a card deck into the ENIAC, and Frances Bilas (right) removing a deck with the results of a computation. (Courtesy of the Charles Babbage Institute, University of Minnesota Libraries, Minneapolis.)

Figure 2. Ethel Marden at the SEAC console (courtesy of the National Institute of Standards and Technology).

the SEAC at the National Bureau of Standards, and Ida Rhodes wrote the first program for the UNIVAC I (*q.v.*).

Betty Holberton's 1951 Sort-Merge Generator was a vital stepping stone toward Hopper's invention of the world's first business programming language, Flow-Matic, a precursor to Cobol. Beatrice Worsley at the University of Toronto was one of the two designers of Transcode, one of the first compilers.

Many of the first programmers were young women because of their participation in the war effort, while most men of their age were in uniform. However, as more men entered the field in the 1950s, the percentage of women fell, although it increased again in the late 1960s.

Women continue to make valuable contributions to computer science. A few female leaders are:

- Dr. Fran Allen, IBM Fellow and Member of the National Academy of Engineering (NAE) and American Academy of Arts and Sciences, credited with establishing the theory and practice of program optimization.
- Dr. Ruzena Bajcsy, a Fellow of the American Association for Artificial Intelligence (AAAI) and Institute of Electrical and Electronics Engineers (IEEE) and Member of the NAE, known for her

work in machine perception, particularly her "Active Perception" paradigm.

- Dr. Adele Goldberg, researcher and laboratory manager at Xerox Palo Alto Research Center (PARC) where she was coinventor of the object-oriented language Smalltalk, and later Chair and Founder of ParcPlace Systems.
- Dr. Shafi Goldwasser, winner of the Gödel prize in theoretical computer science and the ACM Hopper Award for her pioneering work in computational complexity (*q.v.*).
- Dr. Barbara J. Grosz, a Fellow of the American Association for the Advancement of Science (AAAS) and Fellow and former president of AAAI, widely regarded as having established the research field of computational modeling of discourse.
- Dr. Anita Jones, Chair of the Computer Science Department at the University of Virginia, then Director of Defense Research and Engineering for the United States government (1993-1997), a researcher in computer software systems. She is an NAE Member and ACM and IEEE Fellow.
- Dr. Nancy G. Leveson, ACM Fellow and former Editor-in-Chief of *IEEE Transactions on Software Engineering*, a founder of software safety (*q.v.*) research.
- Dr. Barbara Liskov, Member of the NAE, Fellow of the ACM and the American Academy of Arts and Sciences, widely recognized for her contributions toward the methodology of data abstraction.
- Jean E. Sammet, long-time IBM employee and member of the NAE, recognized for many contributions to the development of programming languages including her involvement in the early work on Cobol. She is an ACM Fellow and former president.
- Dr. Mary Shaw, recipient of the 1993 Warnier prize for contributions to software engineering (*q.v.*) and Fellow of the AAAS, ACM, and IEEE.
- "Steve" Shirley, founder and life president of the influential information technology group F. I. Group plc. She was awarded the OBE (Officer of the Order of the British Empire) in 1980 and the Freedom of the City of London in 1987. She also served as President of the British Computer Society (*q.v.*) from 1989 to 1990.

- Carly Fiorina, CEO of Hewlett-Packard, the first woman to lead a large computer company.

Despite a certain number of women in leadership positions, women are greatly underrepresented in computer science. Women received 29% of the bachelor's degrees and 27% of the masters degrees awarded in computing sciences in 1995 in the USA, and 14% of the computer science and computer engineering doctoral degrees in American and Canadian universities in 1998. The figures were virtually the same as of 2002. While women's participation increased in the 1970s and early 1980s, it has since been declining at the bachelor's and master's level. In Ph.D.-granting computer science and computer engineering departments in the USA and Canada, women comprise 19% of assistant professors, 10% of associate professors, and 7% of full professors.

Since the early 1980s, sparked by the release of a report by the women of MIT's computer science labs (MIT, 1983), there has been a growing awareness of sexual bias in computer science and an interest in activities to counter it.

Bibliography

1983. MIT. *Barriers to Equality in Academia: Women in Computer Science at MIT*, prepared by the Laboratory for Computer Science and the Artificial Intelligence Laboratory at MIT.

1995. Gürer, D. W. "Pioneering Women in Computer Science," *Communications of the ACM*, **38**(1), (January), 45–54.

2000. Cuny, J., and Aspray, W. *Recruitment and Retention of Women Graduate Students in Computer Science and Engineering*. Washington, DC: CRA, Inc.

Ellen Spertus and Denise Gürer

WORD PROCESSING

For articles on related subjects, *see*

+ Desktop Publishing
+ Text Editing Systems
+ Spelling Checker
+ T$_E$X
+ Typefont
+ User Interface
+ Window Environments

The term *word processing* was invented by IBM as a way to market a new product, a Selectric typewriter that could record words on magnetic tape. The recording capability meant that corrections and additions could be made to the stored text by re-recording over the original version. It also meant that unlimited perfect copies of the original could be produced, to all appearances personalized and hand-typed, without manually retyping the document.

Early Systems

IBM marketed word processors to business customers as dedicated, single-purpose devices for the creation, revision, storage, and output of text documents. By the mid-1970s, an enthusiastic customer response led to a burgeoning industry. New vendors of word processors, such as Wang Laboratories and others, soon surpassed IBM in sales and product innovation. Vendors enlarged and improved their word processing system's storage media from magnetic tape to magnetic cards to magnetic diskettes (*q.v.*). Cathode-ray tube (CRT) display screens were added that allowed documents to be viewed, revised, and corrected on screen before final versions were printed. In this era, the term *word processor* became a job description as well as a reference to computer-based typing equipment.

The dedicated word processors of this period were quite expensive. A stand-alone fully functioned display word processor with diskette storage and a printer ranged in price from $8 000 to $15 000, including training and vendor support.

Personal Computer Word Processing

The IBM PC (*q.v.*), introduced in 1981, changed the character of word processing. Microprocessor-based PC products were commercially available before the introduction of the IBM PC, but were regarded as chiefly of interest to very small businesses or to hobbyists.

Early microcomputers lacked storage capacity, normally included an inapt data processing-oriented keyboard, offered small screen size with poor resolution, could not be linked in clusters, and were almost exclusively based on limited 8-bit CPU technology. The IBM PC, however, was based on a 16-bit processor and the MS-DOS operating system, which provided software developers with a sufficiently powerful and flexible platform on which to write software applications. As the PC market boomed, the dedicated word processor quickly became obsolete.

Software

The word-processing software market has never been dominated for very long by a single vendor's product. A new hardware platform or technological innovation has often led to a new market, and the lead among word-processing products, in terms of market share, has changed many times. As of 2003, the most popular PC word-processing programs were Microsoft Word, followed by Corel's WordPerfect, and Lotus Word Pro.

Current word-processing products provide a feature set far beyond the standard document creation and error correction of early systems. They will search for certain words or phrases; merge letters with lists of names and addresses; move blocks of text; display italic, bold, underlining, and superscripts and subscripts; display page breaks; allow text to be arranged in multiple columns; display multiple pages on screen at one time; combine text and graphic images; offer shortcuts for keyboard commands; count characters, words, and paragraphs; provide automatic hyphenation and justification; create footnotes, tables of contents, and indexes; correct (some) spelling errors; provide a thesaurus; and, in a few cases, attempt to correct grammar and evaluate the readability of a document according to the reading level of the intended document recipients.

User Interfaces

Early MS-DOS word processors used a character-based *user interface* for interaction (commands and responses) between user and computer. In a character-based interface, the commands given by the user to the computer are made via the keyboard via specific keys or key combinations. The user must know these commands or refer to a manual to find them. Since character commands differ from product to product, each new word-processing package must be learned anew.

Today, most word-processing users benefit by the widespread use of the graphical user interface (GUI), invented by the Xerox Corporation in the mid-1970s, but popularized by the Apple Macintosh, introduced in 1984. Starting in the mid-1980s, Microsoft began to introduce versions of a GUI interface called Windows. With a GUI, pop-up or pull-down menus listing command selections are available to an operator at all times, regardless of what else may be displayed on the screen. There is no need, for example, to close a document and return to a main menu in order to select functions and issue commands. Menus can be activated and functions selected by pointing to them with a cursor controlled by a hand-operated mouse (*q.v.*) rather than by striking keys. Training, beyond identifying proper commands and basic eye–hand mouse operation, is minimal.

Another advantage of a GUI is the so-called WYSIWYG (What You See Is What You Get) display. In the older MS-DOS word processors, the characters displayed on the screen are monospaced; each character, space, or punctuation mark is assigned an equal amount of space, regardless of typeface or size. A WYSIWYG display shows the user proportional typefaces, in different fonts and type sizes, almost exactly as they will appear when printed on paper. A GUI with WYSIWYG display also allows graphic images to be created, positioned, and incorporated with text in compound documents on screen as they will look when printed.

Desktop Publishing

Desktop publishing (DTP) applications typically include many of the text entry features of word processors but add highly sophisticated typesetting and layout functions, such as variable text and display fonts, type styles and sizes, graphics capabilities, and page layout and design features. Where the purpose of word processors is the flexible creation of standard business documents, DTP is intended for the commercial quality design and production of newsletters, brochures, and books. Word processors now include about 85% of the function of a DTP package, and whether you use one or the other largely depends upon whether you are mainly doing word processing or mainly doing elaborate full-color page layouts.

Networking

With a local area network (LAN—*q.v.*), the PCs within a workgroup are linked so that, typically, they are able to communicate electronic messages and share applications and data files that are stored on a dedicated *file server* (*q.v.*). Unlike the earlier Office Automation model, however, the processing power resides in the users' PCs, not in a shared minicomputer (*q.v.*).

Several word processing products are now supporting collaborative work, assuming multiple users working on the same documents simultaneously or sequentially. They do this through supporting multiple versions of the same document, permitting users to mark up documents for approval, and letting multiple users work on different sections of a document simultaneously. This has occurred by building function into the personal word-processing products used on PCs, but linked together by shared files on network servers, now managed by a server-level application such as Lotus Notes or Microsoft's Outlook and Exchange.

Most word-processing products today are not sold alone but rather in software bundles called *office suites*, together with other personal productivity products such as spreadsheets, databases, personal information managers (calendar, scheduler, Rolodex), and graphics/presentation managers.

Amy Wohl

WORKING SET

For articles on related subjects, *see*

+ Memory Management
+ Memory Protection
+ Multiprogramming
+ Operating Systems
+ Virtual Memory

From their beginnings in the 1940s, electronic computers had two-level storage systems. In the 1950s, main memory was magnetic core and secondary memories were magnetic drums. The CPU could address only the main memory. A major part of a programmer's job was to devise a good way to divide a program into blocks and to schedule their moves between the levels. The blocks were called *segments* or *pages* and the movement operations, *overlays* or *swaps*. The contents of main memory were called the "set of working information," or *working set* for short.

In the late 1950s, the designers of the Atlas (*q.v.*) at the University of Manchester introduced *virtual memory*, which made programming considerably easier by automating the arduous acts of planning and implementing overlays. They also invented *multiprogramming*, a method of partitioning main memory among several active programs; multiprogramming increased system throughput (*q.v.*) by maintaining a reserve of ready-to-execute programs. By the middle 1960s, the term "working set" had come to mean the smallest subset of a program's address space that needed to be present in multiprogrammed main memory to maintain acceptable processing efficiency. More precisely, the definition of working set became "the set of pages referenced in a sampling window extending from the current time backwards into the past" (Denning, 1968). The idea of sampling for used pages was already familiar, with usage-bit-based paging algorithms. What was new was that the window was defined in the *virtual time* of the program—that is, CPU time with all interrupts removed—so that the same program with the same input data would have the same working set measurements no matter what the memory size, multi-programming level, or scheduler policy. The window size was the lone parameter: the larger the window, the larger the working set, the lower the probability of paging, and the greater the processing efficiency. Working set theory explained thrashing (repetitive and unproductive memory swaps) and gave a method to prevent it by loading more programs only as long as memory can accommodate their working sets.

The success of working set policies derives from the dynamic property called *locality of reference*. In each phase of virtual time, a program refers to only a subset of the blocks in its address space. When most virtual time is covered by phases that are long compared with the secondary memory access time, the working set is an excellent predictor of memory demand in the immediate future.

Bibliography

1968. Denning, P. J. "The Working Set Model for Program Behavior," *Communications of the ACM*, **11**(5), (May), 323–333.
1980. Denning, P. J. "Working Sets Past and Present," *IEEE Transactions on Software Engineering*, **SE-6**(1), (January), 64–84.
1992. Tanenbaum, A. *Modern Operating Systems.* Upper Saddle River, NJ: Prentice Hall.

Peter J. Denning

WORKSTATION

For articles on related subjects, *see*

+ Computer-Aided Design/Computer-Aided Manufacturing
+ Computer Animation
+ Computer Graphics
+ File Server
+ Local Area Network (LAN)
+ User Interface
+ Virtual Reality
+ Window Environments

A *workstation* is a powerful graphics-oriented micro-computer intended for a single user. When introduced in the early 1980s, workstations were distinguished by their large bitmapped displays and their use of a mouse (*q.v.*) for input, at a time when most systems had relatively small ASCII terminals connected to time-shared mainframes (*q.v.*) or to low-power PCs with keyboard input. By 2000, every PC had a powerful processor and a high-resolution display, and the distinction between workstation and PC has become more a matter of function than of hardware.

Workstations are designed to connect to local area networks using software that allows them to access files located on remote *file servers*. Network access is facilitated by the use of an operating system (*q.v.*) that hides the details of accessing remote files from user programs. They use the TCP/IP (*q.v.*) Internet protocol for easy access to services provided by machines attached to the network. Users send electronic mail (*q.v.*) to persons on remote machines, establish interactive login sessions with remote machines, and send and retrieve files. They commonly run versions of the Unix (*q.v.*) or Windows operating systems. Used initially by scientists and engineers, workstations have become commonplace in educational and business settings where graphics applications and data visualization are important.

Up until a few years ago, it was considered an essential characteristic of a workstation that its software runs under Unix on a RISC microprocessor. The leading machines were made by Sun Microsystems, using its Sparc chip, and Silicon Graphics Incorporated (SGI), which used a MIPS chip (*see* Figs. 1 and 2). Depending on configuration, such workstations were once priced from $3000 to $20 000, while powerful PCs with memory and displays comparable to those of workstations cost from $2000 to $6000. But by the late 1990s, the processing power and storage capacity of high-end PCs overlapped that of many workstations. Aside from cost, another factor in the growing attractiveness of the PC is the maturation

Figure 1. The Sun Microsystems Ultra 80 Workstation (courtesy of Sun Microsystems, UK).

Figure 2. The Silicon Graphics 320 (courtesy of Silicon Graphics, Inc.).

of the Windows operating system, as well as the availability of Linux, the (free) PC version of the Unix *kernel* (*q.v.*).

Bibliography

1994. Bjelland, H. *Configuring a Customized Engineering Workstation.* New York: Windcrest.

1996. Haramundanis, K. *Exploring Workstation Applications with CDE and Motif.* Bedford, MA: Digital Press.

1998. Linthicum, D. S. "Graphics Workstations," *PC Magazine,* **17**(4), (24 February), 148–177.

Thomas Narten

WORLD WIDE WEB

For articles on related subjects, *see*

+ Client-Server Computing
+ Cyberspace
+ Electronic Commerce
+ Electronic Mail (Email)
+ Hypertext
+ Internet
+ Java
+ Markup Languages
+ Networks, Computer
+ Packet Switching
+ TCP/IP

Introduction

The *World Wide Web*, or just "Web," is a rapidly growing collection of over one billion pages linked in a seemingly disorganized topology, which is most dense over the western hemisphere and western Europe, but is nonetheless worldwide in scope. In the sense used here, a *page* is a quantity of information whose size is unrelated to the length of a page of paper or the height of a display screen; those larger than screen size are viewed by scrolling. Pages may contain both text and images that may be animated, and loading a page may invoke sound effects.

Web pages reside on a *server*, a host computer (*q.v.*) that allows general access for computers connected to the host network. The largest network, the Internet, is a collection of thousands of other networks that are interconnected via common network protocols (*q.v.*). The networks that form the Internet may be either local area networks (LANs—*q.v.*) or wide area networks (WANs) and public or private Internet Service Providers (ISPs) such as America Online (AOL).

A *Website* is a coherent cluster of one or more pages, whose *home page* is accessed using a *Uniform Resource Locator* (URL). Websites store information according to the tagging conventions of the HyperText Markup Language (HTML). HTML is an application of Standard Generalized Markup Language (SGML) with one important extension: *hyperlinks* (*see* HYPERTEXT), usually called just *links*. They are conduits to other resources including offsets within documents, other documents, imagery, animation and motion pictures, executable programs called Server-Side Includes (SSIs), Java applets, and so on. Typically, hyperlinks appear in Web documents either as sensitized text (in color) or as sensitized icons, where "sensitized" means that selecting a link (usually by a mouse click) produces some navigational effect. The link uses a URL to specify the location of the hyperlinked resource. The time to access a remote resource depends upon the network bandwidth (*q.v.*) available to its location.

Web Perspectives

Network Perspective

The World Wide Web represents a major paradigm shift in networked computing both in terms of delivery of information and interpersonal, though not in-person, communication. It is the first form of digital communication that has rendering and browsing utilities adequate to allow any person or group with network access to share media-rich information with anyone else. Formally, the Web is a client–server model for packet-switched (*q.v.*), networked computer systems that use a few key Internet protocols. The client handles all of the interaction with other components of the computing environment and temporarily retains information for perusal. The networked servers are information repositories that host software to serve client requests. The procedural "glue" which makes the client–server interactivity possible is the concurrent support, by both client and server, of the protocol-pair HyperText Transfer Protocol (HTTP) and HyperText Markup Language (HTML). The former establishes the basic handshaking (*q.v.*) procedures between client and server, while the latter defines the organization and structure of Web documents to be exchanged.

The rapid growth of the Web is the result of a unique combination of characteristics:

1. *The Web is an enabling technology.* It was the first widespread network technology to extend the notion of a virtual network machine to multimedia (*q.v.*).

2. *The Web is a unifying technology.* This occurred through the Web's accommodation of a wide range of multimedia formats. Since such audio (e.g. .WAV, .AU), graphics (e.g. .GIF, .JPG) and animation (e.g. MPEG) formats are all digital, they were already unified in desktop applications prior to the Web. The Web, however, unified them for distributed network applications.

3. *The Web is a social phenomenon.* This aspect evolved in three stages. Stage one was the phenomenon of Web "surfing." The richness and variety of Web documents and the novelty of the experience made Web surfing the *de facto* standard for curiosity-driven networking behavior. The second stage involved such Web interactive communication forums as Internet Relay Chat (IRC–*see* ONLINE CONVERSATION), which provided a new outlet for interpersonal but not in-person communication. The third stage, still in its infancy, involves the notion of a *virtual community*.

Historical Perspective

The Web was conceived by Tim Berners-Lee and his colleagues at CERN (now called the European Laboratory for Particle Physics) in 1989 as a shared information space for supporting collaborative work. Berners-Lee defined HTTP and HTML at that time, and as a proof of concept developed the first Web browser in 1990 for the NeXTStep platform. Nicola Pellow developed the first cross-platform browser in 1991, while Berners-Lee and Bernd Pollerman developed the first server application—a phone book database. By 1992, the interest in the Web was sufficient to produce four additional browsers—Erwise, Midas, and Viola for the X-Window system, and Cello for Windows. The following year, Marc Andreessen of the National Center for Supercomputing Applications (NCSA) wrote Mosaic for the X-Window system, which soon became

V,W

the browser standard against which all others would be compared.

Most Web resources remain for the most part noninteractive, multimedia downloads (e.g. Java animation applets, movie clips, real-time audio transmissions, text with graphics) augmented with Common Gateway Interface (CGI) forms (*see* SCRIPTING LANGUAGES), and frames for added control of layout. This "rectified" information flow will change in the next decade as software developers and Web content-providers shift their attention to the quality of content as well as the interactive and participatory capabilities of the Internet, the Web, and their successor technologies.

Support of CGI within HTTP in 1993 was the first major step toward adding interactive capability to the Web. CGI forms provide a simple mechanism for input from the Web user–client to be passed to the server for processing without any programming expertise. This opened the area of interactive Web development to the majority of computer users, while the broader use of CGI programming remains within the province of computer programmers.

A second major advance was the advent of "plug-in" technology. This increased the media-rendering capability of browsers while avoiding the time-consuming spawning of so-called "helper apps" (applications) through the browser's launchpad.

Third, the advent of executable content added a high level of animated media rendering and interactive content on the client side. Such object-oriented network programming languages as Java (*q.v.*) produce platform-independent program modules that are executable on enabled Web browsers. This latest extension, which involves executing foreign programs that have been downloaded across the networks, is not without some security risk, although the same is true of such pedestrian applications as email.

Fourth, we have seen advanced information-gathering strategies that go beyond the original "information-pull" concept behind the Web. Where most users, perhaps through autonomous software agents, currently seek to draw information to them,

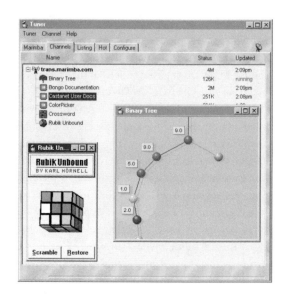

Figure 1. Marimba Corporation's Castanet tuner with two channels open, one which animates binary tree growth as random values are inserted, and the other which supports interactive Rubik cube play.

solicited *push technology* attempts to dispense information routinely and automatically to selected consumers (*see* Fig. 1). Several prototypes of solicited push "netcasting" have been deployed. Some, like Pointcast, consolidate and distribute information via a proprietary server called a *transmitter*. In this case, the client-side software behaves as a dedicated "peruser" for the transmissions. Other solicited push technology, such as Marimba's Castanet, contain a "tuner" that allows the client to connect to an arbitrary number of different servers. Each connection from the client to the transmitter is called a *channel*.

Surfing the Web

The Web itself, as well as its growth and development, would have been impossible without programs called *browsers*, which allow access to the pages of the Web, but in order to search for information efficiently it was necessary to develop utilities called *search engines*. The use of browsers and search engines together is often called *surfing* the Web.

Browsers

General properties

The *browser*, a client-side program, provides the interface capability to the Web. This software opens a window on the desktop that handles the information exchange with the relevant server. Specifically, this includes the formal request of information from the server (via the URL) and the rendering of that information on the desktop. In the earliest days of the Web, this rendering was restricted to text. Since the early 1990s, rendering has been extended to virtually the full range of multimedia.

A Website may contain a cluster of documents (Web pages) and resources. When a Web page is the primary page of an entire Website, it is called a *home page* for that site. Examples of home pages include splash pages, which are best seen as multimedia "enticements" to the site, and pass-through pages, which serve as navigational or routing menus for visitors. The advantage of home pages is that they are frequently mnemonically associated with the host (e.g. `www.ibm.com`, `www.acm.org`) and thus provide a unifying effect on the entire Website.

Commercial Products

In its earliest days, the popularity of the World Wide Web was inextricably linked to one browser, Mosaic, developed at the NCSA. While Mosaic was but one of several competing Web-based browsers available at that time, it quickly displaced the others as the dominant environment for taking in the Web experience. By 1993, Mosaic had more than 90% of the browser market and became the design standard against which all other browsers would be compared for years to come. In 1994, the primary designer and developer of Mosaic, Marc Andreessen, went on to cofound Netscape Communications, whose Netscape Communicator became the *de facto* standard for second-generation Web browsers. In 1998, the browser market was about evenly split between Netscape and Microsoft's later entry called *Internet Explorer*. By 2000, these two browsers had captured 96% of the market, with Explorer holding the far greater share. The principal browsers that

account for the other 4% are Opera, NetPlanet, and Icab.

Search Engines

With millions of Websites and Web pages and an astonishing growth rate, a major issue for users is finding relevant information. To meet the need, several search engines have evolved, such as Google, Yahoo!, Excite, AltaVista, Lycos, Webcrawler, Northern Light, Infoseek, Hotbot, Snap, and many others. Each browser contains a "search" link that leads to a particular search engine, or list of engines. Alternatively, the user who wants to call a particular engine can either recall a link to it from a list of *bookmarked* sites or, if necessary, enter its URL from the keyboard.

Users may query search engines using keywords or key phrases. Most engines support complex Boolean operations. For example, one can ask to find all Websites that refer to "strike AND delivery BUT NOT (baseball OR bowling)." Some engines also have "proximity" operators that allow one to search for occurrences of "encyclopedia NEAR computer." In addition to the general search engines, there are also search engine sites that specialize in searches for a host of applications in such areas as law, medicine, and health. Most search engine companies base their revenue on the sale of advertising which, in turn, is based upon the number of downloads or page hits that they can offer to an advertiser.

The Web as a Social Phenomenon

While definitive conclusions about the social aspects of Web use remain elusive, at least some central issues have been identified (Table 1). Early use convincingly demonstrated that the Web was a popular and worthwhile medium for presenting distributed multimedia, even though we cannot yet quantify the social benefits and institutional costs which result from this use. As CGI was added to the Web, it became clear that the Web would provide important location-independent, multimodal interactivity, although we know little about the motivations behind such interactivity, and even less about how one would measure the long-term utility for the participants and their institutions.

Table 1.   Social issues and Web behavior.

- To what extent can the effects of information overload be avoided by advanced information retrieval methods?
- To what extent will future interactive and participatory Web engagements become enticing and immersive?
- What are the advantages and disadvantages of anonymous engagement?
- What virtues are there in quasi-independent and relative-identity environments?
- To what extent will Web use enhance or supplement alternative modes of information exchange?
- To what extent will the Web increase intellectual quality and economy?
- To what degree will complete geographical transparency be realized? How long will it take before Web access moves beyond technologically advanced nations and regions?
- What rules will govern self-organizing and self-administering virtual communities of the future? How will that affect socialization?
- How will electronic communities of the future enhance and complement their physical counterparts?
- How will human leisure and work performance be affected when the Web becomes ubiquitous?

Virtual Communities

The Web's primary utility is as an information delivery device, but more powerful and robust Web applications are beginning to take hold. Perhaps the most significant future application will involve the construction of *virtual communities*. Virtual, or electronic, communities, are examples of interactive and participatory forums conducted over digital networks for the mutual benefit of participants and sponsors. The first attempts to establish virtual communities dates back to the mid-1980s with the community "freenet" movement. While early freenets offered few services beyond email and Telnet, many quickly expanded to offer access to documents in local libraries and government offices, Internet relay chats, community bulletin boards and so forth, thereby giving participants an enhanced sense of community through another form of connectivity.

Bibliography

1997. Reid, R. H. *Architects of the Web.* New York: John Wiley.

1999. Berghel, H., and Blank, D. "The World Wide Web," in *Advances in Computing* (ed. M. Zaelkowitz), Vol. 48, 178–218. New York: Academic Press.

1999. Berners-Lee, T., and Fischetti, M. *Weaving the Web: The Original Design and Ultimate Destiny of the World Wide Web.* New York: HarperCollins.

Hal Berghel

ZUSE COMPUTERS

For articles on related subjects, see

+ Digital Computers, History of
+ Zuse, Konrad

Konrad Zuse designed and built a number of computers between 1938 and 1969. The first four, which he called Z1 through Z4, have a special place in the history of computing. Because the Second World War isolated him from the Anglo-American computing mainstream, Zuse's early machines embody genuinely different design alternatives to those produced in England and the USA.

The Zuse Z1, begun in 1936 and completed in 1938, used an arrangement of slotted metal plates through which pins passed to store, read, and write binary digits. Calculation was effected by similar mechanical interlocks that provided the fundamental Boolean operations. Zuse independently discovered the relation of binary arithmetic to Boolean logic while working on the arithmetic unit of the Z1, but this computer never worked properly. The failure of Z1 led Zuse to use surplus telephone relays instead of mechanical devices to perform arithmetic for his second machine, the Z2. The Z2, completed in 1939, was built in a workshop at Zuse's parents' Berlin apartment. With funds from the German military, Zuse then built the Z3, the first of his machines to work reliably in all respects. The Z3 used 1800 telephone relays for

memory, 600 for calculation, and 200 for sequence control. Sequences were encoded in 8-bit code by manually punching holes onto strips of discarded 35-mm movie film. The computer executed linear sequences with no provision for conditional jumps. Operations included ordinary arithmetic, square root, store, and recall from memory, and binary–decimal conversion. The Z3 had a memory of 64 22-bit floating-point numbers consisting of 7 bits for the base-2 exponent, 1 bit for the sign, and 14 for the mantissa. Clock speed was about 4 to 5 Hz, with one multiplication taking about 3 to 5 s. The Z3 was completed in early December 1941, but essentially ran only test programs until its destruction in a bombing raid on Berlin in 1944.

From 1942 to 1945, Zuse built the Z4, a machine comparable to the Harvard Mark I and the Bell Labs relay computers as a mature and sophisticated

Figure 1. The Zuse Z4 computer.

digital computer. For the Z4, Zuse returned to the mechanical memory of his first two computers. When the Z4 was completed in 1949, it had a memory of 64 32-bit words and a very sophisticated instruction set (*q.v.*) (Fig. 1). Although it did not store its programs internally, it nonetheless served as the inspiration for much theoretical work in programming and programming languages.

Bibliography

1980. Speiser, A. P. "The Relay Calculator Z4," *IEEE Annals of the History of Computing*, **2**(3), (July), 242–245.

1997. Rojas, R. "Konrad Zuse's Legacy: The Architecture of the Z1 and Z3," *IEEE Annals of the History of Computing*, **19**(2), (April–June), 5–16.

Paul E. Ceruzzi

ZUSE, KONRAD

For articles on related subjects, *see*

+ Digital Computers, History of
+ Zuse Computers

Konrad Zuse (b. 1910 in Berlin, d. 1995 in Bonn; Fig. 1) studied construction engineering at the Technische Hochschule Berlin-Charlottenburg and received the degree Dipl. Ing. in 1935. In 1934, he had already started development work on program-controlled computing machines with electromechanical and mechanical elements. In 1938, he had completed his first model (Z1). In 1941, his first fully working machine (Z3) was operational; it used the binary number system with floating-point arithmetic.

During the next four years, Zuse built a number of special machines and the all-purpose relay computer Z4. The Z3 was destroyed by bombs in 1944, but the Z4 was saved, and in 1950 it was installed at the Eidgenössische Technische Hochschule in Zürich. In 1954, the Z4 was moved to St. Louis, near Basel, where it was used for five years. Around 1945, Zuse designed an (unimplemented) algorithmic language, Plankalkül

Figure 1. Konrad Zuse at the rebuilt Z3 computer, 1984. (Courtesy of Dr. Ing. Horst Zuse, Berlin.)

(Bauer and Wossner, 1972), which he used to describe a full chess program.

In 1949, Zuse formed his own company ZUSE KG. In 1952, he built the largest relay computer in West Germany, the Z5, which consisted of 2400 relays and a 12-word memory with a word length of 36 bits. His first successful serial product was Z11, a relay computer for geodetical and optical applications. His second product was Z22, a vacuum-tube computer (later replaced by its transistorized version Z23); it had an extremely flexible instruction code, achieved by a set of functional bits, an early form of microprogramming (*q.v.*). The first of 50 Z22 computers was delivered in 1958; it was the first tube computer sold commercially in Germany. There were 98 installations of its successor, the Z23. In 1958, Zuse published a design for a field computer, a parallel processor (*q.v.*) especially suited for differential equations. In the same year, he designed a computer-controlled plotter called Z64, or *Graphomat*. After a number of financial difficulties, Zuse left ZUSE KG, which was absorbed by Siemens AG in 1969. Three years before he had become a professor at the University of Göttingen.

In 1956, Zuse received his first of eight honorary doctoral degrees from the Technische Universität Charlottenburg in Berlin. In Bonn in 1964, he received the Werner von Siemens Ring; in 1965, the Harry Goode Memorial Award from AFIPS; in 1969, the German Diesel Medal; in the same year, the Austrian

Exner Medal; and, in 1975, on his 65th birthday, appointment as an Honorary Citizen of Huenfeld. The IEEE Pioneers Award was presented to him in 1982.

The achievements of Zuse can be properly evaluated only if his isolation is taken into account. His background was construction engineering, and he knew practically nothing about computer developments elsewhere until a very late stage. During all his life, Zuse received little understanding and support, but now two ZUSE medals are awarded every year, one by the German Building Industry and one by the Gesellschaft für Informatik (GI).

The editor and the author are grateful to Horst Zuse for new information used in this profile of his father.

Bibliography

1972. Bauer, F. L., and Wössner, H. "The Plankalkül of Konrad Zuse: A Forerunner of Today's Programming Languages," *Communications of the ACM*, **15**, 678–685.

1983. Ceruzzi, P. "Computers in Germany," *Reckoners*, 10–42. Westport, CO: Greenwood Press.

1993. Zuse, K. *The Computer—My Life*. New York: Springer–Verlag.

Heinz Zemanek

Appendix I

ABBREVIATIONS AND ACRONYMS

The Fourth Edition of this Encyclopedia contains an extensive list of acronyms that include ones in common use that may not occur in an article. Websites that maintain extensive acronym lists are www.geocities.com/ikind_babel/babel/babel.html and www.ucc.ie/cgi-bin/acronym. Here, we list only common acronyms that may have been used in an article without repeated elaboration.

2D	Two dimensional
3D	Three-dimensional
ACM	Association for Computing Machinery
A/D	Analog-to-Digital (Conversion)
AI	Artificial Intelligence
ALU	Arithmetic-Logic Unit
AM	Amplitude Modulation
ANSI	American National Standards Institute
AOL	America OnLine
ARPA	Advanced Research Projects Agency
ASCII	American Standard Code for Information Interchange
ATM	Automated Teller Machine
B2B	Business to Business
BCD	Binary-Coded Decimal
BIOS	Basic Input–Output System
BIT	Binary digIT
BNF	Backus–Naur Form
CAD/CAM	Computer-Aided Design/Computer-Aided Manufacturing
CASE	Computer-Aided Software Engineering
CATV	CAble TeleVision
CD	Compact Disc
CD-ROM	Compact Disc–Read Only Memory
CGI	Common Gateway Interface
CISC	Complex Instruction Set Computer
CMOS	Complementary Metal-Oxide Semiconductor

CODASYL	Conference on Data Systems Languages
CPC	Card Programmed Calculator
CP/M	Control Program for Microcomputers
CPM	Critical Path Method
CPU	Central Processing Unit
CRT	Cathode Ray Tube
D/A	Digital-to-Analog (conversion)
DBMS	DataBase Management System
DEC	Digital Equipment Corporation
DES	Data Encryption Standard
DoD	Department of Defense (USA)
DOS	Disk Operating System
DPMA	Data Processing Management Association
DRAM	Dynamic Random Access Memory
DSL	Digital Subscriber {Line|Loop}
DVD	Digital {Versatile|Video} Disc
EDP	Electronic Data Processing
EFT	Electronic Funds Transfer
FIFO	First-In-First-Out
FM	Frequency Modulation
GIGO	Garbage In, Garbage Out
GUI	Graphical User Interface
HTML	HyperText Markup Language
HTTP	HyperText Transfer Protocol
IC	Integrated Circuit
IEEE	Institute of Electrical and Electronics Engineers
IEEE-CS	IEEE-Computer Society
I/O	Input–Output
ISDN	Integrated Systems Digital Network
ISP	Internet Service Provider
IT	Information Technology
LAN	Local Area Network
LCD	Liquid Crystal Display
LED	Light-Emitting Diode
LIFO	Last-In-First-Out
MICR	Magnetic Ink Character Recognition
MIS	Management Information Systems
MIT	Massachusetts Institute of Technology
NASA	National Aeronautics and Space Administration
NSF	National Science Foundation

OCR	Optical Character {Recognition|Reader}
P2P	Peer-to-Peer
PARC	Palo Alto Research Center (Xerox)
PC	Personal Computer
PDA	Personal Digital Assistant
PIN	Personal Identification Number
POL	Problem- {or Procedure-} Oriented Language
QoS	Quality of Service
RAM	Random Access Memory
RISC	Reduced Instruction Set Computer
ROM	Read-Only Memory
SGML	Standard Generalized Markup Language
TCP/IP	Transmission Control Protocol/Internet Protocol
TTY	Teletype
UHF	Ultra-High Frequency
URL	Uniform Resource Locator
VHF	Very High Frequency
VLSI	Very Large Scale Integration
WAN	Wide Area Network
WYSIWYG	What You See Is What You Get
XML	eXtensible Markup Language
Y2K	Year 2K (2000)

Common File Extensions

For a more comprehensive list of over 800 extensions, see `http://filext.com`.

.4th	Forth language source code
.ada	Ada source file
.aif	Audio Interchange Format
.ald	ALDus Pagemaker file
.ani	ANImation file
.api	Adobe Acrobat API file
.arc	ARChive
.art	AOL, Crayola, and Ashton-Tate image format
.asc	ASCii text file
.asm	ASseMbly language source code
.asp	Active Server Page
.au	AUdio format
.awk	AWK program (Unix)
.bak	BAcKup file
.bas	BASic language source file

.bat	BATch file
.bib	BIBliography
.bin	BINary file
.bmp	BitMaP image
.c	C language source file
.cat	CATalog file
.cbl	CoBoL source file
.cdf	Comma-Delineated data File
.cdr	Corel DRaw file
.cfg	ConFiGuration file
.cgi	CGI script
.cgm	Computer Graphics Metafile
.chk	CHecK disk MS file
.clp	CLiPboard
.cmd	OS/2 CoMmanD batch file
.cmf	Creative Music Format
.cob	COBol source file
.com	COMmand file
.cpp	C++ source file
.dat	DATa file
.dbf	DataBase File—several vendors
.dct	DiCTionary file
.dib	Device Independent Bitmap
.dll	DLL file
.doc	DOCument word processing file—several vendors
.dot	DOcument Template
.drv	DRiVer
.drw	DRaW file—Corel Designer
.dwg	DraWinG file—Autocad
.emf	Enhanced MetaFile
.eps	Encapsulated PostScript file
.err	ERRor file
.exe	EXEcutable file
.fax	FAX file
.fif	Fractal Image Format file
.for	FORtran source file
.fpx	Flash PiX
.gif	Graphics Image Format
.glo	LaTeX GLOssary file
.gly	MS Word GLossarY file
.hgl	H-p Graphics Language
.hlp	HeLP file
.htm or. html	HTML text file

.idx	LaTeX and FoxPro InDeX file
.iff	Image File Format—Sun Microsystems
.ini	INItialization file
.jpg or. jpeg	JPEG image format
.js	JavaScript browser information
.lgo	LOGO file
.lib	C++ LIBrary file
.lst	LiSTing
.log	LOG file
.lsp	LiSP source code
.mac	MACpaint graphic file
.mai	or. mail MAIL file
.man	MANual
.map	image MAP
.me	used with self-descriptive file read.me
.mic	Microsoft Image Composition
.mid	or. midi MIDI music file format
.mix	Microsoft Image piX—Picture It! image file
.mme	MIME file
.mpe	MPEG animation file
.mp3	MP3 animation file
.msg	MeSsaGe
.obj	OBJect code file
.ole	MS OLE file
.ovl	OVerLay file
.pas	Pascal language source file
.pcd	Kodak image format
.pct	Macintosh PiCTure file
.pcx	PC paintbrush file
.pdf	Adobe Portable Document Format
.pic	PICture file
.png	Portable Network Graphic image format
.prg	dBase and FoxPro source program
.pro	PROlog source file
.ps	PostScript file
.psd	Adobe PhotoShop Document
.qpw	Quattro Prod Works file
.rgb	Silicon Graphics RGB image format
.rtf	Rich Text Format
.scr	SCRipt
.src	SouRCe code

.sty	STYle sheet
.sys	SYStem file
.tar	Tape ARchive
.tbk	ToolBooK
.tex	TeX or LaTeX file
.tga	Truevision GraphicsArray image format
.ths	THeSaurus
.tif or. tiff	Tagged Image File Format
.tmp	TeMPorary file
.ttf	TrueType Font
.uue	UUEncoded compressed file
.wav	WAVefront music file
.wmf	Windows MetaFile
.wps	MS Works word processing file
.wpw	Word Perfect Works file
.wri	MS WRIte word processing file
.xbm	X-windows BitMap file
.xls	Excel spreadsheet file
.zip	ZIPped (compressed) file

Appendix II

NOTATION AND UNITS
Mathematical Notation

Symbol	Meaning
GENERAL	
$\sum$	Summation $\left(\sum_{i=1}^{n} a_i = a_1 + a_2 + \cdots + a_n \right)$
$\int$	Integral
$\vert\ \vert$	Absolute value ($\vert a \vert = a$ if $a \geq 0$, $= -a$ if $a < 0$)
$\lfloor\ \rfloor$	Floor function (greatest integer less than or equal to: $\lfloor 2.4 \rfloor = 2$, $\lfloor -2.4 \rfloor = -3$)
$\lceil\ \rceil$	Ceiling function (least integer greater than or equal to: $\lceil 2.4 \rceil = 3$, $\lceil -2.4 \rceil = -2$)
$[\ ]$	Closed interval ($[a, b]$ includes all x such that $a \leq x \leq b$)
$(\ )$	Open interval [$\langle a, b \rangle$ includes all x such that $a < x < b$]
$[\ ), (\ ],$	Half-open (half-closed) interval $\{[a, b)$ includes all x such that $a \leq x < b\}$
$\approx, \simeq, \cong, \doteq$	Approximately equal
$\sim$	Asymptotic to
$\times$	Set product [$A \times B$ consists of all pairs (a, b) where $a \in A$, $b \in B$]
Modulo (or mod)	Remainder (x mod y is remainder when x is divided by y; thus, 8 mod 3 is 2)
o	Binary operation (i.e., denotes any operation like $+$ which requires two operands)
fl	Floating point (fl$(x + y)$ denotes the floating-point sum of x and y)
iff	If and only if
$\lg(x)$	$\log_2(x)$
$\ln(x)$	$\log_e(x)$
wrt	With respect to
LOGIC	
$\vee$	Or
$\wedge$	And
$\oplus$	Exclusive or (XOR)
$\sim, \neg$	Not
$\supset, \Rightarrow$	Implication
$\equiv, \Leftrightarrow$	Equivalence

$\neq$	Inequivalence
$\forall x$	For all x (universal quantifier)
$\exists x$	There exists an x or some x (existential quantifier)

SET NOTATION

Let S, S_1, S_2 be sets and P be a predicate:

$x \in S$	x is a member of set S
$\bar{S}$ & macr;	The complement of S relative to a domain; the set of elements of that domain that are not in S
$S_1 \cup S_2$	The union of S_1, and S_2: $\{x \mid x \in S_1 \vee x \in S_2\}$
$S_1 \cap S_2$	The intersection of S_1 and S_2: $\{x \mid x \in S_1 \wedge x \notin S_2\}$
$S_1 - S_2$	The set-difference of S_1 and S_2; the elements of S_1 not in S_2: $\{x \mid x \in S_1 \wedge x \notin S_2\}$
$\{x \mid P(x)\}$	The set of all x such that P is true of x

Notes

1. For a description of the notation used in describing computer language constructs, *see* BACKUS–NAUR FORM.
2. For symbols used in logical circuitry, *see* COMPUTER CIRCUITRY.

Asymptotic Growth Notation Used in the Analysis of Algorithms

If $f(n)$ and $g(n)$ are functions defined on the natural numbers, and are eventually nonnegative, their asymptotic relative growth rates are expressed by the "big-O" and related notations.

$f(n) = O(g(n))$	There are positive constants c, n_0 such that for all $n > n_0$, $0 \le f(n) \le cg(n)$ ($f(n)$ eventually grows no faster than $g(n)$).
$f(n) = \Omega(g(n))$	There are positive constants c, n_0 such that for all $n > n_0$, $0 \le cg(n) \le f(n)$ ($f(n)$ eventually grows at least as fast as $g(n)$).
$f(n) = \Theta(g(n))$	There are positive constants c_1, c_2, n_0 such that for all $n > n_0$, $0 \le c_1 g(n) \le f(n) \le c_2 g(n)$ ($f(n)$ eventually grows at least as fast as $g(n)$).
$f(n) = o(g(n))$	For every constant $c > 0$, there is an $n_0 \gtrless 0$ such that for all $n > n_0$, $0 \le f(n) < cg(n)$($f(n)$ eventually grows more slowly than $g(n)$).
$f(n) = \omega(g(n))$	For every constant $c > 0$, there is an $n_0 \gtrless 0$ such that for all $n > n_0$, $0 \le cg(n) < f(n)$ ($f(n)$ eventually grows faster than $g(n)$).

Units of Measure

This list contains abbreviations of units of measure used in the *Encyclopedia*; these usually appear in their abbreviated form.

General

K	1000 or 1024 ($= 2^{10}$)
M	1 000 000 or 1 048 576 ($= 2^{20}$)
G	2^{30} (approximately 1 US billion)
T	2^{40}
	The powers of two are used primarily in measures of computer main memory.

Time

ms, msec	millisecond (10^{-3} s)
μs, μsec	microsecond (10^{-6} s)
ns, nsec	nanosecond (10^{-9} s)
ps, psec	picosecond (10^{-12} s)
fs, fsec	femtosecond (10^{-15} s)
as, asec	attasecond (10^{-18} s)
zs, zsec	zeptosecond (10^{-21} s)
ys, ysec	yoctosecond (10^{-24} s)

Speed

Megaflops or Mflops	Million floating-point operations per second
Gigaflops or Gflops	Billion floating-point operations per second
Teraflops or Tflops	Trillion floating-point operations per second
BIPS	Billion instructions per second
MIPS	Million instructions per second
LIPS	Logical inferences per second

Electricity

Hz	Hertz (cycles/s)
KHZ	Kilohertz (10^3 cycles/s)
MHz	Megahertz (10^6 cycles/s)
GHz	Gigahertz (10^9 cycles/s)
μW	Microwatt (10^{-6} watts)
mW	Milliwatt (10^{-3} watts)
kW	Kilowatt (10^3 watts)
mV	Millivolt (10^{-3} volt)
mA	Milliamp (10^{-3} amp)
μF	Microfarad (10^{-6} farad)
nF	Nanofarad (10^{-9} farad)
pF	Picofarad (10^{-12} farad)
fF	Femtofarad (10^{-15} farad)
aF	Attafarad (10^{-18} farad)

Storage

Kb	Kilobit (10^3 bits)
Mb	Megabit (10^6 bits)
Gb	Gigabit (10^9 bits)
Tb	Terabit (10^{12} bits)
Pb	Petabit (10^{15} bits)
Eb	Exabit (10^{18} bits)
KB	Kilobyte (10^3 bytes)
MB	Megabyte (10^6 bytes)
GB	Gigabyte (10^9 bytes)
TB	Terabyte (10^{12} bytes)

PB	Petabyte (10^{15} bytes)
EB	Exabyte (10^{18} bytes)
ZB	Zettabyte (10^{21} bytes)
YB	Yottabyte (10^{24} bytes)
L(x)	Location of x (in main memory)
C(A), [A]	Contents of location A (in main memory)

I/O

bps	Bits per second
bpi	Bits per inch
chps	Characters per second
chpi	Characters per inch
lpm	Lines per minute
rpm	Revolutions per minute
KB/s or Kbytes/s	Kilobytes per second
MB/s or Mbytes/s	Megabytes per second
GB/s or Gbytes/s	Gigabytes per second
TB/s or Tbytes/s	Terabytes per second

Miscellaneous

μ	Micron (10^{-6} meter)

Table of important numerical constants

	Decimal (rounded)					Hexadecimal (truncated)				
$\frac{1}{10}$	0.10000	00000	00000	00000	00000	0.1999	9999	9999	9999	9999
$\sqrt{2}$	1.41421	35623	73095	04880	16887	1.6A09	E667	F3BC	C908	B2FB
$\sqrt{3}$	1.73205	08075	68877	29352	74463	1.BB67	AE85	84CA	A73B	2574
$\sqrt{5}$	2.23606	79774	99789	69640	91737	2.3C6E	F372	FE94	F82B	E739
$\sqrt{10}$	3.16227	76601	68379	33199	88935	3.298B	075B	4B6A	5420	9457
$\sqrt[3]{2}$	1.25992	10498	94873	16476	72106	1.428A	2F98	D728	AE22	3DDA
$\ln 2$	0.69314	71805	59945	30941	72321	0.B172	17F7	D1CF	79AB	C9E3
$\ln 10$	2.30258	50929	94045	68401	79915	2.4D76	3776	AAA2	B05B	A95B
$\log_{10} 2$	0.30102	99956	63981	19521	37389	0.4D10	4D42	7DE7	FBCC	47C4
$\log_2 10 = 1/\log_{10} 2$	3.32192	80948	87362	34787	03194	3.5269	E12F	346E	2BF9	24AF
$\log_2 e = 1/\ln 2$	1.44269	50408	88963	40735	99247	1.7154	7642	B82F	E177	7D10
$\log_{10} e = 1/\ln 10$	0.43429	44819	03251	82765	11289	0.6F2D	EC54	9B94	38CA	9AAD
$1° = \pi/180$	0.01745	32925	19943	29576	92369	0.0477	D1AB	94A7	4E45	7076
π	3.14159	26535	89793	23846	26434	3.243F	6A88	85A3	08D3	1319
$1/\pi$	0.31830	98861	83790	67153	77675	0.517C	C1B7	2722	0A94	FE13
π^2	9.86960	44010	89358	61883	44910	9.DE9E	64DF	22EF	2D25	6E26
$\sqrt{\pi}$	1.77245	38509	05516	02729	81675	1.C5BF	891B	4EF6	AA79	C3B0
e	2.71828	18284	59045	23536	02875	2.B7E1	5162	8AED	2A6A	BF71
$1/e$	0.36787	94411	71442	32159	55238	0.5E2D	58D8	B3BC	DF1A	BADE
e^2	7.38905	60989	30650	22723	04275	7.6399	2E35	376B	730C	E8EE
$\sqrt{e}$	1.64872	12707	00128	14684	86508	1.A612	98E1	E069	BC97	2DFE
γ (Euler's constant)	0.57721	56649	01532	86060	65121	0.93C4	67E3	7DB0	C7A4	D1BE
$\varphi = (1+\sqrt{5})/2$ (Golden Ratio)	1.61803	39887	49894	84820	45868	1.9E37	79B9	7F4A	7C15	F39C

Appendix III

TIMELINE OF SIGNIFICANT COMPUTING MILESTONES

The basic idea of this timeline is that those who have seen close to five decades of computing evolve will enjoy the nostalgia of seeing certain developments pass before their eyes as they read. For years that mark multiple accomplishments, there has been no attempt to rank them in any order of perceived importance. The names of computers, languages, algorithms, methods, books, movies, software, etc. have been italicized. Emboldened phrases indicate the names of articles (or portions thereof) that appear in this book.

We trust that readers will be tolerant of the lighthearted nature of some of the early dates, and of the outrageous speculations opposite dates later than 2003 and the frivolous one at 2001.

15 billion BC	Universal computer boots up with a Big Bang.
5 billion BC	First full-scale **analog computer** computes planetary orbits.
500 million BC	First cell, address unknown.
200 million BC	Cells assembled into first **memory** and attached to a rudimentary **central processing unit**.
50,000 BC	Earliest evidence of counting.
2500 BC	Positional number system used in Mesopotamia.
2400 BC	Babylonians use abacus and approximate π as 31/8.
1900 BC	Stonehenge erected.
1650 BC	In the Rhind Papyrus, the Egyptian Ahmes the Scribe states that $\pi = 256/81 \cong 3.1\underline{60}\ldots$
870 BC	A symbol for zero is used in India.
800 BC	I-Ching exhibits binary properties.
600 BC	Abacus used in Greece

550 BC	Pythagoras gets credit for a theorem known to the Chinese a thousand years earlier. When his student Hippasus discovers irrational numbers, Pythagoras, believing the universe to be strictly rational, acts irrationally and has him drowned for heresy.
450 BC	Hippocrates of Chios rediscovers the irrationals but is saved from drowning by clinging to floating-point numbers.
300 BC	Euclid's *Elements*.
230 BC	*Sieve of Eratosthenes*, an early **algorithm**.
215 BC	Archimedes approximates π as 21 1872/67 441 $\cong$ 3.141590. Then he discovers the naked truth and shouts "Eureka."
140 BC	Hipparchus of Rhodes, knowing all the angles, invents trigonometry.
100 BC	Chinese use positive and negative powers of 10 to express magnitudes.
80 BC	The Antikytera calendar mechanism.
44 BC	Caesar, lacking an Antikytera, fails to beware the Ides of March.
AD 150	Ptolemy's *Almagest*.
250	Diophantus's *Arithmetica*.
450	Tsu Ch'ung-chih and his son Tsu Keng-chih compute π as 355/133 $\cong$ 3.1415929..., an accuracy unsurpassed for 1000 years.
600	Decimal number system used in India.
850	*Algebra* of al-Khowarizmi transmits Hindu art of reckoning to the Arabs and thus to Europe; invention of astrolabes.
1050	Chinese scholars arrange the 64 I-Ching hexagrams in a 6-bit binary order called the Fu Hsi arrangement.
1202	Fibonacci sequence.
1261	Yang Hui anticipates "**Pascal**'s" triangle.
1274	Raymond Lull's logic machine.
1430	Baptista Alberti's cipher machine.
1435	Jamshid ben Mas'ud ben Mahmud Ghiath ed-Din al-Kashi invents several special-purpose astronomical calculators, calculates π to 16 places, and is first to express a fraction as a positional decimal.
1489	Use of plus and minus signs by Widmann.
1492	Pellos invents decimal point. Columbus, all at sea, doesn't notice.
1500	Leonardo DaVinci draws sketch of a 13-wheel odometer-like counter, but historians disagree as to whether this was intended to be used in what would have been the first mechanical **calculating machine**; Aldus Manutius develops an italic **typefont**.

1518	First known book of cryptology, *Polygraphiae libri sex* (Six books of polygraphy), by Johannes Trithemius, published posthumously, is later placed on the Falwell Index of Forbidden Books.
1527	Apian publishes "**Pascal**'s" triangle.
1540	Robert Recorde invents the equal sign, " $=$," and, as a matter of **record**(e), turns over in his grave when it is ambiguously used as the replacement operator in ***Fortran*** and ***C++***.
1580	François Vieta causes a sensation by using letters to stand for numerical parameters, thus inventing the concept of a variable; Rabbi Judah ben Loew's automaton.
1610	Edmund Gunter invents several surveying instruments; Ludolph van Ceulen computes π to 35 decimals.
1614	John Napier's *Canon of Logarithms*.
1617	Napier's *Rabdologia* describes "Napier's bones."
1624	Wilhelm Schickard's calculator does automatic addition and subtraction and semiautomatic multiplication and division. Henry Briggs' error-ridden table of logarithms.
1629	William Oughtred and Richard Delamain invent circular slide rule. Adrian Vlacq's first complete set of modern logarithms.
1631	Oughtred's *Clavis Mathematicae* is first to use symbol $\times$ for multiplication and *sin* and *cos* as abbreviations for *sine* and *cosine*.
1637	*Fermat's Last Theorem* is of marginal interest but keeps mathematicians busy for 357 years; Descartes' *Discours de la Méthode* describes analytic geometry, which is indispensable for modern work in **computer graphics**.
1642	**Blaise Pascal**'s calculator, which he names "Pascaline."
1646	Sir Thomas Browne coins the word "electricity" and is first to describe a person who computes as a "computer."
1665	Newton invents calculus but does not publish his discovery.
1672	Samuel Morland's *The Description and Use of Two Arithmetic Instruments*.
1673	René Grillet's adding machine; **Leibniz** invents calculus independently of Newton and, in his spare time, develops the Leibniz "wheel," a calculator that can add, subtract, multiply, and divide, all automatically. He believes that he has invented binary numbers but is later stunned when he learns of the 11th Century Fu Hsi arrangement of the I-Ching.
1687	Newton's *Principia*.
1699	Abraham Sharp computes π to 72 decimal places using the first Sharp calculator (pencil and paper and his head).
1706	Use of the symbol π by William Jones; John Machin computes π to 100 decimal places.

1714	Brook Taylor shows that most basic mathematical functions can be expanded into an infinite series of term that require only pure arithmetic for their computation; Henry Mill receives an English patent for a typewriter.
1730	Stirling's formula for $n!$ which is now so indispensable for the **analysis of algorithms**.
1736	Vaucanson's automata; Euler generalizes and solves the *Seven Bridges of Königsberg* problem and thereby inaugurates modern **Graph Theory**.
1752	Ben Franklin is told to go fly a kite. He does and experiences an electrifying moment.
1761	J. H. Lambert proves that π is irrational.
1774	Phillipp-Matthaus Hahn builds and sells a 12-digit calculator.
1777	Buffon's Needle Problem is first **Monte Carlo** simulation; Earl of Stanhope's "Logic Demonstrator" is first mechanical logic machine.
1786	J. H. Muller's automatic difference engine; Gripenstierna's cipher machine
1801	Gauss's *Disquisitions Arithmeticae*; Jacquard's punched-card-controled loom.
1811	Luddites destroy machines that threaten jobs.
1814	J. H. Hermann's planimeter.
1820	Charles Xavier Thomas's (Thomas de Colmar's) Arithmometer.
1822	**Charles Babbage**'s design and partial construction of a **Difference Engine**.
1829	William Austen Burt is first American to patent a typewriter; Wheatstone uses punched paper tape to store data.
1832	**Babbage** designs his **Analytical Engine**; Menabrea advocates use of **parallel processing**; 20-year old Évariste Galois, on the eve of his death in a duel with the fiancé of his beloved groupie Stéphanie-Félicie Poterine du Motel, frantically writes out an outline of his *group theory*, one of the mathematical foundations for the ultimate proof of *Fermat's Last Theorem*. Ever since, the inns of the kind to which Évariste and Stéphanie journeyed to their trysts by coach are called "motels."
1843	Menabrea's memoir with commentary by Ada Augusta, the Countess of **Lovelace**; Hamilton's quaternions.
1844	Morse sends telegraph message from Washington to Baltimore; Joseph Liouville finds first transcendental number; Johann Dase, a 20-year-old calculating prodigy, occupies himself for two whole months by computing π to 200 decimal places in his head.
1850	Amédée Mannheim designs the logarithmic slide rule that dominated mechanical calculation for the next 100 years.
1853	Pehr Georg and Edvard Scheutz's Tabulating Machine.
1854	George Boole's *Laws of Thought*.
1855	James Clerk Maxwell's improved planimeter.
1860	Boole's *Finite Differences* is first text on subject.

1867	Wheatstone's cipher machine.
1873	Hermite proves that e is transcendental; William Shanks publishes 707 decimal places of π, but only the first 526 prove to be correct.
1876	Alexander Graham Bell's telephone; Lord Kelvin's harmonic analyzer and tide predictor devices.
1878	Thomas Edison, in a letter to a friend, uses "**bug**" in its modern context 65 years before the legendary moth invades Harvard **Mark I** relay circuit.
1880	Baudot's punched paper tape telegraph code, Baudot Code; Ramon Verea's calculator is first to perform direct multiplication rather than using repeated addition.
1882	*Towers of Hanoi* problem invented by Edouard Lucas; Lindemann proves that π is transcendental.
1884	William S. Burroughs' first adding machine.
1885	Marquand's mechanical logic machine; Dorr Felt invents the comptometer, calling it a "Macaroni Box."
1890	**Punched card** machines patented by John Shaw Billings and implemented by **Herman Hollerith**; Leonardo Torres Quevedo builds an electromechanical machine for solving certain endgame problems in chess.
1893	Chess-playing machine envisioned by Ambrose Bierce in his short story "Moxon's Master"; Charles Proteus Steinmetz uses complex arithmetic as a basis for practical calculations in alternating current theory, and develops a Law of Hysteresis that becomes the basis of magnetic core **memory** a half-century later.
1894	Variable-toothed gear invented by Odhner and Baldwin and becomes basis for the Monroe calculator.
1895	Marconi transmits radio signals.
1896	**Hollerith** founds Tabulating Machine Company which later became Computing, Tabulating, and Recording Co. (CTR) in 1911 and then the **IBM** Corporation in 1924; Hadamard and de la Vallée Poussin independently prove the prime number theorem.
1899	Founding of Burroughs Adding Machine Company.
1901	Marconi transmits first transatlantic wireless message but neglects to credit Jagadis Chandra Bose for inventing the "coherer" (receiver) that made it possible.
1904	Diode vacuum tube invented by J. A. Fleming.
1906	Triode vacuum tube invented by Lee De Forest.
1908	Percy Ludgate's analytical engine; through his will, Paul Wolfskehl establishes a prize of 100 000 marks for whoever is able to prove *Fermat's Last Theorem* no later than 2007.
1910	Henry Babbage assembles mill of his father's design and builds a printer to go with it; James Powers develops mechanical **punched card** machinery for use with 1910 census and later forms Powers Accounting Machine Company; Russell and Whitehead's *Principia Mathematica*.

1911	Founding of Computing, Tabulating, and Recording Co. (CTR), the forerunner of IBM; discovery of superconductivity by Kammerlingh Onnes.
1912	Wireless operators on the *Titanic* are first to send a meaningful S.O.S. signal. The *Carpathia*, 58 miles away, responds; the *Californian*, 15 miles away, does not.
1913	Torres Quevedo's electrified arithmometer; Ramanujan develops formulas that form the basis of the fastest algorithms for computing π known to this day.
1917	Armstrong's superheterodyne radio receiver.
1919	Eccles and Jordan's flip-flop circuit.
1921	Karel Čapek coins the word "robot" in his play *R.U.R.*
1924	Computing, Tabulating, and Recording Company is renamed International Business Machines (**IBM**).
1925	Formal establishment of Bell Telephone Laboratories; first public television demonstrations by Philo Farnsworth and, independently, by John Logie Baird.
1926	As a sequel, Baird invents radar, **fiber optics**, and an infrared device for enhancing night vision; early versions of the Hagelin and German *Enigma* cipher machines.
1927	J. A. O'Neill patents magnetic coated tape; newly formed Remington Rand buys Powers Accounting Machine Company.
1928	IBM introduces 80-column **punched card**; L. J. Comrie uses **punched card** machinery to compute Moon orbits.
1929	Vladimir Zworykin of RCA patents first Cathode Ray Tube (CRT); first demonstration of color television; station WRGB in Schenectady, NY begins first regularly scheduled TV broadcasts; Lukasiewicz uses parenthesis-free **Polish notation** in his logic text *Elements of Mathematical Logic*.
1930	Vannevar Bush's Differential Analyzer.
1931	Reynold B. Johnson invents mark-sensed test scoring; Kurt Gödel stuns the mathematical world by enunciating an *Incompleteness Theorem* that states that in any sufficiently rich axiomatic system there are propositions which can neither be proved nor disproved.
1933	Edwin Armstrong and Michael Pupin invent FM broadcasting.
1935	IBM 601 multiplying card punch.
1936	Alonzo Church's lambda calculus and Emil Post's production systems, each of which, together with the following year's **Turing machine**, equivalently embodies the concept of effective computation as enunciated in Church's Thesis; **Konrad Zuse**'s Z1 is first binary (though mechanical) computer.
1937	Bell Labs relay computer project under the direction of George Stibitz; In his paper "On Computable Numbers," **Alan Turing** describes what is now called a **Turing Machine**, which, nine years before the **stored program concept** is credited to **von Neumann**, stores its program on tape (i.e. in memory) in a form indistinguishable from data.

1938   Early computer entrepreneurs William Hewlett and David Packard form Hewlett-Packard (*hp*); xerography invented by Chester F. Carlson.

1939   **Atanasoff-Berry Computer (ABC)** is first electronic computing device to use binary arithmetic; *Zuse* Z2.

1940   Claude Shannon's first paper on communications theory; the Bell Labs Complex Number Calculator is demonstrated by Remote Job Entry, first use of that technique.

1941   **Konrad Zuse**'s electromechanical computer *L3* uses binary and floating-point **computer arithmetic**; Helmut Hoelzer invents first all-electronic general-purpose analog computer.

1943   **Colossus**, a large vacuum tube computer, developed by the British to break the German Lorenz cipher; McCulloch and Pitts's concept of artificial neurons; Curt Herzstark designs the Curta calculator while imprisoned at Buchenwald; first issue of influential journal *Mathematical Tables and Other Aids to Computation*.

1944   *Mark I* relay computer developed at Harvard under direction of **Howard Aiken**; development of the **Monte Carlo method** by Stanislaw Ulam and **John von Neumann**; von Neumann and Morganstern's *Theory of Games and Economic Behavior*.

1945   **Zuse** builds *Z4* and envisions *Plankalkül*, a high-level **programming language** that was never implemented; **Turing** gives a clear exposition of nested subroutines (**subprogram**s) whose calling sequences are based on a pushdown **stack**, floating-point arithmetic, and remote use of a computer over a telephone line; Vannevar Bush envisions **personal computing** and **hypertext** in his historic essay "As We May Think."

1946   *ENIAC*, the first large general-purpose electronic computer, developed by J. Presper Eckert and John Mauchly; publication of the "Princeton Report" by Burks, Goldstine, and **von Neumann** defines **stored-program concept** and uses "flow diagrams" (**flowcharts**); F. C. Williams applies for patent on what is now called Williams Tube Memory; Warren Weaver and Andrew Booth propose **machine translation** of one natural language to another; founding of Engineering Research Associates (ERA); Harvard *Mark II*; IBM 603 Calculating Punch; AIEE appoints Charles Concordia chairman of its Large Scale Computing subcommittee, the forerunner of the **IEEE Computer Society**.

1947   Founding of the **Association for Computing Machinery (ACM)**; Dantzig's Simplex Melhod; Hamming invents **error correcting and detecting codes**; Harvard *Mark II*; first magnetic drum memories; Eckert–Mauchly Computer Corporation, the first company formed with the sole intent to market an electronic digital computer.

1948   The **Manchester University** "baby" machine, a prototype of its later *Mark I*, is built by F. C. Williams and Tom Kilburn using Williams Tube Memory and becomes first electronic **stored program** computer to run a complete program; **index register** (B-box) invented by Newman and Kilburn; transistor invented at Bell Labs by Bardeen, Brattain, and Shockley; **Norbert Wiener**'s *Cybernetics*; **IBM**'s Selective Sequence Electronic Calculator (SSEC); Claude Shannon founds **Information Theory** through publication of his *Mathematical theory of communication*.

1949	*EDSAC*, first practical stored-program computer, becomes operational at Cambridge and uses a "relocating loader"; work begins on *LEO*, an extension of *EDSAC*; Harvard *Mark III; BINAC*, first stored-program computer built in USA; Grosch's Law; An Wang and Jay Forrester independently invent magnetic core **memory**; Edmund Berkeley's *Giant Brains*; *ENIAC* is converted to a stored-program computer by Richard Clippinger and used to compute π to 2,037 decimal places.
1950	Pilot Ace computer; **Wilkes**, Wheeler, and Gill develop concepts of subroutines and subroutine libraries for *EDSAC*; *SEAC*; *Whirlwind*; **Turing test** for machine intelligence; Asimov's "Three Laws of **Robotics**"; Harry Huskey builds *SWAC* for NBS at UCLA; *ERA 1101*; MIT Lincoln Laboratory founded to develop *SAGE*; K. H. Davis builds a **speech recognition** machine.
1951	*Ferranti Mark I* and *Univac I*, first commercial computers; Holberton's sort-merge generator; founding of the Computer Group of the Institute of Radio Engineers (renamed the **IEEE Computer Society** in 1971); **Grace Hopper** proposes use of word "**compiler**" for her *A–0* programming system.
1952	*EDVAC*; *Autocode*, the first working high-level language, is developed by Alick Glennie; *MANIAC* at Los Alamos under direction of Nicholas Metropolis; *ORDVAC* at Aberdeen Proving Grounds; *IAS* under leadership of Julian Bigelow at Institute for Advanced Study at Princeton; *RAYDAC* at NBS; *ABNER* at NSA; Svoboda's *SAPO* in Czechoslovakia is first **fault-tolerant computer**; *ILLIAC I* at University of Illinois; Harvard *Mark IV*; core memory installed on **Whirlwind** and *ENIAC*; Arthur Samuel begins development of a program to play checkers; Huffman encoding.
1953	Nathaniel Rochester's symbolic assembler**; von Neumann** demonstrates the possibility of a self-reproducing automaton; *IBM 701; OMIBAC; ERA 1103*, first commercial computer to use **interrupts**; *BESMl* and *STRELA* in Russia; *JOHNNIAC* at Rand Corporation; **Maurice Wilkes** recommends use of **microprogramming**; B. V. Bowden's *Faster than Thought*.
1954	Eiichi Goto's *Parametron; DYSEAC*; first computor to use **interrupts** for I/O; *NORC; DEUCE*; Laning and Zierler implement first operational **compiler** for *Whirlwind*; *IBM 650*; Masterson's *Uniprinter* prints 600 lines per minute.
1955	*Alwac III-E*, an early minicomputer, time-shares four remote terminals at NSA but its 15-minute time quantum dots not create illusion of simultaneity; **index registers** added to *EDSAC*; first **optical character reader (OCR)**; *IBM SAGE* is first computer to use direct memory access (DMA); Sperry Gyroscope absorbs Remington Rand to form Sperry Rand; SHARE becomes first of many user groups.
1956	*IBM 704* and *Univac 1103* are first commercial computers to use magnetic core storage; **Chomsky hierarchy**; *Ferranti Pegasus* is first computer to use general (purpose) registers; first **operating system** is developed for the *IBM 704* through cooperative effort of General Motors and North American Aviation; *TAC* (Tokyo Automatic Computer) under direction of Hideo Yamashita; *Logic Theorist* of Newell, Shaw, and Simon is the first heuristic program and first to exploit linked lists; John McCarthy coins "**artificial intelligence**"; work on *ATLAS* begins at **Manchester University**

under direction of Tom Kilburn; Doug Ross's *APT* language for numerical control of machine tools becomes an early successful **problem-oriented language**.

1957   *Fortran* developed under leadership of John Backus; Harlan Herrick names its unconditional transfer a *GOTO*; Roy Nutt introduces FORMAT statement into the language; Herb Bright is first *Fortran* user to receive an error message; Yngve's Comit is first **string-processing** language; Bill Norris leaves Sperry to form Control Data Corporation (CDC); Fairchild Semiconductor formed by a group led by Gordon Moore and Robert Noyce; Digital Equipment Corporation (DEC) founded by Ken Olsen and Harlan Anderson. *IBM 305 RAMAC* is first commercial computer to use disk drives; Lejaren Hiller creates first **computer music** composition, the "ILLIAC Suite"; first issue of *Datamation*.

1958   Bernstein's **computer chess** program; CDC 1604; Philco *Transac S-2000* forms base for first family of upward-compatible computers; Jack Kilby's **microcomputer chip**; I/O **interrupt** developed by Morton Astrahan of IBM; **Grace Hopper**'s *Flow-Matic* is first business-oriented high-level language; Daniel McCracken writes first *Fortran* textbook.

1959   *IBM 1400, 7070*, and *7090*; *DEC PDP-1*; CODASYL; **University of Manchester**'s **ATLAS** is first computer to use a paged **virtual memory**; *RPG; ERMA*; McCarthy's *Lisp* **list processing** language based on the lambda calculus of Alonzo Church; John McCarthy and Christopher Strachey independently propose "**time-sharing**"; first Xerox copier.

1960   *Algol 60* language popularizes concepts of **recursion** and **block structure**; Algol 60 Report introduces notation initially called Backus Normal Form (BNF) in honor of John Backus but later renamed **Backus-Naur Form** to give equal honor to Peter Naur; *Cobol; IBM 1620;* first **integrated circuit** patent applied for by Robert N. Noyce of Fairchild; Soviet KIEVcomputer; E. H. Fredkin's *trie* data structure; M. D. McIlroy describes high-level language **macro** expansion; Odo Struger's *programmable logic controller,*which made modern factory **automation** possible; Paul Baran of RAND proposes a global **distributed system** based on what would later be called **packet switching**.

1961   MIT's *Compatible Time Sharing System* (CTSS) under direction of Fernando Corbató; Licklider's DEC **time-sharing** system; E. T. Irons' syntax-directed **compiler**; Newell's *IPL V* **list processing** language; first "**supercomputers**" are IBM's *Stretch*, the first **pipeline**d computer, and Univac's *LARC*; Rosenblatt's self-organizing *perceptron*, an early neural network used for **pattern recognition**; Samuel's checker-playing program attains master rank and is routinely able to defeat its inventor; AFIPS founded; C. A. R. Hoare's *Quicksort* **sorting** algorithm; Unimation markets first industrial robot designed by George Devol; Daniel Shanks and John Wrench use an *IBM 7090* to compute Π to 100 000 decimal places.

1962   **University of Manchester**'s *ATLAS* computer is first to use Tom Kilburn's idea of a two-level memory; Stanford and Purdue establish first departments of **computer science**; Green's question-answering program *Baseball* anticipates modern **database** queries; *Univac 1100* series begun; Steve Russell's *Space War* for the *PDP-1* is the first interactive video game; Iverson's *A Programming Language*; Werner Buchholz's *Planning a Computer System*; Ross Perot founds Electronic Data Systems (EDS); J. C. R. Licklider describes a "Galactic Network," anticipating the **Internet**.

1963   *Burroughs B-5000; Snobol; Forth*; Weizenbaum's *Eliza; LINC; SABRE,*American Airlines reservation system; NEC SX-I and SX-2; Ivan Sutherland's *Sketchpad*, first interactive **computer graphics** system; Cliff Shaw's *JOSS* interactive system at RAND; Lotfi Zadeh begins work on **fuzzy logic**.

1964   *IBM 360*, the first byte-addressable machine; in conjunction with its description, IBM is first to use term "**computer architecture**"; *CDC 6600*, essentially the first **RISC** computer, 16 years prior to coinage of the acronym; Kemeny and Kurtz develop Dartmouth **time-sharing** system and ***Basic*** programming language; *DEC PDP-8; RCA Spectra* series; *Honeywell 200* series; Böhm and Jacopini's paper on the sufficiency of canonical **control structures** is basis for **structured programming**; development of *Formac*, first **computer algebra** program, by an IBM team led by Jean Sammet; *Dendral* is first diagnostic **expert system** program.

1965   Moore's Law; **Wilkes** proposes use of a **cache memory**, attributing the idea to Gordon Scarrott; *PL/I; SPSS*; Dijkstra's semaphores advance state of the art of **concurrent programming**; K. C. Knowlton's *buddy system* for **multiprogramming** storage management; Bachman's Integrated Data Store is forerunner of **database management systems (DBMS)**; Project MAC at MIT; Englebart invents **mouse** at SRI; IBM develops **diskettes** for use with 370 series; Cooley and Tukey's Fast Fourier Transform (FFT) **algorithm**; Donald Davies coins "packet switching" to describe a distributed network similar to that of Paul Baran; Ted Nelson coins "**hypertext**"; first Ph.D. in **computer science** is awarded to Richard Wexelblat by the University of Pennsylvania.

1966   Iverson and Falkoff's ***APL*** language incorporates elastic **data structures** and absence of levels of **operator precedence**; Flynn's classification scheme for **computer architectures**; Hoare invents the "case" **control structure**; IBM **Stretch** is used to compute π to 250,000 decimal places.

1967   ***LOGO***; Greenblatt's chess-playing program, *Mac Huck VI*, is made an honorary member of the US Chess Federation; S. G. Tucker coins term **emulation** to mean hardware-assisted **simulation**; *IBM 360/85* is first commercial computer to use a **cache memory**; Ole-Johan Dahl and Kristen Nygaard's *Simula*, later considered to have been the first **object-oriented programming** (OOP) language; Fred Brooks' **virtual reality** lab at University of North Carolina.

1968   Dijkstra's letter "Goto considered harmful"; a US federal information processing standard that encourages a YYMMDD date standard really *is* harmful, engendering the Year 2000 (Y2K) problem; ACM Curriculum 68; *NCR Century* series; Denning's **working set** model; Arthur C. Clarke's HAL in *2001* alerts world to the possibility of highly intelligent machines; *CDC 7600; Algol 68; Speakeasy; Multics* **operating system** on the *GE* (later *Honeywell) 645* at MIT; Intel founded by Robert Noyce, Andrew

Grove, and Gordon Moore; NATO conference introduces term "**software engineering**"; Volume 1 of Knuth's *Art of Computer Programming*.

1969   *Unix*; Seymour Paper and Marvin Minsky solidify computational limits of the Rosenblatt perceptron; **IBM** "unbundles," pricing software separately from hardware, a decision that spawns a multibillion dollar independent software industry; first use of *ARPANET*.

1970   *IBM 370*; DEC *PDP-ll* uses *Unibus*, first multivendor **bus**; Conway's *Game of Life*, a popular **cellular automaton**; Codd's first paper on **relational database** systems; first "smart" terminal, Jack Frassanito's *Datapoint 2200; DEC PDP 11/20; Sinclair ZX-80*.

1971   Wirth defines **Pascal** language; *Intel 4004* chip inaugurates era of *very large-Scale integration* (VLSI); *CDC Cyber 70*; appearance of electronic handheld **calculators**; Stephen Cook in the USA and Leonid Levin in Russia independently formulate the concept of **NP-complete problems**; Weinberg's *The Psychology of Computer Programming*; formation of the **IEEE Computer Society**.

1972   Founding of Cray Research; *MACSYMA;* David Parnas proposes "**information hiding**"; first vector computers, the *CDC STAR-100* and the Texas Instruments *Advanced Scientific Computer (ASC)*; Ken Thompson of Bell Labs invents a language called *B*, and Dennis Ritchie extends it to form *C*; *Prolog; HP-35* calculator; *PDP 11/45*; Nolan Bushnell founds Atari featuring his *Pong* video game; Ray Tomlinson invents **electronic mail**.

1973   Alan Kay's language *Smalltalk* inaugurates **object-oriented programming** systems (OOPS), but idea doesn't catch fire for 13 more years; first international **computer chess** tournament; *CP/M* microcomputer **operating system**; Robert Metcalfe's **local area network (LAN) Ethernet** protocol.

1974   Hewlett-Packard's programmable **calculator**; Texas Instrument's *SR-50* and *SR-51* calculators; Alto **workstation** at Xerox PARC; Roland Moreno invents "**smart cards**"; July issue of Radio Electronics describes first home computer, Jonathan Titus' *Mark 8*, which uses an *8008* chip; British cryptologists Ellis, Cocks, and Williamson invent a Public Key Cryptosystem based on the difficulty of factoring integers but are not permitted to publish it.

1975   MITS' *Altair*, first persona1 computer kit; *ILLIAC IV*; TCP/IP protocols; Fred Brooks' classic *The Mythical Man-Month*; first laser printer developed by an **Apple** group led by Gary Starkweather.

1976   Introduction of the *CRAY-1* **supercomputer**; Appel and Haken's computer-aided proof of the four-color theorem; Diffie and Hellman rediscover the Public Key Cryptosystem; *Electric Pencil*, Michael Shrayer's **word processing** program for the *Altair* Microcomputer; first network **gateway**; First Edition of the *Encyclopedia of Computer Science*.

1977   IEEE Curriculum in Computer Science and Engineering; Mandelbrot's **fractals**; *DEC VAX-11/780; IBM 303x* series; Erwin Tomash founds the Charles Babbage Institute; Data Encryption Standard (DES); Gates and Allen form **Microsoft** Corporation.

1978	*Apple II* and *Radio Shack TRS-80* achieve wide sales and inaugurate the personal computer era; *DEC VAX-I 1; VISICALC* spreadsheet program; first computer "bulletin board" developed by Ward Christensen and Randy Suess; *Intel 8086*.
1979	*IBM 4300* series; ACM Curriculum 78; Allan M. Cormack and Godfrey N. Hounsfield receive Nobel Prize in Medicine for work in computerized tomography; Boston Computer Museum founded by C. Gordon Bell and Gwen Bell; Knuth's T_EX and *Metafont*; first Hayes **modem**; *Intel 8088*; Compuserve; Philips invents audio CD.
1980	**Ada** language; Patterson and Ditzel coin term **Reduced Instruction Set Computer (RISC)** and advocate this approach to **computer architecture**.
1981	**IBM PC**; *MS-DOS CDC Cyber-205; Commondore VIC-20*; Japan's announcement of a "Fifth Generation" based on **artificial intelligence** is greeted with great skepticism.
1982	AT&T antitrust suit is settled; *Osborne* is first luggable computer; *Turbo Pascal* for the **IBM PC**; *AutoCad*; John Hopfield's theory of neural networks; commercial **electronic mail** to 25 cities; Compaq; Sun Microsystems.
1983	*Cray X-MP; Fujitsu VP100* and *VP200*; first CD-ROM storage; *IBM PC-XT; Lotus 1-2-3* **spreadsheet**; π is computed to 16 million decimal places; Microsoft Word 1.0; Second Edition of the *Encyclopedia of Computer Science and Engineering*.
1984	Introduction of **Apple** *Macintosh popularizes* use of a **mouse**-driven graphical **user interface** (GUI) as inspired by earlier research at XEROX PARC; *IBM PC-AT* and *Tandy 2000* use *Intel 80286* chip; William Gibson coins "**cyberspace**"; Dell Computer founded; introduction of 3.5" **diskette** and the HP laser printer.
1985	John Warnock's ***PostScript***; Paul Brainard's *PageMaker* for the *Macintosh*, first **desktop publishing** software; *Intel 80386* chip; Inmos Transputer; *Windows 1.0*; Thinking Machines Corporation's *Connection Machine*.
1986	Commodore *Amiga*; Burroughs and Sperry merge to form Unisys; *Cray XM-P* **supercomputer** reaches 700 Mflops.
1987	**C++** language stimulates growth of **object-oriented programming**; π is computed to 134 million decimal places by Yasumasa Kannada of the University of Tokyo using a Nippon Electric SX-2 supercomputer.
1988	Foundation of SPEC, the system Performance Evaluation Cooperative, for development and registration of benchmarks; widespread use of **workstation** networks popularizes use of **client/server architecture** in general and **file servers** in particular; *IBM AS/400; Motorola 88000* RISC processor; Robert T. Morris releases **Internet** worm; Wolfram's *Mathematica*.
1989	*Intel 80486* chip; *Soundblaster* sound card.
1990	**Window environments**, long popular on the Apple *Macintosh*, begin to take hold on the **IBM PC** and compatibles (*Windows 3.0*); James Gosling of Sun Microsystems invents a language called *Oak*, later renamed ***Java***; first all-optical processor demonstrated at Bell Labs.

1991	**IBM** and **Apple** announce joint venture; NCR and Tandy market "clipboard" computers that allow input of handwritten printed characters; working version of the original Babbage **Difference Engine** is displayed at the Science Museum in London; Gopher; *Cray Y-MP C90* **supercomputer** reaches 16 Gflops; brothers David and Gregory Chudnovsky, mathematicians at Columbia University, use a formula of their discovery and a low-budget **supercomputer** of their design and construction to compute π to 2.1 billion decimals.
1992	Increasing popularity of lightweight notebook and pen-based **portable computers**; widespread use of **data compression** software to double effective capacity of microcomputer **hard disks**; Michelangelo computer **virus** causes media frenzy but does little actual damage.
1993	**Apple** *Newton* PDA; *Pentium* chip (*Intel 80586*); Leonard Adleman demonstrates DNA computing (**molecular computing**), using it to solve a small traveling salesman problem; Windows NT; Third Edition of the *Encyclopedia or Computer Science*.
1994	Clark and Andreessen's **World Wide Web** browser, *Mosaic* (later *Netscape*); Andrew Wiles' proof of Fermat's last Theorem.
1995	*Windows 95; Lycos, Yahoo!, Webcrawler,* and *AltaVista* search engines; *Toy Story* is first full-length computer-generated movie; Bailey, Borwein, and Plouffe discover a "shocking" formula which allows generation of the nth hexadecimal digit of π without computing all or any prior digits.
1996	Web TV; Yasumasa Kanada temporarily regains world record by computing π to six billion decimal places, but the Chudnovsky brothers reach eight billion shortly thereafter; Joel Armengaud, a member of GIMPS (Great Internet Mersenne Prime Search) uses spare computer time on his PC in a **cooperative computing** effort to find the largest prime known to that date, $2^{1398269}-1$, a *Mersenne prime* of over 400 000 digits.
1997	Gordon Spence, also a member of GIMPS, uses a program written by George Woltman to discover a still larger Mersenne prime, the 895 932 digit number $2^{2976221}-1$; *Intel 80686* (*Pentium II*); MMX chip; IBM's *Deep Blue*, a 32-node *RS/6000* **supercomputer**, defeats World Chess Champion Garry Kasparov; Japan, abandoning the "Fifth Generation," announces the "Sixth Generation" based on **neural networks**; a "farm" of thousands of PCs coordinated over the Internet use **cooperative computing** to decipher a message enciphered in the 56-bit key DES in 140 days; Andrew Wiles accepts the Wolfskehl prize of $50 000, ten years before the deadline; Kanada uses 29 hours of time on a *Hirachi SR2201* to compute π to 51.5 billion decimal places. In tribute, the Chudnovsky brothers record "Oh Kanada" on CD-ROM and vow to reach a trillion places.
1998	Windows 98; *Apple iMac*; IBM Enterprise series; Compaq buys Digital Equipment Corporation for ten gigabucks, becoming, after **IBM**, the world's second-largest computer company; In a three-way deal WorldCom acquires Compuserve and America Online's network service company and AOL acquires Compuserve's **database** and subscriber list. Then AOL buys Netscape with Sun as matchmaker. GIMPS member

	Roland Clarkson discovers 37th Mersenne Prime, the 909, 526 digit number $2^{3021377}-1$.
1999	Intel and Hewlett Packard jointly design and market a 600 MHz chip, the first 64-bit chip and the first Intel chip that is not based on 80×86 architecture. Pentium III; *Linux* becomes a potentially formidable challenger to Windows. GIMPS member Nayan Hajratwala discovers 38th Mersenne prime, the two-million digit number $2^{6972593}-1$.
2000	New Year's Day comes and goes with no serious Y2K problems; Intel/HP and AMD begin to ship gigahertz **microcomputer chips**; AOL announces merger with Time-Warner; Internet users gradually switch from **modems** to cable TV or DSL connectivity; Windows 2000; Microsoft announces a **Java** look-alike called C# ("C sharp); Love Bug **virus** infects 45 million computers in 20 countries within 24 hours. Fourth Edition of the *Encyclopedia of Computer Science*.
2001	GIMPS member Michael Cameron discovers 39th Mersenne prime consisting of over four million digits; HAL writes a bestselling novel about a man named ARTHUR, raising the possibility of there being highly intelligent humans.
2002	Hewlett-Packard (*hp*) buys Compaq, and hence the former Digital Equipment Corporation (DEC).
2003	**Apple** PowerMac G5; Michael Shafer finds 40th Mersenne prime consisting of over six million digits; *Milestones of Computer Science and Information Technology*.
2004	On 14 May, GIMPS member Josh Findley's computer finds the 41st Mersenne prime, which is a million digits longer than the 40th; Concise Edition of the *Encyclopedia of Computer Science*.
2015	Abandoning the "Sixth Generation," Japan announces the "Seventh Generation" based on ESP.
2095	*Pentium XC1* (*Intel 809586*); *Windows 95* redux.
2768	100th Edition of the *Encyclopedia of Computer Science* grows to 30 000 pages, but latest **data compression** techniques allow preparation of a Concise Edition of only 17 pages.
5432	The *Sagan 5000* is used to compute π to "billions and billions" of places beyond the prior record. The middle ten trillion places are found to encode the entire Library of Congress exclusive of certain still-classified works of an obscure 20th Century Congressman whose papers are marked "For eye of Newt only."
9500	Windows 9.5K.
9999	Work begins on the Y10K problem.

Index

Key

A term in parentheses, as in Number base (radix), is an approximate synonym for the indexed term, or a key to its pronunciation, as in Deque ("deck"), or an elaboration of an acronym. A term in brackets, as in Bridge [game] and Bridge [network] describes the context of the term.

Abbreviations used in Index:

| = or
AI = Artificial Intelligence
c. = circa (about)
CAI = Computer-Assisted Instruction
GUI = Graphical User Interface
I/O = Input/Output
IR = Information Retrieval
MT = Machine Translation
n. = noun
op sys = operating system
OCR = Optical Character Recognition
OOP = Object-Oriented Programming
OSI = International Standards Organization
PL = Program Library
SE = Software Engineering
v. = verb

μMath [language], 137
1s complement, 122
2D graphics, 309
2nd generation, 452, 520, 696,
2-out-of-5 code, 108

2s complement, 122
3Com, 585, 624
3D graphics, 309, 517
3rd generation, 262, 265, 523, 694, 696
4-color theorem, 835
45-column card, 368, 654
4GL (4th-Generation Language), 560
5th generation, 836
7 bridges problem, 828
7421 and 742-1 codes, 107
9s complement, 122
10-base-5 [Ethernet], 312
10s complement, 122
45-column card, 654
80-column card, 654
80×86 chip, Intel, 256, 269, 615
8421 code, 106, 107, 456
90-column card, 654
96-column card, 654
9s complement, 122
100-Base-T [Ethernet], 312

A-0/A-2 compilers 362
Abacus 825
Abductive Logic Programming (ALP), 462
ABNER, 832
Absolute address, 12, 570

Absorption law, 70
Abstract algebra, 280
ABSTRACT DATA TYPE, 1, 7, 99, 241, 304, 447, 531, 579, 649, 697
Abstract Windows Toolkit, 430
Accelerated Strategic Computing Initiative (ASCI), 490
Access methods, 581, 776
ACCESS TIME, 3, 144, 326, 495, 502, 504, 509, 520, 706, 774, 785, 803
Accumulator, 10, 12, 39, 40, 144, 264, 305, 401, 472, 474, 486, 518, 640, 668, 767
Accuracy, 626
ACE [computer], 113, 769
Ackermann function, 662
Ackermann, Wilhelm [1896–1962], 662
ACM. *See* **ASSOCIATION FOR COMPUTING MACHINERY.**
ACM Curriculum 68/78, 290
ACM Turing Award. *See* **TURING AWARD WINNERS.**
Acoustic delay line, 294.
ACSL [language], 692
ACTIVATION RECORD, 4, 216, 217, 313, 426, 511, 719
Active matrix display, 531
Active X, 684